Course VOIM112
Office Applications -
Spreadsheets & Databases

Bryant & Stratton College

http://create.mheducation.com

ISBN-10: 1308983190 ISBN-13: 9781308983196

Contents

Credits

Intro Chapter

Windows 10, Office 2016, and File Management

CHAPTER OVERVIEW

Microsoft Office 2016 and Windows 10 introduce many new features, including cloud storage for your files, Office file sharing, and enhanced online content. The integration of Office 2016 and Windows 10 means that files are more portable and accessible than ever when you use *OneDrive*, Microsoft's free online cloud storage. The new user interface for Office 2016 and Windows 10 allows you to work on tablet computers and smartphones in a consistent working environment that resembles that of your desktop or laptop computer.

STUDENT LEARNING OUTCOMES (SLOs)

After completing this chapter, you will be able to:

SLO Intro.1 Explore the features of Windows 10 (p. OI-2).

SLO Intro.2 Use the basic features of Office 2016 and navigate the Office 2016 working environment (p. OI-10).

SLO Intro.3 Create, save, close, and open Office files (p. OI-17).

SLO Intro.4 Customize the view and display size in Office applications and work with multiple Office files (p. OI-25).

SLO Intro.5 Print, share, and customize Office files (p. OI-28).

SLO Intro.6 Use the *Ribbon*, tabs, groups, dialog boxes, task panes, galleries, and the *Quick Access* toolbar (p. OI-33).

SLO Intro.7 Use context menus, mini toolbars, keyboard shortcuts, and function keys in Office applications (p. OI-37).

SLO Intro.8 Organize and customize Windows folders and Office files (p. OI-42).

CASE STUDY

Throughout this book you have the opportunity to put into practice the application features that you are learning. Each chapter begins with a case study that introduces you to the Pause & Practice projects in the chapter. These Pause & Practice projects give you a chance to apply and practice key skills in a realistic and practical context. Each chapter contains three to five Pause & Practice projects.

American River Cycling Club (ARCC) is a community cycling club that promotes fitness. ARCC members include recreational cyclists who enjoy the exercise and camaraderie as well as competitive cyclists who compete in road, mountain, and cyclocross races throughout the cycling season. In the Pause & Practice projects, you incorporate many of the topics covered in the chapter to create, save, customize, manage, and share Office 2016 files.

OFFICE

Pause & Practice Intro-1: Customize the Windows *Start* menu and *Taskbar*, create and save a PowerPoint presentation, create a folder, open and rename an Excel workbook, and use Windows 10 features.

Pause & Practice Intro-2: Modify the existing document, add document properties,

customize the Quick Access toolbar, export the document as a PDF file, and share the document.

Pause & Practice Intro-3: Copy and rename files, create a folder, move files, create a zipped folder, and rename a zipped folder.

SLO INTRO. 1

Using Windows 10

Windows 10 is the ***operating system*** that controls computer functions and the working environment. Windows 10 uses the familiar ***Windows desktop***, ***Taskbar***, and ***Start menu***, and you can customize the working environment. You can install traditional applications (***apps***), such as Microsoft Office, to your computer. Also, you can add modern apps from the Microsoft Store similar to how you add an app to your smartphone. Your ***Microsoft account*** is used to store your Microsoft settings, download apps from the Microsoft Store, and connect you to Microsoft Office, *OneDrive*, and *Office Online*.

Windows 10

The Windows 10 operating system controls interaction with computer hardware and software applications. ***Windows 10*** has a revised user interface that utilizes an updated ***Start menu***, where you can select and open a program. Alternatively, you can use the *Taskbar* on the Windows desktop, which has the familiar look of previous versions of Windows. When you log in to Windows 10 using your Microsoft account, it synchronizes your Windows, Office, and ***OneDrive*** cloud storage among computers.

Microsoft Account

In Windows 10 and Office 2016, your files and account settings are portable. In other words, your Office settings and files can travel with you and be accessed from different computers. You are not restricted to a single computer. When you sign in to Windows 10 using your Microsoft account (user name and password), Microsoft uses this information to transfer your Windows and Office 2016 settings to the computer you are

Intro-1 Create a Microsoft account

using. Your Microsoft account not only signs you in to Windows and Office but also to other free Microsoft online services, such as *OneDrive* and ***Office Online***. If you don't have a Microsoft account, you can create a free account at https://signup.live.com (Figure Intro-1).

> **MORE INFO**
> You will use your Microsoft account for projects in this text.

Windows Desktop and Taskbar

The Windows desktop is the working area of Windows. When you log in to Windows, the desktop displays (Figure Intro-2). The *Taskbar* displays at the bottom of the desktop. You can open programs and folders from the *Taskbar* by clicking on an icon on the *Taskbar* (see Figure Intro-2). You can pin apps and other Windows items, such as the *Control Panel* or *File Explorer*, to the *Taskbar* (see "Customize the Taskbar" later in this section).

Intro-2 Windows desktop and *Taskbar*

Start Menu

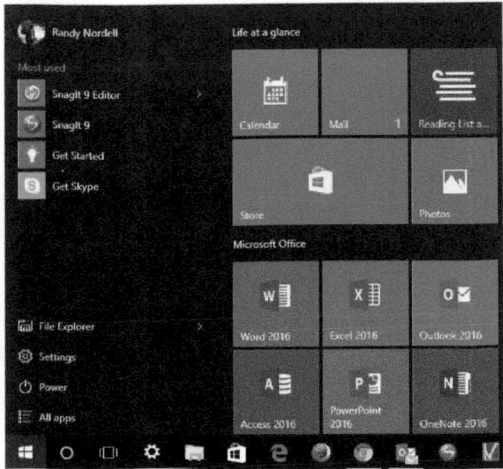

Intro-3 Windows *Start* menu

Windows 10 utilizes a redesigned *Start* menu (Figure Intro-3), that you open by clicking the ***Start button*** located in the bottom left of the *Taskbar*. From the *Start* menu, you can open programs, files, folders, or other Windows resources. The *Start* menu is divided into two main sections. The left side of the *Start* menu displays ***Most Used*** items, buttons to open the ***File Explorer*** and ***Settings*** windows, the ***Power*** button, and ***All apps***, which displays an alphabetical listing of all applications installed on your computer. The right side of the *Start* menu displays apps as tiles (large and small buttons) you can click to open an application or window.

You can customize which apps and items appear on either side of the *Start* menu, arrange and group apps on the *Start* menu, resize the *Start* menu, and display the *Start* menu as a ***Start* page** when you log in to Windows (similar to the *Start* page in Windows 8 and 8.1). See "Customize the Start Menu" later in this section for information about customizing the *Start* menu.

Add Apps

Windows 10 uses the term *apps* generically to refer to applications and programs. Apps include the Windows 10 Weather app, Microsoft Excel program, Control Panel, Google Chrome, or *File Explorer*. Many apps are preinstalled on a Windows 10 computer, and you can add apps to your computer. You can install an app such as Office 2016 or Quicken by downloading it from a web site or from a program DVD. These are referred to as ***traditional apps***.

The ***Microsoft Store*** app is preinstalled on Windows 10 computers. You can also install apps such as Netflix, Trip Advisor, and The Weather Channel from the Microsoft Store. These apps are referred to as ***modern apps*** and look and function similar to apps you install on your smartphone. Many apps in the Microsoft Store are free and others are available for purchase.

▶ **HOW TO:** Add an App from the Microsoft Store

1. Click the **Start** button to open the *Start* menu.
2. Click the **Store** button (tile) to open the Microsoft Store app (Figure Intro-4).
 - If the *Store* tile is not available on the *Start* menu, click **All apps** on the *Start* menu, scroll down, and click **Store** in the alphabetic listing of all apps.
3. Select an app in the Microsoft Store (Figure Intro-5).
 - The Microsoft Store has different categories of apps.
 - You can search for apps by typing key words in the *Search* box in the upper right.
 - When you select an app, a description and screen shots of the app displays.
4. Click the **Free**, **Free trial**, or price button to install the app.
 - You must have a payment method stored in your Microsoft account to purchase apps from the Microsoft Store.
5. Click **Open** to open the installed app.
 - When you install an app, the app is listed in the *Recently added* area on the *Start* menu and *All apps* list of applications.

Intro-4 *Store* button on the *Start* menu

Intro-5 Install an app from the Microsoft Store

Customize the Start Menu

When you start using Windows 10 or after you have installed either traditional or modern apps, you can customize what appears on your *Start* menu and resize the *Start*

menu. When you *pin* an app to the *Start* menu, the app tile remains on the right side of the *Start* menu. Pin the apps you most regularly use, unpin the apps you don't want to display on the *Start* menu, and rearrange and resize apps tiles to your preference.

▶ **HOW TO:** Customize the Start Menu

1. Move an app tile by clicking and dragging the app tile to a new location on the *Start* menu. The other app tiles shuffle to accommodate the placement of the app tile.

2. Remove an app tile from the *Start* menu by right-clicking the app tile you want to remove and selecting **Unpin from Start** from the context menu (Figure Intro-6).
 - The app tile is removed from the *Start* menu, but the program or task is not removed from your computer.

Intro-6 Unpin an app from the *Start* menu

3. Pin an app tile to the *Start* menu by clicking **All apps** at the bottom of the *Start* menu, right-clicking the app to pin, and selecting **Pin to Start** (Figure Intro-7).
 - Drag the newly added app tile to the desired location on the Start menu.

4. Resize an app tile by right-clicking the app tile, selecting **Resize**, and selecting **Small**, **Medium**, **Wide**, or **Large**.
 - Some apps only have *Small*, *Medium*, and *Wide* size options.

Intro-7 Pin an app to the *Start* menu

5. Turn on or off the live tile option by right-clicking the app tile and selecting **Turn live tile on** or **Turn live tile off**.
 - Live tile displays rotating graphics and options on the app tile. When this option is turned off, the name of the app displays on the tile.

6. Uninstall an app by right-clicking the app you want to uninstall and selecting **Uninstall**.
 - Unlike the unpin option, this option uninstalls the program from your computer, not just your *Start* menu.

7. Resize the *Start* menu by clicking and dragging the top or right edge of the *Start* menu.

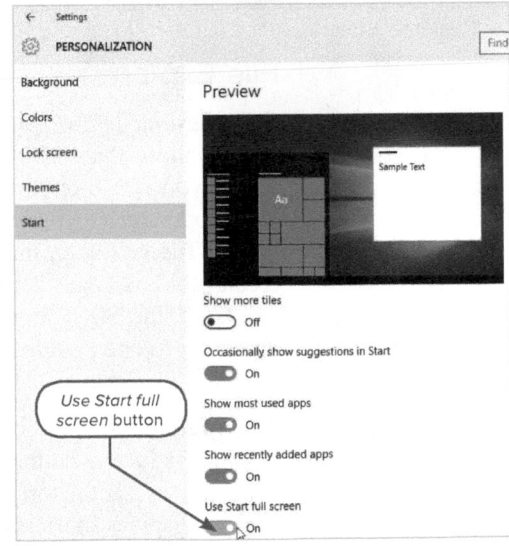

8. Use a full screen *Start* menu by clicking the **Start** button to open the *Start* menu, selecting **Settings** to open the *Settings* window, clicking the **Personalization** button, clicking the **Start** option at the left, selecting **Use Start full screen**, and clicking the **X** in the upper right to close the *Settings* window (Figure Intro-8).
 - The *Start* menu expands to the full screen when opened.

Intro-8 Use full screen *Start* menu

Customize the Taskbar

The *Taskbar* is located at the bottom of the Windows desktop, and you can quickly open an app by clicking a button on the *Taskbar* rather than opening it from the *Start* menu. You can customize the *Taskbar* by pinning, unpinning, and rearranging apps on the *Taskbar*.

▶HOW TO: Customize the Taskbar

1. Pin an app to the *Taskbar* by clicking the *Start* menu, right-clicking an app, clicking **More**, and selecting **Pin to taskbar** (Figure Intro-9).

 • You can also pin an app to the *Taskbar* from the *All apps* list in the *Start* menu.

2. Unpin an app from the *Taskbar* by right-clicking an app on the *Taskbar*, and selecting **Unpin from taskbar** (Figure Intro-10).

 • You can also unpin apps from the *Taskbar* by right-clicking the app in the *Start* menu, clicking **More**, and selecting **Unpin from taskbar**.

3. Rearrange apps on the *Taskbar* by clicking and dragging the app to the desired location on the *Taskbar* and release.

Intro-9 Pin an app to the *Taskbar*

Intro-10 Unpin an app from the *Taskbar*

> ▶ **MORE INFO**
>
> If using a touch screen, you can press and hold an app on the *Start* menu or *Taskbar* to display the app options.

File Explorer

The redesigned *File Explorer* in Windows 10 is a window that opens on your desktop where you can browse for files stored on your computer (Figure Intro-11). You can open a file or folder, move or copy items, create folders, and delete files or folders. Click the **Start** button and select **File Explorer** to open a *File Explorer* window.

The *File Explorer* has different areas:

• *Navigation pane*: The *Navigation* pane displays folders on the left. The ***Quick access*** area at the top of the *Navigation* pane displays shortcuts to favorite folders. You can pin or unpin folders in the *Quick access* area of the *Navigation* pane.

Intro-11 *File Explorer* window

• *Navigation buttons*: The navigation buttons (*Back*, *Forward*, *Recent location*, and *Up*) are located directly above the *Navigation* pane and below the *Ribbon*. Use these buttons to navigate a File Explorer window.

• *Folder pane*: When you select a folder in the *Navigation* pane, the contents of the folder displays in the *Folder* pane to the right of the *Navigation* pane. Double-click a folder or file in the *Folder* pane to open it.

• *Ribbon*: The *Ribbon* at the top of the *File Explorer* is collapsed by default. When you click a tab on the *Ribbon*, it expands to display the options on the tab. The main tabs of

the *Ribbon* are *File*, *Home*, *Share*, and *View*. Other context-sensitive tabs open when you select certain types of files. For example, the *Picture Tool Manage* tab opens when you select a picture file.

- **Quick Access toolbar**: The *Quick Access* toolbar is above the *Ribbon*. From the *Quick Access* toolbar, you can click the **New Folder** button to create a new folder or **Properties** to display the properties of a selected file or folder. You can add buttons, such as *Rename*, to the *Quick Access* toolbar.
- **Search**: The *Search* text box is located on the right of the *File Explorer* window below the *Ribbon*. Type key words in the *Search* text box to find files or folders.

OneDrive

OneDrive is a cloud storage area where you can store files in a private and secure online location that you can access from any computer. When you store your files in *OneDrive*, the files are actually saved on both your computer and on the cloud. *OneDrive* synchronizes your files so when you change a file it is automatically updated on the *OneDrive* cloud.

With Windows 10, the ***OneDrive folder*** is one of your storage location folder options, similar to your *Documents* or *Pictures* folders (Figure Intro-12). You can save, open, and edit your *OneDrive* files from a *File Explorer* folder. Your *OneDrive* folder looks and functions similar to other Windows folders.

In addition to the *OneDrive* folder on your computer, you can also access your *OneDrive* files online using an Internet browser such as Microsoft Edge, Google Chrome, or Mozilla Firefox. When you access *OneDrive* online using a web browser, you can upload files, create folders, move and copy files and folders, and create Office files using *Office Online* (*Office Online* is discussed in *SLO Intro.2: Using Office 2016*).

Intro-12 *OneDrive* folder in a *File Explorer* window

▶ HOW TO: Use OneDrive Online

1. Open an Internet browser window and navigate to the *OneDrive* web site (www.onedrive.live.com), which takes you to the *OneDrive* sign in page.
 - You can use any Internet browser to access *OneDrive* (Microsoft Edge, Google Chrome, Mozilla Firefox).
2. Click the **Sign In** button, type your Microsoft account email address, and click **Next**.
3. Type your Microsoft account password and click **Sign in** (Figure Intro-13). You are taken to your *OneDrive* page.
 - If you are on your own computer, check the **Keep me signed in** box to stay signed in to *OneDrive* when you return to the page.

Intro-13 Log in to *OneDrive* online

- The different areas of *OneDrive* are listed under the *OneDrive* heading on the left (Figure Intro-14).
- Click **Files** to display your folders and files in the folder area.
- At the top of the page, buttons and drop-down menus list the different actions you can perform on selected files and folders.

Intro-14 *OneDrive* online environment

Cortana

In addition to using the search tools in the *File Explorer*, you can also use **Cortana**, which is new in Windows 10. While the search feature in the *File Explorer* searches only for content on your computer, *Cortana* searches for content on your computer, on the Internet, and in the Microsoft Store. You can either type key words for a search or use voice commands to search for content.

When you open *Cortana*, other content, such as weather, upcoming appointments, and popular news stories, displays in the *Cortana* pane.

▶HOW TO: Search Using Cortana

1. Click the **Cortana** button on the *Taskbar* to open the *Cortana* pane (Figure Intro-15).

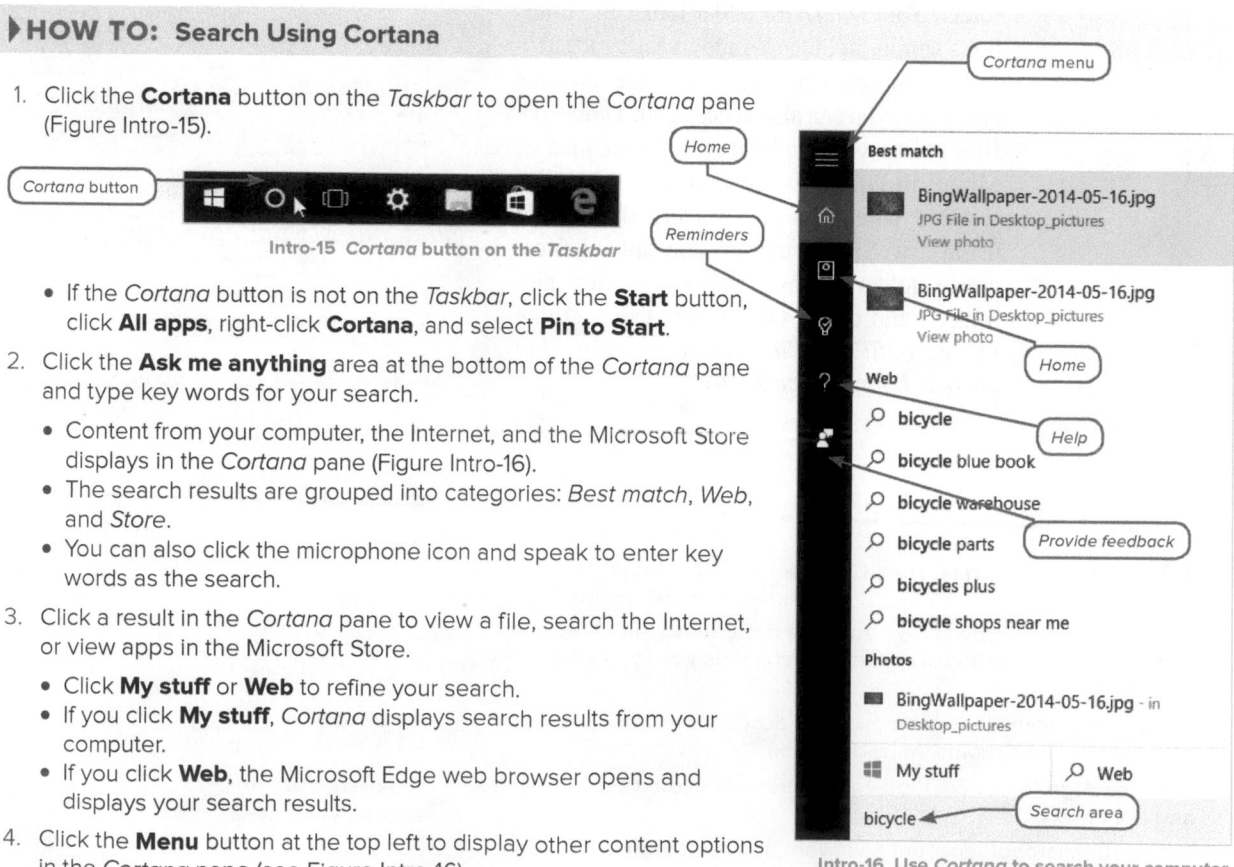

Intro-15 *Cortana* button on the *Taskbar*

- If the *Cortana* button is not on the *Taskbar*, click the **Start** button, click **All apps**, right-click **Cortana**, and select **Pin to Start**.

2. Click the **Ask me anything** area at the bottom of the *Cortana* pane and type key words for your search.

- Content from your computer, the Internet, and the Microsoft Store displays in the *Cortana* pane (Figure Intro-16).
- The search results are grouped into categories: *Best match*, *Web*, and *Store*.
- You can also click the microphone icon and speak to enter key words as the search.

3. Click a result in the *Cortana* pane to view a file, search the Internet, or view apps in the Microsoft Store.

- Click **My stuff** or **Web** to refine your search.
- If you click **My stuff**, *Cortana* displays search results from your computer.
- If you click **Web**, the Microsoft Edge web browser opens and displays your search results.

4. Click the **Menu** button at the top left to display other content options in the *Cortana* pane (see Figure Intro-16).

- The other content options are *Home*, *Notebook*, *Reminders*, *Help*, and *Feedback*.

Intro-16 Use *Cortana* to search your computer, the Internet, and the Microsoft Store

Task View

A new feature to Windows 10 is **Task View**. *Task View* displays all open apps and windows as tiles on your desktop, and you can choose which item to display or close. This feature is very helpful when you have multiple items open and want to select or close one.

▶HOW TO: Use Task View

1. Click the **Task View** button on the *Taskbar* (Figure Intro-17).
 - All open apps and windows display on the desktop (Figure Intro-18).

Intro-17 *Task View* button on the *Taskbar*

Intro-18 *Task View* with open apps and windows displayed on the desktop

2. Select the app or window to open or close.
 - Click a tile to open an app. The app opens and *Task View* closes.
 - Click the **X** in the upper right corner of an app to close an app. *Task View* remains open when you close an app.

Settings

In Windows 10, the **Settings** window is the redesigned *Control Panel* (although the *Control Panel* is still available). The *Settings* window is where you change global Windows settings, customize the Windows environment, add devices, and manage your Microsoft account. Click the **Settings** button on the *Taskbar* or *Start* menu to open the *Settings* window (Figure Intro-19). The following categories are available in the *Settings* window:

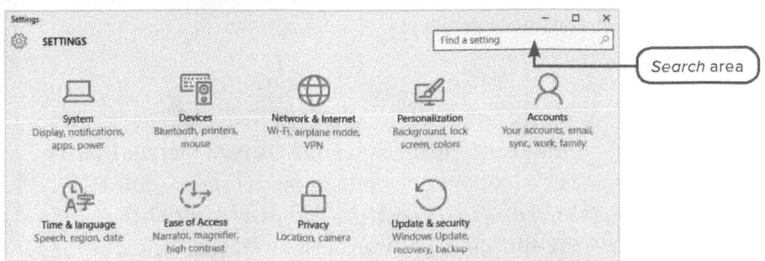

Intro-19 *Settings* window

- *System*: Display, notifications, apps, and power
- *Devices*: Bluetooth, printers, and mouse
- *Network & Internet*: Wi-Fi, airplane mode, and VPN
- *Personalization*: Background, lock screen, and colors
- *Accounts*: Your account, sync settings, work, and family
- *Time & Language*: Speech, region, and date
- *Ease of Access*: Narrator, magnifier, and high contrast
- *Privacy*: Location and camera
- *Update & Security*: Windows Update, recovery, and backup

> **MORE INFO**
>
> If you can't find an item in *Settings*, use the *Search* dialog box (*Find a setting*) in the upper right corner and type key words. If *Settings* is not available on the *Taskbar*, you can find it in the *All apps* list on the *Start* menu.

Action Center

The *Action Center* in Windows 10 provides a quick glance of notifications and buttons to open other commonly used settings and features in Windows. The *Action Center* displays notifications such as emails and Windows update notifications. Or you can click an action button to turn on or off features or open other windows or apps such as the *Settings* menu (*All Settings* button) or OneNote (*Note* button). Click the **Action Center** button on the right side of the *Taskbar* to open the *Action Center* pane on the right side of your screen (Figure Intro-20).

Intro-20 *Action Center*

SLO INTRO. 2

Using Office 2016

Office 2016 includes common software applications such as Word, Excel, Access, and PowerPoint. These applications give you the ability to work with word processing documents, spreadsheets, presentations, and databases in your personal and business projects.

Office 2016 and Office 365

Microsoft Office is a suite of personal and business software applications (Figure Intro-21). *Microsoft Office 2016* and *Microsoft Office 365* are the same software products; the difference is how you purchase the software. Office 2016 is

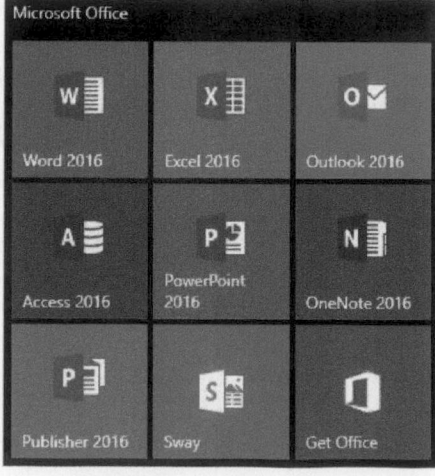

Intro-21 Microsoft Office application tiles on the *Start* menu

the traditional model of purchasing the software, and you own that software for as long as you want to use it. Office 365 is a subscription that you pay monthly or yearly, similar to how you purchase Netflix or Spotify. If you subscribe to Office 365, you automatically receive new versions of the software when they are released.

The common applications typically included in Microsoft Office 2016 and 365 are described in the following list:

- *Microsoft Word*: Word processing software used to create, format, and edit documents such as reports, letters, brochures, and resumes.
- *Microsoft Excel*: Spreadsheet software used to perform calculations on numerical data such as financial statements, budgets, and expense reports.
- *Microsoft Access*: Database software used to store, organize, compile, and report information such as product information, sales data, client information, and employee records.
- *Microsoft PowerPoint*: Presentation software used to graphically present information in slides such as a presentation on a new product or sales trends.
- *Microsoft Outlook*: Email and personal management software used to create and send email and create and store calendar items, contacts, and tasks.
- *Microsoft OneNote*: Note-taking software used to take and organize notes, which can be shared with other Office applications.
- *Microsoft Publisher*: Desktop publishing software used to create professional-looking documents containing text, pictures, and graphics such as catalogs, brochures, and flyers.

Office Desktop Apps, Office Universal Apps, and Office Online

Office desktop apps are the full-function Office 2016 or 365 programs installed on your computer (PC or Mac). Both Office 2016 and Office 365 are considered Office desktop apps. Because of the increased popularity and capabilities of tablets and mobile devices, Office software is also available for both tablets and smartphones. *Office universal apps* are the Office 365 programs that can be installed on tablets or other mobile devices. Office universal apps do not have the full range of advanced features available in Office desktop applications, but Office universal apps provide users the ability to create, edit, save, and share Office files using many of the most common features in the Office suite of programs.

> **MORE INFO**
>
> Office universal apps are also referred to as *Office mobile apps*.

Intro-22 *Office Online*

Office Online is free online software from Microsoft that works in conjunction with your Microsoft account and *OneDrive* (Figure Intro-22). With *Office Online*, you can work with Office files online through a web browser, even on computers that do not have Office 2016 or 365 installed. This is a useful option when you use a computer at a computer lab or use a friend's computer that does not have Office installed.

You can access *Office Online* from your *OneDrive* web page to create and edit Word documents, Excel workbooks, PowerPoint presentations, and OneNote notebooks. *Office Online* is a scaled-down version of Office 2016/365 and not as robust in terms of features, but you can use it to create, edit, print, share, and collaborate on files. If you need more advanced features, you can open *Office Online* files in Office 2016.

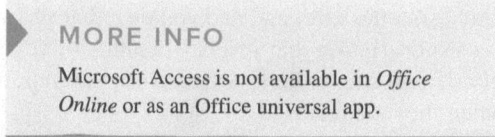

> **MORE INFO**
>
> Microsoft Access is not available in *Office Online* or as an Office universal app.

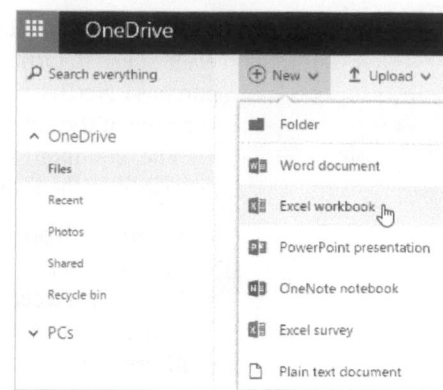

Intro-23 Create an Office Online file from your online *OneDrive* page

▶HOW TO: Create an Office Online File

1. Open an Internet browser Window, navigate to the *OneDrive* web site (www.onedrive.live.com), and log in to *OneDrive*. If you are not already logged in to *OneDrive*, use the following steps.
 - Click the **Sign in** button, type your Microsoft account email address, and click **Next**.
 - Type your Microsoft account password and click **Sign in** to open your *OneDrive* page.
2. Click the **New** button and select the type of *Office Online* file to create (Figure Intro-23).
 - A new file is created and opens in the *Office Online* program.
 - The new file is saved in your *OneDrive* folder (both online and on your computer).
3. Rename the file by clicking on the file name at the top of the file, typing a new file name, and pressing **Enter** (Figure Intro-24).
 - You can also click the **File** tab to open the *Backstage* view, select *Save As*, and choose **Save As** or **Rename**.
 - Click the **OPEN IN [OFFICE APPLICATION]** button (for example **OPEN IN EXCEL**) to open the file in the Office desktop application (see Figure Intro-24).
4. Close the browser tab or window to close the file.
 - *Office Online* automatically saves the file as you make changes.

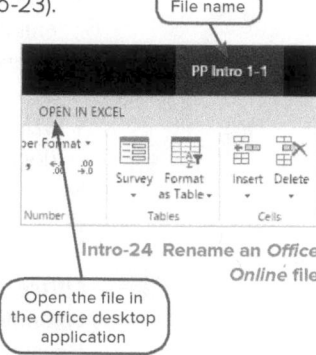

File name

Open the file in the Office desktop application

Intro-24 Rename an *Office Online* file

Open an Office Desktop Application

When using Windows 10, you open an Office desktop application by clicking the application tile on the *Start* menu or the application icon on the *Taskbar*. If your *Start* menu and *Taskbar* do not have the Office applications displayed, click the **Start** button, select **All apps**, and select **Word 2016**, **Excel 2016**, **Access 2016**, or **PowerPoint 2016** to launch the application (Figure Intro-25).

You can also use *Cortana* to quickly locate an Office desktop app (Figure Intro-26).

Intro-25 Open an Office desktop app from the *All apps* area on the *Start* menu

Intro-26 Use *Cortana* to find and open an app

> **MORE INFO**
>
> Add commonly used apps to your Windows *Start* menu and/or *Taskbar* to save you time. See the "Customize the *Start* Menu" and "Customize the *Taskbar*" sections in *SLO Intro.1: Using Windows 10*.

Office Start Page

Most of the Office applications (except Outlook and OneNote) display a ***Start page*** when you launch the application (Figure Intro-27). From this *Start* page, you can create a new blank file (for example a Word document, an Excel workbook, an Access database, or a PowerPoint presentation), create a file from an online template, search for an online template, open a recently used file, or open another file. These options vary depending on the Office application.

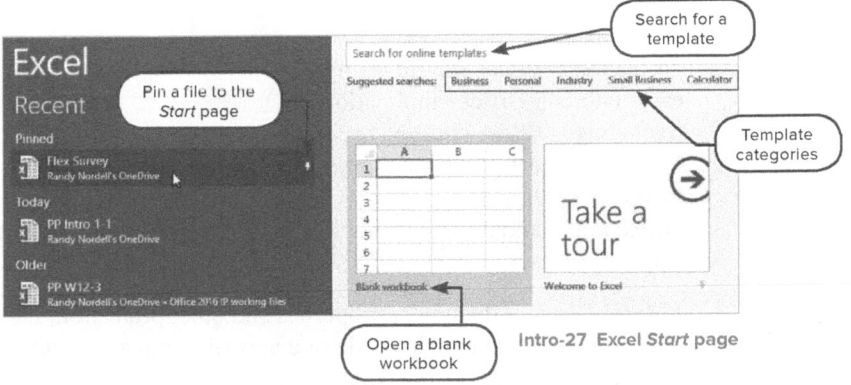

Intro-27 Excel *Start* page

▶HOW TO: Use the Office Start Page

1. Open a file listed in the *Recent* area on the left side of the *Start* menu by clicking the file to open. The file opens in the working area of the Office application.

 • The *Recent* area on the left side of the *Start* page lists files you have recently used and files that are pinned to the *Start* page.

2. Open a new blank file by clicking the **Blank *[file type]*** tile (*Blank workbook*, *Blank document*, etc.) to the right of the *Recent* area.

 • You can also press the **Esc** key to exit the *Start* page and open a new blank file.

3. Open an existing file that is not listed in the *Recent* area by clicking the **Open Other Workbooks** link (Figure Intro-28). The *Open* area on the *Backstage* view displays.

 • Click the **Browse** button to open the *Open* dialog box where you can locate and open a file.
 • You can also select a different location, *OneDrive* or *This PC*, and select a file to open.

4. Open a template by clicking a template file on the right or searching for templates.

 • Search for a template by typing key words in the *Search* area on the *Start* page.
 • Click a link to one of the categories below the *Search* area to display templates in that category.

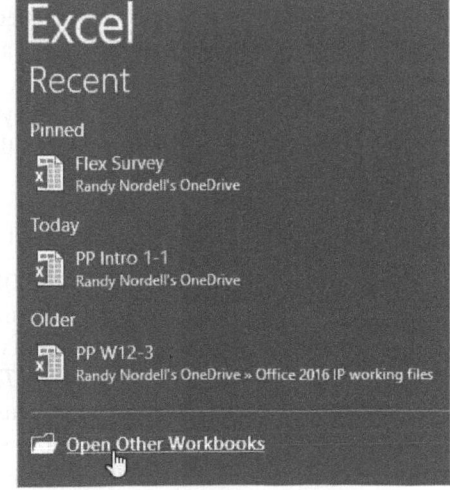

Intro-28 *Open Other Workbooks* link on the *Start* page

5. Pin a frequently used file to the *Start* page by clicking the **Pin** button.
 - The *Pin* button is on the right side of items listed in the *Recent* area and at the bottom right of templates displayed in the *Templates* area (to the right of the *Recent* area).
 - Pinned files display at the top of the *Recent* area.

> **MORE INFO**
>
> In Access, you have to open an existing database or create a new one to enter the program.

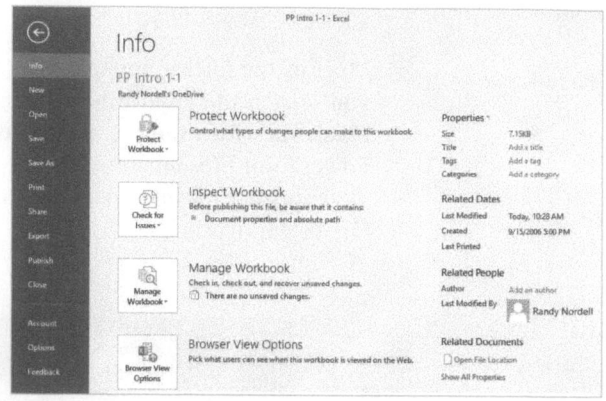

Intro-29 *Backstage* view in Excel

Backstage View

Office incorporates the ***Backstage view*** into all Office applications (including *Office Online* apps). Click the **File** tab on the *Ribbon* to open the *Backstage* view (Figure Intro-29). *Backstage* options vary on the different Office applications. The following list describes common tasks you can perform from the *Backstage* view:

- ***Info***: Displays document properties and other protection, inspection, and version options.
- ***New***: Creates a new blank file or a new file from a template or theme.
- ***Open***: Opens an existing file from a designated location or a recently opened file.
- ***Save***: Saves a file. If the file has not been named, the *Save As* dialog box opens when you select this option.
- ***Save As***: Opens the *Save As* dialog box.
- ***Print***: Prints a file, displays a preview of the file, or displays print options.
- ***Share***: Invites people to share a file or email a file.
- ***Export***: Creates a PDF file from a file or saves as a different file type.
- ***Close***: Closes an open file.
- ***Account***: Displays your Microsoft account information.
- ***Options***: Opens the *[Application] Options* dialog box (for example *Excel Options*).

Office Help—Tell Me

In all the Office 2016/365 applications, ***Tell Me*** is the new help feature (Figure Intro-30). This new help feature displays the commands in the Office application related to your search. The *Help* feature in older versions of Office displayed articles describing the feature and how to use it. The new *Tell Me* feature provides command options that take you directly to a command or dialog box. For example if you type *PivotTable* in the *Tell Me* search box in Excel, the results include the option to open the *Create PivotTable* dialog box, as well as other options such as *Recommended PivotTables* and *Summarize with PivotTable*.

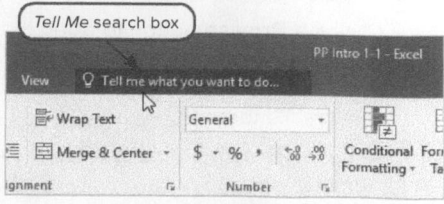

Intro-30 *Tell Me* search box

▶ HOW TO: Use Tell Me

1. Place your insertion point in the **Tell Me** search box at the top of the *Ribbon* (see Figure Intro-30).

2. Type key words for the command or feature for which you are searching.

3. Select an option from the list of displayed search results (Figure Intro-31).

 • When you select a search result, it may apply a command, open a dialog box, or display a gallery of command choices.

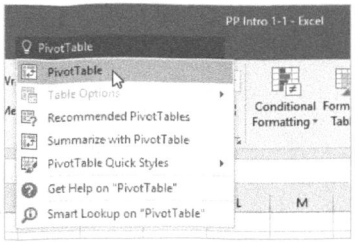

Intro-31 *Tell Me* search results

▶ **ANOTHER WAY**

Alt+Q places the insertion point in the *Tell Me* dialog box.
The previous *Help* feature is still available in Office 2016/365. Press **F1** to open the *Help* dialog box.

Mouse and Pointers

If you are using Office on a desktop or laptop computer, use your mouse (or touch pad) to navigate around files, click tabs and buttons, select text and objects, move text and objects, and resize objects. The following table lists mouse and pointer terminology used in Office:

Mouse and Pointer Terminology

Term	Description
Pointer	When you move your mouse, the pointer moves on your screen. A variety of pointers are used in different contexts in Office applications. The following pointers are available in most of the Office applications (the appearance of these pointers varies depending on the application and the context used): • *Selection pointer:* Select text or an object. • *Move pointer:* Move text or an object. • *Copy pointer:* Copy text or an object. • *Resize pointer:* Resize objects or table columns or rows. • *Crosshair:* Draw a shape.
Insertion point	The vertical flashing line indicating where you type text in a file or text box. Click the left mouse button to position the insertion point.
Click	Click the left mouse button. Used to select an object or button or to place the insertion point in the selected location.
Double-click	Click the left mouse button twice. Used to select text.
Right-click	Click the right mouse button. Used to display the context menu and the mini toolbar.
Scroll	Use the scroll wheel on the mouse to scroll up and down through your file. You can also use the horizontal or vertical scroll bars at the bottom and right of an Office file window to move around in a file.

Touch Mode and Touch Screen Gestures

The new user interface in Windows 10 and Office 2016 has improved touch features to facilitate the use of Windows and the Office applications on a tablet computer or smartphone. On tablets and smartphones, you use a touch screen rather than using a mouse, so the process of selecting text and objects and navigating around a file is different from a computer without a touch screen.

In Office 2016/365, *Touch mode* optimizes the Office working environment when using a computer with a touch screen to provide more space between buttons and commands. Click the **Touch/Mouse Mode** button on the *Quick Access* toolbar (upper left of the Office app window) and select **Touch** from the drop-down list to enable *Touch* mode (Figure Intro-32). To turn off *Touch* mode, select **Mouse** from the *Touch/Mouse Mode* drop-down list.

Intro-32 Turn on *Touch* mode

Quick Access toolbar

> **MORE INFO**
>
> The *Touch/Mouse Mode* button displays on the *Quick Access* toolbar when using a touch-screen computer.

The following table lists common gestures used when working on a tablet or smartphone (these gestures vary depending on the application used and the context):

Touch Screen Gestures

Gesture	Used To	How To
Tap	Select text or an object or position the insertion point. Double tap to edit text in an object or cell.	
Pinch	Zoom in or resize an object.	
Stretch	Zoom out or resize an object.	
Slide	Move an object or selected text.	
Swipe	Select text or multiple objects.	

> **MORE INFO**
>
> Window 10 has a *Tablet mode* that optimizes all of Windows and apps for touch screens. When you turn on the *Tablet mode* feature in Windows, the *Touch mode* in Office apps turns on automatically. Click the **Action Center** button on the Windows *Taskbar* and click the **Tablet mode** button to turn on this feature in Windows.

Creating, Saving, Closing, and Opening Files

Creating, saving, opening, and closing files is primarily done from the *Start* page or *Backstage* view of the Office application you are using. These areas provide you with many options and a central location to perform these tasks. You can also use shortcut commands to create, save, and open files.

Create a New File

When you create a new file in an Office application, you can create a new blank file or a new file based on a template (in PowerPoint, you can also create a presentation based on a theme). On the *Start* page, click **Blank [file type]** to create a new blank file in the application you are using (in Word, you begin with a blank document; in Excel, a blank workbook; in Access, a blank desktop database; and in PowerPoint, a blank presentation).

> **HOW TO: Create a New File from the Start Page**

1. Open the Office application you want to use. The *Start* page displays when the application opens (Figure Intro-33).

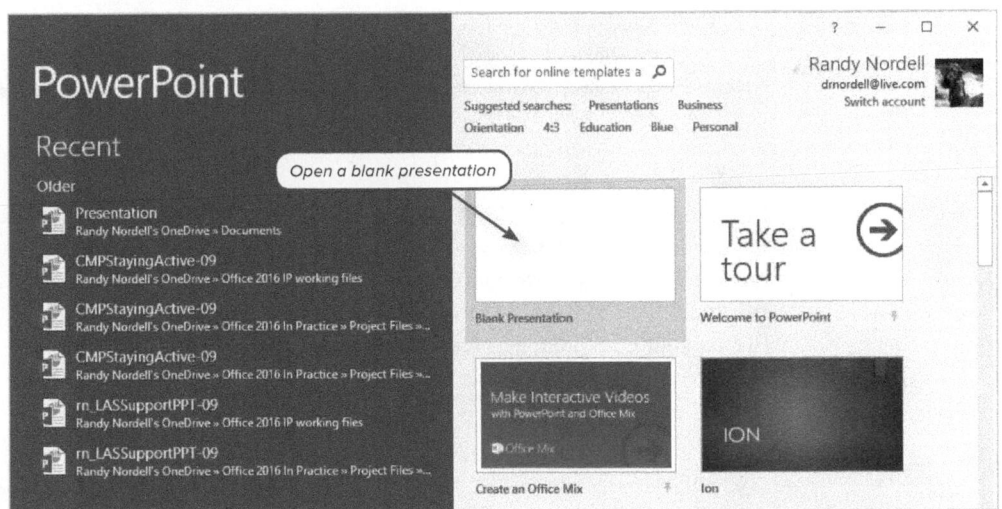

Intro-33 *Start* page in PowerPoint

2. Click **Blank [file type]** or select a template or theme to use for your new blank file. A new file opens in the application you are using.
 - The new file is given a generic file name (for example *Document1*, *Book1*, or *Presentation1*). You can name and save this file later.
 - When creating a new Access database, you are prompted to name the new file when you create it.
 - A variety of templates (and themes in PowerPoint only) display on the *Start* page, but you can search for additional online templates and themes using the *Search* text box at the top of the *Start* page.

> **MORE INFO**
> **Esc** closes the *Start* page and takes you into the Office application (except in Access).

If you have been using an application already and want to create a new file, you create it from the *Backstage* view. From the *Backstage* view, the new file options are available in the *New* area.

▶**HOW TO:** Create a New File from the Backstage View

1. Click the **File** tab to display the *Backstage* view.
2. Select **New** on the left to display the *New* area (Figure Intro-34).
3. Click **Blank [file type]** or select a template or theme to use in your new blank file. A new file opens in the application.
 - The new file is given a generic file name (*Document1*, *Book1*, or *Presentation1*). You can name and save this file later.
 - When you are creating a new Access database, you are prompted to name the new file when you create it.

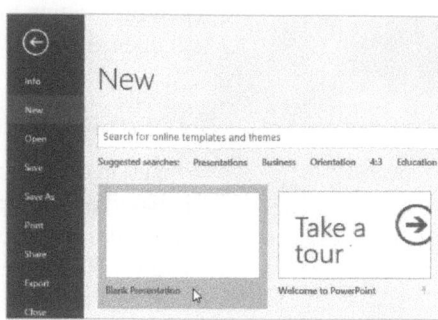

Intro-34 *New* area on the *Backstage* view in PowerPoint

▶ ANOTHER WAY

Ctrl+N opens a new file from within an Office application. In Access, **Ctrl+N** opens the *New* area in the *Backstage* view.

Save a File

In Access, you name a file as you create it, but in Word, Excel, and PowerPoint, you name a file after you have created it. When you save a file, you type a name for the file and select the location to save the file. You can save a file on your computer, an online storage location such as *OneDrive*, or portable device, such as a USB drive.

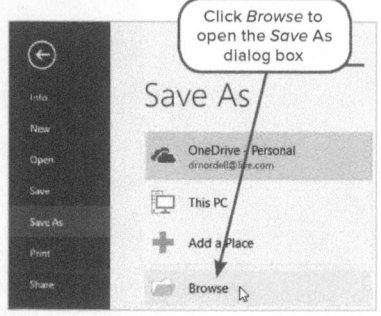

Click *Browse* to open the *Save* As dialog box

Intro-35 *Save As* area on the *Backstage* view in PowerPoint

▶**HOW TO:** Save a File

1. Click the **File** tab to display the *Backstage* view.
2. Select **Save** or **Save As** on the left to display the *Save As* area (Figure Intro-35).
 - If the file has not already been saved, clicking *Save* or *Save As* takes you to the *Save As* area on the *Backstage* view.
3. Click the **Browse** button to open the *Save As* dialog box (Figure Intro-36).
 - You can also select a different location (*OneDrive* or *This PC*) and select a folder from the list of folders at the right to open the *Save As* dialog box.
4. Select a location to save the file in the *Folder* list on the left.

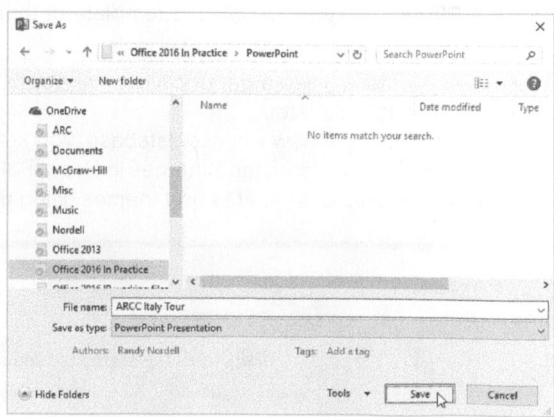

Intro-36 *Save As* dialog box

5. Type a name for the file in the *File name* area.
 * By default, Office selects the file type, but you can change the file type from the *Save as type* drop-down list.
6. Click **Save** to close the dialog box and save the file.

▶ ANOTHER WAY

Ctrl+S opens the *Save As* area on the *Backstage* view when a file has not been named. If a file has already been named, **Ctrl+S** saves the file without opening the *Backstage* view.

▶ MORE INFO

If you save a file in *OneDrive*, you have access to that file from any computer with Internet access. Also, you can share and collaborate on files stored in *OneDrive*. *OneDrive* is one of the folders in the *Save As* dialog box.

Create a New Folder When Saving a File

When saving files, it is a good idea to create folders to organize your files. Organizing your files in folders makes it easier to find your files and saves you time when you are searching for a specific file (see *SLO Intro.8: Organizing and Customizing Folders and Files* for more information on this topic). When you save an Office file, you can also create a folder in which to store that file.

▶ **HOW TO:** Create a New Folder When Saving a File

1. Click the **File** tab to display the *Backstage* view.
2. Select **Save As** on the left to display the *Save As* area.
3. Click **Browse** to open the *Save As* dialog box.
4. Select a location to save the file in the *Folder* list on the left.
5. Click the **New Folder** button to create a new folder (Figure Intro-37).
6. Type a name for the new folder and press **Enter**.

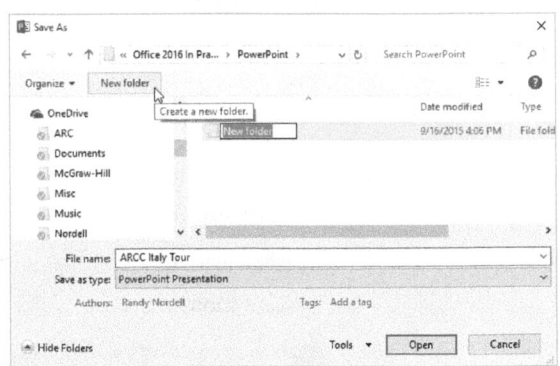

Intro-37 Create a new folder

▶ ANOTHER WAY

F12 opens the *Save As* dialog box (except in Access). On a laptop, you might have to press **Fn+F12**. See more about the *Fn* (Function) key in *SLO Intro.7: Using Context Menus, the Mini Toolbars, and Keyboard Shortcuts*.

Save As a Different File Name

After you have saved a file, you can save it again with a different file name. If you do this, you have preserved the original file, and you can continue to revise the second file for a different purpose.

▶ **HOW TO:** Save as a Different File Name

1. Click the **File** tab to display the *Backstage* view.
2. Select **Save As** on the left to display the *Save As* area.
3. Click the **Browse** button to open the *Save As* dialog box.
4. Select a location to save the file in the *Folder* list on the left.
5. Type a new name for the file in the *File name* area.
6. Click **Save** to close the dialog box and save the file.

Office 2016 File Types

When you save an Office file, by default Office saves the file in the most recent file format for that application. You also have the option of saving files in older versions of the Office application you are using. For example, you can save a Word document as an older version to share with or send to someone who uses an older version of Word. Each file has an extension at the end of the file name that determines the file type. The ***file name extension*** is automatically added to a file when you save it. The following table lists common file types used in the different Office applications:

Office File Types

File Type	Extension	File Type	Extension
Word Document	.docx	Access Database	.accdb
Word Template	.dotx	Access Template	.accdt
Word 97-2003 Document	.doc	Access Database (2000-2003 format)	.mdb
Rich Text Format	.rtf	PowerPoint Presentation	.pptx
Excel Workbook	.xlsx	PowerPoint Template	.potx
Excel Template	.xltx	PowerPoint 97-2003 Presentation	.ppt
Excel 97-2003 Workbook	.xls	Portable Document Format (PDF)	.pdf
Comma Separated Values (CSV)	.csv		

Close a File

You can close a file using the following different methods:

- Click the **File** tab and select **Close** on the left.
- Press **Ctrl+W**.
- Click the **X** in the upper right corner of the file window. This method closes the file and the program if only one file is open in the application.

When you close a file, you are prompted to save the file if it has not been named or if changes were made after the file was last saved (Figure Intro-38). Click **Save** to save and close the file or click **Don't Save** to close the file without saving. Click **Cancel** to return to the file.

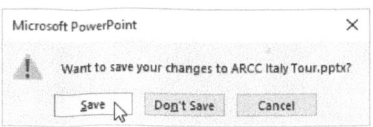

Intro-38 Prompt to save a document before closing

Open an Existing File

You can open an existing file from the *Start* page when you open an Office application or while you are working on another Office file.

▶**HOW TO: Open a File from the Start Page**

1. Open an Office application to display the *Start* page.
2. Select a file to open in the *Recent* area on the left (Figure Intro-39). The file opens in the Office application.
 - If you select a file in the *Recent* area that has been renamed, moved, or on a storage device not connected to the computer, you receive an error message.
3. Alternatively, click the **Open Other [file type]** (for example *Open Other Presentations*) (see Figure Intro-39) link to open the *Open* area of the *Backstage* view (Figure Intro-40).

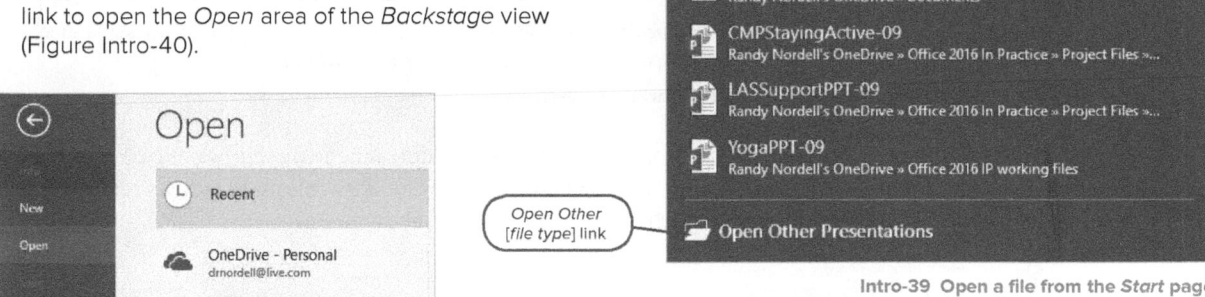

Intro-39 Open a file from the *Start* page

Intro-40 *Open* area on the *Backstage* view

4. Click the **Browse** button to open the *Open* dialog box (Figure Intro-41).
5. Select a location from the *Folder* list on the left.
6. Select the file to open and click the **Open** button.
 - If the file opens in *Protected View*, click the **Enable Editing** button to allow you to edit the file.

Intro-41 *Open* dialog box

When working on a file in an Office application, you might want to open another file. You can open an existing file from within an Office application from the *Open* area on the *Backstage* view.

MORE INFO

When opening a file from an online location, Office may open the file in *Protected* view. If the file opens in *Protected View*, click the **Enable Editing** button to allow you to edit the file.

▶**HOW TO:** Open a File from the Backstage View

1. Click the **File** tab from within an open Office application to open the *Backstage* view.
2. Click **Open** on the left to display the *Open* area on the *Backstage* view (see Figure Intro-40).
3. Click the **Browse** button to open the *Open* dialog box (see Figure Intro-41).
 - You can also select a file to open from the list of *Recent* files on the right of the *Open* area on the *Backstage* view.
4. Select a location from the *Folder* list on the left.
5. Select the file to open and click the **Open** button.
 - If the file opens in *Protected View*, click the **Enable Editing** button to allow you to edit the file.

ANOTHER WAY

Press **Ctrl+F12** to open the *Open* dialog box when you are in the working area of an Office application (except in Access). On some laptops, you might have to press **Fn+Ctrl+F12**.

You can also open a file from a *File Explorer* folder. When you double-click a file in a *File Explorer* folder, the file opens in the appropriate Office application. Windows recognizes the file name extension and launches the correct Office application.

PAUSE & PRACTICE: INTRO-1

For this project, you log in to Windows using your Microsoft account, customize the Windows *Start* menu and *Taskbar*, create and save a PowerPoint presentation, create a folder, open and rename an Excel workbook, and use Windows 10 features.

File Needed: **ARCC2018Budget-Intro.xlsx** *(Student data files are available in the* Library *of your SIMnet account)*
Completed Project File Names: **[your initials] PP Intro-1a.pptx** and **[your initials] PP Intro-1b.xlsx**

1. Log in to Windows using your Microsoft account if you are not already logged in.
 a. If you don't have a Microsoft account, you can create a free account at https://signup.live.com.
 b. If you are using a computer on your college campus, you may be required to log in to the computer using your college user name and password.

2. Customize the *Start* menu to include Office 2016 apps. If these apps tiles are already on the *Start* menu, skip steps 2a–e. You can pin other apps of your choice to the *Start* menu.
 a. Click the **Start** button at the bottom left of your screen to open the *Start* menu.

b. Click **All apps** at the bottom left of the *Start* menu (Figure Intro-42). The list of apps installed on the computer displays on the left side of the *Start* menu.

c. Locate and right-click **Access 2016** and select **Pin to Start** (Figure Intro-43). The app displays as a tile on the right side of the *Start* menu.

d. Repeat step 2c to pin **Excel 2016**, **PowerPoint 2016**, and **Word 2016** apps to the *Start* menu.

e. Display the *Start* menu and drag these Office app tiles so they are close to each other.

f. Click the **Start** button (or press the **Esc** key) to close the *Start* menu.

Intro-42 *All apps* button on the *Start* menu

3. Use *Cortana* and the *Start* menu to pin Office 2016 apps to the *Taskbar*.

a. Click the **Cortana** button (to the right of the *Start* button) on the *Taskbar* and type Access. *Cortana* displays content matching your search.

b. Right-click the **Access 2016** option near the top of the *Cortana* pane and select **Pin to taskbar** (Figure Intro-44). The app pins to the *Taskbar*.

c. Click the **Start** button to open the *Start* menu.

d. Right-click the **Excel 2016** tile on the right side of the *Start* menu, click **More**, and select **Pin to taskbar**. The app pins to the *Taskbar*.

e. Use either of the methods described above to pin the **PowerPoint 2016** and **Word 2016** apps to the *Taskbar*.

f. Drag the Office apps on the *Taskbar* to rearrange them to your preference.

Intro-43 Pin Access 2016 app to *Start* menu

Intro-44 Use *Cortana* to find an Office app and pin it to the *Taskbar*

4. Create a PowerPoint presentation and save the presentation in a new folder.

a. Click the **PowerPoint 2016** app tile on your *Start* menu to open the application.

b. Click **Blank Presentation** on the PowerPoint *Start* page to create a new blank presentation.

c. Click the **Click to add title** placeholder and type American River Cycling Club to replace the place-holder text.

d. Click the **File** tab to open the *Backstage* view and click **Save As** on the left to display the *Save As* area.

e. Click **Browse** to open the *Save As* dialog box (Figure Intro-45).

f. Select a location to save the file from the *Folder* list on the left. If the *OneDrive* folder is an option, select **OneDrive**. If it is not, select the **Documents** folder in the *This PC* folder. You can also save to a portable storage device if you have one.

g. Click the **New Folder** button to create a new folder.

h. Type American River Cycling Club as the name of the new folder and press **Enter** (Figure Intro-46).

i. Double-click the **American River Cycling Club** folder to open it.

Intro-45 *Save As* area on the *Backstage* view in PowerPoint

j. Type [your initials] PP Intro-1a in the *File name* area.

k. Click **Save** to close the dialog box and save the presentation. Leave the file and PowerPoint open.

5. Open an Excel file and save as a different file name.

a. Return to the Windows *Start* menu.

b. Click the **Excel 2016** app button on the *Taskbar* to open it.

c. Click the **Open Other Workbooks** link on the bottom left of the Excel *Start* page to display the *Open* area of the *Backstage* view.

d. Click **Browse** to open the *Open* dialog box (Figure Intro-47).

e. Browse to your student data files and select the *ARCC2018Budget-Intro* file.

f. Click **Open** to open the workbook. If the file opens in *Protected View*, click the **Enable Editing** button.

g. Click the **File** tab to open the *Backstage* view.

h. Click **Save As** on the left to display the *Save As* area and click **Browse** to open the *Save As* dialog box.

i. Locate the **American River Cycling Club** folder (created in step 4h) in the *Folder* list on the left and double-click the folder to open it.

j. Type [your initials] PP Intro-1b in the *File name* area.

k. Click **Save** to close the dialog box and save the workbook. Leave the file and Excel open.

6. Use the *Tell Me* feature in Excel to find a command.

a. Click the **Tell Me** search box on the *Ribbon* of the Excel window and type PivotTable (Figure Intro-48).

b. Click **PivotTable** to open the *Create PivotTable* dialog box.

c. Click the **X** in the upper right corner of the *Create PivotTable* dialog box to close it.

7. Open the *Microsoft Store* app, the *Action Center*, and the *Settings* window.

a. Click the **Cortana** button and type Microsoft Store.

b. Click **Store** at the top of the *Cortana* pane to open the *Store* app.

c. Click **Apps** in the top left and browse the available apps in the Microsoft Store.

d. Click the **Minimize** button in the upper right corner of the *Store* window to minimize this app (Figure Intro-49). The app is still open, but it is minimized on the *Taskbar*.

e. Click the **Action Center** button on the right side of the *Taskbar* to display the *Action Center* pane at the right (Figure Intro-50).

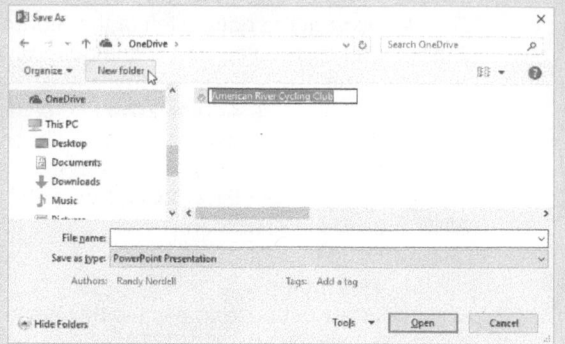

Intro-46 Create a new folder from the *Save As* dialog box

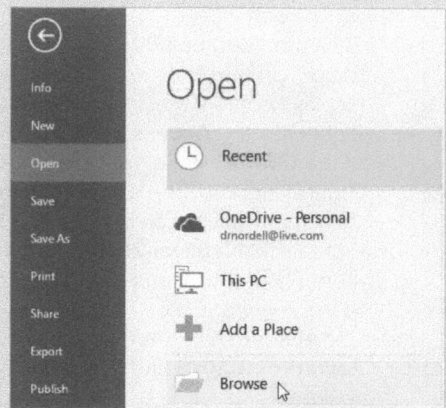

Intro-47 *Open* area on the *Backstage* view

Intro-48 Use the *Tell Me* feature to find a command

Intro-49 *Minimize* button on an app window

Intro-50 Windows 10 *Action Center*

f. Click **All settings** to open the *Settings* window.

g. Click the **Find a setting** search box, type Printer, and view the search results.

h. Click the **Minimize** button to minimize the *Settings* windows to the *Taskbar*.

8. Use the *Task View* feature to open and close apps and windows.

a. Click the **Task View** button on the left side of the *Taskbar* (Figure Intro-51). All of the open apps and windows are tiled on the Windows desktop.

b. Click the **Store** app to open it. *Task View* closes and the *Store* app displays on your Windows desktop.

c. Click the **Task View** button again.

d. Click the **X** in the upper right corner to close each open app and window. You may be prompted to save changes to a file.

e. Click the **Task View** button again or press **Esc** to return to the desktop.

Intro-51 *Task View* button on the *Taskbar*

SLO INTRO. 4

Working with Files

When you work with Office files, a variety of display views are available. You can change how a file displays, adjust the display size, work with multiple files, and arrange the windows to view multiple files. Because most people work with multiple files at the same time, Office makes it easy and intuitive to move from one file to another or to display multiple document windows at the same time.

File Views

Each of the different Office applications provides you with a variety of ways to view your document. In Word, Excel, and PowerPoint, the different views are available on the *View tab* (Figure Intro-52). You can also change views using the buttons on the right side of the *Status bar* at the bottom of the file window (Figure Intro-53). In Access, the differ-

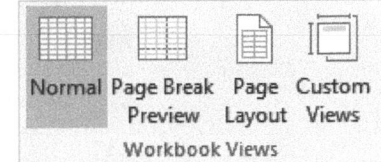

Intro-52 *Workbook Views* group on the *View* tab in Excel

Intro-53 PowerPoint views on the *Status* bar

ent views for each object are available in the *Views* group on the *Home* tab.

The following table lists the views that are available in each of the different Office applications:

File Views

Office Application	Views	Office Application	Views
Word	*Read Mode* *Print Layout* *Web Layout* *Outline* *Draft*	**Access** *(Access views vary depending on active object)*	*Layout View* *Design View* *Datasheet View* *Form View* *SQL View* *Report View* *Print Preview*
Excel	*Normal* *Page Break Preview* *Page Layout* *Custom Views*	**PowerPoint**	*Normal* *Outline View* *Slide Sorter* *Notes Page* *Reading View* *Presenter View*

Change Display Size

You can use the *Zoom* feature to increase or decrease the display size of your file. Using *Zoom* to change the display size does not change the actual size of text or objects in your file; it only changes the size of your display. For example, if you change the *Zoom* level to 120%, you increase the display of your file to 120% of its normal size (100%), but changing the display size does not affect the actual size of text and objects in your file. You could also decrease the *Zoom* level to 80% to display more of your file on the screen.

You can increase or decrease the *Zoom* level several different ways. Your *Zoom* options vary depending on the Office application you are using.

- ***Zoom level*** *on the Status* bar (Figure Intro-54): Click the **+** or **−** button to increase or decrease *Zoom* level in 10% increments.
- ***Zoom group*** *on the View tab* (Figure Intro-55): The *Zoom* group includes a variety of *Zoom* options. The options vary depending on the Office application.
- ***Zoom dialog box*** (Figure Intro-56): Click the **Zoom** button in the *Zoom* group on the *View* tab or click the **Zoom level** on the *Status* bar to open the *Zoom* dialog box.

Intro-54 *Zoom* area on the *Status* bar in PowerPoint

> **MORE INFO**
>
> The *Zoom* feature is only available in Access in *Print Preview* view when you are working with reports.

Intro-55 *Zoom* group in Excel

Manage Multiple Open Files and Windows

When you are working on multiple files in an Office application, each file is opened in a new window. You can *minimize* an open window to place the file on the Windows *Taskbar* (the bar at the bottom of the Windows desktop), *restore down* an open window so it does not fill the entire computer screen, or *maximize* a window so it fills the entire computer screen. The *Minimize, Restore Down/Maximize*, and *Close* buttons are in the upper right of a file window (Figure Intro-57).

Intro-56 *Zoom* dialog box in Word

> **MORE INFO**
>
> You can open only one Access file at a time. If you open another Access file, the first one closes.

Intro-57 Window options buttons

- *Minimize*: Click the **Minimize** button (see Figure Intro-57) to hide the active window. When a document is minimized, it is not closed. It is minimized to the *Taskbar* so the window is not displayed on your screen. Place your pointer on the application icon on the Windows *Taskbar* to display thumbnails of open files. You can click an open file thumbnail to display the file (Figure Intro-58).
- *Restore Down/Maximize*: Click the **Restore Down/Maximize** (see Figure Intro-57) button to decrease the size of an open window or maximize the window to fill the entire screen. This button toggles between *Restore Down* and *Maximize*. When a window is

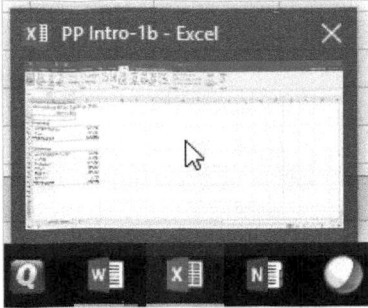

Intro-58 Display minimized file on the *Taskbar*

restored down, you can change the size of a window by clicking and dragging a border of the window. You can also move the window by clicking and dragging the title bar at the top of the window.
- *Close*: Click the **Close** button (see Figure Intro-57) to close the window. If there is only one open file, the Office application also closes when you click the *Close* button on the file.

You can switch between open files or arrange the open files to display more than one window at the same time. The following are several methods to do this:

- *Switch Windows button*: Click the **Switch Windows** button [*View* tab, *Window* group] (not available in Access) to display a drop-down list of open files. Click a file from the drop-down list to display the file.

> **ANOTHER WAY**
>
> Click the Windows **Task View** button on the *Taskbar* to tile all open windows and apps on the desktop.

- *Windows Taskbar*: Place your pointer on an Office application icon on the Windows *Taskbar* to display the open files in that application. Click a file thumbnail to display it (see Figure Intro-58).
- *Arrange All button*: Click the **Arrange All** button [*View* tab, *Window* group] to display all windows in an application. You can resize or move the open file windows.

Snap Assist

The *Snap Assist* feature in Windows provides the ability to position an open window to the left or right side of your computer screen and fill half the screen. When you snap an open window to the left or right side of the screen, the other open windows tile on the opposite side where you can select another window to fill the opposite side of the computer screen (Figure Intro-59).

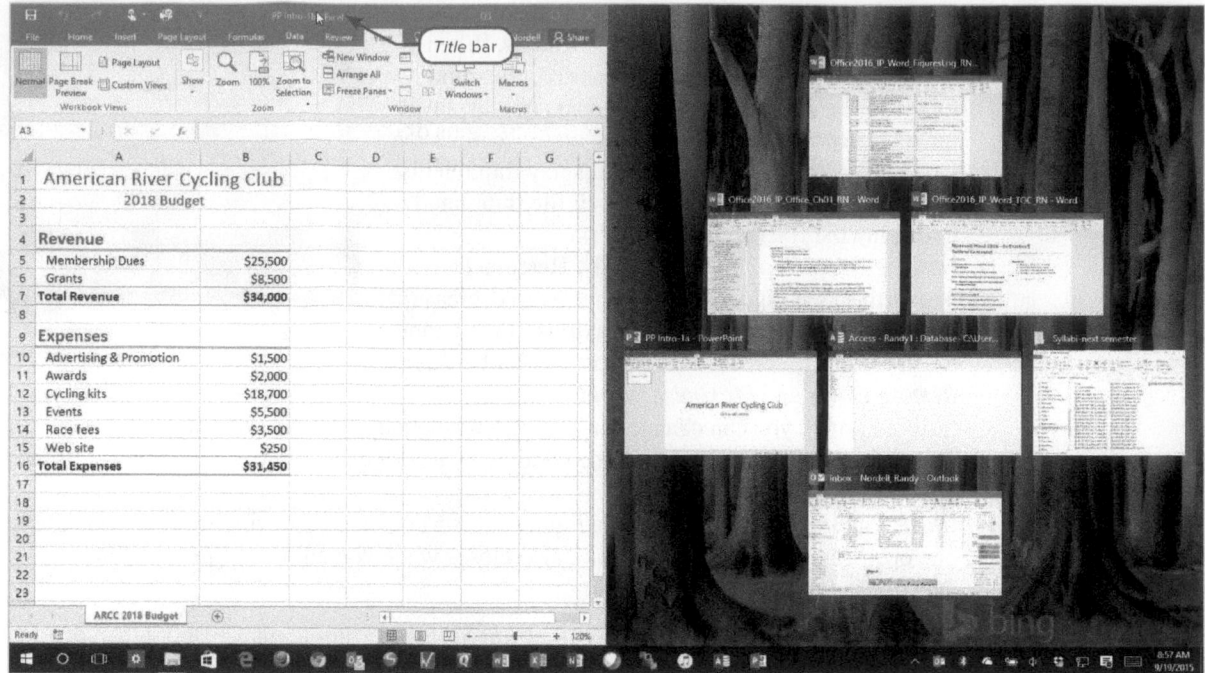

Intro-59 Windows *Snap Assist* feature

▶**HOW TO: Use Snap Assist**

1. Click the **title bar** of an open window.
2. Drag it to the left or right edge of the computer screen and release the pointer.
 - The window snaps to the side of the screen and fills half of the computer screen (see Figure Intro-59).
 - The other open windows and apps display as tiles on the opposite side.
 - If you're using a touch screen computer, you can use *Snap Assist* by pressing and holding the title bar of an open window and dragging to either side of the computer screen.
3. Select a tile of an open window or app to fill the other half of the screen.

▶ MORE INFO

Snap Assist also allows you to snap a window to a quadrant (quarter rather than half) of your screen. Drag the **title bar** of an open window to one of the four corners of your computer screen.

SLO INTRO. 5

Printing, Sharing, and Customizing Files

On the *Backstage* view of any of the Office applications, you can print a file and customize how a file is printed. You can also export an Office file as a PDF file in most of the Office applications. In addition, you can add and customize document properties for an Office file and share a file in a variety of formats.

Print a File

You can print an Office file if you need a hard copy. The *Print* area on the *Backstage* view displays a preview of the open file and many print options. For example, you can choose which page or pages to print and change the margins of the file in the *Print* area. Print settings vary depending on the Office application you are using and what you are printing.

▶ HOW TO: Print a File

1. Open the file you want to print from a Windows folder or within an Office program.
2. Click the **File** tab to open the *Backstage* view.
3. Click **Print** on the left to display the *Print* area (Figure Intro-60).
 - A preview of the file displays on the right. Click the **Show Margins** button to adjust margins or **Zoom to Page** button to change the view in the *Preview* area. The *Show Margins* button is only available in Excel.
4. Change the number of copies to print in the *Copies* area.
5. Click the **Printer** drop-down list to choose from available printers.
6. Customize what is printed and how it is printed in the *Settings* area.
 - The *Settings* options vary depending on the Office application you are using and what you are printing.
 - In the *Pages* area (*Slides* area in PowerPoint), you can select a page or range of pages (slides) to print.
 - By default all pages (slides) are printed when you print a file.
7. Click the **Print** button to print your file.

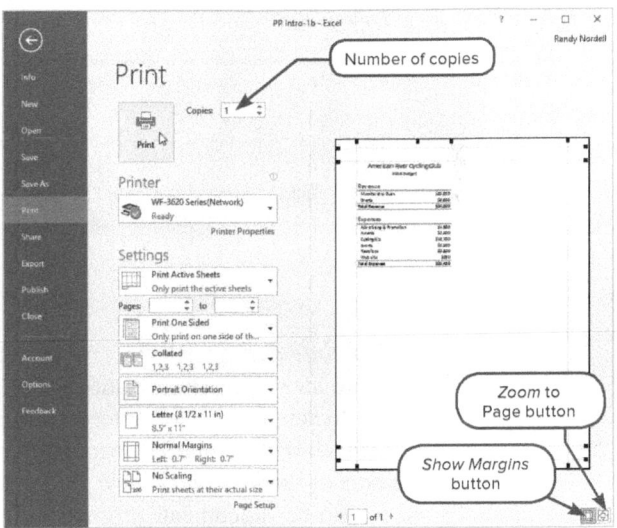

Intro-60 *Print* area on the *Backstage* view

▶ ANOTHER WAY

Press **Ctrl+P** to open the *Print* area on the *Backstage* view.

Export as a PDF File

Portable document format, or *PDF*, is a specific file format that is often used to share files that are not to be changed or to post files on a web site. When you create a PDF file from an Office application file, you are actually exporting a static image of the original file, similar to taking a picture of the file.

The advantage of working with a PDF file is that the format of the file is retained no matter who opens the file. PDF files open in the Windows Reader app or Adobe Reader, which is free software that is installed on most computers. Because a PDF file is a static image of a file, it is not easy for other people to edit your files. When you want people to be able to view a file but not change it, PDF files are a good choice.

▶**HOW TO:** Export a File as a PDF File

1. Open the file you want to export as a PDF file.
2. Click the **File** tab and click **Export** to display the *Export* area on the Backstage view (Figure Intro-61).
3. Select **Create PDF/XPS Document** and click the **Create PDF/XPS**. The *Publish as PDF or XPS* dialog box opens.
 - XPS (XML Paper Specification) format is an alternative to a PDF file. XPS is a Microsoft format and is not widely used.
4. Select a location to save the file.
5. Type a name for the file in the *File name* area.
6. Click **Publish** to close the dialog box and save the PDF file.
 - A PDF version of your file may open. You can view the file and then close it.

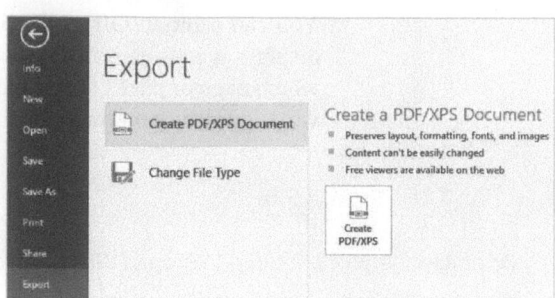

Intro-61 *Export* a file as a PDF file

> **MORE INFO**
>
> Microsoft Word can open PDF files, and you can edit and save the file as a Word document.

Document Properties

Document properties are hidden codes in a file that store identifying information about that file. Each piece of document property information is called a ***field***. You can view and modify document properties in the *Info* area of the *Backstage* view.

Some document properties fields are automatically generated when you work on a file, such as *Size*, *Total Editing Time*, *Created*, and *Last Modified*. Other document properties fields, such as *Title*, *Comments*, *Subject*, *Company*, and *Author*, can be modified. You can use document property fields in different ways such as inserting the *Company* field in a document footer.

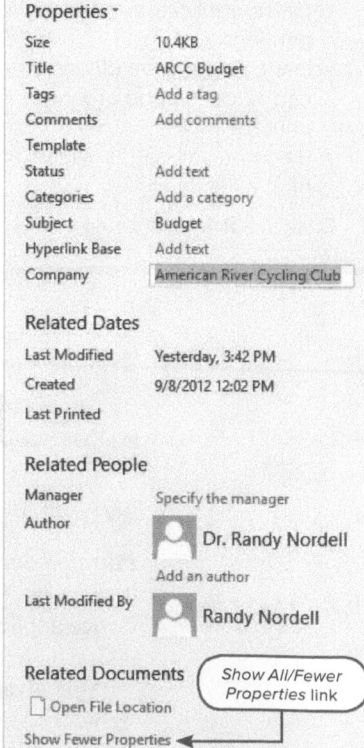

Intro-62 Document properties

▶**HOW TO:** View and Modify Document Properties

1. Click the **File** tab and click **Info**. The document properties display on the right (Figure Intro-62).
2. Click the text box area of a field that can be edited and type your custom document property information.
3. Click the **Show All Properties** link at the bottom to display additional document properties.
 - Click **Show Fewer Properties** to collapse the list and display fewer properties.
 - This link toggles between *Show All Properties* and *Show Fewer Properties*.
4. Click the **Back** arrow to return to the file.

Share a File

Windows 10 and Office 2016 have been enhanced to help you share files and collaborate with others. The *Share* area on the *Backstage* view lists different options for sharing files from within an Office application. When you save a file to your *OneDrive*, Office provides a variety of options to share your file (Figure Intro-63). The two main sharing options are *Share with People* and *Email*. Within these two categories, you have a variety of ways to share a file with others. Your sharing options vary depending on the Office application you are using. The following list describes the sharing options available in the Office applications:

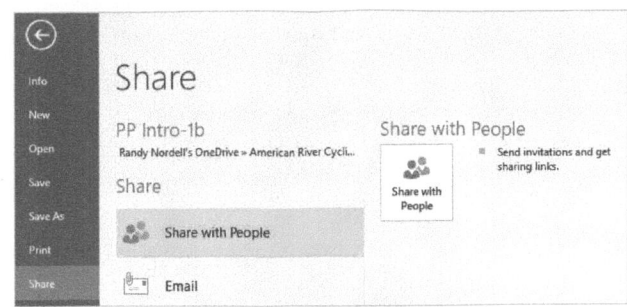

Intro-63 *Share* options on the *Backstage* view

- **Word**: *Share with People, Email, Present Online*, and *Post to Blog*
- **Excel**: *Share with People* and *Email*
- **Access**: No *Sharing* option on the *Backstage* view
- **PowerPoint**: *Share with People, Email, Present Online*, and *Publish Slides*

▶HOW TO: Share a File

1. Click the **File** tab to open the *Backstage* view and select **Share** on the left.
 - If your file is not saved in *OneDrive*, you are directed to first save the file to the cloud (*OneDrive*). Click the **Save to Cloud** button and save your file in *OneDrive*.
 - If your file is not saved to *OneDrive*, you will not have all available sharing options.
2. Share a *OneDrive* file with others by clicking **Share with People** on the left and then clicking the **Share with People** button on the right (see Figure Intro-63).
 - The *Backstage* view closes and the *Share* pane opens on the right side of the file (Figure Intro-64).
 - Alternatively, click the **Share** button in the upper right corner of the Office application window to open the *Share* pane (Figure Intro-65).
 - Type an email address in the *Invite people* text box. If you want to share the file with more than one person, separate email addresses with a semicolon.
 - Select **Can edit** or **Can view** from the permission drop-down list, which controls what others can do with your file.
 - You can include a message the recipients will receive.
 - Click the **Share** button below the message to send a sharing email to recipients.
 - Alternatively, click the **Get a sharing link** option at the bottom of the *Share* pane to create an *edit link* or *view-only link* (Figure Intro-66). You can then copy the sharing link and email it to others or post it in an online location.

Intro-64 *Share* pane

Intro-65 *The Share button* opens the *Share* pane

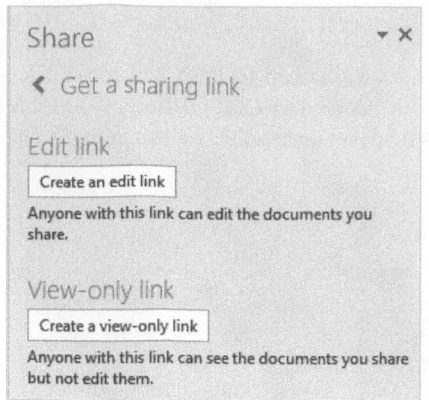

Intro-66 *Get a sharing link* options in the *Share* pane

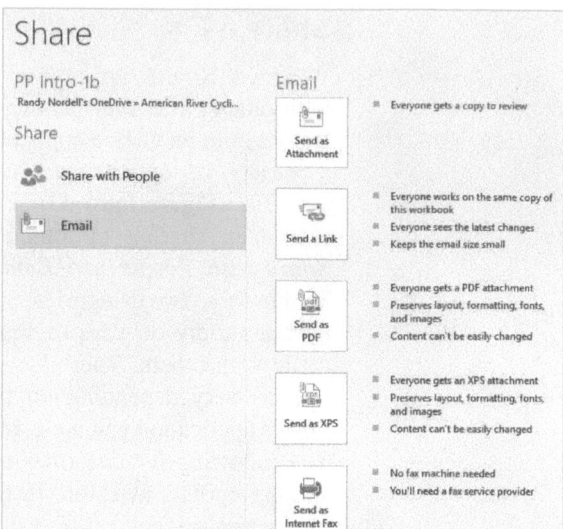

Intro-67 *Email* share options in the *Share* area on the *Backstage* view

3. Share a file through email by clicking the **Email** button on the left side of the *Share* area on the *Backstage* view and selecting an option (Figure Intro-67).

 - These *Email* share options use Microsoft Outlook (email and personal management Office application) to share the selected file through email.
 - The *Email* share options include *Send as Attachment*, *Send a Link*, *Send as PDF*, *Send as XPS*, and *Send as Internet Fax*.
 - A description of each of these *Email* share options are provided to the right of each option.

> **MORE INFO**
>
> Sharing options are also available if you save files to other online storage locations such as **Dropbox** and **Box**.

Program Options

Using the program options, you can apply global changes to the Office program. For example, you can change the default save location to your *OneDrive* folder or you can turn off the *Start* page that opens when you open an Office application.

 Click the **File** tab and select **Options** on the left to open the **[Program] Options** dialog box (Word Options, Excel Options, etc.) (Figure Intro-68). Click one of the categories on the left to display the category options on the right. The categories and options vary depending on the Office application you are using.

Intro-68 *Excel Options* dialog box

SLO INTRO. 6

Using the Ribbon, Tabs, and Quick Access Toolbar

You can use the *Ribbon*, tabs, groups, buttons, drop-down lists, dialog boxes, task panes, galleries, and the *Quick Access* toolbar to modify your Office files. This section describes different tools you can use to customize your files.

The Ribbon, Tabs, and Groups

The **Ribbon**, which appears at the top of an Office file window, displays the many features available to use on your files. The *Ribbon* is a collection of **tabs**. On each tab are **groups** of features. The tabs and groups that are available on each Office application vary. Click a tab to display the groups and features available on that tab.

Some tabs always display on the *Ribbon* (for example the *File* tab and *Home* tabs). Other tabs are **context-sensitive**, which means that they only appear on the *Ribbon* when you select a specific object. Figure Intro-69 displays the context-sensitive *Table Tools Field* tab that displays in Access when you open a table.

Intro-69 Context-sensitive *Table Tools Fields* tab displayed

Ribbon Display Options

The *Ribbon* displays by default in Office applications, but you can customize how the *Ribbon* displays. The **Ribbon Display Options** button is in the upper right corner of an Office application window (Figure Intro-70). Click the **Ribbon Display Options** button to select one of the three options:

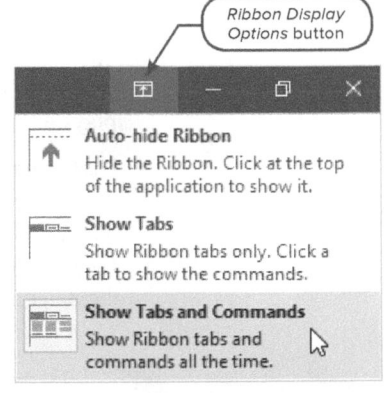

- **Auto-Hide Ribbon**: Hides the *Ribbon*. Click at the top of the application to display the *Ribbon*.
- **Show Tabs**: *Ribbon* tabs display. Click a tab to open the *Ribbon* and display the tab.
- **Show Tabs and Commands**: Displays the *Ribbon* and tabs, which is the default setting in Office applications.

Intro-70 *Ribbon Display Options*

> **MORE INFO**
>
> **Ctrl+F1** collapses or expands the *Ribbon*.

Buttons, Drop-Down Lists, and Galleries

Groups on each of the tabs contain a variety of **buttons**, **drop-down lists**, and **galleries**. The following list describes each of these features and how they are used:

- **Button**: Applies a feature to selected text or object. Click a button to apply the feature (Figure Intro-71).

- *Drop-down list*: Displays the various options available for a feature. Some buttons are drop-down lists only, so when you click one of these buttons the drop-down list of options appears (Figure Intro-72). Other buttons are *split buttons*, which have both a button you click to apply a feature and an arrow you click to display a drop-down list of options (Figure Intro-73).
- *Gallery*: Displays a collection of option buttons. Click an option in a gallery to apply the feature. Figure Intro-74 is the *Styles* gallery. You can click the **More** button to display the entire gallery of options or click the **Up** or **Down** arrow to display a different row of options.

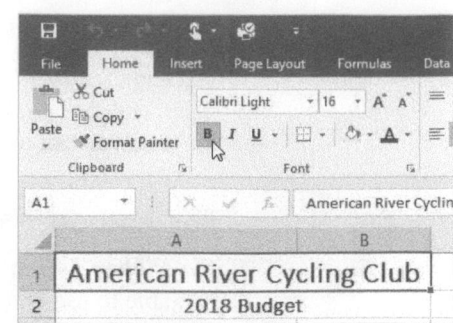

Intro-71 *Bold* button in the *Font* group on the *Home* tab

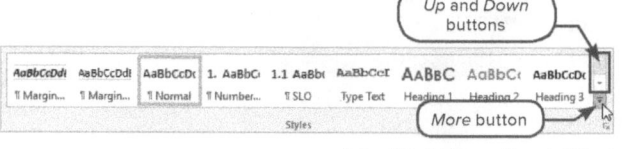

Intro-74 *Styles* gallery in Word

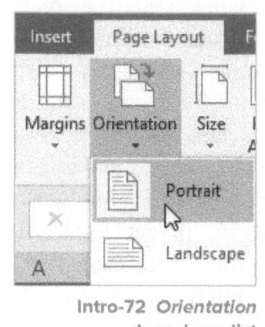

Intro-72 *Orientation* drop-down list

Intro-73 *Merge & Center* split button—button and drop-down list

Dialog Boxes, Task Panes, and Launchers

Not all of the features that are available in an Office application are displayed in the groups on the tabs. Additional options for some groups display in a *dialog box* or *task pane*. A *launcher*, which is a small square in the bottom right of some groups, opens a dialog box or displays a task pane when you click it (see Figure Intro-76).

- *Dialog box*: A new window that opens to display additional features. You can move a dialog box by clicking and dragging the title bar, which is the top of the dialog box where the title is displayed. Figure Intro-75 shows the *Format Cells* dialog box that opens when you click the *Alignment* launcher in Excel.

Intro-75 *Format Cells* dialog box

Intro-76 *Clipboard* pane

- ***Task pane***: Opens on the left or right of the Office application window. Figure Intro-76 shows the *Clipboard* pane, which is available in all Office applications. Task panes are named according to their feature (for example *Clipboard* pane or *Navigation* pane). You can resize a task pane by clicking and dragging its left or right border. Click the **X** in the upper right corner to close a task pane.

ScreenTips

ScreenTips display descriptive information about a button, drop-down list, launcher, or gallery selection. When you place your pointer on an item on the *Ribbon*, a *ScreenTip* displays information about the selection (Figure Intro-77). The *ScreenTip* appears temporarily and displays the command name, keyboard shortcut (if available), and a description of the command.

Intro-77 *Align Left ScreenTip*

Radio Buttons, Check Boxes, and Text Boxes

Dialog boxes and task panes contain a variety of features you can apply using ***radio buttons***, ***check boxes***, ***text boxes***, ***drop-down lists***, and other buttons (Figure Intro-78).

- ***Radio button***: A round button you click to select one option from a list of options. A selected radio button has a solid dot inside the round button.
- ***Check box***: A square button you click to select one or more options. A check appears in a check box you have selected.
- ***Text box***: An area where you can type text.

A task pane or dialog box may also include drop-down lists or other buttons that open additional dialog boxes. Figure Intro-78 shows the *Page Setup* dialog box in Excel, which includes a variety of radio buttons, check boxes, text boxes, drop-down lists, and other buttons that open additional dialog boxes (for example the *Print* and *Options* buttons).

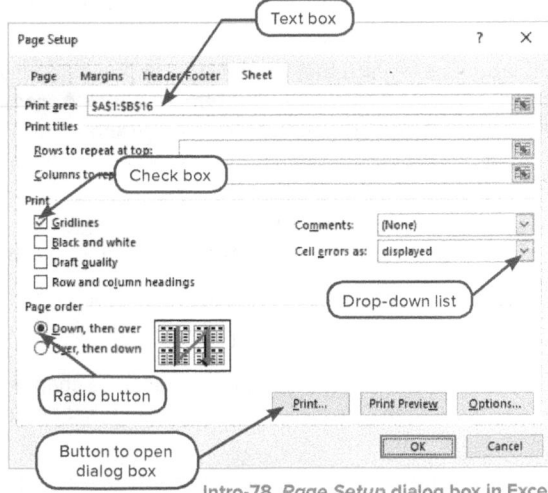

Intro-78 *Page Setup* dialog box in Excel

Quick Access Toolbar

The ***Quick Access toolbar*** is located above the *Ribbon* on the upper left of each Office application window. It contains buttons to apply commonly used commands such as *Save*, *Undo*, *Redo*, and *Open* (Figure Intro-79). The *Undo* button is a split button. You can click the

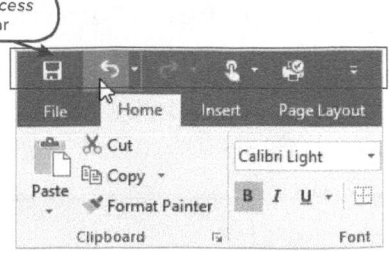

Intro-79 *Quick Access* toolbar

button to undo the last action performed or you can click the drop-down arrow to display and undo multiple previous actions.

Customize the Quick Access Toolbar

You can customize the *Quick Access* toolbar to include features you regularly use, such as *Quick Print*, *New*, and *Spelling & Grammar*. The following steps show how to customize the *Quick Access* toolbar in Word. The customization process is similar for the *Quick Access* toolbar in the other Office applications.

▶**HOW TO:** Customize the Quick Access Toolbar

1. Click the **Customize Quick Access Toolbar** drop-down list on the right edge of the *Quick Access* toolbar (Figure Intro-80).

2. Select a command to add to the *Quick Access* toolbar. The command displays on the *Quick Access* toolbar.

 • Items on the *Customize Quick Access Toolbar* drop-down list with a check mark are commands that are displayed on the *Quick Access* toolbar.
 • Deselect a checked item to remove it from the *Quick Access* toolbar.

3. Add a command that is not listed on the *Customize Quick Access Toolbar* by clicking the **Customize Quick Access Toolbar** drop-down list and selecting **More Commands**. The *Word Options* dialog box opens with the *Quick Access Toolbar* area displayed (Figure Intro-81).

4. Click the **Customize Quick Access Toolbar** drop-down list on the right and select **For all documents** or the current document.

 • If you select *For all documents*, the change is made to the *Quick Access* toolbar for all documents you open in Word.
 • If you select the current document, the change is made to the *Quick Access* toolbar in that document only.

5. Select the command to add from the alphabetic list of commands on the left and click the **Add** button.

 • If you can't find the command you're looking for, click the **Choose commands from** drop-down list and select **All Commands**.
 • The list on the right contains the commands that display on the *Quick Access* toolbar.

6. Rearrange commands on the *Quick Access* toolbar by selecting a command in the list on the right and clicking the **Move Up** or **Move Down** button.

7. Click **OK** to close the *Word Options* dialog box.

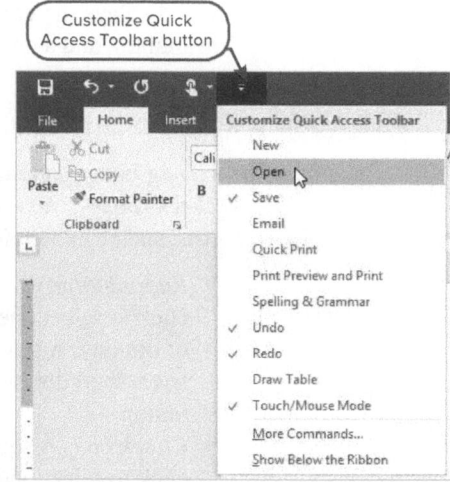

Intro-80 Add a command to the *Quick Access* toolbar

Intro-81 Customize the *Quick Access* toolbar in the *Word Options* dialog box

> **ANOTHER WAY**
>
> To remove an item from the *Quick Access* toolbar, right-click an item and select **Remove from Quick Access Toolbar.**

SLO INTRO. 7

Using Context Menus, the Mini Toolbars, and Keyboard Shortcuts

Most of the commands you use for formatting and editing your files display in groups on the tabs. But many of these features are also available using content menus, mini toolbars, and keyboard shortcuts. You can use these tools to quickly apply formatting or other options to text or objects.

Context Menu

A *context menu* displays when you right-click text, a cell, or an object such as a picture, drawing object, chart, or *SmartArt* (Figure Intro-82). The context menu is a vertical list of options, and the options are context-sensitive, which means they vary depending on what you right-click.

Context menus include options that perform an action (*Cut* or *Copy*), open a dialog box or task pane (*Format Cells* or *Hyperlink*), or display a drop-down list of selections (*Filter* or *Sort*).

Mini Toolbar

The *mini toolbar* is another context menu that displays when you right-click or select text, a cell, or an object in your file (see Figure Intro-82). The

Intro-82 Context menu and mini toolbar

mini toolbar is a horizontal rectangular menu that lists a variety of formatting options. These options vary depending on what you select or right-click. The mini toolbar contains a variety of buttons and drop-down lists. The mini toolbar typically displays above the context menu. The mini toolbar automatically displays when you select text or an object, such as when you select a row of a table in Word or PowerPoint.

Keyboard Shortcuts

You can also use a *keyboard shortcut* to quickly apply formatting or perform commands. A keyboard shortcut is a combination of keyboard keys that you press at the same time. These can include the **Ctrl**, **Shift**, **Alt**, letter, number, and function keys (for example **F1** or **F7**). The following table lists common Office keyboard shortcuts.

Common Office Keyboard Shortcuts

Keyboard Shortcut	Action or Displays	Keyboard Shortcut	Action or Displays
Ctrl+S	Save	Ctrl+Z	Undo
F12	*Save As* dialog *box*	Ctrl+Y	Redo or Repeat
Ctrl+O	*Open* area on the *Backstage* view	Ctrl+1	Single space
Shift+F12	*Open* dialog box	Ctrl+2	Double space
Ctrl+N	New blank file	Ctrl+L	Align left
Ctrl+P	*Print* area on the *Backstage* view	Ctrl+E	Align center
Ctrl+C	Copy	Ctrl+R	Align right
Ctrl+X	Cut	F1	*Help* dialog box
Ctrl+V	Paste	F7	*Spelling* pane
Ctrl+B	Bold	Ctrl+A	Select All
Ctrl+I	Italic	Ctrl+Home	Move to the beginning
Ctrl+U	Underline	Ctrl+End	Move to the end

> **MORE INFO**
> See Appendix A for additional Office 2016 keyboard shortcuts.

Function Keys on a Laptop

When using a laptop computer, function keys perform specific Windows actions on your laptop, such as increase or decrease speaker volume, open Windows *Settings*, or adjust the screen brightness. So when using a numbered function key, such as **F12** as a shortcut to open the *Save As* dialog box in an Office application, you may need to press the ***function key*** (**Fn** or **fn**) on your keyboard in conjunction with a numbered function key to activate the command (Figure Intro-83). The *function key* is typically located near the bottom left of your laptop keyboard next to the *Ctrl* key.

Intro-83 Function key

PAUSE & PRACTICE: INTRO-2

For this project, you work with a document for the American River Cycling Club. You modify the existing document, add document properties, customize the *Quick Access* toolbar, export the document as a PDF file, and share the document.

File Needed: **ARCCTraining-Intro.docx** *(Student data files are available in the* Library *of your SIMnet account)*
Completed Project File Names: *[your initials]* **PP Intro-2a.docx** and *[your initials]* **PP Intro-2b.pdf**

1. Open Word 2016 and open the ***ARCCTraining-Intro*** file from your student data files. If the file opens in *Protected View*, click the **Enable Editing** button.

2. Save this document as [your initials] PP Intro-2a in the *American River Cycling Club* folder in your *OneDrive* folder.
 a. In *Pause & Practice Intro-1*, you created the *American River Cycling Club* folder in *OneDrive* or other storage area. Save this file in the same location.
 b. If you don't save this file in *OneDrive*, you will not be able to complete steps 7 and 9 in this project.

3. Use a button, drop-down list, and dialog box to modify the document.
 a. Select the first heading, "**What is Maximum Heart Rate?**"
 b. Click the **Bold** button [*Home* tab, *Font* group].
 c. Click the **Underline** drop-down arrow and select **Double underline** (Figure Intro-84).
 d. Click the **launcher** in the *Font* group [*Home* tab] to open the *Font* dialog box (Figure Intro-85).
 e. In the *Size* area, select **12** from the list or type 12 in the text box.
 f. In the *Effects* area, click the **Small caps** check box to select it.
 g. Click **OK** to close the dialog box and apply the formatting changes.
 h. Select the next heading, "**What is Target Heart Rate?**"
 i. Repeat steps 3b–g to apply formatting to selected text.

4. Add document properties.
 a. Click the **File** tab to display the *Backstage* view.
 b. Select **Info** on the left. The document properties display on the right.
 c. Click the **Add a title** text box and type ARCC Training.
 d. Click the **Show All Properties** link near the bottom to display additional document properties.
 e. Click the **Specify the subject** text box and type Heart rate training.
 f. Click the **Specify the company** text box and type American River Cycling Club.
 g. Click the **Back** arrow on the upper left to close the *Backstage* view and return to the document.

5. Customize the *Quick Access* toolbar.
 a. Click the **Customize Quick Access Toolbar** drop-down arrow and select **Open** (Figure Intro-86).
 b. Click the **Customize Quick Access Toolbar** drop-down arrow again and select **Spelling & Grammar**.

Intro-84 Apply *Double underline* to selected text.

Intro-85 *Font* dialog box

Intro-86 *Customize Quick Access Toolbar* drop-down list

c. Click the **Customize Quick Access Toolbar** drop-down arrow again and select **More Commands**. The *Word Options* dialog box opens (Figure Intro-87).

d. Select **Insert Comment** in the list of commands on the left.

e. Click the **Add** button to add it to your *Quick Access* toolbar list on the right.

f. Click **OK** to close the *Word Options* dialog box.

g. Click the **Save** button on the *Quick Access* toolbar to save the document.

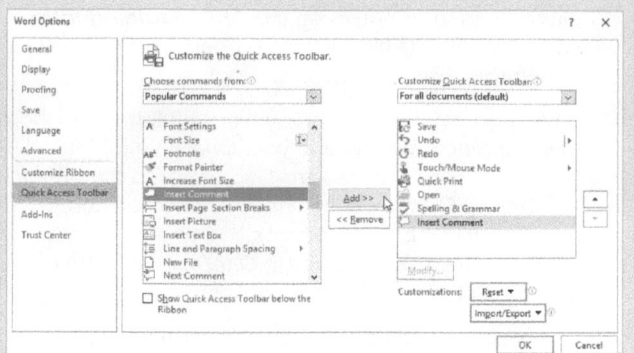

Intro-87 Customize the *Quick Access* toolbar in the *Word Options* dialog box

6. Export the file as a PDF file.

a. Click the **File** tab to go to the *Backstage* view.

b. Select **Export** on the left.

c. Select **Create PDF/XPS Document** and click the **Create PDF/XPS** button. The *Publish as PDF or XPS* dialog box opens (Figure Intro-88).

d. Select the **American River Cycling Club** folder in your *OneDrive* folder as the location to save the file.

e. Type [your initials] PP Intro-2b in the *File name* area.

f. Deselect the **Open file after publishing** check box if it is checked.

g. Select the **Standard (publishing online and printing)** radio button in the *Optimize for* area.

h. Click **Publish** to close the dialog box and create a PDF version of your file.

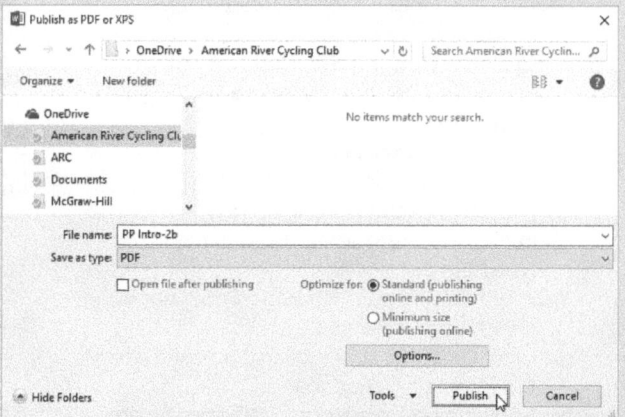

Intro-88 *Publish as PDF or XPS* dialog box

7. Get a link to share a document with your instructor. If your file is not saved in *OneDrive*, skip steps 7 and 9.

a. Click the **Share** button in the upper right of the Word window. The *Share* pane opens on the right side of your document.

b. Click **Get a sharing link** at the bottom of the *Share* pane.

c. Click the **Create an edit link** button.

d. Click **Copy** to copy the edit link (Figure Intro-89).

Intro-89 Copy a sharing link

8. Save and close the document (Figure Intro-90).

American River Cycling Club

www.arcc.org Cycling...a way of life info@arcc.org

WHAT IS MAXIMUM HEART RATE?

The maximum heart rate is the highest your pulse rate can get. To calculate your **predicted maximum heart rate**, use this formula:

(Example: a 40-year-old's predicted maximum heart rate is 180.)

Your actual maximum heart rate can be determined by a graded exercise test. Please note that some medicines and medical conditions might affect your maximum heart rate. If you are taking medicines or have a medical condition (such as heart disease, high blood pressure, or diabetes), always ask your doctor if your maximum heart rate/target heart rate will be affected.

WHAT IS TARGET HEART RATE?

You gain the most benefits and decrease the risk of injury when you exercise in your target heart rate zone. Usually this is when your exercise heart rate (pulse) is 60 percent to 85 percent of your maximum heart rate. Do not exercise above 85 percent of your maximum heart rate. This increases both cardiovascular and orthopedic risk and does not add any extra benefit.

When beginning an exercise program, you might need to gradually build up to a level that is within your target heart rate zone, especially if you have not exercised regularly before. If the exercise feels too hard, slow down. You will reduce your risk of injury and enjoy the exercise more if you don't try to over-do it.

To find out if you are exercising in your target zone (between 60 percent and 85 percent of your maximum heart rate), use your heart rate monitor to track your heart rate. If your pulse is below your target zone (see the chart below), increase your rate of exercise. If your pulse is above your target zone, decrease your rate of exercise.

MAX AND TARGET HEART RATES

AGE	PREDICTED MAX HEART RATE	TARGET HEART RATE (60-85% OF MAX)
20	✓ 200	120-170
25	✓ 195	117-166
30	✓ 190	114-162
35	✓ 185	111-157
40	✓ 180	108-153
45	✓ 175	105-149
50	✓ 170	102-145
55	✓ 165	99-140
60	✓ 160	96-136
65	✓ 155	93-132
70	✓ 150	90-128

Intro-90 PP Intro-2a completed

9. Email the sharing link to your instructor.
 a. Using your email account, create a new email to send to your instructor.
 b. Include an appropriate subject line and a brief message in the body.
 c. Press **Ctrl+V** to paste the link to your document in the body of the email.
 d. Send the email message.

Organizing and Customizing Folders and Files

The more you use your computer to create and use files, the more important it is to stay organized. You can use *folders* to store related files, which makes it easier for you to find, edit, and share your files. For example, you can create a folder for the college you attend. Inside the college folder, you can create a folder for each of your courses. Inside each of the course folders you might create a folder for student data files, solution files, and group projects. Folders can store any type of files; you are not limited to Office files.

Create a Folder

In *SLO Intro.3: Creating, Saving, Closing, and Opening Files*, you learned how to create a new folder when saving an Office file in the *Save As* dialog box. You can also create a Windows folder using *File Explorer*. You can create folders inside other folders.

▶HOW TO: Create a Windows Folder

1. Click the **Start** button and select **File Explorer** to open a *File Explorer* window.
 - Your folders and computer locations are listed on the left.
2. Select the location in the *Navigation* pane on the left where you want to create a new folder.
3. Click **Home** tab, and click the **New folder** button [*New* group]. A new folder is created (Figure Intro-91).
 - The *New Folder* button is also on the *Quick Access* toolbar in the *File Explorer* window.
4. Type the name of the new folder and press **Enter**.

Intro-91 Create a new Windows folder

▶ ANOTHER WAY

Ctrl+Shift+N creates a new folder in a Windows folder.

Move and Copy Files and Folders

Moving a file or folder is cutting it from one location and pasting it in another location. Copying a file or folder creates a copy of it, and you can paste in another location so the file or folder is in two or more locations. If you move or copy a folder, the files in the folder are moved or copied with the folder. Move or copy files and folders using the *Move to* or *Copy to* buttons on the *Home* tab of *File Explorer*, keyboard shortcuts (**Ctrl+X, Ctrl+C, Ctrl+V**), or the drag-and-drop method.

To move or copy multiple folders or files at the same time, press the **Ctrl** key and select multiple items to move or copy. Use the **Ctrl** key to select or deselect multiple non-adjacent files or folders. Use the **Shift** key to select a range of files or folders. Click the first file or folder in a range, press the **Shift** key, and select the last file or folder in the range to select all of the items in the range.

▶HOW TO: Move or Copy a File or Folder

1. Click the **Start** button and select **File Explorer** to open a *File Explorer* window.
2. Select a file or folder to move or copy.
 - Press the **Ctrl** key to select multiple files or folders.
3. Click the **Home** tab in the *File Explorer* window.
4. Click the **Move to** or **Copy to** button [*Organize* group] and select the location where you want to move or copy the file or folder (Figure Intro-92).

Intro-92 Move or copy a selected file or folder

 - If the folder you want is not available, select **Choose location** to open the *Move Items* or *Copy Items* dialog box.
 - To use the keyboard shortcuts, press **Ctrl+X** to cut the file or folder or **Ctrl+C** to copy the file or folder from its original location, go to the desired new location, and press **Ctrl+V** to paste it.
 - To use the drag-and-drop method to move a file or folder, select the file or folder and drag and drop to the new location.
 - To use the drag-and-drop method to copy a file or folder, press the **Ctrl** key, select the file or folder, and drag and drop to the new location.

> **ANOTHER WAY**
> Right-click a file or folder to display the context menu where you can select **Cut**, **Copy**, or **Paste**.

Rename Files and Folders

You can rename a file or folder in a *File Explorer* window. When you rename a file or folder, only the file or folder name changes, and the contents of the file or folder do not change.

▶HOW TO: Rename a File or Folder

1. Click the **Start** button and select **File Explorer** to open a *File Explorer* window.
2. Select the file or folder you want to rename.
3. Click the **Rename** button [*Home* tab, *Organize* group] (see Figure Intro-92).
4. Type the new name of the file or folder and press **Enter**.

> **ANOTHER WAY**
> Select a file or folder to rename, press **F2**, type the new name, and press **Enter**. You can also right-click a file or folder and select **Rename** from the context menu.

Delete Files and Folders

You can also easily delete files and folders. When you delete a file or folder, it is moved from its current location to the ***Recycle Bin*** on your computer where deleted items are stored. If a file or folder is in the *Recycle Bin*, you can restore this item to its original location or move it to a different location. You also have the option to permanently delete a file or folder; the item is deleted and not moved to the *Recycle Bin*. If an item is permanently deleted, you do not have the restore option.

▶HOW TO: Delete Files and Folders

1. Open a *File Explorer* window and select the file or folder you want to delete.
 - You can select multiple files and folders to delete at the same time.
2. Click the **Delete** drop-down arrow [*Home* tab, *Organize* group] to display the list of delete options (Figure Intro-93).
 - The default action when you click the *Delete* button (not the drop-down arrow) is *Recycle*.
3. Delete a file by selecting **Recycle**, which moves it to the *Recycle Bin*.
 - *Recycle* deletes the item(s) and moves it to the *Recycle Bin*.
 - When you *Recycle* an item, you are not by default prompted to confirm the deletion. Select **Show recycle confirmation** from the *Delete* drop-down list to receive a confirmation dialog box each time you delete or recycle an item.
4. Permanently delete a file by selecting **Permanently delete**. A confirmation dialog box opens. Click **Yes** to confirm the deletion.
 - *Permanently delete* deletes the item(s) from your computer.

Intro-93 Delete selected folder

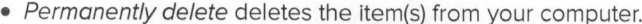

▶ **ANOTHER WAY**

Press **Ctrl+D** or the **Delete** key on your keyboard to recycle selected item(s).
Press **Shift+Delete** to permanently delete selected item(s).

Create a Zipped (Compressed) Folder

If you want to share multiple files or a folder of files with classmates, coworkers, friends, or family, you can **zip** the files into a **zipped folder** (also called a **compressed folder**). For example, you can't attach an entire folder to an email message, but you can attach a zipped folder to an email message. Compressing files and folders decreases their size. You can zip a group of selected files, a folder, or a combination of files and folders, and then share the zipped folder with others through email or in a cloud storage location such as *OneDrive*.

▶HOW TO: Create a Zipped (Compressed) Folder

1. Open a *File Explorer* window.
2. Select the file(s) and/or folder(s) you want to zip (compress).
3. Click the **Zip** button [*Share* tab, *Send* group] (Figure Intro-94). A zipped folder is created.
 - The name of the zipped folder is the name of the first item you selected to zip. You can rename this folder.
 - The icon for a zipped folder looks similar to the icon for a folder except it has a vertical zipper down the middle of the folder.

Intro-94 Create a zipped folder

Extract a Zipped (Compressed) Folder

If you receive a zipped folder via email or download a zipped folder, save the zipped folder to your computer and then you can **extract** its contents. Extracting a zipped folder creates a regular Windows folder from the zipped folder.

▶**HOW TO: Extract a Zipped (Compressed) Folder**

1. Select the zipped folder to extract.
2. Click the **Compressed Folder Tools** tab.
3. Click the **Extract all** button (Figure Intro-95). The *Extract Compressed (Zipped) Folders* dialog box opens (Figure Intro-96).
4. Click **Extract** to extract the folder.
 - Both the extracted folder and the zipped folder display in the folder where they are located.
 - If you check the **Show extracted files when complete** check box, the extracted folder will open after extracting.

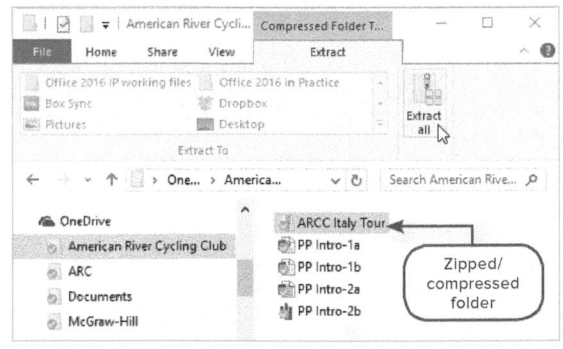

Intro-95 Extract files from a zipped folder

Intro-96 *Extract Compressed (Zipped) Folders* dialog box

For this project, you copy and rename files in your *OneDrive* folder on your computer, create a folder, move files, create a zipped folder, and rename a zipped folder.

Files Needed: *[your initials] PP Intro-1a.pptx, [your initials] PP Intro-1b.xlsx, [your initials] PP Intro-2a.docx, [your initials] PP Intro-2b.docx,* and *ARCC_Membership-Intro.accdb (Student data files are available in the* Library *of your SIMnet account)*
Completed Project File Names: *[your initials] PP Intro-1a.pptx, [your initials] PP Intro-1b.xlsx, [your initials] PP Intro-2a.docx, [your initials] PP Intro-2b.docx, [your initials]PP Intro-3.accdb,* and *ARCC Italy Tour-2018* (zipped folder)

1. Copy and rename a file.
 a. Click the Windows **Start** button and click **File Explorer** to open a *File Explorer* window. If *File Explorer* is not available on the *Start* menu, use *Cortana* to find and open a *File Explorer* window.
 b. Browse the *File Explorer* window to locate your student data files.
 c. Select the **ARCC_Membership-Intro** file.
 d. Click the **Copy to** button [*Home* tab, *Organize* group] and select **Choose location** from the drop-down list to open the *Copy Items* dialog box.
 e. Browse to locate the *American River Cycling Club* folder you created in *Pause & Practice: Intro-1*.
 f. Select the **American River Cycling Club** folder and click the **Copy** button to copy the **ARCC_Membership-Intro** file to the *American River Cycling Club* folder (Figure Intro-97). The *Copy Items* dialog box closes and the file is copied.
 g. In the open *File Explorer* window, browse to locate the *American River Cycling Club* folder and double-click the folder to open it.
 h. Click the **ARCC_Membership-Intro** file in the *American River Cycling Club* folder to select it.
 i. Click the **Rename** button [*Home* tab, *Organize* group], type [your initials] PP Intro-3 as the new file name, and press **Enter** (Figure Intro-98).

2. Create a new folder and move files.
 a. With the *American River Cycling Club* folder still open, click the **New folder** button [*Home* tab, *New* group] (see Figure Intro-98).
 b. Type ARCC Italy Tour as the name of the new folder and press **Enter**.

Intro-97 *Copy Items* dialog box

Intro-98 Rename a file

c. Select the *[your initials] PP Intro-1a* file.

d. Press the **Ctrl** key, select the *[your initials] PP Intro-1b*, *[your initials] PP Intro-2a*, *[your initials] PP Intro-2b*, and *[your initials] PP Intro-3* files, and release the **Ctrl** key. All five files should be selected.

e. Click the **Move to** button [*Home* tab, *Organize* group] and select **Choose location** to open the *Move Items* dialog box (Figure Intro-99).

f. Browse to locate the *ARCC Italy Tour* folder in the *Move Items* dialog box.

g. Select the **ARCC Italy Tour** folder and click the **Move** button to move the selected files to the *ARCC Italy Tour* folder.

h. Double-click the **ARCC Italy Tour** folder to open it and confirm the five files are moved.

i. Click the **Up** or **Back** arrow above the *Navigation* pane to return to the *American River Cycling Club* folder (see Figure Intro-99).

3. Create a zipped folder.

a. Select the **ARCC Italy Tour** folder.

b. Click the **Zip** button [*Share* tab, *Send* group]. A zipped (compressed) folder is created.

c. Place the insertion point at the end of the zipped folder name, type –2018, and press **Enter** (Figure Intro-100).

4. Email the zipped folder to your instructor.

a. Use your email account to create a new email to send to your instructor.

b. Include an appropriate subject line and a brief message in the body.

c. Attach the **ARCC Italy Tour-2018** zipped folder to the email message and send the email message.

Intro-99 Move selected files to a different folder

Intro-100 Create a zipped folder

Chapter Summary

Intro.1 Explore the features of Windows 10 (p. OI-2).

- **Windows 10** is a computer operating system.
- A **Microsoft account** is a free account you create. When you create a Microsoft account, you are given an email address, a **OneDrive** account, and access to **Office Online**.
- The **Windows desktop** is the working area of Windows 10 and the **Taskbar** displays at the bottom of the desktop. You can rearrange icons on and pin applications to the *Taskbar*.
- Use **Start menu** in Windows 10 to select a task. You can pin applications to the *Start* menu and customize the arrangement of apps.
- **Most Used** items, **File Explorer**, **Settings**, the **Power** button, and **All apps** options display to the left of the *Start* menu.
- **Apps** are the applications or programs installed on your computer. App buttons are arranged in tiles on the Windows 10 *Start* menu.
- The **Microsoft Store** is a Windows 10 app you use to search for and install apps on your computer.
- You can install both **traditional apps** and **modern apps** in Windows 10.
- You can customize the *Start* menu and *Taskbar* to add, remove, or arrange apps.
- The *File Explorer* is a window that displays files and folders on your computer.
- *OneDrive* is the cloud storage area where you can store files in a private and secure online location.
- In Windows 10, the **OneDrive folder** is one of your file storage location options.
- You can access your *OneDrive* folders and files using an Internet browser window.
- **Cortana** is a search tool in Windows 10 used to locate information on your computer and the Internet.
- **Task View** displays all open apps and windows as tiles on your desktop where you can select an app or window to display or close.
- **Settings** is the redesigned *Control Panel* where you change many Windows settings.

- The **Action Center** displays notifications and buttons to open many common Windows settings and features.

Intro.2 Use the basic features of Office 2016 and navigate the Office 2016 working environment (p. OI-10).

- **Office 2016** is application software that includes **Word**, **Excel**, **Access**, **PowerPoint**, **Outlook**, **OneNote**, and **Publisher**.
- *Office 2016* and **Office 365** include the same application products, but they differ in how you purchase them.
- **Office desktop apps** are the full-function Office 2016 or 365 products you install on your laptop or desktop computer.
- **Office universal apps** are a scaled-down version of Office applications you install on a tablet or mobile device.
- **Office Online** is free online software that works in conjunction with your online *Microsoft* account.
- When you open each of the Office applications, a **Start page** displays where you can open an existing file or create a new file.
- In the **Backstage view** in each of the Office applications, you can perform many common tasks such as saving, opening an existing file, creating a new file, printing, and sharing.
- **Tell Me** is the Office help feature that displays Office commands related to specific topics.
- Use the mouse (or touch pad) on your computer to navigate the pointer on your computer screen. Use the pointer or click buttons to select text or objects.
- When using Office 2016 on a touch-screen computer, use the touch screen to perform actions. You can choose between **Touch Mode** and **Mouse Mode** in Office applications.

Intro.3 Create, save, close, and open Office files (p. OI-17).

- You can create a new Office file from the *Start* page or *Backstage* view of the Office application you are using.
- When you save a file for the first time, assign the file a file name.

- You can create folders to organize saved files, and you can save a file as a different file name.
- A variety of different file types are used in each of the Office applications.
- You can close an Office file when you are finished working on it. If the file has not been saved or changes have been made to the file, you are prompted to save the file before closing.
- In each of the Office applications, you can open an existing file from the *Start* page or from the *Open* area on *Backstage* view.

Intro.4 Customize the view and display size in Office applications and work with multiple Office files (p. OI-25).

- Each Office application has a variety of display views.
- You can select an application view from the options on the *View tab* or the view buttons on the *Status bar*.
- The *Zoom* feature changes the display size of your file.
- You can **minimize**, **restore down**, or **maximize** an open Office application window.
- You can work with multiple Office files at the same time and switch between open files.
- *Snap Assist* enables you to arrange an open window on one side of your computer screen and select another window to fill the other side of the screen.

Intro.5 Print, share, and customize Office files (p. OI-28).

- You can print a file in a variety of formats. The *Print* area on the *Backstage* view lists your print options and displays a preview of your file.
- You can export a file as a *PDF (portable document format)* file and save the PDF file to post to a web site or share with others.
- *Document properties* store information about a file.
- You can share Office files in a variety of ways and allow others to view or edit shared files. To share a file with others, save the file in *OneDrive*.

- Program options are available on the *Backstage* view. You can use the program options to apply global changes to an Office application.

Intro.6 Use the *Ribbon,* tabs, groups, dialog boxes, task panes, galleries, and the *Quick Access* toolbar (p. OI-33).

- The **Ribbon** appears at the top of an Office window. It contains **tabs** and **groups** with commands to format and edit files.
- The **Ribbon Display Options** provides different ways the *Ribbon* displays in Office applications.
- Within groups on each tab are a variety of **buttons**, **drop-down lists**, and **galleries**.
- **Dialog boxes** contain additional features not always displayed on the *Ribbon*.
- Click the **launcher** in the bottom right corner of some groups to open a dialog box for that group.
- A **ScreenTip** displays information about commands on the *Ribbon*.
- Dialog boxes contain **radio buttons**, **check boxes**, **drop-down lists**, and **text boxes** you can use to apply features.
- The **Quick Access toolbar**, which contains buttons that allow you to perform commands, displays in all Office applications in the upper left.
- You can add or remove commands on the *Quick Access* toolbar.

Intro.7 Use context menus, mini toolbars, keyboard shortcuts, and function keys in Office applications (p. OI-37).

- A **context menu** displays when you right-click text or an object. The context menu contains different features depending on what you right-click.
- The **mini toolbar** is another context menu that displays formatting options.
- You can use **keyboard shortcuts** to apply features or commands.
- Some of the numbered **function keys** perform commands in Office applications. On laptops, you may have to press the function key (**Fn** or **fn**) to activate the numbered function keys.

Intro.8 Organize and customize Windows folders and Office files (p. OI-42).

- **Folders** store and organize your files.
- You can create, move, or copy files and folders. Files stored in a folder are moved or copied with that folder.
- You can rename a file to change the file name.
- When you delete a file or folder, it is moved to the **Recycle Bin** on your computer by

default. Alternatively, you can permanently delete files and folders.

- You can **zip** files and/or folders into a **zipped (compressed) folder** to email or share multiple files as a single file.
- When you receive a zipped folder, you can **extract** the zipped folder to create a regular Windows folder and access its contents.

Check for Understanding

The SIMbook for this text (within your SIMnet account) provides the following resources for concept review:

- Multiple choice questions
- Short answer questions
- Matching exercises

USING MICROSOFT WINDOWS 10 AND OFFICE 2016

For these projects, you use your *OneDrive* to store files. If you don't already have a Microsoft account, see *SLO Intro.1: Using Windows 10* for information about creating a free personal Microsoft account.

Guided Project Intro-1

For this project, you organize and edit files for Emma Cavalli at Placer Hills Real Estate. You extract a zipped folder, rename files, manage multiple documents, apply formatting, and export as a PDF file.
[Student Learning Outcomes Intro.1, Intro.2, Intro.3, Intro.4, Intro.5, Intro.6, Intro.7, Intro.8]

Files Needed: ***CavalliFiles-Intro*** (zipped folder) *(Student data files are available in the* Library *of your SIMnet account)*
Completed Project File Names: ***PHRE*** folder containing the following files: ***BuyerEscrowChecklist-Intro***, ***CavalliProspectingLetter-Intro***, *[your initials]* ***Intro-1a.accdb***, *[your initials]* ***Intro-1b.xlsx***, *[your initials]* ***Intro-1c.docx***, and *[your initials]* ***Intro-1d.docx***

Skills Covered in This Project

- Copy and paste a zipped folder.
- Create a new folder in your *OneDrive* folder.
- Extract a zipped folder.
- Move a file.
- Rename a file.
- Open a Word document.

- Use *Task View* to switch between two open Word documents.
- Save a Word document with a different file name.
- Change display size.
- Use a mini toolbar, keyboard shortcut, context menu, and dialog box to apply formatting to selected text.
- Export a document as a PDF file.

1. Copy a zipped folder and create a new *OneDrive* folder.
 a. Click the Windows **Start** button and click **File Explorer** to open the *File Explorer* window. If *File Explorer* is not available on the *Start* menu, use *Cortana* to find and open the *File Explorer* window.
 b. Browse in the *File Explorer* window to locate your student data files.
 c. Select the ***CavalliFiles-Intro*** zipped folder from your student data files and press **Ctrl+C** or click the **Copy** button [*Home* tab, *Clipboard* group] to copy the folder.
 d. Select your ***OneDrive*** folder on the left of the *File Explorer* window, and click the **New folder** button [*Home* tab, *New* group] to create a new folder. If you don't have *OneDrive* available, create the new folder in a location where you store your files.
 e. Type **PHRE** and press **Enter**.
 f. Press **Enter** again to open the *PHRE* folder or double-click the folder to open it.
 g. Press **Ctrl+V** or click the **Paste** button [*Home* tab, *Clipboard* group] to paste the copied ***CavalliFiles-Intro*** zipped folder in the *PHRE* folder.

2. Extract a zipped folder.
 a. Select the ***CavalliFiles-Intro*** zipped folder.
 b. Click the **Compressed Folder Tools Extract** tab and click the **Extract all** button. The *Extract Compressed (Zipped) Folders* dialog box opens.
 c. Uncheck the **Show extracted files when complete** box if it is checked.
 d. Click the **Extract** button (Figure Intro-101). The zipped folder is extracted, and the *PHRE* folder now=contains two *CavalliFiles-Intro* folders. One folder is zipped and the other is a regular folder.

e. Select the zipped **CavalliFiles-Intro** folder and click the **Delete** button [*Home* tab, *Organize* group] to delete the zipped folder.

3. Move and rename files.
 a. With the *PHRE* folder still open, double-click the **CavalliFiles-Intro** folder to open it.
 b. Click the first file, press and hold the **Shift** key, and click the last file to select all four files.
 c. Press **Ctrl+X** or click the **Cut** button [*Home* tab, *Clipboard* group] to cut the files from the current location (Figure Intro-102).
 d. Click the **Up** arrow to move up to the *PHRE* folder.
 e. Press **Ctrl+V** or click the **Paste** button [*Home* tab, *Clipboard* group] to paste and move the files.
 f. Select the **Cavalli files-Intro** folder and press **Delete** to delete the folder.
 g. Select the **CavalliPHRE-Intro** file and click the **Rename** button [*Home* tab, *Organize* group].
 h. Type [your initials] Intro-1a and press **Enter**.
 i. Right-click the **FixedMortgageRates-Intro** file and select **Rename** from the context menu.
 j. Type [your initials] Intro-1b and press **Enter**.

4. Open two Word documents and rename a Word document.
 a. Press the **Ctrl** key and click the **BuyerEscrowChecklist-Intro** and **CavalliProspectingLetter-Intro** files to select both files.
 b. Press the **Enter** key to open both files in Word. If the files open in *Protected View*, click the **Enable Editing** button.
 c. Press the **Task View** button on your *Taskbar* (Figure Intro-103). All open windows display as tiles on your desktop.
 d. Select the **BuyerEscrowChecklist-Intro** document.
 e. Click the **File** tab to open the *Backstage* view and select **Save As** on the left.
 f. Click the **Browse** button to open the *Save As* dialog box.
 g. Type [your initials] Intro-1c in the *File name* text box and click **Save**. The file is saved in the *PHRE* folder.
 h. Click the **X** in the upper right corner of the Word window to close the document. The *CavalliProspectingLetter-Intro* document remains open.

5. Change display size and edit and rename a Word document.
 a. Press the **Task View** button on your *Taskbar* and select the **CavalliProspectingLetter-Intro** document.

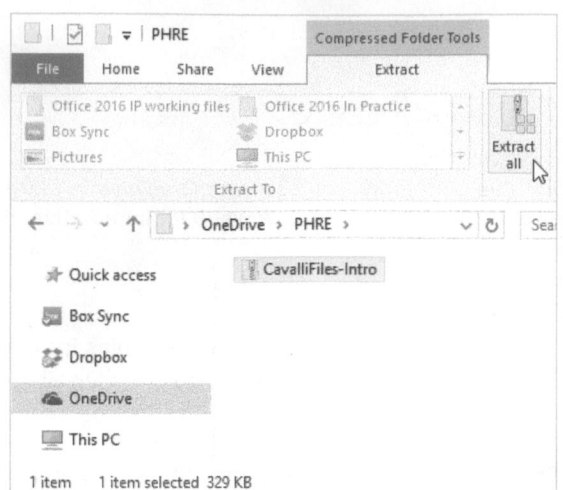

Intro-101 Extract a zipped folder

Intro-102 *Cut* files to move from a folder

Intro-103 *Task View* button on the *Taskbar*

b. Click the **Zoom In** or **Zoom Out** button in the bottom right of the document window to change the display size to **120%** (Figure Intro-104).

Intro-104 Use *Zoom* to change the display size to 120%

c. Select "**Placer Hills Real Estate**" in the first body paragraph of the letter and the mini toolbar displays (Figure Intro-105).

d. Click the **Bold** button on the mini toolbar to apply bold formatting to the selected text.

e. Select "**Whitney Hills resident**" in the first sentence in the second body paragraph and press **Ctrl+I** to apply italic formatting to the selected text.

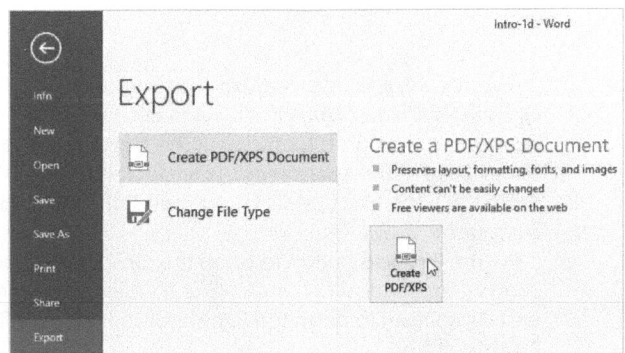

Intro-105 Use the mini toolbar to apply formatting

f. Select the text that reads "**Emma Cavalli**," below "Best regards,".

g. Right-click the selected text and select **Font** from the context menu to open the *Font* dialog box.

h. Check the **Small Caps** box in the *Effects* area and click **OK** to close the *Font* dialog box.

i. With "**Emma Cavalli**" still selected, click the **Bold** button [*Home* tab, *Font* group].

j. Click the **File** tab, select **Save As** on the left, and click the **Browse** button to open the *Save As* dialog box.

k. Type [your initials] Intro-1d in the *File name* text box and click **Save**.

6. Export a Word document as a PDF file.

a. With the *[your initials] Intro-1d* still open, click the **File** tab to open the *Backstage* view.

b. Select **Export** on the left, select **Create PDF/XPS Document** in the *Export* area, and click the **Create PDF/XPS** button (Figure Intro-106). The *Publish as PDF or XPS* dialog box opens.

c. Deselect the **Open file after publishing** check box if it is checked.

d. Select the **Standard (publishing online and printing)** radio button in the *Optimize for* area.

e. Type [your initials] Intro-1e in the *File name* text box and click **Publish**.

f. Click the **File** tab to open the *Backstage* view and select **Save** on the left.

g. Click the **X** in the upper right corner of the Word window to close the document and Word.

7. Your *PHRE* folder should contain the files shown in Figure Intro-107.

Intro-106 Export as a PDF file

Intro-107 Intro-1 completed

Guided Project Intro-2

For this project, you modify an Excel file for Hamilton Civic Center. You create a folder, rename a file, add document properties, use *Tell Me* to search for a topic, share the file, and export a file as a PDF file.
[Student Learning Outcomes Intro.1, Intro.2, Intro.3, Intro.5, Intro.6, Intro.7, Intro.8]

File Needed: **HCCYoga-Intro.xlsx** *(Student data files are available in the* Library *of your SIMnet account)*
Completed Project File Names: **[your initials] Intro-2a.xlsx** and **[your initials] Intro-2b.pdf**

Skills Covered in This Project

- Open Excel and an Excel workbook.
- Create a new folder.
- Save an Excel workbook with a different file name.

- Add document properties to a file.
- Use *Tell Me* to search for a topic.
- Open a Word document.
- Share a file.
- Export a file as a PDF file.

1. Open Excel 2016 and open an Excel workbook.
 a. Click the Windows **Start** button and click **Excel 2016** to open this application. If Excel 2016 is not available on the *Start* menu, click the **Cortana** button on the *Taskbar*, type Excel, and then click **Excel 2016** in the search results to open it.
 b. From the Excel *Start* page, click **Open Other Workbooks** to display the *Open* area of the *Backstage* view.
 c. Click the **Browse** button to open the *Open* dialog box.
 d. Browse to the location where your student data files are stored, select the **HCCYoga-Intro** file, and click **Open** to open the Excel workbook. If the file opens in *Protected View*, click the **Enable Editing** button.

2. Save a file as a different file name in your *OneDrive* folder.
 a. Click the **File** tab to open the *Backstage* view and select **Save As** on the left.
 b. Click the **Browse** button to open the *Save As* dialog box.
 c. Select the **OneDrive** folder on the left and click the **New folder** button to create a new folder (Figure Intro-108). If *OneDrive* is not a storage option, select another location to create the new folder.
 d. Type HCC and press **Enter**.
 e. Double-click the **HCC** folder to open it.
 f. Type [your initials] Intro-2a in the *File name* area and click **Save** to close the dialog box and save the file.

Intro-108 Create a new folder from the *Save As* dialog box

3. Add document properties to the Excel workbook.
 a. Click the **File** button to open the *Backstage* view and select **Info** on the left if it is not already selected. The document properties displays on the right.
 b. Place your insertion point in the *Title* text box ("Add a title") and type Yoga Classes as the worksheet title.

c. Click the **Show All Properties** link at the bottom of the list of properties to display more properties (Figure Intro-109).
d. Place your insertion point in the *Company* text box and type Hamilton Civic Center as the company name.
e. Click the **Back** arrow in the upper left of the *Backstage* window to return to the Excel workbook.

4. Use *Tell Me* to search for a topic.
a. Click the **Tell Me** search box at the top of the *Ribbon* and type Cell formatting (Figure Intro-110).
b. Select **Get Help on "Cell formatting"** to open the *Excel 2016 Help* dialog box.
c. Click the first result link to display information about the topic.
d. Click the **Back** arrow to return to the search list.
e. Click the **X** in the upper right corner to close the *Excel 2016 Help* dialog box.

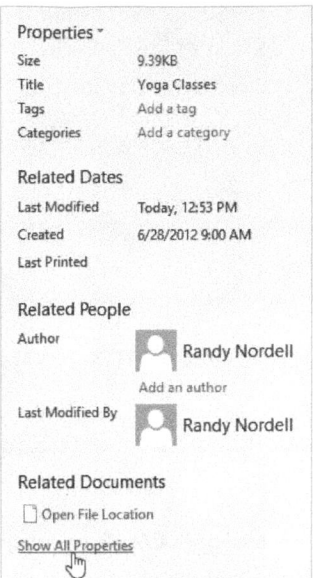

Intro-110 Use *Tell Me* to search for a topic

Intro-109 Add document properties

5. Share an Excel workbook with your instructor. If your file is not saved in *OneDrive*, skip step 5.
a. Click the **Share** button in the upper right of the Excel worksheet. The *Share* pane opens on the right side of the worksheet (Figure Intro-111).
b. Type your instructor's email address in the *Invite people* area.
c. Select **Can edit** from the drop-down list below the email address if it is not already selected.
d. Type a brief message in the body text box.
e. Click the **Share** button.
f. Click the **X** in the upper right corner of the *Share* pane to close the pane.
g. Press **Ctrl+S** to save the worksheet.

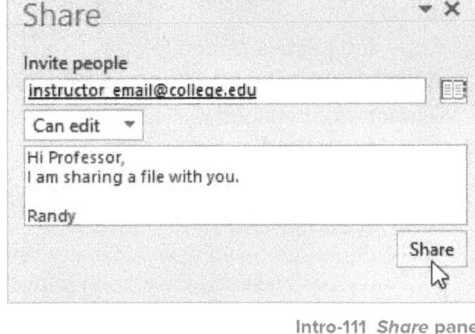

Intro-111 *Share* pane

6. Export an Excel file as a PDF file.
a. Click the **File** tab to open the *Backstage* view.
b. Select **Export** on the left, select **Create PDF/XPS Document** in the *Export* area, and click the **Create PDF/XPS** button (Figure Intro-112). The *Publish as PDF or XPS* dialog box opens.
c. Deselect the **Open file after publishing** check box if it is checked.

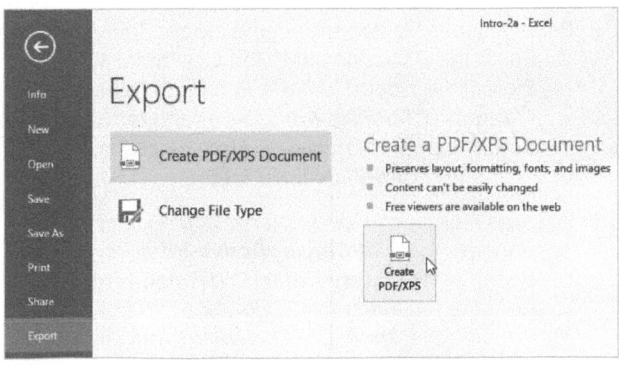

Intro-112 Export as a PDF file

d. Select the **Standard (publishing online and printing)** radio button in the *Optimize for* area.
e. Type [your initials] Intro-2b in the *File name* text box and click **Publish**.

7. Save and close the Excel file.
 a. Click the **File** tab to open the *Backstage* view and select **Save** on the left.
 b. Click the **X** in the upper right corner of the Excel window to close the file and Excel.

Independent Project Intro-3

For this project, you organize and edit files for Courtyard Medical Plaza. You extract a zipped folder, delete a folder, move files, rename files, export a file as a PDF file, and share a file.
[Student Learning Outcomes Intro.1, Intro.2, Intro.3, Intro.5, Intro.8]

File Needed: ***CMPFiles-Intro*** (zipped folder) *(Student data files are available in the Library of your SIMnet account)*
Completed Project File Names: ***[your initials] Intro-3a.pptx, [your initials] Intro-3a-pdf.pdf, [your initials] Intro-3b.accdb, [your initials] Intro-3c.xlsx,*** and ***[your initials] Intro-3d.docx***

Skills Covered in This Project

- Copy and paste a zipped folder.
- Create a new folder in your *OneDrive* folder.
- Extract a zipped folder.
- Delete a folder.
- Move a file.
- Rename a file.
- Open a PowerPoint presentation.
- Export a file as a PDF file.
- Open a Word document.
- Share a file.

1. Copy a zipped folder and create a new *OneDrive* folder.
 a. Open a *File Explorer* window, browse to locate the ***CMPFiles-Intro*** zipped folder in your student data files and copy the zipped folder.
 b. Go to your *OneDrive* folder and create a new folder named Courtyard Medical Plaza within the *OneDrive* folder. If *OneDrive* is not a storage option, select another location to create the new folder.

2. Paste a copied folder, extract the zipped folder, and move files.
 a. Paste the zipped folder in the *Courtyard Medical Plaza* folder.
 b. Extract the zipped folder and then delete the zipped folder.
 c. Open the ***CMPFiles-Intro*** folder and move all of the files to the *Courtyard Medical Plaza* folder.
 d. Return to the *Courtyard Medical Plaza* folder to confirm the four files were moved.
 e. Delete the ***CMPFiles-Intro*** folder.

3. Rename files in the *Courtyard Medical Plaza* folder.
 a. Rename the ***CMPStayingActive-Intro*** PowerPoint file to [your initials] Intro-3a.
 b. Rename the ***CourtyardMedicalPlaza-Intro*** Access file to [your initials] Intro-3b.
 c. Rename the ***EstimatedCalories-Intro*** Excel file to [your initials] Intro-3c.
 d. Rename the ***StayingActive-Intro*** Word file to [your initials] Intro-3d.

4. Export a PowerPoint file as a PDF file.
 a. From the *Courtyard Medical Plaza* folder, open the ***[your initials] Intro-3a*** file. The file opens in PowerPoint. If the file opens in *Protected View*, click the **Enable Editing** button.

b. Export this file as a PDF file. Don't have the PDF file open after publishing and optimize for **Standard** format.

c. Save the file as [your initials] Intro-3a-pdf and save in the *Courtyard Medical Plaza* folder.

d. Close the PowerPoint file and exit PowerPoint.

5. Share a file with your instructor. If your files are not saved in *OneDrive*, skip step 5.

a. Return to your *Courtyard Medical Plaza* folder and open the **Intro-3d** file. The file opens in Word. If the file opens in *Protected View*, click the **Enable Editing** button.

b. Open the *Share* pane.

c. Type your instructor's email address and select **Can edit** from the permission drop-down list.

d. Type a brief message and **Share** the file.

e. Close the *Share* pane.

f. Save and close the document and exit Word.

6. Close the *File Explorer* window containing the files for this project (Figure Intro-113).

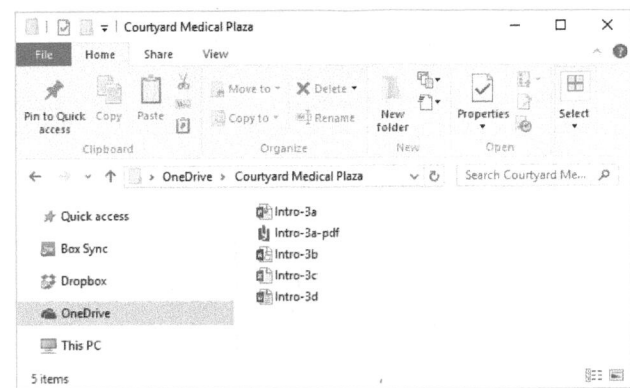

Intro-113 Intro-3 completed

Independent Project Intro-4

For this project, you modify a Word file for Life's Animal Shelter. You create a folder, rename a document, add document properties, modify a document, create a sharing link, export a document as a PDF file, and create a zipped folder.

[Student Learning Outcomes Intro.1, Intro.2, Intro.3, Intro.5, Intro.6, Intro.7, Intro.8]

File Needed: ***LASSupportLetter-Intro.docx*** *(Student data files are available in the* Library *of your SIMnet account)*

Completed Project File Names: ***[your initials] Intro-4a.docx***, ***[your initials] Intro-4b.pdf***, and ***LAS files*** (zipped folder)

Skills Covered in This Project

- Open a Word document.
- Create a new folder.
- Save a file with a different file name.
- Apply formatting to selected text.
- Add document properties to the file.
- Create a sharing link.
- Export a file as a PDF file.
- Create a zipped folder.

1. Open a Word document, create a new folder, and save the document with a different file name.

a. Open Word 2016.

b. From the Word *Start* page, open the ***LASSupportLetter-Intro*** document from your student data files. If the file opens in *Protected View*, click the **Enable Editing** button.

 c. Open the **Save As** dialog box and create a new folder named LAS in your *OneDrive* folder. If *OneDrive* is not a storage option, select another location to create the new folder.

 d. Save this document in the *LAS* folder and use [your initials] Intro-4a as the file name.

2. Apply formatting changes to the document using a dialog box, keyboard shortcut, and mini toolbar.
 a. Select "**To**:" in the memo heading and use the launcher to open the *Font* dialog box.
 b. Apply **Bold** and **All caps** to the selected text.
 c. Repeat the formatting on the other three memo guide words "**From**:," "**Date**:," and "**Subject**:".
 d. Select "**Life's Animal Shelter**" in the first sentence of the first body paragraph and press **Ctrl+B** to apply bold formatting.
 e. Select the first sentence in the second body paragraph ("**Would you again consider** . . .") and use the mini toolbar to apply **italic** formatting.

3. Add the following document properties to the document:
 Title: Support Letter
 Company: Life's Animal Shelter

4. Get a link to share this document with your instructor and email your instructor the sharing link.
 a. Open the *Share* pane and click **Get a sharing link** at the bottom of the *Share* pane.
 b. Create an edit link to send to your instructor.
 c. Copy the edit link.
 d. Open the email you use for this course and create a new email message to send to your instructor.
 e. Type your instructor's email address, include an appropriate subject line, and type a brief message in the body of the email message.
 f. Paste (**Ctrl+V**) the sharing link in the body of the email message and send the message.
 g. Click the **Task View** button on the Windows *Taskbar* and select the ***Intro-4a*** document to display this document.
 h. Close the *Share* pane.
 i. Use the **Save** command on the *Quick Access* toolbar to save the file before continuing.

7. Export this document as a PDF file.
 a. Export this file as a PDF file. Don't have the PDF file open after publishing and optimize for **Standard** format.
 b. Save the file as [your initials] Intro-4b and save in the *LAS* folder.
 c. Save and close the document and exit Word.

8. Create a zipped folder.
 a. Using *File Explorer*, open the ***LAS*** folder in your *OneDrive* folder.
 b. Select the two files and create a zipped folder.
 c. Rename the zipped folder LAS files.

9. Close the open *File Explorer* window (Figure Intro-114).

Intro-114 Intro-4 completed

Challenge Project Intro-5

For this project, you create folders to organize your files for this class and share a file with your instructor.
[Student Learning Outcomes Intro.1, Intro.5, Intro.8]

Files Needed: Student data files for this course
Completed Project File Name: Share a file with your instructor

Using *File Explorer*, create *OneDrive* folders to contain all of the student data files for this class. Organize your files and folders according to the following guidelines:

- Create a *OneDrive* folder for this class.
- Create a *Student data files* folder inside the class folder.
- Copy and paste the student data files in the *Student data files* folder.
- Extract student data files and delete the zipped folder.
- Create a *Solution files* folder inside the class folder.
- Inside the *Solution files* folder, create a folder for each chapter.
- Create a folder to store miscellaneous class files such as the syllabus and other course handouts.
- Open one of the student data files and share the file with your instructor.

Challenge Project Intro-6

For this project, you save a file as a different file name, customize the *Quick Access* toolbar, share a file with your instructor, export a file as a PDF file, and create a zipped folder.
[Student Learning Outcomes Intro.1, Intro.2, Intro.3, Intro.5, Intro.6, Intro.8]

File Needed: Use an existing Office file
Completed Project File Names: *[your initials] Intro-6a* and *[your initials] Intro-6b*

Open an existing Word, Excel, or PowerPoint file. Save this file in a *OneDrive* folder and name it [your initials] Intro-6a. If you don't have any of these files, use one from your Pause & Practice projects or select a file from your student data files.

With your file open, perform the following actions:

- Create a new folder on OneDrive and save the file to this folder using a different file name.
- Customize the *Quick Access* toolbar to add command buttons. Add commands such as *New*, *Open*, *Quick Print*, and *Spelling* that you use regularly in the Office application.
- Share your file with your instructor. Allow your instructor to edit the file.
- Export the document as a PDF file. Save the file as [your initials] Intro-6b and save it in the same *OneDrive* folder as your open file.
- Zip the files in the folder.

Microsoft Excel 2016

Microsoft® Office

IN PRACTICE

excel

CHAPTER

1

Creating and Editing Workbooks

CHAPTER OVERVIEW

Microsoft Excel (Excel) is spreadsheet software for creating an electronic workbook. A workbook consists of rows and columns used to organize data, perform calculations, print reports, and build charts. With Excel, you can create simple to complex personal or business workbooks. This chapter presents basic procedures for creating and editing an Excel workbook.

STUDENT LEARNING OUTCOMES (SLOs)

After completing this chapter, you will be able to:

SLO 1.1 Create, save, and open an Excel workbook (p. E1-3).

SLO 1.2 Enter and edit labels and values in a worksheet (p. E1-6).

SLO 1.3 Use the *SUM* function to build a simple formula (p. E1-19).

SLO 1.4 Format a worksheet with font attributes, borders, fill, cell styles, and themes (p. E1-21).

SLO 1.5 Modify columns and rows in a worksheet (p. E1-31).

SLO 1.6 Insert, delete, and move worksheets in a workbook (p. E1-37).

SLO 1.7 Modify the appearance of a workbook by adjusting zoom size, changing views, and freezing panes (p. E1-42).

SLO 1.8 Review and prepare a workbook for final distribution by spell checking, setting properties, and adjusting page setup options (p. E1-47).

CASE STUDY

Throughout this book you have the opportunity to put into practice the application features that you are learning. Each chapter begins with a case study that introduces you to the Pause & Practice projects in the chapter. These Pause & Practice projects give you a chance to apply and practice key skills in a realistic and practical context. Each chapter contains three to five Pause & Practice projects.

Paradise Lakes Resort (PLR) is a vacation company with properties located throughout northern Minnesota. PLR staff use Excel to track revenue, to monitor expenses, to maintain employee records, and similar tasks. In the Pause & Practice projects for Chapter 1, you create, edit, and format a workbook that displays categories of revenue for one week.

Pause & Practice 1-1: Open, edit, and save a workbook.

Pause & Practice 1-2: Use *SUM* and format data in a worksheet.

Pause & Practice 1-3: Edit columns, rows, and sheets in a workbook.

Pause & Practice 1-4: Finalize a workbook for distribution.

EXCEL

E1-2

SLO 1.1

Creating, Saving, and Opening a Workbook

In Microsoft Excel, the file that you open, edit, and save is a **workbook**. Each workbook contains **worksheets**, which are comparable to individual pages in a Word document. A worksheet is also referred to as a **spreadsheet** or a **sheet**, and you can use these terms interchangeably. This text also uses the terms "workbook" and "file" interchangeably.

Create a New Workbook

By default, a new workbook includes one worksheet, but a workbook can include multiple sheets. The worksheet **tab** is located near the bottom left of the workbook window and is labeled *Sheet1*.

When you first open Excel, the **Excel Start page** displays. From the *Start* page, you can create a new blank workbook, open a recently saved workbook, or create a workbook from an Excel template (a model workbook). Click **Blank workbook** to start a new blank workbook. You can also select *Blank workbook* from the *New* area in the *Backstage* view.

> **ANOTHER WAY**
>
> Press **Esc** to leave the Excel *Start* page and open a blank workbook.

> **HOW TO: Create a New Workbook**
>
> 1. Click the **File** tab to display the *Backstage* view.
> 2. Select **New** on the left to display the *New* area in the *Backstage* view (Figure 1-1).

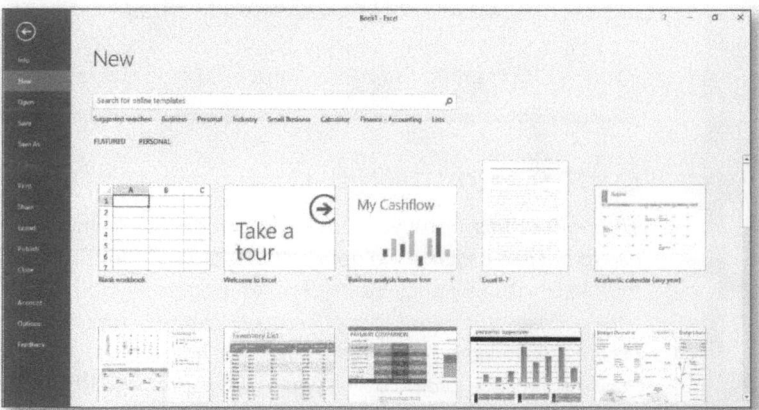

1-1 *Backstage* view for creating new workbooks

> 3. Click **Blank workbook** to create a new blank workbook.

> **ANOTHER WAY**
>
> Press **Ctrl+N** to open a new workbook.

Save and Close a Workbook

When you open a blank workbook, Excel automatically assigns a file name, such as *Book1*. The first time you save a workbook, you should type a descriptive file name for the workbook in the *Save As* dialog box. You can save a workbook on your computer, in a *OneDrive* folder, or on external media.

▶ **HOW TO: Save a New Workbook**

1. Click the **File** tab to display the *Backstage* view.
2. Select **Save As** on the left to display the *Save As* area.
 - You can press **Ctrl+S** to open the *Save As* area in the *Backstage* view for a workbook that has not yet been saved.
3. Select the location to save your workbook.
 - Click **This PC** to see recently used folders.
 - Click **Browse** to open the *Save As* dialog box for further navigation.
 - Click **OneDrive** to see your cloud folder names.
4. Click the folder name to open the *Save As* dialog box (Figure 1-2).
5. Type the file name in the *File name* area.
6. Click **Save** to close the *Save As* dialog box.

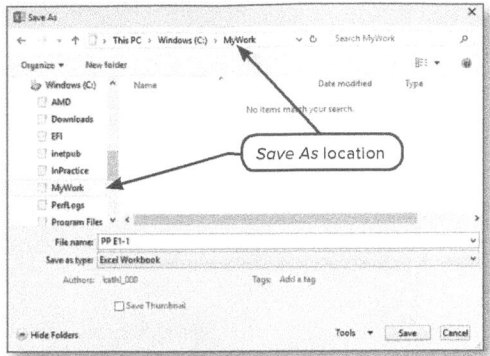

1-2 *Save As* dialog box

▶ **ANOTHER WAY**

Press **F12 (FN+F12)** to open the *Save As* dialog box.

Once a workbook has been saved, you can re-save it with the same file name by pressing **Ctrl+S** or by clicking the **Save** button in the *Quick Access toolbar*.

To close a workbook, click the **File** tab and choose **Close**. You can press **Ctrl+W** or **Ctrl+F4** to close a workbook, too. These commands leave Excel running with a blank screen so that you can open another file or start a new workbook.

You can also click the **X** (**Close** button) in the upper right corner of the window. If the workbook is the only one open, this command closes the file and exits Excel. If multiple workbooks are open, clicking the *Close* button closes only the active workbook.

Open a Workbook

A workbook can be opened from the *Start* page, the *Open* area in the *Backstage* view, or the *Open* dialog box. When a workbook is opened from an Internet or unrecognized source, it opens in ***Protected View***. Click **Enable Editing** when you know that it is safe to work with the file.

▶ **HOW TO: Open a Workbook**

1. Click the **File** tab to open the *Backstage* view.
2. Click **Open** to display the *Open* area.

3. Select the location where the workbook is stored.

- The *Recent* list displays workbook file names on the right.
- The *This PC* option lists recently used folder names.
- Click **Browse** to locate a folder.

4. Click the folder name that stores the file.

5. Select the workbook name and click **Open** (Figure 1-3).

1-3 *Open* dialog box

▶ **ANOTHER WAY**

Ctrl+O displays the *Open* area in the *Backstage* view. **Ctrl+F12** displays the *Open* dialog box.

▶ **MORE INFO**

From an Explorer window, you can double-click a workbook file name to launch Excel and open the workbook.

Save a Workbook with a Different File Name

To preserve an existing workbook, you can open and save it with a different file name, creating a copy of the original file with a new name. Follow the same steps that you would when saving a new workbook.

▶ **HOW TO: Save a Workbook with a Different File Name**

1. Click the **File** tab to open the *Backstage* view.
2. Click **Save As** to display the *Save As* area.
3. Navigate to and select the folder name to open the *Save As* dialog box.
 - You can press **F12** (**FN+F12**) to open the *Save As* dialog box.
4. Type the name in the *File name* area.
5. Click **Save** to close the *Save As* dialog box and save the file.

Workbook File Formats

Excel workbooks are saved as *.xlsx* files, indicated as *Excel Workbook* in the *Save As* dialog box. You can save a workbook in other formats for ease in sharing data. For example, you can save a workbook in *Excel 97-2003* format so that a coworker with an earlier version of Excel can use the data. Or you can create a PDF file of a workbook to provide data to users who do not have Excel.

The *Save as type* area of the *Save As* dialog box lists available formats (Figure 1-4). The following table lists common formats for saving an Excel workbook.

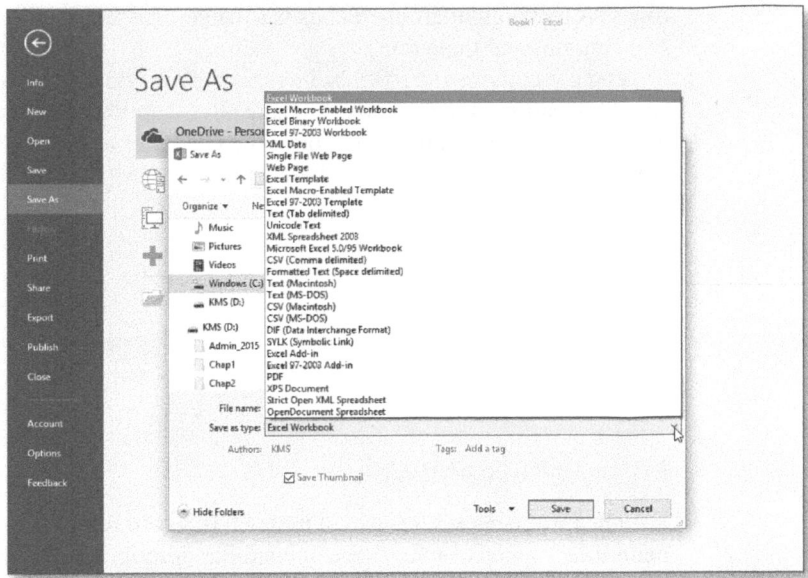

1-4 Workbook file formats

Save Formats

Type of Document	File Name Extension	Uses of This Format
Excel Workbook	.xlsx	Excel workbook compatible with versions 2010 and later
Excel Macro-Enabled Workbook	.xlsm	Excel workbook with embedded macros
Excel 97-2003 Workbook	.xls	Excel workbook compatible with older versions of Microsoft Excel
Excel Template	.xltx	Model or sample Excel workbook stored in the Custom Office Templates folder
Excel Macro-Enabled Template	.xltm	Model or sample Excel workbook with embedded macros stored in the Custom Office Templates folder
Portable Document Format (PDF)	.pdf	An uneditable image of the workbook for viewing that can be opened with free software
Text (tab-delimited)	.txt	Data only with columns separated by a tab character. File can be opened by many applications.
Comma Separated Values (CSV)	.csv	Data only with columns separated by a comma. File can be opened by many applications.
OpenDocument Spreadsheet	.ods	Workbook for the Open Office suite as well as Google Docs
Web Page	.htm, .html	Excel workbook formatted for posting on a web site that includes data, graphics, and linked objects

SLO 1.2

Entering and Editing Data

A worksheet consists of columns and rows. Columns are labeled with letters and rows are labeled with numbers. You enter data in a *cell*, which is the intersection of a column and a row. Each cell is identified with a *cell reference* (or *cell address*), the column letter and row number that represents the location of the cell. Cell A1 is the intersection of column A and

row 1. A rectangular group of cells is a *range*. The range address **A1:B3** identifies six cells in two columns and three rows.

You see column and row headings as well as gridlines on the worksheet to help you identify the location of data. You can change these options from the *View* tab if you prefer to see a cleaner background for your work. The *Gridlines* and *Headings* settings in the *Show* group are toggles that display or hide these features.

> **MORE INFO**
>
> From the *View* tab, you can also display or hide the formula bar and the ruler.

Enter Labels and Values

Data in a worksheet cell is text, a number, or a formula. A *label* is text that displays a name, a main title, row or column titles, and similar descriptive information. Labels are not included in calculations. A *value* is a number that can be used in a calculation or is the result of a calculation. A *formula* is a calculation or expression that displays a result.

When you type data that includes alphabetic characters and numbers, Excel treats that data as a label. Examples include a street address or an ID such as ABC123. When you type data with numbers that are not used in calculations, enter the data as a label by typing an apostrophe (') before the data. Examples of this type of data include a telephone or Social Security number without hyphens.

> **MORE INFO**
>
> If you type a Social Security number *with* hyphens, Excel will identify it as a label.

When a label in a cell is longer or wider than the cell, the label spills into an empty adjacent cell. If adjacent cells are not empty, the label is truncated or cut off in the cell, but the entire entry is visible in the **Formula bar**. The *Formula* bar appears below the *Ribbon* and displays the contents of the selected cell. When a value is too large for the width of the cell, the cell displays a series of # symbols or shows the value in exponential notation (part of the number with E+n as in 1235E+4). You can simply widen the column to see all cell contents.

To enter data, click the cell with the pointer to select and activate the cell. The pointer appears as a solid, white cross (a thick plus sign) when selecting data in the worksheet. The *active cell* displays a solid border, and its address appears in the *Name box* (Figure 1-5).

1-5 **Entering data**

> **HOW TO: Enter Data into a Workbook**

1. Select the cell and type the data.
 - The label or value appears in the cell with an insertion point and in the *Formula* bar.
2. Press **Enter** to complete the entry and activate the cell below.
 - Press **Tab** to complete the entry and activate the cell to the right.
 - Press any keyboard directional arrow key to complete the entry and activate the cell in the direction of the arrow.
 - Press **Ctrl+Enter** to complete the entry and keep the current cell active.
 - Click the **Enter** button in the *Formula* bar to complete the entry and keep the cell active.

Edit Cell Contents

You can edit cell data as you type or after the entry is complete. To edit as you type, press the **Backspace** key to delete characters to the left of the insertion point. Or use arrow keys to move the insertion point and press the **Delete** key to erase characters to the right of the insertion point. To edit a completed entry, start *Edit* mode by double-clicking the cell or by pressing **F2 (FN+F2)**. The word "Edit" appears in the *Status* bar to alert you that data entry is in progress. Position the insertion point either in the cell or in the *Formula* bar, make the change, and press any completion key.

When using some keyboard function keys, you may need to press the **FN** key with the function key to access the command. This depends on the type of computer as well as the keyboard. This text will show a shortcut like this **F2 (FN+F2)** as a reminder to note your keyboard layout.

1-6 *Edit* mode

> **HOW TO: Edit Cell Contents**

1. Double-click the cell to be edited.
 - You can also click the cell and press **F2 (FN+F2)** to start *Edit* mode.
2. Position the insertion point in the cell or the *Formula* bar (Figure 1-6).
3. Edit the data.
4. Press **Enter**.

Replace or Clear Cell Contents

To replace data in a cell, select the cell and type the new data. Then press **Enter**, click the **Enter** button in the *Formula* bar, or press any completion key. The new data displays in the cell. To delete data from a cell, select the cell and press **Delete** or click the **Clear** button [*Home* tab, *Editing* group]. From the **Clear** button options, you can choose *Clear All, Clear Formats,* or *Clear Contents* (Figure 1-7). Pressing the **Delete** key removes the contents and preserves formatting.

▶ HOW TO: Clear Cell Contents

1. Select the cell or cells.
2. Press **Delete** on the keyboard.

 - Click the **Clear** button [*Home* tab, *Editing* group] and choose an option.
 - *Clear All* removes formatting and content.
 - *Clear Formats* only clears formatting and keeps data.
 - *Clear Contents* deletes content but keeps formatting.

1-7 *Clear* button options

Align and Indent Cell Contents

Excel recognizes a combination of letters, numbers, spaces, and other characters as a label. Labels are aligned on the left and bottom of the cell. When you type only numbers into a cell, Excel identifies the entry as a value. Values are aligned on the right and bottom of the cell.

You can change the vertical and horizontal *alignment* of data in a cell from the *Alignment* group on the *Home* tab (Figure 1-8). Horizontal alignment choices are *Align Left*, *Center*, and *Align Right*. Vertical alignment options are *Top Align*, *Middle Align*, and *Bottom Align*.

An *indent* moves cell contents away from the left edge of the cell. In Figure 1-8, labels in rows 5:9 are offset from the label in row 4. The **Increase Indent** button [*Home* tab, *Alignment* group] moves cell contents one space to the right if the data is left-aligned. You can remove an indent by clicking the **Decrease Indent** button [*Home* tab, *Alignment* group].

▶ HOW TO: Align and Indent Text

1. Select the cell.
2. Click a horizontal text alignment button [*Home* tab, *Alignment* group].

 - *Center* positions a label midway between the left and right boundaries of the cell.
 - *Align Left* starts a label at the left boundary of the cell.
 - *Right Align* sets a label to end at the right cell boundary.

3. Click a vertical text alignment button [*Home* tab, *Alignment* group].

 - *Middle Align* positions data midway between the top and bottom cell boundaries.
 - *Top Align* places data at the top cell boundary.
 - *Bottom Align* aligns data at the bottom boundary of the cell.

4. Click an indent button [*Home* tab, *Alignment* group].

 - The *Increase Indent* button moves data toward the right cell boundary.
 - The *Decrease Indent* button moves data toward the left cell boundary.

1-8 Alignment and indent options

In addition to horizontal and vertical settings, the *Alignment* group on the *Home* tab includes the *Orientation* button to display data vertically or at an angle. These settings are also available in the *Format Cells* dialog box on the *Alignment* tab (Figure 1-9).

> ### MORE INFO
>
> Click the **Alignment** launcher [*Home* tab, *Alignment* group] or press **Ctrl+1** to open the *Format Cells* dialog box.

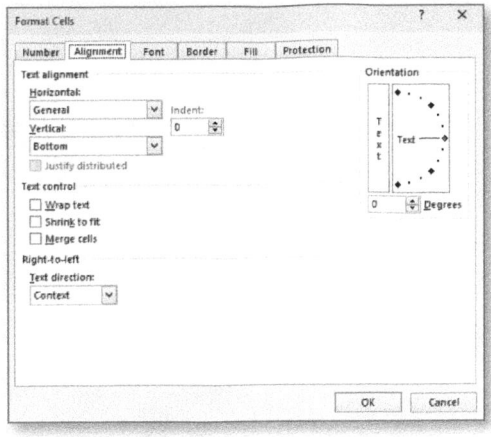

1-9 *Alignment* tab, *Format Cells* dialog box

Select Cells

As you format or edit a worksheet, the first step is to select the cell or cells to be edited. Select a single cell by clicking it. Select a range by clicking the first cell and dragging the pointer in any direction to select adjacent cells. The following table outlines basic selection methods.

Selection Methods

Selection	Instructions
Entire Column or Row	Point to and click the column heading. Point to and click the row heading.
All Worksheet Cells	Press **Ctrl+A** or click the **Select All** button (above the row 1 heading and to the left of the column A heading).
Adjacent Cells by Dragging the Pointer	Click the first cell and drag the selection pointer over the cells to be included. Release the pointer button.
Adjacent Cells Using the Shift Key and the Pointer	Click the first cell, press **Shift**, and click the last cell in the range.
Adjacent Cells Using the Shift and Arrow Keys	Click the first cell, press **Shift**, and press any **Arrow** key.
Nonadjacent Cells	Click a cell or select the first range, press **Ctrl**, and select the next cell or range. Release the pointer button first; then release the **Ctrl** key.
Single Cell or Range Using the *Name Box*	Type a cell or range address in the *Name* box and press **Enter**.

You can see selected cell ranges in Figure 1-10.

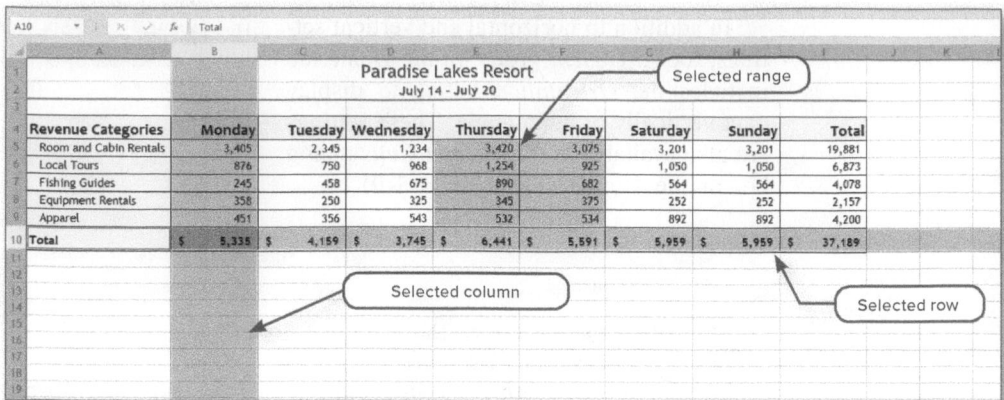

1-10 Selected cells in a worksheet

> **MORE INFO**
>
> To enter data column by column, select the entire cell range, type the first entry, and press **Enter**. Continue to type each entry and press **Enter**. The insertion point moves down each column and to the top of the next column based on the selected range.

The pointer changes shape depending on the current task or mode. The following table describes the shapes and indicates when they appear.

Pointer Shapes

Pointer Icon	Pointer Use
⊹	**Selection pointer** (thick, white cross or plus sign) selects a cell or range; the selection pointer appears when you move the pointer over a cell.
┼	**Fill pointer** (crosshair or thin, black plus sign) copies cell contents or completes a series; it appears when you place the pointer on the *Fill Handle*, the tiny, black square in the bottom right corner of a selected cell or range.
↕	**Move pointer** (solid, white arrow with a black four-pointed arrow) moves data; it appears when you place the pointer on the border of a selected cell or range.
22	**Resize pointer** (two-pointed arrow) adjusts a formula cell range or an object; it appears when you place the pointer on a selection handle in a formula range or on a sizing handle for a selected object.

The Fill Handle

A *series* is a list of labels or values that follows a pattern. An example of a label series is the days of the week or the months of the year. A series of values is 1, 3, 5, 7, 9. Excel recognizes patterns and can complete most series with the ***Fill Handle***. If there is no recognizable series, the *Fill Handle* copies the data.

The *Fill Handle* is a small, black square in the lower right corner of the cell or selected range. You drag this handle across the cell range for the series or to copy data. When you release the pointer button, the data is completed, and the *Auto Fill Options* button displays near the end of the series. This button provides choices for how to complete the series, but you usually need not make any changes.

For series such as the days of the week and the months, you only need enter the first item in the series. For other series, such as 2, 4, 6, 8, you need to enter at least two items for Excel to recognize the pattern.

▶ **HOW TO:** Use the Fill Handle to Create a Series

1. Type the first item in the series and press **Enter**.

 - Press **Ctrl+Enter** to keep the cell active.
 - Type two or three entries to identify a custom series.

2. Select the cell with the entry.

 - Select all cells with data that identify the series.

3. Point to the *Fill Handle* to display the *Fill* pointer (thin, black plus sign) (Figure 1-11).

4. Click and drag the *Fill* pointer through the last cell for the series.

 - A series can be horizontal or vertical.
 - You can double-click the *Fill* pointer to complete data down a column if other columns are already completed to the last row.

5. Release the pointer button.

 - The series is complete and the *Auto Fill Options* button appears.

6. Click the **Auto Fill Options** button.

 - Choose an option as desired (Figure 1-12).

7. Press **Esc** to remove the *Auto Fill Options* button or continue to the next task.

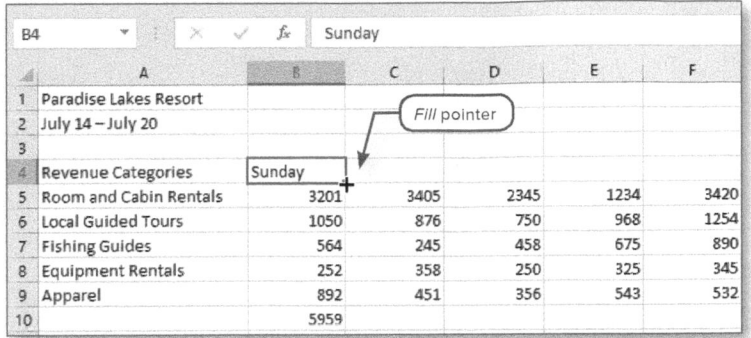

1-11 Use the *Fill Handle* to complete a series

1-12 Completed series with *Auto Fill Options* button

AutoComplete

AutoComplete is an Excel feature that displays a suggested label in a column when the first character or two that you type matches a label already in the column. *AutoComplete* enables you to quickly and accurately complete repetitive data. It works only for data that is alphanumeric, not for a column of values.

In a column that lists city names, for example, a particular city name might be repeated many times. The first time it appears, you type it as usual. On the second and succeeding occurrences of the name, as soon as you type the first character, Excel completes the label but waits for you to accept it. If the *AutoComplete* suggestion is correct, press **Enter**. If the suggestion is not correct, continue typing the label as needed.

Excel usually makes a suggestion after you type a single character in a cell in the column. If the column has more than one entry that begins with that character, type a second character and *AutoComplete* makes another or a better suggestion.

▶ HOW TO: Use AutoComplete

1. Type the first character in a label.
 - A suggested label appears in the cell.
 - Type a second and third character when there are many labels that begin with the same letter.
 - You can type uppercase or lowercase characters to display an *AutoComplete* suggestion.
2. Press **Enter** to accept the *AutoComplete* suggestion (Figure 1-13).
 - Continue typing to ignore an *AutoComplete* suggestion.
 - Press **Enter** to complete a new label.

1-13 *AutoComplete suggestion*

Cut, Copy, and Paste Cell Contents

Excel has the same *Cut*, *Copy*, and *Paste* commands as other Windows applications. Use the **Cut** command to move data from one location to another. The **Copy** command duplicates cell contents to a different location. The **Paste** command places cut or copied data in the selected location. Data is cut or copied from a *source cell* or range and is pasted in a *destination cell* or range. When you cut or copy data, it is usually stored on the Windows *Clipboard* as well as the *Office Clipboard*.

Move or Cut Cell Contents

You can move data using drag and drop, keyboard shortcuts, or *Cut* and *Paste* in the *Clipboard* group on the *Home* tab. Drag and drop is quick when you want to move or copy cells within a visible range on the worksheet. When you use the drag-and-drop method, the source data is not stored on either clipboard.

▶ HOW TO: Move Data Using Drag and Drop

1. Select the cell(s) to be moved.
2. Point to a border of the selection to display a move pointer (white arrow with four-pointed arrow).
3. Click and drag the selection to the new location (Figure 1-14).
 - A preview selection shows the destination address.
4. Release the pointer button.

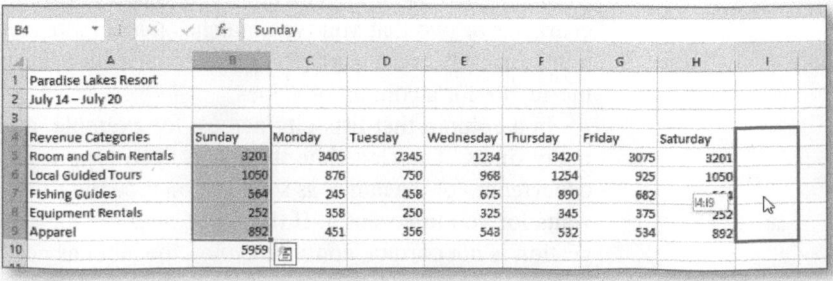

1-14 Drag and drop to move data

When you use the *Cut* command from the *Ribbon* or the keyboard, the selected data is placed on both clipboards. You can paste once from the Windows *Clipboard*. You can paste multiple times from the *Office Clipboard*. There are three methods to cut data:

- *Ribbon* buttons: **Cut** and **Paste** buttons [*Home* tab, *Clipboard* group]
- Shortcut commands: **Ctrl+X** to cut and **Ctrl+V** to paste
- Context menu: Right-click and select **Cut**; right-click and select **Paste**

▶ HOW TO: Move Data Using Cut and Paste

1. Select the cell or range to be moved.
2. Click the **Cut** button [*Home* tab, *Clipboard* group].
 - A moving border surrounds the source cell(s) (Figure 1-15).
3. Select the destination cell.
 - Select the top-left cell in a destination range.
4. Click the **Paste** button [*Home* tab, *Clipboard* group].
 - If the destination cell(s) are not empty, pasted data overwrites existing data.

1-15 Cut data has moving border

The Office Clipboard

The **Office Clipboard** stores cut or copied data from Office applications and makes the data available for pasting in any application. The *Office Clipboard* can hold up to 24 items with each cut or copied item appearing, in turn, at the top of the pane. Click the **Clipboard** launcher to open the *Clipboard* task pane.

▶ HOW TO: Use the Office Clipboard

1. Click the **Home** tab.
2. Click the **Clipboard** launcher to open the *Clipboard* pane (Figure 1-16).
3. Click **Clear All** to empty the *Clipboard*.
 - The button is grayed out if there is no data on the clipboard.

4. Select data to be cut or copied.

5. Click the **Copy** button [*Home* tab, *Clipboard* group].

 - Use any *Cut* or *Copy* command from the *Ribbon* or keyboard.
 - Each item rotates into the first position in the *Clipboard* pane.

6. Select a destination cell.

7. Click the item icon in the *Clipboard* to paste it.

 - You can paste an item multiple times in different locations.

8. Click the **Close** button (X) to hide the *Clipboard*.

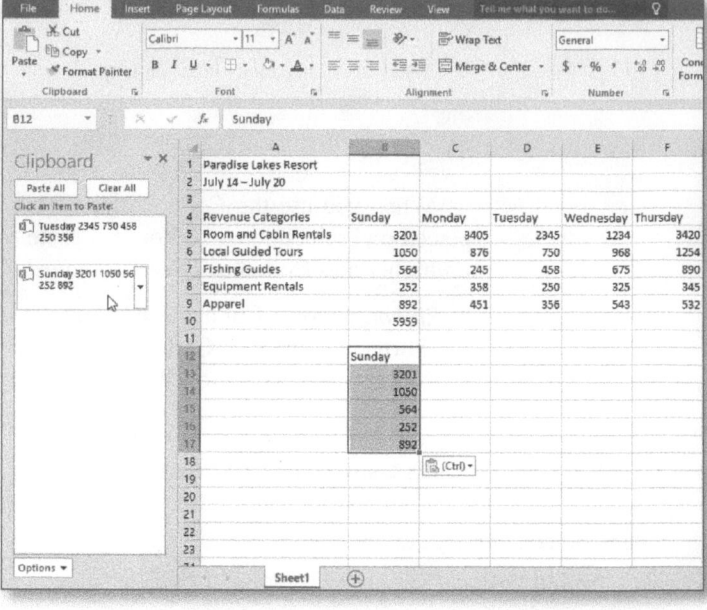

1-16 *Clipboard* pane

> **MORE INFO**
>
> To remove an item from the *Clipboard*
> task pane, click its drop-down arrow
> and choose **Delete**.

Copy Cell Contents

Copying data places a duplicate on the *Clipboard* so that it can be pasted in another location. When you use a *Ribbon*, keyboard, or context menu command, you can paste the data multiple times. You can copy data using the drag-and-drop method and paste it multiple times, even though the copied data is not placed on the *Clipboard*.

The *Copy* command stores data on the *Clipboard*, and the *Paste* command duplicates *Clipboard* contents in the worksheet.

- *Ribbon* buttons: **Copy** and **Paste** buttons [*Home* tab, *Clipboard* group]
- Shortcut commands: **Ctrl+C** to copy and **Ctrl+V** to paste
- Context menu: Right-click and choose **Copy**; right-click and choose **Paste**

▶ HOW TO: Copy Data Using Drag and Drop

1. Select the cell(s) to be copied.

2. Point to a border of the selection to display the move pointer.

3. Press **Ctrl** to display the copy pointer.

 - The copy pointer is a white arrow with a tiny plus sign.

4. Drag the selection to the desired location (Figure 1-17).

 - A preview selection shows where the copy will be pasted.

5. Continue to press **Ctrl** and drag to the next location for another copy.

6. Release the pointer button first and then release **Ctrl**.

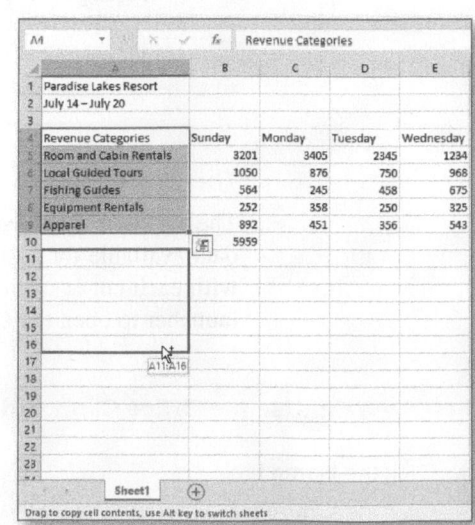

1-17 Copy data using drag and drop

Paste Options

When you paste data, you can choose how it is copied in the new location. You can paste data and formatting, only the data, only the formatting, and so on. To see the options, click the lower half of the **Paste** button [*Home* tab, *Clipboard* group] to open the *Paste Options* gallery. The gallery also displays when you right-click a destination cell.

The table describes the icons in the *Paste Options* gallery:

Paste Options

Group	Paste Icon	Paste Option	Description
Paste		Paste	Copies all data and formatting; this is the default option.
		Formulas	Copies all data and formulas, but no formatting
		Formulas & Number Formatting	Copies all data and formulas with formatting
		Keep Source Formatting	Copies all data and formatting; same as *Paste*
		Match Destination Formatting	Copies data and applies formatting used in the destination
		No Borders	Copies all data, formulas, and formatting except for borders
		Keep Source Column Widths	Copies all data, formulas, and formatting and sets destination column widths to the same width as the source columns
		Transpose	Copies data and formatting and reverses data orientation so that rows are pasted as columns and columns are pasted as rows
		Merge Conditional Formatting	Copies data and *Conditional Formatting* rules. This option is available only if the copied data has conditional formatting.
Paste Values		Values	Copies only formula results (not the formulas) without formatting
		Values & Number Formatting	Copies only formula results (not the formulas) with formatting
		Values & Source Formatting	Copies only formula results (not the formulas) with all source formatting
Other Paste Options		Formatting	Copies only formatting, no data
		Paste Link	Pastes a 3-D reference to data or a formula
		Picture	Pastes a selectable picture object of the data. Data is static, but the object can be formatted like any object.
		Linked Picture	Pastes a selectable picture object of the data. The copied data is dynamic and reflects edits made in the source data. The picture can be formatted like any object.

> **MORE INFO**
>
> The *Paste Special* command opens a dialog box with additional options to paste comments, data validation, themes, and arithmetic operations.

PAUSE & PRACTICE: EXCEL 1-1

In this project, you open an Excel workbook that tracks revenue for one week at Paradise Lakes Resort. You add labels and values to complete the report; align labels; and edit, cut, and paste data. Your worksheet will have deliberate spelling errors for checking in a later Pause & Practice exercise.

File Needed: **ParadiseLakes-01**.xlsx
Completed Project File Name: **[your initials] PP E1-1**.xlsx

1. Open a workbook.
 a. Click the **File** tab and click **Open**.
 b. Navigate to the folder where your data files are stored.
 c. Double-click the name of the folder to open it.
 d. Locate the file name **ParadiseLakes-01** and click to select it.
 e. Click **Open**.
 f. Click **Enable Editing** if the workbook has opened in *Protected View* (Figure 1-18).

1-18 Worksheet opened in *Protected View*

2. Save the workbook with a different name.
 a. Press **F12** (**FN+F12**) to open the *Save As* dialog box.
 b. Select a location to save the workbook.
 c. Change the file name to [your initials] PP E1-1 in the *File name* area.
 d. Click **Save** to save the file and close the *Save As* dialog box.

3. Enter data.
 a. Click cell **A1** and type Paradise Lakes Resort.
 b. Press **Enter**.
 c. Click cell **A10**, type Total, and press **Enter**.
 d. Type the values shown below in cells **G5:H9**.

	G	H
5	3075	3201
6	925	1050
7	682	564
8	375	252
9	534	892

4. Use the *Fill Handle* to complete a series.
 a. Click **B4**.
 b. Point to the *Fill Handle* (small, black square in the lower right corner) until the *Fill* pointer (thin, black plus sign) appears.
 c. Click and drag the *Fill* pointer to reach cell **H4**.
 d. Release the pointer button.

5. Edit worksheet data.
 a. Click cell **B10**.
 b. Press **Delete** to remove the contents.
 c. Double-click cell **A4** to start *Edit* mode.
 d. Click to position the insertion point and delete the "i" in "Categories" to create a deliberate spelling error.
 e. Press **Enter** to accept the edit.
 f. Click cell **A9** and type Aparel with the error. You will correct errors in Pause & Practice 1-4.
 g. Press **Enter** to replace the entry.

6. Indent and align text.
 a. Select cells **A5:A9**.
 b. Click the **Increase Indent** button twice [*Home* tab, *Alignment* group].
 c. Select cells **B4:H4**.
 d. Click the **Center** button [*Home* tab, *Alignment* group].

7. Cut and paste data.
 a. Select cells **B4:B9**.
 b. Click the **Cut** button [*Home* tab, *Clipboard* group].
 c. Click cell **I4**.
 d. Click the **Paste** button [*Home* tab, *Clipboard* group].
 e. Select cells **C4:I9**.
 f. Point to any border of the selected range to display a four-pointed arrow with a white arrow.
 g. Drag the range to start in cell **B4** and release the pointer button.
 h. Click cell **A1**.

8. Save and close the workbook (Figure 1-19).
 a. Press **Ctrl+S** to save the workbook with the same file name.
 b. Click the **Close** button in the upper right corner to exit Excel.

▲	A	B	C	D	E	F	G	H
1	Paradise Lakes Resort							
2	July 14 – July 20							
3								
4	Revenue Categores	Monday	Tuesday	Wednesday	Thursday	Friday	Saturday	Sunday
5	Room and Cabin Rentals	3405	2345	1234	3420	3075	3201	3201
6	Local Tours	876	750	968	1254	925	1050	1050
7	Fishing Guides	245	458	675	890	682	564	564
8	Equipment Rentals	358	250	325	345	375	252	252
9	Aparel	451	356	543	532	534	892	892
10	Total							
11								

1-19 PP E1-1 completed

Using the SUM Function

SLO 1.3

A *formula* calculates a result for numeric data in a cell. A *function* is a built-in formula. *SUM* is a function that adds the values in a cell range. The terms "formula" and "function" are used interchangeably.

To use the *SUM* function, click the cell where you want to show a total. Then click the **AutoSum** button [*Home* tab, *Editing* group]. Excel inserts the function =SUM() with a suggested range of cells to be added between the parentheses. If that range is correct, press **Enter**, **Ctrl+Enter**, or click the **Enter** button in the *Formula* bar to complete the function. If the suggested range is not correct, you can select a different range or choose cells individually and then press a completion key. The sum is shown in the cell, and the function is visible in the *Formula* bar.

> **ANOTHER WAY**
>
> The *Function Library* group on the *Formulas* tab has an *AutoSum* button. You can also enter = SUM() in a cell by pressing **Alt** and the **+/=** key on the top keyboard row.

▶ HOW TO: Use the SUM Function

1. Click the cell for the total.
2. Click the **AutoSum** button [*Home* tab, *Editing* group] (Figure 1-20).
3. Press **Enter** to accept the range and complete the function.
 - Drag the pointer to select a different range before pressing **Enter**.
 - If the row or column of values to be added is adjacent to the formula cell as shown in Figure 1-20, you can double-click the **AutoSum** button to insert and accept the function.

1-20 *SUM* function

> **MORE INFO**
>
> You can display formulas instead of results by clicking the **Show Formulas** button on the *Formulas* tab or by pressing **Ctrl+~**.

Function Syntax

An Excel function has *syntax*, the required elements and the order of those elements for the function to work. Every function starts with the equals sign [=] followed by the name of the function and a set of parentheses. Within the parentheses, you enter the argument(s). An

argument is the cell reference or value required to complete the function. A function can have a single or multiple arguments. In = SUM(B5:B9), the argument is the range B5:B9. Multiple arguments in a function are separated by commas. There are three arguments in this function: =SUM(B5, B10, B15).

<div style="border:1px solid">

SUM(B5:B9)

SUM(B5, B10, B15)

</div>

Copy the SUM Function

The *SUM* function can be copied using regular copy and paste commands as well as the *Fill Handle*. When *SUM* is used to total data in rows or columns, you can enter the formula in the first column or row and copy it to the other locations. In Figure 1-21, for example, the same function is used in cells B10 through H10, each with its own argument. The formula in cell B10 is =SUM(B5:B9), the formula for cell C10 is =SUM(C5:C9) and so on. When a function is copied into adjacent cells, use the *Fill Handle*. Excel copies the formula and adjusts each argument based on the location in the worksheet.

▶ **HOW TO: Use the Fill Handle to Copy a Function**

1. Click the cell with the function to be copied.
2. Point to the *Fill Handle* in the lower right corner.

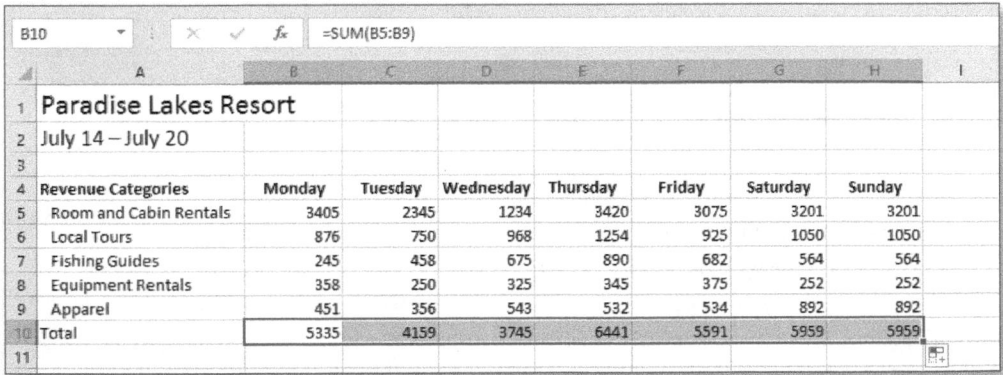

B10		✕ ✓ *fx*	=SUM(B5:B9)					
▲	A	B	C	D	E	F	G	H
1	Paradise Lakes Resort							
2	July 14 – July 20							
3								
4	Revenue Categories	Monday	Tuesday	Wednesday	Thursday	Friday	Saturday	Sunday
5	Room and Cabin Rentals	3405	2345	1234	3420	3075	3201	3201
6	Local Tours	876	750	968	1254	925	1050	1050
7	Fishing Guides	245	458	675	890	682	564	564
8	Equipment Rentals	358	250	325	345	375	252	252
9	Apparel	451	356	543	532	534	892	892
10	Total	5335	4159	3745	6441	5591	5959	5959
11								

1-21 Use the *Fill Handle* to copy a function

3. Click and drag the *Fill* pointer across the cells where the function should be pasted (Figure 1-21).

▶ **ANOTHER WAY**

You can use regular copy and paste commands to copy a function or formula to any location on the worksheet.

Edit the Function Argument

If you edit a value in a cell that is referenced in a formula or function, the results are automatically recalculated. If you must change a cell or range argument in a function, however, you use *Edit* mode to enter new references. In *Edit* mode, you can make a change in the *Formula* bar or in the cell. You can often use the **Range Finder** to drag or select a new range, too. The *Range Finder* is an Excel feature that highlights and color-codes formula cells as you enter or edit a formula or function.

▶ **HOW TO:** Edit an Argument Range in the Formula Bar

1. Select the cell with the function.
2. Click the argument cell range in the *Formula* bar.
 - The *Range Finder* highlights the argument range in the worksheet.
 - The range is color-coded in the *Formula* bar to match the highlighted range (Figure 1-22)
3. Type the new cell references in the *Formula* bar.
4. Press **Enter**.
 - You can click the **Enter** button in the *Formula* bar to complete the edit.

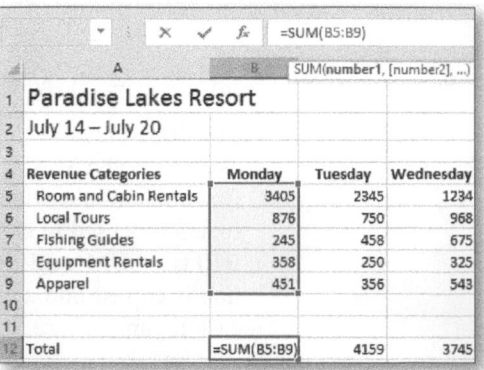

1-22 Argument range is color-coded

You can drag a *Range Finder* handle to select a different argument range, expanding or shrinking the number of included cells. This is easy to do when the formula cell is not adjacent to the range.

> ### ANOTHER WAY
> Double-click the cell with the function and edit the argument in the cell.

▶ **HOW TO:** Edit an Argument Range by Dragging

1. Double-click the cell with the function.
 - *Edit* mode starts (Figure 1-23).
2. Drag the selection handle down to expand the argument range.
 - Drag the selection handle up to shrink the argument range.
3. Press **Enter** to complete the change.
 - Click the **Enter** button in the *Formula* bar.

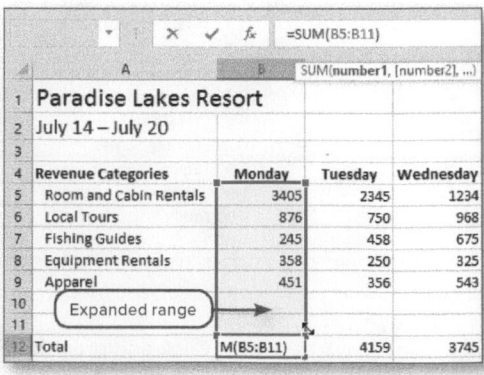

1-23 Edit a cell reference range by dragging

SLO 1.4

Formatting a Worksheet

A new workbook uses a default **theme** named *Office* which is a collection of fonts, colors, and special effects. The default theme applies the 11 point Calibri font and the *General* number format to all cells. You can change the theme as well as individual font attributes, or you can add fill and borders to highlight or emphasize data.

Font Face, Size, Style, and Color

A *font* is a type design for alphanumeric characters, punctuation, and keyboard symbols. *Font size* specifies the size of the character, measured in *points* (pt.). A point is equal to 1/72 of an inch. The *font style* refers to the thickness or angle of the characters and includes settings such as **bold**, <u>underline</u> or *italic*. *Font color* is the hue of the characters in the cell. You can apply any of these font attributes to a single cell or a range of cells.

Default font attributes for Excel 2016 workbooks are:

- Font: Calibri
- Font size: 11 point
- Font color: Black, Text 1

> ### MORE INFO
>
> The font list displayed on your computer depends on your Windows installation and other applications that are installed.

▶ **HOW TO:** Customize Font, Style, Font Size, and Font Color

1. Select the cell or range to be formatted.
 - You can format cells before any data is entered if you prefer.
2. Click the **Font** drop-down list [*Home* tab, *Font* group].
 - A list of available fonts is displayed.
3. Point to a font name.
 - *Live Preview* shows the selected data with the new font applied (Figure 1-24).
4. Click the **Font Size** drop-down list [*Home* tab, *Font* group] and select a size.
 - *Live Preview* shows the selected data in the new size.
 - You can type a custom size in the *Font Size* area.
 - You can also click the **Increase Font Size** or **Decrease Font Size** button [*Home* tab, *Font* group] to adjust the font size in 1-point increments.
5. Click the **Bold**, **Italic**, or **Underline** button [*Home* tab, *Font* group] to apply a style.
 - You can apply multiple styles.
6. Click the **Font Color** drop-down list [*Home* tab, *Font* group] and select a color.
 - Click the **Font Color** button (not the arrow) to apply the most recent font color shown on the button.

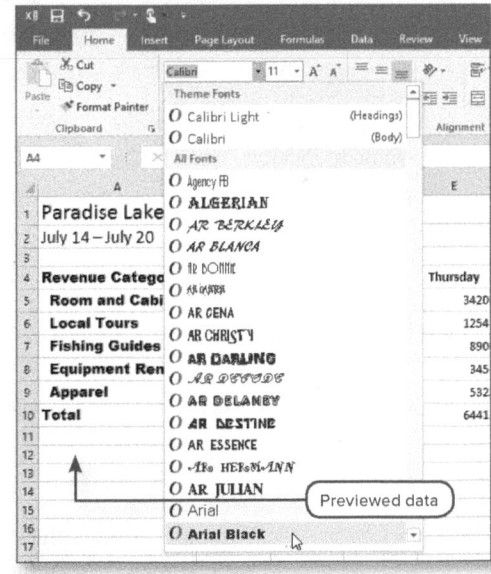

1-24 *Live Preview* when selecting a font name

The *mini toolbar* includes common commands from the *Font*, *Alignment*, and *Number* groups. It appears when you right-click a cell or selected range (Figure 1-25).

1-25 Mini toolbar

The *Format Cells* dialog box includes basic format settings and more. It has six tabs: *Number, Alignment, Font, Border, Fill,* and *Protection.*

- Mini toolbar: Right-click a cell or selected range.
- *Format Cells* dialog box: Click the **Font** launcher in the *Font* group, press **Ctrl+1** or right-click a selected cell and choose **Format Cells** (Figure 1-26).

The Format Painter

The ***Format Painter*** copies formatting attributes and styles from one cell to another cell or range. You can apply your custom formats without having to redefine each attribute, saving time and ensuring an exact duplicate.

1-26 *Format Cells* dialog box

▶ HOW TO: Use the Format Painter

1. Select a cell that contains the formatting you want to copy.
2. Click the **Format Painter** button [*Home* tab, *Clipboard* group].
 - The pointer changes to a thick, white cross with a tiny paint brush.
 - Double-click the **Format Painter** button to lock it for painting formats to multiple areas in the worksheet.
3. Click the cell or drag across the range to be formatted (Figure 1-27).
4. Release the pointer button.
 - The *Format Painter* is canceled.
 - If the *Format Painter* command is locked, click the **Format Painter** button or press **Esc** to turn it off.

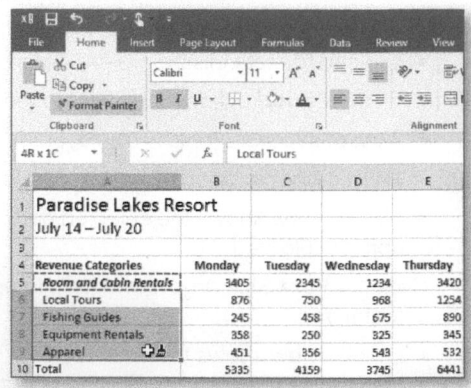

1-27 Copy formats to a range using *Format Painter*

Number Formats

You can format values with currency symbols, decimal points, commas, percent signs, and more so that data is quickly recognized and understood. The *Number* group on the *Home* tab includes command buttons for *Accounting, Percent,* and *Comma* styles as well as command buttons to *Increase Decimal* or *Decrease Decimal.* Dates and times are values, and *Date* and *Time* formats are included in the *Number* group. From the *Format Cells* dialog box, you can apply and customize these number formats or create your own format.

▶ HOW TO: Format Numbers

1. Select the cell or range of values.
2. Click a command button [*Home* tab, *Number* group] (Figure 1-28).

- Click the **Number Format** drop-down list to choose a format.
- Press **Ctrl+1** to open the *Format Cells* dialog box and click the **Number** tab to select a format.

3. Click the **Increase Decimal** or **Decrease Decimal** button to control the number of decimal places.

 - When a cell displays a series of pound or number symbols (#####), you can widen the column to see the value.

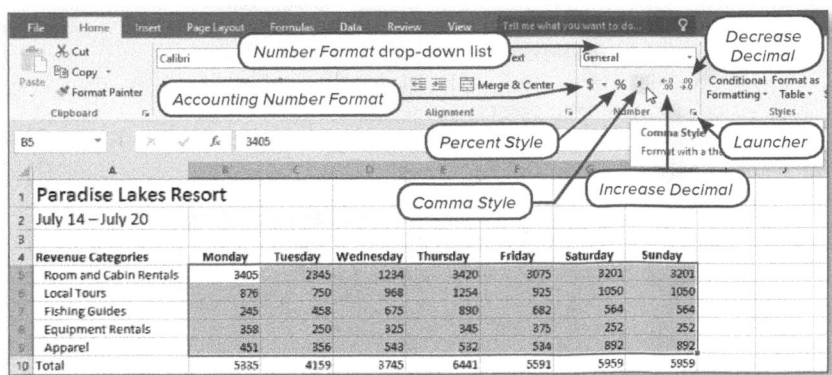

1-28 *Number* group on the *Home* tab

Borders and Fill

A *border* is an outline for a cell or a range. You can design a border to separate main or column headings, to emphasize totals, or to group data. *Fill* is a background color or pattern and is used to highlight or draw attention to data. You can use the *Ribbon* or the *Format Cells* dialog box to apply borders and fill color.

▶**HOW TO:** Add Borders and Fill Using the Ribbon

1. Select the cell or range.

2. Click the arrow next to the **Borders** button [*Home* tab, *Font* group].

 - The **Borders** button shows the most recently used border style.

3. Select a border option from the list (Figure 1-29).

 - To remove a border, choose **No Border**.

4. Click the arrow for the **Fill Color** button [*Home* tab, *Font* group].

 - Click the **Fill Color** button to apply the most recently selected color.
 - To remove a fill, choose **No Fill**.

1-29 *Borders* drop-down list

5. Select a color tile in the palette (Figure 1-30).

 - *Live Preview* displays the cell or range with the color applied.
 - Click **More Colors** to build a custom color.

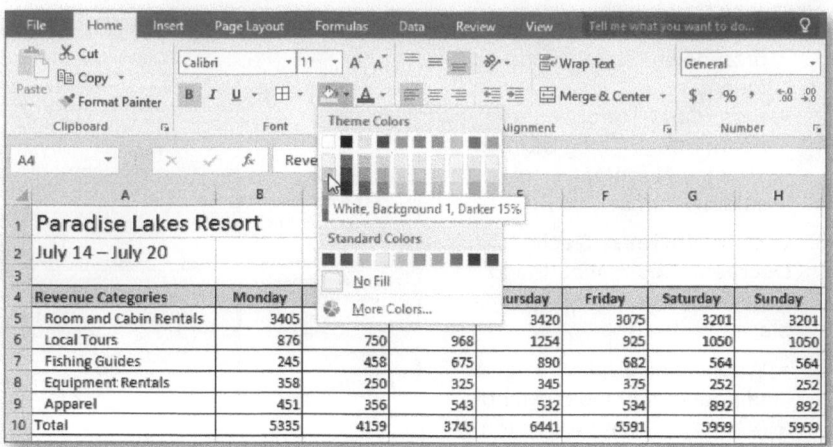

1-30 *Fill Color* palette

The *Format Cells* dialog box has a *Border* tab and a *Fill* tab. From the *Border* tab, you can choose a different line style, a different color, or different positions for the border. From the *Fill* tab, you can design patterned or gradient fills. A ***pattern*** fill uses crosshatches, dots, or stripes. A ***gradient*** is a blend of two or more colors. Use fill choices carefully, because they affect the readability of your data.

▶ **HOW TO:** Add Borders and Fill Using the Format Cells Dialog Box

1. Select the cell or range.

2. Click the **Font** launcher [*Home* tab, *Font* group] to open the *Format Cells* dialog box.

 - Press **Ctrl+1** to open the *Format Cells* dialog box.
 - Right-click a cell in the range and select **Format Cells**.

3. Click the **Border** tab (Figure 1-31).

 - Click **None** to remove all borders.

4. Choose a color from the *Color* drop-down list.

 - Select the color before choosing a line style or location.

5. Select a line style in the *Style* area.

6. Click **Outline** in the *Presets* area to apply an outside border.

 - The *Preview* area shows the border.
 - Build a custom border by clicking the desired icons in the *Border* area or by clicking the desired position in the *Preview* area.

7. Click the **Fill** tab (Figure 1-32).

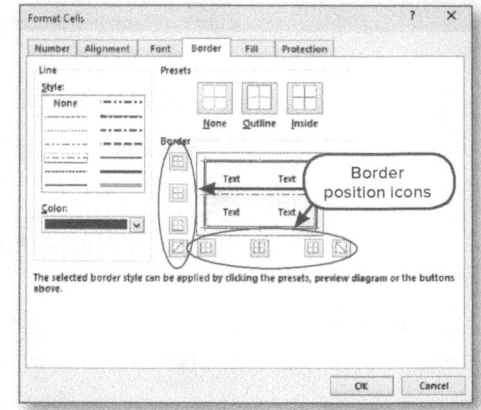

1-31 Build a custom border in the *Format Cells* dialog box

1-32 *Fill* tab in the *Format Cells* dialog box and *Fill Effects* dialog box

8. Select a color tile in the *Background Color* area.
 - Select a color from the *Pattern Color* list and select a pattern from the *Pattern Style* list.
 - Click **Fill Effects** to apply a gradient. Choose two colors, a shading style, and a variant.
9. Click **OK** to close the *Format Cells* dialog box.

Cell Styles

A **cell style** is a set of formatting elements that includes font style, size, color, alignment, borders, and fill as well as number formats. Like other formatting, you select the cell or range and then apply a cell style. When you apply a cell style, the style format overwrites individual formatting already applied. After a cell style is applied, however, you can individually change any of the attributes. The *Cell Styles* gallery is located in the *Styles* group on the *Home* tab.

> ### MORE INFO
> Your screen size and settings determine if you see part of the *Cell Styles* gallery in the *Ribbon* or only the *Cell Styles* button.

▶ HOW TO: Apply Cell Styles

1. Select the cell or range.
2. Click the **More** button in the *Cell Styles* gallery.
 - Click the **Cell Styles** button [*Home* tab, *Styles* group] to open the gallery (Figure 1-33).

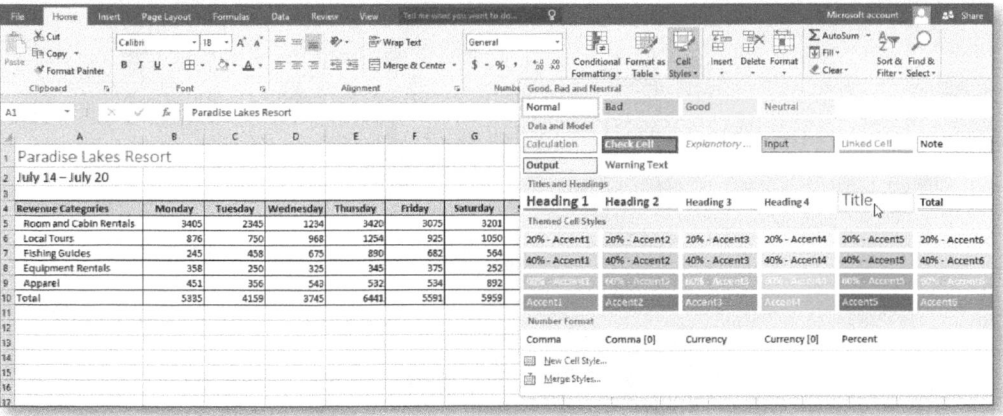

1-33 *Cell Styles* gallery and *Live Preview* for selected cell

3. Point to a style name to see a *Live Preview* in the worksheet.
4. Click a style name to apply it.

Workbook Themes

A workbook **theme** is a professionally designed set of fonts, colors, and effects. When you change the workbook theme, data formatted with theme settings are reformatted with the new

theme fonts, colors, and effects. You can change the theme to quickly restyle a worksheet without having to individually edit cell formats throughout the sheet.

A theme includes a font name for headings and one for body text, and some themes use the same font for both. You can see the names of *Theme Fonts* at the top of the *Font* list. *Theme Colors* are identified in the color palettes for the **Fill** and **Font Color** buttons [*Home* tab, *Font* group]. Cell styles use font and color settings from the theme.

The *Themes* gallery lists built-in themes, and there are additional themes available online. You can also create and save your own theme.

▶ **HOW TO: Change the Workbook Theme**

1. Click the **Theme** button [*Page Layout* tab, *Themes* group]
 • The *Themes* gallery opens.
2. Point to a theme name.
 • *Live Preview* displays the worksheet with new format settings (Figure 1-34).

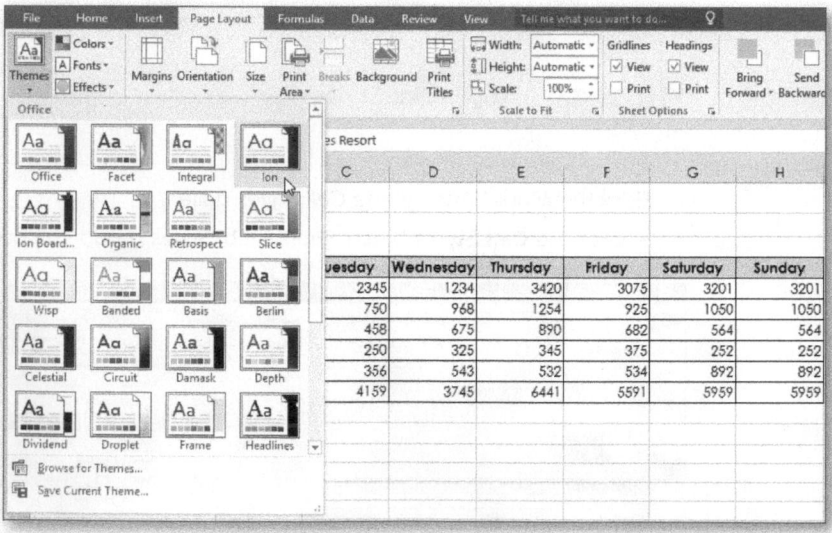

1-34 *Themes* gallery and a *Live Preview* in the worksheet

3. Click a theme icon to apply a different theme.
 • Display the **Font** button list [*Home* tab, *Font* group] to see the new theme font names at the top of the list.
 • Display the **Font Color** and **Fill Color** button galleries [*Home* tab, *Font* group] to see new theme colors.

▶ MORE INFO

Rest the pointer on the **Themes** button [*Page Layout* tab, *Themes* group] to see the name of the current theme.

PAUSE & PRACTICE: EXCEL 1-2

In this project, you open the workbook you created in *Pause & Practice Excel 1-1*. You add totals using *SUM* and copy the function using *AutoFill*. Your format changes result in truncated or cutoff data; you learn how to adjust column widths in the next learning objective and will fix this problem in the next Pause & Practice project.

File Needed: ***[your initials] PP E1-1****.xlsx*
Completed Project File Name: ***[your initials] PP E1-2****.xlsx*

1. Open a workbook and save it as a different name.
 a. Click the **File** tab and choose **Open**. If you have just started Excel and the file name appears in the *Recent* list in the Excel *Start* page, click the name to open it. Otherwise, click **Open Other Workbooks** at the bottom of the *Start* page.
 b. Locate the folder where your file is stored.
 c. Open ***[your initials] PP E1-1***. (Click **Enable Editing** if the workbook has opened in *Protected View*).
 c. Press **F12 (FN+F12)** to open the *Save As* dialog box.
 d. Locate the folder where your files are saved.
 e. Edit the file name to [your initials] PP E1-2 and click **Save**.

2. Calculate daily totals using *SUM*.
 a. Click cell **B10**.
 b. Click the **AutoSum** button [*Home* tab, *Editing* group].
 c. Press **Enter** to accept the suggested range and to complete the formula.

3. Copy a function using the *Fill Handle*.
 a. Click cell **B10**.
 b. Point to the *Fill Handle* in the lower right corner of the cell.
 c. Click and drag the *Fill* pointer to cell **H10** (Figure 1-35). Release the pointer button.

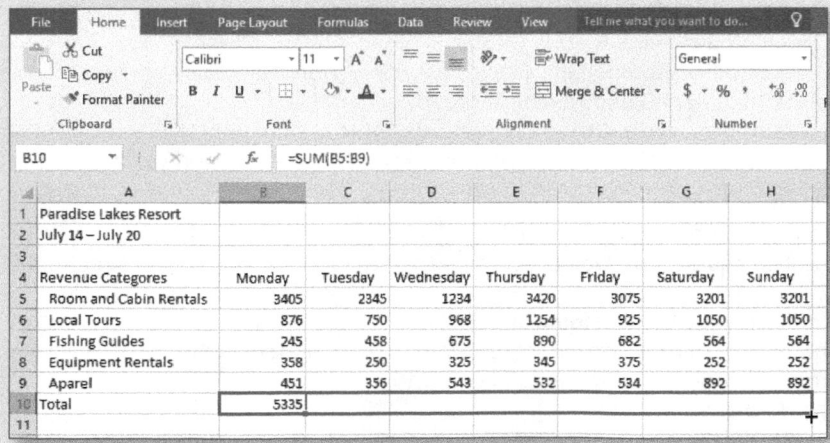

1-35 Copy a function with the *Fill* pointer

4. Calculate sales category totals.
 a. Click cell **J5**.
 b. Double-click the **AutoSum** button [*Home* tab, *Editing* group] to accept and complete the formula.

E1-28

5. Edit the argument cell range.
 a. Click cell **J5**.
 b. Click the *Formula* bar within the range **B5:I5**.
 c. Position the insertion point and edit the range to **B5:h5**. When you type the "h," you will see a *Formula AutoComplete* list which you can ignore (Figure 1-36).
 d. Press **Enter** to accept the new range.

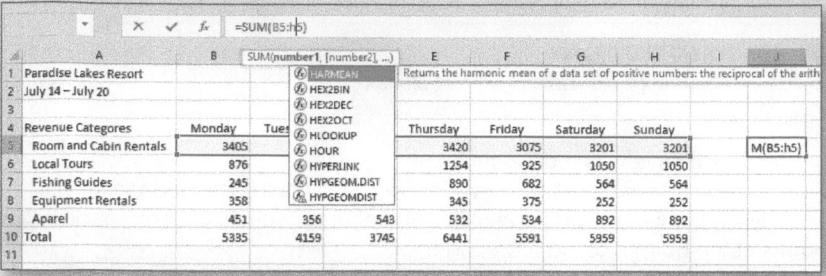

1-36 Edit the cell reference in the *Formula* bar

6. Copy a function using the *Fill Handle*.
 a. Select cell **J5** and point to the *Fill Handle*.
 b. Click and drag the *Fill* pointer to cell **J10**. Release the pointer button.

7. Drag and drop to move a cell range.
 a. Select cells **J5:J10**.
 b. Point to any border of the selected range to display the move pointer.
 c. Drag the range to cells **I5:I10**.
 d. In cell **I4**, type Total.

8. Apply cell styles.
 a. Select cell **A1** and click the **Cell Styles** button or the **More** button [*Home* tab, *Styles* group] to open the *Cell Styles* gallery.
 b. Click **Title** in the *Titles and Headings* group.
 c. Select cell **A2** and click the **Cell Styles** button or the **More** button [*Home* tab, *Styles* group].
 d. Select **Heading 2** in the *Titles and Headings* group.
 e. Select cells **A10:I10** and open the *Cell Styles* gallery [*Home* tab, *Styles* group].
 f. Select **Total** in the *Titles and Headings* group.
 g. Select cells **A4:A10**, press **Ctrl**, and select cells **B4:I4** to add them to the selection.
 h. Open the *Cells Style* gallery and select **20%, Accent1** in the *Themed Cell Styles* category.
 i. Click cell **F1** to deselect cells and view the styles.

9. Change the theme and apply font attributes.
 a. Click the **Themes** button [*Page Layout* tab, *Themes* group] and choose **Facet** from the gallery.
 b. Select cell **A4** and click the **Home** tab.
 c. Click the **Font** drop-down list [*Font* group] and select **Candara** in the *All Fonts* section.
 d. Click the **Font Size** drop-down list and select **16 pt**.
 e. Click the **Bold** button [*Font* group].
 f. Select cells **A5:I10**.
 g. Click the **Font Size** drop-down list and choose **12 pt**.

10. Use the *Format Painter*.
 a. Click cell **A4**.
 b. Click the **Format Painter** button [*Home* tab, *Clipboard* group].
 c. Drag to paint cells **B4:I4** and release the pointer button (Figure 1-37).

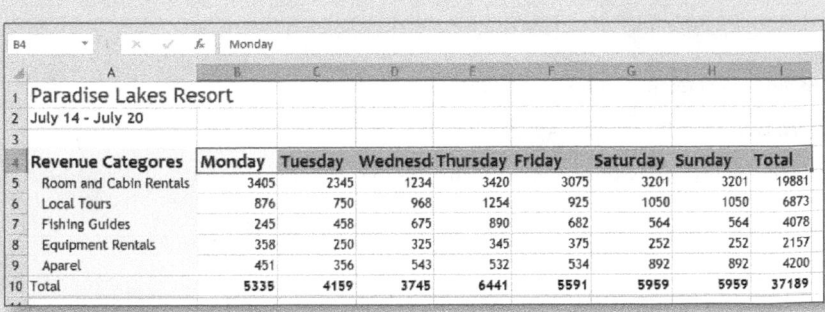

	A	B	C	D	E	F	G	H	I
1	Paradise Lakes Resort								
2	July 14 - July 20								
3									
4	Revenue Categores	Monday	Tuesday	Wednesd	Thursday	Friday	Saturday	Sunday	Total
5	Room and Cabin Rentals	3405	2345	1234	3420	3075	3201	3201	19881
6	Local Tours	876	750	968	1254	925	1050	1050	6873
7	Fishing Guides	245	458	675	890	682	564	564	4078
8	Equipment Rentals	358	250	325	345	375	252	252	2157
9	Aparel	451	356	543	532	534	892	892	4200
10	Total	5335	4159	3745	6441	5591	5959	5959	37189

1-37 Paint the format from cell A4

11. Apply number formats and align text.
 a. Select cells **B5:I9**.
 b. Click the **Comma Style** button [*Home* tab, *Number* group] and leave cells B5:I9 selected.
 c. Click the **Decrease Decimal** button [*Home* tab, *Number* group] two times while cells B5:I9 are selected.
 d. Select cells **B10:I10**.
 e. Click the **Accounting Number Format** button [*Home* tab, *Number* group]. You may see a series of # symbols in the cells.
 f. Click the **Decrease Decimal** button [*Home* tab, *Number* group] two times.
 g. Select cells **B4:I4**.
 h. Click the **Align Right** button [*Home* tab, *Alignment* group]. Not all labels are visible with this alignment setting.
 i. Apply **Bold** to cell **A10**.

12. Add borders.
 a. Select cells **A4:I10** and click the **Border** button arrow [*Home* tab, *Font* group].
 b. Select **All Borders**. The border format from the *Total* cell style in row 10 is overwritten with the *All Borders* format.
 c. Select cells **A10:I10** and press **Ctrl+1** to open the *Format Cells* dialog box.
 d. Click the **Border** tab.
 e. Click the bottom border icon In the *Border* preview area to remove the border (Figure 1-38).
 f. Click the double solid line style (second column, seventh style).
 g. In the preview area, click the bottom border position to reset the border (Figure 1-39).
 h. Click **OK** to close the *Format Cells* dialog box and to apply the new border.
 i. Select cells **A2:I2** and open the *Format Cells* dialog box.
 j. Click the **Border** tab and click the bottom border position two times to remove the bottom border.
 k. Click the **Color** drop-down list, and select **Dark Green, Accent 2, Darker 25%**.

1-38 Remove the bottom border

1-39 Reset the bottom border

l. Select the thick, solid line style (second column, fifth style).

m. In the preview area, click the bottom border location to reset the border.

n. Click **OK** and then click cell **A1**.

13. Click the **Save** button in the *Quick Access* toolbar.

14. Click the **File** tab and click **Close**, or press **Ctrl+W** to close the workbook (Figure 1-40).

Paradise Lakes Resort								
July 14 - July 20								
Revenue Categores	**Monday**	**Tuesday**	**ednesday**	**Thursday**	**Friday**	**Saturday**	**Sunday**	**Total**
Room and Cabin Rentals	3,405	2,345	1,234	3,420	3,075	3,201	3,201	19,881
Local Tours	876	750	968	1,254	925	1,050	1,050	6,873
Fishing Guides	245	458	675	890	682	564	564	4,078
Equipment Rentals	358	250	325	345	375	252	252	2,157
Aparel	451	356	543	532	534	892	892	4,200
Total	$ 5,335	$ 4,159	$ 3,745	$ 6,441	$ 5,591	$ 5,959	$ 5,959	$ 37,189

1-40 PP E1-2 completed

Modifying Columns and Rows

A worksheet has a default number of rows and columns, each in the default width and height for the workbook theme. There are over 1 million rows and more than 16,000 columns available for use. You can modify the width of a column, insert columns, change the height of a row, delete a column, and more.

 MORE INFO

Unused rows and columns are ignored when you print a worksheet with default print settings.

Adjust Column Width and Row Height

The default width for a column in a worksheet using the Office theme is 8.43 characters (64 pixels) in the default font. Column width can be set to any value between 0 and 255 characters. The default height of each row is 15 points (20 pixels). A *pixel* measures one screen dot. You can change *column width* or *row height* by dragging the border between column or row headings, by using the context menu, or by selecting a command from the **Format** button list [*Home* tab, *Cells* group]. You can adjust one or more columns or rows at the same time.

▶ **HOW TO:** Change Column Width or Row Height

1. Select one or more cells in the same column.
 - The cells need not be in adjacent rows.
2. Click the **Format** button [*Home* tab, *Cells* group].
3. Select **Row Height**.
 - The *Row Height* dialog box opens.

4. Enter a height in points and click **OK**.
 - The row height is adjusted for the rows in which you selected cells.
5. Select one or more cells in the same row.
 - The cells need not be in adjacent columns.
6. Click the **Format** button [*Home* tab, *Cells* group].
7. Select **Column Width**.
 - The *Column Width* dialog box opens.
8. Enter a new width in characters and click **OK** (Figure 1-41).

1-41 Change the column width for several columns

> **MORE INFO**
>
> Click the **Format** button [*Home* tab, *Cells* group] and select **Default Width** to change the default column width for the entire worksheet.

You can quickly change column widths and row heights using the worksheet headings. Point to the border between two column or row headings and click and drag to set a new width or height. When you point to a border, the pointer changes to a resize arrow, and you will see a *ScreenTip* with the setting as you drag. You can use this method with multiple columns or rows, too. Drag across the headings to select the number of columns or rows to be adjusted, and then click and drag any border in the selected group.

AutoFit Columns and Rows

The *AutoFit* feature resizes column width or row height to fit the width or height of the longest or tallest entry. The quickest way to *AutoFit* a column is to double-click the right border of the column heading (Figure 1-42). To *AutoFit* a row, double-click the bottom border of the row heading. You can *AutoFit* multiple columns or rows by first selecting them and double-clicking any border within the selection. You can also use the *AutoFit Column Width* or the *AutoFit Row Height* commands on the **Format** button in the *Cells* group on the *Home* tab.

> **HOW TO: AutoFit Column Width or Row Height**

1-42 Double-click a column border to *AutoFit* its width to the longest item

1. Point to the border to the right of the column heading or below the row heading.
 - Drag to select more than one column or row.
2. Double-click the resize arrow.
 - All selected columns and rows are set to fit the longest or tallest entry.

Wrap Text, Merge Cells, and Center Across Selection

When a label is too long for the column width, it spills into an empty adjacent cell. If that adjacent cell is not empty, a long label may be cut off within the cell. You can widen the column, or you can wrap text. Wrapped text is often used to show lengthy column titles on more than one line (Figure 1-43).

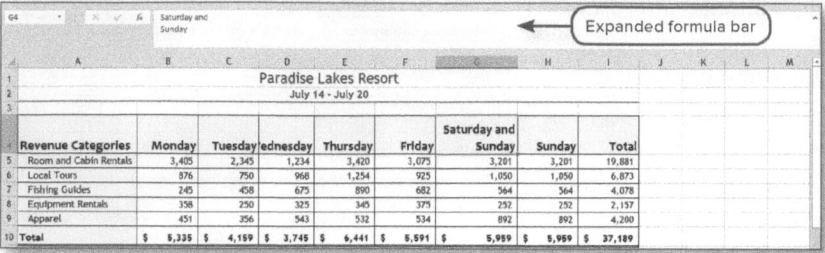

1-43 Label in cell G4 is wrapped to two lines; *Formula* bar is expanded

The **Wrap Text** command displays a label on multiple lines within the cell, splitting the label between words to fit the width of the column. You can control where the label splits by inserting a manual **line break**. Press **Alt+Enter** after the word where you want a new line to start. When using multi-line labels, you can expand the *Formula* bar by clicking the **Formula Bar** expand or collapse button at the right edge of the *Formula* bar.

> **MORE INFO**
>
> After using the *Wrap Text* command, you may need to adjust the column width or row height to better display the label.

> ▶ **HOW TO:** Wrap Text in a Cell

1. Select the cell with the label.
2. Click the **Home** tab.
3. Click the **Wrap Text** button in the *Alignment* group.
 - To control the split, edit the cell and click at the desired location. Press **Alt+Enter** to insert a manual line break and then press **Enter** to finish.
4. Adjust the column width and row height as desired.

> ▶ **ANOTHER WAY**
>
> As you type a label, press **Alt+Enter** at the point where a new line should start, finish the label, and press **Enter**. The *Wrap Text* command is automatically enabled.

The **Merge & Center** command combines two or more cells into one cell and centers the data within the combined cell. This command is a quick way to center a main label over multiple columns. Because the result is one large cell, you can format the area with special fill effects. When you use *Merge & Center*, the data must be in the upper left cell of the selection.

The *Merge & Center* button [*Home* tab, *Alignment* group] includes options to merge cells without centering and to unmerge cells.

▶ HOW TO: Merge and Center

1. Select the cells to be merged and centered.

 - You can merge and center the cells first and then enter the data.

2. Click the **Home** tab.

3. Click the **Merge & Center** button [*Alignment* group] (Figure 1-44).

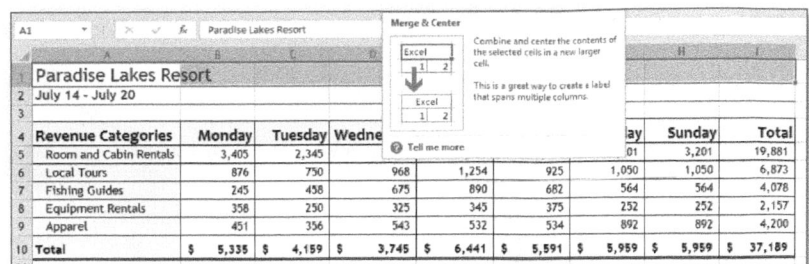

1-44 Select cells to merge and center

The ***Center Across Selection*** command horizontally centers multiple rows across multiple columns. When you have two or three rows of labels to center, you can select the entire range and center them with one command. This command does not merge cells, and you can still insert and delete rows and columns in the centered area.

The *Center Across Selection* command is on the *Alignment* tab in the *Format Cells* dialog box.

▶ HOW TO: Center Across a Selection

1. Select the cell range that includes the data to be centered.

 - Select all rows with data to be centered.
 - Select columns to identify the range over which the labels should be centered.

2. Click the **Alignment** launcher [*Home* tab, *Alignment* group].

3. Click the **Horizontal** drop-down arrow and choose **Center Across Selection** (Figure 1-45).

4. Click **OK**.

1-45 Selection identifies area for centering

Insert and Delete Columns and Rows

You can insert or delete rows or columns in a worksheet. When you do, Excel moves existing data to make room for new data or to fill the gap left by deleted data. Functions or formulas are automatically updated to include an inserted row or column, and they reflect deleted rows or columns in the argument or range.

You can insert rows and columns from options on the **Insert** button [*Home* tab, *Cells* group]. You can also right-click a column or row heading and choose **Insert** from the context menu. To insert multiple columns or rows, first select the number of columns or rows that you want to insert. For example, if you want to insert two columns to the left of column A, select columns A:B. Then use any **Insert** command to insert two new columns.

▶ HOW TO: Insert a Column or a Row

1. Select a cell in the column to the right of where a new column is to be inserted.
2. Click the arrow on the **Insert** button [*Home* tab, *Cells* group].
3. Select **Insert Sheet Columns**.
 - A column is inserted to the left of the current column.
4. Right-click the row heading below the row where a new row should appear.
5. Choose **Insert** from the context menu (Figure 1-46).
 - A row is inserted above the selected row.

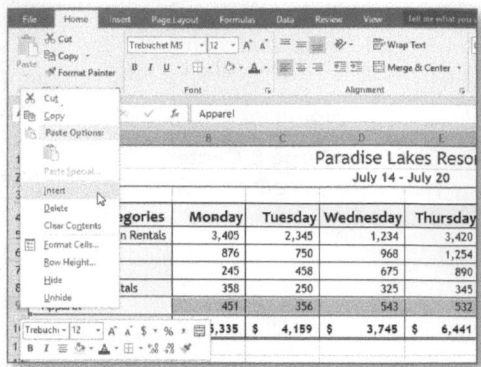

1-46 Insert a row above row 9

When you delete a column or row, data is deleted and remaining columns and rows shift to the left or up. Most functions or formulas are updated if you delete a row or column that is within the argument range.

You can delete rows and columns from the **Delete** button [*Home* tab, *Cells* group] or from the context menu. To delete multiple columns or rows, select them and use the **Delete** command.

> **ANOTHER WAY**
>
> Select a cell and press **Ctrl+plus sign (+)** in the numeric keypad. Choose **Entire Column** or **Entire Row** and press **Enter**. Press **Ctrl+minus sign (−)** in the numeric keypad to delete a column or row.

▶ HOW TO: Delete Columns or Rows

1. Select a cell in the column to be deleted.
2. Click the arrow on the **Delete** button [*Home* tab, *Cells* group].
3. Select **Delete Sheet Columns**.
 - The entire column is deleted.
 - Remaining columns shift to the left.
4. Right-click the row heading for the row to be deleted.
 - The context menu opens.
5. Choose **Delete**.
 - The entire row is deleted.
 - Remaining rows shift up.

> **MORE INFO**
>
> You can delete or insert cells with the **Insert Cells** or **Delete Cells** commands [*Home* tab, *Cells* group]. Be careful with these commands, because they delete only cells, move adjacent data, and can have unexpected results in a worksheet.

Hide and Unhide Columns and Rows

If a worksheet has more data than necessary for your current task, you can hide data to optimize screen space. In a checkbook register with data for several years, you might want to hide rows from two years ago so that you only see the current year's data. You should not delete the old data because it is necessary for record-keeping.

Hidden rows and columns are available and included in calculations and can be shown whenever necessary. The ***Hide*** and ***Unhide*** commands apply to columns or rows; you cannot hide cells. When a column or row is hidden, there is a tiny gap between the column or row headings. In addition, column or row headings are not consecutive, so you can quickly identify what is hidden.

▶ HOW TO: Hide and Unhide Columns or Rows

1. Click the row or column heading of the row or column to be hidden.
 - Select multiple row or column headings as desired.
 - Rows or columns need not be adjacent.
2. Right-click one of the selected row or column headings.
 - The context menu opens.
3. Select **Hide** (Figure 1-47).
 - The entire row or column is hidden.
 - Formula references to hidden cells are maintained.
4. Drag across the column or row headings where there are hidden columns or rows.
 - Drag from the column to the left of a hidden column to one column to the right of a hidden column.
 - Drag from the row above hidden rows to one row below hidden rows.
5. Right-click one of the selected row or column headings.
 - The context menu opens.
6. Select **Unhide**.

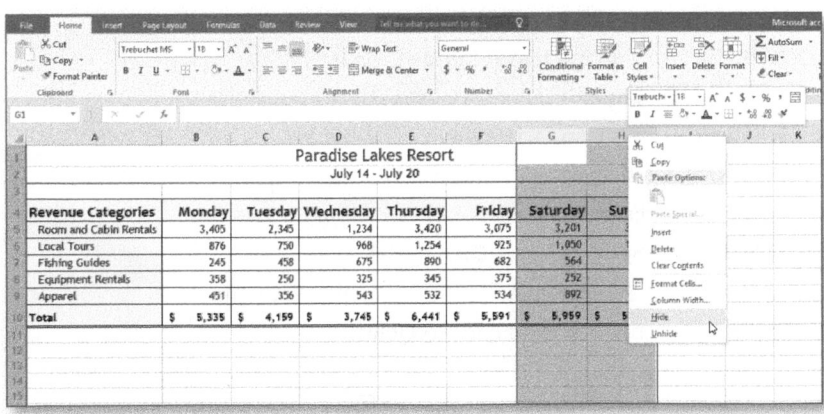

1-47 Hide two columns

> **ANOTHER WAY**
>
> To hide or unhide columns or rows, select the column or row headings, click the **Format** button [*Home* tab, *Cells* group], choose **Hide & Unhide**, and select the desired command.

SLO 1.6

Modifying Worksheets

Each worksheet in an Excel workbook has a worksheet tab near the bottom left of the Excel window that displays the name of the sheet. A new workbook starts with one sheet, but the number of worksheets is limited only by the size of memory on the computer. You can insert and delete sheets, rename them, and change the tab color. You can also hide, copy, or move sheets.

Insert and Delete Worksheets

You can keep related worksheets in a single workbook for ease in managing your files and tasks. For example, a monthly workbook could include revenue and expense, payroll, and customer data sheets. When there are multiple worksheets in a workbook, activate a sheet by clicking its tab name.

You can insert worksheets from the **Insert** button [*Home* tab, *Cells* group] or by simply clicking the **New Sheet** button to the right of the tab names. You can also right-click an existing sheet tab and choose **Insert** to open an *Insert* dialog box. Inserted worksheets are named *SheetN*, where *N* is the next available number.

To delete the active worksheet, right-click the sheet tab and select **Delete**. You can also click the arrow on the **Delete** button [*Home* tab, *Cells* group] and select **Delete Sheet**.

> **MORE INFO**
>
> Press **Ctrl+Page Down** to move to the next worksheet in the tab order. Press **Ctrl+Page Up** to move to the previous sheet.

> **HOW TO:** Insert and Delete Worksheets

1. Click the **New Sheet** button (plus sign) to the right of the worksheet tabs (Figure 1-48).
 • A new sheet is inserted to the right of the active sheet.
2. Click the arrow on the **Insert** button [*Home* tab, *Cells* group].
3. Select **Insert Sheet**.
 • A new sheet is inserted to the left of the active sheet.
4. Right-click a tab and select **Insert**.
 • The *Insert* dialog box opens.
5. Select **Worksheet** and click **OK**.
 • The new sheet is inserted to the left of the active sheet.
6. Right-click a sheet tab and choose **Delete**.
 • The sheet is deleted.
7. Click the arrow on the **Delete** button [*Home* tab, *Cells* group] and select **Delete Sheet**.
 • The sheet is deleted.

New Sheet button

1-48 *New Sheet* button

> **ANOTHER WAY**
>
> Press **Shift+F11** to insert a worksheet to the left of the active sheet.

> **MORE INFO**
>
> To delete or insert multiple sheets, select multiple tabs. Then right-click one of the selected tabs and choose **Delete** or **Insert**.

Rename Worksheets and Change Tab Color

New worksheets are named *Sheet1*, *Sheet2*, and so on, but you can rename a worksheet to identify its contents and purpose. The tab width adjusts to display the name, so if you use lengthy names, you limit the number of tabs visible at the same time. When you cannot see all the tabs, use the ***tab scrolling buttons*** located to the left of the leftmost tab name. Move forward and backward through the tabs, or you can right-click a tab scrolling button to display the *Activate* dialog box with a list of existing worksheet names (Figure 1-49). The tab scrolling buttons are enabled when needed.

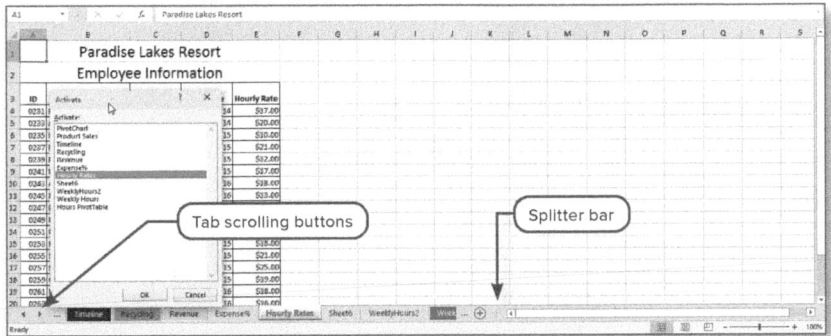

1-49 Activate dialog box and tab scrolling buttons

> **MORE INFO**
>
> The number of tab names visible at one time depends on the width of the horizontal scroll bar. Use the tab splitter to resize the horizontal scroll bar.

You can apply a ***tab color*** to further distinguish a particular sheet. The color palette includes tiles for theme and standard colors as well as an option to build a custom color.

▶ HOW TO: Rename a Worksheet and Apply a Tab Color

1. Double-click the worksheet tab.
 - You can right-click the tab and select **Rename**.
2. Type the new name on the tab and press **Enter**.
 - You can click the **Format** button [*Home* tab, *Cells* group] and select **Rename Sheet**.
3. Right-click the worksheet tab.
4. Choose **Tab Color** from the context menu to open the palette (Figure 1-50).
 - You can click the **Format** button [*Home* tab, *Cells* group] and select **Tab Color**.

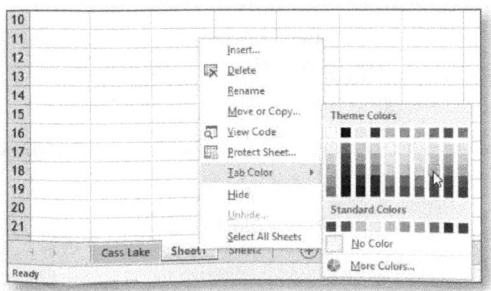

1-50 Change the tab color

5. Select a color.

6. Click another tab to better see the tab color.

Move and Copy Worksheets

You can rearrange (move) tabs to display the worksheets in your preferred left-to-right order. You can also move worksheets to another workbook.

You can copy a worksheet to make an exact duplicate of the data and formatting. When you copy a worksheet, the copy is named with the same name as the original followed by a number in parentheses (i.e., *January (2)*).

When moving sheets within a workbook, you simply drag the tab to the desired location. When moving or copying to another workbook, however, use the ***Move or Copy*** dialog box.

You can move or copy multiple sheets, too. Select sheet names using **Ctrl** or **Shift**. The word *[Group]* displays in the title bar. After you complete the move or copy command, right-click any tab in the group and choose **Ungroup**.

▶**HOW TO: Move and Copy Worksheets**

1. Point to the worksheet tab to be moved.

2. Drag the pointer to the desired location in the tab names.

 • A triangle and a worksheet icon preview where the worksheet will be moved (Figure 1-51).

3. Release the pointer button.

4. Right-click the worksheet tab to be copied.

5. Select **Move or Copy**.

 • The *Move or Copy* dialog box opens.
 • You can also click the **Format** button [*Home* tab, *Cells* group] to select **Move or Copy Sheet**.

6. Click the **To book** drop-down arrow and choose a workbook name.

 • To copy the sheet in the same workbook, choose its name.
 • To copy the worksheet into a different workbook, choose its name; the workbook must be open.

7. In the *Before sheet* list, choose a sheet name as desired.

 • Choose **(move to end)** to place the copied sheet as the last tab.

8. Select the **Create a copy** box (Figure 1-52).

9. Click **OK** to close the dialog box.

 • The copied worksheet has the same name as the original followed by *(2)*.

10. Rename the copied sheet as desired.

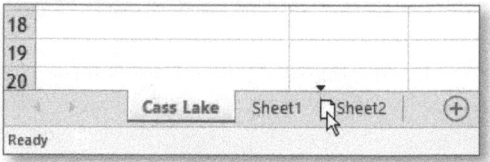

1-51 Drag a sheet tab to a position

1-52 *Move or Copy* dialog box

▶**ANOTHER WAY**

To copy a worksheet by dragging, press **Ctrl** and drag the tab to the desired location for the copy.

In this project, you open *[your initials] PP E1-2* and adjust column heights and row widths, insert a row, merge and center cells, and add borders. You also copy and rename sheets, apply tab colors, and delete worksheets.

File Needed: *[your initials] PP E1-2.xlsx*
Completed Project File Name: *[your initials] PP E1-3.xlsx*

1. Open the *[your initials] PP E1-2* workbook completed in *Pause & Practice 1-2*.

2. Save the file as [your initials] PP E1-3.

3. Change the width of columns B through I.
 a. Point to the column **B** heading to display a down-pointing arrow.
 b. Click and drag to reach column **I**.
 c. Click the **Format** button [*Home* tab, *Cells* group].
 d. Select **Column Width** from the menu.
 e. Enter 14 in the *Column Width* dialog box.
 f. Click **OK** to set the new width for the selected columns.

4. Change the row height for rows 4 and 10.
 a. Click the row **4** heading.
 b. Press **Ctrl** and click the row **10** heading. Two rows are selected.
 c. Right-click the row **4** heading.
 d. Choose **Row Height** from the menu.
 e. Enter 24 as the new height.
 f. Click **OK** to set the row height for both rows.

5. Insert a row.
 a. Right-click row heading **9**.
 b. Choose **Insert**. The inserted row is row 9, and the remaining rows have shifted down.
 c. In cell **A9**, type Food & Beverage. The new row uses the same format as the other rows (Figure 1-53).
 d. Press **Enter**.

A10	▾	✕ ✓ *fx*	Aparel						
	A	**B**	**C**	**D**	**E**	**F**	**G**	**H**	**I**
1	Paradise Lakes Resort								
2	July 14 - July 20								
3									
4	Revenue Categores	Monday	Tuesday	Wednesday	Thursday	Friday	Saturday	Sunday	Total
5	Room and Cabin Rentals	3,405	2,345	1,234	3,420	3,075	3,201	3,201	19,881
6	Local Tours	876	750	968	1,254	925	1,050	1,050	6,873
7	Fishing Guides	245	458	675	890	682	564	564	4,078
8	Equipment Rentals	358	250	325	345	375	252	252	2,157
9	Food & Beverage								
10	Aparel	451	356	543	532	534	892	892	4,200
11	Total	$ 5,335	$ 4,159	$ 3,745	$ 6,441	$ 5,591	$ 5,959	$ 5,959	$ 37,189
12									

1-53　New row and label inserted

6. Hide a row.
 a. Select cell **A9**.
 b. Click the **Format** button [*Home* tab, *Cells* group].
 c. Select **Hide & Unhide** in the *Visibility* category.
 d. Select **Hide Rows**. The selected row is hidden.

7. Center titles across a selection.
 a. Select cells **A1:I2**.
 b. Click the **Alignment** launcher [*Home* tab, *Alignment* group].

c. Click the **Horizontal** drop-down arrow and choose **Center Across Selection**.
d. Click **OK**.

8. Rename a worksheet and change the tab color.
 a. Double-click the **Sheet1** tab name.
 b. Type Cass Lake.
 c. Press **Enter**.
 d. Right-click the **Cass Lake** tab name and select **Tab Color**.
 e. Select **Green Accent 1, Darker 50%** (fifth column).

9. Copy and rename a worksheet.
 a. Right-click the **Cass Lake** tab.
 b. Choose **Move or Copy**. The *Move or Copy* dialog box opens.
 c. Choose **(move to end)** in the *Before Sheet* list.
 d. Select the **Create a copy** box.
 e. Click **OK**. The copied sheet is named *Cass Lake (2)*.
 f. Double-click the **Cass Lake (2)** tab, type Breezy Point, and press **Enter**.
 g. Right-click the **Breezy Point** tab and choose **Tab Color**.
 h. Format the tab color to **Orange, Accent 4, Darker 25%**.
 i. Select cells **B5:H10** and press **Delete** (Figure 1-54).
 j. Press **Ctrl+Home**.

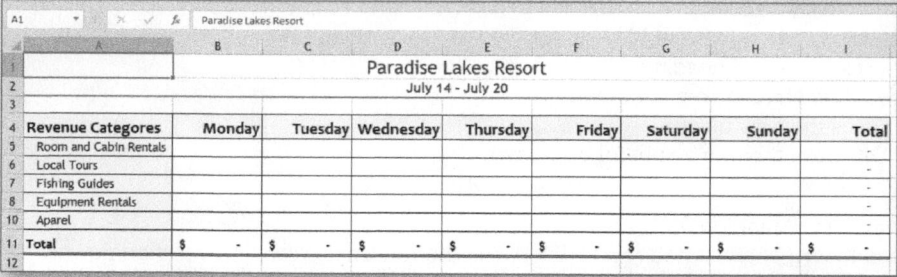

1-54 Data deleted on copied sheet

10. Click the **Cass Lake** tab and press **Ctrl+Home**.

11. Press **Ctrl+S** to save the workbook.

12. Click the **File** tab and click **Close** to close the workbook (Figure 1-55).

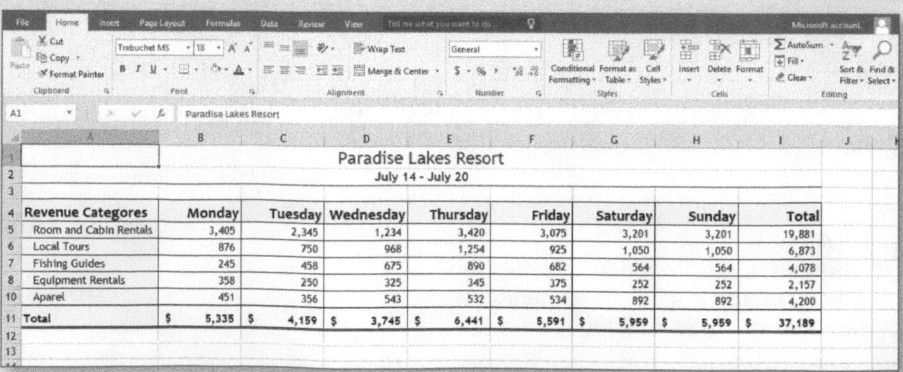

1-55 PP E1-3 completed worksheet

| SLO 1.7 | **Modifying the Appearance of the Workbook** |

You can adjust how you see data in a worksheet to make your work as easy as possible. You can select a view, zoom in or out on the data, freeze parts of the screen, split the worksheet into two panes, and switch between multiple open windows.

Workbook Views

The *View* tab has a *Workbook Views* group with three main views or layouts for working in an Excel worksheet. The views are **Normal**, **Page Layout**, and **Page Break Preview**.

- *Normal* view is the default and is used to create and modify a worksheet.
- *Page Layout* view opens the header and footer areas, indicates margin areas, and shows rulers.
- *Page Break Preview* displays printed pages with dashed or dotted lines to mark where new pages start.

There are buttons for *Normal* view, *Page Layout* view, and *Page Break Preview* on the right side of the *Status* bar.

> **MORE INFO**
>
> The **Ribbon Display Options** button (on the right of the workbook title bar) can be used to hide the *Ribbon* for maximum screen space in any workbook view.

▶ **HOW TO:** Switch Workbook Views Using the Status Bar

1. Click the **View** tab.
 - The *Normal* button is activated in the *Workbook Views* group.
2. Click the **Page Layout** button in the *Status* bar.
 - This view displays the header, the footer, and margin areas (Figure 1-56).

1-56 *Page Layout* view

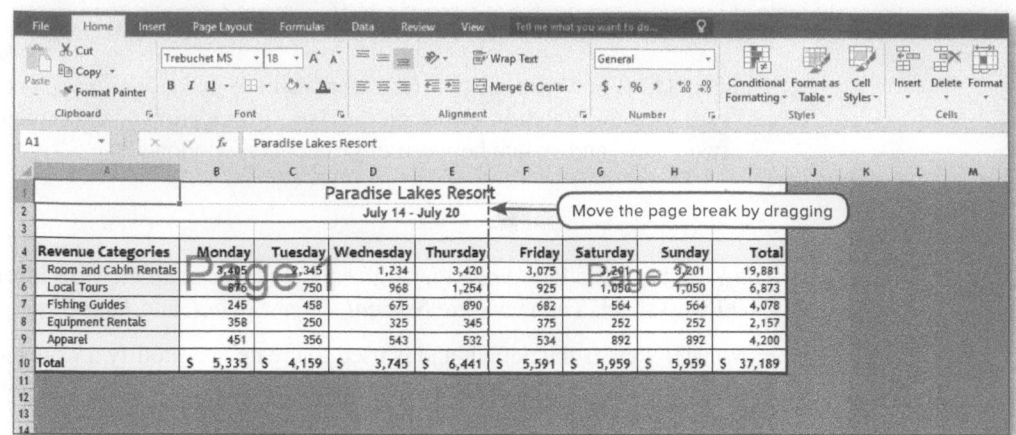

1-57 *Page Break Preview*

3. Click the **Page Break Preview** button in the *Status* bar.

 • If the data does not fit on a single page, a dashed line indicates where the second page will start (Figure 1-57).

4. Click the **Normal** button in the *Status* bar.

Zoom Options

You can change a sheet's magnification to see more of the data at once (zoom out) or to scrutinize content more carefully (zoom in). There is a *Zoom* group on the *View* tab as well as *Zoom* controls in the *Status* bar.

The *Status* bar controls include a **Zoom In** button, a **Zoom Out** button, and the **Zoom** slider. The slider is the vertical bar in the middle of the horizontal line which you can drag to change the magnification level.

▶ HOW TO: Change Zoom Levels

1. Click the **Zoom In** button in the *Status* bar.

 • The magnification is increased in 10% increments with each click.

2. Click the **Zoom Out** button in the *Status* bar.

 • The magnification is decreased in 10% increments with each click.

3. Drag the **Zoom** slider in the middle of the horizontal line to the left or right to set a value (Figure 1-58).

 • The magnification percentage is displayed to the right of the line.

1-58 *Zoom* slider

4. Click the **Zoom** button [*View* tab, *Zoom* group].

 • The *Zoom* dialog box includes preset values.

5. Click a radio button to choose a *Magnification* level.

 • Select **Fit selection** for a selected range to fill the screen.
 • Choose **Custom** to enter any magnification value.

6. Click **OK**.

> **ANOTHER WAY**
>
> The *Zoom* group [*View* tab] has **100%** and *Zoom to Selection* buttons.

Freeze Panes

In a worksheet with many rows and columns of information, it is not possible to see all the data at once. As you scroll to see information on the right, related labels or values on the left scroll out of view. The *Freeze Panes* command locks rows or columns in view so that you can position data for easy review. The worksheet is divided into two or four panes (sections) with a thin, black border to indicate the divisions.

The active cell becomes the top left corner of the moving pane. For example, if you select cell B5 and select the *Freeze Panes* command, column A and rows 1:4 are stationary.

▶ HOW TO: Freeze and Unfreeze Panes

1. Select a cell in the worksheet.
 - Click a cell one row below the last row to be frozen.
 - Click a cell one column to the right of the last column to be locked.
2. Click the **Freeze Panes** button [*View* tab, *Window* group].
 - Select **Freeze Top Row** to lock row 1 in view, regardless of the active cell.
 - Choose **Freeze First Column** to keep the first column in view, regardless of the active cell.
3. Select **Freeze Panes**.
 - All rows above and all columns to the left of the active cell are locked in position.
 - A thin, black border identifies frozen rows and columns.
4. Scroll the data in any direction (Figure 1-59).
5. Click the **Freeze Panes** button [*View* tab, *Window* group].
6. Select **Unfreeze Panes**.
 - The black border is removed.

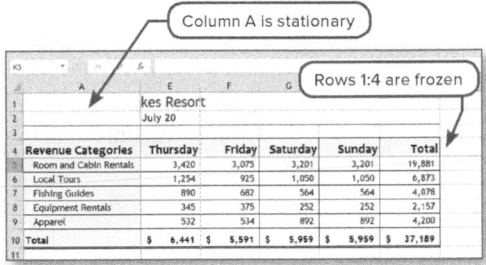

1-59 *Freeze Panes* results when cell B5 is selected and columns B:D are scrolled left

Split a Worksheet into Panes

The *Split* command divides a worksheet into two or four display panes. Each pane shows the same sheet, but you can arrange each pane to show different or the same rows and columns. There is only one active cell, and you may not see it in all the panes. Because it is one work-sheet, an edit can be made in any pane.

The panes are split based on the position of the active cell when you give the command. A *splitter bar* is a light gray bar that spans the window, either horizontally, vertically, or both. You can drag a splitter bar to resize the panes.

▶ HOW TO: Split a Worksheet

1. Select the cell for the location of a split.
 - Click a cell in column A (except cell A1) to split the worksheet into two horizontal panes.
 - Click a cell in row 1 (but not cell A1) to split the worksheet into two vertical panes.
 - Click a cell to split the worksheet into four panes.
2. Click the **Split** button [*View* tab, *Window* group].

3. Drag a splitter bar to resize a pane (Figure 1-60).

4. Click the **Split** button [*View* tab, *Window* group] to remove the split.

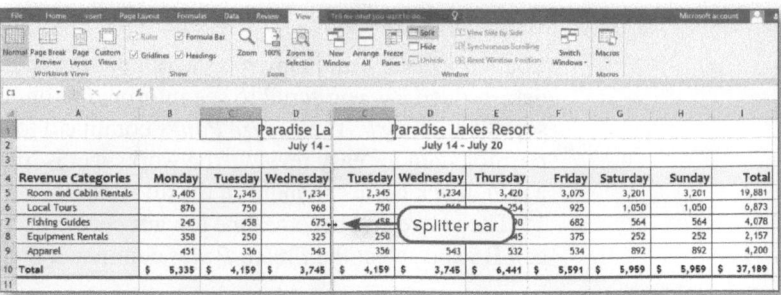

1-60 Split worksheet

> **ANOTHER WAY**
>
> You can remove a window split by double-clicking the splitter bar.

Hide or Unhide Worksheets

A ***hidden worksheet*** is a worksheet whose tab is not displayed. It is part of the workbook and can be referenced in calculations. A worksheet might be hidden to prevent accidental changes to it, or it might hold data that should not be easily visible. You can hide a worksheet using the **Format** button [*Home* tab] or by right-clicking the sheet tab. You cannot hide a worksheet if it is the only sheet in the workbook.

> **MORE INFO**
>
> The command to print an *Entire Workbook* does not print a hidden worksheet.

> **HOW TO:** Hide and Unhide Worksheets

1. Right-click the sheet tab to hide.

 - Press **Ctrl** to select multiple sheets, then right-click any one of the selected tabs.

2. Select **Hide**.

 - The worksheet tab is hidden.

3. Right-click any worksheet tab.

4. Select **Unhide**.

 - The *Unhide sheet* dialog box opens.

5. Select the tab name to unhide (Figure 1-61).

6. Click **OK**.

1-61 *Unhide sheet* dialog box

> **MORE INFO**
>
> The *Hide* command on the *View* tab hides a workbook. A hidden workbook can be used to store programming routines such as macros or external reference data that should be protected from viewing or accidental editing.

Switch Windows Command

When more than one workbook is open, the *Switch Windows* command changes or cycles through open workbooks. You can switch windows from the *Ribbon*, from the Windows task-bar, or with the keyboard shortcut **Ctrl+F6**. When you click the **Switch Windows** button [*View* tab, *Window* group], a menu lists the names of open workbooks so that you can select one. To use the Windows taskbar, point to the Excel icon to see a thumbnail with the file name of each open workbook and click the one to be edited. The keyboard shortcut toggles between the last two viewed workbooks.

When only two workbooks are open, you can view them side by side. The *View Side by Side* button is grayed out when only one workbook is open. For side-by-side viewing, you can scroll the windows together or separately. *Synchronous Scrolling* moves both workbooks in the same direction at the same time. This is especially helpful when worksheets have the same types of data in the same locations. Synchronous scrolling is automatically enabled when you choose the *View Side by Side* command.

> ▶ **HOW TO:** Switch Windows Using the Ribbon
>
> 1. Open two or more workbooks.
> 2. Click the **Switch Windows** button [*View* tab, *Window* group].
> - The names of open workbooks are listed.
> 3. Click the name of the workbook to view.

> ▶ **MORE INFO**
>
> If three or more workbooks are open when you select the *View Side by Side* command, the *Compare Side by Side* dialog box opens with the names of open workbooks. The one you select is displayed side by side with the active workbook.

View Multiple Worksheets

The *New Window* command opens a new separate window with the same workbook. The new window displays the workbook name in the title bar followed by a colon and number. Combined with the *Arrange All* command, you can position different parts of the workbook to make comparisons or monitor changes as you work. Figure 1-62 shows different sheets in the same workbook.

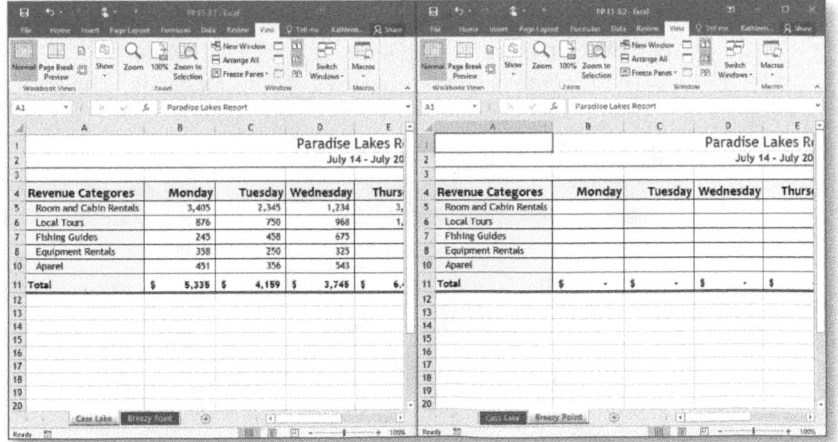

1-62 Two windows for a workbook

> ▶ **MORE INFO**
>
> You can open as many windows as needed and arrange them all.

▶ **HOW TO:** View Multiple Worksheets at the Same Time

1. Click the **View** tab and click the **New Window** button [*Window* group].
 - A second window opens for the same workbook and is active.
 - Both windows are maximized.
2. Click the **Arrange All** button [*View* tab, *Window* group].
 - The *Arrange Windows* dialog box opens.
3. Choose an option for arranging the windows.
 - The active window is arranged on the left (vertically tiled) or at the top (horizontally tiled).
 - If several workbooks are open but only the active workbook has multiple windows, choose **Windows of active workbook** so that only those windows are arranged.
4. Click **OK**.
 - The active window is arranged on the left or at the top.
5. Click the **Maximize** button in either title bar.
 - The window is full size.
6. Click the **Close** button (**X**) in the title bar to close the window.
 - The other window is displayed at its tiled size.
7. Click the **Maximize** button.

SLO 1.8

Finalizing a Workbook

Before you distribute your work to others, make sure that it is ready for sharing. A quick spell check can help locate and correct misspelled labels. You can enter document properties or insert headers and footers to help identify your work. You can control how your worksheet prints by setting margins, changing the orientation, or adjusting page breaks.

Check Spelling

The *Spelling* command scans a worksheet and locates words that do not match entries in the main Office dictionary; it also finds duplicate words. The dictionary is shared among all Office applications, and you can add labels to it, such as unusual or technical words. You can spell check the entire worksheet or a selected range.

The *Spelling* dialog box includes options for handling an error as shown in the following table:

Spelling Dialog Box Options

Option	Action
Ignore Once	Skips the occurrence of the label
Ignore All	Skips all occurrences of the same spelling of the label
Add to Dictionary	Adds the label to the default dictionary
Change	Changes the label to the highlighted entry in the *Suggestions* box
Change All	Same as *Change*, but changes the same label throughout the worksheet
Delete	Appears for *Repeated Word*. Click to delete one occurrence of the label.
AutoCorrect	Adds the label to the *AutoCorrect* list
Options	Opens the *Excel Options* dialog box to the *Proofing* tab for changing default settings
Undo Last	Reverses the most recent correction
Cancel	Discontinues spell checking

▶ **HOW TO:** Spell Check a Worksheet

1. Press **Ctrl+Home** to move to cell **A1**.
 - Start at the beginning of the worksheet.
 - Select a range to limit spell checking to that group of cells.
2. Click the **Review** tab and click the **Spelling** button [*Proofing* group].
 - The first error is located.
 - A list of suggested corrections is displayed.
3. Select the correct spelling in the list.
 - If there is no acceptable suggestion, click the **Not in Dictionary** box and type the correct spelling of the label.
4. Click **Change** to replace the misspelled label (Figure 1-63).
5. Click **Close** when spelling is complete.

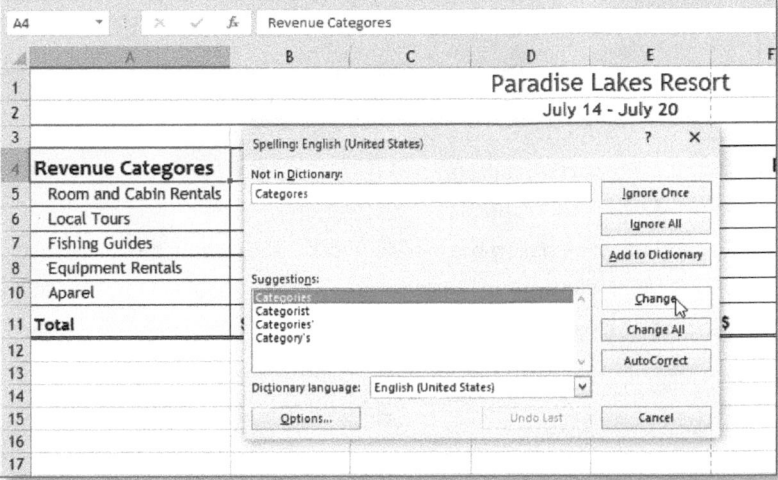

1-63 *Spelling* dialog box

Document Properties

A *document property* or *metadata* is a field of information. Metadata are settings and content including the author name, the date the file was created, the type and size of file, and more. Some properties are uneditable such as dates and file size; these settings are automatically updated. You can edit other document properties, including *Title*, *Author*, and *Subject*. A partial list of properties is available in the *Backstage* view on the right in the *Info* pane.

▶ **HOW TO:** Add Document Properties in Backstage View

1. Click the **File** tab to display the *Backstage* view.
2. Select **Info** if it is not already selected.
 - Property field names are listed.
 - An editable property has an entry box.
3. Click an entry box to enter or edit an item (Figure 1-64).
4. Return to the workbook and save the file.

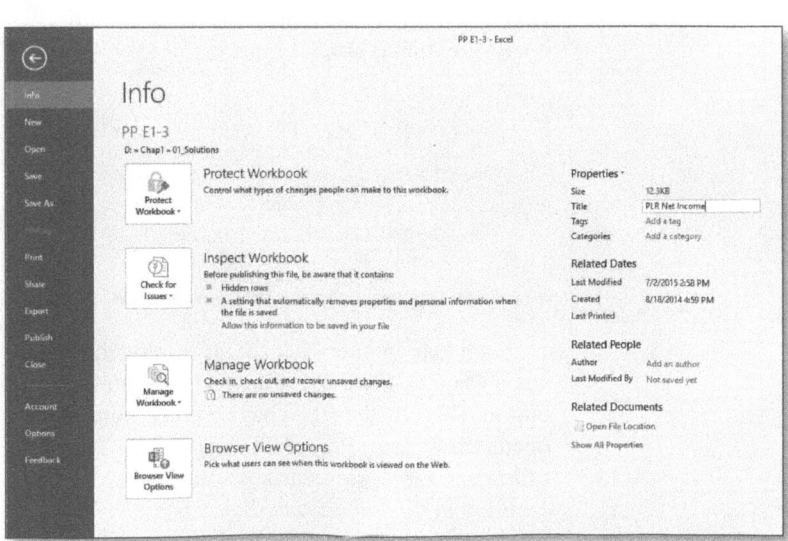

1-64 Workbook properties

The Properties Dialog Box

You can review all properties in the *Properties* dialog box. The *General, Statistics,* and *Contents* tabs list uneditable metadata. The *Summary* tab has properties such as the title, subject, and keywords. Keywords are used in file search commands. On the *Custom* tab, you can choose an additional property and type a default value.

> ▶ **HOW TO: Open the Properties Dialog Box**
>
> 1. Display the *Backstage* view and click **Info**.
> 2. Click the **Properties** button.
> 3. Select **Advanced Properties**.
> • The *Properties* dialog box opens (Figure 1-65).
> 4. Click a tab to view or edit a property.
> 5. Click **OK** to close the dialog box.

1-65 *Properties* dialog box

The Page Setup Dialog Box

The *Page Setup* dialog box offers several command groups for controlling how a worksheet prints. The commands are from the *Sheet Options, Scale to Fit,* and *Page Setup* groups on the *Page Layout* tab as well as commands for setting headers and footers. The ***Page Setup*** launcher [*Page Layout* tab, *Page Setup* group] opens the dialog box.

> ▶ **ANOTHER WAY**
>
> Open the *Page Setup* dialog box by clicking the launcher in the *Scale to Fit* or the *Sheet Options* group on the *Page Layout* tab.

Each tab in the *Page Setup* dialog box has a *Print,* a *Print Preview,* and an *Options* button (Figure 1-66). The *Options* button opens the *Printer Properties* dialog box. The following table summarizes commands on each tab in the *Page Setup* dialog box:

1-66 *Page* tab in the *Page Setup* dialog box

Page Setup Dialog Box Options

Tab	Available Settings
Page	Set the *Orientation* to *Portrait* or *Landscape*. Use *Scaling* to shrink or enlarge the printed worksheet to the paper size. Choose a *Paper size* or set *Print quality*. Define the *First page number*.
Margins	Adjust *Top*, *Bottom*, *Left*, and *Right* worksheet margins. Set *Header* and *Footer* top and bottom margins. *Center on page* horizontally and/or vertically.
Header/Footer	Choose a preset header or footer layout. Create a custom header or footer. Specify first and other page headers. Set header and footers to scale with worksheet and to align with margins.
Sheet	Identify a *Print area* other than the entire worksheet. Identify *Print titles* to repeat on each page. Print *Gridlines*, *Row and column headings*, *Comments*, and *Error messages*.

> **MORE INFO**
>
> You can make changes to multiple worksheets at the same time from the *Page Setup* dialog box. Select the tabs first to group the worksheets.

> **ANOTHER WAY**
>
> Open the *Page Setup* dialog box by clicking the *Page Setup* link in the *Print* area on the *Backstage* view.

Margins, Page Orientation, and Paper Size

A new Excel workbook uses the following default settings:

- Top and bottom margins: 0.75"
- Left and right margins: 0.7"
- Header and footer margins: 0.3"
- Portrait orientation
- Letter size paper

The *Margins* button [*Page Layout* tab, *Page Setup* group] lists *Normal*, *Wide*, and *Narrow* for margin settings as well as *Custom Margins*. When you select **Custom Margins**, the *Page Setup* dialog box opens to the *Margins* tab. Here you can set any value for any margin area, including the header and the footer. You can also center the page horizontally or vertically from this tab.

The *Orientation* button [*Page Setup* group, *Page Layout* tab] has two choices, *Portrait* or *Landscape*. A portrait page is taller than it is wide. A landscape page is wider than it is tall. The *Size* button lists paper sizes, but your printer must be able to accommodate the size.

You can modify settings for one worksheet or for several worksheets at a time. To format multiple worksheets, you need to group the worksheet tabs. Do this by clicking the first tab name, holding down **Shift**, and clicking the last tab name to select all sheets between those two names. You can also click the first tab name, press **Ctrl**, and click nonadjacent sheet names to create a group.

▶ **HOW TO:** Set Margins, Page Orientation, and Paper Size

1. Click the **Margins** button [*Page Layout* tab, *Page Setup* group].
2. Select **Custom Margins** to open the *Page Setup* dialog box (Figure 1-67).
 - The dialog box opens to the *Margins* tab.
3. Type each margin setting as desired.
 - You can use the spinner buttons to change the margin value.
4. Select the **Horizontally** box in the *Center on page* area.
 - This command centers the data between the left and right margins.
 - You can also vertically center the data on the page.
5. Click the **Page** tab in the *Page Layout* dialog box.
6. Select the radio button for **Portrait** or **Landscape**.
7. Click the **Paper size** arrow and select a paper size.
 - The default paper size is 8½ × 11", which is called *Letter*.
8. Click **OK** to close the dialog box.

1-67 *Margins* tab in the *Page Setup* dialog box

▶ **MORE INFO**

Top and bottom margins must be greater than header and footer margins. If they are not, worksheet data prints over header and footer text.

▶ **ANOTHER WAY**

In *Page Layout* view, you can set margins using the ruler. Display the rulers by clicking the *View* tab and selecting the *Ruler* box [*Show* group]. Point to a margin boundary to display a two-pointed arrow and drag the pointer to a new setting.

Headers and Footers

A *header* is information that prints at the top of each page. A *footer* is data that prints at the bottom of each page. You can use a header or a footer to display identifying information such as a company name or logo, page numbers, the date, or the file name.

Each header or footer has left, middle, and right sections. Information in the left section is left aligned, data in the middle section is centered, and material in the right section is right aligned. You can select a predefined header and footer, or you can create your own.

▶ **MORE INFO**

Predefined headers and footers include one, two, or three elements, separated by commas. One element prints in the center section. Two elements print in the center and right sections. Three elements use all three sections.

Headers and footers are not visible in *Normal* view, but you can see them in *Page Layout* view or *Print Preview*. Headers and footers are inserted and edited in *Page Layout* view at the top or bottom of the worksheet.

▶ HOW TO: Insert a Header and Footer Using the Ribbon

1. Select the worksheet.
 - You can select more than one worksheet to apply the same header or footer.
2. Click the **Insert** tab.
3. Click the **Header & Footer** button [*Text* group].
 - The view changes to *Page Layout* view.
 - Three header sections are visible at the top of the worksheet.
 - The *Header & Footer Tools Design* tab is active.
4. Click a header section.
5. Click an element name in the *Header & Footer Elements* group [*Header & Footer Tools Design* tab].
 - A code is inserted with an ampersand (&) and the element name enclosed in square brackets (Figure 1-68).
 - You can type your own label in a section.
 - You can select and delete codes and text in a section.

1-68 Header section in *Page Layout* view

6. Click the **Go To Footer** button [*Header & Footer Tools Design* tab, *Navigation* group].
7. Click a footer section.
8. Click an element name in the *Header & Footer Elements* group [*Header & Footer Tools Design* tab].
 - The related code is inserted.
 - You can type your own label in a footer section.
 - You can select and delete codes and text in a section.
9. Click any worksheet cell.
 - The header and footer appear as they will print.
 - The *Header & Footer Tools Design* tab is hidden.
10. Click the **Normal** button in the *Status* bar.
 - The header and footer are not visible in *Normal* view.

▶ **ANOTHER WAY**

To insert a built-in header or footer, click the **Header or Footer** button [*Header & Footer Tools Design* tab, *Header & Footer* group] and make a selection.

▶ **MORE INFO**

In a typed header or footer label such as "Research & Development," type two ampersands in the section like this: *Research && Development*. This distinguishes the required ampersand from the one used in an element code such as &[Date].

You can also use the *Page Setup* dialog box to insert a header or a footer. There is a *Header & Footer* tab which includes the preset headers and footers as well as a *Custom Header* or *Custom Footer* option.

▶ HOW TO: Insert Headers or Footers on Multiple Sheets

1. Select a single or multiple worksheet tabs.
 - Click the first worksheet tab for the group, press **Shift**, and click the last tab.
 - Click a worksheet tab, press **Ctrl**, and click a nonadjacent tab.
 - Right-click any tab and click **Select All Sheets**.
2. Click the **Page Setup** launcher [*Page Layout* tab, *Page Setup* group].
 - The *Page Setup* dialog box opens.
3. Click the **Header/Footer** tab.
4. Click the arrow for the *Header* or the *Footer* text box (Figure 1-69).
 - A list of built-in header or footer layouts opens.
 - Choose **(none)** to remove a header or footer.
5. Choose a predefined header or footer.
 - The header or footer is displayed in the preview area.
6. Click **Custom Header** or **Custom Footer** to open the *Header* or *Footer* dialog box (Figure 1-70).
7. Click a section.
8. Click a button to insert an element.
 - Point to a button to see its *ScreenTip*.
 - The text or code appears in the section.
9. Click **OK** to close the *Header* or *Footer* dialog box.
 - The custom header or footer is displayed in the preview area.
10. Click **OK** to close the *Page Setup* dialog box.
11. Right-click a sheet tab and choose **Ungroup Sheets**.

1-69 Select a built-in header or footer in the *Page Setup* dialog box

1-70 *Footer* dialog box

You can remove a header or footer in *Page Layout* view or from the *Page Setup* dialog box. To remove headers and footers from multiple worksheets, select the sheet tabs so that they are grouped. In *Page Layout* view, click the header or footer section and delete labels and codes. From the *Page Setup* dialog box, you can simply select **(none)** from the *Header* or *Footer* drop-down list.

▶ HOW TO: Remove Headers and Footers

1. Select the worksheet(s).
2. Click the **Page Setup** launcher [*Page Layout* tab, *Page Setup* group].
3. Click the **Header/Footer** tab.
4. Click the **Header** or **Footer** drop-down list and select **(none)**.
5. Click **OK** to close the *Page Setup* dialog box.
6. Ungroup sheets if needed.

Page Breaks

A *page break* is a printer code that starts a new page. When worksheet data spans more than one printed page, automatic page breaks are inserted based on the paper size, the margins, and scaling. Automatic page breaks readjust as you add or delete data. You can insert manual page breaks, too. Manual page breaks do not adjust as you make edits.

In *Page Break Preview*, an automatic page break displays as a dotted or dashed blue line. A manual page break appears as a solid, blue line.

▶ HOW TO: Insert a Page Break

1. Select the cell for the location of a page break.
 - Select a cell in column A below the row where you want to start a new page.
 - Select a cell in row 1 to the right of the column where you want to start a new page.
 - Select a cell below and to the right of where new pages should start.
2. Click the **Page Layout** tab.
3. Click the **Breaks** button.
4. Select **Insert Page Break** (Figure 1-71).
 - A manual page break is shown as a thin, solid line in the worksheet in *Normal* view.

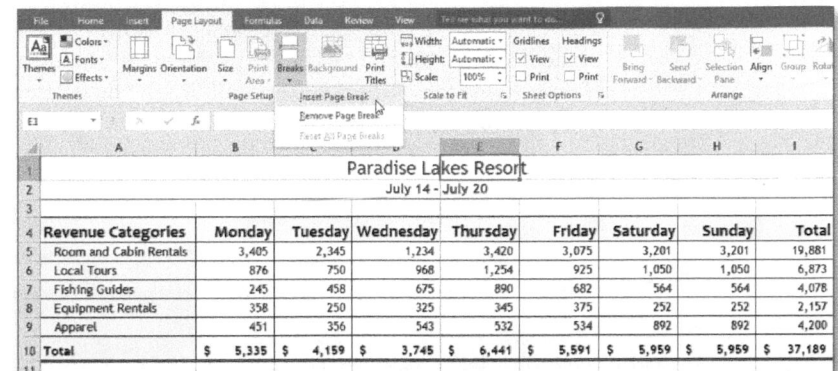

1-71 Page break inserted after column D

Preview and Move a Page Break

In *Page Break Preview*, you can move an automatic or a manual page break by dragging its blue line. You can see how the data is affected and evaluate the new printed pages. Depending on the amount of data, as you move one page break, another automatic break may be inserted. When you move an automatic page break, it becomes a manual page break.

> ▶ MORE INFO
>
> To move a page break in *Normal* view, you must delete the existing break and insert a new one; you cannot drag the line.

▶ HOW TO: Preview and Move a Page Break

1. Click the **Page Break Preview** button in the *Status* bar.
 - You can adjust the zoom size in *Page Break Preview*.
2. Point to the page break (dashed or solid, blue line) to display a two-pointed arrow.
3. Drag the pointer to a new location (Figure 1-72).
 - You cannot drag an automatic page break to the right of its current location.

4. Release the pointer button.

- A manual page break appears as a solid, blue line.
- Another automatic page break may be inserted if the data requires it.

5. Click the **Normal** button in the *Status* bar.

1-72 Drag a page break line to a new position

Remove a Manual Page Break

You can remove a manual page break in *Normal* view or *Page Break Preview*. Click a cell immediately to the right of or below the break and then click the **Remove Page Break** button [*Page Layout* tab, *Page Setup* group]. When you delete a manual page break, Excel may insert a new automatic page break.

> **MORE INFO**
>
> An automatic page break can be "deleted" by inserting a manual page break before it.

> **HOW TO: Remove a Manual Page Break**

1. Click the **Page Break Preview** button in the *Status* bar.

2. Click a cell immediately to the right of or below the page break to be removed.

3. Click the **Breaks** button [*Page Layout* tab, *Page Setup* group].

- You can select **Reset All Page Breaks** to remove all manual page breaks.

4. Click **Remove Page Break** (Figure 1-73).

- An automatic page break is inserted if required.

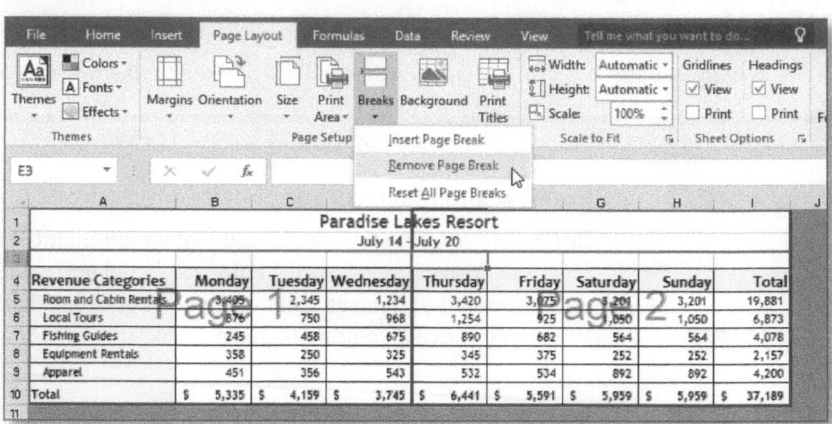

1-73 Remove a manual page break

> **ANOTHER WAY**
>
> In *Page Break Preview*, you can drag a manual page break off the page to the right. Excel will insert an automatic page break if required by the margins and other settings.

Customize Print Settings

You can print the entire workbook, the current worksheet, or a selected cell range by making a choice in the *Settings* area in the *Backstage view* for the *Print* command. The *Sheet Options* and *Page Setup* groups on the *Page Layout* command tab include additional options for repeating titles, displaying a background image, and printing gridlines, column letters, and row numbers.

Gridlines, the vertical and horizontal lines that form the columns and rows, are a visual guide to your working on the sheet. Row and column headings serve a similar purpose—to

help you navigate in a worksheet. By default, the gridlines and headings do not print but you can print them from an option on the *Page Layout* tab.

A **print title** is a row or column of data that is repeated on each printed page. For example, you can print main labels from rows 1:3 and from column A on each printed page of a 20-page worksheet.

▶ **HOW TO:** Print Gridlines, Print Titles, and Column and Row Headings

1. Click the **Page Layout** tab.

2. Select the **Print** box under *Gridlines* in the *Sheet Options* group.

3. Select the **Print** box under *Headings* in the *Sheet Options* group.

4. Click the **Print Titles** button *[Page Layout* tab, *Page Setup* group].

 • The *Page Setup* dialog box opens to the *Sheet* tab.

5. Select the **Rows to repeat at top** box.

6. Drag to select the heading(s) for the row(s) to print on each page.

 • The dialog box collapses as you select row headings.
 • The dialog box expands when you release the pointer button.
 • You can type a reference such as $1:$3 to repeat data in the first three rows.

7. Select the **Columns to repeat at left** box (Figure 1-74).

8. Drag to select the heading(s) for the column(s) to print on each page.

 • The dialog box collapses as you select column headings.
 • You can type a reference such as $A:$A to repeat data in column A.

9. Click **OK**.

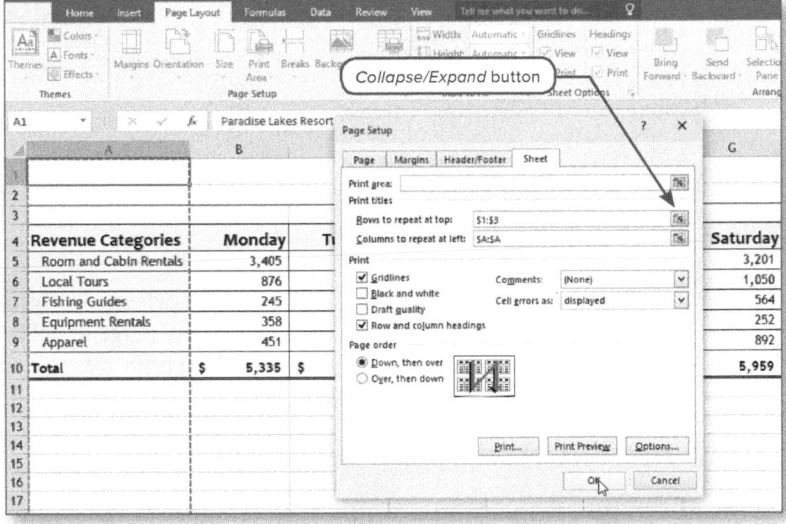

1-74 *Sheet* tab in the *Page Setup* dialog box

▶ **ANOTHER WAY**

You can print *Gridlines* and *Row and column headings* from an option in the *Page Setup* dialog box.

Scale to Fit

The **Scale to Fit** command enlarges or shrinks printed data to fit a specific number of pages or a particular paper size. You can scale printed data as a percentage of normal size or by setting the number of pages. Normal size is how the data would print in the current font size and is shown as *Automatic* in the *Scale to Fit* group *[Page Layout* tab].

▶ **HOW TO:** Scale to Fit

1. Click the **Page Layout** tab.

2. Click the **Width** drop-down list *[Scale to Fit* group] and select an option.

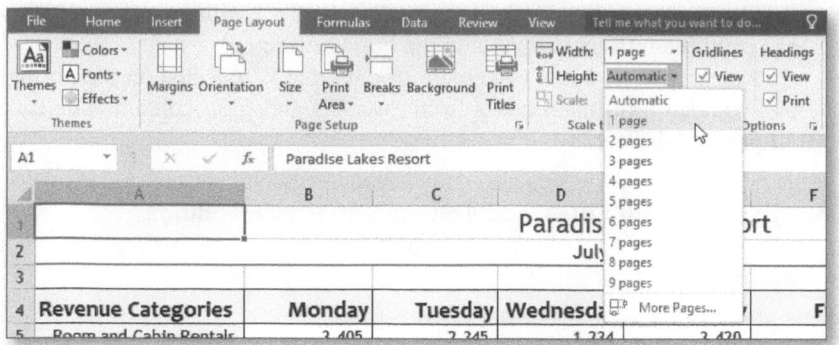

1-75 *Scale to Fit* options

3. Click the **Height** drop-down list [*Scale to Fit* group] and select an option (Figure 1-75).

 • You can click the **Scale** button spinner arrows to set a percentage of the normal size.

> **ANOTHER WAY**
>
> Click the **Scale to Fit** launcher [*Page Layout* tab, *Scale to Fit group*] to open the *Page Setup* dialog box and set options in the *Scaling* area.

Print Area

A ***print area*** is the data that prints when you give a *Print* command. The default is the entire worksheet, but you can identify any range of cells as a print area. You can add adjacent data to a print area, and you can clear a print area to return to the default.

▶ **HOW TO: Set and Clear a Print Area**

1. Select the cells to print.

 • You can select nonadjacent ranges but they print on separate pages.
2. Click the **Page Layout** tab.
3. Click the **Print Area** button [*Page Setup* group] (Figure 1-76).
4. Select **Set Print Area**.

 • You can see the print area in the *Backstage view* for the *Print* command and in *Page Break Preview*.
 • A print area is saved with the workbook.
5. Click the **Print Area** button [*Page Layout* tab, *Page Setup* group].
6. Select **Clear Print Area**.

 • All print areas are cleared.
 • The default print area of the entire sheet is reset.

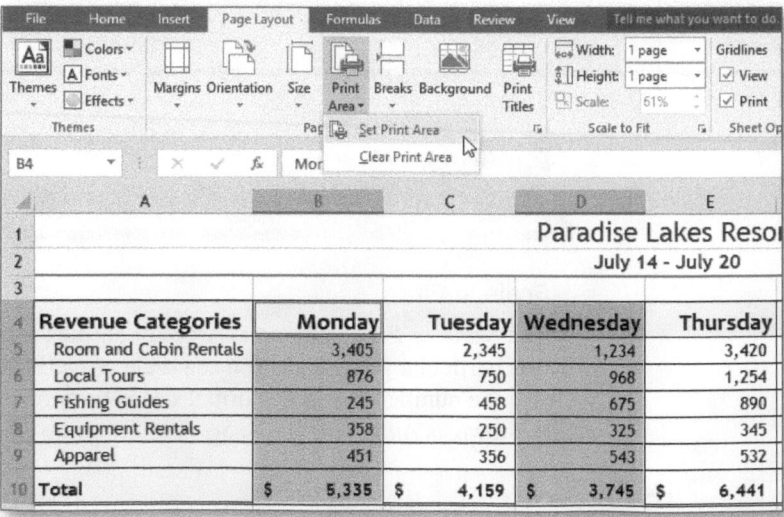

1-76 **Nonadjacent print areas**

> **MORE INFO**
>
> You can select one or more ranges and choose **Print Selection** in the *Settings* area for the *Print* command in the *Backstage* view. Nonadjacent ranges print on separate pages. These selections are not saved with the workbook.

> **ANOTHER WAY**
>
> You can define a print area from the *Sheet* tab in the *Page Setup* dialog box.

Print a Worksheet or Workbook

The *Print* command in the *Backstage view* provides a preview so that you can make changes before actual printing. The *Show Margins* button toggles the display of margin and column markers which can be dragged to new settings. The *Zoom to Page* button toggles between two zoom settings for the preview.

▶HOW TO: Preview and Print a Worksheet

1. Click the **File** tab and select **Print**.
 - You can also click **Print Preview** in the *Page Setup* dialog box to open the *Print* command in the *Backstage* view.
2. Click **Show Margins** to display margin and column markers (Figure 1-77).
3. Click **Zoom to Page** to toggle between zoom sizes.
4. Set the number of *Copies*.
 - Type a number or use the spinner arrows.
5. Click the **Printer** arrow.
 - Choose the printer name.
 - Make sure the printer is ready.

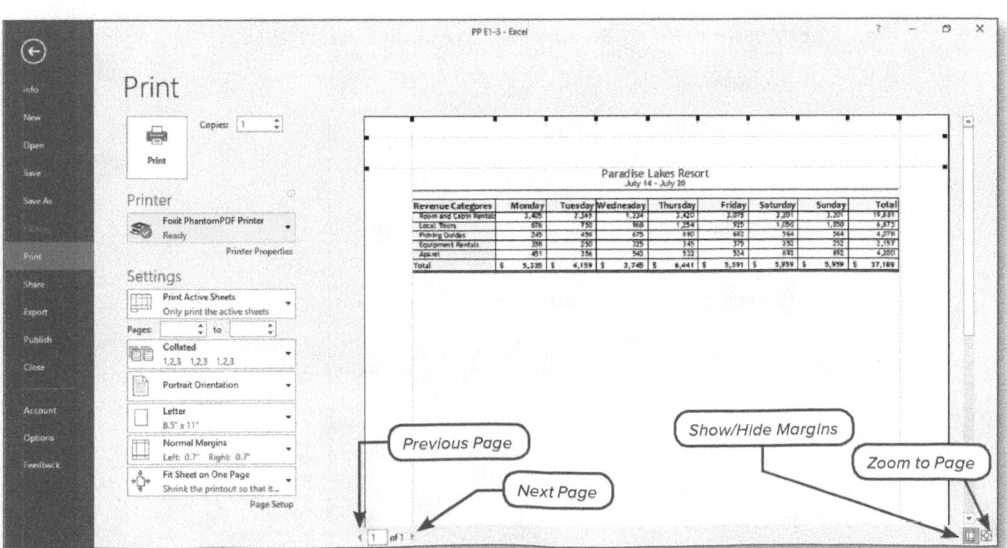

1-77 *Backstage* view for *Print*

6. Click the **Settings** arrow.
 - The active sheets are the default.
 - Cell ranges must be selected in order to print a selection.
 - The workbook setting prints all worksheets.

7. Specify which pages to print.
 - The default is all pages of the worksheet.
 - Click the **Next Page** or **Previous Page** arrow to navigate through multiple pages.

8. Verify orientation, paper size, margin settings, and scaling.
 - You can make changes from the *Page Setup* dialog box by clicking the **Page Setup** link at the bottom of the *Settings* area.

9. Click **Print**.
 - The data is sent to the printer.
 - The *Backstage view* closes.

> **ANOTHER WAY**
>
> Press **Ctrl+P** to open the *Print* command in the *Backstage view*.

PAUSE & PRACTICE: EXCEL 1-4

In this project, you open *[your initials] PP E1-3.xlsx* to unhide a row, add data, and hide a sheet. You also spell check a worksheet, set document properties, and finalize the workbook for distribution.

File Needed: *[your initials] PP E1-3.xlsx*
Completed Project File Name: *[your initials] PP E1-4.xlsx*

1. Open *[your initials] PP E1-3* completed in *Pause & Practice 1-3*.

2. Save the workbook as [your initials] PP E1-4.

3. Select the **Cass Lake** worksheet.

4. Unhide row 9.
 a. Click and drag to select row headings **8:10**.
 b. Right-click either of the selected row headings.
 c. Choose **Unhide** from the context menu.

5. Enter the following data in cells **B9:H9**. The data is formatted the same as row 8.

	B	C	D	E	F	G	H
Food & Beverage	254	209	198	402	519	677	399

6. Hide a worksheet.
 a. Right-click the **Breezy Point** tab.
 b. Choose **Hide**.

7. Check spelling.
 a. Press **Ctrl+Home**.
 b. Click the **Spelling** button [*Review* tab, *Proofing* group].
 c. Click **Change** to accept the suggested correction for "Categores."
 d. Click **Change** to accept the suggested correction for "Aparel."
 e. Click **OK** when spell checking is finished.
 f. Press **Ctrl+Home**.

8. Enter document properties.
 a. Click the **File** tab to display the *Backstage* view.
 b. Click the **Show All Properties** link at the bottom of the properties list.
 c. Click the *Title* text box and type PP Excel 1-4.
 d. Click the *Subject* text box and type Weekly Revenue.
 e. In the *Status* text box, type Draft (Figure 1-78).

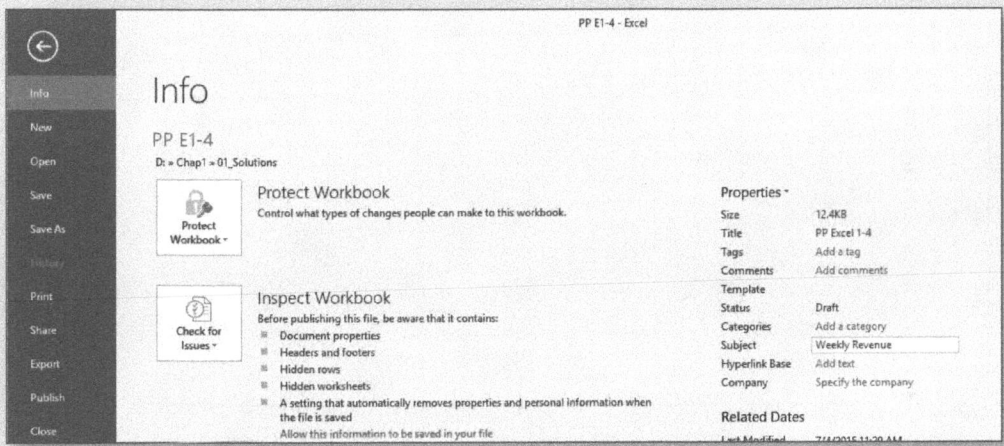

1-78 Properties in *Backstage* view

 f. Click the **Show Fewer Properties** link at the bottom of the properties list.
 g. Return to the worksheet.

9. Change page setup options.
 a. Click the **Page Layout** tab.
 b. Click the **Orientation** button and select **Landscape**.
 c. Click the **Page Setup** launcher to open the *Page Setup* dialog box.
 d. On the **Page** tab, click the **Fit to** button.
 e. Set **1** page wide and **1** page tall.
 f. Click the **Margins** tab.
 g. Select the **Horizontally** box in the *Center on page* area.
 h. Do not close the dialog box.

10. Add a header and footer.
 a. Click the **Header/Footer** tab.
 b. Click the **Header** drop-down list and select *[your initials]* **PP E1-4**. The file name displays in the preview center section.
 c. Click the **Footer** drop-down list and select **Cass Lake** to insert the sheet name in the center section of the footer.
 d. Click **OK** to close the *Page Setup* dialog box.

11. Preview and print the worksheet.
 a. Click the **File** tab and select **Print**. *Print Preview* displays how the worksheet will print.
 b. Select the printer.
 c. Click **Print** to print the worksheet.

12. Save and close the workbook (Figure 1-79).

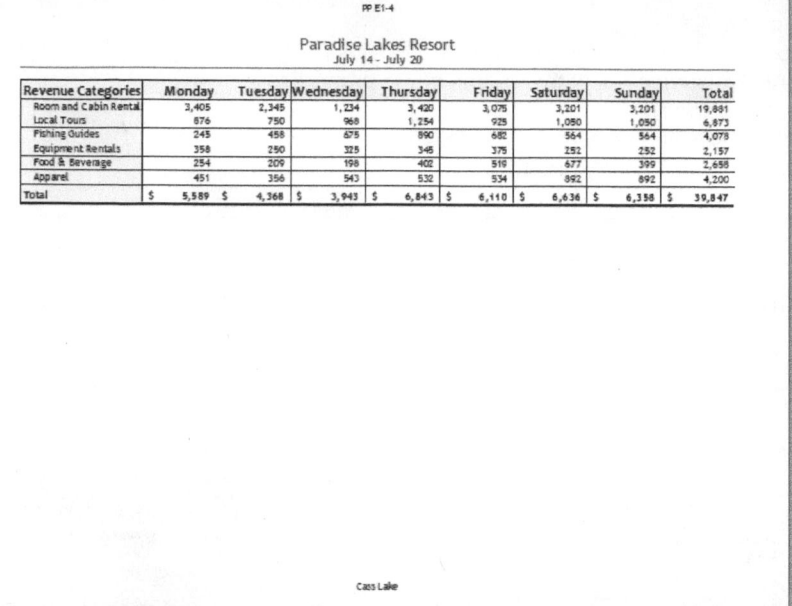

PP E1-4

Paradise Lakes Resort
July 14 - July 20

Revenue Categories	Monday	Tuesday	Wednesday	Thursday	Friday	Saturday	Sunday	Total
Room and Cabin Rental	3,405	2,345	1,234	3,420	3,075	3,201	3,201	19,881
Local Tours	876	750	968	1,254	925	1,050	1,050	6,873
Fishing Guides	245	458	675	890	682	564	564	4,078
Equipment Rentals	358	250	325	346	375	252	252	2,157
Food & Beverage	254	209	198	402	519	677	399	2,658
Apparel	451	356	543	532	534	892	892	4,200
Total	$ 5,589	$ 4,368	$ 3,943	$ 6,843	$ 6,110	$ 6,636	$ 6,356	$ 39,847

Cass Lake

1-79 PP E1-4 completed

Chapter Summary

1.1 Create, save, and open an Excel workbook (p. E1-3).

- A new Excel workbook has one worksheet and is named *BookN*, with numbers assigned in order throughout a work session.
- Save a workbook with a descriptive name that identifies the contents and purpose.
- Create a new workbook from the *Excel Start* page or from the *New* command on the *File* tab.
- A workbook that is opened or copied from an online source will open in **Protected View**.
- An Excel workbook is an *.xlsx* file, but it can be saved in other formats for easy sharing of data.

1.2 Enter and edit labels and values in a worksheet (p. E1-6).

- Data is entered in a cell which is the intersection of a column and a row. Each cell has an address or reference.
- Data is recognized as a label or a value. Labels are not used in calculations. A label is left-aligned in the cell; a value is right-aligned.
- A **formula** is a calculation that displays a value as its result in the worksheet.
- Press **F2 (FN+F2)** or double-click a cell to start *Edit* mode. After making the change, press **Enter** to complete the edit.
- Horizontal alignment options for cell data include *Align Left, Center,* and *Align Right.* Data can also be indented from the cell border. Vertical alignment choices are *Top Align, Middle Align,* and *Bottom Align.*
- A group or selection of cells is a **range**. You can use the pointer and keyboard shortcuts to select a range.
- Use the **Fill Handle** to create a series that follows a pattern. The *Fill Handle* copies data when there is no pattern.
- **AutoComplete** supplies a suggestion for a column entry that begins with the same character as a label already in the column.
- Cut, copy, and paste commands include drag and drop as well as regular Windows **Cut, Copy,** and **Paste** buttons on the *Home* tab, context menus, and keyboard shortcuts.

1.3 Use the *SUM* function to build a simple formula (p. E1-19).

- A **function** is a built-in formula. Results appear in the worksheet cell, but the function is displayed in the *Formula* bar.
- The *AutoSum* button [*Home* tab, *Editing* group] inserts the *SUM* function in a cell to add the values in a selected range.
- Each function has **syntax** which is its required parts in the required order. A function begins with an equals sign (=), followed by the name of the function. After the name, the function **argument** is shown in parentheses.
- You can change a function argument by entering new cell references in the *Formula* bar or by dragging the range border in the worksheet.
- When you copy a function, Excel adjusts cell references to match their locations in the worksheet.

1.4 Format a worksheet with font attributes, borders, fill, cell styles, and themes (p. E1-21).

- Apply font attributes from the *Font* group on the *Ribbon* or from the *Format Cells* dialog box.
- Font attributes include the **font** name or face, the **font size**, font styles such as bold, italic, and underline, and the **font color**.
- Number formats include decimals, commas, currency symbols, and percent signs. They also determine how negative values appear in the worksheet.
- Number formats are applied from the *Ribbon* or the *Format Cells* dialog box.
- The **Format Painter** copies formatting from one cell to another.
- Add borders or fill color to cells for easy identification, clarification, and emphasis.
- A **cell style** is a preset collection of font, font size, alignment, color, borders, and fill color and is based on the theme.
- A **theme** is a collection of fonts, colors, and special effects for a workbook.
- You can use themes and cell styles to quickly format a worksheet with consistent, professionally designed elements.

1.5 Modify columns and rows in a worksheet (p. E1-31).

- The default column width and row height depend on the font size defined by the workbook theme.
- You can change the width of a column or the height of a row by dragging the border between the headings.
- *AutoFit* a column or row by double-clicking the border between the headings.
- The *Format* button [*Home* tab, *Cells* group] includes commands to change *row height* and *column width*.
- Insert or delete a column or a row by right-clicking the column or row heading and choosing *Insert* or *Delete*.
- The *Insert* and *Delete* buttons include commands for inserting and deleting rows and columns.
- Display a label on multiple lines in a cell using the *Wrap Text* command to split the label.
- The *Merge & Center* command combines two or more cells into one and centers the data within that new cell.
- The *Center Across Selection* command can be used to center multiple rows of data across the same range.
- One or multiple rows or columns can be hidden, but they are still available for use in a formula.

1.6 Insert, delete, and move worksheets in a workbook (p. E1-37).

- The number of worksheets in a workbook is limited only by the amount of computer memory.
- You can click the *New Sheet* button next to the worksheet tabs to insert a new sheet in a workbook.
- The *Insert* and *Delete* buttons include options to insert and delete worksheets.
- You can double-click a worksheet tab, type a name, and press **Enter** to rename a sheet.
- You can apply a *tab color* to distinguish a particular sheet by changing the background color.

- Move a worksheet tab to another location in the list of tabs by dragging it to that location.
- You can create an exact duplicate of a worksheet in the same or another workbook with the *Move or Copy* command or the context menu.

1.7 Modify the appearance of a workbook by adjusting zoom size, changing views, and freezing panes (p. E1-42).

- A workbook can be viewed in three ways: *Normal*, *Page Layout*, and *Page Break Preview*.
- Switch views from the *Status* bar buttons or from the *Workbook Views* group on the *View* tab.
- Adjust the zoom size to display more or less data on screen. Zoom controls are available in the *Status* bar and from the *View* tab.
- Use the *Freeze Panes* command to lock selected rows or columns on screen so that you can scroll data while keeping important data in view.
- The *Split* command divides the screen into multiple sections so that you can see different areas of a large worksheet at once.
- You can hide a worksheet from view and unintended editing.
- When multiple workbooks are open, the *Switch Windows* command lists the open workbook names.
- You can switch among open workbooks from the Windows taskbar.
- The *New Window* command displays the same workbook in a second window. Use this command with the *Arrange All* command to view different areas or sheets of a workbook at the same time.

1.8 Review and prepare a workbook for final distribution by spell checking, setting properties, and adjusting page setup options (p. E1-47).

- Spell checking a workbook follows the same steps as other Office applications.
- A *document property* is *metadata* stored with the file.

- Some properties are supplied by Excel and cannot be edited. Other document properties are added or edited by the user.
- Several properties are visible and can be edited in the *Info* area in the *Backstage* view.
- You can open the *Properties* dialog box to build or edit properties.
- The *Page Layout* tab includes commands to set page margins and orientation.
- **Headers** and **footers** can be added to print at the top and bottom of each page.
- When a worksheet fills more than one printed page, Excel inserts automatic page breaks.
- You can insert manual **page breaks** to change where a new page starts.
- From commands on the *Page Layout* tab or in the *Page Setup* dialog box, you can print **gridlines** as well as row and column headings.

- You can make additional changes to the printed worksheet from the **Print** area in the *Backstage* view. These include choosing to print only a selection or the entire workbook.

Check for Understanding

The SIMbook for this text (within your SIMnet account) provides the following resources for concept review:

- Multiple choice questions
- Matching exercises
- Short answer questions

USING MICROSOFT EXCEL 2016

Guided Project 1-1

Life's Animal Shelter (LAS) maintains data in an Excel workbook that tracks daily expenses for categories that include supplies, animal food, and wages. You will create a new workbook for the current week, enter and format the data, and prepare the workbook for distribution.
[Student Learning Outcomes 1.1, 1.2, 1.3, 1.4, 1.5, 1.6, 1.7, 1.8]

File Needed: None
Completed Project File Name: *[your initials] Excel 1-1.xlsx*

Skills Covered in This Project

- Create and save a workbook.
- Enter labels and values.
- Use the *Fill Handle*.
- Set column widths and row heights.
- Merge and center labels.
- Apply a workbook theme and cell styles.

- Apply font attributes and insert borders.
- Use *SUM* and set number formatting.
- Copy and rename worksheets.
- Set worksheet tab color.
- Change page setup options.
- Use spell check.
- Adjust zoom size and freeze panes.

1. Create and save a workbook.
 a. Click the **File** tab to open the *Backstage* view.
 b. Select **New** and then click **Blank workbook**.
 c. Click the **Save** button on the *Quick Access* toolbar to open the *Save As* dialog box.
 d. Select the folder to save the workbook, or **Browse** to a location on *OneDrive*, your computer, or external media.
 e. Name the workbook [your initials] Excel 1-1 in the *File name* area.
 f. Click **Save**.

2. Enter data with deliberate errors.
 a. In cell **A1**, type Life's Aminal Shelter with the spelling error and press **Enter**.
 b. In cell **A2**, type Setember 1 through 7 with the spelling error and press **Enter**.
 c. In cell **A4**, type Expens Categories and press **Enter**.

3. Adjust column width.
 a. Point to the border between the column **A** and column **B** headings to display a two-pointed arrow.
 b. Double-click to *AutoFit* column **A**.

4. Enter labels and values as shown in Figure 1-80.

	A	B	C	D	E	F	G	H
1	Life's Aminal Shelter							
2	Setember 1 through 7							
3								
4	Expens Categories	Monday						
5	Pet nutrition	55.25	47.5	38.55	27.45	42.5	35.25	51.75
6	Veterinary supplies	27.85	32.35	35	25	28.5	38.75	44.85
7	Shelter supplies	78	56.45	65.35	55	70	60.25	45.35
8	Salaries and wages	475						
9	Utilities (prorated)	45						
10								

1-80 Labels and values to be entered with errors in cells A1:A2 and A4

5. Use the *Fill Handle* to fill a series and copy data.
 a. Select cell **B4**.
 b. Click and drag the *Fill* pointer to cell **H4**.
 c. Select cells **B8:B9**. There is one *Fill Handle* shown in cell B9.
 d. Click and drag the *Fill* pointer to cell **H9**. When there is no discernible pattern, the *Fill Handle* copies data.
 e. Point to the border between the column **D** and column **E** headings to display a two-pointed arrow.
 f. Double-click to *AutoFit* column **D**.

6. Merge and center labels.
 a. Select cells **A1:H1** and click the **Merge & Center** button [*Home* tab, *Alignment* group].
 b. Select cells **A2:H2** and click the **Merge & Center** button [*Home* tab, *Alignment* group].
 c. Select cells **B4:H4**.
 d. Click the **Center** button [*Home* tab, *Alignment* group].

7. Choose a workbook theme.
 a. Click the **Themes** button [*Page Layout* tab, *Themes* group].
 b. Choose **Integral** from the gallery.
 c. Click the **Home** tab. All labels and values are set in the **Tw Cen MT** font.

8. Apply cell styles.
 a. Select cell **A1** and click the **Cells Styles** button or the **More** button [*Home* tab, *Styles* group].
 b. Select **Title** in the *Titles and Headings* category. For the *Integral* theme, a title is format in the *Tw Cen MT Condensed* font, 18 points.
 c. Select cell **A2** and click the **Cells Styles** or the **More** button [*Home* tab, *Styles* group].
 d. Select **Heading 2** in the *Titles and Headings* category. The second level heading uses *Tw Cen MT* bold, 13 points. Both styles use a dark blue color.
 e. Select cells **A4:A9**.
 f. Press **Ctrl** and select cells **B4:H4**. Two ranges are selected.
 g. Click the **Cells Styles** or the **More** button [*Home* tab, *Styles* group].
 h. Select **40%, Accent 1** in the *Themed Cell Styles* category.
 i. Click the **Bold** button [*Home* tab, *Font* group].
 j. Select cell **A10**.
 k. Type Total and press **Enter**. The format from the column is automatically applied.

9. Apply font attributes.
 a. Select cells **A4:H10**.
 b. Click the **Font size** drop-down list [*Home* tab, *Font* group] and select **12**.
 c. Change the font size for cell **A2** to **14**.
 d. Select cells **A5:A9**.
 e. Click the **Increase Indent** button [*Home* tab, *Alignment* group] two times.
 f. Select cell **A10** and click the **Align Right** button [*Home* tab, *Alignment* group].

10. Use the *SUM* function and copy a formula.
 a. Select cell **B10**.
 b. Click the **AutoSum** button [*Home* tab, *Editing* group] and press **Enter** to accept the suggested range.
 c. Select cell **B10** and drag the *Fill* pointer to cell **H10**.

11. Apply number formatting.
 a. Select cells **B5:H10**.
 b. Click the **Accounting Number Format** button [*Home* tab, *Number* group]. Column widths are adjusted to accommodate the values.
 c. Click the **Decrease Decimal** button [*Home* tab, *Number* group] two times. Column widths do not adjust.

12. Change row heights.
 a. Click the heading for row **4**.
 b. Press **Ctrl** and click the row **10** heading. Two rows are selected.
 c. Right-click the row **4** heading.
 d. Choose **Row Height** and type 25 as the new height.
 e. Click **OK**.
 f. Click the heading for row **5** and drag down to select rows **5:9**.
 g. Point to the bottom border of the row **9** heading to display the resize arrow.
 h. Drag the pointer down to reach a height of **21.00 (28 pixels)** and release the pointer button (Figure 1-81).

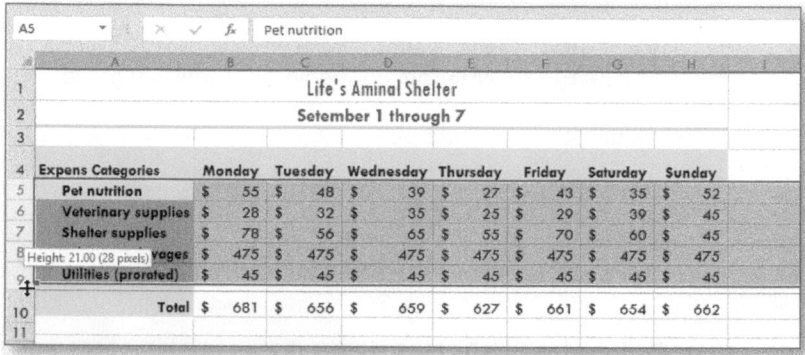

1-81 Change row heights for rows 5:9

13. Insert a row and change column width.
 a. Select cell **A9** and then right-click row heading **9**.
 b. Choose **Insert** from the context menu. The new row is located above the selected row; other rows shift down.
 c. In cell **A9**, type Cages and equipment.
 d. Point to the border between columns **A** and **B** to display the resize arrow.
 e. Drag the pointer to a width of **22.50 (185 pixels)** and release the pointer button.

14. Enter the following data in row **9**. A zero (0) is displayed as a small dash.

	B	C	D	E	F	G	H
Cages and equipment	35	35	25	0	0	35	40

15. Insert borders and change the font size.
 a. Select cells **A4:H11**.
 b. Click the **Borders** button drop-down list and choose **All Borders**.
 c. Select cell **A2** and press **Ctrl+1** to open the *Format Cells* dialog box.
 d. Click the **Border** tab.
 e. Click the blue bottom border in the preview area to remove it.
 f. Click the **Color** drop-down arrow and select **Black, Text 1**.
 g. Click to select the solid, thick line (second column, sixth style) in the *Style* group,
 h. Click the bottom border In the preview area (Figure 1-82).
 i. Click **OK**.
 j. Select cell **A1** and change the font size to **24**.

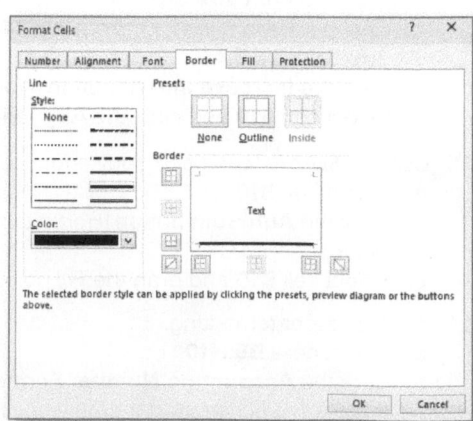

1-82 Create a custom border

16. Rename the sheet and set the tab color.
 a. Double-click the **Sheet1** tab name.
 b. Type Week 1 and press **Enter**.
 c. Click the **Format** button [*Home* tab, *Cells* group].
 d. Select **Tab Color** in the *Organize Sheets* category.
 e. Select **Blue Accent 2, Darker 50%**.

17. Spell check a worksheet.
 a. Press **Ctrl+Home** to go to cell **A1**.
 b. Click the **Spelling** button [*Review* tab, *Proofing* group].
 c. Type Animal in the *Not in Dictionary* box and click **Change**.
 d. Choose "September" in the *Suggestions* list and click **Change**.
 e. Correct "Expens" when the error is located.
 f. Click **OK**.
 g. Press **Ctrl+Home**.

18. Change page setup options.
 a. Click the **Page Layout** tab and click the **Page Setup** launcher.
 b. On the **Page** tab, select the **Landscape** radio button.
 c. Click the **Margins** tab.
 d. Select the **Horizontally** box under *Center on page*.
 e. Click the **Header/Footer** tab.
 f. Click the **Header** drop-down list and choose *[your initials] Excel 1-1* to insert the file name in the center section.
 g. Click **OK**.
 h. Press **Ctrl+F2** to preview the worksheet.
 i. Press **Esc** to close the *Backstage* view.

19. Copy and edit a worksheet.
 a. Right-click the **Week 1** tab name.
 b. Select **Move or Copy** from the menu.
 c. Select **(move to end)** in the *Before sheet* list.
 d. Select the **Create a copy** box and click **OK**.
 e. On the copied worksheet, select cells **B5:H10** and delete the data.
 f. Double-click cell **A2** to start *Edit* mode.
 g. Change "September 1 through 7" to September 8 through 14.
 h. Double-click the **Week 1 (2)** tab name.
 i. Type Week 2 and press **Enter**.
 j. Right-click the **Week 2** tab name and choose **Tab Color**.
 k. Select **Green Accent 4, Darker 50%**.

20. Click the **Week 1** sheet tab.

21. Click the **File** tab and select **Print** to preview the **Week 1** worksheet.

22. Change the zoom size and freeze panes.
 a. Select cell **B5**.
 b. Click the **Zoom In** button in the *Status* bar five times.
 c. Click the **Freeze Panes** button [*View* tab, *Window* group].
 d. Choose **Freeze Panes**.
 e. Scroll the window on the right so that column **F** is immediately to the right of column **A** (Figure 1-83).
 f. Select cell **A1**.

Expense Categories	Friday	Saturday	Sunday
Pet nutrition	$ 43	$ 35	$ 52
Veterinary supplies	$ 29	$ 39	$ 45
Shelter supplies	$ 70	$ 60	$ 45
Salaries and wages	$ 475	$ 475	$ 475
Cages and equipment	$ -	$ 35	$ 40
Utilities (prorated)	$ 45	$ 45	$ 45
Total	$ 661	$ 689	$ 702

1-83 Panes frozen and positioned

23. Save and close the workbook (Figure 1-84).

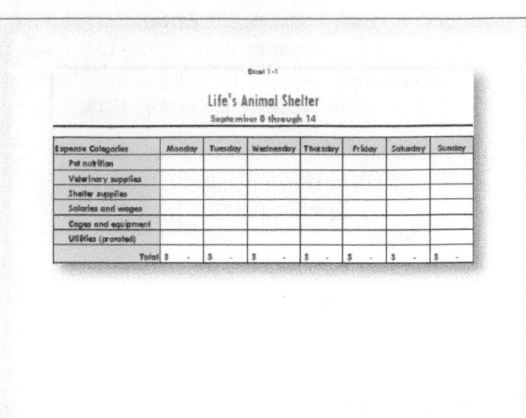

1-84 Excel 1-1 completed

Guided Project 1-2

In this project, you edit a worksheet for Eller Software Services representative Adam White. He maintains client data with sales revenue and specific products or services. You plan to format the data, complete the calculation, and prepare the worksheet for sharing with management.
[Student Learning Outcomes 1.1, 1.2, 1.3, 1.4, 1.5, 1.6, 1.8]

File Needed: **EllerSoftwareServices-01.xlsx** [Student data files are available in the Library of your SIMnet account.]
Completed Project File Name: **[your initials] Excel 1-2.xlsx**

Skills Covered in This Project

- Open and save a workbook.
- Choose a workbook theme.
- Enter and copy labels using the *Fill Handle*.
- Set font attributes and number formats.
- Use *SUM*.
- Center labels across a selection.
- Change page orientation and scale a worksheet for printing.
- Design borders.
- Insert a row and hide a column.
- Rename and apply color to sheet tabs.
- Adjust page setup options.

1. Open the workbook **EllerSoftwareServices-01.xlsx** from your student data files. If the workbook has opened in *Protected View*, click **Enable Editing** in the security bar.

2. Save the workbook with a new file name.
 a. Press **F12 (FN+F12)** to open the *Save As* dialog box.
 b. Navigate to the folder where your files are stored.
 c. Rename the file [your initials] Excel 1-2.
 d. Click **Save**.

3. Choose a workbook theme.
 a. Click the **Themes** button [*Page Layout* tab, *Themes* group].
 b. Choose **Ion** from the gallery. A different font, *Century Gothic*, is used for all data in the worksheet.
 c. Double-click the border between the column **C** and column **D** headings to *AutoFit* column **C**.

4. Enter and copy data.
 a. Select cell **F5**, type **MN**, and press **Enter**.
 b. Select cell **F5** and point to the *Fill Handle*.
 c. Click and drag the *Fill* pointer to cell **E13**.

5. Format data.
 a. Select cells **D5:D13**.
 b. Press **Ctrl+1** to open the *Format Cells* dialog box.
 c. Click the **Number** tab.
 d. In the *Category* list, click **Special**.
 e. Select **Phone Number** in the *Type* list and click **OK** (Figure 1-85).
 f. Select cells **I6:I13**.
 g. Click the **Comma Style** button [*Home* tab, *Number* group].
 h. Select cell **I5**.
 i. Click the **Accounting Number Format** button [*Home* tab, *Number* group]. A series of # symbols means the column is not wide enough to display the data (Figure 1-86).

1-85 Special number format

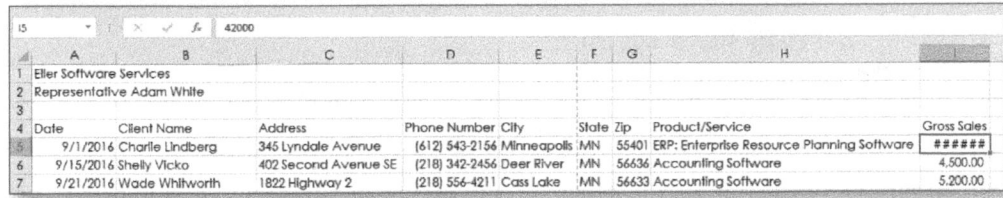

1-86 Column I is not wide enough

 j. Double-click the border between the column **I** and column **J** headings to *AutoFit* column **I**.

6. Enter and edit the reference range for the *SUM* function.
 a. Click cell **A15**, type Total, and press **Enter**.
 b. Select cell **I15**.
 c. Click the **AutoSum** button [*Home* tab, *Editing* group]. The suggested range includes an empty row.
 d. Click cell **I5** and drag to select cells **I5:I13**. Your selected range is highlighted and shown in the *Formula* bar and in the cell (Figure 1-87).
 e. Press **Enter** to accept the range. The *Accounting Number* format is applied.

7. Center labels across a selection.
 a. Select cells **A1:I2** and click the **Alignment** launcher [*Home* tab, *Alignment* group].
 b. Click the **Horizontal** arrow and select **Center Across Selection**.
 c. Click **OK**.

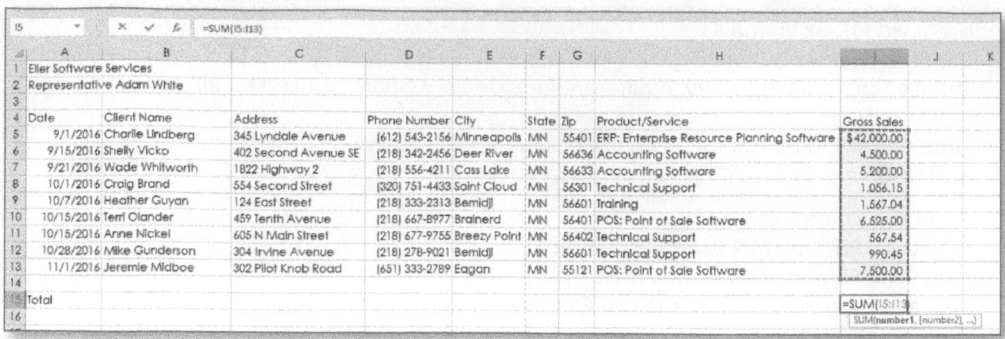

1-87 New range selected for *SUM*

8. Apply font attributes and cell styles.
 a. Select cell **A1**, click the **Font Size** drop-down list [*Home* tab, *Font* group], and select **24**.
 b. Select cell **A2** and change the font size to **18**.
 c. Select cells **A4:A15**, press **Ctrl**, and then select cells **B4:I4**.
 d. Click the **Cell Styles** button or the **More** button and select **40% - Accent3** in the *Themed Cell Styles* category.
 e. While the cells are selected, click the **Bold** button [*Home* tab, *Font* group].
 f. Select cell **I15** and apply the **Total** cell style.
 g. Select cells **A4:I4**.
 h. Click the **Font Size** drop-down list [*Home* tab, *Font* group] and select **12**.
 i. Click the **Center** button [*Home* tab, *Alignment* group].
 j. *AutoFit* column **D**.
 k. Select cell **A15** and click the **Align Right** button [*Home* tab, *Alignment* group].

9. Edit a label.
 a. Double-click cell **H9** to start *Edit* mode.
 b. Press **Home** to position the insertion point before the word "Training".
 c. Type ERP and press **Spacebar**.
 d. Press **Enter**.

10. Insert a row.
 a. Right-click row heading **10**.
 b. Choose **Insert** from the context menu.
 c. In cell **A10**, type 10/10/16 and press **Tab**.
 d. Complete the data as shown here. For the phone number, do not type any spaces; it is automatically formatted when you press **Tab** to move to the next cell.

 B10 Hillary Marschke
 C10 245 West Third Avenue
 D10 3203555443(press **Tab**)
 E10 sa (press **Tab**)
 F10 m (press **Tab**)
 G10 56301
 H10 t (press **Tab**)
 I10 750

11. Apply borders.
 a. Select cells **A4:I14**.
 b. Click the **Border** drop-down arrow [*Home* tab, *Font* group] and choose **All Borders**.

c. Select cells **A16:I16**.
d. Press **Ctrl+1** to open the *Format Cells* dialog box and click the **Border** tab.
e. Select the solid, single line (first column, sixth option) in the *Style* list.
f. Click the top border In the *Border* preview area.
g. Select the solid, double line (second column, seventh option) in the *Style* list.
h. Click the bottom border In the *Border* preview area (Figure 1-88).
i. Click **OK**.
j. Select cells **A15:I16**.
k. Click the **Border** arrow [*Home* tab, *Font* group] and choose **Left Border**.
l. Click the **Border** arrow [*Home* tab, *Font* group] and choose **Right Border**.

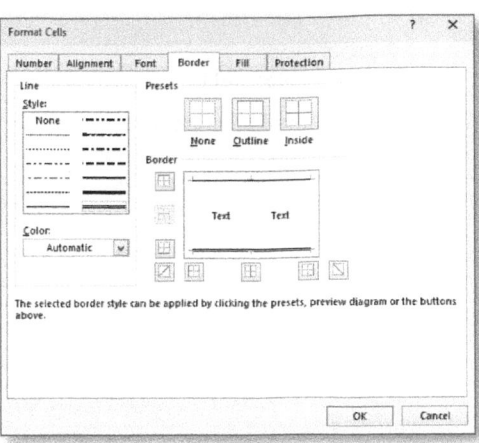

1-88 Design a double border

12. Hide a column.
 a. Right-click the column **F** heading.
 b. Select **Hide**.
 c. Press **Ctrl+Home**.

13. Rename and color a sheet tab.
 a. Double-click the **Sheet1** tab.
 b. Type MN Clients and press **Enter**.
 c. Right-click the **MN Clients** tab.
 d. Select **Tab Color** and choose **Gold, Accent 3**.

14. Change page setup options.
 a. Click the **Page Layout** tab.
 b. Click the **Orientation** button [*Page Setup* group] and choose **Landscape**.
 c. In the *Scale to Fit* group, click the **Width** arrow and choose **1 page**.
 d. Click the **Insert** tab.
 e. Click the **Header & Footer** button In the *Text* group. The view switches to *Page Layout* with the insertion point in the center header section. The *Header & Footer Tools Design* toolbar displays.
 f. Click the **Go to Footer** button in the *Navigation* group.
 g. Click the **Footer** button in the *Header & Footer* group (Figure 1-89).

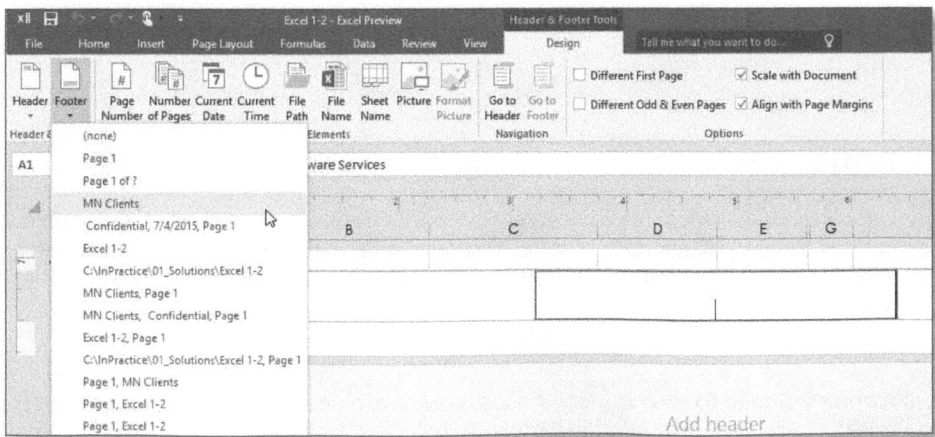

1-89 Select a built-in footer

h. Choose **MN Clients** to insert the sheet name in the footer. The *Header & Footer Tools Design* toolbar closes.

i. Click the **Normal** button in the *Status* bar. The footer is not visible in this view.

15. Preview and print the worksheet.
 a. Select **Print** from the *File* tab.
 b. Review the worksheet layout.
 c. Click **Print** or press **Esc** to return to the workbook.

16. Save and close the workbook (Figure 1-90).

Eller Software Services
Representative Adam White

Date	Client Name	Address	Phone Number	City	Zip	Product/Service	Gross Sales
9/1/2016	Charlie Lindberg	345 Lyndale Avenue	(612) 543-2156	Minneapolis	55401	ERP: Enterprise Resource Planning Software	$ 42,000.00
9/15/2016	Shelly Vickro	402 Second Avenue SE	(218) 342-2456	Deer River	56636	Accounting Software	4,500.00
9/21/2016	Wade Whitworth	1822 Highway 2	(218) 556-4211	Cass Lake	56633	Accounting Software	5,200.00
10/1/2016	Craig Brand	554 Second Street	(320) 751-4435	Saint Cloud	56301	Technical Support	1,056.15
10/7/2016	Heather Guyan	124 East Street	(218) 333-2513	Bemidji	56601	ERP Training	1,567.04
10/10/2016	Hilary Manchke	245 West Third Avenue	(320) 355-5445	Saint Cloud	56301	Technical Support	750.00
10/15/2016	Terri Olander	459 Tenth Avenue	(218) 667-8977	Brainerd	56401	POS: Point of Sale Software	6,525.00
10/15/2016	Anne Nickel	605 N Main Street	(218) 677-9755	Breezy Point	56402	Technical Support	567.54
10/28/2016	Mike Gunderson	304 Irvine Avenue	(218) 278-9021	Bemidji	56601	Technical Support	990.45
11/1/2016	Jeremie Midboe	302 Pilot Knob Road	(651) 333-2789	Eagan	55121	POS: Point of Sale Software	7,500.00
Total							**$ 70,656.18**

MN Clients

1-90 Excel 1-2 completed

Guided Project 1-3

In this project, you edit a worksheet for Wear-Ever Shoes that tracks their product inventory. You change the zoom size, reset the panes, and format data. You copy an existing formula to calculate the value of the current stock and insert a column for new data. After adjusting print options, you set a print area for a specific product line.
[Student Learning Outcomes 1.1, 1.2, 1.4, 1.5, 1.6, 1.7, 1.8]

File Needed: ***WearEverShoes-01.xlsx*** *[Student data files are available in the Library of your SIMnet account.]*
Completed Project File Name: *[your initials] Excel 1-3.xlsx*

Skills Covered in This Project

- Open and save a workbook.
- Change zoom size and remove a split.
- Freeze panes.
- Format labels and values.
- Use the *Fill Handle* to copy a formula and fill a series.
- Check spelling.
- Apply a workbook theme, cell styles, and font attributes.
- Merge and center labels.
- Insert a column and adjust column widths and row heights.
- Adjust alignment, indents, and borders.
- Rename the sheet tab.
- Use *Page Layout* view to insert a footer.

1. Open and rename a workbook.
 a. Open the workbook *WearEverShoes-01.xlsx* from your student data files. If the workbook has opened in *Protected View*, click **Enable Editing** in the security bar.
 b. Press **F12** (**FN+F12**) and locate the folder where your files are saved.
 c. Save the workbook as [your initials] Excel 1-3.

2. Remove a split and freeze panes.
 a. Click the **Split** button [*View* tab, *Window* group]. The split is removed.
 b. Click cell **A4** to freeze the column titles at this position.
 c. Click the **Freeze Panes** button [*View* tab, *Window* group].
 d. Choose **Freeze Panes**. There is a solid border between rows 3 and 4 to mark the pane.
 e. Scroll to row **31** and click cell **E31**. The column titles are frozen.
 f. Type 3 and press **Enter** (Figure 1-91).
 g. Press **Ctrl+Home**. The insertion point returns to cell **A4**.

E31		×	✓	fx	3			
	A	B	C	D	E	F	G	H
1	Wear-Ever Shoes							
2	Current Stock							
3	Product ID	Product	Color	Size	Quantity	Men's or \	Cost	Value
16	WE013	Comfy Walking Shoes	Taupe	7.5	2	W	47.5	
17	WE014	Comfy Walking Shoes	Brown	8	3	W	47.5	
18	WE015	Lazy Flip-Flops	Pink	6	4	W	7.5	
19	WE016	Lazy Flip-Flops	Pink	7	0	W	7.5	
20	WE017	Lazy Flip-Flops	Pink	8	2	W	7.5	
21	WE018	Lazy Flip-Flops	White	6	3	W	7.5	
22	WE019	Lazy Flip-Flops	White	7	1	W	7.5	
23	WE020	Lazy Flip-Flops	White	8	2	W	7.5	
24	WE021	Lazy Flip-Flops	Brown	8	2	M	7.5	
25	WE022	Lazy Flip-Flops	Brown	9	4	M	7.5	
26	WE023	Lazy Flip-Flops	Brown	10	2	M	7.5	
27	WE024	Lazy Flip-Flops	Brown	11	2	M	7.5	
28	WE025	Seriously Tall Boots	Black	6	0	W	42.5	
29	WE026	Seriously Tall Boots	Black	6.5	0	W	42.5	
30	WE027	Seriously Tall Boots	Black	7	1	W	42.5	
31	WE028	Seriously Tall Boots	Black	7.5	3	W	42.5	

1-91 Panes frozen at cell A4

3. Change zoom size and unfreeze the pane.
 a. Click the **100%** button [*View* tab, *Window* group].
 b. Click the **Freeze Panes** button [*View* tab, *Window* group].
 c. Choose **Unfreeze Panes**.
 d. Click cell **A1**.

4. Check spelling in the worksheet.
 a. Click the **Spelling** button [*Review* tab, *Proofing* group]. The first occurrence of "Hikin" is found as misspelled.
 b. Select **Hiking** in the *Suggestions* list.
 c. Click **Change All** to correct all occurrences of the misspelled word (Figure 1-92).
 d. Click **OK**.

5. Use the *Fill Handle* to copy a formula.
 a. Click **H4**. The formula is visible in the *Formula* bar. The formula multiplies the quantity by the cost to calculate the value of the current stock (Figure 1-93).
 b. Point to the *Fill Handle* for cell **H4**.
 c. Double-click the *Fill* pointer. The formula is copied down the entire column.
 d. Press **Ctrl+Home**.

1-92 Change all occurrences of a misspelled word

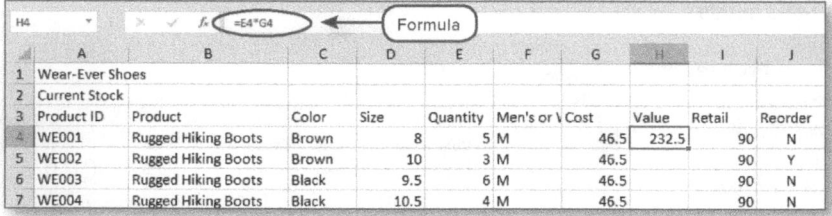

1-93 Formula to be copied

6. Click the **Themes** button [*Page Layout* tab, *Themes* group] and choose **Ion** from the gallery.

7. Merge and center the titles.
 a. Select cells **A1:J1** and click the **Merge & Center** button [*Home* tab, *Alignment* group].
 b. Merge and center cells **A2:J2**.

8. Apply cell styles and adjust row height.
 a. Select cell **A1**, click the **Cell Styles** button or the **More** button [*Home* tab, *Styles* group], and select **Title** in the *Titles and Headings* category.
 b. Select cell **A2** and apply the **Heading 4** style.
 c. Click the **Font Size** arrow [*Home* tab, *Font* group] and select **14 pt**. Your font size change overwrites the font size of the cell style.
 d. Point to the row **1** heading and drag to select row headings **1:2**.
 e. Click the **Format** button [*Home* tab, *Cells* group] and choose **Row Height**.
 f. Type 22 as the new row height and press **Enter**.
 g. Select cells **A3:J3**.
 h. From the *Cell Styles* gallery [*Home* tab], select **40% - Accent3**.
 i. Apply **bold** to the selected cells.
 j. Click the row **3** heading.
 k. Point to the bottom border of the row heading to display the resize arrow.
 l. Drag the resize arrow to **21.00 (28 pixels)** as the new row height and release the pointer button (Figure 1-94).
 m. Click the **Zoom Out** button in the *Status* bar if necessary so that you can see all rows (1:39).

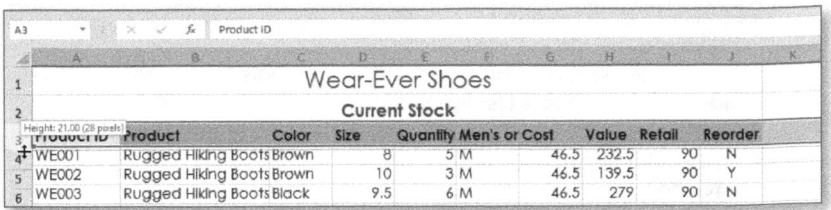

1-94 Adjust row height from the row heading

9. Change alignment, format values, apply borders, and increase the indent.
 a. Select cells **D4:F39**.
 b. Click the **Center** button [*Home* tab, *Alignment* group].
 c. Select cells **G4:H39**.
 d. Click the **Accounting Number Format** button [*Home* tab, *Alignment* group].
 e. Click cells **A3:J39**.
 f. Click the **Borders** drop-down arrow [*Home* tab, *Font* group] and select **All Borders**.
 g. While the cells are selected, click the **Font size** drop-down arrow [*Home* tab, *Font* group] and choose **12**.
 h. Select cells **B4:C39** and click the **Increase Indent** button [*Home* tab, *Alignment* group] one time. This moves the label away from the border for easier reading.
 i. Click and drag to select columns **A:J**.
 j. Double-click the border between columns J and K to *AutoFit* the selected columns (Figure 1-95).
 k. Select and **center** align the labels in row **3**.

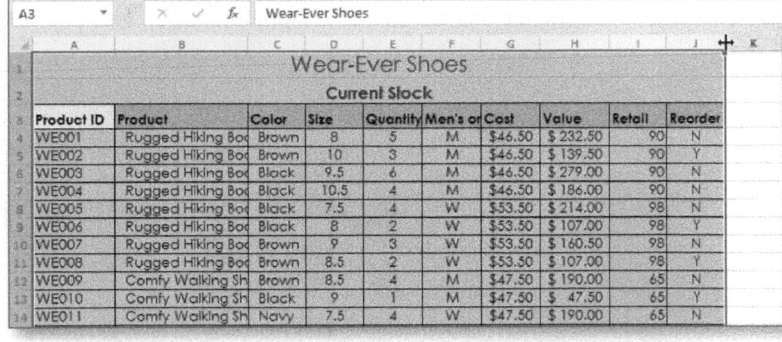

1-95 Select column headings to *AutoFit*

10. Insert a column and fill data.
 a. Right-click column heading **B**.
 b. Choose **Insert** from the context menu.
 c. In cell **B3**, type Disc? and press **Enter**.
 d. In cell **B4**, type No and press **Enter**.
 e. In cell **B5**, type No and press **Enter**.
 f. In cell **B6**, type Yes and press **Enter**.
 g. Select cells **B4:B6** and increase the indent twice.
 h. Select cells **B4:B6** and double-click the *Fill* pointer (Figure 1-96).
 i. Select cells **A4:A39** and increase the indent one time.
 j. Press **Ctrl+Home**.

11. Rename the sheet tab.
 a. Double-click the **Sheet1** tab.
 b. Type Inventory and press **Enter**.

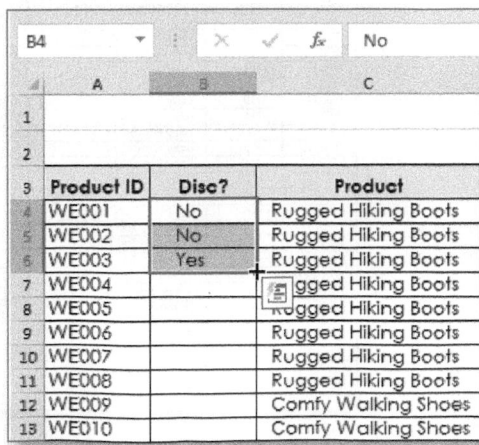

1-96 Double-click the *Fill* pointer to complete a series

12. Use *Page Layout* view to insert a footer.
 a. Click the **Page Layout** button in the *Status* bar.
 b. Click the center header section. The *Header & Footer Tools Design* tab is active.
 c. Click the **Header & Footer Tools Design** tab.
 d. Click the **Go to Footer** button [*Header & Footer Tools Design* tab, *Navigation* group].
 e. Click the middle section if necessary.
 f. Click the **File Name** button in the *Header & Footer Elements* group. The code is *&[File]*.
 g. Click a worksheet cell to see the file name.
 h. Switch to *Normal* view and press **Ctrl+Home**.

13. Change page setup options.
 a. Click the **Page Layout** tab and click the **Page Setup** launcher.
 b. Display the *Page* tab and select the **Landscape** radio button under *Orientation*.
 c. Select the **Fit to** radio button and enter 1 page wide by 1 tall.
 d. Click **OK**.

14. Set a print area.
 a. Select cells **A1:K11**.
 b. Click the **Page Layout** tab.
 c. Click the **Print Area** button [*Page Setup* group] and select **Set Print Area**.
 d. Press **Ctrl+Home**.
 e. Click the **File** tab and select **Print** to preview the worksheet print area.
 f. Print the area and return to *Normal* view.

15. Click the **Save** button in the *Quick Access* toolbar to save the workbook changes. The print area is saved.

16. Close the workbook (Figure 1-97).

Product ID	Disc?	Product	Color	Size	Quantity	Men's or Women's	Cost	Value	Retail	Reorder
WE001	No	Rugged Hiking Boots	Brown	8	5	M	$ 46.50	$ 232.50	90	N
WE002	No	Rugged Hiking Boots	Brown	10	3	M	$ 46.50	$ 139.50	90	Y
WE003	Yes	Rugged Hiking Boots	Black	9.5	6	M	$ 46.50	$ 279.00	90	N
WE004	No	Rugged Hiking Boots	Black	10.5	4	M	$ 46.50	$ 186.00	90	N
WE005	No	Rugged Hiking Boots	Black	7.5	4	W	$ 53.50	$ 214.00	98	N
WE006	Yes	Rugged Hiking Boots	Black	8	2	W	$ 53.50	$ 107.00	98	Y
WE007	No	Rugged Hiking Boots	Brown	9	3	W	$ 53.50	$ 160.50	98	N
WE008	No	Rugged Hiking Boots	Brown	8.5	2	W	$ 53.50	$ 107.00	98	Y
WE009	Yes	Comfy Walking Shoes	Brown	8.5	4	M	$ 47.50	$ 190.00	65	N
WE010	No	Comfy Walking Shoes	Black	9	1	M	$ 47.50	$ 47.50	65	Y
WE011	No	Comfy Walking Shoes	Navy	7.5	4	W	$ 47.50	$ 190.00	65	N
WE012	Yes	Comfy Walking Shoes	Black	8	1	W	$ 47.50	$ 47.50	65	Y
WE013	No	Comfy Walking Shoes	Taupe	7.5	2	W	$ 47.50	$ 95.00	65	N
WE014	No	Comfy Walking Shoes	Brown	8	3	W	$ 47.50	$ 142.50	65	Y
WE015	Yes	Lazy Flip-Flops	Pink	6	4	W	$ 7.50	$ 30.00	14	N
WE016	No	Lazy Flip-Flops	Pink	7	0	W	$ 7.50	$ -	14	N
WE017	No	Lazy Flip-Flops	Pink	8	2	W	$ 7.50	$ 15.00	14	Y
WE018	Yes	Lazy Flip-Flops	White	6	3	W	$ 7.50	$ 22.50	14	N
WE019	No	Lazy Flip-Flops	White	7	1	W	$ 7.50	$ 7.50	14	N
WE020	No	Lazy Flip-Flops	White	8	2	W	$ 7.50	$ 15.00	14	Y
WE021	Yes	Lazy Flip-Flops	Brown	8	2	M	$ 7.50	$ 15.00	14	Y
WE022	No	Lazy Flip-Flops	Brown	9	4	M	$ 7.50	$ 30.00	14	N
WE023	No	Lazy Flip-Flops	Brown	10	2	M	$ 7.50	$ 15.00	14	Y
WE024	Yes	Lazy Flip-Flops	Brown	11	2	M	$ 7.50	$ 15.00	14	Y
WE025	No	Seriously Tall Boots	Black	6	0	W	$ 42.50	$ -	80	Y
WE026	No	Seriously Tall Boots	Black	6.5	0	W	$ 42.50	$ -	80	Y
WE027	Yes	Seriously Tall Boots	Black	7	1	W	$ 42.50	$ 42.50	80	Y
WE028	No	Seriously Tall Boots	Black	7.5	3	W	$ 42.50	$ 127.50	80	Y
WE029	No	Seriously Tall Boots	Black	8	2	W	$ 42.50	$ 85.00	80	Y
WE030	Yes	Seriously Tall Boots	Black	8.5	1	W	$ 42.50	$ 42.50	80	Y
WE031	No	Glide Running Shoes	White	8	6	M	$ 48.00	$ 288.00	75	N
WE032	No	Glide Running Shoes	White	9	6	M	$ 48.00	$ 288.00	75	N
WE033	Yes	Glide Running Shoes	White	10	6	M	$ 48.00	$ 288.00	75	N
WE034	No	Glide Running Shoes	Black	8	2	M	$ 48.00	$ 96.00	75	N
WE035	No	Glide Running Shoes	Black	9	3	M	$ 48.00	$ 144.00	75	N
WE036	Yes	Glide Running Shoes	Black	10	1	M	$ 48.00	$ 48.00	75	Y

Wear-Ever Shoes
Current Stock

Excel 1-3

1-97 Excel 1-3 completed

Independent Project 1-4

As staff at Blue Lake Sports Company, you are expected to prepare the monthly sales worksheet. You edit and format data, complete calculations, and prepare the workbook for distribution. You also copy the sheet for next month's data.
[Student Learning Outcomes 1.1, 1.2, 1.3, 1.4, 1.5, 1.6, 1.8]

File Needed: ***BlueLakeSports-01.xlsx*** [*Student data files are available in the Library of your SIMnet account.*]
Completed Project File Name: *[your initials] **Excel 1-4**.xlsx*

Skills Covered in This Project

- Open and save a workbook.
- Choose a workbook theme.
- Edit and format data.
- Center labels across a selection.

- Use *SUM* and the *Fill Handle*.
- Adjust column width and row height.
- Insert a header and a footer.
- Adjust page layout options.
- Copy and rename a worksheet.

1. Open ***BlueLakeSports-01.xlsx*** from your student data files. If the workbook has opened in *Protected View*, click **Enable Editing** in the security bar.

2. Save the workbook as [your initials] Excel 1-4 in your usual location.

3. Apply the **Slice** theme to the worksheet.

4. Edit worksheet data.
 a. Edit the title in cell **A2** to display Monthly Sales by Department.
 b. Edit cell **D6** to 1950.

5. Select cells **A1:F2** and apply the *Center Across Selection* command.

6. Select and delete row **8**.

7. Use the *Fill Handle* to complete a series.
 a. Select cell **B3**.
 b. Use the *Fill Handle* to complete the series to **Week 4** in column **E**.
 c. *AutoFit* the columns to display the complete label.

8. Use *SUM* and the *Fill Handle* to calculate totals.
 a. Use the **AutoSum** button to build a *SUM* function in cell **F4**.
 b. Use the *Fill Handle* to copy the formula in cell **F4** to cells **F5:F16**.
 c. Delete the contents of cell **F17** if you copied the formula to that cell.
 d. Select cells **B17:F17** and click the **AutoSum** button. The *SUM* formula is inserted, and a **Quick Analysis** options button appears (Figure 1-98).
 e. Press **Esc** to ignore the *Quick Analysis* options.

B17		✕ ✓ fx	=SUM(B4:B16)				
	A	B	C	D	E	F	G
1		Blue Lake Sports					
2		Monthly Sales by Department					
3	Department	Week 1	Week 2	Week 3	Week 4	Total	
4	Apparel	2600	3200	3800	3700	13300	
5	Baseball	3500	1200	1350	2100	8150	
6	Basketball	1800	1800	1950	1400	6950	
7	Bike & Skate	1500	1325	1225	2450	6500	
8	Fitness	2650	2875	3250	3775	12550	
9	Footwear	1875	2675	3575	3250	11375	
10	Game Room	1300	1500	1900	1050	5750	
11	Golf	4750	875	925	5400	11950	
12	Hockey	850	1875	1950	750	5425	
13	Hunting	2000	*Quick Analysis button*				
14	Lacrosse	1750					
15	Running	1925	2400	2800	2650	9775	
16	Winter Sports	1250	34350	2750	550	38900	
17	Total	27750	56875	27875	29175	141675	
18							
19							

1-98 *AutoSum* complete with *Quick Analysis* button

9. Format labels and values.
 a. Select cells **A1:A2** and increase the font size to **18**.
 b. Increase the row height of rows **1:2** to **24 (32 pixels)**.
 c. Format cells **A3:F3** as **Bold** and increase the row height to **18 (24 pixels)**.
 d. Center the data in cells **B3:F3**.
 e. Format all values with **Comma Style** and decrease the decimal two times.
 f. Apply the **All Borders** format to cells **A3:F17**.
 g. Select cells **B17:F17** and apply the **Accounting Number Format** with no decimal places.
 h. *AutoFit* each column that does not display all data.

10. Finalize the worksheet.
 a. Click the **Insert** tab and click the **Header & Footer** button.
 b. In the right header section, insert the **Sheet Name** field.
 c. Go to the footer and click the right section.
 d. Type [your first and last name] (Figure 1-99).

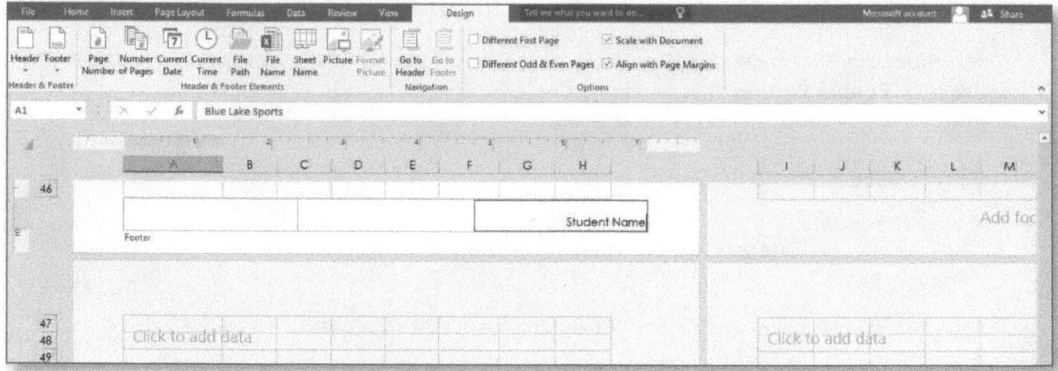

1-99 Add a footer in *Page Layout* view

 e. Click a cell in the worksheet and return to *Normal* view.
 f. Center the worksheet horizontally on the page.

11. Copy and rename a worksheet.
 a. Right-click the *January* sheet tab and choose **Move or Copy**.
 b. Make a copy of the sheet at the end.
 c. Rename the copied sheet February.
 d. Format the *February* sheet tab color to **Dark Blue, Accent 1**.
 e. Delete the values in cells **B4:E16** and press **Ctrl+Home**.
 f. Return to the *January* sheet.

12. Preview the *January* sheet.

13. Save and close the workbook (Figure 1-100).

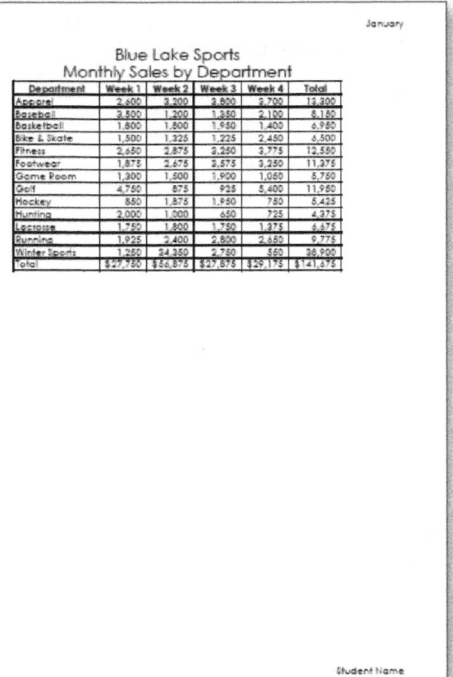

1-100 Excel 1-4 completed

Independent Project 1-5

Clemenson Imaging employs certified staff to perform mobile medical imaging at several hospitals state-wide. Your worksheet maintains a log of which hospitals were visited and what images were made. You need to format the data and finalize the worksheet.
[Student Learning Outcomes 1.1, 1.2, 1.3, 1.4, 1.5, 1.6, 1.7, 1.8]

File Needed: *ClemensonImaging-01.xlsx* [*Student data files are available in the Library of your SIMnet account.*]
Completed Project File Name: *[your initials] Excel 1-5.xlsx*

Skills Covered in This Project

- Open and save a workbook.
- Use *SUM*.
- Unfreeze panes and change the zoom size.
- Format data.

- Merge and center labels.
- Adjust column width and row height.
- Design borders.
- Copy a sheet and rename a tab.
- Add document properties.
- Change page layout options.

1. Open **ClemensonImaging-01.xlsx** from your student data files and save it as [your initials] Excel 1-5. If the workbook has opened in *Protected View*, click **Enable Editing** in the security bar.

2. Edit the label in cell **A1** to insert LLC after "Clemenson Imaging." Edit the label in cell **A2** to show "Second Quarter . . ." instead of "First Quarter."

3. Merge and center the label in cell **A1** across the worksheet data and then do the same for the label in cell **A2**.

4. Scroll to and select cell **A41**. Type Total. Right-align this label and apply bold format.

5. Use *SUM* in cell **F41** to add the values in cells **F5:F40**.

6. Unfreeze the panes and set a zoom size to display rows 1:30.

7. *AutoFit* columns **D** and **G**.

8. Format data.
 a. Click cell **A1** and set the font size to **18**.
 b. Change the label in cell **A2** to a font size of **14**.
 c. Select cells **A4:H4** and apply bold and center.
 d. Format cells **A4:H4** to use the **White, Background 1, Darker 15%** fill color.
 e. Format the row height for row **4** to **21.00 (28 pixels)**.
 f. Select cells **A4:H41** and apply **All Borders**.
 g. Select cells **A41:H41** and apply the fill color **White, Background 1, Darker 15%**.
 h. Make the value in cell **F41** bold.

9. Set page layout options.
 a. Change the page orientation to **Landscape**.
 b. Center the worksheet horizontally.
 c. Scale the sheet to fit on a single page.
 d. Add a footer that displays the current date in the left section and your first and last name in the right section.
 e. *Autofit* columns that do not display all the data.

10. Add document properties.
 a. Click the **File** tab and select **Info**.
 b. Click the **Properties** drop-down arrow and select **Advanced Properties**.
 c. Click the **Title** box and type Procedures.
 d. Click the **Author** box and type your first and last name (Figure 1-101).
 e. Return to the worksheet.

1-101 *Properties* dialog box

11. Rename *Sheet1* as Qtr 2.

12. Copy the *Qtr 2* sheet and place it at the end. Name the copy Qtr 3. Set this tab color to **Blue, Accent 1, Darker 50%**.

13. On the *Qtr 3* sheet, edit the label in cell **A2** to show "Third Quarter . . .".

14. Delete the contents of cells **A5:H40** on the *Qtr 3* sheet.

15. Select cell **A5** and return to the *Qtr 2* sheet.

16. Press **Ctrl+Home** and preview the entire workbook (Figure 1-102).

17. Save and close the workbook (Figure 1-103).

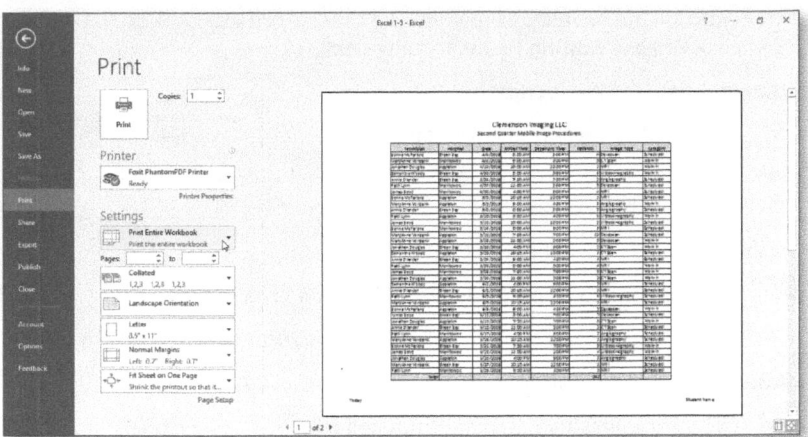

1-102 Entire workbook selected for preview and print

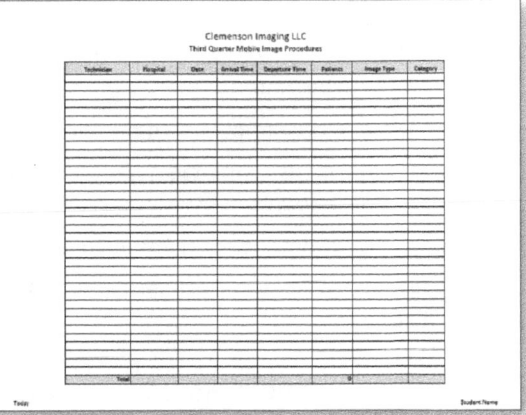

1-103 Excel 1-5 completed

Independent Project 1-6

As accounts receivable clerk for Livingood Income Tax & Accounting, you track daily payments from clients in an Excel worksheet. After entering the data, you format the worksheet and prepare it for distribution to coworkers.

[Student Learning Outcomes 1.1, 1.2, 1.3, 1.4, 1.5, 1.6, 1.8]

File Needed: None
Completed Project File Name: *[your initials] Excel 1-6.xlsx*

Skills Covered in This Project

- Create and save a workbook.
- Enter labels, dates, and values.
- Use the *Fill Handle* to build series.
- Use *SUM*.
- Change font size and attributes.
- Adjust column width and row height.
- Choose a theme and cell styles.
- Choose page layout options.
- Rename and apply color to sheet tabs.

1. Create a new workbook and save it as [your initials] Excel 1-6. If the workbook has opened in *Protected View*, click **Enable Editing** in the security bar.

2. Apply the **Organic** theme for the workbook.

3. In cell **A1**, type Livingood Income Tax and Accounting and press **Enter**

4. In cell **A2**, type Accounts Receivable and press **Enter**.

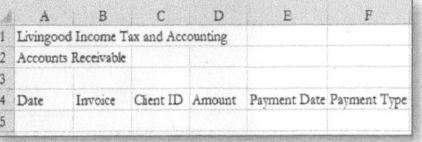

1-104 Data to be entered

5. In row **4**, type the labels as shown here in Figure 1-104:

6. *AutoFit* or widen the columns to display each label in row 4 in its cell.

7. In cell **A5**, type 8/18/17 to enter the date. In cell **A6**, type 8/20/17 to set a pattern for the dates.

8. Select cells **A5:A6** and use the *Fill Handle* to fill in dates to cell A15.

9. In cell **B5**, type 1001 for the first invoice number. In cell **B6**, type 1002 to set a pattern for the invoice numbers.

10. Select cells **B5:B6** and use the *Fill Handle* to fill in invoice numbers to reach cell B15.

11. In cell **C5**, type LITA001 as the first client ID. In cell **C6**, type LITA002 to set a pattern.

12. Use the *Fill Handle* to complete the client ID numbers.

13. Type 425 in cell **D5**. In cell **D6**, type 450 to set the pattern and fill in the amounts.

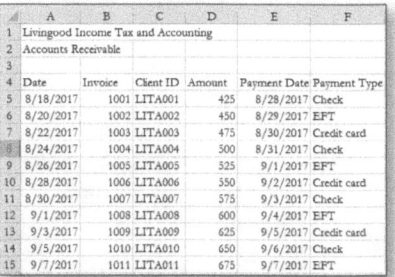

1-105 All columns filled

14. Type the first two payment dates in column **E** and fill the cells (Figure 1-105).

15. Type the first three payment types in cells **F5:F7** and then use the *Fill Handle* to complete the cells in column F.

16. Format data.
 a. Select cells **C5:C15**, increase the indent one time, and *AutoFit* the column. Do the same for the payment type data.
 b. Format the values in column **D** as **Accounting Number Format**.
 c. Select cells **A1:A2** and change the font size to **18**. Center the labels across cells **A1:F2**.
 d. Select the labels in row **4** and apply bold format center alignment.
 e. *AutoFit* columns that do not show all the data.
 f. Apply **All Borders** to cells **A4:F15**. Apply an **Outside Border** for cells **A1:F2**.
 g. Apply the **Green, Accent 1, Lighter 60%** fill color to cells **A1:F2** and **A4:F4**.
 h. Apply the **Green, Accent 1, Lighter 60%** fill color to cells **A6:F6**.
 i. Use the **Ctrl** key to select the data in rows **8**, **10**, **12**, and **14** and apply the same fill color.

17. Rename *Sheet1* as AR and set the tab color to **Green, Accent 1**.

18. Define page layout and add document properties.
 a. Center the worksheet horizontally on the page.
 b. Create a header with the sheet name in the left section and your name in the right section.
 c. Delete an existing author name and key your first and last name as *Author* in the *Properties* dialog box.
 d. Type Receivables in the *Title* box (Figure 1-106).
 e. Preview your worksheet.

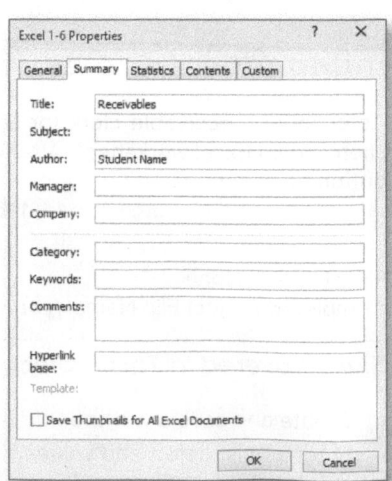

1-106 Properties entered in dialog box

E1-83

19. Save and close the workbook (Figure 1-107).

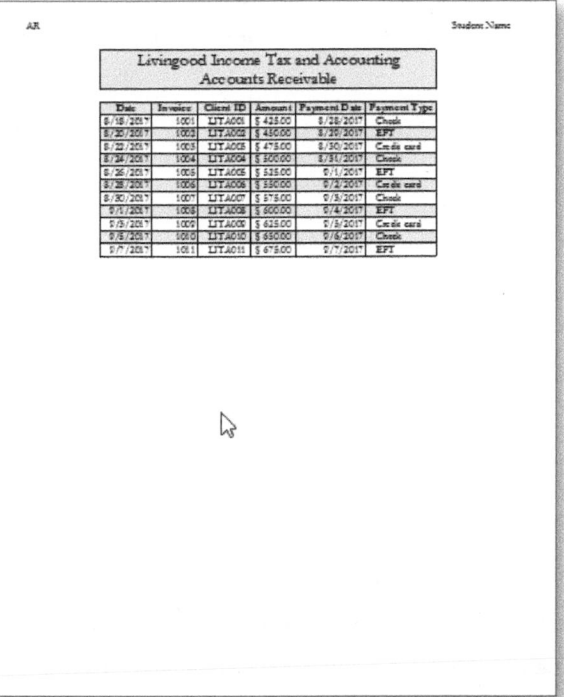

1-107 Excel 1-6 completed

Improve It Project 1-7

In this project, you complete a worksheet that maintains flight statistics for Boyd Air. The data has been imported from the reservation system, and you now need to add finishing touches.
[Student Learning Outcomes 1.1, 1.2, 1.3, 1.4, 1.5, 1.6, 1.7, 1.8]

File Needed: ***BoydAir-01.xlsx*** [*Student data files are available in the Library of your SIMnet account.*]
Completed Project File Name: ***[your initials] Excel 1-7.xlsx***

Skills Covered in This Project

- Open and save a workbook.
- Change the zoom level and remove a split.
- Enter and merge and center labels.
- Insert a row and set column width.

- Format data.
- Use *SUM*.
- Apply cell styles.
- Rename and color the sheet tab.
- Adjust page layout options.
- Add document properties.

1. Open the workbook ***BoydAir-01.xlsx*** from your student data files. If the workbook has opened in *Protected View*, click **Enable Editing** in the security bar.

2. Save the workbook as [your initials] Excel 1-7.

3. Remove the split from the window.

4. Type Boyd Air in cell **A1** and Flight Statistics in cell **A2**.

5. Merge and center the labels in cells **A1** and **A2**. Change the font size for both labels to **16**.

6. Insert a row at row **3**.

7. Select the labels in row **4** and make them bold and centered. *AutoFit* columns to show each label in row 4.

8. Change the zoom size to **100%**.

9. Select cells **B5:D18**, press **Ctrl**, and select cells **G5:G18**. Increase the indent one time.

10. Apply **All Borders** for cells **A4:H19**.

11. Calculate the total number of passengers in cell **H19**.

12. Apply the **Accent2** cell style to cells **A3:H3** and cells **A20:H20**.

13. Select cells **A3:H3** and **A20:H20**and apply an **Outside Border**.

14. Modify page layout options.
 a. Change the orientation to **Landscape**.
 b. Center the worksheet horizontally on the page.
 c. Show the file name in the left header section.
 d. Type your first and last name in the right header section.

15. Name the sheet tab Feb-Mar and format the tab color as **Orange, Accent 2**.

16. Set the document properties to show your first and last name as the *Author*. In the *Title* field, type Flight Stats.

17. Preview your worksheet.

18. Save and close the workbook (Figure 1-108).

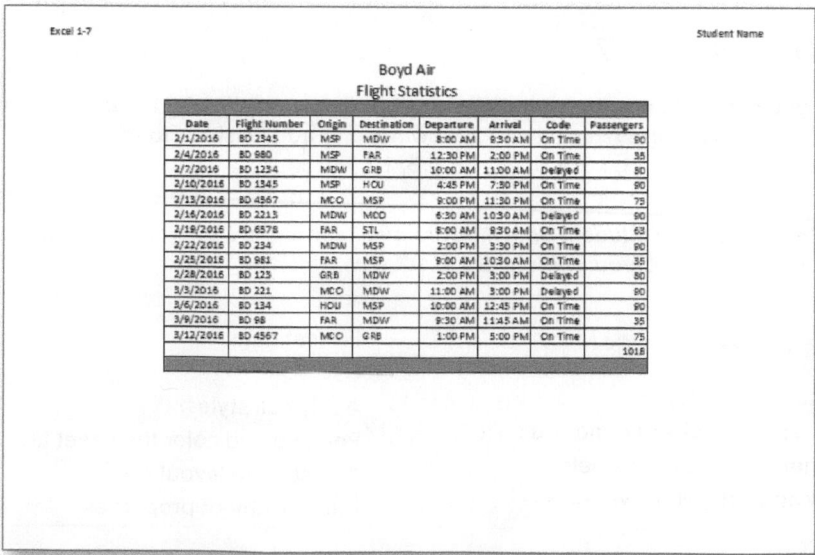

1-108 Excel 1-7 completed

Challenge Project 1-8

In this project, you create a workbook that lists and tracks candy and beverage sales at a gourmet chocolate store for selected holidays or special events. You enter and format the data and then finalize the workbook for distribution.
[Student Learning Outcomes 1.1, 1.2, 1.3, 1.4, 1.5, 1.6, 1.8]

File Needed: None
Completed Project File Name: *[your initials] Excel 1-8.xlsx*

Create a new workbook and save it as [your initials] Excel 1-8. Modify your workbook according to the following guidelines:

- Choose a workbook theme.
- Determine and type a name for the store in cell **A1**. In cell **A2**, type Sales by Holiday.
- Starting in cell **B3**, type names of four chocolate candies and one chocolate beverage (cells B3:F3).
- Type the names of five holidays, celebrations, or special events in cells **A4:A8**.
- Fill in values to reflect dollar or unit sales, and format these values appropriately.
- Calculate a total for each holiday and a total for each candy or beverage. Add labels for these values.
- Use cell styles, borders, fill color, or other formatting to design your worksheet.
- *AutoFit* columns and adjust row heights as needed.
- Insert a footer that includes your name in one section and the date in another section.
- Use portrait orientation and fit the worksheet to a single page. Center it horizontally.
- Name the sheet tab and set a tab color.
- Enter the company name in the *Title* field in the document properties.

Challenge Project 1-9

In this project, you create a worksheet for a photography club that rents retail space for selling used equipment. The equipment includes camera bodies, lenses, tripods, cases, accessories, books, and more. You are building the worksheet so that expected selling prices can be entered each month for each item.
[Student Learning Outcomes 1.1, 1.2, 1.4, 1.5, 1.6, 1.7, 1.8]

File Needed: None
Completed Project File Name: *[your initials] Excel 1-9.xlsx*

Create a new workbook and save it as [your initials] Excel 1-9. Modify your workbook according to the following guidelines:

- Create and type a name for the photography club as a main label. As a second label, type a label that specifies the purpose of the worksheet.
- In cell **B3**, type Jan. Fill the months to **Dec** in column **M**.
- Starting in cell **A4**, type the names of ten items related to any type of photography equipment in column **A**. Research a web site that sells similar items.

- As the January price for the first item, type a value that makes sense as a resale price. For the February price, type a value that is a few dollars more than the January price. Select these two cells and fill prices for the remaining months.
- Repeat the tasks in the previous step for each of the ten items to fill in values for all the items.
- Use cell styles, borders, fill color, or other formatting to design the worksheet.
- Adjust column widths and row heights.
- Insert a header that includes your name in the right section.
- Use landscape orientation and fit the worksheet to a single page.
- In the document properties, enter the club's name in the *Author* field.
- Name the worksheet tab and choose a tab color.
- Split the sheet at cell **G1**. Arrange the data so that you see cell **A1** in each window.

Challenge Project 1-10

In this project, you create a spreadsheet that details your expected monthly income and expenses. [Student Learning Outcomes 1.1, 1.2, 1.3, 1.4, 1.5, 1.6, 1.8]

File Needed: None
Completed Project File Name: *[your initials] Excel 1-10.xlsx*

Create a new workbook and save it as [your initials] Excel 1-10. Modify your workbook according to the following guidelines:

- **Type the main label** Expected Monthly Income and Estimated Expenses. Type your name as a second label.
- Type Income in cell **A3**. In cells **A4:A7**, enter labels for four categories of income. For example, you may have regular wages from one or more jobs, interest from a certificate of deposit, rent from property that you own, income from Internet sales, etc. Include descriptive labels, enter values in column **B**, and include a total income calculation using *SUM*.
- In cell **D3**, type Expenses. In cells **D4:D9**, enter labels for six categories of expenses. These include rent, a mortgage payment, insurance, loan payments, food, clothing, entertainment, transportation, and so on. Complete labels, enter values in column **E**, and use *SUM* to calculate total expenses.
- Format the data with borders, fill color, font styles, and number formats. Adjust page layout options so that the sheet fits on a single portrait page.
- Spell check the sheet.
- Name the sheet Jan and choose a tab color.
- Copy the sheet and name the copy Feb. Choose a different tab color.
- Delete the expense amounts on the *Feb* sheet.
- Make a copy of the *Feb* sheet to create a worksheet for March.
- Add document properties to identify the workbook.

CHAPTER

2

Working with Formulas and Functions

CHAPTER OVERVIEW

With its capabilities in mathematical, scientific, engineering, and other calculations, Excel is a valuable tool for business, government, education, and you. You can use Excel to create a simple addition formula or a sophisticated calculation with layers of arithmetic. In this chapter, you learn how to build a basic formula and how to use mathematical rules. You also explore Excel function categories.

STUDENT LEARNING OUTCOMES (SLOs)

After completing this chapter, you will be able to:

SLO2.1 Build and edit basic formulas (p. E2-89).

SLO2.2 Set mathematical order of operations in a formula (p. E2-91).

SLO2.3 Use absolute, mixed, relative, and 3D references in a formula (p. E2-93).

SLO2.4 Use formula auditing tools in a worksheet (p. E2-99).

SLO2.5 Work with *Statistical* and *Date & Time* functions (p. E2-106).

SLO2.6 Work with functions from the *Financial, Logical*, and *Lookup & Reference* categories (p. E2-114).

SLO2.7 Build functions from the *Math & Trig* category (p. E2-122).

CASE STUDY

In the Pause & Practice projects in this chapter, you work with a multi-sheet workbook for Paradise Lakes Resort (PLR), the northern Minnesota chain of resorts. You build formulas to complete a simple income statement, to calculate data for the boutique division, and to track information about the youth camp.

Pause & Practice 2-1: Build and audit formulas in a worksheet.

Pause & Practice 2-2: Insert *Statistical* and *Date & Time* functions in a workbook.

Pause & Practice 2-3: Use *Financial, Logical, Lookup*, and *Math & Trig* functions in a workbook.

SLO 2.1

Building and Editing a Formula

An Excel *formula* is an expression or statement that uses common arithmetic operations to carry out a calculation. Basic arithmetic operations are addition, subtraction, multiplication, and division. The formula is entered in a cell and refers to other cells or ranges in the worksheet or workbook. The formula appears in the *Formula* bar, but the results appear in the cell.

You learned in Chapter 1 that a function is a built-in formula. Like a function, a formula begins with an equals sign (=). After the equals sign, you enter the address of the first cell, followed by the arithmetic operator, followed by the next cell in the calculation. An example of a simple addition formula is **=B5+B6** which adds the values in cells B5 and B6.

Basic arithmetic operators are listed in the table. Enter arithmetic operators using the numeric keypad or the symbols on the number keys at the top of the keyboard.

In the multiplication formula **=C5*C6**, the value in cell C5 is multiplied by the value in cell C6. You can use cell references in a formula or a value known as a *constant*. In the formula **=D5*85%**, the constant is 85%.

Character	Arithmetic Operator
+	Addition
–	Subtraction
*	Multiplication
/	Division

Type a Formula

For a simple formula, you can easily type it. Click the cell, type the equals sign, type the first cell address, type the operator, type the next cell address, and so on. Press any completion key when the formula is finished. Formulas are not case sensitive, so you can type cell addresses in lowercase letters. Excel automatically converts cell references to uppercase when the formula is completed. If you press **Esc** before completing a formula, it is canceled and nothing is entered in the cell.

As you type a cell address after the equals sign, *Formula AutoComplete* displays a list of functions and range names that match the character that you typed. You can ignore the list and continue typing. In addition, the *Range Finder* highlights and color codes each cell as you type its address.

▶ **HOW TO:** Type a Formula

1. Click the cell for the formula.
2. Type an equals sign (=) to begin the formula.
3. Type the column letter for the first cell reference (Figure 2-1).
 - *Formula AutoComplete* displays a list of functions and range names.
 - You can type a lowercase or uppercase character.
4. Type the row number for the cell reference.
 - The *Range Finder* color codes the cell and its reference.
5. Type the arithmetic operator.
6. Type the cell address for the next reference.

2-1 *Formula AutoComplete* while typing a formula

7. Press **Enter**.

- The result displays in the cell where the formula is located (Figure 2-2).
- The *Formula* bar displays the formula.
- You can click the **Enter** button (the check mark) on the *Formula* bar to complete a formula.
- You can press **Ctrl+Enter** to complete a formula.

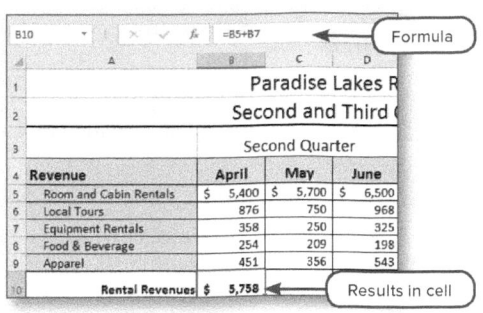

2-2 Formula and result

Point and Click to Build a Formula

Instead of typing a cell address, you point to and click the cell to enter its address in a formula. This method guards against your typing the wrong address. You will not see a *Formula AutoComplete* list, but the *Range Finder* will highlight and color code the cells.

▶**HOW TO:** Point and Click to Build a Formula

1. Click the cell for the formula.

2. Type an equals sign (=) to start the formula.

3. Point to and click the first cell for the formula.

- The reference is entered in the cell and in the *Formula* bar.
- The *Range Finder* highlights and color codes the reference.
- If you click the wrong cell, click the correct cell to replace the address.

4. Type the arithmetic operator.

5. Point to and click the next cell for the formula (Figure 2-3).

- The reference is entered in the cell and in the *Formula* bar.
- The *Range Finder* highlights and color codes the reference.

6. Press **Enter**.

- The result displays in the cell.
- The *Formula* bar displays the formula.
- Click the **Enter** button on the *Formula* bar or press **Ctrl+Enter** to complete a formula.

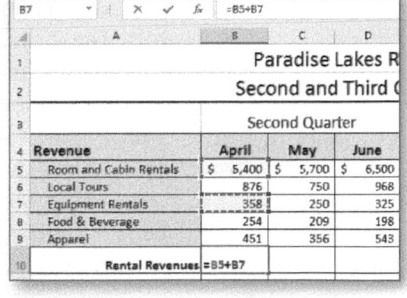

2-3 Point and click to build a formula

Edit a Formula

You edit a formula in *Edit* mode by double-clicking its cell or by clicking the *Formula* bar while the cell is active. The *Range Finder* highlights and color codes the formula cell as well as the cells used in the formula. You can add or remove cells and operators to build a new formula in the cell or in the *Formula* bar.

ANOTHER WAY

Click the cell and press **F2 (FN+F2)** to start *Edit* mode.

▶ HOW TO: Edit a Formula

1. Double-click the formula cell.
 - The *Range Finder* highlights and color codes the cells.
2. Edit the formula in the cell (Figure 2-4).
 - Edit the cell address or type a different operator.
 - Select a cell address and click a different cell to replace the reference.
 - You can make the same edits in the *Formula* bar.
3. Press **Enter**.
 - Click the **Enter** button on the *Formula* bar or press **Ctrl+Enter** to complete a formula.

2-4 Edit a formula in the cell

SLO 2.2

Setting Mathematical Order of Operations

A formula can have more than one operator, such as a combination of addition and multiplication. Figure 2-5 illustrates two formulas a restaurant might use to calculate a bill for a couple who ordered the same items. The formula in cell B6 lists the additions first and multiplies by 2; the total of $24 is incorrect. The formula in cell B8 is the same except for the parentheses; the correct amount is $42.

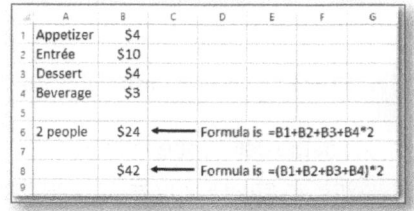

2-5 Formulas with multiple operators

Excel follows ***mathematical order of operations***, which is the sequence of arithmetic calculations. The order in which the mathematics in a formula is carried out depends on the operator as well as left-to-right order. The basic sequence is left to right, but multiplication and division are done before addition and subtraction. This concept is also known as ***order of precedence*** or ***math hierarchy***.

You control the order of operations with parentheses. The formula in cell B8 (Figure 2-5) uses parentheses to reorder the calculation. The parentheses group the addition ($4+$10+$4+$3 = 21) and then multiplies by 2 ($21*2 = 42).

In a formula with multiple operators, references enclosed in parentheses are calculated first. If a value with an exponent exists, it is calculated next. Multiplication and division follow and finally addition and subtraction. When two operators have the same precedence, Excel calculates them from left to right.

Mathematical Order of Precedence

Operator	Operation	Order or Precedence
()	**Parentheses**	First
^	**Exponent**	Second
*	**Multiplication**	Third
/	**Division**	Third
+	**Addition**	Fourth
−	**Subtraction**	Fourth

Exponents raise a number to a power. The formula **3^3** multiplies 3 * 3 * 3, 27. Use the caret symbol (^) to build a formula with an exponent.

Multiple Operators in a Formula

When different operators are used in a formula, you must determine how the calculation should be completed and if parentheses are necessary to set the proper order. Here are formulas with two operators. Since addition and subtraction are equal in priority, Excel calculates from left to right.

$$2 + 5 - 3 = 4 \qquad 5 + 1 - 3 = 3$$

Below are formulas with two operators with different priority. Excel calculates the multiplication first and then follows left to right order.

$$2 + 5 * 3 = 17 \qquad 2 * 5 + 3 = 13$$

Consider this formula with three different operators. Since multiplication and division are equal priority but higher than addition, the multiplication is first, followed by the division (left to right). The result of those calculations is added to 5.

$$= 2 * 5/2 + 5 = 10$$

▶ HOW TO: Use Multiple Operators in a formula

1. Type = to start the formula.
2. Type ((left parenthesis) to start the calculation that should have priority.
 - The calculation in parentheses can occur anywhere in the formula.
3. Click the first cell for the calculation to be enclosed in parentheses.
4. Type the arithmetic operator.
5. Click the next cell for the calculation to be enclosed in parentheses.
6. Type) (right parenthesis) to end the calculation with priority (Figure 2-6).
 - You must have matching parentheses.
7. Complete the formula.
8. Press **Enter**.

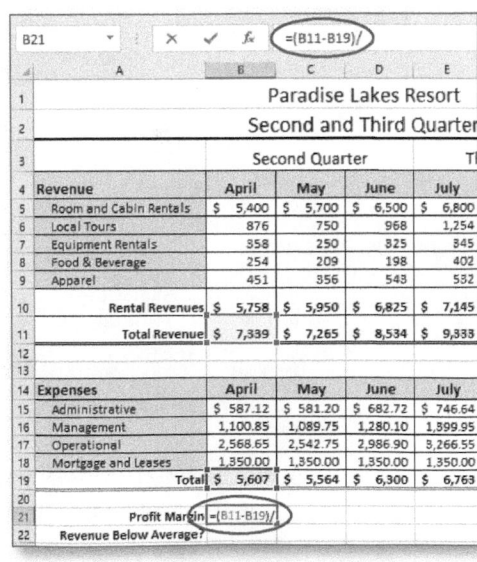

2-6 Set the order of operation with parentheses

SLO 2.3

Using Absolute, Mixed, Relative, and 3D References

Cell references in a formula are identified in different ways. How a cell reference is identified affects how the formula is adjusted when it is copied.

- A *relative cell reference* is the location of a cell, such as cell **B2**. In column B, the formula is **=B5+B7**, but when copied to column C, it is **=C5+C7**. When you copy a formula with relative references, copied references are updated to the new locations.
- An *absolute cell reference* is indicated with dollar signs as in cell **B2**. When an absolute reference is copied, it does not change. In the formula **=B6−C7**, B6 would not change when copied anywhere in the workbook. C7, on the other hand, would reflect where the copy is located. You can type the dollar signs in an absolute reference, but it is easier to use the **F4 (FN+F4)** function key. When building a formula, enter the cell address and then press **F4 (FN+F4)**.
- A *mixed cell reference* has one relative and one absolute reference. Cell **$B2** is a mixed reference. When it is copied, it always refers to column B, but the row number updates relative to where the copy is located. The formula **=$B5+C$6** has two mixed references. When copied, this formula will always show column B for the first address and row 6 for the second address.
- A *3D cell reference* is a cell located in another worksheet in the same workbook. It can be absolute, mixed, or relative. A 3D reference includes the name of the sheet as in **Sheet2!B2** or **Inventory!$B2**. The sheet name is followed by an exclamation point. When you point and click to build a 3D reference, the sheet name and exclamation point are automatically entered. When the sheet name includes special characters (@, #, &, etc.), the name is enclosed in single quotes as in **'Inventory#'!$B2**. When you type a 3D reference, you must spell the sheet name correctly and include the exclamation point and single quotes.

The following table illustrates each cell reference type:

Cell Reference Types

Cell Reference	Reference Type	Behavior When Copied
B2	Relative	Cell address updates to new location(s).
B2	Absolute	Cell address does not change.
$B2	Mixed	Column does not change; row updates to new location(s).
B$2	Mixed	Row does not change; column updates to new location(s).
Sheet2!B2	3D Relative	Cell address updates to new location(s).

> **MORE INFO**
>
> When used in a reference, the dollar sign ($) and the exclamation point (!) are identifiers. The dollar sign is not treated as a currency symbol, and the exclamation point is not considered punctuation.

Copy a Formula with a Relative Reference

When a formula with relative references is copied, the copied formulas use cell addresses that reflect their locations in the worksheet. In the Paradise Lakes worksheet shown in Figure 2-7, the formula to calculate rental revenue in cell B10 is **=B5+B7**. The formula for cell C10 is **=C5+C7**. The formula in cell B10 can be copied to cells C10:G10 and will automatically adjust for each column.

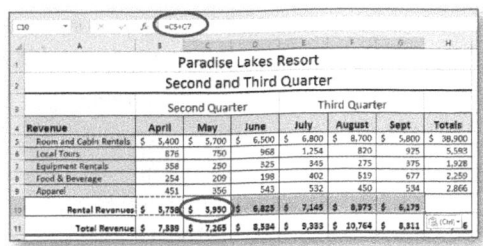

2-7 Copy a formula with a relative reference

▶**HOW TO:** Copy a Formula with a Relative Reference

1. Select the cell with the formula.
 • You can select multiple adjacent cells.
2. Press **Ctrl+C** to copy the formula(s).
 • Click and drag the *Fill* pointer if the copies are adjacent to the original formula(s).
 • Use the **Copy** button on the *Home* tab if you prefer.
3. Select the destination cell or range.
 • Click the first cell in a destination range when pasting multiple cells.
4. Press **Ctrl+V** to paste the formula (see Figure 2-7).
 • The pasted formula reflects its location on the worksheet.
 • Ignore the **Paste Options** button.
 • Use the **Paste** button on the *Home* tab if you prefer.

Build and Copy a Formula with an Absolute Reference

An absolute reference in a formula maintains that address when copied. An example is a worksheet in which expenses are calculated as a percentage of revenue. You type the percentage once in a worksheet cell, use an absolute reference to that cell in the first formula, and copy the formula.

To change a cell address to an absolute reference, press the **F4 (FN+F4)** function key while keying or editing the formula. The first press of the key inserts dollar signs for the row and column reference. Another press of the **F4 (FN+F4)** key makes it a mixed reference, and each press of the key cycles through the next option.

▶**HOW TO:** Build and Copy a Formula with an Absolute Reference

1. Click the cell for the formula.
2. Type an equals sign (=) to begin the formula.
3. Click the cell to be referenced in the formula.
4. Press **F4 (FN+F4)**.
 • The reference becomes absolute (Figure 2-8).
5. Complete the formula and press **Enter**.

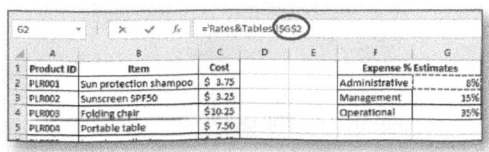

2-8 Make a reference absolute

6. Select the cell with the formula.

7. Press **Ctrl+C** to copy the formula(s).

 - Click and drag the *Fill* pointer if the copies are adjacent to the original formula.
 - Use the **Copy** button on the *Home* tab if you prefer.

8. Select the destination cell or range.

9. Press **Ctrl+V** to paste the formula.

 - The pasted formula uses the same cell reference as the original.
 - Use the **Paste** button on the *Home* tab if you prefer.
 - Ignore the **Paste Options** button.

> ▶ **MORE INFO**
>
> When you type a constant in a formula, such as **=B7*12**, the constant (12) is treated as an absolute value.

Build and Copy a Formula with a Mixed Reference

A mixed cell reference has one relative and one absolute reference in the cell address. Part of the copied formula is unchanged and part is updated. A mixed reference has one dollar sign. You still use the **F4 (FN+F4)** function key, because each press of the key cycles through displaying the dollar signs in different combinations.

▶ HOW TO: Build and Copy a Formula with a Mixed Reference

1. Click the cell for the formula.

2. Type an equals sign (=) to begin the formula.

3. Click the cell to be referenced in the formula.

4. Press **F4 (FN+F4)**.

 - The reference is absolute.

5. Press **F4 (FN+F4)** again.

 - The column reference is relative and the row reference is absolute.

6. Press **F4 (FN+F4)** again (Figure 2-9).

 - The row reference is relative and the column reference is absolute.

7. Complete the formula and press **Enter**.

8. Select the formula cell.

9. Press **Ctrl+C** to copy the formula(s).

 - Drag the *Fill* pointer if copies are adjacent to the original formula.
 - You can use the **Copy** button on the *Home* tab.

10. Click the destination cell or range.

11. Press **Ctrl+V** to paste the formula.

 - The pasted formula keeps the absolute part of the reference but updates the relative part.
 - Use the **Paste** button on the *Home* tab if you prefer.

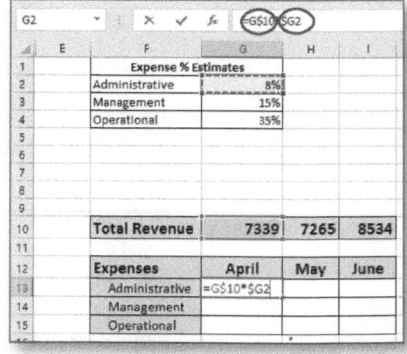

2-9 Formula with a mixed reference

Create a Formula with a 3D Reference

An important feature of an Excel workbook is that you can refer to data on any sheet in a formula. This type of formula is called a *3D reference*, because it uses more than one sheet or surface to calculate a result.

A 3D reference includes the name of the worksheet and can be absolute, mixed, or relative.

Sample 3D References

Cell on Sheet1	Formula on Sheet1	Results
B4	=B3+Sheet2!B3+Sheet3!B3	Adds the values in cell B3 on Sheet1, Sheet2, and Sheet3
B7	=SUM(B4:B6)+Sheet2!A12	Adds the values in cells B4:B6 on Sheet1 to the value in cell A12 on Sheet2
C8	=C7*Sheet2!D4	Multiplies the value in cell C7 by the value in cell D4 on Sheet2
D10	=Sheet2!B2/Sheet3!B2	Divides the value in cell B2 on Sheet2 by the value in cell B2 on Sheet3

> **MORE INFO**
>
> An external reference formula refers to a cell in another workbook. It can be absolute, mixed, or relative. An external reference includes the name of the workbook in square brackets as in **[PLRSales]Sheet!B$2**.

▶ HOW TO: Create a Formula with a 3D Reference

1. Click the cell for the formula.
2. Type =.
3. Select the sheet tab with the cell to be used in the formula.
4. Click the required cell.
 - Press **F4 (FN+F4)** to make the reference absolute or mixed as needed.
5. Type the operator (Figure 2-10).
6. Click the next cell for the formula.
 - The next cell can be on the same or another sheet.
7. Type the next operator and complete the formula as needed.
8. Press **Enter** or any completion key.

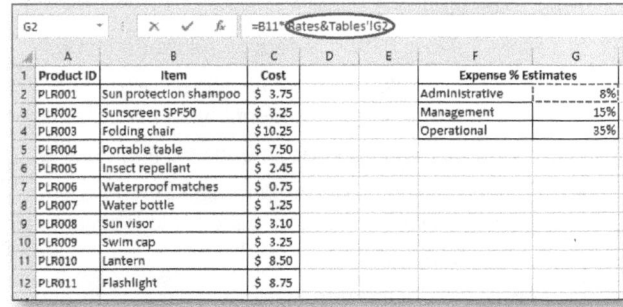

2-10 3D cell reference

Range Names and Formula AutoComplete

A *range name* is a label assigned to a single cell or a group of cells. You can use range names instead of cell references in a formula. Instead of **=B11*10%**, you can name cell B11 as "Revenue" to build the formula **=Revenue*10%**. Descriptive range names help you interpret

a formula. In addition, named cell ranges appear in the *Formula AutoComplete* list for ease in building formulas. A named cell range is an absolute reference in a formula.

You create a range name from the *Name* box or from the *Defined Names* group on the *Formulas* tab. The *Name Manager* command in this group enables you to create, edit, and delete range names. If you alter a range name, Excel automatically updates formulas that use that range name. There is also a command that enables you to name a range and apply it to existing formulas that refer to those cells.

Follow these basic rules for naming a cell range:

- Begin a range name with a letter.
- Use a short, descriptive name.
- Do not use spaces or special characters in a range name.
- Separate words in a range name with an underscore as in "First_Qtr," or use initial caps for each word such as "FirstQtr."
- Do not name a range with a single character such as "N."
- Do not name a range with a cell reference such as "B2."

To use the name in a formula, type the first character of the name when it is required to display the *Formula AutoComplete* list. You may need to type a second character to see the name in a workbook that has many range names. Select the range name in the list and press **Tab**, or double-click the name to enter it in the formula. Range names are automatically substituted in formulas when you select the named cell range in the worksheet while building a formula.

▶HOW TO: Name a Range and Use Formula AutoComplete

1. Select the cell or range to be named.
2. Click the **Name** box at the left of the *Formula* bar.
3. Type the name and press **Enter** (Figure 2-11).
4. Click the cell for the formula.
5. Type = to start the formula
6. Type the first one or two letters of the range name.
 - The *Formula AutoComplete* list shows range and function names.
 - The list is alphabetical, and function names are uppercase.
7. Find the range name and double-click it (Figure 2-12).
 - The name is inserted in the formula.
 - You can also click the name in the list to highlight it and press **Tab**.
8. Complete the formula.
9. Press **Enter** when the formula is complete.

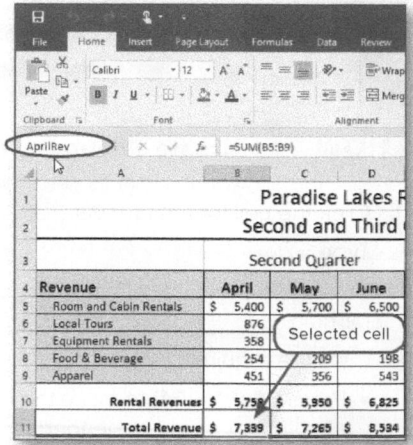

2-11 Name a range in the *Name* box

Expenses	April	May
Administrative	=to	
Management	*fx* TODAY	
Operational	Total_Revenue	
Mortgage and Leases	1350	1350
Total	$ 1,350	$ 1,350

2-12 Use *Formula AutoComplete* with a range name

In addition to selecting cell ranges to name them, you can use row and column labels to create range names. The *Create from Selection* button on the *Formulas* tab automatically assigns range names based on labels in the top row, the left column, or both.

▶ HOW TO: Create Names from a Selection

1. Select the range including row or column labels (or both) (Figure 2-13).
 - Values and related labels must be adjacent.
2. Click the **Create from Selection** button [*Formulas* tab, *Defined Names* group].
 - The *Create Names from Selection* dialog box opens.
3. Select the **Top row** or **Left column** box.
 - You can choose both options if appropriate for the data.
 - There are options for the bottom row and right column.
4. Click **OK**.
5. Click the **Name box** arrow on the *Formula* bar.
 - All range names are listed.

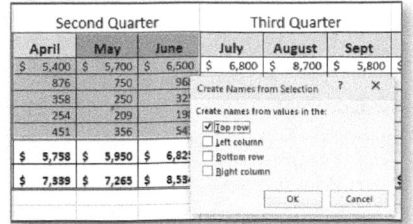

2-13 *Create Names from Selection* dialog box

The **Define Name** button [*Formulas* tab, *Defined Names* group] opens the *New Name* dialog box. Here you can type the name, enter a comment, select the cells, and specify a *scope*. The scope determines if the range applies to a particular sheet or to the entire workbook. By default, a range name applies to the workbook. If you use the name "JanSales" on Sheet1, you cannot use it again on Sheet2, unless you scope each name to a particular sheet. When you scope names to a worksheet, you can use the name multiple times in the workbook.

▶ HOW TO: Define and Scope a Range Name

1. Select the cell range to be named.
2. Click the **Define Name** button [*Formulas* tab, *Defined Names* group].
 - The *New Name* dialog box opens.
3. Type the range name in the *Name* box.
4. Click the **Scope** drop-down list (Figure 2-14).
 - Choose the name of a worksheet as desired.
5. Select or edit the *Refers to* entry.
 - The selected cell range address displays.
 - If no cells are selected, you can type or select the range address.
6. Click **OK**.

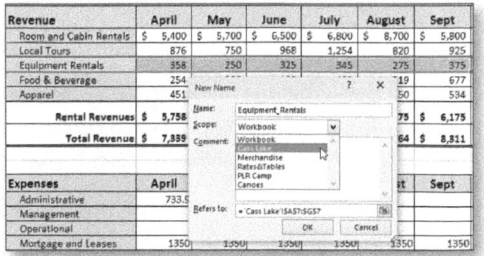

2-14 *New Name* dialog box

The *Use in Formula* button [*Formulas* tab, *Defined Names* group] displays a list of range names for insertion in a formula. You can do the same from the *Paste Name* dialog box, opened when you press the **F3 (FN+F3)** function key.

▶ HOW TO: Paste a Range Name in a Formula and Paste a List

1. Click the formula cell and type =.
2. Press **F3 (FN+F3)** to open the *Paste Name* dialog box.
 - Range names are listed in alphabetical order.

E2-98

3. Find the range name and double-click it (Figure 2-15).

 - You can also highlight the range name and press **Enter** or click **OK**.
 - The range name displays in the formula.
 - The worksheet displays the highlighted range.

4. Complete the formula and press **Enter**.

5. Click a blank cell in an unused area of the worksheet.

 - You can select a cell on another worksheet.

6. Click the **Use in Formula** button [*Formulas* tab, *Defined Names* group].

7. Select **Paste Names**.

 - The *Paste Name* dialog box opens.

8. Click **Paste List**.

 - A list of range names and cell references is pasted.
 - You can edit and format these cells.

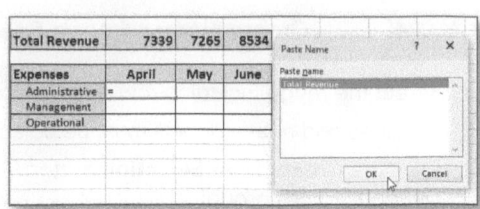

2-15 Choose a range name for the formula

Using Formula Auditing Tools

Formula auditing is the process of reviewing formulas for accuracy. Excel automatically audits formulas as you enter them and when you open a workbook based on its error checking rules [*File* tab, *Options*, *Formulas* pane]. Excel recognizes many errors, but not all of them. For example, if you type a formula that multiplies the values in two cells when it should add the values, you must find that error on your own. There are also circumstances when Excel identifies an error, but the formula is correct.

> ### MORE INFO
>
> You can set whether automatic error checking is enabled and you can select which rules are used in the *Excel Options* dialog box.

When Excel finds an error in a formula, it displays a small green error triangle in the top left corner of the cell. Click the cell to see the *Trace Error* button and point to the button to see a *ScreenTip* about the error. The *Trace Error* button has a drop-down list with options for dealing with the error.

▶ HOW TO: Trace an Error

1. Click the cell with the triangle error.

 - The *Trace Error* button appears.

2. Point to the **Trace Error** button to display a *ScreenTip*.

3. Click the **Trace Error** drop-down list (Figure 2-16).

 - Options for handling the error are listed.

4. Choose an option for the error.

 - The options depend on the type of error.
 - Select **Ignore Error** if the formula is correct.

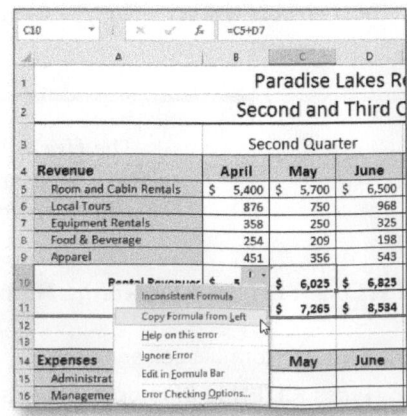

2-16 *Trace Error* button and its drop-down list

In addition to the green triangle error, Excel functions can result in a standard error message in the cell. For example, if you create a division formula that divides by a blank cell, the result is *#DIV/0!* When you click the **Trace Error** button, it is identified as a division by zero error. Excel error messages occur for a syntax error, such as spelling a function name incorrectly, using an incorrect operator or symbol, having the wrong number of arguments, and so on. A standard error message starts with the number sign (#) and ends with an exclamation point (!).

 MORE INFO

From the *Go to Special* dialog box [**Find & Select** button, *Home* tab, *Editing* group], you can highlight cells with formula errors, blank cells, and cells with precedents and dependents. This command helps identify potential problems in a workbook.

The Formula Auditing Group

The *Formula Auditing* group on the *Formulas* tab has tools to check formulas for logic, consistency, and accuracy. These commands enable you to examine what contributes to a formula and analyze if the formula is correct. The tools are helpful but they do require that you correct the problem.

Button	Description
Trace Precedents	Displays lines with arrows to identify all cells referenced in the formula in the active cell
Trace Dependents	Displays lines with arrows to all cells that use the active cell directly or indirectly in a formula
Remove Arrows	Removes all lines and arrows from the *Trace Precedents* or *Trace Dependents* buttons
Show Formulas	Displays formulas in the cells
Error Checking	Checks data against the error rules in Excel Options
Evaluate Formula	Steps through each part of a formula and displays an outcome for each part so that an error can be isolated
Watch Window	Opens a floating window that displays selected cells and values for monitoring

Trace Precedents and Dependents

A ***precedent*** is a cell that contributes to the formula results. Excel displays lines from the formula cell to each precedent cell for an easy way to audit your formula. A ***dependent*** is a cell that is affected by the active cell. Excel displays lines from the active cell to each cell that depends on the value in that cell. When the lines and arrows are blue, the precedents or dependents do not have an error. If the lines and arrows are red, the precedents or dependents have some type of recognized error. If a precedent or dependent cell is located on a different worksheet, a black line and arrow point to a small worksheet icon, but this does not identify the actual error cell address.

▶ HOW TO: Use Formula Auditing Tools

1. Click the **Show Formulas** button [*Formulas* tab, *Formula Auditing* group].
 - Each formula displays in its cell.
 - Show or hide formulas by pressing **Ctrl+~**.
2. Select the formula cell.

3. Click the **Trace Precedents** button [*Formulas* tab, *Formula Auditing* group].

- Lines and arrows identify cells that contribute to the formula results (Figure 2-17).
- You can trace precedents and dependents with formulas shown or hidden.

4. Click the **Remove Arrows** button [*Formulas* tab, *Formula Auditing* group].

- Clicking the button removes all arrows.
- Click the **Remove Arrows** drop-down list to specify the type of arrow to remove.

5. Click a cell that is referenced in a formula.

- The cell need not have a formula.

2-17 *Trace Precedents* arrows with formulas shown

6. Click the **Trace Dependents** button [*Formulas* tab, *Formula Auditing* group].

- Lines and arrows trace to cells that are affected by the active cell.

7. Click the **Remove Arrows** button [*Formulas* tab, *Formula Auditing* group].

8. Click the **Show Formulas** button [*Formulas* tab, *Formula Auditing* group].

- Formulas are hidden.
- Show or hide formulas by pressing **Ctrl+~**.

> **MORE INFO**
>
> In a complex worksheet with sophisticated formulas, click the **Trace Precedents** button [*Formulas* tab, *Formula Auditing* group] once to trace the first layer of precedents. Then click the button again to trace the precedents of the precedents.

The Formula Correction Message Window

As you complete a formula with a minor error (e.g. typing "5c" as a cell address), Excel displays a message box with information about the error (Figure 2-18). For many of these types of errors, review the suggested correction and select **Yes**. For an error that Excel finds but cannot offer a solution, a message box opens with suggestions but you need to solve the problem on your own.

2-18 Formula correction message window

Circular Reference

A *circular reference* is an error that occurs when a formula includes the cell address of the formula. For example, if the formula in cell **B10** is **=B5+B10**, the reference is circular. When you try to complete such a formula, a message box opens as shown in Figure 2-19. The *Status* bar displays the location of circular references, but Excel does not correct this type of error. You can keep a circular reference in a worksheet, but the formula results are inaccurate.

2-19 Circular reference and its message window

> **MORE INFO**
>
> A workbook can be saved with a circular reference. When you open it, you will see the message box, and the reference is noted in the *Status* bar.

PAUSE & PRACTICE: EXCEL 2-1

For this project, you build formulas in a Paradise Lakes Resort worksheet. You use mixed and absolute references, a 3D reference, and set order of precedence. You also name cell ranges and use auditing tools.

File Needed: ***ParadiseLakes-02.xlsx*** *[Student data files are available in the* Library *of your SIMnet account.]*
Completed Project File Name: ***[your initials] PP E2-1.xlsx***

1. Open the ***ParadiseLakes-02.xlsx*** workbook from your student data files.

2. Save the workbook as [your initials] PP E2-1. (If the workbook opens in *Protected View*, click **Enable Editing**.)

3. Enter and copy an addition formula.
 a. Click cell **B10** on the **Cass Lake** sheet.
 b. Type = to start a formula.
 c. Click cell **B5** to insert the first rental item in the formula.
 d. Type + as the mathematical operator.
 e. Click cell **B7** to add the second rental item. The formula is =B5+B7 (Figure 2-20).
 f. Press **Enter** or click the **Enter** button on the *Formula* bar. The result is $5,758.
 g. Select cell **B10** and point to the *Fill* handle.
 h. Drag the *Fill* pointer to copy the formula to cells **C10:H10**. Ignore the *Auto Fill Options* button.

2-20 Point and click to build a formula

4. Create and copy a 3D formula with absolute cell references.
 a. Select cell **B15**. Administrative expense is calculated by multiplying the total revenue for the month by a set percentage.
 b. Type = to start the formula.
 c. Click cell **B11**, the total revenue for April.
 d. Type * to indicate multiplication.
 e. Click the **Rates&Tables** sheet tab. The sheet name is inserted in the *Formula* bar with single quotes and an exclamation point.
 f. Click cell **G2**, the percentage for administrative expenses. The cell address is added to the formula.
 g. Press **F4 (FN+F4)** to make the reference absolute (Figure 2-21).
 h. Press **Enter**. The formula is complete and the *Cass Lake* sheet is active.
 i. Select cell **B15** and drag the *Fill* pointer to copy the formula to cells **C15:G15**. The reference to cell G2 does not change, but the reference to cell B11 does (Figure 2-22).

2-21 Absolute 3D reference in the formula

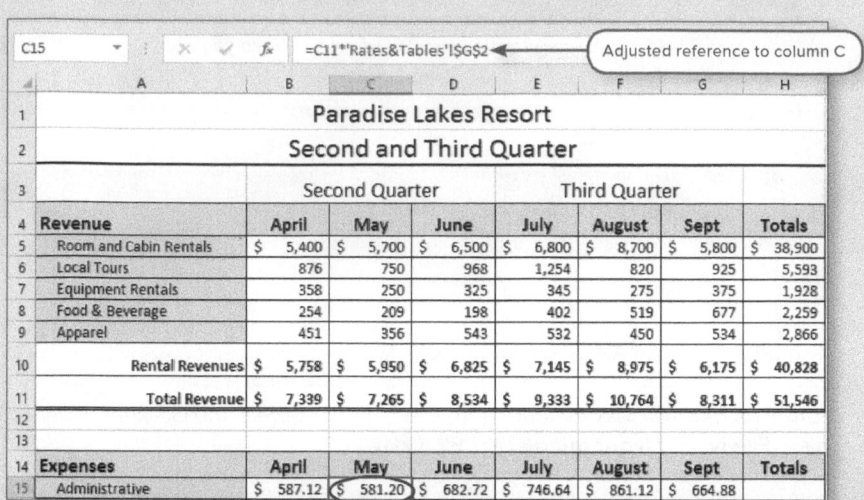

2-22 Copied formula with absolute reference

5. Create and copy a 3D formula with mixed references.
 a. Select cell **B16**. Management expense is calculated by multiplying the total revenue for the month by the set percentage.
 b. Type = to start the formula.
 c. Click cell **B11**, the total revenue for April.
 d. Press **F4 (FN+F4)** to make the reference absolute (B11).
 e. Press **F4 (FN+F4)** to make the reference mixed with the row reference absolute (B$11). When the formula is copied, the row will not change but the column reference will (Figure 2-23).
 f. Type * for multiplication.
 g. Click the **Rates&Tables** sheet tab. The sheet name is inserted in the *Formula* bar.
 h. Click cell **G3**, the percentage for management expenses.
 i. Press **F4 (FN+F4)** to make the reference absolute (G3).
 j. Press **F4 (FN+F4)** to make the reference mixed with the row reference absolute (G$3).
 k. Press **F4 (FN+F4)** to make the reference mixed with the column reference absolute ($G3) (Figure 2-24). When the formula is copied, the column will not change but the row will.

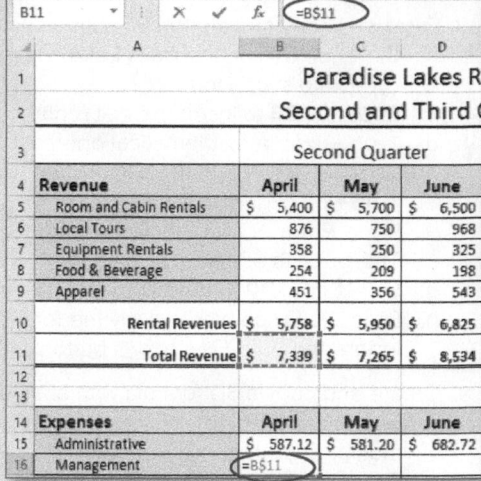

2-23 Mixed cell reference

G3		f_x	=B$11*'Rates&Tables'!$G3				
	A	B	C	D	E	F	G
1	Product ID	Item	Cost			Expense % Estimates	
2	PLR001	Sun protection shampoo	$ 3.75			Administrative	8%
3	PLR002	Sunscreen SPF50	$ 3.25			Management	15%
4	PLR003	Folding chair	$10.25			Operational	35%
5	PLR004	Portable table	$ 7.50				

2-24 Absolute reference to column G

l. Press **Enter**. The formula is complete and the *Cass Lake* sheet is active.

m. Select cell **B16** and drag its *Fill* pointer to cell **B17**.

n. Keep cells **B16:B17** selected and drag the *Fill* pointer for cell B17 to copy the formulas to cells **C16:G17**.

6. Use *Formula Auditing* tools.

a. Click cell **D17** to view how the mixed reference formula has been copied.

b. Click the **Trace Precedents** button [*Formulas* tab, *Formula Auditing* group]. The formula refers to cell D11 on the **Cass Lake** sheet and to the **Tables&Rates** sheet.

c. Click cell **E16** and click the **Trace Precedents** button. The formula refers to cell E11 on the **Cass Lake** sheet and to the **Tables&Rates** sheet (Figure 2-25).

d. Click the **Remove Arrows** button [*Formulas* tab, *Formula Auditing* group].

e. Click the **Show Formulas** [*Formulas* tab, *Formula Auditing* group] to see all formulas. This view does not display number formatting (Figure 2-26).

2-25 Formula precedents

2-26 Formulas displayed in worksheet

f. Click the **Show Formulas** [*Formulas* tab, *Formula Auditing* group] to hide the formulas.

7. Edit a formula and correct an error.
 a. Select cells **H15:H18** and click the **AutoSum** button [*Home* tab, *Editing* group]. The *SUM* function displays in each cell.
 b. Widen column **H** to display all data.
 c. Double-click cell **H16** to start *Edit* mode.
 d. Edit the cell range to **B15:G16** and press **Enter** to create a deliberate error. The green error triangle appears in the upper right corner of the cell.
 e. Click cell **H16** to display the **Trace Error** button and then click the button. This formula is now inconsistent with others in the column (Figure 2-27).

H16	▾	× ✓ *fx*	=SUM(B15:G16)				

	A	B	C	D	E	F	G	H
1				Paradise Lakes Resort				
2				Second and Third Quarter				
3			Second Quarter			Third Quarter		
4	Revenue	April	May	June	July	August	Sept	Totals
5	Room and Cabin Rentals	$ 5,400	$ 5,700	$ 6,500	$ 6,800	$ 8,700	$ 5,800	$ 38,900
6	Local Tours	876	750	968	1,254	820	925	5,593
7	Equipment Rentals	358	250	325	345	275	375	1,928
8	Food & Beverage	254	209	198	402	519	677	2,259
9	Apparel	451	356	543				2,866
10	Rental Revenues	$ 5,758	$ 5,950	$ 6,825	Inconsistent Formula			$ 40,828
11	Total Revenue	$ 7,339	$ 7,265	$ 8,534	Copy Formula from Above			$ 51,546
12					Help on this error			
13					Ignore Error			
14	Expenses	April	May	June	Edit in Formula Bar			Totals
15	Administrative	$ 587.12	$ 581.20	$ 682.72	Error Checking Options...			$ 4,123.68
16	Management	$ 1,100.85	$ 1,089.75	$ 1,280.10	$ 1,399.95	$ 1,614.60	$ 1,24 ▾	$ 11,855.58
17	Operational	$ 2,568.65	$ 2,542.75	$ 2,986.90	$ 3,266.55	$ 3,767.40	$ 2,908.85	$ 18,041.10

2-27 *Trace Error* button and options

 f. Select **Copy Formula from Above** to correct the error.
 g. Click cell **H16** and click the **Trace Precedents** button [*Formulas* tab, *Formula Auditing* group]. The formula refers to the correct cells in row 16.
 h. Click the **Remove Arrows** button [*Formulas* tab, *Formula Auditing* group].

8. Set mathematical order of operations.
 a. Select cell **B21**. Profit margin, as a percentage, is revenue minus expenses divided by revenue. The formula is **=(B11—B19)/B11**; the parentheses are necessary so that the subtraction is done before the division.
 b. Type **=(** to start the formula and insert the opening parenthesis.
 c. Click cell **B11**, the total revenue for April.
 d. Type **—** for subtraction.
 e. Click cell **B19**, total expenses for April.
 f. Type **)** to set the precedence with the closing parenthesis.
 g. Type **/** for division and click cell **B11** (Figure 2-28).
 h. Press **Enter**. The result is formatted as *Accounting Number* format to match the source cells and displays a zero due to rounding.

B11	▾	× ✓ *fx*	=(B11-B19)/B11	

	A	B	C	D	E
2			Second and Third Quarter		
3			Second Quarter		Th
4	Revenue	April	May	June	July
5	Room and Cabin Rentals	$ 5,400	$ 5,700	$ 6,500	$ 6,800
6	Local Tours	876	750	968	1,254
7	Equipment Rentals	358	250	325	345
8	Food & Beverage	254	209	198	402
9	Apparel	451	356	543	532
10	Rental Revenues	$ 5,758	$ 5,950	$ 6,825	$ 7,145
11	Total Revenue	$ 7,339	$ 7,265	$ 8,534	$ 9,333
12					
13					
14	Expenses	April	May	June	July
15	Administrative	$ 587.12	$ 581.20	$ 682.72	$ 746.64
16	Management	$ 1,100.85	$ 1,089.75	$ 1,280.10	$ 1,399.95
17	Operational	$ 2,568.65	$ 2,542.75	$ 2,986.90	$ 3,266.55
18	Mortgage and Leases	1350	1350	1350	1350
19	Total	$ 5,607	$ 5,564	$ 6,300	$ 6,763
20					
21	Profit Margin	=(B11-B19)/B11			
22	Revenue Below Average?				

2-28 Set arithmetic order

i. Click cell **B21** and click the **Percent Style** button [*Home* tab, *Number* group].

j. Copy the formula in cell **B21** to cells **C21:G21**.

9. Name a cell range.

 a. Select cell **H11** and click the **Name** box.

 b. Type TotalRevenue in the *Name* box and press **Enter**.

 c. Select cells **B11:G11**.

 d. Click the **Define Name** button [*Formulas* tab, *Defined Names* group].

 e. Type Monthly_Rev in the *Name* box and click **OK** (Figure 2-29).

 f. Click cell **A1**.

 g. Click the **Name box** arrow and choose **TotalRevenue**. Cell H11 is selected.

 h. Click the **Name box** arrow and choose **Monthly_Rev**. Cells B11:G11 are selected.

New Name	? ✕
Name:	Monthly_Rev
Scope:	Workbook ⌄
Comment:	
Refers to:	='Cass Lake'!B11:G11
	OK Cancel

2-29 Use the *New Name* dialog box to name a range

10. Format cells **B16:H18** as **Comma Style**. Decrease the decimal two times.

11. Select cells **B15:H15** and decrease the decimal two times.

12. Press **Ctrl+Home**. Save and close the workbook (Figure 2-30).

	Paradise Lakes Resort						
	Second and Third Quarter						
	Second Quarter			Third Quarter			
Revenue	April	May	June	July	August	Sept	Totals
Room and Cabin Rentals	$ 5,400	$ 5,700	$ 6,500	$ 6,800	$ 8,700	$ 5,800	$ 38,900
Local Tours	876	750	968	1,254	820	925	5,593
Equipment Rentals	358	250	325	345	275	375	1,928
Food & Beverage	254	209	198	402	519	677	2,259
Apparel	451	356	543	532	450	534	2,866
Rental Revenues	$ 5,758	$ 5,950	$ 6,825	$ 7,145	$ 8,975	$ 6,175	$ 40,828
Total Revenue	$ 7,339	$ 7,265	$ 8,534	$ 9,333	$ 10,764	$ 8,311	$ 51,546
Expenses	April	May	June	July	August	Sept	Totals
Administrative	$ 587	$ 581	$ 683	$ 747	$ 861	$ 665	$ 4,124
Management	1,101	1,090	1,280	1,400	1,615	1,247	$ 7,732
Operational	2,569	2,543	2,987	3,267	3,767	2,909	$ 18,041
Mortgage and Leases	1350	1350	1350	1350	1350	1350	$ 8,100
Total	$ 5,607	$ 5,564	$ 6,300	$ 6,763	$ 7,593	$ 6,170	$ 37,997
Profit Margin	24%	23%	26%	28%	29%	26%	
Revenue Below Average?							

2-30 PP E2-1 completed

 SLO 2.5

Working with Statistical and Date & Time Functions

A function is a built-in formula. Like a formula, a function starts with an equals sign (=) followed by the name of the function. Each function has its own syntax, its set of rules for correct execution. The syntax includes arguments, which are cell references and other elements necessary for the function to work properly.

> **MORE INFO**
>
> A formula such as **=B2+B3−B6** is usually not called a function since it has no function name.

Excel functions are grouped into categories on the *Formulas* command tab in the *Function Library* group. This group also has an *Insert Function* button which opens the *Insert Function*

dialog box. From this dialog box, you can display an alphabetical list of all functions, a list by category, or a recently used list. You can also search for a function by name in this dialog box.

The *Statistical* function category includes calculations that determine an average, a maximum, a minimum, and a count. These common functions are options on the *AutoSum* button on the *Home* tab. The *Formulas* tab also has an *AutoSum* button with the same options.

AVERAGE Function

The *AVERAGE* function calculates the arithmetic **mean** of a range of cells. The mean is determined by adding all the values and dividing the result by the number of values. The *AVERAGE* function ignores empty cells or cells that include labels. When calculating an average, do not include total values in the range to be averaged.

The *AVERAGE* function has one argument, *numberN*. A number argument can be a range such as B11:G11. You can average up to 255 numbers (or ranges). The proper syntax for an *AVERAGE* function is:

=AVERAGE(number1, [number2], [number3], . . .)

The *Number1* argument is required and others are optional.

When you choose a function from the *AutoSum* button, you will see the function name, an assumed range within parentheses, and an **Argument ScreenTip** below the cell that displays the syntax. When you choose to type a function, the *ScreenTip* shows the next argument in bold type as a guideline.

> **HOW TO: Use the AVERAGE Function**

1. Click the cell for the function.
2. Click the **AutoSum** button arrow [*Formulas* tab, *Function Library* group].
3. Select **Average**.
 - The function and an assumed argument range display in the *Formula* bar and in the cell.
4. Select the correct cell range (Figure 2-31).
 - You can type cell addresses rather than selecting cells.
 - When the selected cells have been named, the range name is substituted in the formula.

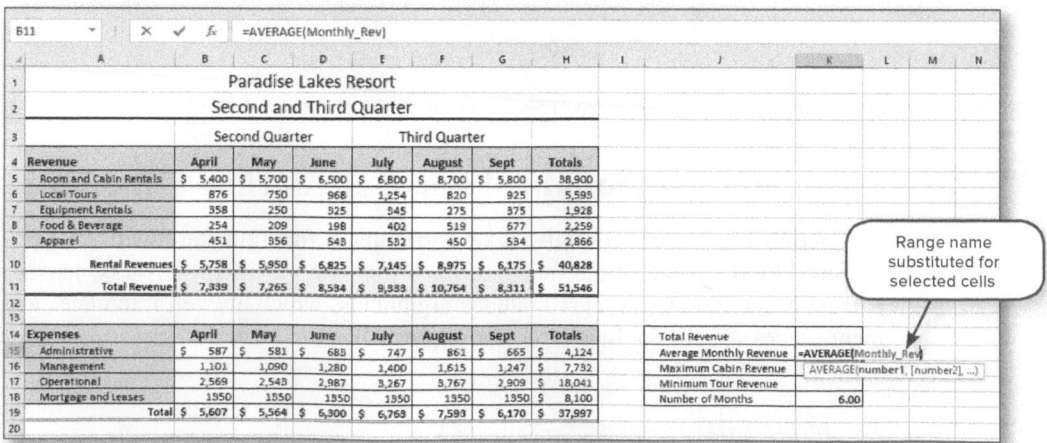

2-31 *AVERAGE* function

5. Press **Enter**.
 - You can use any completion key.

 MORE INFO

The *MEDIAN* function in the *Statistical* category determines the precise middle value in the range.

COUNT Functions

There are five functions in the *Statistical* category that are *COUNT* functions which tally the number of items in a range. The basic *COUNT* function is an option on the *AutoSum* button, but it appears in the list as *Count Numbers*. The *COUNT* function includes only cells with values in its result.

From the *Statistical* group, you can choose *COUNTA* which includes cells with values and labels. There is a *COUNTBLANK* function that counts cells that are empty. The following table describes the *Statistical COUNT* functions.

MORE INFO

In the *Database* function category, there are *DCOUNT* and *DCOUNTA* functions. This category is available from the *Insert Function* dialog box.

Statistical COUNT Functions

Count Functions	Description	Example Syntax
COUNT (Count Numbers)	Counts the cells in a range that contain values	=COUNT(A1:A15)
COUNTA	Counts the cells in a range that contain any data type	=COUNTA(A1:A15)
COUNTBLANK	Counts empty cells in a range	=COUNTBLANK(A1:A15)
COUNTIF	Counts the cells in a range that meet the criteria argument	=COUNTIF(A1:A15, "Services")
COUNTIFS	Counts the cells in one or more criteria ranges that meet respective criteria arguments	=COUNTIFS(B2:B5, "=A", C2:C5, "=21")

The *COUNT* function has one argument, *valueN*. You can count up to 255 cells or ranges. The proper syntax for a *COUNT* function is:

=COUNT(value1, [value2], [value3], . . .)

The *Value1* argument is required.

▶ **HOW TO: Use the COUNT Function**

1. Click the cell for the function.
2. Click the **AutoSum** button arrow [*Formulas* tab, *Function Library* group].
3. Select **Count Numbers**.
 - The *COUNT* function is inserted with an assumed range.
 - The function appears in the cell and in the *Formula* bar (Figure 2-32).

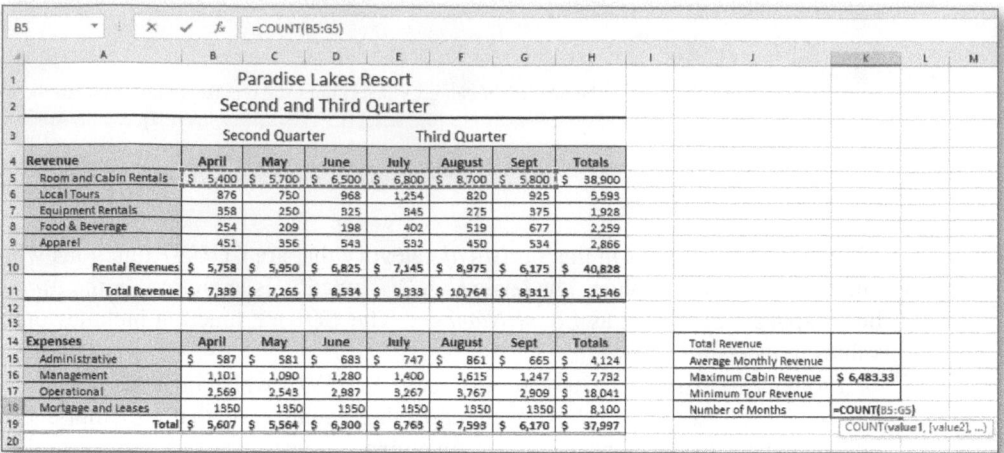

| B5 | ▼ | × ✓ ƒx | =COUNT(B5:G5) | | | | | | | | | | |

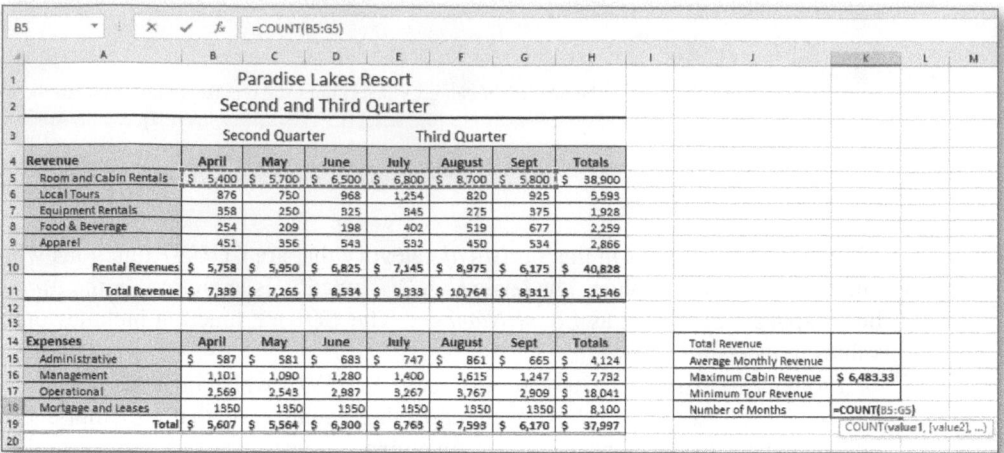

2-32 *COUNT* function

4. Select the correct cell range.

 • You can type cell addresses rather than selecting cells.

5. Press **Enter** or any completion key.

> **MORE INFO**
>
> If you use *COUNT* with a range of labels, the result is zero (0).

MAX and MIN Functions

The *MAX* function finds the largest value in a range, and the *MIN* function finds the smallest value. Both functions are options on the *AutoSum* button. Each has one argument, the cells to be evaluated.

The proper syntax for *MAX* and *MIN* functions is:

=MAX(number1, [number2], [number3], . . .)
=MIN(number1, [number2], [number3], . . .)

In many worksheets, an argument range is a group of adjacent cells such as B11:G11, but the cells need not be next to each other. You can select individual cells anywhere in the worksheet for an argument, and they are separated by commas as in =MAX(B11, B15, B18).

▶**HOW TO: Use the MAX Function with Nonadjacent Cells**

1. Click the cell for the function.

2. Click the **AutoSum** button arrow [*Formulas* tab, *Function Library* group].

3. Select **Max** (Figure 2-33).

- The function displays in the cell and in the *Formula* bar.
- The *Argument ScreenTip* shows the next argument in bold **number1**.

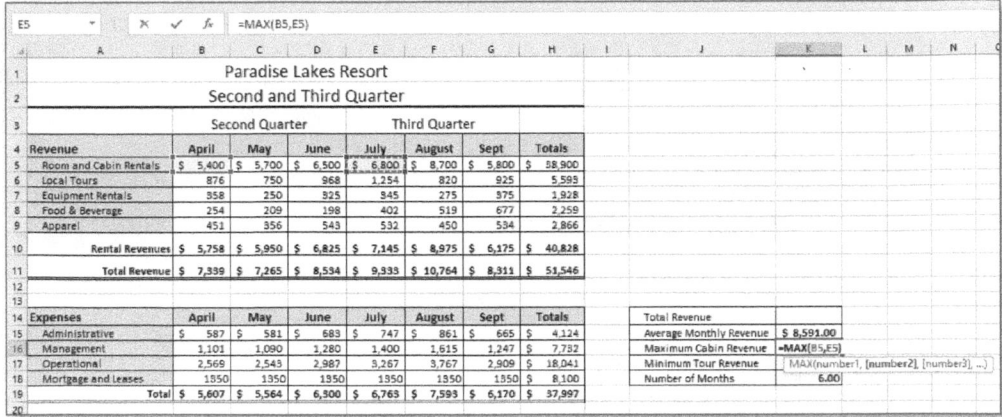

2-33 Use nonadjacent cells for *MAX*

4. Click the first cell to be evaluated.

5. Type , (a comma) to separate the arguments.

- The *Argument ScreenTip* shows the next argument in bold **number2**.

6. Click the next cell to be evaluated.

7. Type a comma , to add additional cells to the argument.

8. Press **Enter** when all the cells are listed.

AutoCalculate

The ***AutoCalculate*** feature is located on the right side of the *Status* bar where statistical and mathematical results are displayed for selected cells. The calculations are *Average*, *Count*, *Numerical Count*, *Maximum*, *Minimum*, and *Sum*. The *Count* calculation is the equivalent of *COUNTA*, and *Numerical Count* is the same as *COUNT*. AutoCalculate allows you to see results without inserting a function in the worksheet. You can see and change which calculations are visible by right-clicking that area of the *Status* bar to open the *Customize Status Bar* menu.

▶ **HOW TO:** Use AutoCalculate

1. Select the cell range or individual cells in the worksheet.

2. View the results on the *Status* bar (Figure 2-34).

- Selected options appear on the *Status* bar when appropriate; there is no *SUM* when you select labels.

3. Right-click the right side of the *Status* bar.

- The *Customize Status Bar* menu opens.
- If a function has a check mark to the left, it is active.

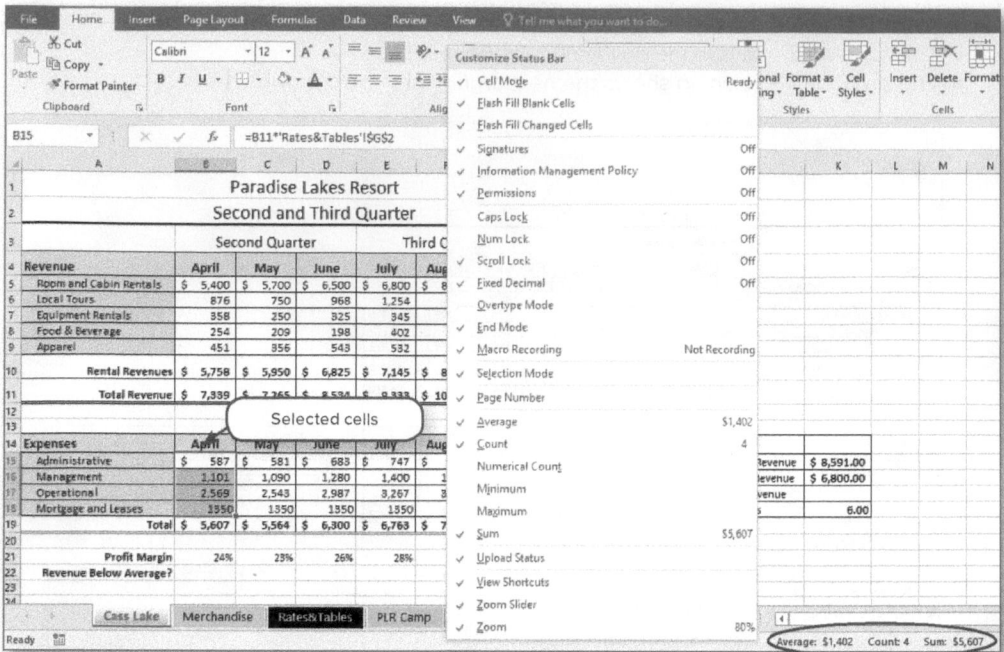

2-34 *AutoCalculate* results and other *Status* bar options

4. Select a calculation name to activate it and show it on the *Status* bar.

5. Select a calculation name with a check mark to hide it from the *Status* bar.

TODO and NOW Functions

The *Date & Time* category has many functions for date and time arithmetic, for converting dates and times to values, and for controlling how dates and times are displayed.

The *TODAY* function inserts the current date in the cell and updates each time the workbook is opened. It uses the computer's clock, and the syntax is =TODAY(). The parentheses are necessary, but there are no arguments. The *NOW* function uses the syntax =NOW() and has no arguments. These two functions are **volatile** which means that the result depends on the current date, time, and computer.

After either function is inserted, you can format results to show both the date and the time. The *Format Cells* dialog box has a *Date* category and a *Time* category with many preset styles. There are also two date formats available from the *Number Format* list [*Home* tab, *Number* group], *Short Date* and *Long Date*.

In its handling of dates, Excel treats each date as a **serial number**, a unique value assigned to each date. Excel starts by setting January 1, 1900, as number 1; January 2, 1900 is number 2, and so on. January 1, 2018, is number 43101. You can see the serial number for any date by applying the *General* format to the cell.

> ### MORE INFO
>
> On the *Advanced* pane in the *Excel Options* dialog box [*File* tab], you can set a 1904 date system which matches the date system in the Macintosh operating system.

You can select **TODAY** or **NOW** from the *Date & Time* function category. Since they are widely used and have no arguments, you may prefer to type either with the help of *Formula AutoComplete*.

▶ **HOW TO:** Insert TODAY with Formula AutoComplete

1. Click the cell.
2. Type =to to display a filtered *Formula AutoComplete* list (Figure 2-35).

 2-35 *Formula AutoComplete* list

 - The list appears as soon as you type a character.
 - Each additional character further limits the list of names.
3. Point to the function name and double-click.
 - Instead of double-clicking the name, point and click once to select it and press **Tab**.
 - The name and parentheses are inserted.
 - If you accidentally press **Enter** to select a name and see an error in the cell, delete the cell contents and try again.
4. Press **Enter** to complete the function (Figure 2-36).

 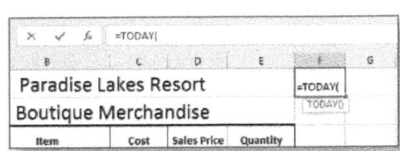

 2-36 TODAY inserted in cell

 - Excel supplies the closing parenthesis.
 - The current date is shown in the cell.
 - The *TODAY* function has no arguments.

PAUSE & PRACTICE: EXCEL 2-2

For this project, you open your Pause & Practice file and insert Excel functions to complete more of the worksheet. You insert functions from the *AutoSum* button and by typing. You also use *AutoCalculate* to check results.

File Needed: *[your initials] PP E2-1.xlsx*
Completed Project File Name: *[your initials] PP E2-2.xlsx*

1. Open the *[your initials] PP E2-1.xlsx* workbook completed in *Pause & Practice 2-1* and save it as [your initials] PP E2-2.
2. Enter functions using the *AutoSum* button.
 a. Click the **Cass Lake** worksheet tab and select cell **K14**.
 b. Click the **AutoSum** arrow button [*Formulas* tab, *Function Library* group].
 c. Choose **Sum**. The function name and parentheses are inserted, and a *Function ScreenTip* is visible.
 d. Select cells **B11:G11**. The range is highlighted on screen, and Excel has substituted the defined name that you set in *Pause & Practice 2-1* (Figure 2-37).
 e. Press **Enter**.
 f. Select cell **K15** and click the **AutoSum** arrow button [*Formulas* tab, *Function Library* group].
 g. Choose **Average**. The name and parentheses are inserted.
 h. Select cells **B11:G11**. The range is highlighted, but the range name is substituted.
 i. Press **Enter**. Average sales are $8,591.

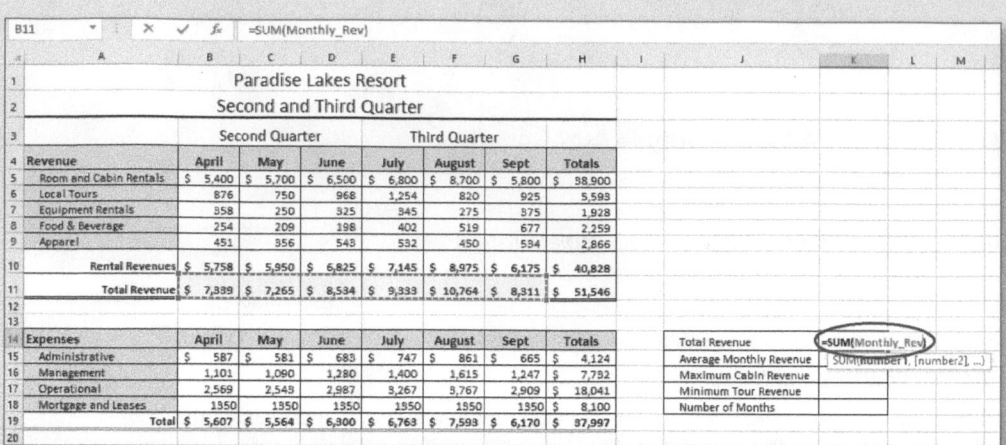

2-37 Range name substituted in formula

3. Enter the *MAX* function by typing.
 a. Select cell **K16**.
 b. Type =ma to display the *Formula AutoComplete* list. You only need type as many characters as necessary to see the function name.
 c. Point to **MAX** in the list, click to select it, and press **Tab** (Figure 2-38).
 d. Select cells **B5:G5** for the *number1* argument. This range is not named.
 e. Press **Enter**. Excel supplies the closing parenthesis.

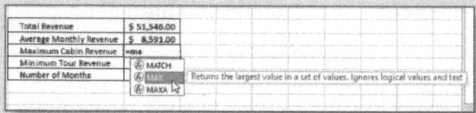

2-38 Choose *MAX* from *Formula AutoComplete* list

4. Copy and edit a function.
 a. Select cell **K16** and use the *Fill* pointer to copy the formula to cell **K17**.
 b. Double-click cell **K17**. Note that the argument cell range was updated because it was a relative reference.
 c. Replace the function name *MAX* in the cell with **min** (Figure 2-39).
 d. Press **Enter**. The minimum value is $750.

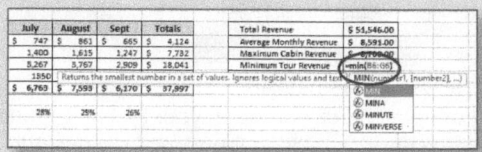

2-39 Edit a function name

5. Type the *COUNT* function.
 a. Select cell **K18**.
 b. Type =cou to display the *Formula AutoComplete* list.
 c. Double-click **COUNTA** in the list. This function counts cells with labels and values. The *ScreenTip* shows the first argument as *value1*.
 d. Select cells **B4:G4** to count the months. The formula is =COUNTA(B4:G4).
 e. Press **Enter**. The final parenthesis is supplied, and the result is 6.00.
 f. Select cells **K14:K18** and decrease the decimal two times.
 g. Apply the **General** format to cell **K18** [*Home* tab, *Number* group, *Number Format* drop-down list].

6. Check results with *AutoCalculate*.
 a. Select cells **B11:G11**.
 b. Right-click near the middle of the *Status* bar to display the options.
 c. Verify that **Average, Count,** and **Sum** are checked.
 d. Left-click anywhere in the *Status* bar to close the menu.
 e. Compare the values shown in the *Status* bar with the results in column K.

7. Insert the *TODAY* function.
 a. Select cell **A25**.
 b. Click the **Formulas** tab.
 c. Click the **Date & Time** button [*Function Library* group].
 d. Find and select **TODAY**. A *Function Arguments* dialog box notes that this function does not have any arguments and that it is volatile (Figure 2-40).
 e. Click **OK**. The current date is inserted.
 f. Press **Ctrl+Home**.

9. Save and close the workbook (Figure 2-41).

2-40 *Function Arguments* dialog box for *TODAY*

2-41 PP E2-2 completed

SLO 2.6

Working with Financial, Logical, and Lookup Functions

The *Financial* category includes functions that determine loan payments, the amount of interest earned, the rate of return on an investment, and more. Most of the functions in the *Logical* category display TRUE or FALSE as the result, but the *IF* function is in this group. An *IF* function can test if monthly revenue is above or below average and display "Yes" or "No" in the cell. The *Lookup & Reference* category is used to find and display information from a list in the workbook. For example, you might use a *Lookup* function to insert a price from a price list.

The Function Arguments Dialog Box

Functions require arguments in a particular order. They are easy to learn and build when you use the *Function Arguments* dialog box. This dialog box opens when you choose a function name from a category on the *Formulas* tab or when you use the *Insert Function* dialog box.

The *Function Arguments* dialog box shows each argument with an entry box and an explanation (Figure 2-42). You can select cells to enter an address, or you can type directly in the entry box. In addition to doing the work for you, the *Function Arguments* dialog box helps you learn the proper syntax for a function.

Function arguments may be required or optional. Optional arguments generally add some level of refinement to the calculation. In the *Function Arguments* dialog box and the

ScreenTip, a required argument name is shown in bold. When you use *Formula AutoComplete* to build a function, the *ScreenTip* shows optional arguments in square brackets (e.g., [type]).

When you are not sure about a function's name or category, you can search for it in the *Insert Function* dialog box. Open this dialog box by clicking the **Insert Function** button on the *Formulas* tab [*Function Library* group] or the same button to the left of the *Formula* bar. In the search area, type the name of the function or a brief description of what you want the function to do. For example, you can type "rate of return" to list *Financial* functions that calculate a rate of return for an investment.

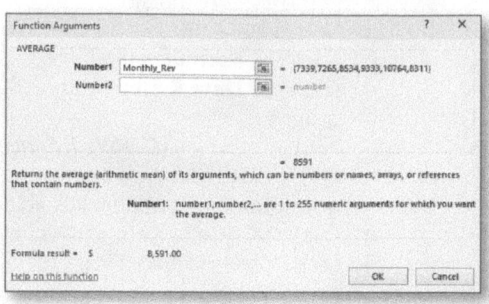

2-42 *Function Arguments* dialog box for *AVERAGE*

> **ANOTHER WAY**
>
> **Shift+F3** opens the *Insert Function* dialog box.

PMT Function

The *PMT* function is in the *Financial* category. It calculates a constant loan payment amount for a period of time at a stated interest rate. When you borrow money for tuition or to buy a car, you can use the *PMT* function to determine your monthly payment for a selected payback time.

The *PMT* function has five arguments. Three of them are required: *rate*, *nper*, and *pv*. The other arguments are optional, *fv* and *type*. The proper syntax for a *PMT* formula is:

=PMT(rate, nper, pv, [fv], [type])

- **Rate** is the interest rate, a percentage of the amount borrowed. Most rates are set at a yearly rate. To determine monthly payments, you must divide the rate by 12.
- **Nper** is the total number of periods for repayment. If you make monthly payments for five years, the *nper* argument is 60.
- **Pv** is the present value, the amount borrowed.
- **Fv** is any future value after the last payment, an amount still owed at the end of the loan. When the *fv* argument is omitted, it means zero or that you have paid back the entire amount.
- **Type** indicates if payments are made at the beginning or the end of the period. Most loan payments are at the beginning of the period, because the interest amount is less. The number *1* is used to set payment at the beginning of the period.

Figure 2-43 shows a PMT function in cell B7 **=PMT(B6/12,B5*12,B4,,1)**. In the *Formula* bar, arguments are separated by commas. Where there are two commas with nothing between them, an argument has been omitted. In this case, it is the *fv* argument.

B6/12 is the interest *rate* divided by 12 to determine a monthly payment.

B5*12 is the *nper* argument, the number of years times 12, to determine the total number of payments.

B4 is the *pv* argument, the amount of money borrowed.

1 is the *type* argument and indicates that payment occurs at the beginning of the period.

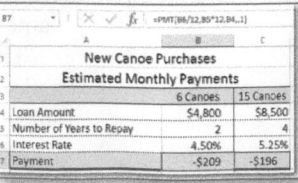

The *PMT* result is a negative number, because the function is calculated from the borrower's point of view. It is money paid out.

2-43 *PMT* function is in cell B7

▶ HOW TO: Use the PMT Function

1. Click the cell where the function results should display.

2. Click the **Insert Function** button to the left of the *Formula* bar.

 - The *Insert Function* dialog box opens.

3. Type payment in the *Search for a function* box.

4. Click **Go** (Figure 2-44).

 - A list of functions that include some type of payment displays.

5. Select **PMT** and click **OK**.

 - The *Function Arguments* dialog box opens.
 - The dialog box includes a description of the function.

6. Click the **Rate** box and click the cell with the interest rate.

 - You can type the rate in the entry box with the percent sign.
 - An explanation of the argument is displayed.

7. Type /12 immediately after the address in the *Rate* box.

 - Divide by 12 for monthly payments.
 - If payments are quarterly, divide by 4.

8. Click the **Nper** box and click the cell that contains the loan term.

9. Type *12 immediately after the address in the *Nper* box.

 - If the loan term is years and payments are quarterly, multiply by 4.
 - If the cell already displays the total number of payments, just click to enter the address.

10. Click the **Pv** box and click the cell that contains the amount of the loan.

11. Click the **Type** box.

 - The *Fv* argument is usually omitted, because loans require a zero balance at the end.

12. Type 1 in the *Type* box to set a payment at the beginning of the period (Figure 2-45).

 - Most loan payments are at the beginning, because the payment is less than if it were at the end of the period.

13. Click **OK**.

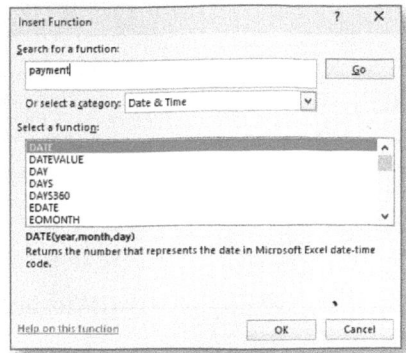

2-44 *Insert Function* dialog box

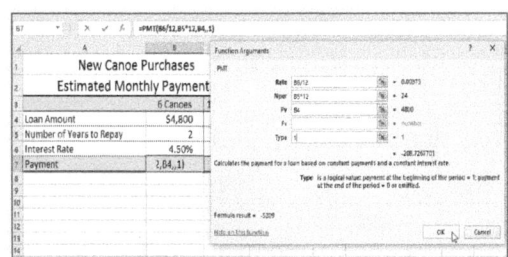

2-45 *Function Arguments* dialog box for *PMT*

▶ **MORE INFO**

To show the payment as a positive value, type a minus sign (−) before the loan amount in the worksheet or before its cell address in the *Function Arguments* dialog box.

▶ **ANOTHER WAY**

Choose the *PMT* function from the **Financial** button [*Formulas* tab, *Function Library* group].

IF Function

The *IF* function tests a condition or statement; if it is true, there is a specified result; if it is false, there is an alternative result. In the Paradise Lakes revenue worksheet, you can use an

IF formula to determine if each month's revenue is above average. If it is, you can display "Yes," in the cell, and if it is not, you can display "No."

> **MORE INFO**
>
> An *IF* function is similar to an *IF* statement in many programming languages.

An *IF* function has three arguments, and its syntax is:

=IF(logical_test, value_if_true, value_if_false)

- The **logical_test** is the value or statement to be evaluated.
- The **value_if_true** is the result displayed in the cell when the *logical_test* is true. You can select a cell, enter text, or use a formula for this argument.
- The **value_if_false** is the result displayed in the cell when the *logical_test* is false. You can select a cell, enter text, or use a formula for this argument.

An *IF* function can use comparison or logical operators in its arguments. The following table describes the comparison operators:

Comparison Operators

Operator	Description
=	Equal to
<>	Not equal to
>	Greater than
>=	Greater than or equal to
<	Less than
<=	Less than or equal to

Figure 2-46 has an *IF* function in cell D5 **=IF(B5>=4,18,20)**. When you use the *Function Arguments* dialog box to build a function, the commas to separate arguments are entered automatically.

B5>=4 is the *logical_test*. It determines if the value in cell B5 is equal to or greater than 4. Cell B5 is a relative reference so when the formula is copied, it will update to show the new row. The *value_if_true* argument is **18**. If the age is 4 or higher, the fee is $18. This value is a constant. It does not change when the formula is copied. The *value_if_false* argument is **20**, another constant. If the age is not 4 or higher, it must be lower and the fee is $20. The constant does not change when the formula is copied.

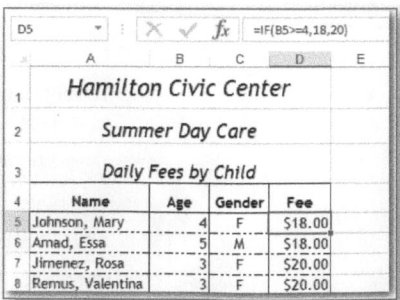

2-46 *IF* function in cell D5

You can insert the *IF* function from the *Logical* category on the *Formulas* tab, from the *Insert Function* button, or by typing it. When you type an *IF* function, you must type the commas to separate arguments, and you must enclose text arguments within quotation marks.

▶ HOW TO: Build an IF Function

1. Click the cell for the function.
2. Click the **Logical** button [*Formulas* tab, *Function Library* group].
 - The list of *Logical* functions opens.
3. Select **IF** in the list.
 - The *Function Arguments* dialog box for *IF* opens.
4. Click the **Logical_test** box.
5. Click the cell that will be evaluated.
 - Make the reference absolute if you know that the formula will be copied and that the reference should not change.
6. Type a comparison operator immediately after the cell address.
7. Type a value or click a cell to complete the expression to be tested.
 - You can build a statement such as B11=K15 or B11<10000.
 - Make a cell reference absolute or mixed if necessary.
8. Click the **Value_if_true** box.
9. Type the label or click a cell that contains data that should be displayed if the *logical_test* is true.
 - You can type a value in the text box.
10. Click the **Value_if_false** box.
11. Type the label or click a cell that contains data that should be displayed if the *logical_test* is false (Figure 2-47).
 - Results for the current cell are displayed in the *Function Arguments* dialog box.

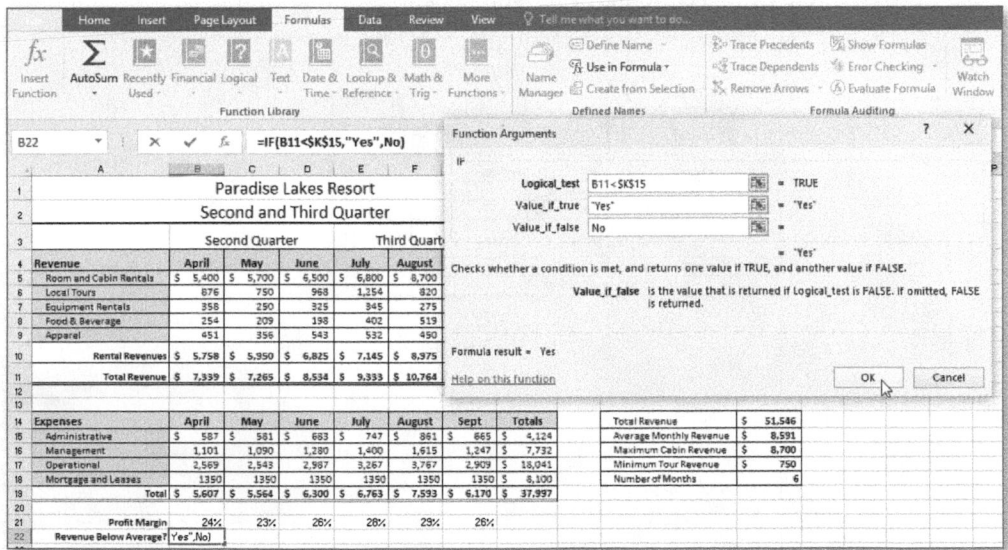

2-47 *Function Arguments* dialog box for *IF*

12. Click **OK**.

▶ MORE INFO

The *value_if_false* argument for the *logical_test* can be another *IF* function which allows you to test for more than one possibility.

Lookup Functions

A *Lookup* function displays a piece of data from a range of cells in another part of the work-book. There are two *Lookup* functions: *VLOOKUP* (vertical) and *HLOOKUP* (horizontal). These two functions have the same syntax and similar arguments. *VLOOKUP* uses a lookup table that is organized in columns, and *HLOOKUP* uses a lookup range that is laid out in rows.

A *VLOOKUP* function has four arguments, and the syntax is:

=VLOOKUP (lookup_value, table_array, col_index_num, [range_lookup])

- The ***lookup_value*** is the data to be found or looked up. It is usually a cell address, but you can type a value or a text string. The function locates this *lookup_value* in the first column of the table array. It then displays data from the designated column in the same row as the *lookup_value*.
- The ***table_array*** is a range of cells, sorted in ascending order by the first column. The range can be located on a different worksheet or in a different workbook. It is good practice to name the range so that its reference is absolute.
- The ***col_index_num*** sets which column in the *table_array* contains the data to be displayed in the result. The columns are counted from left to right.
- The ***[range lookup]*** is optional and is often omitted. This argument is either TRUE or FALSE. TRUE means that Excel finds the closest match to the *lookup_value*, not always a good choice. If the data in the table array is sorted, TRUE will generally return the correct match. When you set this argument to FALSE, the data can be in any order.

Figure 2-48 shows a *VLOOKUP* function in cell D3 in the worksheet on the left. The result (250) is from the third column in row 6 in the table array in the worksheet on the right. These are two sheets in the same workbook.

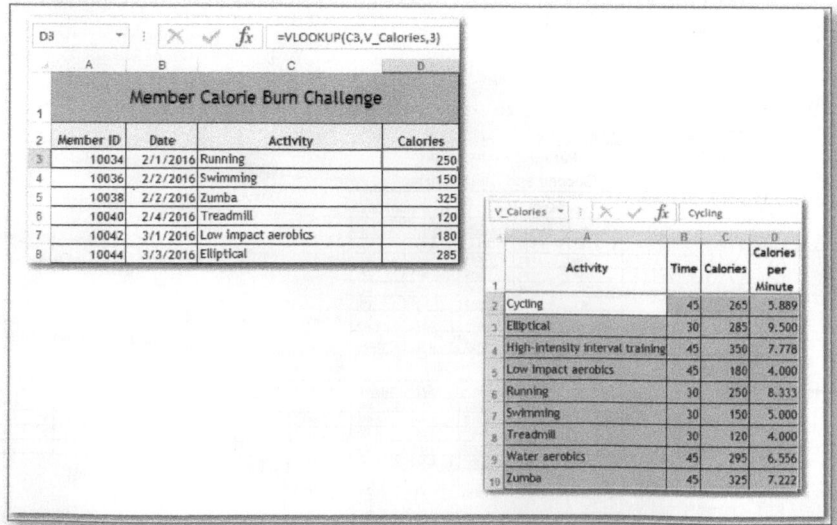

2-48 *VLOOKUP* function in cell D3 on the left

=VLOOKUP(C3,V_Calories,3)

The *lookup_value* argument is cell C3 ("Running").

The *table_array* argument is a named cell range, *V_Calories*. The "V" is a reminder that this range is a vertical lookup table. The *V_Calories* range is cells A2:D10 in the sheet on the right. The *col_index_num* argument is *3* so that the result is from the third column, the "Calories" column, in the *V_Calories* range.

The *range_lookup* argument is omitted or TRUE. The data in the table array (on the right) is sorted so TRUE is acceptable for this argument.

You can insert the *VLOOKUP* function from the *Lookup & Reference* category on the *Formulas* tab or by searching for it in the *Insert Function* dialog box. When you are experienced using the function, you can type it in the cell and use *Formula AutoComplete*.

▶ HOW TO: Enter the VLOOKUP Function

1. Click the cell for the function.
2. Click the **Lookup & Reference** button [*Formulas* tab].
3. Select **VLOOKUP**.
 - The *Function Arguments* dialog box opens.
 - Move the dialog box if it covers data that you need to see or select.
4. Click the **Lookup_value** box.
5. Click the cell to be matched.
 - The *lookup_value* is typically a cell in the same row as the function.
 - This reference is usually relative.
6. Click the **Table_array** box.
7. Select the cell range with the lookup data.
 - When the lookup table is named, the range name is substituted.
 - The *Function Arguments* dialog box collapses while you select cells.
8. Press **F4 (FN+F4)** to make the reference absolute if cell addresses are used.
 - When a range name has been substituted, you need not do this.
9. Click the **Col_index_num** box.
10. Type the column number, counting from the left, that contains the data to be displayed (Figure 2-49).
 - The result for the current cell is displayed in the dialog box.

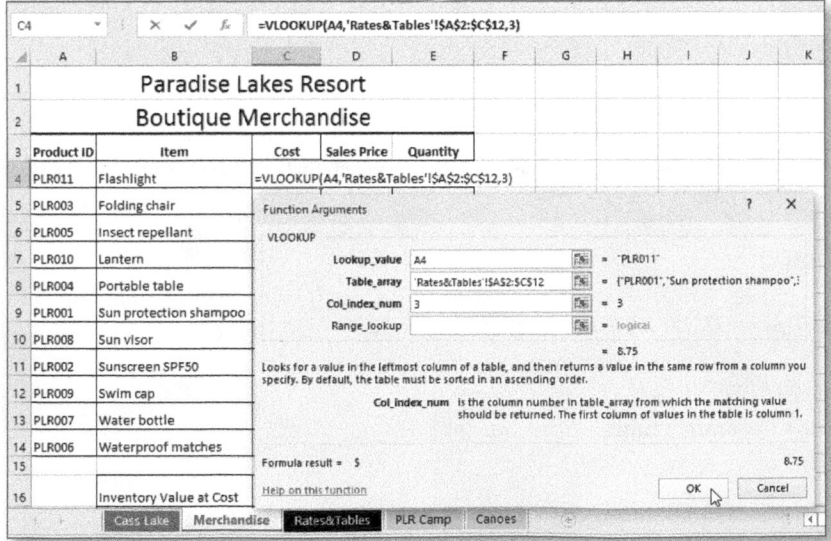

2-49 *Function Arguments* dialog box for *VLOOKUP*

11. Leave the *Range_lookup* argument box empty if the data in the table array is sorted.
12. Click **OK**.

The *HLOOKUP* function has a *row_index_num* argument instead of the *col_index_num* argument. *The table_array* is set up horizontally as seen in Figure 2-50, and the first row is arranged in alphabetical order from left to right. The *HLOOKUP* function is in cell C6 in the sheet on the left. The lookup table is named *H_Fees*, shown in the sheet on the right.

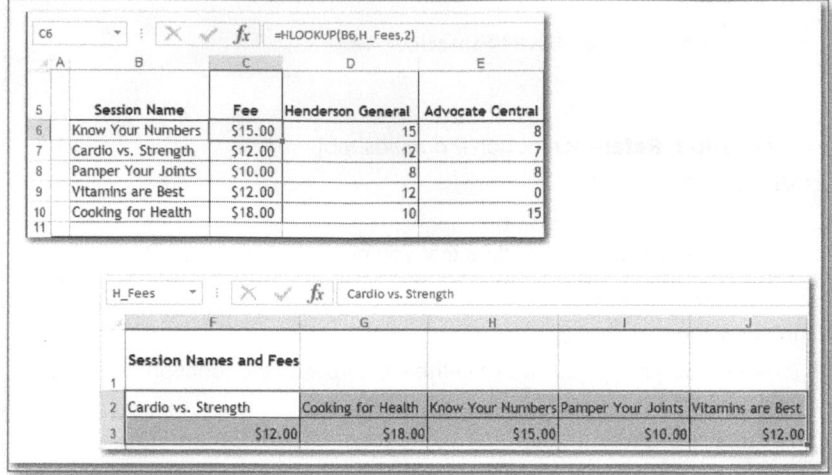

2-50 *HLOOKUP* in cell C6

=HLOOKUP(B6,H_Fees,2)

The *lookup_value* argument is cell B6 ("Know Your Numbers").
The *table_array* argument is a named cell range, *H_Fees*. The "H" is a visual cue for a horizontal lookup table. The *H_Fees* range is cells F2:J3 on the right.
The *row_index_num* argument is *2* so that the data shown in cell C6 is from the second row of the *H_Fees* range.
The *range_lookup* argument is omitted, because the data range is sorted alphabetically from left to right.

> **MORE INFO**
>
> The *range_lookup* argument TRUE (or omitted) finds the largest value that is less than or equal to the *lookup_value*.

▶ **HOW TO: Use The HLOOKUP Function**

1. Click the cell for the function.
2. Click the **Lookup & Reference** button [*Formulas* tab].
3. Select **HLOOKUP**.
 - The *Function Arguments* dialog box opens.
4. Click the **Lookup_value** box.
5. Click the cell to be matched.
 - The *lookup_value* is typically a cell in the same row as the function.
 - This reference is usually relative.
6. Click the **Table_array** box.

7. Select the cell range with the lookup data.
 - When the lookup table is named, the range name is substituted.
 - The *Function Arguments* dialog box collapses while you select cells.
8. Press **F4 (FN+F4)** to make the reference absolute when cell addresses are used.
9. Click the **Row_index_num** box.
10. Type the row number, counting the first row of the *table_array* as 1 (Figure 2-51).
 - The result for the current cell is displayed in the dialog box.

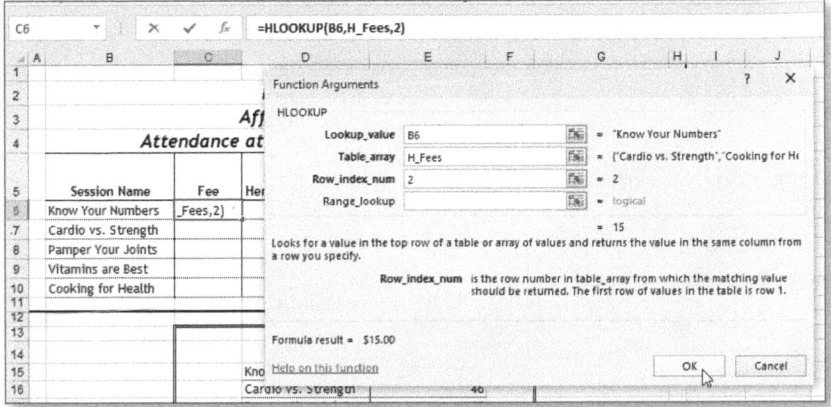

2-51 *HLOOKUP Function Arguments* dialog box

11. Leave the *Range_lookup* argument box empty if the data in the table array is sorted.
12. Click **OK**.

SLO 2.7

Using Math & Trig Functions

You have already used *SUM* from the *Math & Trig* function category. There are functions in this category to display the absolute value of data, one to calculate the cosine of an angle, or one that returns the power of a number. You might recognize the function *PI* or π from a math class. Three *Math & Trig* functions that are often used in business or personal calculations are *ROUND*, *SUMIF*, and *SUMPRODUCT*.

ROUND Function

Rounding means that a value is adjusted to display a specified number of decimal places or a whole number. You can round the numbers on your tax return in the United States which means that you need not show any cents, just dollars.

The *ROUND* function has two arguments, *number* and *num_digits*.

=ROUND(number, num_digits)

- The ***number*** is the cell or the value to be adjusted.
- The ***num_digits*** sets the number of decimal places for rounding. When this argument is zero (0), the value is displayed as the nearest whole number. When the *num_digits* argument is greater than zero, the value is rounded to that number of decimal places. You can use a negative number for the *num_digits* argument which rounds the value to the left of the decimal point. Make sure you understand the results when you round to the left of the decimal point.

When a value used in rounding is 5 or greater, results round up to the next digit. If you round 5.523 to show zero (0) decimal places, it rounds up to display as 6 because the value after the decimal point is 5. If you round 5.423 to two places, it rounds to 5.42 because the value used for rounding is 3. The *Increase Decimal* and *Decrease Decimal* buttons follow these rounding principles for displaying values in the cell as do the *Accounting Number* and *Currency* formats. These formats, however, keep the full unrounded value in the cell and use that value in calculations.

> **MORE INFO**
>
> When a value is rounded, the rounded value is used in calculations, not the full unrounded number.

HOW TO: Use the ROUND Function

1. Click the cell for the function.
2. Type =rou and press **Tab**.
 - *Formula AutoComplete* inserts the function in the cell.
 - The *number* argument is bold in the *ScreenTip*.
3. Select the cell to be rounded.
 - The cell address appears in the cell and in the *Formula* bar.
 - You can type a value if there is no cell reference.
4. Type , (a comma) to separate the arguments.
 - The *num_digits* argument is bold in the *ScreenTip*.
5. Type a number to set the number of decimal places (Figure 2-52).
6. Press **Enter**.

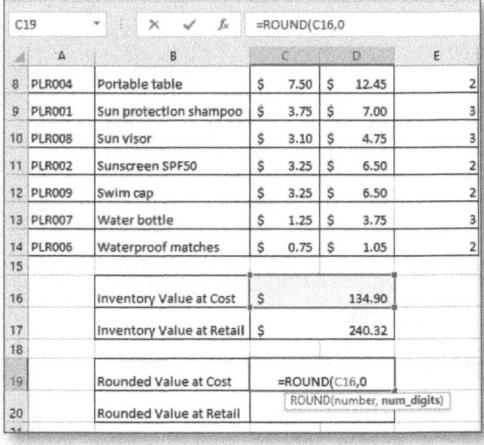

2-52 Type the *ROUND* function

> **MORE INFO**
>
> Excel has a *ROUNDDOWN* function that always rounds a number down. The *ROUNDUP* function rounds a value up.

SUMIF Function

The *SUMIF* function controls which data in a range is included in the total. It allows you to eliminate cells from the calculation by criteria that you set. **Criteria** are restrictions, conditions, or rules that must be met. In a *SUMIF* function, cell values are included in the sum only if they match the criteria.

The *SUMIF* function has three arguments.

=SUMIF (range, criteria, [sum_range])

- The **range** is the range of cells to be evaluated or searched, the values that are compared to the criteria.
- The **criteria** argument defines which cells from the range should be included in the sum. You can use comparison operators, cell references, a value, or text. When you use text or a comparison operator, the criteria must be enclosed in quotation marks.

- The *[sum_range]* is the cell range to be summed. This argument is optional, because it is omitted when the range to be summed is the same as the *range* argument.

Figure 2-53 illustrates a *SUMIF* function in cell I5 that totals sales for products that have a price greater than $10.

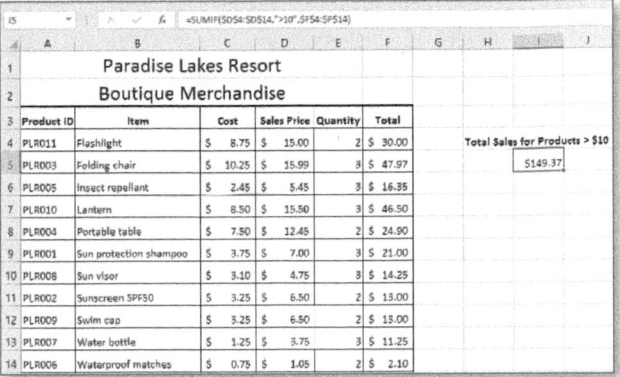

2-53 *SUMIF* function in cell I5

=SUMIF(D4:D14,">=10",F4:F14)

The *range* argument is the sales price column, cells D4:D14. It is an absolute reference so that the formula can be copied.

The *criteria* argument is >=10, shown in quotation marks. The quotation marks are added automatically when you use the *Function Arguments* dialog box.

The *sum_range* argument is cells F4:F14, the cells to be added if the price is greater than 10.

> **MORE INFO**
>
> You can use wildcards (* or ?) in a criteria argument. For example, to sum sales for all items that begin with the letter S, use **s*** as the criteria. Criteria are not case-sensitive.

HOW TO: Build a SUMIF Function

1. Click the cell for the function.
2. Click the **Math & Trig** button [*Formulas* tab, *Function Library* group].
3. Select **SUMIF**.
4. Click the **Range** box.
5. Select the cell range to be compared against the criteria.
 - Make the reference absolute if the formula might be copied.
 - Press **F3 (FN+F3)** to paste a range name rather than selecting the range.
6. Click the **Criteria** box.
 - Type text to be compared or a value to be matched.
 - Type an expression with operators to be evaluated.
 - Quotation marks are automatically supplied.

7. Click the **Sum_range** box (Figure 2-54).
 - Select the cells to be added.
 - If the cells to be added are the same as those in the *range* argument, leave the entry blank.

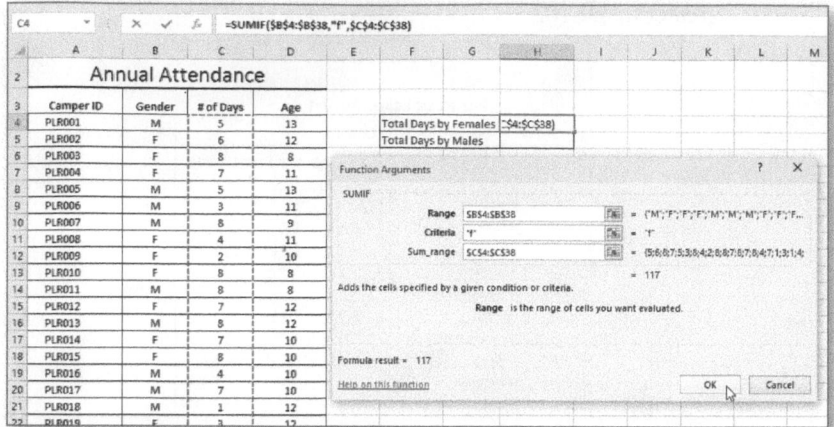

2-54 *Function Arguments* dialog box for *Sumif*

8. Click **OK**.

SUMPRODUCT Function

The *SUMPRODUCT* function calculates the sum of the product of several ranges. It multiplies the cells identified in its *array* arguments and then it totals those individual products. A ***product*** is the result of a multiplication problem; 4 is the product of 2 times 2. An ***array*** is a range of cells in a row or a column. An array has a ***dimension***, which is the number of columns or rows. The arrays A1:A5 and C1:C5 have the same dimension, five rows and one column.

The *SUMPRODUCT* function has the following syntax.

=SUMPRODUCT(array1, array2, [arrayN])

- The ***array1*** argument is the first range of cells for the multiplication.
- The ***array2*** argument is the range that is multiplied by the corresponding cells in the *array1* range. These two ranges must have the same number of cells, the same dimension.

It is possible to use more than two arrays so that you could have an *array3* argument or even more.

In Figure 2-55, the *SUMPRODUCT* function in cell C22 multiplies the first array C6:C20 by the corresponding values in cells F6:F20 and totals those products.

=SUMPRODUCT(C6:C20,F6:F20)

The value in cell C6 is multiplied by cell F6, cell C7 is multiplied by cell F7, and so on. Those individual products are summed, and the result is $249.15.

2-55 *SUMPRODUCT* in cell C22

▶ HOW TO: Build a SUMPRODUCT Function

1. Click the cell for the function.
2. Click the **Math & Trig** button [*Formulas* tab, *Function Library* group].
3. Select **SUMPRODUCT**.
 - The *Function Arguments* dialog box opens.
4. Click the **Array1** box.
5. Select the first cell range to be multiplied.
6. Click the **Array2** box.
7. Select the next cell range to be multiplied (Figure 2-56).
 - Both arrays must have the same number of cells and rows.
 - Use as many arrays as required for the calculation.

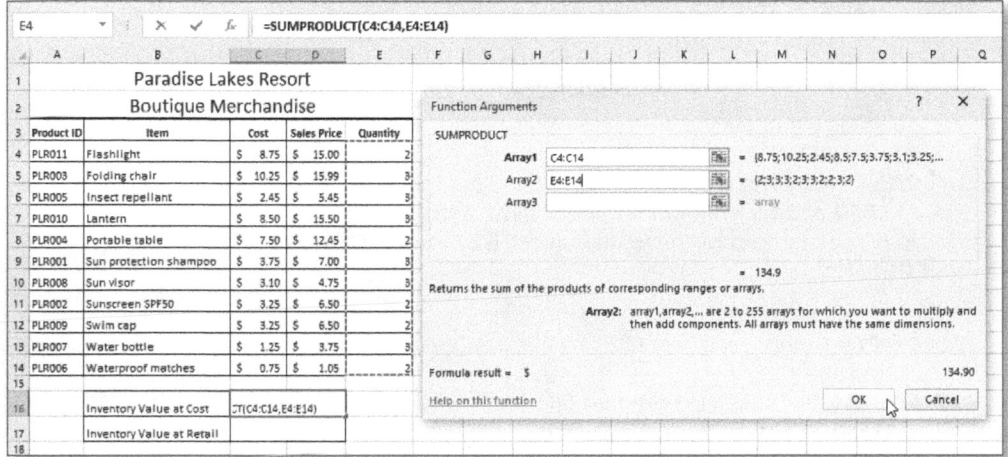

2-56 *Function Arguments* dialog box for *SUMPRODUCT*

8. Click **OK**.

> ### MORE INFO
>
> If an array in a *SUMPRODUCT* formula includes an empty cell, Excel treats that value as 0, but the multiplication by zero does not affect the sum.

PAUSE & PRACTICE: EXCEL 2-3

For this project, you continue working on the workbook for Paradise Lakes. You calculate totals related to camp attendance and merchandise inventory using functions from the *Math & Trig*, *Financial*, *Logical*, *Lookup & Reference*, and *Date & Time* categories.

File Needed: **[your initials] PP E2-2.xlsx**
Completed Project File Name: **[your initials] PP E2-3.xlsx**

1. Open the **[your initials] PP E2-2.xlsx** workbook completed in *Pause & Practice 2-2* and save it as [your initials] PP E2-3.

2. Click the **Cass Lake** worksheet tab.

3. Enter an *IF* function to determine if a month's revenue was below average.
 a. Click cell **B22** and click the **Formulas** tab.
 b. Click the **Logical** button In the *Function Library* group and select **IF**. The *Function Arguments* dialog box opens.
 c. Click the **Logical_test** text box and click cell **B11**.
 d. After "B11" in the *Logical_test* box, type < for a less than operator.
 e. Click cell **K15** and press **F4 (FN+F4)** to make this an absolute reference.
 f. Click the **Value_if_true** box and type Yes. You need not type quotation marks when you use the *Function Arguments* dialog box.
 g. Press **Tab** to move to the *Value_if_false* box. Excel supplies the quotation marks for "Yes."
 h. Type No (Figure 2-57).
 i. Click **OK**. For April, the result is *Yes*.
 j. Click cell **B22** and click the **Center** button [*Home* tab, *Font* group].
 k. Use the *Fill* pointer to copy the formula in cell **B22** to cells **C22:G22**.
 l. Press **Ctrl+Home**.

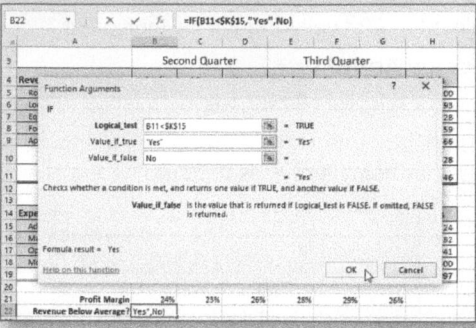

2-57 Build an *IF* function

4. Use *SUMIF* to calculate results.
 a. Click the **PLR Camp** worksheet tab. The number of attendees is tracked with the camper's ID, gender, and age.
 b. Select cell **H4**, and click the **Formulas** tab.
 c. Click the **Math & Trig** button in the *Function Library* group and select **SUMIF**.
 d. Click the **Range** text box and select cells **B4:B38**.
 e. Press **F4 (FN+F4)** to make the reference absolute.
 f. Press **Tab** and type f in the *Criteria* box. Criteria are not case-sensitive. The cells in column B will be checked to determine if they show "F."
 g. Click the **Sum_range** box, select cells **C4:C38**, and press **F4 (FN+F4)**. The values in this range will be summed for those rows in which the gender is F (Figure 2-58).
 h. Click **OK**. Female camp days are 117.
 i. Click cell **H4** and use the *Fill* pointer to copy the formula to cell **H5**.
 j. Edit the formula in cell **H5** to show m instead of "f."

2-58 Build a *SUMIF* function

5. Use *VLOOKUP* to display costs.
 a. Click the **Merchandise** sheet tab and select cell **C4**. Individual costs are missing, but they are listed on the **Rates&Tables** sheet.
 b. Click the **Lookup & Reference** button [*Formulas* tab, *Function Library* group].
 c. Select **VLOOKUP**.
 d. Click the **Lookup_value** box and select cell **A4**.
 e. Click the **Table_array** box. The table with the costs is on the **Rates&Tables** sheet.
 f. Click the **Rates&Tables** worksheet tab and select cells **A2:C12**. This array or range includes the ID, the name, and the cost. The costs are in column C, the third column from the left.

g. Press **F4 (FN+F4)** to make the array an absolute reference.

h. Click the **Col_index_num** box and type 3. The ID in cell A4 will be located in cells A2:C12 on the **Rates&Tables** sheet, and the cost in the third column will be displayed.

i. Click the **Range_lookup** box and type false (Figure 2-59).

j. Click **OK**. The cost for the first item is $8.75.

k. Copy the formula in cell **C4** to cells **C5:C14**.

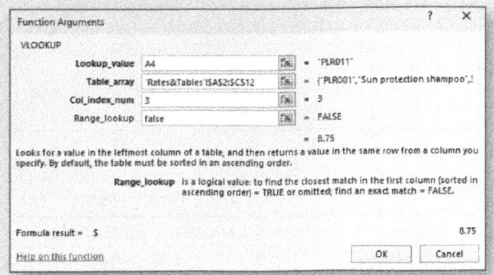

2-59 Build a *VLOOKUP* function

6. Use *SUMPRODUCT* to calculate inventory values.
 a. Click cell **C16**. This is a merged and centered cell.
 b. Click the **Formulas** tab.
 c. Click the **Math & Trig** button in the *Function Library* group and select **SUMPRODUCT**.
 d. Click the **Array1** box and select cells **C4:C14**. There are 11 values in this range.
 e. Click the **Array2** box and select cells **E4:E14**. There are 11 values in this range, and each one will be multiplied by the corresponding value in the same row in column C.
 f. Click **OK**. The value of the inventory at cost is 134.9.
 g. Click cell **C17**, type =sump, and press **Tab**. The function is inserted and the *ScreenTip* shows the next argument, *array1*.
 h. Select cells **D4:D14** and type , (a comma) to separate the first argument from the second.
 i. Select cells **E4:E14** (Figure 2-60). You need not type the closing parenthesis.
 j. Press **Enter**. The value is 240.32.
 k. Select cells **C16:C17** and apply the **Accounting Number** format.

2-60 Type a *SUMPRODUCT* function

7. Use the *ROUND* function.
 a. Select cell **C19**.
 b. Click the **Math & Trig** button [*Formulas* tab, *Function Library* group].
 c. Select **ROUND**.
 d. In the *Number* text box, click cell **C16**.
 e. Type 0 in the *Num_digits* text box.
 f. Press **Enter**. The value is rounded up to $135.00.
 g. Copy the formula in cell **C19** to cell **C20**. The value from cell C17 is rounded down to $240.00.

8. Use the PMT function to determine payments for new canoe purchases.
 a. Click the **Canoes** sheet tab and click cell **B7**.
 b. Click the **Formulas** tab and the **Financial** button [*Function Library* group].
 c. Select **PMT**.
 d. Click the **Rate** box and click cell **B6**.
 e. Immediately after "B6," type /12 to divide the rate by 12 for monthly payments.

f. Click the **Nper** box and click cell **B5**. Type *12 to multiply by 12 for 12 months per year.

g. Click the **Pv** box and click cell **B4**. This is the amount of the loan.

h. Click the **Fv** box. Leave this blank to indicate no balance due at the end of the loan term.

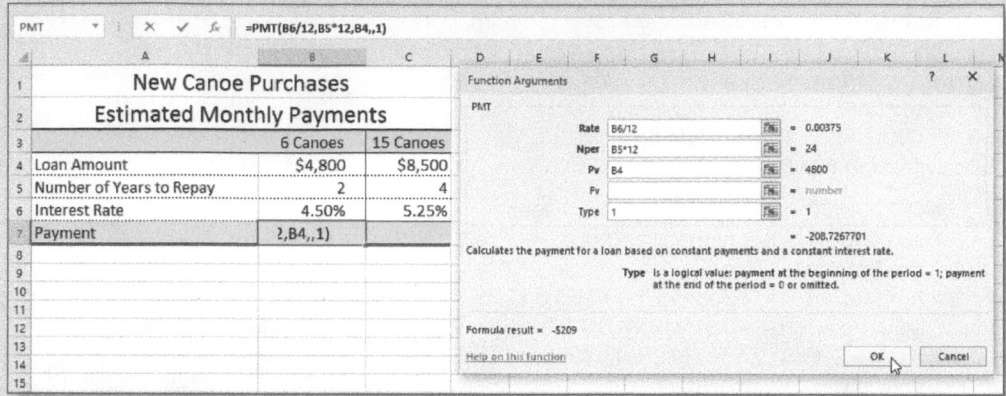

2-61 PMT function for payment at the beginning of the period

i. Click the **Type** box and type 1. The payment will made at the beginning of the month (Figure 2-61).

j. Click **OK**. The payment is −$209, a negative value because it is money paid out. This cell was formatted to show no decimal places.

9. Type the PMT function.

a. Click cell **C7**.

b. Type =pm, and press **Tab**. The *ScreenTip* shows the first argument, *rate*.

c. Click cell **C6** and type /12,. This divides the rate by 12 and enters a comma to separate the arguments (Figure 2-62).

d. Click cell **C5** for the *nper* argument, type *12, to multiply by 12 and enter a comma to separate the arguments.

e. Click cell **C4** for the *pv* argument, the amount of the loan.

f. Type , (a comma) to move to the *fv* argument.

g. Type , (another comma) to move to the *type* argument. *Formula AutoComplete* lists two options for the argument (Figure 2-63).

h. Double-click **1-beginning of the period** in the *ScreenTip*.

i. Press **Enter**. The payment is −$196.

j. Press **Ctrl+Home**.

2-62 Type a PMT function

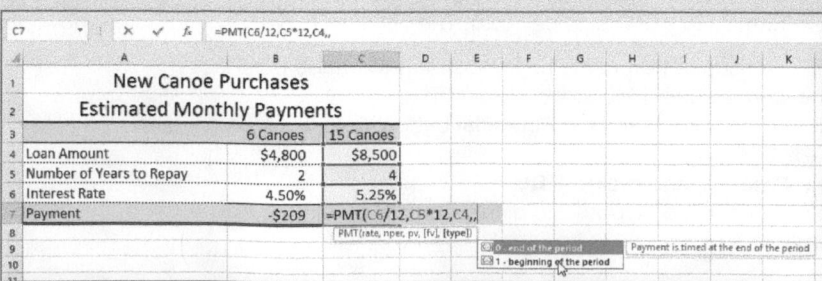

2-63 *Formula AutoComplete* for argument choices

10. Save and close the workbook (Figure 2-64).

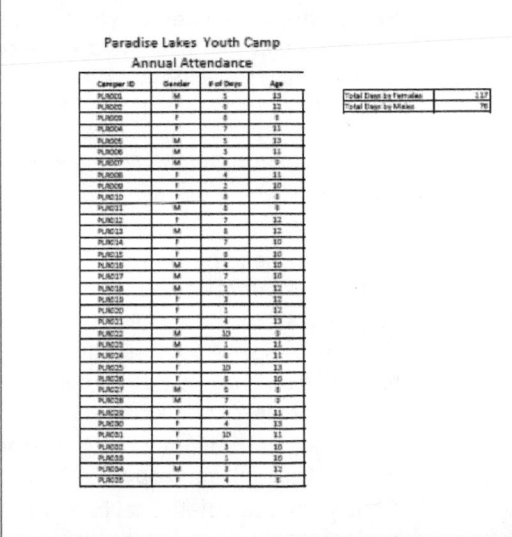

2-64 PP 2-3 completed

Chapter Summary

2.1 Build and edit basic formulas (p. E2-89).

- A *formula* is a calculation that uses arithmetic operators, worksheet cells, and constant values. Basic arithmetic operations are addition, subtraction, multiplication, and division.
- You can type a formula in the cell or you can point and click to select cells.
- When you type a formula, *Formula AutoComplete* displays suggestions for completing the formula.
- Formulas are edited in the *Formula* bar or in the cell to change cell addresses, use a different operator, or add cells to the calculation.

2.2 Set mathematical order of operations (p. E2-91).

- Excel follows mathematics rules for the order in which operations are carried out when a formula has more than one operator.
- You can control the sequence of calculations by placing operations that should be done first within parentheses.
- Use the following acronym to help remember the order of arithmetic operations: **P**lease **E**xcuse **M**y **D**ear **A**unt **S**ally (**P**arentheses, **E**xponentiation, **M**ultiplication, **D**ivision, **A**ddition, **S**ubtraction).

2.3 Use absolute, mixed, relative, and 3D references in a formula (p. E2-93).

- A *relative cell reference* in a formula is the cell address which, when copied, updates to the address of the copy.
- An *absolute cell reference* is the cell address with dollar signs as in A5. This reference does not change when the formula is copied.
- A *mixed cell reference* contains one relative and one absolute address as in $B5 or B$5. When copied, the absolute part of the reference does not change.
- A *3D cell reference* is a cell in another worksheet in the same workbook. It includes the name of the worksheet followed by an exclamation point as in *Inventory!B2*.
- You can name a single cell or a group of cells with a defined *range name*.
- You can use range names in formulas instead of cell addresses.

- *Formula AutoComplete* displays range names so that you can paste them in a formula.
- A named range is an absolute reference.

2.4 Use formula auditing tools in a worksheet (p. E2-99).

- Excel highlights several types of formula errors as you work, but you still need to review errors and make corrections.
- Excel automatically error-checks formulas based on its internal rules. A potential error is marked in the upper left corner of the cell with a small triangle.
- *Formula auditing* tools include several commands to aid your review of workbook formulas and functions.
- The *Formula Auditing* group on the *Formulas* tab includes the *Trace Precedents* and *Trace Dependents* buttons.
- A *circular reference* is an error that occurs when a formula includes the address of the formula.
- Some errors are noted as you press a completion key and can be quickly corrected by accepting the suggested correction in the message window.

2.5 Use *Statistical* and *Date & Time* functions (p. E2-106).

- The *AVERAGE* function calculates the arithmetic mean by adding values and dividing by the number of values.
- The *COUNT* function tallies the number of cells in a range. There are different *COUNT* functions based on whether cell contents are labels, values, or blank.
- *MAX* and *MIN* functions find the largest and the smallest values, respectively, in a range.
- Commonly used statistical functions are options on the *AutoSum* button.
- The *AutoCalculate* feature displays numerical results such as *Sum*, *Average*, and *Count* on the *Status* bar for selected cells.
- The *Date & Time* category includes a *TODAY* function and a *NOW* function that display the current date and time.

2.6 Work with functions from the *Financial*, *Logical*, and *Lookup & Reference* categories. (p. E2-114).

- Use the *Function Arguments* dialog box for help in completing an Excel function.

- The *Function Arguments* dialog box includes a description of the function and an explanation of each argument.
- The *PMT* function from the *Financial* category calculates a constant payment amount for a loan.
- The *Logical* function *IF* evaluates a statement or condition and displays a particular result when the statement is true and another result when the condition is false.
- A *Lookup* function displays data from a cell located in another part of the workbook.
- Two widely used *Lookup* functions are *VLOOKUP* (vertical) and *HLOOKUP* (horizontal).

2.7 Build functions from the *Math & Trig* category (p. E2-122).

- The *ROUND* function adjusts a value up or down based on the number of decimal places.

- The *SUMIF* function includes cells in a total only if they meet a set criteria or condition.
- The *SUMPRODUCT* function multiplies corresponding cells from an **array** and then totals the results of each multiplication.

Check for Understanding

The SIMbook for this text (within your SIMnet account) provides the following resources for concept review:

- Multiple choice questions
- Matching exercises
- Short answer questions

Guided Project 2-1

Courtyard Medical Plaza (CMP) has doctor offices, a pharmacy, x-ray and lab services, insurance and billing support, optometry and dental facilities, and onsite dining. You will complete an inventory worksheet for the pharmacy as well as insurance and payment data for the optometry group.
[Student Learning Outcomes 2.1, 2.2, 2.3, 2.4, 2.5, 2.6, 2.7]

File Needed: ***CourtyardMedical-02.xlsx*** [Student data files are available in the Library of your SIMnet account.]
Completed Project File Name: ***[your initials] Excel 2-1.xlsx***

Skills Covered in This Project

- Build and copy formulas.
- Name cell ranges.
- Use *AVERAGE*, *MAX*, and *MIN*.
- Use relative, mixed, absolute, and 3D cell references in formulas.
- Use *SUMIF*.

- Check results with *AutoCalculate*.
- Use the *VLOOKUP* function.
- Set mathematical order of operations.
- Use formula auditing tools.
- Use the *PMT* and *SUMPRODUCT* functions.
- Insert the *TODAY* function.

1. Open the ***CourtyardMedical-02.xlsx*** workbook from your student data files and save it as [your initials] Excel 2-1.

2. Enter and copy subtraction formulas.
 a. Click cell **E2** on the **Lookup_Data** worksheet. To calculate the dollar amount of the margin, subtract the cost from the retail price.
 b. Type an equals sign (=) to start the formula.
 c. Click cell **D2**, the retail price.
 d. Type a minus sign, or hyphen (–) to subtract, and click cell **C2**, the cost.
 e. Click the **Enter** button (check mark) on the *Formula* bar. The pointer stays in the formula cell. The margin for acetaminophen is $1.49.
 f. Drag the *Fill* pointer to copy the formula in cell **E2** to cells **E3:E16**. The *Auto Fill Options* button appears near cell E16.
 g. Click the **Auto Fill Options** button and choose **Fill Without Formatting** (Figure 2-65). This option copies the formula without the top border from cell E2.
 h. Format cells **E3:E16** as **Currency**.
 i. Click the **Optometry** sheet tab and select cell **G5**.
 j. Type = to start the formula to subtract the deductible amount from the billed amount.
 k. Click cell **E5**, the billed amount.
 l. Type –, click cell **F5**, the deductible amount, and press **Enter**.
 m. Copy the formula in cell **G5** to cells **G6:G24** without formatting to maintain the fill color.

E2	▾	× ✓	*fx*	=D2-C2		
	A	B	C	D	E	F
1	Product ID	Description	Cost	Retail	Margin	
2	CMP-006	Acetaminophen	$2.50	$3.99	$1.49	
3	CMP-001	Tongue depressor	$0.55	$1.99	$1.44	
4	CMP-002	Cough drops	$0.85	$1.29	$0.44	
5	CMP-003	Nasal spray	$3.45	$5.99	$2.54	
6	CMP-004	Antiseptic wash	$2.75	$4.99	$2.24	
7	CMP-005	Disinfectant wipes	$1.25	$3.99	$2.74	
8	CMP-007	Bandage, 1 inch strips	$1.25	$3.99	$2.74	
9	CMP-008	Bandage, 2 inch strips	$1.25	$3.99	$2.74	
10	CMP-009	Bandage, assorted	$1.75	$4.99	$3.24	
11	CMP-010	Ibuprofen	$2.50	$3.99	$1.49	
12	CMP-011	Cough syrup	$2.25	$4.99	$2.74	
13	CMP-012	Antibiotic ointment	$2.25	$5.99	$3.74	
14	CMP-013	Moisture lotion	$1.55	$4.99	$3.44	
15	CMP-014	Dandruff shampoo	$2.75	$5.99	$3.24	
16	CMP-015	Insect bite gel	$3.55	$6.99	$3.44	
17						

- Copy Cells
- Fill Formatting Only
- Fill Without Formatting
- Flash Fill

2-65 Copy without formatting to preserve borders

3. Name cell ranges.
 a. Select cells **E5:E24**. This named range will refer to the billable amounts.
 b. Click the **Name** box.
 c. Type Billables in the *Name* box and press **Enter**.
 d. Click the **Lookup_Data** worksheet tab.
 e. Select cells **A2:D16**. This named range will not include the calculated margin.
 f. Click the **Name** box.
 g. Type Costs in the *Name* box and press **Enter**.
 h. Select cells **H2:I5** and click the **Formulas** tab.
 i. Click the **Create from Selection** button [*Defined Names* group]. Excel will create range names based on the labels in the column on the left.
 j. Select the **Left column** box and click **OK**.
 k. Click cell **A1** and click the **Name** box arrow to see the range names in the worksheet (Figure 2-66).

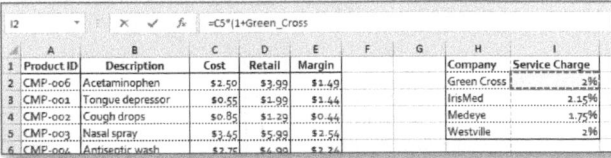

2-66 **Range names in the worksheet**

4. Use range names with *AVERAGE*, *MIN*, and *MAX*.
 a. Click the **Optometry** sheet tab and select cell **D27**.
 b. Type =aver and press **Tab**.
 c. Select cells **E5:E24** and press **Enter**. The range name is substituted in the formula when you select the cells in the worksheet.
 d. Select cell **D28**, click the **AutoSum** button arrow [*Home* tab, *Editing* group], and select **Max**.
 e. Select cells **E5:E24** and press **Enter**.
 f. Use *MIN* in cell **D29** with the same cell range.

5. Set the order of operations in a 3D formula.
 a. Click the **Insurance** sheet tab and select cell **D5**. The total with service charge is calculated by multiplying 1 plus the percentage times the billed amount. The percentages are on the **Lookup_Data** sheet in named ranges.
 b. Type = and click cell **C5**.
 c. Type *(immediately after **C5**. The next part of the formula will be calculated first.
 d. Type 1+ immediately after the left parenthesis. The calculation is (1+ the percentage).
 e. Click the **Lookup_Data** sheet tab. The sheet name is displayed in the *Formula* bar.
 f. Click cell **I2**. The range name is substituted. Because it is an absolute reference, the sheet name is removed (Figure 2-67).
 g. Press **Enter**. Because the formula refers to another sheet and a range name, the missing parenthesis is not automatically supplied (Figure 2-68).
 h. Click **Yes** to accept the suggested correction.
 i. Copy the formula to cells **D5:D9** for the Green Cross patients.

2-67 **3D formula with a range name**

6. Edit and copy a formula.
 a. Click cell **D9** and copy the formula to cell **D10**.
 b. Double-click cell **D10** to start *Edit* mode.
 c. Select the range name **Green_Cross** in the cell or *Formula* bar (Figure 2-69).
 d. Click the **Lookup_Data** sheet tab and select cell **I3**. The *IrisMed* range name replaces *Green_Cross*, and the parenthesis is maintained.

2-68 **Formula correction message window**

e. Press **Enter**. Four decimal places are shown for some results.

f. Copy the formula in cell **D10** to cells **D11:D16**.

g. Double-click cell **D16** and select **IrisMed** in the cell or in the *Formula* bar.

h. Press **F3 (FN+F3)** to open the *Paste Name* dialog box.

i. Select **Medeye** in the list and click **OK**.

j. Press **Enter**.

k. Copy the formula in cell **D16** to cells **D17:D20**.

l. Complete the formulas for Westville insurance.

7. Format cells **D5:D24** as **Currency** from the *Number Format* drop-down list. The values are rounded to two decimals places.

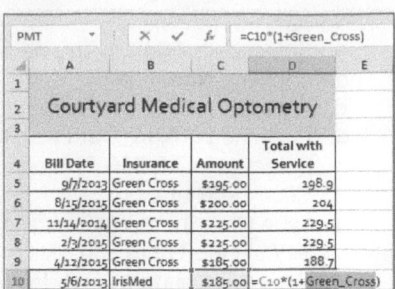

2-69 Edit the range name in a formula

8. Use the *SUMIF* function to calculate billable amounts by insurance company.

a. Click the **Optometry** worksheet tab and select cell **D31**.

b. Click the **Math & Trig** button [*Formulas* tab, *Function Library* group].

c. Select **SUMIF**.

d. Click the **Range** box and select cells **C5:C24**.

e. Click the **Criteria** box and select cell **C31** to use a relative reference to the company name.

f. Click the **Sum_range** text box and select cells **E5:E24**. The range name is substituted (Figure 2-70).

g. Click **OK**. The result is 1030, the total amount billed to Green Cross.

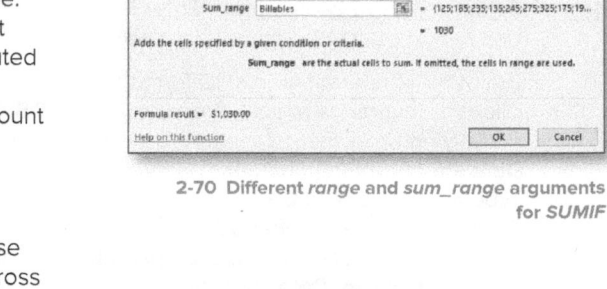

2-70 Different *range* and *sum_range* arguments for *SUMIF*

9. Verify results with *AutoCalculate*.

a. Select cells **E13:E15**.

b. Press **Ctrl** and select cells **E20:E21**. These are the billable amounts for the Green Cross insurance company.

c. Compare the *SUM* in the *Status* bar with the result in cell **D31** (Figure 2-71).

10. Copy the *SUMIF* function with a relative reference.

a. Select cell **D31**.

b. Drag the *Fill* pointer to copy the formula in cell **D31** to cells **D32:D34**. The *Auto Fill Options* button appears near cell D34.

c. Select cell **D32**. The reference to cell C31 in the original formula is updated to cell C32 in the copied formula (Figure 2-72).

	A	B	C	D	E	F	G	H	I	J	K
11	OP0007	3/7/2015	IrisMed	Soft	$325.00	$100.00	$225.00				
12	OP0008	12/3/2014	Westville	Gas Permeable	$175.00	$75.00	$100.00				
13	OP0009	9/7/2013	Green Cross	Gas Permeable	$195.00	$50.00	$145.00				
14	OP0010	8/15/2015	Green Cross	Soft	$200.00	$75.00	$125.00				
15	OP0011	11/14/2014	Green Cross	Soft	$225.00	$100.00	$125.00				
16	OP0012	6/8/2015	IrisMed	Soft	$200.00	$100.00	$100.00				
17	OP0013	5/3/2014	Medeye	Glasses	$475.00	$100.00	$375.00				
18	OP0014	4/18/2014	IrisMed	Soft	$235.00	$75.00	$160.00				
19	OP0015	3/17/2014	IrisMed	Soft	$235.00	$75.00	$160.00				
20	OP0016	2/3/2015	Green Cross	Soft	$225.00	$75.00	$150.00				
21	OP0017	4/12/2015	Green Cross	Gas Permeable	$185.00	$50.00	$135.00				
22	OP0018	3/21/2015	Westville	Gas Permeable	$195.00	$50.00	$145.00				
23	OP0019	2/18/2015	Westville	Soft	$225.00	$75.00	$150.00				
24	OP0020	10/5/2014	Medeye	Glasses	$375.00	$100.00	$275.00				
25											
26											
27			Average Billable	$233.50							
28			Maximum Billable	$475.00							
29			Minimum Billable	$125.00							
30											
31			Green Cross	1030							

Lookup_Data | Pharmacy | Optometry | Insurance | Payments

Ready Average: $206.00 Count: 5 Sum: $1,030.00

2-71 *AutoCalculate* results in Status bar

11. Format cells **D31:D34** as **Currency** from the *Number Format* drop-down list. Press **Ctrl+Home**.

12. Use *VLOOKUP* with a range name to display costs.
 a. Click the **Pharmacy** worksheet tab and select cell **C6**. Cost and retail prices are missing.
 b. Click the **Lookup & Reference** button [*Formulas* tab, *Function Library* group] and select **VLOOKUP**.
 c. Click the **Lookup_value** box and click cell **A6**. The ID in column A will be located in the table array.
 d. Click the **Table_array** box. All prices are in the *Lookup_Data* sheet.
 e. Click the **Lookup_Data** sheet tab and select cells **A2:D16**. This range *Costs* is substituted when you select the cells; the range name is not substituted if you type the range address. Notice that the cost is in the third column.
 f. Click the **Col_index_num** box and type 3 (Figure 2-73).

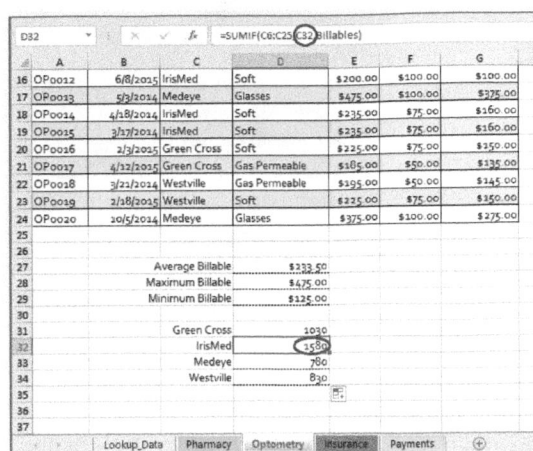

2-72 Relative reference is adjusted after copying

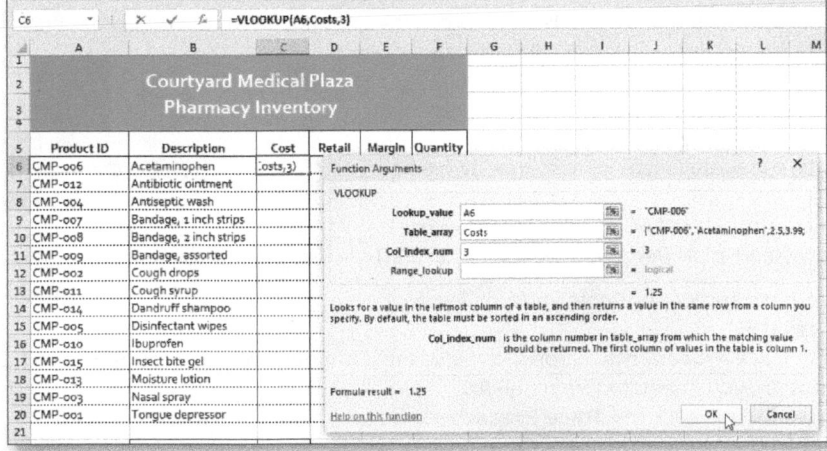

2-73 *VLOOKUP* and its arguments

 g. Click **OK**. The acetaminophen cost is 1.25.
 h. Copy the formula in cell **C6** to cells **C7:C20** without formatting. Format cells **C6:C20** as **Currency**.

13. Type the *VLOOKUP* function.
 a. Click cell **D6**.
 b. Type =vl and press **Tab**. The first argument is *lookup_value*.
 c. Select cell **A6** and type a comma (,) to separate the arguments. The next argument is *table_array*.
 d. Type costs,. You can type the name or select it in the *Formula AutoComplete* list (Figure 2-74).

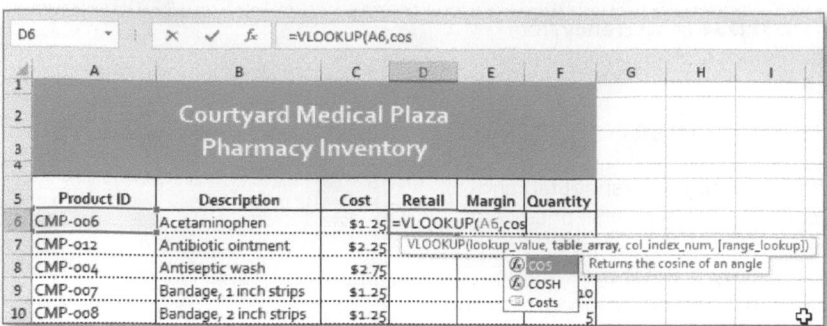

2-74 *Formula AutoComplete* shows range names

e. Type 4 for the *Col_index_num* argument, because the retail price is in the fourth column of the *Costs* range.

f. Press **Enter**. The closing parenthesis is supplied, and the retail price for acetaminophen is 3.99.

g. Copy the formula in cell **D6** to cells **D7:D20** without formatting and then format the cells as **Currency**.

14. Set order of precedence in a formula.
 a. Click cell **E6**. The formula to calculate the margin subtracts the cost from the retail price and then divides by the cost. The margin is shown as a markup percentage.
 b. Type =(to start the formula and enter the opening parenthesis.
 c. Click cell **D6** for the retail price.
 d. Type − and click cell **C6** to subtract the cost from the retail price.
 e. Type) for the closing parenthesis. This forces the subtraction to be carried out first.
 f. Type / for division and click cell **C6** to divide the results by the cost (Figure 2-75).
 g. Press **Enter**. The results are formatted as currency.
 h. Apply **Percent Style** to cell **E6**. A margin of 219% means that the retail price is more than two times the cost.
 i. Copy the formula in cell **E6** to cells **E7:E20** without formatting; then apply **Percent Style** to cells **E7:E20**.

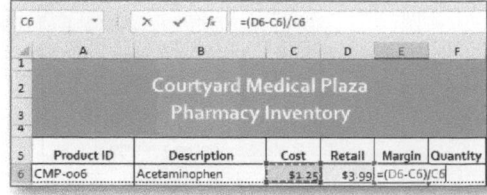

2-75 Formula with multiple operators

15. Trace precedents and dependents for formulas.
 a. Select cell **C6**.
 b. Click the **Trace Precedents** button [*Formulas* tab, *Formula Auditing* group]. The formula uses data from another worksheet and from cell **A6**.
 c. Select cell **E6** and click the **Trace Precedents** button.
 d. Select cell **D7** and click the **Trace Dependents** button. The arrow points to cell **E7**.
 e. Click the **Remove Arrows** button [*Formulas* tab, *Formula Auditing* group].

16. Enter a *SUMPRODUCT* function to calculate inventory values.
 a. Click cell **C22**.
 b. Click the **Math & Trig** button [*Formulas* tab, *Function Library* group] and select **SUMPRODUCT**.
 c. Click the *Array1* box and select cells **C6:C20**.
 d. Click the *Array2* box and select cells **F6:F20**. Both arrays have the same dimension (Figure 2-76).
 e. Click **OK**. The result in E22 is 249.15. Each value in column C is multiplied by its corresponding value in column E, and those results are summed.

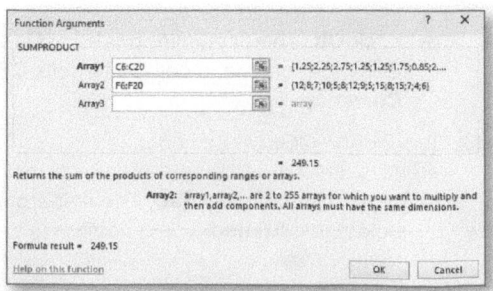

2-76 Two arrays for SUMPRODUCT

E2-137

17. Type the *SUMPRODUCT* function.
 a. Click cell **D23**.
 b. Type =sump and press **Tab**. The first argument is *array1*.
 c. Select cells **D6:D20** and type a comma (,) to separate the arguments. The next argument is *array2*.
 d. Select cells **F6:F20** and press **Enter** (Figure 2-77). The result is 588.29.
 e. Format cells **D22:D23** as **Currency**. Press **Ctrl+Home**.

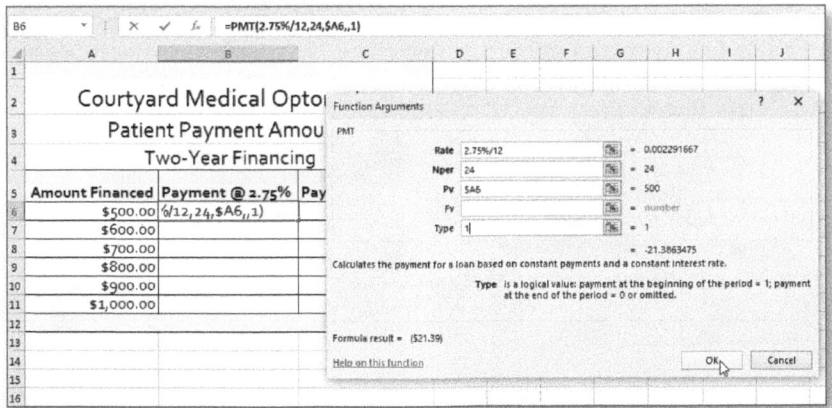

A	B	C	D	E	F	G
5 **Product ID**	**Description**	**Cost**	**Retail**	**Margin**	**Quantity**	
6 CMP-006	Acetaminophen	$3.25	$3.99	229%	12	
7 CMP-012	Antibiotic ointment	$2.25	$5.99	166%	8	
8 CMP-004	Antiseptic wash	$2.75	$4.99	81%	7	
9 CMP-007	Bandage, 1 inch strips	$1.25	$3.99	219%	10	
10 CMP-008	Bandage, 2 inch strips	$1.25	$3.99	219%	5	
11 CMP-009	Bandage, assorted	$1.75	$4.99	185%	8	
12 CMP-002	Cough drops	$0.85	$1.29	52%	22	
13 CMP-011	Cough syrup	$2.25	$4.99	122%	9	
14 CMP-014	Dandruff shampoo	$2.75	$5.99	118%	6	
15 CMP-005	Disinfectant wipes	$1.25	$3.99	219%	15	
16 CMP-010	Ibuprofen	$2.50	$3.99	60%	8	
17 CMP-015	Insect bite gel	$3.55	$6.99	97%	26	
18 CMP-013	Moisture lotion	$1.55	$4.99	222%	7	
19 CMP-003	Nasal spray	$3.45	$5.99	74%	4	
20 CMP-001	Tongue depressor	$0.55	$1.99	262%	6	
21						
22	Total Value at Cost	249.35				
23	Total Value at Retail	=SUMPRODUCT(D6:D20,F6:F20				
24		SUMPRODUCT(array1, [array2], [array3], [array4] ...)				

2-77 Both arrays have the same dimension

18. Use *PMT* to calculate patient payments.
 a. Click the **Payments** sheet tab and select cell **B6**.
 b. Click the **Financial** button [*Formulas* tab, *Function Library* group] and select **PMT**.
 c. Click the **Rate** box and type 2.75%/12. You can type the rate when it is not shown in a cell. Yearly rates are divided by 12 for monthly payments.
 d. Click the **Nper** box and type 24. The length of the loan is indicated in the label in cell A4. Two-year financing means 24 monthly payments.
 e. Click the **Pv** box and click cell **A6**, the amount of a loan.
 f. Press **F4 (FN+F4)** to make the reference absolute (A6). Press **F4 (FN+F4)** again to make a mixed reference A$6.
 g. Press **F4 (FN+F4)** once more to make the reference mixed $A6.
 h. Click the **Type** box and type 1 for payment at the beginning of the month. The *Fv* argument is blank (Figure 2-78).
 i. Click **OK**. The payment for financing $500 is ($21.39).
 j. Copy the formula to cells **B7:B11**. The reference to cell $A6 is mixed, and the *rate* and *nper* values that you typed are absolute.

B6 × ✓ fₓ =PMT(2.75%/12,24,$A6,,1)

	A	B	C	D	E	F	G	H	I	J
1										
2	Courtyard Medical Opto									
3	Patient Payment Amou									
4	Two-Year Financing									
5	Amount Financed	Payment @ 2.75%	Pay							
6	$500.00	%/12,24,$A6,,1)								
7	$600.00									
8	$700.00									
9	$800.00									
10	$900.00									
11	$1,000.00									
12										
13										
14										
15										
16										

Function Arguments ? ×

PMT

Rate 2.75%/12 = 0.002291667
Nper 24 = 24
Pv $A6 = 500
Fv = number
Type 1 = 1

= -21.3863475

Calculates the payment for a loan based on constant payments and a constant interest rate.

Type is a logical value: payment at the beginning of the period = 1; payment at the end of the period = 0 or omitted.

Formula result = ($21.39)

Help on this function OK Cancel

2-78 PMT arguments

19. Copy and edit a *PMT* function with a mixed reference.
 a. Copy the formula in cell **B6** to cell **C6**. The reference to cell $A6 is correct, but you need to edit the *Rate* argument.
 b. Select cell **C6** and click the **Insert Function** button in the *Formula* bar. The *Function Arguments* dialog box opens with the formula.
 c. Click the **Rate** text box and edit the calculation to 3.25%/12.
 d. Click **OK**. The payment for financing $500 at 3.25% is ($21.49).
 e. Copy the formula to cells **C7:C11**.

20. Enter the TODAY function.
 a. Select cell **A14**.
 b. Type =to, press **Tab**, and press **Enter**.
 c. Press **Ctrl+Home**.

21. Save and close the workbook (Figure 2-79).

Courtyard Medical Optometry

Patient ID	Initial Visit	Insurance	Prescription	Billable	Deductible	Patient Responsibility
OP0001	3/3/2014	Medeye	Gas Permeable	$125.00	$50.00	$75.00
OP0002	5/6/2013	IrisMed	Soft	$185.00	$50.00	$135.00
OP0003	8/12/2014	Medeye	Glasses	$235.00	$75.00	$160.00
OP0004	4/4/2014	Westville	Glasses	$135.00	$75.00	$60.00
OP0005	7/8/2014	Medeye	Soft	$245.00	$50.00	$195.00
OP0006	2/1/2014	IrisMed	Soft	$275.00	$100.00	$175.00
OP0007	3/7/2015	IrisMed	Soft	$325.00	$100.00	$225.00
OP0008	12/3/2014	Westville	Gas Permeable	$275.00	$75.00	$200.00
OP0009	9/7/2013	Green Cross	Gas Permeable	$195.00	$50.00	$145.00
OP0010	8/14/2014	Green Cross	Soft	$200.00	$75.00	$125.00
OP0011	11/14/2014	Green Cross	Soft	$225.00	$100.00	$125.00
OP0012	6/8/2015	IrisMed	Soft	$200.00	$100.00	$100.00
OP0013	5/3/2014	Medeye	Glasses	$475.00	$100.00	$375.00
OP0014	4/18/2014	IrisMed	Soft	$235.00	$75.00	$160.00
OP0015	3/17/2014	IrisMed	Soft	$235.00	$75.00	$160.00
OP0016	2/3/2015	Green Cross	Soft	$225.00	$75.00	$150.00
OP0017	4/12/2015	Green Cross	Gas Permeable	$185.00	$50.00	$135.00
OP0018	3/21/2014	Westville	Gas Permeable	$195.00	$50.00	$145.00
OP0019	2/18/2015	Westville	Soft	$225.00	$75.00	$150.00
OP0020	10/5/2014	Medeye	Glasses	$375.00	$100.00	$275.00

Average Billable	$233.50
Maximum Billable	$475.00
Minimum Billable	$135.00
Green Cross	$1,020.00
IrisMed	$1,455.00
Medeye	$1,455.00
Westville	$720.00

Courtyard Medical Optometry

Bill Date	Insurance	Amount	Total with Service Charge
9/7/2013	Green Cross	$195.00	$198.90
8/15/2015	Green Cross	$200.00	$204.00
11/14/2014	Green Cross	$225.00	$229.50
2/3/2015	Green Cross	$225.00	$229.50
4/12/2015	Green Cross	$185.00	$188.70
5/6/2013	IrisMed	$185.00	$188.98
2/1/2015	IrisMed	$275.00	$280.91
3/7/2015	IrisMed	$325.00	$331.99
6/8/2015	IrisMed	$200.00	$204.30
4/18/2014	IrisMed	$235.00	$240.05
3/17/2014	IrisMed	$235.00	$239.11
3/3/2014	Medeye	$125.00	$127.19
8/12/2014	Medeye	$235.00	$239.11
7/8/2014	Medeye	$245.00	$249.29
5/3/2014	Medeye	$475.00	$483.31
10/5/2014	Medeye	$375.00	$381.56
4/4/2014	Westville	$135.00	$137.70
12/3/2014	Westville	$175.00	$178.50
3/21/2014	Westville	$195.00	$198.90
2/18/2015	Westville	$225.00	$229.50

Courtyard Medical Optometry
Patient Payment Amounts
Two-Year Financing

Amount Financed	Payment @ 1.75%	Payment @ 2.25%
$100.00	$4.24	$4.27
$400.00	$16.96	$17.07
$700.00	$29.68	$29.87
$800.00	$33.92	$34.14
$900.00	$38.16	$38.42
$1,000.00	$42.40	$42.69

2-79 Completed Excel 2-1

Courtyard Medical Plaza Pharmacy Inventory

Product ID	Description	Cost	Retail	Margin	Quantity
CMP-006	Acetaminophen	$1.25	$3.99	219%	12
CMP-012	Antibiotic ointment	$2.25	$5.99	166%	8
CMP-004	Antiseptic wash	$2.75	$4.99	81%	7
CMP-007	Bandage, 1 inch strips	$1.25	$3.99	219%	10
CMP-008	Bandage, 2 inch strips	$1.25	$3.99	219%	8
CMP-009	Bandage, assorted	$1.75	$4.99	185%	8
CMP-002	Cough drops	$0.85	$1.29	52%	12
CMP-011	Cough syrup	$2.25	$4.99	122%	9
CMP-014	Dandruff shampoo	$2.75	$5.99	118%	7
CMP-005	Disinfectant wipes	$1.25	$3.99	219%	15
CMP-010	Ibuprofen	$2.50	$3.99	60%	8
CMP-015	Insect bite gel	$3.55	$6.99	97%	15
CMP-013	Moisture lotion	$3.55	$4.99	223%	7
CMP-003	Nasal spray	$3.45	$5.99	74%	6
CMP-001	Tongue depressor	$0.55	$1.99	262%	6

Total Value at Cost	$349.55
Total Value at Retail	$588.29

Guided Project 2-2

Hamilton Civic Center (HCC) is a nonprofit community fitness center with an indoor pool, sauna, indoor track, project room, racquetball courts, meeting rooms, and a boutique. In this workbook, you complete tasks related to health seminars, a member challenge, and the daycare program.
[Student Learning Outcomes 2.1, 2.2, 2.3, 2.4, 2.5, 2.6, 2.7]

File Needed: **HamiltonCivic-02.xlsx** *[Student data files are available in the* Library *of your SIMnet account.]*
Completed Project File Name: ***[your initials] Excel 2-2.xlsx***

Skills Covered in This Project

- Create and copy formulas.
- Name cell ranges.
- Use relative and absolute references.
- Set mathematical order of operations.
- Use *AutoCalculate* and formula auditing tools.
- Use *VLOOKUP* and *HLOOKUP*.
- Create an *IF* function.
- Create a *SUMIF* function.
- Use the *TODAY* function.

1. Open the **HamiltonCivic-02.xlsx** workbook from your student data files and save it as [your initials] Excel 2-2.

2. Name cell ranges.
 a. On the *Seminars* sheet, select cells **B6:B10**, and click the **Name** box.
 b. Type Seminars in the *Name* box and press **Enter**.
 c. Click the **Data** sheet tab. You will name the cell ranges used in the *Lookup* functions.
 d. Select cells **A2:D10** and click the **Name** box.
 e. Type V_Calories in the *Name* box and press **Enter**. This will remind you that this range is a vertical table array.
 f. Select cells **F2:J3** and click the **Name** box.
 g. Type H_Fees and press **Enter**. This range is a horizontal table array.

3. Enter and copy a division formula.
 a. Select cell **D2** on the **Data** worksheet. To calculate calories per minute, divide the total calories by the number of minutes.
 b. Type an equals sign (=) to start the formula.
 c. Click cell **C2**, the total number of calories. This formula uses relative references.
 d. Type / for division.
 e. Click cell **B2**, the number of minutes, and press **Enter**. As many decimal places as fit in the cell are displayed (Figure 2-80).
 f. Drag the *Fill* pointer to copy the formula in cell **D2** to cells **D3:D10**. Ignore the *Auto Fill Options* button.
 g. While cells **D2:D10** are selected, click the **Decrease Decimal** button [*Home* tab, *Number* group] two times. The sets the same number of decimal positions for all results.

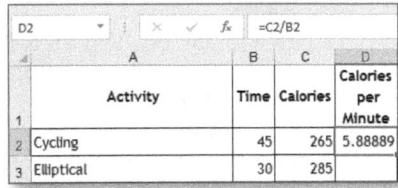

2-80 Decimal positions fill the cell

4. Use *HLOOKUP* with a range name to display fees.
 a. Click the **Seminars** worksheet tab and select cell **C6**. Fees are in the *H_Fees* range.
 b. Click the **Lookup & Reference** button [*Formulas* tab, *Function Library* group] and select **HLOOKUP**.
 c. Click the **Lookup_value** box and click cell **B6**.
 d. Click the **Table_array** box.

e. Type **h_fees** the name of the range. It is not case sensitive, and quotation marks are not necessary.

f. Click the **Row_index_num** box and type **2** because the fees are in the second row of the *H_Fees* range (Figure 2-81).

g. Click **OK**. The fee is $15.00.

h. Copy the formula in cell **C6** to cells **C7:C10**.

5. Enter and copy an addition formula.

a. Click cell **E15** and type an equals sign (=) to start the formula.

b. Click cell **D6**, the number of attendees for the seminar in Hendersonville.

c. Type **+** for addition.

d. Click cell **E6** to add the number of attendees for Advocate Central.

e. Type **+**, click cell **F6**, type **+**, and click cell **G6** (Figure 2-82).

f. Press **Enter**.

g. Drag the *Fill* pointer to copy the formula in cell **E15** to cells **E16:E19**. Ignore the *Auto Fill Options* button.

h. Click cell **E20**, click the **AutoSum** button [*Home* tab, *Editing* group], and press **Enter**. The total is 209 attendees.

6. Set order of operations in a formula.

a. Select cell **E24**. The fee is multiplied by the sum of the attendees at each hospital. Cells D6:G6 must be added first and that result is multiplied by cell C6.

b. Type **=** to start the formula and click cell **C6**.

c. Type ***** to multiply.

d. Type **(** for the opening parenthesis. This forces the addition to be carried out first.

e. Click cell **D6**, type **+**, click cell **E6**, type **+**, click cell **F6**, type **+**, and click cell **G6**.

f. Type **)** for the closing parenthesis (Figure2-83).

g. Press **Enter**. The result is 705.

h. Format cell **E24** as **Currency** and copy the formula to cells **E25:E28**.

i. Click cell **E29**, click the **AutoSum** button [*Home* tab, *Editing* group], and press **Enter**.

7. Use *AutoCalculate* and formula auditing tools.

a. Select cells **E24:E28**.

b. Compare the *SUM* in the *Status* bar with the result in cell E29.

c. Select cell **E15**.

2-81 Arguments for *HLOOKUP*

2-82 Simple addition formula

2-83 Addition done before multiplication

d. Click the **Trace Precedents** button [*Formulas* tab, *Formula Auditing* group].

e. Click the **Trace Dependents** button. The formula in cell E15 has both precedent and dependent cells (Figure 2-84).

f. Click the **Remove Arrows** button [*Formulas* tab, *Formula Auditing* group].

2-84 Precedent and dependent cells

8. Use *VLOOKUP* with a range name to display calories expended.

a. Click the **Data** sheet tab.

b. Click the **Name** box arrow and select **V_Calories**. Notice that total calories are in the third column.

c. Click the **Calorie Tracking** sheet tab and select cell **D3**. Calories by activity are within the range *V_Calories*.

d. Click the **Lookup & Reference** button [*Formulas* tab, *Formula Auditing* group] and select **VLOOKUP**.

e. Click the **Lookup_value** box and click cell **C3**. The activity name in column C will be located in the table array.

f. Click the **Table_array** box and press **F3 (FN+F3)** to open the *Paste Name* dialog box.

g. Double-click **V_Calories** to insert it.

h. Click the **Col_index_num** box and type 3 (Figure 2-85).

i. Click **OK**. Calories for the first activity are 250.

j. Copy the formula in cell **D3** to cells **D4:D23**.

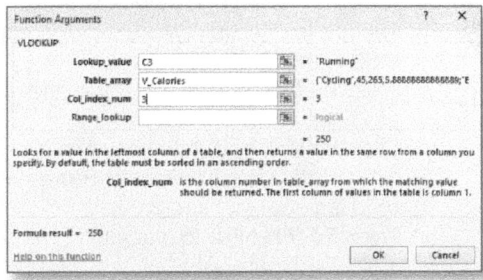

2-85 Arguments for the *VLOOKUP* function

9. Build a *SUMIF* formula with absolute and relative references.

a. Select cell **D28** on the **Calorie Tracking** sheet.

b. Click the **Recently Used** button [*Formulas* tab, *Function Library* group].

c. Look for and choose **SUMIF**. (If you do not see *SUMIF* in the list, click the **Math & Trig** button to find and select **SUMIF**.)

d. Click the **Range** box and select cells **C3:C23**, the range that will be evaluated.

e. Press **F4 (FN+F4)** to make the cell references absolute.

f. Click the **Criteria** box and select cell **C28** to find rows with "cycling" as the activity.

g. Click the **Sum_range** box and select cells **D3:D23**, the values to be summed if the activity is cycling.

h. Press **F4 (FN+F4)** to make the references absolute (Figure 2-86).
i. Click **OK**. The result is 795 calories.

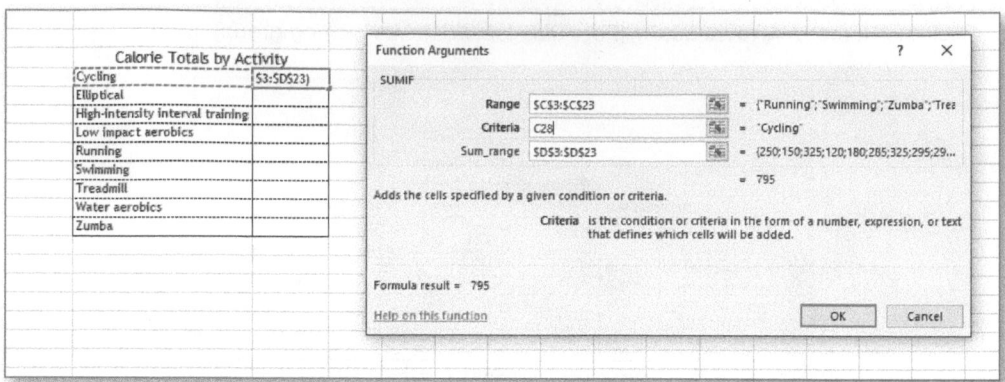

2-86 *SUMIF* **function for cycling**

10. Copy the formula in cell **D28** to cells **D29:D36** without formatting (Figure 2-87).

11. Create an *IF* function to calculate a fee based on age.
 a. Click the **Day Care** sheet tab and select cell **D5**.
 b. Click the **Logical** button [*Formulas* tab, *Function Library* group] and select **IF**.
 c. Click the **Logical_test** box and click cell **B5**.
 d. Type >=4 to test if the child is 4 years old or greater.
 e. Click the **Value_if_true** box and click cell **I9**. The fee for a child 4 years old or greater is $18.
 f. Press **F4 (FN+F4)** to make the reference absolute.
 g. Click the **Value_if_false** box and click cell **I8**. If the child is not 4 years old or greater, the child is between 1 and 3 years old.
 h. Press **F4 (FN+F4)** to make the reference absolute (Figure 2-88).
 i. Click **OK**. The fee for Mary is $18.
 j. Format the result as **Currency**.
 k. Copy the formula in cell **D5** to cells **D6:D14**.

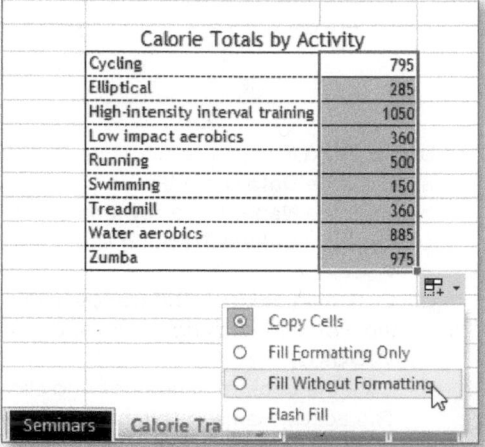

2-87 **Copy the formula without formatting**

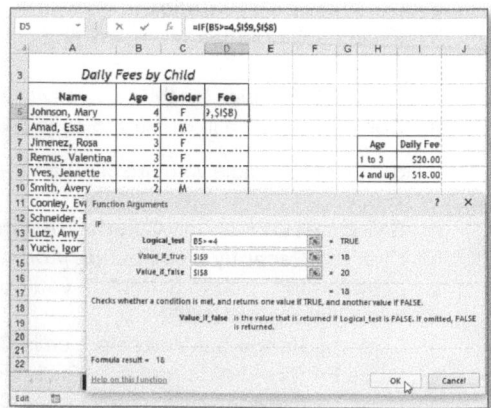

2-88 *IF* **function to determine the fee**

12. Insert the current date as a function.
 a. Click the **Data** sheet tab and click cell **A12**.
 b. Type =to and press **Tab** to select the function.
 c. Press **Enter**.
 d. Press **Ctrl+Home**.

13. Paste range names.
 a. Click the **New sheet** button in the sheet tab area.
 b. Click the **Use in Formula** button [*Formulas* tab, *Defined Names* group] and select **Paste Names**.
 c. Click the **Paste List** button in the *Paste Name* dialog box.
 d. *AutoFit* each column and name the tab Range Names.

14. Save and close the workbook (Figure 2-89).

2-89 Excel 2-2 completed

Guided Project 2-3

Sierra Pacific Community College District (SPCCD) consists of four individual community colleges. The workbook for this project includes an amortization schedule for student loans and a fee and credit hour summary for several departments.
[Student Learning Outcomes 2.1, 2.2, 2.3, 2.4, 2.5, 2.6, 2.7]

File Needed: **SierraPacific-02.xlsx** *[Student data files are available in the* Library *of your SIMnet account.]*
Completed Project File Name: **[your initials] Excel 2-3.xlsx**

Skills Covered in This Project

- Name cell ranges.
- Create and copy formulas.
- Set mathematical order of operations.
- Use absolute references in formulas.

- Insert the current date as a function.
- Use the *PMT* function.
- Audit formulas.
- Use *SUMIF* and *SUMPRODUCT*.

1. Open the **SierraPacific-02.xlsx** workbook from your student data files and save it as [your initials] Excel 2-3.

2. Set range names for the workbook.
 a. On the **Student Loan** sheet, select cells **B5:C8**.
 b. Click the **Create from Selection** button [*Formulas* tab, *Defined Names* group].
 c. Verify that the **Left column** box in the *Create Names from Selection* dialog box is selected.
 d. Deselect the **Top row** box if it is checked and click **OK**.
 e. Select cells **E5:F7**. Repeat steps a–d to create range names.
 f. Click the **Name Manager** button [*Formulas* tab, *Defined Names* group] to view the names in the *Name Manager* dialog box (Figure 2-90).
 g. Click **Close**.

2-90 *Name Manager* dialog box

3. Enter a *PMT* function.
 a. Select **C8**.
 b. Click the **Financial** button [*Formulas* tab, *Function Library* group] and select **PMT**.
 c. Click the **Rate** box and click cell **C7**. The range name *Rate* is substituted.
 d. Type /12 immediately after **Rate** to divide by 12 for monthly payments.
 e. Click the **Nper** box and click cell **C6**. The substituted range name is *Loan_Term*.
 f. Type *12 after **Loan_Term** to multiply by 12.
 g. Click the **Pv** box and type a minus sign (–) to set the argument as a negative amount.
 h. Click cell **C5** (*Loan_Amount*) for the *pv* argument. A negative loan amount reflects the lender's perspective, since the money is paid out now (Figure 2-91).

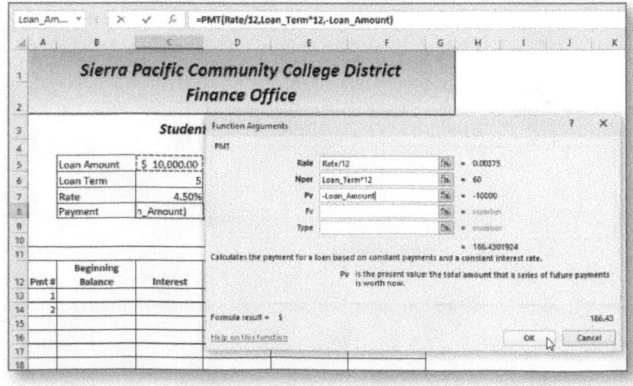

2-91 *Pv* argument is negative in the *PMT* function

 i. Leave the *Fv* and *Type* boxes empty.

 j. Click **OK**. The payment for a loan at this rate is **$186.43**, shown as a positive value.

4. Create a total interest formula.

 a. Click cell **F5** (*Total_Interest*). This value is calculated by multiplying the monthly payment by the total number of payments to determine total outlay. From this amount, you subtract the loan amount.

 b. Type = and click cell **C8** (the *Payment*).

 c. Type * to multiply and click cell **C6** (*Loan_Term*).

 d. Type *12 to multiply by 12 for monthly payments.

 e. Type − immediately after ***12** to subtract.

 f. Click cell **C5** (the *Loan_Amount*). The formula is *Payment*Loan_Term*12−Loan_Amount*. Parentheses are not required, because the multiplications are done from left to right, followed by the subtraction (Figure 2-92).

 g. Press **Enter**. The result is **$1,185.81**.

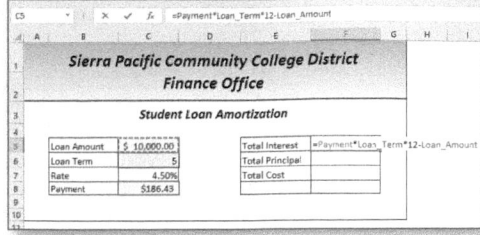

2-92 Left-to-right operations

5. Create the total principal formula and the total loan cost.

 a. Select cell **F6** (*Total_Principal*). This value is calculated by multiplying the monthly payment by the total number of payments. From this amount, subtract the total interest.

 b. Type = and click cell **C8** (the *Payment*).

 c. Type * to multiply and click cell **C6** (*Loan_Term*).

 d. Type *12 to multiply by 12 for monthly payments.

 e. Type − immediately after ***12** to subtract.

 f. Click cell **F5** (the *Total_Interest*). The formula is *Payment*Loan_Term*12−Total_Interest*.

 g. Press **Enter**. Total principal is the amount of the loan.

 h. Click cell **F7**, the *Total_Cost* of the loan. This is the total principal plus the total interest.

 i. Type =, click cell **F5**, type +, click cell **F6**, and then press **Enter**.

6. Build an amortization schedule.

 a. Click cell **B13**. The beginning balance is the total cost of the loan.

 b. Type =, click cell **F7**, and press **Enter**.

 c. Format the value as **Accounting Number Format**.

 d. Select cell **C13**. The interest for each payment is calculated by multiplying the balance in column B by the rate divided by 12.

 e. Type = and click cell **B13**.

 f. Type *(and click cell **C7**.

 g. Type /12). Parentheses are necessary so that the division is done first (Figure 2-93).

 h. Press **Enter** and format the results as **Accounting Number Format**.

 i. Select cell **D13**. The portion of the payment that is applied to the principal is calculated by subtracting the interest portion from the payment.

 j. Type =, click cell **C8** (the *Payment*).

 k. Type −, click cell **C13**, and press **Enter**.

 l. Click cell **E13**. The total payment is the interest portion plus the principal portion.

 m. Type =, click cell **C13**, type +, click cell **D13**, and then press **Enter**. The value matches the amount in cell **C8**.

 n. Select cell **F13**. The ending balance is the beginning balance minus the payment.

 o. Type =, click cell **B13**, type −, click cell **E13**, and then press **Enter**. The ending balance is **$10,999.38**.

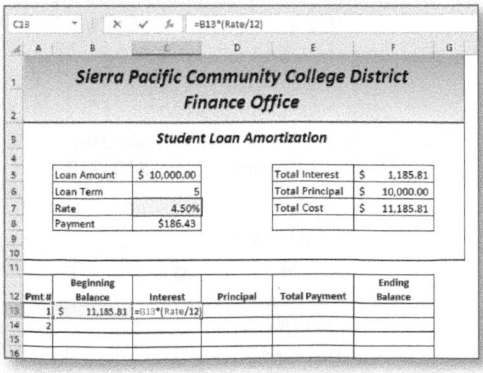

2-93 The interest formula

B13	=Total_Cost
C13	=B13*(Rate/12)
D13	=Payment−C13
E13	=C13+D13
F13	=B13−E13

7. Fill data and copy formulas.
 a. Select cells **A13:A14**. This is a series with an increment of 1.
 b. Drag the *Fill* pointer to reach cell **A72**. This sets 60 payments for a five-year loan term.
 c. Select cell **B14**. The beginning balance for the second payment is the ending balance for the first payment.
 d. Type =, click cell **F13**, and press **Enter**.
 e. Double-click the *Fill* pointer for cell **B14** to fill the formula down to row **72**. The results are zero until the rest of the schedule is complete.
 f. Select cells **C13:F13**.
 g. Double-click the *Fill* pointer at cell **F13**. All of the formulas are filled (copied) to row **72** (Figure2-94).
 h. Scroll to see the values in row **72**. The loan balance reaches 0.
 i. Press **Ctrl+Home**.

8. Build a multiplication formula and set order of mathematical operations.
 a. Click the **Fees & Credit** sheet tab and select cell **F7**. Credit hours times number of sections times the fee calculates the total fees from a course.
 b. Type =, click cell **C7**, type *, click cell **D7**, type *, click cell **E7**, and then press **Enter**. No parentheses are necessary because multiplication is done in left to right order.
 c. Select cell **G7**. Fee collected per credit hour is determined by dividing the value in cell F7 by the number of sections times credit hours times average enrollment.
 d. Type =, click cell **F7**, and type / (. Parentheses are necessary so that left to right order is overridden.
 e. Click cell **C7**, type *, and click cell **D7**.
 f. Type *, click cell **C20**, and press **F4 (FN+F4)** to make the reference absolute (Figure 2-95).
 g. Press **Enter**. A message box notes that the closing parenthesis is missing.
 h. Click **Yes** in the message box.
 i. Select cells **F7:G7** and double-click the *Fill* pointer to copy the formulas.
 j. Format cells **G7:G18** as **Currency** and set a bottom border for cells **F18:G18**.

9. Use *SUMIF*.
 a. Select cell **D26**. Fees by department can be calculated.
 b. Click the **Math & Trig** button [*Formulas* tab, *Function Library* group] and select **SUMIF**.
 c. Click the **Range** box and select cells **A7:A18**. This range will be matched against the criteria.
 d. Press **F4 (FN+F4)** to make the reference absolute.
 e. Click the **Criteria** box and type bio.
 f. Click the **Sum_range** box, select cells **F7:F18**, and press **F4 (FN+F4)**.

2-94 Formulas copied down columns

2-95 Formula to calculate fee per credit hour

g. Click **OK**. Total fees for the Biology department are 13350.

h. Format the results as **Currency**.

10. Copy a *SUMIF* function and check formula errors.

a. Click cell **D26** and drag its *Fill* pointer to copy the formula to cells **D27:D29** without formatting.

b. Double-click cell **D27**. You need to change the criteria.

c. Edit the criteria argument in the *Formula* bar or in the cell to display frl. Do not change the quotation marks or any other punctuation (Figure 2-96).

d. Press **Enter** or click the **Enter** button in the *Formula* bar. An error triangle appears in the top left corner of cell **D27**.

e. Click cell **D27** and point to its **Trace Error** button to see the *ScreenTip* (Figure 2-97). The formula has different criteria than the immediately preceding formula, but this is correct.

f. Click the **Trace Error** button and choose **Ignore Error**.

g. Double-click cell **D28** and edit the criteria argument to display ims.

h. Edit the argument in cell **D29** to show the department initials.

i. Format cells **D27:D29** as **Currency**.

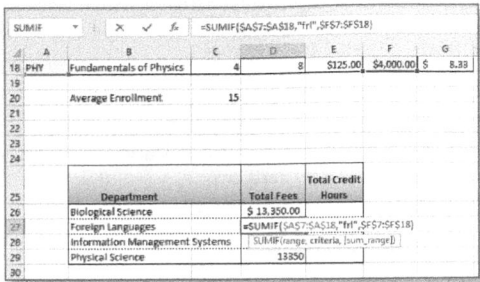

2-96 Edit the SUMIF criteria in the cell or in the *Formula* bar

11. Use *SUMPRODUCT* and trace an error.

a. Select cell **E26** and click the **Formulas** tab.

b. Click the **Math & Trig** button in the *Function Library* group and select **SUMPRODUCT**.

c. Click the **Array1** box and select cells **C7:C9**, credit hours for courses in the Biology Department.

d. Click the **Array2** box and select cells **D7:D9**, the number of sections for the Biology Department.

e. Click **OK**. The Biology Department has 98 total credit hour offerings.

f. Click cell **E26** and point to its **Trace Error** button. The formula omits adjacent cells in columns C and D, which is correct.

g. Click the **Trace Error** button and select **Ignore Error**.

2-97 *Trace Error* button and its *ScreenTip*

12. Copy and edit *SUMPRODUCT*.

a. Click cell **E26** and drag its *Fill* pointer to copy the formula to cells **E27:E29** without formatting.

b. Click cell **E27** and click the **Insert Function** button in the *Formula* bar.

c. Select and highlight the range in the *Array1* box and select cells **C10:C12**. The range you select replaces the range in the dialog box (Figure 2-98).

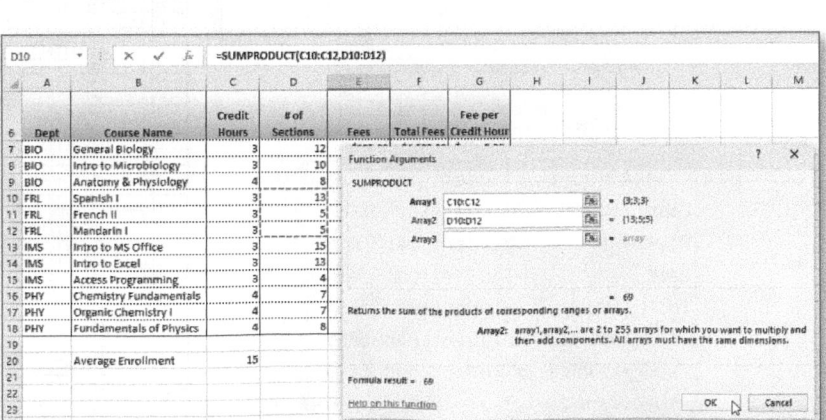

2-98 Replace the *ArrayN* arguments

 d. Select the range in the *Array2* box and select cells **D10:D12**.

 e. Click **OK**.

 f. Edit and complete the formulas in cells **E28:E29** and ignore errors.

13. Insert the current date as a function.
 a. Select cell **G30**.
 b. Type =to and press **Tab** to select the function.
 c. Press **Enter**.
 d. Press **Ctrl+Home**.

14. Paste range names.
 a. Click the **New sheet** button in the sheet tab area.
 b. Name the new sheet **Range Names**.
 c. Press **F3 (FN+F3)** to open the *Paste Name* dialog box.
 d. Click the **Paste List** button.
 e. *AutoFit* each column.

15. Save and close the workbook (Figure 2-99).

Sierra Pacific Community College District
Finance Office

Student Loan Amortization

Loan Amount	$ 10,000.00		Total Interest	$ 1,185.81
Loan Term	5		Total Principal	$ 10,000.00
Rate	4.50%		Total Cost	$ 11,185.81
Payment	$186.43			

Pmt #	Beginning Balance	Interest	Principal	Total Payment	Ending Balance
1	$ 11,185.81	$ 41.95	$ 144.48	$ 186.43	$ 10,989.38
2	$ 10,989.38	$ 41.25	$ 145.18	$ 186.43	$ 10,812.95
3	$ 10,812.95	$ 40.55	$ 145.88	$ 186.43	$ 10,626.52
4	$ 10,626.52	$ 39.85	$ 146.58	$ 186.43	$ 10,440.09
5	$ 10,440.09	$ 39.15	$ 147.28	$ 186.43	$ 10,253.66
6	$ 10,253.66	$ 38.43	$ 147.98	$ 186.43	$ 10,067.23
7	$ 10,067.23	$ 37.75	$ 148.68	$ 186.43	$ 9,880.80
8	$ 9,880.80	$ 37.05	$ 149.38	$ 186.43	$ 9,694.37
9	$ 9,694.37	$ 36.35	$ 150.08	$ 186.43	$ 9,507.94
10	$ 9,507.94	$ 35.63	$ 150.79	$ 186.43	$ 9,321.51
11	$ 9,321.51	$ 34.96	$ 151.47	$ 186.43	$ 9,135.08
12	$ 9,135.08	$ 34.26	$ 152.17	$ 186.43	$ 8,948.85
13	$ 8,948.85	$ 33.56	$ 152.87	$ 186.43	$ 8,762.22
14	$ 8,762.22	$ 32.86	$ 153.57	$ 186.43	$ 8,575.79
15	$ 8,575.79	$ 32.16	$ 154.27	$ 186.43	$ 8,389.36
16	$ 8,389.36	$ 31.46	$ 154.97	$ 186.43	$ 8,202.93
17	$ 8,202.93	$ 30.76	$ 155.67	$ 186.43	$ 8,016.50
18	$ 8,016.50	$ 30.06	$ 156.37	$ 186.43	$ 7,830.07
19	$ 7,830.07	$ 29.36	$ 157.07	$ 186.43	$ 7,643.64
20	$ 7,643.64	$ 28.66	$ 157.77	$ 186.43	$ 7,457.21
21	$ 7,457.21	$ 27.96	$ 158.47	$ 186.43	$ 7,270.78
22	$ 7,270.78	$ 27.27	$ 159.16	$ 186.43	$ 7,084.35
23	$ 7,084.35	$ 26.57	$ 159.86	$ 186.43	$ 6,897.92
24	$ 6,897.92	$ 25.87	$ 160.56	$ 186.43	$ 6,711.48
25	$ 6,711.48	$ 25.17	$ 161.26	$ 186.43	$ 6,525.06
26	$ 6,525.06	$ 24.47	$ 161.96	$ 186.43	$ 6,338.63
27	$ 6,338.63	$ 23.77	$ 162.66	$ 186.43	$ 6,152.20
28	$ 6,152.20	$ 23.07	$ 163.36	$ 186.43	$ 5,965.77
29	$ 5,965.77	$ 22.37	$ 164.06	$ 186.43	$ 5,779.34
30	$ 5,779.34	$ 21.67	$ 164.76	$ 186.43	$ 5,592.91
31	$ 5,592.91	$ 20.97	$ 165.46	$ 186.43	$ 5,406.48
32	$ 5,406.48	$ 20.27	$ 166.16	$ 186.43	$ 5,220.05
33	$ 5,220.05	$ 19.58	$ 166.86	$ 186.43	$ 5,033.62
34	$ 5,033.62	$ 18.88	$ 167.55	$ 186.43	$ 4,847.19
35	$ 4,847.19	$ 18.18	$ 168.25	$ 186.43	$ 4,660.75
36	$ 4,660.75	$ 17.48	$ 168.95	$ 186.43	$ 4,474.32
37	$ 4,474.32	$ 16.78	$ 169.65	$ 186.43	$ 4,287.89
38	$ 4,287.89	$ 16.08	$ 170.35	$ 186.43	$ 4,101.46
39	$ 4,101.46	$ 15.38	$ 171.05	$ 186.43	$ 3,915.03
40	$ 3,915.03	$ 14.68	$ 171.75	$ 186.43	$ 3,728.60
41	$ 3,728.60	$ 13.98	$ 172.45	$ 186.43	$ 3,542.17
42	$ 3,542.17	$ 13.28	$ 173.15	$ 186.43	$ 3,355.74
43	$ 3,355.74	$ 12.58	$ 173.85	$ 186.43	$ 3,169.31
44	$ 3,169.31	$ 11.88	$ 174.55	$ 186.43	$ 2,982.88
45	$ 2,982.88	$ 11.19	$ 175.24	$ 186.43	$ 2,796.45
46	$ 2,796.45	$ 10.49	$ 175.94	$ 186.43	$ 2,610.02
47	$ 2,610.02	$ 9.79	$ 176.64	$ 186.43	$ 2,423.59
48	$ 2,423.59	$ 9.09	$ 177.34	$ 186.43	$ 2,237.16
49	$ 2,237.16	$ 8.39	$ 178.04	$ 186.43	$ 2,050.73
50	$ 2,050.73	$ 7.69	$ 178.74	$ 186.43	$ 1,864.30
51	$ 1,864.30	$ 6.99	$ 179.44	$ 186.43	$ 1,677.87
52	$ 1,677.87	$ 6.29	$ 180.14	$ 186.43	$ 1,491.44
53	$ 1,491.44	$ 5.59	$ 180.84	$ 186.43	$ 1,305.01
54	$ 1,305.01	$ 4.89	$ 181.54	$ 186.43	$ 1,118.58
55	$ 1,118.58	$ 4.19	$ 182.24	$ 186.43	$ 932.15
56	$ 932.15	$ 3.50	$ 182.93	$ 186.43	$ 745.72
57	$ 745.72	$ 2.80	$ 183.63	$ 186.43	$ 559.29
58	$ 559.29	$ 2.10	$ 184.33	$ 186.43	$ 372.86
59	$ 372.86	$ 1.40	$ 185.03	$ 186.43	$ 186.43
60	$ 186.43	$ 0.70	$ 185.73	$ 186.43	$ 0.00

Sierra Pacific Community College District
Credit Hours and Fees by Department

Dept	Course Name	Credit Hours	# of Sections	Fees	Total Fees	Fee per Credit Hour
BIO	General Biology	3	12	$125.00	$4,500.00	$ 8.33
BIO	Intro to Microbiology	3	10	$135.00	$4,050.00	$ 9.00
BIO	Anatomy & Physiology	4	8	$150.00	$4,800.00	$ 10.00
FRL	Spanish I	3	13	555.00	$2,145.00	$ 3.67
FRL	French II	3	5	555.00	$825.00	$ 3.67
FRL	Mandarin I	3	5	555.00	$825.00	$ 3.67
IMS	Intro to MS Office	3	15	575.00	$3,375.00	$ 5.00
IMS	Intro to Excel	3	13	575.00	$2,925.00	$ 5.00
IMS	Access Programming	3	4	575.00	$900.00	$ 5.00
PHY	Chemistry Fundamentals	4	7	$125.00	$3,500.00	$ 8.33
PHY	Organic Chemistry I	4	7	$150.00	$4,200.00	$ 10.00
PHY	Fundamentals of Physics	4	8	$125.00	$4,000.00	$ 8.33

Average Enrollment 15

Department	Total Fees	Total Credit Hours
Biological Science	$ 13,350.00	98
Foreign Languages	$ 3,795.00	69
Information Management Systems	$ 7,200.00	96
Physical Science	$ 11,700.00	88

Loan_Amount	='Student Loan'!C5
Loan_Term	='Student Loan'!C6
Payment	='Student Loan'!C8
Rate	='Student Loan'!C7
Total_Cost	='Student Loan'!F7
Total_Interest	='Student Loan'!F5
Total_Principal	='Student Loan'!F6

2-99 Completed Excel 2-3

Independent Project 2-4

Central Sierra Insurance (CSI) sets bonus percentages based on commissions earned by each agent and calculates totals by branch office. This workbook also tracks fundraising efforts of employees for a community event.
[Student Learning Outcomes 2.1, 2.2, 2.3, 2.5, 2.6, 2.7]

File Needed: **CentralSierra-02.xlsx** *[Student data files are available in the Library of your SIMnet account.]*
Completed Project File Name: **[your initials] Excel 2-4.xlsx**

Skills Covered in This Project

- Create, copy, and edit formulas.
- Name cell ranges.
- Set mathematical order of operations.

- Set cell references to be absolute.
- Use the *NOW* function.
- Use *HLOOKUP* and *VLOOKUP* functions.
- Use the *SUMIF* function.
- Build an *IF* function.

1. Open the **CentralSierra-02.xlsx** workbook from your student data files and save it as [your initials] Excel 2-4. Review the data on each sheet.

2. On the **Tables** sheet, select cells **A6:B10** and create range names from this selection.

3. Select cells **B1:F2** and click the **Name** box. Name this as H_Rates.

4. Create an *HLOOKUP* function to display the bonus rate.
 a. Click the **Commissions** sheet tab and select cell **F5**.
 b. Start the *HLOOKUP* function and use cell **E5** as the *lookup_value*.
 c. For the *table_array* argument, use the **H_Rates** range.
 d. Use the second row for the *row_index_num* argument (Figure 2-100).

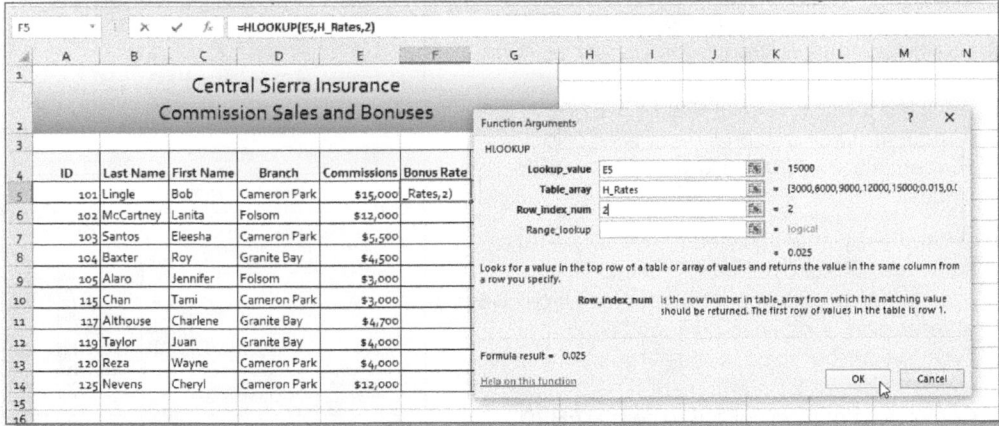

2-100 *HLOOKUP* function to display bonus rate

5. Format the results as **Percent Style** with two decimal places.

6. Copy the formula in cell **F5** to cells **F6:F14**.

7. Set order of operations to calculate total earnings.
 a. Select cell **G5**.
 b. Build a formula to add the commissions amount (E5) to the commissions amount times the rate (F5*E5). Use parentheses to set the multiplication as the first calculation.
 c. Copy the formula in cell **G5** to cells **G6:G14**.

8. Create and copy a *SUMIF* function to calculate total earnings by branch office.
 a. Select cell **E18**.
 b. Start the *SUMIF* function with cells **D5:D14** as the *Range* argument.
 c. The *Criteria* argument is a relative reference to cell **C18**.
 d. Select cells **G5:G14** for the *Sum_range* argument and make the references absolute.
 e. Copy the formula in cell **E18** to cells **E19:E20** without formatting.
 f. Format cells **E18:E20** as **Currency**.

9. Total the earnings in cell **E21**.

10. Create and format the current date.
 a. Select cell **G23** and insert the *NOW* function.
 b. Select cell **G23** and click the **Number** group launcher [*Home* tab]. On the *Number* tab, select the **Date** category.
 c. Scroll the *Type* list to find the date that displays the month spelled out, the date, a comma, and a four-digit year (Figure 2-101).
 d. Click **OK**. Press **Ctrl+Home**.

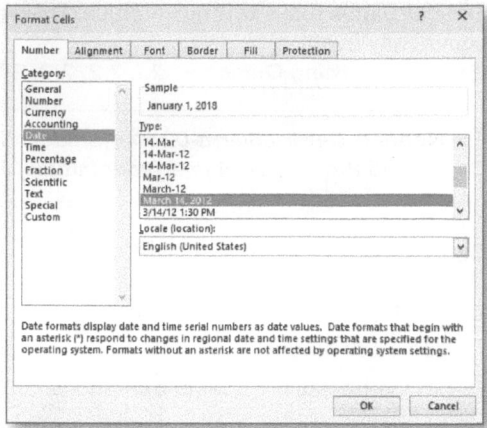

2-101 Date format selected

11. Create and copy a *VLOOKUP* function to display goals for each funding source.
 a. Click the **Family Day** sheet tab and select cell **F6**.
 b. Start the *VLOOKUP* function and use cell **E6** as the *lookup_value*.
 c. Click the **Tables** sheet tab for the *table_array* argument and use cells **A6:B10**.
 d. Use the second column as the *col_index_num* argument.
 e. Copy the formula in cell **F6** to cells **F7:F20** without formatting to preserve the fill color.
 f. Format cells **F7:F20** as **Currency** with no decimal places.

12. Create and copy an *IF* function.
 a. Select cell **H6** and start an *IF* function.
 b. Type a *logical_argument* to determine if cell **G6** is greater than or equal to (>=) cell **F6**.
 c. Type **Yes** as the *Value_if_true* argument and **No** as the *Value_if_false* argument.
 d. Copy the formula in cell **H6** to cells **H7:H20** without formatting to maintain the fill color.
 e. Center align cells **H6:H20**.
 f. Press **Ctrl+Home**.

13. Insert a new sheet at the end of the tab names and paste the range names starting in cell A1. Name the worksheet as Range Names.

14. Save and close the workbook (Figure 2-102).

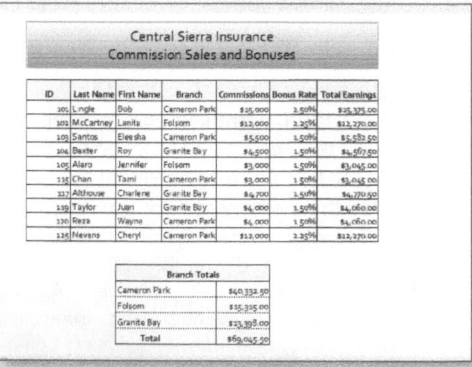

2-102 Excel 2-4 completed

Independent Project 2-5

San Diego Sailing keeps data about its fleet of rental and charter boats in a workbook. One of the sheets is missing a piece of data and another sheet has circular reference errors. You will complete work on these sheets, calculate projected rates for each boat, and build basic statistics about past rentals. [Student Learning Outcomes 2.1, 2.2, 2.3, 2.4, 2.5, 2.6, 2.7]

File Needed: **SanDiegoSailing-02.xlsx** [Student data files are available in the Library of your SIMnet account.]
Completed Project File Name: **[your initials] Excel 2-5.xlsx**

Skills Covered in This Project

- Create and copy formulas.
- Use formula auditing tools.
- Set mathematical order of operations.
- Use relative, mixed, and 3D cell references.
- Use *COUNTIF* and *SUMIF* functions.
- Build an *IF* formula.
- Insert the *TODAY* function.

1. Open the **SanDiegoSailing-02.xlsx** workbook from your student data files. When a workbook has a circular reference, a message box appears immediately as you open it (Figure 2-103).

2-103 Circular reference message

2. Click **OK** in the message box. There is a message in the *Status* bar that there are *Circular References*.

3. Save the workbook as [your initials] Excel 2-5. Review the data on each sheet.

4. Use formula auditing tools.
 a. Click the **New Prices** sheet tab and review the *Status* bar.
 b. Click cell **D5**. The formula should be 1 plus the value in cell D4.
 c. Click the **Formulas** tab and click the **Trace Precedents** button in the *Formula Auditing* group. The worksheet icon means that the formula has a 3D reference to another sheet.
 d. Click the **Evaluate Formula** button [*Formula Auditing* group]. The circular reference is identified (Figure 2-104).
 e. Click **Close** and click the **Remove Arrows** button [*Formula Auditing* group].

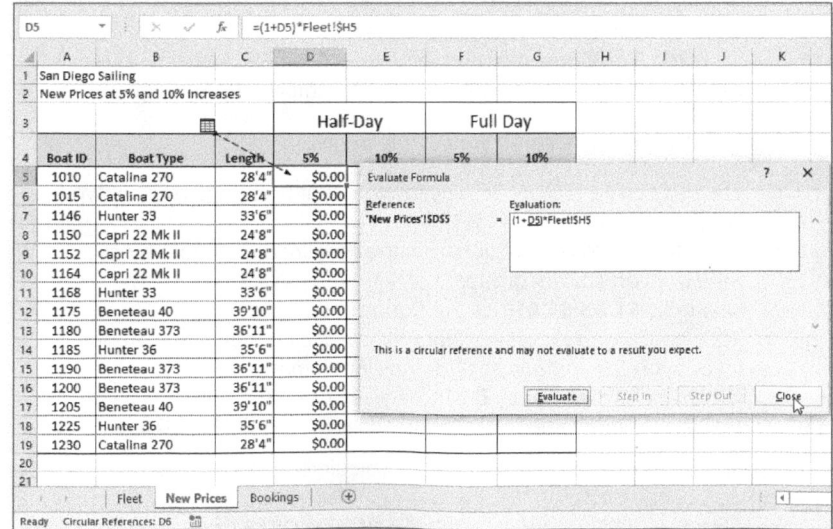

2-104 *Evaluate Formula* dialog box

5. Edit and copy a formula with mixed references.
 a. Edit the formula in cell D5 to show D$4 instead of "D5." The formula multiplies one plus the percentage value in cell D4 by the current rate on the **Fleet** sheet ($H5). With an absolute reference to row 4 and column H on the **Fleet** sheet, you can copy the formula down the column (Figure 2-105).
 b. Copy the formula in cell **D5** to cells **D6:D19** without formatting to preserve the border. When the circular reference message box opens, click **OK**.
 c. Select cells **D5:D19** and drag the *Fill* pointer to copy the formulas to cells **E5:E19**.
 d. Click cell **E6**. The formula is adjusted to use the percentage value in cell E4. Note also that the reference on the **Fleet** sheet ($H6) is adjusted to show the correct row.

2-105 Mixed reference in the edited formula

6. Build a formula with mixed references.
 a. Click cell **F5** and type =(1+ to start the formula.
 b. Select cell **F4** and make it an absolute reference to the row but not the column.
 c. Type)* for the closing parenthesis and multiplication.
 d. Click cell **I5** on the **Fleet** sheet, and make the reference absolute for the column but not the row (Figure 2-106).
 e. Copy the formula down column F without formatting to preserve the border.
 f. Format cells **F5:F19** as **Currency** and then copy cells **F5:F19** to cells **G5:G19**.

2-106 Mixed references in the new formula

7. Build an *IF* function formula.
 a. Click the **Fleet** sheet tab and select cell **G5**. Rental boats must be able to seat 8 or more people to have a stove in the galley.
 b. Create an *IF* function in which the *logical_test* argument determines if there are 8 or more seats.
 c. Use **Yes** for the *value_if_true* argument. Use **No** for the *value_if_false* argument.
 d. Copy the formula to cells **G6:G19** without formatting and then center the data in column G.

8. Insert the *TODAY* function in cell **B21**. Format the date to show the month spelled out, the date, and four digits for the year.

9. Create a division formula.
 a. Click the **Bookings** sheet tab and select cell **F5**. Average revenue per passenger can be determined by dividing the fee by the number of passengers.
 b. Build the division formula.
 c. Copy the formula in cell **F5** to cells **F6:F19**.

10. Create and copy a *COUNTIF* function to count bookings by boat type.
 a. Select cell **D27**.
 b. Start the *COUNTIF* function from the *Statistical* category by clicking the **More Functions** button in the *Function Library* group.
 c. Use cells **C5:C19** as the *Range* argument.
 d. To set a *Criteria* argument that will select all boats in the "Beneteau" group, the criteria is **ben***. If you type the formula, include quotation marks.
 e. Copy the formula in cell **D27** to cells **D28:D30**.
 f. Edit the criteria in each copied formula in cells **D28:D30** to reflect the boat type.

11. Create and copy a *SUMIF* function to calculate total revenue by boat type.
 a. Select cell **E27**.
 b. Start the *SUMIF* function with cells **C5:C19** as the *Range*.

 c. The *Criteria* is ben*.

 d. The *Sum_range* is cells **E5:E19**.

 e. Copy the formula in cell **E27** to cells **E28:E30**.

 f. Edit the criteria in each copied formula in cells **E28:E30** as needed.

12. Complete formatting.

 a. Apply the **Currency** format to all values that represent money.

 b. Format the labels in cells **A1:A2** as **18** point.

 c. Select cells **A1:F2** and center them across the selection.

 d. Merge and center the label in cell **C25** over cells C25:E25 and format it at **16** points.

 e. Bold and center the labels in rows **4** and **26**.

 f. Select cells **A4:F19** and apply **All Borders**. Do the same for cells **C25:E30**.

 g. Center the page horizontally.

13. Save and close the workbook (Figure 2-107).

San Diego Sailing Bookings
Revenue per Passenger

Date	Boat ID	Boat Type	# of Passengers	Total Fees	Revenue per Passenger
4/5/2016	1010	Catalina 270	4	$525.00	$131.25
4/8/2016	1015	Catalina 270	6	$850.00	$141.67
4/11/2016	1146	Hunter 33	6	$500.00	$83.33
4/14/2016	1150	Capri 22 Mk II	6	$525.00	$87.50
4/17/2016	1152	Capri 22 Mk II	4	$325.00	$81.25
4/20/2016	1164	Capri 22 Mk II	3	$475.00	$158.33
4/23/2016	1168	Hunter 33	6	$725.00	$120.83
4/26/2016	1175	Beneteau 40	10	$850.00	$85.00
4/29/2016	1180	Beneteau 373	8	$350.00	$43.75
5/2/2016	1185	Hunter 36	8	$650.00	$81.25
5/5/2016	1190	Beneteau 373	10	$625.00	$62.50
5/8/2016	1200	Beneteau 373	8	$725.00	$90.63
5/11/2016	1205	Beneteau 40	12	$850.00	$70.83
5/14/2016	1225	Hunter 36	8	$725.00	$90.63
5/17/2016	1230	Catalina 270	6	$675.00	$112.50

Bookings by Type

	Count	Total Revenue
Beneteau	5	$3,400.00
Capri 22 Mk II	3	$1,325.00
Catalina 270	3	$2,050.00
Hunter	4	$2,600.00

San Diego Sailing
Rental and Charter Fleet

Boat ID	Boat Type	Length	Model Year	Seats	Sleeps	Galley with Stove	Half-Day Rate	Full Day Rate
1010	Catalina 270	28'4"	2000	8	6	Yes	$375.00	$650.00
1015	Catalina 270	28'4"	2001	8	6	Yes	$425.00	$725.00
1146	Hunter 33	33'6"	2004	10	6	Yes	$350.00	$500.00
1150	Capri 22 Mk II	24'8"	2005	6	4	No	$325.00	$500.00
1152	Capri 22 Mk II	24'8"	2005	6	4	No	$325.00	$500.00
1164	Capri 22 Mk II	24'8"	2006	6	4	No	$325.00	$500.00
1168	Hunter 33	33'6"	2007	10	6	Yes	$425.00	$725.00
1175	Beneteau 40	39'10"	2008	12	6	Yes	$489.00	$750.00
1180	Beneteau 373	36'11"	2009	10	6	Yes	$369.00	$725.00
1185	Hunter 36	35'6"	2009	10	6	Yes	$349.00	$550.00
1190	Beneteau 373	36'11"	2010	10	6	Yes	$369.00	$625.00
1200	Beneteau 373	36'11"	2010	10	6	Yes	$369.00	$625.00
1205	Beneteau 40	39'10"	2012	12	6	Yes	$489.00	$750.00
1225	Hunter 36	35'6"	2012	10	6	Yes	$349.00	$725.00
1230	Catalina 270	28'4"	2012	8	6	Yes	$439.00	$675.00

San Diego Sailing
New Prices at 5% and 10% increases

Boat ID	Boat Type	Length	Half-Day 5%	Half-Day 10%	Full Day 5%	Full Day 10%
1010	Catalina 270	28'4"	$393.75	$412.50	$682.50	$715.00
1015	Catalina 270	28'4"	$446.25	$467.50	$761.25	$797.50
1146	Hunter 33	33'6"	$367.50	$385.00	$525.00	$550.00
1150	Capri 22 Mk II	24'8"	$341.25	$357.50	$525.00	$550.00
1152	Capri 22 Mk II	24'8"	$341.25	$357.50	$525.00	$550.00
1164	Capri 22 Mk II	24'8"	$341.25	$357.50	$525.00	$550.00
1168	Hunter 33	33'6"	$446.25	$467.50	$761.25	$797.50
1175	Beneteau 40	39'10"	$513.45	$537.90	$787.50	$825.00
1180	Beneteau 373	36'11"	$387.45	$405.90	$761.25	$797.50
1185	Hunter 36	35'6"	$366.45	$383.90	$577.50	$605.00
1190	Beneteau 373	36'11"	$387.45	$405.90	$656.25	$687.50
1200	Beneteau 373	36'11"	$387.45	$405.90	$656.25	$687.50
1205	Beneteau 40	39'10"	$513.45	$537.90	$787.50	$825.00
1225	Hunter 36	35'6"	$366.45	$383.90	$761.25	$797.50
1230	Catalina 270	28'4"	$460.95	$482.90	$708.75	$742.50

2-107 Excel 2-5 completed

Independent Project 2-6

Placer Hills Real Estate has regional offices throughout central California, and each office tracks its listings and sales data. In the workbook, you need to insert agent names, calculate market days, and determine sale price as a percentage of list price. You also calculate summary statistics.
[Student Learning Outcomes 2.1, 2.3, 2.5, 2.6, 2.7]

File Needed: **PlacerHills-02.xlsx** *[Student data files are available in the Library of your SIMnet account.]*
Completed Project File Name: ***[your initials] Excel 2-6.xlsx***

Skills Covered in This Project

- Create and copy formulas.
- Use dates in a subtraction formula.
- Name cell ranges.

- Use relative and 3D cell references in formulas.
- Use the *VLOOKUP* function.
- Use *AVERAGE*, *MAX*, *MIN*, and *COUNT*.
- Use *COUNTIF*.

1. Open the **PlacerHills-02.xlsx** workbook from your student data files and save it as [your initials] Excel 2-6. Review the data on each sheet.

2. Build a subtraction formula with dates.
 a. Select cell **N4** on the **Listings** sheet. You can subtract the older date from the later date to determine the number of days on the market.
 b. Type = and click cell **M4**, the sold date.
 c. Type − for subtraction and click cell **B4**, the listing date.
 d. Press **Enter**. The result is formatted as a date (Figure 2-108).

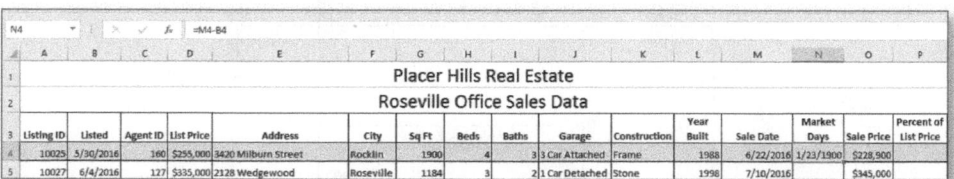

2-108 Result is formatted as a date

 e. Copy the formula in cell **N4** to cells **N5:N12** without formatting to preserve the fill color.
 f. Format cells **N4:N12** as **General**.

3. Calculate the sold price as a percentage of the list price.
 a. Select cell **P4** and type =.
 b. Build a formula to divide the selling price by the list price.
 c. Copy the formula without formatting and format the column as **Percent Style** with **two** decimal places.

4. Use the *VLOOKUP* function to insert the agent's last name in a new column.
 a. Insert a column at column **D**.
 b. Type Name in cell **D3** and click cell **D4**.
 c. Start a *VLOOKUP* function and set the agent ID (C4) as the *lookup_value* argument.
 d. Use an absolute reference to cells **A2:B7** on the **Agents** sheet for the *table_array* argument. Do not include column titles in a table array.
 e. Enter the appropriate number for the *col_index_num* argument to display the agent's last name.
 f. Copy the formula without formatting to display each agent's name and *AutoFit* the column width.

5. Name cell ranges.
 a. Select cells **E3:E12**.
 b. Press **Ctrl** and select cells **G3:G12**, **L3:L12**, and **P3:P12**.
 c. Click the **Create from Selection** button [*Formulas* tab, *Defined Names* group] and use the **Top row** to create range names.

d. Press **Ctrl+Home**.

e. Set this sheet to fit one page, landscape orientation.

f. Insert a footer that displays your name in the right section.

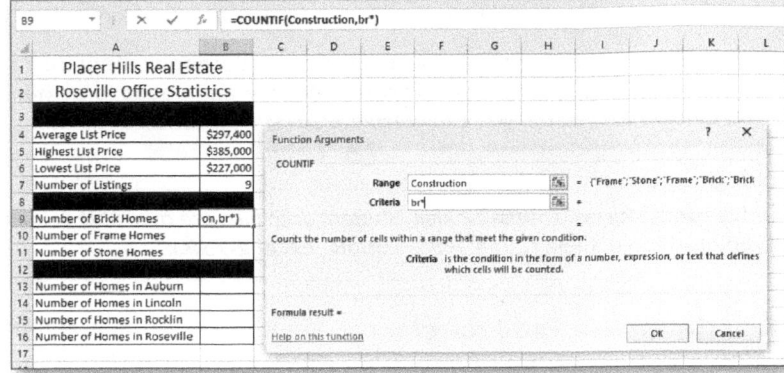

2-109 Arguments for COUNTIF

6. Calculate statistics for the agency.

a. Click the **Statistics** sheet tab and select cell **B4**.

b. Click the **AutoSum** button arrow and choose *Average*. There is no assumed range.

c. Press **F3 (FN+F3)** to open the *Paste Name* dialog box.

d. Choose **List_Price** and click **OK**. Press **Enter**.

e. Continue on this sheet to calculate the highest and lowest list prices as well as the number of listings. Be careful to select the correct range name.

7. Use *COUNTIF* to calculate statistics.

a. Select cell **B9**.

b. Click the **More Functions** button in the *Function Library* group, choose **Statistical**, and select **COUNTIF**.

c. For the *Range* argument, use the range name **Construction** (Figure 2-109).

d. Type br* for the *Criteria* and click **OK**.

e. Copy the formula and edit the criteria for cells **B10:B11**.

f. Start a new *COUNTIF* function in cell **B13** with the appropriate range name. Then copy and edit the formula for cells **B14:B16**. Be sure to use criteria that will distinguish between the two city names that begin with "ro."

8. Center the sheet horizontally. Add a footer with your name in the center section.

9. Save and close the workbook (Figure 2-110).

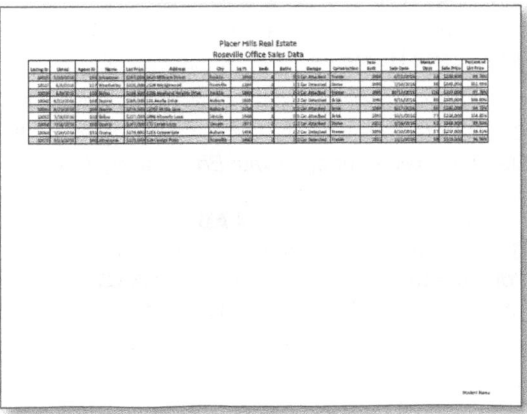

2-110 Excel 2-6 completed

Improve It Project 2-7

Mary's Rentals serves light-to-heavy equipment rental needs of contractors as well as the general public. Data has been imported from an Access database and needs to be handled for better management in Excel. Once that is done, you can calculate several statistics for the company.
[Student Learning Outcomes 2.1, 2.3, 2.4, 2.5, 2.7]

File Needed: ***MarysRentals-02.xlsx*** *[Student data files are available in the* Library *of your SIMnet account.]*
Completed Project File Name: ***[your initials] Excel 2-7.xlsx***

Skills Covered in This Project

- Use formula auditing tools.
- Name cell ranges.
- Create, copy, and edit formulas.

- Use relative references and range names in formulas.
- Use *Statistical* functions.
- Use functions from the *Math & Trig* category.

1. Open the ***MarysRentals-02.xlsx*** workbook from your student data files and save it as [your initials] Excel 2-7. The *Equipment* sheet is an inventory of equipment available for rental.

2. Correct errors on the *Rentals* sheet.
 a. Click the **Rentals** tab. This data was imported from an Access database, and there are error triangles in many cells.
 b. Select cells **A2:A47** and click the **Trace Error** button near cell A2 (Figure 2-111). This data was imported as text (labels) but should be set as values.
 c. Select **Convert to Number**. The data is formatted as a value and is right-aligned.
 d. Repeat for cells **B2:C47**.
 e. Center align cells **E2:E47**. This column specifies whether the rental was daily, weekly, or monthly.
 f. Press **Ctrl+Home**.

3. Name cell ranges.
 a. Select cells **B1:B47**, press **Ctrl**, and select cells **E1:E47** and cells **I1:I47**.
 b. Create names from the selection.
 c. Press **Ctrl+Home**.

4. Create and copy a *SUMIF* function with a relative reference.
 a. Click the **Generators** sheet tab and select cell **C5**.
 b. Start the *SUMIF* function with *Equipment_ID* as the *Range* argument.
 c. The *Criteria* argument is cell **A5**.
 d. The *Sum_range* argument is the *Total_Cost* range.
 e. Copy the formula in cell **C5** to cells **C6:C7**. The relative cell reference to cell A5 is adjusted.
 f. Format cells **C5:C7** as **Currency** with no decimal places.

5. Build a custom border.
 a. Select cells **A4:C7**.
 b. Press **Ctrl+1** to open the *Format Cells* dialog box and click the **Border** tab.
 c. In the *Presets* section, click the **Outline** button.
 d. In the *Style* section, click the dotted line style (second option, first column, just below *None*).

2-111 *Trace Error* button for a selected range

 e. Click the middle horizontal position in the *Border* preview area.

 f. In the *Style* section, click the single solid line style (last option, first column).

 g. Click the middle vertical position in the *Border* preview area (Figure 2-112).

 h. Click **OK**.

6. Complete formatting.

 a. Apply bold and centering to cells **A4:C4**.

 b. Format cells **A1:A2** to **16** points.

 c. Select cells **A1:C2** and use **Center Across Selection**.

 d. Center the sheet horizontally.

 e. Insert a header with your name in the right section.

2-112 Build a custom border in the *Format Cells* dialog box

7. Use *SUMIF* to calculate daily, weekly, and monthly income rentals.

 a. Click the **Income Data** sheet tab and select cell **B4**.

 b. Start the *SUMIF* function with **Type** as the *Range* argument.

 c. Type d for daily income as the *Criteria* argument.

 d. The *Total_Cost* range is the *Sum_range* argument.

 e. In cells **B5:B6**, enter *SUMIF* formulas or copy and edit the formula in cell B4.

 f. Use *SUM* in cell **B7**.

 g. Format cells **B4:B7** as **Currency** with no decimal places.

8. Use *COUNTIF* to count rentals by type.

 a. Select cell **B9** and start the *COUNTIF* function from the *Statistical* category.

 b. Use the range name **Type** as the *Range* argument. The *Criteria* is d.

 c. Create a separate formula in cells **B10:B11**, or copy and edit the formula in cell B9.

9. Add a border and fill.

 a. Select cells **A3:B12**.

 b. Click the **Font** group launcher [*Home* tab] and click the **Border** tab.

 c. Click the **Outline** button in the *Presets* section.

 d. In the *Style* section, click the single solid line style (last option, first column).

 e. Click the middle vertical position in the *Border* preview area.

 f. In the *Style* section, click the dotted line style (second option, first column).

 g. Click the middle horizontal position in the *Border* preview area.

 h. Click **OK**.

 i. Select cells **A3:B3, A8:B8**, and **A12:B12**.

 j. Click the arrow with the **Fill Color** button and choose **Black, Text 1, Lighter 50%**.

 k. Select cells **A1:B2** and use **Center Across Selection**.

 l. Increase the font size for cells **A1:B2** to **16**.

 m. Center the sheet horizontally.

 n. Insert a footer with your name in the right section.

10. Save and close the workbook (Figure 2-113).

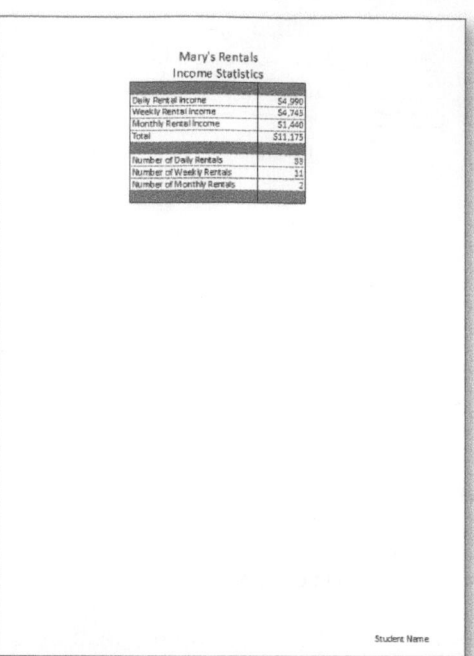

Mary's Rentals
Income Statistics

Daily Rental Income	54,990
Weekly Rental Income	54,745
Monthly Rental Income	51,440
Total	$11,175
Number of Daily Rentals	33
Number of Weekly Rentals	11
Number of Monthly Rentals	2

Student Name

Rental ID	Equipment ID	Customer ID	Date Out	Type	# of Units
2512	9063	27	04-Jan-17	D	1
2513	10233	80	04-Jan-17	D	2
2513	10389	80	04-Jan-17	D	2
2514	10236	102	05-Jan-17	D	2
2514	10237	102	05-Jan-17	D	1
2515	10283	83	05-Jan-17	W	1
2516	10047	15	06-Jan-17	D	4
2517	10103	21	06-Jan-17	W	1
2518	9063	102	07-Jan-17	W	1
2519	10015	44	07-Jan-17	D	3
2520	10388	73	07-Jan-17	D	2
2521	10426	17	08-Jan-17	D	4
2522	10237	56	08-Jan-17	W	1
2522	10425	56	08-Jan-17	W	1
2523	10426	8	08-Jan-17	D	2
2524	10015	31	09-Jan-17	D	2
2525	10398	124	10-Jan-17	D	3
2526	10233	111	10-Jan-17	D	1
2527	10013	30	12-Jan-17	D	3
2527	10047	30	12-Jan-17	D	3
2527	10233	30	12-Jan-17	D	3
2527	10281	30	12-Jan-17	D	3
2528	10236	39	13-Jan-17	W	1
2529	10389	27	13-Jan-17	D	2
2530	10233	94	13-Jan-17	D	1
2530	10427	94	13-Jan-17	D	1
2531	10283	15	13-Jan-17	W	1
2532	9063	73	15-Jan-17	D	1
2533	10103	62	15-Jan-17	M	1
2534	10426	68	15-Jan-17	D	1
2535	10426	91	16-Jan-17	D	1
2536	10047	46	17-Jan-17	W	1
2537	10233	102	17-Jan-17	D	2
2538	10237	63	17-Jan-17	D	3
2538	10389	83	17-Jan-17	D	3
2539	10388	31	17-Jan-17	D	2
2540	10426	21	17-Jan-17	D	1
2541	9063	38	17-Jan-17	M	1
2542	10013	31	18-Jan-17	W	1
2543	9063	44	19-Jan-17	W	1
2544	10388	124	19-Jan-17	W	1
2545	10233	27	19-Jan-17	D	2
2546	10423	111	20-Jan-17	D	3
2547	10426	30	20-Jan-17	W	1
2548	10427	113	20-Jan-17	D	2
2549	10236	94	20-Jan-17	D	2

Date Due	Rate	Total Cost
05-Jan-17	$160.00	$160.00
07-Jan-17	$10.00	$30.00
07-Jan-17	$60.00	$180.00
06-Jan-17	$35.00	$35.00
06-Jan-17	$200.00	$200.00
12-Jan-17	$480.00	$480.00
10-Jan-17	$225.00	$900.00
13-Jan-17	$360.00	$360.00
14-Jan-17	$640.00	$640.00
10-Jan-17	$30.00	$90.00
09-Jan-17	$15.00	$30.00
12-Jan-17	$35.00	$140.00
16-Jan-17	$800.00	$800.00
16-Jan-17	$120.00	$120.00
11-Jan-17	$40.00	$80.00
12-Jan-17	$30.00	$30.00
13-Jan-17	$15.00	$45.00
11-Jan-17	$10.00	$10.00
15-Jan-17	$30.00	$90.00
15-Jan-17	$225.00	$675.00
15-Jan-17	$10.00	$30.00
15-Jan-17	$120.00	$360.00
19-Jan-17	$140.00	$140.00
15-Jan-17	$60.00	$120.00
14-Jan-17	$10.00	$10.00
14-Jan-17	$120.00	$120.00
22-Jan-17	$480.00	$480.00
16-Jan-17	$160.00	$160.00
13-Feb-17	$1,080.00	$1,080.00
16-Jan-17	$35.00	$35.00
17-Jan-17	$40.00	$40.00
24-Jan-17	$900.00	$900.00
18-Jan-17	$10.00	$10.00
20-Jan-17	$200.00	$600.00
20-Jan-17	$60.00	$180.00
18-Jan-17	$15.00	$15.00
18-Jan-17	$35.00	$35.00
18-Jan-17	$160.00	$160.00
19-Feb-17	$360.00	$360.00
26-Jan-17	$640.00	$640.00
26-Jan-17	$45.00	$45.00
21-Jan-17	$10.00	$20.00
23-Jan-17	$30.00	$90.00
27-Jan-17	$140.00	$140.00
22-Jan-17	$120.00	$240.00
22-Jan-17	$35.00	$70.00

Student Name

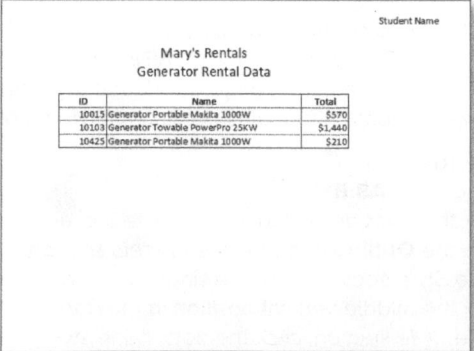

Mary's Rentals
Generator Rental Data

ID	Name	Total
10015	Generator Portable Makita 1000W	$570
10103	Generator Towable PowerPro 25KW	$1,440
10425	Generator Portable Makita 1000W	$210

2-113 Excel 2-7 completed

Challenge Project 2-8

For this project, you create a workbook for a hair products company that includes an inventory list and an invoice form. You use *VLOOKUP* to enter the cost of the product on the invoice and then calculate a total with taxes for each product.
[Student Learning Outcomes 2.1, 2.2, 2.3, 2.5, 2.6]

File Needed: None
Completed Project File Name: *[your initials] Excel 2-8.xlsx*

Create and save a workbook as [your initials] Excel 2-8. Modify your workbook according to the following guidelines:

- In cell **A1**, type a name for the hair products company. In cell **A2**, type Customer Invoice. In cells **A4:D4**, enter these labels: Product ID, Cost, Quantity, and Total with Tax. Do not include a comma or a period. Name this sheet tab Invoice.
- Insert a new sheet and name it Stock. In cells **A1:C1**, enter labels for Product ID, Name, and Cost with no punctuation.
- In cells **A2:C11**, enter data for ten products that can be purchased from your company. Use *AutoFill* to create a series for the *Product ID*. Since this range will be used as the table array in a *VLOOKUP* function, the product IDs must be in ascending order, either A to Z or low value to high value. Name the cell range Stock (without the labels in row 1).
- Below the *Stock* range, enter Tax Rate as a label. In a cell either to the right or below the label, enter 3.75% as the rate.
- On the *Invoice* sheet, type any three of the product IDs in cells **A5:A7**. Use *VLOOKUP* in column B to display the cost. In the *Quantity* column, type three values to indicate the number ordered.
- In the *Total with Tax* column, build a formula to multiply the cost by the quantity ordered. This result should be multiplied by one plus the tax rate on the *Stock* sheet. Show a grand total in row 8.
- Use the *TODAY* function in cell **A10** on the *Invoice* sheet and format the date to show the date, the month with a three-letter abbreviation, and the year as two-digits.
- Complete formatting on the *Invoice* sheet. Select a workbook theme if desired, use cell styles, or build your own designs.
- Add a header that shows your name in the right section.
- Set document properties to show your name as the author and the company name as the title. Spell check the workbook if necessary.

Challenge Project 2-9

For this project, you create a workbook for a mobile services provider to calculate revenue from purchased mobile apps. You enter and format data and use *SUMPRODUCT* to determine revenue by category.
[Student Learning Outcomes 2.1, 2.3, 2.5, 2.7]

File Needed: None
Completed Project File Name: *[your initials] Excel 2-9.xlsx*

Create and save a workbook as [your initials] Excel 2-9. Modify your workbook according to the following guidelines:

- In cell **A1**, enter a name for your mobile services company.
- In cell **A2**, type Last Month's Activity.
- In cells **B3:D3**, enter the labels App Name, Times Downloaded, and Cost.
- In cell **A4**, type Books as the first category. In cells **A7, A10,** and **A13**, type the names of three other categories of mobile applications. Examples might be Travel, Entertainment, Games, Health, Sports, and so on.
- In cells **B5:D6**, complete data for two apps in the *Books* category. Then do the same for the other categories.
- Starting in row **18**, create a section that calculates revenue from each app category using the *SUMPRODUCT* function.
- In a cell below the data, use the *TODAY* function and format the date to show a short date.
- Select a workbook theme if desired, use cell styles, or set your own formatting.
- Add a footer that shows the current date in the left section and your name in the right section.
- Set document properties to show your name as the author and a title of your choice. Spell check the workbook if necessary.

Challenge Project 2-10

In this project, you create a workbook that calculates monthly payments for a major purchase at four possible interest rates and different payback times.
[Student Learning Outcomes 2.1, 2.3, 2.4, 2.5, 2.6]

File Needed: None
Completed Project File Name: *[your initials] Excel 2-10.xlsx*

Create and save a workbook as [your initials] Excel 2-10. Modify your workbook according to the following guidelines:

- Enter main labels that identify the worksheet and your proposed purchase.
- Build the first section for a *PMT* formula with the labels Loan, Rate, Term, and Payment. Since you plan to copy the section to show other possibilities, do not use range names.
- Fill in values for the loan amount, an interest rate, and the term. Include the percent sign when you type the interest rate. For the term, you can use the number of years or the number of months.
- Use *PMT* to calculate the payment made at the beginning of the month (*Type* argument). If you set months for the term, do not multiply the *Nper* argument by 12.
- Copy the entire section once below the current location with a blank row or two between. Then copy these two groupings one or two columns to the right. You should have four possible payment scenarios on the sheet.
- Edit the interest rate and term for each of the copied sections. Be consistent in how you indicate the term of the loan (years or months). Assume that the loan amount is the same.
- In a row below the data, use the *TODAY* function and format the date to show a short date.
- Make formatting choices to building an easy-to-read report for your possibilities.
- Add a footer with your name in the right section.
- Set document properties to show your name as the author, and spell check the workbook if necessary.

CHAPTER

3

Creating and Editing Charts

CHAPTER OVERVIEW

In addition to building formulas and functions in a worksheet, you can use Excel to graph or chart data. After selecting values and labels, you can quickly create a professional looking chart with a few clicks of the mouse. This chapter introduces you to the basics of creating, editing, and formatting Excel charts.

STUDENT LEARNING OUTCOMES (SLOs)

After completing this chapter, you will be able to:

SLO 3.1 Create Excel chart objects and chart sheets (p. E3-163).

SLO 3.2 Use quick layouts and chart styles to design a chart (p. E3-167).

SLO 3.3 Edit chart elements including titles, data labels, and source data (p. E3-172).

SLO 3.4 Format chart elements with shape styles, fill, outlines, and special effects (p. E3-179).

SLO 3.5 Use pictures, shapes, and *WordArt* in a chart (p. E3-183).

SLO 3.6 Build pie charts and combination charts (p. E3-188).

SLO 3.7 Create sunburst and waterfall charts (p. E3-191).

SLO 3.8 Insert and format sparklines in a worksheet (p. E3-194).

CASE STUDY

In the Pause & Practice projects in this chapter, you use data in a Paradise Lakes Resort workbook to build charts that compare revenue categories for two quarters. You build column and pie charts as objects and separate sheets. You also add trendlines and sparklines to further illustrate aspects of the data.

Pause & Practice 3-1: Create and edit column and bar charts.

Pause & Practice 3-2: Edit and format charts and chart elements.

Pause & Practice 3-3: Create and format pie, combo, and sunburst charts and insert sparklines.

E3-162

Creating a Chart Object and a Chart Sheet

SLO 3.1

An Excel *chart* is a visual representation of numeric data in a worksheet. A chart helps you identify trends, make comparisons, and recognize patterns in the numbers. Charts are dynamic and linked to the data, so when values in the worksheet change, the chart is automatically redrawn. You can display a chart in the worksheet with its data, or you can place a chart on its own sheet.

There are different kinds of charts, and Excel can recommend the best chart type based on your selected data. It is essential, however, that you select appropriate data for a chart, because it is possible to build charts that illustrate nothing of any consequence. With experience and practice, you will learn how to create charts that have meaning to your work.

Create a Chart Object

A *chart object* is a selectable item surrounded by a square border that is separate from worksheet data. A chart object contains chart elements such as titles, axes, and gridlines, and each element is selectable, too. You can size and position a chart object in a worksheet, and you can size and position each chart element on the chart.

Source data are the cells that contain values and labels to be graphed in a chart. When you select data for a chart, you usually do not include sums, averages, or similar calculations. In Figure 3-1, the source data includes the series names in column A, the category names in row 4,

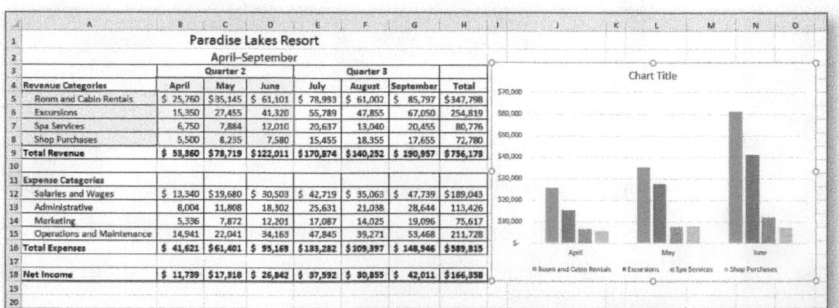

3-1 Chart object and its source data

and four values for each of three months. Each of the values is a *data point*, a cell containing a value. Each group of data points or values is a *data series*. In this example, there are four data series, one for each revenue category. Each data series has a name or label.

The text label that describes a data series is a *category label*. In Figure 3.1, the category labels are the month names.

> **ANOTHER WAY**
> You can create a default chart object by selecting the data and pressing **Alt+F1**.

Data for a chart is best arranged with labels and values in adjacent cells and no empty rows. If you do not include labels for the source data, there are no labels in the chart to describe the data. An empty row within the source data is graphed as a data point with a value of zero (0) and will distort the chart's ability to illustrate a comparison or trend.

When you select contiguous source data (all cells are next to each other), the **Quick Analysis** button appears in the lower right corner of the selection. The *Quick Analysis* tool

lists command groups you would be likely to use for the selected data, such as *Formatting, Charts,* or *Totals.* When you select the *Charts* command, Excel shows recommended chart types. As you point to each type, you see a preview of the chart. Click the preferred type to create the chart object in the worksheet.

▶ **HOW TO:** Create a Chart Object from the Quick Analysis Tool

1. Select the source data range with labels and values.
 - The *Quick Analysis* button appears at the lower right corner of the range.
2. Click the **Quick Analysis** button.
 - A dialog box with command categories opens.
3. Select **Charts**.
 - Possible chart types are listed (Figure 3-2).
4. Point to a chart type.
 - A preview of the chart object is displayed.
5. Click to select the chart type.
 - The chart object displays in the worksheet.

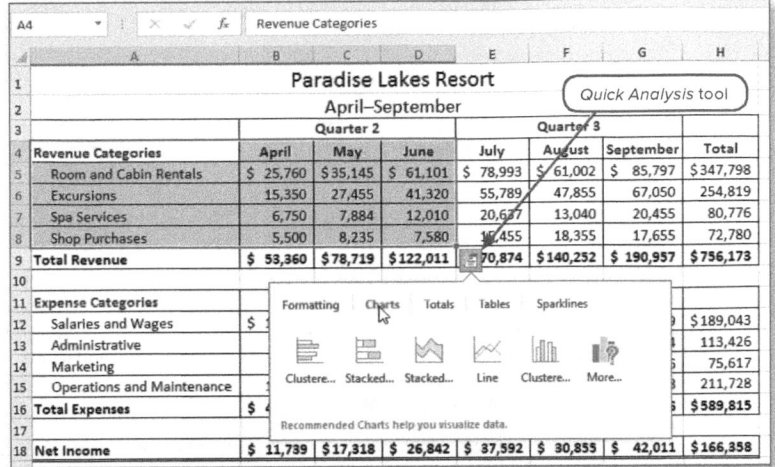

3-2 Chart options for selected data

Excel Chart Types

Excel has many chart types and most types have subtypes or variations. The most common chart types are column or bar, line, and pie, but Excel can build powerful scientific and statistical charts. The following table describes Excel chart types:

Excel Chart Types

Chart Type	Purpose	Data Example	Categories (Labels)	Values (Numbers)
Column	Illustrates data changes over a period of time or shows comparisons among items	Monthly sales data for three automobile models	Horizontal axis	Vertical axis
Bar	Displays comparisons among individual items or values at a specific period of time	Number of pairs sold for eight shoe styles	Vertical axis	Horizontal axis
Pie	Uses one data series to display each value as a percentage of the whole	Expenses or revenue by department for one quarter		One data series shown by slice size
Line	Displays trends in data over time, emphasizing the rate of change	Number of weekly web site views over a ten-week period	Horizontal axis	Vertical axis
Area	Displays the magnitude of change over time and shows the rate of change	Yearly consumption of apples, bananas, and pears over a ten-year period	Horizontal axis	Vertical axis

Continued

Chart Type	Purpose	Data Example	Categories (Labels)	Values (Numbers)
XY (Scatter) or Bubble	Displays relationships among numeric values in two or more data series; these charts do not have a category.	Number of times a patient visits a doctor, amount billed to insurance, and cost billed to patient	Horizontal axis (value 1-x)	Vertical axis (value 2-y)
Stock	Displays three series of data to show fluctuations in stock prices from high to low to close	Opening, closing, and high price for Microsoft stock each day for 30 days	Horizontal axis	Vertical axis
Surface	Displays optimum combinations of two sets of data on a surface	Perceived outside temperature at ten temperature and ten humidity levels	Horizontal axis (value 1-x)	Horizontal axis (value 1-x)
Radar	Displays the frequency of multiple data series relative to a center point. There is an axis for each category.	Style, comfort, and value ratings for three snow boot styles	NA	NA
TreeMap	Displays a hierarchical view of data with different sized and colored rectangles and sub-rectangles to compare the sizes of groups	Soda sales by product name, continent, country, and city	NA	NA
Sunburst	Displays a hierarchical view of data with concentric rings. The top hierarchy is the inner ring and each outer ring is related to its adjacent inner ring.	Tablet sales by screen size, continent, country, and city	NA	NA
Histogram	Column-style chart that shows frequencies within a distribution	Number of students in each of five grade categories for an exam	Horizontal axis	Vertical axis
Box & Whisker	Displays the distribution of data with minimum, mean, maximum, and outlier values	Sales prices of home in five suburbs during a three-week period	Horizontal axis	Vertical axis
Waterfall	Plots each element in a running total and displays negative and positive effects of each on the total	Banking or savings account register	Horizontal axis	Vertical axis
Funnel	Plots values that progressively decrease from one stage or process to the next	Job applications received, applications selected, initial interviews, team interviews, HR interview, job offer	Vertical axis	Horizontal axis
Combo Chart	Uses two types of charts to graph values that are widely different	Line chart for number of monthly web site visits and a column chart for monthly sales of online golf gloves	Either	Either

Size and Position a Chart Object

When you select a chart object, it is active and surrounded by eight selection handles. A **selection handle** is a small circle shape on each corner and in the middle of each side. To select the chart object, point to its border and click. When the chart object is selected, the *Range Finder* highlights the source data in the worksheet. When you point to a selection handle, you will see a two-pointed resize arrow. Drag a corner handle to size the height and width proportionally.

To move a chart object, point to the chart border to display a four-pointed move pointer. Then drag the chart object to the desired location.

When a chart is active or selected, the *Chart Tools Design* and *Format* tabs are available in the *Ribbon* and three *Quick Chart Tools* are available in the top right corner of the object: *Chart Elements, Chart Styles,* and *Chart Filters.*

> **MORE INFO**
>
> You can select individual elements or parts of the chart, and each element has its own selection handles.

▶**HOW TO: Move and Size a Chart Object**

1. Select the chart object.
 - Point to the border of the chart and click.
2. Point to the outside border of the chart to display a move pointer.
 - Point anywhere along the border.
3. Drag the chart object to a new location and release the pointer button (Figure 3-3).
4. Point to a corner selection handle to display a resize arrow.
5. Drag the pointer to resize the chart proportionally.

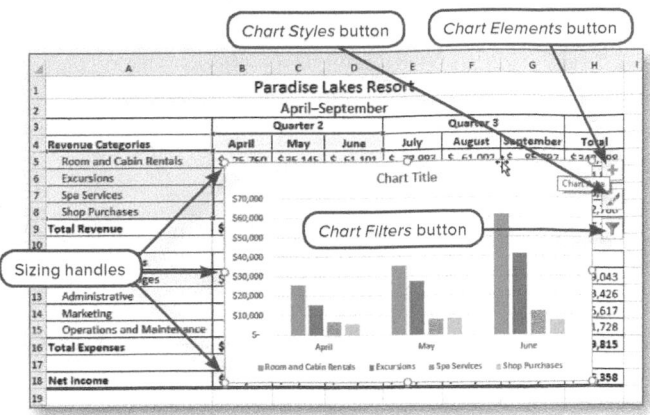

3-3 Selected chart object and move pointer

Create a Chart Sheet

A *chart sheet* is an Excel chart that is displayed on its own sheet in the workbook. A chart sheet does not have rows, columns, and cells, but the chart is linked to its data on the source worksheet.

From the *Quick Analysis* tool or the *Insert* tab, Excel creates a chart object. You must move the chart object to its own sheet with the *Move Chart* button on the *Chart Tools Design* tab. Excel uses default sheet names *Chart1, Chart2,* and so on, but you can type a descriptive name in the *Move Chart* dialog box, or you can rename the sheet at any time.

You can create an automatic column chart sheet by selecting the data and pressing the **F11** (**FN+F11**) function key.

> ▶ **MORE INFO**
>
> When the *Recommended Charts* button does not recommend a chart type, select the source data again in a left-to-right order. If there are still no suggestions, click the **All Charts** tab and choose a type.

Source data for a chart need not be contiguous. The *Quick Analysis* tool does not appear for noncontiguous data, but you can click the **Recommended Charts** button in the *Charts* group on the *Insert* tab. The *Insert Chart* dialog box opens and recommends chart types.

▶**HOW TO: Create a Chart Sheet for Noncontiguous Cells**

1. Select the values and labels for the chart.
 - Select the first range, press the **Ctrl** key, and select each range (Figure 3-4).
2. Click the **Recommended Charts** button [*Insert* tab, *Charts* group].
 - The *Insert Chart* dialog box opens.
 - You can click the **All Charts** tab to select any chart type.
3. Click the thumbnail for a chart type to preview the results.

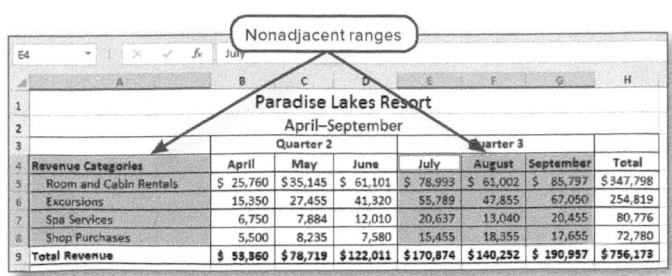

3-4 Source data ranges that are not next to each other

4. Click the preferred chart type and click **OK**.
 - The chart object is active.
 - The *Chart Tools* tabs are available.
5. Click the **Move Chart** button [*Chart Tools Design* tab, *Location* group].
6. Click the **New sheet** radio button (Figure 3-5).
7. Type a descriptive name for the chart sheet.
8. Click **OK**.

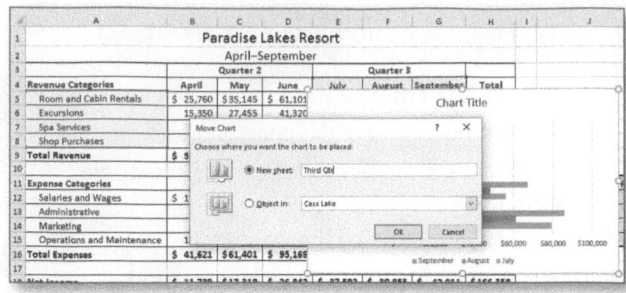

3-5 *Move Chart* dialog box

SLO 3.2 ## Using Quick Layouts and Chart Styles

A newly created chart has a default layout, color, and style. Excel has various tools to help you enhance the appearance of your chart for originality, readability, and appeal. The *Chart Tools Design* tab includes commands for selecting a chart layout, choosing a chart style, or changing the color scheme.

Apply a Quick Layout

A ***chart layout*** is a set of elements and the location of those elements. Elements are individual parts of a chart such as a main title, a legend, and axis titles. The *Quick Layout* button [*Chart Tools Design* tab, *Chart Layouts* group] opens a gallery of predefined layouts (Figure 3-6). As you point to an option in the gallery, *Live Preview* redraws the chart. When a chart layout adds an element such as a title, the element displays a generic label like "Chart Title." You can add or remove individual elements, as well as edit placeholder text.

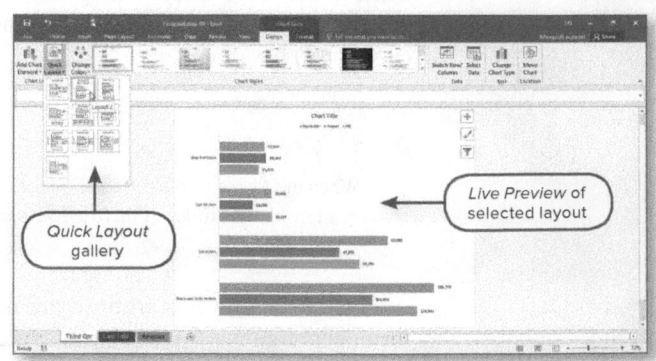

3-6 *Quick Layout* gallery

▶ HOW TO: Apply a Quick Layout to a Chart

1. Select the chart object or the chart sheet tab.
2. Click the **Quick Layout** button [*Chart Tools Design* tab, *Chart Layouts* group].
 - The gallery displays thumbnail images of each layout.
 - Quick layouts are named *Layout 1* through the last number.
3. Point to a layout to preview it in the chart.
4. Click a thumbnail to select it.
 - The chart is reformatted with the *Quick Layout* elements.

Apply a Chart Style

A ***chart style*** is a preset combination of colors and effects for a chart, its background, and its elements. The chart styles that are available for a chart are based on the current workbook theme. If you change the theme, the chart style colors are updated, and your chart reflects the new color palette. You can find chart styles in the *Chart Styles* group on the *Chart Tools Design* tab. Like a chart layout, you can preview the effects of a chart style as you point to each style in the gallery.

> **HOW TO: Apply a Chart Style**

1. Select the chart object or the chart sheet tab.
2. Click the *Chart Styles* **More** button to open the gallery or point to a *Style* thumbnail [*Chart Tools Design* tab, *Chart Styles* group].

 - The number of styles depends on the chart type (Figure 3-7).
 - Chart styles are named *Style 1* through the last number.

3. Point to a style thumbnail to see a *Live Preview* in the chart.
4. Click to select a style.

 - The chart is redrawn with the selected style.

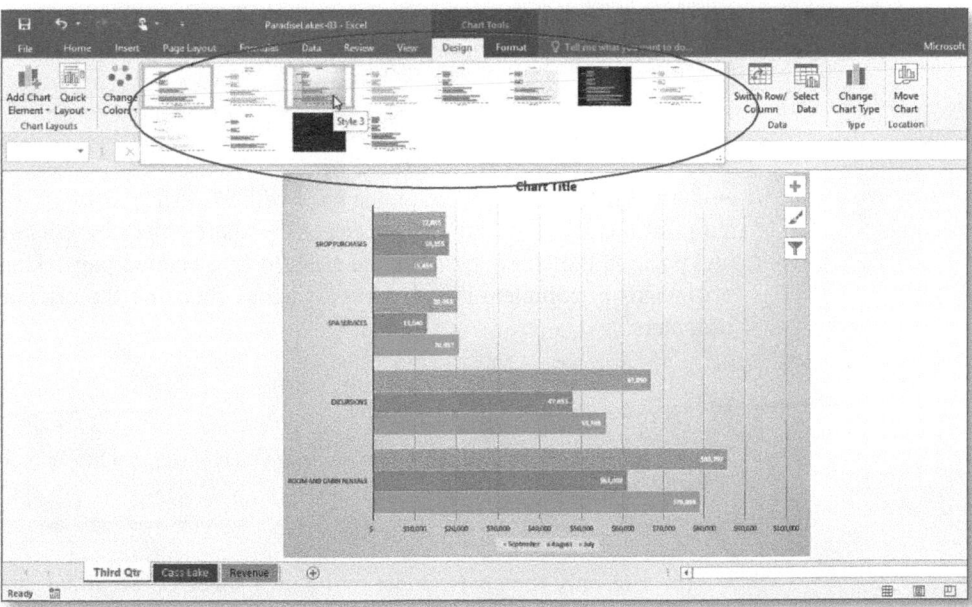

3-7 *Chart Styles* gallery and preview of selected style

Change Chart Colors

The workbook theme and the chart style form the basis for a chart's color scheme. The *Chart Styles* group [*Chart Tools Design* tab] includes a *Change Colors* button with optional color palettes. These palettes are divided into *Colorful* and *Monochromatic* groups.

▶ **HOW TO: Change Chart Colors**

1. Select the chart object or the chart sheet tab.
2. Click the **Change Colors** button [*Chart Tools Design* tab, *Chart Styles* group].
 * A gallery of color palettes opens (Figure 3-8).
 * Color schemes are named *Color 1* through the last number.
3. Point to a palette to see a *Live Preview* in the chart.
4. Click to select a palette.
 * The chart is formatted with new colors.

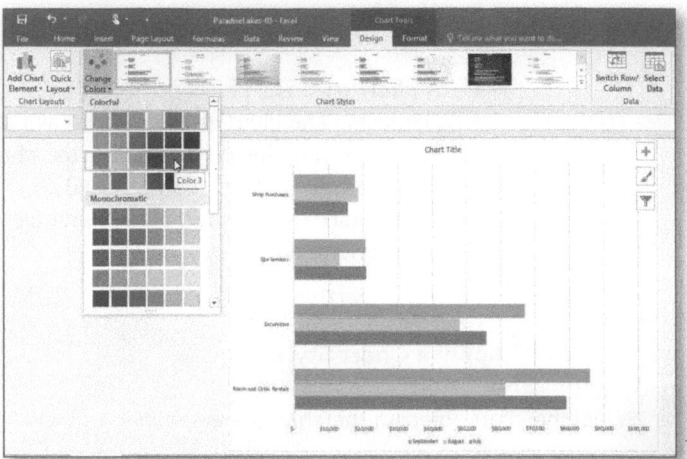

3-8 *Change Colors* gallery

Print a Chart

A chart object can be printed on the page with worksheet data, or it can be printed separately. To print a chart with the data, deselect the chart object by clicking a worksheet cell. Size and position the chart and scale the sheet to fit a printed page. Then use regular *Page Setup* commands to complete the print task, such as choosing the orientation or inserting headers or footers.

▶ MORE INFO

When you insert a header or footer in a selected chart object, that header or footer is not inserted on the worksheet.

To print only the chart object on its own sheet, select it and use regular *Print* and *Page Setup* options. A selected chart object, by default, prints scaled to fit a landscape page. A chart sheet also prints in landscape orientation fit to the page.

▶ **HOW TO: Print a Chart with Its Source Data**

1. Click any cell in the worksheet.
 * Size and position the chart object as needed.
2. Click the **File** tab to open the *Backstage* view (Figure 3-9).
3. Select **Print**.

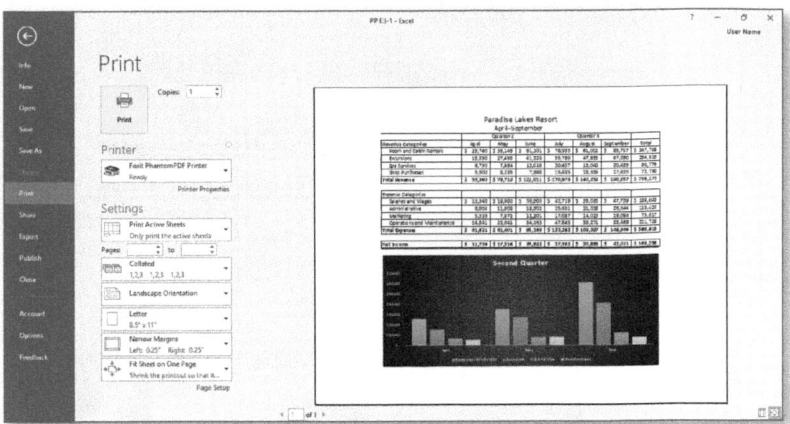

3-9 Print a chart with the data

4. Choose print settings as needed.
 - Set margins and scale the sheet to fit.
5. Click **Print**.

PAUSE & PRACTICE: EXCEL 3-1

In this project, you insert a clustered column chart object in a worksheet that tracks revenue and expenses for Paradise Lakes Resort. You also insert a clustered bar chart sheet to highlight second quarter results.

File Needed: *ParadiseLakes-03.xlsx* [*Student data files are available in the Library of your SIMnet account.*]
Completed Project File Name: *[your initials] PP E3-1.xlsx*

1. Open the ***ParadiseLakes-03*** workbook from your student data files and save it as [your initials] PP E3-1.

2. Create a chart object.
 a. Select cells **A4:D8** on the **Cass Lake** sheet. These are labels and values for the chart.
 b. Click the **Quick Analysis** button and select **Charts**.
 c. Click **Clustered Column**.

3. Position and size the chart object.
 a. Click the chart object if it is not selected.
 b. Point to the chart border to display a move pointer.
 c. Drag the chart object so that its top left corner is at cell **A20**.
 d. Point to the lower right selection handle to display a resize arrow.
 e. Drag the pointer to reach cell **H35**.

4. Choose a quick layout.
 a. Select the chart object if necessary.
 b. Click the **Quick Layout** button [*Chart Tools Design* tab, *Chart Layouts* group].
 c. Click **Layout 3** (Figure 3-10).

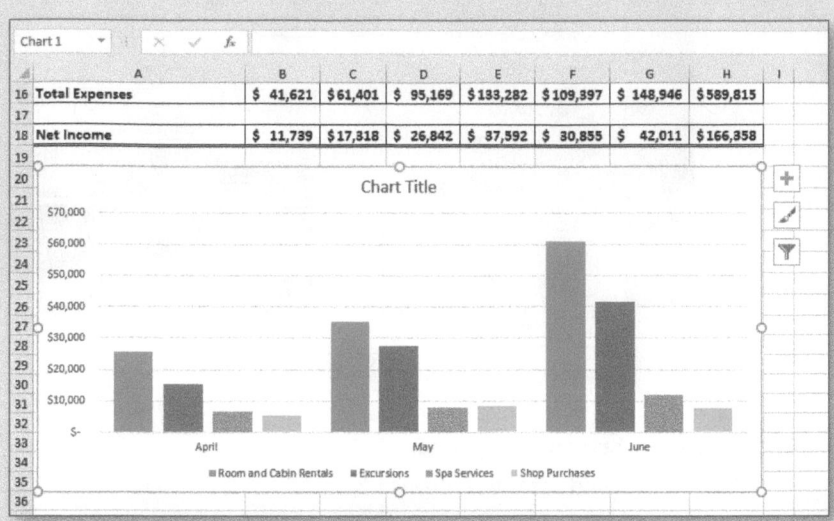

3-10 Chart object sized and positioned

5. Create a chart sheet.
 a. Select cells **A4:A8**.
 b. Press **Ctrl** and select cells **E4:G8**.
 c. Click the **Recommended Charts** button [*Insert* tab, *Charts* group].
 d. Select **Clustered Bar**.
 e. Click **OK**. The chart object is inserted and selected.
 f. Click the **Move Chart** button [*Chart Tools Design* tab, *Location* group].
 g. Click the **New sheet** radio button.
 h. Type Qtr 3 as the sheet name.
 i. Click **OK**. The chart sheet tab is active.

6. Choose a chart style.
 a. Click the **More** button to open the *Chart Styles* gallery [*Chart Tools Design* tab, *Chart Styles* group].
 b. Select **Style 7**.

7. Preview the charts.
 a. Select the **Qtr 3** sheet if necessary.
 b. Click the **File** tab to open the *Backstage* view.
 c. Choose **Print** to preview the chart sheet (Figure 3-11).
 d. Click the **Back** button to return to the worksheet.
 e. Click the **Cass Lake** worksheet tab and select cell **A1**.
 f. Click the **File** tab and select **Print**. The worksheet and chart are previewed on a single page.
 g. Click the **Back** button to return to the worksheet.

3-11 Print preview for chart sheet

8. Save and close the workbook (Figure 3-12).

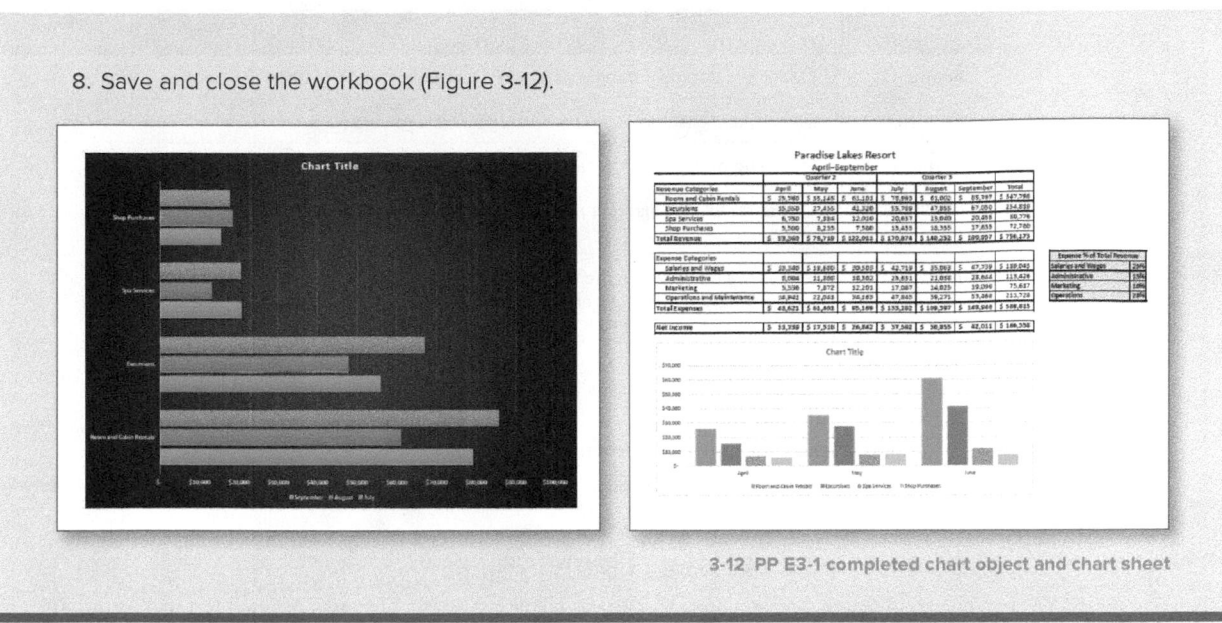

3-12 PP E3-1 completed chart object and chart sheet

SLO 3.3

Editing Chart Elements and Data

A **chart element** is a separate, clickable, editable object. The chart layout and style affects which elements are initially displayed, but you can add, remove, format, size, and position elements as you design a chart. The following table describes common chart elements:

Excel Chart Elements

Element	Description
Axis	Horizontal or vertical boundary that identifies what is plotted
Axis title	Optional description for the categories or values
Chart area	Background for the chart; can be filled with a color, gradient, or pattern
Chart floor	Base or bottom for a 3D chart
Chart title	Optional description or name for the chart
Chart wall	Vertical background for a 3D chart
Data label	Optional element that displays values with the marker for each data series
Data marker	Element that represents individual values. The marker is a bar, a column, a slice, or a point on a line.
Data point	A single value or piece of data from a data series
Data series	Group of related values that are in the same column or row and translate into the columns, lines, pie slices, and other markers
Gridline	Horizontal or vertical line that extends across the plot area to help in identifying values
Horizontal (category) axis	Describes what is shown in the chart and is created from row or column headings. In a bar chart, the category axis is the vertical axis; the category axis is the horizontal axis in a column chart.

Continued

Element	Description
Legend	Element that explains symbols, textures, or colors used to differentiate data series
Plot area	Rectangular area bounded by the horizontal and vertical axes
Tick mark	Small line or marker on an axis to guide in reading values
Trendline	Line or curve that displays averages in the data and can be used to forecast future averages
Vertical (value) axis	Shows the numbers on the chart. In a bar chart, the vertical axis is along the bottom; in a column chart, the vertical axis is along the side.

> **MORE INFO**
>
> Not all charts have all elements. For example, a pie chart does not have any axes or axes titles.

Add and Remove Chart Elements

When you point to a chart element, a *ScreenTip* describes it. When you click the element, it is active and surrounded by selection handles, as shown for the legend in Figure 3-13. In addition to clicking, you can select an element from the *Chart Elements* drop-down list on the *Chart Tools Format* tab. The name of the selected element appears in the *Chart Elements* box.

You show or hide chart elements from the *Chart Elements* button in the top right corner of a chart. When you click the button, the *Chart Elements* pane opens with a list of available elements for the chart type. In this pane, select or deselect the box to show or remove an element. To hide the pane, click the **Chart Elements** button again.

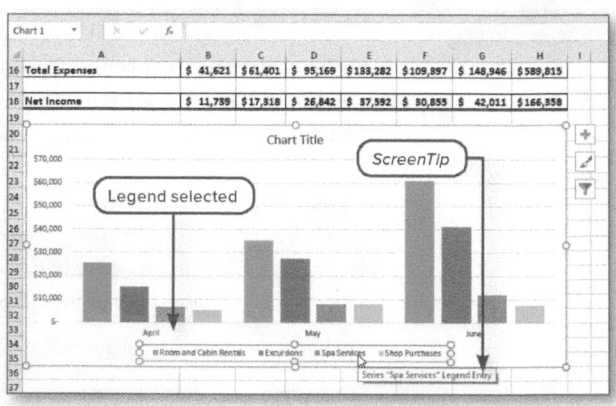

3-13 Selected legend and ScreenTip for a data series

> **ANOTHER WAY**
>
> Click the **Add Chart Element** button [*Chart Tools Design* tab, *Chart Layouts* group] to show a chart element.

Chart and Axes Titles

Chart layouts may include placeholders, which are text box objects, for a main chart title and for axes titles. If the quick layout does not include titles, you can add them. In either case, you must edit the placeholder text.

A main chart title is usually positioned above the chart, but within the chart area. Once you insert the text box, you can select it and move it anywhere on the chart. You might use an axis title to clarify what is represented by the categories or the values. If the chart represents the data well, axes titles are often not necessary.

▶ HOW TO: Insert a Chart Title

1. Click the chart object or the chart sheet tab.
2. Click the **Chart Elements** button in the top right corner of the chart.
3. Select the **Chart Title** box.
 - The *Chart Title* placeholder displays above the chart.
4. Click the **Chart Title** arrow in the *Chart Elements* pane to select a position for the title.
5. Triple-click the *Chart Title* placeholder text to select it (Figure 3-14).
 - The mini toolbar opens.
6. Type a title to replace the placeholder text.
7. Click the chart border.
 - The title object is deselected.
 - If you press **Enter** while typing in the text box, you insert a new line in the title. Press **Backspace** to remove it and then click the chart border.

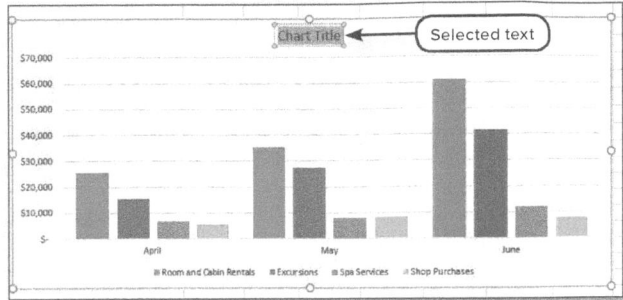

3-14 Placeholder text to be edited

To edit placeholder text, you can also select the object and type text in the *Formula* bar. Then press **Enter**, or click the **Enter** button in the *Formula* bar to complete it. The label appears in the *Formula* bar as you type, and you will not see it on the chart until you press **Enter**.

All text within an object can be formatted with font attributes from the *Font* and *Alignment* groups [*Home* tab] when the element is selected. When you want to apply a format to a portion of the text, click to place an insertion point inside the element and select the characters to be changed.

> ### MORE INFO
>
> When you double-click a chart element, its *Format* pane opens with format and design choices for that element.

Removing a chart element makes more room for the actual chart. In Figure 3-15, for example, the vertical axis title "Dollars" is probably not necessary. By removing it, the chart resizes to fit the chart area. You can always show the element again if you change your mind.

To delete a chart element, select it and press **Delete**. You can confirm which element is selected in the *Chart Elements* box on the *Chart Tools Format* tab [*Current Selection* group].

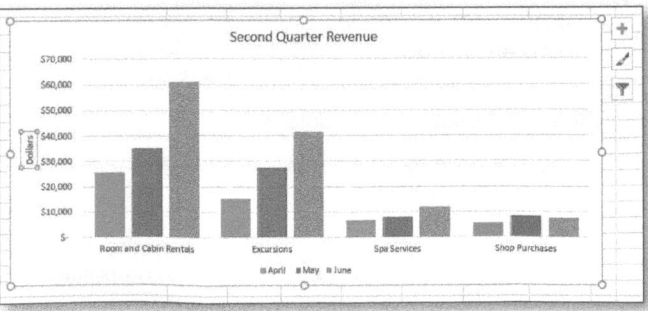

3-15 Delete an axis title to make more room for the chart

▶**HOW TO:** Delete a Chart Element

1. Click the chart element.
 - The element displays selection handles.
 - Confirm which element is selected in the *Chart Elements* list box [*Chart Tools Format* tab, *Current Selection* group].
2. Press **Delete**.
 - The chart resizes to fit the area.
 - You can also right-click the chart element and choose **Delete**.

> ▶ **ANOTHER WAY**
>
> To remove an element, click the **Chart Elements** button in the top right corner of the chart and deselect the box for that element.

Data Labels

Data labels display the number represented by a column, bar, pie slice, or other marker on the chart. Because the value axis uses a scale, it cannot show a precise value, but a data label can display that number. Data labels should be used when there are not too many data series because they can clutter a chart. Or you can select just one or two of the data points (the individual bars or columns) and show labels for only that data.

Data labels are displayed from the *Chart Elements* button on the chart or from the same button on the *Chart Tools Design* tab [*Chart Layouts* group].

▶**HOW TO:** Add Data Labels

1. Select the chart object or the chart sheet tab.
2. Click the **Chart Elements** button in the top right corner of the chart.
3. Select the **Data Labels** box.
 - *Live Preview* shows data labels for each data point in the data series
4. Point to **Data Labels** in the pane and point to its arrow (Figure 3-16).
 - Position choices for the labels are listed.
 - *Live Preview* updates as you point to each option.
5. Choose a location for the data labels.

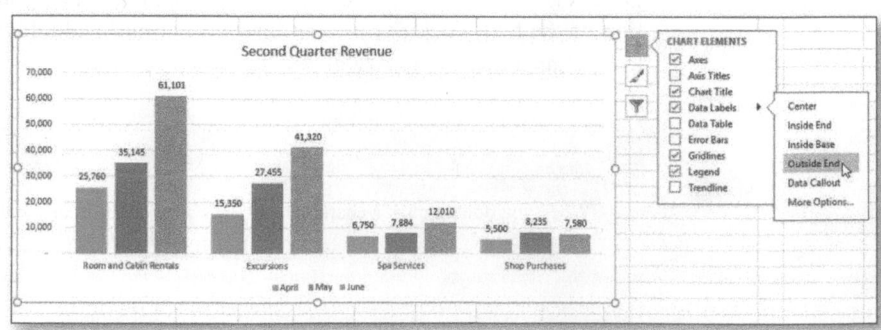

3-16 Data labels shown outside bar markers

Data Table

A chart **data table** is a columnar display of the values for each data series in a chart, located just below the chart. When your readers do not have access to the source data for a chart, a data table can supply valuable information.

To include a data table below your chart, you can use the *Add Chart Element* button on the *Chart Tools Design* tab in the *Chart Layouts* group or the *Chart Elements* button on the

chart. You can show a data table with or without legend markers, a mini legend to the left of the table (Figure 3-17).

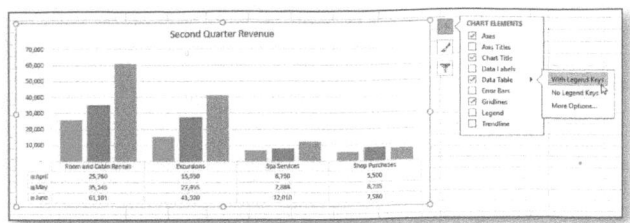

3-17 Data table element for a chart

Trendlines

A *trendline* is a chart element that plots patterns using a moving average of the current data. It uses a straight or curved line and can extend past the data to predict future averages. Some charts cannot display a trendline, such as a stacked chart, a pie chart, or a 3D chart. A basic linear trendline is appropriate for values that tend to increase or decrease as time passes. A trendline traces data for one data series as seen in

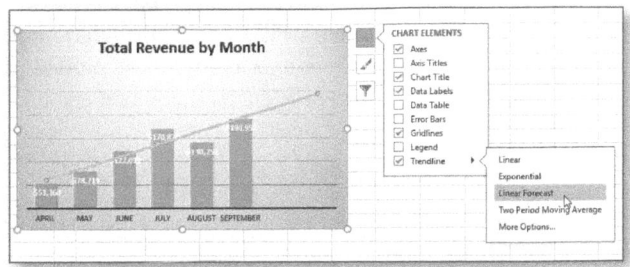

3-18 Column chart with "Total Revenue" linear trendline

Figure 3-18. If you have multiple data series, as in a typical column chart, you can add a trendline for each series.

> **ANOTHER WAY**
>
> Right-click a data series marker (its column) and choose **Add Trendline** to open the *Format Trendline* task pane and build a trendline.

▶ **HOW TO: Add a Trendline to a Chart**

1. Click the chart object or the chart sheet tab.
2. Click the **Chart Elements** button in the top right corner of the chart.
3. Select the **Trendline** box in the *Chart Elements* pane.
 - The *Add Trendline* dialog box lists the names of the data series.
 - When there is only one data series, the trendline is added to the chart.
4. Choose a data series for the trendline and click **OK** (Figure 3-19).
5. Point to the **Trendline** arrow in the *Chart Elements* pane.
 - Choose **Linear** to show a line for existing data.
 - Choose **Linear Forecast** to build a line for current and future data.

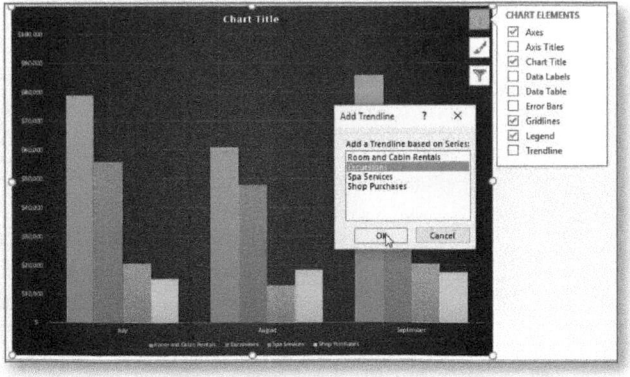

3-19 *Add Trendline* dialog box for chart with multiple data series

> **MORE INFO**
>
> Excel uses logarithmic and other statistical concepts as it builds a trendline. Explore these options in the *Trendline Format* task pane if your work often requires trendlines.

Switch Row and Column Data

Excel plots the data series based on the number of rows and columns selected in the worksheet and the chart type. Based on your choices, Excel determines if the labels are along the bottom or the side of the chart. When necessary, you can change which data series is plotted on the x-axis and which is plotted on the y-axis. In a column chart, the x-axis is along the bottom of the chart; the y-axis is along the left.

▶ HOW TO: Switch Row and Column Data

1. Click the chart object or the chart sheet tab.
2. Click the **Switch Row/Column** button [*Chart Tools Design* tab, *Data* group] (Figure 3-20).
 - The data series become the categories.
 - You can toggle between how columns and rows are plotted.

3-20 Column and row data switched

> **ANOTHER WAY**
>
> Click the **Chart Filters** button in the top right corner of the chart and choose **Select Data** at the bottom of the pane to open the *Select Data Source* dialog box and switch row and column data.

Change the Chart Type

When a chart does not depict what you intended, you need a variety of chart types for a project, or you simply prefer a different chart, you can easily change the chart type. Changing the type assumes that the source data is the same and that it can be graphed in the new chart. You should not, for example, change a column chart with three data series into a pie chart, because a pie chart has only one series. The resulting chart would not represent the data as expected.

The *Change Chart Type* button is on the *Chart Tools Design* tab in the *Type* group. For a selected chart object or sheet, you can also right-click and choose **Change Chart Type** from the context menu. The *Change Chart Type* dialog box has *Recommended Charts* and *All Charts* tabs like the *Insert Chart* dialog box.

▶ HOW TO: Change the Chart Type

1. Click the chart object or chart sheet.
2. Click the **Change Chart Type** button [*Chart Tools Design* tab, *Type* group].
 - The *Change Chart Type* dialog box opens.

3. Click the **Recommended Charts** tab.
 - Click **All Charts** tab if the recommended charts are not adequate.
4. Click a thumbnail image to preview the chart in the dialog box.
5. Select a chart type and click **OK**.

Filter Source Data

A chart displays all the categories and all the data series. You can, however, filter or refine which data is displayed by hiding categories or series. A *filter* is a requirement or condition that identifies which data is shown and which is hidden. Chart filters do not change the underlying cell range for a chart, but they enable you to focus on particular data.

You filter chart data from the *Chart Filters* button in the top right corner of the chart or in the *Select Data Source* dialog box.

▶ HOW TO: Filter Source Data

1. Select the chart object or chart sheet tab.
2. Click the **Chart Filters** button in the top right corner.
 - The *Chart Filters* pane shows a check mark for series and categories that are shown.
3. Deselect the box for a series or category to be hidden.
4. Click **Apply** (Figure 3-21).
 - The chart is redrawn.
5. Click the **Chart Filters** button to close the pane.
 - You can show the hidden data when desired.

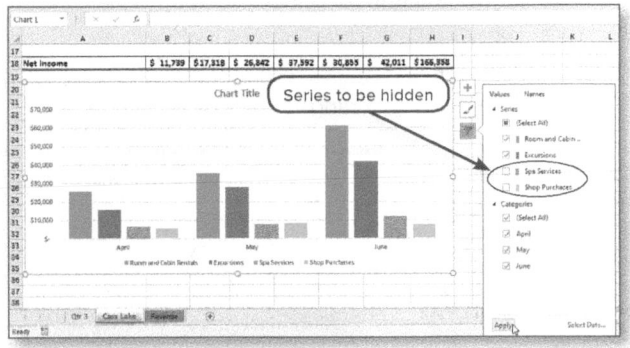

3-21 *Chart Filters* pane

Edit Source Data

The cells used to build a chart are its source data. This data can be edited to change, add, or remove cells. In a column chart, for example, you can add a data series, or another column. To add or delete a data series in a chart object, select the chart and drag the sizing arrow in the lower right corner of the highlighted cell range to expand or shrink the data range, as shown in Figure 3-22. Removing cells from the data range deletes that data series from the chart.

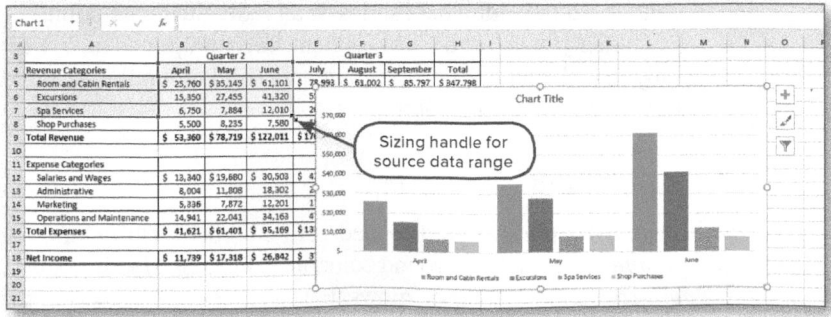

3-22 The "Shop Purchases" column will be removed from chart

To edit the source data for a chart sheet, click the **Select Data** button on the *Chart Tools Design* tab [*Data* group] to open the *Select Data Source* dialog box.

▶**HOW TO:** Add a Data Series in a Chart Sheet

1. Click the chart sheet tab.

2. Click the **Select Data** button [*Chart Tools Design* tab, *Data* group].

 • The *Select Data Source* dialog box opens.
 • The worksheet is active, and the source cells are highlighted.

3. Select the new cell range in the worksheet (Figure 3-23).

 • If the cell ranges are not adjacent, select the first one, type a comma, and select the next range.
 • You can type cell addresses in the *Chart data range* box rather than selecting cells.

4. Click **OK**.

 • The chart sheet is active and redrawn with the edited source data range.

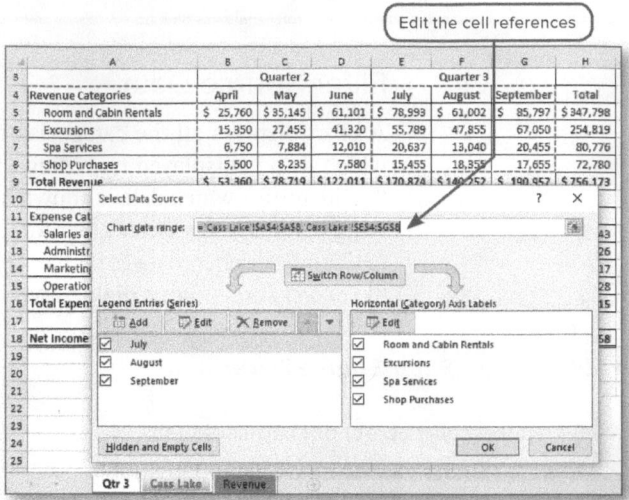

3-23 *Select Data Source* dialog box for a chart sheet

▶ **ANOTHER WAY**

You can open the *Select Data Source* dialog box by clicking **Select Data** at the bottom of the *Chart Filters* pane. You can define filters from this dialog box by selecting or deselecting a series or category name box.

SLO 3.4

Formatting Chart Elements

Quick Layout and *Chart Styles* apply formatting, but you can change most attributes to personalize your work. Making your own format choices enables you to distinguish your charts from those of other Excel users. You can also use company, association, or school colors and images to further differentiate your charts.

Some chart elements consist of a group of related elements. A data series, for example, is the group of values for a particular item. Within each data series, there are data points. You can format the entire data series or an individual data point.

When you select a chart element, certain options on the *Chart Tools Design* tab apply to only that element. When the chart area (background) is selected, for example, you can change only its fill or border color.

Apply a Shape Style

A *shape style* is a predesigned set of borders, fill colors, and effects for a chart element. *Shape fill* is the background color, and *shape outline* is the border around the element. *Shape effects* include shadows, glows, bevels, or soft edges. All of these commands are available in the *Shape Styles* group on the *Chart Tools Format* tab.

<table>
<tr><td>

</td><td>

Shape styles are shown in a gallery and are grouped as *Theme Styles* or *Presets*. Point to an icon to see a *ScreenTip* with a descriptive name and click an icon to apply it to the selected element. *Live Preview* is available for a chart object but not for a chart sheet.

</td></tr>
</table>

▶ HOW TO: Apply a Shape Style

1. Select the chart element.
 - Confirm or select a chart element by clicking the **Chart Elements** drop-down arrow [*Chart Tools Format* tab, *Current Selection* group] and choosing the name.
 - If you accidentally open the *Format* task pane for a chart element, close it.
2. Click the **More** button [*Chart Tools Format* tab, *Shape Styles* group].
 - Each icon in the *Shape Styles* gallery displays fill, outline, and effects (Figure 3-24).
 - Point to an icon to see its name and *Live Preview* in a chart object.
3. Click a shape style icon.
 - The chart element is reformatted.

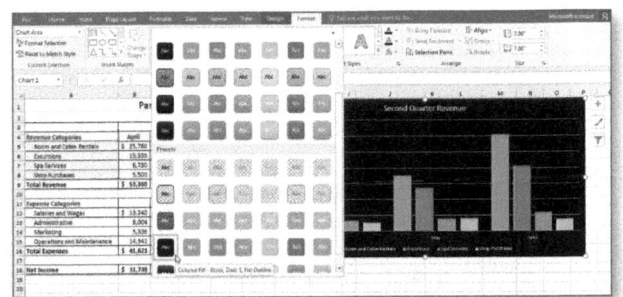

3-24 Shape Style gallery for the chart area

Apply Shape Fill, Outline, and Effects

Fill color, outline width and color, and special effects are available separately, and your choices override shape style settings already applied.

For fill color, you choose from the gallery, standard colors, or a custom color. After you choose a color, you can refine it to use a gradient, a variegated blend of the color.

▶ HOW TO: Apply Gradient Fill to a Chart Element

1. Select the chart element.
 - Confirm or select a chart element from the **Chart Elements** list [*Chart Tools Format* tab, *Current Selection* group].
2. Click the **Shape Fill** button [*Chart Tools Format* tab, *Shape Styles* group].
 - The gallery and menu options are listed.
3. Point to a color tile to see its name in a *ScreenTip*.
 - *Live Preview* applies the color to an element in a chart object.
4. Select a color tile to apply the color.
5. Click the **Shape Fill** [*Chart Tools Format* tab, *Shape Styles* group].
6. Choose **Gradient** to open the gallery (Figure 3-25).
7. Point to a tile to see its description.
8. Click the preferred gradient.

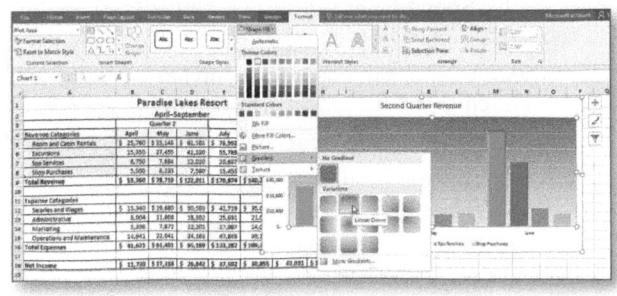

3-25 Shape Fill and Gradient galleries

▶ **ANOTHER WAY**

You can apply most formats from the *Home* tab for a selected chart element.

The outline for a shape is a border that surrounds or encircles the element. Not all chart elements are suited to an outline, but elements such as the chart or plot area often benefit from the use of an outline. When you add an outline to a chart element, you can select a weight or thickness for the line as well as a color. The thickness of an outline is measured in points, like fonts. Excel provides a gallery of weights to help you visualize the width. After you apply an outline, it is easier to see the effect if you deselect the chart object.

▶ HOW TO: Apply an Outline to a Chart Element

1. Select the chart element.
2. Click the **Shape Outline** button [*Chart Tools Format* tab, *Shape Styles* group].
 - The gallery and menu options are listed.
3. Choose a color.
4. Click the **Shape Outline** button [*Chart Tools Format* tab, *Shape Styles* group].
5. Click **Weight** to open its gallery.
6. Choose a width for the outline (Figure 3-26).
7. Click a worksheet cell or another chart element to see the outline.

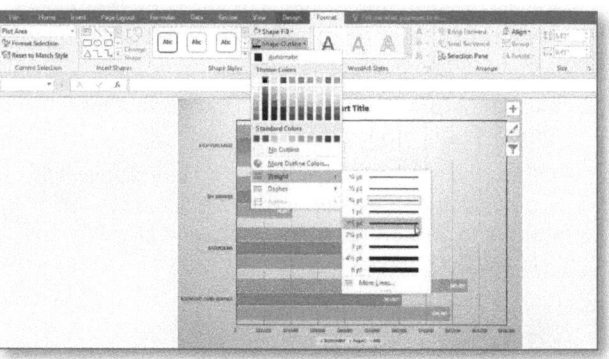

3-26 *Outline color* and *Weight* galleries

▶ **MORE INFO**

To remove shape fill or outline, select the object, click the command button, and choose **No Fill** or **No Outline**.

Special effects that are commonly used are bevels and shadows, because they give an element a realistic, three-dimensional look. These effects are best used on larger elements, such as the chart area, because they can overwhelm smaller elements.

To remove an effect, select the element and click the **Shape Effects** button. Choose the effect group to select the first option such as **No Shadow** or **No Bevel**.

▶ HOW TO: Apply an Effect to a Chart Element

1. Select the chart element.
2. Click the **Shape Effects** button [*Chart Tools Format* tab, *Shape Styles* group].
 - The gallery lists effect groups and then variations for each group.
3. Select a group for the effect (Figure 3-27).
 - If a group name is grayed out, it is not available for the selected element.
4. Point to an icon to see its name.
5. Click to choose an effect.
6. Click a worksheet cell or another chart element to see the outline.

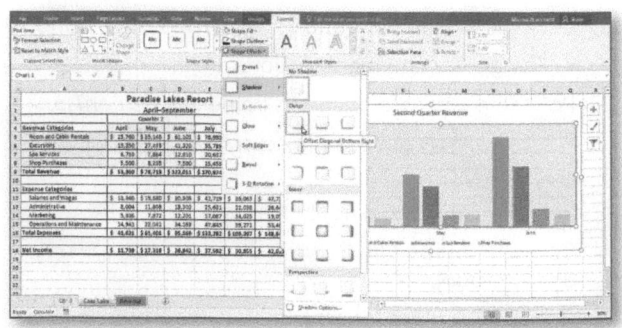

3-27 *Shape Effects* gallery for the plot area

The Format Task Pane

Every chart element has a *Format* task pane that consolidates shape, fill, and color options and provides custom commands for the element. To open the *Format* pane for a chart element, double-click the element or right-click it and choose **Format** [*Element Name*] from the menu. The *Format* pane opens to the right of the workbook window and automatically updates to reflect the selected element.

> **ANOTHER WAY**
>
> Open a *Format* task pane for a selected object by clicking the **Format Selection** button [*Chart Tools Format* tab, *Selection* group].

A task pane lists command options at the top of the pane. In Figure 3-28, *Title Options* and *Text Options* are available because the selected element is a chart title. The small triangle next to the first *Options* name enables you to choose a different chart element.

For each options group, most *Format* task panes have at least two buttons. The *Fill & Line*, *Effects,* and *Options* buttons are common, but there are other buttons for selected elements. Point to a button to see its *ScreenTip*. When you click a button, the pane displays relevant commands.

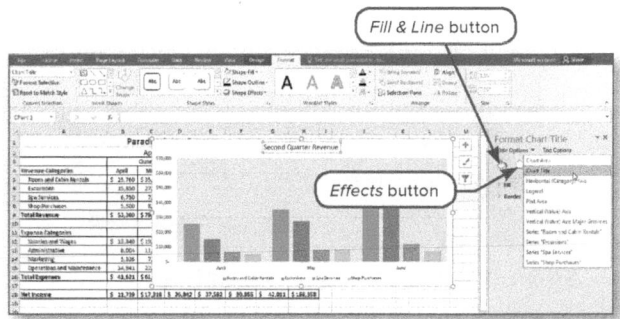

3-28 *Format Chart Title* pane

> **MORE INFO**
>
> Expand or collapse a command group in the *Format* task pane by clicking the command name.

▶ **HOW TO: Use the Format Task Pane to Change Shape Fill**

1. Double-click the chart element.
 - The *Format* task pane for the element opens on the right.
 - Select another element in the chart to see its task pane.
 - You can also select an element and click the **Format Selection** button [*Chart Tools Format* tab, *Current Selection* group] to open the task pane.
2. Click the name of the *Options* group at the top of task pane.
 - For some chart elements, there is only one group.
3. Click the **Fill & Line** button in the *Format* task pane.
4. Click **Fill** to expand the group.
5. Click the **Fill Color** button to open the gallery (Figure 3-29).
6. Choose the desired color.

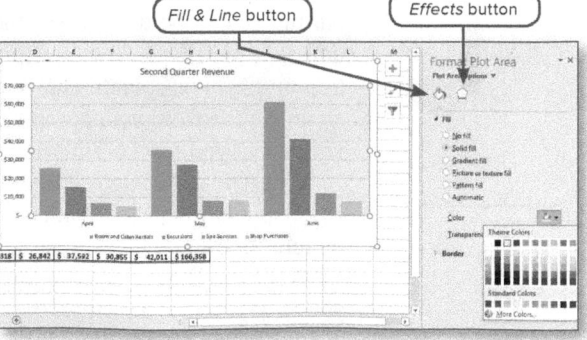

3-29 *Fill & Line* command in the *Format Plot Area* task pane

While the *Fill & Line* and *Effects* buttons offer similar commands for all elements, the *Options* button in a *Format* task pane is specific to the element. For a data series in a column chart, for example, these commands determine whether numbers are shown to the right or left of the chart (secondary or primary axis), or whether the columns overlap. A pie chart, on the other hand, has options that allow you to rotate the pie or explode slices.

▶ **HOW TO:** Use the Format Task Pane to Format Data Labels

1. Double-click a data label element in the chart.
 - Right-click an element and choose **Format Data Labels**.
 - All data labels for one series are selected.
2. Choose **Label Options** at the top of the task pane.
 - Point to a button to see a *ScreenTip*.
 - *Text Options* are also available.
3. Click the **Label Options** button.
4. Click **Label Options** or **Number** to expand the command group.
5. Select format options for the labels (Figure 3-30).
 - Formats are applied as you select them.
6. Close the task pane.

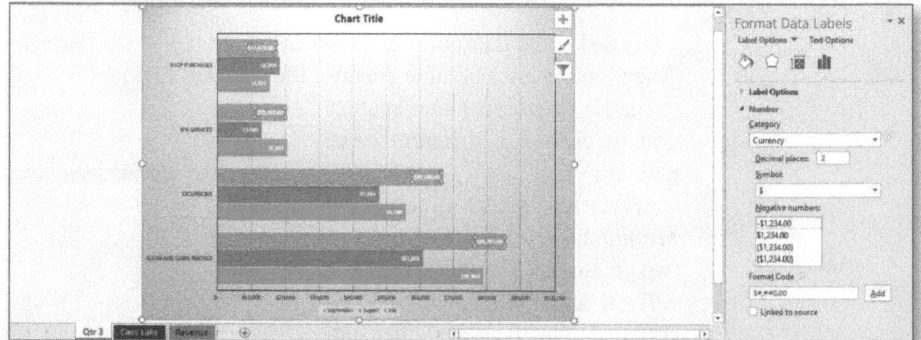

3-30 *Format Data Labels* pane

Using Pictures, Shapes, and WordArt in a Chart

A chart can be enhanced with pictures, shapes, or *WordArt*. Pictures can be inserted as separate design objects on the chart, or they can be used as fill for a chart element. You can draw a shape such as an arrow or a lightning bolt to highlight a particular data point on a chart. *WordArt* is often applied to a chart title for a distinctive look.

Use a Picture as Shape Fill

An image can be used to fill the chart area, the plot area, or a marker, especially bars, columns, or pie slices. You have probably seen bar charts with stick figures to illustrate population numbers or column charts with tiny automobile images to show auto sales. You can use an image file from your computer, from external media, or from an online source. And always verify that you have permission to use an image in your work.

The size and design of the picture is important, and you should guard against making the chart appear busy. You can edit some attributes of a picture in Excel, but this depends on the picture format.

A picture is inserted from the **Fill** command on the *Format* task pane for the element. After you have inserted a picture, the task pane displays *Stretch* and *Stack* options. *Stretch* enlarges and elongates a single copy of a picture to fill the element. The *Stack* choice sizes and repeats the image to fill the area. There is also a *Stack and Scale* setting for precise matching of the number of images used per unit of value.

> **MORE INFO**
>
> When you select the *Picture or texture fill* command for a chart element, it displays the most recently used image, if any, in the element.

▶ HOW TO: Use a Picture as Fill

1. Double-click the chart element for the fill.

 - The *Format* task pane opens.
 - You can also right-click the element and choose **Format [*Element Name*]**.

2. Click the **Fill & Line** button in the *Format* task pane.

3. Click **Fill** to expand the group.

4. Select the **Picture or texture fill** radio button.

 - If the last-used picture or texture displays in the chart element, ignore it. It will be replaced.

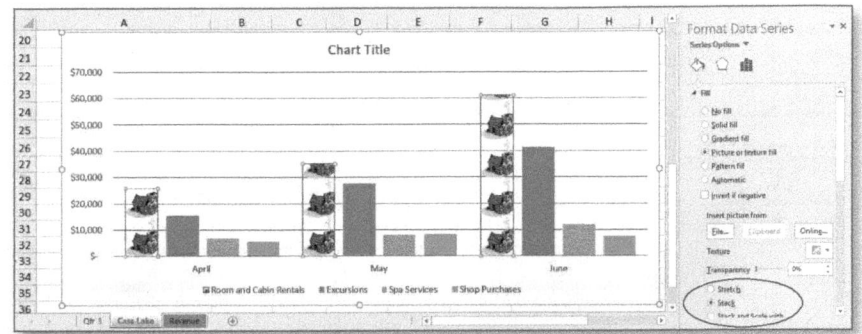

3-31 Image used as fill for data series

5. Click **Online** to search for an image or click **File** to choose a stored image.

6. Find and insert the image.

 - The picture is placed in the chart element.

7. Click the **Stack** button in the task pane (Figure 3-31).

 - Copies of the picture fill the element.

> **MORE INFO**
>
> Insert an image as a separate design element on a chart from the *Insert* tab and edit it from the *Picture Format* tab.

Insert Shapes

The *Shapes* gallery is located in the *Insert Shapes* group on the *Chart Tools Format* tab. These predefined shapes include arrows, lines, circles, and other basic figures. Shapes can be used to highlight or emphasize a point in the chart. They can be drawn anywhere on the chart, but are usually placed on the background or the plot area so they do not obscure any data. A shape, once drawn, is a clickable, selectable object. When it is selected, the *Picture Tools Format* tab is available with commands for altering the appearance of the shape and there is also the *Format Shape* task pane.

▶ HOW TO: Insert a Shape in a Chart

1. Select the chart object or the chart sheet tab.

2. Click the **More** button [*Chart Tools Format* tab, *Insert Shapes* group].

3. Select the shape.

4. Click and drag to draw the shape on the chart (Figure 3-32).

 - The shape is selected.

5. Type text for the shape.

 - Text is optional.
 - Some shapes cannot display text.

6. Click the **Drawing Tools Format** tab to format the shape.

 - You can also apply formatting from the *Format Shape* task pane.

7. Click a worksheet cell or another chart element to deselect the shape.

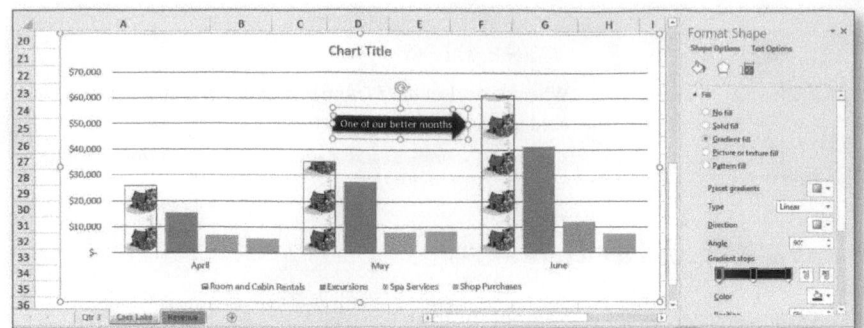

3-32 Shape inserted in chart

> **ANOTHER WAY**
>
> Insert a shape from the *Shapes* button on the *Insert* tab [*Illustrations* group].

Use WordArt in a Chart

WordArt is a text box with preset font style, fill, and effects. *WordArt* is best used for main titles, because it can make smaller elements unreadable. You apply a *WordArt* style from the *Chart Tools Format* tab, *WordArt Styles* group. You can further design a *WordArt* style by individually changing its fill, outline, and effects.

> **MORE INFO**
>
> You can insert a *WordArt* text box from the *Insert* tab [*Text* group] and position it on the chart.

▶ HOW TO: Use WordArt in a Chart

1. Select the chart title object.

 - You can also apply *WordArt* to an axis title, a data label, or the legend.

2. Click the **More** button to open the *WordArt Styles* gallery [*Chart Tools Format* tab, *WordArt Styles* group].

3. Point to a style icon to see a *ScreenTip* with a description.

 - The styles use colors and effects from the workbook theme.
 - *Live Preview* works in a chart object but not on a chart sheet.

4. Click the preferred style (Figure 3-33).

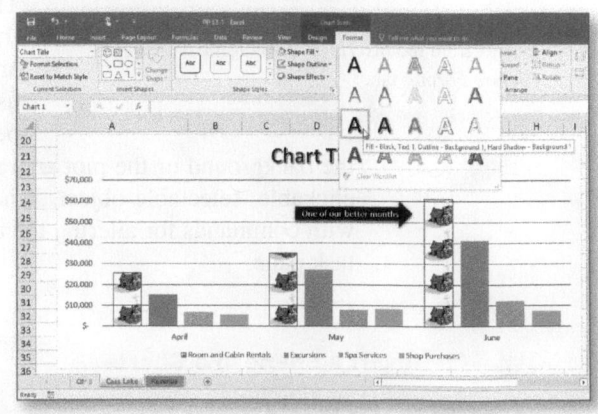

3-33 *WordArt Style* gallery for selected chart title

PAUSE & PRACTICE: EXCEL 3-2

For this project, you open your Pause & Practice file to edit and format the Paradise Lakes Resort charts. You switch row and column data, remove chart elements, and change the chart type. Finally, you format the charts for increased visual appeal.

File Needed: *[your initials] PP E3-1.xlsx*
Completed Project File Name: *[your initials] PP E3-2.xlsx*

1. Open the *[your initials] PP E3-1* workbook completed in *Pause & Practice 3-1* and save it as [your initials] PP E3-2.

2. Switch the row and column data in the chart object.
 a. Click the **Cass Lake** worksheet tab.
 b. Point to the border or edge of the chart object and click to select it.
 c. Click the **Switch/Row Column** button [*Chart Tools Design* tab, *Data* group].

3. Edit, add, and remove chart elements.
 a. Click to select the chart title box.
 b. Point to the placeholder text and triple-click to select all of it.
 c. Type Second Quarter Activity.
 d. Click the chart border to deselect the title.
 e. Click the **Chart Elements** button in the top right corner of the chart.
 f. Select the **Axis Titles** box.
 g. Select the horizontal *Axis Title* placeholder below the columns and press **Delete**.
 h. Select the vertical *Axis Title* placeholder.
 i. Click the *Formula* bar, type Revenue, and press **Enter** (Figure 3-34).
 j. Click a worksheet cell to deselect the chart object.

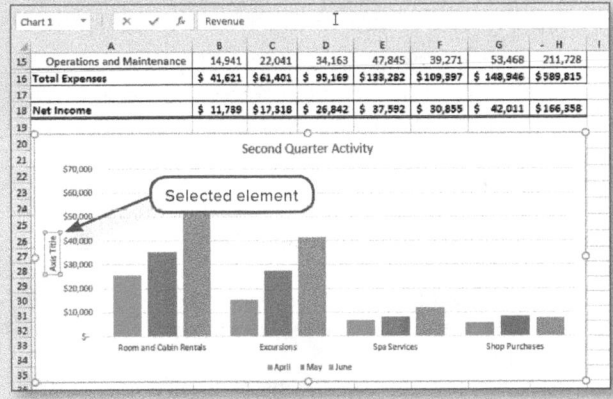

3-34 Edit the text in the *Formula* bar

4. Change the chart type.
 a. Click the **Qtr 3** sheet tab.
 b. Click the **Change Chart Type** button [*Chart Tools Design* tab, *Type* group].
 c. Click the **Recommended Charts** tab.
 d. Find and select the first **Clustered Column** in the pane on the left.
 e. Click **OK**.

5. Filter the source data.
 a. Click the **Chart Filters** button at the top right corner of the chart.
 b. Deselect the **Excursions** box in the *Series* area.
 c. Click **Apply**.
 d. Click the **Chart Filters** button to close the pane (Figure 3-35).

3-35 Filtered data in chart

E3-186

6. Apply shape styles and outlines to chart elements.
 a. Click the **Cass Lake** tab and select the chart object.
 b. Click the **Chart Elements** drop-down arrow [*Chart Tools Format* tab, *Current Selection* group].
 c. Choose **Plot Area** to select the plot area of the chart.
 d. Click the **More** button [*Chart Tools Format* tab, *Shape Styles* group].
 e. Click **Subtle Effect – Gold**, **Accent 4** in the fourth row in the *Theme Styles* group.
 f. Click the drop-down arrow for the **Shape Outline** button [*Chart Tools Format* tab, *Shape Styles* group].
 g. Choose **Black**, **Text 1** in the top row of the *Theme Colors*.
 h. Click the **Chart Elements** drop-down arrow [*Chart Tools Format* tab, *Current Selection* group].
 i. Choose **Vertical (Value) Axis Major Gridlines** to select the major gridlines in the plot area.
 j. Click the icon with the **Shape Outline** button [*Chart Tools Format* tab, *Shape Styles* group] to apply the last-used color (**Black**, **Text 1**).
 k. Click the **Chart Elements** drop-down arrow [*Chart Tools Format* tab, *Current Selection* group] and choose **Chart Area**.
 l. Apply **Black**, **Text 1** for the outline (Figure 3-36).
 m. Click a worksheet cell.

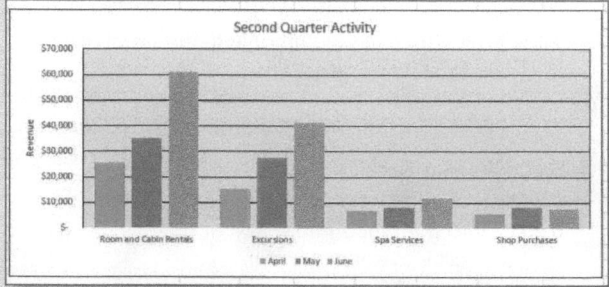

3-36 Plot area formatted

7. Use a picture as fill.
 a. Click the **Qtr 3** tab.
 b. Double-click one of the "Room and Cabin Rentals" columns to open the *Format Data Series* task pane.
 c. Click the **Fill & Line** button.
 d. Click **Fill** to expand the command group.
 e. Select the **Picture or texture fill** button.
 f. Click **Online**, type log cabin in the *Bing Image Search* box, and press **Enter**.
 g. Choose an image and insert it (Figure 3-37). If you choose an image that cannot be used as fill, a message appears in the columns; just select a different picture.
 h. Select the **Stack** radio button in the *Format Data Series* task pane.
 i. Click **Fill** to collapse the command group and click **Border** to expand its group.
 j. Select the **Solid line** button.
 k. Click the **Color** button and choose **Black**, **Text 1**.
 l. Close the task pane.

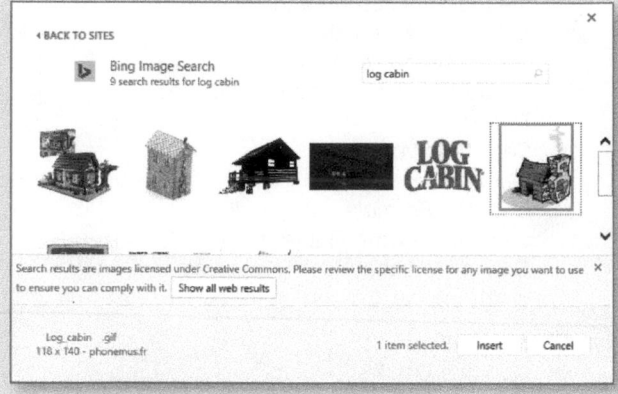

3-37 Online search for a picture as fill

8. Use *WordArt* in a chart.
 a. Triple-click the **Chart Title** placeholder text to select the text.
 b. Type Third Quarter Activity.
 c. Triple-click the new label and change the font size to **32 pt**.
 d. Click the border area of the chart title to display the selection handles.
 e. Click the **More** button [*Chart Tools Format* tab, *WordArt Styles* group].
 f. Choose **Fill – Gray-25%**, **Background 2**, **Inner Shadow** (third row).

9. Format the legend.
 a. Click to select the legend.
 b. Click the **Home** tab and change the font size to **12 pt**.
 c. Click the chart border to deselect the legend.
 d. Click a worksheet cell and press **Ctrl+Home**.

10. Save and close the workbook (Figure 3-38).

3-38 PP E3-2 completed worksheet and chart sheet

<div style="SLO 3.6"></div>

Building Pie and Combination Charts

A pie chart represents one set of related values and shows the proportion of each value to the total. A combination chart uses at least two sets of values and plots each data series with a different chart type. A combination chart can also have two value axes, one on the left and one on the right.

Create a 3-D Pie Chart

A pie chart graphs one data series and illustrates how each number relates to the whole. Be cautious about the number of categories, because a pie chart with hundreds of slices is difficult to interpret and does not depict the relationship among the values.

As you develop chart-building skills, you can choose a type from the *Charts* group on the *Insert* tab. When you select a chart type button, you see a gallery with available subtypes. As you point to each subtype, *Live Preview* previews the chart.

From the *Insert Pie or Doughnut Chart* button on the *Insert* tab, you can select from a gallery of 2-D or 3-D pie types as well as a doughnut shape (Figure 3-39). A doughnut chart is a pie chart with a hollow center. There are also options for a pie chart with a bar or another pie chart.

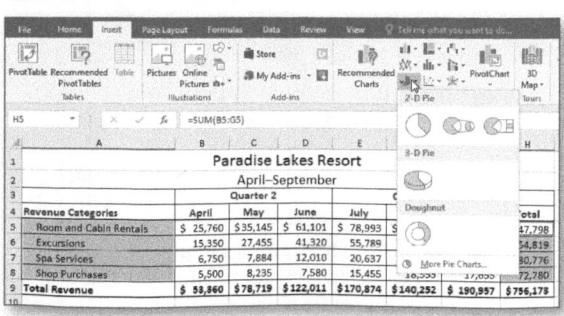

3-39 Selected data series and categories for a pie chart

▶ HOW TO: Create a 3-D Pie Chart Sheet

1. Select the cells that include the values and the category labels.
 - The labels and values need not be adjacent.
2. Click the **Insert Pie or Doughnut Chart** button [*Insert* tab, *Charts* group].
3. Choose **3-D Pie**.
 - A pie chart object is placed in the worksheet.
4. Click the **Move Chart** button [*Chart Tools Design* tab, *Location* group].
5. Click the **New sheet** button.
6. Type a name for the chart sheet.
7. Click **OK**.

Pie Chart Elements and Options

In a pie chart, the data series is represented by the whole pie. A data point is a slice of the pie. You can format the data series as a whole, or you can format individual slices.

A pie chart can display a legend and a title. It does not, however, have axes and does not use axes titles. Data labels can be used in place of a legend, because they show the same information.

Custom commands for a pie chart are the angle of the first slice and the percent of explosion. These commands are available on the *Format* task pane for the data series (the whole pie) or for a selected data point (one slice). The angle of the first slice allows you to rotate the pie. The first slice starts at the top of the chart at 0° (zero degrees). As you increase that value, the slice arcs to the right. *Live Preview* displays the results, too.

Exploding a pie slice emphasizes that slice, because it moves the slice away from the rest of the pie. This uses more white space in the chart, and the pie gets smaller. You set explosion as a percentage.

▶ HOW TO: Rotate a Pie Chart and Explode a Slice

1. Double-click the pie shape.
 - The *Format Data Series* task pane opens.
 - You can also right-click the pie shape and choose **Format Data Series**.
2. Click the **Series Options** button.
3. Drag the vertical slider to set the *Angle of first slice.*
 - The percentage is shown in the entry box.
 - You can also type a percentage or use the spinner arrows to set a value.
4. Click the data point (slice) to explode.
 - The *Format Data Point* task pane opens.
5. Drag the vertical slider to set the *Pie Explosion* (Figure 3-40).
 - The percentage is shown in the entry box.
 - The larger the percentage, the farther the slice is from the rest of the pie.
 - You can type a percentage or use the spinner arrows to set a value.

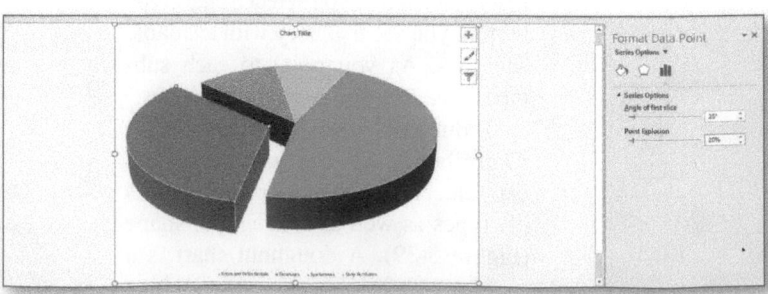

3-40 Exploded pie slice with angle of first slice changed

> **MORE INFO**
>
> You can explode all the slices in a pie chart by selecting the data series, not a data point.

Create a Combination Chart

A combination chart includes at least two chart types such as a line chart and a column chart. Paradise Lakes Resort can use a combination chart to compare revenue from cabin and room rentals to total revenue. These two values reflect a different scale of numbers, so showing one series as a line and the other as a column focuses the comparison (Figure 3-41).

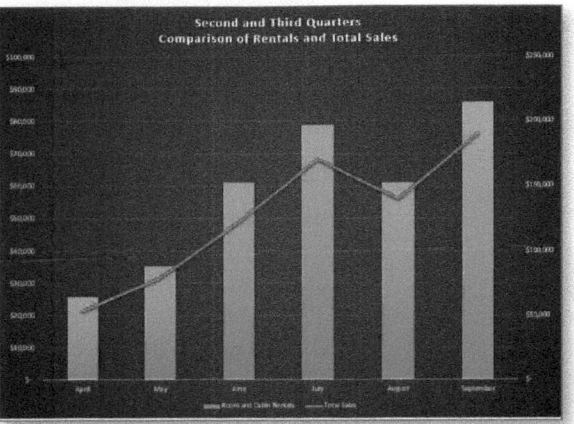

> **MORE INFO**
>
> A line and column combination chart resembles a column chart with a trendline, but the combination chart uses actual values. The trendline predicts values.

3-41 Line-Column combination chart

The most common combination of chart types is line and column, but you can also use a line and area combination. Excel offers an option to create a custom combination, but it is best to use this only after you have experience charting your data.

> **MORE INFO**
>
> Not all chart types can be combined. If you try to do so, Excel opens a message box to inform you.

Create a combination chart from the *Insert Combo Chart* button in the *Charts* group on the *Insert* tab as well as from the *All Charts* tab in the *Insert Chart* dialog box.

▶ HOW TO: Create a Combination Chart

1. Select the cell ranges for the chart.
 - The cell ranges need not be contiguous.
2. Click the **Insert Combo Chart** button [*Insert* tab, *Charts* group].
 - Suggested combinations are displayed.
 - Point to a subtype to see a description and a *Live Preview* (Figure 3-42).
3. Select the chart subtype.
 - A combo chart object displays in the worksheet.
 - You can move the chart to its own sheet if desired.

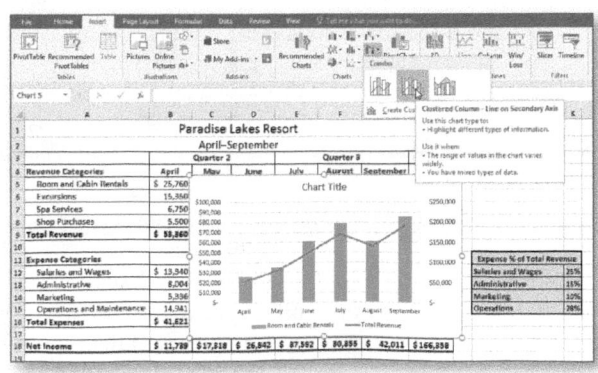

3-42 Insert Combo Chart button options

Combination Chart Elements and Options

A combination chart has at least two data series, each graphed in its own chart type. Keep this type of chart relatively simple, because its purpose is to compare unlike items and too many data series complicate what viewers see.

In a combination chart, you can display values on two vertical axes. The axis on the left is the primary

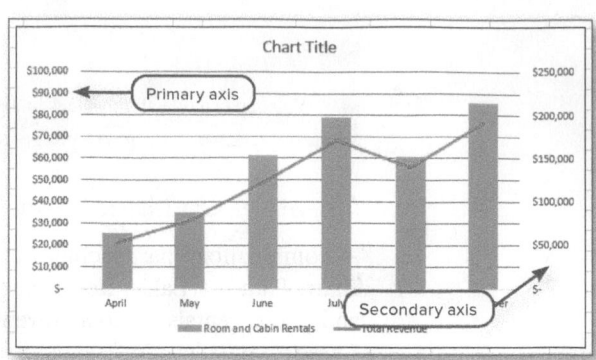

3-43 Secondary axis for a combo chart

axis; the one on the right is secondary (Figure 3-43). This option is best when the values are very different or use a different scale.

For the secondary axis, Excel builds the number scale based on the data. Select the data series to be plotted on the secondary axis and choose the option from the *Series Options* command group in the *Format* task pane. You can also define a secondary axis in the *Insert Chart* or the *Change Chart Type* dialog boxes.

A combination chart has the same elements and commands as a regular column or line chart. You can apply chart styles and layouts, as well as shape fill, outline, effects, pictures, shapes, and *WordArt*.

▶ **HOW TO: Display a Secondary Axis on a Combination Chart**

1. Select the chart object or the chart sheet tab.
2. Select the data series to be shown on the secondary axis.
 - Select the line or any column in a line-column combo chart.
 - You can also choose the data series from the *Chart Elements* box [*Chart Tools Format* tab, *Current Selection* group].
3. Click the **Format Selection** button [*Chart Tools Format* tab, *Current Selection* group].
4. Click the **Series Options** button in the task pane (Figure 3-44).
5. Click the **Secondary Axis** radio button.
 - Additional options for the axis depend on the chart type.
6. Close the *Format Data Series* task pane.

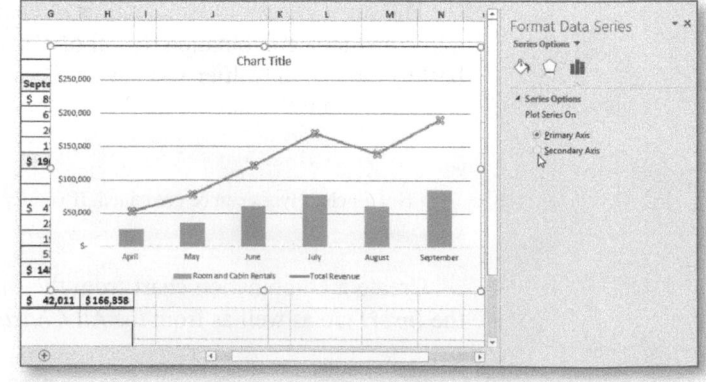

3-44 *Format Data Series* task pane to define a secondary axis

SLO 3.7

Creating Sunburst and Waterfall Charts

New chart types in Excel 2016 visualize data in ways that previously required engineering or similar specialized software. With a sunburst chart, you can show relationships between multiple categories of data. A waterfall chart depicts a running total for financial data so that you can assess the impact of negative and positive cash flows. These charts have many characteristics of standard Excel charts, but they have a few limitations related to requirements for the data they plot.

Create a Sunburst Chart

A *sunburst chart* is a hierarchy chart that illustrates the relationship among categories and subcategories of data. It resembles a doughnut chart with concentric rings for each layer of data as shown in Figure 3-45. A *hierarchy* is a division of data that identifies a top group followed by lesser groups. The student population at your college can be illustrated in a hierarchy with gender at the top, followed by age group, then home city, followed by area of study, and so on.

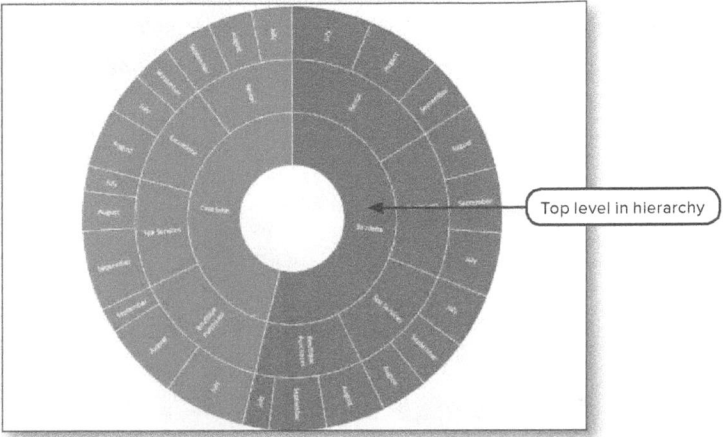

3-45 Sunburst chart for third quarter revenue for two locations

Paradise Lakes Resort keeps a record of revenue by location, category, and month. The inner ring in Figure 3-45 is the top level of the hierarchy, the location. The second level is the revenue category (Rentals, Excursions, etc.), and the outside ring is the month's revenue. From the chart, you can see that Baudette contributed slightly more than half of the total revenue and that the boutique purchases at Cass Lake were high.

A sunburst chart has one data series and no axes. It can display a title, data labels, and a legend. The *Chart Tools Design* and *Format* tabs provide basic options for fine-tuning the appearance of the chart.

The *Insert Hierarchy Chart* button [*Insert* tab, *Charts* group] has two subtypes, *Sunburst* and *TreeMap*. These subtypes can handle large amounts of data, but be careful not to build charts that are difficult to interpret due to their size.

> **MORE INFO**
>
> A *TreeMap* chart illustrates hierarchical data using rectangles of various sizes and colors to represent the divisions and subdivisions.

▶ **HOW TO: Create a Sunburst Chart**

1. Select the source data with labels and values.
 - The **Quick Analysis** button appears, but the *Charts* group does not include the *Sunburst* chart type.
2. Click the **Insert Hierarchy Chart** button [*Insert* tab, *Charts* group].
 - A menu lists the subtypes.
3. Point to **Sunburst** to see a *Live Preview*.

4. Click **Sunburst** to select it.
 - A chart object is placed in the worksheet.
5. Click the **Move Chart** button [*Chart Tools Design* tab, *Location* group].
6. Select **New sheet**.
7. Type a name for the chart sheet and click **OK**.
 - The *Chart Tools Design* and *Format* tabs are available.
8. Click the sunburst shape to select the circle.
9. Point to a category name in the inner ring and click to select the data point.
 - The category and its related items are selected (Figure 3-46).

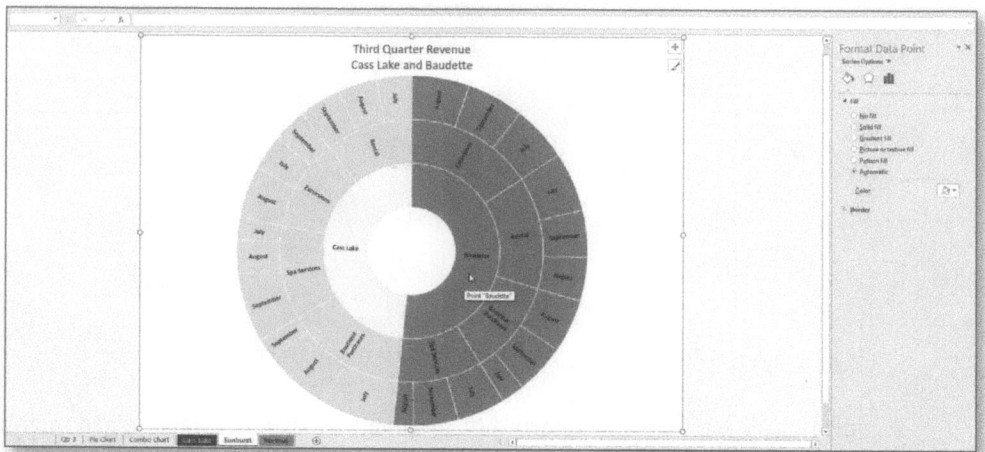

3-46 Sunburst chart sheet with selected data point

10. Format the data point as desired.
 - If the *Format Data Point* task pane is not open, click the **Format Selection** button [*Chart Tools Format* tab, *Current Selection* group].
11. Click outside the chart background to deselect the chart.

> **MORE INFO**
>
> The *Hierarchy* charts do not appear in any *Recommended Charts* list, but they are listed on the *All Charts* tab.

Create a Waterfall Chart

A **waterfall chart** is a financial chart that displays a moving total for positive and negative values. A waterfall chart graphs how each expense or outlay affects the account. You might, for example, build a waterfall chart to visualize your monthly income sources (inflows) and expenditures (outlays) to watch how you spend your resources.

In Figure 3-47, it is obvious that payroll consumes most of the cash account for Paradise Lakes Resort. In a waterfall chart, the depth or height of the marker indicates the value. In the figure, the beginning balance and ending total markers rest on the bottom axis. The other amounts are described as floating.

A waterfall chart plots one data series and has a legend that clarifies the increase, decrease, and total colors. A waterfall chart can also include axes, titles, gridlines, and data labels.

The *Insert Waterfall or Stock Chart* button is in the *Charts* group on the *Insert* tab. These charts do not appear in the *Recommended Charts* list, but they are available on the *All Charts* tab.

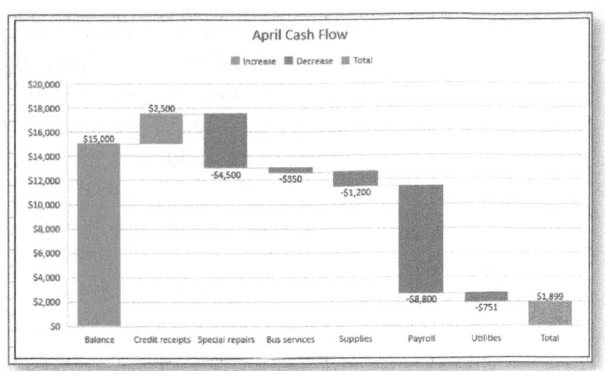

3-47 Waterfall chart for cash flow

▶ HOW TO: Create a Waterfall Chart Sheet

1. Select the source data with labels and values.
 - The *Quick Analysis* button appears but does not have an option for a waterfall chart.
2. Click the **Insert Waterfall or Stock Chart** button [*Insert* tab, *Charts* group].
 - A menu lists the subtypes.
3. Click **Waterfall**.
 - A chart object is placed in the worksheet.
4. Click the **Move Chart** button [*Chart Tools Design* tab, *Location* group].
5. Select **New sheet**.
6. Type a name for the chart sheet and click **OK**.
 - The *Chart Tools Design* and *Format* tabs are available.
7. Click a column marker to select the data series.
8. Click the ending marker to select only it.
9. Click the **Format Selection** button [*Chart Tools Format* tab, *Current Selection* group].
10. Click the **Series Options** button in the task pane.
11. Expand the *Series Options* group.
12. Select the **Set as total** box (Figure 3-48).
 - The marker rests on the bottom axis and is no longer floating.
13. Close the task pane and click outside the chart to deselect it.

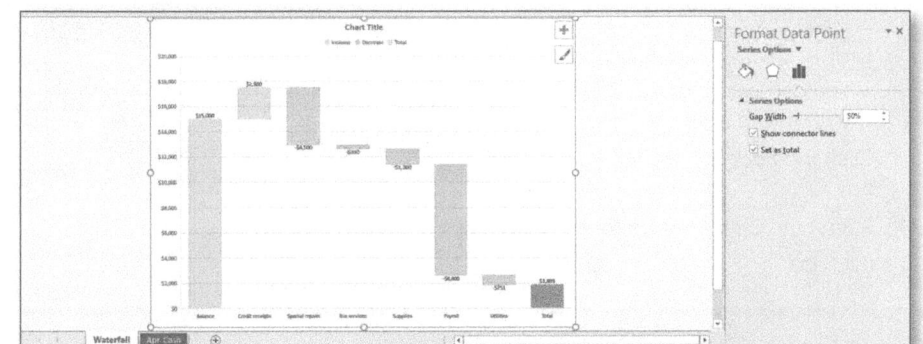

3-48 Set a marker as a total

Inserting and Formatting Sparklines

Sparklines are miniature charts in a cell or cell range. They can be used to illustrate trends and patterns without adding a separate chart object or sheet. They do not have the same characteristics as an Excel chart.

Sparklines are created from a selected data range and placed in a location range, usually next to the data (Figure 3-49). They are embedded in the cell, almost like a background. If you enter a label or value in a cell with a sparkline, that data appears on top of the sparkline.

3-49 Column sparklines in a worksheet

Insert Sparklines

There are three sparkline types: *Line*, *Column*, and *Win/Loss*. The *Sparklines* commands are located on the *Insert* tab of the worksheet. The *Data Range* is the range of cells to be graphed, and the *Location Range* is the cell or range for the sparklines. The **Sparkline Tools Design** tab opens when you select the sparkline group.

▶ **HOW TO:** Insert Column Sparklines in a Worksheet

1. Select the cell range of data to be graphed.

2. Click the **Column Sparkline** button [*Insert* tab, *Sparklines* group].

 - The selected range address is shown in the *Data Range* entry box.
 - You can select or edit the data range here.

3. Click the *Location Range* box.

4. Select the cell or range for the sparklines (Figure 3-50).

5. Click **OK**.

3-50 *Create Sparklines* dialog box

Sparkline Design Tools

When sparklines are selected, the *Sparkline Tools Design* tab opens. This context-sensitive tab includes several options for changing the appearance of the sparklines. There is a *Sparkline Style* option that changes the color scheme for the sparkline group, but you can also change colors with the *Sparkline Color* command. The *Marker Color* command enables you to choose a different color for identified values. A **marker** for a sparkline is the data point value. You can use different colors to highlight the high, low, first, or last value as well as negative values.

When you define a location range for sparklines, they are embedded as a group. If you select any cell in the sparkline range, the entire group is selected. Subsequent commands affect all sparklines in the group. From the *Group* section on the *Sparkline Tools Design* tab, you can ungroup the sparklines so that you can format them individually.

From the *Sparkline Tools Design* tab, you can also change the type of sparkline, such as making a column sparkline into a line sparkline. The *Show* group lists the marker values that can be highlighted. When you select one of these options, that marker in the sparkline is formatted with a different color.

▶**HOW TO: Format Sparklines**

1. Click a cell with a sparkline.
 - The sparkline group is selected.
2. Click the *Sparkline Line Tools Design* tab.
3. Click the **More** button [*Sparkline Tools Design* tab, *Style* group].
4. Choose a sparkline style.
 - The sparkline group is recolored.
5. Select the **High Point** box in the *Show* group (Figure 3-51).
 - A default color based on the sparkline style is applied to the highest value in the sparkline for each row.

3-51 *High Point* marker selected for sparklines

6. Click the **Sparkline Color** button [*Sparkline Tools Design* tab, *Style* group].
7. Choose a color for the sparkline group.
 - The sparkline group is recolored, and the color from the *Sparkline Style* is overridden.
8. Click the **Marker Color** button [*Sparkline Tools Design* tab, *Style* group].
9. Choose **High Point** and select a color.
 - The color for the highest value is reset.

Clear Sparklines

You can remove sparklines from a worksheet with the *Clear* command in the *Group* group on the *Sparkline Tools Design* tab. After sparklines are cleared, you may also need to delete the column where they were located or reset row heights and column widths.

▶**HOW TO: Clear Sparklines**

1. Select any cell in the sparklines range.
2. Click the arrow with **Clear Selected Sparklines** button [*Sparkline Tools Design* tab, *Group* group].
3. Choose **Clear Selected Sparklines Groups**.

▶ MORE INFO

When you ungroup sparklines, you can select a single sparkline cell and clear it.

PAUSE & PRACTICE: EXCEL 3-3

For this project, you complete Paradise Lakes' revenue report by inserting a pie chart that shows the proportion of each revenue category. You also insert a combination chart sheet to compare rentals with total revenue and a sunburst chart to analyze third quarter revenue. Finally, you insert sparklines in the worksheet.

File Needed: *[your initials] PP E3-2.xlsx*
Completed Project File Name: *[your initials] PP E3-3.xlsx*

1. Open the **[your initials] PP E3-2** workbook completed in *Pause & Practice 3-2* and save it as [your initials] PP E3-3.

2. Create a pie chart for total sales revenue.
 a. Select the **Cass Lake** tab.
 b. Select cells **A5:A8** as the category.
 c. Press **Ctrl** and select cells **H5:H8** as the data series.
 d. Click the **Insert Pie or Doughnut Chart** button [*Insert* tab, *Charts* group].
 e. Choose **3-D Pie**.
 f. Click the **Move Chart** button [*Chart Tools Design* tab, *Location* group].
 g. Click the **New sheet** button and type Pie Chart as the sheet name.
 h. Click **OK**.

3. Format a pie chart.
 a. Select the **Pie Chart** tab.
 b. Click the **Chart Title** placeholder to select it and then triple-click the **Chart Title** placeholder text.
 c. Type Second and Third Quarters and press **Enter**.
 d. Type Sources of Revenue on the second line.
 e. Drag to select the first line of the title.
 f. Use the mini toolbar to change the font size to **24 pt**.
 g. Drag to select the second line of the title.
 h. Use the mini toolbar to change the font size to **18 pt**. (Figure 3-52).
 i. Click the chart border to deselect the title.
 j. Double-click the pie to open the *Format Data Series* task pane.
 k. Click the **Series Options** button in the *Format Data Series* task pane.
 l. Click the **Room and Cabin Rentals** slice to change to the *Format Data Point* task pane.
 m. Set the pie explosion percentage at **10%**.
 n. Close the task pane.
 o. Select the legend at the bottom of the chart to display selection handles.
 p. Click the **Home** tab and change the font size to **14 pt** (Figure 3-53).

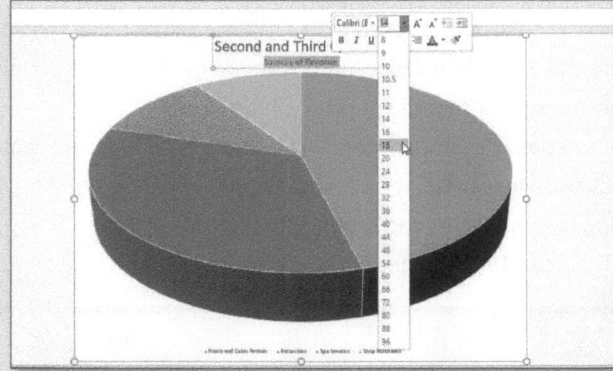

3-52 Chart titles typed and font size changed

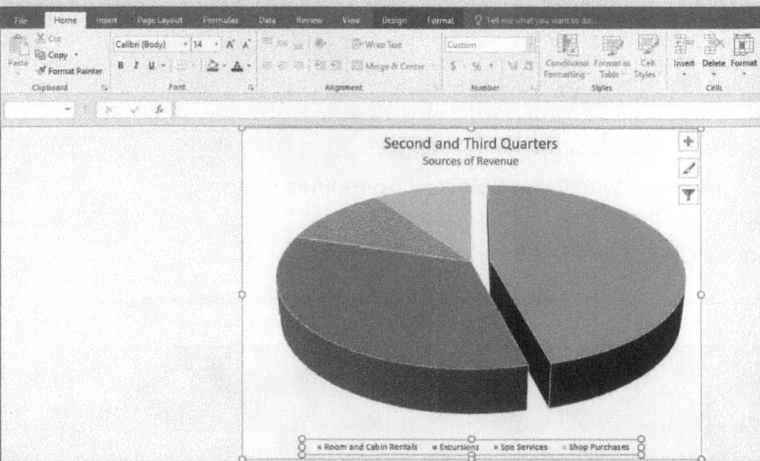

3-53 Selected legend with new font size

4. Create a combination chart for total sales revenue and room and cabin rentals.
 a. Select the **Cass Lake** tab.
 b. Select cells **A4:G5** as one data series and category.

 c. Press **Ctrl** and select cells **A9:G9** as another data series and category.

 d. Click the **Insert Combo Chart** button [*Insert* tab, *Charts* group].

 e. Choose **Clustered Column – Line on Secondary Axis**.

 f. Click the **Move Chart** button [*Chart Tools Design* tab, *Location* group].

 g. Click the **New sheet** button and type Combo Chart as the sheet name.

 h. Click **OK**.

5. Format a combination chart.

 a. Select the **Combo Chart** tab, select the **Chart Title** placeholder, and then triple-click the placeholder text.

 b. Type Second and Third Quarters and press **Enter**.

 c. Type Comparison of Rentals and Total Revenue on the second line.

 d. Click the chart border to deselect the chart title.

 e. Choose **Style 6** [*Chart Tools Design* tab, *Chart Styles* group] (Figure 3-54).

 f. Click the background to deselect the chart.

3-54 Combo chart with Style 6

6. Create a sunburst chart for third quarter revenue analysis.

 a. Select the **Revenue** tab.

 b. Select cells **A5:D28** as the data series and categories. This chart will illustrate revenue for Cass Lake and Baudette.

 c. Click the **Insert Hierarchy Chart** button [*Insert* tab, *Charts* group].

 d. Choose **Sunburst**.

 e. Click the **Move Chart** button [*Chart Tools Design* tab, *Location* group].

 f. Click the **New sheet** button and type Sunburst as the sheet name.

 g. Click **OK**.

 h. Select the **Chart Title** placeholder and type Third Quarter Revenue.

 i. Press **Enter** and type Cass Lake and Baudette on the second line (Figure 3-55).

 j. Click the chart border to deselect the title object.

 k. Click to select the title object and change its font size to **16 pt**.

 l. Click the background to deselect the chart.

3-55 Sunburst chart with edited title

7. Insert sparklines in a worksheet.
 a. Select the **Cass Lake** tab.
 b. Right-click the column **H** heading and choose **Insert** to insert a new column.
 c. Select the cell range **B5:G8** as the data to be charted with sparklines.
 d. Click the **Column Sparkline** button [*Insert* tab, *Sparklines* group].
 e. Click the **Location Range** box, and select cells **H5:H8**.
 f. Click **OK**.

8. Format sparklines.
 a. Click the **Sparkline Color** button [*Sparkline Tools Design* tab, *Style* group] and select **Green**, **Accent 6**, **Darker 25%**.
 b. Select the sparkline group if necessary, click the **Format** button [*Home* tab, *Cells* group], and change the **Row Height** to **30 (40 pixels)**.
 c. Format column **H** to a width of **16.00 (117 pixels)**.
 d. Press **Ctrl+Home**.

9. Save and close the workbook (Figure 3-56).

		Quarter 2			Quarter 3				
Revenue Categories	April	May	June	July	August	September			Total
Room and Cabin Rentals	$ 25,760	$35,145	$ 61,101	$ 78,993	$ 61,002	$ 85,797			$347,798
Excursions	15,350	27,455	41,320	55,789	47,855	67,050			254,819
Spa Services	6,750	7,884	12,010	20,637	13,040	20,455			80,776
Shop Purchases	5,500	8,235	7,580	15,455	18,355	17,655			72,780
Total Revenue	$ 53,360	$78,719	$122,011	$170,874	$140,252	$ 190,957			$756,173
Expense Categories									
Salaries and Wages	$ 13,340	$19,680	$ 30,503	$ 42,719	$ 35,063	$ 47,739			$189,043
Administrative	8,004	11,808	18,302	25,631	21,038	28,644			113,426
Marketing	5,336	7,872	12,201	17,087	14,025	19,096			75,617
Operations and Maintenance	14,941	22,041	34,163	47,845	39,271	53,468			211,728
Total Expenses	$ 41,621	$61,401	$ 95,169	$133,282	$109,397	$ 148,946			$589,815

Paradise Lakes Resort
April–September

3-56 PP E3-3 completed worksheet

Chapter Summary

3.1 Create Excel chart objects and chart sheets (p. E3-163).

- A *chart* is a visual representation of worksheet data.
- A *chart object* is a selectable item or element in a worksheet.
- A *chart sheet* is an Excel chart on its own tab in the workbook.
- The cells with values and labels used to build a chart are its *source data*.
- Chart objects and sheets are linked to their source data and contain editable chart elements such as data labels or a chart title.
- Commonly used chart types are *Column, Line, Pie,* and *Bar,* and Excel can build sophisticated statistical, financial, and scientific charts.
- You can size and position a chart object in a worksheet, or move it to its own sheet using the *Move Chart* button in the *Location* group on the *Chart Tools Design* tab.
- The *Quick Analysis* tool includes a command group for charts, and it appears when the selected source data is contiguous.

3.2 Use Quick layouts and chart styles to design a chart (p. E3-167).

- A *chart layout* is a set of elements and their locations in a chart.
- The *Quick Layout* button [*Chart Tools Design* tab, *Chart Layouts* group] includes predefined layouts for the current chart type.
- A *chart style* is a predefined combination of colors and effects for chart elements.
- Chart styles are based on the current workbook theme.
- The *Change Colors* command [*Chart Tools Design* tab, *Chart Styles* group] provides quick color palettes for customizing a chart.
- A chart object can be printed with its worksheet data or on its own sheet.
- A chart sheet prints on its own page in landscape orientation.

3.3 Edit chart elements including titles, data labels, and source data (p. E3-172).

- A *chart element* is a selectable and editable part or item in the chart.

- Chart elements include chart and axes titles, data labels, legends, gridlines, and more, depending on the type of chart.
- Excel plots data based on the number of rows and columns selected and the chart type, but you can switch the row and column data.
- You can change some chart types into another type using the *Change Chart Type* button on the *Chart Tools Design* tab.
- Chart data can be filtered to hide and display values or categories without changing the source data.
- Source data for a chart can be edited to use a different cell range or to add or remove a data series.

3.4 Format chart elements with shape styles, fill, outlines, and special effects (p. E3-179).

- A *shape style* is a predesigned set of fill colors, borders, and effects.
- *Shape fill, outline,* and *effects* can also be applied to a chart element from the *Chart Tools Format* tab.
- A chart element has a *Format* task pane that includes fill, outline, and effects commands as well as specific options for the element.
- Most formats can also be applied to a selected chart element from the *Home* tab.

3.5 Use pictures, shapes, and *WordArt* in a chart (p. E3-183).

- For chart shapes that have a fill color, you can use a picture as fill.
- Images used as fill can be from your own or online sources, but not all pictures work well as fill.
- Shapes are predefined outline drawings available from the *Insert Shapes* group on the *Chart Tools Format* tab or from the *Illustrations* group on the *Insert* tab.
- Shapes can be placed on a chart to highlight or draw attention to a particular element.
- *WordArt* is a text box with a preset design, often used to format a chart title.

3.6 Build pie charts and combination charts (p. E3-188).

- A pie chart has one data series and shows each data point as a slice of the pie.

- A pie chart does not have axes, but it does have options to rotate or explode slices.
- A combination chart uses at least two chart types to highlight, compare, or contrast differences in data or values.
- You can format a combination chart to show a secondary axis when values are widely different or use different scales.

3.7 Create sunburst and waterfall charts (p. E3-191).

- A *sunburst chart* has one data series that is grouped in a *hierarchy*.
- A sunburst chart illustrates the relationship among the hierarchies in a pie-like chart with concentric rings.
- A *waterfall chart* depicts a running total for positive and negative values.
- A waterfall chart is used for financial or other data that shows inflows and outlays of resources.

- A waterfall chart resembles a column chart and has category and value axes.
- You can place a sunburst chart or a waterfall chart as an object or on a separate sheet.

3.8 Insert and format sparklines in a worksheet (p. E3-194).

- A *sparkline* is a miniature chart in a cell or range of cells in the worksheet.
- Three sparkline types are available: *Line*, *Column*, and *Win/Loss*.
- When inserted in a range of cells, sparklines are grouped and can be ungrouped.
- The *Sparkline Tools Design* tab is visible when a sparkline is selected and includes formatting options such as setting the color or identifying high and low values.

Check for Understanding

The SIMbook for this text (within your SIMnet account) provides the following resources for concept review:

- Multiple choice questions
- Matching exercises
- Short answer questions

USING MICROSOFT EXCEL 2016

Guided Project 3-1

Life's Animal Shelter (LAS) is an animal care and adoption agency that accepts unwanted and abandoned domestic animals. For this project, you create expense charts and insert sparklines to help the agency track expenses for the first six months of the year. You also build a waterfall chart to graph cash flow for a month.
[Student Learning Outcomes 3.1, 3.2, 3.3, 3.4, 3.5, 3.6, 3.7, 3.8]

File Needed: **LAS-03.xlsx** [Student data files are available in the Library of your SIMnet account.]
Completed Project File Name: **[your initials] Excel 3-1.xlsx**

Skills Covered in This Project

- Create a chart object.
- Create a chart sheet.
- Apply *Quick Layout* and chart styles.
- Add and format chart elements.
- Change the chart type.

- Filter the data series.
- Insert a shape in a chart.
- Create and format a combination chart.
- Insert and format sparklines in a worksheet.
- Create and format a waterfall chart.

1. Open the **LAS-03** workbook from your student data files and save it as [your initials] Excel 3-1.

2. Create a pie chart object.
 a. Select the **Jan-June** sheet and select cells **A5:A10**. Press **Ctrl** and select cells **I5:I10**.
 b. Click the **Insert Pie or Doughnut Chart** button [*Insert* tab, *Charts* group].
 c. Select the **2D-Pie** chart subtype.

3. Create a chart sheet.
 a. Select the pie chart object.
 b. Click the **Move Chart** button [*Chart Tools Design* tab, *Location* group].
 c. Click the **New sheet** button.
 d. Type Pie Chart in the text box.
 e. Click **OK**.

4. Apply a chart style.
 a. Click the **More** button [*Chart Tools Design* tab, *Chart Styles* group].
 b. Select **Style 12**.

5. Edit and format chart elements.
 a. Click the chart title element.
 b. Click the *Formula* bar, type January through June Expenses, and press **Enter**.
 c. Triple-click the new label in the chart and change the font size to **28 pt**.
 d. Click the legend element to select it and to deselect the title element.
 e. Click the **Font Size** arrow [*Home* tab, *Font* group] and change the legend size to **12 pt**.
 f. Select the *Chart Area* element, the chart background.
 g. Click the **Shape Outline** button [*Chart Tools Format* tab, *Shape Styles* group].
 h. Choose **Black, Text 1** as the color.
 i. Click the **Shape Outline** button again.

j. Choose **Weight** and select **1 pt**.
k. Click outside the chart background to see the outline (Figure 3-57).

6. Create a bar chart object.
 a. Click the **Jan-June** sheet tab.
 b. Select cells **A4:G9** as source data, omitting the *Rent* expense.
 c. Click the **Quick Analysis** button and select **Charts**.
 d. Select **Clustered Bar**.
 e. Point to the chart border to display a move pointer.
 f. Drag the chart object so that its top left corner is at cell **A13**.
 g. Point to the bottom right selection handle to display a resize arrow.
 h. Drag the pointer to reach cell **I30** (Figure 3-58).

7. Change the chart type.
 a. Click the bar chart object.
 b. Click the **Change Chart Type** button [*Chart Tools Design* tab, *Type* group].
 c. Click the **Recommended Charts** tab.
 d. Choose **Clustered Column** in the left pane.
 e. Click **OK**.

8. Filter the source data.
 a. Click the column chart object.
 b. Click the **Chart Filters** button in the top right corner of the chart.
 c. Deselect the **January**, **February**, and **March** boxes.
 d. Click **Apply** in the *Chart Filters* pane (Figure 3-59).
 e. Click the **Chart Filters** button to close the pane.

9. Edit, format, and add chart elements.
 a. Click the chart title object.
 b. Click the *Formula* bar.
 c. Type Second Quarter Variable Expenses and press **Enter**.
 d. Click the **Chart Elements** arrow [*Chart Tools Format* tab, *Current Selection* group] and choose **Chart Area**.
 e. Click the **Shape Outline** button [*Chart Tools Format* tab, *Shape Styles* group].
 f. Choose **Black, Text 1** as the color.
 g. Click the **Shape Outline** button again and choose **Weight** and **1 pt**.

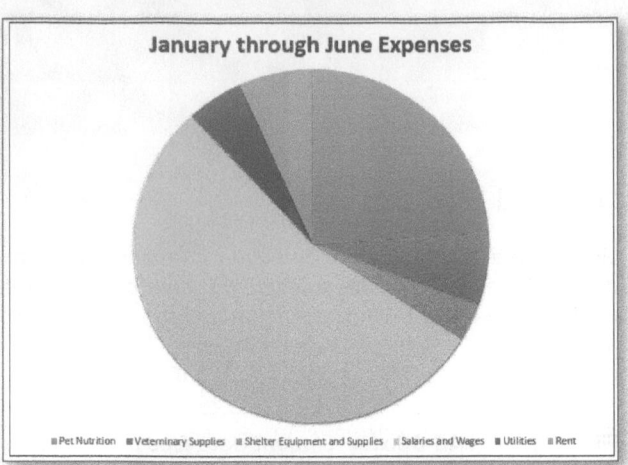

3-57 Pie Chart sheet with format changes

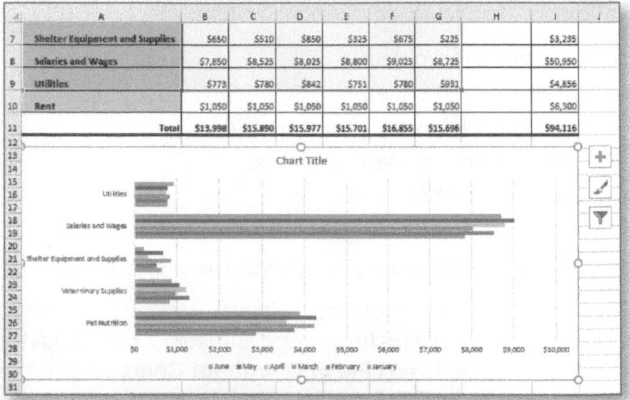

3-58 Bar chart object sized and positioned

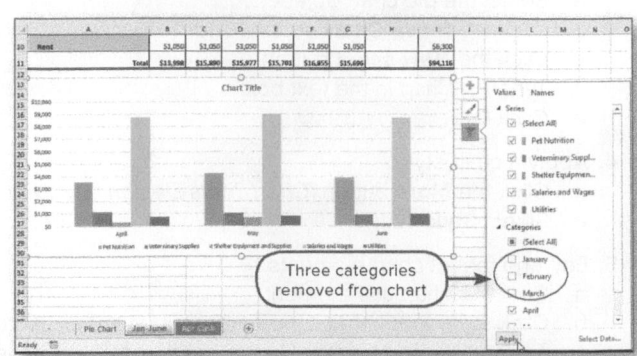

Three categories removed from chart

3-59 Chart filters applied

 h. Click the **Change Colors** button [*Chart Tools Design* tab, *Chart Styles* group].
 i. Choose **Color 3** in the *Colorful* group.
 j. Click the **Chart Elements** arrow [*Chart Tools Format* tab, *Current Selection* group] and choose **Plot Area**.
 k. Click the **Shape Fill** button [*Chart Tools Format* tab, *Shape Styles* group].
 l. Choose **Gold**, **Accent 4**, **Lighter 80%** as the color.
 m. Click a worksheet cell.

10. Create a combination chart sheet.
 a. Select cells **A9:G9**. Press **Ctrl** and select cells **A11:G11**.
 b. Click the **Insert Combo Chart** button [*Insert* tab, *Charts* group].
 c. Select the **Clustered Column-Line** chart subtype.
 d. Click the **Move Chart** button [*Chart Tools Design* tab, *Location* group].
 e. Click the **New sheet** button, type Combo Chart as the name, and click **OK**.
 f. Double-click the line marker in the chart.
 g. Click the **Series Options** button in the *Format Data Series* task pane.
 h. Select the **Secondary Axis** box in the task pane (Figure 3-60).
 i. Close the task pane.

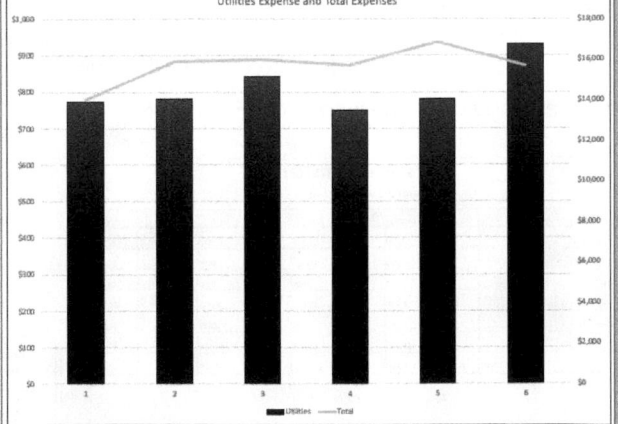

3-60 Combo chart and a secondary axis

11. Edit and format chart elements.
 a. Edit the chart title placeholder to Utilities Expense and Total Expenses.
 b. Select the chart area.
 c. Apply a **1 pt**. **Black, Text 1** outline to the chart area.
 d. Click one of the column markers to select the data series.
 e. Click the **More** button [*Chart Tools Format* tab, *Shape Styles* group].
 f. Select **Moderate Effect – Black**, **Dark 1** in the *Theme Styles* group.
 g. Click the line marker.
 h. Click the **Shape Outline** button [*Chart Tools Format* tab, *Shape Styles* group].
 i. Choose **Gold**, **Accent 4** as the color.
 j. Click the **Shape Outline** button again and choose **Weight** and **3 pt** (Figure 3-61).

12. Insert sparklines in the worksheet.
 a. Click the **Jan-June** sheet tab.
 b. Select cells **B5:G9** as the data range.
 c. Click the **Column Sparkline** button [*Insert* tab, *Sparklines* group].
 d. Select cells **H5:H9** for the *Location Range* and click **OK**.
 e. Click the **Sparkline Color** button [*Sparkline Tools Design* tab, *Style* group].
 f. Choose **White, Background 1, Darker 50%**.

3-61 Line and column formatted in combo chart

13. Insert a shape in a chart.
 a. Select the column chart object.
 b. Click the **More** button [*Chart Tools Format* tab, *Insert Shapes* group].
 c. Select the **Text Box** shape [*Basic Shapes* group].
 d. Draw a text box like the one shown in Figure 3-62.
 e. Type Utilities are to be removed from an updated chart per management request.
 f. Drag a selection handle to size the text box shape if necessary.
 g. Point to a border of the *Text Box* shape to display a four-pointed arrow and position it if needed.

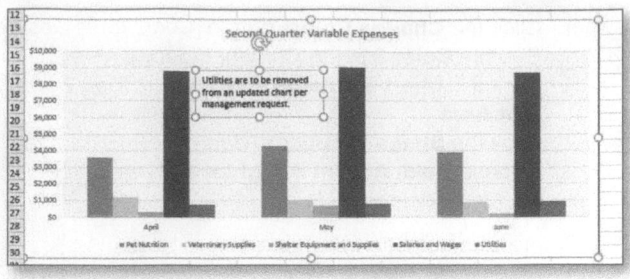

3-62 Text box shape inserted in chart

14. Click a worksheet cell and press **Ctrl+Home**.

15. Create a waterfall chart object.
 a. Select the **Apr Cash** sheet tab.
 b. Select cells **A5:B14**. This data represents cash coming in and going out for April.
 c. Click the **Insert Waterfall or Stock Chart** button [*Insert* tab, *Charts* group].
 d. Select **Waterfall**.

16. Size and position a chart object.
 a. Point to the chart border to display the move pointer.
 b. Drag the chart object so that its top left corner is at cell **C1**.
 c. Point to the bottom right selection handle to display the resize arrow.
 d. Drag the pointer to cell **L20**.

17. Format chart elements.
 a. Double-click the Net Cash column marker and then click the marker again to open the *Format Data Point* pane.
 b. Click the **Series Options** button in the task pane and expand the *Series Options* group.
 c. Select the **Set as total** box.
 d. Triple-click the chart title placeholder text and type April Cash Flow.
 e. Select the chart area and apply a **1 pt**. **black** outline.
 f. Click a worksheet cell and press **Ctrl+Home**.

18. Save and close the workbook (Figure 3-63).

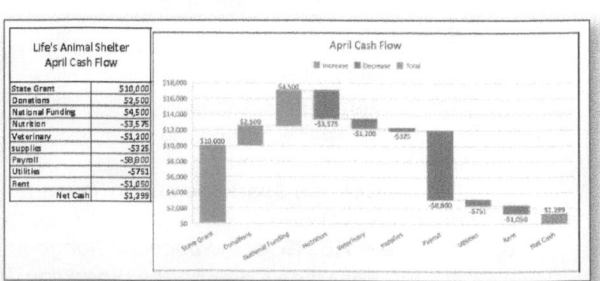

3-63 Excel 3-1 completed worksheets and charts

Guided Project 3-2

Wear-Ever Shoes is a shoe outlet with several locations. In a worksheet that tracks sales of popular items for the past six months, you create a bar chart to compare the number of pairs sold by style. You also create a combination chart to compare number of pairs sold and unit cost for each style. For another set of data, you create a sunburst chart to illustrate sales by shoe style, gender, and color.
[Student Learning Outcomes 3.1, 3.2, 3.3, 3.4, 3.5, 3.6, 3.7]

File Needed: **WearEverShoes-03.xlsx** [Student data files are available in the Library of your SIMnet account.]
Completed Project File Name: **[your initials] Excel 3-2.xlsx**

Skills Covered in This Project

- Create a chart sheet.
- Change the chart type.
- Apply a chart style.
- Add and format chart elements.
- Use a picture as fill.
- Create and format a combination chart.
- Use *WordArt* in a chart.
- Create and format a sunburst chart.

1. Open the **WearEverShoes-03** workbook from your student data files and save it as [your initials] Excel 3-2.

2. Create a column chart sheet.
 a. Select cells **A5:B16** on the **Unit Sales** sheet.
 b. Click the **Quick Analysis** button and choose **Charts**.
 c. Select **Clustered Column**.
 d. Click the **Move Chart** button [*Chart Tools Design* tab, *Location* group].
 e. Click the **New sheet** button.
 f. Type Sales Chart and click **OK**.

3. Change the chart type.
 a. Click the **Sales Chart** sheet tab if necessary.
 b. Click the **Change Chart Type** button [*Chart Tools Design* tab, *Type* group].
 c. Click the **Recommended Charts** tab.
 d. Choose **Clustered Bar** in the left pane and click **OK**.

4. Apply a chart style.
 a. Click the **Chart Styles** button in the top right corner of the chart.
 b. Select **Style 7**.
 c. Click the **Chart Styles** button to close the pane.

5. Add fill color to a data series.
 a. Double-click one of the bars to open the *Format Data Series* task pane.
 b. Click the **Fill & Line** button in the task pane.
 c. Click **Fill** to expand the command group.
 d. Select the **Vary colors by point** box.

6. Use a picture as fill for a data point.
 a. Click the "Classy Pumps" bar to display its *Format Data Point* task pane.
 b. Click the **Fill & Line** button in the task pane.
 c. Click **Fill** to expand the command group.
 d. Click the **Picture or texture fill** button.
 e. Click **Online** to open the *Insert Pictures* dialog box.
 f. Type heels in the *Bing Image Search* box and press **Enter** (Figure 3-64).

g. Select an image and click **Insert**.

h. Click the **Stack** radio button in the task pane.

i. Close the task pane and click the chart border.

7. Create a combination chart sheet.

a. Click the **Unit Sales** sheet tab.

b. Select cells **A5:A16**. Press **Ctrl** and select cells **E5:F16**.

c. Click the **Insert Combo Chart** button [*Insert* tab, *Charts* group].

d. Select the **Clustered Column-Line on Secondary Axis** chart subtype.

e. Click the **Move Chart** button [*Chart Tools Design* tab, *Location* group].

f. Click the **New sheet** button.

g. Type Cost&Retail and click **OK**.

3-64 Online image search for fill in a data point

8. Edit chart elements.

a. Click the chart title placeholder.

b. Type Cost and Selling Price Comparison in the *Formula* bar and press **Enter**.

c. Select the chart title box.

d. Click the **Home** tab and change the font size to **20 pt**.

e. Select the chart area and apply a **¾ pt. black** outline.

f. Select one of the column shapes.

g. Click the **More** button [*Chart Tools Format* tab, *Shapes Styles* group].

h. Choose **Intense Effect - Blue**, **Accent 1** in the bottom row of the *Theme Styles* gallery.

i. Select the line marker.

j. Click the **Shape Outline** button [*Chart Tools Format* tab, *Shape Styles* group] and choose **Black**, **Text 1** as the color.

k. Change the weight of the line to **3 pt**.

9. Use *WordArt* in a chart.

a. Click the chart title.

b. Click the **More** button [*Chart Tools Format* tab, *WordArt Styles* group].

c. Choose **Fill - Black**, **Text 1**, **Shadow** in the first row of the gallery.

d. Click the chart border to deselect the title.

10. Create a sunburst chart.

a. Click the **Grouped Sales** sheet tab.

b. Select cells **A5:D24**.

c. Click the **Insert Hierarchy Chart** button [*Insert* tab, *Charts* group].

d. Click **Sunburst** to select it.

e. Click the **Move Chart** button [*Chart Tools Design* tab, *Location* group].

f. Select **New sheet**, type Sunburst, and click **OK**.

11. Format a sunburst chart.

a. Click the chart title element.

b. Triple-click the placeholder text to select it.

c. Type Sales by Style, Color, and Gender.

d. Click the sunburst shape to select the circle.

e. Point to the **Comfy Walking Shoes** arc in the inner ring and click twice to select the data point. The data point is the wedge that represents two colors of the style. You can confirm your selection on the *Chart Tools Format* tab in the *Current Selection* group. It should display "Branch Comfy Walking."

f. Click the **Format Selection** button [*Chart Tools Format* tab, *Current Selection* group].

g. Click the **Fill & Line** button.

h. Click **Fill** to expand the command group.

i. Choose **Solid fill** and click the **Color** button.

j. Choose **Orange**, **Accent 6**, **Lighter 40%**.

k. Close the task pane.

l. Click outside the chart background to deselect the chart.

12. Save and close the workbook (Figure 3-65).

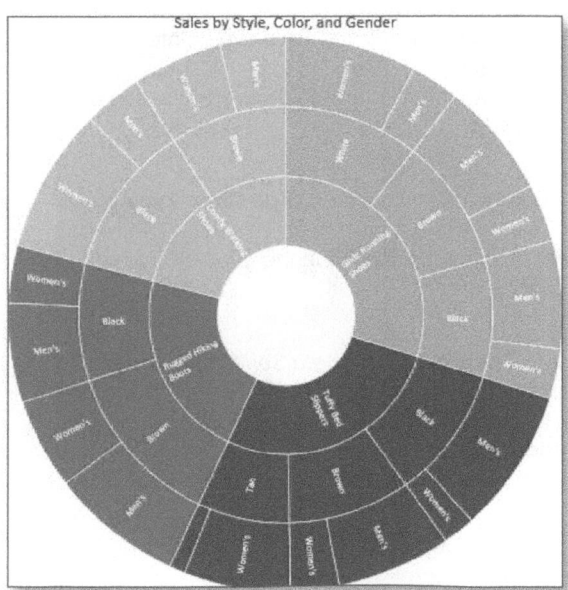

3-65 Excel 3-2 completed chart sheets

Guided Project 3-3

Blue Lake Sports has locations in several major cities and tracks sales by department in each store. For this project, you create a pie chart that shows each store's share of golf-related sales for the first quarter. You also create a line chart to illustrate week-to-week sales for specific departments in one of the stores and insert sparklines in the data.
[Student Learning Outcomes 3.1, 3.2, 3.3, 3.4, 3.6, 3.8]

File Needed: **BlueLakeSports-03.xlsx** [Student data files are available in the Library of your SIMnet account.]
Completed Project File Name: **[your initials] Excel 3-3.xlsx**

Skills Covered in This Project

- Create, size, and position a pie chart object.
- Apply a chart style.
- Change the chart type.
- Add and format chart elements.
- Create a line chart sheet.
- Apply a chart layout.
- Insert and format sparklines in a worksheet.

1. Open the **BlueLakeSports-03** workbook from your student data files and save it as [your initials] Excel 3-3.

2. Create a pie chart object.
 a. Select the **Revenue by Department** sheet, select cells **A4:F4**, press **Ctrl**, and select cells **A13:F13**.
 b. Click the **Recommended Charts** button [Insert tab, Charts group].
 c. Choose **Pie** and click **OK**.

3. Apply a chart style.
 a. Select the chart object.
 b. Click the **More** button [Chart Tools Design tab, Chart Styles group].
 c. Select **Style 12**.

4. Size and position a chart object.
 a. Point to the chart object border to display the move pointer.
 b. Drag the chart object so its top left corner is at cell **A21**.
 c. Point to the bottom right selection handle to display the resize arrow.
 d. Drag the pointer to cell **G36**.

5. Change the chart type.
 a. Select the pie chart object and click the **Change Chart Type** button [Chart Tools Design tab, Type group].
 b. Select the **All Charts** tab and choose **Pie** in the left pane.
 c. Choose **3-D Pie** and click **OK**.

6. Format pie chart elements.
 a. Double-click the pie to open its Format Data Series task pane.
 b. Click the **Atlanta** slice to update the pane to the Format Data Point task pane. (Rest the pointer on a slice to see its identifying ScreenTip.)
 c. Click the **Series Options** button in the Format Data Series task pane.
 d. Set the pie explosion percentage at **10%**.
 e. Close the task pane.
 f. Click the chart object border to deselect the **Atlanta** slice.

7. Add and format chart elements in a pie chart.
 a. Click the **Chart Elements** button in the top right corner of the chart.
 b. Select the **Data Labels** box.

c. Click the **Data Labels** arrow to open its submenu and choose **More Options**.
d. Click the **Label Options** button In the *Format Data Labels* pane.
e. Click **Label Options** to expand the group.
f. Select the **Percentage** box.

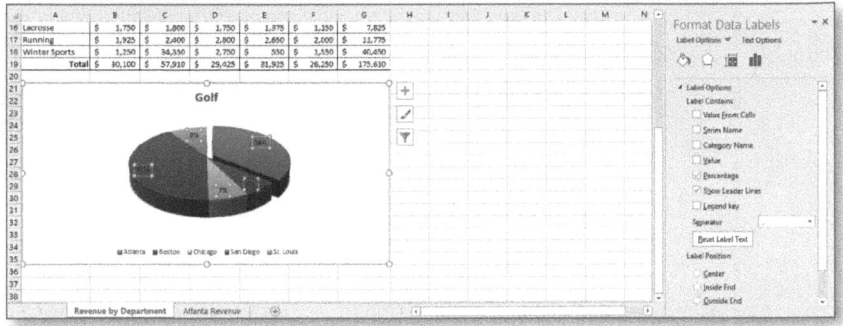

3-66 *Format Data Point* task pane for data labels

g. Deselect the **Value** box (Figure 3-66).
h. Press **Ctrl+B** to apply bold.
i. Change the font size to **12 pt** [*Home* tab, *Font* group].
j. Click the chart object border to select it.
k. Click the **Shape Outline** button [*Chart Tools Format* tab, *Shape Styles* group] and choose **Purple, Accent 4, Darker 50%**.
l. Click the **Shape Outline** button and choose **Weight** and **1 pt**.
m. Click a worksheet cell.

8. Create a line chart sheet.
 a. Select the **Atlanta Revenue** sheet tab.
 b. Select cells **A4:E7**.
 c. Click the **Quick Analysis** button and choose **Charts**.
 d. Select **Line**.
 e. Click the **Move Chart** button [*Chart Tools Design* tab, *Location* group].
 f. Click the **New sheet** button.
 g. Type Promo Depts and click **OK**.

9. Apply a chart layout.
 a. Click the **Quick Layout** button [*Chart Tools Design* tab, *Chart Layouts* group].
 b. Select **Layout 5** to add a data table to the chart sheet (Figure 3-67).

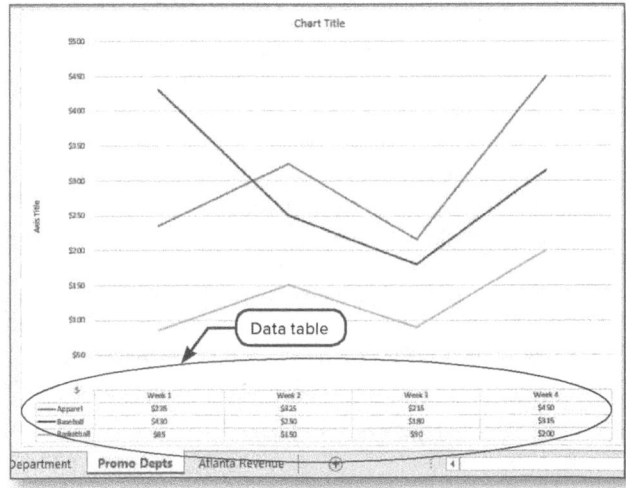

3-67 Data table added by *Quick Layout*

10. Change the chart type.
 a. Click the **Change Chart Type** button [*Chart Tools Design* tab, *Type* group].
 b. Select the **All Charts** tab and choose **Line with Markers** in the *Line* category.
 c. Click **OK**.

11. Edit chart elements in a line chart.
 a. Click the chart title placeholder.
 b. Type Special Promotion Departments in the formula bar and press **Enter**.
 c. Click the vertical axis title placeholder.
 d. Type Dollar Sales in the formula bar and press **Enter**.
 e. Click the **Chart Elements** drop-down arrow [*Chart Tools Format* tab, *Current Selection* group].
 f. Choose **Series "Apparel"** to select the line in the chart.

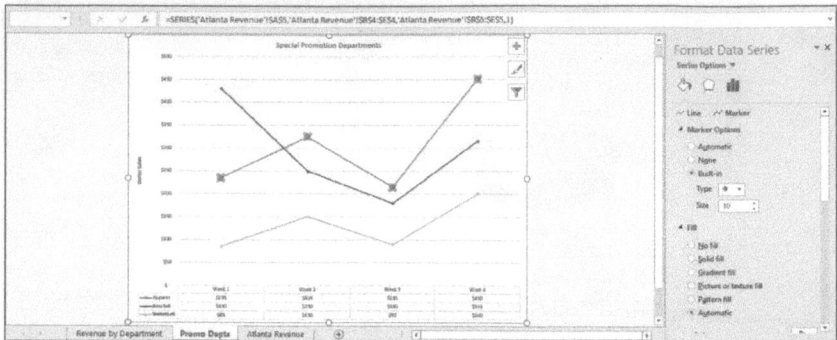

3-68 Marker options for the data series

 g. Click the **Format Selection** button [*Chart Tools Format* tab, *Current Selection* group].
 h. Click the **Fill & Line** button in the *Format Data Series* task pane.
 i. Click **Marker** and then click **Marker Options** to expand the group (Figure 3-68).
 j. Choose **Built-in** and select **10 pt**.
 k. Click the *Series Options* triangle at the top of the task pane and choose **Series "Baseball"** (Figure 3-69).
 l. Apply the same marker changes for the baseball series.
 m. Select the basketball series and make the same marker changes.
 n. Close the task pane and click outside the chart.

12. Insert sparklines in the worksheet.
 a. Click the **Atlanta Revenue** tab.
 b. Right-click the column **F** heading and choose **Insert**.
 c. Select cells **B5:E18** as the data range.
 d. Click the **Line Sparkline** button [*Insert* tab, *Sparklines* group].
 e. Select cells **F5:F18** in the *Location Range* box.
 f. Click **OK**.

13. Format sparklines in worksheet.
 a. Click the **Format** button [*Home* tab, *Cells* group] and change the **Row Height** to **24**.
 b. Click the **Format** button [*Home* tab, *Cells* group] and set the **Column Width** to **35**.
 c. Select the **Markers** box in the *Show* group in the *Sparkline Tools Design* tab.
 d. Click the **Sparkline Color** button [*Sparkline Tools Design* tab, *Style* group].
 e. Choose **Black**, **Text 1** for the line color.
 f. Click cell **A1**.

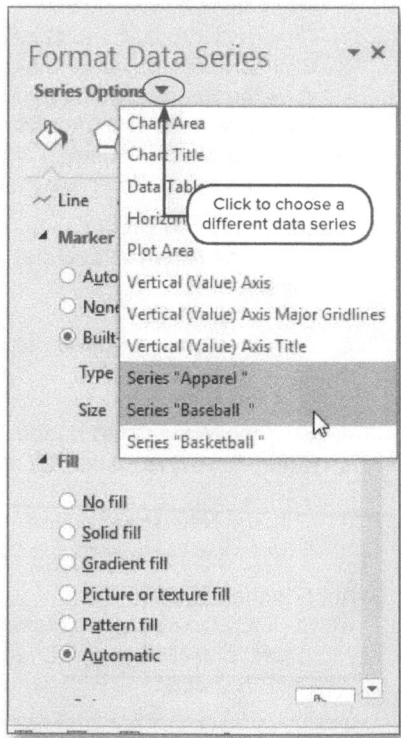

3-69 New data series selected

14. Change the page orientation to landscape.

15. Save and close the workbook (Figure 3-70).

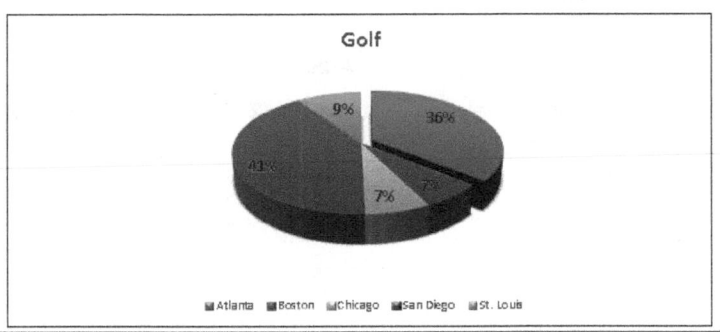

Blue Lake Sports
First Quarter Sales by City

Department	Atlanta	Boston	Chicago	San Diego	St. Louis	Total
Apparel	$ 2,600	$ 3,200	$ 3,800	$ 3,700	$ 3,200	$ 16,500
Baseball	$ 3,500	$ 1,200	$ 1,950	$ 2,100	$ 2,475	$ 10,625
Basketball	$ 1,800	$ 1,800	$ 2,250	$ 1,400	$ 1,750	$ 9,000
Bike & Skate	$ 1,500	$ 1,325	$ 1,225	$ 2,450	$ 1,650	$ 8,150
Exercise	$ 2,650	$ 2,875	$ 3,250	$ 3,775	$ 2,950	$ 15,500
Fishing	$ 2,350	$ 1,035	$ 1,250	$ 2,750	$ 1,450	$ 8,835
Footwear	$ 1,875	$ 2,675	$ 3,575	$ 3,250	$ 2,950	$ 14,325
Game Room	$ 1,300	$ 1,500	$ 1,900	$ 1,050	$ 1,275	$ 7,025
Golf	$ 4,750	$ 875	$ 925	$ 5,400	$ 1,250	$ 13,200
Hockey	$ 850	$ 1,875	$ 1,950	$ 750	$ 1,650	$ 7,075
Hunting	$ 2,000	$ 1,000	$ 650	$ 725	$ 950	$ 5,325
Lacrosse	$ 1,750	$ 1,800	$ 1,750	$ 1,375	$ 1,150	$ 7,825
Running	$ 1,925	$ 2,400	$ 2,800	$ 2,650	$ 2,000	$ 11,775
Winter Sports	$ 1,250	$ 34,350	$ 2,750	$ 550	$ 1,550	$ 40,450
Total	$ 30,100	$ 57,910	$ 29,425	$ 31,925	$ 26,250	$ 175,610

Golf

9% 36% 41% 7% 7%

☐ Atlanta ☐ Boston ☐ Chicago ☐ San Diego ☐ St. Louis

Special Promotion Departments

Blue Lake Sports
January Sales in Atlanta

Department	Week 1	Week 2	Week 3	Week 4		Total
Apparel	$ 295	$ 325	$ 215	$ 450		$ 1,225
Baseball	$ 430	$ 250	$ 180	$ 315		$ 1,175
Basketball	$ 85	$ 150	$ 90	$ 200		$ 525
Bike & Skate	$ 200	$ 325	$ 75	$ 175		$ 775
Exercise	$ 150	$ 160	$ 180	$ 170		$ 660
Fishing	$ 75	$ 150	$ 85	$ 200		$ 510
Footwear	$ 500	$ 350	$ 275	$ 330		$ 1,455
Game Room	$ 45	$ 75	$ 35	$ 15		$ 170
Golf	$ 175	$ 950	$ 580	$ 200		$ 1,905
Hockey	$ 85	$ 125	$ 50	$ 35		$ 295
Hunting	$ 125	$ 350	$ 475	$ 450		$ 1,400
Lacrosse	$ 200	$ 50	$ 65	$ 75		$ 390
Running	$ 165	$ 235	$ 325	$ 180		$ 905
Winter Sports	$ 75	$ 15	$ -	$ 15		$ 105
Total	$ 2,645	$ 2,910	$ 2,630	$ 2,810		$ 10,895

3-70 Excel 3-3 completed worksheet and charts

Independent Project 3-4

For this project, you create a column chart to illustrate April–September revenue for Classic Gardens and Landscapes. You also build a pie chart sheet to graph the proportion that each category contributes to total revenue.
[Student Learning Outcomes 3.1, 3.2, 3.3, 3.4, 3.5, 3.6]

File Needed: *ClassicGardens-03.xlsx* [Student data files are available in the Library of your SIMnet account.]
Completed Project File Name: *[your initials] Excel 3-4.xlsx*

Skills Covered in This Project

- Create a chart object.
- Size and position a chart object.
- Edit and format chart elements.

- Edit the source data for a chart.
- Build a pie chart sheet.
- Use texture as fill.
- Add and format data labels in a chart.

1. Open the ***ClassicGardens-03*** workbook from your student data files and save it as [your initials] Excel 3-4.

2. Create a **Clustered Column** chart object for cells **A4:G9**.

3. Move the chart object so that its top left corner is at cell **A12**. Size the bottom of the chart to reach cell **H30**.

4. Edit the chart title to display CGL Major Sales Revenue on one line and Second and Third Quarters on the second line.

5. Apply chart **Style 14** to the chart.

6. Format the first line of the chart title to a font size of **20 pt**. Format the second title line as **16 pt**.

7. Apply a ½ **point Black**, **Text 1** outline to the chart area.

8. Verify that the chart is still selected. In the highlighted range in the worksheet, drag the resize pointer to remove the *Design Consulting* data series from the chart (Figure 3-71).

9. Create a *3-D Pie* chart for cells **A4:A9** and cells **H4:H9**. Move the chart to its own sheet named Revenue Breakdown.

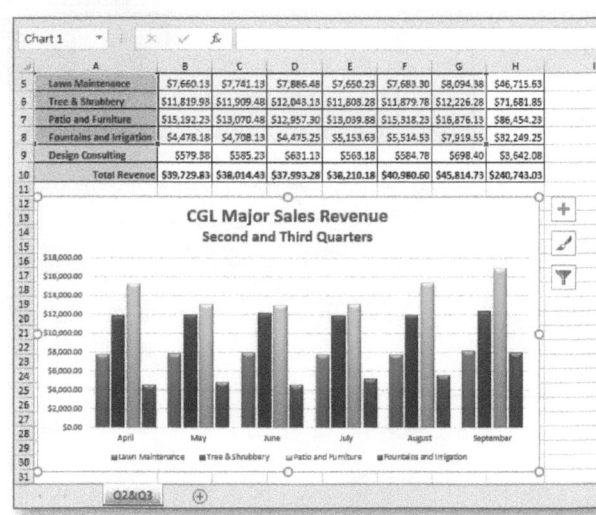

3-71 Resize the chart by dragging the resize pointer

10. Edit the chart title to display Revenue by Category. Change the font size to **32**.

11. Select the legend and change the font size to **12**.

12. Apply the **Woven mat** texture fill to the *Patio and Furniture* slice.

13. Add data labels to display in the center of each slice.
 a. Display the *Format Data Labels* task pane, choose the **Accounting** format, and set **0** decimal places.
 b. While the data labels are selected, change the font size to **14 pt** and apply **bold** [*Home* tab, *Font* group].

14. Deselect the chart.

15. Save and close the workbook (Figure 3-72).

Classic Gardens and Landscapes (CGL)
Revenue for Quarters 2 and 3

Revenue Categories	April	May	June	July	August	September	Total
Lawn Maintenance	$7,660.13	$7,741.13	$7,886.48	$7,650.25	$7,683.30	$8,094.38	$46,715.63
Tree & Shrubbery	$11,819.93	$11,909.48	$12,043.13	$11,805.28	$11,879.78	$12,226.28	$71,681.85
Patio and Furniture	$15,192.23	$13,070.48	$12,957.30	$13,039.88	$15,318.23	$16,876.13	$86,454.23
Fountains and Irrigation	$4,478.18	$4,708.13	$4,475.25	$5,153.68	$5,514.53	$7,919.55	$32,249.25
Design Consulting	$579.38	$585.23	$631.13	$563.13	$684.78	$698.40	$3,642.08
Total Revenue	$39,729.85	$38,014.43	$37,993.28	$38,210.18	$40,980.60	$45,814.73	$240,743.03

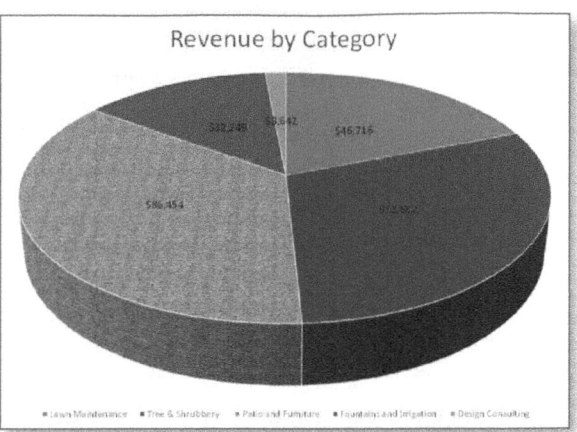

3-72 Excel 3-4 completed chart sheets

For this project, you create a stacked bar chart to illustrate projected tuition and fee amounts for Sierra Pacific Community College District (SPCCD). You also create a pie chart to show total projected revenue for the time period and add sparklines to the worksheet.
[Student Learning Outcomes 3.1, 3.2, 3.3, 3.4, 3.6, 3.8]

File Needed: **SierraPacific-03.xlsx** *[Student data files are available in the* Library *of your SIMnet account.]*
Completed Project File Name: **[your initials] Excel 3-5.xlsx**

Skills Covered in This Project

- Create a chart object.
- Size and position a chart object.
- Apply a chart style.
- Switch row and column data.
- Edit chart source data.
- Create a pie chart sheet.
- Edit and format chart elements.
- Insert and format sparklines in a sheet.

1. Open the **SierraPacific-03** workbook from your student data files and save it as [your initials] Excel 3-5.

2. Select cells **A3:E7** and use the *Quick Analysis* tool to create a stacked bar chart object.

3. Size and position the chart below the worksheet data in cells **A10:G28**.

4. Apply **Chart Style 6**.

5. Edit the chart title to display Tuition Revenue Projection.

6. Apply a **½ pt Dark Blue**, **Text 2** outline to the chart object.

7. Edit the source data to remove the utilization and facilities fees from the chart.

8. Switch the row and column data for the chart so that semester names are shown on the vertical axis.

9. Create a 3-D pie chart sheet for cells **A4:A7** and cells **F4:F7**. Move the chart to a new sheet named Total Revenue.

10. Apply **Chart Style 3** and a **black ½ pt** outline.

11. Edit the chart title to Projected Revenue Sources.

12. Format the legend font size to **12 pt**.

13. Create a column sparkline with cell **G8** as the location range for cells **B8:E8**. Format cell **G8** with an **Outside Border** [*Home* tab, *Font* group].

14. Save and close the workbook (Figure 3-73).

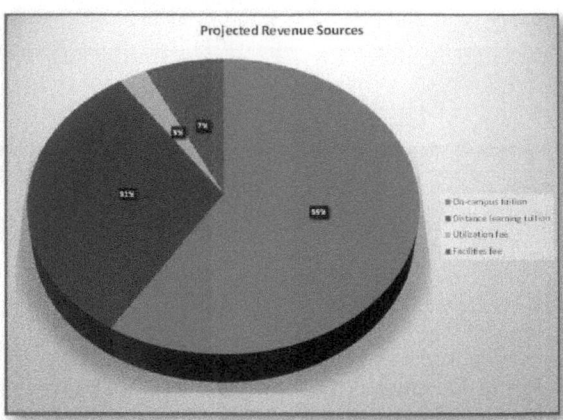

3-73 Excel 3-5 completed worksheet and chart

Independent Project 3-6

Courtyard Medical Plaza (CMP) is a full-service medical office complex providing customers with a variety of medical services in one location. For this project, you create charts to illustrate data about the number of procedures performed at CMP as well as how patients came to the facility. Your final task is to prepare a waterfall chart for the operations account.
[Student Learning Outcomes 3.1, 3.2, 3.3, 3.4, 3.5, 3.7]

File Needed: *CourtyardMedical-03.xlsx* [*Student data files are available in the* Library *of your SIMnet account.*]
Completed Project File Name: *[your initials] Excel 3-6.xlsx*

Skills Covered in This Project

- Create a column chart sheet.
- Add and edit chart elements.
- Add and format a trendline in a chart.

- Insert a text box shape in a chart.
- Display gridlines in a chart.
- Use gradient fill for a chart object.
- Create a waterfall chart.

1. Open the **CourtyardMedical-03** workbook from your student data files and save it as [your initials] Excel 3-6.

2. Select the **Patient Arrivals** worksheet. Create a clustered column chart sheet for cells **A5:M5** and cells **A7:M7**. Move the chart to its own sheet named Immed Care.

3. Edit the chart title to display Immediate Care Patient Count.

4. Click the **Chart Elements** button and select **Trendline**.

5. Click the options arrow next to **Trendline** and select **More Options** to open the *Format Trendline* task pane.
 a. In the *Forecast* group, set the **Forward** value to **12**.
 b. Choose **Olive Green, Accent 3, Darker 50%** for the line color.
 c. Set the **Width** of the trendline to **4 pt**.

6. Draw a *Text Box* shape between the 300 and 400 gridlines and type The number of patients who come in for Immediate Care services will continue to grow. (Figure 3-74).

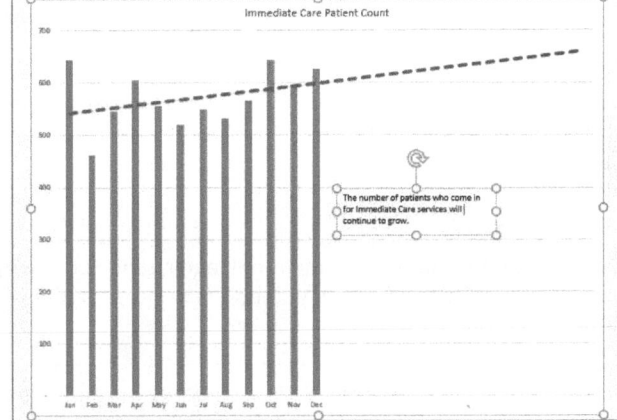

3-74 Text box shape in a chart

7. Select the **Procedures Count** worksheet and use the *Quick Analysis* tool to create a clustered column chart for cells **A5:D16** on its own sheet named Procedures Chart.

8. Edit the chart title to Number of Procedures on the first line and Three-Month Period on the second line.

9. Change the chart type to a clustered bar chart.

10. Click the **Chart Elements** button. Show **Primary Major Vertical**, **Primary Major Horizontal** and **Primary Minor Vertical** gridlines. Format each gridline element to use **Black, Text 1, Lighter 50%**.

11. Use the **Shape Fill** button to format the plot area to **Tan, Background 2**.

12. Select the **Operations** sheet tab and create a waterfall chart object for cells **A3:B9**.

13. Position the waterfall chart object so that its top left corner is at cell **A11**. Size the object to reach cell **I28**.

14. Select the ending balance marker and set it as a total.

15. Edit the chart title placeholder to CMP Operations Account.

16. Select the chart area and apply a **1 pt black** outline.

17. Click a worksheet cell and press **Ctrl+Home**.

18. Save and close the workbook (Figure 3-75).

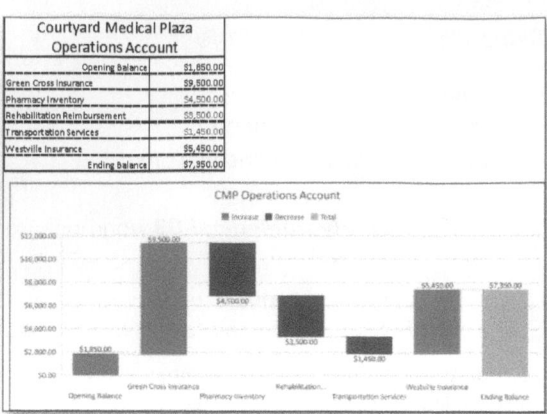

3-75 Excel 3-6 completed worksheet and charts

Improve It Project 3-7

Central Sierra Insurance is a multi-office insurance company that handles commercial and personal insurance products. In this project, you add missing data and verify that the charts are updated.
[Student Learning Outcomes 3.2, 3.3, 3.4]

File Needed: ***CentralSierra-03.xlsx*** *[Student data files are available in the* Library *of your SIMnet account.]*
Completed Project File Name: *[your initials] Excel 3-7.xlsx*

Skills Covered in This Project

- Edit source data.
- Switch row and column data.

- Change chart colors.
- Apply a chart style.
- Add and format elements in a chart.
- Change the chart type.

1. Open the ***CentralSierra-03*** workbook from your student data files and save it as [your initials] Excel 3-7. There are two chart objects on the worksheet.

2. Insert a new row at row 8.

3. Type Motorcycle in cell **A8**. In cells **B8:D8**, type these values: 15, 82, and 24.

4. Change the pie chart object to a **3-D Pie** and apply **Chart Style 3**. Notice that a data series for "Motorcycle" has been added.

5. Switch the row and column data for the column chart. The data series for "Motorcycle" is not included.

6. Click the **Select Data** button [*Chart Tools Design* tab, *Data* group] and reset the source data to show cells **A5:D10**.

7. Change the column chart color scheme to **Color 11** in the *Monochromatic* list.

8. Format chart elements.
 a. Use the **Shape Fill** button [*Chart Tools Format* tab, *Shape Styles* group] to apply **Olive Green, Accent 3** fill for the **Side Wall** of the column chart.
 b. Use the **Shape Fill** button to apply the **Linear Down** gradient in the *Light Variations* group to the side wall.

c. Apply the same fill and gradient to the **Walls** element.

d. Apply the **Olive Green**, **Accent 3**, **Lighter 60%** with no gradient to the **Floor** element.

e. Select the horizontal gridlines and use the **Shape Outline** button to format them with **Black**, **Text 1**, **Lighter 50%**.

9. Select the pie chart object and change the colors to **Color 11** in the *Monochromatic* group.

10. Use **Olive Green**, **Accent 3** as shape fill for the pie chart area with a **Linear Down** gradient from the light variations.

11. Apply a **½ pt Olive Green**, **Accent 3**, **Darker 25%** outline to both chart objects.

12. Save and close the workbook (Figure 3-76).

3-76 Excel 3-7 Completed worksheet with charts

Challenge Project 3-8

For this project, you build a worksheet by copying a worksheet from one of the student data files, editing data, and creating a TreeMap chart.
[Student Learning Outcomes 3.1, 3.2, 3.3, 3.7]

File Needed: ***WearEverShoes-03.xlsx*** *[Student data files are available in the* Library *of your SIMnet account.]*
Completed Project File Name: *[your initials] Excel 3-8.xlsx*

Create a new workbook and save it as [your initials] Excel 3-8. Modify your workbook according to the following guidelines:

- Open the ***WearEverShoes-03*** workbook from your student data files.
- Copy the **Grouped Sales** sheet to *[your initials] Excel 3-8*. Close ***WearEverShoes-03***.
- Rename the *Grouped Sales* sheet as My Groups.
- Delete column **C** to create two levels in the hierarchy, the style name and the color. Each item has a value.
- Select a topic of interest or relevance to you that can be placed in a two-level hierarchy like the worksheet. Examples are college department and course name; company name and functional area; state and city; music type and song title. Assign different values if appropriate to your data.
- Edit the data in the worksheet to reflect your groups and subgroups. Edit the title labels also.
- Type a main and secondary title for your data. Format your worksheet.
- Select the appropriate data and create a *TreeMap* hierarchy chart on its own sheet.
- Edit the chart title and apply a chart style.
- Edit the source data to increase or decrease values and see how the *TreeMap* is adjusted.

Challenge Project 3-9

For this project, you create a worksheet and accompanying charts to track daily usage of your smartphone, tablet, or smart watch.
[Student Learning Outcomes 3.1, 3.2, 3.3, 3.4, 3.5, 3.6]

File Needed: None
Completed Project File Name: *[your initials] Excel 3-9.xlsx*

Create a new workbook and save it as [your initials] Excel 3-9. Modify your workbook according to the following guidelines:

- Enter the days of the week as column headings, starting in cell B2.
- As row headings starting in cell A3, type the names of five daily tasks or activities for your device. Examples are "Send text," "Receive phone call," "Use GPS," "View video," or similar tasks.
- Enter a value for the number of times you perform each task on each day.
- Type a main title for your data in row 1. Format your data.
- Create a column chart object that compares the number of times for each task on Monday.

- Size and position the chart object below the worksheet data.
- Change the layout or apply a chart style.
- Edit the chart title placeholder to display an appropriate title.
- Format chart elements to create an attractive, easy-to-understand chart of your data.
- For the task with the greatest Monday value, create another column chart that displays daily numbers for that one task.
- Size and position this chart object below the first chart.
- Format the second chart to complement the first chart.

Challenge Project 3-10

For this project, you create a worksheet with a column/line combo chart that compares air temperature and humidity level in your city or town for 10 days. You also insert a single sparkline in the data.
[Student Learning Outcomes 3.1, 3.2, 3.3, 3.4, 3.6, 3.8]

File Needed: None
Completed Project File Name: *[your initials] Excel 3-10.xlsx*

Create a new workbook and save it as [your initials] Excel 3-10. Modify your workbook according to the following guidelines:

- In a worksheet, enter dates in cells **A4:A13** for each of the last 10 days or each of the next 10 days.
- In column B, enter a recorded or predicted temperature in degrees for each date at 12 noon. Use an online weather reference or a weather app.
- In column C, enter corresponding humidity levels as percentages. Use the same weather reference or make an estimate.
- Type a main title for the data as well as column labels.
- Create a clustered column/line combo chart with a secondary axis for the percentages. Move the chart to its own sheet.
- Change the layout or apply a chart style.
- Edit and format the chart elements as needed.
- In the worksheet, select the range of temperature values as the data range for a line sparkline. As the location range, select cell **D14**. Format column D as **32.00 (229 pixels)** wide.
- Format the sparkline and adjust row heights to better display the data and the sparkline.

CHAPTER 4

Formatting, Organizing, and Getting Data

CHAPTER OVERVIEW

Excel can use data from many sources as well as provide data to other programs. When data is shared among applications, the data is usually in a list or table layout like a database. This chapter covers how to format data as an Excel table, how to sort and filter data, how to get data from other sources, and how to build a *PivotTable*.

STUDENT LEARNING OUTCOMES (SLOs)

After completing this chapter, you will be able to:

SLO 4.1 Create and format a list as an Excel table (p. E4-222).

SLO 4.2 Apply *Conditional Formatting* rules as well as *Color Scales, Icon Sets,* and *Data Bars* (p. E4-228).

SLO 4.3 Sort data by one or more columns or by attribute (p. E4-234).

SLO 4.4 Filter data by using *AutoFilters* and by creating an *Advanced Filter* (p. E4-238).

SLO 4.5 Use subtotals, groups, and outlines for tabular data in a worksheet (p. E4-242).

SLO 4.6 Import data into an Excel worksheet from a text file, a database file, and other sources (p. E4-248).

SLO 4.7 Export Excel data as a text file and into a Word document (p. E4-254).

SLO 4.8 Build and format a *PivotTable* (p. E4-258).

CASE STUDY

For the Pause & Practice projects in this chapter, you create worksheets for Paradise Lakes Resort. To complete the work, you format a list as an Excel table, sort and filter data, import and clean data, and create a *PivotTable*.

Pause & Practice 4-1: Format data as an Excel table and set conditional formatting.

Pause & Practice 4-2: Sort, filter, and subtotal data.

Pause & Practice 4-3: Import and *Flash Fill* data in a workbook.

Pause & Practice 4-4: Create and format a *PivotTable* and a *PivotChart*.

SLO 4.1

Creating and Formatting an Excel Table

An Excel *table* is a list of related pieces of information that is formatted with a title row followed by rows of data (Figure 4-1). When data is in table format, you can organize, sort, filter, and calculate data easily and quickly, much like a database.

The *header row* is the first row of a table with descriptive titles or labels. Each row of data is a *record* and each column is a *field.* The label in the header row is sometimes referred to as the *field name.* When you format Excel data as a table, follow these guidelines to optimize your tables for use of Excel commands:

4-1 Excel table

- Type descriptive labels in the first row and begin each label with a letter, not a number.
- Assign each header a unique label; do not repeat any of the descriptive labels.
- Keep the same type of data within each column (e.g., text or values).
- Do not leave blank rows within the data.
- Keep the table separate from other data on the worksheet.

Create an Excel Table

When data is arranged as a list and conforms to the guidelines just described, a simple format command creates an Excel table. Select the data and click the **Format as Table** button in the *Styles* group on the *Home* tab to open the *Table Styles* gallery. Choose a style and click **OK** in the *Format as Table* dialog box. When the data is selected, you can also click the **Table** button in the *Tables* group on the *Insert* tab to open the *Format as Table* dialog box and create the table with a default style.

After your data is formatted as a table, each label in the header row displays an *AutoFilter* arrow, and the *Table Tools Design* tab opens with command groups for modifying the table. Recall from Chapter 3 that a filter is criteria that determines which data is shown and which is hidden. From *AutoFilter* arrows, you can show records for employees in a particular location or for revenue from certain months.

> **MORE INFO**
>
> *AutoFilter* arrows replace the worksheet column headings when you scroll down in a table with many records. *AutoFilter* arrows do not print.

▶ **HOW TO: Create an Excel Table**

1. Select the cells to be formatted as a table.
 - Include the header row with column titles.
2. Click the **Format as Table** button [*Home* tab, *Styles* group] to open the table gallery.
3. Choose a table style from the *Table Styles* gallery (Figure 4-2).

4-2 *Table Styles* gallery and selected data

- Table styles are organized in light, medium, and dark categories.

4. Confirm the cell range in the *Format As Table* dialog box.

- You can drag to select a different range, if necessary.

5. Select the **My table has headers** box in the *Format As Table* dialog box.

- When the selected range does not have column titles, Excel inserts a row above the data with the labels *Column1, Column2,* and so on. You can edit these names.

6. Click **OK**.

- When the selected range includes data from an outside source, you will see a message box asking to remove the data connection. Click **Yes** to create the table (Figure 4-3).

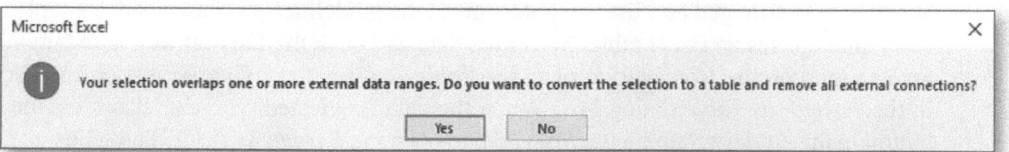

4-3 Message box for data from an outside source

ANOTHER WAY

Select the header and data rows, click the **Quick Analysis** tool, and choose **Tables**. Then click the **Table** button to format the data in a default table style. This method is not available for data from an outside source.

Table Styles and Options

A *table style* is a predesigned set of format settings with a color scheme, alternating fill for rows and columns, vertical and horizontal borders, and more. You select a style when you create a table from the **Format as Table** button, but you can apply a different style at any time. Predefined table styles are classified as *Light, Medium,* and *Dark* and use colors based on the workbook theme. You can remove a style by selecting *None* in the *Light* group.

▶**HOW TO:** Apply a Table Style

1. Click any cell within the table.
 - The *Table Tools Design* tab opens.
2. Click the **More** button [*Table Tools Design* tab, *Table Styles* group].
 - The *Table Styles* gallery opens.
 - Styles are named *Table Style Light 1, Table Style Medium 4, Table Style Dark 8,* and so on.
 - The *None* style is the first icon in the *Light* group.
3. Point to a style icon to see a *Live Preview* in the table.
4. Click to select and apply a style.

▶ **MORE INFO**

You can create and save a custom table style by clicking the **More** button in the *Table Styles* group [*Table Tools Design* tab] and choosing **New Table Style**.

The *Table Style Options* group on the *Table Tools Design* tab includes commands for showing or hiding various parts of the table such as the header row or a total row. When you show a total row, a blank row inserts as the last row, and you can choose which calculation displays in each column. Other options are banded columns or rows, which alternate fill or borders. There is also a command to apply bold to data in the first or last column, or both. You can also hide the *AutoFilter* arrows.

▶**HOW TO:** Display a Total Row in a Table

1. Click any cell within the table.
 - The *Table Tools Design* tab opens.
2. Select the **Total Row** box [*Table Tools Design* tab, *Table Style Options* group].
 - The total row displays as the last row in the table.
3. Click a cell in the total row and click its arrow to open the calculation list.
 - The default calculation is *Sum* for numeric data.
4. Choose the calculation for the column (Figure 4-4).
 - You can use *Count* for alphanumeric columns.

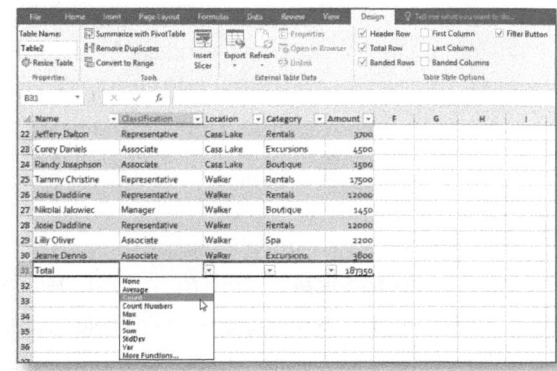

4-4 Table with total row

The Table Tools and Properties Groups

The *Tools* group on the *Table Tools Design* tab includes commands to remove duplicate records and to convert the table to a regular cell range. The *Insert Slicer* command opens a filter window for hiding or showing records in the table. The *Properties* group includes the table name and a command to resize the table.

A *duplicate row* is a record in a table that has exactly the same information in one or more columns. The *Remove Duplicates* command scans a table to locate and delete rows with repeated data in the specified columns. In the *Remove Duplicates* dialog box, you set which columns might have duplicate data. If you check all the columns, a row must have the same data in every column as another row.

▶ HOW TO: Remove Duplicates

1. Click any cell within the table.
2. Click the **Remove Duplicates** button [*Table Tools Design* tab, *Tools* group] (Figure 4-5).
3. Select the box for each column that might have duplicate data.
 * Click **Unselect All** to remove all check marks and select a single label.
 * Excel recognizes headers and does not scan them for duplicate content.
4. Click **OK**.
 * A message box indicates how many duplicate values were removed and how many unique values remain.
5. Click **OK**.
 * The rows are removed from the table.
 * The command does not preview which rows are deleted.
 * You can **Undo** this command if needed.

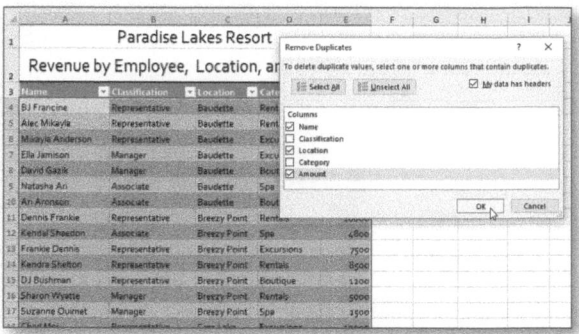

4-5 *Remove Duplicates* dialog box

The *Insert Slicer* command opens a floating window that is used as a visual filter, allowing you to work with smaller pieces of large datasets. If a table has 10,000 records but you are concerned with one location or category, you can insert a slicer to control which records display in the table. A *Slicer* window is an object that can be sized and positioned, and it displays selection handles like other objects. The *Slicer Tools Options* tab is available when a slicer object is active with settings to customize the floating window.

▶ HOW TO: Insert a Slicer

1. Click any cell within the table.
2. Click the **Insert Slicer** button [*Table Tools Design* tab, *Tools* group] (Figure 4-6).
 * The *Insert Slicers* dialog box lists all field names in the table.
3. Select the box for the field to be used for filtering.
 * You can select more than one field to open multiple slicers.
4. Click **OK**.
 * The *Slicer* window is a selectable object.
 * All records display in the table.
5. Click an item name to filter the data.
 * The records are filtered.
 * You can press **Ctrl** and click another item to use more than one filter.
 * You can also toggle the **Multi-Select** button in the *Slicer* title bar so that you can click or tap to select multiple items for filtering.

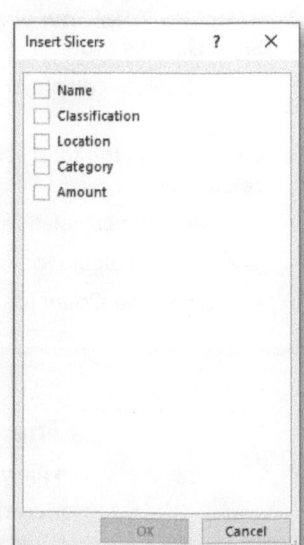

4-6 *Insert Slicers* dialog box

6. Click the **Clear Filter** button in the *Slicer* title bar.

 • All the records display.

7. Click the **More** button [*Slicer Tools Options* tab, *Slicer Styles* group].

8. Select a style for the *Slicer.*

9. Click the **Columns** spinner button [*Slicer Tools Options* tab, *Buttons* group] to set the number of columns in the *Slicer* (Figure 4-7).

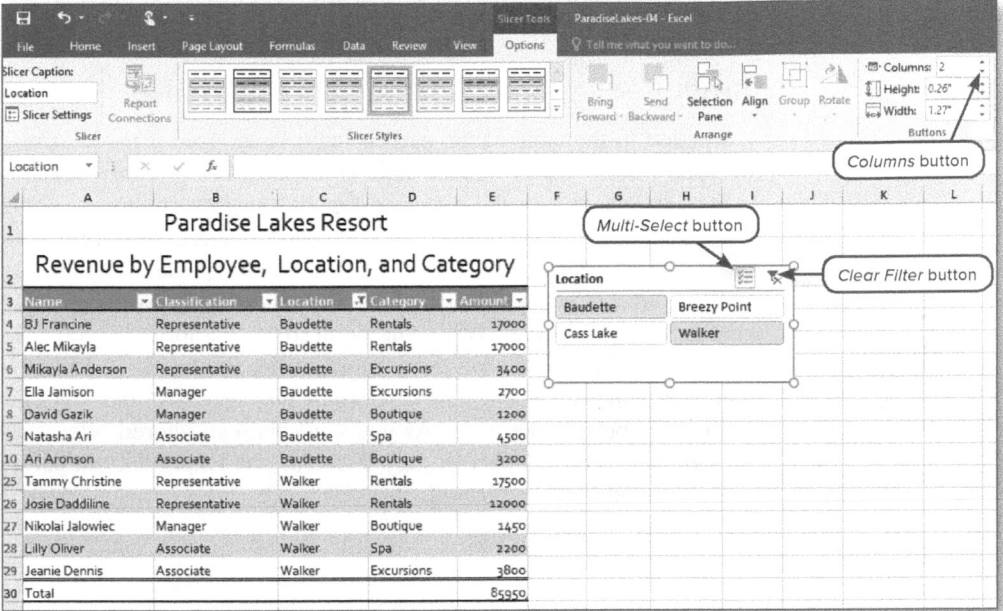

4-7 *Slicer* window for a table

10. Click and drag a corner selection handle to resize the *Slicer.*

 • You can set a specific size in the *Size* group [*Slicer Tools Options* tab].

11. Press **Delete** to remove the *Slicer* window.

 • The *Slicer* window must be selected to be deleted.

The *Convert to Range* command removes table formatting and options, but it does keep font style and fill colors. You may need to convert a table to a range when combining data from different sources or when sharing data with applications that require unformatted data.

▶ **HOW TO: Convert a Table to a Range**

1. Click any cell within the table.

2. Click the **Convert to Range** button [*Table Tools Design* tab, *Tools* group] (Figure 4-8).

3. Click **Yes** in the message box.

 • The data is shown as a regular range of cells.
 • Font size, font style, and colors remain.
 • You can format the data as needed.

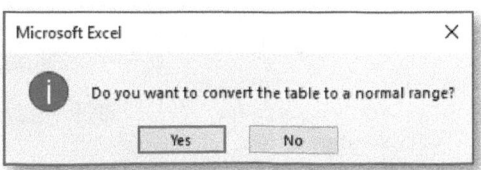

4-8 *Convert to Normal Range* message box

Tables are named automatically as *TableN* where *N* is a number. To change the name to a more descriptive label, click the **Table Name** box in the *Properties* group on the *Table Tools Design* tab and type the name. You cannot use spaces in a table name, and table names in a workbook must be unique. From the *Properties* group, you can also open the *Resize Table* dialog box to select an expanded or reduced cell range for the table. A table also has a resize arrow in its bottom right cell that you can drag to grow or shrink the table. Tables grow automatically when you press **Tab** after the last item in the last row to start a new record.

Structured References and Table Formulas

In addition to the table name, each column is assigned a name using the label in its header row. The column name with its table name is known as a ***structured reference.*** An example is *Table1[Category]* as the reference for the category column in *Table1*. Column names are enclosed in square brackets. In addition to column names, there are specific item names. They are *#All, #Data, #Headers, #This Row,* and *#Totals,* each preceded by the # symbol as an identifier.

Structured references are supplied automatically in formulas making it easy to identify what is being calculated. When you point to build a formula, you will see [*@ColumnName*] as the reference with @ inserted as an identifier (Figure 4-9). The table name and structured reference names appear in *Formula AutoComplete* lists, and you can refer to those ranges in formulas outside the table. As you work with structured references, you can expand the *Formula* bar to better see a lengthy formula. The **Expand/Collapse Formula Bar** button is on the right edge of the *Formula* bar.

MORE INFO

To enter cell references in a table formula instead of structured references, disable **Use table names in formulas** in Excel *Options* [*File* tab, *Options, Formulas* pane].

Tables are automatically expanded to include a new column when you type a label adjacent to the last row heading. As part of its *Table AutoExpansion* feature, Excel copies a formula to complete a column with a calculation.

▶ **HOW TO:** Add a Calculation Column in a Table

1. Select the cell to the right of the last column heading in the table.
2. Type the new column label and press **Enter**.
 • A column is added to the table.
3. Select the cell below the new label.
4. Type = to start a formula.
5. Click the table cell with the value to be used in the formula.
 • The column name in square brackets preceded an @ symbol is inserted.
6. Complete the formula (Figure 4-9).

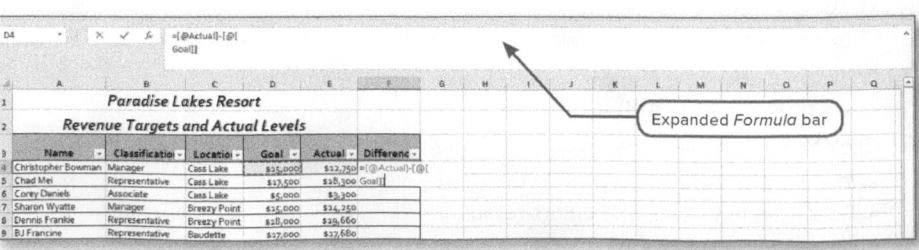

4-9 Structured references in a table

- You can refer to other cells in the table or the worksheet or type a constant.

7. Press **Enter**.

- The formula is copied down the entire column.
- You can enter the formula in any row in the column for it to be copied.

> **MORE INFO**
>
> You can disable automatic copying of table formulas in the *AutoCorrectOptions, AutoFormat As You Type* tab [*File* tab, *Options, Proofing* pane].

SLO 4.2

Applying Conditional Formatting

Conditional formatting commands apply formats to cells only when the cells meet the criteria. For example, you can use conditional formatting to display revenue amounts below a certain level in a bold red font. Conditional formatting is dynamic; the formatting adapts if the data changes.

Basic conditional formatting commands are *Highlight Cells Rules* and *Top/Bottom Rules*. For these commands, you set the rule or criteria in a dialog box and choose the format. Another type of conditional formatting is *data visualization*, in which the cell displays a fill color, a horizontal bar, or an icon.

Highlight Cells Rules

Highlight Cells Rules use relational or comparison operators to determine if the value or label should be formatted. *Highlight Cells Rules* include common operators such as *Equal To* and *Greater Than*. You can also create your own rule using other operators or a formula.

You can access all of the conditional formatting options from the *Conditional Formatting* button in the *Styles* group on the *Home* tab (Figure 4-10). You can also choose a default conditional formatting rule from the *Quick Analysis* tool options.

4-10 Highlight Cells Rules menu

▶ **HOW TO: Create a "Less Than" Highlight Cells Rule**

1. Select the cell range.
2. Click the **Conditional Formatting** button [*Home* tab, *Styles* group].
3. Select **Highlight Cells Rules** and select **Less Than**.
 - The *Less Than* dialog box opens.
4. Type a value in the *Format cells that are LESS THAN* box.
 - *Live Preview* applies the default format to cells that meet the criteria.

E4-228

5. Click the arrow for the *with* box.
 - A list of preset formats is available.
6. Choose a format (Figure 4-11).
 - You can choose *Custom Format* to open the *Format Cells* dialog box and build a format.
7. Click **OK**.
 - Formatting is applied to cells that meet the criteria.
 - Click a cell away from the range to better see the formatting.

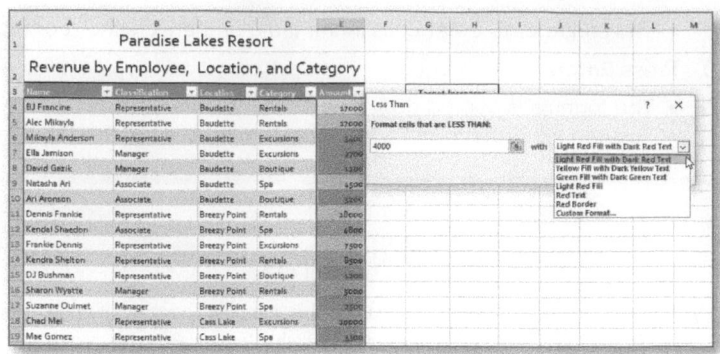

4-11 *Less Than* dialog box

Top/Bottom Rules

Top/Bottom Rules use ranking to format the highest (top) or lowest (bottom) items, either by number or percentage. You set the number or percentage in the dialog box as well as the format. You can also set a rule to format values that are above or below average (Figure 4-12).

For a selected range, the *Formatting* group in the *Quick Analysis* tool provides the most likely conditional formatting choices.

▶ **HOW TO:** Create a Top 10% Rule

1. Select the cell range.
 - The *Quick Analysis* button appears in the bottom right cell of the range.
2. Click the **Quick Analysis** button.
3. Choose **Formatting**.
 - Commonly used conditional format choices are listed.
4. Choose **Top 10%** (Figure 4-13).
 - The number of cells equal to the *Top 10%* of the number of cells in the column are formatted with a default format.
 - You can edit the format to use different attributes.

4-12 *Top/Bottom Rules*

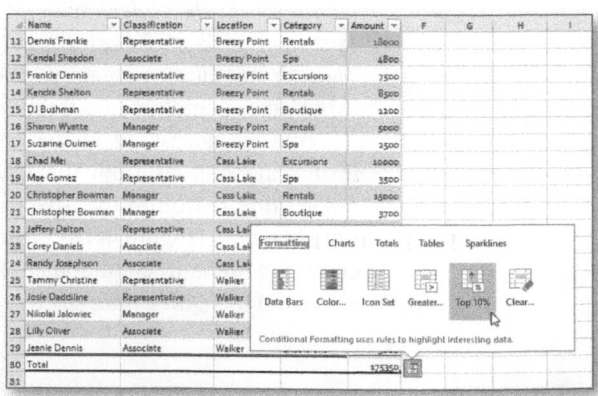

4-13 *Quick Analysis* options for conditional formatting

Use a Formula for a Rule

In addition to the *Highlight Cells* or *Top/Bottom* rules, you can create a conditional formatting formula using operators, criteria, and settings in the *New Formatting Rule* dialog box. You can, for example, build a rule to format cells in the amount column if the location is Baudette. A formula must result in either TRUE or FALSE (a Yes or No question) to be used as criteria.

▶ **HOW TO:** Use a Formula in a Conditional Formatting Rule

1. Select the cell range.
2. Click the **Conditional Formatting** button [*Home* tab, *Styles* group].
3. Select **New Rule**.
 - The *New Formatting Rule* dialog box opens.
 - The choices in the dialog box update based on the rule type.
4. Choose **Use a formula to determine which cells to format** in the *Select a Rule Type* list.
5. In the *Edit the Rule Description* area, type = in the *Format values where this formula is true* box.
 - You must start the formula with an equals sign (=).
 - The formula must be built so that the result is either TRUE or FALSE.
6. Type the formula.
 - Use relative cell references to the first row of data (Figure 4-14).
 - When you click to enter the cell reference, it is absolute; press **F4 (FN+F4)** to make it relative.
 - Text in the formula must be enclosed in quotation marks.
7. Click **Format** to open the *Format Cells* dialog box.
8. Build the format and click **OK**.
9. Click **OK** to close the *New Formatting Rule* dialog box.
 - Cells that meet the formula condition are formatted.

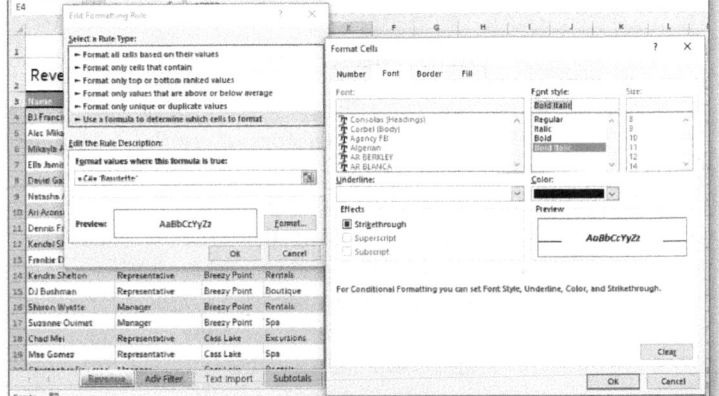

4-14 *New Formatting Rule* and *Format Cells* dialog boxes

Data Bars, Color Scales, and Icon Sets

Data visualization formats cells with icons, fill color, or shaded bars to distinguish values. Visualization formats highlight low, middle, or top values or compare the values to each other. Data visualization commands are *Data Bars, Color Scales,* and *Icon Sets.*

These three commands are part of the conditional formatting group, because they apply a rule for determining what is shown in the cell. You can choose which colors or icons are applied from the *Conditional Formatting* button [*Home* tab, *Styles* group]. When you select an option from the *Quick Analysis* button, however, a default choice is applied.

▶ **HOW TO:** Format Data with Data Bars

1. Select the cell range.
2. Click the **Quick Analysis** button.
3. Choose **Formatting**.
 - *Data Bars* compare the value in each cell to the other values in the range by the length of the bar.
 - *Color Scales* use a variation of two or three colors to indicate low, middle, and high values.

- *Icon Sets* inserts icons that represent the upper, middle, or lower values of the cell range.

4. Choose **Data Bars** (Figure 4-15).

- A default data bar style and color is applied.

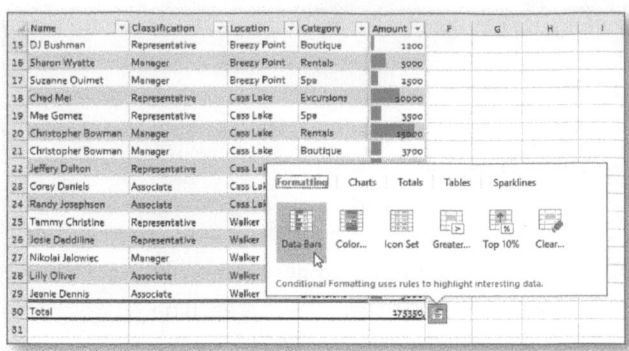

4-15 Setting *Data Bars* from the *Quick Analysis* button

Manage Conditional Formatting Rules

You can edit any conditional formatting rule, including data visualization commands, from the *Conditional Formatting Rules Manager* dialog box. From this dialog box, you can reset the range to be formatted, change the actual format, change the rule, or delete the rule.

If you select the formatted range before you start the *Manage Rules* command, the rule for that selection is shown in the *Conditional Formatting Rules Manager* dialog box. You can also show all the rules in the current or another sheet (Figure 4-16).

When you click **Edit Rule**, the *Edit Formatting Rule* dialog box opens. This dialog box is similar to the *New Formatting Rule* dialog box, and you set options the same way.

4-16 *Conditional Formatting Rules Manager* dialog box

▶ HOW TO: Manage Conditional Formatting Rules

1. Select the formatted cell range.
2. Click the **Conditional Formatting** button [*Home* tab, *Styles* group].
3. Choose **Manage Rules**.
 - *Current Selection* is listed in the *Show formatting rules for* box.
 - Choose **This Worksheet** to list all rules in the worksheet.
4. Select the rule name to be modified.
5. Select **Edit Rule**.
 - The *Edit Formatting Rule* dialog box opens.
 - The current *Rule Description* displays.
 - You can select another rule type in the top half of the dialog box.
6. Make choices to change the rule in the *Edit the Rule Description* area.
 - The options depend on the rule type (Figure 4-17).
 - Click **Format** when available to open the *Format Cells* dialog box.

4-17 *Edit Formatting Rule* dialog box for data bars

7. Click **OK** to close the *Edit Formatting Rule* dialog box.
8. Click **OK** to close the *Conditional Formatting Rules Manger* dialog box.

You can clear conditional formatting from a selected range or from the entire sheet. For a selected range, click the **Quick Analysis** button and choose **Clear...** You can also choose **Clear Rules** from the *Conditional Formatting* button menu.

PAUSE & PRACTICE: EXCEL 4-1

For this project, you format data as a table, add a total row, and remove duplicate records. As you complete formulas on the sheet, you see structured references. You also set conditional formatting with data bars.

File Needed: ***ParadiseLakes-04.xlsx*** *[Student data files are available in the Library of your SIMnet account.]*
Completed Project File Name: ***[your initials] PP E4-1.xlsx***

1. Open the ***ParadiseLakes-04*** workbook from your student data files and save it as [your initials] PP E4-1.

2. Click the **Revenue** sheet tab.

3. Format data as an Excel table.
 a. Select cells **A3:E30**.
 b. Click the **Format as Table** button [*Home* tab, *Styles* group].
 c. Select **Table Style Medium 20** from the gallery.
 d. Verify that the **My table has headers** box is selected in the *Format As Table* dialog box.
 e. Click **OK**.

4. Add a total row to a table.
 a. Click a cell within the table.
 b. Select the **Total Row** box [*Table Tools Design* tab, *Table Style Options* group].
 c. Click cell **D31** and choose **Count** from the drop-down list.
 d. Select cells **E4:E31** and format them as **Currency**. Decrease the decimal two times to show zero decimal places (Figure 4-18).

5. Remove duplicate rows in a table.
 a. Click a cell within table.
 b. Click the **Remove Duplicates** button [*Table Tools Design* tab, *Tools* group].
 c. Click **Unselect All** to deselect all the boxes.
 d. Select the **Name** box and the **Amount** box. When you can look for duplicate data in specific columns, you can speed up search activities.
 e. Click **OK** in the *Remove Duplicates* dialog box. There is one record that will be removed, the one for Josie Daddiline. The records for Christopher Bowman are not duplicated in the selected columns.
 f. Click **OK** in the message box.

	A	B	C	D	E
1		Paradise Lakes Resort			
2		Revenue by Employee, Location, and Category			
3	Name	Classification	Location	Category	Amount
4	BJ Francine	Representative	Baudette	Rentals	$17,000
5	Alec Mikayla	Representative	Baudette	Rentals	$17,000
6	Mikayla Anderson	Representative	Baudette	Excursions	$3,400
7	Ella Jamison	Manager	Baudette	Excursions	$2,700
8	David Gazik	Manager	Baudette	Boutique	$1,200
9	Natasha Ari	Associate	Baudette	Spa	$4,500
10	Ari Aronson	Associate	Baudette	Boutique	$3,200
11	Dennis Frankie	Representative	Breezy Point	Rentals	$18,000
12	Kendal Shaedon	Associate	Breezy Point	Spa	$4,800
13	Frankie Dennis	Representative	Breezy Point	Excursions	$7,500
14	Kendra Shelton	Representative	Breezy Point	Rentals	$8,500
15	DJ Bushman	Representative	Breezy Point	Boutique	$1,200
16	Sharon Wyatte	Manager	Breezy Point	Rentals	$5,000
17	Suzanne Ouimet	Manager	Breezy Point	Spa	$2,500
18	Chad Mei	Representative	Cass Lake	Excursions	$10,000
19	Mae Gomez	Representative	Cass Lake	Spa	$3,500
20	Christopher Bowman	Manager	Cass Lake	Rentals	$15,000
21	Christopher Bowman	Manager	Cass Lake	Boutique	$3,700
22	Jeffery Dalton	Representative	Cass Lake	Rentals	$3,700
23	Corey Daniels	Associate	Cass Lake	Excursions	$4,500
24	Randy Josephson	Associate	Cass Lake	Boutique	$1,500
25	Tammy Christine	Representative	Walker	Rentals	$17,000
26	Josie Daddiline	Representative	Walker	Rentals	$12,000
27	Nikolai Jalowiec	Manager	Walker	Boutique	$1,450
28	Josie Daddiline	Representative	Walker	Rentals	$12,000
29	Lilly Oliver	Associate	Walker	Spa	$2,200
30	Jeanie Dennis	Associate	Walker	Excursions	$3,800
31	Total			27	$187,350

4-18 Data formatted as a table

6. Apply conditional formatting using data bars.
 a. Select cells **E4:E29**.
 b. Click the **Conditional Formatting** button [*Home* tab, *Styles* group].
 c. Point to **Data Bars** to see its menu.
 d. Select **Blue Data Bar** in the *Gradient Fill* group (Figure 4-19).

4-19 Choose a gradient fill for data bars

7. Manage conditional formatting rules.
 a. Select cells **E3:E29**.
 b. Click the **Conditional Formatting** button [*Home* tab, *Styles* group].
 c. Choose **Manage Rules**.
 d. Click **Edit Rule**.
 e. Click the **Color** arrow for **Fill** in the *Bar Appearance* area.
 f. Choose **Gold, Accent 3**.
 g. Click the arrow for **Border** in the *Bar Appearance* area.
 h. Choose **No Border** (Figure 4-20).
 i. Click **OK** to close the *Edit Formatting Rule* dialog box.
 j. Click **OK** to close the *Conditional Formatting Rules Manager* dialog box.

8. Refer to a structured reference in a formula.
 a. Select cell **H4** and type = to start a formula.
 b. Click cell **E30** to insert a structured reference to the total in the Amount column.
 c. Type * (1+, click cell **G4**, and type) to calculate a new total that reflects a 2% increase (Figure 4-21).

4-20 Edit the rule for data bars

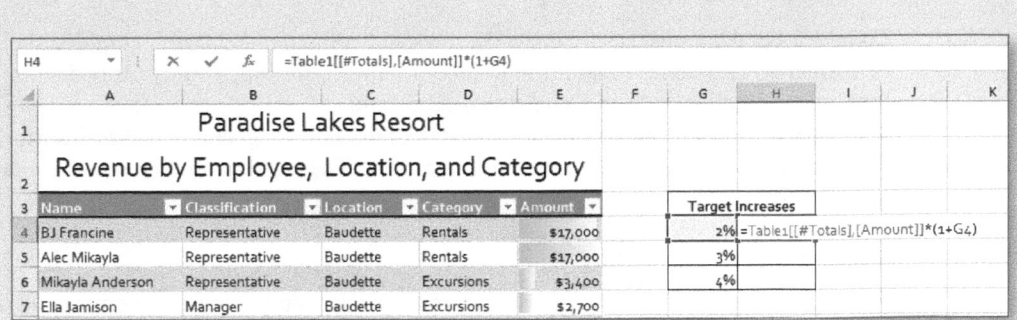

4-21 Structured reference in a formula

d. Press **Enter**. The target total is $178,857.
e. Copy the formula to cells **H5:H6**.

9. Save and close the workbook (Figure 4-22).

4-22 Completed PP E 4-1

Sorting Data

Sorting is the process of arranging rows of data in an identified order. For Paradise Lakes Resort, you can arrange the revenue table by employee classification to compare results for a particular job title. Or you may want to order the rows from highest amount to lowest.

You sort data in ascending or descending order. *Ascending* order sorts data alphabetically from A to Z or numerically from smallest to largest value. In a *descending* sort, data are arranged alphabetically Z to A or numerically from largest to smallest value.

Sort Options

To be sorted, data must be organized in rows and columns like an Excel table, but it need not be formatted as a table. In addition to text or number sorting, you can sort data by fill color, font color, or cell icon from *Conditional Formatting*.

The *Sort & Filter* button on the *Home* tab in the *Editing* group lists *A to Z* sort, *Z to A* sort, and *Custom Sort* (multiple columns) commands. The same commands are available in the *Sort & Filter* group on the *Data* tab as separate buttons.

Sort Data by One Column

When data has a header row followed by rows of data with at least one empty row above and below the data, you can click any cell in the column you want to sort and choose a sort command. Excel recognizes and sorts the entire dataset.

Data to be sorted can be text, numbers, or dates. Dates are treated as values. An ascending sort (smallest to largest) arranges dates so that the earliest date is first. A descending date sort organizes the data so that the most current date is first.

You can undo a sort task by clicking the **Undo** button [*Quick Access* toolbar]. You can also sort data many times to arrange it in your preferred order.

▶ **HOW TO:** Sort Data by a Single Column

1. Select a cell in the column to be used for sorting.
 - Click a cell with data, not the column header.
2. Click the **Sort A to Z** button [*Data* tab, *Sort & Filter* group] (Figure 4-23).
 - The records are arranged in alphabetical or smallest-to-largest order based on the first character in each cell in the column.
 - If the first character in an alphanumeric column is a value or special character, that record is sorted at the top.
3. Click the **Sort Z to A** button [*Data* tab, *Sort & Filter* group].
 - The records are arranged in reverse alphabetical or largest-to-smallest order based on the first character.
 - If the first character in an alphanumeric column is a value or special character, that record is sorted at the bottom.

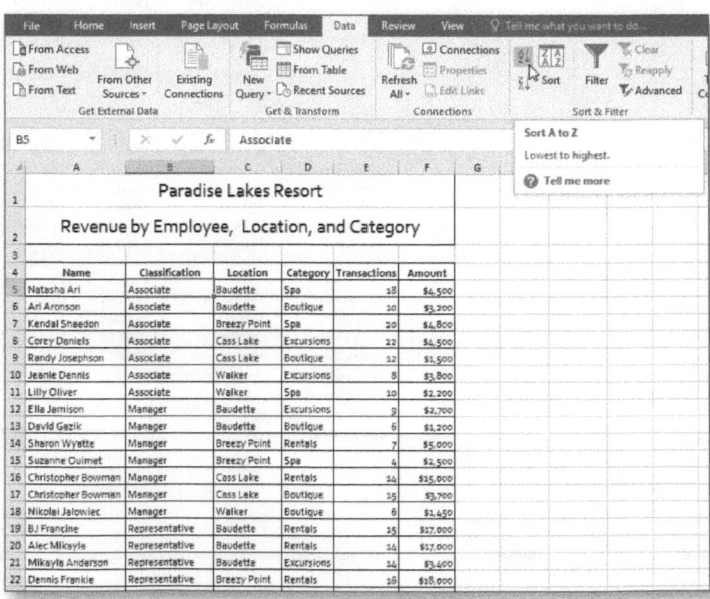

4-23 "Classification" column sorted A to Z

▶ **ANOTHER WAY**

To sort by a single column, right-click a cell in the column, choose **Sort**, and then choose the type of sort.

Sort Data by Multiple Columns

You can sort data by more than one column. An example of data that is often sorted by two columns is a list with cities in one column and states or provinces in another. Such data is sorted by state so that Alabama is before Arizona, and within a particular state, the cities are also sorted alphabetically. When you use the *Sort & Filter* button [*Home* tab, *Editing* group] or a sort button on the *Data* tab, you sort first by the least important field. You can also use the *Sort* dialog box which opens when you click the **Sort** button [*Data* tab, *Sort & Filter* group] or when you choose **Custom Sort** from the *Sort & Filter* button options.

The data in Figure 4-24 are sorted by two columns, classification and amount. When you use the *Sort* dialog box, you set the *Classification* field first and then the *Amount*. When you use the *Sort & Filter* button, you sort first by the *Amount* and then by the *Classification*.

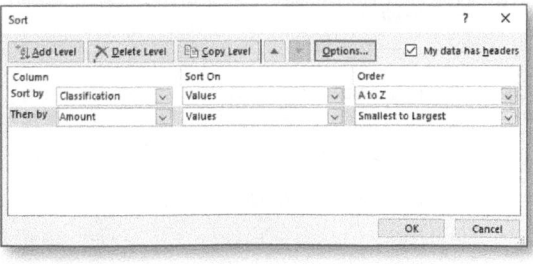

	Name	Classification	Location	Category	Transactions	Amount
	Revenue by Employee, Location, and Category					
5	Randy Josephson	Associate	Cass Lake	Boutique	12	$1,500
6	Lilly Oliver	Associate	Walker	Spa	10	$2,200
7	Ari Aronson	Associate	Baudette	Boutique	10	$3,200
8	Jeanie Dennis	Associate	Walker	Excursions	8	$3,800
9	Natasha Ari	Associate	Baudette	Spa	18	$4,500
10	Corey Daniels	Associate	Cass Lake	Excursions	22	$4,500
11	Kendal Shaedon	Associate	Breezy Point	Spa	20	$4,800
12	David Gazik	Manager	Baudette	Boutique	6	$1,200
13	Nikolai Jalowiec	Manager	Walker	Boutique	6	$1,450
14	Suzanne Ouimet	Manager	Breezy Point	Spa	4	$2,500
15	Ella Jamison	Manager	Baudette	Excursions	9	$2,700
16	Christopher Bowman	Manager	Cass Lake	Boutique	15	$3,700
17	Sharon Wyatte	Manager	Breezy Point	Rentals	7	$5,000
18	Christopher Bowman	Manager	Cass Lake	Rentals	14	$15,000
19	DJ Bushman	Representative	Breezy Point	Boutique	5	$1,200
20	Mikayla Anderson	Representative	Baudette	Excursions	14	$3,400
21	Mae Gomez	Representative	Cass Lake	Spa	12	$3,500
22	Jeffery Dalton	Representative	Cass Lake	Rentals	5	$3,700
23	Frankie Dennis	Representative	Breezy Point	Excursions	16	$7,500
24	Kendra Shelton	Representative	Breezy Point	Rentals	10	$8,500

4-24 Data sorted by "Classification" and "Amount"

▶ HOW TO: Sort Data by Multiple Columns

1. Select a cell in the range to be sorted.
 - Click a cell with data, not the column header.
2. Click the **Sort** button [*Data* tab, *Sort & Filter* group].
 - The *Sort* dialog box opens.
 - The range is highlighted in the worksheet.
 - You can click the **Sort & Filter** button [*Home* tab, *Editing* group] and select **Custom Sort**.
3. Select the **My data has headers** box if your data has a header row.
4. Click the **Sort by** arrow and select the column heading for the first sort level.
5. Click the **Sort On** arrow.
 - Use *Values* for text or numbers.
 - If the data has a cell attribute such as a font color, select the name of the attribute.
6. Click the **Order** arrow and choose a sort option.
 - For columns with numbers or dates, the options are *Smallest to Largest* and *Largest to Smallest.*
 - The *Custom List* option provides special sorting orders for days of the week and months of the year so that data is sorted chronologically.
7. Click **Add Level** to add a second sort column.
8. Click the **Then by** arrow and select the second column heading.
9. Click the **Sort On** arrow and choose **Values** or an attribute.
10. Click the **Order** arrow and choose a sort order (Figure 4-25).
 - Click the **Options** button in the *Sort* dialog box to specify case-sensitive sorting or to change the orientation of ascending and descending sorts.
11. Click **OK**.

4-25 *Sort* dialog box

Sort Data by Cell Attribute

An **attribute** is a setting or property. Cell attributes that can be used for sorting are font color, fill color, and cell icon. These choices are options for the *Sort On* choice in the *Sort* dialog box, and they are listed when you choose **Sort** from a cell's context menu.

When you sort by font or cell color, the *Order* choices are the colors used in the column. You choose a color and set its position in the sorted column.

A cell icon is the symbol placed in a cell by conditional formatting. Column E in Figure 4-26 has an icon set sorted with hollow icons on the top.

	A	B	C	D	E
2	Revenue by Employee, Location, and Category				
3					
4	Name	Classification	Location	Category	Amount
5	Mikayla Anderson	Representative	Baudette	Excursions	☆ $3,400
6	Ella Jamison	Manager	Baudette	Excursions	☆ $2,700
7	Nikolai Jalowiec	Manager	Walker	Boutique	☆ $1,450
8	Lilly Oliver	Associate	Walker	Spa	☆ $2,200
9	Jeanie Dennis	Associate	Walker	Excursions	☆ $3,800
10	Natasha Ari	Associate	Baudette	Spa	☆ $4,500
11	Kendal Shaedon	Associate	Breezy Point	Spa	☆ $4,800
12	Frankie Dennis	Representative	Breezy Point	Excursions	☆ $7,500
13	Sharon Wyatte	Manager	Breezy Point	Rentals	☆ $5,000
14	Corey Daniels	Associate	Cass Lake	Excursions	☆ $4,500
15	BJ Francine	Representative	Baudette	Rentals	☆ $17,000
16	Alec Mikayla	Representative	Baudette	Rentals	☆ $17,000
17	Dennis Frankie	Representative	Breezy Point	Rentals	☆ $18,000
18	Kendra Shelton	Representative	Breezy Point	Rentals	☆ $8,500
19	Chad Mei	Representative	Cass Lake	Excursions	☆ $10,000
20	Christopher Bowman	Manager	Cass Lake	Rentals	☆ $15,000
21	Tammy Christine	Representative	Walker	Rentals	☆ $17,500

4-26 Data sorted by the cell icon in "Amount" column

▶ **HOW TO:** Sort Data by Cell Attribute

1. Select a cell in the column to sort.
2. Click the **Sort** button [*Data* tab, *Sort & Filter* group].
 - The *Sort* dialog box opens.
 - You can also click the **Sort & Filter** button [*Home* tab, *Editing* group] and select **Custom Sort**.
3. Select the for **My data has headers** box if the data has a header row.
4. Click the **Sort by** arrow and select the column heading.
5. Click the **Sort On** arrow and choose the attribute.
 - The column must have data with different font colors, cells with different fill colors, or cell icons.
6. Click the leftmost **Order** arrow and choose a color or icon.
7. Click the rightmost **Order** arrow and choose **On Top** or **On Bottom**.
8. Click **Add Level**.
9. Click the **Then by** arrow and select the same column heading.
10. Click the **Sort On** arrow and choose the attribute.
11. Click the leftmost **Order** arrow and choose a color or icon.
12. Click the rightmost **Order** arrow and choose **On Top** or **On Bottom** (Figure 4-27).
 - Add and define as many sort levels as there are colors or icons to be sorted.
13. Click **OK**.

4-27 Cell icon order in the *Sort* dialog box

Sort Data in an Excel Table

When data is formatted as a table, you can sort from the *AutoFilter* arrows with each label in the header row. Sort choices are listed at the top of the pane that opens when you click an *AutoFilter* arrow.

▶ **HOW TO: Sort Data in an Excel Table**

1. Click the **AutoFilter** arrow for the column heading that represents the lowest sort level.
 - The *AutoFilter* pane lists sort choices at the top.
2. Choose **Sort A to Z** or **Sort Smallest to Largest** (Figure 4-28).
 - *Sort Smallest to Largest* appears for numeric data.
 - The table is sorted by the column.
3. Click the **AutoFilter** arrow for the column heading that represents the top sort level.
4. Choose **Sort A to Z** or **Sort Smallest to Largest**.
 - The table maintains the sort order from the first selected column within the sorted data for the top-level column.

4-28 *AutoFilter* arrow sort choices

Filtering Data

You can usually work more efficiently when you filter large amounts of data to show rows of importance to your task. You can, for example, filter data to show records for the year, the month, the individual, the product, or similar grouping. When you filter data, information that does not meet the requirements is temporarily hidden. A filter specifies which data are shown and which are hidden.

AutoFilters

In list-type data or an Excel table, the *Filter* button [*Data* tab, *Sort & Filter* group] displays or hides the *AutoFilter* arrow for each label in the header row. When you click an *AutoFilter* arrow, a pane displays sort options, filter types based on the data type, and check boxes for every piece of data. You can select boxes to mark which records display, or you can build a filter.

▶ **HOW TO:** Display and Use AutoFilters

1. Select a cell in the list.
2. Click the **Filter** button [*Data* tab, *Sort & Filter* group].
 - *AutoFilter* arrows appear in the header row with each label.
 - *AutoFilter* arrows display by default in an Excel table.
3. Click the **AutoFilter** arrow for the column used for filtering.
 - All items are selected and displayed in the data.
 - Filter options depend on the type of data in the column.
4. Click the **(Select All)** box to remove all check marks.
5. Select the box for each item to be shown (Figure 4-29).
6. Click **OK**.
 - Records that meet the criteria display with row headings in blue.
 - Records that do not meet the criteria and their row numbers are hidden.
 - A filter symbol appears with the column *AutoFilter* arrow.

4-29 *AutoFilter* for "Category" column

To remove a filter and display the complete list, click the **AutoFilter** arrow for the column and choose **Clear Filter From (ColumnName)**. You can also click the **Clear** button in the *Sort & Filter* group on the *Data* tab.

Custom AutoFilter

A *custom AutoFilter* is criteria that you build in a dialog box. A custom *AutoFilter* gives you more options for how rows display, because you can use multiple criteria with *AND* and *OR*. For a column with alphanumeric data, *Text Filters* are available, and there are *Number Filters* and *Date Filters* for columns with those types of data. Operators use common words such as *Equals, Begins With*, or *Contains* (Figure 4-30).

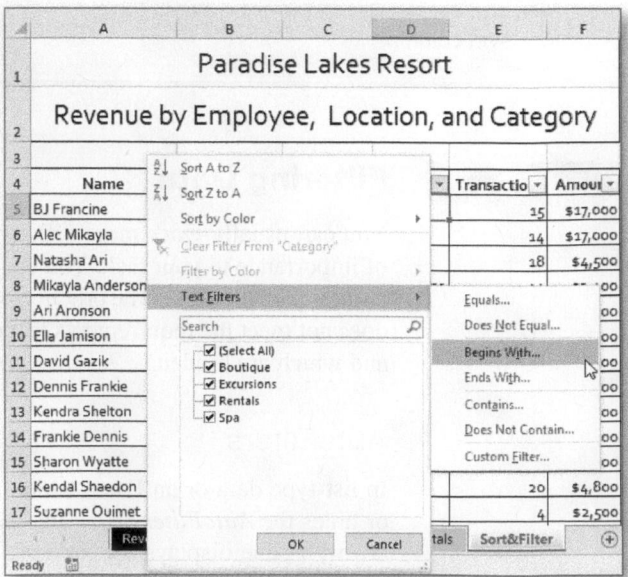

4-30 Text filters for a custom *AutoFilter*

▶**HOW TO:** Create a Custom Text AutoFilter

1. Select a cell in the data to filter.
2. Click the **Filter** button [*Data* tab, *Sort & Filter* group] to display *AutoFilter* arrows for the header row.
3. Click the **AutoFilter** arrow for the column used for filtering.
4. Select **Text Filters** and choose an operator.
 - The *Custom AutoFilter* dialog box opens.
5. Type criteria for the first operator in the box on the right.
 - You can also select a value from the drop-down list.
 - You can use wildcard characters.
6. Click the **And** or **Or** radio button.
 - *Or* conditions include rows that match either criteria.
 - *And* conditions are more restrictive and require that both criteria be met.
7. Click the arrow to choose a second operator.
 - A second operator is optional.
8. Type or select criteria for the second operator (Figure 4-31).
9. Click **OK**.
 - Rows in the data are filtered.

4-31 *Custom AutoFilter* dialog box

Advanced Filter

For an *Advanced Filter,* you build a criteria range separate from the data and type the conditions within that range. You can show the results in the data range, or you can display filtered data in another location on the sheet. Using another location for results allows you to create separate reports with filtered rows while the main list displays all data. An *Advanced Filter* requires more set-up work but allows you to apply more complex filters. You can even use a formula in the criteria.

A *criteria range* is at least two rows in which the first row must use the same column names as the data; the second row is where criteria is entered. You need not use all column names, and you can use more than one row for criteria. You can create a criteria range in empty rows anywhere on the worksheet or on another sheet. In Figure 4-32, the criteria range is cells G5:K6.

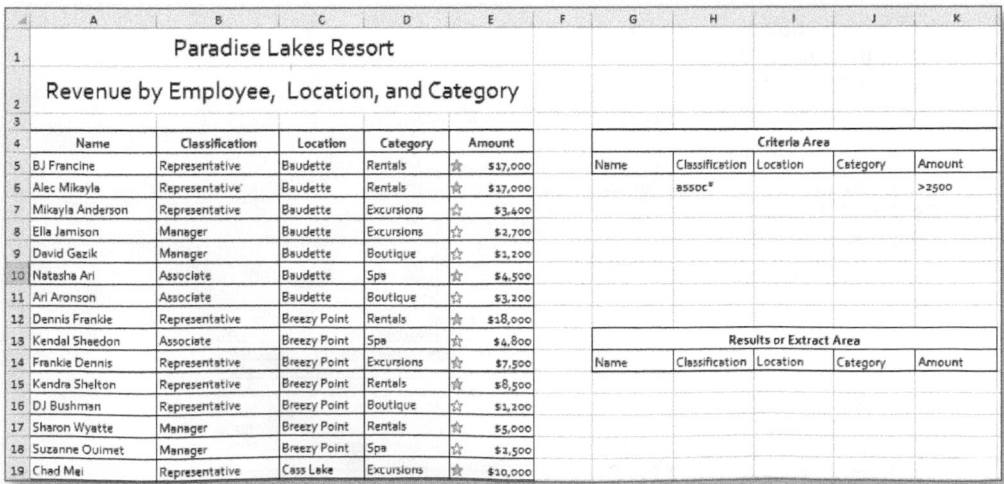

4-32 *Advanced Filter* set up

E4-240

Multiple rows below the header row in the criteria range set *AND* or *OR* conditions. If you enter criteria on the same row, they are treated as *AND* conditions. In Figure 4-32, "assoc*" in cell H6 and ">2500" in cell K6 are criteria. Both criteria must be met for a record to be displayed. For an *OR* condition, use a second (or third) row in the criteria range. An *OR* filter displays a record if any one of the requirements is met.

To show filtered results in another location, you also create an ***output*** or ***extract range***. You specify one row for this range, and it should include the same column headings as the data. In Figure 4-32, the extract range is cells G14:K14. Filtered rows are copied below these headings and take up as many rows as necessary. The output range must be on the same worksheet as the data, but you can copy the results to another sheet or another workbook.

▶ HOW TO: Create an Advanced Filter

1. Select labels in the header row for fields that will be used for filtering.
 - You can copy all the labels in the header row if preferred.
2. Copy the labels to a *Criteria* area.
 - The criteria area can be on the same or another sheet in the workbook.
 - If the criteria range is above the data, leave at least one blank row between it and the data.
3. Copy the labels again to an *Extract* area.
 - The output or extract area must be on the same sheet as the data.
 - Leave blank rows below the labels for the filtered results.
4. Type criteria in the criteria range.
 - Criteria is not case sensitive.
 - You can use wildcard characters in the criteria.
5. Click a cell in the data range.
6. Click the **Advanced** button [*Data* tab, *Sort & Filter* group].
 - The *Advanced Filter* dialog box opens.
7. Select **Copy to another location** In the *Action* group.
8. Verify or select the range (including the header row) in the *List range* box.
 - If the data range is named, press **F3 (FN+F3)** and select the name.
9. Select the criteria cell range with its header row in the *Criteria range* box.
 - If the criteria range is named, press **F3 (FN+F3)** and select the name.
 - You can type cell references to identify the criteria range.
10. Select the extract range in the *Copy to* box.
 - This range is the row of labels.
11. Click **OK** (Figure 4-33).

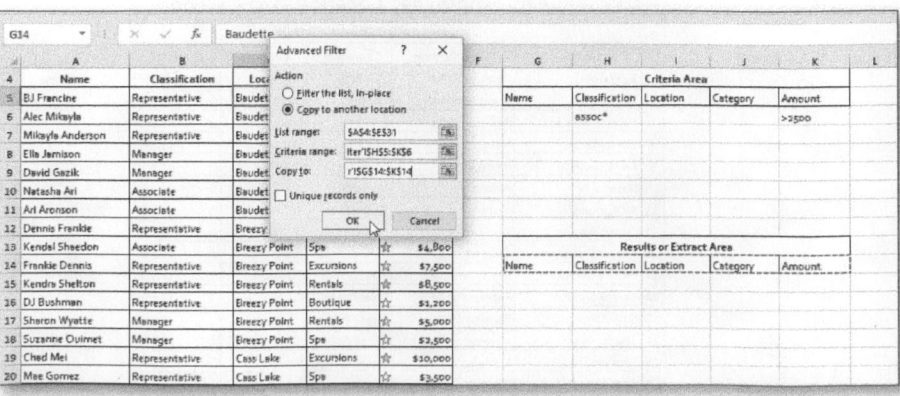

4-33 *Advanced Filter* dialog box

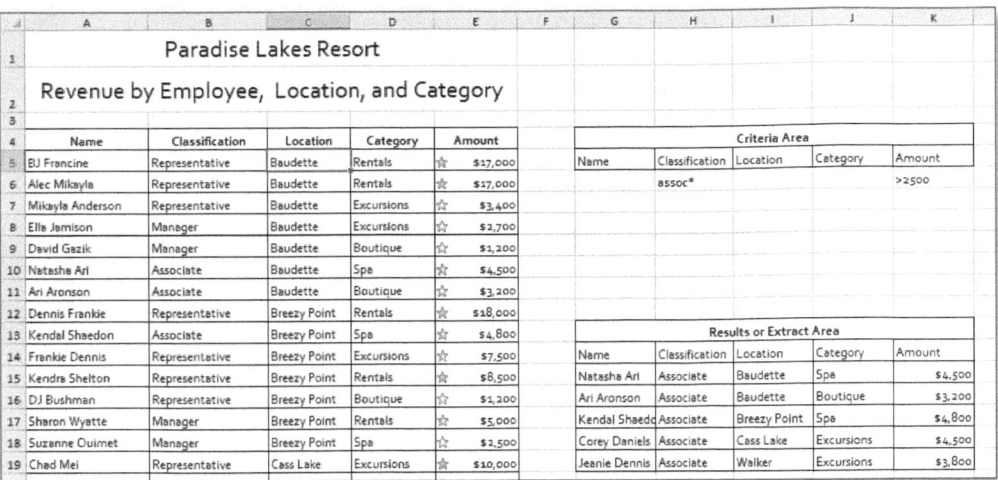

	Name	Classification	Location	Category	Amount				

Paradise Lakes Resort
Revenue by Employee, Location, and Category

Criteria Area

Name	Classification	Location	Category	Amount
	assoc*			>2500

Name	Classification	Location	Category	Amount
BJ Francine	Representative	Baudette	Rentals	$17,000
Alec Mikayla	Representative	Baudette	Rentals	$17,000
Mikayla Anderson	Representative	Baudette	Excursions	$3,400
Ella Jamison	Manager	Baudette	Excursions	$2,700
David Gazik	Manager	Baudette	Boutique	$1,200
Natasha Ari	Associate	Baudette	Spa	$4,500
Ari Aronson	Associate	Baudette	Boutique	$3,200
Dennis Frankie	Representative	Breezy Point	Rentals	$18,000
Kendal Shaedon	Associate	Breezy Point	Spa	$4,800
Frankie Dennis	Representative	Breezy Point	Excursions	$7,500
Kendra Shelton	Representative	Breezy Point	Rentals	$8,500
DJ Bushman	Representative	Breezy Point	Boutique	$1,200
Sharon Wyatte	Manager	Breezy Point	Rentals	$5,000
Suzanne Ouimet	Manager	Breezy Point	Spa	$2,500
Chad Mei	Representative	Cass Lake	Excursions	$10,000

Results or Extract Area

Name	Classification	Location	Category	Amount
Natasha Ari	Associate	Baudette	Spa	$4,500
Ari Aronson	Associate	Baudette	Boutique	$3,200
Kendal Shaedo	Associate	Breezy Point	Spa	$4,800
Corey Daniels	Associate	Cass Lake	Excursions	$4,500
Jeanie Dennis	Associate	Walker	Excursions	$3,800

4-34 *Advanced Filter* results copied to another location

- Filtered rows are copied to the output range below the copied labels (Figure 4-34).

> **MORE INFO**
>
> Enter < > as criteria to display records that have any entry in the column. Enter = as criteria to show rows that have no entry in the column.

SLO 4.5

Using Subtotals, Groups, and Outlines

A *subtotal* is a summary row for data that is grouped. A *group* is a set of data that has the same entry in one or more columns. You can see groups by "Location" with a subtotal in the "Amount" column in Figure 4-35. An *outline* is a summary that groups records so that individual groups can be displayed or hidden from view. These three features are Excel commands that make it easy to organize and calculate results for worksheets with large sets of data.

Paradise Lakes Resort
Revenue by Employee, Location, and Category

Name	Classification	Location	Category	Transactions	Amount
BJ Francine	Representative	Baudette	Rentals	15	$17,000
Alec Mikayla	Representative	Baudette	Rentals	14	$17,000
Natasha Ari	Associate	Baudette	Spa	18	$4,500
Mikayla Anderson	Representative	Baudette	Excursions	14	$3,400
Ari Aronson	Associate	Baudette	Boutique	10	$3,200
Ella Jamison	Manager	Baudette	Excursions	9	$2,700
David Gazik	Manager	Baudette	Boutique	6	$1,200
		Baudette Total		86	$49,000
Dennis Frankie	Representative	Breezy Point	Rentals	16	$18,000
Kendra Shelton	Representative	Breezy Point	Rentals	10	$8,500
Frankie Dennis	Representative	Breezy Point	Excursions	16	$7,500
Sharon Wyatte	Manager	Breezy Point	Rentals	7	$5,000
Kendal Shaedon	Associate	Breezy Point	Spa	20	$4,800
Suzanne Ouimet	Manager	Breezy Point	Spa	4	$2,500
DJ Bushman	Representative	Breezy Point	Boutique	5	$1,200
		Breezy Point Total		78	$47,500

4-35 Grouped rows with a subtotal in "Amount" column

The Subtotal Command

The *Subtotal* command in the *Outline* group on the *Data* tab inserts summary rows for a sorted list and formats the data as an *outline*. The *Subtotal* command is available for a normal range of cells, not an Excel table. The *Subtotal* command includes *SUM, AVERAGE, MAX,* or *MIN* as well as other *Statistical* functions.

To use the *Subtotal* command, the data should have a header row with data rows following, and you must sort the rows by the main field (column) to be summarized or totaled. To display revenue numbers by location, for example, sort the data by location. The *Subtotal* command groups the rows by this field but can show subtotals for any column.

> **MORE INFO**
>
> If data is formatted as an Excel table, convert it to a normal cell range [*Table Tools Design* tab, *Tools* group] to use the *Subtotal* command.

▶ HOW TO: Display Subtotals

1. Sort the data by the column by which subtotals will be calculated.
2. Click a cell in the data range.
3. Click the **Subtotal** button [*Data* tab, *Outline* group].
 - When data has a header row followed by data rows, the range is selected.
4. Click the **At each change in** arrow.
5. Choose the column heading name that was used for sorting.
 - Subtotals need not be shown for this column.
6. Click the **Use function** arrow and select the function.
7. In the **Add subtotal to** list, select each field that should display a subtotal.
 - Make sure the function applies to the column data type; for example, do not use *Sum* for a text column.
8. Choose **Replace current subtotals**.
 - If the range already has subtotals, they are replaced.
9. Choose **Summary below data** (Figure 4-36).
 - The "Summary" row can be placed above the data if you prefer.
 - You can also allow a group to split across pages.
 - You can remove subtotals from this dialog box.
10. Click **OK** (Figure 4-37).
 - A subtotal row appears below each group.
 - A grand total appears after the last row of data.
 - Outline buttons appear to the left of the column and row headings.
 - The outline is expanded, showing all details.

4-36 *Subtotal* dialog box

	A	B	C	D	E	F
4	**Name**	**Classification**	**Location**	**Category**	**Transactions**	**Amount**
5	Ari Aronson	Associate	Baudette	Boutique	10	$3,200
6	David Gazik	Manager	Baudette	Boutique	6	$1,200
7	DJ Bushman	Representative	Breezy Point	Boutique	5	$1,200
8	Christopher Bowm	Manager	Cass Lake	Boutique	15	$3,700
9	Randy Josephson	Associate	Cass Lake	Boutique	12	$1,500
10	Nikolai Jalowiec	Manager	Walker	Boutique	6	$1,450
11				**Boutique Total**		$12,250
12	Mikayla Anderson	Representative	Baudette	Excursions	14	$3,400
13	Ella Jamison	Manager	Baudette	Excursions	9	$2,700
14	Frankie Dennis	Representative	Breezy Point	Excursions	16	$7,500
15	Chad Mei	Representative	Cass Lake	Excursions	24	$10,000
16	Corey Daniels	Associate	Cass Lake	Excursions	22	$4,500
17	Jeanie Dennis	Associate	Walker	Excursions	8	$3,800
18				**Excursions Total**		$31,900
19	BJ Francine	Representative	Baudette	Rentals	15	$17,000
20	Alec Mikayla	Representative	Baudette	Rentals	14	$17,000
21	Dennis Frankie	Representative	Breezy Point	Rentals	16	$18,000
22	Kendra Shelton	Representative	Breezy Point	Rentals	10	$8,500
23	Sharon Wyatte	Manager	Breezy Point	Rentals	7	$5,000
24	Christopher Bowm	Manager	Cass Lake	Rentals	14	$15,000
25	Jeffery Dalton	Representative	Cass Lake	Rentals	5	$3,700
26	Tammy Christine	Representative	Walker	Rentals	16	$17,500
27	Josie Daddiline	Representative	Walker	Rentals	10	$12,000
28	Josie Daddiline	Representative	Walker	Rentals	12	$12,000
29				**Rentals Total**		$125,700
30	Natasha Ari	Associate	Baudette	Spa	18	$4,500
31	Kendal Shaedon	Associate	Breezy Point	Spa	20	$4,800
32	Suzanne Ouimet	Representative	Breezy Point	Spa	4	$2,500
33	Mae Gomez	Representative	Cass Lake	Spa	12	$3,500
34	Lilly Oliver	Associate	Walker	Spa	10	$2,200
35				**Spa Total**		$17,500
36				**Grand Total**		$187,350

4-37 "Amount" subtotals for each category

The *Subtotal* command inserts the *SUBTOTAL* function in each cell with a result. Its arguments are *Function_num* and *RefN*. *Function_num* is a number from 1 through 11 that specifies which calculation was selected in the *Subtotal* dialog box. If you chose *Sum*, for example, the function is =SUBTOTAL(9,F5:F11). *Ref1* is the range to be summed.

> **MORE INFO**
>
> The *Function_num* arguments are in alphabetical order, so that *AVERAGE* is 1, *COUNT* is 2, and so on. You can see the argument list in Excel *Help* for the function.

Outline Buttons

An outline groups and summarizes data. A worksheet can have only one outline; the outline can include all of the worksheet data or a portion of the data. Outlines have levels, indicated by the numbered buttons to the left of the column headings. Each *Outline Level* button shows an increasing level of detail. An outline can have up to eight levels. The worksheet in Figure 4-37 has three levels: a grand total (1), a category total for each group (2), and all the rows (3).

Each group has an *Expand/Collapse* button, shown to the left of the row headings. This button is a toggle and shows a minus sign (−) or a plus sign (+). When an individual group is collapsed, you do not see details for that group, only the subtotal.

▶ HOW TO: Use Outline Buttons

1. Click a collapse button (−) to hide details for a group.
 - Only the subtotal row displays.
2. Click an expand button (+) to display details for a group.
3. Click the **Level 1** button (1) to reveal the grand total.
4. Click the **Level 2** button (2) to see the second outline level details (Figure 4-38).
5. Click the **Level 3** button (3) to display all details.

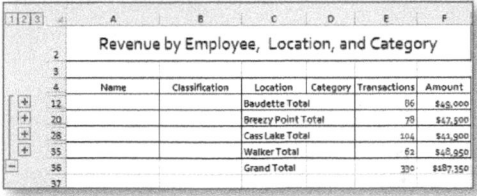

4-38 Level 2 outline results

Create an Auto Outline

An **Auto Outline** inserts groups based on where formulas are located. Consistent data and formulas that follow a pattern are necessary, and the formulas can be in specific rows or columns. The data in Figure 4-39 is grouped by location, and there is a *SUM* formula after each group in column E and F.

When data is not properly formatted, Excel displays a message that an *Auto Outline* cannot be created.

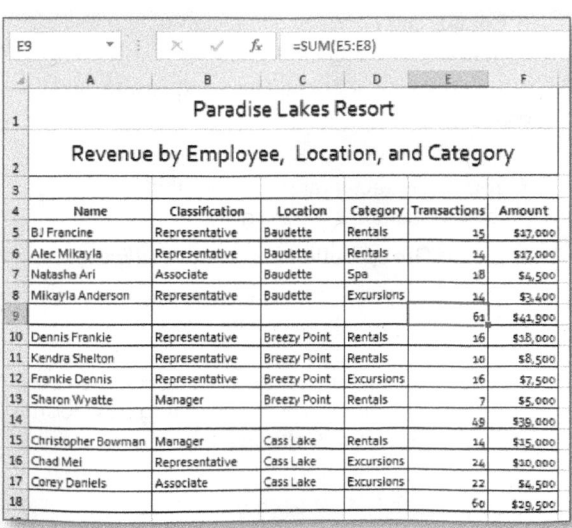

4-39 Data sorted by location with formulas for each group

▶ **HOW TO:** Create an Auto Outline

1. Click a cell within the data range.
2. Click the **Group** button arrow [*Data* tab, *Outline* group].
3. Select **Auto Outline**.
 - Outline level buttons are inserted.
 - The outline is expanded.
4. Click each collapse button to hide details (Figure 4-40).

4-40 *Auto Outline* with two levels

Define Groups

You can create a group, by rows or columns, for data that does not have totals or formulas. This can be a time-consuming task for a large set of records, but you can use groups to hide irrelevant records and concentrate on groups that require editing.

To define groups, data must be sorted or arranged so that you can select a range of cells to indicate the group. In addition, you must insert a blank summary row either above or below the group (or a blank column to the left or right of the group). You can use blank rows to enter subtitles for the data before or after grouping.

The data in Figure 4-41 is sorted by the "Classification" column, so that groups can be created for each job title. Note that a blank row has been inserted after each group.

▶ **HOW TO:** Define a Group

1. Sort the data (or arrange columns) based on the preferred grouping.
2. Insert a blank row at the end of each sort group (or at the start of each group).
 - Insert the blank row above the group if you want to label each group.
 - For column data, the summary column is usually to the right of the group.
3. Select the row or column headings for the first group.
 - Do not include the blank row or column.
 - You can select a range of cells that spans the rows or columns for the group.
4. Click the **Group** button [*Data* tab, *Outline* group].
 - The rows or columns are grouped.
 - Outline level buttons are inserted.
 - The data is expanded.
 - When you select a range of cells, not the row or column headings, the *Group* dialog box opens. Choose **Rows** or **Columns** if the dialog box opens and click **OK**.
5. Repeat steps 1–4 for each group (see Figure 4-41).

4-41 Data sorted by "Classification"; blank rows inserted after each title

> **MORE INFO**
>
> To clear an *Auto Outline* or remove all groups, click a cell within the group. Then click the **Ungroup** button arrow [*Data* tab, *Outline* group] and select **Clear Outline**.

PAUSE & PRACTICE: EXCEL 4-2

For this project, you sort and filter data for Paradise Lakes Resort based on location. You use a *Number Filter* to displays records within a range of values, build an advanced filter, and include subtotals in the workbook.

File Needed: **[your initials] PP E4-1.xlsx**
Completed Project File Name: **[your initials] PP E4-2.xlsx**

1. Open the **[your initials]PP E4-1** workbook completed in *Pause & Practice 4-1* and save it as [your initials] PP E4-2.

2. Click the **Sort&Filter** sheet tab.

3. Sort data in a worksheet.
 a. Click cell **A5**.
 b. Click the **Sort** button [*Data* tab, *Sort & Filter* group].
 c. Select the **My data has headers** box, if necessary.
 d. Click the **Sort by** arrow and select **Location**.
 e. Choose **Values** for *Sort On* and **A to Z** for *Order.*
 f. Click **Add Level**.
 g. Click the **Then by** arrow and select **Amount**.
 h. Choose **Values** for *Sort On* and **Largest to Smallest** for *Order* (Figure 4-42).
 i. Click **OK**. The data in is sorted alphabetically by location and then by amount in descending order.

4. Use a *Number AutoFilter.*
 a. Click cell **A5**.
 b. Click the **Filter** button [*Data* tab, *Sort & Filter* group] to display *AutoFilter* arrows.
 c. Click the *AutoFilter* arrow for "Amount."
 d. Point to **Number Filters** and select **Between**.
 e. Type 5000 in the **is greater than or equal to** box.
 f. Type 10000 in the **is less than or equal to** box (Figure 4-43).
 g. Click **OK**.

5. Click the **Adv Filter** sheet tab.

6. Set a criteria range.
 a. In cell **H6**, type assoc*.
 b. Type >1500 in cell **K6**.

7. Run an *Advanced Filter.*
 a. Click cell **A5**.
 b. Click the **Advanced** button [*Data* tab, *Sort & Filter* group].
 c. Select the **Copy to another location** radio button.
 d. Verify that cells **A4:E31** are identified in the **List range** box.

4-42 Multiple column sort with text and numeric data

4-43 *Custom AutoFilter* dialog box for "Amount" between $5,000 and $10,000

e. Click the **Criteria range** box and select cells **G5:K6**.

f. Click the **Copy to** box and select cells **G14:K14** (Figure 4-44).

g. Click **OK**. Six records are extracted and displayed.

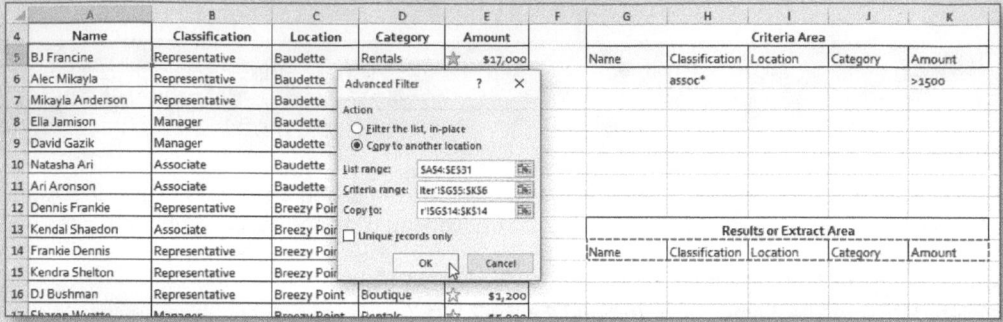

4-44 Criteria and extract ranges; *Advanced Filter* dialog box

8. Click the **Subtotals** sheet tab.

9. Show subtotals in a list.

a. Click a cell in the **Location** column. The records are sorted by this column.

b. Click the **Subtotal** button [*Data* tab, *Outline* group].

c. Click the **At each change in** arrow and choose **Location**.

d. Click the **Use function** arrow and choose **Sum**.

e. Select **Transactions** and **Amount** in the **Add subtotal to list** box.

f. Click **OK** (Figure 4-45).

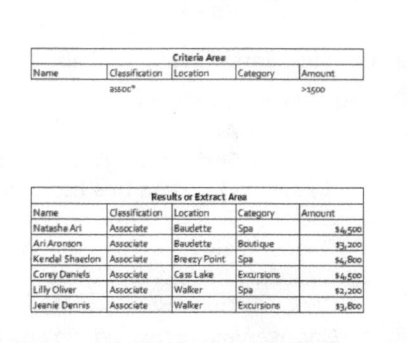

4-45 Completed PP E4-2 worksheets

10. Save and close the workbook.

SLO 4.6

Importing Data

Importing is the process of getting data from an outside source into an Excel worksheet. For example, you can probably import data from your bank into a worksheet so that you can analyze your transactions. *External data* is data that originated in another program or format. You import or copy external data into Excel from a *source,* which might be a text file, a database, or a web location. Imported data in a worksheet is almost always in list or table format.

The *Get External Data* command group on the *Data* tab establishes a connection to the source so that data can be refreshed. When you copy data into a worksheet using a *Copy and Paste* command, there is no connection to the source. Data connections are discussed later in this section.

Text Files

A *text file* is a document that includes raw data with no formatting. Text files are *.txt* (text) documents such as those created in NotePad or WordPad. Another widely used text format is *.csv* (comma separated values); you might see this type of file when you download a bank statement.

Text files separate data into *fields.* In one method, a character such as a comma or a tab separates the fields, and the file is described as *delimited* (e.g., tab-delimited file). A *delimiter* is the character used to separate the data. Common delimiters are the tab, space, and comma characters.

A second way to separate fields in a text file is by *fixed width*. Each field is a specified number of characters followed by a space. If the first name field is set at 25 characters, the name "Tom," is imported as 3 characters plus 22 spaces. The second field always starts at position 26.

When you click the **From Text** button in the *Get External Data* group on the *Data* tab, the **Text Import Wizard** guides you through the importing steps.(Figure 4-46).

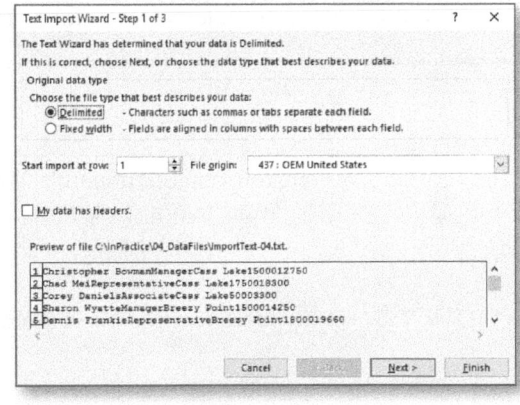

> **MORE INFO**
>
> Many legacy or mainframe computer systems use fixed width files for data.

4-46 Text Import Wizard – Step 1

▶ **HOW TO:** Import a Tab-Delimited Text File into a Worksheet

1. Select the cell in which imported data should begin.
2. Click the **From Text** button [*Data* tab, *Get External Data* group].
3. Navigate to and select the text file name in the *Import Text File* dialog box.
4. Click **Import** (Figure 4-47).
5. Select the **Delimited** radio button in the *Text Import Wizard – Step 1 of 3* window.
 - A preview of the data displays.

4-47 Import Text File dialog box

6. Click the spinner arrow for **Start import at row** to set the first row of imported text.

7. Click **Next**.

8. Select the **Tab** box in the *Text Import Wizard – Step 2 of 3* window.

 • The *Data preview* shows how the data will be separated into columns.

9. Click **Next**.

 • The *Step 3 of 3* window allows you to set formats as the data is imported.
 • This is optional; you can format data after it is imported.

10. Click **Finish**.

11. Select the radio button for **Existing worksheet** in the *Import Data* dialog box.

 • You can change or select the beginning cell location.
 • When you choose **New worksheet**, imported data starts at cell A1.

12. Click **OK**.

 • The data is available in the worksheet.

13. Right-click a cell within the imported data and select **Data Range Properties**.

 • The *External Data Range Properties* dialog box opens (Figure 4-48).
 • The *Name* is the name for the data connection.
 • You can specify when and how data is refreshed or updated.

14. Click **OK** to close the *External Data Range Properties* dialog box.

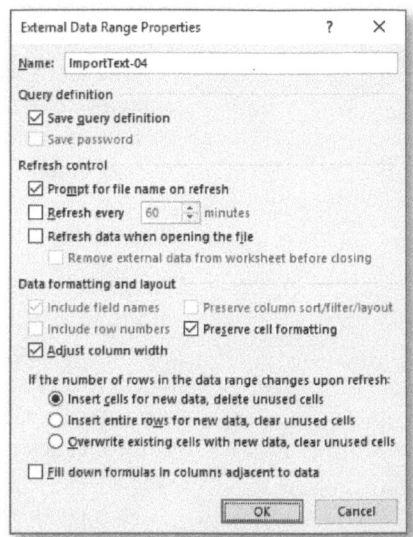

4-48 *External Data Range Properties* **dialog box**

Word Documents

You cannot "import" a Word document into Excel, but you can copy and paste data from Word into a worksheet. You can keep the Word formatting, or you can choose the current worksheet format.

▶ HOW TO: Copy Data from a Word Document

1. Select the cell in which imported data should begin.

2. Start Word and open the document.

3. Select the data to be copied.

4. Click the **Copy** button [*Home* tab, *Clipboard* group].

5. Switch to the Excel worksheet.

6. Click the arrow with the **Paste** button [*Home* tab, *Clipboard* group].

7. Choose **Match Destination Formatting** from the *Paste* gallery.

 • The data is pasted in the worksheet.
 • If you click the **Paste** button, data is pasted with the Word format.

> **ANOTHER WAY**
> Save a Word document as a text file (*.txt*) and import the text file into Excel.

Access Database Files

Most organizations and enterprises maintain large amounts of data in a database. A **database** is a collection of related tables, queries, forms, and reports. **Microsoft Access** is a relational database management system that is part of the Office suite. You can import a table or a query from an Access database into an Excel worksheet. In Access, a table is a data list, and a query is a subset of the list.

> **MORE INFO**
>
> If a database has a single table or query, it is automatically imported into Excel; the *Select Table* dialog box does not open.

When a database includes many tables and queries, the *Select Table* dialog box opens so that you can choose the table or query to import. Access data is imported as an Excel table, a *PivotTable,* or a *PivotChart.*

▶HOW TO: Import an Access Table into a Worksheet

1. Select the cell in which imported data should begin.
2. Click the **From Access** button [*Data* tab, *Get External Data* group].
3. Navigate to and select the database name in the *Select Data Source* dialog box.
4. Click **Open**.
 - If only one table or query exists in the database, it is imported.
5. Select the name of the table or query in the *Select Table* dialog box (Figure 4-49).
6. Click **OK**.
7. Select **Table** and **Existing worksheet** in the *Import Data* dialog box.
 - You can choose a new worksheet for imported data or select a different cell.
 - You can also import data as a *PivotTable,* a *PivotChart,* or as a connection for later use.
8. Click **OK**.
 - The data is imported in an Excel table.
 - Field names from the Access table or query are column headings in the Excel table.
9. Click the *Table Tools Design* tab.
10. Click the **Properties** button [*External Table Data* group].
 - The *External Data Properties* dialog box opens (Figure 4-50).
 - You can adjust formatting and refresh options.
11. Click the **Connection Properties** button (to the right of the *Name* box).
 - The *Connection Properties* dialog box opens.
 - You can type a description for the data connection.
 - You can set how the data is refreshed or updated.
 - The *Definition* tab identifies the source of the imported data.
12. Click **OK** to close the *Connection Properties* dialog box.
13. Click **OK** to close the *External Data Properties* dialog box.

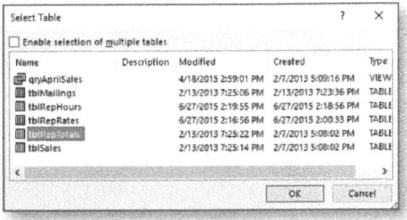

4-49 *Select Table* dialog box

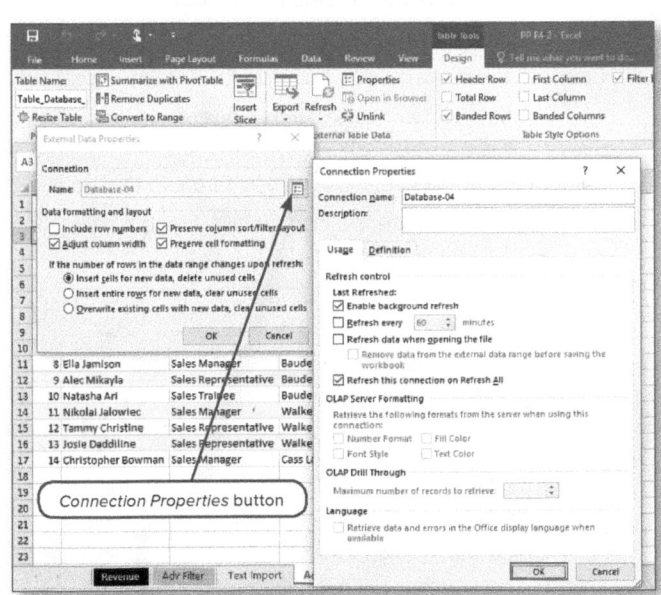

4-50 *External Data Properties* and *Connection Properties* dialog boxes

> **MORE INFO**
>
> You can import tables and queries from relational data bases such as SQL Server with the *From Other Sources* button [*Data* tab, *Get External Data* group].

Web Site Data

Web sites that deal with research, statistics, demographics, and similar public data often have downloadable text or Excel files for importing. Most web sites, however, have protected multimedia content with images, video, and audio, not list-type data for importing into Excel.

> **MORE INFO**
>
> You can copy web page data and paste it in Excel. This data includes links, images, and other elements. There is no data connection.

When you use the *From Web* command, data are identified by a small red arrow in a yellow-orange box. When you click the arrow, the importable data is selected, and the arrow changes to a blue check mark. Data from a web page establishes a connection to the URL that you can refresh. If the URL changes, you must edit the query to find the new address.

> **HOW TO: Create a Web Query to Import Data**

1. Navigate to the web site and select the URL in the *Address* bar.
2. Press **Ctrl+C** to copy the URL to the Windows *Clipboard*.
3. Select the cell in which imported data should begin.
4. Click the **From Web** button [*Data* tab, *Get External Data* group].
 - The *New Web Query* dialog box opens.
 - Use the resize arrow at the bottom right corner to resize the dialog box.
5. Select the default URL in the *Address* bar in the *New Web Query* dialog box.
6. Press **Ctrl+V** to paste the copied URL in the *Address* bar.
7. Click **Go** or press **Enter**.
 - If an error message box opens about scripts that cannot be run, click **Yes**.
8. Navigate to the data to be imported.
9. Click the **Click to select this table** arrow (yellow-orange arrow) next to data to import (Figure 4-51).
 - The arrow changes to a blue check mark, the **Click to deselect this table** arrow.
10. Click **Import**.
 - The *Import Data* dialog box opens.

4-51 *New Web Query* dialog box

11. Click **OK**.
- You may see a brief screen message as data is imported.
- The imported data is unformatted.

Workbook Connections

When you use the *Get External Data* group on the *Data* tab, Excel establishes a connection that you can edit, refresh, name, or remove. A ***connection*** is an identifier and a link for data that originated outside the workbook. All connections are listed in the *Workbook Connections* dialog box. In this dialog box, you can select the connection name and open its *Properties* dialog box to edit various settings.

A data connection to an Internet location is named *Connection*. A data connection to a text or database file is named the same as the original file. You can change the name of a data connection to a descriptive name in the *Properties* dialog box.

When you open a workbook that has data connections, you will usually see a security warning bar at the top of the worksheet. When you are sure that the connection is safe, click **Enable Content** to work with the data.

▶HOW TO: Manage Data Connections

1. Click the **Connections** button [*Data* tab, *Connections* group].
 - The *Workbook Connections* dialog box lists current connections.
2. Select the name of the connection.
3. Click the link **Click here to see where the selected connections are used** in the lower pane.
 - This identifies where the data is located in the workbook (Figure 4-52).

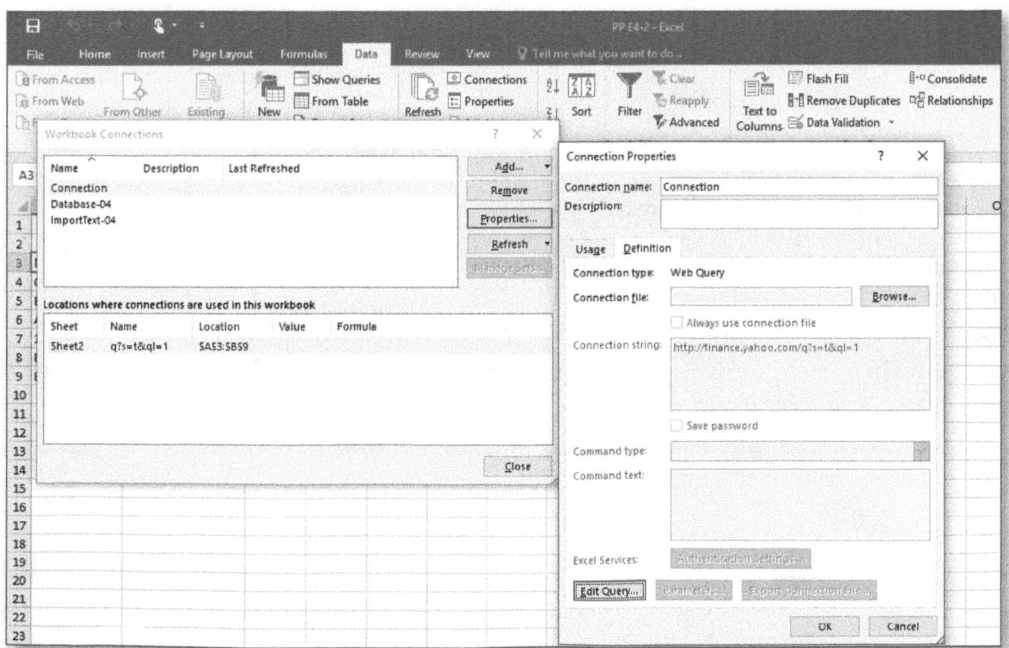

4-52 *Workbook Connections* and *Connection Properties* dialog boxes

4. Click **Refresh** to update the selected connection.

- The *Import Text File* dialog box opens for a text file so that you can import it again.
- A database source is automatically refreshed if the file is accessible.
- An Internet source updates if the URL is accessible.

5. Click **Properties** to open the *Connection Properties* dialog box.

- You can set how the data are refreshed, change the connection name, or add a description.
- Click the *Definition* tab to edit a web query to update a URL.

6. Click **OK** to close the *Connection Properties* dialog box.

7. Click **Close** to save changes.

Flash Fill

Imported data often needs to be "cleaned" because it may not be in the correct sort order, it may have missing or incorrect data, and so on. *Flash Fill* is a feature that recognizes a pattern in the first cell and suggests data for the remaining rows in a column. It can be used to quickly complete new, missing, or incorrect data. For example, imagine that imported data lists first and last names in a single column, but you want first and last names in separate columns. Type the first person's name in an empty column next to the original column. As you start to type a second name below the first one, *Flash Fill* previews the completed column. Just press **Enter** to complete the column. Then do the same for the person's last name in the next column to the right. The *Flash Fill Options* button appears after you press **Enter** so that you can undo the fill if necessary or accept all the suggestions.

▶ **HOW TO: Flash Fill Data in a Worksheet**

1. Click the first cell in an empty column next to the original data.

- The first *Flash Fill* column must be adjacent to the original data.
- Use an empty column or insert a column.

2. Type the data as you want it to appear.

3. Press **Enter** and type data in the cell below the first cell.

- The suggested list is previewed.
- If the suggested list does not appear, try typing a third item in the column (Figure 4-53).
- The data must be consistent and follow a recognizable pattern.

4. Press **Enter** to complete the *Flash Fill*.

- If there is no *Flash Fill* suggestion list, click the **Flash Fill** button [*Data* tab, *Data Tools* group] with the insertion point in the column.

4-53 *Flash Fill* suggestion list

▶ **ANOTHER WAY**

To split data into separate columns, insert blank columns to the right. Select the column to be split and click the **Text to Columns** button [*Data* tab, *Data Tools* group]. Complete the *Convert Text to Columns Wizard*.

SLO 4.7 Exporting Data

Exporting is the process of saving data in a format that can be used by another program or application. This can be as simple as providing a PDF file for viewing, copying data into Word, or saving worksheet data as a text file.

Export Data as a Text File

Most software applications can read a text file, a common way to transfer or share data. You can save Excel data as a tab-delimited, space-delimited, or comma-delimited file. When you save worksheet data as a text file, Excel renames the sheet with the same file name that you type for the text file. You can save only one worksheet in a text file. If a workbook has multiple sheets, a message box will alert you that only the current sheet will be saved.

▶ HOW TO: Save Excel Data as a Tab-Delimited File

1. Click the worksheet tab with data to export.
 - The insertion point can be in any cell.
2. Click the **File** tab and select **Export**.
3. Select **Change File Type**.
4. Select **Text (Tab delimited)** as the file type (Figure 4-54).

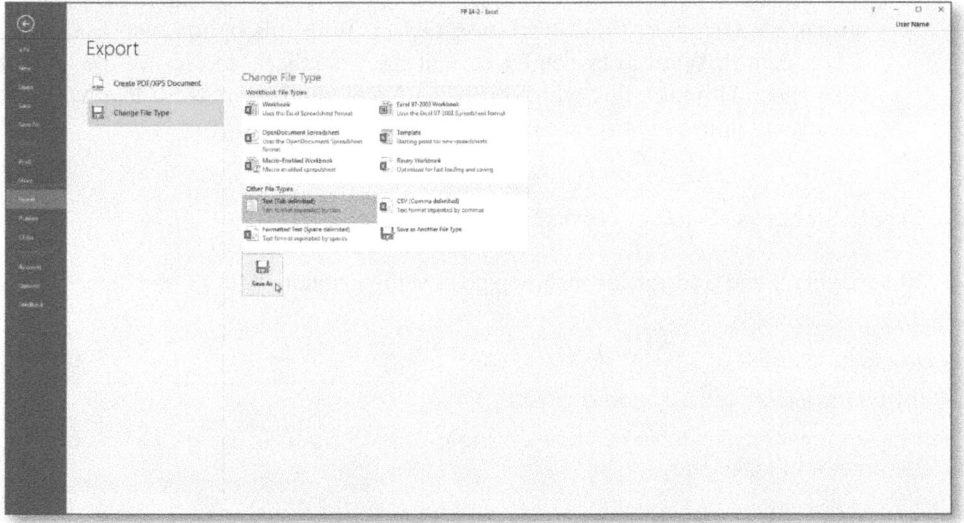

4-54 *Export* command in *Backstage* view

5. Click **Save As**.
 - The *Save As* dialog box opens with *Text (tab-delimited)* as the *Save as type*.
6. Navigate to the location for the exported data.
7. Type a file name for the text file in the *File name* box.
8. Click **Save**.
 - If a workbook has more than one sheet, a message box reminds you that only one sheet can be exported. Click **OK** in this message box.
9. Click **Yes** to acknowledge that Excel features may be lost.
 - The worksheet tab has the same name as the exported file.
10. Rename the sheet tab as desired.

11. Click the **File** tab and choose **Save As**.

12. Select **Excel Workbook** as the *Save as type* in the *Save As* dialog box.

13. Navigate to the folder for saved work.

14. Select or type the original workbook file name and click **Save**.

15. Click **Yes** to replace the file.

16. Close the workbook.

 - The exported text file is available in the folder selected for saving.
 - The original workbook is unchanged and resaved.

> **MORE INFO**
>
> To use Excel data in an Access table, export the data as a text file. You can then import the text file into an Access table.

Export Data via the Clipboard

Excel data can be copied and pasted into a Word document as well as other applications. The *Paste* button gallery in Word has options to paste a table, to paste text separated by tabs or spaces, and to paste a picture object. The *Paste Special* command in the gallery has an option to paste a *Microsoft Excel Worksheet Object*. With this option, you can paste a link to the Excel data in Word to launch Excel, edit the worksheet, and resave the Excel file. You can also paste without a link which opens an Excel window in Word that has most Excel commands but does not affect the original Excel file.

▶ HOW TO: Create a Microsoft Excel Worksheet Object

1. Open the Word document and position the insertion point at the location for the Excel data.

2. Switch to the Excel worksheet.

3. Select the cells to be copied.

4. Click the **Copy** button [*Home* tab, *Clipboard* group].

 - The data can be formatted as a table or a normal range.
 - You can also press **Ctrl+C** to copy.

5. Switch to the Word document.

6. Click the arrow with the **Paste** button [*Home* tab, *Clipboard* group] and choose **Paste Special**.

7. Select **Microsoft Excel Worksheet Object** in the *Paste Special* dialog box.

8. Select **Paste link** in the *Paste Special* dialog box (Figure 4-55).

9. Click **OK**.

 - The data is pasted as a worksheet object.

10. Complete work in the Word document.

 - Use horizontal alignment commands to position the object, if necessary.
 - You can double-click anywhere in the object to launch Excel and open the source workbook.

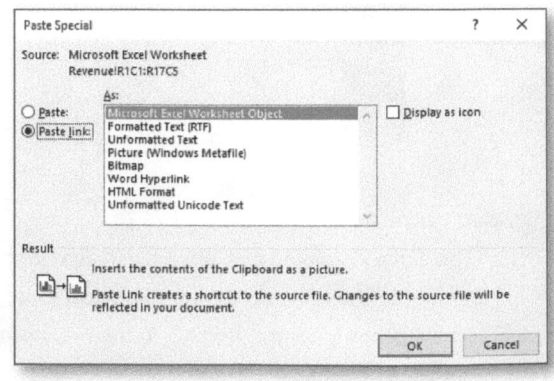

4-55 *Paste Special* dialog box

SharePoint Lists

A **SharePoint server** is a web platform that runs *Microsoft SharePoint,* a family of products that allows for collaboration and simultaneous work by groups of people via the Internet. You can export data in an Excel table to a SharePoint list so that others in your work circle have access to the data. The *Export* button is in the *External Table Data* group on the *Table Tools Design* tab, and it launches the *Export Table to SharePoint List Wizard.* To work with a SharePoint server, you must have an Internet connection and permission from the network administrator.

PAUSE & PRACTICE: EXCEL 4-3

For this project, you import data from a text file into an Excel worksheet, format the data as an Excel table, copy data from a Word document, and use *Flash Fill* to complete the worksheet for Paradise Lakes Resort.

Files Needed: *[your initials] PP E4-2.xlsx, ImportText-04.txt*, and **CopyWord-04.docx** *[Student data files are available in the* Library *of your SIMnet account.]*
Completed Project File Name: *[your initials] PP E4-3.xlsx*

1. Open the *[your initials] PP E4-2* workbook completed in *Pause & Practice 4-2* and save it as [your initials] PP E4-3.

2. Import data from a text file.
 a. Select cell **A4** on the **Text Import** tab.
 b. Click the **From Text** button [*Data* tab, *Get External Data* group].
 c. Navigate to and select *ImportText-04.txt* from your student data files in the *Import Text File* dialog box.
 d. Click **Import**.
 e. Select **Delimited** in the *Text Import Wizard – Step 1 of 3* dialog box and click **Next**.
 f. Select the **Tab** box in the *Text Import Wizard – Step 2 of 3* dialog box and click **Next**.
 g. Click **Finish** to accept the *General* format.
 h. Click **OK** in the *Import Data* dialog box.

3. Copy data from a Word document.
 a. Select cell **A18**.
 b. Open Microsoft Word and open the **CopyWord-04** document from your student data files.
 c. Select all the data and click the **Copy** button [*Home* tab, *Clipboard* group].
 d. Switch to the Excel window.
 e. Click the arrow with the **Paste** button [*Home* tab, *Clipboard* group] and choose **Match Destination Formatting** (Figure 4-56).

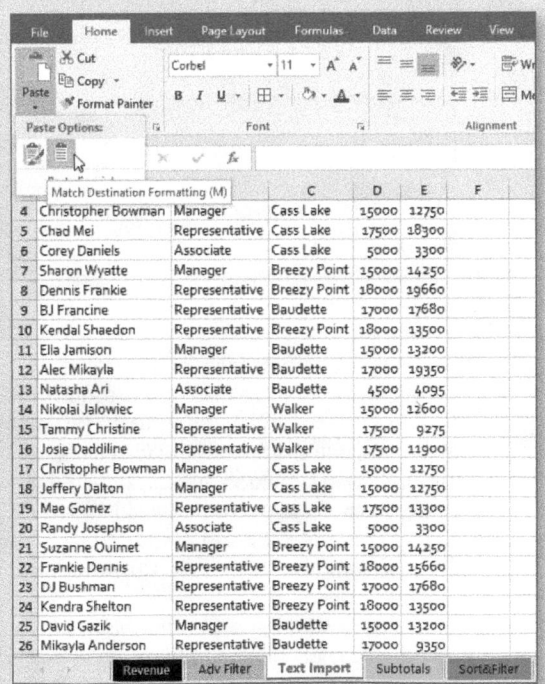

4-56 *Paste Options* for copied data

f. Select cells **D4:E27** and apply the **Currency** number format with zero decimals.

g. Adjust the widths of columns **C:E** to **11.43 (85 pixels)**.

4. Use *Flash Fill* to create an email address column.

a. Insert a column between columns **A** and **B**.

b. Type Email Address in cell **B3**.

c. Increase the width of the "Email Address" column to **31.00 (222 pixels)**.

d. In cell **B4** type c.bowman@somewhere.com and press **Enter**.

e. Select cell **B5** and type c.m to start the second address and display the *Flash Fill* suggested list.

f. Press **Enter**. If the *Flash Fill* suggestion list did not appear, click the **Flash Fill** button [*Data* tab, *Data Tools* group].

5. Format data as an Excel table.

a. Select cells **A3:F27**. Since the data was imported from different sources, you must select the range.

b. Click the **Format as Table** button [*Home* tab, *Styles* group].

c. Choose **Table Style Light 1** and click **OK**. The data connections must be removed to create an Excel table.

d. Choose **Yes** in the message box (Figure 4-57).

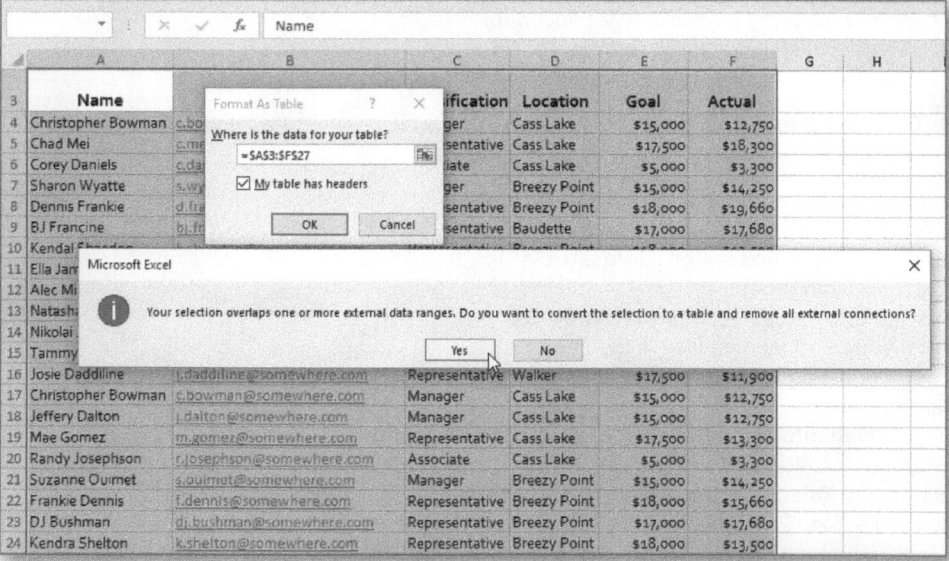

4-57 Message box to remove data connections

6. Add a column with a calculation to a table.

a. Type Difference in cell **G3** and press **Enter**.

b. Change the column width to **10.70 (80 pixels)** and use a black bottom border for the cell.

c. Type = in cell **G4** to start the formula and click cell **F4**.

d. Type − for subtraction and click cell **E4** (Figure 4-58).

e. Press **Enter** to copy the formula in the column.

f. Select cells **G4:G27** and press **Ctrl+1** to open the *Format Cells* dialog box.

g. On the *Number* tab, choose **Currency** with zero decimal places and negative numbers in red, and close the dialog box.

h. Select cells **A1:G1** and click the **Merge & Center** button [*Home* tab, *Alignment* group] to remove the centering. Then click the **Merge & Center** button again to re-center the cells over the new range.

i. Repeat the steps to re-center cells **A2:G2**.

j. Change the orientation to **Landscape**.

4-58 Structured references in a table formula

7. Save and close the workbook. Close the Word document (Figure 4-59).

Paradise Lakes Resort
Revenue Target and Actual Levels

Name	Email Address	Classification	Location	Goal	Actual	Difference
Christopher Bowman	c.bowman@somewhere.com	Manager	Cass Lake	$15,000	$12,750	$2,250
Chad Mei	c.mei@somewhere.com	Representative	Cass Lake	$17,500	$18,300	$800
Corey Daniels	c.daniels@somewhere.com	Associate	Cass Lake	$5,000	$3,300	$1,700
Sharon Wyatte	s.wyatte@somewhere.com	Manager	Breezy Point	$15,000	$14,250	$750
Dennis Frankie	d.frankie@somewhere.com	Representative	Breezy Point	$18,000	$19,660	$1,660
BJ Francine	bj.francine@somewhere.com	Representative	Baudette	$17,000	$17,680	$680
Kendal Shaedon	k.shaedon@somewhere.com	Representative	Breezy Point	$18,000	$13,500	$4,500
Ella Jamison	e.jamison@somewhere.com	Manager	Baudette	$15,000	$13,200	$1,800
Alec Mikayla	a.mikayla@somewhere.com	Representative	Baudette	$17,000	$19,350	$2,350
Natasha Ari	n.ari@somewhere.com	Associate	Baudette	$4,500	$4,095	$405
Nikolai Jalowiec	n.jalowiec@somewhere.com	Manager	Walker	$15,000	$12,600	$2,400
Tammy Christine	t.christine@somewhere.com	Representative	Walker	$17,500	$9,275	$8,225
Josie Daddiline	j.daddiline@somewhere.com	Representative	Walker	$17,500	$11,900	$5,600
Christopher Bowman	c.bowman@somewhere.com	Manager	Cass Lake	$15,000	$12,750	$2,250
Jeffery Dalton	j.dalton@somewhere.com	Manager	Cass Lake	$15,000	$12,750	$2,250
Mae Gomez	m.gomez@somewhere.com	Representative	Cass Lake	$17,500	$13,300	$4,200
Randy Josephson	r.josephson@somewhere.com	Associate	Cass Lake	$5,000	$3,300	$1,700
Suzanne Ouimet	s.ouimet@somewhere.com	Manager	Breezy Point	$15,000	$14,250	$750
Frankie Dennis	f.dennis@somewhere.com	Representative	Breezy Point	$18,000	$15,660	$2,340
DJ Bushman	dj.bushman@somewhere.com	Representative	Breezy Point	$17,000	$17,680	$680
Kendra Shelton	k.shelton@somewhere.com	Representative	Breezy Point	$18,000	$13,500	$4,500
David Gazik	d.gazik@somewhere.com	Manager	Baudette	$15,000	$13,200	$1,800
Mikayla Anderson	m.anderson@somewhere.com	Representative	Baudette	$17,000	$9,350	$7,650
Ari Aronson	a.aronson@somewhere.com	Associate	Baudette	$4,500	$4,095	$405

4-59 PP E4-3 completed worksheet

SLO 4.8

Building and Formatting PivotTables

A *PivotTable* is a cross tabulation report based on list-type data. It is a separate worksheet in which you can sort, filter, and calculate large amounts of data. *PivotTables* are analysis tools, an important part of *Business Intelligence (BI)*. Business intelligence is a combination of applications and processes that enable you to "drill-down" into data and assess various types of results or changes. In a table or list with thousands of records, you can build a *PivotTable*

to quickly show average revenue by state, by city, or other criteria, and, just as quickly, return to the entire list (Figure 4-60).

PivotTables are interactive, because you rearrange the report for analysis by clicking or dragging. Rearranging data is *pivoting* the data so that you can look at it from a different perspective. It takes time and practice to create and understand all the features of a *PivotTable*, but it is easy to experiment placing fields, sorting data, or filtering results.

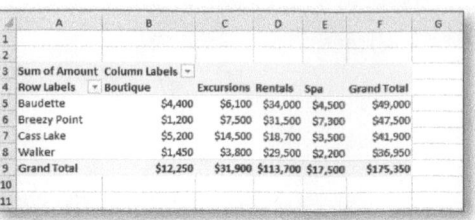

4-60 An Excel *PivotTable*

Create a PivotTable

Data for a *PivotTable* should follow the same guidelines as those recommended for an Excel table in the beginning of this chapter. Data can be formatted as a table but need not be. A *PivotTable* is placed on its own sheet in the workbook.

The *Tables* group on the *Insert* tab includes the *PivotTable* button as well as the *Recommended PivotTables* button. When you are first learning about *PivotTables,* the *Recommended PivotTables* button may help you gain experience building these reports.

After you create a *PivotTable,* the *PivotTable Tools Analyze* and *Design* tabs are available for additional format choices and data commands.

▶ HOW TO: Create a PivotTable

1. Click a cell in the data range.
 - The data range must have a header row.
2. Click the **Recommended PivotTables** button [*Insert* tab, *Tables* group] (Figure 4-61).
 - A data range is assumed and highlighted in the worksheet.
3. Point to a preview tile on the left to see a *ScreenTip* for the proposed *PivotTable.*
4. Select the preferred *PivotTable* and click **OK**.
 - The *PivotTable* report is created on a separate sheet.

4-61 *RecommendedPivotTables* for a data range

The PivotTable Fields Pane

A *PivotTable* is created on a new sheet in the workbook, and the *PivotTable Fields* pane opens at the right. From this pane, you can add and remove fields from the report and drag field names into different areas in the pane to reset how the data are organized (Figure 4-62).

There are *Filters, Columns, Rows,* and *Values* areas in the pane. Each item from a field in the *Rows* area appears in its own row in the *PivotTable.* Each item in a field in the *Columns* area displays as a column. Columns and rows are usually the categories of data, not the actual values. Fields in the *Values* area are the ones that are summed, averaged, counted, or

otherwise used in a calculation. *Filters* are fields placed as separate buttons above the *PivotTable* which act like *AutoFilter* arrows. Row and column labels include a filter arrow in the body of the *PivotTable,* and row data have collapse/expand buttons for certain field layouts. You can filter data from the filter arrows with a field, or you can insert a *Slicer* window.

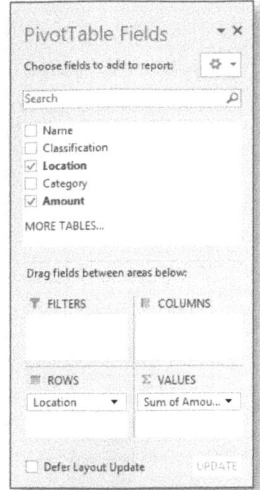

4-62 *PivotTable Fields* pane

▶ HOW TO: Adjust Fields in a PivotTable

1. Click a cell in the body of the *PivotTable*.
2. Drag a field name from the *Choose fields to add to report* area into the *Columns* area in the *PivotTable Fields* pane and release the pointer button.
 - Columns for the field items are added to the report.
 - A grand total column is added.
3. Drag a field name into the *Filters* area and release the pointer button (Figure 4-63).

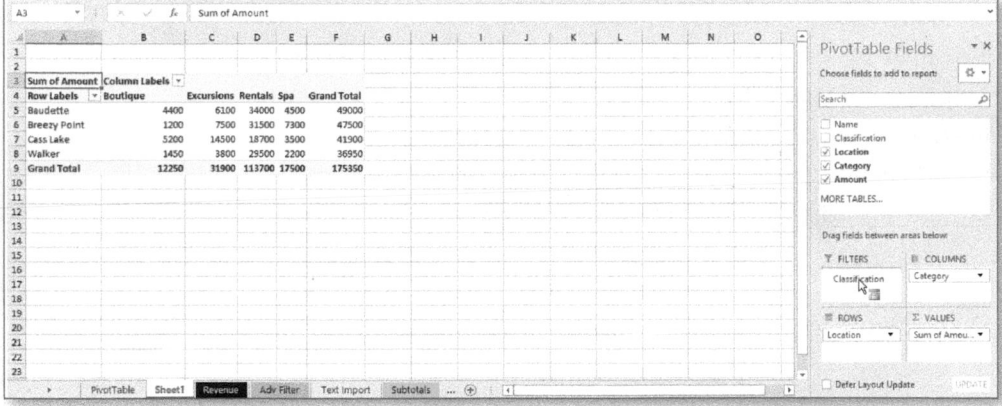

4-63 Drag fields in the *PivotTable Fields* pane

 - The field is added as a filter button in row 1 of the *PivotTable*.
 - No filter is applied.
4. Drag a field name from the *Rows* area to the left and into the worksheet area.
 - The field is removed from the *PivotTable.*
5. Drag a field name from one area in the *PivotTable Fields* pane to another area.
 - The *PivotTable* is updated after each change.

Field Settings

Fields in a *PivotTable* include various settings that depend on the type of data. ***Field Settings*** for a text field include layout and print options as well as subtotal and filter choices. The *Layout* group on the *PivotTable Tools Design* tab includes many of the same commands as the *Field Settings* dialog box.

The ***Value Field Settings*** for a *PivotTable Values* field determine how data is summarized. The default function is *SUM,* but you can change the function or select a custom percentage, difference, or ranking. From the *Value Field Settings* dialog box, you can edit the label that

appears in the *PivotTable,* choose a function, and set how numbers are formatted. To select a field in a *PivotTable,* click the field name in the *Row Labels* row or any cell in the column.

> **ANOTHER WAY**
>
> You can right-click a field in the *PivotTable* and select **Field Settings** or **Value Field Settings** to open the dialog box.

> **MORE INFO**
>
> You can show a field more than once in a *PivotTable* and choose different settings for each occurrence.

▶ **HOW TO: Change Value Field Settings in a PivotTable**

1. Click the arrow for *Sum of [Field Name]* in the *Values* area in the *PivotTable Fields* pane.
2. Select **Value Field Settings** from the menu.
 - The *Value Field Settings* dialog box opens.
 - You can also click one of the field values in the *PivotTable* and click the **Field Settings** button [*PivotTable Tools Analyze* tab, *Active Field* group] to open the dialog box.
3. Click the **Custom Name** box and type a new label as desired.
 - The label cannot be the same as the field name in the *PivotTable Fields* pane.
4. Select the **Summarize Values By** tab, if necessary.
5. Choose the function from the *Summarize value field by* list.
6. Click **Number Format**.
7. Select the preferred number format in the *Format Cells* dialog box (Figure 4-64).

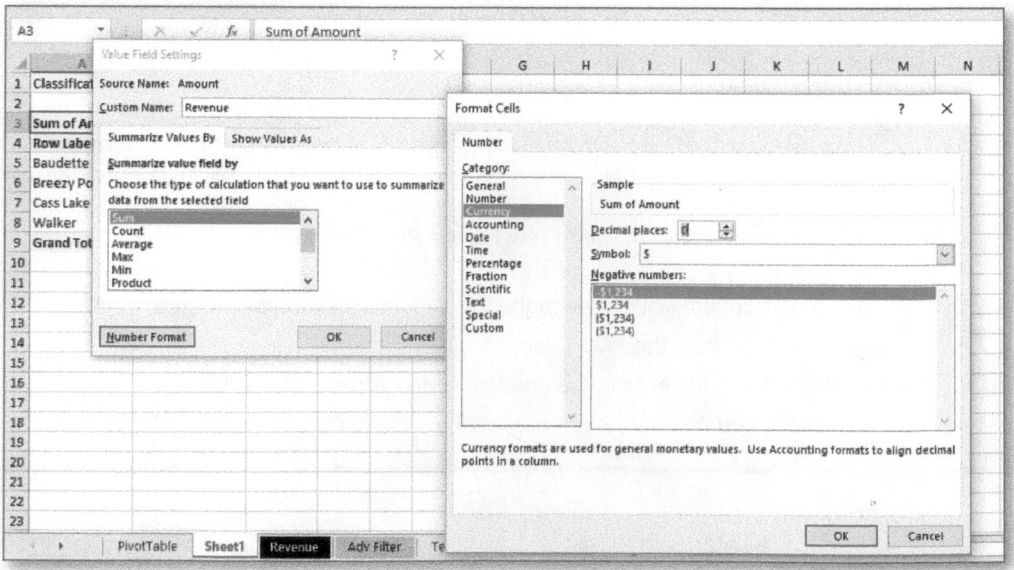

4-64 *Value Field Settings* dialog box and *Number Format* options

8. Click **OK** to close the *Format Cells* dialog box.
9. Click **OK** to close the *Value Field Settings* dialog box.
 - The new label displays in the *PivotTable* and in the task pane.
 - The entire field is reformatted.

Format a PivotTable

A *PivotTable* can be formatted from the *PivotTable Tools Design* tab or from the *Home* tab. The *PivotTable Tools Design* tab includes *PivotTable* styles and layout options. *PivotTable* styles are similar to Excel table styles. You can choose from a gallery to apply fill, border, and font color. Changes made from the *PivotTable Tools Design* tab affect the entire table.

The *Layout* group on the *PivotTable Tools Design* tab provides options for displaying subtotals and grand totals. The *Report Layout* command offers choices for the report design and selections for repeated labels. From the *PivotTable Style Options* group, you can choose whether row and column headings are bold and filled and whether columns and rows are banded with fill or borders. These style options are dependent on the *PivotTable* style.

From the *Home* tab, you can change the font size and style, set alignment, and more. When you apply changes from the *Home* tab, the format is applied to the selected cell or cells.

▶ **HOW TO: Format a PivotTable**

1. Click a cell in the *PivotTable*.
2. Click the **More** button for the *PivotTable Styles* group [*PivotTable Tools Design* tab].
 - The style gallery is categorized by light, medium, and dark colors.
3. Point to a style icon to see a *Live Preview*.
 - The styles are named *Pivot Style Light 1, Pivot Style Light 2,* and so on.
 - You can design your own style.
4. Click to select a style.
5. Select the box for **Banded Rows** in the *PivotTable Styles Options* group [*PivotTable Tools Design* tab].
 - The rows are filled or a border is applied, based on the selected *PivotTable* style.
6. Select the box for **Banded Columns** in the *PivotTable Styles Options* group [*PivotTable Tools Design* tab].
 - The columns are filled or a border is applied.
7. Click the **Grand Totals** button [*PivotTable Tools Design* tab, *Layout* group] (Figure 4-65).

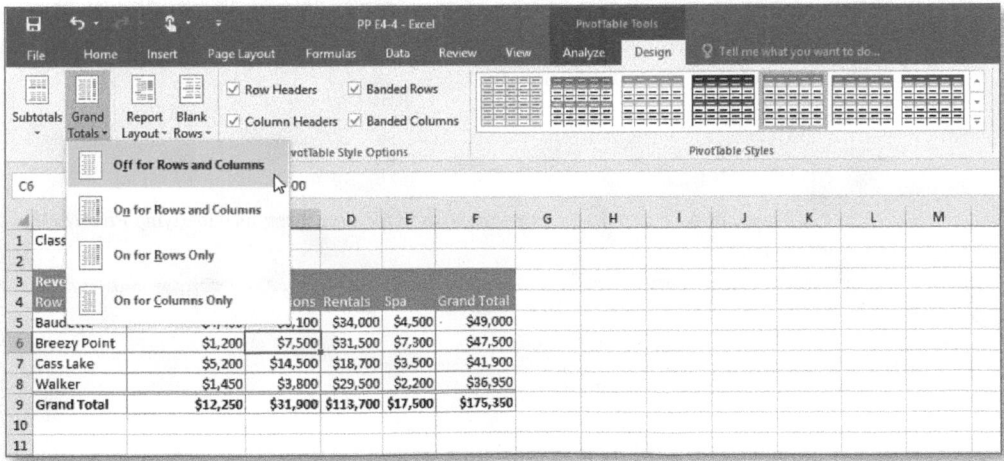

4-65 Display or hide total column and row

8. Choose **Off for Rows and Columns**.
 - The total column and row are removed.
 - You can show totals by selecting **On for Columns and Rows**.

Refresh a PivotTable

Although a *PivotTable* is based on worksheet data, the *PivotTable* is not automatically updated if the data are edited. This is a security measure because a *PivotTable* can be associated with data in a different workbook or an external source such as a database. You can use the context-sensitive menu for any cell in the *PivotTable* and choose **Refresh**, or you can click the **Refresh** button in the *Data* group on the *PivotTable Tools Analyze* tab.

 MORE INFO

There is a *PivotTable* option to automatically refresh the data each time the workbook is opened. Click the **Options** button [*PivotTable Tools Analyze* tab, *PivotTable* group] and select the **Data** tab.

▶ HOW TO: Refresh Data in a PivotTable

1. Click any cell in the *PivotTable*.
2. Click the **Refresh** button [*PivotTable Tools Analyze* tab, *Data* group].
 - The *PivotTable* data is updated.
 - You can refresh all data connections in the workbook by clicking the arrow for the **Refresh** button and selecting **Refresh All**.

Create a PivotChart

A ***PivotChart*** contains charted data that updates with the *PivotTable* and has the same field buttons and filter options. The *PivotChart* button is on the *PivotTable Tools Analyze* tab.

A *PivotChart* can be formatted like an Excel chart from its *PivotChart Tools Design* and *Format* tabs. You can select a style, switch row and column data, change the chart type, and so on. When the chart object is selected, you will also see the *PivotChart Tools Analyze* tab with the same commands as the *PivotTable Tools Analyze* tab, and the *PivotChart Fields* pane on the right. A *PivotChart* and its *PivotTable* are linked, and you can make changes from command tabs for the table or the chart.

 MORE INFO

You can create a *PivotChart* directly from a list in the worksheet; its underlying *PivotTable* is automatically created.

▶ HOW TO: Create a PivotChart

1. Click a cell in the *PivotTable*.
2. Click the **PivotChart** button [*PivotTable Tools Analyze* tab, *Tools* group].
 - The *Insert Chart* dialog box opens.
3. Select a chart type from the list on the left.
4. Select a subtype for the chart.
5. Click **OK** (Figure 4-66).

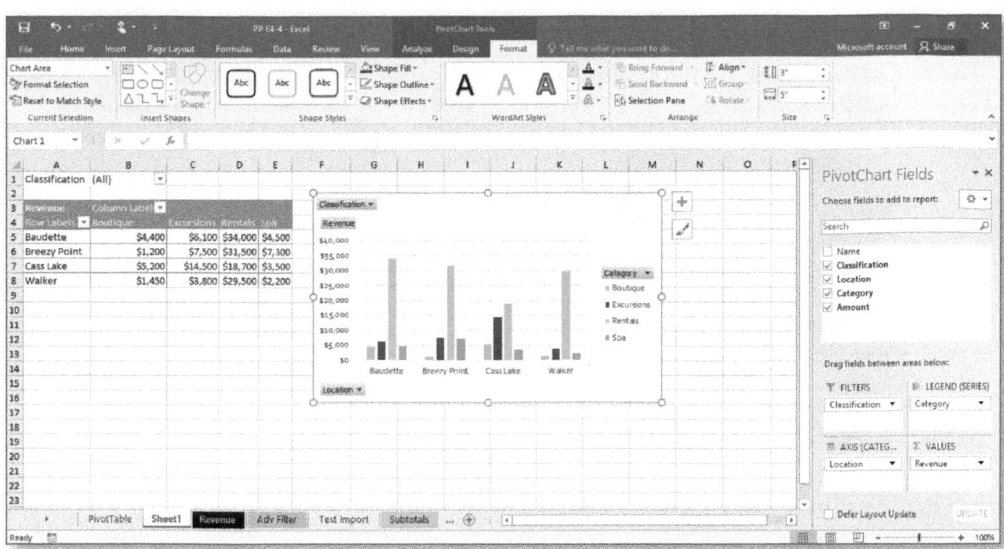

4-66 *PivotChart* inserted as chart object

- The chart displays as a chart object.
- The *PivotChart Tools Analyze, Design,* and *Format* tabs are available.
- The *PivotChart Fields* pane is similar to the *PivotTable Fields* pane.

PAUSE & PRACTICE: EXCEL 4-4

For this project, you create a *PivotTable* for Paradise Lakes Resort using the Excel table as its source. You also create a *PivotChart* and add a slicer to the worksheet. Your workbook now has data connections, so you may see a security warning when you open the file, depending on the settings of your computer.

File Needed: *[your initials] PP E4-3.xlsx*
Completed Project File Name: *[your initials] PP E4-4.xlsx*

1. Open the *[your initials] PP E4-3* workbook completed in *Pause & Practice 4-3.* The security bar informs you that the data connections have been disabled (Figure 4-67).

2. Click **Enable Content**. (If you did not see the security bar, continue to step 3.)

3. Save the workbook as [your initials] PP E4-4.

4. Create a *PivotTable.*
 a. Click cell **A4** on the **Revenue** sheet tab.
 b. Click the **Recommended PivotTables** button [*Insert* tab, *Tables* group].

4-67 Security warning for a workbook with data connections

c. Locate and click the **Sum of Amount by Location** preview tile.
d. Click **OK**.
e. Name the worksheet tab PivotTable.

5. Add a field and a *Slicer* window in a *PivotTable*.
 a. Drag the **Category** field from the *Choose fields to add to report* group to the *Columns* area in the *PivotTable Fields* pane.
 b. Click the **Insert Slicer** button [*PivotTable Tools Analyze* tab, *Filter* group].
 c. Select the **Classification** box and click **OK** (Figure 4-68).
 d. Select and drag the *Slicer* window to position it below the *PivotTable*.

6. Format fields in a *PivotTable*.
 a. Right-click cell **B5**.
 b. Choose **Value Field Settings** from the menu.
 c. Click **Number Format** and set **Currency** format with zero decimal places.
 d. Click **OK** to close each dialog box.

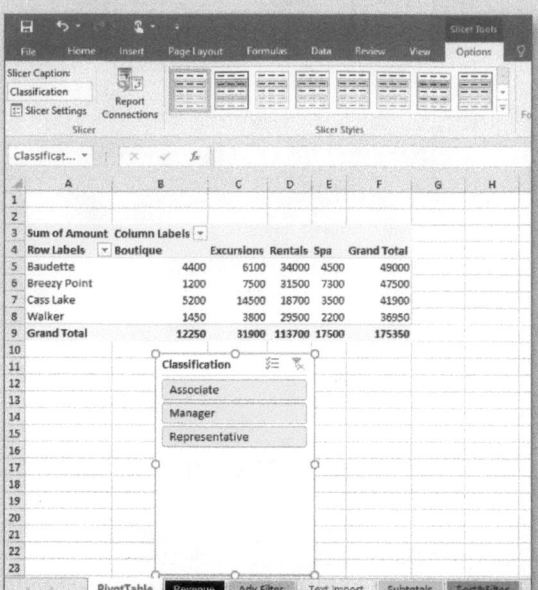

4-68 Field added to *Columns* area and *Slicer* window inserted

7. Create a *PivotChart*.
 a. Click the **PivotChart** button [*PivotTable Tools Analyze* tab, *Tools* group].
 b. Select **Clustered Column** from the *Column* group and click **OK**.
 c. Click the **Quick Layout** button [*PivotChart Tools Design* tab, *Chart Layouts* group].
 d. Select **Layout 3**.
 e. Click to select the **Chart Title** placeholder.
 f. Click the *Formula* bar, type Revenue by Category, and press **Enter**.
 g. Position the chart object so that its top left corner is at cell **H3**.

8. Adjust fields in a *PivotTable* and *PivotChart*.
 a. Click **Representative** in the *Slicer* window. The data is filtered in the *PivotTable* and in the *PivotChart*.
 b. Click the **Category** button in the chart.
 c. Deselect **(Select All)** to remove all the check marks (Figure 4-69).
 d. Select the **Excursions** and **Rentals** boxes and click **OK**.

4-69 Data is filtered in the chart and the table

9. Click cell **A1**.

10. Save and close the workbook (Figure 4-70).

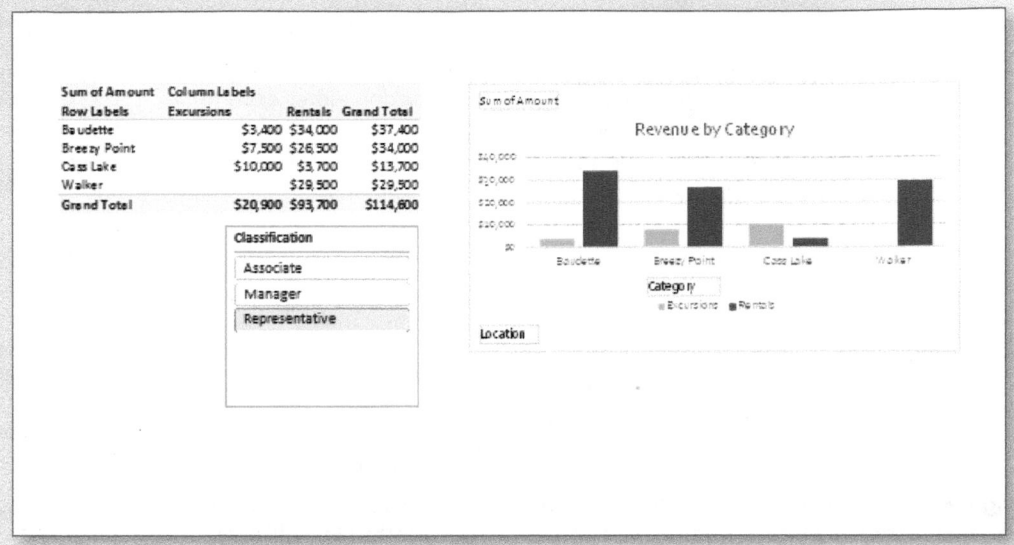

4-70 Completed worksheet for PP E4-4

Chapter Summary

4.1 Create and format a list as an Excel table (p. E4-222).

- An Excel *table* provides enhanced commands for sorting, filtering, and calculating data.
- A table is a list with a *header row,* AutoFilter arrows with the labels in the header row, and the same type of data in each column.
- When any cell in a table is selected, the *Table Tools Design* tab is available with commands for editing and formatting the table.
- A *table style* is a preset combination of colors and borders.
- Table style options enable you to display a total row, to emphasize the first or last column, and to add shading to rows or columns.
- The *Table Tools* group on the *Table Tools Design* tab has commands to remove duplicate rows, to convert a table to a normal cell range, or to insert a *slicer* window for filtering the data.
- The automatic name for a table and several of its parts are *structured references.*
- Structured references appear in *Formula AutoComplete* lists and are substituted automatically in formulas that refer to certain cell ranges in the table.

4.2 Apply *Conditional Formatting* rules as well as *Color Scales, Icon Sets,* and *Data Bars* (p. E4-228).

- *Conditional formatting* formats only cells that meet specified criteria.
- *Highlight Cells Rules* use relational or comparison operators such as *Greater Than* or *Equals* to determine which cells are formatted.
- *Top/Bottom Rules* use ranking or averages to format cells.
- In the *New Rule* dialog box, you can create a rule that uses a formula to determine which cells are formatted.
- *Data visualization* uses rules to format cells with *Icon Sets, Color Scales,* or *Data Bars.*
- You can edit any conditional formatting rule with the *Manage Rules* command.
- Conditional formatting can be removed from a selected cell range or from the entire sheet with the *Clear Rules* command.

4.3 Sort data by one or more columns or by attribute (p. E4-234).

- *Sorting* is a process that arranges data in order, either *ascending* (A to Z) or *descending* (Z to A).
- Data can be sorted by one or by multiple columns.
- For a single column sort, use the *Sort A to Z* or *Sort Z to A* button in the *Sort & Filter* group on the *Data* tab.
- For a multiple column sort, use the *Sort* dialog box by clicking the *Sort* button on the *Data* tab.
- You can perform a multiple column sort within the data by sorting in lowest to highest sort priority.
- From the *Sort* dialog box, data can also be sorted by cell attribute including font color, cell color, or cell icon.
- Data in an Excel table can be sorted from the *AutoFilter* arrows with labels in the header row.

4.4 Filter data by using *AutoFilters* and by creating an *Advanced Filter* (p. E4-238).

- The *Filter* button [*Data* tab, *Sort & Filter* group] displays an *AutoFilter* arrow for each column heading in list-type data.
- From an *AutoFilter* arrow, you can select records to be shown or hidden or build a custom filter.
- A custom *AutoFilter* uses operators such as *Equals* or *Greater Than* as well as AND and OR conditions.
- An *Advanced Filter* provides filter options such as using a formula in the filter definition.
- An *Advanced Filter* requires a criteria range in the same workbook and can display filtered results separate from the data.

4.5 Use subtotals, groups, and outlines for tabular data in a worksheet (p. E4-242).

- The *Subtotal* command inserts summary rows for sorted data using *SUM* or a statistical function.
- The *Subtotal* command formats the data as an *outline,* which groups records so that they can be displayed or hidden.

- Outline buttons appear next to row and column headings and determine the level of detail shown in the data.
- An **Auto Outline** creates groups based on formulas that are located in a consistent pattern in a list.
- Groups can be defined by sorting data, inserting blank rows, and using the *Group* button in the *Outline* group on the *Data* tab.

4.6 Import data into an Excel worksheet from a text file, a database file, and other sources (p. E4-248).

- To save time and increase accuracy, you can **import** text files into a worksheet.
- Common text file formats include *.txt* (text) and *.csv* (comma separated values).
- Data in a text file is **delimited** or **fixed width.**
- The **Text Import Wizard** guides you through the steps of importing data.
- You can copy data from a Word document into a worksheet.
- From a **Microsoft Access database,** you can import a table or a query into a worksheet.
- If a web site has table-formatted data, you can use the *From Web* command on the *Data* tab to import data into a worksheet.
- Data that has been imported from a command in the *Get External Data* group establishes a data connection so that the data can be refreshed.
- The **Flash Fill** command recognizes and copies typing actions from one or more cells and suggests data for the remaining rows in the same column.

4.7 Export Excel data as a text file and into a Word document (p. E4-254).

- Data in a worksheet can be exported for use in another program or application.
- Excel data can be exported as a text file.
- Text file formats can be tab-, space-, or comma-delimited.
- The Windows or Office *Clipboard* can be used to copy data from Excel into Word and other programs.

4.8 Build and format a *PivotTable* (p. E4-258).

- A **PivotTable** is a cross-tabulated summary report on its own worksheet.
- When a *PivotTable* is active, the *PivotTable Tools Analyze* and *Design* tabs are available.
- When any cell in a *PivotTable* is selected, the *PivotTable Fields* pane is open on the right side of the window.
- The *PivotTable Fields* pane includes a list of available fields and areas in the report in which the fields can be positioned.
- You can drag field names in the *PivotTable Fields* pane to reposition them and analyze data from a different perspective.
- Fields in a *PivotTable* can be modified and formatted from the *Field Settings* dialog box.
- *PivotTables* can be formatted from the *PivotTable Tools Design* tab, and selected cells can be formatted from the *Home* tab.
- A **PivotChart** is a chart based on a *PivotTable* with the same features as the *PivotTable*.

Check for Understanding

The SIMbook for this text (within your SIMnet account) provides the following resources for concept review:

- Multiple choice questions
- Matching exercises
- Short answer questions

Guided Project 4-1

For this project, you import a text file to complete the inventory worksheet for Wear-Ever Shoes. You use *Flash Fill* to enter product codes and sort the data by supplier and code. You use *AutoFilter* for several tasks, format data as an Excel table, prepare subtotals, build a *PivotTable,* and export data as a text file.
[Student Learning Outcomes 4.1, 4.2, 4.3, 4.4, 4.5, 4.6, 4.7, 4.8]

Files Needed: **WearEver-04.xlsx** and **WearEver-04.txt** *[Student data files are available in the* Library of *your SIMnet account.]*
Completed Project File Names: **[your initials] Excel 4-1.xlsx** and **[your initials] Excel 4-1.txt**

Skills Covered in This Project

- Import a text file.
- Use *Flash Fill* to complete data.
- Sort data.
- Use an *AutoFilter*.

- Set conditional formatting.
- Create an Excel table.
- Use the *Subtotal* command.
- Create and format a *PivotTable*.
- Export data as a tab-delimited file.

1. Open the **WearEver-04** workbook from your student data files and save it as [your initials] Excel 4-1.

2. Import a text file.
 a. Select cell **I4**.
 b. Click the **From Text** button [*Data* tab, *Get External Data* group].
 c. Find and select the **WearEver-04.txt** file from your student data files in the *Import Text File* window.
 d. Click **Import**.
 e. Verify that the **Delimited** button is selected in the first *Wizard* window and click **Next**.
 f. Verify that the **Tab** box is selected and click **Next**.
 g. Do not change any formats and click **Finish**.
 h. Click **OK** in the *Import Data* dialog box. The supplier name and phone number are imported and added to the list.

3. Use the **Format Painter** button to copy formatting from cell **H4** to cells **I4:J4**.

4. *AutoFit* columns **I:J**.

5. Select cells **A1:J2** and click the **Launcher** in the *Alignment* group [*Home* tab]. From the *Horizontal* list, choose **Center Across Selection**.

6. Use *Flash Fill* to insert product codes.
 a. Insert a column between columns **B** and **C**.
 b. Type Code in cell **C4**.
 c. Type RHB in cell **C5**.
 d. Type r and press **Enter** in cell **C6**. Regular *AutoComplete* completes the entries based on what is already in the column.
 e. In cell **C7**, type r and press **Enter**.

f. Click the **Fill** button [*Home* tab, *Editing* group]. The *Flash Fill* suggestion list did not appear because there is no recognizable pattern.

g. Choose **Flash Fill**.

h. *AutoFit* column **C**.

7. Sort data in multiple columns.

a. Click cell **A5**.

b. Click the **Sort** button [*Data* tab, *Sort & Filter* group].

c. Select the **My data has headers** box, if necessary.

d. Click the **Sort by** arrow and choose **Supplier**.

e. Verify that **Values** is selected for *Sort On*.

f. Choose **A to Z** for *Order*.

g. Click **Add Level**.

h. Click the **Then by** arrow and choose **Code**.

i. Verify that **Values** is selected for *Sort On* and that **A to Z** is selected for *Order*.

j. Click **OK** (Figure 4-71).

8. Apply conditional formatting.

a. Select cells **F5:F40**, the quantity in stock.

b. Click the **Conditional Formatting** button [*Home* tab, *Style* group].

c. Click **Highlight Cells Rules** and select **Less Than**.

d. Type 2 in the *Format cells that are LESS THAN* box.

e. Click **OK** to accept the *Light Red Fill with Dark Red Text* format.

4-71 Data sorted by "Supplier" and "Code"

9. Use an *AutoFilter*.

a. Click cell **A5**.

b. Click the **Filter** button [*Data* tab, *Sort & Filter* group].

c. Click the *AutoFilter* arrow for the **Supplier** column.

d. Deselect the **(Select All)** box to remove all the check marks.

e. Select the **Jennifer's Closet** box.

f. Click **OK**. The data is filtered to show only records from one supplier.

10. Copy the **Inventory** worksheet to the right and name the copy Women's. Set the tab color to **Gold, Accent 4**.

11. Clear a filter and conditional formatting.

a. On the **Women's** sheet, click the *AutoFilter* arrow for the **Supplier** column.

b. Select **Clear Filter from "Supplier."**

c. Click the **Filter** button [*Data* tab, *Sort & Filter* group] to hide the *AutoFilter* arrows.

d. Click the **Conditional Formatting** button [*Home* tab, *Style* group].

e. Select **Clear Rules** and select **Clear Rules From Entire Sheet**.

12. Create an Excel table.

a. Select cells **A4:K40** on the **Women's** sheet.

b. Click the **Format as Table** button [*Home* tab, *Styles* group].

c. Choose **Table Style Medium 5** in the *Table Styles* gallery.

d. Confirm the range in the *Format as Table* dialog box and click **OK**.

e. Select **Yes** in the message box to remove the data connection (Figure 4-72).

13. Add a calculated column to a table.
 a. Insert a column at column **J**.
 b. Type Markup in cell **J4** and press **Enter**.
 c. Type = in cell **J5** to start the formula and click cell **I5**.
 d. Type − for subtraction and click cell **H5**.
 e. Press **Enter** to copy the formula.

4-72 Data connection will be removed to create the table

14. Filter data in a table.
 a. Click the *AutoFilter* arrow for the **Men's or Women's** column.
 b. Deselect the **(Select All)** box to remove all the check marks.
 c. Select the **W** box and click **OK**.
 d. Press **Ctrl+Home** (Figure 4-73).

15. Copy the **Inventory** worksheet to the end and name the copy Subtotals. Set the tab color to **Orange, Accent 6**.

16. Clear a filter and conditional formatting.
 a. On the **Subtotals** sheet, clear the filter for the **Supplier**.
 b. Click the **Filter** button [*Data* tab, *Sort & Filter* group] to hide the *AutoFilter* arrows.
 c. Click the **Conditional Formatting** button [*Home* tab, *Style* group] and clear rules from the sheet.

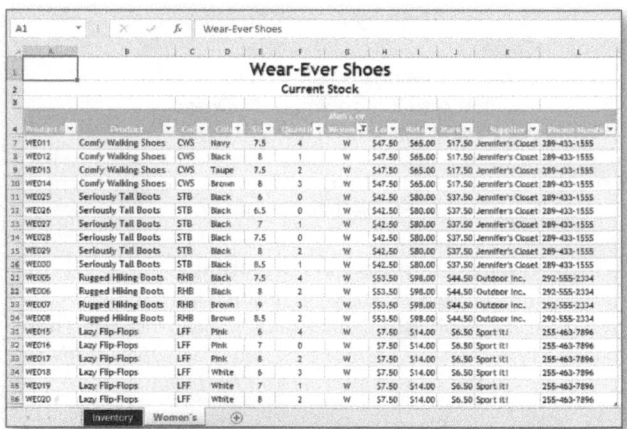

4-73 Table filtered to show women's products

17. Use the *Subtotal* command.
 a. On the **Subtotals** sheet, select cell **J5**. The records are sorted by the "Supplier" column.
 b. Click the **Subtotal** button [*Data* tab, *Outline* group].
 c. Click the **At each change in** arrow and choose **Supplier**.
 d. Click the **Use function** arrow and choose **Count**.
 e. Check the **Supplier** box in the *Add subtotal to* area.
 f. Deselect any other selected fields in the *Add subtotal to* list (Figure 4-74).
 g. Click **OK**. A subtotal row displays at the bottom of each group and shows how many products are available from each supplier.
 h. Format the label in cell **I17** as **right-aligned**.

4-74 *Subtotal* dialog box to count number of products by supplier

i. **Right-align** the remaining subtotal labels in column **I** (Figure 4-75).

18. Create a *PivotTable*.
 a. Click the **Inventory** sheet tab and select cell **A5**.
 b. Click the **PivotTable** button [*Insert* tab, *Tables* group].
 c. Verify that the *Table/Range* is **A4:K40** in the *Create PivotTable* dialog box and that the *New Worksheet* button is selected (Figure 4-76).
 d. Click **OK**. A blank *PivotTable* layout displays on a new sheet.

19. Add fields in a *PivotTable*.
 a. Select the **Product** box in the *PivotTable Fields* pane to place it in the *Rows* area.
 b. Select the **Quantity** box to place it in the *Values* area.
 c. Drag the **Supplier** field name into the *Columns* area.

20. Format a *PivotTable*.
 a. Click the **More** button in the *PivotTable Styles* group [*PivotTable Tools Design* tab].
 b. Select **PivotTable Style Medium 7**.
 c. Select the **Banded Rows** box [*PivotTable Tools Design* tab, *PivotTable Style Options* group].
 d. Select the **Banded Columns** box [*PivotTable Tools Design* tab, *PivotTable Style Options* group] (Figure 4-77).
 e. Name the sheet PivotTable.

21. Copy the **Inventory** worksheet to the end and do not rename it.

22. On the copied sheet, clear the filter from the **Supplier** column and remove the *AutoFilter* arrows.

23. Export data as a tab-delimited file.
 a. Click cell **A1** in the copied sheet.
 b. Click the **File** tab and select **Export**.
 c. Select **Change File Type**.
 d. Select **Text (Tab delimited)** as the file type.
 e. Click **Save As**.
 f. Navigate to the save location for the exported data in the *Save as type* dialog box.
 g. Type Excel 4-1 as the file name.

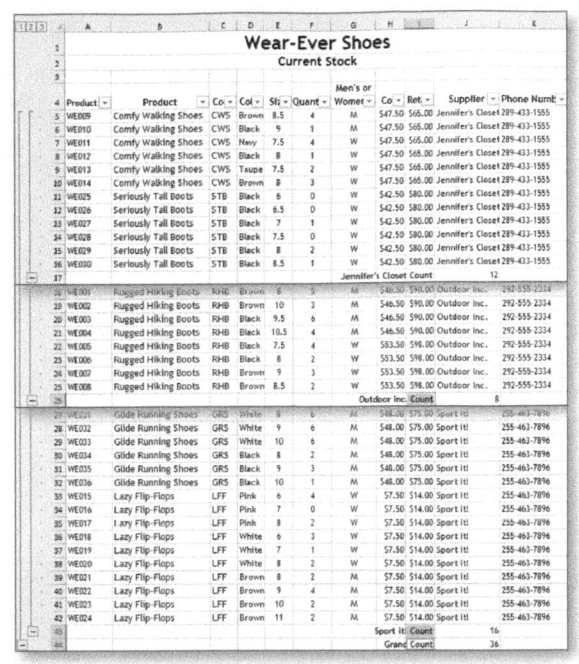

4-75 Subtotals inserted for each group

4-76 *Create PivotTable* dialog box

	A	B	C	D	E
1					
2					
3	Sum of Quantity	Column Labels ▾			
4	Row Labels ▾	Jennifer's Closet	Outdoor Inc.	Sport it!	Grand Total
5	Comfy Walking Shoes	15			15
6	Glide Running Shoes			24	24
7	Lazy Flip-Flops			22	22
8	Rugged Hiking Boots		29		29
9	Seriously Tall Boots	4			4
10	Grand Total	19	29	46	94

4-77 Formatted *PivotTable*

h. Click **Save**.
i. Click **OK** in the message box to save only the current sheet (Figure 4-78).

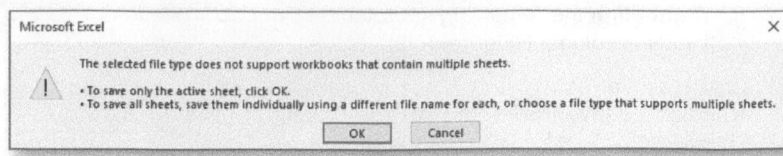

Microsoft Excel ✕

⚠ The selected file type does not support workbooks that contain multiple sheets.

• To save only the active sheet, click OK.
• To save all sheets, save them individually using a different file name for each, or choose a file type that supports multiple sheets.

[OK] [Cancel]

4-78 Only the current sheet is saved as a text file

j. Click **Yes** in the message box about features being lost. The sheet is renamed and the data is exported to a *.txt* file.

24. Save the workbook with the same file name.
 a. Click the **File** tab and choose **Save As**.
 b. Navigate to the folder for saved work.
 c. Select **Excel Workbook** as the *Save as type* in the *Save As* dialog box.
 d. Select *[your initials] Excel 4-1* from the list.
 e. Click **Save** and select **Yes** to replace the *.xlsx* file that you saved at the beginning of this project.
 f. Close the workbook (Figure 4-79).

	A	B	C	D	E	F	G	H	I	J	K
1					**Wear-Ever Shoes**						
2					**Current Stock**						
3											
4	Product ▾	Product ▾	Co ▾	Col ▾	Si ▾	Quant ▾	Men's or Women ▾	Co ▾	Ret ▾	Supplier ▾	Phone Numb ▾
5	WE009	Comfy Walking Shoes	CWS	Brown	8.5	4	M	$47.50	$65.00	Jennifer's Closet	289-433-1555
6	WE010	Comfy Walking Shoes	CWS	Black	9	1	M	$47.50	$65.00	Jennifer's Closet	289-433-1555
7	WE011	Comfy Walking Shoes	CWS	Navy	7.5	4	W	$47.50	$65.00	Jennifer's Closet	289-433-1555
8	WE012	Comfy Walking Shoes	CWS	Black	8	1	W	$47.50	$65.00	Jennifer's Closet	289-433-1555
9	WE013	Comfy Walking Shoes	CWS	Taupe	7.5	2	W	$47.50	$65.00	Jennifer's Closet	289-433-1555
10	WE014	Comfy Walking Shoes	CWS	Brown	8	3	W	$47.50	$65.00	Jennifer's Closet	289-433-1555
11	WE025	Seriously Tall Boots	STB	Black	6	0	W	$42.50	$80.00	Jennifer's Closet	289-433-1555
12	WE026	Seriously Tall Boots	STB	Black	6.5	0	W	$42.50	$80.00	Jennifer's Closet	289-433-1555
13	WE027	Seriously Tall Boots	STB	Black	7	1	W	$42.50	$80.00	Jennifer's Closet	289-433-1555
14	WE028	Seriously Tall Boots	STB	Black	7.5	0	W	$42.50	$80.00	Jennifer's Closet	289-433-1555
15	WE029	Seriously Tall Boots	STB	Black	8	2	W	$42.50	$80.00	Jennifer's Closet	289-433-1555
16	WE030	Seriously Tall Boots	STB	Black	8.5	1	W	$42.50	$80.00	Jennifer's Closet	289-433-1555
41											

4-79 Excel 4-1 completed inventory worksheet

Guided Project 4-2

Classic Gardens and Landscapes is building a workbook with data about revenue and promotion campaigns. You copy data from Word and import data from an Access database. You set conditional formatting, format an Excel table, sort and filter data, and build a *PivotTable* and *PivotChart*.
[Student Learning Outcomes 4.1, 4.2, 4.3, 4.4, 4.5, 4.6, 4.7, 4.8]

Files Needed: ***ClassicGardens-04.xlsx, Database-04.accdb,*** and ***ClassicGardens-04.docx*** *[Student data files are available in the* Library *of your SIMnet account.]*
Completed Project File Names: *[your initials] Excel 4-2.xlsx* and *[your initials] Excel 4-2.csv*

Skills Covered in This Project

- Copy data from Word.
- Use conditional formatting with an icon set.
- Prepare data for an *Auto Outline*.
- Import a table from a database file.
- Apply a table style and show a total row.
- Sort and filter data in a table.
- Build and format a *PivotTable*.
- Build a *PivotChart*.
- Filter data in a *PivotChart*.
- Export data as a comma-separated text file.

E4-273

1. Open the ***ClassicGardens-04*** workbook from your student data files and save it as [your initials] Excel 4-2.

2. Select the **Quarterly** sheet; insert six columns between columns **G** and **H**.

3. Copy data from Word.
 a. Open the Word document ***ClassicGardens-04. docx*** from your student data files.
 b. Select all the data in Word and copy it.
 c. Select cell **H4** in the Excel workbook.
 d. Click the **Paste** button arrow [*Home* tab, *Clipboard* group] and choose **Match Destination Formatting**.
 e. Select cell **N5** and click the **AutoSum** button [*Home* tab, *Editing* group].
 f. Verify or select the range **B5:M5** and press **Enter**.
 g. Double-click the *Fill* handle for cell **N5** to copy the formula to cells **N6:N10**.
 h. Select cells **H10:M10** and click the **AutoSum** button [*Home* tab, *Editing* group].

4. Apply conditional formatting.
 a. Select cells **N5:N9**.
 b. Click the **Quick Analysis** button.
 c. Verify that **Formatting** is selected.
 d. Choose **Icon Set** (Figure 4-80).The cells display an icon to represent the upper, middle, or lower values of the range.

4-80 Icon set conditional formatting

5. *AutoFit* the columns and make sure all data is visible.

6. Click the **AutoOutline** sheet tab.

7. Use *AutoSum* to calculate subtotals and totals.
 a. Select cells **E5:E18**, press **Ctrl** and select cells **I5:I18**, **M5:M18**, and **Q5:Q18** (Figure 4-81).
 b. Click the **AutoSum** button [*Home* tab, *Editing* group].
 c. Select cells **R5:R18** and click the **AutoSum** button [*Home* tab, *Editing* group]. Excel sums the *Qtr 1, Qtr 2, Qtr 3,* and *Qtr 4* columns.
 d. Select cells **B19:R19** and click the **AutoSum** button [*Home* tab, *Editing* group].
 e. *AutoFit* columns as needed.
 f. Select cells **E21:E25**, press **Ctrl** and select cells **I21:I25**, **M21:M25**, and **Q21:Q25**.
 g. Click the **AutoSum** button [*Home* tab, *Editing* group].

4-81 *SUM* function used in a consistent pattern

h. Use *AutoSum* in cells **R21:R25**, in cells **E28:E33**, **I28:I33**, **M28:M33**, **Q28:Q33**, and in cells **R28:R33** to complete the worksheet.

i. *AutoFit* the columns.

8. In cell **B35**, type = to start a formula.

9. Click cell **B19**, type +, click cell **B26**, type +, click cell **B34**, and press **Enter**. The formula is =**B19+ B26+B34**.

10. Copy the formula in cell **B35** to cells **C35:R35**. *AutoFit* the columns, if necessary.

11. Create an *Auto Outline*.

a. Click cell **B5**.

b. Click the arrow for the **Group** button [*Data* tab, *Outline* group] and choose **Auto Outline** (Figure 4-82). The *Auto Outline* command uses column and row formulas to group the data.

c. Click the **Level 2** column outline button (above the column headings).Only the quarter totals display (Figure 4-83).

12. Import a table from an Access database.

a. Click the **Table** sheet tab.

b. Select cell **A4**.

c. Click the **From Access** button [*Data* tab, *Get External Data* group].

d. Find and select ***Database-04.accdb*** from your student data files in the *Select Data Source* window.

e. Click **Open**.

f. Click **tblMailings** in the *Select Table* dialog box (Figure 4-84).

g. Click **OK**.

h. Select **Table** and **Existing worksheet** if necessary and click **OK**.

13. Apply a table style and show a total row.

a. Click cell **B5** in the table.

b. Click the **More** button [*Table Tools Design* tab, *Table Styles* group].

c. Choose **Table Style Medium 15**.

d. Select the **Total Row** box [*Table Tools Design* tab, *Table Style Options* group].

e. Click cell **C30** and choose **Sum**. Then copy the formula to cells **D30:M30**.

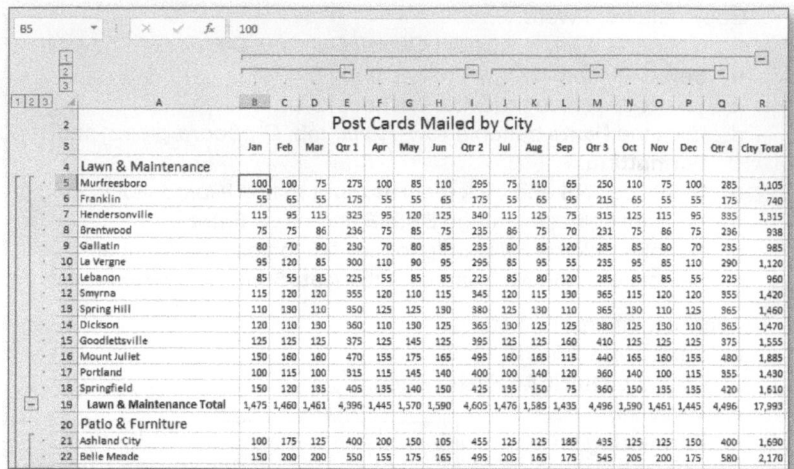

4-82 *AutoOutline* with three row levels and three column levels

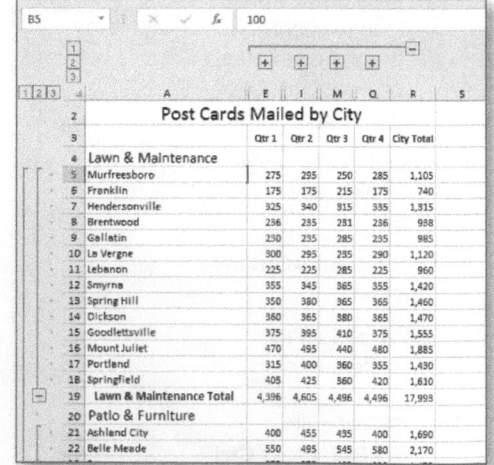

4-83 Outline collapsed at Level 2 column group

4-84 *Select Table* dialog box for an Access database

14. Sort and filter data in an Excel table.
 a. Click the *AutoFilter* arrow for **City**.
 b. Choose **Sort A to Z**.
 c. Click the *AutoFilter* arrow for **City**.
 d. Select **Text Filters** and **Equals**.
 e. Type c* in the first criteria box to select cities that begin with "C."
 f. Select the **Or** radio button.
 g. Verify that **equals** is selected as the second operator.
 h. Type m* in the second criteria box to select cities that begin with "M" (Figure 4-85).
 i. Click **OK**.

15. Merge and center the labels in rows **1:2** and set them to a font size of **18 pt**. (Figure 4-86).

16. Select the **Pivot Source** sheet tab.

17. Create a *PivotTable*.
 a. Select cell **A5**.
 b. Click the **Recommended PivotTables** button [*Insert* tab, *Tables* group].
 c. Select the **Sum of # of Responses by Department** thumbnail and click **OK**.
 d. Select the **City** and **# Mailed** boxes in the *Choose fields to add to report* area to add them to the report.
 e. Drag the **Department** field from the *Rows* area to the *Filters* area in the *PivotTable Fields* pane (Figure 4-87).

18. Format a *PivotTable*.
 a. Right-click cell **B4** and select **Value Field Settings** from the context menu.
 b. Click **Number Format**.
 c. Choose **Number** as the *Category*.
 d. Select zero decimal places.
 e. Select the **Use 1000 Separator (,)** box.
 f. Click **OK** to close each dialog box.
 g. Apply the same number format for "Sum of # Mailed" field.
 h. Click the **More** button [*PivotTable Tools Design* tab, *PivotTable Styles* group].
 i. Select **PivotTable Style Medium 9** [*PivotTable Tools Design* tab, *PivotTable Styles* group].
 j. Select the **Banded Rows** box [*PivotTable Tools Design* tab, *PivotTable Styles Options* group].

4-85 *Custom AutoFilter for cities that begin with "C" or "M"*

ID	City	Jan	Feb	Mar	Apr	May	Jun	Jul	Aug	Sep	Oct	Nov	Dec
18	Carthage	75	85	95	95	125	100	110	105	105	110	95	125
19	Centerville	150	100	85	100	85	150	85	150	100	85	85	85
20	Charlotte	150	175	205	175	215	135	205	175	255	135	205	205
21	Coopertown	150	225	200	235	200	145	195	250	200	145	200	235
22	Cross Plains	200	200	210	200	215	210	210	200	265	215	210	210
12	Mount Juliet	150	160	160	155	175	165	160	165	115	165	160	155
1	Murfreesboro	100	100	75	100	85	110	75	110	65	110	75	100
Total		975	1045	1030	1060	1100	1015	1040	1155	1105	965	1030	1115

4-86 *Imported data sorted and filtered*

4-87 *PivotTable layout*

k. Select the **Banded Columns** box [*PivotTable Tools Design* tab, *PivotTable Styles Options* group] (Figure 4-88).

19. Create and format a *PivotChart*.
 a. Click the **PivotChart** button [*PivotTable Tools Analyze* tab, *Tools* group].
 b. Select **Bar** as the chart type and **Clustered Bar** as the subtype.
 c. Click **OK**.
 d. Position the chart object so that its top-left corner is at cell **E3**.
 e. Drag the bottom-right selection handle to reach cell **O24**.
 f. Click the **More** button [*PivotChart Tools Design* tab, *Chart Styles* group].
 g. Choose **Style 5**.
 h. Click the **Shape Outline** button [*PivotChart Tools Format* tab, *Shape Styles* group].
 i. Select **Blue**, **Accent 1**.

20. Filter data in a *PivotChart*.
 a. Click the **Department** filter button in the chart.
 b. Select the **Select Multiple Items** box.
 c. Deselect the **(All)** box.
 d. Select the **Landscape Design** box and click **OK**.
 e. Select cell **A13** to deselect the *PivotTable* and *PivotChart* (Figure 4-89).
 f. Name the sheet PivotTable.

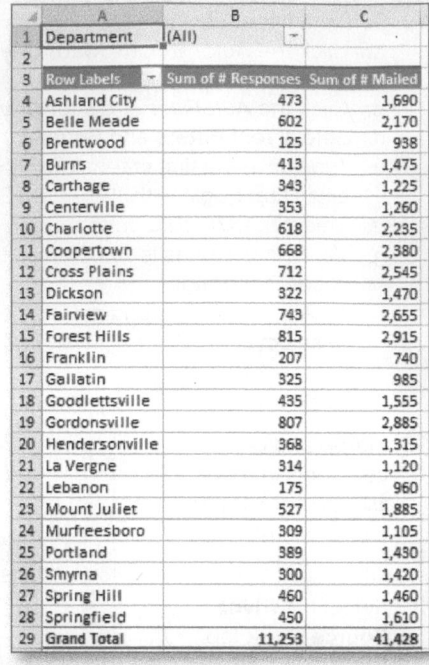

	A	B	C
1	Department	(All)	
2			
3	Row Labels	Sum of # Responses	Sum of # Mailed
4	Ashland City	473	1,690
5	Belle Meade	602	2,170
6	Brentwood	125	938
7	Burns	413	1,475
8	Carthage	343	1,225
9	Centerville	353	1,260
10	Charlotte	618	2,235
11	Coopertown	668	2,380
12	Cross Plains	712	2,545
13	Dickson	322	1,470
14	Fairview	743	2,655
15	Forest Hills	815	2,915
16	Franklin	207	740
17	Gallatin	325	985
18	Goodlettsville	435	1,555
19	Gordonsville	807	2,885
20	Hendersonville	368	1,315
21	La Vergne	314	1,120
22	Lebanon	175	960
23	Mount Juliet	527	1,885
24	Murfreesboro	309	1,105
25	Portland	389	1,430
26	Smyrna	300	1,420
27	Spring Hill	460	1,460
28	Springfield	450	1,610
29	Grand Total	11,253	41,428

4-88 Formatted *PivotTable*

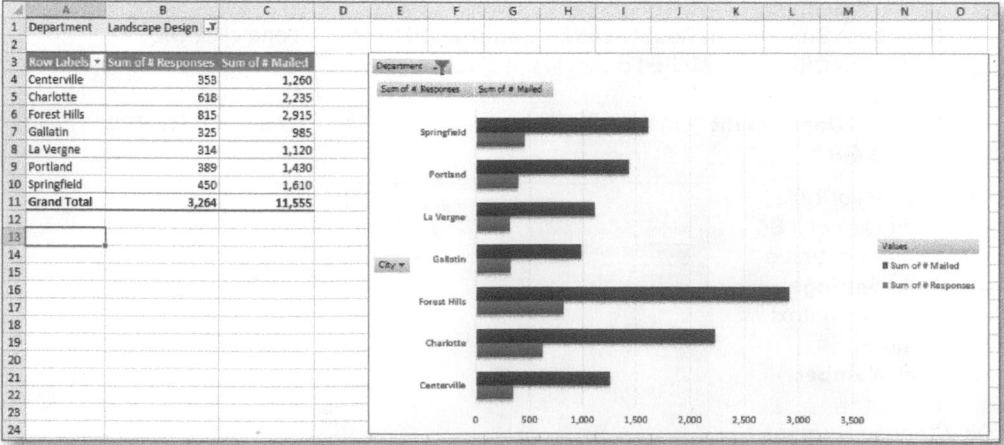

4-89 Filtered data in *PivotChart* and *PivotTable*

21. Export data as a comma-separated file.
 a. Click the **Quarterly** sheet tab.
 b. Click the **File** tab and select **Export**.
 c. Select **Change File Type**.
 d. Select **CSV (Comma delimited)** as the file type.
 e. Click **Save As**.
 f. Navigate to the save location for the exported data in the *Save as type* dialog box.

g. Type Excel 4-2 as the file name.
h. Click **Save**.
i. Click **OK** in the message box to save the current sheet.
j. Click **Yes** in the message box about lost features. The sheet is renamed and the data is exported to a *.csv* file.
k. Rename the sheet as Quarterly.

22. Save the workbook with the same file name.
 a. Click the **File** tab and choose **Save As**.
 b. Navigate to the folder for saved work.
 c. Select **Excel Workbook** as the *Save as type* in the *Save As* dialog box.
 d. Select *[your initials] Excel 4-2* from the list.
 e. Click **Save** and click **Yes** to replace the file.

23. Save and close the workbook. Close Word.

Guided Project 4-3

Clemenson Imaging analyzes expense reports from field representatives as well as patient and image data. To complete the worksheets, you format data as a table and build an advanced filter. You import a comma-separated text file (*.csv*) and use the *Subtotal* command. Finally, you display data in a *PivotTable*.
[Student Learning Outcomes 4.1, 4.2, 4.3, 4.4, 4.5, 4.6, 4.7, 4.8]

Files Needed: **ClemensonImaging-04.xlsx, ClemensonImaging-04.csv,** and **ClemensonImaging.docx**
[Student data files are available in the Library *of your SIMnet account.]*
Completed Project File Names: *[your initials] Excel 4-3.xlsx* and *[your initials] Excel 4-3.docx*

Skills Covered in This Project

- Format data as an Excel table.
- Build an *Advanced Filter*.
- Apply conditional formatting to filtered results.
- Sort data by multiple columns.
- Import a comma-separated text file.
- Use the *Subtotal* command.
- Export data via the *Clipboard*.
- Create a *PivotTable*.

1. Open the **ClemensonImaging-04** workbook from your student data files and save it as [your initials] Excel 4-3.

2. Copy the **Past&Projected** sheet before the **Criteria** sheet and name the copied sheet Adv Filter.

3. Create and format an Excel table.
 a. Select cells **A4:E60** on the **Adv Filter** sheet.
 b. Click the **Quick Analysis** tool and choose **Tables**.
 c. Click **Table**.

4. Apply a table style.
 a. Click cell **A5** in the table.
 b. Click the **More** button [*Table Tools Design* tab, *Table Styles* group].
 c. Select **Table Style Medium 15**.

5. Create an output range for an *Advanced Filter*.
 a. Select cells **A4:E4** and copy and paste them to cell **G4**.
 b. Type Extract Range in cell **G3** and set the font to **Cambria 16 pt**.
 c. Adjust column widths to show the labels.

6. Create an *Advanced Filter*.
 a. Click the **Criteria** sheet tab.
 b. Type >12/31/16 in cell **A3** to find records after 2016.
 c. Type mri in cell **B3**.
 d. Type >12/31/14 in cell **A4** to find records after 2014.
 e. Type ct scan in cell **B4**. This criteria will find records dated 2017 or later for MRIs *and* records for CT scans after 2014 (Figure 4-90).

	A	B	C	D	E
1	**Criteria Range**				
2	Month	Image	Patients	Total Hours	# of Employees
3	>12/31/16	mri			
4	>12/31/14	ct scan			

4-90 Criteria for *Advanced Filter*

 f. Click cell **A5** on the **Adv Filter** sheet.
 g. Click the **Advanced** button [*Data* tab, *Sort & Filter* group].
 h. Select the **Copy to another location** radio button.
 i. Verify that the **List range** is cells **A4:E60**. If the range is incorrect, click and drag to select the range including the header row.
 j. Click the **Criteria range** box and select cells **A2:B4** on the **Criteria** sheet.
 k. Click the **Copy to** box and select cells **G4:K4**.
 l. Click **OK** in the *Advanced Filter* dialog box.

7. Sort data in the output range.
 a. Right-click cell **H5**, choose **Sort**, and select **Sort A to Z**.
 b. Right-click cell **G5**, choose **Sort**, and select **Sort Oldest to Newest**. This sorts the results by date, earliest date first.

8. Apply conditional formatting and borders.
 a. Select cells **I5:I14**.
 b. Click the **Conditional Formatting** button [*Home* tab, *Styles* group].
 c. Choose **Highlight Cells Rules** and **Greater Than**.
 d. Type 750 and choose **Green Fill with Dark Green Text**.
 e. Click **OK**.
 f. Select cells **G5:K14** and apply **All Borders** (Figure 4-91).
 g. Press **Ctrl+Home**.

Extract Range

Month	Image	Patients	Total Hours	# of Employees
Apr 2015	CT Scan	1000	1800	5
Aug 2015	CT Scan	500	2400	3
Dec 2015	CT Scan	500	2400	2
Apr 2016	CT Scan	500	2400	3
Aug 2016	CT Scan	750	2400	3
Dec 2016	CT Scan	500	1800	4
Jan 2017	MRI	1000	1800	3
Apr 2017	CT Scan	750	2400	2
May 2017	MRI	750	3000	4
Aug 2017	CT Scan	500	2400	3

4-91 *Advanced Filter* results

9. Import a comma-separated values text file.
 a. Click the **Expense Info** sheet tab.
 b. Select cell **A5**.
 c. Click the **From Text** button [*Data* tab, *Get External Data* group].
 d. Find and select the ***ClemensonImaging-04.csv*** file from your student data files in the *Import Text File* window.
 e. Click **Import**.
 f. Select the **Delimited** button in the first *Wizard* window and click **Next**.
 g. Deselect the **Tab** box and select the **Comma** box.
 h. Click **Next**.
 i. Click the date column in the *Data preview* area in the third *Wizard* window.
 j. Click the **Date** radio button in the *Column data format* group (Figure 4-92).

k. Click **Finish**, deselect the **Add this data to the Data Model** box in the *Import Data* dialog box, and click **OK**.

l. Select columns **A:D** and size each column to **12.14 (90 pixels)** wide.

m. Deselect the columns.

10. Use the *Subtotal* command.
 a. Click cell **A5**.
 b. Click the **Sort A to Z** button [*Data* tab, *Sort & Filter* group] to sort by last name.
 c. Click the **Subtotal** button [*Data* tab, *Outline* group].
 d. Verify that **Last Name** is selected for **At each change in**.
 e. Click the **Use function** arrow and choose **Average**.
 f. Check the **Amount** box in the *Add subtotal to* area.
 g. Click **OK**.
 h. Format the values in column **D** as **Currency** with zero decimal places.

11. Collapse outline groups.
 a. Click the collapse symbol (−) for Allen in row **8**.
 b. Click the collapse symbol (−) for McAllister (Figure 4-93).

12. Create a *PivotTable*.
 a. Click the **Past&Projected** sheet tab.
 b. Select cells **A4:E60**.
 c. Click the **Quick Analysis** tool and choose **Tables**.
 d. Point to each *PivotTable* option to see the *Live Preview*.
 e. Choose the option that shows a sum of the employees, the total hours, and the patients (Figure 4-94).
 f. Rename the sheet *PivotTable*.
 g. Drag the **Month** field in the *Rows* area in the *PivotTable Fields* pane out of the pane and into the worksheet.

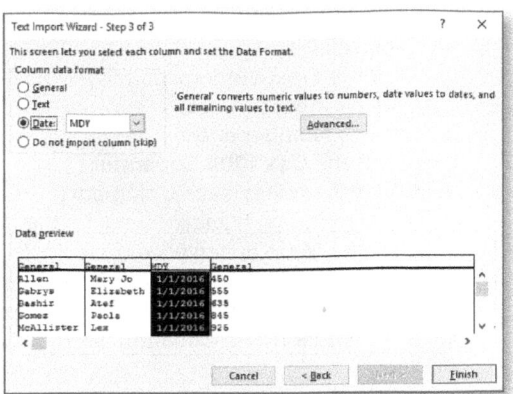

4-92 *Text Import Wizard* to set format

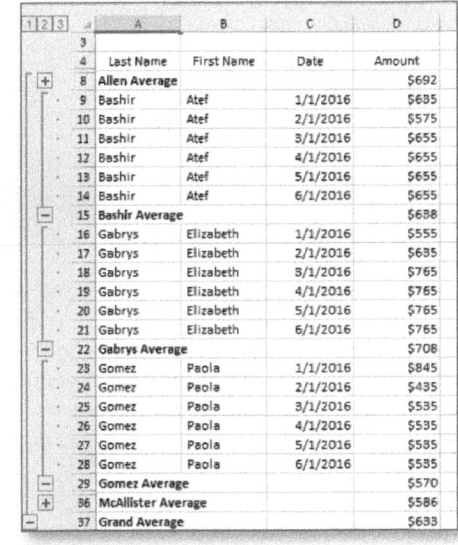

4-93 Subtotals added and outline collapsed for two groups

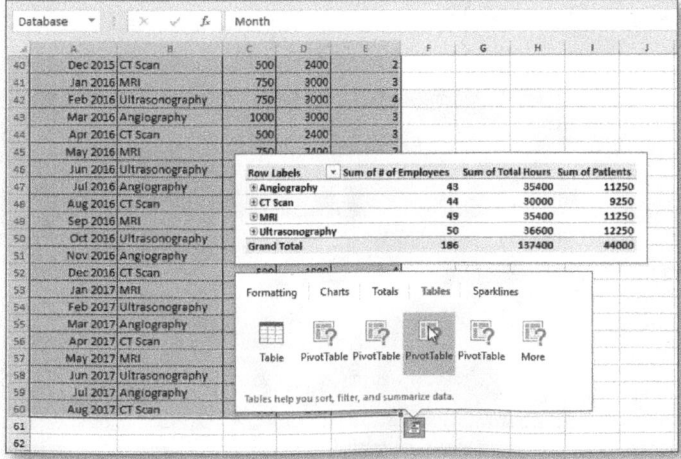

4-94 Suggested *PivotTable* choices from the *Quick Analysis* tool

13. Format a *PivotTable*.
 a. Click cell **C4**.
 b. Click the **Field Settings** button [*PivotTable Tools Analyze* tab, *Active Field* group].
 c. Click **Number Format**.
 d. Choose **Number** as the *Category*.
 e. Select the **Use 1000 Separator (,)** box and set zero decimal places.
 f. Click **OK** to close each dialog box.
 g. Apply the same number format for the "Sum of Patients" field.
 h. Click the **More** button [*PivotTable Tools Design* tab, *PivotTable Styles* group].
 i. Select **PivotTable Style Dark 9** [*PivotTable Tools Design* tab, *PivotTable Styles* group].
 j. Select the **Banded Rows** box [*PivotTable Tools Design* tab, *PivotTable Styles Options* group].
 k. Select the **Banded Columns** box [*PivotTable Tools Design* tab, *PivotTable Styles Options* group] (Figure 4-95).

14. Create and format a *PivotChart*.
 a. Click the **PivotChart** button [*PivotTable Tools Analyze* tab, *Tools* group].
 b. Select **Bar** as the chart type and **Stacked Bar** as the subtype.
 c. Click **OK**.
 d. Position the chart object so that its top-left corner is at cell **A12**.
 e. Drag the bottom-right selection handle to reach cell **J30**.
 f. Click the **More** button [*PivotChart Tools Design* tab, *Chart Styles* group] and choose **Style 8**.
 g. Click the **Change Colors** button [*PivotChart Tools Design* tab, *Chart Styles* group].
 h. Select **Color 5** in the *Monochromatic* group.
 i. Deselect the **# of Employees** box in the *PivotChart Fields* pane (Figure 4-96).
 j. Click cell **A1**.

	A	B	C	D
1				
2				
3	Row Labels ▼	Sum of # of	Sum of Total Hours	Sum of Patients
4	Angiography	43	35,400	11,250
5	CT Scan	44	30,000	9,250
6	MRI	49	35,400	11,250
7	Ultrasonography	50	36,600	12,250
8	Grand Total	186	137,400	44,000

4-95 *PivotTable* with new settings

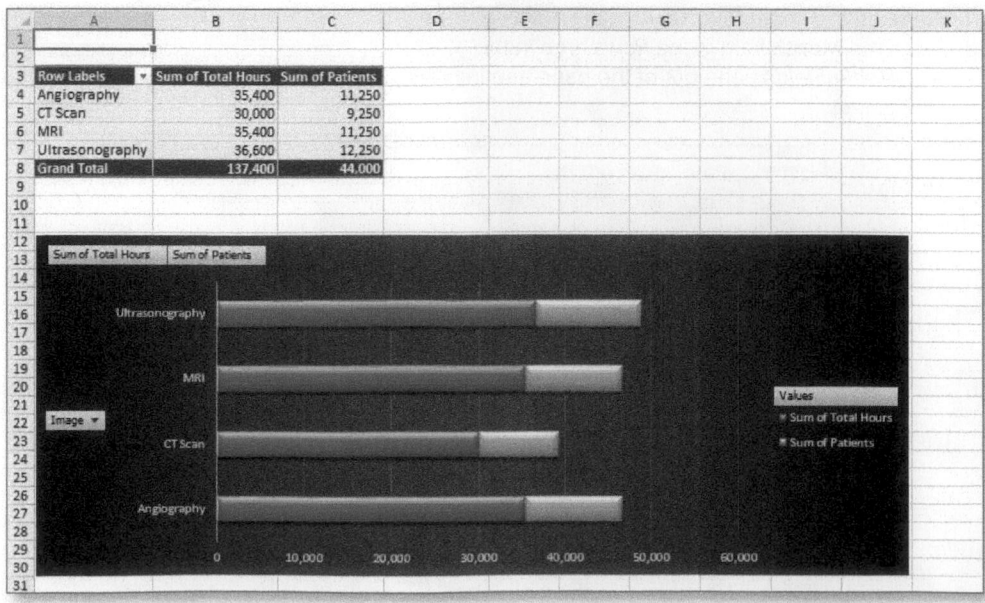

4-96 *PivotChart* object

15. Export data using the *Clipboard*.
 a. Click the **Adv Filter** sheet tab.
 b. Select cells **G4:K14** and click the **Copy** button [*Home* tab, *Clipboard* group].
 c. Open the **ClemensonImaging-04** Word document from your student data files.
 d. Press **Ctrl+End** to position the insertion point.
 e. Click the arrow with the **Paste** button [*Home* tab, *Clipboard* group] and choose **Paste Special**.
 f. Select **Microsoft Excel Worksheet Object** in the *Paste Special* dialog box.
 g. Select the **Paste link** radio button in the *Paste Special* dialog box and click **OK**.
 h. Click the **Center** button [*Home* tab, *Paragraph* group].
 i. Save the Word document as *[your initials] Excel 4-3* in your usual folder (Figure 4-97).
 j. Close Word.

16. Save and close the Excel workbook.

Clemenson Imaging
3454 Monroe Avenue South
Green Bay, WI 54301

August 2, 2015

Here is data about CT Scan and MRI hours, filtered from our master list. Please review and let us know our next steps.

Month	Image	Patients	Total Hours	# of Employees
Apr 2015	CT Scan	1000	1800	5
Aug 2015	CT Scan	500	2400	3
Dec 2015	CT Scan	500	2400	2
Apr 2016	CT Scan	500	2400	3
Aug 2016	CT Scan	750	2400	3
Dec 2016	CT Scan	500	1800	4
Apr 2017	CT Scan	750	2400	2
Aug 2017	CT Scan	500	2400	3
Jan 2017	MRI	1000	1800	3
May 2017	MRI	750	3000	4

4-97 Word document with pasted Excel object

Independent Project 4-4

Eller Software Services has received contract revenue information in a text file. You import, sort, and filter the data. You also create a *PivotTable*, prepare a worksheet with subtotals, and format related data as an Excel table.
[Student Learning Outcomes 4.1, 4.3, 4.4, 4.5, 4.6, 4.8]

Files Needed: ***EllerSoftware-04.xlsx*** and ***EllerSoftware-04.txt*** [*Student data files are available in the Library of your SIMnet account.*]
Completed Project File Name: *[your initials] Excel 4-4.xlsx*

Skills Covered in This Project

- Import a text file.
- Use *AutoFilters*.
- Sort data by multiple columns.
- Create a *PivotTable*.

- Format fields in a *PivotTable*.
- Use the *Subtotal* command.
- Format data in an Excel table.
- Sort data in an Excel table.

1. Open the ***EllerSoftware-04*** workbook from your student data files and save it as [your initials] Excel 4-4.

2. Import the ***EllerSoftware-04.txt*** file from your student data files beginning in cell **A4**. The text file has a header row and is tab-delimited.

3. Format the values in column **H** as **Currency** with zero decimal places.

4. Click cell **G4** and show *AutoFilter* arrows.

5. Use the *AutoFilter* arrow to sort by date with the earliest date first. Then use the *AutoFilter* arrow to sort by product/service name in ascending order.

6. Filter the *Date* column to show only contracts for **September** using the **All Dates in the Period** option.

7. Select cells **A1:H2** and press **Ctrl+1** to open the *Format Cells* dialog box. On the *Alignment* tab, choose **Center Across Selection**.

8. Change the font size for cells **A1:H2** to **20 pt** (Figure 4-98).

4-98 Imported data sorted and filtered

9. Copy the **Contracts** sheet to the end and name the copy Data.

10. Clear the date filter and hide the *AutoFilter* arrows.

11. Select cell **A5** and click the **PivotTable** button [*Insert* tab] to create a blank *PivotTable* layout on its own sheet named PivotTable.

12. Show the **Product/Service** and **Contract** fields in the *PivotTable*.

13. Drag the **Contract** field from the *Choose fields to add to report* area below the **Sum of Contract** field in the *Values* area so that it appears twice in the report layout and the pane (Figure 4-99).

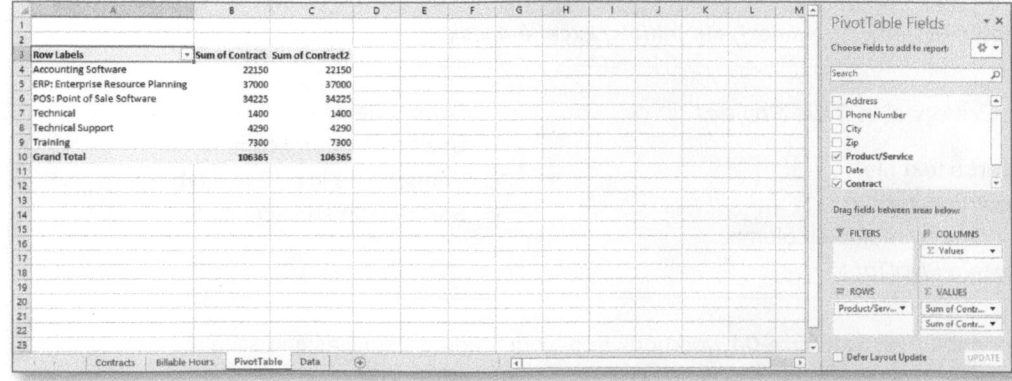

4-99 "Contract" field appears twice in the report

14. Select cell **C4** and click the **Field Settings** button [*PivotTable Tools Analyze* tab, *Active Fields* group]. Type Average Contract as the *Custom Name,* choose **Average** as the calculation, and set the *Number Format* to **Currency** with zero decimal places.

15. Select cell **B4** and set its *Custom Name* to Total Contracts and the number format to **Currency** with zero decimal places.

16. Apply **PivotTable Style Dark 3**.

17. Select the **Data** sheet tab and copy cells **A1:A2**. Paste them in cell **A1** on the **PivotTable** sheet. Set **Align Left** for both cells and **16 pt** as the font size (Figure 4-100).

18. Copy the **Data** sheet to the end and name the copy Subtotals.

19. Select cell **D5** and sort by **City** in **A to Z** order.

20. Use the *Subtotal* command to show a **SUM** for the contract amounts for each city.

21. Click the **Billable Hours** sheet tab and select cell **A4**.

22. Click the **Format as Table** button [*Home* tab, *Styles* group], use **Table Style Medium 10**, and remove the data connections.

23. Type 5% Add On in cell **E4** and press **Enter**.

24. Build a formula in cell **E5** to multiply cell **D5** by **105%**.

25. Select cells **A1:E2** and center them across the selection.

26. Use the *AutoFilter* arrows to sort first by date in oldest to newest order and then by client name in ascending order.

27. Save and close the workbook (Figure 4-101).

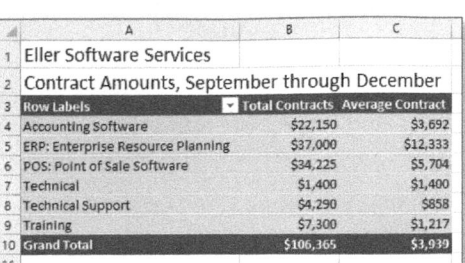

	A	B	C
1	Eller Software Services		
2	Contract Amounts, September through December		
3	Row Labels	Total Contracts	Average Contract
4	Accounting Software	$22,150	$3,692
5	ERP: Enterprise Resource Planning	$37,000	$12,333
6	POS: Point of Sale Software	$34,225	$5,704
7	Technical	$1,400	$1,400
8	Technical Support	$4,290	$858
9	Training	$7,300	$1,217
10	Grand Total	$106,365	$3,939
11			

4-100 Completed *PivotTable*

Eller Software Services
Contract Amounts, September through December

Client Name	Address	Phone Number	City	Zip	Product/Service	Date	Contract
Martin Green	127 Oak Street	218-555-2363	Bemidji	56601	Accounting Software	12/15/2016	$850
Mike Gunderson	304 Irvine Avenue	218-555-9021	Bemidji	56601	Technical Support	10/28/2016	$890
Heather Guyan	124 East Street	218-555-2513	Bemidji	56601	Training	10/7/2016	$1,500
Paula Valentine	127 Oak Street	218-555-2513	Bemidji	56601	Training	10/15/2016	$950
			Bemidji Total				$4,390
Jerri Selzman	800 Lake Avenue	218-555-8977	Brainerd	56401	POS: Point of Sale Software	9/15/2016	$7,000
Terri Olander	459 10th Avenue	218-555-8977	Brainerd	56401	POS: Point of Sale Software	10/15/2016	$6,525
Christine Barton	902 Clinton Street	218-555-8977	Brainerd	56401	POS: Point of Sale Software	11/15/2016	$3,500
Michelle Cronin	800 Lake Avenue	218-555-8977	Brainerd	56401	POS: Point of Sale Software	12/15/2016	$4,500
Patricia Glunz	902 Gunter Street	218-555-8900	Brainerd	56401	POS: Point of Sale Software	12/15/2016	$3,200
			Brainerd Total				$26,725
Glenn Ladewig	1600 Highway 2	218-555-6211	Cass Lake	56633	Accounting Software	9/1/2016	$4,500
Karen Talon	1600 Highway 3	218-555-6287	Cass Lake	56633	Accounting Software	9/1/2016	$4,000
Wade Whitworth	1822 Highway 2	218-555-6211	Cass Lake	56633	Accounting Software	9/21/2016	$5,200
Thomas Larson	1044 Highway 2	218-555-1254	Cass Lake	56633	Training	10/15/2016	$2,500
			Cass Lake Total				$16,200
Shelly Vicko	402 2nd Avenue SE	218-555-2456	Deer River	56636	Accounting Software	9/15/2016	$1,050
Arnold Robert	500 2nd Avenue SW	218-555-2596	Deer River	56636	Accounting Software	9/15/2016	$5,000
			Deer River Total				$7,500
Jeremie Midboe	Pilot Knob Road	651-555-2789	Eagan	55121	POS: Point of Sale Software	11/1/2016	$7,500
			Eagan Total				$7,500
Charlie Lindberg	345 Lyndale Avenue	612-555-2156	Minneapolis	55401	ERP: Enterprise Resource Planning	9/1/2016	$12,000
Robert Gneiss	245 Western Avenue	612-555-2566	Minneapolis	55401	ERP: Enterprise Resource Planning	9/1/2016	$10,000
Susan Charlotte	507 Lyndale Avenue	612-555-2177	Minneapolis	55401	ERP: Enterprise Resource Planning	11/1/2016	$13,000
Robert Lawlor	245 Western Avenue	612-555-2376	Minneapolis	55401	Technical	9/1/2016	$1,400
			Minneapolis Total				$38,400
Craig Brand	554 2nd Street	320-555-4483	Saint Cloud	56301	Technical Support	10/1/2016	$1,000
Arthur Weston	554 3rd Street	320-555-4483	Saint Cloud	56301	Technical Support	10/1/2016	$750
Richard Malinowski	309 Fifth Street	320-555-4483	Saint Cloud	56301	Technical Support	10/1/2016	$750
Elisabeth Jones	450 Fifth Street	320-555-4422	Saint Cloud	56301	Technical Support	10/1/2016	$750
Hilary Marschke	245 West 3rd Avenue	320-555-5443	Saint Cloud	56301	Training	11/15/2016	$750
Juan Garcia	400 South Avenue	320-555-5443	Saint Cloud	56301	Training	11/15/2016	$800
Amir Atef	300 South Avenue	320-555-5443	Saint Cloud	56301	Training	12/15/2016	$600
			Saint Cloud Total				$5,650
			Grand Total				$106,365

Eller Software Services
Billable Hours

Client Name	Product/Service	Date	Billable	5% Add On
Amir Atef	Training	12/15/2016	4.00	4.2
Arnold Robert	Accounting Software	9/15/2016	5.00	5.25
Arthur Weston	Technical Support	10/1/2016	3.00	3.15
Arthur Weston	Technical Support	5/5/2017	6.00	6.3
Charlie Lindberg	ERP: Enterprise Resource Planning	9/1/2016	4.00	4.2
Charlie Lindberg	ERP: Enterprise Resource Planning	4/5/2017	6.00	6.3
Christine Barton	POS: Point of Sale Software	11/15/2016	4.00	4.2
Christine Barton	POS: Point of Sale Software	11/15/2016	2.00	2.1
Craig Brand	Technical Support	10/1/2016	5.00	5.4
Elisabeth Jones	Technical Support	10/1/2016	3.50	3.675
Glenn Ladewig	Accounting Software	9/1/2016	5.00	5.25
Heather Guyan	Training	10/7/2016	3.25	3.4125
Heather Guyan	Training	2/3/2017	4.50	4.725
Hilary Marschke	Training	11/15/2016	5.00	5.25
Hilary Marschke	Training	11/15/2016	5.00	5.25
Hilary Marschke	Training	3/8/2017	5.00	5.25
Jeremie Midboe	POS: Point of Sale Software	11/1/2016	3.50	3.675
Jerri Selzman	POS: Point of Sale Software	3/9/2017	4.50	4.725
Juan Garcia	Training	11/15/2016	4.00	4.2
Karen Talon	Accounting Software	9/1/2016	3.50	3.675
Karen Talon	Accounting Software	10/1/2016	5.50	5.775
Martin Green	Accounting Software	12/15/2016	5.00	5.25
Martin Green	Accounting Software	3/7/2017	4.00	4.2
Michelle Cronin	POS: Point of Sale Software	12/15/2016	4.00	4.2
Michelle Cronin	POS: Point of Sale Software	12/15/2016	5.00	5.25
Mike Gunderson	Technical Support	10/28/2016	4.75	4.9875
Mike Gunderson	Technical Support	12/15/2016	4.50	4.725
Patricia Glunz	POS: Point of Sale Software	12/15/2016	3.25	3.4125
Paula Valentine	Training	10/15/2016	4.00	4.2
Paula Valentine	Training	10/15/2016	4.00	4.2
Paula Valentine	Training	11/15/2016	4.00	4.2
Paula Valentine	Training	4/5/2017	4.00	4.2
Richard Malinowski	Technical Support	10/1/2016	4.50	4.725
Richard Malinowski	Technical Support	1/5/2017	3.00	3.15
Robert Gneiss	ERP: Enterprise Resource Planning	9/1/2016	6.00	6.3
Robert Gneiss	ERP: Enterprise Resource Planning	2/5/2017	7.00	7.35
Robert Lawlor	Technical Support	1/5/2017	2.75	2.8875
Shelly Vicko	Accounting Software	9/15/2016	5.00	5.25
Shelly Vicko	Accounting Software	11/16/2016	5.00	5.25
Susan Charlotte	ERP: Enterprise Resource Planning	11/1/2016	6.00	6.3
Susan Charlotte	ERP: Enterprise Resource Planning	1/5/2017	5.00	5.4
Terri Olander	POS: Point of Sale Software	10/15/2016	6.50	6.825
Thomas Larson	Training	12/5/2016	3.00	3.15
Thomas Larson	Training	3/14/2017	4.00	4.2
Wade Whitworth	Accounting Software	11/24/2016	5.00	5.25
Wade Whitworth	Accounting Software	2/1/2017	6.00	6.3
Wade Whitworth	Accounting Software	5/11/2017	5.00	5.25

4-101 Completed Excel table and *Subtotals* sheet

Independent Project 4-5

Boyd Air is monitoring flight arrival status as well as capacities. Before formatting the data as an Excel table, you will export it as a text file for use in the reservation software. You will filter the data in the table, build a *PivotTable,* and create a *PivotChart.*
[Student Learning Outcomes 4.1, 4.2, 4.3, 4.4, 4.7, 4.8]

File Needed: ***BoydAir-04.xlsx*** *[Student data files are available in the Library of your SIMnet account.]*
Completed Project File Names: ***[your initials] Excel 4-5.xlsx*** and ***[your initials] Excel 4-5.txt***

Skills Covered in This Project

- Export data as a text file.
- Format data as an Excel table.
- Use a number filter in a table.

- Set conditional formatting with an icon set.
- Filter data by cell icon.
- Create and format a *PivotTable.*
- Create and format a *PivotChart.*

1. Open ***BoydAir-04*** workbook from your student data files and save it as [your initials] Excel 4-5.

2. Export the data to a tab-delimited text file named ***[your initials] Excel 4-5*** in your usual location for saving work.

3. Rename the sheet tab Stats after the data is exported.

4. Use the *Save As* command to save and replace ***[your initials] Excel 4-5*** as an **Excel Workbook**.

5. Select cell **A4** and format the data as an Excel table using **Table Style Medium 21**.

6. Copy the **Stats** sheet to the end and name the copy PM Flights.

7. Select the **PM Flights** sheet and use a *Greater Than* filter to display flights with a departure time after 12:00 PM (Figure 4-102).

8. Select the **Stats** worksheet, select cells **I5:I32**, and set conditional formatting to use **3 Stars** from the *Icon Sets.*

9. Build a two-level *Custom Sort* for the *Capacity* column to sort by icon. Show the solid gold star at the top, followed by the half-gold star. The silver star will default to the bottom (Figure 4-103).

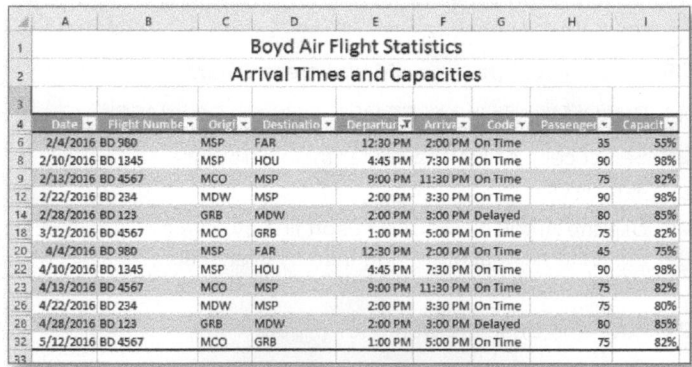

4-102 Filter results for *Departure Time* field

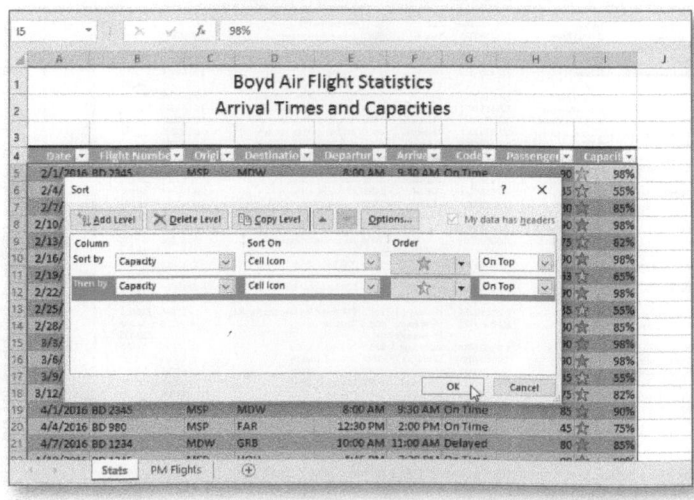

4-103 Custom sort for the *3 Stars* icon set

10. Select the **Stats** worksheet, select cells **A4:I32**, and use the *Quick Analysis* tool to create a *PivotTable* to display average of capacity by origin (Figure 4-104).

11. Select cell **B3** in the *PivotTable* and use **Field Settings** to set a **Number Format** of **Percentage** with two decimal places. Edit the *Custom Name* to display **Average Capacity**.

12. Add the **Passengers** field to the *PivotTable VALUES* area with a sum calculation. Edit the field settings to display **# of Passengers** as the custom name. Set the number format to **Number** with zero decimals and a thousand's separator.

13. Use **PivotTable Style Light 8** for the *PivotTable* and show banded columns and rows.

14. Add a **3-D Pie PivotChart** to the sheet and position the chart object to start in cell **E3**. Size the chart to reach cell **N22**.

15. Select the legend in the chart and set its font size to **11** from the *Home* tab.

16. Show **Data Labels** on the chart positioned at the **Inside End**. Select a data label and format all labels from the *Home* tab as **bold** and **10 pt**.

17. Select cell **A1** and rename the sheet PivotTable&Chart (Figure 4-105).

18. Save and close the workbook.

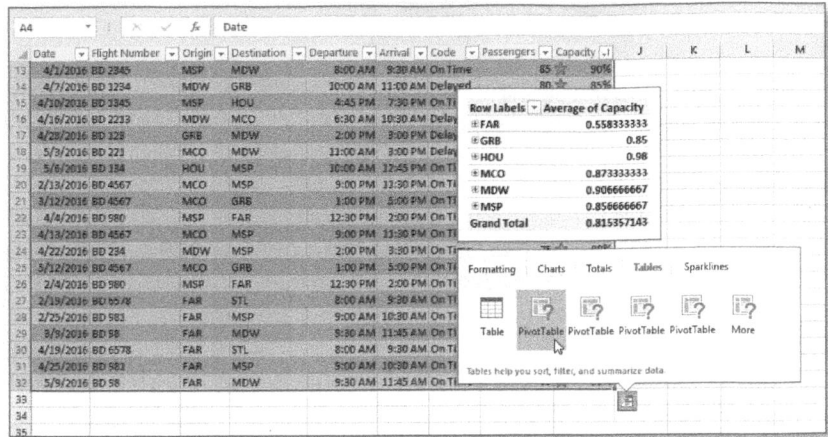

4-104 *PivotTable* suggestions from the *Quick Analysis* tool

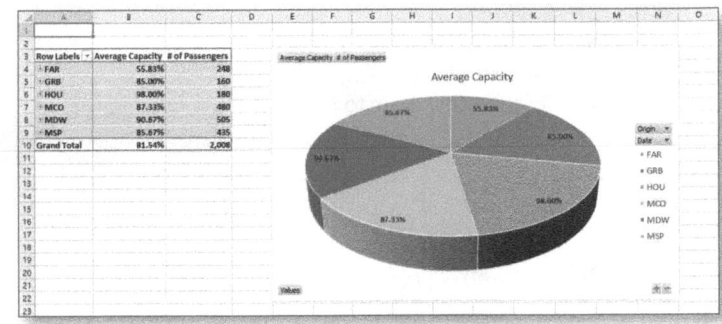

4-105 Excel 4-5 completed sheets

Independent Project 4-6

Life's Animal Shelter has a list of suppliers in a worksheet which must be copied to Word for use by another staff member. You will build an advanced filter to show suppliers for specific product categories and define groups based on supplier name. Your final task is to create an Excel table for sorting and filtering.

[Student Learning Outcomes 4.1, 4.3, 4.4, 4.5, 4.7]

File Needed: **LAShelter-04.xlsx** [Student data files are available in the Library of your SIMnet account.]
Completed Project File Names: **[your initials] Excel 4-6.xlsx** and **[your initials] Excel 4-6.docx**

Skills Covered in This Project

- Copy Excel data to Word.
- Create an advanced filter.
- Use *Flash Fill* to complete a column.

- Format data as a table.
- Filter data.
- Define groups in a worksheet.

1. Open the **LAShelter-04** workbook from your student data files and save it as [your initials] Excel 4-6.

2. Select the **LAS Suppliers** sheet, select cells **A4:D32**, and copy them to the Windows *Clipboard*.

3. Open Word and create a new document.

4. Paste the data into Word with the **Use Destination Styles** option (Figure 4-106).

5. Save the Word document as [your initials] Excel 4-6.docx.

6. Close the Word document and exit Word.

7. Click the **Criteria** sheet tab.

8. Type *cage* in cell **A2** and type *carrier* in cell **A3**. This is *OR* criteria that will find products that include either the word "cage" or the word "carrier."

9. Select the **LAS Suppliers** sheet and format the labels in row **4** as **bold** and **centered** to distinguish the header row from other data.

10. Click cell **A5** on the **LAS Suppliers** sheet.

11. Build an advanced filter that uses the data on the **LAS Suppliers** sheet, the criteria range on the **Criteria** sheet, and cells **F6:G6** as the output range. In the *Advanced Filter* dialog box, select the **Unique records only** box (Figure 4-107).

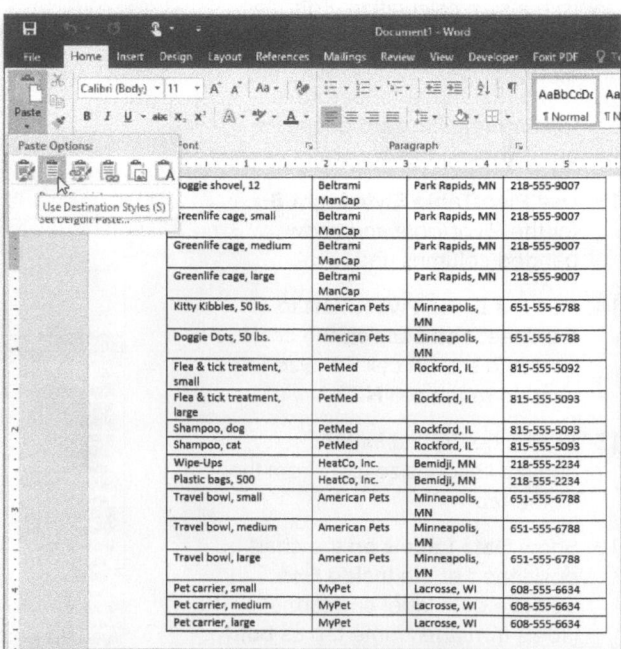

4-106 Word *Paste Options* for Excel data

12. Replace the criteria with *bowl* and *collar* to build a second advanced filter and show the filtered results as indicated on the worksheet.

13. Select cells **A4:D32** and copy them to cell **A4** on the **Table** sheet. Remove all borders.

14. Select cells **A5:A32** and sort the data by product name in ascending order.

15. Type (651) 555-6788 in cell **E5**.

16. Type (2 in cell **E6** and press **Enter** when the *Flash Fill* suggestion appears.

17. Type Phone in cell **E4** and delete column **D**. Set column **D** to a width of **15.71 (115 pixels)**.

18. Format the data as a table using **Table Style Medium 2**.

19. Filter the data to show the suppliers located in Minnesota.

20. Select cells **A1:A2** and remove the **Merge & Center** command. Set both cells to **Align Left**. Then select cells **A1:D2** and use the **Center Across Selection** command (Figure 4-108).

21. Select the **By City** worksheet tab.

22. Sort by **City** in **A to Z** order.

23. Insert a row at row **5** and type Bemidji in cell **A5**. Left-align the label.

24. Insert a row at row **10** and type Houston in cell **A10**. **Bold** the label.

25. Insert blank rows and type labels for the remaining cities.

26. Select the row headings for rows **6:9** and click the **Group** button [*Data* tab, *Outline* group]. Do not include the row with the city name in the group.

27. Repeat the command to group the rows for each city (Figure 4-109).

28. Select and delete column **C**.

29. Collapse the *Houston* and *Minneapolis* groups (Figure 4-110).

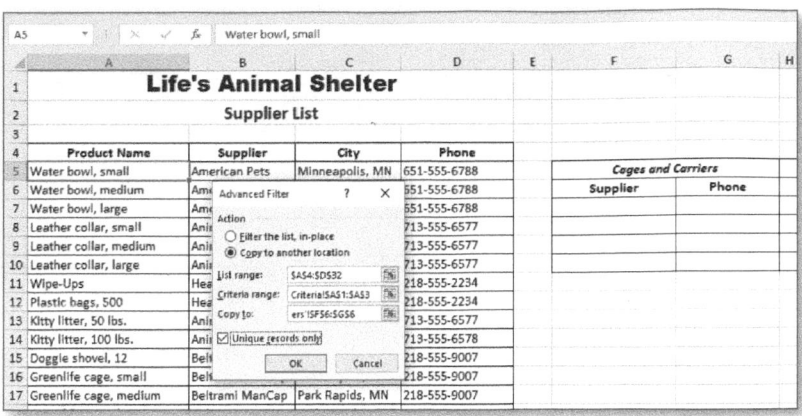

4-107 Advanced filter to select unique records

4-108 Completed table

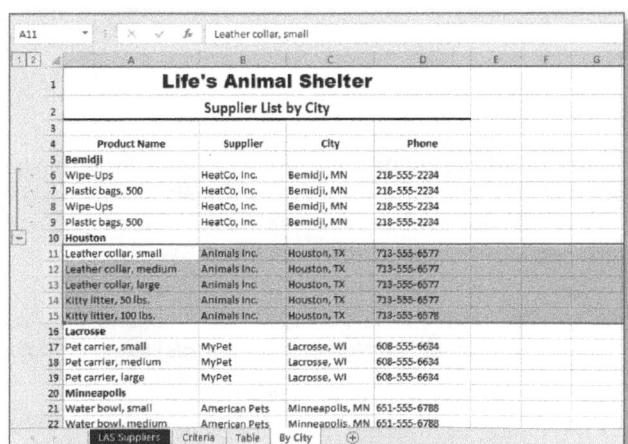

4-109 Data manually defined in groups

4-110 Excel 4-6 completed worksheets

30. Save and close the workbook.

Improve It Project 4-7

Placer Hills Real Estate wants its latest *PivotTable* to show sales by agent listing, but the table needs additional work. In the source data, you also need to highlight certain listings for insurance purposes. In a separate table, you plan to create a calculation column to show the number of market days.
[Student Learning Outcomes 4.1, 4.2, 4.8]

File Needed: ***PlacerHills-04.xlsx*** [*Student data files are available in the* Library *of your SIMnet account.*]
Completed Project File Name: **[your initials]** *Excel 4-7.xlsx*

Skills Covered in This Project

- Pivot fields in a *PivotTable*.
- Format fields in a *PivotTable*.
- Add a field to a table.
- Set conditional formatting with a formula.

1. Open the **PlacerHills-04** workbook from your student data files and save it as [your initials] Excel 4-7.

2. Select the **Listings** sheet and use a formula to set conditional formatting for cells **A5:A26**. The formula is **=k5="frame"** to determine if the construction is frame. Set the format to use light blue fill.

3. Select the **PivotTable** sheet, drag the **City** field out of the *Rows* area, and drag the **Agent ID** field to the *Rows* area.

4. Drag the **Sale Price** field into the *Values* area so that it is shown twice in the *PivotTable*.

5. Format the first occurrence of the **Sales Price** field to show a sum with **Currency** format, zero decimals, and a custom name of Total Sales. Format the second occurrence to show an average with the same **Currency** format and the name Average Sale.

6. Apply **PivotTable Style Light 15**.

7. Select cells **A3:C9** in the *PivotTable*. Click the **Border** button [*Home* tab, *Font* group] and apply **All Borders**. Select cell **A1**.

8. Select the **Table** sheet tab.

9. Type Days in cell **O4**. In cell **O5**, build an *IF* formula to display the number of days on the market. The *logical_test* determines if the sale date is greater than the list date. The *value_if_true* argument is the sale date minus the list date. For the *value_if_false* argument, press **Spacebar** once to leave the cell blank when there is no sale date.

10. Save and close the workbook (Figure 4-111).

4-111 Excel 4-7 completed worksheets

Challenge Project 4-8

For this project, you build a worksheet for a company that sells four varieties of socks in four eastern states. When the data is complete, you will format the data as an Excel table.
[Student Learning Outcomes 4.1, 4.2, 4.3]

File Needed: None
Completed Project File Name: *[your initials] Excel 4-8.xlsx*

Create a new workbook and save it as [your initials] Excel 4-8. Modify your workbook according to the following guidelines:

- Type the labels State, Model, Month, Pairs, and Price in cells **A4:E4**.
- In cells **A5:A8**, type Connecticut, Maine, New Hampshire, and Vermont.
- In cell **B5**, type the style name for one type of sock sold by the company. Copy the name to cells **B6:B8**.
- In cells **C5**, type January and copy the month to cells **C6:C8**.
- In cells **D5:D8**, enter values for how many pairs were sold in each state in January. In column E, enter and copy a price for this sock style.
- Copy cells **A5:E8** and paste the range in cell **A9** to create a February group. Edit the month and the number of pairs sold.
- Copy cells **A5:E12** and paste the range in cell **A13** to create the data for another sock style. In this range, edit the style name, the number of pairs sold, and the price. The price is the same for all rows in this group.
- Copy and paste to complete two more ranges for two sock styles, so that you have January and February data for four sock styles for each state.
- Set conditional formatting to show one of the state names in a format different from the other states.
- Name the sheet Data and make a copy named Table.
- On the **Table** sheet, format the data as an Excel table with a light table style.
- Type Total in cell **F4** and create a formula to calculate the dollar amount of sales in the column.
- Show a total row for the table with results for the number of pairs and sales dollars.
- Add additional formatting to the table as needed.
- Use the *AutoFilter* arrows to sort by style and then by state.
- Enter a name for the company in cell **A1**. Enter a label in cell **A2** that describes the data.

Challenge Project 4-9

For this project, you explore the Bureau of Labor Statistics web site to download data for use in a worksheet. After you have arranged and formatted the data, you copy it to a Word document.
[Student Learning Outcomes 4.1, 4.2, 4.6, 4.7]

File Needed: None
Completed Project File Names: *[your initials] Excel 4-9.xlsx* and *[your initials] Excel 4-9.docx*

Create a new workbook and save it as [your initials] Excel 4-9. Modify your workbook according to the following guidelines:

- Go to www.bls.gov/data.
- Review the subject areas and choose one to explore. Find a topic and subtopic which provides an *.xlsx* file for download.
- Download or copy the data into your worksheet.
- Format the data as an Excel table if it is not already formatted, or apply a different table style.
- Determine and apply conditional formatting for some aspect of the data.
- Determine and set a different sort order.
- Add a main title to your worksheet and set other format attributes to effectively display your information.
- Copy the data to a new Word document and save the Word document as [your initials] Excel 4-9.docx.

Challenge Project 4-10

For this project, you create a worksheet that lists names, birth dates, and hair color for 20 people. You format the list as a table for sorting and filtering. You convert the table to a range and use the *Subtotal* command.
[Student Learning Outcomes 4.1, 4.3, 4.4, 4.5]

File Needed: None
Completed Project File Name: *[your initials] Excel 4-10.xlsx*

Create a new workbook and save it as [your initials] Excel 4-10. Modify your workbook according to the following guidelines:

- Type your first name, your last name, your birthdate, and your hair color in a row using one column for each item.
- Type data for **19** more people, using fictitious or real data. Use birthdates that are the same year as yours as well as four other years, so that your list has only five different years. Use at least three hair colors in your list, such as brown, blond, red.
- Format the data as a table and apply a table style.
- Sort the date by birthdate with the youngest people listed first. Then filter the data to show only those records from the first year listed in the data.
- Make a copy of the sheet and convert the table to a normal range. Use the *Subtotal* command to count the number of persons with each hair color.

CHAPTER
5

Consolidating and Linking Data and Inserting Objects

CHAPTER OVERVIEW

When multiple worksheets have identical layouts and labels, you can summarize data with the *Consolidate* command. You can also link to data in a different workbook to build a formula or display information. In this chapter, you will learn how to consolidate data from multiple sheets in the same workbook and how to link multiple workbooks with an external reference formula. You will also insert *SmartArt* graphics, screenshots, and hyperlinks in a worksheet.

STUDENT LEARNING OUTCOMES (SLOs)

After completing this chapter, you will be able to:

SLO 5.1 Create a static data consolidation (p. E5-294).

SLO 5.2 Create a dynamic data consolidation (p. E5-296).

SLO 5.3 Consolidate data by category (p. E5-298).

SLO 5.4 Group worksheets for editing and formatting (p. E5-299).

SLO 5.5 Link workbooks to consolidate data (p. E5-303).

SLO 5.6 Insert illustrations using *SmartArt*, screenshots, and pictures in a worksheet (p. E5-309).

SLO 5.7 Insert hyperlinks in a worksheet (p. E5-316).

SLO 5.8 Safeguard work by marking it as final or by setting a password (p. E5-318).

CASE STUDY

In the Pause & Practice projects in this chapter, you build consolidated worksheets and link workbooks for Paradise Lakes Resort. You create an illustration to accompany the data and add basic security to the workbook.

Pause & Practice 5-1: Create static and dynamic data consolidations and format grouped sheets.

Pause & Practice 5-2: Link workbooks.

Pause & Practice 5-3: Insert *SmartArt*, hyperlinks, and a screenshot in a workbook; mark a workbook as final.

EXCEL

SLO 5.1

Creating a Static Data Consolidation

A *consolidated worksheet* summarizes data from multiple sheets with a mathematical or statistical function. The *Consolidate* command on the *Data* tab calculates totals, averages, or other functions for data from multiple worksheets. Worksheets must have common data in the same rows and columns on each sheet for consolidation *by position*.

Each location for Paradise Lakes Resort follows the same layout for its net income worksheet, but the values are different. Figure 5-1 shows the worksheets for two locations. Revenue items and values are in cells A5:D8 on each sheet. When worksheets use the same pattern, the *Consolidate* command gathers data from each sheet to calculate a total, an average, or similar function.

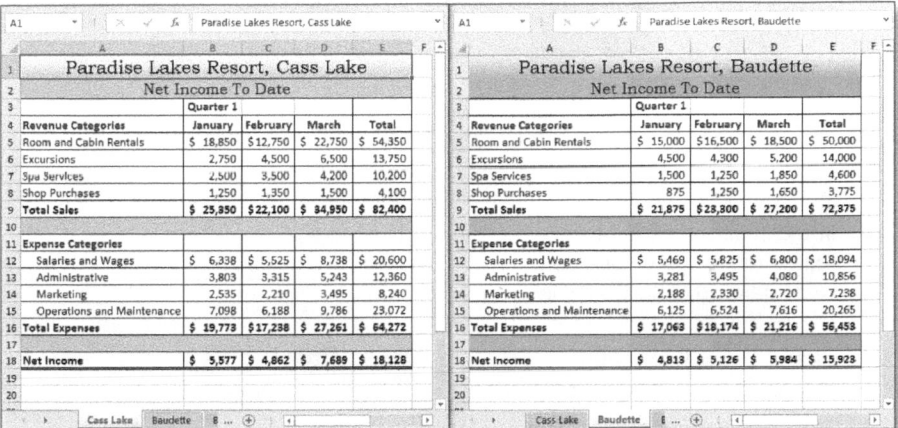

5-1 Two sheets prepared for consolidation by position

A *consolidation worksheet* is a separate summary sheet in the workbook. You create a consolidation sheet by copying one of the *source worksheets*. On the consolidation sheet, delete the contents of cells to be consolidated. You must create the consolidation worksheet before you start the *Consolidate* command.

▶HOW TO: Prepare a Consolidation Sheet

1. Copy one of the source worksheets in the workbook.
2. Rename the copied sheet as desired.
3. Delete the contents of cells to be consolidated (Figure 5-2).
 - Do not delete formulas that will be used on the consolidation sheet.

5-2 Copied sheet ready for consolidation

Static Data Consolidation

A *static consolidation* summarizes the data and displays a result on the consolidated sheet. The result does not change when a value on any source worksheet is edited. A static consolidation for the data in Figure 5-1 displays 2,125 in cell B8 on the consolidation sheet. If cell B8 on the Cass Lake sheet is changed after consolidation, cell B8 on the consolidation sheet does not recalculate. When you know that source data is final and will not be edited, you can use a static consolidation.

> ### MORE INFO
>
> If values are edited in source worksheets used in a static consolidation, run the *Consolidate* command again to update results.

▶ HOW TO: Create a Static Consolidation

1. Select the cell range to be summarized on the consolidation worksheet.
 - You can also click the first cell in the range.
 - This is the range whose contents were deleted (cells B5:D8 in Figure 5-3).
2. Click the **Consolidate** button [*Data* tab, *Data Tools* group].
 - The *Consolidate* dialog box opens.
 - If recently used cell ranges are listed in the *All references* box, select each reference and click **Delete** in the dialog box.
3. Click the **Function** arrow and choose the function (Figure 5-3).
4. Click the *Reference* box.
5. Click the first worksheet tab name with data to be consolidated.
 - The sheet name displays in the *Reference* box.
 - Move the *Consolidate* dialog box if necessary to select cells.
6. Select the cells to be summarized on the source sheet (Figure 5-4).
 - The *Consolidate* dialog box collapses as you select the range.
 - The reference appears in the *Reference* box.
7. Click **Add** in the *Consolidate* dialog box.
 - The first reference displays in the *All references* list.
 - The first selected sheet tab is active with the range selected.

5-3 *Consolidate* dialog box

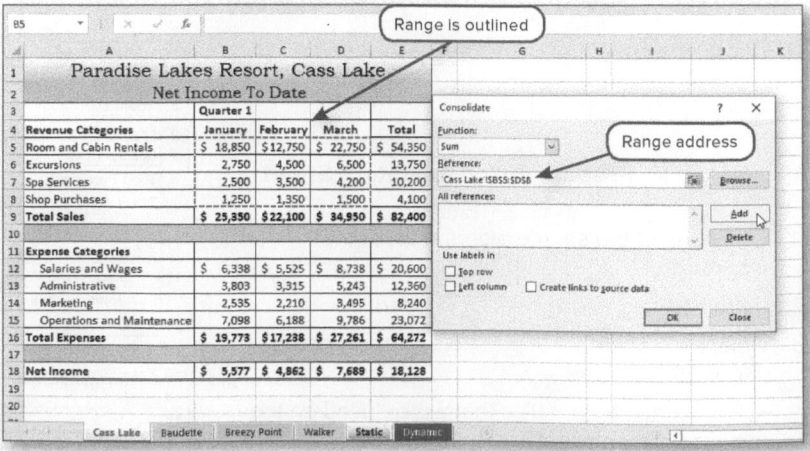

5-4 Range selected on first sheet

8. Click the next worksheet tab name with data to be consolidated.

 • The same cell range is selected.

9. Click **Add**.

 • The reference is placed in the *All references* list.

10. Repeat steps 8 and 9 for each worksheet to include in the consolidation (Figure 5-5).

11. Click **OK**.

 • The data is summarized.
 • The consolidated sheet displays a result in each cell (Figure 5-6).

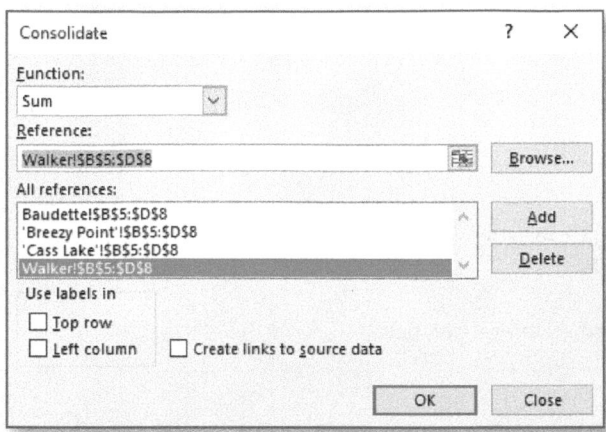

5-5 Data to be consolidated by SUM on four worksheets

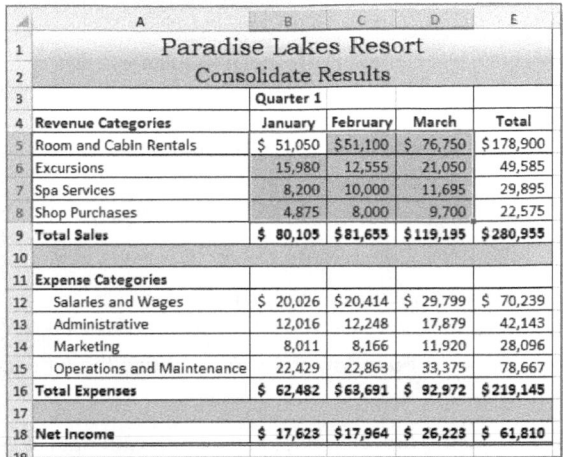

5-6 Consolidated results

Creating a Dynamic Data Consolidation

A *dynamic consolidation* places formulas on the consolidated sheet in an outline. When data on a source worksheet is edited, the formula recalculates. You should use dynamic consolidation when data on source worksheets might be edited after you have created the consolidation worksheet.

> **MORE INFO**
>
> An Excel outline can show or hide details as discussed in *SLO 4.5: Using Subtotals, Outlines, and Groups.*

Dynamic Data Consolidation

You build a dynamic consolidation sheet the same way that you build a static consolidation sheet. In the *Consolidate* dialog box, however, choose the option to create links to the source data. The resulting outline in the consolidation sheet uses 3D reference formulas (Figure 5-7). The formulas identify the sheet name and cell used for consolidation. In a dynamic consolidation, you can expand outline items to display individual values that are summarized.

> **ANOTHER WAY**
>
> You can dynamically consolidate data by using 3D references in your own formulas.

Outline level buttons

Expanded item

3D reference

5-7 Consolidated results in outline view with 3D references

▶ HOW TO: Create a Dynamic Consolidation

1. Select the cell range to be summarized.
 - The cell contents should be blank.
 - You can also click the first cell in the range.

2. Click the **Consolidate** button [*Data* tab, *Data Tools* group].
 - The *Consolidate* dialog box opens.
 - Select and delete recently used reference ranges in the *All references* box.

3. Click the **Function** arrow and choose the function.

4. Click the *Reference* box.

5. Click the first worksheet tab name with data to be consolidated.
 - The sheet name displays in the *Reference* box.
 - Move the *Consolidate* dialog box if necessary to select cells.
 - You can scroll sheet names as needed.

6. Select the cells to be summarized.
 - The *Consolidate* dialog box collapses as you select the range.
 - The reference appears in the *Reference* box.

7. Click **Add** in the *Consolidate* dialog box.
 - The first reference is listed in the *All references* box.
 - The first selected sheet tab is active with the range selected.

8. Click the next worksheet tab name with data to be consolidated.
 - The same cell range is selected.

9. Click **Add**.
 - The second reference is listed in the *All references* box.

10. Repeat steps 8 and 9 for each worksheet to include in the consolidation.

11. Select the **Create links to source data** box (Figure 5-8).

12. Click **OK** (Figure 5-9).
 - The data is consolidated in outline format.
 - Each item is collapsed.
 - The consolidated sheet displays a 3D reference in each cell above the result cell when the outline is expanded.

5-8 Data to be consolidated by *SUM* with links

5-9 Dynamic data consolidation results

| SLO 5.3 | # Consolidating Data by Category |

When data in multiple worksheets is arranged differently but has the same row and column labels, you can build a consolidation *by category*. Category refers to the row or column labels. Consolidation by category can be static or dynamic.

Data Consolidation by Category

The worksheets shown in Figure 5-10 have data for January, February, and March. The month names are not arranged in the same way, but they are spelled alike on both sheets.

To consolidate data by category, copy one of the source worksheets. On the consolidation sheet, delete the contents of cells to be consolidated including the labels. For example, in a consolidation for the data in Figure 5-10, delete cells B4:D8 on the consolidation sheet including the month names. When you select the range on each source sheet, select the same range (B4:D8). In the *Consolidate* dialog box, you activate the option to use the top row or left column labels or both.

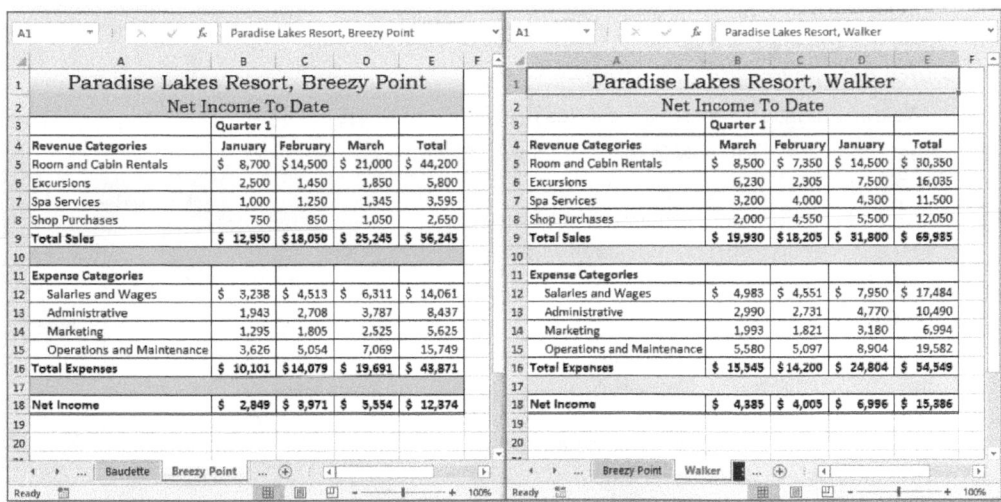

5-10 Data has same labels in different order

▶ HOW TO: Create a Dynamic Data Consolidation by Category

1. Delete the contents of the cells to be summarized including labels on the consolidation sheet.

2. Select the range of cells to be summarized including label cells (Figure 5-11).

3. Click the **Consolidate** button [*Data* tab, *Data Tools* group].

 - The *Consolidate* dialog box opens.
 - Select and delete references in the *All references* box.

4. Click the **Function** arrow and choose the function.

5. Click the first sheet tab name with data to be consolidated.

 - The sheet name displays in the *Reference* box.

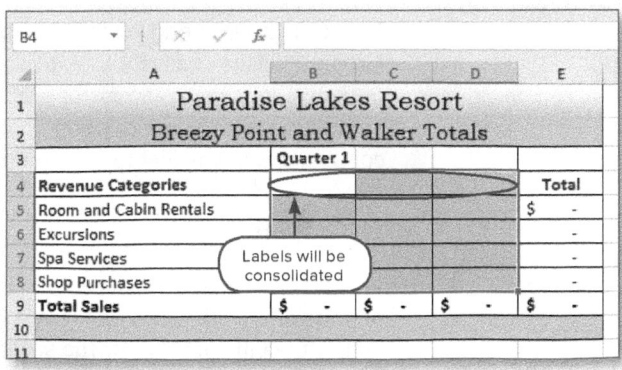

5-11 Consolidation sheet with labels and data deleted

6. Select data and label cells to be summarized.

7. Click **Add** in the *Consolidate* dialog box.

 - The first reference appears in the *All references* list.

8. Click the next worksheet tab name.

 - The same cell range is selected.

9. Click **Add**.

 - The second reference appears in the *All references* list.

10. Repeat steps 8 and 9 for each worksheet to include in the consolidation.

11. Select the **Create links to source data** box.

 - The consolidation can be static if desired.

12. Select the box for **Top row** in the *Use labels in* group (Figure 5-12).

 - Use *Left column* when required.
 - You can select both label positions when needed.

13. Click **OK** (Figure 5-13).

 - Labels display in the consolidated sheet in the same order as the first sheet listed in the *Consolidate* dialog box.
 - The data is consolidated in outline format.
 - Each item is collapsed.
 - The 3D references indicate the cells used for each result on the consolidation sheet.

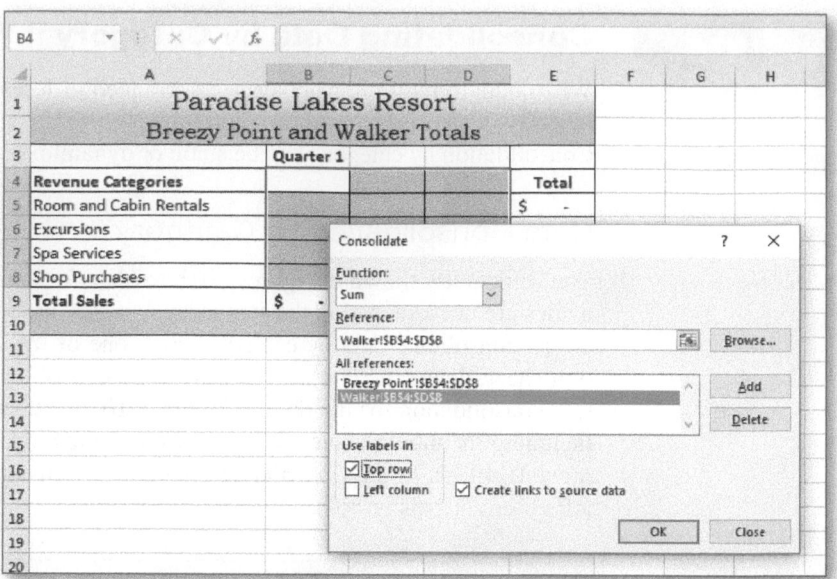

5-12 *Consolidate* dialog box choices for consolidation by category

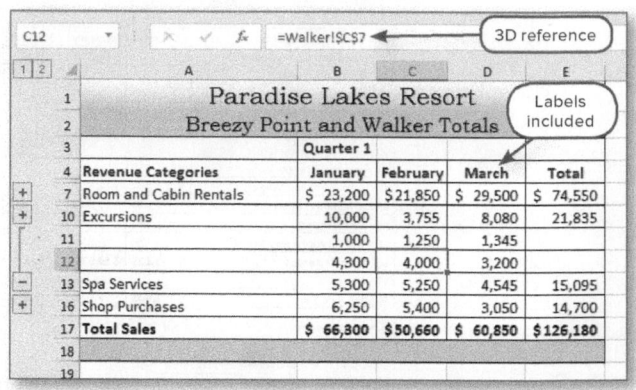

5-13 Consolidation results

<image>SLO 5.4</image> **Working with Grouped Worksheets**

You can group worksheets that have identical layouts for common editing or formatting. Group sheets to change a font, to apply a fill color, to set alignment, to edit data, and more.

Not all commands work for grouped worksheets. For example, you cannot insert a graphic on grouped sheets, nor can you apply conditional formatting. When sheets are grouped and a command is not available, the command button or option is grayed out in the *Ribbon*.

Group Worksheets

When worksheets are grouped, the title bar shows *[Group]* after the file name, and commands or edits affect all sheets in the group. The tabs for grouped worksheets appear white with a hint of the tab color below the sheet name. When grouping sheets, you may find it helpful to set different tab colors so that it is easier to recognize grouped sheets.

To group worksheets, press **Ctrl** or **Shift** to select multiple tab names. Select all sheets in a workbook from the context menu for any tab. To ungroup sheets, click any tab name that is not part of the group. When all sheets are grouped, right-click any tab name and choose **Ungroup Sheets**.

▶ **HOW TO:** Group Worksheets

1. Click the first sheet tab to be included in the group.

2. Press **Shift** and click the last tab name for the group to select adjacent sheets.

 • The first sheet remains visible.

3. Press **Ctrl** and click each tab name to select nonadjacent sheets (Figure 5-14).

4. Right-click any sheet tab and choose **Select All Sheets** to group all sheets in a workbook.

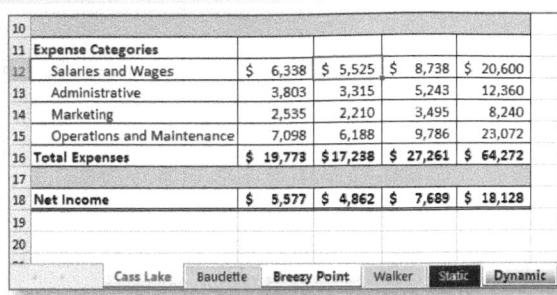

5-14 Nonadjacent grouped worksheets

▶ MORE INFO

If you save a workbook while sheets are grouped, the workbook opens with grouped sheets.

Edit and Format Grouped Worksheets

All worksheets in a group are affected by a command, so worksheets should be identical in layout. If they are not, you might make changes that are not appropriate for every sheet in the group.

One command that you *can* apply to grouped sheets that are not identical is a header or footer command. You can also change page orientation for multiple sheets that are not identical.

▶ **HOW TO:** Edit and Format Grouped Sheets

1. Group the worksheets.

2. Click a cell to be edited.

 • Any sheet in the group can be active or visible.

3. Enter data and press **Enter**.

 • The edit is made on all sheets in the group.

4. Select cells to be formatted.

5. Apply the format.

 • The format displays on all sheets in the group.

6. Ungroup the sheets.

PAUSE & PRACTICE: EXCEL 5-1

For this project, you create a static data consolidation for Paradise Lakes Resort to sum income data. You also create a dynamic consolidation to average income data and group sheets for formatting.

File Needed: **ParadiseLakes-05.xlsx** *(Student data files are available in the Library of your SIMnet account)*
Completed Project File Name: **[your initials] PP E5-1.xlsx**

1. Open the **ParadiseLakes-05** workbook from your student data files and save it as [your initials] PP E5-1.

2. Create a static data consolidation.
 a. Click the **Static** sheet tab.
 b. Select cells **B5:D8** and press **Delete**. The formulas calculate to zero which displays as a hyphen in this worksheet.
 c. Click the **Consolidate** button [*Data* tab, *Data Tools* group].
 d. Verify that the **SUM** function is selected.
 e. If there are references in the *All references* box, select and delete each one.
 f. Click the **Reference** box and click the **Cass Lake** sheet tab.
 g. Select cells **B5:D8**.
 h. Click **Add** in the *Consolidate* dialog box.
 i. Click the **Baudette** sheet tab. Verify that the same cell range (B5:D8) is selected. If it is not selected, select it.
 j. Click **Add** (Figure 5-15).
 k. Click **OK**.

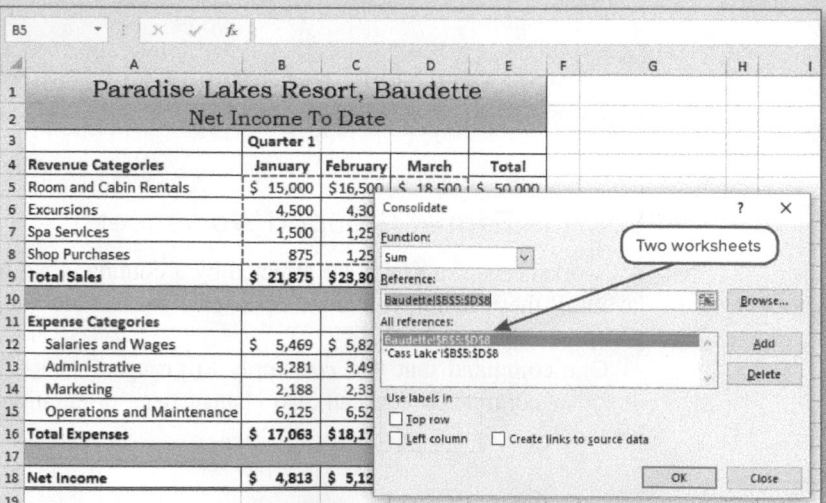

5-15 *Consolidate dialog box for two worksheets in a static consolidation*

3. Create a dynamic data consolidation by category.
 a. Click the **Dynamic** sheet tab.
 b. Select and delete cells **B4:D8**. The labels in row 4 will be consolidated.
 c. Click the **Consolidate** button [*Data* tab, *Data Tools* group].
 d. Click the **Function** drop-down list and choose **AVERAGE**.
 e. If there are references in the *All references* box, select and delete each one.
 f. Click the **Reference** box and click the **Breezy Point** sheet tab.
 g. Select cells **B4:D8** and click **Add** in the *Consolidate* dialog box.
 h. Click the **Walker** sheet tab. Note that the month names are in different order.
 i. Click **Add**.

j. Select the **Top row** box in the *Consolidate* dialog box.

k. Select the **Create links to source data** box (Figure 5-16).

l. Click **OK**. The labels are consolidated in the same order as the **Breezy Point** sheet.

4. Group, format, and edit sheets.

a. Click the **Cass Lake** sheet tab.

b. Press **Shift** and click the **Dynamic** sheet tab to group all sheets.

c. Select cells **A5:A8**.

d. Click the **Increase Indent** button [*Home* tab, *Alignment* group] two times.

e. Select cells **B3:D3**.

f. Click the **Merge & Center** button [*Home* tab, *Alignment* group].

g. Select cell **A9** and edit the label to show Total Revenue.

h. Format columns **B:E** to be **10.00 (75 pixels)** wide.

i. Press **Ctrl+Home**.

j. Right-click the **Cass Lake** sheet tab and choose **Ungroup Sheets**.

k. Select the **Dynamic** sheet. The labels on this sheet are not indented because the outline format uses different row numbers.

l. Select cell **A10**. Press Ctrl and select cell **A13** and then cell **A16**. Increase the indent two times.

m. Press **Ctrl+Home**.

5. Save and close the workbook (Figure 5-17).

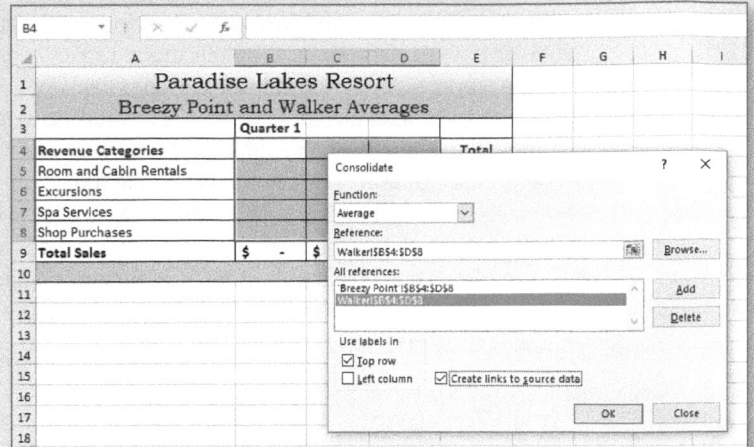

5-16 *Consolidate dialog box for a dynamic consolidation by category*

Paradise Lakes Resort				
Cass Lake and Baudette Net Income				
		Quarter 1		
Revenue Categories	January	February	March	Total
Room and Cabin Rentals	$ 33,850	$ 29,250	$ 41,250	$ 104,350
Excursions	7,250	8,800	11,700	27,750
Spa Services	4,000	4,750	6,050	14,800
Shop Purchases	2,125	2,600	3,150	7,875
Total Revenue	$ 47,225	$ 45,400	$ 62,150	$ 154,775
Expense Categories				
Salaries and Wages	$ 11,806	$ 11,350	$ 15,538	$ 38,694
Administrative	7,084	6,810	9,323	23,216
Marketing	4,723	4,540	6,215	15,478
Operations and Maintenance	13,223	12,712	17,402	43,337
Total Expenses	$ 36,836	$ 35,412	$ 48,477	$ 120,725
Net Income	$ 10,390	$ 9,988	$ 13,673	$ 34,051

Expense % of Total Revenue	
Salaries and Wages	25%
Administrative	15%
Marketing	10%
Operations	28%

Paradise Lakes Resort, Cass Lake				
Net Income To Date				
		Quarter 1		
Revenue Categories	January	February	March	Total
Room and Cabin Rentals	$ 18,850	$ 12,750	$ 22,750	$ 54,350
Excursions	2,750	4,500	6,500	13,750
Spa Services	2,500	3,500	4,200	10,200
Shop Purchases	1,250	1,350	1,500	4,100
Total Revenue	$ 25,350	$ 22,100	$ 34,950	$ 82,400
Expense Categories				
Salaries and Wages	$ 6,338	$ 5,525	$ 8,738	$ 20,600
Administrative	3,803	3,315	5,243	12,360
Marketing	2,535	2,210	3,495	8,240
Operations and Maintenance	7,098	6,188	9,786	23,072
Total Expenses	$ 19,773	$ 17,238	$ 27,261	$ 64,272
Net Income	$ 5,577	$ 4,862	$ 7,689	$ 18,128

Expense % of Total Revenue	
Salaries and Wages	25%
Administrative	15%
Marketing	10%
Operations	28%

Paradise Lakes Resort				
Breezy Point and Walker Averages				
		Quarter 1		
Revenue Categories	January	February	March	Total
Room and Cabin Rentals	$ 11,600	$ 10,925	$ 14,750	$ 37,275
Excursions	5,000	1,878	4,040	10,918
Spa Services	2,650	2,625	2,273	7,548
Shop Purchases	3,125	2,700	1,525	7,350
Total Sales	$ 43,925	$ 32,533	$ 38,263	$ 63,090

5-17 Completed PP E5-1 worksheets

SLO 5.5

Linking Workbooks

Linking workbooks is the process of referring to data in another workbook. Linking may display data, or it may reference data for a formula. Linked workbooks are referred to as *dependent* and *source workbooks*. A dependent workbook includes or refers to data from another workbook. A source workbook includes data that is referenced in a dependent workbook. For workbooks to be linked, they must be accessible over a network, on the same computer, or in the cloud.

Paradise Lakes Resort maintains a consolidated income workbook (a dependent workbook), but each location builds its own workbook (source workbooks). The consolidated workbook displays up-to-the-minute data because it includes links to each of the individual workbooks.

Link workbooks using the *Consolidate* command, or build formulas that refer to cells in other workbooks. Whether the reference is entered in the *Consolidate* dialog box or in a formula, it is an *external reference* because it refers to cells in another workbook.

Link Workbooks Using the Consolidate Command

An external reference includes the name of the workbook in square brackets, the sheet name, cell address(es), and *identifiers*. An identifier is a character such as an exclamation point that marks or signifies a component of the reference. The complete syntax for an external reference is:

='[WorkbookName]WorksheetName'!CellRange

All workbooks must be open when you use the *Consolidate* command.

▶**HOW TO:** Link Workbooks with a Dynamic Data Consolidation

1. Open the dependent workbook.
 - This is the workbook that will refer to another workbook.
2. Delete the contents of cells to be consolidated.
3. Open the source workbook.
 - This is workbook with data that is needed to complete the dependent workbook.
 - If there are multiple source workbooks, open each of them.
4. Return to the dependent workbook.
5. Select the range of cells to be consolidated.
6. Click the **Consolidate** button [*Data* tab, *Data Tools* group].
7. Click the **Function** arrow and choose the function.
8. Select and delete references in the *All references* list.
9. Click the *Reference* box.
10. Click the workbook icon on the Windows taskbar for the first source workbook (Figure 5-18).
 - You can also press **Ctrl+F6** to switch to the next open workbook.

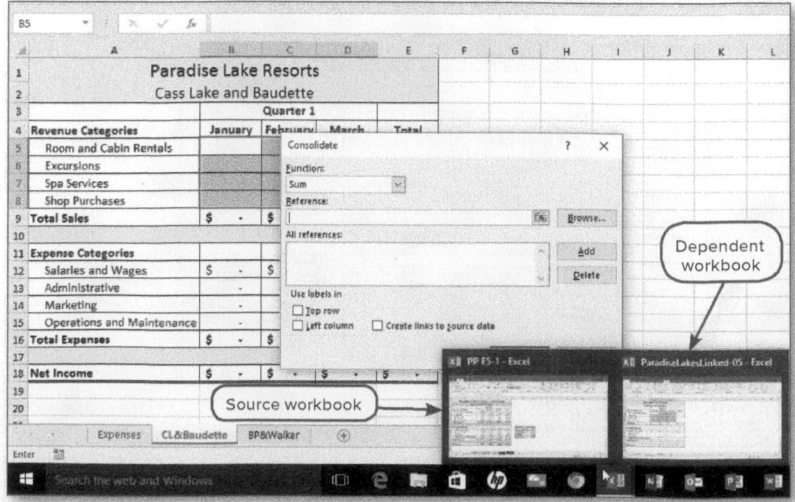

5-18 Open workbook icons on the Windows task bar

11. Select the sheet tab with data to be consolidated.

12. Select the cell range and click **Add**.

 • The reference includes the workbook and sheet names.

13. Click the next tab name and click **Add** (Figure 5-19).

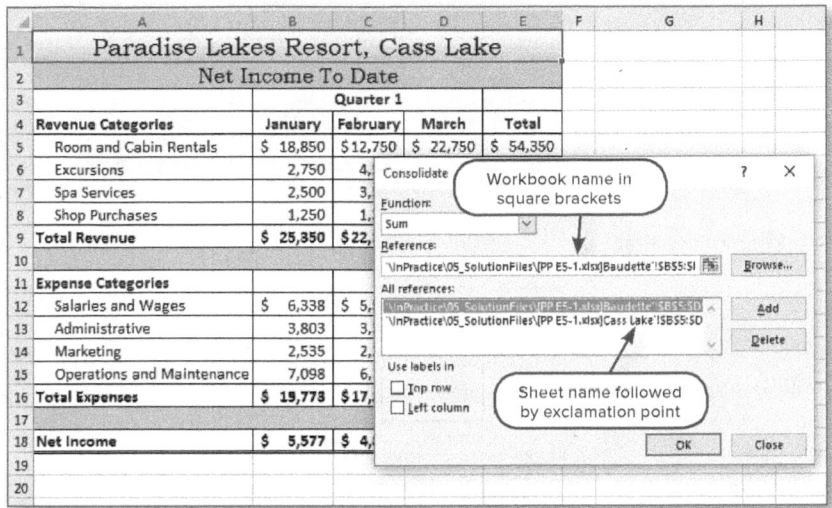

5-19 References with identifiers to another workbook

• If multiple workbooks are used, click the *Reference* box and click the icon for the next source workbook on the Windows taskbar.

• Repeat this step for each sheet or workbook to be used as a source in the consolidation.

14. Select the **Create links to source data** box.

15. Click **OK**.

16. Switch to the dependent workbook.

 • The outline is collapsed.

 • External references are placed above the result cell.

 • External references include the name of the workbook, the sheet name, and the cell address or range (Figure 5-20).

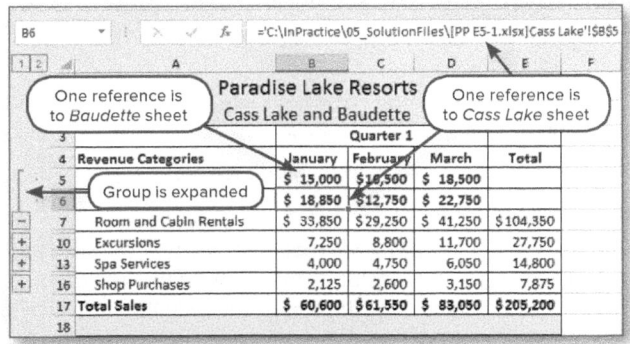

5-20 Dynamic data consolidation with another workbook

Link Workbooks Using a Formula

The *Consolidate* command includes a limited list of functions and requires that the same cell range be referenced in all worksheets. These limitations do not apply in an external reference or linking formula.

An external reference formula refers to cells in another workbook and establishes a link to the source workbook. When the source workbook is open, you can point to build the formula. The source workbook need not be open to build an external reference formula, but you must type the formula with proper syntax and all identifiers.

When you point to create an external reference, it is built with absolute references. You can edit the references to be relative or mixed when you plan to copy the formula.

▶ HOW TO: Link Workbooks with an Addition Formula

1. Open the dependent workbook.
 - This is the workbook that will include a formula with references to another workbook.
2. Open all source workbooks.
3. Return to the dependent workbook.
4. Click the cell for the formula.
5. Type = to start the formula.
 - You can enter an Excel function in the dependent workbook.
6. Click the icon on the Windows taskbar for the first source workbook.
7. Click the sheet tab and click the cell for the first argument.
 - The formula displays in the *Formula* bar with identifiers.
8. Type + for addition.
 - You can use any mathematical operator in a formula.
9. Click the next sheet tab.
 - If the next reference is in another workbook, click its icon on the taskbar.
10. Click the cell for the next formula argument (Figure 5-21).
 - The cell address need not be in the same location as the first sheet or workbook.
11. Repeat these steps to build the formula.
12. Press **Enter** (Figure 5-22).
 - The dependent workbook displays the formula result.
 - The reference includes the name of the workbook, the sheet name, and absolute cell references.
 - You can also click the **Enter** button in the *Formula* bar to complete the formula and return to the dependent workbook.

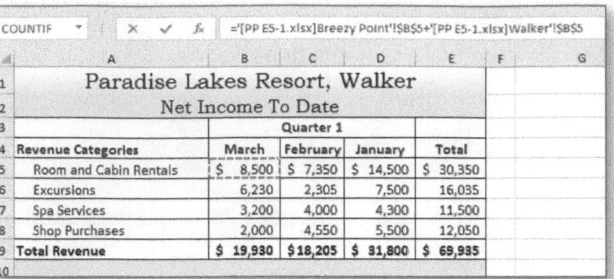

5-21 Formula to link workbooks

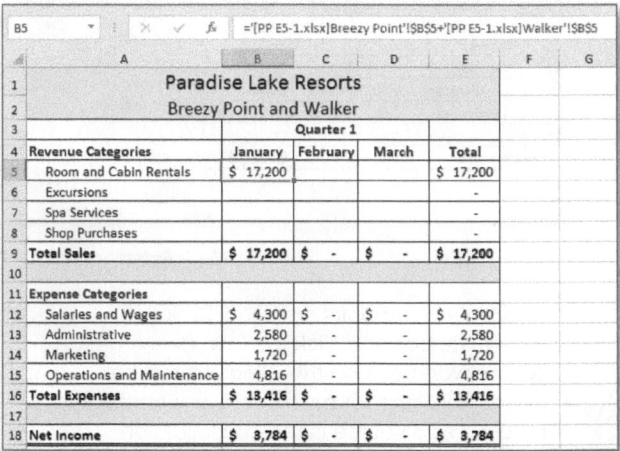

5-22 An external reference formula in the dependent workbook

▶ **ANOTHER WAY**

Arrange open workbooks side by side or horizontally tiled and switch between them by pointing and clicking.

Examine and Edit Links

An external reference formula creates a ***link*** to the source workbook, a data connection. The link specifies the file name and location at the time the formula was created. You can choose how links are handled when a workbook is opened from the *Trust Center Settings* for *External Content* (Excel *Options*) (Figure 5-23).

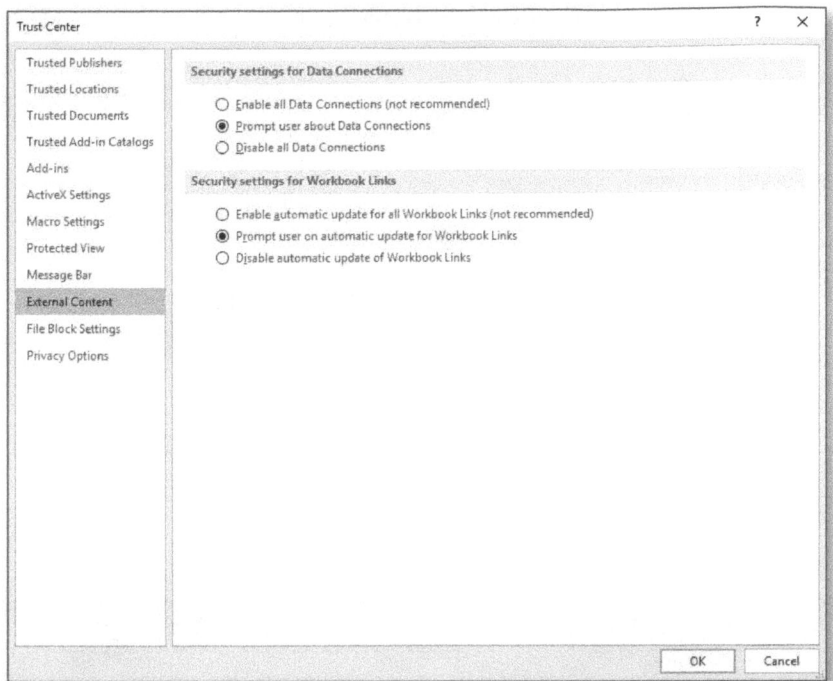

5-23 *Trust Center Settings for* External Content

Links can be updated when the source workbook is accessible. If a source workbook was renamed or moved to another location, the link cannot be updated. When this happens, a dependent workbook shows a result for the formula, but it may not be accurate until you edit the link.

You can break a link to remove the data connection but keep formula results as values in the dependent workbook.

▶ **HOW TO: Update Links in a Workbook**

1. Open the dependent workbook.
 - This workbook has a formula that refers to another workbook.
 - The source workbook need not be open.

5-24 Message box when opening linked workbooks

2. Click **Enable Content** in the security message bar.

3. Click **Update** in the message box (Figure 5-24).
 - If the source workbook is accessible, the data is refreshed.
 - If the source workbook is not accessible, a message box displays options to continue or edit the links.

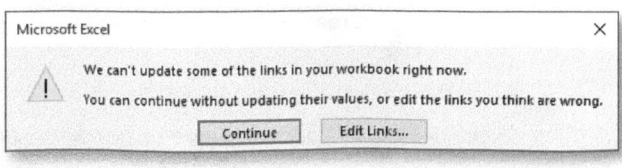

5-25 Message box when links are not accessible

4. Click **Continue** if the links cannot be updated (Figure 5-25).

5. Click the **Edit Links** button [*Data* tab, *Connections* group].

 - The *Edit Links* dialog box opens.
 - You can open this dialog box at any time to examine links (Figure 5-26).

6. Click **Change Source**.

 - You can find a file that has been moved to change its *Location*.

7. Navigate to find the file and click to select its name.

8. Click **OK** to update the location.

9. Click **Update Values**.

10. Click **Close**.

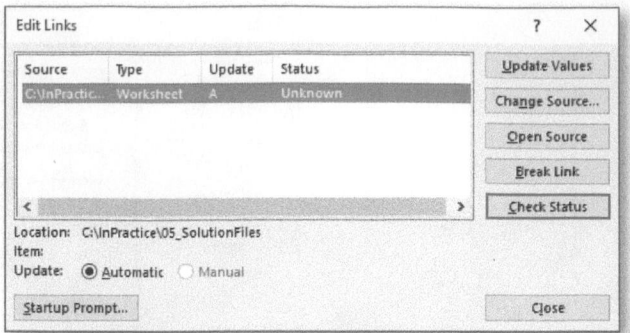

5-26 *Edit Links* dialog box

PAUSE & PRACTICE: EXCEL 5-2

For this project, you create a dynamic consolidation with links to another workbook. You also create and copy an external reference formula.

Files Needed: *[your initials] PP E5-1.xlsx* and *ParadiseLakesLinked-05.xlsx (Student data files are available in the* Library *of your SIMnet account)*
Completed Project File Name: *[your initials] PP E5-2.xlsx*

1. Open the *ParadiseLakesLinked-05* workbook from your student data files.

2. Save the workbook as [your initials] PP E5-2. This is the dependent workbook.

3. Open the *[your initials] PP E5-1* workbook completed in *Pause & Practice 5-1*. This is the source workbook.

4. Use the *Consolidate* command to link workbooks.
 a. Return to the *[your initials] PP E5-2* workbook and click the **CL&Baudette** sheet tab.
 b. Select cells **B5:D8**.
 c. Click the **Consolidate** button [*Data* tab, *Data Tools* group].
 d. Select and delete any references in the *All references* list.
 e. Verify that **SUM** is selected as the function.
 f. Click the *Reference* box.
 g. Click the icon on the Windows taskbar for *[your initials] PP E5-1*.
 h. Click the **Cass Lake** sheet tab and select cells **B5:D8**.
 i. Click **Add**.
 j. Click the **Baudette** sheet tab and click **Add**.
 k. Select the **Create links to source data** box.
 l. Click **OK**.

5. Switch to the *[your initials] PP E5-2* workbook and format columns **B:E** to be **10.00 (75 pixels)** wide.

6. Click the *Expand* button for row **7** and click cell **B6** (Figure 5-27).

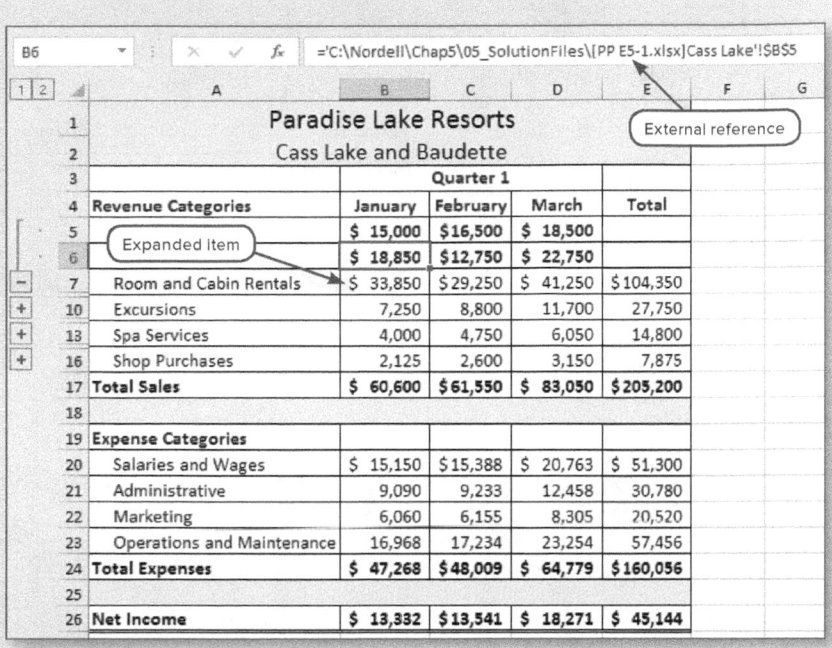

5-27 Dynamic consolidation

7. Link workbooks using a formula.
 a. Click the **BP&Walker** sheet tab in *[your initials]* **PP E5-2**.
 b. Click cell **B5**.
 c. Type = to start the formula.
 d. Press **Ctrl+F6** or click the icon on the Windows taskbar for *[your initials]* **PP E5-1**.
 e. Click the **Breezy Point** worksheet tab.
 f. Select cell **B5** and type + for addition.
 g. Click the **Walker** sheet tab (Figure 5-28).
 h. Select cell **D5** for the January amount and press **Enter**.

8. Edit and copy the formula.
 a. Select cell **B5** in the **BP&Walker** sheet.
 b. Click the *Formula* bar.
 c. Delete the dollar signs in **B5** to display **B5** and in **D5** to display **D5**, both relative references (Figure 5-29).
 d. Press **Enter**.
 e. Copy the formula in cell **B5** to cells **B6:B8**.

9. Create, edit, and copy linking formulas.
 a. Select cell **C5** in the **BP&Walker** sheet and type = to start the formula.
 b. Press **Ctrl+F6** or click the icon on the Windows taskbar for *[your initials]* **PP E5-1**.

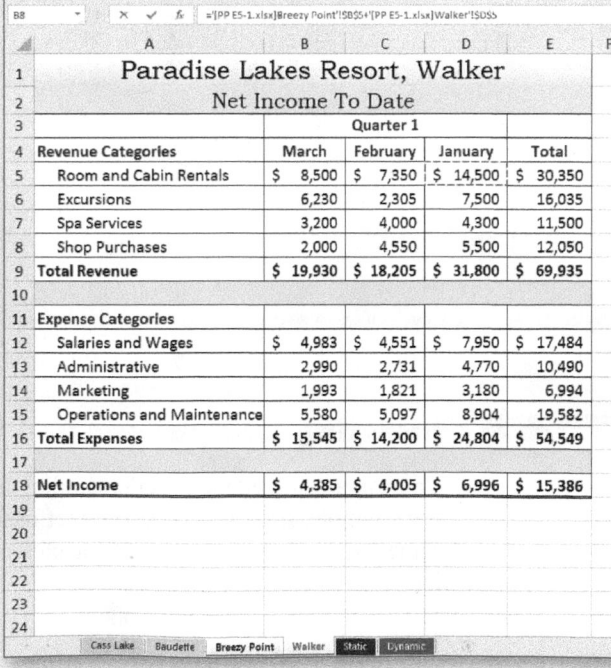

5-28 Point to build an external reference formula

c. Click the **Breezy Point** worksheet tab, select cell **C5** and type + for addition.
d. Click the **Walker** sheet tab, select cell **C5**, and press **Enter**. The linking formula is calculated in the **BP&Walker** sheet.
e. Select cell **C5** and click the *Formula* bar.
f. Delete the dollar signs in both occurrences of **C5** to display **C5**, and press **Enter**.
g. Select cell **D5** and type = to start the formula.
h. Press **Ctrl+F6** or click the icon on the Windows taskbar for *[your initials]* **PP E5-1**.
i. Click the **Breezy Point** worksheet tab, select cell **D5**, and type + for addition.
j. Click the **Walker** sheet tab, select cell **B5** for March, and press **Enter**.
k. Select cell **D5**, click the *Formula* bar, delete the dollar signs in **D5** and **B5** to create relative references, and press **Enter**.
l. Select cells **C5:D5** and copy the formulas to cells **C6:D8**.
m. Select and format cells **B6:D8** as **Comma Style** with no decimals.

10. Save and close the workbook (Figure 5-30).

11. Close *[your initials]* **PP E5-1** without saving it.

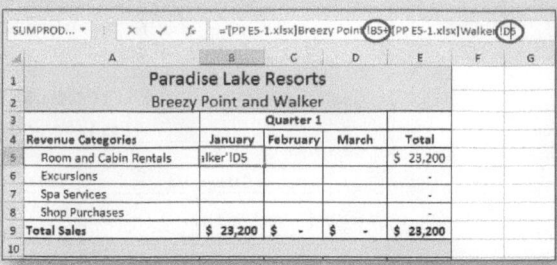

5-29 Linking formula edited to use relative references

Paradise Lake Resorts				
Cass Lake and Baudette				
		Quarter 1		
Revenue Categories	January	February	March	Total
	$ 15,000	$ 16,500	$ 18,500	
	$ 18,850	$ 12,750	$ 22,750	
Room and Cabin Rentals	$ 33,850	$ 29,250	$ 41,250	$ 104,350
Excursions	7,250	8,800	11,700	27,750
Spa Services	4,000	4,750	6,050	14,800
Shop Purchases	2,125	2,600	3,150	7,875
Total Sales	$ 60,600	$ 61,550	$ 83,050	$ 205,200
Expense Categories				
Salaries and Wages	$ 15,150	$ 15,388	$ 20,763	$ 51,300
Administrative	9,090	9,233	12,458	30,780
Marketing	6,060	6,155	8,305	20,520
Operations and Maintenance	16,968	17,234	23,254	57,456
Total Expenses	$ 47,268	$ 48,009	$ 64,779	$ 160,056
Net Income	$ 13,332	$ 13,541	$ 18,271	$ 45,144

Paradise Lake Resorts				
Breezy Point and Walker				
		Quarter 1		
Revenue Categories	January	February	March	Total
Room and Cabin Rentals	$ 23,200	$ 21,850	$ 29,500	$ 74,550
Excursions	$ 10,000	$ 3,755	$ 8,080	21,835
Spa Services	$ 5,300	$ 5,250	$ 4,545	15,095
Shop Purchases	$ 6,250	$ 5,400	$ 3,050	14,700
Total Sales	$ 44,750	$ 36,255	$ 45,175	$ 126,180
Expense Categories				
Salaries and Wages	$ 11,188	$ 9,064	$ 11,294	$ 31,545
Administrative	6,713	5,438	6,776	18,927
Marketing	4,475	3,626	4,518	12,618
Operations and Maintenance	12,530	10,151	12,649	35,330
Total Expenses	$ 34,905	$ 28,279	$ 35,237	$ 98,420
Net Income	$ 9,845	$ 7,976	$ 9,939	$ 27,760

5-30 Completed PP E-2 worksheets

SLO 5.6

Inserting Illustrations in a Worksheet

You can assist readers in understanding and navigating through your work in different ways. For example, include a link to direct users to another worksheet or to other locations in the same sheet. You might include a picture of folder contents to help a coworker learn file location.

SmartArt Graphics

A *SmartArt* graphic is an illustration, usually with text, in an Excel worksheet. Examples of *SmartArt* are organization charts, matrices, pyramids, bulleted lists, and similar diagrams.

SmartArt graphics are text-focused but some may include pictures. Figure 5-31 is a *SmartArt* graphic with text and pictures.

A *SmartArt* graphic has a pane for entering text, but you can also type directly inside the component shapes. The text pane appears on the left or right side of the graphic depending where the graphic is positioned. As you type an entry, the text and its shape are sized to fit the content.

A *SmartArt* graphic is not linked to worksheet data.

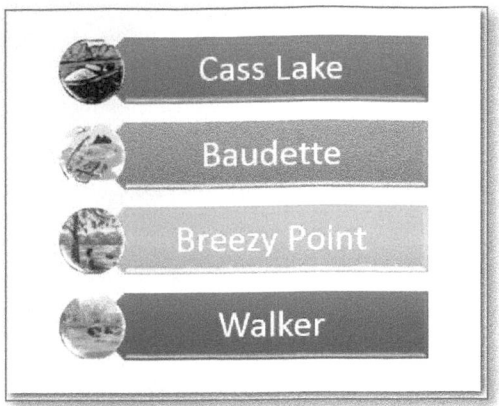

5-31 *SmartArt* graphic with four shapes and pictures

▶ HOW TO: Insert a SmartArt Graphic

1. Click the worksheet tab for the *SmartArt*.

2. Click the **Insert a SmartArt Graphic** button [*Insert* tab, *Illustrations* group].

 • The *Choose a SmartArt Graphic* dialog box opens (Figure 5-32).

3. Choose the category from the list on the left.

 • The *All* category displays all available designs.
 • Click a thumbnail image to see a preview and a description on the right.

4. Select the *SmartArt* graphic and click **OK** (Figure 5-33).

 • A default object is placed at a default size in the worksheet.
 • The *Name* box displays *Diagram N*, where "N" is a number.
 • Display or hide the text pane by clicking the control at the left or right edge of the graphic frame

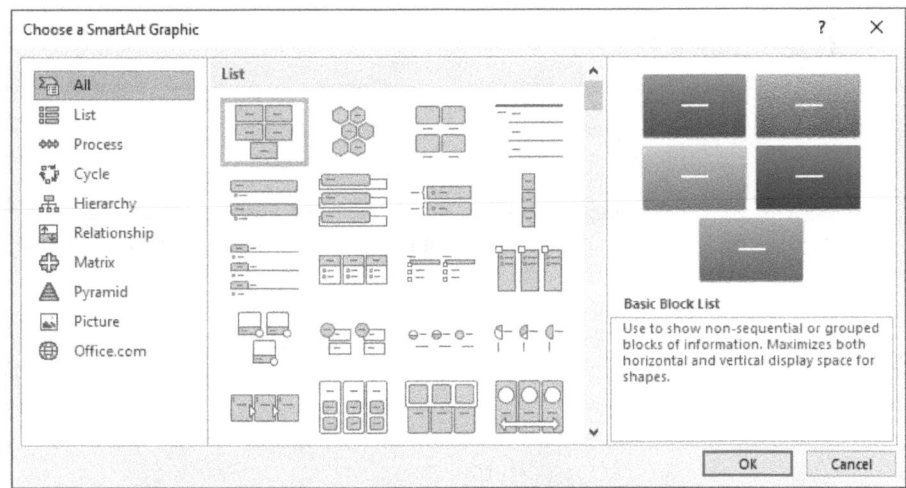

5-32 *Choose a SmartArt Graphic* dialog box

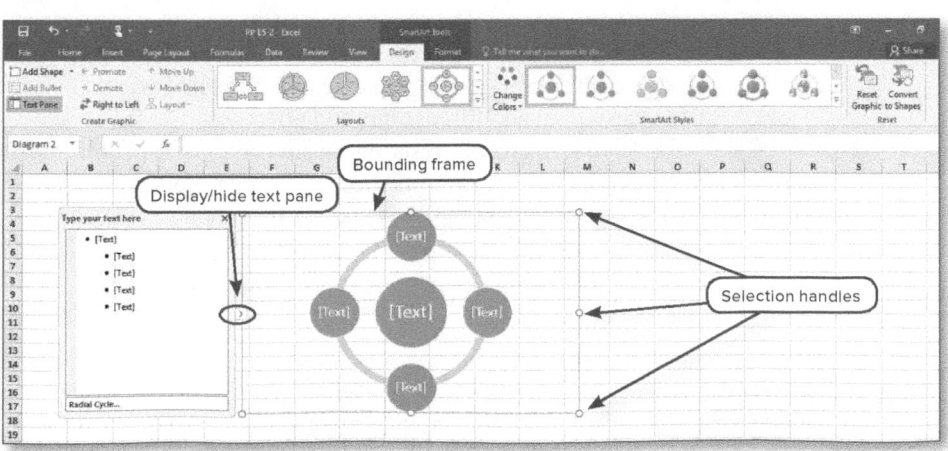

5-33 *SmartArt* graphic with text frame

or by clicking the **Text Pane** button [*SmartArt Tools Design* tab, *Create Graphic* group].

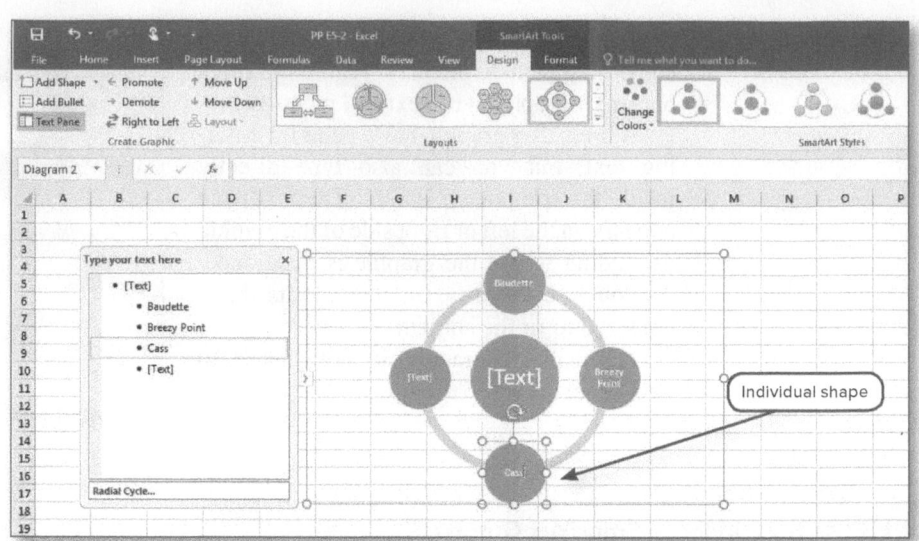

5-34 Text entered in *SmartArt* graphic

5. Click a shape and type the text (Figure 5-34).

 - The entry appears in the shape and in the text pane.
 - The label is sized to fit the shape as you type.
 - You can edit text within the shape or the text pane.
 - Each shape has its own selection handles and frame.

6. Click another shape or click the frame of the *SmartArt* object.

SmartArt Tools

A *SmartArt* graphic is an object that you can select, size, and format. It has selection and sizing handles as well as a bounding frame, similar to a chart object. A *SmartArt* graphic is one object that consists of several smaller shapes.

When you insert a *SmartArt* image, it is placed with the default number of shapes. For many *SmartArt* diagrams, you can add or remove shapes. Each individual shape in a *SmartArt* object has its own selection handles, a rotation handle, and a bounding frame.

> **MORE INFO**
>
> A few *SmartArt* shapes are limited in the number of smaller shapes they contain due to the layout and purpose of the diagram.

When a *SmartArt* object is selected, the *SmartArt Tools Design* and *Format* tabs are available. From the tabs, you can change to a different image, choose a style, add a shape, reposition shapes, and add fill, outline, and effects.

A *SmartArt* graphic rests on an invisible, transparent layer in the worksheet, covering cells. You can activate a worksheet cell that appears within the frame of the *SmartArt* by typing the cell address in the *Name* box or by moving the image.

▶ HOW TO: Format a SmartArt Graphic

1. Select the *SmartArt* graphic.

 - Click near one of the shapes to select the diagram.
 - The bounding frame is a rectangle that surrounds the graphic.

2. Click the **More** button [*SmartArt Tools Design* tab, *SmartArt Styles* group] to open the gallery.

3. Point to a style thumbnail to see a *Live Preview*.

4. Click a style icon to apply it.

5. Click the **Change Colors** button [*SmartArt Tools Design* tab, *SmartArt Styles* group].

6. Point to a color thumbnail to see a *Live Preview*.

7. Click a color scheme to apply it.

8. Click an individual shape in the graphic.

9. Click the arrow with the **Shape Fill** button [*SmartArt Tools Format* tab, *Shape Styles* group].

10. Choose a color from the gallery (Figure 5-35).

11. Point to a corner sizing handle on the *SmartArt* frame.

 - The pointer displays a resize arrow.

12. Drag the resize arrow to make the graphic larger or smaller.

13. Point to the *SmartArt* frame.

 - The pointer displays a move arrow.

14. Drag the graphic to the desired location.

15. Click a worksheet cell to deselect the *SmartArt* graphic.

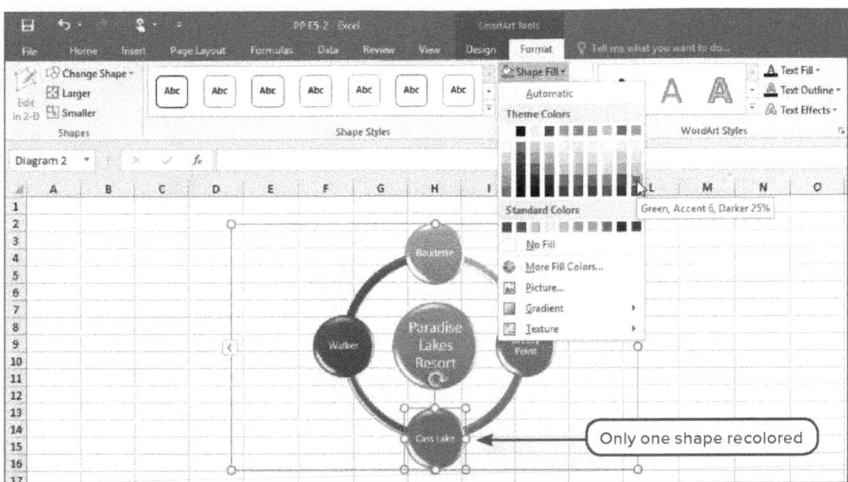

5-35 Shape Fill color gallery for a *SmartArt* shape

Screenshots

A **screenshot** is a picture of a full or partial computer screen inserted as an object in a worksheet. You can capture an image of an open window or select a portion of a document or text from a web site. When capturing screenshots of web pages or another person's work, you should have permission from the author or owner to use the image.

The *Take a Screenshot* button is located on the *Insert* tab in the *Illustrations* group. When you click the button, you see a gallery of open application windows (Figure 5-36). If you select one of the thumbnail windows, a capture of the full screen is placed in your worksheet. To select part of the window, choose **Screen Clipping** from the gallery.

Once you place a screenshot in the worksheet, it is a picture object that you can format, position, and size.

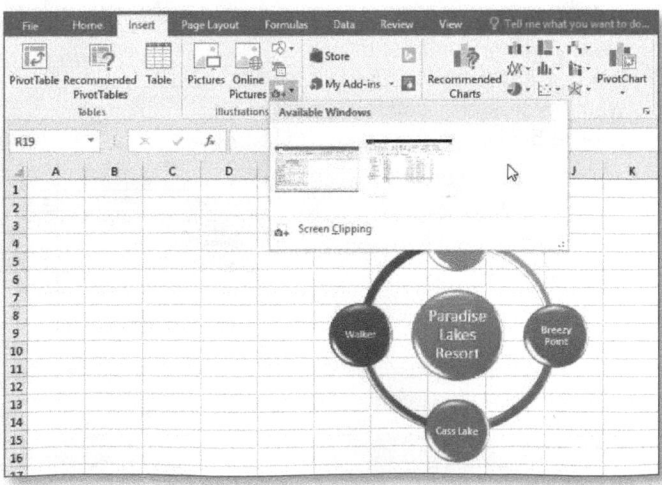

5-36 Screenshot gallery with two available windows

> **MORE INFO**
>
> When you take a screen clipping, open only two windows, one to hold the screenshot and the other to provide the image.

▶ HOW TO: Insert a Screenshot Clipping in a Worksheet

1. Click the sheet tab where the screenshot will be inserted.

2. Open the workbook, document, or web site that contains the content to be captured.
 - Open only two windows or applications.
 - Open another window for the same workbook to capture an image from another worksheet.

3. Click a cell in the worksheet that will hold the captured image.

4. Click the **Take a Screenshot** button [*Insert* tab, *Illustrations* group].

5. From the gallery, choose **Screen Clipping**.
 - The focus switches to the next open window.
 - The entire screen dims in a few seconds.
 - The pointer shape in the dimmed window is a crosshair.

6. Draw a rectangle around the content to be captured with the crosshair pointer. (Figure 5-37).
 - The selected area is no longer dim.

7. Release the mouse button (Figure 5-38).
 - The focus returns to the worksheet.
 - The screenshot displays at a default size and position.

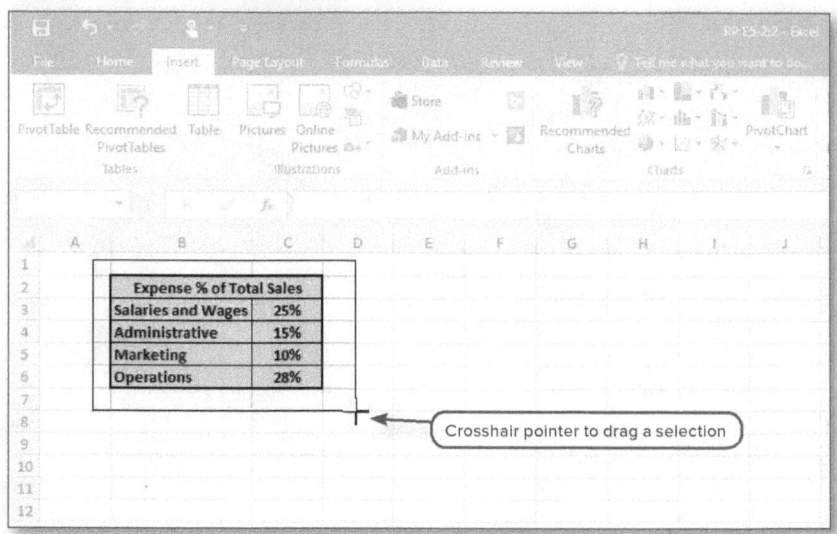

5-37 Dimmed screen for screenshot

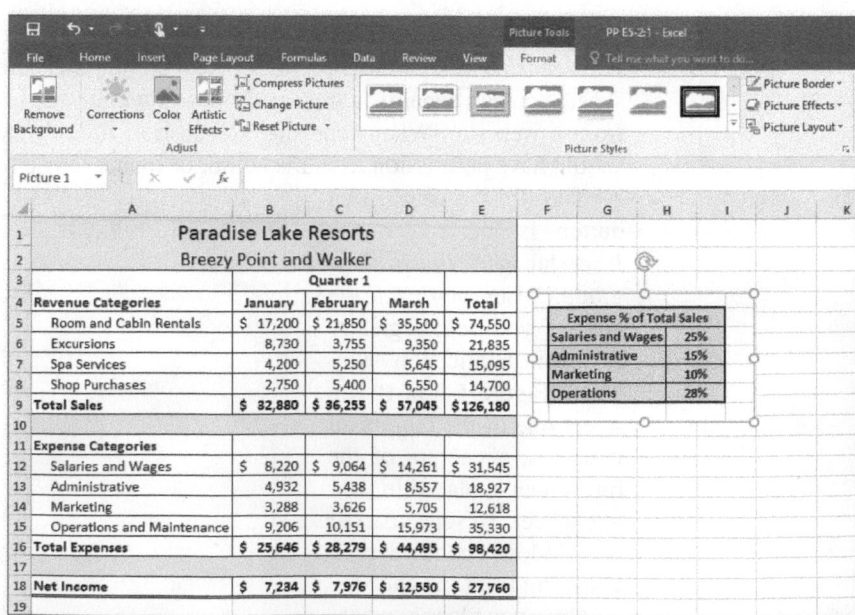

5-38 Screenshot image placed in worksheet

Picture Tools

A screenshot graphic is a picture object with selection and sizing handles, a rotation handle, and a bounding frame. When the object is selected, the *Picture Tools Format* tab is available with command groups for altering the appearance of the image.

Like a *SmartArt* graphic, a screenshot image is placed on the invisible, transparent layer of the worksheet.

▶ HOW TO: Work with Picture tools

1. Select the screenshot or picture object.
 - The bounding frame is rectangular.
 - Selection and sizing handles appear on the bounding frame.
2. Click the **More** button [*Picture Tools Format* tab, *Picture Styles* group].
 - The gallery includes preset combinations of border, fill, and rotation settings.
3. Point to a thumbnail to see a *Live Preview*.
4. Click an icon to apply the style (Figure 5-39).
5. Click the **Artistic Effects** button [*Picture Tools Format* tab, *Adjust* group].

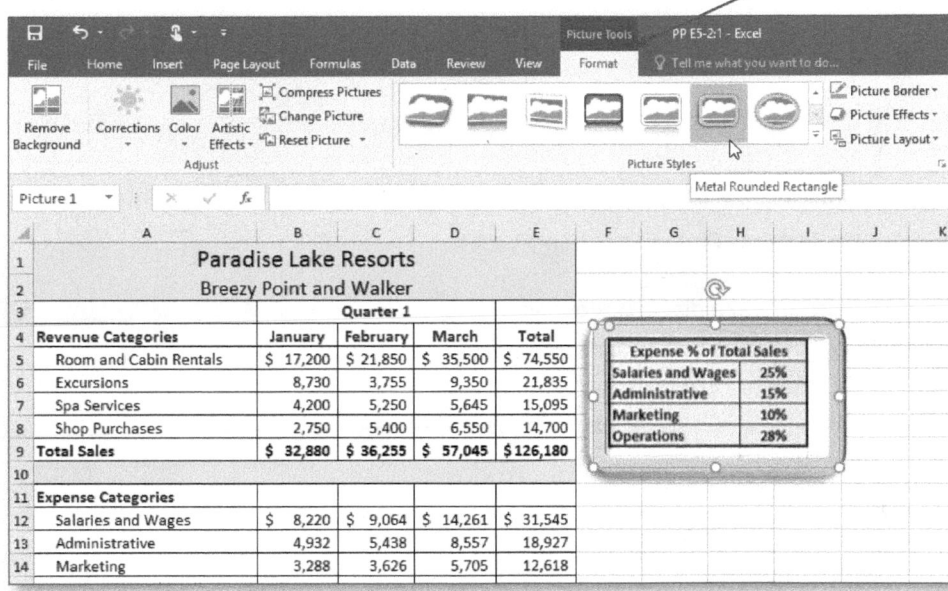

5-39 Style applied to a screenshot

6. Point to a thumbnail to see a *Live Preview*.
 - Many effects may not be appropriate for worksheet images.
7. Click an icon to apply an effect.
8. Click the **Rotate** button [*Picture Tools Format* tab, *Arrange* group].
9. Point to a menu choice to see a *Live Preview*.
10. Click a rotation option to apply the setting.
11. Point to a corner sizing handle on the picture border to display a resize arrow.
 - Use a corner handle to size proportionally.
12. Drag the resize arrow to make the picture larger or smaller.
13. Point to the picture border.
 - The pointer displays a move arrow.
14. Drag the picture to the desired location.
15. Click a worksheet cell to deselect the picture object.

Pictures

You can place pictures in an Excel worksheet for clarification, emphasis, or visual appeal. Insert pictures from a file or online sources. Always investigate copyright issues when you use pictures from outside sources.

The *Pictures* and *Online Pictures* buttons are located on the *Insert* tab in the *Illustrations* group. The *Pictures* command inserts an image from your network, your computer, or your cloud sources. The *Online Pictures* command opens a dialog box in which you search for pictures related to a key term. Excel can use popular image formats such as JPEG, PNG, and TIFF, and you can do simple editing such as changing colors or adding shadows.

> **MORE INFO**
>
> Do not use too many pictures in a worksheet so that you do not draw attention away from the data.

▶ HOW TO: Insert a Picture from a File

1. Click a blank cell in the worksheet.
2. Click the **Pictures From File** button [*Insert* tab, *Illustrations* group].
 - The *Insert Picture* dialog box opens.
3. Navigate to the location with the image file.
4. Select the image file (Figure 5-40).
 - Adjust the view to show icons if you want to see a thumbnail of the picture.
5. Click **Insert**.
 - The picture appears in the worksheet at a default size and position (Figure 5-41).

5-40 Select a picture from a file

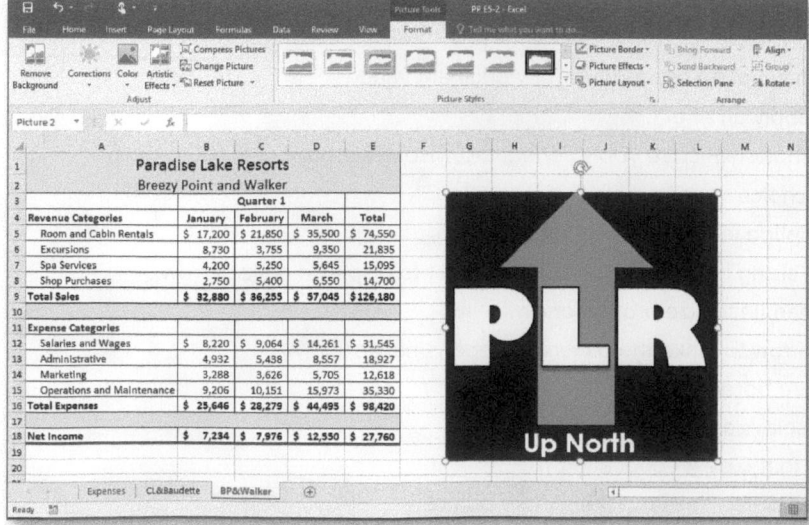

5-41 Picture placed at default size and position

- The picture object is selected.
- The *Picture Tools Format* tab displays.

6. Point to a corner selection handle to display a resize arrow and drag the pointer to shrink or enlarge the image.

7. Point to the image frame to display a move pointer and drag the picture to the desired location in the sheet.

SLO 5.7

Inserting Hyperlinks in a Worksheet

A *hyperlink* is a clickable text string or object that, when clicked, moves the pointer to another location. A hyperlink can also open another workbook or a web page. You might use a hyperlink to open a source workbook, to switch to another worksheet, or to navigate to a *SmartArt* image.

Cell Hyperlinks

A cell hyperlink is a text shortcut or jump term in a cell. It appears as underlined text in the color set in the document theme for hyperlinks. After a hyperlink is created, you can change the font color, font name, and font size from the mini toolbar or from the *Font* group on the *Home* tab.

> **ANOTHER WAY**
>
> The keyboard shortcut to insert a hyperlink is **Ctrl+K**.

The *Hyperlink* button is located on the *Insert* command tab. You can also insert a hyperlink from the shortcut menu for a cell.

> **MORE INFO**
>
> You can choose the hyperlink text color by clicking the *Colors* button on the *Page Layout* tab and selecting *Customize Colors*.

▶ **HOW TO:** Create a Cell Hyperlink

1. Click the cell where the hyperlink text should appear.
2. Click the **Hyperlink** button [*Insert* tab, *Links* group].
 - The *Insert Hyperlink* dialog box opens.
3. Select **Place in This Document** in the *Link to* list on the left.
 - The *Or select a place in this document* box displays locations in the workbook.
 - The names of existing sheets are listed in the *Cell Reference* group.
 - The *Defined Names* group displays range names in the workbook.
 - The *Cell Reference* and *Defined Names* groups have expand and collapse buttons.
4. Select a worksheet name to jump to that sheet.
 - Choose the name of the current sheet if the hyperlink will move to a location on this sheet.
5. Click the *Type the cell reference* box.

6. Type the cell address that should be selected when the hyperlink is clicked.
 - The default is cell **A1**.

7. Click the *Text to display* box and enter text for the hyperlink cell.
 - Select and delete default text.

8. Click the **ScreenTip** button (Figure 5-42).
 - The *Set Hyperlink ScreenTip* dialog box opens.

9. Type an optional *ScreenTip*.
 - The default *ScreenTip* identifies the file and provides basic instructions for a hyperlink.

10. Click **OK** to close the *Set Hyperlink ScreenTip* dialog box.

11. Click **OK** to close the *Insert Hyperlink* dialog box (Figure 5-43).
 - The underlined hyperlink text appears in the cell.
 - When you point to the link, the *ScreenTip* displays.

12. Click the hyperlink to navigate to the location.

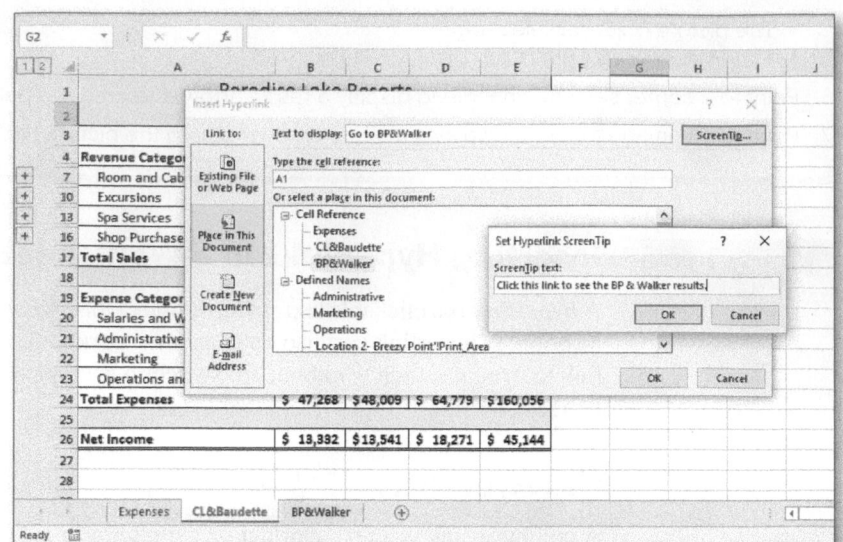

5-42 *Hyperlink* and custom *ScreenTip* dialog boxes

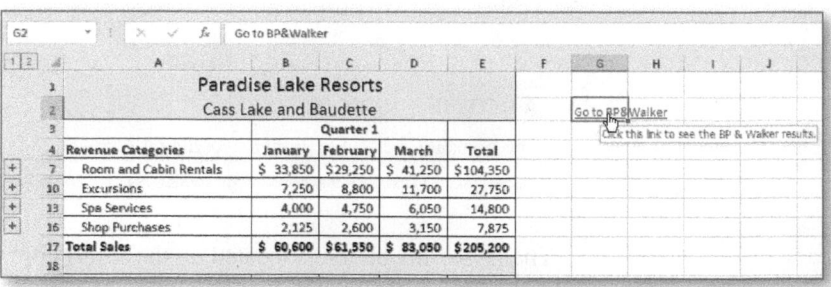

5-43 *Hyperlink* text and its *ScreenTip*

When you choose *Existing File or Web Page* in the *Insert Hyperlink* dialog box, you browse to the location for the file or the web page. The path to the file or the URL for the web address appears in the *Address* box.

Object Hyperlinks

An object hyperlink is a shortcut assigned to an object such as a *SmartArt* graphic, a chart, or a picture. There is no underlined text, but you can use the hyperlink *ScreenTip* to provide information.

▶ **HOW TO:** Create a Hyperlink to Open a File

1. Select the image or object.
 - The selection handles should be visible.

2. Click the **Hyperlink** button [*Insert* tab, *Links* group].
 - The *Insert Hyperlink* dialog box opens.

3. Select **Existing File or Web Page** in the *Link to* list on the left.

- The *Look in* box displays the name of the current folder.
- The names of workbooks in the current folder are listed.
- You can navigate to other folders in this dialog box.

4. Select a workbook name.

- The file name is entered in the *Address* box (Figure 5-44).

5. Click the **ScreenTip** button.

6. Type text for a *ScreenTip* to describe the action.

7. Click **OK** to close the *Set Hyperlink ScreenTip* dialog box.

8. Click **OK** to close the *Insert Hyperlink* dialog box (Figure 5-45).

9. Click a worksheet cell to deselect the object.

10. Point to the object to see the *ScreenTip*.

11. Click the object to open the file.

- The file opens with the active sheet and cell based on its last save command.

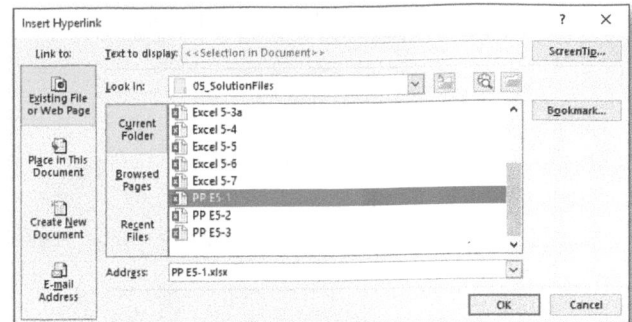

5-44 Workbook name selected for hyperlink

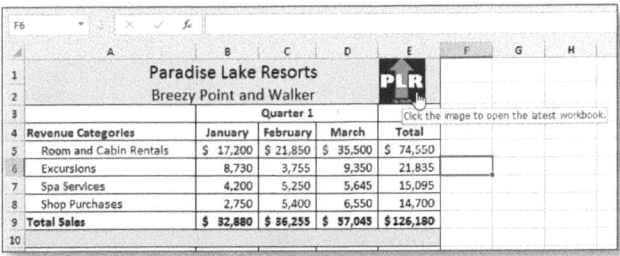

5-45 Object hyperlink in worksheet

To remove a hyperlink from a cell or from an object, right-click the cell or the object and choose **Remove Hyperlink**. You can also edit a hyperlink from the shortcut menu to change the *ScreenTip*, reset the file, or change a URL address.

SLO 5.8 Safeguarding a Workbook

Excel has two commands that provide a simple level of security to protect your work from unwanted changes. One command is a courtesy message or warning and one command is the assignment of a password.

Mark a Workbook as Final

To let others know that your work is complete and should not be edited, use the *Mark as Final* command which sets a read-only file property. When the workbook opens, you will see a security message bar, an icon in the *Status* bar, and a *[Read-Only]* label in the title bar. You and others can remove the property by clicking the *Edit Anyway* button in the security message bar.

> **ANOTHER WAY**
>
> Remove the *Mark as Final* property by clicking the *Protect Workbook* button [*File* tab, *Info* option] and choosing *Mark as Final*.

▶**HOW TO:** Mark a Workbook as Final

1. Save the workbook.
2. Click the **Protect Workbook** button [*File* tab, *Info* option].
 • Protection commands display.
3. Select **Mark as Final**.
 • A message box informs you that the file will be marked and saved (Figure 5-46).
4. Click **OK**.
 • The workbook is resaved with the same file name.
 • If the workbook has not yet been saved, the *Save As* dialog box opens so that you can choose the file location and name.
 • A second message box provides details about the *Mark as Final* command (Figure 5-47). (There is an option to hide this message box, so you may not see it).
5. Click **OK**.
 • The security bar shows the property (Figure 5-48).
 • The icon on the *Status* bar indicates that the workbook is final.

5-46 Message box that workbook will be saved and marked as final

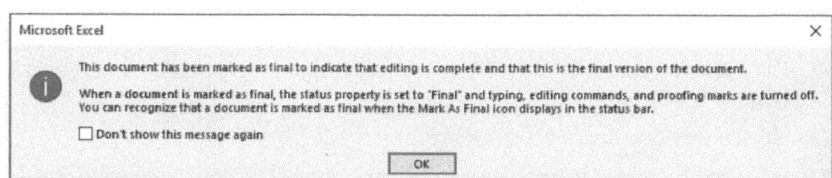

5-47 Details about the *Mark as Final* property

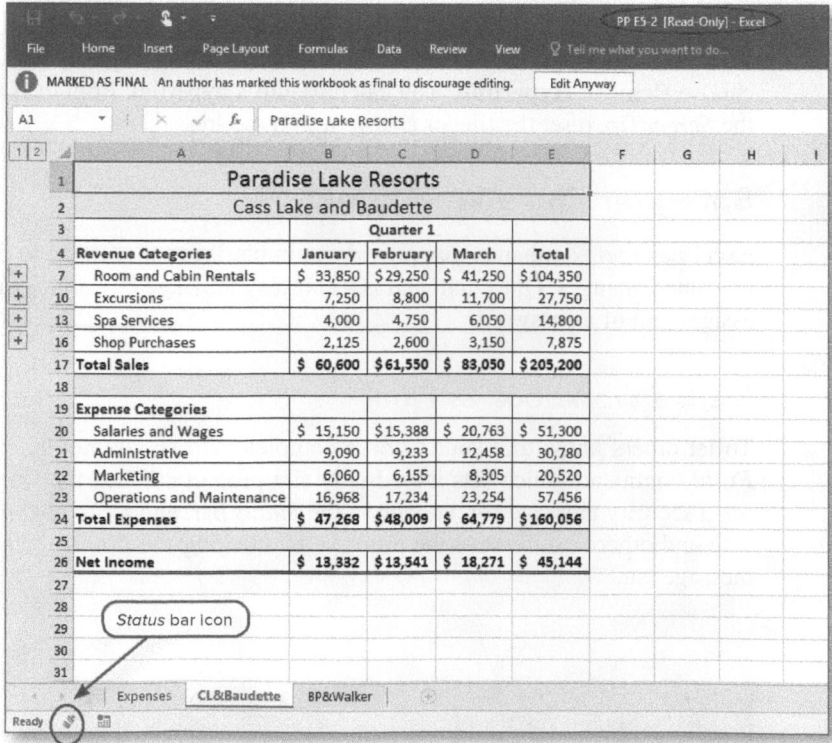

5-48 Workbook that is marked as final

Encrypt a Workbook with a Password

Password protection requires that you type the password as you open the workbook. After you set a password, the *Protect Workbook* button [*File* tab, *Info* pane] indicates that the workbook requires a password as shown in Figure 5-49.

To remove a password, you must open the workbook and enter the password. Then click the **Protect Workbook** button, select **Encrypt with Password**, delete the password, leave the *Password* box empty, and resave the workbook.

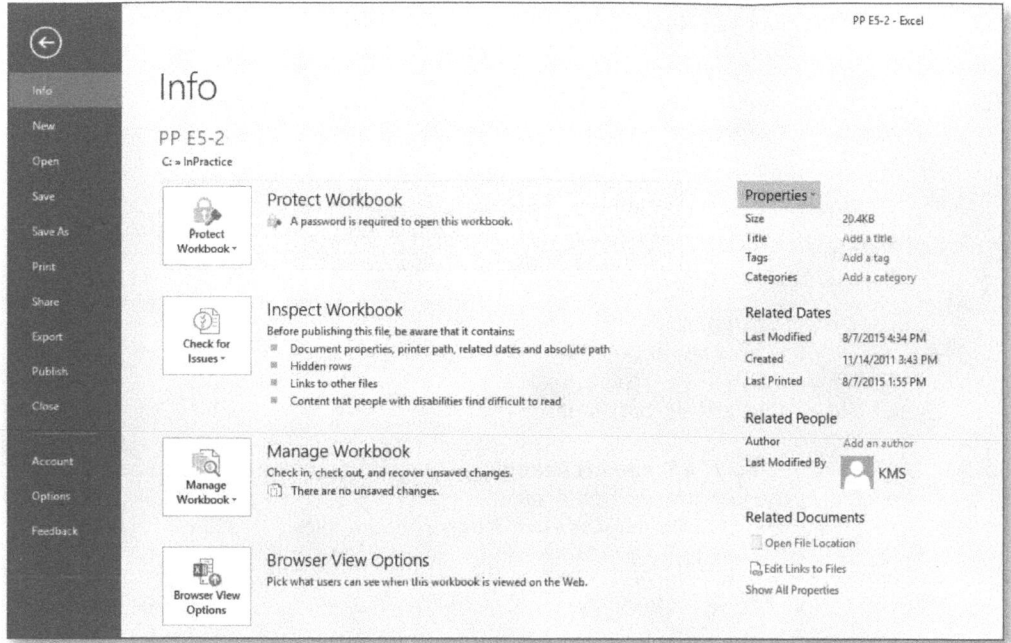

5-49 *Info* pane for a workbook with a password

▶ **HOW TO: Password Protect a Workbook**

1. Click the **Protect Workbook** button [*File* tab, *Info* pane].
2. Select **Encrypt with Password**.
 - The *Encrypt Document* dialog box opens.
3. Type a password in the *Password* box (Figure 5-50).
 - Passwords are hidden as you type them.
 - Passwords are case sensitive.
4. Click **OK**.
 - The *Confirm Password* dialog box requires that you retype the same password.
5. Retype the password and click **OK**.
6. Click **Close**.
7. Click **Save**.

5-50 Passwords are case-sensitive and are hidden as you type them.

For this project, you insert a *SmartArt* graphic to illustrate how revenue results are consolidated for Paradise Lakes Resort. You insert a hyperlink to the *SmartArt*, add the company logo to a sheet, and mark your work as final.

Files Needed: *[your initials] PP E5-2.xlsx* and *PLR.png (Student data files are available in the* Library of *your SIMnet account)*
Completed Project File Name: *[your initials] PP E5-3.xlsx*

1. Open the *[your initials] PP E5-2.xlsx* workbook completed in *Pause & Practice 5-2*. Because the workbook includes links, you will see a security warning or a message box (Figure 5-51).

2. Click *Enable Editing* or *Update* to edit the workbook. The message box choice depends on your computer and file management procedures.

3. Save the workbook as [your initials] PP E5-3.

5-51 Security message for workbook with links

4. Insert a *SmartArt* graphic.
 a. Click the **New sheet** button.
 b. Name the new sheet SmartArt and position it at the end of the tab names.
 c. Click the **Insert a SmartArt Graphic** button [*Insert* tab, *Illustrations* group].
 d. Select **Cycle** in the list on the left.
 e. Locate and click **Radial Venn** in the gallery of graphics.
 f. Click **OK**. If the text pane for the graphic is open, close it.

5. Add text to a *SmartArt* graphic.
 a. Click the top circle shape.
 b. Type Room and Cabin Rentals. Do not press **Enter**; if you did, press **Backspace**.
 c. Click the leftmost circle shape and type Excursions. If you make an error, click again in the shape and make the correction.
 d. Type Spa Purchases in the bottom circle shape.
 e. Type Shop Purchases in the rightmost shape.
 f. In the center shape, type Total Revenue (Figure 5-52).
 g. Click a cell near the center circle to deselect the shape.

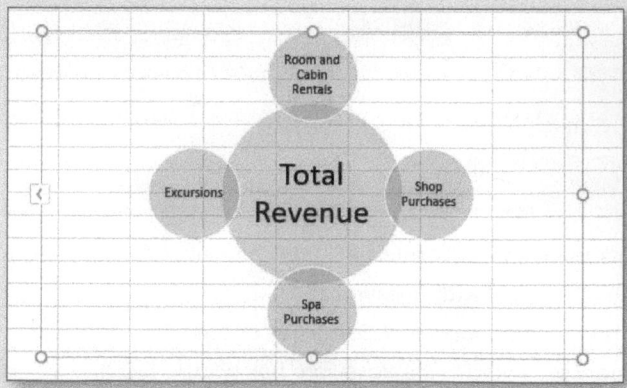

5-52 Text entered in shapes in *SmartArt* graphic

6. Format, position, and size a *SmartArt* graphic.
 a. Click the frame of the *SmartArt* graphic to select it.
 b. Click the **More** button [*SmartArt Tools Design* tab, *SmartArt Styles* group].
 c. Choose **Inset** in the *3-D* group.
 d. Click the **Change Colors** button [*SmartArt Tools Design* tab, *SmartArt Styles* group].
 e. Choose **Colorful – Accent Colors**.
 f. Point to the *SmartArt* frame to display a move pointer.

g. Drag the graphic to position the top left selection handle in cell **A1**. When a *SmartArt* graphic is selected, you can also use a keyboard directional arrow key to nudge the object into position.

h. Point to the bottom right selection handle to display a resize arrow.

i. Drag the frame to reach cell **I22** (Figure 5-53).

j. Click cell **K1** to deselect the *SmartArt*.

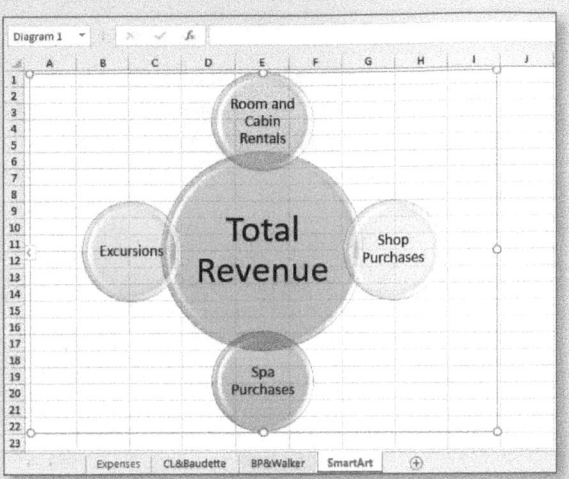

5-53 Styled and positioned *SmartArt*

7. Insert a hyperlink.

a. Click the **BP&Walker** sheet tab.

b. Select cell **G2**.

c. Click the **Hyperlink** button [*Insert* tab, *Links* group].

d. Select **Place in This Document**.

e. Select the sheet name **SmartArt** in the *Or select a place in this document* list.

f. Select the default text In the *Text to display* box and type View Illustration.

g. Click the **ScreenTip** button and type Click this link to view the graphic. (Figure 5-54).

h. Click **OK** in the *Set Hyperlink ScreenTip* dialog box.

i. Click **OK** in the *Insert Hyperlink* dialog box.

j. Click cell **G3**.

k. Click the link to test it.

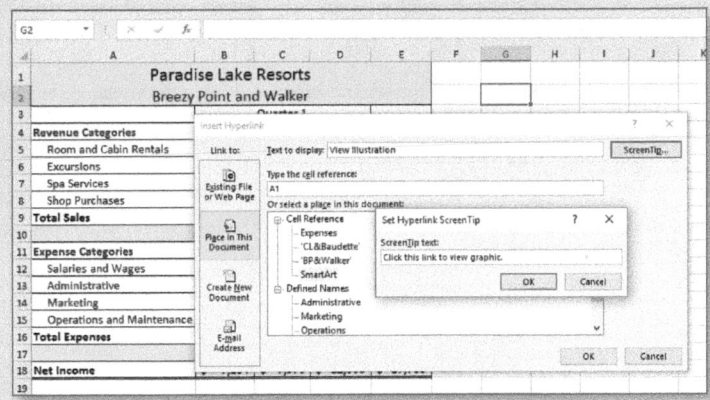

5-54 Hyperlink text and *ScreenTip*

8. Insert a picture.

a. Click the **CL&Baudette** sheet tab.

b. Click the **Pictures** button [*Insert* tab, *Illustrations* group].

c. Navigate to the folder with your student data files.

d. Choose **PLR** and click **Insert**.

e. Click the **Height** box [*Picture Tools Format* tab, *Size* group].

f. Replace the default height with .55 and press **Enter**.

g. Click the **Color** button [*Picture Tools Format* tab, *Adjust* group].

h. Select **Gold, Accent color 4 Dark** in the *Recolor* group.

i. Drag and position the image as shown in Figure 5-55.

9. Click cell **A3**.

	A	B	C	D	E
1	**PLR**	Paradise Lake Resorts			
2		Cass Lake and Baudette			
3			Quarter 1		
4	**Revenue Categories**	January	February	March	Total
7	Room and Cabin Rentals	$ 33,850	$29,250	$ 41,250	$104,350
10	Excursions	7,250	8,800	11,700	27,750
13	Spa Services	4,000	4,750	6,050	14,800
16	Shop Purchases	2,125	2,600	3,150	7,875
17	**Total Sales**	$ 60,600	$61,550	$ 83,050	$205,200
18					
19	**Expense Categories**				
20	Salaries and Wages	$ 15,150	$15,388	$ 20,763	$ 51,300
21	Administrative	9,090	9,233	12,458	30,780
22	Marketing	6,060	6,155	8,305	20,520
23	Operations and Maintenance	16,968	17,234	23,254	57,456
24	**Total Expenses**	$ 47,268	$48,009	$ 64,779	$160,056
25					
26	**Net Income**	$ 13,332	$13,541	$ 18,271	$ 45,144

5-55 Image inserted in worksheet

10. Mark a workbook as final.
 a. Click the **File** tab.
 b. Click the **Protect Workbook** button and select **Mark as Final**.
 c. Click **OK** to resave the file.
 d. Click **OK** to close the message box.

11. Close the workbook (Figure 5-56).

Paradise Lake Resorts				
Breezy Point and Walker				View Illustration
		Quarter 1		
Revenue Categories	January	February	March	Total
Room and Cabin Rentals	$ 17,200	$ 21,850	$ 35,500	$ 74,550
Excursions	8,730	3,755	9,350	21,835
Spa Services	4,200	5,250	5,645	15,095
Shop Purchases	2,750	5,400	6,550	14,700
Total Sales	$ 32,880	$ 36,255	$ 57,045	$ 126,180
Expense Categories				
Salaries and Wages	$ 8,220	$ 9,064	$ 14,261	$ 31,545
Administrative	4,932	5,438	8,557	18,927
Marketing	3,288	3,626	5,705	12,618
Operations and Maintenance	9,206	10,151	15,973	35,330
Total Expenses	$ 25,646	$ 28,279	$ 44,495	$ 98,420
Net Income	$ 7,234	$ 7,976	$ 12,550	$ 27,760

5-56 Completed worksheet for PP E5-3

Chapter Summary

5.1 Create a static data consolidation (p. E5-294).

- A *consolidated worksheet* combines data from multiple worksheets using a mathematical or statistical function.
- When labels and values are in the same position on all worksheets, the consolidation is by position.
- A *static consolidation* places a non-changing result in the consolidation sheet. If the source data is edited, the consolidated sheet is not updated.
- The **Consolidate** button is located on the *Data* tab in the *Data Tools* group.

5.2 Create a dynamic data consolidation (p. E5-296).

- A *dynamic consolidation* places formulas in the consolidation worksheet. If the source data is edited, the consolidated sheet is automatically updated.
- A dynamic data consolidation formats the results as an Excel outline.
- To build a dynamic consolidation, choose the *Create links to source data* option in the *Consolidate* dialog box.

5.3 Consolidate data by category (p. E5-298).

- When labels and values are not in the same position on all worksheets, you may be able to consolidate data by category.
- A category is a row or column label.
- A consolidate by category command includes the label cells on the source worksheets.
- The consolidated sheet displays labels in the same order as the first sheet listed in the *Consolidate* dialog box.
- Consolidation by category can be static or dynamic.

5.4 Group worksheets for editing and formatting (p. E5-299).

- When worksheets are grouped, editing and format commands affect all sheets in the group.
- You can apply formats, enter formulas, or enter data in grouped sheets.
- Not all commands are available in grouped sheets.
- When a command is not available, it is grayed out in the *Ribbon*.
- Press **Shift** or **Ctrl** to group contiguous or non-contiguous sheets.

- Ungroup sheets when finished editing to guard against applying a command in error to the group.

5.5 Link workbooks to consolidate data (p. E5-303).

- *Linking* workbooks is the process of referring to data in another workbook.
- A *dependent workbook* refers to data in another workbook.
- A *source workbook* supplies data to another workbook.
- An *external reference* formula is in a dependent workbook and refers to cells in a source workbook.
- An external reference includes the name of the workbook, the sheet name, cell addresses, and *identifiers*.
- You can *link* workbooks by using the *Consolidate* command on the *Data* tab if all source workbooks are open.
- You can link workbooks by building a formula that refers to another workbook.
- You can point to build an external reference formula if the source workbook is open.
- If the source workbook is not open, build an external reference formula by typing the complete path and file name, the sheet name, cell addresses, and all identifiers.
- The *Excel Trust Center* includes security options for workbooks with links.

5.6 Insert illustrations using *SmartArt*, screenshots, and pictures in a worksheet (p. E5-309).

- A *SmartArt* graphic is an illustration such as a matrix, a cycle diagram, an organization chart, or a process chart.
- A *SmartArt* graphic is a selectable object that you can size, position, and style.
- *SmartArt* graphics are not linked to worksheet data; they contain descriptive text.
- When a *SmartArt* graphic is selected, the *SmartArt Tools Design* and *Format* tabs are available.
- A *SmartArt* graphic consists of several smaller shapes; you can format an individual shape separately.
- A *screenshot* is an image of data on the screen that is inserted as a picture object in a worksheet.

- The **Take a Screenshot** button displays thumbnails of open windows that you can capture as images.
- You can take a *Screen Clipping* by drawing a rectangle around the desired area.
- Pictures can be inserted in a worksheet from a file or from online sources.
- When a picture object is selected, the *Picture Tools Format* tab is available with commands for changing the appearance of the image.

5.7 Insert hyperlinks in a worksheet (p. E5-316).

- A *hyperlink* is a clickable line of text in a cell or a clickable object in a worksheet.
- A hyperlink acts as a jump term or a shortcut to another location in the workbook, on the computer, or in the cloud.
- A cell hyperlink is underlined text in the color specified by the document theme.
- An object hyperlink is a shortcut assigned to an image, a *SmartArt* graphic, or another object.
- The *Hyperlink* button is located in the *Links* group on the *Insert* tab.

5.8 Safeguard work by marking it as final or by setting a password (p. E5-318).

- You can assign a simple level of security to a workbook by marking it as final.
- The *Mark as Final* command is a reminder that the work is complete and should not be edited.
- You can remove the *Mark as Final* setting by clicking **Enable Editing** in the security message bar.
- The *Encrypt with Password* command allows you to assign a password to a workbook.
- You must type the password before the workbook can be opened.
- The *Mark as Final* and *Encrypt with Password* commands are available from the **Protect Workbook** button [*File* tab, *Info* pane].

Check for Understanding

The SIMbook for this text (within your SIMnet account) provides the following resources for concept review:

- Multiple choice questions
- Matching exercises
- Short answer questions

Guided Project 5-1

Blue Lake Sports has maintained sales data about specialty departments. For this project, you reformat worksheets as a group, insert the *SUM* function, build static and dynamic consolidation sheets, insert a *SmartArt* graphic, and create a hyperlink.
[Student Learning Outcomes 5.1, 5.2, 5.4, 5.5, 5.6, 5.7, 5.8]

Files Needed: ***BlueLakeSports-05.xlsx*** and ***BlueLakeSportsLinked-05.xlsx*** (*Student data files are available in the* Library *of your SIMnet account*)
Completed Project File Names: ***[your initials] Excel 5-1.xlsx*** and ***[your initials] Excel 5-1a.xlsx***

Skills Covered in This Project

- Group and format worksheets.
- Edit grouped worksheets.
- Enter a *SUM* function in grouped worksheets.
- Create a static data consolidation.

- Create a dynamic consolidation.
- Link workbooks using the *Consolidate* command.
- Encrypt a workbook with a password.
- Insert and format a *SmartArt* graphic.
- Insert and format a hyperlink.

1. Open the ***BlueLakeSports-05*** workbook from your student data files and save it as [your initials] Excel 5-1.

2. Group and format worksheets.
 a. Right-click the **Quarter 1** tab and choose **Select All Sheets**.
 b. Select cell **A2** and change the font to **Calibri**.
 c. Select cells **A4:E8** and apply **All Borders**.
 d. Select cells **A8:E8** and apply a **Top and Double Bottom Border**.
 e. Click the **Launcher** in the *Page Setup* group on the *Page Layout* tab.
 f. Select the **Horizontally** box on the *Margins* tab to center the data on the page.
 g. Click the **Header/Footer** tab.
 h. Click the *Footer* drop-down arrow and select ***[your initials] Excel 5-1***.
 i. Click **OK**.

3. Enter a formula for grouped sheets.
 a. Click cell **E5** and enter a *SUM* function to add cells **B5:D5**.
 b. Select cell **E5** and copy the formula to cells **E6:E7**.
 c. Select cells **B5:E5** and cells **B8:E8**.
 d. Click the **Accounting Number Format** button [*Home* tab, *Number* group].
 e. Click the **Decrease Decimal** button twice [*Home* tab, *Number* group].
 f. Select cells **B6:E7** and click the **Decrease Decimal** button twice [*Home* tab, *Number* group].
 g. Press **Ctrl+Home** (Figure 5-57).
 h. Right-click the **Static** tab and choose **Ungroup Sheets**.

4. Create a static data consolidation.
 a. Select cell **B5** on the **Static** sheet.
 b. Click the **Consolidate** button [*Data* tab, *Data Tools* group].
 c. Choose the **SUM** function.

d. Select each reference, if any, in the *All references* box and click **Delete**.

e. Click the *Reference* box and click the **Quarter 1** worksheet tab.

f. Select cells **B5:D7**.

g. Click **Add** in the *Consolidate* dialog box.

h. Click the **Quarter 2** tab. Verify that cells B5:D7 are selected.

i. Click **Add** in the *Consolidate* dialog box.

j. Add cells **B5:D7** from the **Quarter 3** and **Quarter 4** worksheets to the *All references* list in the *Consolidate* dialog box.

k. Click **OK**. (Figure 5-58).

5. Select cell **A1**.

6. Open the ***BlueLakeSportsLinked-05.xlsx*** workbook from your student data files and save it as [your initials] Excel 5-1a.

7. Tile the windows.

a. Click the **Arrange All** button [*View* tab, *Window* group].

b. Choose **Vertical** and click **OK**.

8. Create a dynamic data consolidation by linking workbooks.

a. Click cell **B5** in *[your initials] Excel 5-1a*.

b. Click the **Consolidate** button [*Data* tab, *Data Tools* group].

c. Choose the **SUM** function.

d. Select each reference in the *All references* box and click **Delete**.

e. Click the *Reference* box and double-click the **Quarter 1** tab in *[your initials] Excel 5-1*. The first click activates the window; the second click selects the tab.

f. Select cell **E5** and click **Add** in the *Consolidate* dialog box.

g. Click the **Quarter 2** tab in *[your initials] Excel 5-1*.

h. Verify that cell **E5** is selected and click **Add** in the *Consolidate* dialog box.

i. Add cell **E5** from the **Quarter 3** and **Quarter 4** worksheets to the *All references* list.

j. Select the **Create links to source data** box (Figure 5-59).

k. Click **OK**. The result is $2,182,906.

9. Repeat step 8 for the **Golf** and **Winter Sports** categories (cells **E6** and **E7**).

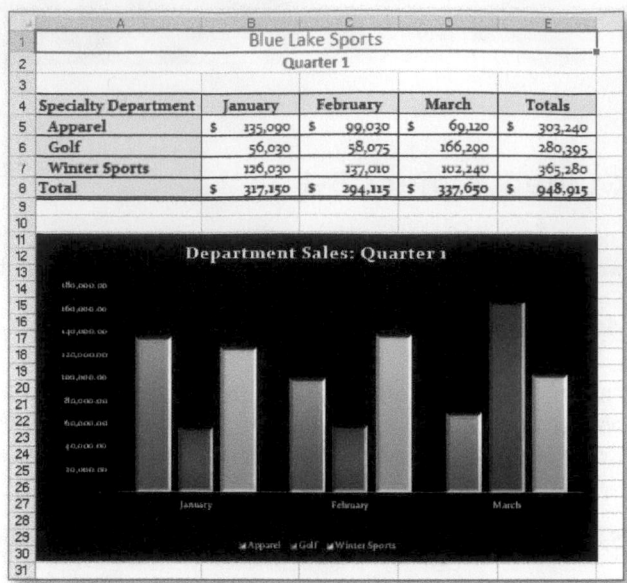

5-57 Completed *Quarter 1* sheet; other sheets are the same

5-58 Consolidated results

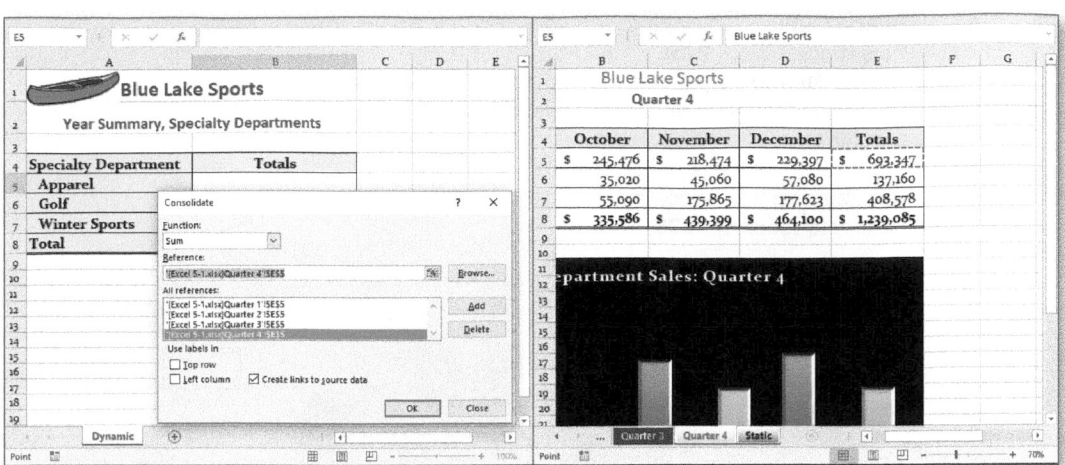

5-59 Dynamic consolidation for Apparel group

10. Click cell **B20** in **[your initials] Excel 5-1a** and click the **AutoSum** button [*Home* tab, *Editing* group].

11. Insert a *SmartArt* graphic.
 a. Click cell **D2** on the **Dynamic** sheet. Maximize the window.
 b. Click the **Insert a SmartArt Graphic** button [*Insert* tab, *Illustrations* group].
 c. Click **Process** in the list at the left.
 d. Find and click **Vertical Equation** in the gallery of graphics.
 e. Click **OK** to insert the *SmartArt* graphic. Close the text pane if necessary.
 f. Click the top left circle shape and type Apparel. Do not press **Enter;** if you did, press **Backspace**.
 g. Click the shape below *Apparel* and type Golf.
 h. Click the **Add Shape** button [*SmartArt Tools Design* tab, *Create Graphic* group] (Figure 5-60).
 i. Click the bottom shape and type Winter Sports.
 j. Click the large circle shape on the right and type Specialty Departments.

12. Format, position, and size a *SmartArt* graphic.
 a. Click the frame of the *SmartArt* graphic to select it.
 b. Click the **More** button [*SmartArt Tools Design* tab, *SmartArt Styles* group].
 c. Choose **Polished** in the *3-D* group.
 d. Click the **Change Colors** button [*SmartArt Tools Design* tab, *SmartArt Styles* group].
 e. Choose **Colored Fill – Accent 1** in the *Accent 1* group.
 f. Click the **Shape Fill** button [*SmartArt Tools Format* tab, *Shapes Styles* group].
 g. Choose **White, Background 1, Darker 15%**.

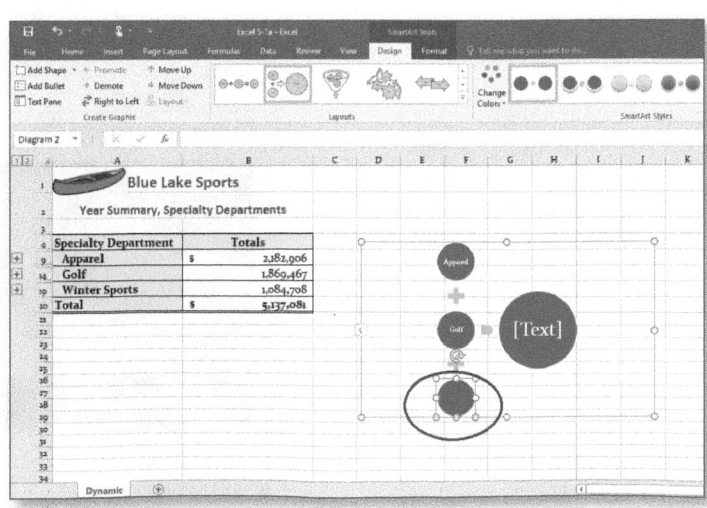

5-60 Shape added to *SmartArt* graphic

h. Click the **Shape Outline** button [*SmartArt Tools Format* tab, *Shapes Styles* group].
i. Choose **Weight** and select **½ pt**.
j. Click the **Shape Outline** button again and choose **Blue, Accent 1**.
k. Point to the *SmartArt* frame to display a move pointer.
l. Drag the graphic to position the top left selection handle in cell **C1**. While the graphic is selected, press the *Up* or *Left* keyboard directional arrow to fine-tune the position of the graphic.
m. Point to the bottom right selection handle to display a resize pointer.
n. Drag the pointer to reach cell **J35**.

13. Click cell **B3** to deselect the *SmartArt*.

14. Save and close the workbook (Figure 5-61).

15. Maximize the window for *[your initials] Excel 5-1*.

16. Insert a hyperlink.
 a. Click the **Quarter 4** sheet tab and select cell **F9**.
 b. Click the **Hyperlink** button [*Insert* tab, *Links* group].
 c. Select **Place in This Document** in the *Insert Hyperlink* dialog box.
 d. In the *Or select a place in this document* list, select **Static** in the *Cell Reference* group.
 e. Select the default text in the *Text to display* box and type See totals.
 f. Click **OK** in the *Insert Hyperlink* dialog box.

17. Format a hyperlink.
 a. Right-click the cell hyperlink.
 b. Format the font size to **16 pt**. from the mini toolbar.
 c. Format the font color to **Blue, Accent 1**.
 d. Click cell **G7** (Figure 5-62).

18. Click the hyperlink to test it.

19. Encrypt a workbook with a password.
 a. Click the **Protect Workbook** button [*File* tab, *Info* pane].

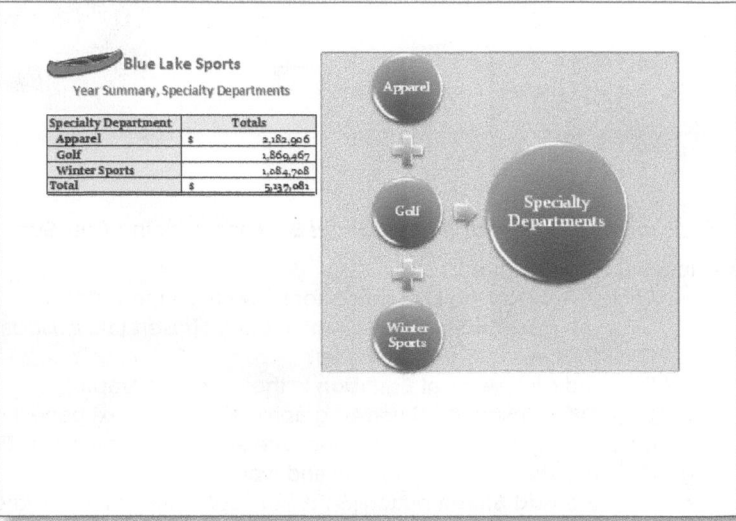

5-61 Completed *SmartArt* graphic and worksheet

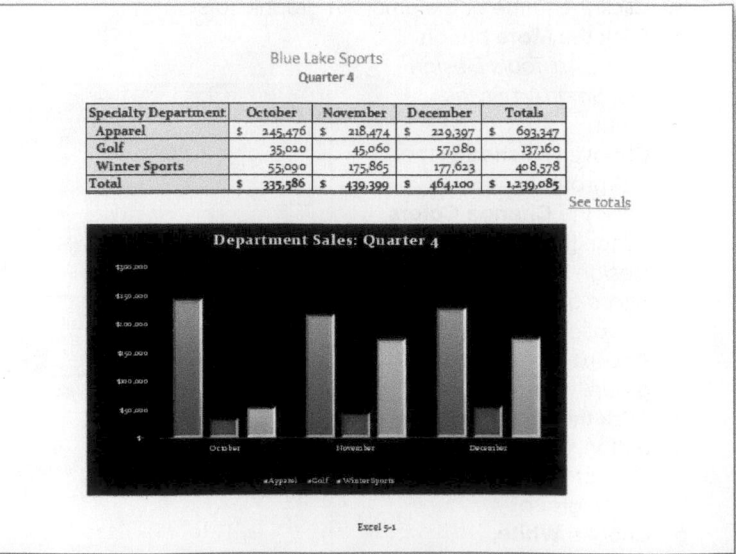

5-62 Completed hyperlink for Excel 5-1

b. Select **Encrypt with Password**.
c. Type 123 in the *Password* box.
d. Click **OK**.
e. Retype 123 to confirm the password and click **OK**.
f. Click **Close**.
g. Click **Save**.

Guided Project 5-2

Eller Software Services has collected monthly data for products and services and can consolidate and link to create management reports. You also format grouped sheets.
[Student Learning Outcomes 5.1, 5.2, 5.3, 5.4, 5.5, 5.6, 5.7, 5.8]

Files Needed: ***EllerSoftware-05.xlsx*** and ***EllerSoftwareLinked-05.xlsx*** *(Student data files are available in the* Library *of your SIMnet account)*
Completed Project File Names: [***your initials***] ***Excel 5-2.xlsx*** and [***your initials***] ***Excel 5-2a.xlsx***

Skills Covered in This Project

- Group and format worksheets.
- Build a static consolidation by category.
- Build a dynamic data consolidation by position.

- Link workbooks with a formula.
- Insert a screenshot in a worksheet.
- Size and format a screenshot.
- Insert an object hyperlink.
- Mark a workbook as final.

1. Open ***EllerSoftware-05.xlsx*** from your student data files and save it as [your initials] Excel 5-2.

2. Group and format worksheets.
 a. Right-click the **2015** sheet tab and choose **Select All Sheets**.
 b. Select cells **B4:F4** and **B9:F9**.
 c. Click the **Accounting Number Format** button [*Home* tab, *Number* group].
 d. Click the **Decrease Decimal** button [*Home* tab, *Number* group] two times.
 e. Select cells **B5:F8** and apply **Comma Style** with no decimals.
 f. Select cells **B9:F9** and click the **AutoSum** button [*Home* tab, *Editing* group].
 g. Select cell **A9** and **right-align** it.
 h. Select cell **A1**.
 i. Right-click the **2015** tab and choose **Ungroup Sheets**.

3. Click the **2017** sheet tab. Notice that the month names are not in January to April order.

4. Make a copy of the **2017** sheet at the end of the tabs and name the copy as Static.

5. Create a static consolidation by category.
 a. Select cells **B3:E8** on the **Static** sheet and press **Delete**.
 b. Click the **Consolidate** button [*Data* tab, *Data Tools* group].
 c. Select and delete references in the *All references* box, if any.
 d. Verify that **Sum** is the selected function.
 e. Click the *Reference* box and select the **2015** sheet tab.
 f. Select cells **B3:E8** on the **2015** sheet.
 g. Click **Add** in the *Consolidate* dialog box.

h. Click the **2016** tab name and add the same range to the *All references* list.

i. Repeat for the *2017* sheet.

j. Select the **Top row** box in the *Use labels in* group (Figure 5-63).

k. Click **OK**. The months are consolidated in the same order as the months on the first sheet used in the consolidation (2015).

l. Press **Ctrl+Home**.

6. Make a copy of the **2017** sheet at the end and name the copy as Dynamic.

7. Create a dynamic consolidation by category.

a. Select cells **B3:E8** on the **Dynamic** sheet and press **Delete**.

b. Click the **Consolidate** button [*Data* tab, *Data Tools* group].

c. Click the **Function** arrow and choose **Average**.

d. Verify the references in the *All references* box or select the same cells as those used in Step 5 (cells **B3:E8** on the **2015**, **2016**, and **2017** sheets).

e. Verify that the **Top row** box is selected.

f. Select the **Create links to source data** box and click **OK** (Figure 5-64).

8. Edit the label in cell **A2** to insert the word Average before "Billings."

5-63 Consolidating by category

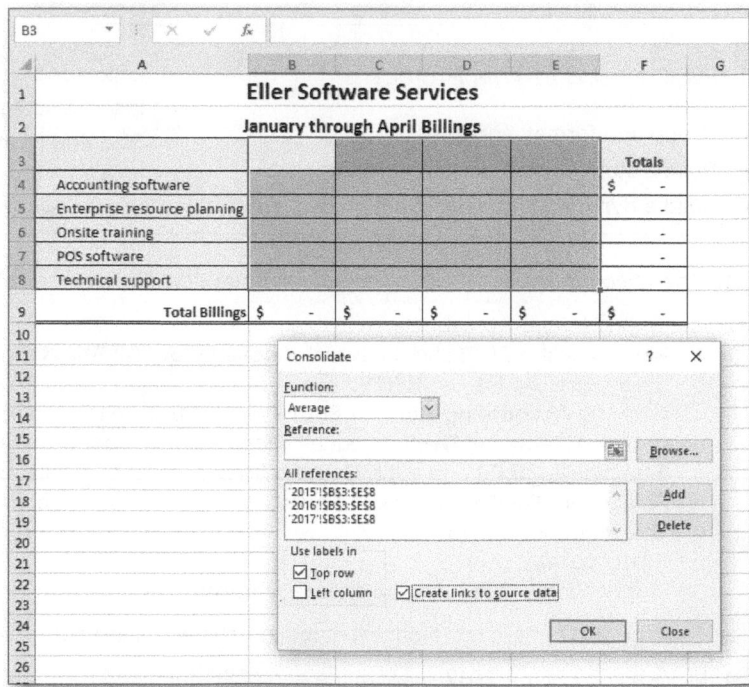

5-64 Dynamic consolidation by category

9. Right-click the column **F** heading and delete the column. Right click the row **24** heading and delete it (Figure 5-65).

10. Open *EllerSoftwareLinked-05.xlsx* from your student data files and save it as [your initials] Excel 5-2a.

11. Click the **Arrange All** button [*View* tab, *Window* group]. Choose **Vertical** and click **OK**. It does not matter which workbook is in the left pane.

12. Link workbooks with a formula.
 a. Select cell **B5** in the *[your initials] Excel 5-2a* workbook and type =.
 b. Double-click the **Static** sheet tab in *[your initials] Excel 5-2* to activate it and select cell **E4** (Figure 5-66).
 c. Press **Enter**. The reference is placed with an absolute reference.

13. Copy and edit a linked formula.
 a. Select cell **B5** in *[your initials] Excel 5-2a*.
 b. Click the *Formula* bar and delete both dollar signs. Click after **E4**, type *125% to multiply by 125%, and press **Enter** (Figure 5-67).
 c. Copy the formula in cell **B5** to cells **B6:B9** without formatting to preserve the borders.

		A	B	C	D	E
1		**Eller Software Services**				
2		January through April Average Billings				
3			January	February	March	April
7	Accounting software	$ 1,400	$ 1,200	$ 842	$ 492	
11	Enterprise resource planning	1,128	333	783	767	
15	Onsite training	458	392	509	478	
19	POS software	525	575	482	592	
23	Technical support	603	542	258	658	

Sheet tabs: 2015 2016 2017 **Static** **Dynamic**

5-65 Completed *Dynamic* sheet

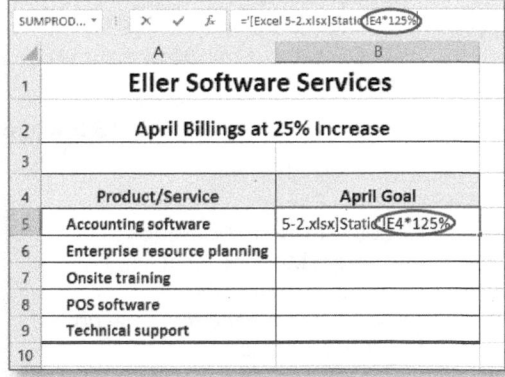

5-66 External reference with absolute reference

d. Format cells **B5:B9** as **Currency** with zero decimal places.
e. Maximize the *[your initials] Excel 5-2a* window.

14. Insert and format a screenshot in a workbook.
 a. Switch to the *[your initials] Excel 5-2* workbook and maximize the window.
 b. Select the **Static** sheet tab.
 c. Deselect the **Gridlines** box [*View* tab, *Show* group].
 d. Switch to *[your initials] Excel 5-2a* and select cell **A11**. (It is easier to take screenshots when only the two windows of interest are open, so if you have other programs running, close them and return to *[your initials] Excel 5-2a*.)
 e. Click the **Take a Screenshot** button [*Insert* tab, *Illustrations* group].
 f. Choose **Screen Clipping** from the gallery. The focus switches to *[your initials] Excel 5-2* and the screen dims after a few seconds.
 g. With the crosshair pointer, draw a rectangle to frame cells **A1:F9** for the screenshot and release the mouse button.

SUMPROD... ▾ | × ✓ fx | ='[Excel 5-2.xlsx]Static'!E4*125%

	A	B
1	**Eller Software Services**	
2	April Billings at 25% Increase	
3		
4	**Product/Service**	**April Goal**
5	Accounting software	5-2.xlsx]Static'!E4*125%
6	Enterprise resource planning	
7	Onsite training	
8	POS software	
9	Technical support	
10		

5-67 Edit the formula

h. Click the **More** button [*Picture Tools Format* tab, *Picture Styles* group].
i. Find and select **Center Shadow Rectangle** (Figure 5-68).

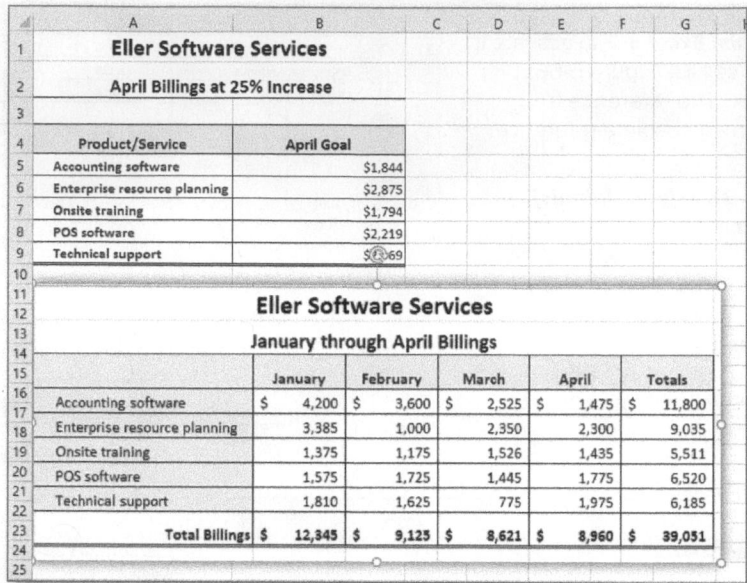

5-68 Screenshot placed in worksheet

15. Insert an object hyperlink.
 a. Select the screenshot if necessary.
 b. Click the **Hyperlink** button [*Insert* tab, *Links* group].
 c. Select **Existing File or Web Page** in the *Insert Hyperlink* dialog box.
 d. Select **Current Folder** in the *Look in* group.
 e. Select *[your initials] Excel 5-2* in the file name list. If your file is not listed, navigate to the correct folder to locate it.
 f. Click **ScreenTip** and type Click to open source file (Figure 5-69).
 g. Click **OK** in the *Set Hyperlink ScreenTip* dialog box.
 h. Click **OK** in the *Insert Hyperlink* dialog box.
 i. Select cell **A1**.

16. Switch to the *[your initials] Excel 5-2* window.

17. Mark a workbook as final.
 a. Click the **File** tab.
 b. Click the **Protect Workbook** button and select **Mark as Final**.
 c. Click **OK** to resave the file.
 d. Click **OK** to close the message box.
 e. Close the workbook.

18. Click the hyperlink in *[your initials] Excel 5-2a* to test it. The *[your initials] Excel 5-2* workbook opens in *Read Only* mode because it is marked as final.

19. Close *[your initials] Excel 5-2*. Save and close *[your initials] Excel 5-2a*.

5-69 Hyperlink to open another workbook

Guided Project 5-3

Hamilton Civic Center tracks the number of participants enrolled in classes and seminars. You will create a dynamic consolidation to link data, prepare monthly sheets for consolidation, copy the company logo, and complete work for the summary workbook.
[Student Learning Outcomes 5.1, 5.2, 5.3, 5.4, 5.5, 5.6]

Files Needed: **HamiltonCC-05.xlsx**, **HamiltonCCLinked-05.xlsx**, and **HCC.png** *(Student data files are available in the* Library *of your SIMnet account)*
Completed Project File Names: *[your initials] Excel 5-3.xlsx* and *[your initials] Excel 5-3a.xlsx*

Skills Covered in This Project

- Group and format worksheets.
- Create a static data consolidation by category.
- Sort consolidated data.
- Copy a picture.
- Break links in a workbook.
- Link workbooks in the *Consolidate* dialog box.
- Create a dynamic data consolidation.
- Insert, size, and position a picture.

1. Open the **HamiltonCC-05** workbook from your student data files and save it as [your initials] Excel 5-3.

2. Group the worksheets.
 a. Click the **January** worksheet tab.
 b. Press **Shift** and click the **March** tab.

3. Format grouped worksheets.
 a. Select cells **A5:F12**.
 b. Click the arrow with the **Borders** button [*Home* tab, *Font* group] and select **More Borders**.
 c. Click the **Color** arrow and choose **Black, Text 1**.
 d. Click the thin solid line **Style** (bottom choice in the first column of styles).
 e. Click the **vertical middle** of the preview box. If you place a border in the wrong location, click the line in the preview to remove it.
 f. Click the second line **Style** in the first column (two below **None**).
 g. Click the **horizontal middle** of the preview box. This border will appear between rows.
 h. Click the bottom line **Style** in the second column (a double border).
 i. Click the **bottom** of the preview area to place a bottom horizontal border (Figure 5-70).
 j. Click **OK**.

5-70 *Border* tab in *Format Cells* dialog box

4. Enter *SUM* in grouped worksheets.
 a. Select cells **F6:F11**.
 b. Click the **AutoSum** button [*Home* tab, *Editing* group].
 c. Use *SUM* in cells **B12:F12**.
 d. Click cell **A1**.
 e. Right-click the **February** sheet tab and choose **Ungroup Sheets**.

5. Copy a picture.
 a. Click to select the organization logo picture on the **February** sheet.
 b. Press **Ctrl+C** to copy the picture.
 c. Click the **January** sheet tab.
 d. Press **Ctrl+V** to paste the picture.
 e. Point to the picture frame to display a move pointer.
 f. Drag the picture so that it appears in column A to the left of "Hamilton Civic Center." You can nudge the image with any keyboard directional arrow key.
 g. Click cell **B1**.

6. Make a copy of the **March** sheet at the end and name it Quarter 1.

7. Set the tab color to **Black, Text 1**.

8. Edit cell **A3** to read First Quarter Enrollment.

9. Create a static data consolidation by category.
 a. Delete the contents of cells **A6:E11** on the **Quarter 1** sheet. The labels in column A are not in the same order on the quarterly sheets.
 b. Click the **Consolidate** button [*Data* tab, *Data Tools* group].
 c. Choose the **SUM** function.
 d. Select and delete references in the *All references* box.
 e. Click the *Reference* box and click the **January** tab.
 f. Select cells **A6:E11** and click **Add** in the *Consolidate* dialog box.
 g. Click the **February** tab, verify that cells A6:E11 are selected, and click **Add**.
 h. Add the **March** worksheet data to the *All references* list.
 i. Select the **Left column** box in the *Use labels in* group (Figure 5-71).
 j. Click **OK**.

5-71 *Consolidate* dialog box to consolidate by category

10. Sort consolidated data.
 a. Select cells **A6:E11** on the **Quarter 1** sheet.
 b. Click the **Sort & Filter** button [*Home* tab, *Editing* group].
 c. Choose **Sort A to Z**.
 d. Click cell **B1**.

11. Save the *[your initials] Excel 5-3* workbook and leave it open.

12. Open the *HamiltonCCLinked-05* workbook from your student data files. Click **Enable Editing** if updating of links is disabled, or click *Update* or *Continue* without updating. The message box depends on file management procedures on your computer.

13. Save the workbook as [your initials] Excel 5-3a.

14. View and break links in the workbook.
 a. Click cell **D7**. The link is incorrect; it should refer to the **Quarter 1** sheet in *[your initials] Excel 5-3*.
 b. Click the **Edit Links** button [*Data* tab, *Connections* group].

c. Click **Break Link**. When you break a link, formulas are replaced with values and the command cannot be undone (Figure 5-72).

d. Click **Break Links**. Formulas are removed, but the cells display the values.

e. Click **Close**.

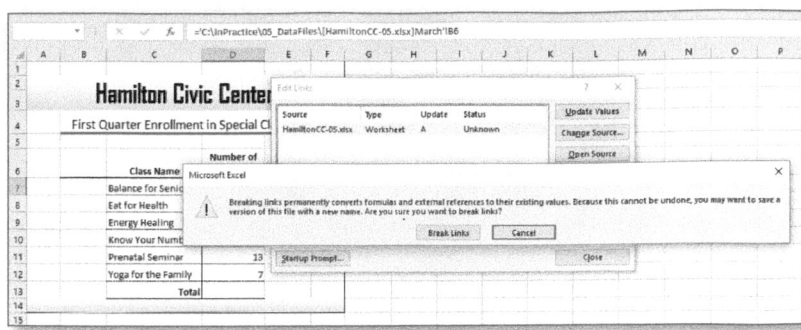

5-72 *Edit Links* dialog box and *Break Links* message box

15. Create a dynamic data consolidation to link workbooks.

a. Select cells **D7:D12** on the **FirstQuarter** sheet.

b. Click the **Consolidate** button [*Data* tab, *Data Tools* group].

c. Choose the **SUM** function.

d. Select and delete references in the *All references* box.

e. Click the *Reference* box and press **Ctrl+F6** to switch to the *[your initials] Excel 5-3* workbook.

f. Click the **Quarter 1** sheet tab if necessary.

g. Select cells **F6:F11**. When there is only one reference, you don't need to click **Add**.

h. Select the **Create links to source data** box (Figure 5-73).

i. Click **OK**.

j. Switch to the *[your initials] Excel 5-3a* workbook if necessary.

k. Select cell **D19**, click the **AutoSum** button [*Home* tab, *Editing* group], and press **Enter**.

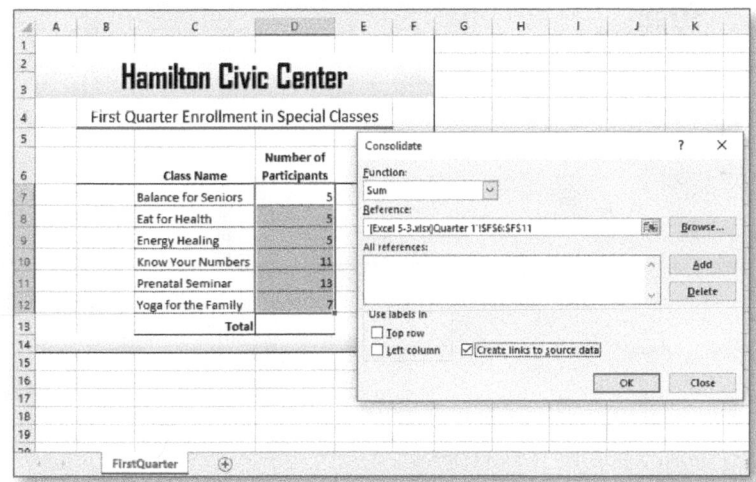

5-73 *Consolidate* dialog box to link workbooks

16. Insert a picture from a file.

a. Click cell **G2** on the **FirstQuarter** sheet.

b. Click the **Pictures** button [*Insert* tab, *Illustrations* group].

c. Find and select **HCC** from your student data files (Figure 5-74).

d. Click **Insert**. The picture is placed at a default size.

5-74 *Insert Picture* dialog box

 e. Click the **Height** box [*Picture Tools Format* tab, *Size* group].

 f. Type .5 to replace the default height and press **Enter**. The image is proportionally resized.

 g. Point to the logo frame to display a move pointer.

 h. Drag the image to cover cells **A1:B3**.

 i. Click cell **C1**.

17. Save and close the *[your initials] Excel 5-3a* workbook. Save and close the *[your initials] Excel 5-3* workbook (Figure 5-75).

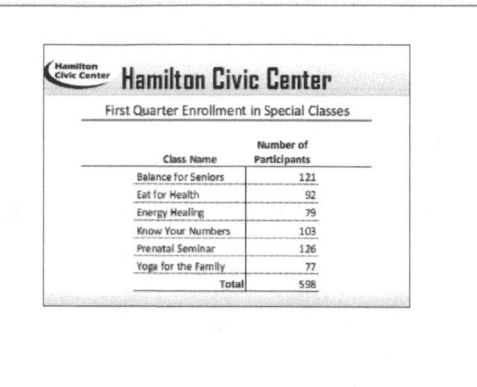

5-75 Completed worksheets for Excel 5-3a

Independent Project 5-4

Wilson Home Entertainment Systems monitors cash flow at their locations separately and consolidates data at the end of the quarter. After the summary is complete, you insert hyperlinks to each of the supporting worksheets.
[Student Learning Outcomes 5.1, 5.2, 5.4, 5.6, 5.7, 5.8]

Files Needed: ***WilsonHome-05.xlsx*** and ***WHES.png*** *(Student data files are available in the* Library *of your SIMnet account)*
Completed Project File Name: *[your initials] Excel 5-4.xlsx*

Skills Covered in This Project

- Group and format worksheets.
- Create a static data consolidation with *SUM*.
- Create a dynamic data consolidation with *AVERAGE*.

- Insert a picture from a file.
- Insert a hyperlink.
- Copy a hyperlink.
- Encrypt a workbook with a password.

1. Open the ***WilsonHome-05*** workbook from your student data files and save it as [your initials] Excel 5-4.

2. Group the **Cash Flow**, **Peoria**, **Champaign**, and **Rockford** sheets.

3. Edit and format grouped sheets.
 a. Select cells **A2:B2** and click the **Launcher** in the *Alignment* group [*Home* tab]. Choose **Center Across Selection** from the *Horizontal* list and click **OK**.
 b. Edit the contents of cell **A10** to read Cash paid for marketing.
 c. Select cell **A1** and ungroup the sheets.

4. Select the **CashFlow** sheet.

5. Build a static consolidation for the *Cash flow from operations* section.
 a. Select cells **B4:B12**.
 b. Use **Sum** to consolidate the data from the three location sheets without links. (Figure 5-76).

6. Build a static consolidation for the *Cash flow from banking and investment* section in cells **B15:B21**. Delete the references in the *Consolidate* dialog box and use **Sum** as the function.

7. Build a static consolidation for the *Cash balance at the beginning of the quarter* amounts in cell **B24** with **Sum** as the function.

8. Insert a picture from a file.
 a. Delete the contents of cell **A1** on the **CashFlow** sheet.
 b. Click cell **D2**.
 c. Click the **Pictures** button [*Insert* tab, *Illustrations* group].
 d. Find and select **WHES** from your student data files.
 e. Click **Insert**. The picture is placed at a default size.
 f. Click the **Height** box [*Picture Tools Format* tab, *Size* group].
 g. Type 1.2 to replace the default height and press **Enter**.
 h. Format the height of row **1** to **86.25 (115 pixels)**.
 i. Point to the logo frame to display a move pointer.
 j. Drag the image to appear in cell **A1** as a main label for the worksheet (Figure 5-77).
 k. Click cell **D2**.

9. Create a dynamic consolidation for *Cash flow from operations* data.
 a. Click the **Averages** sheet tab.
 b. Select cells **B4:B12**.
 c. Use **Average** as the function to consolidate data from the **Peoria**, **Champaign**, and **Rockford** sheets with links to the source data.
 d. Expand the *Cash paid for salaries and wages* group (Figure 5-78).
 e. Select cell **A1**.

5-76 *Consolidate* dialog box for cash flow

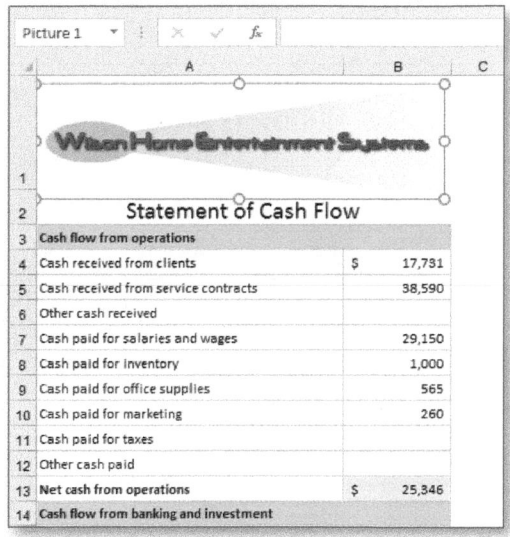

5-77 Image positioned as title

5-78 Completed *Averages* worksheet

10. Insert and copy a hyperlink.
 a. Click cell **D3** on the **Peoria** worksheet.
 b. Create a hyperlink that displays Company Averages and switches to cell **A1** on the **Averages** worksheet.
 c. Right-click cell **D3** and choose **Copy** from the menu.
 d. Select the **Champaign** sheet tab and paste the hyperlink in cell **D3**.
 e. Select the **Rockford** sheet tab and paste the hyperlink in cell **D3**.
 f. Select the **Peoria** sheet, and press **Esc** to remove the copy marquee if it is still visible.
 g. Select cell **D5** and click the hyperlink to test it.
11. Encrypt the workbook with the password abc.
12. Save and close the workbook (Figure 5-79).

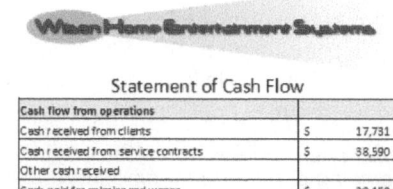

5-79 *Peoria* worksheet with hyperlink and completed *CashFlow* sheet for Excel 5-4

Independent Project 5-5

At Sierra Pacific Community College, student assignment and exam points are listed on a single sheet but in different name order. You will consolidate by category and copy the results to another sheet. You will also insert the school logo in a footer.
[Student Learning Outcomes 5.1, 5.3, 5.6, 5.8]

Files Needed: **SierraPacific-05.xlsx** and **SPCCD.png** (Student data files are available in the Library of your SIMnet account)
Completed Project File Name: **[your initials] Excel 5-5.xlsx**

Skills Covered in This Project

- Remove the *Mark as Final* property.
- Create a static data consolidation.
- Consolidate data by category.
- Insert a picture from a file in a header.
- Size a picture.
- Change the color of a picture.

1. Open the **SierraPacific-05** workbook and click **Edit Anyway** to remove the *Read-Only* property from the *Mark as Final* command.

2. Save the workbook as [your initials] Excel 5-5. On the **PPT&Access** sheet, student names and points are listed for each segment but not in the same order.

3. Consolidate points by category.
 a. Select cells **I3:K25**. Consolidated data will be placed in this range.
 b. Open the *Consolidate* dialog box.
 c. Select and delete any references in the *All references* list.
 d. Choose **Sum** as the function.
 e. Click the *Reference* box, select cells **A3:C25**, and click **Add**.
 f. Select cells **E3:G25** and click **Add**.
 g. Select the **Top row** and **Left column** boxes (Figure 5-80).
 h. Do not use links.
 i. Click **OK**. The columns are consolidated, and the names are in alphabetical order. The label for the last name column is missing.

4. Copy and format consolidation results.
 a. Select cells **J4:K25** and click the **Copy** button [*Home* tab, *Clipboard* group] (Figure 5-81).
 b. Click the **Total** sheet tab. Student names are already entered in alphabetical order.
 c. Click cell **C4** and click the **Paste** button [*Home* tab, *Clipboard* group].

5-80 Consolidating by both label groups

5-81 Copy consolidated values to another sheet

 d. Select cell **A4** and click the **Format as Table** button [*Home* tab, *Styles* group].
 e. Use **Table Style Medium 16**.
 f. Show the **Total Row** with **Average** as the function in the **Points** and **Exams** columns.
 g. Format cell **A1** with a **16 pt**. font size.
 h. Format row **1** as **22.50 (30 pixels)** high.
 i. Type Total in cell **E3**.
 j. In cell **E4**, enter a formula to add cells **C4** and **D4**.
 k. Show **Average** in the **Total Row** for column **E**.
 l. Type Average in cell **A26**, and format it bold and right-aligned.
 m. **Center** cells **A3:E3**.

5. Insert a picture from a file in a header.
 a. Click the **Page Layout** view button on the *Status* bar.
 b. Click the right header section.
 c. Click the **Picture** button [*Header & Footer Tools Design* tab, *Header & Footer Elements* group].
 d. In the *Insert Pictures* dialog box, click **Browse** for the *From a file* group.
 e. Find and select **SPCCD** in the folder with your data files.
 f. Click **Insert**. The *&[Picture]* code is placed in the section (Figure 5-82).
 g. Click a worksheet cell. In *Page Layout* view, you can see the picture.

6. Format a picture in a header.
 a. Click the right header section to display the *&[Picture]* code.
 b. Click the **Format Picture** button [*Header & Footer Tools Design* tab, *Header & Footer Elements* group].
 c. Click the **Height** box on the *Size* tab and type .50 to replace the default Height.
 d. Press **Tab**. to move to the *Width* box. When *Lock aspect ratio* is active, the image is automatically proportionally sized.
 e. Click the **Picture** tab in the dialog box.
 f. Click the arrow for **Color** and choose **Grayscale**.
 g. Click **OK** and click a worksheet cell (Figure 5-83).
 h. Click the **Normal** view button on the *Status* bar. You do not see headers in this view.
 i. Press **Ctrl+Home**.

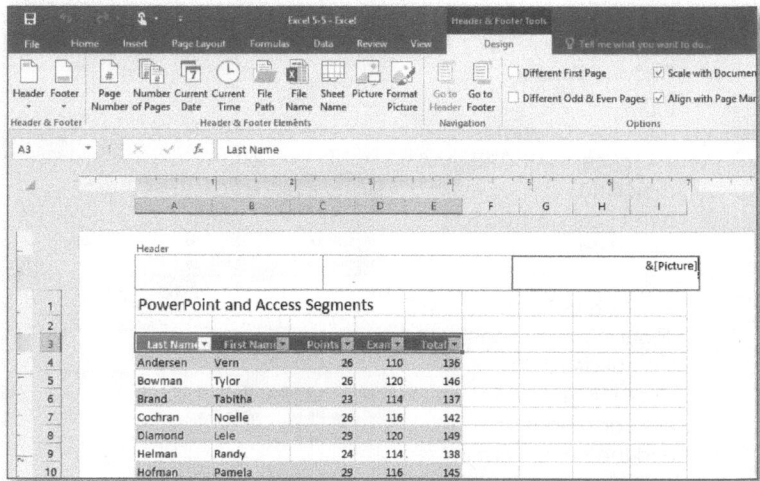

5-82 Picture code in header

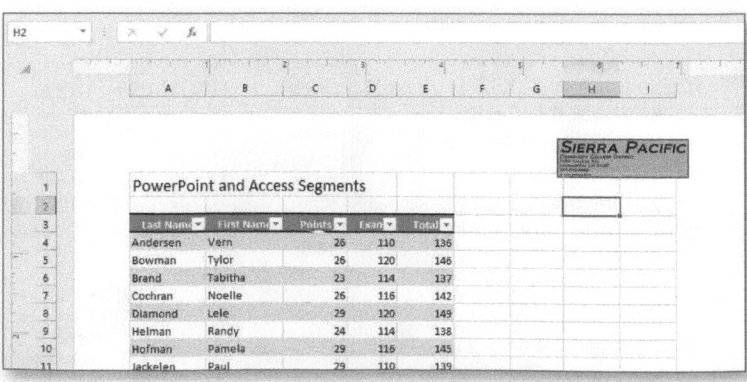

5-83 Reformatted picture

7. Save and close the workbook (Figure 5-84).

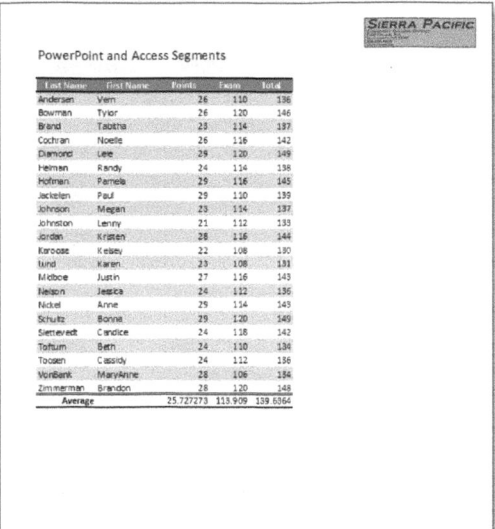

5-84 Completed worksheets for Excel 5-5

Independent Project 5-6

Wear-Ever Shoes plans to link a new workbook to an existing workbook with best-seller data. Your linking formula will use addition, and you plan to use a hyperlink to open the source workbook. You will also illustrate the process to build an external reference formula in a *SmartArt* graphic.
[Student Learning Outcomes 5.5, 5.6, 5.7]

File Needed: *WearEver-05.xlsx (Student data files are available in the* Library *of your SIMnet account)*
Completed Project File Name: *[your initials] Excel 5-6.xlsx*

Skills Covered in This Project

- Link workbooks with an addition formula.
- Edit and copy an external reference formula.
- Insert a hyperlink.
- Insert a *SmartArt* graphic.

1. Create a new workbook and save it as [your initials] Excel 5-6.

2. Open the *WearEver-05* workbook from your student data files.

3. Arrange the two workbooks to be vertically tiled.

4. Copy the **North** worksheet in the *WearEver-05* workbook to *[your initials] Excel 5-6* by selecting your workbook name from the *To book* list in the *Move or Copy* dialog box. The fill color for the copied sheet is different.

5. In *[your initials] Excel 5-6*, rename the copied sheet as Totals, and delete **Sheet1**.

6. Prepare the linked workbook.
 a. In *[your initials] Excel 5-6*, delete the contents of cells **B6:B16**.
 b. Select and delete columns **C:D**.
 c. Edit the label in cell **A3** to display Best Sellers All Regions.
 d. Change the sheet tab color to **Orange, Accent 2** and the **Fill Color** for cells **A1:F4** to **Orange, Accent 2, Lighter 60%**.

7. Link workbooks with an addition formula.
 a. Click cell **B6** in *[your initials] Excel 5-6* and type = to start the formula.
 b. Add the contents of cell **B6** from each of the sheets in the **WearEver-05** workbook in the formula (Figure 5-85). Press **Enter** after the last cell reference.

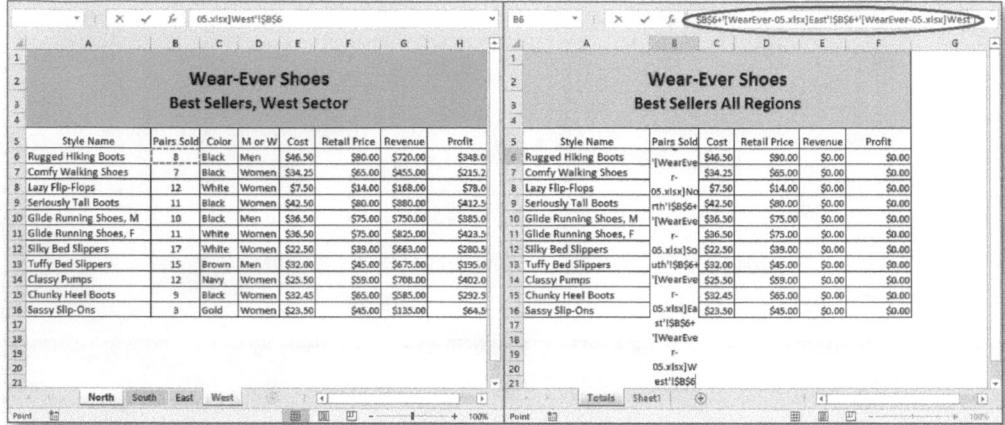

5-85 External reference formula to link workbooks

8. Close the **WearEver-05** workbook without saving and maximize your workbook window.

9. Edit and copy an external reference formula.
 a. Click cell **B6** in *[your initials] Excel 5-6*.
 b. Edit the formula to change each absolute reference to a relative reference. Note that the external reference shows the complete path for the source workbook because it is no longer open (Figure 5-86).
 c. Copy the formula to complete the pairs sold column.

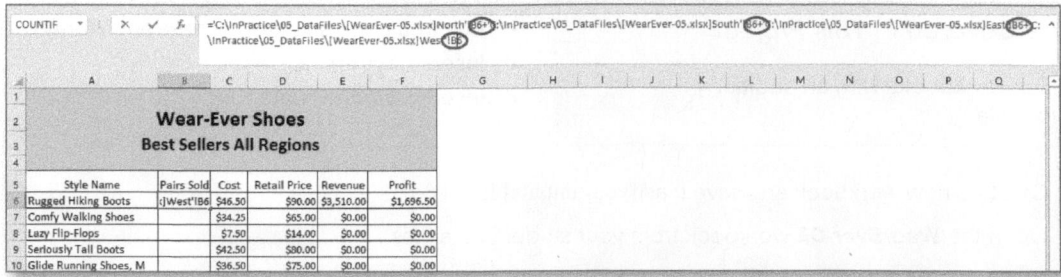

5-86 Formula edited for copying

10. Insert a hyperlink to open the source workbook **WearEver-05**.
 a. Click cell **G3**.
 b. Create a cell hyperlink and edit the display text to read Open source data.

c. Navigate to the folder with the **WearEver-05** workbook to enter its location in the dialog box.

d. Right-click the hyperlink and format its text color to **Orange, Accent 2**.

e. Test the hyperlink and close the source workbook without saving.

11. Insert a *SmartArt* graphic.

a. Insert a **Basic Process** graphic on the **Totals** sheet.

b. In the leftmost text box, type Create new workbook. Do not press **Enter** after typing the label.

c. Type Open source file in the middle box.

d. Type Copy sheet and delete data in the rightmost box.

e. Click the **Add Shape** button [*SmartArt Tools Design* tab, *Create Graphic* group] (Figure 5-87).

f. Type Build formula in the new shape.

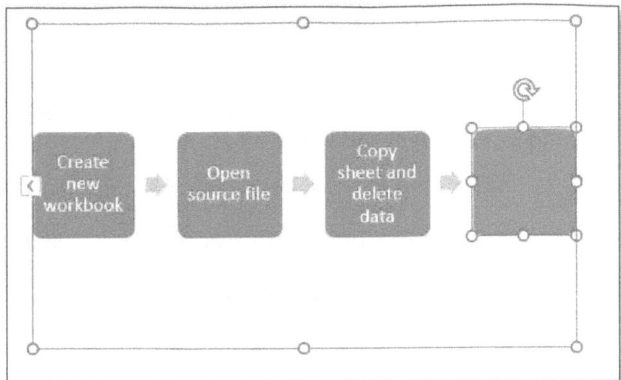

5-87 Fourth shape added to *SmartArt*

12. Format a *SmartArt* graphic.

a. Click the frame of the *SmartArt* graphic to select it.

b. Click the **More** button [*SmartArt Tools Design* tab, *SmartArt Styles* group].

c. Choose **Brick Scene** in the *3-D* group.

d. Click the **Change Colors** button [*SmartArt Tools Design* tab, *SmartArt Styles* group].

e. Choose **Colorful Range – Accent Colors 2 to 3** in the *Colorful* group.

f. Format the *SmartArt* frame with a **½ pt black** outline.

g. Point to the *SmartArt* frame and drag the graphic to position the top left selection handle in cell **A18**.

h. Point to the bottom right selection handle and resize the frame to reach cell **F35**.

i. Select cell **A1**.

13. Save and close the workbook (Figure 5-88).

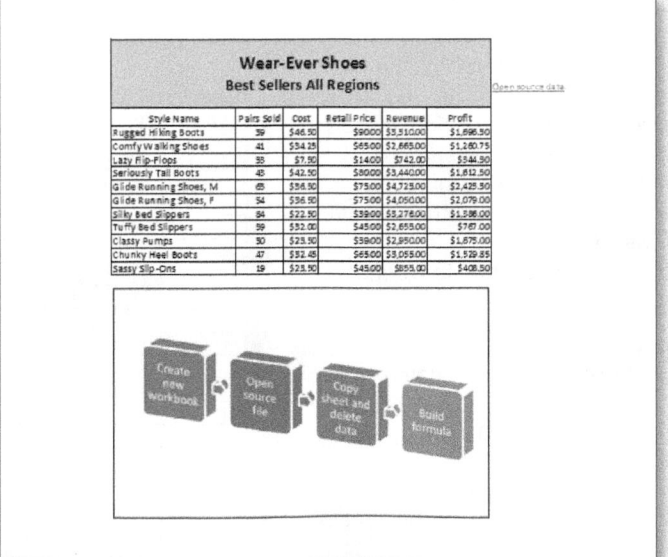

5-88 Completed worksheet for Excel 5-6

Improve It Project 5-7

American River Cycling Club has consolidated data about competitions from April through June. It is a dynamic consolidation but should be static. For this project, you redo the consolidation, improve formatting, and insert the club's logo in a footer.
[Student Learning Outcomes 5.1, 5.2, 5.4, 5.6]

Files Needed: **AmRiverCycling-05.xlsx** and **ARRC.png** (Student data files are available in the Library of your SIMnet account)
Completed Project File Name: **[your initials] Excel 5-7.xlsx**

Skills Covered in This Project

- Remove a dynamic consolidation.
- Create a static data consolidation.
- Insert a picture in a footer.
- Group and format worksheets.

1. Open the **AmRiverCycling-05** workbook from your student data files and save it as [your initials] Excel 5-7.

2. On the **Static** sheet, click the Level **2** outline button to expand the outline.

3. Select cells **A4:D7**, turn off the bold font, and use **No Fill**.

4. Select and delete the contents of cells **A4:D48**.

5. Click the arrow with the **Ungroup** button [*Data* tab, *Outline* group] and clear the outline.

6. Select cells **B4:D12** on the **Static** sheet and create a static data consolidation using **Sum** and cells **E4:G12** on each of the supporting worksheets.

7. Format all results as right-aligned. Note that the dates are missing (Figure 5-89).

8. Select the headings for rows **13:48** (to the left of column A) and right-click one of the headings. Choose **Delete** to delete those rows and select cell **A1**.

9. Insert a picture in a footer.
 a. Switch to *Page Layout* view and click the center footer section.
 b. Click the **Picture** button [*Header & Footer Tools Design* tab, *Header & Footer Elements* group].
 c. Click **Browse** in the *From a file* group.
 d. Find and select **ARRC** from your student data files and click **Insert**.
 e. Click a worksheet cell and return to *Normal* view.

10. Group and format worksheets.
 a. Group the four sheets with a state name as the tab name.
 b. Select and delete columns **C:D** in the grouped sheets.
 c. In cell **A1** on the grouped sheets, type American River Cycling Club. Format the font size as **20 pt**.
 d. Type April-June Race Participation in cell **A2** and format the font size as **18 pt**.

5-89 Outline cleared; dates missing

 e. Select cells **A1:E2** and use the *Format Cells* dialog box to center across the selection.

 f. *AutoFit* columns **A:C**.

 g. Format the labels in row **3** bold and centered.

 h. Apply **All Borders** to cells **A3:E12**. Apply **Outside Borders** to cells **A1:E2**.

 i. Format the **Height** of rows **3:12** to **21.00 (28 pixels)**.

 j. Select the dates in column **A** and use the *Format Cells* dialog box to apply a *Date* format that displays the date as *1-Apr*.

 k. Open the *Page Setup* dialog box to the *Margins* tab. Center the sheets horizontally on the page.

11. Click cell **A1** and ungroup the sheets.

12. Copy the dates in column **A** on the **Washington** sheet to cell **A4** on the **Static** sheet.

13. Save and close the workbook (Figure 5-90).

American River Cycling Club
April-June Race Participation

Date	City	# of Riders	Male	Female
1-Apr	Algonquin	35	18	17
4-Apr	Blue Island	27	14	13
14-Apr	Cicero	28	12	16
23-Apr	Midlothian	28	12	16
1-May	Peoria	32	16	16
8-May	Rockford	39	20	19
21-May	Salem	35	15	20
1-Jun	Springfield	39	18	21
5-Jun	Urbana	33	18	15

American River Cycling Club
April-June Race Participation

Date	City	# of Riders	Male	Female
1-Apr	Addison	21	11	10
4-Apr	Arlington	21	9	12
14-Apr	Denton	32	20	12
23-Apr	Fort Worth	27	14	13
1-May	Grand Prairie	27	15	12
8-May	Irving	33	18	15
21-May	Plano	27	21	6
1-Jun	River Oaks	29	15	14
5-Jun	San Antonio	22	11	11

American River Cycling Club
April-June Race Participation

Date	City	# of Riders	Male	Female
1-Apr	Arlington	40	24	16
4-Apr	Brookline	37	20	17
14-Apr	Cambridge	28	19	9
23-Apr	Chestnut Hill	38	18	20
1-May	Everett	35	20	15
8-May	Framingham	29	19	10
21-May	Foxboro	29	18	11
1-Jun	Revere	35	21	14
5-Jun	Watertown	39	22	17

American River Cycling Club
Race Participation Totals

Date	# of Riders	Male	Female
1-Apr	117	68	49
4-Apr	115	59	56
14-Apr	114	69	45
23-Apr	121	59	62
1-May	134	72	61
8-May	135	75	60
21-May	121	72	49
1-Jun	132	69	63
5-Jun	121	67	54

AMERICAN RIVER CYCLING CLUB

American River Cycling Club
April-June Race Participation

Date	City	# of Riders	Male	Female
1-Apr	Bainbridge Island	21	15	6
4-Apr	Bellevue	30	16	14
14-Apr	Bothell	26	18	8
23-Apr	Kirkland	28	15	13
1-May	Lynnwood	40	21	19
8-May	Parkland	34	18	16
21-May	Poulsbo	30	18	12
1-Jun	Redmond	29	15	14
5-Jun	Tacoma	27	16	11

5-90 Completed worksheets for Excel 5-7

 Challenge Project 5-8

For this project, you work with a classmate (or on your own) to develop source and dependent workbooks. The source workbook includes details about the time spent each weekday on each of five activities for four weeks. The dependent workbook uses external reference formulas to summarize the week's activities.
[Student Learning Outcomes 5.4, 5.5, 5.7]

File needed: None
Completed Project File Names: *[your initials] Excel 5-8.xlsx* and *[your initials] Excel 5-8a.xlsx*

Create a new workbook and save it as [your initials] Excel 5-8. **Modify your workbook according to the following guidelines:**

- Type the names of the five weekdays as column labels, starting in cell B3.
- Type the names of five tasks or activities as row labels, starting in cell A4. Choose activities such as Prepare meals, Work on class assignments, Exercise or workout, and other daily tasks.
- Name the sheet Week 1 and enter the number of minutes spent each day on each activity.
- Copy the sheet to create separate sheets for weeks 2–4.
- Group the sheets and enter main labels in rows 1:2 to describe the data. Use a formula to total each activity for the week.
- Format the grouped sheets in an attractive, easy-to-view style.
- Ungroup the sheets and edit three values on each of the worksheets for weeks 2–4.
- Create a new workbook named [your initials] Excel 5-8a.
- Copy one of the sheets from *[your initials] Excel 5-8* into this workbook and name the sheet Month.
- Create an external reference formula to add the first task minutes for Monday using *[your initials] Excel 5-8* as the source workbook. Edit and copy the formula.
- Insert a hyperlink in the dependent workbook to open the source workbook.

 Challenge Project 5-9

For this project, you build worksheets with data about an activity or concept from your neighborhood or your workplace. You will group sheets for formatting, copy a sheet from one workbook to the other, and insert a *SmartArt* graphic.
[Student Learning Outcome 5.2, 5.4, 5.5, 5.6, 5.7]

File Needed: None
Completed Project File Names: *[your initials] Excel 5-9.xlsx* and *Excel 5-9a.xlsx*

Create a new source workbook and save it as [your initials] Excel 5-9. **Modify your workbook according to the following guidelines:**

- Key labels and values to illustrate a concept of interest to you. For example, build a worksheet to track the average number of automobiles owned by street in your community, the number of workers by department at your office, travel distances to campus by your classmates, etc.

- Copy the sheet and change one value in each column in the copied sheet.
- Group the sheets and apply formatting that suits both sheets.
- Review the *SmartArt* categories to find a graphic to illustrate a concept related to your data. Place the *SmartArt* on its own sheet. If necessary, add or remove shapes from the graphic.
- Format the *SmartArt* graphic with a style, change the colors, or add fill or a border. Size and position the graphic.
- On each worksheet, insert a hyperlink that switches to the *SmartArt* sheet.
- Save the workbook and leave it open.
- Create a second workbook and save it as [your initials] Excel 5-9a.
- Copy either sheet from *[your initials] Excel 5-9* to *[your initials] Excel 5-9a*.
- Name the copied sheet in *[your initials] Excel 5-9a* to indicate that it is a consolidation worksheet.
- Dynamically consolidate data from the two sheets in *[your initials] Excel 5-9*.
- Save and close both workbooks.

Challenge Project 5-10

For this project, you create a timesheet workbook for five employees. After four weeks, you consolidate data to create a worksheet that displays average number of hours worked on a given day by each employee.
[Student Learning Outcomes 5.1, 5.4, 5.6, 5.8]

File Needed: None
Completed Project File Name: *[your initials] Excel 5-10.xlsx*

Create a new workbook and save it as [your initials] Excel 5-10. Modify your workbook according to the following guidelines:

- Insert worksheets so that you have five worksheets in the workbook. Name the sheets Week 1, Week 2, Week 3, Week 4, and Averages.
- Group all the sheets and type the names of five employees in a column as row labels. Use a five- or seven-day workweek, typing the day names as column headings.
- Add a main title to indicate a company name. Enter the number of hours worked by each employee for each day worked (all employees have the same number of hours). Include values that are decimals, such as 5.5 or 6.25, and enter zero (0) in at least five cells.
- Total weekly hours by employee and show the total hours worked by day.
- Apply formatting to the grouped sheets.
- Ungroup the sheets and prepare the *Averages* sheet for consolidation without links. Edit labels as needed and delete the total column and row.
- On the *Averages* sheet, insert a picture from an online source to complement your company name. Size and format the image to enhance the overall appearance of the worksheet.
- Mark the workbook as final.

CHAPTER

6

Exploring the Function Library

CHAPTER OVERVIEW

The Excel *Function Library* includes functions that perform complex and sophisticated calculations for use in business, government, education, and research. In this chapter, you learn about functions in the *Database, Logical, Date & Time, Financial,* and *Text* categories. You also nest functions and build time, date, and statistical calculations.

STUDENT LEARNING OUTCOMES (SLOs)

After completing this chapter, you will be able to:

SLO 6.1 Use *Database* functions such as *DSUM* and *DAVERAGE* (p. E6-350).

SLO 6.2 Build *AND, OR,* nested, and *IFS* functions (p. E6-352).

SLO 6.3 Explore the *Lookup & Reference* category with *INDEX, MATCH,* and *TRANSPOSE* (p. E6-364).

SLO 6.4 Build date, time, and statistical calculations (p. E6-368).

SLO 6.5 Use *Financial* functions such as *PV, FV,* and *NPV* (p. E6-380).

SLO 6.6 Work with *Text* functions including *TEXTJOIN, CONCAT, EXACT,* and *REPLACE* (p. E6-384).

SLO 6.7 Use multiple criteria in *SUMIFS, AVERAGEIFS,* and *COUNTIFS* functions (p. E6-391).

SLO 6.8 Monitor and edit functions with the *Watch Window* and *Find and Replace* (p. E6-394).

CASE STUDY

In the Pause & Practice projects in this chapter, you work on revenue, inventory and forecasting, financial planning, and human resources worksheets for Paradise Lakes Resort (PLR) using Excel functions.

Pause & Practice 6-1: Use *Database* and *Logical* functions.

Pause & Practice 6-2: Work with date and time calculations and *Lookup & Reference* functions.

Pause & Practice 6-3: Build *Financial* and *Text* functions.

Pause & Practice 6-4: Use multiple criteria, the *Watch Window,* and *Find and Replace.*

SLO 6.1

Working with Database Functions

A *database function* performs a mathematical or statistical calculation only for data that meet the criteria. In a worksheet with revenue numbers for Paradise Lakes Resort, for example, you can use a database function to total results only for Cass Lake.

Database Function Syntax

The term *database* refers to a range of cells that includes a header row and rows of data, like a list or a table. Each row in a database is a *record* and includes the same information for each entity. A column is a *field*.

Database functions use the following syntax:

FunctionName(database, field, criteria)

The first argument, *database*, is the range of cells to be analyzed. You can use a named range or cell addresses. In Figure 6-1, the *database* argument is the named range *List*.

> **MORE INFO**
>
> Press **F3 (FN+F3)** to paste a range name as an argument.

The *field* argument refers to the column used for the calculation. You can type the column label or the position number of the column in the list. The first column is 1, the second is 2, and so on.

The third argument is *criteria*, a cell range on the same or another sheet where you type specifications. The *criteria* argument includes labels in one row and criteria in the row below. In Figure 6-1, the criteria range is cells B2:B3. Labels in the criteria range must be spelled exactly like those in the database. In Figure 6-1, the *DMAX* function in cell D21 calculates the highest value in the "Goal" column for cells that show "Cass Lake" in the "Location" column.

You can specify *AND* criteria in the same row, build *OR* criteria in separate rows, and use wildcard characters in the criteria.

The following table explains popular *Database* functions.

D21			✓	fx	=DMAX(List,"goal",B2:B3)

	A	B	C	D	E	F
1	Criteria					
2	Name	Location	Goal	Actual		
3		cas*				
4						
5	Revenue Data by Employee					
6	Name	Location	Goal	Actual	Met Goal?	Both Goals?
7	B.J Francine	Baudette	$17,000	$21,500	Yes	TRUE
8	Christopher Bowman	Cass Lake	$15,000	$12,750	No	FALSE
9	Nikolai Jaiowiec	Walker	$15,000	$15,600	Yes	TRUE
10	Chad Meison	Cass Lake	$17,500	$15,000	Yes	TRUE
11	Dennis Omang	Breezy Point	$18,000	$21,000	Yes	TRUE
12	Corey Daniels	Cass Lake	$5,000	$3,300	No	FALSE
13	Natasha Nelson	Baudette	$0	$4,050	Yes	FALSE
14	Tammy Christine	Walker	$75,000	$81,000	Yes	TRUE
15	Wyatte Mockentune	Breezy Point	$15,000	$14,200	No	FALSE
16	Kendal Shaedon	Breezy Point	21000S	$18,500	No	FALSE
17	Ella Jamison	Baudette	$15,000	$13,200	No	FALSE
18	Alec Jones	Baudette	$17,000	$9,350	No	FALSE
19	Josie Daddiline	Walker	$42,500	$56,000	Yes	TRUE
20						
21		Maximum Goal, Cass Lake		$17,500		
22		Average Goal, Cass Lake		$12,500		
23		Total Goal, Cass Lake		$37,500		
24						
25						

6-1 *DMAX* function for tabular data

Database Functions

Function Name	Explanation
DAVERAGE	Averages the values of cells in the field (column) that meet the criteria
DCOUNT	Counts cells with values in the field (column) that meet the criteria
DCOUNTA	Counts cells in the field (column) that are not empty that meet the criteria

Function Name	Explanation
DMAX	Displays the largest value in the field (column) that meets the criteria
DMIN	Displays the smallest value in the field (column) that meets the criteria
DSUM	Sums the values of cells in the field (column) that meet the criteria

The *Database* function category is listed in the *Insert Function* dialog box. You can also type = and a few characters of the function name to choose it from the *Formula AutoComplete* list.

▶ HOW TO: Build a DSUM Function

1. Copy the labels that are used to specify criteria.
2. Enter criteria below the label in the criteria range.
3. Click the cell for *DSUM* results.
4. Click the **Insert Function** button [*Formulas* tab, *Function Library* group].
5. Choose **Database** in the *Or select a category* list (Figure 6-2).
 - Click a function name in the list to display its description and syntax.
6. Select **DSUM** and click **OK**.
 - The *Function Arguments* dialog box opens.
7. Click the **Database** box.
8. Select the cells in the worksheet.
 - Include the header row and all data rows.
 - Press **F3** (**FN+F3**) to paste a range name instead of selecting cells.
9. Click the **Field** box.
10. Type the field name (column label).
 - The argument is not case sensitive.
 - Quotation marks are automatically supplied when you use the *Function Arguments* dialog box.
 - Type a number to indicate the column's position in the database instead of typing the label.
11. Click the **Criteria** box.
12. Select the criteria range (Figure 6-3).

6-2 *Insert Function* dialog box and the *Database* category

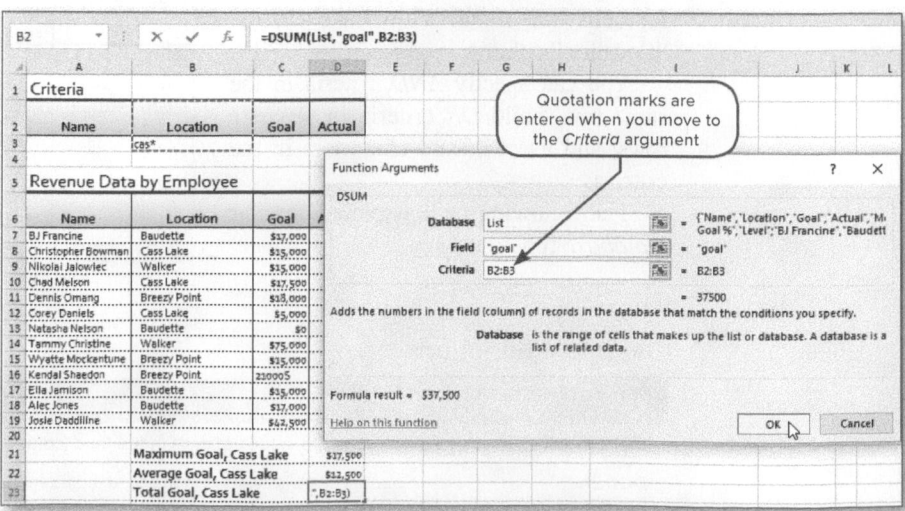

6-3 *Function Arguments* dialog box for *DSUM*

- You can key the range address.
- The criteria range can be located on a different worksheet.

13. Click **OK**.

- Results appear in the cell.
- You can press **Enter** to close the dialog box.

 SLO 6.2

Building AND, OR, Nested, and IFS Functions

Functions in the *Logical* group determine if one or all conditions are met and display TRUE or FALSE as the result. The *IFS* function can display text or calculated results as well as TRUE or FALSE.

The AND Function

The *AND* function defines multiple conditions that must be met for a TRUE result. Paradise Lakes Resort can use an *AND* function to determine if an employee met an individual sales goal as well as a department goal.

The syntax for an *AND* function is:

= AND(LogicalN)

An *AND* function has one argument named *LogicalN*. *N* is a number; arguments are named *Logical1, Logical2, Logical3*, up to *Logical255*. In each *LogicalN* argument, you build a simple statement. An argument such as **D7<C7** means that the value in cell D7 must be less than the value in cell C7 for the result to be TRUE. If you build five *LogicalN* arguments, every statement must be true for the result to display TRUE. If one of those five statements is not true, the result in the cell is FALSE.

> **MORE INFO**
>
> *AND* functions with many arguments are restrictive or limiting.

> **HOW TO:** Build an AND Function

1. Click the cell for the result.
2. Click the **Logical** button [*Formulas* tab, *Function Library* group].
3. Choose **AND**.

 - Two *LogicalN* argument boxes are listed in the dialog box.
 - Additional arguments become available as you complete the previous argument.

4. Click the **Logical1** box.
5. Build the first statement to be evaluated.

 - You can type the statement.
 - You can select cells in the worksheet or use range names.
 - If the statement includes text, you must enclose the text in quotation marks.

6. Click the **Logical2** box.

 - A third argument box opens.

7. Build the second statement to be evaluated (Figure 6-4).

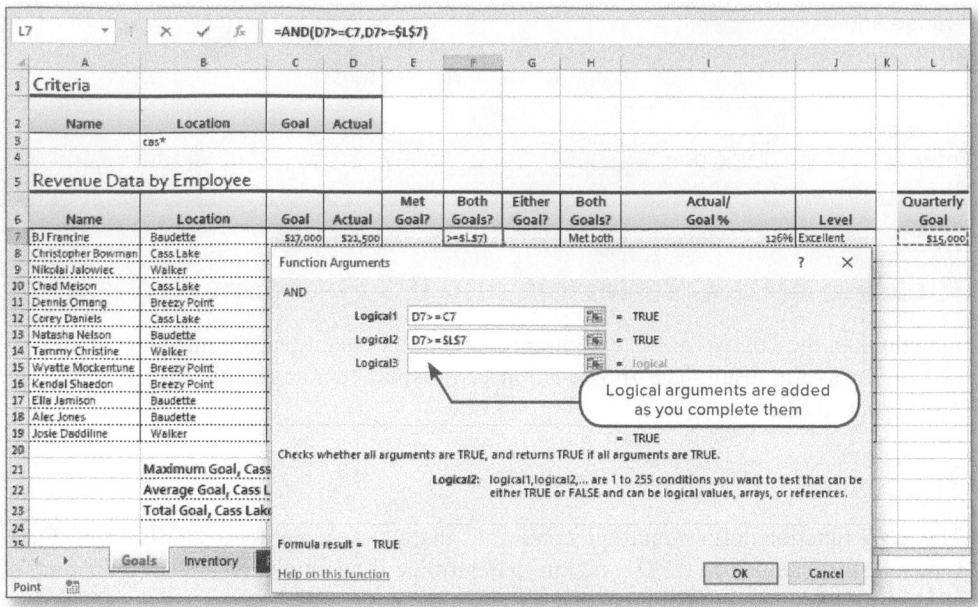

6-4 *AND* function in the *Function Arguments* dialog box

8. Build additional *LogicalN* arguments as needed.

9. Click **OK** or press **Enter**.

- If all statements are true, the word TRUE appears in the cell.
- If one of the statements is false, the word FALSE displays in the cell.

The OR Function

An *OR* function is less restrictive than an *AND* statement. In an *OR* function, if one of the arguments is true, the result is TRUE. All arguments must be false for FALSE to display as the result. You can use up to 255 *LogicalN* arguments.

The syntax for an *OR* function is:

= OR(LogicalN)

> **MORE INFO**
>
> Use absolute or relative cell references in *AND* or *OR* functions as required if the formula will be copied.

▶ HOW TO: Type an OR Function

1. Click the cell for the result.

2. Type =or and press **Tab**.

- **=OR(** displays in the cell.
- The first argument *logical1* is bold in the *ScreenTip*.

3. Build the first statement to be evaluated.

- You can type the statement.
- Select cells in the worksheet or press **F3 (FN+F3)** to paste a range name.
- If the statement includes text, enclose the text in quotation marks.

4. Type a comma , to separate the arguments.

 - The next argument *logical2* appears bold in the *ScreenTip*.

5. Build the second statement to be evaluated (Figure 6-5).

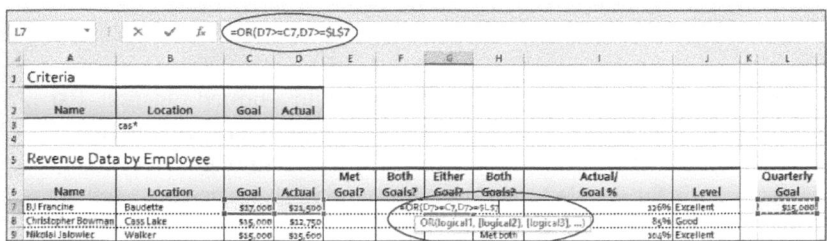

6-5 *OR* function with two arguments

6. Type a comma , to add another *logicaln* argument.

 - Build additional *logicaln* arguments as needed.

7. Press **Enter** when all arguments are typed.

 - If one statement is true, the word TRUE displays in the cell.
 - If no statement is true, the word FALSE appears in the cell.

The IF Function with AND and OR

A ***nested function*** is a function within a function. Logical functions are commonly nested. For example, use *AND* and *OR* with an *IF* function to build a statement that specifies multiple requirements. You can display a result other than TRUE or FALSE, because the *Value_if_true* and *Value_if_false* arguments in the *IF* function determine the results.

The following table illustrates examples of nesting *AND* or *OR* within an *IF* function in cell D4.

Sample Nested Functions

Function	Arguments	Explanation
=IF(C4>15000, 5000,0)	Logical_test = C4>15000 Value_if_true = 5000 Value_if_false = 0	If the value in cell C4 is greater than 15,000, cell D4 displays 5,000. If the value in cell C4 is less than 15,000, cell D4 displays 0.
=IF(AND(C4>15000,C7>12500), 5000,0)	Logical_test = C4>15000 and C7>12500 Value_if_true = 5000 Value_if_false = 0	If the value is cell C4 is greater than 15,000 **and** if the value in cell C7 is greater than 12,500, cell D4 displays 5,000. If either of these conditions is false, cell D4 displays 0.
=IF(OR(C4>15000,C7>12500), 5000,0)	Logical_test = C4>15000 or C7>12500 Value_if_true = 5000 Value_if_false = 0	If the value is cell C4 is greater than 15,000 **or** if the value in cell C7 is greater than 12,500, cell D4 displays 5,000. Cell D4 displays 0 when the value in cell C4 is equal to or less than 15,000 **and** the value in cell C7 is equal to or less than 12,500.

> MORE INFO
>
> Do not type commas as thousand separators in formulas, because Excel mistakes the comma for an argument separator.

When you use the *Function Arguments* dialog box to build a nested function, Excel supplies separators and parentheses. Whether you use the dialog box or type a nested function, parentheses are color-coded to help you follow formula syntax. Although Excel automatically enters a closing parenthesis for simple formulas, it may not do so for nested functions. When a parenthesis is missing, Excel may display a message box with a suggested fix.

When using the *Function Arguments* dialog box to build nested functions, you toggle among functions by clicking the function name in the *Formula* bar. The *Function Arguments* dialog box displays arguments for the function that has the focus.

> MORE INFO
>
> You must use opening and closing parentheses in pairs in nested functions.

▶HOW TO: Nest AND and IF Functions

1. Click the cell for the result.
2. Type =if(to open the *ScreenTip*.
 - The *logical_test* argument appears bold.
 - The *logical_test* argument is the *AND* function.
3. Type and and press **Tab**.
 - The *ScreenTip* displays arguments for the *AND* function.
4. Type the first *logicalN* statement and type a comma , (Figure 6-6).

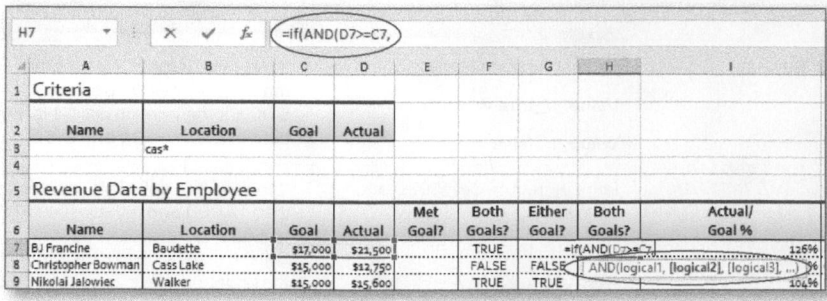

6-6 *AND* function is *logical_test* argument

 - You can select a worksheet cell rather than type the reference.
 - Use absolute or relative references as required.
5. Enter each *logicalN* argument followed by a comma.
6. Type the closing parenthesis and a comma), after the last argument for the *AND* function (Figure 6-7).
 - The focus returns to the *IF* function.

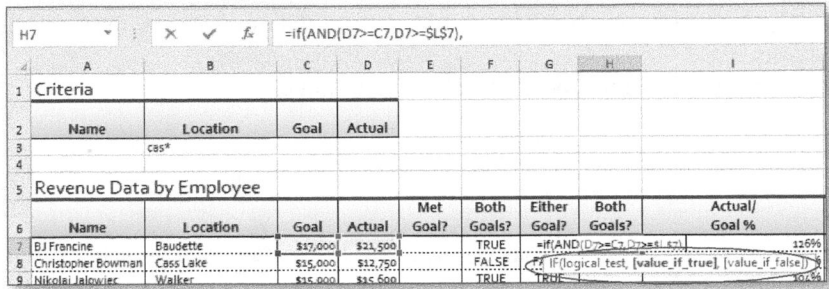

6-7 Closing parenthesis returns focus to *IF* function

7. Enter the *value_if_true* argument.
 - If the argument is text, enclose it in quotation marks.
 - You can select a cell or type its address.
 - Use absolute or relative references as required.

8. Type a comma , to move to the *value_if_false* argument.

9. Enter the *value_if_false* argument.

10. Type the closing parenthesis) (Figure 6-8).

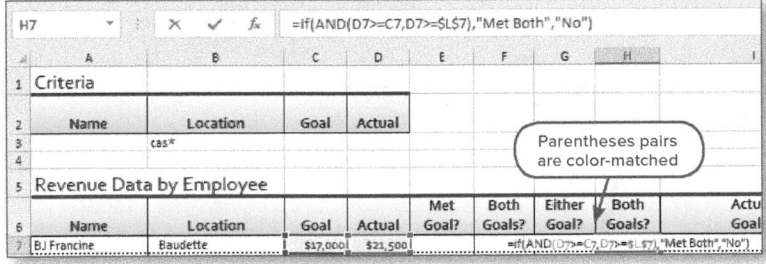

6-8 *AND* function nested within *IF*

11. Press **Enter**.
 - You can click the **Enter** button on the *Formula* bar.

The IFS Function

An *IFS* function has one or more logical tests with corresponding results for each test. The result that displays in the cell represents the first logical test that evaluates to TRUE. Your course grade can be calculated with an *IFS* function as follows:

=IFS(D2>=92,"A",D2>=84,"B",D2>=76,"C",D2<76,"D")

If you receive 92 or more points, the first logical test is TRUE, you receive an A grade, and the *IFS* function ends. When that is not true, the next logical test runs to determine if your score is 84 or higher (but not 92 points or higher). When that is true, the *IFS* function ends, and the result cell displays a B. The third logical test uses 76 points or higher (but not 84 points or higher), and the last test uses fewer than 76 points.

The syntax for an *IFS* function is:

=IFS(logical_test1, value_if_true1, [logical_test2, value_if_true2], ⋯)

Each *logical_testN* argument must have a *value_if_trueN* argument, and there can be up to 127 logical tests.

IFS functions are usually built from high value to low value.

> **MORE INFO**
>
> In earlier versions of Excel, a nested *IF* formula checked multiple logical tests. In a nested *IF* formula, the number of outcomes minus 1 is the number of logical tests required.

▶ HOW TO: Create an IFS Function

1. Click the cell for the *IFS* function.
2. Click the **Logical** button [*Formulas* tab, *Function Library* group].
3. Choose **IFS** to open the *Function Arguments* dialog box.
4. Enter the *logical_test1* argument.
 - You can click a cell or type its address.
 - You can use an operator to build a statement or expression.
5. Enter the *value_if_true1* result (Figure 6-9).
 - If the *logical_test1* argument is true, this result appears and no more logical tests are run.
 - The *Function Arguments* dialog box enters parentheses and quotation marks as needed.
 - Use uppercase and lowercase as preferred for results.

6-9 First logical test in an *IFS* formula

6. Enter the *logical_test2* argument.
 - If the *logical_test1* argument is false, the second test runs.
7. Enter the *value_if_true2* result.
 - If the *logical_test2* argument is true, this result appears and the function ends.
8. Enter *logical_testN* arguments as needed.

9. Enter *value_if_trueN* results for each *logical_testN* argument (Figure 6-10).

- You can use up to 127 *logical_test* arguments.

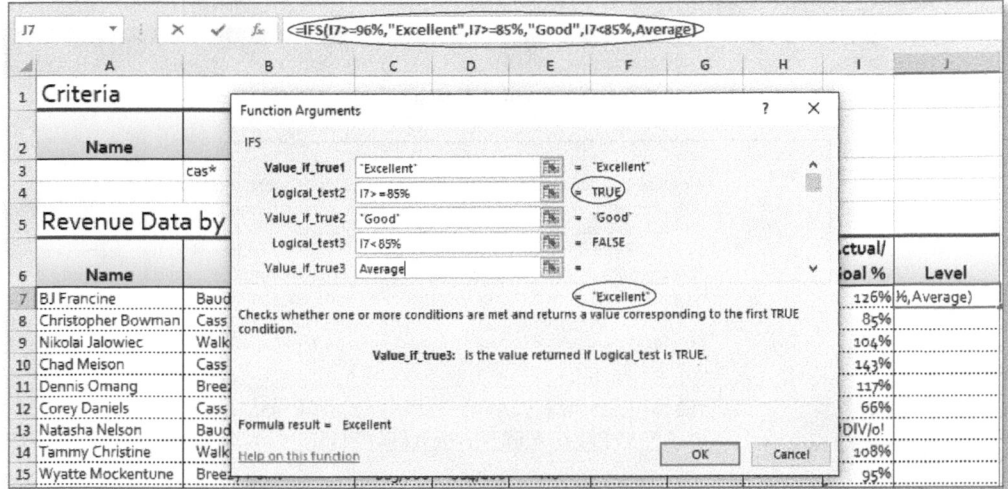

6-10 Three logical tests and results for an *IFS* formula

10. Click **OK**.

- The *value_if_true* argument for the first *logical_test* that is TRUE displays in the cell.

The IFERROR Function

A formula syntax error results in an Excel error value message in the cell. Common syntax errors include typing the letter "o" instead of a zero (0) or typing a letter as part of a value as shown in row 16 in Figure 6-11. Excel displays #VALUE! in the formula cell. When you anticipate an error that you or someone else might make, use the *IFERROR* function to display a specific, custom error message such as "Check that all entries are numbers."

5	Revenue Data by Employee									
6	Name	Location	Goal	Actual	Met Goal?	Both Goals?	Either Goal?	Both Goals?	Actual/ Goal %	Level
7	BJ Francine	Baudette	$17,000	$21,500		TRUE	TRUE	Met Both	126%	Excellent
8	Christopher Bowman	Cass Lake	$15,000	$12,750		FALSE	FALSE		85%	Good
9	Nikolai Jalowiec	Walker	$15,000	$15,600		TRUE	TRUE		104%	Excellent
10	Chad Meison	Cass Lake	$17,500	$25,000		TRUE	TRUE		143%	Excellent
11	Dennis Omang	Breezy Point	$18,000	$21,000		TRUE	TRUE		117%	Excellent
12	Corey Daniels	Cass Lake	$5,000	$3,300		FALSE	FALSE		66%	Average
13	Natasha Nelson	Baudette	$0	$4,050		FALSE	TRUE		#DIV/o!	#DIV/o!
14	Tammy Christine	Walker	$75,000	$81,000		TRUE	TRUE		108%	Excellent
15	Wyatte Mockentune	Breezy Point	$15,000	$14,200		FALSE	FALSE		95%	Good
16	Kendal Shaedon	Breezy Point	21000S	$18,500		FALSE	TRUE		#VALUE!	#VALUE!
17	Ella Jamison	Baudette	$15,000	$13,200		FALSE	FALSE		88%	Good
18	Alec Jones	Baudette	$17,000	$9,350		FALSE	FALSE		55%	Average
19	Josie Daddiline	Walker	$42,500	$56,000		TRUE	TRUE		132%	Excellent

6-11 Standard, default error messages

The *IFERROR* function works only for formulas that can return a standard Excel error value message. When a formula uses incorrect mathematics or the wrong cell address, an

error may not be identified or may result in an error triangle, and *IFERROR* is not relevant. The following table lists error values and descriptions.

Excel Error Messages

Error Value	Description
#N/A	A value or an argument is missing.
#VALUE!	An incorrect data type is used (for example a label is used instead of a value).
#REF!	A cell reference is empty, usually because cells were deleted.
#DIV/0!	The formula divides by zero (0) or an empty cell.
#NUM!	The formula uses an invalid numeric entry (for example, it could be a wrong data type or a negative number instead of a required positive value).
#NAME?	The formula uses unrecognized text such as a misspelled function, sheet, or range name.
#NULL!	The formula refers to an intersection of two cell ranges that do not intersect, or uses an incorrect range separator (for example, a semicolon or comma instead of a colon).

An *IFERROR* function has two arguments. The *value* argument is the formula that might display an error message. The *value_if_error* argument is the text that should appear in place of the default Excel error message.

=IFERROR(value, value_if_error)
=IFERROR(A7/A9, "Check the values in column A.")

▶ HOW TO: Create an IFERROR Function

1. Click the cell for the result.
 - This is a formula cell that may display a standard error message.
2. Delete the cell contents if the formula is already entered in the cell.
3. Click the **Logical** button [*Formulas* tab, *Function Library* group].
4. Choose **IFERROR**.
5. Enter the *Value* argument.
 - You can key the formula using lowercase letters or select cells in the worksheet.
 - You don't need to key an equals sign when you use the *Function Arguments* dialog box.
6. Enter the *Value_if_error* argument (Figure 6-12).
 - Use uppercase, lowercase, and punctuation as you want it to appear in your message.
 - Quotation marks are supplied when you use the *Function Arguments* dialog box.

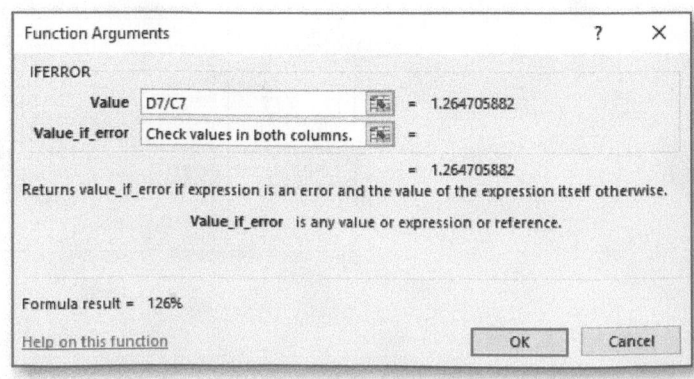

6-12 *IFERROR* with both arguments complete

7. Click **OK**.
 - The error message appears only when there is an error that would have resulted in a standard error message (Figure 6-13).

| 5 | Revenue Data by Employee | | | | | | | | | |
|---|---|---|---|---|---|---|---|---|---|
| 6 | Name | Location | Goal | Actual | Met Goal? | Both Goals? | Either Goal? | Both Goals? | Actual/ Goal % | Level |
| 7 | BJ Francine | Baudette | $17,000 | $21,500 | | TRUE | TRUE | Met Both | 126% | Excellent |
| 8 | Christopher Bowman | Cass Lake | $15,000 | $12,750 | | FALSE | FALSE | No | 85% | Good |
| 9 | Nikolai Jalowiec | Walker | $15,000 | $15,600 | | TRUE | TRUE | Met Both | 104% | Excellent |
| 10 | Chad Meison | Cass Lake | $17,500 | $25,000 | | TRUE | TRUE | Met Both | 143% | Excellent |
| 11 | Dennis Omang | Breezy Point | $18,000 | $21,000 | | TRUE | TRUE | Met Both | 117% | Excellent |
| 12 | Corey Daniels | Cass Lake | $5,000 | $3,300 | | FALSE | FALSE | No | 66% | Average |
| 13 | Natasha Nelson | Baudette | $0 | $4,050 | | FALSE | TRUE | No | Check values in both columns | Excellent |
| 14 | Tammy Christine | Walker | $75,000 | $81,000 | | TRUE | TRUE | Met Both | 108% | Excellent |
| 15 | Wyatte Mockentune | Breezy Point | $15,000 | $14,200 | | FALSE | FALSE | No | 95% | Good |
| 16 | Kendal Shaedon | Breezy Point | 21000S | $18,500 | | FALSE | TRUE | No | Check values in both columns | Excellent |
| 17 | Ella Jamison | Baudette | $15,000 | $13,200 | | FALSE | FALSE | No | 88% | Good |
| 18 | Alec Jones | Baudette | $17,000 | $9,350 | | FALSE | FALSE | No | 55% | Average |
| 19 | Josie Daddiline | Walker | $42,500 | $56,000 | | TRUE | TRUE | Met Both | 132% | Excellent |

6-13 Custom error message appears in place of Excel default message

PAUSE & PRACTICE: EXCEL 6-1

In this project, you complete calculations for Paradise Lakes Resort using *Database* functions. You also use *Logical* functions to calculate results about employees' revenue accomplishments.

File Needed: ***ParadiseLakes-06.xlsx*** *(Student data files are available in the* Library *of your SIMnet account)*
Completed Project File Name: ***[your initials] PP E6-1.xlsx***

1. Open ***ParadiseLakes-06.xlsx*** from your student data files and save it as [your initials] PP E6-1.

2. Build a *DSUM* function using the *Function Arguments* dialog box.
 a. Click the **Goals** sheet tab and select cell **B3**.
 b. Type cas*. Criteria is not case-sensitive, and wildcard characters are acceptable.
 c. Click cell **C23** and click the **Insert Function** button in the *Formula* bar.
 d. Choose **Database** in the *Or select a category* list.
 e. Select **DSUM** and click **OK**.
 f. Press **F3** (**FN+F3**) in the *Database* box to open the *Paste Names* dialog box.
 g. Choose **List** and click **OK**.
 h. Click the **Field** box and type goal. Entries are not case sensitive.
 i. Click the **Criteria** box and select cells **B2:B3** (Figure 6-14). Quotation marks are entered for the *Field* argument.
 j. Click **OK**. The total for Cass Lake is $37,500.

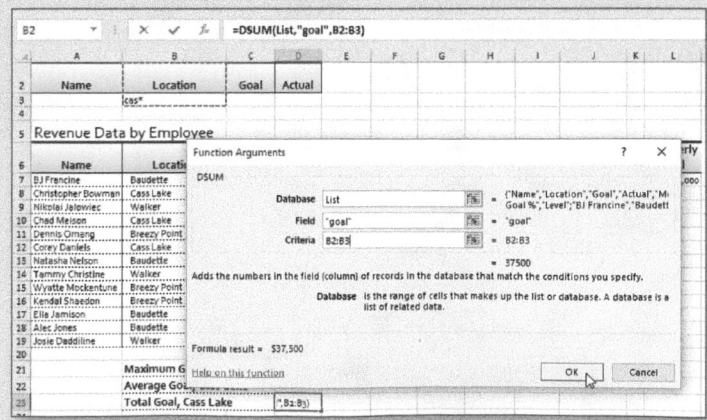

6-14 *DSUM* and its arguments

3. Type a *DAVERAGE* function.
 a. Click cell **C22**.
 b. Type =dav to display the *Formula AutoComplete* list and press **Tab**.
 c. Type a lowercase L l for the *database* argument and to open *Formula AutoComplete* again.

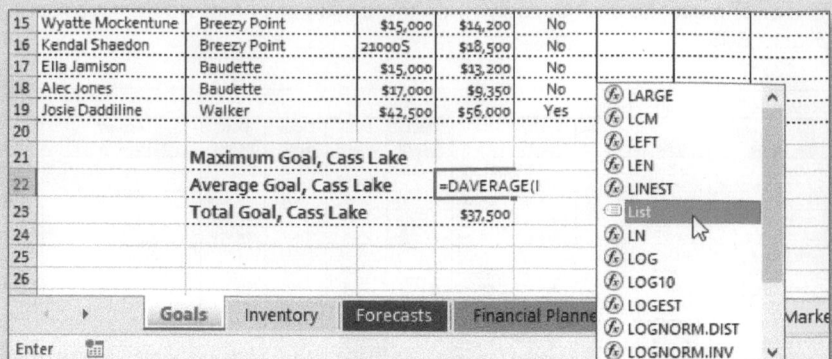

6-15 *DAVERAGE* and *Formula AutoComplete*

 d. Double-click **List** (Figure 6-15).
 e. Type a comma , to move to the *field* argument.
 f. Type "goal" including the quotation marks.
 g. Type a comma , to move to the *criteria* argument.
 h. Select cells **B2:B3** and press **Enter**. The closing parenthesis is supplied. The average for Cass Lake is $12,500.

4. Use the *Function Arguments* dialog box or type to create a *DMAX* function in cell **C21** with the same arguments as used in step 3. The maximum value for Cass Lake is $17,500.

5. Use the *Function Arguments* dialog box to build an *AND* function.
 a. Select cell **F7** and click the **Logical** button [*Formulas* tab, *Function Library* group].
 b. Choose **AND**.
 c. Click the **Logical1** argument box.
 d. Select cell **D7**, type >=, and select cell **C7**. The first condition is that the value in cell D7 be greater than or equal to the value in cell C7.
 e. Click the **Logical2** box.
 f. Select cell **D7**, type >=, select cell **L7**, and press **F4** (**FN+F4**). The reference to cell L7 must be absolute for copying the formula (Figure 6-16).

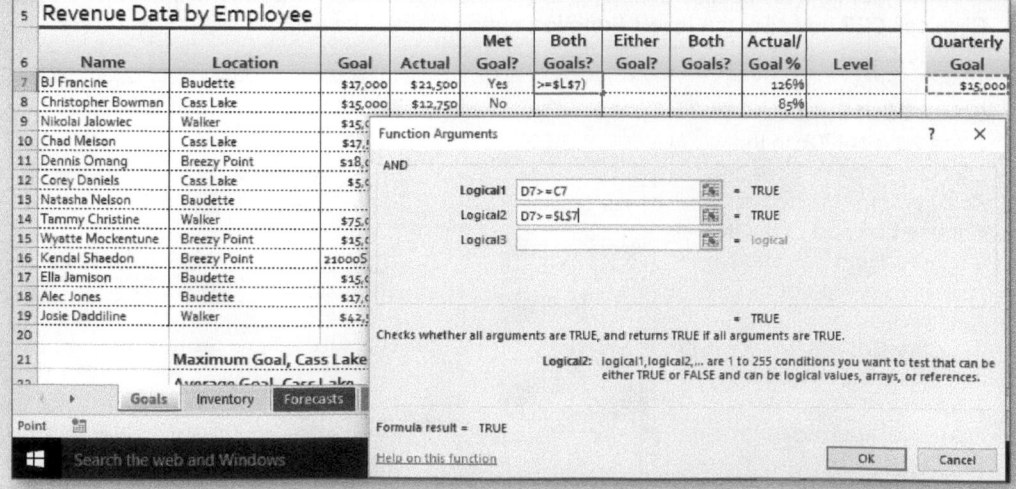

6-16 *AND* function being built

g. Click **OK**. The result for cell F7 is TRUE.
h. Copy the formula in cell **F7** to cells **F8:F19**.

6. Type an *OR* function.
 a. Select cell **G7**.
 b. Type =or and press **Tab**.
 c. Type d7>=c7 for the *logical1* argument.
 d. Type a comma , to move to the *logical2* argument.
 e. Type d7>=, select cell **L7**, and press **F4** (**FN+F4**) (Figure 6-17).

6-17 *OR function typed in the worksheet*

f. Press **Enter**. The result for cell G7 is TRUE.
g. Copy the formula in cell **G7** to cells **G8:G19**. *OR* functions are less restrictive than *AND* functions, so more TRUE results display.

7. Nest *AND* and *IF* functions.
 a. Select cell **H7**.
 b. Type =if(an and press **Tab** (Figure 6-18). The focus is on the *AND* formula as is the *ScreenTip*.

6-18 *AND function as logical test for IF function*

c. Type d7>=c7 for the *logical1* argument.
d. Type a comma , to move to the *logical2* argument.
e. Type d7>=L7 and press **F4** (**FN+F4**) for the *logical2* argument. (You can type a lowercase L).
f. Type a closing parenthesis). The focus and *ScreenTip* return to the *IF* function.
g. Type a comma , to complete the *logical_test* argument for the *IF* function.
h. Type "Met both" including the quotation marks for the *value_if_true* argument.
i. Type a comma , to move to the *value_if_false* argument.
j. Type "No" (Figure 6-19).

6-19 *Arguments for the IF function*

k. Type a closing parenthesis) and press **Enter**.
l. Copy the formula in cell **H7** to cells **H8:H19**.

8. Create an *IFS* function.
 a. Select cell **J7**, click the **Logical** button [*Formulas* tab, *Function Library* group], and choose **IFS**.
 b. Select cell **I7** and type >=96% in the *Logical_test1* box.

c. Click the **Value_if_true1** box and type Excellent. If the percentage in cell I7 is 96% or higher, the formula displays *Excellent* and no additional logical tests are run.

d. Click the **Logical_test2** box, select cell **I7**, and type >= 85%.

e. Click the **Value_if_true2** box and type Good. If the percentage in cell I7 is 85% or higher up to 96%, the formula displays *Good* and no more logical tests are run (Figure 6-20).

f. Click the **Logical_test3** box, select cell **I7**, and type <85%.

g. Click the **Value_if_true3** box and type Average. If the percentage in cell I7 is less than 85%, the formula displays *Average*.

h. Click **OK**.

i. Increase the indent one time for cell **J7**.

j. Copy the formula in cell **J7** to cells **J8:J19**. Widen the column to show all data if necessary (Figure 6-21).

6-20 First *logical_test* returns TRUE so result is "Excellent"

	A	B	C	D	E	F	G	H	I	J
4										
5	Revenue Data by Employee									
6	Name	Location	Goal	Actual	Met Goal?	Both Goals?	Either Goal?	Both Goals?	Actual/Goal %	Level
7	BJ Francine	Baudette	$17,000	$21,500	Yes	TRUE	TRUE	Met both	126%	Excellent
8	Christopher Bowman	Cass Lake	$15,000	$12,750	No	FALSE	FALSE	No	85%	Good
9	Nikolai Jalowiec	Walker	$15,000	$15,600	Yes	TRUE	TRUE	Met both	104%	Excellent
10	Chad Meison	Cass Lake	$17,500	$25,000	Yes	TRUE	TRUE	Met both	143%	Excellent
11	Dennis Omang	Breezy Point	$18,000	$21,000	Yes	TRUE	TRUE	Met both	117%	Excellent
12	Corey Daniels	Cass Lake	$5,000	$3,300	No	FALSE	FALSE	No	66%	Average
13	Natasha Nelson	Baudette	$0	$4,050	Yes	FALSE	TRUE	No	#DIV/o!	#DIV/o!
14	Tammy Christine	Walker	$75,000	$81,000	Yes	TRUE	TRUE	Met both	108%	Excellent
15	Wyatte Mockentune	Breezy Point	$15,000	$14,200	No	FALSE	FALSE	No	95%	Good
16	Kendal Shaedon	Breezy Point	210005	$18,500	No	FALSE	TRUE	No	#VALUE!	#VALUE!
17	Ella Jamison	Baudette	$15,000	$13,200	No	FALSE	FALSE	No	88%	Good
18	Alec Jones	Baudette	$17,000	$9,350	No	FALSE	FALSE	No	55%	Average
19	Josie Daddiline	Walker	$42,500	$56,000	Yes	TRUE	TRUE	Met both	132%	Excellent

6-21 *IFS* function results in "Level" column

9. Create an *IFERROR* function.

a. Select cell **I7**. The formula is =**D7/C7**.

b. Delete the contents of cell **I7**.

c. Click the **Logical** button [*Formulas* tab, *Function Library* group] and choose **IFERROR**.

d. In the *Value* argument box, click cell **D7**, type /, and click cell **C7**.

e. Click the *Value_if_error* box.

f. Type Check values in columns C and D. including the period. If the formula results in an error, your message displays instead of a standard error value message.

g. Click **OK**.

h. Copy the formula in cell **I7** to cells **I8:I19**. *AutoFit* column I (Figure 6-22). Column J displays "Excellent" for cells I13 and I16, but the *IFS* formula recalculates when corrections are made in columns C or D.

10. Save and close the workbook.

	Name	Location	Goal	Actual	Met Goal?	Both Goals?	Either Goal?	Both Goals?	Actual/ Goal %	Level	Quarterly Goal
1	Criteria										
2	Name	Location	Goal	Actual							
3		cas*									
4											
5	Revenue Data by Employee										
6	Name	Location	Goal	Actual	Met Goal?	Both Goals?	Either Goal?	Both Goals?	Actual/ Goal %	Level	Quarterly Goal
7	BJ Francine	Baudette	$17,000	$21,500	Yes	TRUE	TRUE	Met both	126%	Excellent	$15,000
8	Christopher Bowman	Cass Lake	$15,000	$12,750	No	FALSE	FALSE	No	85%	Good	
9	Nikolai Jalowiec	Walker	$15,000	$15,600	Yes	TRUE	TRUE	Met both	104%	Excellent	
10	Chad Meison	Cass Lake	$17,500	$25,000	Yes	TRUE	TRUE	Met both	143%	Excellent	
11	Dennis Omang	Breezy Point	$18,000	$21,000	Yes	TRUE	TRUE	Met both	117%	Excellent	
12	Corey Daniels	Cass Lake	$5,000	$3,300	No	FALSE	FALSE	No	66%	Average	
13	Natasha Nelson	Baudette	$0	$4,050	Yes	FALSE	TRUE	No	Check values in columns C and D.	Excellent	
14	Tammy Christine	Walker	$75,000	$81,000	Yes	TRUE	TRUE	Met both	108%	Excellent	
15	Wyatte Mockentune	Breezy Point	$15,000	$14,200	No	FALSE	FALSE	No	95%	Good	
16	Kendal Shaedon	Breezy Point	21000S	$18,500	No	FALSE	TRUE	No	Check values in columns C and D.	Excellent	
17	Elia Jamison	Baudette	$15,000	$13,200	No	FALSE	FALSE	No	88%	Good	
18	Alec Jones	Baudette	$17,000	$9,350	No	FALSE	FALSE	No	55%	Average	
19	Josie Daddiline	Walker	$42,500	$56,000	Yes	TRUE	TRUE	Met both	132%	Excellent	
20											
21			Maximum Goal, Cass Lake	$17,500							
22			Average Goal, Cass Lake	$12,500							
23			Total Goal, Cass Lake	$37,500							
24											

6-22 Completed PP E6-1 worksheet

Exploring the Lookup & Reference Category

The functions in the *Lookup & Reference* group are used to find, refer to, or manipulate data. These functions do not perform a calculation; they enable you to work with large datasets that might otherwise be unmanageable.

The INDEX Function

The *INDEX* function displays the contents of the cell at the intersection of a specified column and row. In a large inventory sheet that is sorted many times throughout the day, you can use *INDEX* to determine the product name in the third row, fourth column, at any given time. The *INDEX* function is rarely used alone and is generally nested with the *MATCH* function.

The *INDEX* function has two arguments lists. The first list is the array form of the function and includes an array or range of cells, the row number, and the column number as arguments. The syntax for an INDEX function (array form) is:

=INDEX(array, row_num, column_num)

The *array* argument is a cell range to be searched. You can select cells or enter a range name. The *row_num* argument is a row number in the array. The *column_num* argument identifies the column location, counting left to right. When the array consists of one column, a *column_num* argument is not necessary.

The second argument list for *INDEX* is referred to as the reference form, because it has a reference argument to identify multiple cell ranges. The syntax for an INDEX function (reference form) is:

=INDEX(reference, row_num, [column_num], [area_num])

▶ **HOW TO:** Create an INDEX (Array Form) Function

1. Select the cell for the result.

2. Click the **Lookup & Reference** button [*Formulas* tab, *Function Library* group].

3. Choose **INDEX**.

 - The *Select Arguments* dialog box shows two argument lists (Figure 6-23).

4. Select the first list **array, row_num, column_num** and click **OK**.

5. Select the cell range in the worksheet for the *Array* argument.

 - You can press **F3** (**FN+F3**) and paste a range name.

6. Click the **Row_num** box and type the row number.

7. Click the **Column_num** box and type the column number (Figure 6-24).

8. Click **OK**.

 - The result displays the contents of the cell identified by the *Row_num* and *Column_num* arguments.

6-23 *Select Arguments* dialog box for *INDEX*

6-24 *Function Arguments* dialog box for *INDEX*

The MATCH Function

The *MATCH* function looks for data that matches your specifications and displays the location of the data within a list. It is similar to *VLOOKUP*, but *MATCH* shows a row or column identifier, not the data. The syntax for a *MATCH* function is:

=MATCH(lookup_value, lookup_array, [match_type])

The *lookup_value* argument is the text or value that you want to locate. You can enter a cell address that contains the data or type a label or value. *Lookup_array* is a range, either a single row or a single column. You can select the range or use a defined name. These two arguments are required.

The *match_type* argument establishes how the *lookup_value* is compared to values in the *lookup_array*. The *match_type* argument is optional, but it is best to use *0* as the *match_type* for an exact match. The following table explains options for the *match_type* argument.

Match_type Argument	Result
1 or omitted	The function finds the largest value that is less than or equal to the lookup_value. The lookup_array must be sorted in ascending order.
0	The function finds the first value that exactly matches the lookup_value. The lookup_array can be in any order.
−1	The function finds the smallest value that is greater than or equal to the lookup_value. The lookup_array must be sorted in descending order.

> **ANOTHER WAY**
>
> Click the **Recently Used** button in the *Function Library* group [*Formulas* tab] to choose a function that you have recently selected.

▶ **HOW TO: Build a MATCH Function**

1. Select the cell for the result.
2. Click the **Lookup & Reference** button [*Formulas* tab, *Function Library* group].
3. Choose **MATCH**.
4. Select the cell with data to be located and matched for the *Lookup_value* argument.
 - You can type a text entry; quotation marks are entered automatically.
 - This data is located in the lookup array.
5. Click the **Lookup_array** box and select the cell range in the worksheet.
 - The range is a single column or a single row that includes the data you are looking for.
 - If the range has been named, press **F3** (**FN+F3**) to paste the name.
6. Click the **Match_type** box.
7. Type 0 to find an exact match (Figure 6-25).
 - Type 1 or leave the text box empty when the array is sorted in ascending order and you want to find the closest match that is greater than the lookup value.
8. Click **OK**. The relative position of the *lookup_value* in the *lookup_array* displays in the cell.

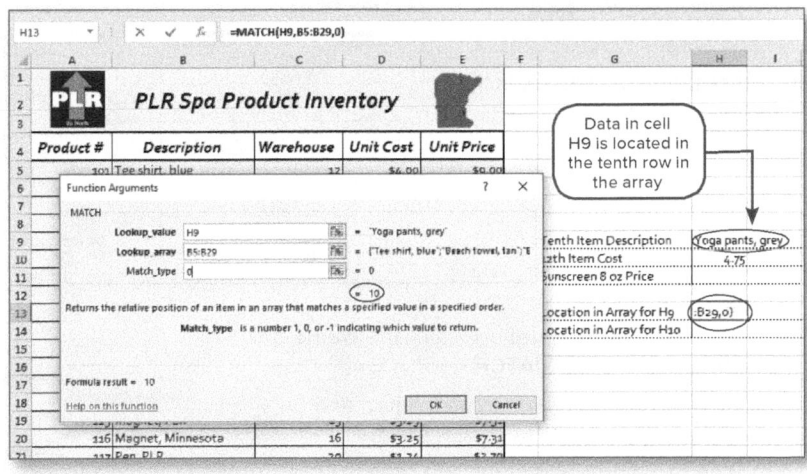

6-25 *Function Arguments* dialog box for *MATCH*

MATCH Nested in INDEX

The *INDEX* and *MATCH* functions, when used together, work quickly on large sets of data. Although you can often accomplish the same task by sorting, filtering, or using a *LOOKUP* function, these methods can take a long time in a worksheet with millions of records.

Below is an *INDEX* function that nests *MATCH* for the *row_num* and *column_num* arguments. The *INDEX array* argument is the named range "Inventory." The *INDEX row_num* argument is a *MATCH* function that finds and exactly matches the data in cell B15 in cells B5:B29. The *INDEX column_num* argument is a second *MATCH* function that finds and matches the data in cell E4 in cells A4:E4.

=INDEX(Inventory,MATCH(B15,B5:B29,0),MATCH(E4,A4:E4,0))

▶**HOW TO:** Nest MATCH in INDEX

1. Select the cell for the result.
2. Click the **Lookup & Reference** button [*Formulas* tab, *Function Library* group].
3. Choose **INDEX**.
4. Select the first argument list **array, row_num, column_num** and click **OK**.
5. For the *Array* argument, select the cells in the worksheet.
 - This range is the entire list.
 - Press **F3 (FN+F3)** to paste a range name.
6. Click the **Row_num** box, click the **Name** box arrow, and choose **MATCH**.
 - Click **More Functions** if necessary to find and select *MATCH*.
7. Select the cell with data to be located and matched as the *Lookup_value* argument for *MATCH*.
 - You can type a text entry.
8. Click the **Lookup_array** box and select the cell range in the worksheet.
 - The range is a single column or a single row that includes the *lookup_value*.
 - If the range has been named, press **F3 (FN+F3)** to paste the name.
9. Click the **Match_type** box and type 0 (Figure 6-26).
10. Click the name **INDEX** in the *Formula* bar.
 - The *Function Arguments* dialog box presents the *INDEX* function again.
 - Ignore the *Select Arguments* list dialog box if it opens.

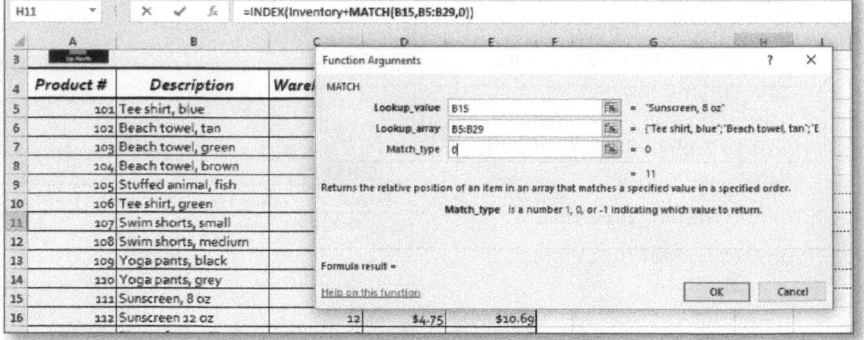

6-26 Complete arguments for the first nested *MATCH*

11. Click the **Column_num** box, click the **Name** box arrow, and choose **MATCH**.
12. Select the cell with data to be located and matched for the *Lookup_value* argument.
 - You can type a text entry.
13. Click the **Lookup_array** box and select the cell range.
 - The range is the single row or column that includes the *lookup_value* argument.
14. Click the **Match_type** box and type 0.
15. Click the name **INDEX** in the *Formula* bar and click **OK** (Figure 6-27).

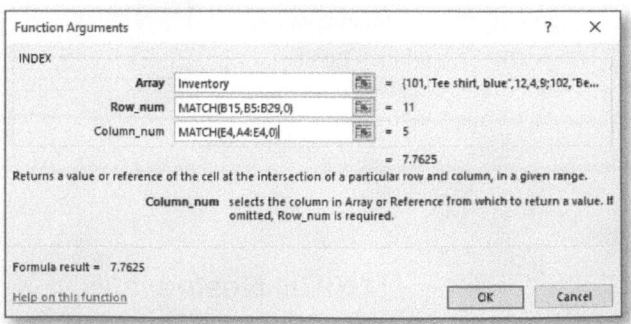

6-27 *MATCH* nested as *column_num* argument

The TRANSPOSE Function

The *TRANSPOSE* function displays columnar data in rows and vice versa, and results are located in multiple cells. An **array formula** is a formula that calculates results across a range of cells. Many Excel functions can be executed as array formulas by pressing **Ctrl+Shift+Enter** as completion keys. These types of formulas are referred to as **CSE** formulas.

An array formula appears in each cell of the results range. The formula includes an equals sign, the name of the function, and the argument in parentheses. The entire function is enclosed in curly braces to indicate that it is an array formula.

{=TRANSPOSE(SheetName!B1:S1)}

The *TRANSPOSE* function has one argument, *array*, which are the cells to be rearranged. To use *TRANSPOSE*, first select the range that will hold the transposed data. If the data occupies 15 columns in a row, select 15 cells in a column to transpose the data.

> **ANOTHER WAY**
>
> The *Paste Special* dialog box includes an option to transpose copied data.

▶ HOW TO: Create a TRANSPOSE Function

1. Select the cells for transposed results.

2. Click the **Lookup & Reference** button [*Formulas* tab, *Function Library* group].

3. Choose **TRANSPOSE**.

4. Select the cells that are to be transposed for the *Array* argument (Figure 6-28).

 • The cells can be on a different sheet.

5. Press **Ctrl+Shift+Enter**.

 • The formula is inserted in each cell in the selected range.

 • If you press **Enter**, only the first result is calculated.

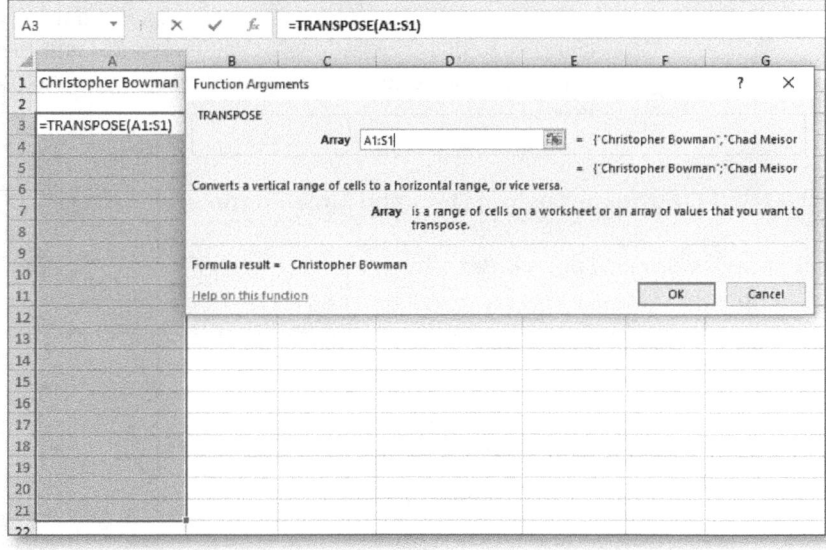

6-28 *TRANSPOSE* arguments

Building Date, Time, and Statistical Calculations

Date and time calculations enable you to determine arrival dates, to age accounts receivable, or to figure hours worked. If you depend on market research for your work, concepts such as a mean absolute deviation or a standard deviation are important numbers. These types of tasks can be handled by an Excel formula.

Date and Time Formats

For ease in building date and time calculations, you must understand how dates and times are entered, formatted, and recognized. Excel uses serial numbers for dates which set January 1,

1900, as 1; January 2, 1900, as 2; and so on. For years between 1900 and 1929, you must key "19" to identify the twentieth century; otherwise Excel assumes the twenty-first century.

Dates are often entered in *mm/dd/yy* format in the United States. Excel recognizes a date typed in this style and applies the *Short Date* format. Depending on how you key a date, however, the onscreen format might be different because Excel applies the closest format from its list of preset formats.

> ### MORE INFO
>
> International and military dates are often entered in *dd/mm/yy* or *yy/mm/dd* format.

Excel uses a 24-hour day in time calculations but can display results using a 12-hour or a 24-hour clock. If you key 14:30 in a cell, Excel displays 2:30 PM in the *Formula* bar. If you key 1:30, the *Formula* bar shows 1:30 AM.

The *Date*, *Time*, and *Custom* categories in the *Format Cells* dialog box provide preset and special display formats for dates and times. From the *Custom* category, scroll a list of formats, choose one that is close to what you prefer, and edit the codes in the *Type* box. When time or date calculations display unexpected results, you should always check and reset the format as needed.

▶ HOW TO: Create Custom Date and Time Formats

1. Type the date and press **Enter**.
 - The date is formatted if it is recognized as a date.
2. Select the cell with the date.
3. Click the **Launcher** for the *Number* group [*Home* tab].
4. Choose **Custom** in the *Category* list.
 - Choose **Date** in the list to select a preset format instead.
5. Scroll the *Type* list and choose a format.
 - The codes for a date are *d*, *y*, and *m* for day, year, and month (Figure 6-29).
 - The *Sample* box previews the formatted date.
6. Click the **Type** box above the list and edit the format codes as desired.
 - You can enter special characters in the *Type* box such as a hyphen or a comma.
7. Press **Enter** or click **OK**.
8. Type the time and press **Enter**.
 - Include **AM** or **PM** to use a 12-hour clock.
 - A colon is required for times not on the hour such as 1:30.
9. Select the cell with the time.
10. Click the **Launcher** for the *Number* group [*Home* tab].
11. Choose **Custom** in the *Category* list.
 - Choose **Time** in the list to select a preset format instead.

6-29 Build a custom date format

12. Scroll the *Type* list and choose a format.

 • The *Sample* box previews the formatted time.

13. Click the **Type** box and edit the format codes as desired.

 • The codes for a time are *h, m,* and *s* for hour, minute, and second (Figure 6-30).

14. Press **Enter** or click **OK**.

6-30 Build a custom time format

Date Calculations

Date calculations include determining your age, counting the days until your next holiday, or estimating expiration dates. Formula results calculate the number of days, but you can convert days into years (or months). Be careful about mathematical order of preference in date calculations, because formulas typically include multiple operators.

Many date formulas use the *TODAY* function to calculate how much time has passed. To determine your age, for example, subtract your birth date from *TODAY* and divide by 365.25. When you use *TODAY* in a date calculation, you can refer to a cell with the function or enter the function as part of the formula.

> **MORE INFO**
>
> It is common practice to use 365.25 as the number of days in a year which accounts for a leap year every four years.

▶ HOW TO: Calculate Years Passed

1. Enter the *TODAY* function in a cell in the worksheet.

2. Click the cell for the calculated results.

3. Type =(to start the formula.

 • The opening parenthesis is necessary so that the subtraction is done first.

4. Click the cell with the *TODAY* function and press **F4** (**FN+F4**).

 • The reference should be absolute if you plan to copy the formula.

5. Type – to subtract the next date.

6. Select the cell with the starting date.

 • *TODAY* minus the start date is the subtraction.
 • You can also type the starting date in *mm/dd/yy* format.

7. Type)/ for the closing parenthesis and division.

8. Type 365.25 to convert the result to years (Figure 6-31).

 • Without the division, the result displays the number of days.

9. Press **Enter**.

 • The result displays as many decimals as will fit in the cell.
 • Format the results with decimal places as desired.

D3	▼	:	× ✓ fx	=(F1-C3)/365.25			
▲	A	B	C	D	E	F	G
1	PLR Employee Hire Dates					1/1/2018	
2	First Name	Last Name	Hire Date	Length			
3	BJ	Francine	03/15/14	=(F1-C3)/365.25			
4	Alec	Jones	09/18/14				
5	Mikayla	Anderson	07/15/15				
6	Ella	Jamison	05/11/15				
7	David	Gazik	11/14/15				
8	Natasha	Nelson	10/24/15				
9	Ari	Aronson	05/10/16				
10	Dennis	Omang	04/15/16				
11	Kendal	Shaedon	06/14/16				
12	Frankie	Dennis	08/18/16				

6-31 Build a date calculation

Time Calculations

Time calculations include calculating hours worked, upload or delivery times, or processing time. As long as you have a start time and end time, you can determine how many hours have passed. Excel shows time results as a fraction of a 24-hour day, and you can convert to hours by multiplying by 24.

▶ HOW TO: Calculate Time Passed

1. Click the cell for the result.

2. Type =(to start the formula and enter the opening parenthesis.

 • The parentheses set the subtraction as the first operation.

3. Click the cell with the ending time.

4. Type – to subtract.

5. Select the cell with the beginning time (Figure 6-32).

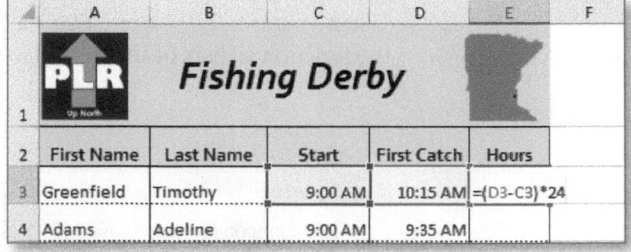

▲	A	B	C	D	E	F
1	PLR Up North	Fishing Derby				
2	First Name	Last Name	Start	First Catch	Hours	
3	Greenfield	Timothy	9:00 AM	10:15 AM	=(D3-C3)*24	
4	Adams	Adeline	9:00 AM	9:35 AM		

6-32 Build a time calculation

6. Type)* for the closing parenthesis and multiplication.

7. Type 24 to convert the result to hours by multiplying by 24.

8. Press **Enter**.

 • The result may be formatted as a time.

9. Select the cell and apply the **General** format [*Home* tab, *Number* group, *Number Format* drop-down list].

 • The time passed is shown with as many decimals as will fit in the cell.
 • Format the results with decimal places as desired.

> ▶ **MORE INFO**
>
> Convert time displayed in hours into minutes by multiplying by 60 or format time with fractions instead of decimals.

The DATEVALUE and TIMEVALUE Functions

Two functions in the *Date & Time* category convert text data into date or time values, *DATEVALUE* and *TIMEVALUE*. This is a common task for date and time data from external sources, because the data often is imported as text. Data to be converted must be in a Microsoft-acceptable arrangement for a date or time.

▶ **HOW TO:** Use DATEVALUE

1. Click the cell where the converted date should display.
2. Click the **Date & Time** button [*Formulas* tab, *Function Library* group].
3. Choose **DATEVALUE**.
 • The argument is *Date_text*.
4. Select the cell with a date as text (Figure 6-33).
 • You can also type a date in the argument box.
5. Click **OK** or press **Enter**.
 • The date is converted to a serial number.
6. Select the cell and apply a date format.

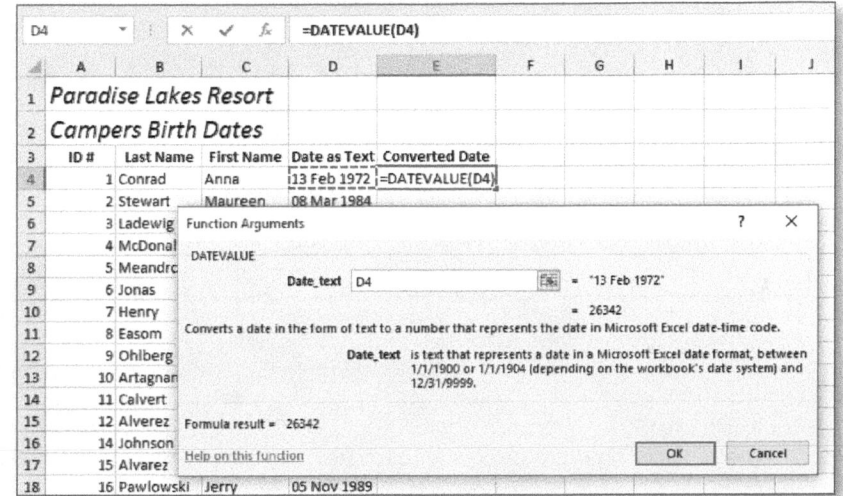

6-33 *DATEVALUE Function Arguments* dialog box

Forecast Errors and MAD Calculations

A *forecast error* is the difference between actual amounts and predicted values, an important analysis tool for business and research. A forecast error is a *deviation*, a simple subtraction formula. Paradise Lakes Resort can compare the number of products sold with predicted sales to manage inventory. A small forecast error or deviation means good inventory procedures while a large error signifies better control is needed.

A popular measure of how spread out a set of values is from the average (the mean) is the *mean absolute deviation*. Its acronym is **MAD**, and it is a calculation that uses two Excel functions, *ABS* and *AVERAGE*.

When analyzing deviations, it generally is not important whether the value is positive or negative. The *ABS* function displays the numeric value of a number–the value without any sign, the *absolute* value. A MAD formula calculates the absolute difference for each cell and then averages those values.

▶ **HOW TO:** Build a MAD Calculation

1. Click the cell for the first absolute result.
2. Type =ab and press **Tab**.
 • The *ScreenTip* shows the *number* argument.
3. Click the cell with the forecasted or planned value.

4. Type – and click the cell with the actual value (Figure 6-34).

5. Press **Enter**.

6. Copy the *ABS* formula as needed.

7. Click the cell for the MAD calculation.

8. Type =aver and press **Tab**.

9. Select the cells with absolute values.

10. Press **Enter** (Figure 6-35).

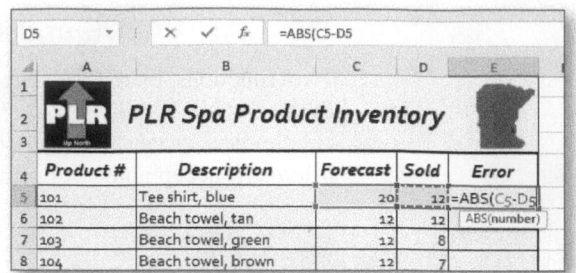

6-34 *ABS* function and argument

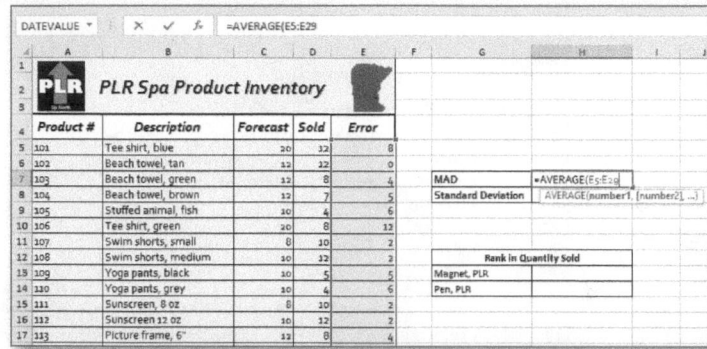

6-35 Calculate the mean absolute deviation

- The result is, on average, how far each deviation or error is from the mean of those errors.

 ANOTHER WAY

The *AVEDEV* function in the *Statistical* category calculates the average deviation of the absolute values in a range.

Standard Deviation

A *standard deviation* measures how broadly values deviate from the mean or average value in a range of numbers, a popular statistical calculation. The *STDEV*.S function applies to sample populations and ignores text and logical values. A *sample* is a subset of a population; a *population* is all the data.

MORE INFO

To calculate the standard deviation for an entire population instead of a sample, use the function **STDEV.P**.

The syntax for a *STDEV*.S function is:

=STDEV.S(number1,[number2],...)

The required argument is *number1*, the first value or range. When the values to be analyzed are not adjacent, you use additional *number* arguments to include each cell in the formula.

▶ HOW TO: Use the STDEV.S Function

1. Click the cell for the result.
2. Click the **More Functions** button [*Formulas* tab, *Function Library* group] and choose **Statistical**.
3. Find and choose **STDEV.S**.
4. Select the cells to be analyzed for the *Number1* argument. (Figure 6-36).
5. Click **OK**.

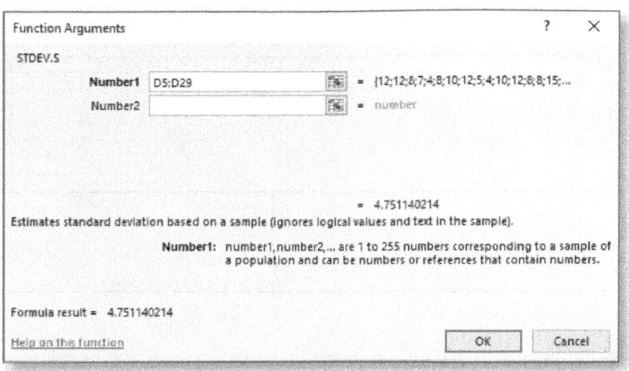

6-36 *STDEV.S Function Arguments* dialog box

▶ MORE INFO

The mean square error (MSE) is a measure of variability that uses *SUMSQ* and *COUNT* to sum the squares of the values and divide by the number of values in the range.

The RANK.EQ Function

In a large set of data, use the *RANK.EQ* or the *RANK.AVG* function to calculate where a particular value appears in the dataset. The *RANK* functions identify where the value is relative to all the other values.

The syntax for a *RANK.EQ* function is:

=RANK.EQ(number, ref,[order])

The *Number* is the cell that you want to rank. *Ref* is the range of values in which the *Number* lies. *Order* identifies whether you want the values to be considered in ascending or descending order. Values in descending order place the highest value as rank 1.

When duplicate values exist in the range, *RANK.EQ* shows the lower rank. The *RANK.AVG* function calculates duplicate values with an average rank.

▶ HOW TO: Use the RANK.EQ Function

1. Click the cell for the rank result.
2. Click the **More Functions** button [*Formulas* tab, *Function Library* group] and choose **Statistical**.
3. Find and choose **RANK.EQ**.
4. In the *Number* box, select the cell to be ranked.

5. Click the **Ref** box and select the cells with related values (Figure 6-37).

• This is the range in which the cell to be ranked is located.

6. Leave the **Order** box empty to indicate descending order (top rank is 1).

7. Click **OK**.

• The value's position in relation to the other values is indicated.

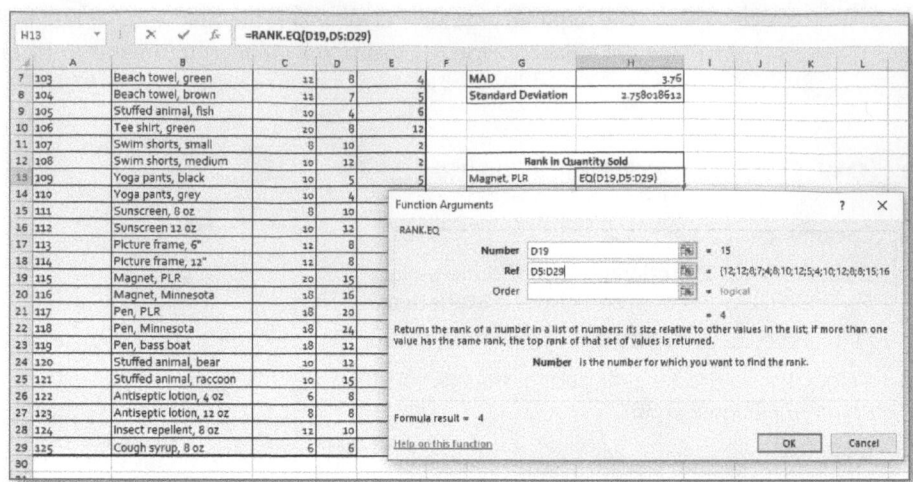

6-37 *RANK.EQ Function Arguments* dialog box

PAUSE & PRACTICE: EXCEL 6-2

In this project, you nest *INDEX* and *MATCH* functions to display information on the inventory worksheet for Paradise Lakes Resort. You transpose data, calculate statistics for inventory data, and prepare time and date calculations.

File Needed: *[your initials] PP E6-1.xlsx*
Completed Project File Name: *[your initials] PP E6-2.xlsx*

1. Open *[your initials] PP E6-1.xlsx* completed in *Pause & Practice 6-1* and save it as [your initials] PP E6-2.

2. Click the **Inventory** worksheet tab.

3. Use the *INDEX* function with one column of data.
 a. Select cell **H9**.
 b. Click the **Lookup & Reference** button [*Formulas* tab, *Function Library* group] and choose **INDEX**.
 c. Select the first argument list **array, row_num, column_num** and click **OK**.
 d. Select cells **B5:B29** for the *Array* argument.
 e. Click the **Row_num** box and type 10 to show data from the tenth row in the range. When using a single column as the array, there is no *Column_num* argument (Figure 6-38).
 f. Click **OK**. *Yoga pants, grey* is the description.

6-38 *INDEX* function to show data from tenth row

4. Use the *INDEX* function with a range name.
 a. Select cell **H10**.
 b. Click the **Recently Used** button [*Formulas* tab, *Function Library* group] and choose **INDEX**.
 c. Select the first argument list and click **OK**.
 d. Press **F3** (**FN+F3**) to open the *Paste List* dialog box in the *Array* argument box.
 e. Choose **Inventory** and click **OK**.
 f. Click the **Row_num** box and type 12 to show data from the twelfth row.
 g. Click the **Column_num** box and type 4 to display data from the Cost column, the fourth column (Figure 6-39).
 h. Click **OK** and format cell **H10** as **Currency**. The cost of the twelfth item, 12 oz. sunscreen, is $4.75.

6-39 *INDEX* function to show data from twelfth row, fourth column

5. Use the *MATCH* function.
 a. Select cell **H13**.
 b. Click the **Lookup & Reference** button [*Formulas* tab, *Function Library* group] and choose **MATCH**.
 c. Select cell **H9** for the *Lookup_value* argument.
 d. Click the **Look_up array** box and select cells **B5:B29**. These two arguments will find a match in cells B5:B29 for the data in cell H9.
 e. Click the **Match_type** argument and type 0 to look for an exact match (Figure 6-40).
 f. Click **OK**. The data in cell H9 is located in the tenth row in the array.
 g. Select cell **H14**, type =m and press **Tab**.
 h. Click cell **H10** and type a comma , to move to the array argument.
 i. Select cells **D5:D29** for the *look_up array* and type a comma ,.
 j. Type 0 to look for an exact match.
 k. Press **Enter**. The price in cell H10 is first located in the fifth row.

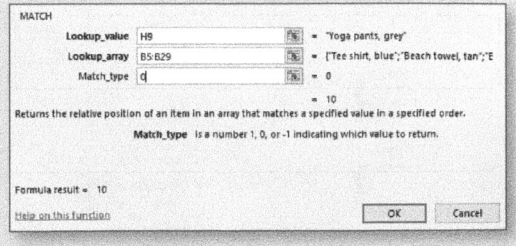

6-40 *MATCH* function for an exact match

6. Nest *INDEX* and *MATCH* functions.
 a. Select cell **H11**.
 b. Click the **Recently Used** button [*Formulas* tab, *Function Library* group] and choose **INDEX**.

c. Select the first argument list and click **OK**.
d. Press **F3** (**FN+F3**) for the *Array* argument, choose **Inventory**, and click **OK**.
e. Click the **Row_num** box, click the **Name** box arrow, and choose **MATCH**.
f. Select cell **B15**, the 8 oz. sunscreen, for the *Lookup_value*.
g. Click the **Lookup_array** box and select cells **B5:B29**.
h. Click the **Match_type** box and type 0. This completes the nested *MATCH* function for the *Row_num* argument (Figure 6-41).

6-41 Nested *MATCH* and *INDEX*

i. Click the word **INDEX** in the *Formula* bar.
j. Click the **Column_num** box for the *INDEX* function.
k. Click the **Name** box arrow and choose **MATCH**.
l. Select cell **E4**, the *Unit Price* label, for the *Lookup_value*.
m. Click the **Lookup_array** box and select cells **A4:E4**, the label row.
n. Click the *Match_type* box and type 0. This is the nested *MATCH* function for the *Column_num* argument.
o. Click the word **INDEX** in the *Formula* bar (Figure 6-42).

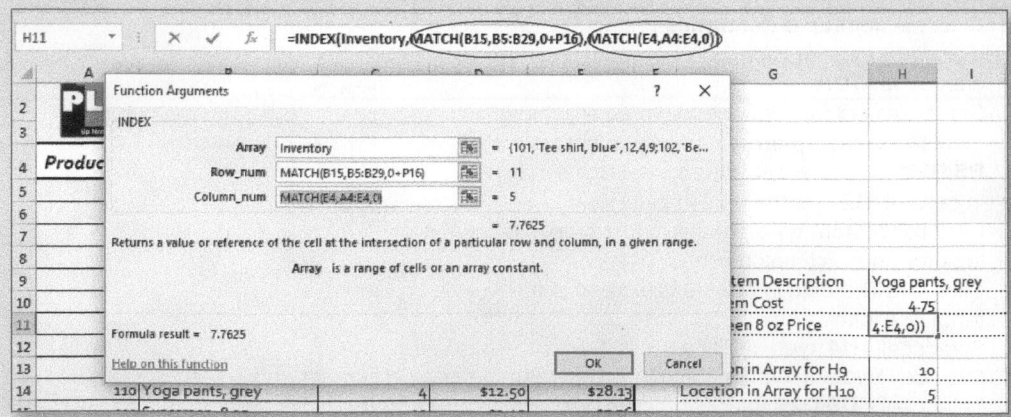

6-42 *MATCH* is *Row_num* and *Column_num* arguments

p. Click **OK**. The price for the 8 oz. sunscreen displays unrounded as 7.7625.
q. Format cell **H11** as **Currency**.

7. Calculate the mean absolute deviation (MAD) for forecast errors.
 a. Click the **Forecasts** sheet tab and select cell **E5**.
 b. Type =ab and press **Tab**.
 c. Type c5-d5 and press **Enter**. The closing parenthesis is provided.
 d. Copy the formula in cell **E5** to cells **E6:E29** without formatting. Absolute values do not show any signs.
 e. Select cell **H7**.
 f. Use the *AVERAGE* function with cells **E5:E29** as the argument.

8. Calculate a standard deviation for number sold.
 a. Select cell **H8**.
 b. Type =std, select **STDEV.S** from the list, and press **Tab**.
 c. Select cells **D5:D29** and press **Enter**.

9. Rank products by quantity sold.
 a. Select cell **H13**.
 b. Click the **More Functions** button [*Formulas* tab, *Function Library* group] and choose **Statistical**.
 c. Select **RANK.EQ**.
 d. Select cell **D19**, the number of magnets sold, for the *Number* argument.
 e. Click the **Ref** box and select cells **D5:D29** (Figure 6-43).

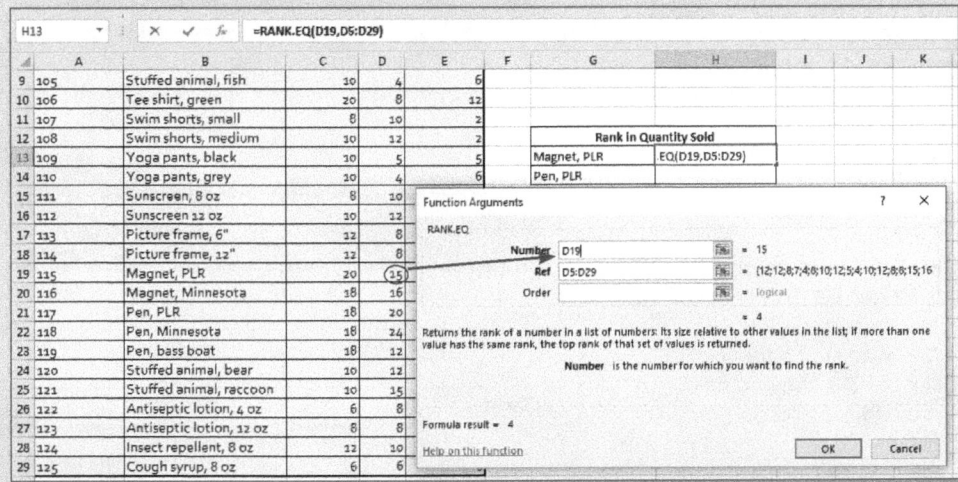

6-43 Rank a value in the list

 f. Click **OK**.
 g. Select cell **H14** and use *RANK.EQ* to rank the quantity sold for the pen.

10. Transpose data using *TRANSPOSE*.
 a. Click the **Transpose** worksheet tab. The data occupies 19 columns in a single row.
 b. Click the **Marketing** worksheet tab.
 c. Select cells **A3:A21**, 19 rows in a single column.
 d. Click the **Lookup & Reference** button [*Formulas* tab, *Function Library* group] and select **TRANSPOSE**.
 e. For the *Array* argument, click the **Transpose** sheet tab and select cells **A1:S1**.
 f. Press **Ctrl+Shift+Enter** to create an array formula (Figure 6-44).

11. Format dates and calculate days employed.
 a. Click the **Hire Dates** sheet tab.
 b. Select cells **C3:C25**. These are serial numbers that represent hire dates.
 c. Click the **Launcher** in the *Number* group [*Home* tab] and select the *Date* category.
 d. Select the format that shows a leading zero **03/14/12** and click **OK**.
 e. Enter the *TODAY* function in cell **A27**.
 f. Select cell **D3**.
 g. Type =(to start a formula.
 h. Click cell **A27** and press **F4** (**FN+F4**) to make it absolute.
 i. Type – to subtract and click cell **C3**.
 j. Type)/ for a closing parenthesis and division.
 k. Type 365.25 to convert results to years and press **Enter** (Figure 6-45).
 l. Copy cell **D3** to cells **D4:D25** without formatting.
 m. Format cells **D3:D25** with the **Number** format.

12. Calculate time.
 a. Click the **Derby** sheet tab.
 b. Select cell **E3**. The ending time is the time of the first catch.
 c. Type =(to start a formula.
 d. Click cell **D3**, the end time.
 e. Type – to subtract and click cell **C3**.
 f. Type)* for a closing parenthesis and multiplication.
 g. Type 24 to convert days to hours.
 h. Type *60 to convert hours to minutes (Figure 6-46).
 i. Press **Enter**.
 j. Copy cell **E3** to cells **E4:E8** without formatting.
 k. Format the results as **General** from the *Number Format* list [*Home* tab, *Number* group].

13. Save and close the workbook (Figure 6-47).

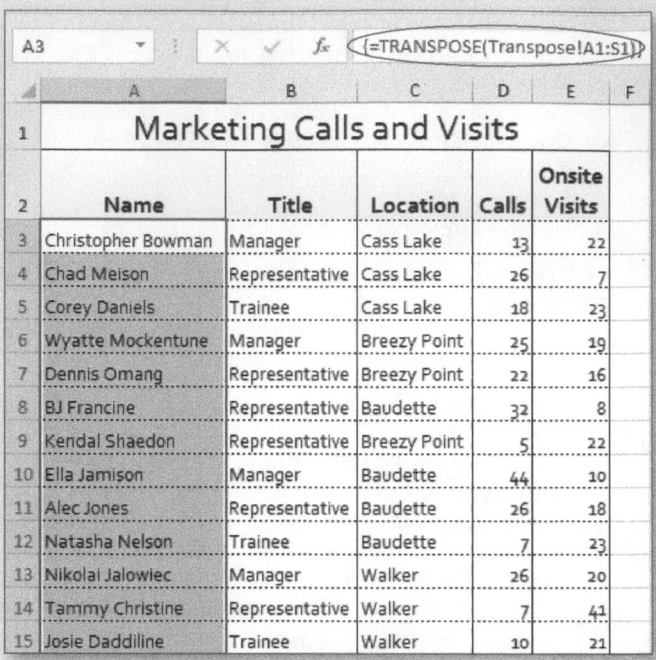

6-44 *TRANSPOSE* in an array formula

6-45 Calculate years employed

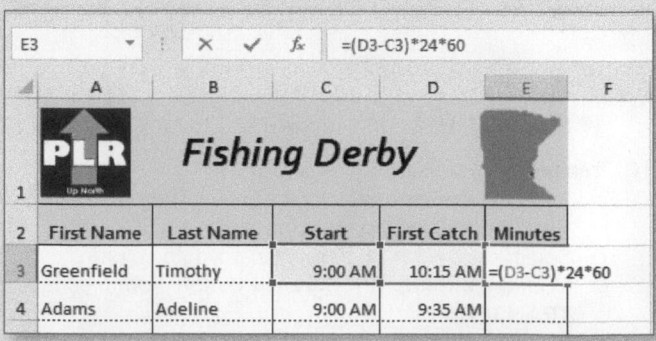

6-46 Calculate time as minutes

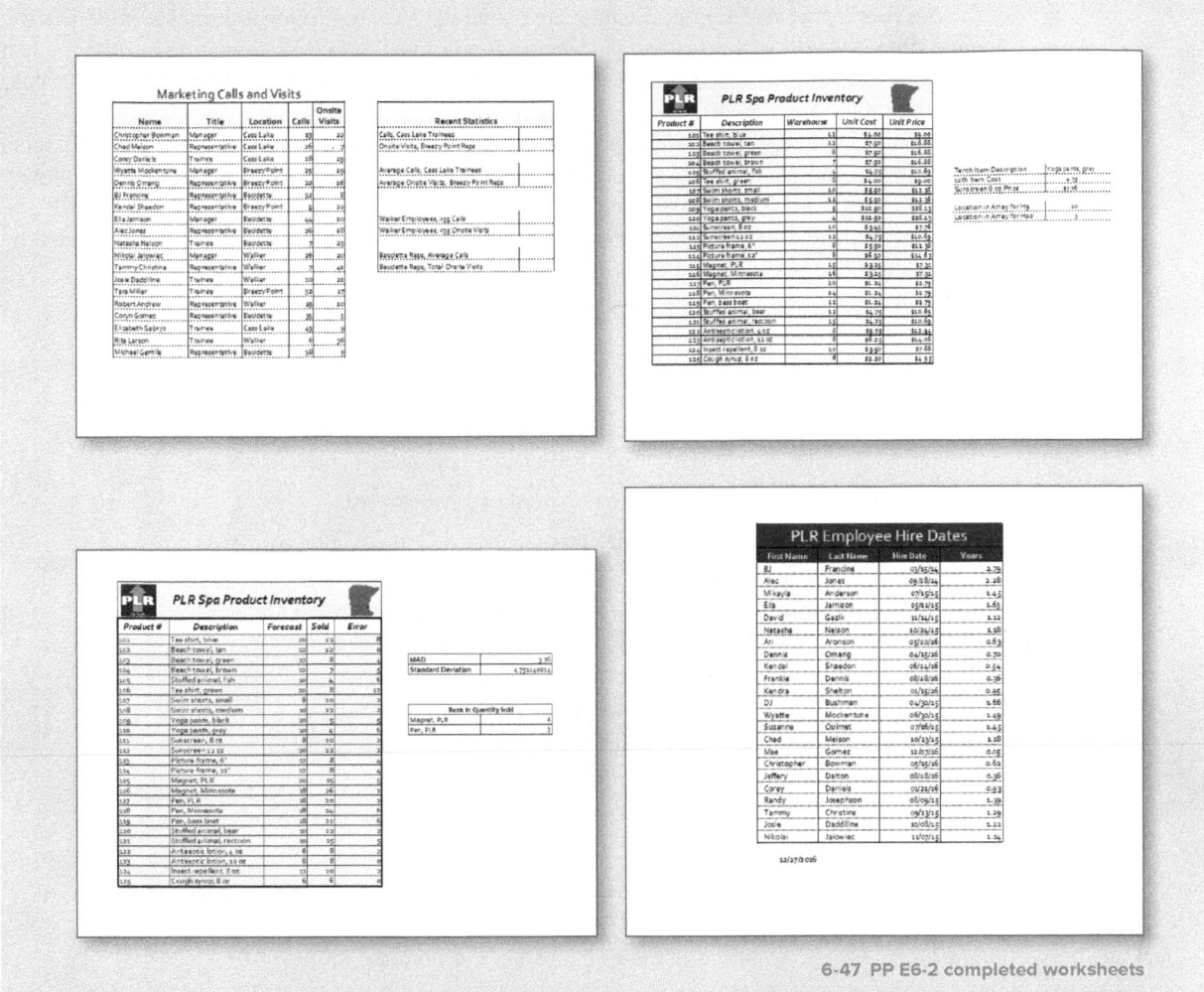

6-47 PP E6-2 completed worksheets

SLO 6.5

Using Financial Functions

Functions in the *Financial* category analyze money transactions such as loans, bond purchases, depreciation, and mortgage amortization. Many *Financial* functions use common arguments including *rate* and *nper*. **Rate** is an interest rate for the time period. **Nper** is the total number of payments or deposits.

The PV Function

The *PV* function calculates the *present value* of a money transaction. If you buy an insurance policy that will pay a specified amount in 20 years, you can use the *PV* function to determine if a lump sum premium paid now is a good value. The *PV* function uses the concept of an **annuity**, a series of equal payments made at the same time of the month or year for a specified period of time.

The syntax for a *PV* function is:

=PV(rate,nper,pmt,[fv],[type])

The *rate*, *nper*, and *pmt* arguments are required. *Rate* and *nper* arguments must use the same time division such as months or years. If you make monthly payments but the interest rate is an annual rate, the rate must be divided by 12. The *pmt* argument is the amount paid each period.

Two optional arguments are *fv* and *type*. The *fv* argument, future value, is a cash balance, if any, at the end of the last period. In the insurance policy example, an *fv* amount is money that you would allow the insurance company to keep. The *type* argument specifies if the payment is made at the beginning or the end of the period. When you receive payments, the beginning of the period is preferable.

▶ HOW TO: Use the PV Function

1. Click the cell for the result.
2. Click the **Financial** button [*Formulas* tab, *Function Library* group] and choose **PV**.
3. Select the cell that contains the interest rate for the *Rate* box.
 - If the interest rate is an annual rate and payments are monthly, type /12 after the cell address.
 - If the interest rate is an annual rate and payments are quarterly, type /4 after the cell address.
 - You can type the interest rate in the entry box as a percent or its decimal equivalent.
4. Click the **Nper** box and select the cell that contains the number of years.
 - If the term is shown in years and payments are monthly, type *12 after the cell address.
 - If the term is shown in years and payments are quarterly, type *4 after the cell address.
 - You can type the total number of payments.
5. Click the **Pmt** box and select the cell that contains the payment amount.
6. Click the **Fv** box and click the cell with the cash balance amount, if any.
 - Type a value in the entry box instead of selecting a cell.
 - Type a zero (0) or leave the entry blank to indicate no cash balance.
7. Click the **Type** box and type 1 if the payment is at the beginning of the period (Figure 6-48).
 - Type 0 or leave the entry blank to indicate payment at the end of the period.

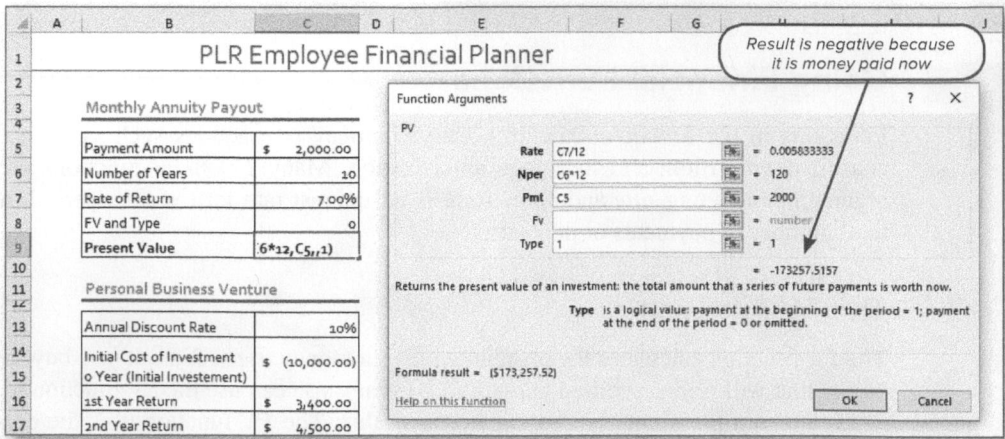

6-48 *Function Arguments* dialog box for *PV*

8. Click **OK**.

> ► MORE INFO
>
> The *PV* function can be calculated from the payee's or the payer's perspective. When payments are made *to you*, the payment amount is a positive number. The *PV* result is a negative number, because you pay out that amount now.

The FV Function

The *FV* function determines the *future value* of a series of payments at the same interest rate for a specified period of time. You can use this function to calculate results for an investment or savings plan in which you plan to deposit a specific amount each period.

The syntax for an *FV* function is:

=FV(rate,nper,pmt,[pv],[type])

Rate, *nper*, and *pmt* are required; *pv* and *type* are optional. The *pv* argument, the present value, might be a required initial investment or an amount already in the account. In a savings or investment plan, the *pv* argument is the amount that you start with.

The *type* argument is either 1 or 0 (or omitted) to indicate if payment is made at the beginning or the end of the period. In a savings plan, payment at the beginning of the period earns interest for the entire period.

► HOW TO: Use the FV Function

1. Click the cell for the result.
2. Click the **Financial** button [*Formulas* tab, *Function Library* group] and choose **FV**.
3. Select the cell that contains the interest rate for the *Rate* box.

 - If the interest rate is an annual rate and payments are monthly, type /12 after the cell address.
 - If the interest rate is an annual rate and payments are quarterly, type /4 after the cell address.
 - Type the interest rate in the *Rate* box instead of selecting a cell.

4. Click the **Nper** argument box and select the cell that contains the number of years.

 - If the term is years and payments are monthly, type *12 after the cell address.
 - If the term is years and payments are quarterly, type *4 after the cell address.
 - You can type the total number of payments in the *Nper* box.

5. Click the **Pmt** box and select the cell that contains the payment amount.

 - The payment amount can be formatted as a negative value, because it is money you pay each period.

6. Click the **Pv** box and select the cell with a starting amount, if any.

 - Type a value in the box if the value is not shown in the worksheet.
 - Type a zero (0) or leave the entry blank to indicate no starting amount.

7. Click the **Type** box and type 1 if the payment is at the beginning of the period (Figure 6-49).

 - Type 0 or leave the entry blank to indicate payment at the end of the period.

8. Click **OK**.

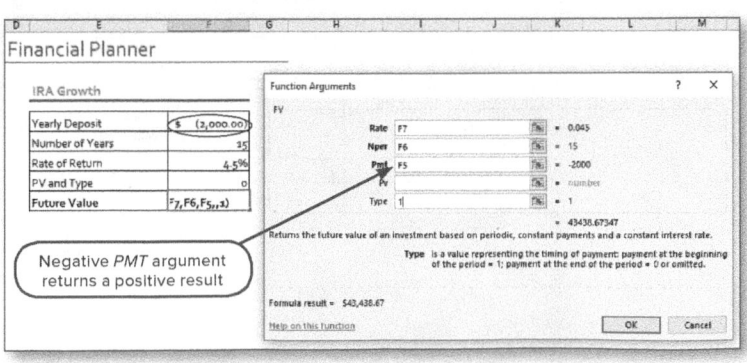

6-49 *Function Arguments* dialog box for *FV*

The NPV Function

The *NPV* function calculates the *net present value* of an investment using a discount rate and a series of future payments and receipts. A ***discount rate*** represents the cost of financing or the rate of return possible with a competing investment. In the *NPV* function, the series of payments and receipts can vary, unlike the payment amount in *PV* and *FV* functions.

The syntax for a *NPV* function is:

=NPV(rate,value1,value2,. . .)

Rate is the discount rate, an interest rate. The *valueN* arguments are positive and negative ***cash flows***, payments or receipts. *Value* arguments are listed in the order in which they occur. For example, if you earn $3,400 in the first period, that amount is the *value1* argument. The *value2* argument is the next payment or receipt, and so on. A separate initial payment or cost is not a *value* argument but is added to the result of the *NPV* function as a negative amount.

> **MORE INFO**
>
> The *NPV* function assumes that cash flows occur at the end of each period.

▶ **HOW TO: Use the NPV Function**

1. Click the cell for the result.
2. Click the **Financial** button [*Formulas* tab, *Function Library* group] and choose **NPV**.
3. Click the cell that contains the discount interest rate for the *Rate* box.
 - Use a percentage (10%) or its decimal equivalent (.1).
 - You can type a value instead of selecting a cell.
4. Click the **Value1** box and select the cell that contains the amount of cash flow at the end of the first period.
 - Cash flow amounts can be negative or positive values.
5. Click the **Value2** argument box and select the cell that contains the amount of cash flow at the end of the second period.
6. Click each additional **Value** box and select the cell (Figure 6-50).
 - For a year with neither a positive or negative cash flow, type a zero (0) as the *ValueN* argument to prevent the sequence of cash flows from moving forward one year.

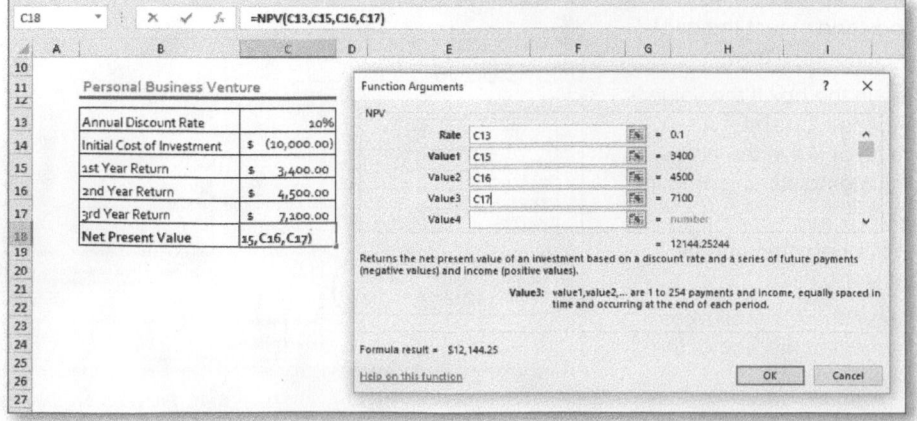

6-50 *Function Arguments* dialog box for *NPV*

7. Click **OK**.

8. To include an initial payment, click the *Formula* bar to edit the formula.

 - The initial payment should be formatted as a negative value.

9. Press **End** to position the insertion point after the closing parentheses and type +.

10. Click the cell with the initial payment and press **Enter** (Figure 6-51).

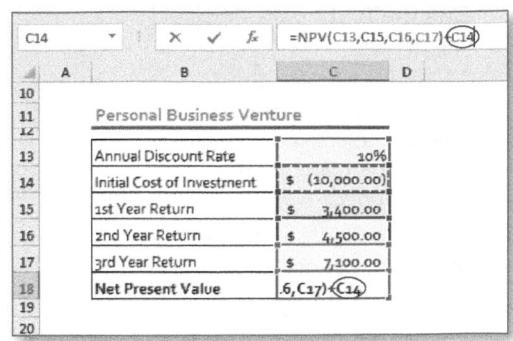

6-51 Edited *NPV* function to include initial cost

SLO 6.6

Working with Text Functions

Text functions split, join, or convert labels and values in a worksheet. With a *Text* function, you can format a value as a label to control alignment or display labels in uppercase or lower case letters.

The TEXTJOIN Function

The *TEXTJOIN* function combines strings of text, values, or characters. A common use of *TEXTJOIN* is to display a person's full name in a single cell by joining two or more cells.

The syntax for a *TEXTJOIN* function is:

=TEXTJOIN(delimiter, ignore_empty, text1, [text2], . . .)

The *delimiter* argument specifies the character used to separate the *TextN* arguments. There can be up to 252 *TextN* arguments but only one delimiter. A *Text* argument can be a cell reference or data that you type.

When you combine text strings, such as first and last names or city, state, and ZIP code, the delimiter is a space character. *TEXTJOIN* results are usually placed in a separate column or row to preserve the original data.

▶**HOW TO:** Use the TEXTJOIN Function

1. Click the cell for the result.

2. Click the **Text** button [*Formulas* tab, *Function Library* group] and choose **TEXTJOIN**.

3. Press **Spacebar** to insert a space character in the *Delimiter* box.

4. Click the **Ignore_empty** box.

 - Leave this box empty for the default TRUE option.
 - A cell with no data is ignored in the function results.
 - The *Delimiter* space character displays with quotation marks.

5. Click the **Text1** argument box.

6. Select the cell with the first text string to be joined.

 - You can also type a text string, a value, or a punctuation character.

7. Click the **Text2** box and select the cell with data to be joined (Figure 6-52).

- You can use a combination of cell references and typed data among the *TextN* arguments.

8. Complete *TextN* argument boxes as needed.

9. Click **OK**.

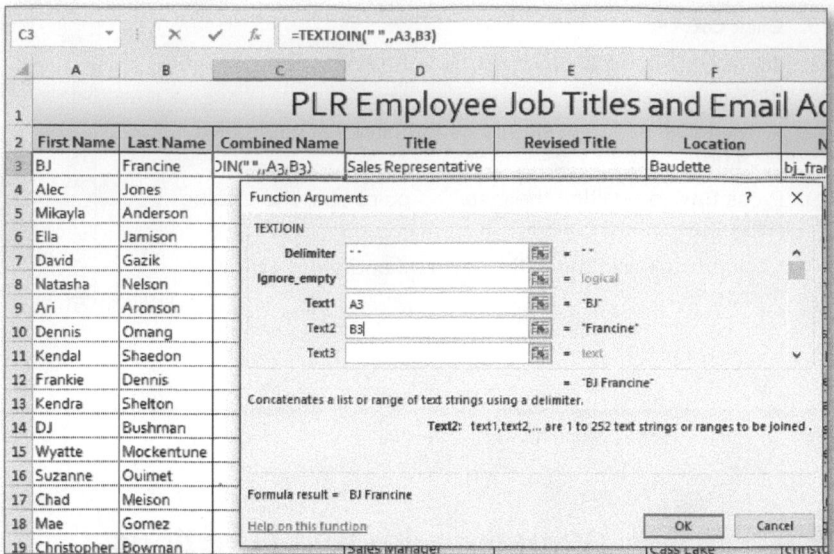

6-52 *Function Arguments* dialog box for *TEXTJOIN*

The CONCAT Function

To **concatenate** means to link or join; the *TEXTJOIN* function concatenates text strings. Excel has another *Text* function *CONCAT* that joins or combines data strings. The *CONCAT* function does not have a *delimiter* argument which enables you to specify a different delimiter between each two *TextN* arguments in the formula.

The syntax for a *CONCAT* function is:

=CONCAT(text1, [text2], . . .)

The *CONCAT* function has one argument *TextN*, where *N* is a number from 1 to 255. The *Text* argument can be a cell reference, data that you type, or a delimiter character.

> **ANOTHER WAY**
>
> You can join data in a formula using the & operator. The formula **=A1&B1** returns the same result as **=CONCAT(A1,B1)**.

When you concatenate text strings, such as first and last names, you must include space characters to separate words or values. Concatenated results are placed in a separate column or row to preserve original data.

In previous versions of Excel, *CONCAT* was named *CONCATENATE*.

▶HOW TO: Use the CONCAT Function

1. Click the cell for the result.

2. Click the **Text** button [*Formulas* tab, *Function Library* group] and choose **CONCAT**.

3. Select the cell with the first text string for the *Text1* argument.

- Type a text string rather than selecting a cell.
- You do not need to include quotation marks when you use the *Function Arguments* dialog box.

4. Click the **Text2** box and enter the next string to be concatenated.
 - You can type a delimiter such as a space, a period, or a comma.
 - You can click a cell with the second text string.
5. Click the **Text3** box and select or type next text string (Figure 6-53).
6. Complete *TextN* argument boxes as needed.

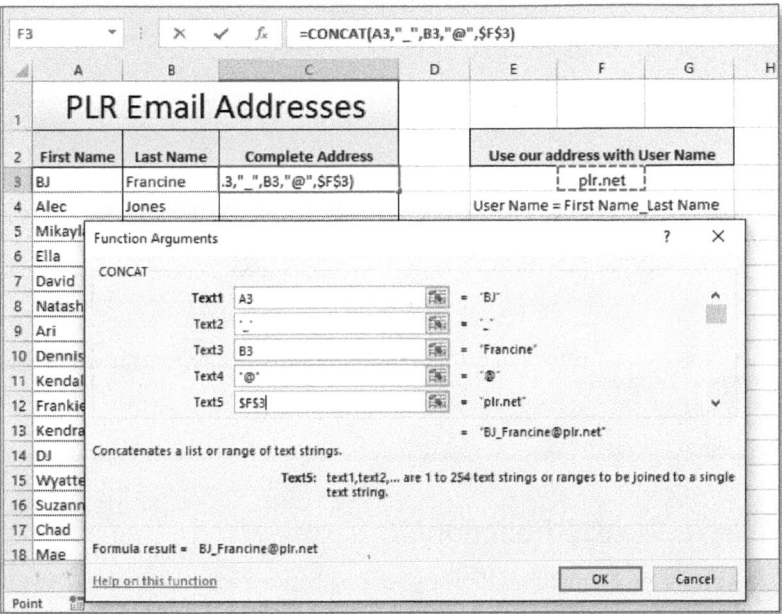

6-53 *Function Arguments* dialog box for *CONCAT*

7. Click **OK**.

> **ANOTHER WAY**
>
> You can include a space or punctuation character immediately after a cell reference in a *TextN* argument box.

> **MORE INFO**
>
> Use *TEXTJOIN* when the same delimiter is necessary for all *TextN* arguments. Use *CONCAT* to build a unique combination of *TextN* arguments and delimiters.

The EXACT Function

The *EXACT* function compares two text strings, values, or characters to determine if they are identical. For example, if you import email names, you can compare imported names to your current list.

The syntax for an *EXACT* function is:

=EXACT(text1, text2)

The *EXACT* function has two required arguments, *Text1* and *Text2*. *Text1* is the first text string, and *Text2* is the second text string. The arguments are case-sensitive, but the function does not check formatting. The result for an *EXACT* function is TRUE or FALSE.

▶ **HOW TO:** Use the EXACT Function

1. Click the cell for the result.
2. Type =ex and press **Tab**.
 • The *text1* argument is bold in the *ScreenTip*.
3. Select the cell or type the text string.
 • If you type the text string, enclose it within quotation marks and use upper- and lowercase as used in the data.
4. Type a comma (,) to move to the *text2* argument.
 • The *text2* argument is bold in the *ScreenTip*.
5. Select the cell or type the second text string (Figure 6-54).
6. Press **Enter**.
 • The closing parenthesis is supplied.
 • The result is TRUE or FALSE.

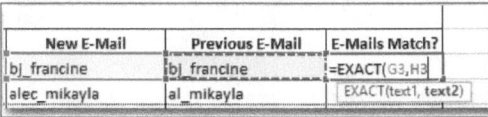

6-54 *EXACT* function has two arguments

The REPLACE Function

The *REPLACE* function allows you to substitute characters for a specified number of characters in existing data. This command is helpful when data in a column follows a pattern. For example, if Paradise Lakes Resort products have an ID that starts with PAR, use the *REPLACE* function to change each ID to PLR.

> ▶ **ANOTHER WAY**
>
> Use the *SUBSTITUTE* function in the *Text* category to replace specified text within a cell.

The syntax for a *REPLACE* function is:

=REPLACE(old_text, start_num, num_chars, new_text)

The *old_text* argument is the cell with data that you want to change. The *start_num* argument is the position in the cell of the first character to be replaced. If you want to replace the first three characters in a cell, the *start_num* is 1. However, if you want to replace characters in the second word in the cell, you must count each character position, including spaces, to determine the number.

The *num_chars* argument determines how many characters from the *start_num* position are replaced, and the *new_text* argument is the replacement text.

▶ **HOW TO:** Use the REPLACE Function

1. Click the cell for the result.
2. Click the **Text** button [*Formulas* tab, *Function Library* group] and choose **REPLACE**.
3. Select the cell with data to be replaced for the *Old_text* argument.

4. Click the **Start_num** box.
 - Count character positions from the first character on the left.
5. Type a number to indicate the position at which replacement should begin.
6. Click the **Num_chars** box.
 - Count how many characters are to be replaced.
7. Type the number of replacement characters.
8. Click the **New_text** box.
9. Type the replacement text (Figure 6-55).
 - The new text can have more or fewer characters than the *num_chars* argument.
 - Quotation marks are not necessary when you use the *Function Arguments* dialog box.
 - Use upper- and lowercase as required.
10. Press **Enter** or click **OK**.
 - The new text displays in the cell.

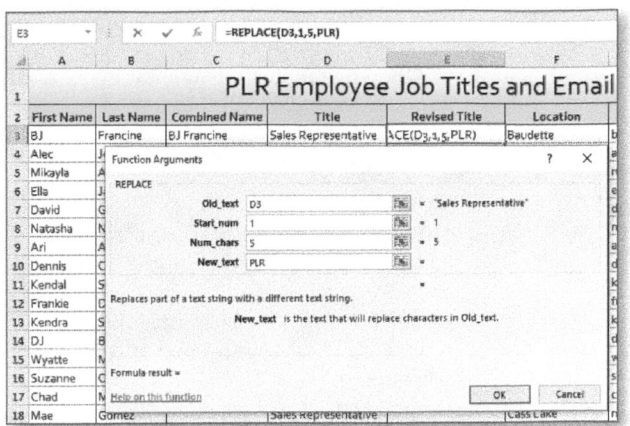

6-55 *REPLACE* function has four arguments

PAUSE & PRACTICE: EXCEL 6-3

In this project, you complete a financial planning worksheet for Paradise Lakes Resort staff. You also update the employee data sheet using *Text* functions.

File Needed: *[your initials] PP E6-2.xlsx*
Completed Project File Name: *[your initials] PP E6-3.xlsx*

1. Open *[your initials] PP E6-2.xlsx* completed in *Pause & Practice 6-2* and save it as [your initials] PP E6-3.

2. Click the **Financial Planner** sheet tab.

3. Use the *PV* function.
 a. Select cell **C9**.
 b. Click the **Financial** button [*Formulas* tab, *Function Library* group] and choose **PV**.
 c. Select cell **C7** for the *Rate* argument and type /12 after **C7**, because the payments are monthly.
 d. Click the **Nper** argument box and select cell **C6**.
 e. Type *12 after **C6**, because the term is years but payments are monthly.
 f. Click the **Pmt** box and select cell **C5**.
 g. Press **Tab** two times to skip the *Fv* box and move to the *Type* box.
 h. Type 1 in the *Type* box to indicate payment at the beginning of the period (Figure 6-56).

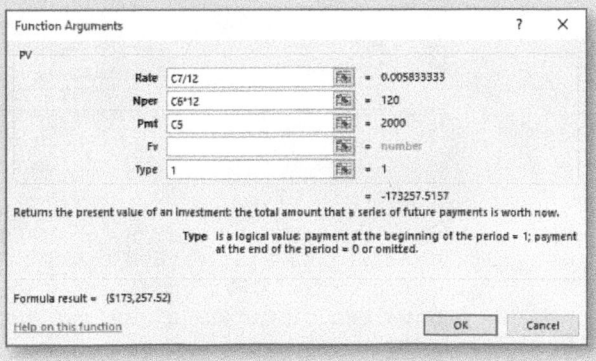

6-56 Payment is made at beginning of period

i. Click **OK**. An annuity or insurance policy costs over $173,000 to pay-out $2,000 monthly for 10 years.

4. Use the *FV* function.
 a. Select cell **F9**.
 b. Click the **Financial** button [*Formulas* tab, *Function Library* group] and choose **FV**.
 c. Click cell **F7** for the *Rate* argument. The payment is once a year and the rate is annual.
 d. Click the **Nper** argument box and select cell **F6**. There is only one payment per year.
 e. Click the **Pmt** box and select cell **F5**. The amount is negative, because you must pay it each year.
 f. Press **Tab** two times to skip the *Pv* box and move to the *Type* box. Leave both boxes empty (Figure 6-57).
 g. Click **OK**. If you invest $2,000 a year in an IRA account that earns 4.5% per year, you will have over $40,000 at the end of 15 years.

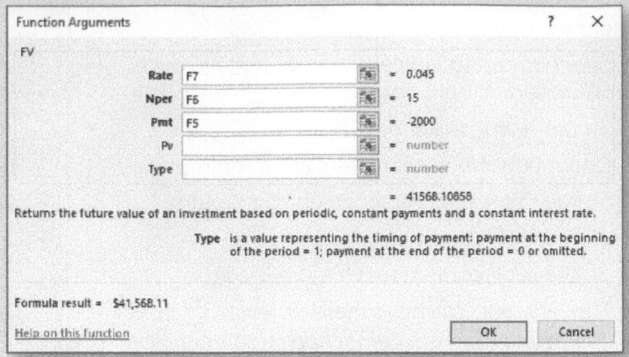

6-57 Rate and payment are yearly

5. Use the *NPV* function.
 a. Select cell **C18**.
 b. Click the **Financial** button [*Formulas* tab, *Function Library* group] and choose **NPV**.
 c. Select cell **C13** for the *Rate* argument.
 d. Click the **Value1** box and select cell **C15**.
 e. Click the **Value2** box and select cell **C16**.
 f. Click the **Value3** box and select cell **C17** (Figure 6-58).

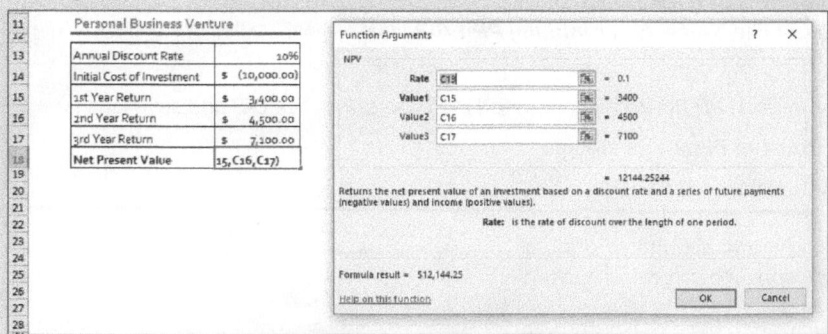

6-58 Initial investment is not a *value* argument

g. Click **OK**.
h. Click the *Formula* bar and press **End** to position the insertion point.
i. Type **+** and select cell **C14** to add the cost of the investment.
j. Press **Enter**. Based on projected cash flows, the investment has a present value of $2,144.25.

6. Use the *TEXTJOIN* function.
 a. Click the **Title&EMail** sheet tab and select cell **C3**.
 b. Click the **Text** button [*Formulas* tab, *Function Library* group] and choose **TEXTJOIN**.

c. Press **Spacebar** for the *Delimiter* argument.

d. Click the **Text1** box and select cell **A3**. The *Ignore_empty* argument is blank which means empty cells are ignored.

e. Click the **Text2** box and select cell **B3**.

f. Click **OK**.

g. Copy the *TEXTJOIN* formula in cell **C3** to cells **C4:C25** without formatting.

h. Make column C **19.29 (140 pixels)** wide (Figure 6-59).

7. Use the *REPLACE* function.

a. Select cell **E3**.

b. Click the **Text** button [*Formulas* tab, *Function Library* group] and choose **REPLACE**.

c. Click cell **D3** for the *Old_text* argument.

d. Click the **Start_num** box and type 1.

e. Click the **Num_chars** box and type 5. This preserves the space after the word "Sales."

f. Click the **New_text** box.

g. Type PLR.

h. Press **Enter** or click **OK**.

i. Copy the *REPLACE* formula in cell **E3** to cells **E4:E25** without formatting.

j. Hide column **D** and *AutoFit* column **E**.

8. Use the *EXACT* function.

a. Select cell **I3**.

b. Type =ex and press **Tab**.

c. Select cell **G3** for the *text1* argument and type a comma , to move to the *text2* argument.

d. Select cell **H3** and press **Enter**.

e. Copy the *EXACT* formula in cell **I3** to cells **I4:I25** without formatting.

f. Apply a *Highlight Cells* rule to cells **I4:I25** to show FALSE values in **Light Red Fill with Dark Red Text**.

9. Save and close the workbook (Figure 6-60).

A	B	C
First Name	**Last Name**	**Combined Name**
BJ	Francine	BJ Francine
Alec	Jones	Alec Jones
Mikayla	Anderson	Mikayla Anderson
Ella	Jamison	Ella Jamison
David	Gazik	David Gazik
Natasha	Nelson	Natasha Nelson
Ari	Aronson	Ari Aronson
Dennis	Omang	Dennis Omang
Kendal	Shaedon	Kendal Shaedon
Frankie	Dennis	Frankie Dennis
Kendra	Shelton	Kendra Shelton
DJ	Bushman	DJ Bushman
Wyatte	Mockentune	Wyatte Mockentune
Suzanne	Ouimet	Suzanne Ouimet
Chad	Meison	Chad Meison
Mae	Gomez	Mae Gomez
Christopher	Bowman	Christopher Bowman
Jeffery	Dalton	Jeffery Dalton
Corey	Daniels	Corey Daniels
Randy	Josephson	Randy Josephson
Tammy	Christine	Tammy Christine
Josie	Daddiline	Josie Daddiline
Nikolai	Jalowiec	Nikolai Jalowiec

6-59 *TEXTJOIN* formula shows results in single cell

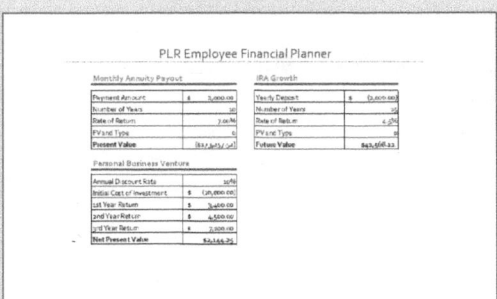

6-60 Completed worksheets for PP E6-3

SLO 6.7

Using Multiple Criteria in Functions

You have used multiple arguments in functions and multiple criteria in filters. Three functions combine multiple arguments with multiple criteria: *SUMIFS* in the *Math & Trig* category and *AVERAGEIFS* and *COUNTIFS* in the *Statistical* category.

The SUMIFS Function

The *SUMIFS* function adds or totals cells only if they meet the criteria. In the data shown in Figure 6-61, *SUMIFS* can be used to sum the cells in the "Calls" column if the location is Breezy Point (first criteria) and if the title is Trainee (second criteria).

Marketing Calls and Visits

Name	Title	Location	Calls	Onsite Visits
Christopher Bowman	Manager	Cass Lake	13	22
Chad Meison	Representative	Cass Lake	26	7
Corey Daniels	Trainee	Cass Lake	18	23
Wyatte Mockentune	Manager	Breezy Point	25	39
Dennis Omang	Representative	Breezy Point	22	36
BJ Francine	Representative	Baudette	32	8
Kendal Shaedon	Representative	Breezy Point	5	22
Ella Jamison	Manager	Baudette	44	10
Alec Jones	Representative	Baudette	26	18
Natasha Nelson	Trainee	Baudette	7	23
Nikolai Jalowiec	Manager	Walker	26	20
Tammy Christine	Representative	Walker	7	41
Josie Daddiline	Trainee	Walker	10	21
Tara Miller	Trainee	Breezy Point	32	37
Robert Andrew	Representative	Walker	15	10
Coryn Gomez	Representative	Baudette	35	5
Elizabeth Gabrys	Trainee	Cass Lake	43	9
Rita Larson	Trainee	Walker	6	36
Michael Gentile	Representative	Baudette	38	9

6-61 Criteria from more than one column can be used in *SUMIFS*, *AVERAGEIFS*, or *COUNTIFS*

> **MORE INFO**
>
> The *SUMIFS* function is best used in large lists for which it would be time-consuming to calculate these types of results.

The syntax for a *SUMIFS* function is:

=SUMIFS(sum_range, criteria_range1, criteria1, [criteria_range2, criteria2], . . .)

The three required arguments are *sum_range*, *criteria_range1*, and *criteria1*. The *sum_range* is the cell range to be added. *Criteria_rangeN* is the range of cells that holds the criteria; it must have the same number of rows and columns as the *sum_range*. The *criteriaN* argument is a cell or typed data that must be matched for the cells to be included in the total.

A *SUMIFS* formula includes one *sum_range* and up to 127 *criteria_rangeN* arguments, each with a corresponding *criteriaN* argument.

 HOW TO: Use SUMIFS

1. Click the cell for the result.
2. Click the **Math & Trig** button [*Formulas* tab, *Function Library* group] and choose **SUMIFS**.
3. Select the cells with data to be totaled for the *Sum_range* argument.
 - You can type cell references instead of selecting them.
4. Click the **Criteria_range1** argument box.
5. Select the range of cells with the first set of data to be matched with criteria.
 - This range must be the same size as the *sum_range*.
6. Click the **Criteria1** argument box.
7. Type the data to be used as a condition.
 - You can use wildcard characters in the criteria.
 - Text criteria are not case-sensitive.
 - If the criteria are located in a cell on the worksheet, you can select the cell.

8. Click the **Criteria_range2** argument box.

9. Select the range with the next set of data to be matched.
 - This range must be the same size as the *sum_range*.

10. Click the **Criteria2** argument box.

11. Type the second requirement or condition (Figure 6-62).

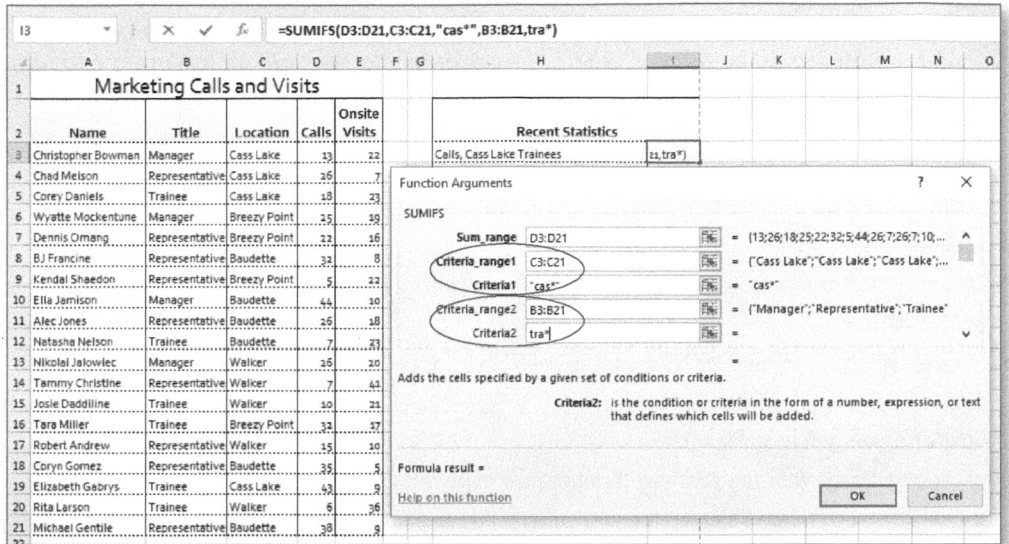

6-62 Data is included in sum only if it meets both criteria

12. Add *Criteria_range* and *Criteria* arguments as needed.
 - The size of each *criteria_range* must match the size of the *sum_range*.
 - Each *criteria_range* argument must have a corresponding *criteria* argument.

13. Click **OK**.

The AVERAGEIFS and COUNTIFS Functions

AVERAGEIFS and *COUNTIFS* perform their computations only when the data meets multiple criteria, like the *SUMIFS* function. For the data in Figure 6-63, use *AVERAGEIFS* to calculate the average number of onsite visits made by Walker representatives.

> **ANOTHER WAY**
>
> Results calculated by *SUMIFS*, *AVERAGEIFS*, or *COUNTIFS* can also be determined by filtering and sorting data in an Excel table.

The syntax for the *AVERAGEIFS* function is:

=AVERAGEIFS(average_range, criteria_range1, criteria1, [criteria_range2, criteria2] . . .)

The three arguments in an *AVERAGEIFS* calculation are *average_range*, *criteria_rangeN*, and *criteriaN*. There is one *average_range*, and the *criteria_range* arguments must be the same size as the *average_range*. You can use up to 127 criteria ranges, and each one must have corresponding criteria.

The syntax for the *COUNTIFS* function is:

=COUNTIFS(criteria_range1, criteria1, [criteria_range2, criteria2] . . .)

The *COUNTIFS* function has multiple *criteria_range* arguments, which are the cell ranges with data to be counted. There is a corresponding *criteria* argument for each *criteria_range* argument, up to 127.

▶ HOW TO: Use AVERAGEIFS

1. Click the cell for the result.
2. Click the **More Functions** button [*Formulas* tab, *Function Library* group] and choose **Statistical**.
3. Choose **AVERAGEIFS**.
4. Select the cells with data to be averaged for the *Average_range* argument.
 - You can type the range address.
5. Click the **Criteria_range1** argument box.
6. Select the range of cells with the first set of data to be matched with criteria.
 - This range must be the same size as the *average_range* argument.
7. Click the **Criteria1** box.
8. Type the data to be used as a condition.
 - Text criteria are not case-sensitive, and you can use wildcard characters.
 - If criteria are located in a worksheet cell, select the cell.
9. Click the **Criteria_range2** argument box.
10. Select the range of cells with the next set of data to be matched.
 - This range must be the same size as the *average_range* argument.
11. Click the **Criteria2** box.
12. Type the second requirement or condition (Figure 6-63).

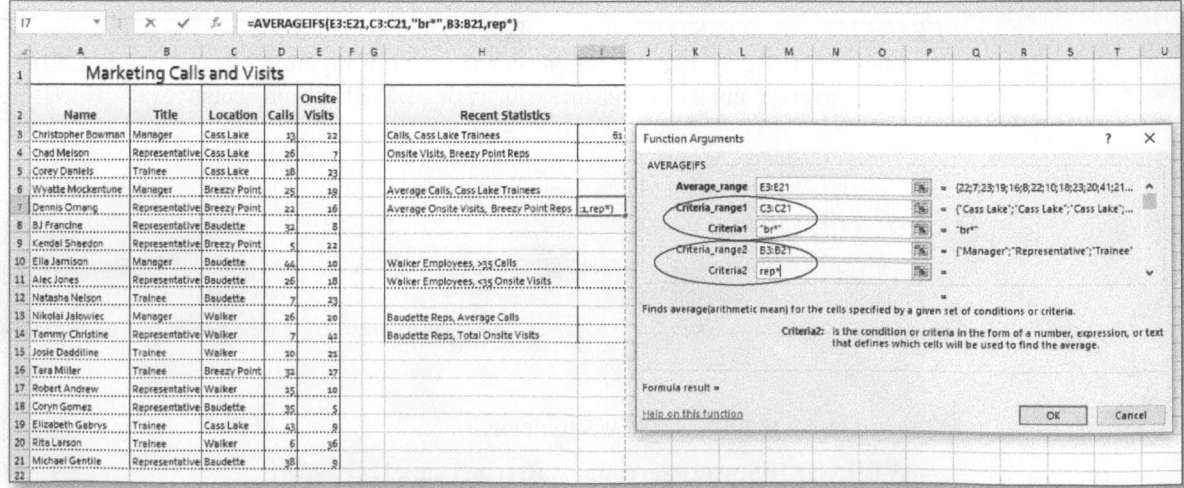

6-63 Data is included in average only if it meets both criteria

13. Add *Criteria_range* and *Criteria* arguments as needed.
 - The size of each *criteria_range* must match the size of the *average_range*.
 - Each *criteria_range* argument must have a corresponding *criteria* argument.
14. Click **OK**.

SLO 6.8

Monitoring and Editing Functions

With the *Find and Replace* command, you can make batch changes to functions or formulas. You can monitor results in different parts of a large worksheet or in a multi-sheet workbook from the *Watch Window*.

Find and Replace

You can use *Find and Replace* to change a function or an argument throughout a worksheet. In a nested *IF* function used in thousands of rows, use *Find and Replace* to edit a *value_if_true* argument. Or, if you mistakenly used *DAVERAGE* many times when you should have used *DSUM*, find and replace the incorrect function names.

▶**HOW TO: Replace a Function Argument**

1. Select the cell range with data to be replaced.
2. Click the **Find & Select** button [*Home* tab, *Editing* group] and choose **Replace**.
3. Click **Options >>** to expand the *Find and Replace* options.
4. Click the **Find what** box.
 - Delete existing search strings.
 - If necessary, click the **Format** arrow and clear the find format.
5. Type the data to be replaced.
 - Use uppercase if it will be necessary to match case.
 - Use wildcard characters to shorten a find string.
6. Click the **Replace with** box and type the replacement data.
 - Use uppercase for characters when new text should be capitalized.
7. Select the **Match case** box if appropriate.
8. Select the **Match entire cell contents** box if required.
 - Do not use this choice when looking for a specific part of cell data.
9. Verify or select **Within**, **Search**, and **Look In** options.
10. Click **Find All** (Figure 6-64).
 - Size the *Find and Replace* dialog box to view the results.
11. Click **Replace All**.
 - You can also replace occurrences one at a time if preferred.

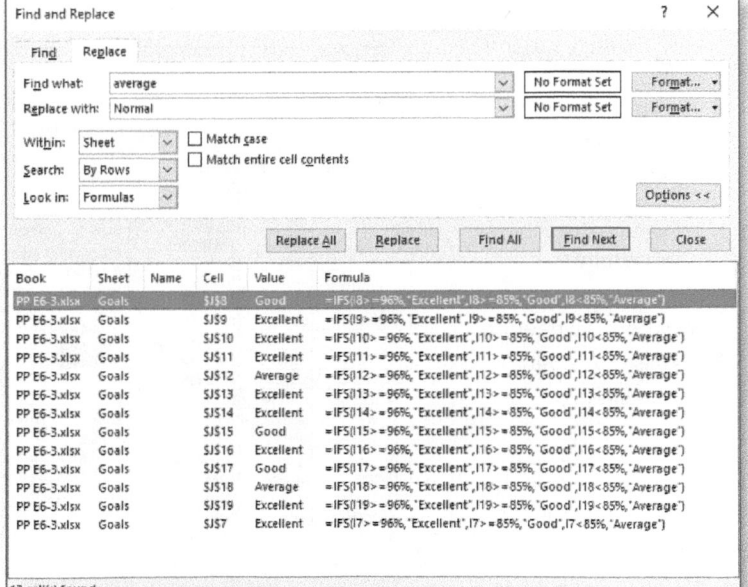

6-64 All occurrences that will be replaced

12. Click **OK** in the message box.

13. Close the *Find and Replace* dialog box.

- You can undo a *Find and Replace* task by pressing **Ctrl+Z** or by clicking the Undo button in the *Quick Access* toolbar.

> **ANOTHER WAY**
>
> Use the *Find and Replace* command to replace formats such as font name, fill color, or border style.

The Watch Window

The *Watch Window* is a floating dialog box with cell addresses and content to monitor while you work in another part of the workbook or worksheet. The *Watch Window* enables you to observe the effects of changes without having to scroll through a large sheet or switch between multiple sheets. You can position and size the *Watch Window* like any dialog box. In addition, when you double-click a cell address in the *Watch Window*, the insertion point moves to that location, like a bookmark.

▶ HOW TO: Monitor Changes in the Watch Window

1. Click the **Watch Window** button [*Formulas* tab, *Formula Auditing* group].
 - The *Watch Window* opens.
2. Select the first cell or range to monitor and click **Add Watch** in the floating window.
3. Click **Add** in the *Add Watch* dialog box.
4. Repeat steps 2–3 to add cells or ranges to the *Watch Window*.
 - Size the *Watch Window* and its columns to see the contents (Figure 6-65).
 - Position the window as desired.
5. Edit data in the workbook as needed.
 - Switch to another worksheet if necessary.
6. Select a watch in the *Watch Window* and click **Delete Watch** in the floating window.
 - Use regular selection methods to select more than one watch.
7. Close the *Watch Window*.

6-65 Resized *Watch Window*

PAUSE & PRACTICE: EXCEL 6-4

In this project, you use functions from the *Math & Trig* and *Statistical* categories with multiple critieria ranges to analyze Paradise Lakes Resort marketing data. You also update an argument in an *IFS* function and watch changes in transposed data.

File Needed: *[your initials] PP E6-3.xlsx*
Completed Project File Name: *[your initials] PP E6-4.xlsx*

1. Open *[your initials] PP E6-3.xlsx* completed in *Pause & Practice 6-3* and save it as [your initials] PP E6-4.

2. Click the **Marketing** sheet tab.

3. Use the *SUMIFS* function.
 a. Select cell **I3**.
 b. Click the **Math & Trig** button [*Formulas* tab, *Function Library* group] and choose **SUMIFS**.
 c. Select cells **D3:D21** for the *Sum_range* argument.
 d. Click the **Criteria_range1** box and select cells **C3:C21**, the location column.
 e. Click the **Criteria1** box and type cas* to include cells with data for Cass Lake.
 f. Click the **Criteria_range2** box and select cells **B3:B21**, the job title column.
 g. Click the **Criteria2** box and type tr* to include trainee data (Figure 6-66).
 h. Click **OK**. The number of calls made by Cass Lake trainees is 61.
 i. Select cell **I4** and use *SUMIFS* to total the number of onsite visits made by Breezy Point representatives.

6-66 *SUMIFS* with two criteria ranges

4. Use the *AVERAGEIFS* function.
 a. Select cell **I6**.
 b. Click the **More Functions** button [*Formulas* tab, *Function Library* group] and choose **Statistical**.
 c. Choose **AVERAGEIFS**.
 d. Select cells **D3:D21** for the *Average_range* argument.
 e. Click the **Criteria_range1** box and select cells **C3:C21** for the location.
 f. Click the **Criteria1** box and type cas* for Cass Lake as the location.
 g. Click the **Criteria_range2** box and select cells **B3:B21** for the job title.
 h. Click the **Criteria2** box and type tr* (Figure 6-67).

i. Click **OK**. The average number of calls made by Cass Lake trainees is 30.5.
j. Click cell **I7** and use *AVERAGEIFS* to find the average number of onsite visits made by Breezy Point representatives.

5. Use *COUNTIFS*.
 a. Select cell **I10**.
 b. Click the **More Functions** button [*Formulas* tab, *Function Library* group], **Statistical**, and select **COUNTIFS**.
 c. Select cells **C3:C21** for the *Criteria_range1* argument.
 d. Click the **Criteria1** box and type wa* to include Walker data.
 e. Click the **Criteria_range2** box and select cells **D3:D21**. The function will count the number of cells in which the location is Walker and the number of calls is greater than 35.
 f. Click the **Criteria2** box and type >35 (Figure 6-68).
 g. Click **OK**. No Walker representatives made more than 35 calls.
 h. Click cell **I11** and use *COUNTIFS* to count the number of Walker representatives who made fewer than 35 onsite visits.

6-67 *AVERAGEIFS* with two criteria ranges

6-68 *COUNTIFS* with two criteria ranges

6. Click cell **I13** and use *AVERAGEIFS* based on the data in cell **H13**.

7. Click cell **I14** and use *SUMIFS*.

8. Watch edits in the *Watch Window*.
 a. Select cells **A3:A21**.
 b. Click the **Watch Window** button [*Formulas* tab, *Formula Auditing* group].
 c. Select and delete any previous watches.
 d. Click **Add Watch**, verify the selection, and click **Add**.
 e. Size the columns in the *Watch Window* to see more data in each column.
 f. Click the **Transpose** sheet tab.
 g. Click cell **B1**, change the name to **Barton Miles**, and press **Enter**. (Figure 6-69). The name is updated on the **Marketing** sheet as shown in the *Watch Window*.
 h. Select the first watch in the *Watch Window*.
 i. Press **Shift** and select the last watch.
 j. Click **Delete Watch** and close the *Watch Window*.

9. Use *Find and Replace*.
 a. Click the **Goals** sheet tab.
 b. Click the **Find & Select** button [*Home* tab, *Editing* group] and choose **Replace**.
 c. Click **Options>>**. When the dialog box is expanded, this command appears as **<<Options**.
 d. If necessary, click the **Format** arrow and clear previous find format settings.

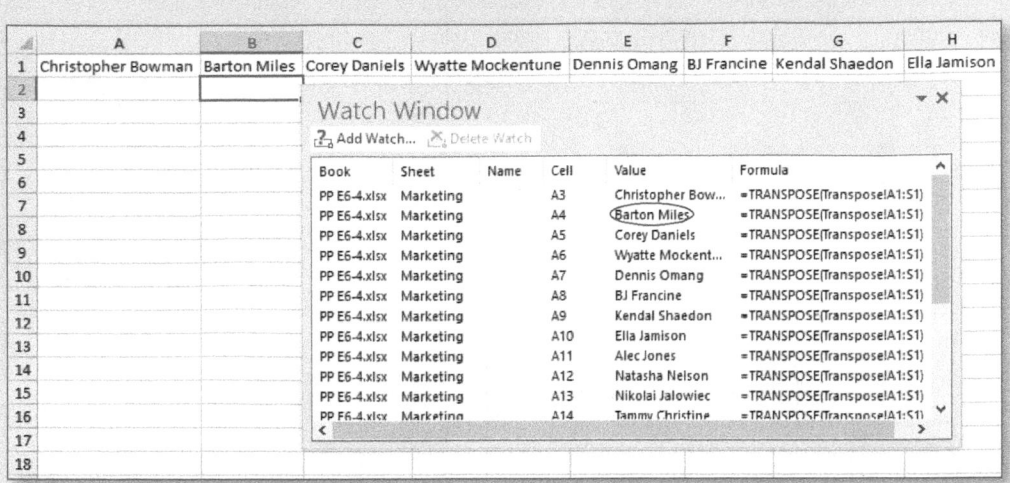

6-69 Name is changed on *Marketing* sheet

e. Click the **Find what** box and delete previous search strings.
f. Type average. The *Find what* string is not case-sensitive.
g. Click the ***Replace with*** box and type Normal.
h. Verify that the **Within** choice is **Sheet**, the **Search** choice is **By Rows**, and the **Look In** choice is **Formulas**.
i. Click **Find All** and size the dialog box to see the listed references.
j. Select the reference for cell **J7** in the *Find and Replace* dialog box.
k. Scroll the list, press **Shift**, and select the reference for cell **J19**. The selected references exclude cells B22 and D22 (Figure 6-70).
l. Click **Replace All** and then click **OK**.
m. Close the *Find and Replace* dialog box.

6-70 Select references to be replaced

10. Save and close the workbook (Figure 6-71).

Marketing Calls and Visits

Name	Title	Location	Calls	Onsite Visits
Christopher Bowman	Manager	Cass Lake	13	22
Barton Miles	Representative	Cass Lake	26	7
Corey Daniels	Trainee	Cass Lake	18	23
Wyatte Mockentune	Manager	Breezy Point	25	19
Dennis Omang	Representative	Breezy Point	22	16
BJ Francine	Representative	Baudette	32	8
Kendal Shaedon	Representative	Breezy Point	5	22
Ella Jamison	Manager	Baudette	44	10
Alec Jones	Representative	Baudette	26	18
Natasha Nelson	Trainee	Baudette	7	23
Nikolai Jalowiec	Manager	Walker	26	20
Tammy Christine	Representative	Walker	7	41
Josie Daddiline	Trainee	Walker	10	21
Tara Miller	Trainee	Breezy Point	32	17
Robert Andrew	Representative	Walker	15	10
Coryn Gomez	Representative	Baudette	35	5
Elizabeth Gabrys	Trainee	Cass Lake	43	9
Rita Larson	Trainee	Walker	6	36
Michael Gentile	Representative	Baudette	38	9

Recent Statistics	
Calls, Cass Lake Trainees	61
Onsite Visits, Breezy Point Reps	38
Average Calls, Cass Lake Trainees	30.5
Average Onsite Visits, Breezy Point Reps	19
Walker Employees, >35 Calls	0
Walker Employees, <35 Onsite Visits	3
Baudette Reps, Average Calls	32.75
Baudette Reps, Total Onsite Visits	40

Revenue Data by Employee

Name	Location	Goal	Actual	Met Goal?	Both Goals?	Either Goal?	Both Goals?	Actual/ Goal %	Level	Quarterly Goal
										$15,000
BJ Francine	Baudette	$17,000	$21,500	Yes	TRUE	TRUE	Met both	126%	Excellent	
Christopher Bowman	Cass Lake	$15,000	$13,750	No	FALSE	FALSE	No	85%	Good	
Nikolai Jalowiec	Walker	$15,000	$15,600	Yes	TRUE	TRUE	Met both	104%	Excellent	
Chad Meison	Cass Lake	$17,500	$25,000	Yes	TRUE	TRUE	Met both	143%	Excellent	
Dennis Omang	Breezy Point	$18,000	$21,000	Yes	TRUE	TRUE	Met both	117%	Excellent	
Corey Daniels	Cass Lake	$5,000	$3,300	No	FALSE	FALSE	No	66%	Normal	
Natasha Nelson	Baudette	$0	$4,050	Yes	FALSE	TRUE	No	Check values in columns C and D.	Excellent	
Tammy Christine	Walker	$75,000	$81,000	Yes	TRUE	TRUE	Met both	108%	Excellent	
Wyatte Mockentune	Breezy Point	$15,000	$14,200	No	FALSE	FALSE	No	95%	Good	
Kendal Shaedon	Breezy Point	21000.5	$18,500	No	FALSE	TRUE	No	Check values in columns C and D.	Excellent	
Ella Jamison	Baudette	$15,000	$13,200	No	FALSE	FALSE	No	88%	Good	
Alec Jones	Baudette	$17,000	$9,350	No	FALSE	FALSE	No	55%	Normal	
Josie Daddiline	Walker	$42,500	$56,000	Yes	TRUE	TRUE	Met both	132%	Excellent	

Maximum Goal, Cass Lake	$17,500
Average Goal, Cass Lake	$12,500
Total Goal, Cass Lake	$37,500

6-71 Completed worksheets for PP E6-4

Chapter Summary

6.1 Use *Database* functions such as *DSUM* and *DAVERAGE* (p. E6-350).

- Functions in the *Database* category perform a calculation only when data meet the criteria.
- **Database functions** are used with list or table-type data.
- The syntax for a *Database* function is *FunctionName (database, field, criteria)*.
- The *criteria* argument is a range of cells with labels in one row and criteria below the label row on the same or another sheet.
- The criteria range can use *AND* conditions in the same row or *OR* criteria in separate rows.

6.2 Build *AND*, *OR*, nested, and *IFS* functions (p. E6-352).

- *AND* and *OR* functions return TRUE or FALSE as a result.
- An *AND* function tests multiple conditions and shows TRUE only when all conditions are met.
- An *OR* function tests multiple conditions and shows TRUE if one condition is met and shows FALSE only when all statements are false.
- *AND* and *OR* functions have one argument, *logicalN*, but there can be up to 255 *logicalN* statements.
- A **nested function** is a function within another function.
- *AND* or *OR* are nested within *IF* to check for multiple conditions by using an *AND* or *OR* function as the *logical_test* argument.
- An *IFS* function can use multiple *logical_test* arguments with a corresponding *value_if_true* argument for each test.
- A formula syntax error results in a default error message in the cell such as #N/A or #VALUE!
- For formulas that may result in a default error message, use the *IFERROR* function to display a custom message.

6.3 Explore the *Lookup & Reference* category with *INDEX*, *MATCH*, and *TRANSPOSE* (p. E6-364).

- An *INDEX* function displays the contents of the cell at the intersection of a specified column and row.
- The *MATCH* function returns the relative location of data in a list.

- *MATCH* and *INDEX* are nested to accomplish the same tasks as a *VLOOKUP* formula but at a faster speed.
- Nested *MATCH* and *INDEX* formulas are well-suited to datasets with millions of rows.
- The *TRANSPOSE* function displays columnar data in rows and vice versa.

6.4 Build date, time, and statistical calculations (p. E6-368).

- Date arithmetic is possible because Excel uses a serial numbering system for dates.
- Date and time calculations are straightforward, but an unsuitable format can disguise the results.
- The *Date & Time* function category includes functions that convert text into dates, determine workdays in a range of dates, or display the day of the week for a date.
- Use Excel functions to build common statistical forecasting calculations.
- A **forecast error** is the deviation or difference between actual values and predicted or forecasted values.
- The **mean absolute deviation (MAD)** is a statistical measure of how spread out a group of values is from the average.
- A **standard deviation** measures how broadly values vary from the mean (average) value, a common statistical calculation.

6.5 Use *Financial* functions such as *PV*, *FV*, and *NPV* (p. E6-380).

- Financial functions analyze money transactions.
- Many functions in the *Financial* category include **rate** and **nper** arguments and use the concept of an **annuity**, a series of equal payments.
- The *PV* function calculates the current value of regular payments at a set interest rate for a specified period of time.
- The *FV* function calculates the future value of regular payments or deposits invested at a constant interest rate for a specified period of time.
- The *NPV* function calculates the net present value of an investment using a **discount rate** and a series of **cash flows** which can be receipts or payments.

6.6 Work with *Text* functions including *TEXTJOIN*, *CONCAT*, *EXACT*, and *REPLACE* (p. E6-384).

- Text functions join, convert, and split labels and values in a worksheet.
- The *TEXTJOIN* function combines up to 252 strings of text, values, or characters in a single cell and uses a delimiter to separate the strings.
- The *CONCAT* function combines up to 255 strings of text, values, or characters in a single cell, and delimiters must be included in the arguments.
- The *EXACT* function compares two text, value, or character strings and displays TRUE if they are identical.
- The *REPLACE* function removes characters in a data string and replaces them with new characters.

6.7 Use multiple criteria in *SUMIFS*, *AVERAGEIFS*, and *COUNTIFS* functions (p. E6-391).

- The *SUMIFS* function is in the *Math & Trig* category and sums values for cells that meet up to 127 criteria.
- *AVERAGEIFS* and *COUNTIFs* are both in the *Statistical* category.

- *AVERAGIFS* averages values for cells that meet the criteria and *COUNTIFS* counts them.

6.8 Monitor and edit functions with the *Watch Window* and *Find and Replace* (p. E6-394).

- Use the *Find and Replace* command to locate and replace function arguments as well as function names in a workbook.
- The **Watch Window** is a floating dialog box, sized and positioned to show as much data as necessary.
- Add cell references to the *Watch Window* to observe changes in another part of the worksheet or workbook.

Check for Understanding

The SIMbook for this text (within your SIMnet account) provides the following resources for concept review:

- Multiple choice questions
- Matching exercises
- Short answer questions

USING MICROSOFT EXCEL 2016

Guided Project 6-1

In this project, you use *Database* functions to calculate results for the Boyd Air flight schedule. You complete projected versus actual passenger numbers and build a worksheet that tracks flight hours. You also work with *Text* and *Financial* functions.
[Student Learning Outcomes 6.1, 6.2, 6.3, 6.4, 6.5, 6.6, 6.7, 6.8]

File Needed: ***BoydAir-06.xlsx*** *(Student data files are available in the Library of your SIMnet account)*
Completed Project File Name: *[your initials] Excel 6-1.xlsx*

Skills Covered in this Project

- Use *Database* functions *DAVERAGE*, *DCOUNTA*, and *DMIN*.
- Use *COUNTIFS* and *SUMIFS*.
- Nest *MATCH* and *INDEX* functions.
- Build time and deviation calculations.

- Build *Logical* functions with *IF*, *AND*, and *OR*.
- Create an *IFERROR* formula.
- Build an *IFS* formula.
- Use and nest *Text* functions.
- Create formulas with *Financial* functions.
- Find and replace function arguments.

1. Open the ***BoydAir-06*** workbook from your student data files and save it as [your initials] Excel 6-1.

2. Use *DCOUNTA* to determine the number of flights originating in Chicago.
 a. Click the **Flight Stats** sheet tab.
 b. Select cells **A4:H18** and name the range Flights. The range includes the labels in row 4.
 c. Click the **Criteria** sheet tab.
 d. Click cell **C2** and type mdw for Midway airport in Chicago.
 e. Click the **Flight Stats** sheet, select cell **E22**, and click the **Insert Function** button on the *Formula* bar.
 f. Choose **Database** in the *Or select a category* list.
 g. Select **DCOUNTA** and click **OK**.
 h. Press **F3 (FN+F3)** for the *Database* argument to open the *Paste Name* dialog box.
 i. Choose **Flights** and click **OK**.
 j. Click the **Field** argument box and type origin.
 k. Click the **Criteria** argument box and select cells **C1:C2** on the **Criteria** sheet. (Figure 6-72).
 l. Click **OK**. The result is 3.

6-72 *DCOUNTA function to count flights that originated at MDW*

3. Use *DCOUNTA* to determine the number of flights terminating in Minneapolis.
 a. Click the **Criteria** sheet tab.
 b. Click cell **D2** and type msp for the Minneapolis-St. Paul airport.
 c. Click the **Flight Stats** sheet tab and select cell **E23**.
 d. Click the **Recently Used** button [*Formulas* tab, *Function Library* group] and select **DCOUNTA**.
 e. Press **F3** (**FN+F3**) for the *Database* argument, choose **Flights**, and click **OK**.
 f. Click the **Field** argument box and type 4 for the fourth column from the left in the range.
 g. Click the **Criteria** box, click the **Criteria** sheet tab, and select cells **D1:D2**.
 h. Click **OK**. The result is 4.

4. Copy cells **A1:H2** on the **Criteria** sheet to cells **A4:H5** and again to cells **A7:H8**. Delete the contents of cells **C5:D5** and **C8:D8**.

5. Select cell **D5** and type grb for the Green Bay airport.

6. Click the **Flight Stats** sheet and select cell **E24**. Start a *DAVERAGE* formula, select the **Flights** range name, and use the "passengers" column. The criteria is located in cells **D4:D5** on the **Criteria** sheet; the result is 77.5

7. Click the **Criteria** sheet tab, select cell **D8**, and type mdw.

8. Click the **Flight Stats** sheet, select cell **E25** and use *DMIN*. The result is 35.

9. Use *COUNTIFS* to count flights delayed into Chicago.
 a. Select cell **E26** on the **Flight Stats** sheet.
 b. Click the **More Functions** button [*Formulas* tab, *Function Library* group] and choose **Statistical**.
 c. Choose **COUNTIFS**.
 d. Select cells **D5:D18** for the *Criteria_range1* argument.
 e. Click the **Criteria1** box and type mdw for Midway airport.
 f. Click the **Criteria_range2** box and select cells **G5:G18**.
 g. Click the **Criteria2** box and type del* for "Delayed" (Figure 6-73).
 h. Click **OK**. The result is 2.

10. Use *SUMIFS* to count total passengers delayed into Chicago.
 a. Select cell **E27**.
 b. Click the **Math & Trig** button [*Formulas* tab, *Function Library* group] and choose **SUMIFS**.
 c. Select cells **H5:H18** for the *Sum_range* argument.
 d. Click the **Criteria_range1** box and select cells **D5:D18**, the destination field.
 e. Click the **Criteria1** box and type mdw.
 f. Click the **Criteria_range2** box and select cells **G5:G18**, the code field.
 g. Click the **Criteria2** box and type del*.
 h. Click **OK**. The count is 170 passengers.

11. Nest *MATCH* with *INDEX* function to display an arrival time.
 a. Select cell **D31**.
 b. Click the **Lookup & Reference** button [*Formulas* tab, *Function Library* group] and choose **INDEX**.
 c. Select the first argument list **array, row_num, column_num** and click **OK**.
 d. Paste the **Flights** range name for the *Array* argument.
 e. Click the **Row_num** box and click the **Name** box arrow.

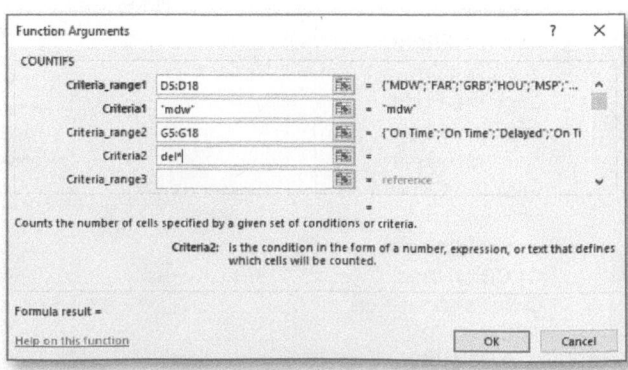

6-73 *COUNTIFS* with two criteria

f. Choose **MATCH** in the list or choose **More Functions** to find and select **MATCH**.

g. Select cell **C31** for the *Lookup_value* box.

h. Click the **Lookup_array** box and select cells **D4:D18**. When the named range includes the header row, the label row is included in the lookup array.

i. Click the **Match_type** box and type 0 to use an exact match.

j. Click the function name **INDEX** in the *Formula* bar. (If an argument lists box opens, click **OK**).

k. Click the **Column_num** box, click the **Name** box arrow, and choose **MATCH**.

l. Select cell **F4** for the *Lookup_value* argument.

m. Click the **Lookup_array** box and select cells **A4:H4**.

n. Click the **Match_type** argument and type 0.

o. Click **INDEX** in the *Formula* bar to see the complete nested formula (Figure 6-74).

p. Click **OK**. The result is formatted as a number.

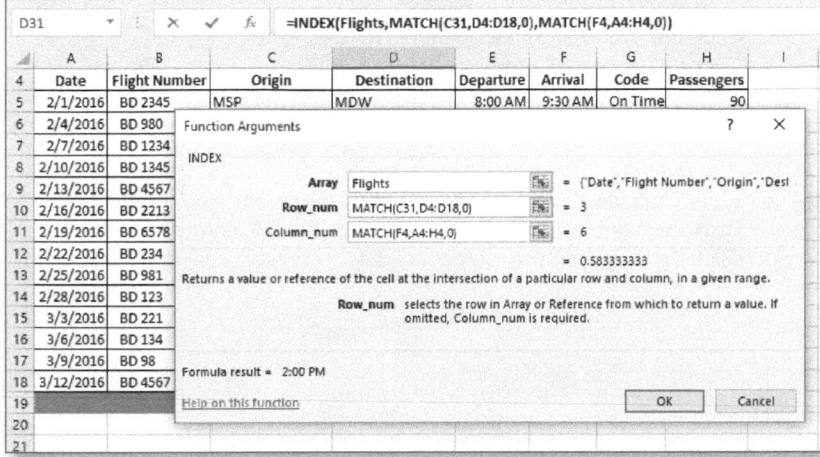

6-74 *MATCH* nested for both *INDEX* arguments

12. Select cell **D31** and click the **Launcher** in the *Number* group [*Home* tab].

13. Choose the **Time** category and the **1:30 PM** style. Click **OK**.

14. Press **Ctrl+Home**.

15. Calculate the difference between scheduled and actual arrival time.

a. Click the **Time Deviations** worksheet tab and select cell **G5**.

b. Type =(and select cell **F5**.

c. Type a minus sign –, select cell **E5**, and type the closing parenthesis).

d. Type *24*60 to convert the result to days and then to minutes (Figure 6-75).

e. Press **Enter**. A negative number of minutes means the flight was early.

f. Copy the formula in cell **G5** to cells **G6:G24**.

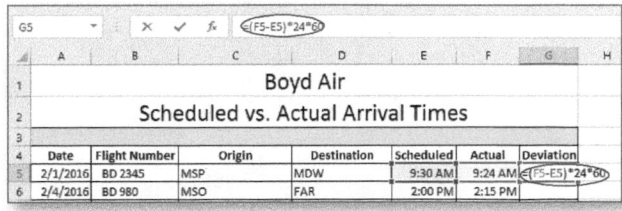

6-75 Time difference is converted to minutes

16. Calculate the mean absolute deviation (MAD) for arrival times.

a. Select cell **I5**.

b. Click the **Math & Trig** button [*Formulas* tab, *Function Library* group] and choose **ABS**.

c. Select cell **G5** for the *Number* argument and click **OK**.

d. Copy the formula in cell **I5** to cells **I6:I24**.

e. Select cell **D27**.

f. Use the *AVERAGE* function to calculate the mean (or average) for cells **I5:I24**. The result is 10.35.

g. Right-click the column **I** heading and choose **Hide**.

17. Calculate the standard deviation for arrival times.
 a. Select cell **D28**.
 b. Click the **More Functions** button [*Formulas* tab, *Function Library* group], choose **Statistical**, and choose **STDEV.S**.
 c. Select cells **G5:G24** and press **Enter**. The result is 13.3111548.
 d. Press **Ctrl+Home**.

18. Build an *IF* function.
 a. Click the **Flight Hours** sheet tab and select cell **F4**.
 b. Click the **Logical** button [*Formulas* tab, *Function Library* group] and choose **IF**.
 c. Click the **Logical_test** argument box, select cell **D4**, and type >20.
 d. Click the **Value_if_true** box and type Yes.
 e. Click the **Value_if_false** box and type No.
 f. Click **OK** or press **Enter**.
 g. Copy the formula to cells **F5:F18** without formatting to preserve the borders.
 h. Center cells **F4:F18**.

19. Use the *Function Arguments* dialog box to enter an *OR* function.
 a. Select cell **G4**, click the **Logical** button [*Formulas* tab, *Function Library* group], and choose **OR**.
 b. Click the **Logical1** argument box, select cell **D4**, and type >20.
 c. Click the **Logical2** box, select cell **E4**, and type >20 (Figure 6-76).

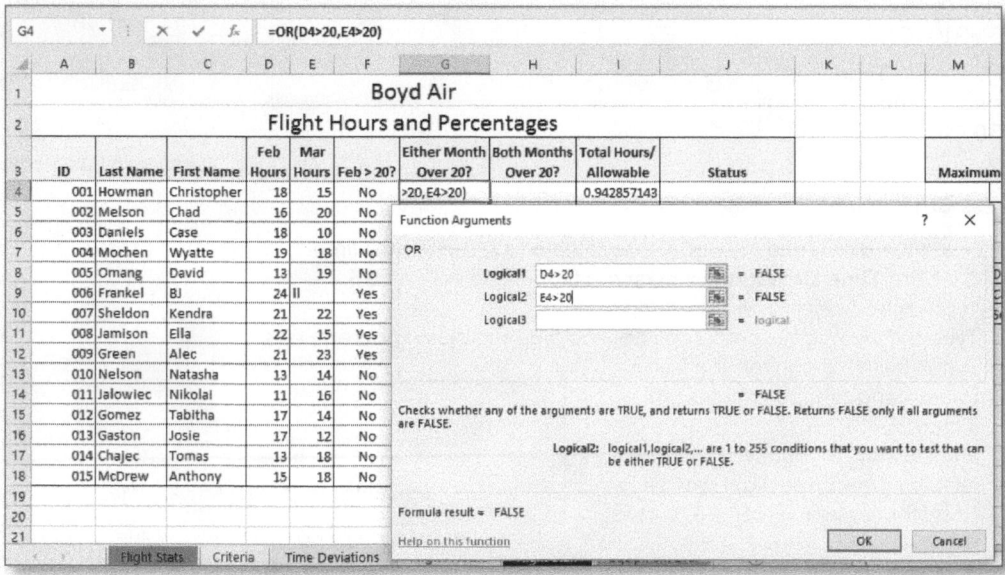

6-76 *OR* formula

 d. Click **OK**. The first result is FALSE.
 e. Copy the formula in cell **G4** to cells **G5:G18** without formatting.

20. Create an *AND* function.
 a. Select cell **H4**, click the **Logical** button [*Formulas* tab, *Function Library* group], and choose **AND**.
 b. Click the **Logical1** box, select cell **D4**, and type >20.
 c. Click the **Logical2** box, select cell **E4**, and type >20.
 d. Click **OK**. The first result is FALSE.
 e. Copy the formula in cell **H4** to cells **H5:H18** without formatting.

21. Use *IFERROR* to display a custom message.
 a. Select cell **I4**. The formula adds the hours for February and March and then divides by the allowable hours in cell N4. There is a standard Excel error message in cell **I9** because the data in cell E9 is text.
 b. Delete the formula in cell **I4**.
 c. Click the **Logical** button [*Formulas* tab, *Function Library* group] and choose **IFERROR**.
 d. Type a left parenthesis (in the *Value* argument box, select cell **D4**, type +, and select cell **E4**.
 e. Type a right parenthesis and a forward slash for division)/, click cell **N4**, and press **F4 (FN+F4)** to make it absolute.
 f. Click the **Value_if_error** box and type Check values. (Figure 6-77).
 g. Click **OK**.

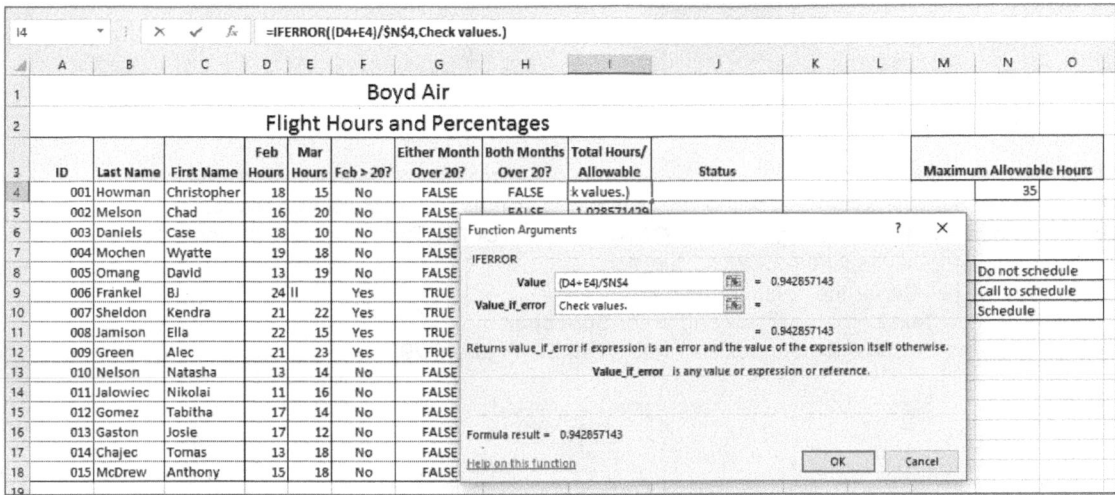

6-77 *IFERROR* formula

 h. Copy the formula in cell **I4** to cells **I5:I18** without formatting. Widen the column to display the complete message.
 i. Format cells **I4:I18** with **Percent Style** and two decimal places.

22. Create an *IFS* function.
 a. Select cell **J4**, click the **Logical** button [*Formulas* tab, *Function Library* group] and choose **IFS**.
 b. Select cell **I4** for the *Logical_test1* box and type >=100%.
 c. Click the **Value_if_true1** box, select cell **N8**, and press **F4 (FN+F4)**.
 d. Click the **Logical_test2** box, select cell **I4**, and type >=91%.
 e. Click the **Value_if_true2** box, select cell **N9**, and press **F4 (FN+F4)**.
 f. Click the **Logical_test3** box, select cell **I4**, and type >=70%.
 g. Press **Tab** to move to the *Value_if_true3* box, select cell **N10**, and press **F4 (FN+F4)** (Figure 6-78).
 h. Click **OK**.
 i. Copy the formula in cell **I4** to cells **I5:I18** without formatting.
 j. Increase the indent one time for the data in column **J**.
 k. Press **Ctrl+Home**.

23. Create a nested *Text* function with *UPPER* and *CONCAT*.
 a. Click the **Flight Staff** sheet tab and select cell **D4**. Printed labels display first and last names in uppercase characters.
 b. Click the **Text** button [*Formulas* tab, *Function Library* group] and choose **UPPER**. The argument is the *Text* to be shown in uppercase letters.

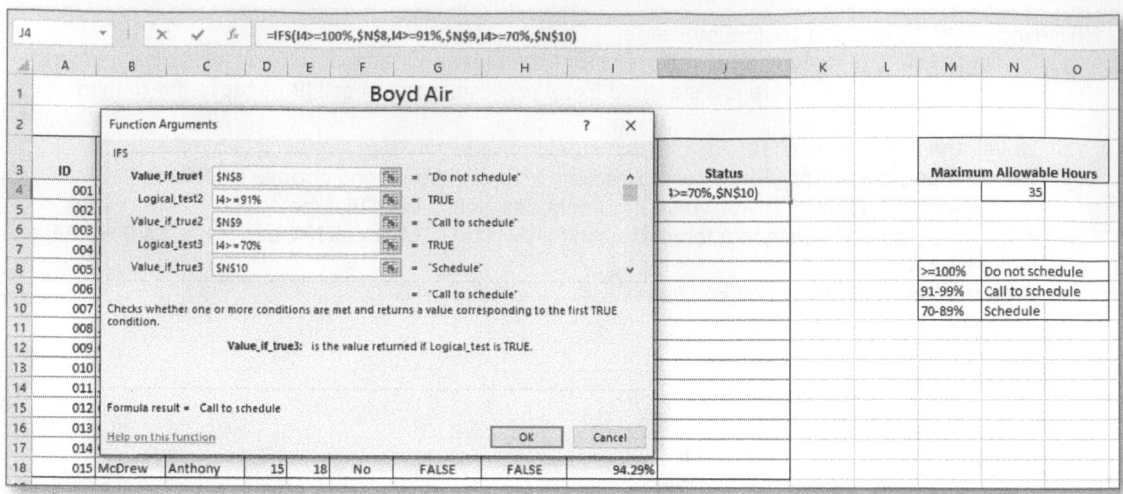

6-78 *IFS function*

c. For the *Text* argument, click the **Name** box arrow, and choose **More Functions**.
d. Choose **Text** as the category, select **CONCAT**, and click **OK**. The *Function Arguments* dialog box shows arguments for the *CONCAT* function.
e. Select cell **C4** for the *Text1* argument.
f. Click the **Text2** argument box and press **Spacebar**.
g. Click the **Text3** argument box and select cell **B4** (Figure 6-79).

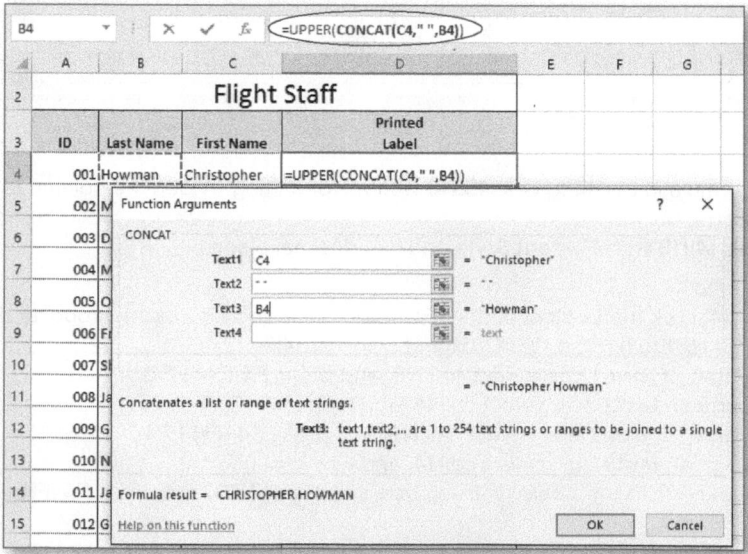

6-79 *CONCAT and UPPER functions*

h. Click **OK**.
i. Copy the formula in cell **D4** to cells **D5:D18** without formatting.
j. Press **Ctrl+Home**.

24. Determine the net present value of new equipment purchases.
 a. Click the **Equipment Eval** sheet tab and select cell **C12**.
 b. Click the **Financial** button [*Formulas* tab, *Function Library* group] and choose **NPV**.

c. Select cell **C5** for the *Rate* argument.

d. Click the **Value1** box and select cell **C8**, the expected savings in the first year.

e. Click the **Value2** box and select cell **C9**, expected savings in the second year.

f. For the **Value3** argument, select cell **C10**. (Figure 6-80).

g. Click **OK**.

h. Double-click cell **C12**. Press **End** to position the insertion point at the end of the formula.

i. In the cell or in the *Formula* bar, type +, select cell **C6**, and press **Enter** (Figure 6-81). The cost is added to the formula results because it is incurred before savings start.

j. Select cell **C24** and build an *NPV* calculation for an investment at an 8% discount.

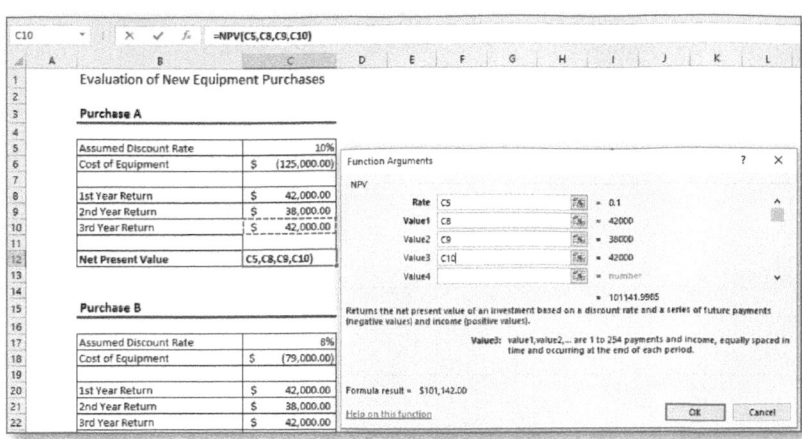

6-80 *NPV* function does not include initial cost

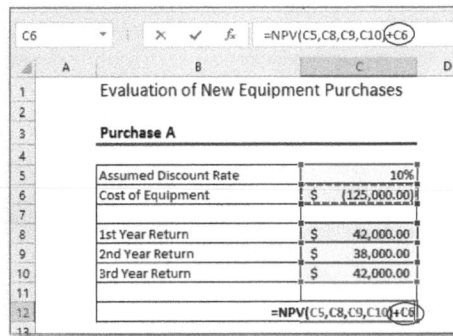

6-81 Add cost to results of *NPV* formula

25. Use *Find and Replace*.

a. Click the **Flight Hours** sheet tab and select cells **J4:J18**.

b. Click the **Find & Select** button [*Home* tab, *Editing* group] and choose **Replace**.

c. Click **Options > >** to expand the options.

d. Click the **Format** arrow and select **Clear Find Format** if it is available.

e. Click the **Find what** box, select previous data if any, and press **Delete**.

f. Type 91% to locate "91%" in the *IFS* formula.

g. Click the **Replace with** box and type 90%.

h. Verify that the **Within** choice is **Sheet**, the **Search** choice is **By Columns**, and the **Look In** choice is **Formulas**.

i. Click **Find All**. Fifteen cells are found (Figure 6-82).

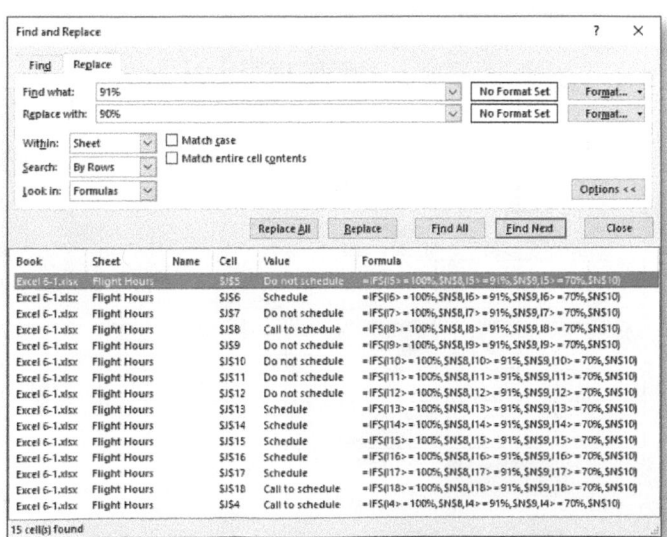

6-82 Arguments to be replaced

j. Click **Replace All** and click **OK**. Close the *Find and Replace* dialog box.

k. Edit cell **M9** to show 90 as the starting percentage.

26. Save and close the workbook (Figure 6-83).

Boyd Air
Scheduled vs. Actual Arrival Times

Date	Flight Number	Origin	Destination	Scheduled	Actual	Deviation
2/1/2016	BD 2345	MSP	MDW	9:30 AM	9:26 AM	-4
2/4/2016	BD 990	MSO	FAR	2:00 PM	2:15 PM	15
2/7/2016	BD 1234	MDW	GRB	11:00 AM	11:02 AM	2
2/10/2016	BD 1345	MSP	HOU	7:30 PM	7:56 PM	26
2/13/2016	BD 6578	FAR	STL	9:30 AM	9:14 AM	-16
2/23/2016	BD 234	MDW	MSP	9:30 PM	9:20 PM	-10
2/25/2016	BD 981	FAR	MSP	10:30 AM	10:15 AM	-15
2/28/2016	BD 123	GRB	MDW	9:00 PM	9:24 PM	24
3/5/2016	BD 134	HOU	MSP	12:45 PM	1:15 PM	30
3/9/2016	BD 98	FAR	MDW	11:45 AM	11:52 AM	7
4/1/2016	BD 2345	MSP	MDW	9:30 AM	9:32 AM	2
4/4/2016	BD 990	MSP	FAR	2:00 PM	2:14 PM	14
5/7/2016	BD 1234	MDW	GRB	11:00 AM	10:48 AM	-12
5/16/2016	BD 1345	MSP	HOU	7:30 PM	7:41 PM	11
5/19/2016	BD 6578	FAR	STL	9:30 AM	9:27 AM	-3
6/23/2016	BD 234	MDW	MSP	3:30 PM	3:30 PM	0
6/25/2016	BD 981	FAR	MSP	10:30 AM	10:30 AM	0
6/28/2016	BD 123	GRB	MDW	3:00 PM	2:55 PM	-5
7/6/2016	BD 134	HOU	MSP	12:45 PM	12:42 PM	-3
7/9/2016	BD 98	FAR	MDW	11:45 AM	11:51 AM	6

MAD	10.35
Standard Deviation	13.3111345

Boyd Air
Flight Hours and Percentages

(table of flight hours and percentages — small, partially illegible)

Evaluation of New Equipment Purchases

Purchase A

Assumed Discount Rate	10%
Cost of Equipment	$ (125,000.00)
1st Year Return	$ 42,000.00
2nd Year Return	$ 38,000.00
3rd Year Return	$ 42,000.00
Net Present Value	($23,858.00)

Purchase B

Assumed Discount Rate	8%
Cost of Equipment	$ (79,000.00)
1st Year Return	$ 42,000.00
2nd Year Return	$ 38,000.00
3rd Year Return	$ 42,000.00
Net Present Value	$25,808.72

Boyd Air
Flight Staff

ID	Last Name	First Name	Printed Label
001	Howman	Christopher	CHRISTOPHER HOWMAN
002	Melson	Chad	CHAD MELSON
003	Daniels	Case	CASE DANIELS
004	Mochen	Wyatte	WYATTE MOCHEN
005	Omang	David	DAVID OMANG
006	Frankel	BJ	BJ FRANKEL
007	Sheldon	Kendra	KENDRA SHELDON
008	Jamison	Ella	ELLA JAMISON
009	Green	Alec	ALEC GREEN
010	Nelson	Natasha	NATASHA NELSON
011	Jalowiec	Nikolai	NIKOLAI JALOWIEC
012	Gomez	Tabitha	TABITHA GOMEZ
013	Gaston	Josie	JOSIE GASTON
014	Chajec	Tomas	TOMAS CHAJEC
015	McDrew	Anthony	ANTHONY MCDREW

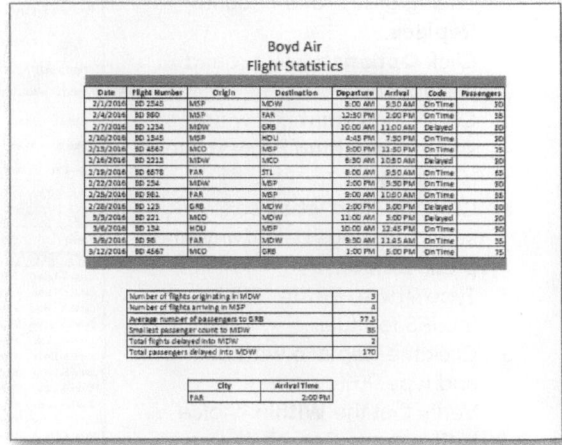

Boyd Air
Flight Statistics

Date	Flight Number	Origin	Destination	Departure	Arrival	Code	Passengers
2/1/2016	BD 2345	MSP	MDW	8:00 AM	9:30 AM	On Time	30
2/4/2016	BD 990	MSP	FAR	12:30 PM	2:00 PM	On Time	18
2/7/2016	BD 1234	MDW	GRB	10:00 AM	11:00 AM	Delayed	30
2/10/2016	BD 1345	MSP	HOU	4:45 PM	7:30 PM	On Time	30
2/13/2016	BD 4560	MCO	MSP	9:00 PM	11:30 PM	On Time	75
2/16/2016	BD 2313	MDW	MCO	8:30 AM	10:30 AM	Delayed	30
2/19/2016	BD 6578	FAR	STL	8:00 AM	9:30 AM	On Time	55
2/22/2016	BD 234	MDW	MSP	2:00 PM	3:30 PM	On Time	30
2/25/2016	BD 981	FAR	MSP	9:00 AM	10:00 AM	On Time	18
2/28/2016	BD 123	GRB	MDW	2:00 PM	3:00 PM	Delayed	30
3/3/2016	BD 221	MCO	MDW	11:00 AM	3:00 PM	Delayed	30
3/6/2016	BD 134	HOU	MSP	10:00 AM	12:45 PM	On Time	30
3/9/2016	BD 98	FAR	MDW	9:30 AM	11:45 AM	On Time	55
3/12/2016	BD 4567	MCO	GRB	1:00 PM	5:00 PM	On Time	75

Number of flights originating in MDW	3
Number of flights arriving in MSP	4
Average number of passengers to GRB	37.5
Smallest passenger count to MDW	85
Total flights delayed into MDW	2
Total passengers delayed into MDW	170

City	Arrival Time
FAR	2:00 PM

6-83 Completed worksheets for Excel 6-1

Guided Project 6-2

In a workbook for Eller Software Services, you calculate deviation statistics for sales by product and city. You verify phone numbers using a *Text* function, develop a worksheet with projected return on investment, and determine representative assignments.
[Student Learning Outcomes 6.1, 6.2, 6.3, 6.4, 6.5, 6.6, 6.7, 6.8]

File Needed: ***EllerSoftware-06.xlsx*** *(Student data files are available in the* Library *of your SIMnet account)*
Completed Project File Name: *[your initials] Excel 6-2.xlsx*

Skills Covered in this Project

- Calculate the mean absolute deviation (MAD).
- Use the *STDEV.S* function.
- Nest *MATCH* and *INDEX* functions.
- Build *SUMIFS* formulas.
- Use functions from the *Database* category.

- Use *EXACT* to match data.
- Calculate the net present value of an expenditure.
- Create a nested *IF* and *AND* formula.
- Use *Find and Replace* with the *Watch Window*.
- Calculate the number of days between two dates.

1. Open the ***EllerSoftware-06*** workbook from your student data files and save it as [your initials] Excel 6-2.

2. Calculate the mean absolute deviation (MAD) for the difference between estimated and actual sales.
 a. Click the **Revenue** sheet and select cell **I5**.
 b. Type =ab and press **Tab**.
 c. Select cell **H5** for the *number* argument, type – to subtract, select cell **G5**, and press **Enter**.
 d. Copy the formula to cells **I6:I17** without formatting to preserve the fill color.
 e. Select cell **D20** and use the *AVERAGE* function with the cell range **I5:I17**.
 f. Format the results as **Number** from the *Number Format* drop-down list [*Home* tab, *Number* group].

3. Calculate the standard deviation for actual sales.
 a. Select cell **D21**.
 b. Type =std and double-click **STDEV.S** in the list.
 c. Select cells **G5:G17** and press **Enter**. The closing parenthesis is supplied, and the result is 12871.23785.

4. Create a nested function using *INDEX* and *MATCH* to display a phone number.
 a. Select cell **D24** and type Jeremie Midboe.
 b. Select cell **D25**. Click the **Lookup & Reference** button [*Formulas* tab, *Function Library* group] and choose **INDEX**.
 c. Select the first argument list **array, row_num, column_num** and click **OK**.
 d. For the *Array* argument, press **F3** (**FN+F3**) and select **Clients**.
 e. Click the **Row_num** box, click the **Name** box arrow, and choose **More Functions**.
 f. Choose **Lookup & Reference** as the category, select **MATCH**, and press **Enter**. The *Function Arguments* dialog box shows *MATCH* arguments.
 g. Select cell **D24** for the *Lookup_value* argument.
 h. Click the **Lookup_array** box and select cells **A5:A17**. The *MATCH* function finds the value that matches cell D24 in column A.
 i. Click the **Match_type** box and type 0.
 j. Click the name **INDEX** in the *Formula* bar. If the *Select Arguments* dialog box opens, click **OK**.
 k. Click the **Column_num** box, click the **Name** box arrow, and choose **MATCH**.
 l. Type phone number in the *Lookup_value* box.
 m. Click the **Lookup_array** box and select cells **A4:I4**. This *MATCH* function will locate the Phone Number column (Figure 6-84).

6-84 Nested *MATCH* and *INDEX* functions

n. Click the **Match_type** box and type 0. The formula is
 =INDEX(Clients,MATCH(D24,A5:A17,0), MATCH("phone number",A4:I4,0)).
o. Click **OK**.
p. Select cell **D24**, type Anne Nickel, and press **Enter**. The phone number changes.

5. Use *SUMIFS* to total revenue by category and city.
 a. Select cell **G20**.
 b. Click the **Math & Trig** button
 [*Formulas* tab, *Function Library*
 group] and choose **SUMIFS**.
 c. Select cells **G5:G17 f**or the
 Sum_range argument and press
 F4 (FN+F4) to make it absolute.
 d. Click the **Criteria_range1** box,
 select cells **D5:D17**, the City field,
 and press **F4 (FN+F4)**.
 e. Click the **Criteria1** box and type
 eag*.
 f. Click the **Criteria_range2** box,
 select cells **F5:F17**, and press
 F4 (FN+F4).
 g. Click the **Criteria2** box, type pos*
 (Figure 6-85).
 h. Click **OK**.

6-85 *SUMIFS* with its arguments

 i. Copy the *SUMIFS* function in cell **G20** to cell **G21**. Edit the formula criteria to show the ERP total
 for Minneapolis.
 j. Format cells **G20:G21** as **Currency** with no decimal places.

6. Use *DAVERAGE* to calculate average sales in Bemidji.
 a. Select cells **A4:I17** and name the range SalesData. The range includes column labels.
 b. Select cell **G24** and note the label in cell **F24**.
 c. Click the **Criteria** sheet tab.
 d. Click cell **D2** and type be*.
 e. Click the **Revenue** sheet tab.

E6-411

f. In cell **G24**, click the **Insert Function** button in the *Formula* bar.

g. Choose **Database** in the *Or select a category* list.

h. Select **DAVERAGE** and click **OK**.

i. Press **F3** (**FN+F3**) in the *Database* box, choose **SalesData**, and click **OK**.

j. Click the **Field** box and type actual sales.

k. Click the **Criteria** argument box and select cells **D1:D2** on the **Criteria** sheet (Figure 6-86).

l. Click **OK**.

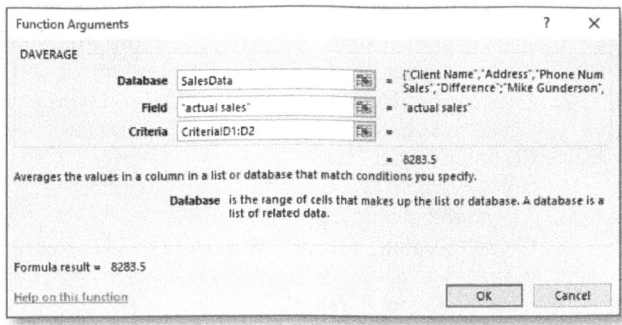

6-86 *DAVERAGE* and its arguments

7. Copy cells **A1:I2** on the **Criteria** sheet to cells **A4:I5** and again to cells **A7:I8**. Delete the contents of cells **D5** and **D7**.

8. Select cell **D5** and type min*. Select cell **D7** and type de*.

9. Click the **Revenue** sheet tab. Select cell **G25** and use *DMAX* to display the top sale in Minneapolis.

10. Select cell **G26** and use *DMIN*.

11. Format cells **G24:G26** as **Currency** with no decimal places and press **Ctrl+Home**.

12. Create a *Text* function with *EXACT*.
 a. Click the **Phone Numbers** sheet tab and select cell **D5**. The phone numbers on this sheet will be compared to those on the **Revenue** sheet.
 b. Click the **Text** button [*Formulas* tab, *Function Library* group] and choose **EXACT**.
 c. Select cell **C5** for the *Text1* argument.
 d. Click the **Text2** argument, click the **Revenue** sheet tab, and select cell **C5**.
 e. Click **OK**. If the phone number is an exact match, the result is TRUE.
 f. Copy the formula in cell **D5** to cells **D6:D17**.
 g. Apply a *Highlight Cells* rule to cells **D5:D17** to show FALSE in **Light Red Fill with Dark Red Text**.
 h. Press **Ctrl+Home**.

13. Determine the net present value (*NPV*) for client purchases.
 a. Click the **Product ROR** sheet tab and select cell **F6**.
 b. Click the **Financial** button [*Formulas* tab, *Function Library* group] and choose **NPV**.
 c. Select cell **J5** for the *Rate* argument and press **F4 (FN+F4)**.
 d. Click the **Value1** box and select cells **B6:E6**, costs and projected savings per year. The cost is paid in increments during the first year and is included as a *Value* argument.
 e. Click **OK**. The projected return is $3,729.56.
 f. Copy the formula in cell **F6** to cells **F7:F9**.
 g. Press **Ctrl+Home**.

14. Create a nested *IF* function with *AND* functions as the logical tests.
 a. Click the **Rep Assignments** sheet tab and select cell **F6**.
 b. Click the **Logical** button [*Formulas* tab, *Function Library* group] and choose **IF**.
 c. In the *Logical_test* box, click the **Name** box arrow, and choose **AND** from the list, or choose **More Functions** to find and select **AND**.
 d. Click the **Logical1** argument box, select cell **B6** and type ="yes". Quotations marks are required, but the argument is not case-sensitive.
 e. Click the **Logical2** box, select cell **D6**, and type ="yes". The *AND* formula determines if both cells B6 and D6 show "Yes."
 f. In the *Formula* bar, click the word **IF** to return to the *IF Function Arguments* dialog box (Figure 6-87).
 g. Click the **Value_if_true** box, select cell **I5**, and press **F4 (FN+F4)**. If cells B6 and D6 show "Yes," the rep's name in cell I5 displays.

h. Click the **Value_if_false** box. If the *Logical_test* is false, a second *IF* statement runs.

i. Click **IF** in the *Name* box or choose **More Functions** to find and select **IF**.

j. For the *Logical_test* for the second *IF* statement, click the **Name** box arrow and choose **AND**.

k. Click the **Logical1** box, select cell **C6**, and type ="yes".

l. Click the **Logical2** box, click cell **D6**, and type ="yes". This *AND* formula determines if both cells C6 and D6 show "Yes."

m. In the *Formula* bar, click the second occurrence of **IF** to return to the nested *IF Function Arguments* dialog box (Figure 6-88).

n. Click the **Value_if_true** box, select cell **I6**, and press **F4 (FN+F4)**. If cells C6 and D6 show "Yes," the rep's name in cell I6 displays.

o. Click the **Value_if_false** box, select cell **I7**, and press **F4 (FN+F4)**. If neither *IF* logical test is true, the rep's name in cell I7 displays.

p. Click **OK** and copy the formula in cell **F6** to cells **F7:F18** without formatting.

15. Use *Find and Replace*.

a. Click the **Projects** sheet and select cells **B5:B17**.

b. Click the **Watch Window** button [*Formulas* tab, *Formula Auditing* group].

c. Click **Add Watch** and click **Add**.

d. Click the **Revenue** sheet tab.

e. Click the **Find & Select** button [*Home* tab, *Editing* group] and choose **Replace**.

f. Click **Options>>** to expand the options. If necessary, click the **Format** arrow and clear previous find format settings.

g. Delete previous search strings in the *Find what* box.

h. Click the **Find what** box and type acc*.

i. Click the **Replace with** box and type AR/AP for accounts receivable and accounts payable.

j. Verify that the **Within** choice is **Workbook**.

k. Click **Find All**. Nine occurrences display in the dialog box (Figure 6-89).

l. Click **Replace All**. Close the *Find and Replace* dialog box.

m. Select the first reference in the *Watch Window*, press **Shift**, and click the last reference.

n. Click **Delete Watch** and close the *Watch Window*.

o. Press **Ctrl+Home**.

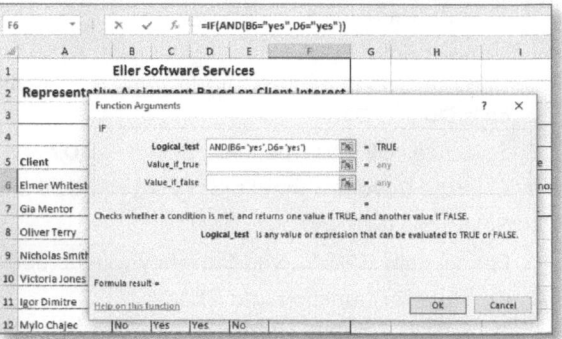

6-87 First *IF* function and its logical_test argument

6-88 The second *IF* function in the nested formula

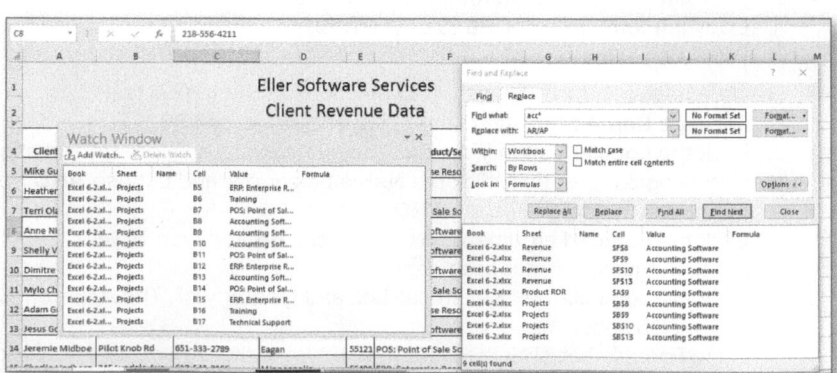

6-89 *Find and Replace* dialog box and *Watch Window*

16. Calculate project duration in days.
 a. Click the **Projects** sheet tab and select cell **E5**.
 b. Type = and click cell **D5**, the ending date.
 c. Type – to subtract and click cell **C5**, the starting date.
 d. Press **Enter**. The result is formatted as a date.
 e. Copy the formula in cell **E5** to cells **E6:E17** without formatting to preserve the fill color.
 f. Format cells **E5:E17** with the **General** format [*Number Format* drop-down list, *Home* tab].
 g. Press **Ctrl+Home**.

17. Save and close the workbook (Figure 6-90).

Eller Software Services
Representative Assignment Based on Client Interest

	Product Group						Assignment Plan	
Client	ERP	HR	POS	AR/AP	Assigned Rep		ERP and POS	Adam White
Elmer Whitestead	Yes	No	Yes	No	Adam White		HR and POS	Barbara Munoz
Gia Mentor	No	No	Yes	No	Josh Haines		Others	Josh Haines
Oliver Terry	Yes	Yes	No	Yes	Josh Haines			
Nicholas Smith	Yes	Yes	Yes	No	Adam White			
Victoria Jones	No	Yes	Yes	No	Barbara Munoz			
Igor Dimitre	Yes	Yes	Yes	Yes	Adam White			
Mylo Chajec	No	Yes	Yes	No	Barbara Munoz			
Lester Simmons	No	Yes	No	Yes	Josh Haines			
Kelly MacNeil	Yes	No	Yes	No	Adam White			
Jerome Decker	No	No	Yes	No	Josh Haines			
Charlie Strom	No	Yes	No	No	Josh Haines			
Clinton Olmstead	Yes	No	Yes	Yes	Adam White			
Michael Conover	Yes	Ys	Yes	No	Adam White			

Eller Software Services
Updated Phone List

Client Name	Address	Phone Number	OK?
Mike Gunderson	304 Irvine Ave	218-278-9021	TRUE
Heather Guyan	124 East Street	218-333-2312	FALSE
Terri Olander	459 10th Avenue	218-667-8977	TRUE
Anne Nickel	1822 Highway 2	218-556-4211	TRUE
Shelly Vicko	402 2nd Ave SE	218-342-2456	TRUE
Dimitre Ivanov	1344 Highway 3	218-556-3009	TRUE
Mylo Chajec	544 West Main	651-345-9000	FALSE
Adam Greenfield	123 Oak Street	612-543-0090	TRUE
Jesus Gomez	500 5th Ave	218-342-8765	TRUE
Jeremie Midboe	Pilot Knob Rd	651-333-2789	TRUE
Charlie Lindberg	345 Lyndale Ave	612-543-3290	FALSE
Hilary Marschke	245 West 3rd Ave	320-355-5443	TRUE
Craig Brand	554 2nd Street	320-751-4433	TRUE

Eller Software Services
Projected Return on Client Investment after 3 Years

		Savings/Increase in Productivity			
Product/Service	Typical Sale	Year 1	Year 2	Year 3	Return
ERP: Enterprise Resource Planning	-$20,000	$8,000	$9,000	$10,000	$3,729.56
Training	-$2,000	$1,500	$2,000	$2,000	$2,711.63
POS: Point of Sale Software	-$4,500	$2,500	$3,500	$3,500	$3,690.70
AR/AP	-$5,000	$2,000	$3,000	$4,500	$3,146.29

Eller Software Services
Project Duration

Project ID	Product/Service	Start	End	Time
ESS014	ERP: Enterprise Resource Planning	5/1/16	6/2/16	32
ESS016	Training	6/3/16	8/5/16	63
ESS018	POS: Point of Sale Software	7/7/16	7/10/16	3
ESS020	AR/AP	9/7/16	11/7/16	61
ESS022	AR/AP	10/2/16	12/21/16	80
ESS024	AR/AP	2/3/17	5/8/17	94
ESS026	POS: Point of Sale Software	4/2/17	4/5/17	3
ESS028	ERP: Enterprise Resource Planning	5/1/17	8/13/17	104
ESS030	AR/AP	5/5/17	8/12/17	99
ESS032	POS: Point of Sale Software	6/6/17	6/10/17	4
ESS034	ERP: Enterprise Resource Planning	7/1/17	8/30/17	60
ESS036	Training	8/5/17	8/15/17	10
ESS038	Technical Support	10/1/17	10/10/17	9

Eller Software Services
Client Revenue Data

Client Name	Address	Phone Number	City	Zip	Product/Service	Actual Sales	Estimated Sales	Difference
Mike Gunderson	304 Irvine Ave	218-278-9021	Bemidji	56601	ERP: Enterprise Resource Planning	$15,000	$10,000	$5,000
Heather Guyan	124 East Street	218-333-2312	Bemidji	56601	Training	$1,569	$1,175	$392
Terri Olander	459 10th Avenue	218-667-8977	Brainerd	56401	POS: Point of Sale Software	$6,329	$6,156	$1,631
Anne Nickel	1822 Highway 2	218-556-4211	Cass Lake	56630	AR/AP	$5,230	$5,480	$780
Shelly Vicko	402 2nd Ave SE	218-342-2456	Deer River	56636	AR/AP	$4,500	$3,375	$1,125
Dimitre Ivanov	1344 Highway 3	218-556-3009	Cass Lake	56630	AR/AP	$750	$925	$175
Mylo Chajec	544 West Main	651-345-9071	Eagan	55121	POS: Point of Sale Software	$3,500	$2,800	$700
Adam Greenfield	123 Oak Street	612-543-0090	Minneapolis	55402	ERP: Enterprise Resource Planning	$31,000	$21,000	$10,000
Jesus Gomez	500 5th Ave	218-342-8765	Deer River	56636	AR/AP	$5,000	$3,500	$1,000
Jeremie Midboe	Pilot Knob Rd	651-333-2789	Eagan	55121	POS: Point of Sale Software	$7,500	$5,975	$1,675
Charlie Lindberg	345 Lyndale Ave	612-543-2156	Minneapolis	55401	ERP: Enterprise Resource Planning	$42,000	$48,900	$6,900
Hilary Marschke	245 West 3rd Ave	320-355-5443	Saint Cloud	56301	Training	$750	$992	$189
Craig Brand	554 2nd Street	320-751-4433	Saint Cloud	56301	Technical Support	$1,096	$1,320	$264

| MAX | 23401.75 |
| Standard Deviation | 11971.19785 |

| Find Phone for: | Anne Nickel |
| | 218-556-4211 |

| POS Sales, Eagan | $11,000 |
| ERP, Minneapolis | $74,000 |

Average Sale, Bemidji	$8,284
Highest Sale, Minneapolis	$42,000
Lowest Sale, Deer River	$4,500

6-90 Completed worksheets for Excel 6-2

Guided Project 6-3

The Wear-Ever Shoes company maintains inventory data and customer satisfaction survey results in your workbook. You use *Lookup & Reference*, *Database*, and *Logical* functions to complete the data. You also use a *Financial* function to calculate depreciation and a *Text* function to enter email addresses. [Student Learning Outcomes 6.1, 6.2, 6.3, 6.5, 6.6, 6.7]

File Needed: ***WearEverShoes-06.xlsx*** *(Student data files are available in the* Library *of your SIMnet account)* Completed Project File Name: ***[your initials] Excel 6-3.xlsx***

Skills Covered in this Project

- Nest the *INDEX* and *MATCH* functions.
- Use *SUMIFS* from the *Math & Trig* category.

- Use *DAVERAGE*.
- Create an *IFS* formula.
- Use a *Text* function to concatenate text strings.
- Calculate depreciation with the *DB* function.

1. Open the ***WearEverShoes-06*** workbook from your student data files and save it as [your initials] Excel 6-3.
2. Click the **Inventory** sheet tab.
3. Select cells **A3:I39**, click the **Name** box, type Inventory as the range name, and press **Enter**.
4. Select cell **L5** and type WE006.
5. Create a nested function with *INDEX* and *MATCH* to display inventory for a product.
 a. Select cell **L6**.
 b. Click the **Lookup & Reference** button [*Formulas* tab, *Function Library* group] and choose **INDEX**. Select the first argument list **array, row_num, column_num** and click **OK**.
 c. For the *Array* argument, press **F3** (**FN+F3**) and select **Inventory**.
 d. Click the **Row_num** box and click the **Name** box arrow. Choose **MATCH** in the list or choose **More Functions** to find and select **MATCH**. The *INDEX* function uses this *MATCH* statement to find the row.
 e. Click cell **L5** for the *Lookup_value* argument.
 f. Click the **Lookup_array** box and select cells **A3:A39**. This *MATCH* function finds the row that matches cell L5 in column A.
 g. Click the **Match_type** argument and type 0.
 h. Click **INDEX** in the *Formula* bar.
 i. Click the **Column_num** argument, click the **Name** box arrow, and choose **MATCH** (Figure 6-91).

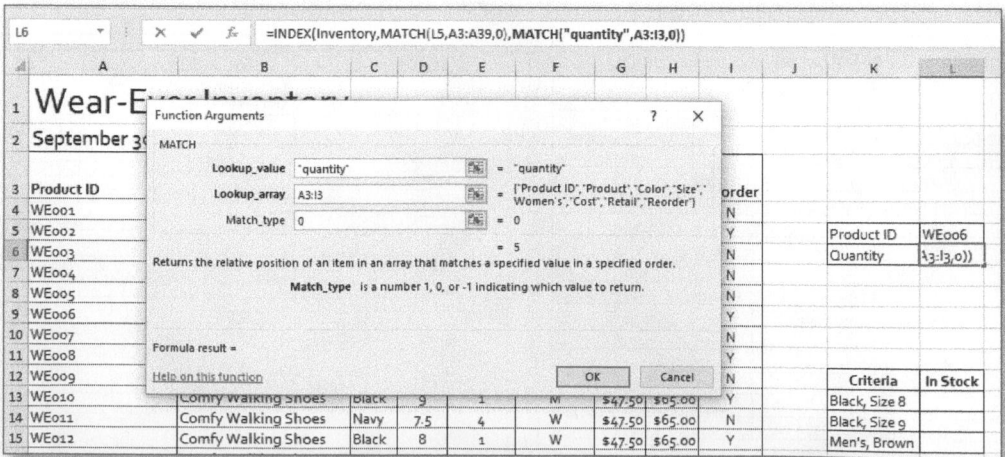

6-91 *MATCH* is nested twice

 j. Type quantity in the *Lookup_value* box.

 k. Click the **Lookup_array** box and select cells **A3:I3**. This *MATCH* function finds the cell in the "Quantity" column after the row is located by the first *MATCH* function.

 l. Click the **Match_type** box and type 0. The formula is **=INDEX(Inventory,MATCH(L5,A3:A39,0),MATCH("quantity",A3:I3,0))**.

 m. Click **OK**. The result is 2.

 n. Click cell **L5**, type WE010, and press **Enter**. The quantity is updated.

6. Use *SUMIFS* to calculate total pairs in stock by specific criteria.

 a. Select cell **L13**.

 b. Click the **Math & Trig** button [*Formulas* tab, *Function Library* group] and choose **SUMIFS**.

 c. Select cells **E4:E39** for the *Sum_range* argument and press **F4** (**FN+F4**).

 d. Click the **Criteria_range1** box, select cells **C4:C39**, the Color field, and press **F4** (**FN+F4**).

 e. Click the **Criteria1** box and type bla*.

 f. Click the **Criteria_range2** box, select cells **D4:D39**, and press **F4** (**FN+F4**).

 g. Click the **Criteria2** box and type 8. This criteria specifies the number of black pairs, size 8 (Figure 6-92).

6-92 *SUMIFS to calculate number by color and size*

 h. Click **OK**. The result is 7.

 i. Select cell **L14** and use *SUMIFS* to sum black, size 9 shoes in stock.

 j. Select cell **L15** and use SUMIFS to sum men's brown shoes in stock.

7. Click the **Satisfaction Survey** worksheet tab and review the data.

8. Select cells **A4:H40** and name the range as Survey.

9. Use *DAVERAGE* to summarize customer survey data.

 a. Click the **Average Ratings** worksheet tab and select cell **C5** to calculate an average comfort rating for the Rugged Hiking Boots.

 b. Click the **Criteria** sheet tab.

 c. Select cell **B2** and type rug*.

 d. Click the **Average Ratings** sheet tab and verify that cell **C5** is selected.

 e. Click the **Insert Function** button [*Formulas* tab, *Function Library* group].

 f. Choose **Database** in the *Or select a category* list.

 g. Select **DAVERAGE** and click **OK**.

 h. Press **F3** (**FN+F3**), choose **Survey** for the *Database* argument, and click **OK**.

 i. Click the **Field** box and type comfort.

j. Click the **Criteria** box, select the **Criteria** sheet tab, select cells **B1:B2**, and press **F4** (**FN+F4**) (Figure 6-93).

k. Click **OK**. The result is 7.75.

l. Copy the formula in cell **C5** to cells **D5:F5**.

m. Select cell **D5** and edit the *Field* argument in the formula to show "fit."

n. Repeat step m for cells **E5:F5** to use the correct *Field* argument.

10. Use *DAVERAGE* to summarize survey data.

a. Select the **Criteria** sheet tab.

b. Select cell **B5** and type com* to specify the Comfy Walking Shoes.

c. Click the **Average Ratings** sheet tab and select cell **C6**.

d. Click the **Recently Used** button [*Formulas* tab, *Function Library* group] and select **DAVERAGE**.

e. Press **F3** (**FN+F3**) and choose **Survey** for the *Database* argument.

f. Click the **Field** argument box and type comfort.

g. Click the **Criteria** box, select cells **B4:B5** on the **Criteria** sheet, and press **F4** (**FN+F4**).

h. Click **OK**. The result is 7.5.

i. Copy the formula in cell **C6** to cells **D6:F6**.

j. Edit the formulas in cells **D6:F6** to use the correct *Field* argument.

11. Build *DAVERAGE* functions for the remaining shoe styles on the **Average Ratings** sheet.

12. Select cells **G5:G9** on the **Average Ratings** sheet, click the **AutoSum** arrow [*Home* tab, *Editing* group], and choose **Average**.

13. Create an *IFS* function.

a. Select cell **H5**, click the **Logical** button [*Formulas* tab, *Function Library* group], and choose **IFS**.

b. Click the **Logical_test1** argument, select cell **G5**, and type >=9.

c. Click the **Value_if_true1** box, click cell **J5**, and press **F4** (**FN+F4**) (Figure 6-94).

6-93 *DAVERAGE* for comfort rating

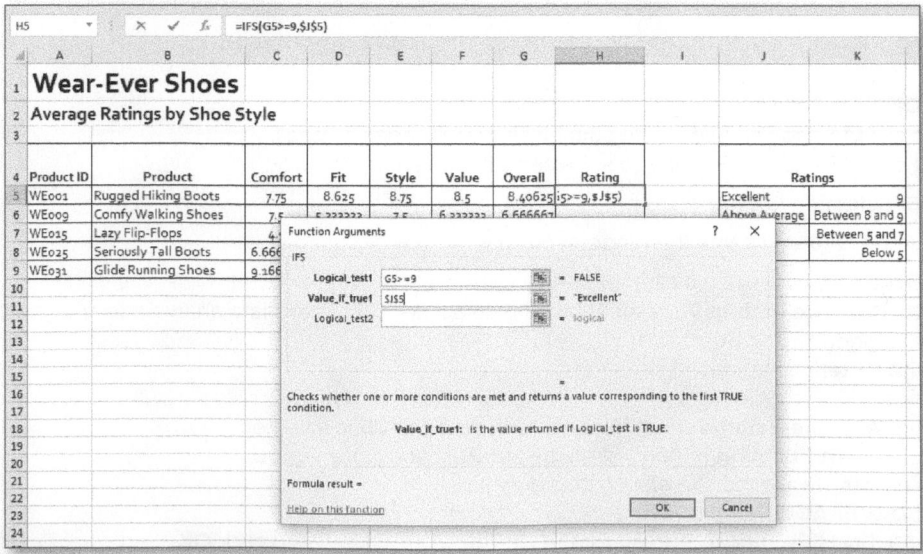

6-94 First logical test and result for *IFS*

d. Click the **Logical_test2** box, click cell **G5**, and type >= 8.

e. Click the **Value_if_true2** box, click cell **J6**, and press **F4 (FN+F4)**.

f. Click the **Logical_test3** box, click cell **G5**, and type >= 5.

g. Click the down scroll arrow to reveal the *Value_if_true3* box, click cell **J7**, and press **F4 (FN+F4)**.

h. Click the down scroll arrow to reveal the *Logical_test4* box, click cell **G5**, and type <5.

i. Click the down scroll arrow to reveal the *Value_if_true4* box, click cell **J8**, and press **F4 (FN+F4)** (Figure 6-95). The complete formula is:

6-95 *IFS* function with four logical tests

=IFS(G5>=9,J5,G5>=8,J6,G5>=5,J7,G5<5,J8)

j. Click **OK** and copy the formula to cells **H6:H9**.

k. Make column **H 13.57 (100 pixels)** wide.

14. Calculate depreciation for an asset using a *Financial* function.

a. Click the **Depreciation** sheet tab and select cell **C11**. Depreciation is the decrease in the value of an asset as it ages. The **DB** function calculates the loss in value over a specified period of time at a fixed rate.

b. Click the **Financial** button [*Formulas* tab, *Function Library* group] and choose **DB**.

c. For the *Cost* argument, select cell **C6** and press **F4 (FN+F4)**.

d. Click the **Salvage** box, select cell **C7**, and press **F4 (FN+F4)**. This is the expected value of the equipment at the end of its life.

e. Click the **Life** box, select cell **C8**, and press **F4 (FN+F4)**. This is how long the equipment will be in use.

f. Click the **Period** box and select cell **B11**. The first formula calculates depreciation for the first year (Figure 6-96).

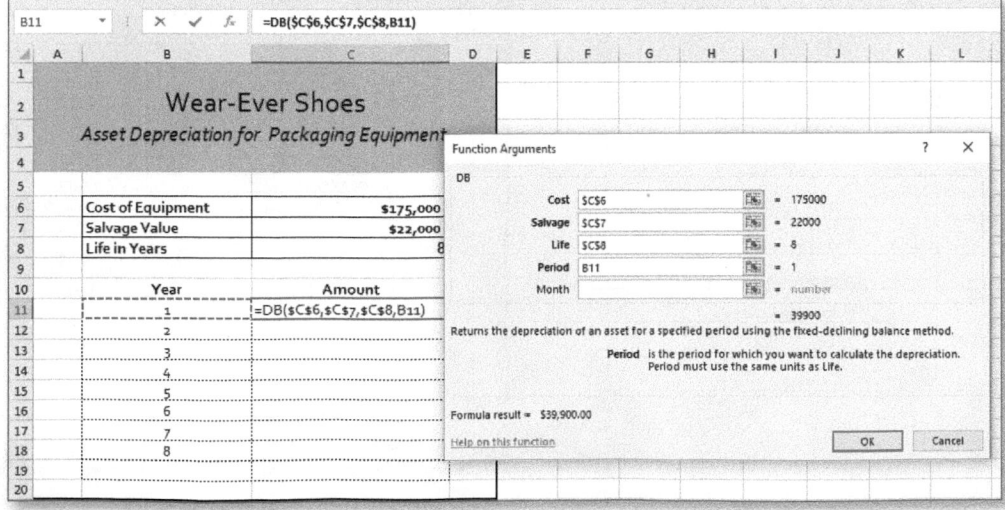

6-96 *DB* function to calculate asset depreciation

g. Click **OK**.

h. Copy the formula in cell **C11** to cells **C12:C18**. Each year's depreciation is less than the previous year's.

i. Select cell **C19** and use **AutoSum**. The total depreciation plus the salvage value is approximately equal to the original cost. It is not exact due to rounding.

15. Use *CONCAT* to build an email address.

a. Right-click any worksheet tab, choose **Unhide**, select **E-Mail**, and click **OK**.

b. Select cell **C5**, type =con, and press **Tab**. The *text1* argument is first.

c. Select cell **A5** and type a comma (,) to move to the *text2* argument.

d. Select cell **B5** and type a comma (,) to move to the *text3* argument.

e. Type "@weshoes.org" including the quotation marks (Figure 6-97).

f. Type the closing parenthesis) and press **Enter**.

g. Copy the formula in cell **C5** to cells **C6:C9**.

16. Save and close the workbook (Figure 6-98).

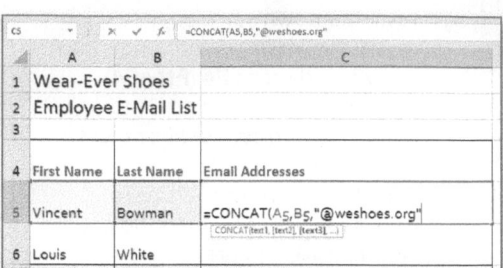

6-97 *CONCAT* references and typed data

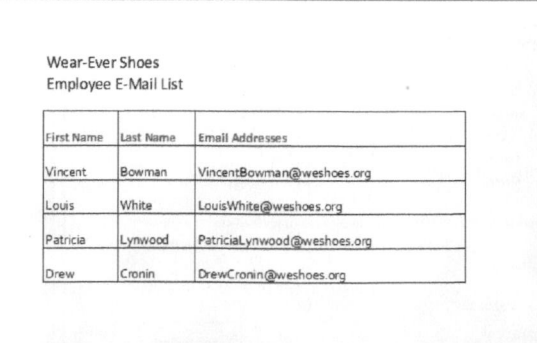

6-98 Completed worksheets for Excel 6-3

Independent Project 6-4

Blue Lake Sports is analyzing the net present value of installing solar panels. They also plan to calculate statistics related to inventory using *Database* and other functions.
[Student Learning Outcomes 6.1, 6.2, 6.4, 6.5, 6.6, 6.8]

File Needed: ***BlueLakeSports-06.xlsx*** *(Student data files are available in the* Library *of your SIMnet account)*
Completed Project File Name: *[your initials]* ***Excel 6-4.xlsx***

Skills Covered in this Project

- Calculate the net present value of an investment.
- Use the *REPLACE Text* function.
- Build a MAD calculation.

- Use *RANQ.EQ* to rank sales for a product.
- Use *DAVERAGE* to summarize data.
- Create an *IFS* function.
- Use *Find and Replace* to edit a function argument.

1. Open the ***BlueLakeSports-06*** workbook from your student data files and save it as [your initials] Excel 6-4.

2. Determine the net present value for solar panel installation.
 a. Select cell **C12** on the **Solar Install** sheet and start an *NPV* formula.
 b. Select cell **C10** for the *Rate* argument. This is the interest rate that could be earned if panels are not installed.
 c. Click the **Value1** box and select cell **C5**, the savings during the first year.
 d. For the *Value2* through *Value5* arguments, use cells **C6:C9** (Figure 6-99). (Press **Tab** or click the down scroll arrow to reveal each *Value* box.)

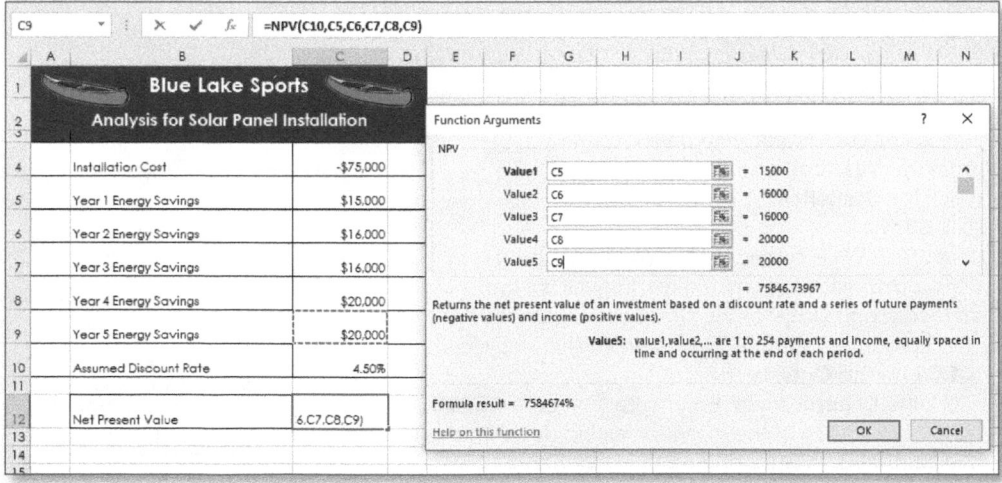

6-99 *Value* arguments for *NPV*

 e. Click **OK**.
 f. Edit the formula to add cell **C4** to the results. The initial cost is added to the results, because the cost is incurred before any savings. (Figure 6-100).

3. Use the *REPLACE* function to update product IDs.
 a. Click the **Inventory** sheet tab and select cell **B5**. New IDs in column B will display "BLS" as the beginning characters instead of "STL" as shown in column A.

b. Use *REPLACE* from the *Text* function category to replace the first three characters in cell **A5** with BLS in uppercase letters (Figure 6-101).

c. Copy the formula and preserve the borders.

4. Calculate the mean absolute deviation (MAD) for differences and the standard deviation for actual sales.

a. Click the **Unit Sales** sheet tab and select cell **G6**.

b. Calculate the absolute value of the difference between the estimated and actual amounts.

c. Click cell **G22** and calculate the mean absolute deviation (MAD).

d. Format the results in cell **G22** to display three decimal positions.

e. Click cell **G23** and use *STDEV.S* to calculate the standard deviation for the actual sales amounts.

5. Click cell **G25** and use *RANK.EQ* to determine the rank in actual sales for the titanium driver.

6. Use *DAVERAGE* to summarize survey data.

a. Click the **Product Evaluation** tab and name cells **A4:E19** as Data. Notice that the "Overall Rating" column is the fifth column in the range.

b. Click the **Criteria** sheet and type ap* in cell **C2** to reference data from the "Apparel" department.

c. Click the **Statistics** tab and select cell **B5**.

d. Use *DAVERAGE* to calculate an overall average for product satisfaction by department. Use the named range **Data** for the *Database* argument. For the *Field* argument, type 5. The *Criteria* argument is cells **C1:C2** on the **Criteria** sheet.

e. Click the **Criteria** sheet. Enter criteria in cells **C5**, **C8**, and **C11** for each of the three remaining departments on the **Statistics** sheet.

f. Click the **Statistics** sheet tab and select cell **B6**. Use DAVERAGE and your criteria ranges for cells **B6:B8**.

7. On the **Statistics** sheet, set columns **A:B** each to **16 (133 pixels)** wide.

8. Select cells **A1:B3** and open the *Format Cells* dialog box. Choose **Center Across Selection** on the *Alignment* tab.

9. Center align the labels in row **4** and apply **All Borders** to cells **A4:B8** (Figure 6-102).

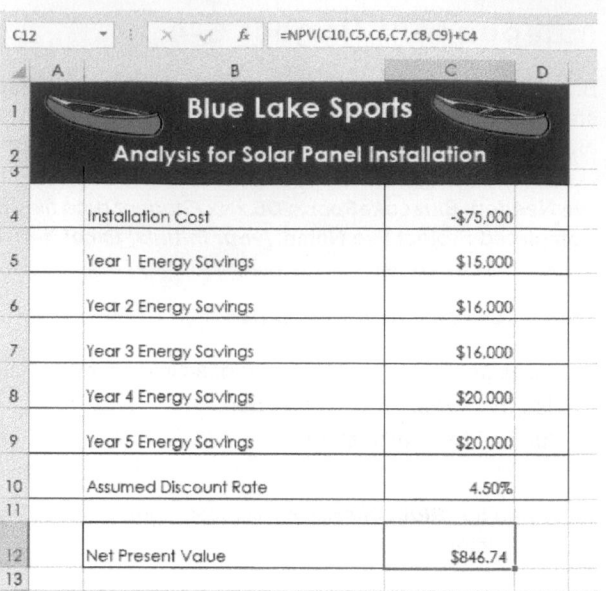

6-100 Positive *NPV* is good

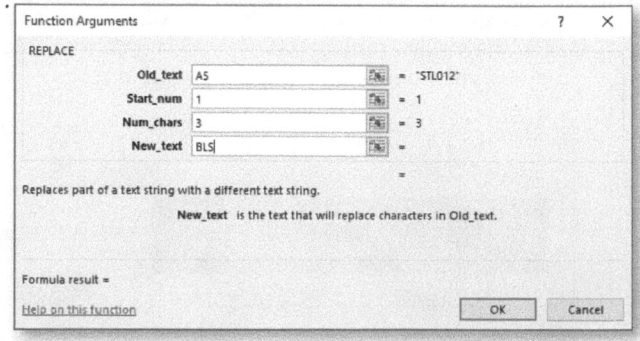

6-101 *REPLACE* function to change three characters

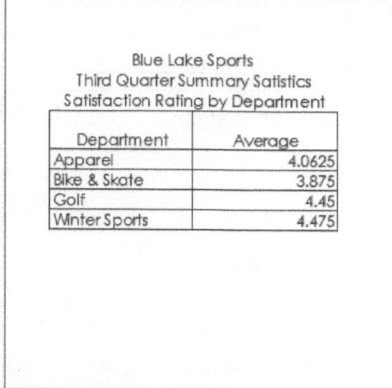

6-102 Completed *Statistics* worksheet

10. Create an *IFS* function.
 a. Click the **Product Evaluation** sheet tab and select cell **F5**. Evaluation criteria and ratings are displayed in rows 21:24.
 b. Start an *IFS* function in cell **F5**, select cell **E5** for the *Logical_test1* box, and type >=4.85.
 c. Click the **Value_if_true1** box, click cell **E21**, and press **F4** (**FN+F4**).
 d. Click the **Logical_test2** box, click cell **E5** and type >=4.35.
 e. Click the **Value_if_true2** box, click cell **E22**, and press **F4** (**FN+F4**).
 f. Click the **Logical_test3** box. Complete the statement and its corresponding *value_if_true* argument.
 g. Complete the fourth logical test and *value_if_true* argument (Figure 6-103) and click **OK**.
 h. Copy the formula in cell **F5** to cells **F6:F19**.

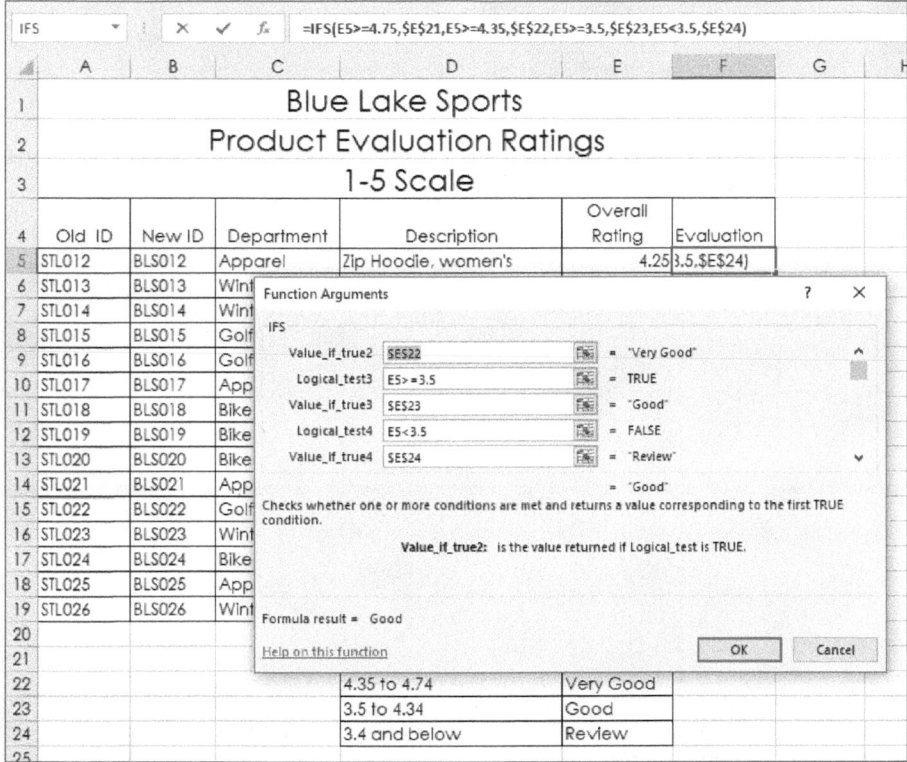

6-103 *IFS* function displays the evaluation

11. Apply **All Borders** to cells **A4:F19** and to cells **D21:E24**.

12. Use **Center Across Selection** for the labels in rows **1:3** and set the font size to **20 pt**.

13. *AutoFit* columns that do not show all the data.

14. Use *Find and Replace* to edit a function argument.
 a. Start a **Replace** command, expand the options, and clear any find format settings.
 b. Replace 4.85 with 4.75 in the worksheet.
 c. Replace 4.84 with 4.74 in the worksheet.
 d. Close the *Find and Replace* dialog box.

15. Save and close the workbook (Figure 6-104).

Blue Lake Sports
Product Evaluation Ratings
1-5 Scale

Old ID	New ID	Department	Description	Overall Rating	Evaluation
STL012	BLS012	Apparel	Zip Hoodie, women's	4.25	Good
STL013	BLS013	Winter Sports	Snowboard, men's	5	Excellent
STL014	BLS014	Winter Sports	Snowboard, women's	4.75	Excellent
STL015	BLS015	Golf	Full Set, Ladies	4.35	Very Good
STL016	BLS016	Golf	Titanium Driver, Men's	4	Good
STL017	BLS017	Apparel	Rain Jacket, girls	5	Excellent
STL018	BLS018	Bike & Skate	Biking helmet, women's	4.75	Excellent
STL019	BLS019	Bike & Skate	Biking helmet, child's	3.25	Review
STL020	BLS020	Bike & Skate	Bicycle Trailer, single	3.5	Good
STL021	BLS021	Apparel	Fleece Sweatshirt, men's	4	Good
STL022	BLS022	Golf	Rangefinder	5	Excellent
STL023	BLS023	Winter Sports	Snow Tube, 44"	4.15	Good
STL024	BLS024	Bike & Skate	Bike Rack, double	4	Good
STL025	BLS025	Apparel	Soft Shell Jacket, boy's	3	Review
STL026	BLS026	Winter Sports	Hockey Facemask, men's	4	Good

4.75 and above	Excellent
4.35 to 4.74	Very Good
3.5 to 4.34	Good
3.4 and below	Review

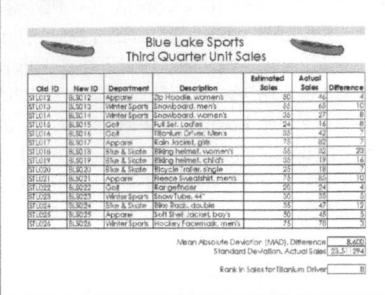

Blue Lake Sports
Third Quarter Unit Sales

Old ID	New ID	Department	Description	Estimated Sales	Actual Sales	Difference
STL012	BLS012	Apparel	Zip Hoodie, women's	50	46	4
STL013	BLS013	Winter Sports	Snowboard, men's	55	65	10
STL014	BLS014	Winter Sports	Snowboard, women's	35	27	8
STL015	BLS015	Golf	Full Set, Ladies	24	16	8
STL016	BLS016	Golf	Titanium Driver, Men's	55	42	7
STL017	BLS017	Apparel	Rain Jacket, girls	75	82	7
STL018	BLS018	Bike & Skate	Biking helmet, women's	55	32	23
STL019	BLS019	Bike & Skate	Biking helmet, child's	35	19	16
STL020	BLS020	Bike & Skate	Bicycle Trailer, single	20	18	2
STL021	BLS021	Apparel	Fleece Sweatshirt, men's	73	63	10
STL022	BLS022	Golf	Rangefinder	20	24	4
STL023	BLS023	Winter Sports	Snow Tube, 44"	50	55	5
STL024	BLS024	Bike & Skate	Bike Rack, double	55	47	8
STL025	BLS025	Apparel	Soft Shell Jacket, boy's	50	45	5
STL026	BLS026	Winter Sports	Hockey Facemask, men's	75	78	3

Mean Absolute Deviation (MAD), Difference 8.600
Standard Deviation, Actual Sales 23.3 294
Rank in Sales for Titanium Driver 8

Blue Lake Sports Warehouse Inventory

Old ID	New ID	Department	Description	Qty on Hand
STL012	BLS012	Apparel	Zip Hoodie, women's	24
STL013	BLS013	Winter Sports	Snowboard, men's	34
STL014	BLS014	Winter Sports	Snowboard, women's	22
STL015	BLS015	Golf	Full Set, Ladies	8
STL016	BLS016	Golf	Titanium Driver, Men's	12
STL017	BLS017	Apparel	Rain Jacket, girls	20
STL018	BLS018	Bike & Skate	Biking helmet, women's	25
STL019	BLS019	Bike & Skate	Biking helmet, child's	35
STL020	BLS020	Bike & Skate	Bicycle Trailer, single	15
STL021	BLS021	Apparel	Fleece Sweatshirt, men's	25
STL022	BLS022	Golf	Rangefinder	18
STL023	BLS023	Winter Sports	Snow Tube, 44"	13
STL024	BLS024	Bike & Skate	Bike Rack, double	9
STL025	BLS025	Apparel	Soft Shell Jacket, boy's	14
STL026	BLS026	Winter Sports	Hockey Facemask, men's	16

6-104 Completed worksheets for Excel 6-4

Independent Project 6-5

Classic Gardens and Landscapes counts responses to mail promotions to determine effectiveness. You use *SUMIFS* and a nested *IF* formula to complete the summary. You also calculate insurance statistics and convert birth dates from text to dates.
[Student Learning Outcomes 6.1, 6.2, 6.3, 6.4, 6.7]

File Needed: ***ClassicGardens-06.xlsx*** *(Student data files are available in the Library of your SIMnet account)*
Completed Project File Name: ***[your initials] Excel 6-5.xlsx***

Skills Covered in this Project

- **Nest** *MATCH* and *INDEX* functions.
- **Create** *DSUM* formulas.

- Build an *IFS* function.
- Build *SUMIFS* formulas.
- Use *DATEVALUE* to convert text to dates.

1. Open the ***ClassicGardens-06*** workbook from your student data files and save it as [your initials] Excel 6-5.
2. Create a nested *INDEX* and *MATCH* function to display the number of responses from a city.
 a. Click the **Mailings** sheet tab and select and name cells **A3:D28** as Responses.

b. Click the **Mailing Stats** sheet tab.

c. Click cell **B21** and type Carthage.

d. Click cell **C21**, start an **INDEX** function, and select the first argument list option.

e. Choose the **Responses** range for the *Array* argument.

f. Click the **Row_num** box and nest a **MATCH** function. Select cell **B21** for the *Lookup_value* and cells **A3:A28** on the **Mailings** sheet for the *Lookup_array*. Click the **Match_type** argument box and type 0.

g. Click **INDEX** in the *Formula* bar. Click the **Column_num** box and nest a second **MATCH** function to look up cell **D3** on the **Mailings** sheet in the lookup array **A3:D3**.

h. Click the **Match_type** box and type 0 (Figure 6-105).

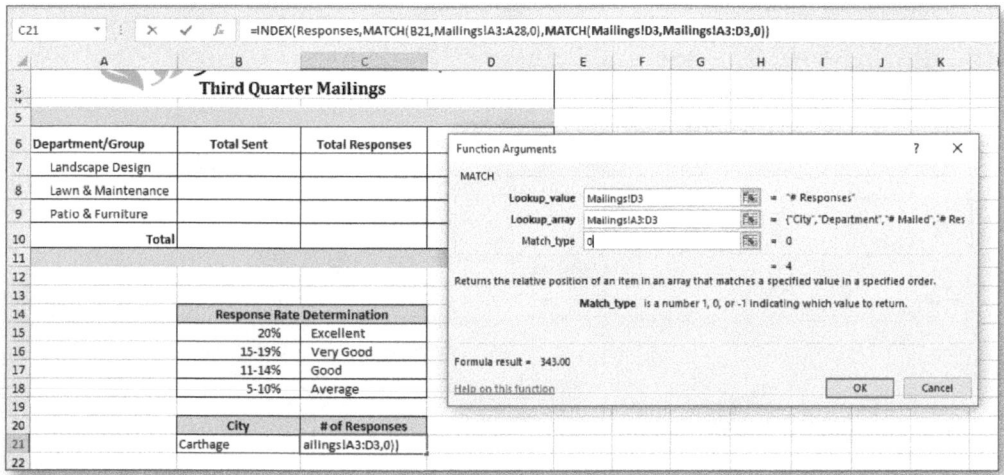

6-105 Nested *MATCH* and *INDEX* functions

i. Format the results to show zero decimal places.

j. Type Smyrna in cell **B21**.

3. Use *DSUM* to summarize mailing data.

a. On the **Mailings** sheet, note that number sent is located in the third column and response data is in the fourth column.

b. Click the **Criteria** sheet tab. Select cell **B2** and type lan* to select data for the Landscape Design department.

c. Click the **Mailing Stats** sheet tab and select cell **B7**.

d. Use **DSUM** with the range name **Responses** as the *Database* argument. Type 3 for the *Field* argument, and use an absolute reference to cells **B1:B2** on the **Criteria** sheet as the *Criteria* argument.

e. Copy the formula to cell **C7** and edit the *Field* argument to use the fourth column.

f. Complete criteria for the two remaining departments on the **Criteria** sheet.

g. Click the **Mailing Stats** sheet tab and select cell **B8**.

h. Use *DSUM* in cells **B8:C9** to calculate results for the two departments.

4. Use *SUM* in cells **B10:C10**.

5. Format all values as **Comma Style** with no decimal places.

6. Create an *IFS* function to display a response rating.

a. Click cell **D7**. The response rate and ratings are shown in rows 14:18.

b. Start an *IFS* function and select **C7** for the *Logical_test1* argument. Type / for division and select cell **B7**. Type >= 20% to complete the test.

c. Click the **Value_if_true1** box, select **C15**, and press **F4 (FN+F4)** (Figure 6-106).

6-106 First logical test and value_if_true arguments

d. Click the **Logical_test2** box, select **C7**, type /, select cell **B7**, and type >=15%

e. Click the **Value_if_true2** box, click cell **C16**, and press **F4 (FN+F4)**.

f. Complete the third and fourth logical tests and *value_if_true* arguments (Figure 6-107).

g. Copy the formula in cell **D7** to cells **D8:D10**.

7. Use *SUMIFS* to total insurance claims and dependents by city and department.

a. Click the **Employee Insurance** sheet tab and select cell **E25**.

b. Use *SUMIFS* with an absolute reference to cells **F4:F23** as the *Sum_range* argument.

c. The *Criteria_range1* argument is an absolute reference to cells **E4:E23** with *Criteria1* that will select the city of Brentwood.

d. The *Criteria_range2* argument is an absolute reference to the department column with criteria that will select the Landscape Design department.

e. Complete *SUMIFS* formulas for cells **E26:E28**.

f. Format borders to remove inconsistencies, if any, and adjust column widths to display data.

8. Use *DATEVALUE* to convert text data to dates.

a. Click the **Birth Dates** sheet tab and select cell **D4**. The dates were imported as text and cannot be used in date arithmetic.

b. Select cells **D4:D23** and cut/paste them to cells **G4:G23**.

6-107 Completed *IFS* function arguments

c. Select cell **H4** and use *DATEVALUE* to convert the date in cell **G4** to a serial number.

d. Copy the formula to cells **H5:H23**.

e. Select cells **H4:H23** and copy them to the *Clipboard*.

f. Select cell **D4**, click the arrow with the **Paste** button [*Home* tab, *Clipboard* group], and choose **Values** (Figure 6-108).

g. Format the values in column **D** to use the **Short Date** format.

h. Hide columns **G:H**.

i. Apply **All Borders** to the data and make columns **B:D** each **13.57 (100 pixels)** wide.

6-108 Only values are pasted

9. Save and close the workbook (Figure 6-109).

Classic Gardens and Landscape (CGL) Employee Birth Dates

ID #	Last Name	First Name	Date
1	Conrad	Anna	2/13/1972
2	Stewart	Maureen	3/8/1984
3	Ladewig	Lisle	5/8/1978
4	McDonald	Alphonse	9/5/1981
5	Meandro	Juan	10/13/1985
6	Jonas	Keiko	4/17/1990
7	Henry	Conrad	1/30/1992
8	Easom	Nassar	7/18/1991
9	Ohlberg	Sarah	9/15/1987
10	Artagnan	George	3/21/1988
11	Calvert	Maria	6/16/1976
12	Alverez	Beryl	11/21/1994
14	Johnson	Burton	12/8/1990
15	Alvarez	José	10/4/1989
16	Pawlowski	Jerry	11/5/1989
17	Lopez	Anita	2/21/1991
18	Gaylord	David	3/14/1992
19	Yager	Bobbi	8/8/1994
20	Hughes	Delores	12/6/1990
21	Svenson	Imre	2/28/1975

6-109 Completed worksheets for Excel 6-5

Independent Project 6-6

Clemenson Imaging LLC analyzes increased revenue from the purchase and use of CT scan equipment. You determine the number of patients and procedures by technician and location and transpose technician names.
[Student Learning Outcomes 6.3, 6.4, 6.5, 6.6, 6.7]

File Needed: ***ClemensonImaging-06.xlsx*** *(Student data files are available in the* Library *of your SIMnet account)*
Completed Project File Name: *[your initials] **Excel 6-6.xlsx***

Skills Covered in this Project

- Calculate the net present value of a purchase.
- Use *TRANSPOSE* to rearrange labels into a column.

- Concatenate cells to display names.
- Use *SUMIFS* to summarize data.
- Calculate procedure times.
- Format times with fractions.

1. Open the ***ClemensonImaging-06*** workbook from your student data files and save it as [your initials] Excel 6-6.

2. Determine the net present value of a new equipment purchase.
 a. Click the **Financials** sheet tab and select cell **H5**.
 b. Use **NPV** with a *Rate* argument of **4.25%**. For the *Value1* argument, select cells **D7:D13**. This is the same as entering each value argument separately.
 c. Edit the formula to add both investment costs (cells **D4** and **D5**) at the end of the formula.

3. Use *TRANSPOSE* to arrange technician names.
 a. Click the **Technicians** sheet tab. The names are in rows.
 b. Select cells **A4:A10**, seven rows in one column.
 c. Select **TRANSPOSE** from the *Lookup & Reference* category and select cells **A1:G1** for the *Array* argument.
 d. Press **Ctrl+Shift+Enter** to complete the array formula.
 e. Repeat the *TRANSPOSE* task for the first names in cells **B4:B10**.
 f. Select cells **A4:B10** and copy them to the *Clipboard*.
 g. Select cell **D4**, click the arrow with the **Paste** button [*Home* tab, *Clipboard* group], and choose **Values** (Figure 6-110).

4. Use *CONCAT* to display technician names.
 a. Click the **Summary** sheet tab.
 b. Select cell **A5** and use *CONCAT* with cell **D4** on the **Technicians** sheet as the *Text1* argument.
 c. The *Text2* argument is a comma and a space.
 d. The *Text3* argument is cell **E4** on the **Technicians** sheet (Figure 6-111).
 e. Copy the formula to display the remaining names and preserve the borders.

6-110 Transposed and copied data

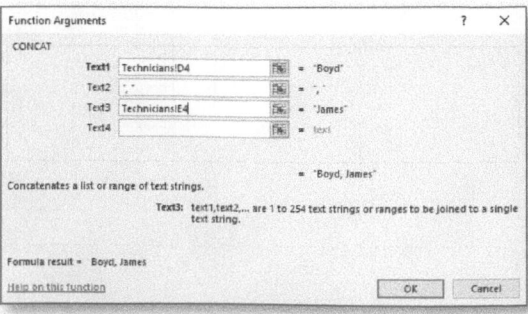

6-111 *CONCAT* with 3D references

5. Use *SUMIFS* to total number of patients by procedure and technician.
 a. Click the **Procedures** tab and name cells **A5:F41** as Data.
 b. Click the **Summary** sheet tab and select cell **C5**.
 c. Use *SUMIFS* with an absolute reference to cells **D5:D41** on the **Procedures** sheet for the *Sum_range*. Since the range name includes the column label, you must include the label in each *CriteriaN* range.
 d. The first criteria range is an absolute reference to the image type column on the **Procedures** sheet. Its corresponding criteria is mri.
 e. The second criteria range is an absolute reference to the technician names column on the **Procedures** sheet.
 f. Type **boyd** for the *Criteria2* argument. This string means that any character(s) can precede or follow "boyd" (Figure 6-112).

6. Copy and edit the *SUMIFS* formula or start a new formula to complete data in cells **C6:C11**.

7. Use *SUMIFS* to total number of patients by category and location in cells **C14:C15**.

8. Look for and correct format inconsistencies.

9. Calculate procedure times.
 a. Click the **Times** sheet tab and select cell **F6**.
 b. Build a formula to subtract the start time from the end time and multiply those results by 24. The result is shown in hours.
 c. Copy the formula to row **41**.
 d. Select cells **F6:F41** and open the *Format Cells* dialog box. On the *Number* tab, choose **Fraction** with a *Type* of **Up to one digit** (Figure 6-113).

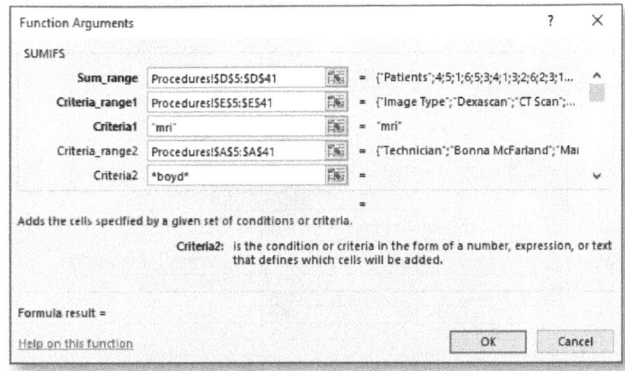

6-112 Wildcard characters in the argument

6-113 Time results formatted with fractions

10. Save and close the workbook (Figure 6-114).

Clemenson Imaging
Time Duration for Procedures in Hours

Patient ID	Location	Image Type	Start	End	Duration
CL024	Green Bay	Dexascan	9:15 AM	9:30 AM	1/4
CL027	Manitowoc	CT Scan	1:00 PM	1:45 PM	3/4
CL030	Appleton	MRI	10:15 AM	11:30 AM	1 1/4
CL033	Green Bay	Ultrasonography	9:00 AM	10:00 AM	1
CL036	Green Bay	Angiography	2:30 PM	4:15 PM	1 3/4
CL039	Manitowoc	Dexascan	10:30	11:00 AM	1/2
CL042	Manitowoc	MRI	2:45 PM	4:15 PM	1 1/2
CL045	Appleton	MRI	8:00 AM	10:30 AM	2 1/2
CL048	Appleton	Angiography	1:30 PM	3:45 PM	2 1/4
CL051	Green Bay	Angiography	3:00 PM	4:45 PM	1 3/4
CL054	Appleton	Ultrasonography	1:00 PM	1:45 PM	3/4
CL057	Manitowoc	Ultrasonography	11:30 AM	1:45 PM	2 1/4
CL060	Manitowoc	MRI	10:15 AM	11:30 AM	1 1/4
CL063	Appleton	Dexascan	10:30	11:00 AM	1/2
CL066	Appleton	Dexascan	11:00 AM	11:20 AM	1/3
CL069	Green Bay	CT Scan	2:15 PM	3:30 PM	1 1/4
CL072	Appleton	CT Scan	3:30 PM	5:00 PM	1 1/2
CL075	Green Bay	MRI	8:00 AM	11:00 AM	3
CL078	Manitowoc	MRI	9:00 AM	11:30 AM	2 1/2
CL081	Manitowoc	CT Scan	4:00 PM	5:30 PM	1 1/2
CL084	Appleton	CT Scan	8:00 AM	9:45 AM	1 3/4
CL087	Appleton	MRI	12:00 PM	2:30 PM	2 1/2
CL090	Green Bay	MRI	2:15 PM	4:45 PM	2 1/2
CL093	Manitowoc	Ultrasonography	1:00 PM	1:45 PM	3/4
CL096	Appleton	MRI	10:15 AM	11:30 AM	1 1/4
CL099	Appleton	Dexascan	11:00 AM	11:20 AM	1/3
CL102	Green Bay	Dexascan	8:00 AM	8:10 AM	1/3
CL105	Appleton	CT Scan	2:00 PM	3:30 PM	1 1/2
CL108	Green Bay	CT Scan	3:00 PM	3:45 PM	3/4
CL111	Manitowoc	Angiography	4:00 PM	4:45 PM	3/4
CL114	Appleton	Angiography	3:45 PM	5:00 PM	1 1/4
CL117	Green Bay	Ultrasonography	11:00 AM	11:20 AM	1/3
CL120	Manitowoc	Ultrasonography	12:00 PM	1:30 PM	1 1/2
CL123	Appleton	Angiography	4:00 PM	4:45 PM	3/4
CL126	Green Bay	MRI	10:15 AM	11:30 AM	1 1/4
CL129	Manitowoc	MRI	9:00 AM	11:15 AM	2 1/4

Clemenson Imaging, LLC
Purchase and Training Cost Analysis

Cost of CT Scan Equipment	-$200,000			
Cost of Staff Training	-$25,000	Net Present Value	$22,933.93	
Additional Revenue Year 1	$30,000			
Additional Revenue Year 2	$30,000			
Additional Revenue Year 3	$45,000			
Additional Revenue Year 4	$45,000			
Additional Revenue Year 5	$48,000			
Additional Revenue Year 6	$48,000			
Additional Revenue Year 7	$50,000			

Clemenson Imaging
Second Quarter Summary

Technician	Procedure	# of Patients
Boyd, James	MRI	4
Douglas, Jonathan	CT Scan	13
Lynfield, Patti	Angiography	2
McFarland, Donna	Angiography	0
Olander, Annie	MRI	5
Vonbank, MaryAnne	MRI	2
Woods, Samantha	CT Scan	1

Patient Category	Location	# of Patients
Scheduled	Appleton	22
Walk-In	Green Bay	17

6-114 Completed worksheets for Excel 6-6

Improve It Project 6-7

In the Livingood Income Tax and Accounting workbook, you use *IFERROR* to replace a standard error with a custom message. You correct the spelling of a client name throughout the worksheet, incorporate the *TODAY()* function in a concatenated statement, and calculate data about overdue accounts.
[Student Learning Outcomes 6.2, 6.4, 6.6, 6.8]

File Needed: **Livingood-06.xlsx** *(Student data files are available in the Library of your SIMnet account)*
Completed Project File Name: *[your initials] Excel 6-7.xlsx*

Skills Covered in this Project

- Use *IFERROR* to display a custom message.
- Add cell references to the *Watch Window*.
- Monitor *Find and Replace* in the *Watch Window*.

- Create a *SUMIF* formula.
- Build a *COUNTIF* formula.
- Concatenate *TODAY()* with text.
- Use date format codes in a function.

1. Open the **Livingood-06** workbook from your student data files and save it as [your initials] Excel 6-7.
2. Select cell **E6** on the **Accounts Aging** sheet and review the formula. The formula subtracts the invoice date from today's date in cell G1.
3. Use an *IFERROR* formula in cell **E6** that displays Re-enter date instead of a standard error message.
4. Copy the *IFERROR* formula to cells **E7:E20** and *AutoFit* the column.
5. Select cells **C6:C20** and add them as a watch to the *Watch Window*.
6. Click the **Aging Detail** sheet tab. Build a *Find and Replace* command to replace all occurrences of "accoustaff, inc." with AccounStaff, Inc. throughout the workbook. Close the *Watch Window*.
7. Use *SUMIFS* to calculate totals that are late by 30 days or more.
 a. Click the **Aging Detail** sheet tab.
 b. Name cells **A5:E20** as Detail.
 c. Use *SUMIFS* in cell **H6** to calculate the total due from *AccounStaff* that is 30 or more days late.
 d. Copy or enter a *SUMIFS* formula for *Custom Tax* in cell **H7**.
 e. Format cells **H6:H7** as **Currency**.
8. Use *COUNTIFS* to calculate how many invoices are late by 30 days or more.
 a. Use *COUNTIFS* in cell **I6** to calculate the number of *AccounStaff* invoices that are 30 or more days overdue.
 b. Copy or enter a *COUNTIFS* formula for *Custom Tax* in cell **I7**.
9. Use *CONCAT* to display a sentence about the current date.
 a. Click cell **A22** on the **Aging Detail** sheet and start a *CONCAT* formula.
 b. Type Today is with a space after the word "is" for the *Text1* argument.
 c. Click the **Text2** box and nest the **TEXT** function from the *Text* category.
 d. Type today() for the *Value* argument. The equals sign is not necessary when the function is used as an argument.
 e. Click the **Format_text** box and type mmmm d, yyy. This format spells out the month, uses four digits for the year, and shows the date without leading zeros (Figure 6-115).
 f. Click **OK**.

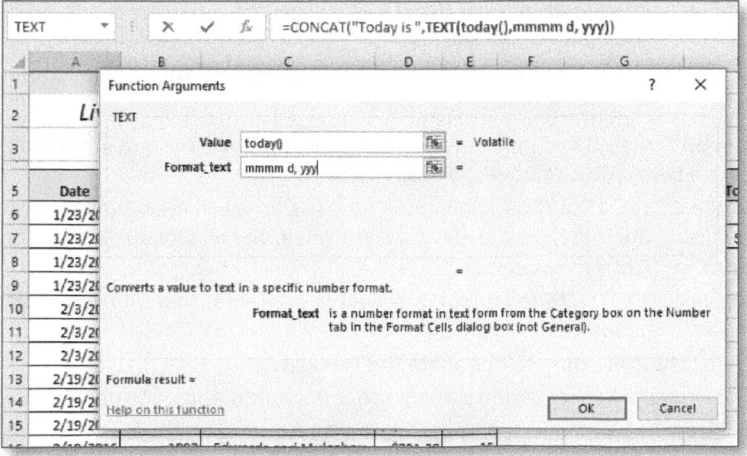

6-115 Nested *TEXT* function with custom date format

10. Save and close the workbook (Figure 6-116).

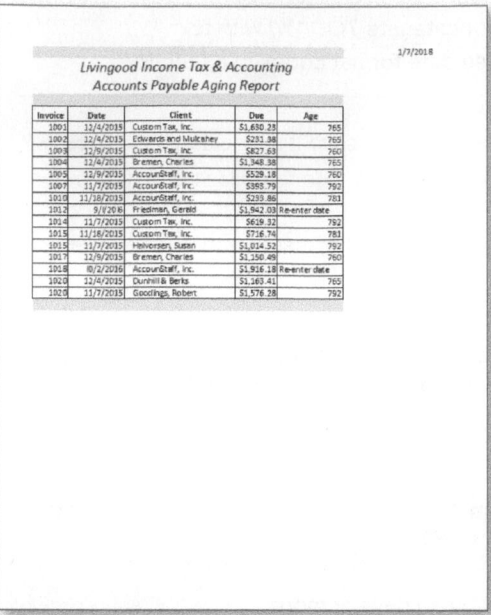

Livingood Income Tax & Accounting
Accounts Payable Aging Report

6-116 Completed worksheets for Excel 6-7

Challenge Project 6-8

In this project, you build a list of names and use *Text* functions to create email addresses. You also use the *SUBSTITUTE* function to update the email address list to display a revised name.
[Student Learning Outcome 6.6]

File Needed: None
Completed Project File Name: *[your initials] Excel 6-8.xlsx*

Create and save a workbook as [your initials] Excel 6-8. Modify your workbook according to the following guidelines:

- In cells **A3:B8**, type first and last names for six persons, first names in column A, last names in column B. Names can be friends, relatives, or colleagues.
- In cells **C3:C8**, use *CONCAT* to display an email address for each individual that consists of the first name, an underscore, the last name, and @ with a domain name. Use the same domain name for all, such as "abc.com" or "CompanyA.com."
- In cells **D3:D8**, use *SUBSTITUTE* to change the **Text** in column **C** to a different domain name. For example, change "CompanyA.com" to "CompanyB.com."
- Type labels and apply formatting to complete the worksheet.
- Insert a footer that displays the current date in the left section and your name in the right section.
- Set document properties to show your name as the author and a title of your choice. Spell check the workbook if necessary.

Challenge Project 6-9

In this project, you calculate net present value and internal rate of return for an electric car purchase. You include the increased cost of this type of automobile, a tax credit from your state government, and gasoline cost savings for five years of ownership.
[Student Learning Outcome 6.5]

File Needed: None
Completed Project File Name: *[your initials] Excel 6-9.xlsx*

Create and save a workbook as [your initials] Excel 6-9. Modify your workbook according to the following guidelines:

- Enter the following labels in column A: Price Premium, Tax Credit, Year 1 Fuel Savings. Enter labels for fuel savings for years 2–5.
- In column B, enter a value as the price premium for an electric car. This is a negative amount and is how much more an electric car costs than a gasoline-powered car.
- Enter a value for a tax credit that is half the premium value; this is a positive value because it is a savings for you.
- For the fuel savings, estimate a yearly amount based on driving an electric car rather than a gasoline-powered car.
- Enter labels below the data for Net Present Value and Internal Rate of Return.
- Use *NPV* to calculate the net present value of the purchase. For the discount rate, enter a percentage that is close to the percentage you might earn for a moderately safe investment.
- Explore the *IRR* and the *MIRR* functions. Then use either to determine a return rate on the purchase, if any.
- Insert main labels to identify the purpose of the sheet and apply formatting.
- Insert a header that shows the current date in the center section and your name in the right section.
- Edit document properties to show your name as the author.

Challenge Project 6-10

In this project, you create a worksheet that compares year-to-year usage for text messages, tweets, or blog posts. You calculate the percentage change and use *IFERROR* to identify incomplete data.
[Student Learning Outcome 6.2]

File Needed: None
Completed Project File Name: *[your initials] Excel 6-10.xlsx*

Create and save a workbook as [your initials] Excel 6-10. Modify your workbook according to the following guidelines:

- Starting in cell **A3**, enter the names of the months from January to December in the column.
- In cells **B2:D2**, enter labels for Year 1, Year 2, and % Change.

- Enter values for January through September for both years. These values can represent the number of tweets, text messages, or other posts of interest to you. Do not enter values for October through December.
- In column D, enter the formula to calculate the percentage change. The formula is year 2's value minus year 1's value divided by year 1's value. Set the order of precedence so that the subtraction is calculated before the division. Format the results as **Percent Style** with two decimal places.
- Copy the formula for all months, including October through December, to display the standard error message *#DIV/0!* in the rows without values.
- Edit or replace the formulas in column D with an *IFERROR* formula to display Missing Data instead of the standard error.
- Insert main labels to identify the purpose of the sheet and complete formatting.
- Insert a header with your name in the right section.
- Edit document properties to show your name as the author.

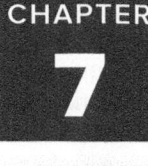

CHAPTER 7

Working with Templates and Sharing Work

CHAPTER OVERVIEW

Excel templates are model workbooks. When you create a new workbook, you use a template with basic settings, including a document theme, a font name and size, and default margins. You can build an easy-to-use, error-free workbook with a template and commands such as data validation and form controls.

STUDENT LEARNING OUTCOMES (SLOs)

After completing this chapter, you will be able to:

SLO 7.1 Use a template to create a workbook and save a workbook as a template (p. E7-435).

SLO 7.2 Set data validation, input messages, and error alerts (p. E7-437).

SLO 7.3 Use the *Form* button and *Form Controls* (p. E7-443).

SLO 7.4 Set worksheet and workbook protection to manage editing (p. E7-448).

SLO 7.5 Share a workbook, track changes, and compare and merge workbooks (p. E7-455).

SLO 7.6 Inspect a workbook for metadata, check compatibility, and define a trusted location (p. E7-460).

CASE STUDY

In the Pause & Practice projects in this chapter, you work with inventory and guest worksheets for Paradise Lakes Resort (PLR). You save the workbook as a template, add data validation and an option button, and check the workbook for distribution issues.

Pause & Practice 7-1: Create an Excel template and add data validation settings to a worksheet.

Pause & Practice 7-2: Create a workbook from a template, use a data form, add a form control, and set worksheet and workbook protection.

Pause & Practice 7-3: Share and merge workbooks and prepare a workbook for distribution.

EXCEL

SLO 7.1

Using Excel Templates

A **template** is a prototype or sample workbook. A template can include data, formulas, formatting, charts, images, controls, and more. Templates are best for work that requires the same layout, the same design, and the same data pattern each time you prepare a workbook.

Create a Workbook from a Template

The *Backstage* view for the *New* command displays recently published and popular templates in its *Featured* group. Excel has thousands of templates, and *Backstage* view lists suggested search categories. When you create a workbook from a template, a copy of the template opens as an Excel workbook with the same name as the template followed by a number.

▶ HOW TO: Create a Workbook from a Template

1. Click the **New** button [*File* tab].
 - *Backstage* view for *New* displays a thumbnail and name for *Featured* templates.
 - The *Blank workbook* template creates a new workbook.
 - The *Suggested searches* categories locate online templates.
 - Select **PERSONAL** to use a template that you created.
2. Click the thumbnail for the template you want to use.
 - A preview window describes the template (Figure 7-1).
3. Click **Create**.
 - A workbook with the same name as the template followed by a number opens (Figure 7-2).
 - A template can include sample data and multiple sheets.
4. Save the workbook in your usual location with a descriptive name.

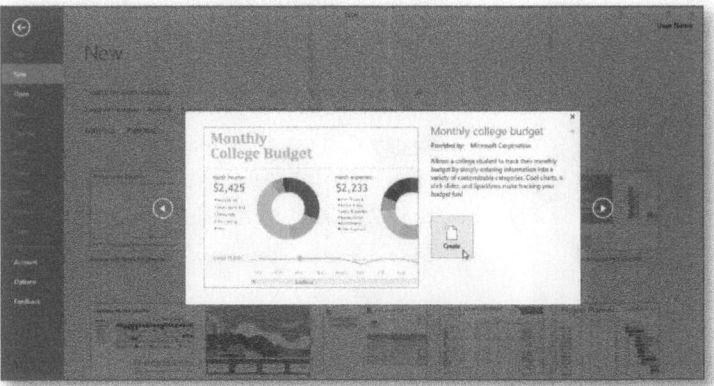

7-1 Preview of selected template in *Backstage* view

7-2 Workbook created from a template

Save a Workbook as a Template

Published and online templates provide a starting point for a new workbook, but you can create a template from any Excel workbook. When you use the same design, formulas, and objects for a task, you can create a model, save it as a template, and build new workbooks from the template.

When you save a workbook as an Excel template, it is saved in the *Custom Office Templates* folder in the *Documents* folder for the current user at your computer. Your saved templates are

available in the *Personal* category in *Backstage* view for the *New* command [*File* tab]. Excel templates are saved with the .xltx file name extension.

> **MORE INFO**
>
> You can save templates in any folder but their names do not appear in the *Personal* category and they do not open as copies. Change the default folder for personal templates in the *Excel Options* dialog box in the *Save* pane.

Check the *Save Thumbnail* box before you choose the *Save as type* to include a preview for a template. A ***thumbnail*** is a tiny image of the active sheet.

> **MORE INFO**
>
> A default setting to save thumbnails with all workbooks appears in the *Properties* dialog box on the *Summary* tab. Thumbnails are visible in the *Open* dialog box when you set view options to show icons.

▶ **HOW TO:** Save a Workbook as a Template

1. Click the **File** tab and choose **Save As**.
2. Choose **This PC**.
3. Click the **More Options** link.
 - The *Save As* dialog box opens.
 - The default name in the *File name* box is highlighted.
4. Type the template name.
5. Click the **Save as type** arrow.
6. Select **Excel Template** (Figure 7-3).
 - Excel selects the default *Custom Office Templates* folder.
 - You can navigate to another folder.
7. Select the **Save Thumbnail** box.
8. Click **Save**.
9. Close the template.

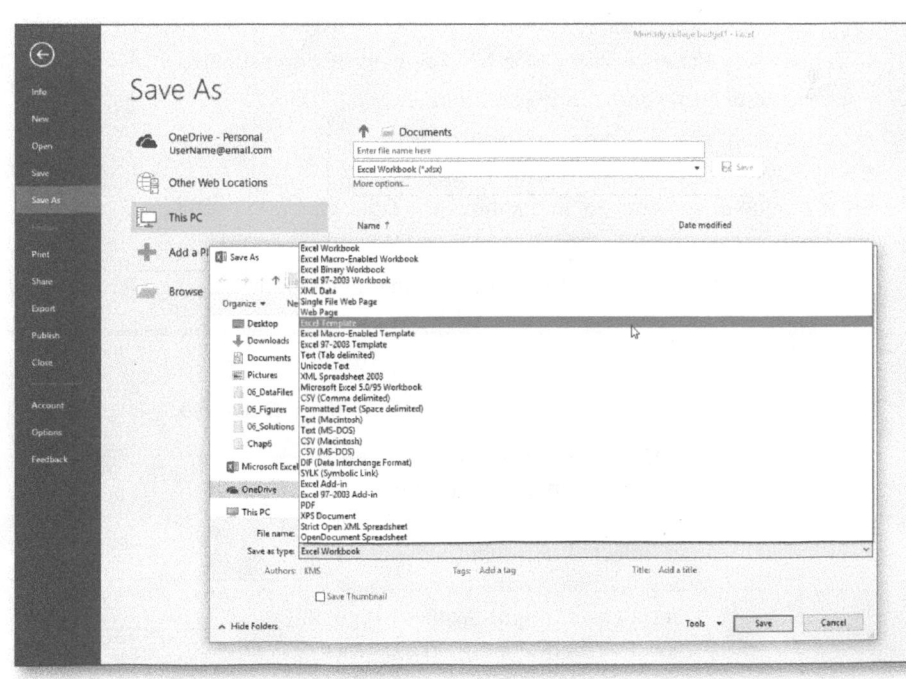

7-3 *Save as type* sets the default templates folder

SLO 7.2

Setting Data Validation

Data validation is a process in which Excel checks data as it is entered to verify that it matches established requirements. In an inventory worksheet, Paradise Lakes Resort can set a data validation rule that requires the stock quantity to be a positive number. If a user enters a negative number, a pop-up message reminds the person about the error.

Validation Settings

Validation settings are rules applied to data as it is entered. You can build a simple condition using relational operators, such as requiring that the data be a whole number within a range of values or that data be greater than or less than a value. You can allow or prohibit decimal values, specify date or time limits, or limit the length of a text entry. It is also possible to use a list or a formula in a data validation setting.

You usually set data validation for a range of cells before any data is entered. You can set validation after data is entered but already-entered data that does not meet the rule is not automatically identified.

▶ HOW TO: Set Data Validation with an Operator

1. Select the cell or the cell range where data validation settings are required.
2. Click the **Data Validation** button [*Data* tab, *Data Tools* group].
 - The *Data Validation* dialog box has three tabs.
3. Click the **Settings** tab.
4. Click the **Allow** arrow and choose an option.
 - Choose **Whole Number** to set a particular value or range of values.
 - Choose **Any Value** or click **Clear All** to clear validation settings.
5. Click the **Data** arrow and choose an operator.
 - *Data* options are based on the *Allow* choice.
 - Dialog box choices depend on the operator.
6. Enter a value or select a cell to complete the *Data Validation* settings (Figure 7-4).
7. Click **OK**.
 - Cells with data that do not match the criteria are not identified.

7-4 Data validation settings

Create a Data Validation Input Message

An ***input message*** is a comment box that appears on screen as soon as a cell with data validation is selected. An input message is a guideline for the person entering data. It might display "Type a value between 1 and 10," or "Choose a name from this list." Figure 7-5 shows an input message before data is entered.

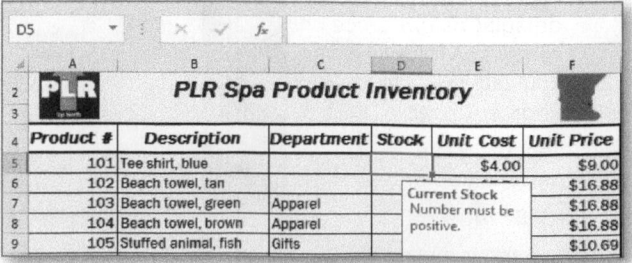

7-5 Input message when the cell is selected

▶ **HOW TO:** Create an Input Message

1. Select the cell or the range with data validation settings.
2. Click the **Data Validation** button [*Data* tab, *Data Tools* group].
3. Click the **Input Message** tab.
4. Verify that the **Show input message when cell is selected** box is selected.
5. Click the **Title** box and type a name or title for the message box.
 - A title is optional.
6. Click the **Input message** box and type the message to appear on screen (Figure 7-6).
 - Use capitalization and punctuation as desired.
 - Be brief to keep the input box small.
7. Click **OK**.

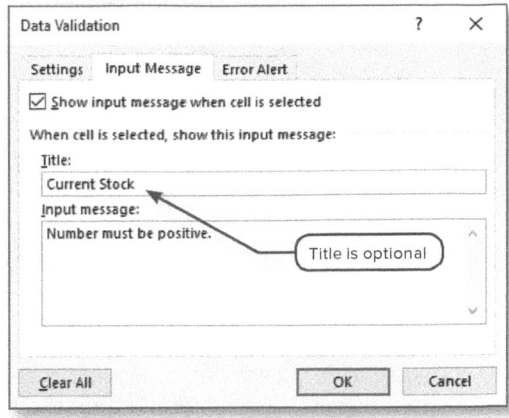

7-6 Input message for data validation

▶ MORE INFO

You can create a custom *ScreenTip* by creating an input message without a data validation setting.

Create a Data Validation Error Alert

An ***error alert*** is a pop-up message that appears after invalid data is entered, as shown in Figure 7-7. You can set an error alert as well as an input message for each data validation setting in a worksheet.

When you create an error alert, you specify the type of warning box. With a *Stop* warning, the user is prohibited from making an entry and can cancel the task or retry. A *Stop* warning displays a white **X** in a red circle.

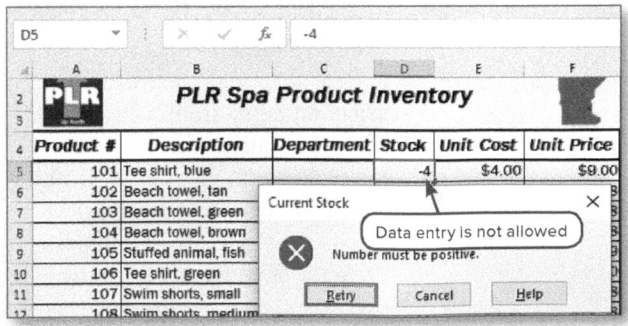

7-7 *Stop* style error alert

When you select a *Warning* box, the message box shows an exclamation point (!) in a yellow triangle. With this type of warning, the entry is allowed or can be edited or canceled. The third warning style is *Information* which allows the entry to be made. This message box includes a lowercase **i** in a blue circle.

▶ MORE INFO

When you allow invalid entries, you can set conditional formatting to highlight invalid entries for review.

After you set the type of warning, you can type an optional title for the message box. The *Error message* is text that appears on screen. The message should clearly and briefly explain what the user should do to create a valid entry.

> **HOW TO: Create an Error Alert**

1. Select the cell or the range with data validation settings.
2. Click the **Data Validation** button [*Data* tab, *Data Tools* group].
3. Click the **Error Alert** tab.
4. Verify that the **Show error alert after invalid data is entered** box is selected.
5. Click the **Style** arrow and choose a warning type.
 - Use a *Stop* style if the entry should not be allowed.
 - Use a *Warning* or *Information* style if the entry is permissible.
6. Click the **Title** box and type a label for the message box.
 - The title is optional.
7. Click the **Error message** box and type the message to appear in the warning box (Figure 7-8).
 - Use capitalization and punctuation as you want it to appear on screen.
 - Check spelling and grammar carefully.
8. Click **OK**.

7-8 Warning style error alert

Validation Lists

Data validation includes an option that requires users to select an entry from a list. You can type entries for the list in the dialog box, separating items with commas, or you can select a cell range in the workbook.

With a validation list, the user sees a drop-down arrow when he or she selects the cell as shown in Figure 7-9. It is good practice to enter data in alphabetical or other logical order so that it is easy for the user to find his or her choice.

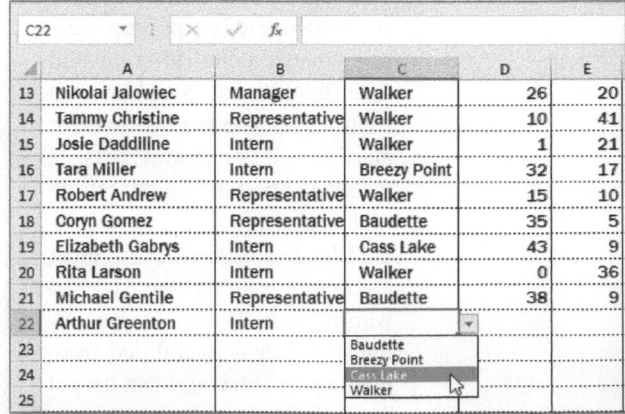

7-9 A data validation list

> **HOW TO: Set a Data Validation List**

1. Select the cell or range for data validation.
2. Click the **Data Validation** button [*Data* tab, *Data Tools* group].
3. Click the **Settings** tab.
4. Click the **Allow** arrow and choose **List**.

5. Click the **Source** entry box and do one of the following:
 - Select the range of cells with the list.
 - Press **F3** (**FN+F3**) to open the *Paste Name* dialog box, choose the name, and click **OK** (Figure 7-10).
 - Type each entry for the list, followed by a comma.
6. Click **OK**.

7-10 Validation settings for a list

Circle Invalid Data

Invalid data is a value or label that does not conform to validation criteria. Invalid data can occur because it is possible to copy data into a range with validation settings and because you can set validation after data is already entered.

You can highlight invalid data with the *Circle Invalid Data* command. This command places a red ***ellipse*** (an elongated circle) around each cell in which the data does not match the validation criteria. The *Circle Invalid Data* command highlights cells. It does not edit or correct the data.

▶ HOW TO: Circle Invalid Data

1. Select the cell or range with validation settings.
2. Click the **Data Validation** button [*Data* tab, *Data Tools* group].
3. Select **Circle Invalid Data**.
 - A red ellipse highlights each cell with invalid data (Figure 7-11).
4. Type or select valid data for each invalid entry.
 - The ellipse is removed after valid data is entered.
5. Click the **Data Validation** button [*Data* tab, *Data Tools* group].
6. Select **Clear Validation Circles** to remove ellipses if necessary.

Product #	Description	Department	Stock	Unit Cost	Unit Price
	PLR Spa Product Inventory				
101	Tee shirt, blue		12	$4.00	$9.00
102	Beach towel, tan		12	$7.50	$16.88
103	Beach towel, green	Apparel	-8	$7.50	$16.88
104	Beach towel, brown	Apparel	7	$7.50	$16.88
105	Stuffed animal, fish	Gifts	4	$4.75	$10.69
106	Tee shirt, green	Apparel	8	$4.00	$9.00
107	Swim shorts, small	Apparel	10	$5.50	$12.38
108	Swim shorts, medium	Apparel	12	$5.50	$12.38
109	Yoga pants, black	Apparel	5	$12.50	$28.13
110	Yoga pants, grey	Apparel	4	$12.50	$28.13
111	Sunscreen, 8 oz	Health Aids	10	$3.45	$7.76
112	Sunscreen 12 oz	Health Aids	12	$4.75	$10.69
113	Picture frame, 6"	Gifts	8	$5.50	$12.38
114	Picture frame, 12"	Gifts	8	$6.50	$14.63
115	Magnet, PLR	Gifts	15	$3.25	$7.31
116	Magnet, Minnesota		-16	$3.25	$7.31
117	Pen, PLR		20	$1.24	$2.79
118	Pen, Minnesota	Gifts	24	$1.24	$2.79

7-11 Invalid data is circled

PAUSE & PRACTICE: EXCEL 7-1

In this project, you save a workbook as a template, set data validation rules, circle invalid data, and remove invalidation circles. You also use input and error alert messages.

File Needed: ***ParadiseLakes-07.xlsx*** (Student data files are available in the Library of your SIMnet account)
Completed Project File Name: ***[your initials] PP E7-1Template.xltx***

1. Open the *ParadisesLakes-07* workbook from your student data files.

2. Save a workbook as a template.
 a. Click the **File** tab and choose **Save As**.
 b. Select **This PC** and click the **More Options** link to open the *Save As* dialog box.
 c. Type [your initials] PP E7-1Template in the *File name* box.
 d. Select the **Save Thumbnail** box.
 e. Click the **Save as type** arrow and choose **Excel Template**. The default folder for templates is opened.
 f. Click **Save**.

3. Create data validation settings with an operator to require a positive value.
 a. Select cells **D5:D29** on the **Inventory** sheet.
 b. Click the **Data Validation** button [*Data* tab, *Data Tools* group].
 c. Click the **Allow** arrow and choose **Whole Number**.
 d. Click the **Data** arrow and choose **greater than**.
 e. Click the **Minimum** box and type 0.
 f. Do not click **OK**.

4. Create an input message for data validation settings.
 a. Click the **Input Message** tab.
 b. Verify that the **Show input message when cell is selected** box is selected.
 c. Click the **Title** box and type Current Stock.
 d. Click the **Input message** box and type Number must be positive. including the period (Figure 7-12).
 e. Click **OK**. The input message appears because the range is selected.
 f. Select cell **E5** to remove the input message.

5. Circle and delete invalid data.
 a. Click the arrow for the **Data Validation** button [*Data* tab, *Data Tools* group].
 b. Choose **Circle Invalid Data**.
 c. Select each cell with invalid data and press **Delete**. The validation setting requires a value greater than zero, so the circles are not removed (Figure 7-13).
 d. Click the arrow for the **Data Validation** button [*Data* tab, *Data Tools* group] and choose **Clear Validation Circles**.

6. Create data validation settings with a list.
 a. Click the **Validation Lists** sheet tab and select cells **A2:A4**.
 b. Sort the cells in ascending order (A-Z).
 c. Click the **Inventory** sheet tab and select cells **C5:C29**.

7-12 Input message for the stock number

7-13 Invalid data is circled

d. Click the **Data Validation** button [*Data* tab, *Data Tools* group].

e. Select the **Settings** tab, click the **Allow** arrow, and choose **List**.

f. Click the **Source** box and click the **Validation Lists** worksheet tab.

g. Select cells **A2:A4** and click **OK**.

7. Select cell **C5** and choose **Apparel** from the validation list. Select cell **C6** and choose **Apparel**.

8. Select cell **C20** and choose **Gifts** from the validation list.

9. For cells **C21** and **C23**, choose **Gifts**.

10. For cells **C28:C29**, choose **Health Aids**.

11. Type the list for validation settings and add an error alert.

a. Select the **Responses** sheet tab and select cells **B3:B39**.

b. Click the **Data Validation** button [*Data* tab, *Data Tools* group].

c. Click the **Allow** arrow and choose **List**.

d. Click the **Source** box.

e. Type Intern,Manager,Representative with no space after each comma (Figure 7-14).

f. Click the **Error Alert** tab.

g. Verify that the **Show error alert after invalid data is entered** box is selected.

h. Click the **Style** arrow and choose **Warning**. This style will allow an invalid entry to be made.

i. Click the **Title** box and type Wait!.

j. Click the **Error message** box and type Please choose from the list.

k. Click **OK**.

12. Select cell **B4** and choose **Intern**.

13. Select cell **B5**, type Staff, and press **Enter** to display the error alert (Figure 7-15).

14. Choose **Yes** to allow the entry.

15. Choose **Manager** in cell **B6**.

16. Press **Ctrl+Home**. Click the **Save** button on the *Quick Access* toolbar to save the template with the same name.

17. Close the workbook (Figure 7-16).

7-14 Typed validation list

7-15 Error alert after invalid entry

Paradise Lakes Resort
Web and Phone Responses

Name	Title	Location	Web	Phone
Christopher Bowman	Representative	Cass Lake	13	22
Chad Meison	Intern	Cass Lake	26	7
Corey Daniels	Staff	Cass Lake	18	23
Wyatte Mockentune	Manager	Breezy Point	25	19
Dennis Omang	Representative	Breezy Point	22	16
BJ Francine	Representative	Baudette	32	8
Kendal Shaedon	Representative	Breezy Point	5	22
Ella Jamison	Manager	Baudette	44	10
Alec Jones	Representative	Baudette	26	18
Natasha Nelson	Intern	Baudette	0	23
Nikolai Jalowiec	Manager	Walker	26	20
Tammy Christine	Representative	Walker	10	41
Josie Daddiline	Intern	Walker	1	21
Tara Miller	Intern	Breezy Point	32	17
Robert Andrew	Representative	Walker	15	10
Coryn Gomez	Representative	Baudette	35	5
Elizabeth Gabrys	Intern	Cass Lake	43	9
Rita Larson	Intern	Walker	0	36
Michael Gentile	Representative	Baudette	38	9

PLR Spa Product Inventory

Product #	Description	Department	Stock	Unit Cost	Unit Price
101	Tee shirt, blue	Apparel	12	$4.00	$9.00
102	Beach towel, tan	Apparel	12	$7.50	$16.88
103	Beach towel, green	Apparel		$7.50	$16.88
104	Beach towel, brown	Apparel	7	$7.50	$16.88
105	Stuffed animal, fish	Gifts	4	$4.75	$10.69
106	Tee shirt, green	Apparel	8	$4.00	$9.00
107	Swim shorts, small	Apparel	10	$5.50	$12.38
108	Swim shorts, medium	Apparel	12	$5.50	$12.38
109	Yoga pants, black	Apparel	5	$12.50	$28.13
110	Yoga pants, grey	Apparel	4	$12.50	$28.13
111	Sunscreen, 8 oz	Health Aids	10	$3.45	$7.76
112	Sunscreen 12 oz	Health Aids	12	$4.75	$10.69
113	Picture frame, 6"	Gifts	8	$5.50	$12.38
114	Picture frame, 12"	Gifts	8	$6.50	$14.63
115	Magnet, PLR	Gifts	15	$3.25	$7.31
116	Magnet, Minnesota	Gifts		$3.25	$7.31
117	Pen, PLR	Gifts	20	$1.24	$2.79
118	Pen, Minnesota	Gifts	24	$1.24	$2.79
119	Pen, bass boat	Gifts	12	$1.24	$2.79
120	Stuffed animal, bear	Gifts	12	$4.75	$10.69
121	Stuffed animal, raccoon	Gifts	15	$4.75	$10.69
122	Antiseptic lotion, 4 oz	Health Aids	8	$5.75	$12.94
123	Antiseptic lotion, 12 oz	Health Aids	8	$6.25	$14.06
124	Insect repellent, 8 oz	Health Aids	10	$3.50	$7.88
125	Cough syrup, 8 oz	Health Aids	6	$2.20	$4.95

7-16 Completed worksheets for PP E7-1

SLO 7.3

Using the Form button and Form Controls

Excel has commands, buttons, and tools that enable you to streamline data entry in a template so that users can quickly complete their work. Many of these tools are available from the *Developer* command tab which is not displayed on the *Ribbon* by default.

The Form Button and the Developer Tab

The *Form* button creates a screen form for data entry. The button can be displayed on the *Quick Access* toolbar or in a custom tab or group. The *Developer* tab has command groups for working with macros, controls, and add-ins, and it appears when it is toggled on in Excel *Options* (Figure 7-17).

7-17 *Form* button and *Developer* tab on the *Ribbon*

> **ANOTHER WAY**
>
> Click the arrow on the *Quick Access* toolbar and choose **More Commands** to open the *Excel Options* dialog box.

7. Protect the worksheet for data entry.
 a. Select cells **D4:E4**.
 b. Press **Ctrl** and select cells **C9:C12**, **H9**, **H11**, **H13:H14**, **H16**, **H22**, and **E22**.
 c. Click the **Format** button [*Home* tab, *Cells* group].
 d. Select **Lock Cell** to remove the *Locked* property.
 e. Click the **Protect Sheet** button [*Review* tab, *Changes* group].
 f. Allow the options to select locked and unlocked cells. Do not use a password.
 g. Click **OK**.

8. Delete the contents of cells **C9:C10**, **H9** and **H16**.

9. Select cell **D4** to position the insertion point on the template.

10. Save and close the template.

11. Create a workbook from a template.
 a. Click the **New** button [*File* tab] and click **PERSONAL** near the top of the gallery.
 b. Click *[your initials] Excel 7-3Template*.
 c. Save the workbook as a regular Excel workbook named [your initials] Excel 7-3 in your usual location for saving files.

12. Select cell **C9**, type 450000, and press **Enter**. The cells are formatted and formulas are calculated.

13. Type 275000 in cell **C10** and press **Enter**.

14. Select cell **H9**, type 485000, and press **Enter**.

15. Type 75000 in cell **H11**.

16. Enter data in cells **H13**, **H14**, and **H16** as shown in Figure 7-73.

17. Click the spin box control arrows to select **3** as the agent ID.

18. Select cell **E22**, type 1875, and select cell **D4**.

19. Save and close the workbook.

20. Move the template from the default folder.
 a. Click the **File** tab, choose **Open**, and click **Browse**.
 b. Expand the *Quick access* list in the left pane and select **Documents**.
 c. Double-click **Custom Office Templates**.
 d. Right-click *[your initials] Excel 7-3Template* and choose **Cut**.
 e. Navigate to and open your folder for saving files.
 f. Right-click an unused area of the dialog box and choose **Paste**.
 g. Click **Cancel** to close the dialog box.

21. Remove the *Developer* tab.
 a. Click the **Options** button [*File* tab] and click **Customize Ribbon** in the left pane.
 b. Deselect the **Developer** box in the *Main Tabs* group and click **OK**.

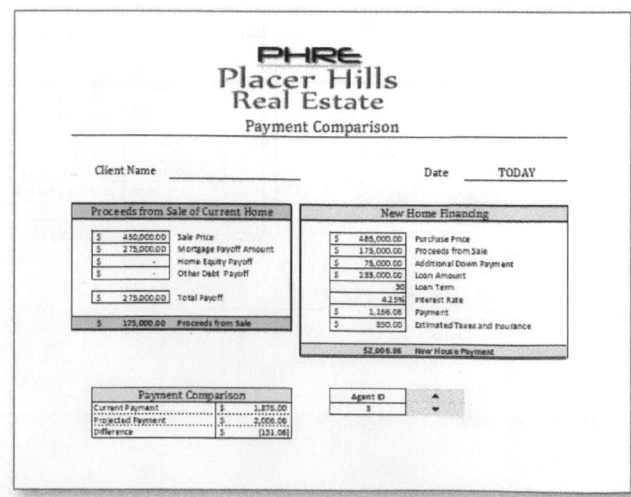

7-73 Completed worksheet for Excel 7-3

▶**HOW TO: Show the Form Button and the Developer Tab**

1. Click the **Options** button [*File* tab].
2. Select **Quick Access Toolbar** in the left pane.
3. Choose **All Commands** from the drop-down list for the *Choose commands from* box.
4. Choose **Form** in the list of commands.
5. Click **Add** to add the command to the *Customize Quick Access Toolbar* list on the right (Figure 7-18).
6. Click **Customize Ribbon** in the left pane.
7. Select the **Developer** box in the *Main Tabs* group.
8. Click **OK**.

 • The *Developer* tab displays at the right end of the *Ribbon*.
 • The **Form** button is located at the right on the *Quick Access* toolbar.

7-18 Excel *Options* dialog box to add *Form* button to *Quick Access* toolbar

Use a Data Input Form

The *Form* button creates a data input screen for list-type data. A ***data input form*** is a window or dialog box with labels and entry boxes in a vertical layout. Many users find it quicker and easier to enter data in a screen form than in a worksheet row. A data input form is a temporary view of worksheet data and is created each time you want to use it. After you complete data in one form and move to the next form, worksheet data is updated.

A data input form can display up to 32 fields or columns and shows one row (record) at a time. In the form, you can delete or add a record as well as filter the records.

▶**HOW TO: Create and Use a Data Input Form**

1. Select the cell range including column headings.
2. Click the **Form** button on the *Quick Access Toolbar* (Figure 7-19).

 • A data entry form opens and displays the first record (row) in the range.
 • When there are more fields than can be displayed at one time, a scroll bar is available for viewing all fields.

3. Click **New** to open a blank form.
4. Enter data for the new record and click **New**.

 • The row is added to the list.

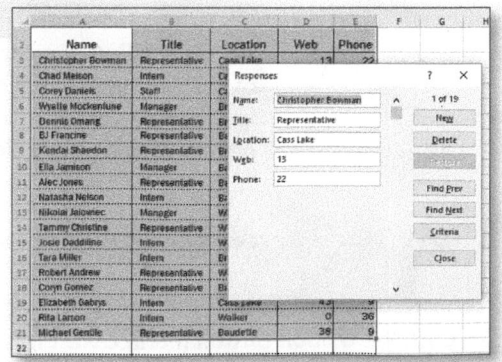

7-19 Selected range and data entry form

5. Click **Criteria** to open a blank form.

6. Click the field to be used for filtering data.

7. Type the criteria (Figure 7-20).

 • You can use wildcard characters.
 • Criteria are not case-sensitive.

8. Click *Find Next* or *Find Prev* to find a matching record.

 • The search begins at the current form.
 • The first matching record displays in the form.

9. Click **Close** to close the form.

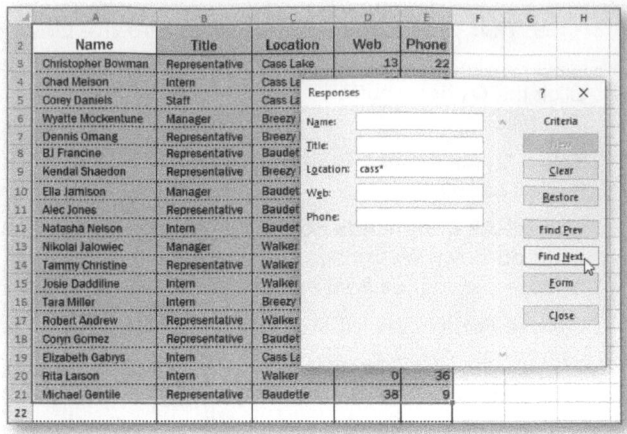

7-20 Data entry criteria form

Form Controls

A **form control** is an object that you can use to display a choice, to run a command, or to perform an action in a worksheet. Form controls make data entry easier and can improve the appearance of your work. You use form controls when you select from a drop-down list, choose an option button, or click a check box.

Two categories, *Form Controls* and *ActiveX Controls*, are available from the **Insert Controls** button in the *Controls* group on the *Developer* tab. ActiveX Controls require that you write code in **VBA (Visual Basic for Applications)** a programming language for enhanced commands and features in Excel. *Form Controls* accomplish similar tasks without programming.

A selected form control has handles for sizing, a move arrow for positioning, and a context menu. The *Format Control* dialog box includes properties and settings specific to each type of control. When a form control is selected, the *Drawing Tools Format* tab is available, too.

> **MORE INFO**
>
> If a control's context menu shows *Assign Macro*, it is a *Form* control. If the context menu includes *Properties*, it is an *ActiveX* control.

Option Button Control

An **Option Button** control is a radio button that allows the user to select one choice from a set of possibilities. An option button control has a default label "Option Button N" in which "n" is a number. You edit the label to specify the option names. Option button controls are usually organized in a **Group Box** control or a rectangle shape.

▶ **HOW TO: Insert an Option Button Form Control**

1. Click the **Insert Controls** button [*Developer* tab, *Controls* group].

2. Click the **Option Button (Form Control)** button in the *Form Controls* group (Figure 7-21).

 • The pointer is a thin cross or plus sign.

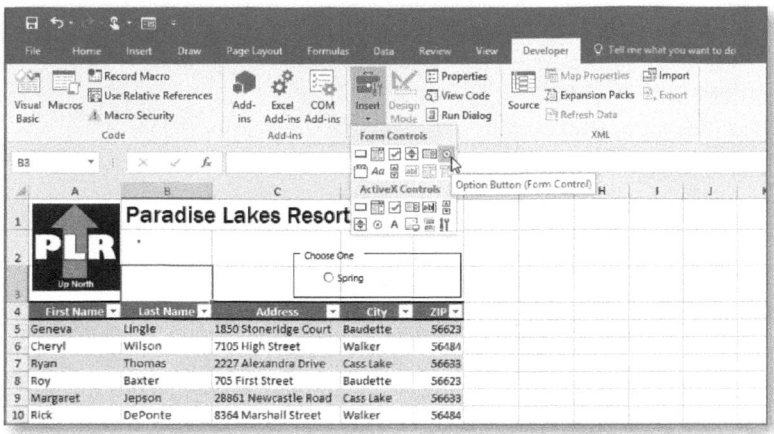

7-21 Form controls gallery

3. Click and drag the pointer to draw the control.

 - The control is selected immediately after it is created.
 - An option button control includes a default label.
 - To select a control, point to display the link select pointer and right-click.

4. Click the **Properties** button [*Developer* tab, *Controls* group].

 - The *Format Control* dialog box opens.

5. Verify that the **Control** tab is selected.

6. Select the **Unchecked** button for *Value*.

 - Options depend on the type of control.

7. Select the **3-D shading** box (Figure 7-22).

8. Click **OK**.

9. Point to the control and right-click.

10. Select **Edit Text**.

 - The insertion point displays next to the default label.

11. Delete the default label.

12. Type a new label for the option button (Figure 7-23).

13. Select a worksheet cell to deselect the control.

 - You can drag the control to the desired position on the sheet.
 - You can use *Drawing Tools* to align multiple controls.

7-22 *Format Control* dialog box

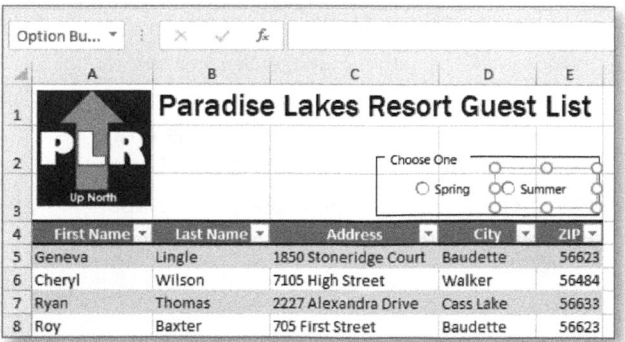

7-23 New control in worksheet

Combo Box Control

A ***Combo Box*** control creates a drop-down list from which you select one option. The options in the list are from a cell range in the workbook. You link the control to a cell which displays a value that represents the position of the choice in the range. You can display the result displayed in the combo box in a worksheet cell by using an *INDEX* command.

▶ HOW TO: Use a Combo Box Form Control with Index

1. Click the **Insert Controls** button [*Developer* tab, *Controls* group].
2. Click the **Combo Box (Form Control)** button in the *Form Controls* group.
 - The pointer is a thin cross or plus sign.
3. Click and drag the pointer to draw the control.
 - The control is selected immediately after it is created.
 - To select a control, point to display the link select pointer and right-click.
4. Right-click the control and select **Format Control**.
 - The *Format Control* dialog box opens.
 - You can also click the **Properties** button in the *Controls* group [*Developer* tab].
5. Verify that the **Control** tab is selected.
6. Click the **Input range** box and select the cells with data for the combo box drop-down list.
 - You can type a range name, but you cannot paste a range name.
7. Click the **Cell link** box.
8. Click the worksheet cell where the choice made in the combo box will display.
 - You can type a cell address.
 - The linked cell can be hidden by positioning the control over it.
9. Click the **Drop down lines** box and enter the number of lines to display in the combo box.
10. Select the **3-D shading** check box (Figure 7-24).
11. Click **OK**.
12. Select the cell for the *INDEX* function.
 - Select a cell other than the *Cell link* cell.
 - The control is deselected.
13. Start an *INDEX* function and select the **array, row_number, column_ num** argument list.
14. Select the same cell range used as the input range in the combo box for the *Array* argument.
 - You can type or paste a range name.
15. Click the **Row_num** box.
16. Select the same cell used as the *Cell link* in the control.
 - You can type the cell address.
17. Click **OK** to complete the *INDEX* formula.
18. Click the combo box arrow and make a choice.
 - The number indicating the position of your choice displays in the linked cell.
 - The *INDEX* formula returns the text of the choice (Figure 7-25).

7-24 *Format Object* dialog box for a combo box

7-25 **Combo box selection and** *INDEX* **result**

Reset the Ribbon

You can hide the *Form* button or the *Developer* tab and reset the *Ribbon* to its previous settings.

> **HOW TO: Hide the Form Button and the Developer Tab**

1. Click the **File** tab and select **Options**.
2. Click **Quick Access Toolbar** in the left pane.
3. Choose **Form** in the *Customize Quick Access Toolbar* list on the right.
4. Click **Remove**.
5. Click **Customize Ribbon** in the left pane.
6. Deselect the **Developer** box in the *Main Tabs* group.
7. Click **OK**.
 - The *Developer* tab is removed from the *Ribbon*.
 - The *Form* button is removed from the *Quick Access* toolbar.

> **SLO 7.4**

Setting Worksheet and Workbook Protection

Worksheet protection allows you to choose which cells can be edited. When you share work with others, worksheet protection safeguards your work from accidental changes by others. You can also prohibit changes to the size and position of workbook windows as well as not permit the addition or deletion of worksheets.

Worksheet Protection

Worksheet protection is a simple way to prevent changes to your work. When the *Protect Sheet* command is enabled, you can select a cell but you cannot edit it. If you attempt to edit a cell, you see an error message box as shown in Figure 7-26. Many *Ribbon* commands are grayed out when a worksheet is protected.

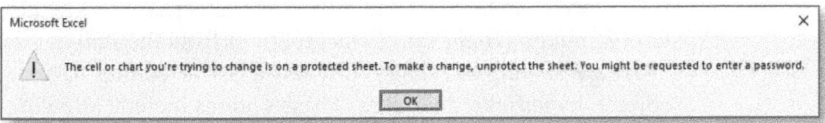

Microsoft Excel ×

⚠ The cell or chart you're trying to change is on a protected sheet. To make a change, unprotect the sheet. You might be requested to enter a password.

[OK]

7-26 Message box when cells are not editable

The *Protect Sheet* command works in conjunction with the ***Locked*** cell property which is active for all cells and objects by default. Setting worksheet protection requires you to determine which cells and objects should be unlocked for editing.

Unlock Worksheet Cells

After you have completed the template for Paradise Lakes, you do not want labels, images, product IDs, and descriptions to be changed. Data such as the number in stock and the price, however, can be edited. Cells that are editable must be unlocked before setting worksheet protection.

You can toggle the *Locked* property on and off from the *Format* button menu [*Home* tab, *Cells* group]. When a cell is locked, the icon with the *Locked* command name in the menu is outlined. The *Locked* property is also available on the *Protection* tab in the *Format Cells* dialog box.

▶ HOW TO: Unlock Cells for Editing

1. Select the cell(s) to be unlocked.
 - You can select noncontiguous cells or ranges.
2. Click the **Format** button [*Home* tab, *Cells* group].
 - The icon for *Lock Cell* is outlined to indicate that cells are locked (Figure 7-27).
 - All cells are locked by default.
3. Choose **Lock Cell**.
 - The selected cells are unlocked for editing.
4. Click the **Format** button [*Home* tab, *Cells* group].
 - The icon for *Lock Cell* is not outlined.
5. Click a cell to close the menu.

7-27 All cells are locked by default

MORE INFO

The *Locked* property should be enabled for formula cells in a protected sheet so that formulas are not accidentally changed or deleted.

Protect a Worksheet

The *Locked* property setting has no effect until you add worksheet protection. The *Protect Sheet* button is in the *Changes* group on the *Review* tab. The *Protect Sheet* button becomes the *Unprotect Sheet* button when a sheet is protected. You can also protect a worksheet from the *Format* button [*Home* tab, *Cells* group] or from the *Info* command on the *File* tab.

The *Protect Sheet* dialog box has a list of editing options for locked cells, *PivotTables*, objects, hyperlinks, and more. These options include allowing cells to be selected or formatted, permitting rows and columns to be modified, and allowing *PivotTables* to be used.

As you activate worksheet protection, you can set an optional password. Worksheet protection without a password is not very secure, because you only need know how to unprotect the sheet.

▶ HOW TO: Protect a Worksheet

1. Unlock cells as needed.
2. Click the **Protect Sheet** button [*Review* tab, *Changes* group].
 - The *Protect Sheet* dialog box opens.
3. Type a password, as desired.
 - You see placeholders as you type a password.

4. Select the box for each editing capability that should be available (Figure 7-28).

5. Click **OK**.

 - The *Confirm Password* dialog box opens if you set a password.

6. Retype the password.

 - Passwords are case sensitive.

7. Click **OK**.

 - The *Protect Sheet* button displays *Unprotect Sheet*.

7-28 *Protect Sheet* dialog box

> **MORE INFO**
>
> You cannot recover a lost or forgotten password without the use of a password recovery program.

Unprotect a Worksheet

Sheet protection must be removed to edit a protected sheet. Click the **Unprotect Sheet** button [*Review* tab, *Changes* group]. If a password was used, enter the password in the *Unprotect Sheet* dialog box and click **OK**.

> **HOW TO: Unprotect a Worksheet**

1. Click the **Unprotect Sheet** button [*Review* tab, *Changes* group].

 - Protection is removed if no password exists.
 - The *Unprotect Sheet* dialog box opens if a password exists.

2. Type the password.

3. Click **OK**.

Protect Workbook Structure

Workbook structure includes the number and arrangement of sheet tabs. By setting this protection, you can prohibit others from deleting or inserting a sheet, from moving a tab, or from unhiding a worksheet. When workbook protection is active, unavailable commands are grayed out or cannot be selected.

You can protect workbook structure with or without a password. You can remove workbook structure protection by clicking the **Protect Workbook** button [*File* tab].

> **ANOTHER WAY**
>
> You can set and remove workbook protection by clicking the *Protect Workbook* button [*Review* tab, *Changes* group].

▶**HOW TO:** Protect Workbook Structure

1. Arrange worksheet tabs and hide sheets as desired.
2. Click the **Protect Workbook** button [*Review* tab, *Changes* group].
 - The *Protect Structure and Windows* dialog box opens.
 - The *Windows* setting is disabled by default.
3. Verify that the **Structure** box is selected (Figure 7-29).
4. Type a password in the *Password* box.
 - A password is optional.
 - If you include a password, click **OK**, and retype it in the *Confirm Password* dialog box.
5. Click **OK** in the *Protect Structure and Windows* dialog box.
 - The **Protect Workbook** button [*Review* tab, *Changes* group] is highlighted.
6. Click the **File** tab.
 - The *Info* command describes the current protection setting.
7. Click the **Protect Workbook** button.
8. Select **Protect Workbook Structure**.
 - Enter the password if needed and click **OK**.
 - The protection is removed.

7-29 *Protect Structure and Windows* dialog box

PAUSE & PRACTICE: EXCEL 7-2

In this project, you create a workbook from a template and use a data input form. You add a combo box control, unlock cells, and set worksheet protection.

File Needed: *[your initials] PP E7-1Template.xltx*
Completed Project File Name: *[your initials] PP E7-2.xlsx*

1. Create a workbook from a template.
 a. Click the **File** tab and select **New**.
 b. Click **PERSONAL** (Figure 7-30).
 c. Select *[your initials] PP E7-1Template* completed in *Pause & Practice 7-1* to create a workbook based on the template. (If your template is not available in the *Personal* category, open it from your usual location for saving files.)
 d. Save the workbook as an Excel workbook named [your initials] PP E7-2 in your usual location.

2. Display the *Form* button and the *Developer* tab.
 a. Click the **Customize Quick Access Toolbar** arrow at the right edge of the *Quick Access* toolbar.
 b. Choose **More Commands** to open the *Excel Options* dialog box.
 c. Select **All Commands** in the *Choose commands from* list.
 d. Scroll to find **Form. . .** in the list and select it.
 e. Click **Add**.
 f. Click **Customize Ribbon** in the left pane.

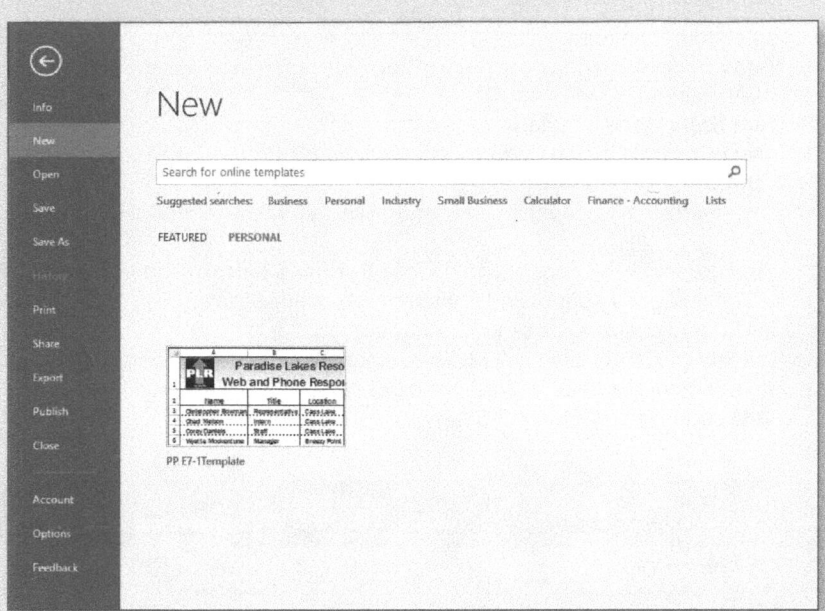

7-30 User-created templates are in the *PERSONAL* category

 g. Select the **Developer** box in the *Main Tabs* group.

 h. Click **OK**.

3. Verify that the **Responses** sheet is selected.

4. Create and use a data input form.

 a. Select cells **A2:E21**.

 b. Click the **Form** button on the *Quick Access* toolbar. The form displays the first of 19 records.

 c. Click **Find Next** in the data form. The second record (row) displays in the form.

 d. Click **Criteria** in the form to open a blank form.

 e. Type tam* in the *Name* box to find the record for Tammy Christine.

 f. Click **Find Next**. The record displays in the form.

 g. Click **Delete** and select **OK**. The record is deleted from the worksheet.

 h. Click **New** in the data form to display a blank form.

 i. Type John Jones in the *Name* box and press **Tab**. (If you accidentally press **Enter**, the form is completed. Click **Criteria**, type john*, and click **Find Next** to find the incomplete form.)

 j. Type Intern in the *Title* box and press **Tab**. Data validation settings do not function in a simple data form.

 k. Type Walker in the *Location* box and press **Tab**.

 l. Type 12 in the *Web* box and press **Tab**.

 m. Type 10 in the *Phone* box and press **Enter**. A new blank form opens, and data is added as the last row (Figure 7-31).

 n. Click **Close** to close the data form and press **Ctrl+Home**.

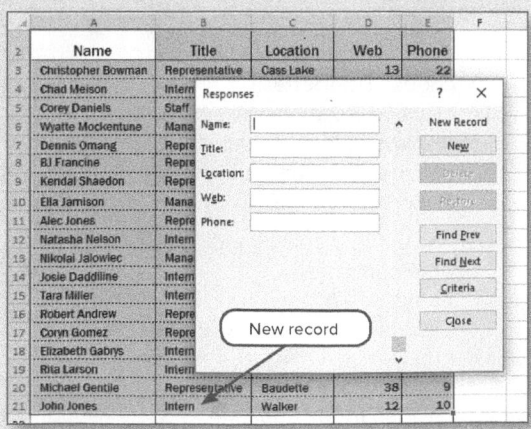

7-31 One record deleted and one added in the data form

5. Insert a combo box form control.
 a. Click the **Name** box arrow and choose **Location**. This range includes the four location names for Paradise Lakes Resort.
 b. Click the **Data Entry** worksheet tab.
 c. Click the **Insert Controls** button [*Developer* tab, *Controls* group].
 d. Click the **Combo Box (Form Control)** button.
 e. Draw a control directly over and the same width and height as cells **G2:H2** (Figure 7-32).
 f. Right-click any border of the control and choose **Format Control**. If the command is not listed, click a cell to deselect the control and right-click the control again.
 g. Type location in the *Input range* box on the *Control* tab.
 h. Click the **Cell link** box and select cell **I2**. The selection made in the combo box will display in this cell as a value to mark the relative position of the choice in the range.
 i. Select the **3-D shading** box (Figure 7-33).

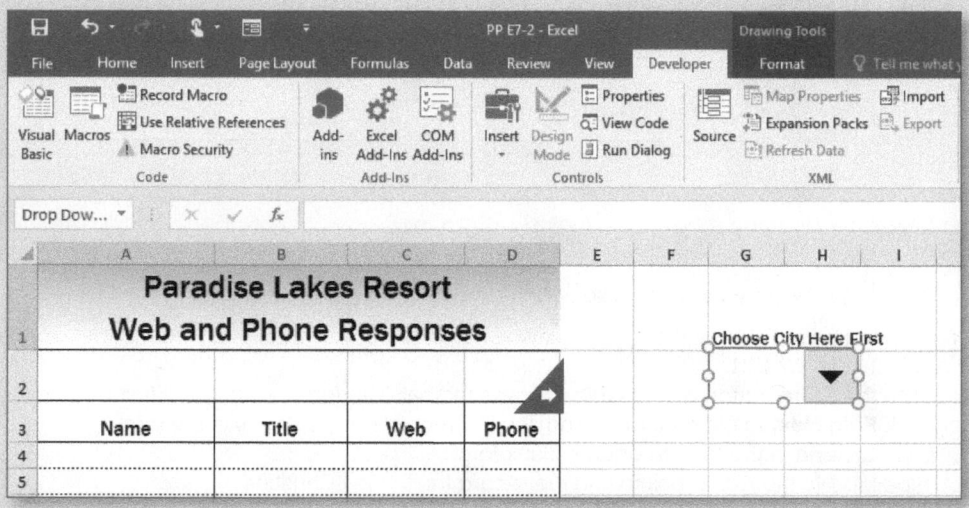

7-32 Combo box drawn on sheet

j. Click **OK**. Click cell **H3** to deselect the combo box control.
k. Click the **combo box** arrow and choose **Baudette**. The label displays in the control and **1** displays in the linked cell (I2), because Baudette is the first item in the input range.

6. Use *INDEX* to display the city name from the combo box.
 a. Select cell **A2**.
 b. Click the **Lookup & Reference** button [*Formulas* tab, *Function Library* group].
 c. Choose **Index** and choose the **array, row_num, column_num** argument group.

7-33 Combo box defined in *Format Control* dialog box

d. Press **F3** (**FN+F3**) and select **Location** for the *Array* argument.

e. Click the **Row_num** box, select cell **I2**, and click **OK**. The city name represented by the value in cell I2 displays in cell A2 and in the combo box.

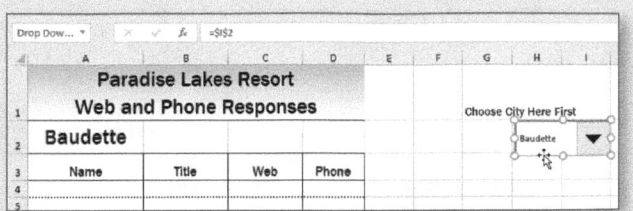

7-34 Combo box covers linked cell

f. Right-click the combo box control to display its context menu.

g. Point to a border of the control and left-click to hide the menu.

h. With the four-pointed move arrow, drag the control to cells **H2:I2** so that it covers the linked cell (Figure 7-34).

i. Deselect the control object.

j. Click the combo box arrow and choose **Cass Lake**.

7. Unlock cells and protect a sheet.
 a. Click the **Inventory** sheet tab.
 b. Select cells **C5:D29**.
 c. Click the **Format** button [*Home* tab, *Cells* group] and select **Lock Cell**. Data in columns C and D are unlocked and editable.
 d. Select cell **A5**.
 e. Click the **Protect Sheet** button [*Review* tab, *Changes* group].
 f. Verify that the **Select locked cells** and **Select unlocked cells** boxes are selected.
 g. Click **OK**.

8. Protect workbook structure.
 a. Right-click the **Validation Lists** sheet tab and choose **Hide**.
 b. Click the **File** tab and choose **Info**.
 c. Click the **Protect Workbook** button and select **Protect Workbook Structure**.
 d. Click **OK** to protect the structure without a password.

9. Save and close the workbook (Figure 7-35).

10. Move the template from the default folder and hide the **Form** button and the *Developer* tab.
 a. Click the **File** tab and choose **Open**.
 b. Click **Browse**.

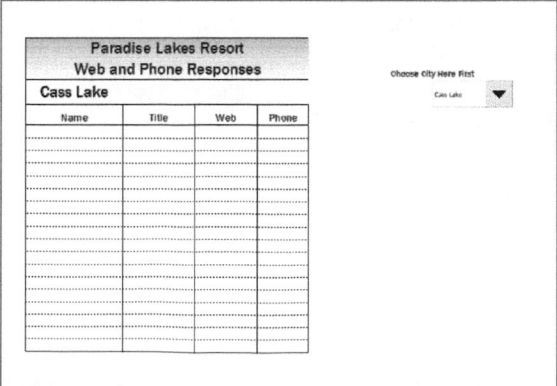

Name	Title	Location	Web	Phone
Paradise Lakes Resort				
Web and Phone Responses				
Christopher Bowman	Representative	Cass Lake	13	22
Chad Meison	Intern	Cass Lake	26	7
Corey Daniels	Staff	Cass Lake	18	23
Wyatte Mockentune	Manager	Breezy Point	25	19
Dennis Omang	Representative	Breezy Point	22	16
BJ Francine	Representative	Baudette	32	8
Kendal Shaedon	Representative	Breezy Point	5	22
Ella Jamison	Manager	Baudette	44	10
Alec Jones	Representative	Baudette	26	18
Natasha Nelson	Intern	Baudette	0	23
Nikolai Jalowiec	Manager	Walker	26	20
Josie Daddiline	Intern	Walker	1	21
Tara Miller	Intern	Breezy Point	32	17
Robert Andrew	Representative	Walker	15	10
Coryn Gomez	Representative	Baudette	35	5
Elizabeth Gabrys	Intern	Cass Lake	43	9
Rita Larson	Intern	Walker	0	36
Michael Gentile	Representative	Baudette	38	9
John Jones	Intern	Walker	12	10

7-35 Completed worksheets for PP E7-2

c. Expand the *Quick access* list in the left pane and select **Documents**.
d. Double-click **Custom Office Templates** in the pane on the right.
e. Right-click ***[your initials] PP E7-1Template*** and choose **Cut**.
f. Navigate to and open your folder for saving files.
g. Right-click an unused area of the *Open* dialog box and choose **Paste**.
h. Click **Cancel** to close the dialog box.
i. Click the **File** tab and choose **Options**.
j. Click **Customize Ribbon** in the left pane and deselect the **Developer** box in the *Main Tabs* group.
k. Click **Quick Access Toolbar** in the left pane.
l. Click **Form . . .** on the right and click **Remove**.
m. Click **OK**.

SLO 7.5

Sharing and Merging Workbooks

A ***shared workbook*** is one that multiple people edit, either simultaneously or at different times. When a shared workbook is maintained on a network and all users have access to it, each person can work on it as needed. In other cases, a shared workbook is copied so that each user has his or her own copy. After all members of the work group have completed their work, the copies are combined into a merged workbook.

Paradise Lakes Resort can use a shared workbook for inventory or customer management. As representatives work from various locations, they record their own data, and all copies are merged to create a final report with the latest data.

Not all commands are available in a shared workbook such as deleting sheets, merging cells, inserting or editing charts, setting conditional formatting or data validation, setting worksheet protection, and using passwords. Most of these tasks, however, can be completed before the workbook is shared.

Share a Workbook

When a workbook is shared, any user who has access permission can edit it. Most shared workbooks are stored on a network so that editing is live. When that is not possible, each person in the work group simply makes a copy of the workbook.

One person shares the workbook and is considered the "owner." When a workbook is shared, the word *[Shared]* appears after the file name in the title bar. As you edit a shared workbook, the user name of the computer identifies each change.

The *Share Workbook* dialog box has two tabs, *Editing* and *Advanced*. On the *Editing* tab, you indicate that the workbook is to be shared (Figure 7-36). The *Advanced* tab includes settings that determine how changes are tracked. You can set the number of days that edits are kept, when edits are saved, and what happens if two users make conflicting edits at

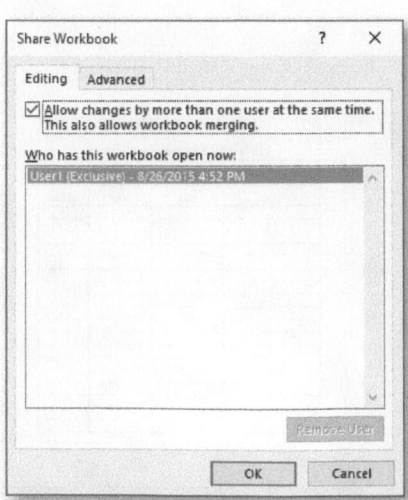

7-36 *Editing* tab in the *Share Workbook* dialog box

the same time. A shared workbook maintains a ***change history***, a record of each edit. This history includes the name of the user, the date, and a brief description of the change. When multiple copies of a shared workbook are combined, the change history helps you decide which changes should be accepted for the final report.

> **MORE INFO**
>
> Set the change history to ensure enough time for all users to complete their work.

▶HOW TO: Share a Workbook

1. Click the **Share Workbook** button [*Review* tab, *Changes* group].
2. Select the **Allow changes by more than one user at the same time** box on the *Editing* tab.
 - The user name is shown as the person who has the workbook open.
3. Click the **Advanced** tab (Figure 7-37).
4. Set the number of days for keeping the change history in the *Track changes* group.
 - You can also indicate that the change history not be kept.
5. Choose how often edits are saved in the *Update changes* group.
 - You can save edits only when the file is saved.
 - If you set an automatic save at a specific time interval, you can further manage changes.
6. Choose how to handle conflicts in the *Conflicting changes between users* group.
 - You can review each conflicting edit to accept or reject it.
 - You can keep only those edits being saved by you.
 - The *Include in personal view* group enables each user to save print and filter choices for the workbook.
7. Click **OK**.
 - The message box notes that the workbook will be saved, using the same file name.
8. Click **OK**.
 - The file name in the title bar displays **[Shared]**.
 - If a shared workbook has features that are not editable, a pop-up window may alert you to that information.

7-37 Advanced tab in the *Share Workbook* dialog box

Protect a Shared Workbook

When you protect a shared workbook, no user can delete the change history. If the number of days set in the *Advanced* tab of the *Share Workbook* window has been reached and you have not added this protection, the change history is deleted and you will not be able to combine individual copies of the workbook into a final report.

The *Protect Shared Workbook* button is on the *Review* tab in the *Changes* group. It is a toggle that shows *Unprotect Shared Workbook* when protection is active.

▶ **HOW TO:** **Protect a Shared Workbook**

1. Click the **Protect Shared Workbook** button [*Review* tab, *Changes* group].

 • The *Protect Shared Workbook* dialog box opens.

2. Select the **Sharing with track changes** box (Figure 7-38).

 • You can encrypt a workbook with a password before sharing it.

3. Click **OK**.

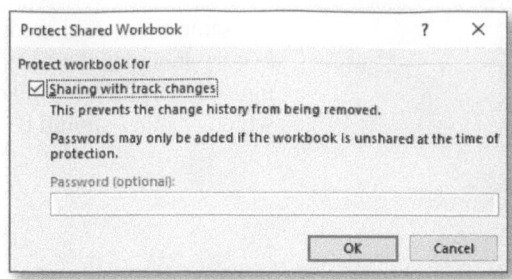

7-38 *Protect Shared Workbook* dialog box

Insert Comments

A ***comment*** is a pop-up text box attached to a cell (Figure 7-39). A default comment is automatically inserted in a shared workbook for each edit. You can insert your own comments, too, for clarification or discussion. Comments are useful when you or a member of your team wants to add an explanation or ask a question.

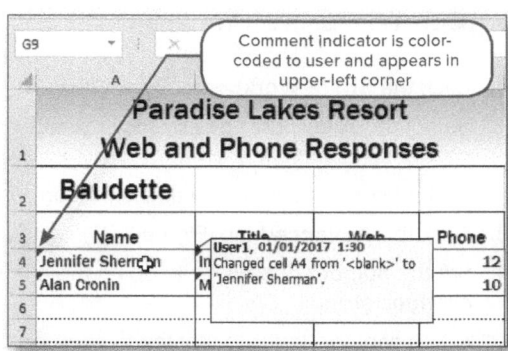

7-39 A comment is attached for each edit in a shared workbook

You insert comments from the *Review* tab or from a cell's context menu. After you add a comment to a cell, a small red triangle (called an ***indicator***) appears in the upper-right corner of the cell. To view the comment, hover the pointer over a cell with an indicator.

▶ **ANOTHER WAY**

Display all comments in a sheet by clicking the *Show All Comments* button on the *Review* tab.

Open the Excel *Options* and select the **Advanced** tab. Scroll to the *Display* group and set whether comments display or if only the indicator displays in the cell. You can also display or hide comments from the *Review* tab.

▶ **MORE INFO**

Comments do not print by default. Choose the option to print them on the *Sheet* tab in the *Page Setup* dialog box.

After a comment is created, you can edit or delete it by selecting the cell and the desired command on the *Review* tab. You can also execute comment-related commands by right-clicking the comment cell and choosing from the context menu.

▶ HOW TO: Insert a Comment

1. Select the cell for the comment.
2. Click the **New Comment** button [*Review* tab, *Comments* group].
 - A comment box opens and displays the user name.
 - You can delete or replace the user name.
3. Type the text of the comment (Figure 7-40).
4. Click any cell away from the comment cell.
5. Click the **Show All Comments** button [*Review* tab, *Comments* group] to toggle on/off the display of all comments in the worksheet.
 - A small red triangle displays in the upper-right corner of the cell with the comment.
6. View the comment by hovering the pointer over the cell.

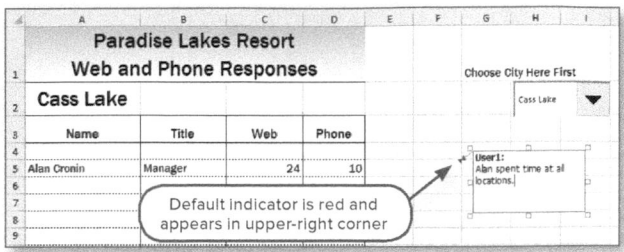

7-40 Comment text for a user-defined comment

Compare and Merge Workbooks

When multiple copies of a shared workbook exist, the copies are combined using the *Compare and Merge Workbooks* command to create a final report. Here are the requirements for workbooks to be merged:

- The original shared workbook must have the change history active.
- Each copy must have been made from the original shared workbook.
- Each copy must have a different file name and cannot have a password.

Customize the *Quick Access* toolbar to add the *Compare and Merge Workbooks* button or add the button to a custom group on the *Ribbon*.

▶ HOW TO: Compare and Merge Workbooks

1. Click the **File** tab and choose **Options**.
2. Click **Quick Access Toolbar** in the left pane.
3. Choose **All Commands** from the *Choose commands from* list.
4. Select **Compare and Merge Workbooks** from the list.
5. Click **Add** to add the command to the *Customize Quick Access Toolbar* list.
6. Click **OK**.
 - The **Compare and Merge Workbooks** button appears on the right of the *Quick Access* toolbar (Figure 7-41).
7. Open the original shared workbook.
8. Click the **Compare and Merge Workbooks** button.
9. Click **OK** to save the workbook.
 - The *Select Files to Merge into Current Workbook* dialog box opens.

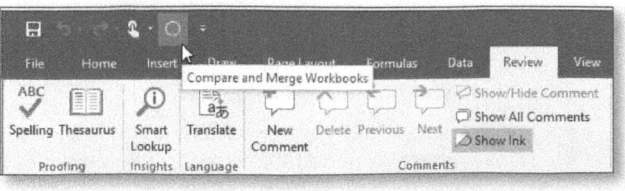

7-41 *Compare and Merge Workbooks*
button on the *Quick Access* toolbar

10. Navigate to the folder with the first file to be merged and select the file name (Figure 7-42).

 - You can select multiple files from the same folder using the **Ctrl** key.

11. Click **OK**.

 - If a workbook has no changes, you see a notification message box.

12. Click the **File** tab and choose **Options**.

13. Click **Quick Access Toolbar** in the left pane.

14. Choose **Compare and Merge Workbooks** on the right.

15. Click **Remove** and then click **OK**.

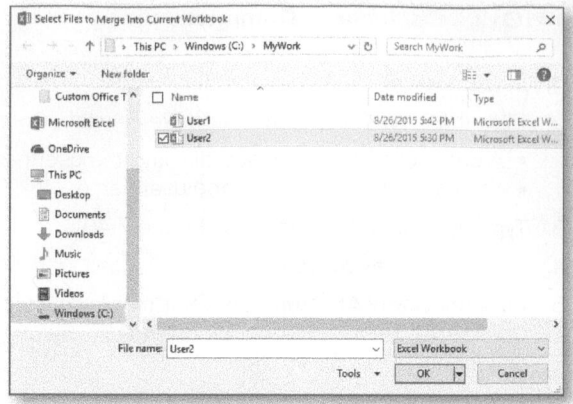

7-42 *Select Files to Merge into Current Workbook* dialog box

Highlight Changes

After a workbook has been shared or merged, you can track changes to accept or reject edits. Each user's edits are highlighted by colored cell borders and triangles in the upper left corners. A comment box displays for each change and identifies the user name and the edit. To see the comment, click a highlighted cell.

In the *Highlight Changes* dialog box, you specify which changes should be highlighted. The *When* setting provides options that include seeing all edits or edits made since a particular date. The *Who* option can be set to show changes by everyone including you, by everyone else, or by a specific user. The *Where* setting is used to select a range of cells for review rather than the entire worksheet.

You can choose to see the changes on screen or in a printed change history sheet. The history sheet is a generated sheet that is automatically deleted when the workbook is saved.

> ▶**HOW TO:** Highlight Changes in a Shared Workbook

1. Click the **Track Changes** button [*Review* tab, *Changes* group].

2. Choose **Highlight Changes** (Figure 7-43).

 - The *Highlight Changes* dialog box opens.
 - Verify that the **Track changes while editing** box is selected.

3. Verify that the **When** box is selected.

 - You can use *When*, *Who*, and *Where* or just one of these categories.

4. Click the **When** arrow and select an option.

 - *Not yet reviewed* shows all edits that you have not seen.

5. Select the **Who** box and click its arrow.

 - Choose *Everyone* to review edits by all users.
 - Choose a user name to review only those edits.

6. Select the **Where** box to limit highlighted edits to a cell range.

 - Select the range in the worksheet or type the range address.

7-43 *Highlight Changes* dialog box

7. Verify that the **Highlight changes on screen** box is selected.

 • You can print the change history by selecting the *List changes on a new sheet* box.

8. Click **OK**.

 • If there are no edits, click **OK** to close the message box.

9. Hover at a cell with a revision triangle to see a description of the edit.

Accept or Reject Changes

The *Accept or Reject Changes* command opens a dialog box for each change, and you choose to accept or reject the edit. If you reject a change, the data is reset to the original content. When there have been multiple edits to the same cell, the *Accept or Reject Changes* dialog box lists each change so that you can select one to accept or keep the original value.

▶**HOW TO: Accept or Reject Changes in a Shared Workbook**

1. Click the **Track Changes** button [*Review* tab, *Changes* group].

2. Choose **Accept/Reject Changes**.

 • If the workbook has not yet been saved, you must save it.
 • The *Select Changes to Accept or Reject* dialog box is similar to the *Highlight Changes* dialog box.

3. Click the **When** arrow and choose **Not yet reviewed**.

4. Click **OK**.

 • The first change is detailed in the *Accept or Reject Changes* dialog box (Figure 7-44).
 • If there are multiple edits for the cell, the changes are listed in the dialog box.

5. Click **Accept** to accept the edit and move to the next edit.

 • Click **Accept All** to accept all changes in the workbook without further review.

6. Click **Reject** to reject the edit and move to the next edit.

 • Click **Reject All** to reject all changes without further review.
 • The dialog box closes after all edits have been accepted or rejected.

7. Save the workbook.

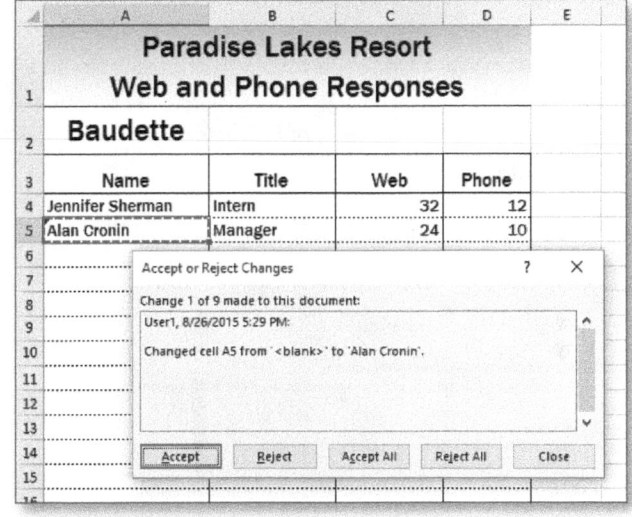

7-44 Each edit is shown in the *Accept or Reject Changes* dialog box

Checking a Workbook for Distribution Issues

Before distributing a workbook to clients or coworkers, you can ensure that the workbook does not include properties that should not be shared and that the workbook is compatible with all Excel versions. There is even a command to gauge how much of your work is accessible for persons with visual impairment.

Inspect a Workbook

The **Inspect Document** command looks for metadata and personal information in a workbook. **Metadata** are embedded file properties such as user name and date at the time of creation, the original file location, and user comments. Some metadata can be removed. For example, if you insert comments for your team members while working on a shared workbook, you can remove those comments before a customer sees the workbook. The **Document Inspector** is the dialog box that lists properties and data that can be removed.

▶ **HOW TO: Inspect a Workbook**

1. Click the **Check for Issues** button [*File* tab].
2. Choose **Inspect Document**.
3. Click **Yes** to save the workbook.

 - The *Document Inspector* lists categories of content that can be searched (Figure 7-45).
 - All categories are selected by default.
 - Deselect the box for any category that should not be searched.

4. Click **Inspect**.

 - The *Document Inspector* identifies what is included in the workbook.
 - Not all metadata can be removed.

5. Click **Remove All** for each category of content to be cleared (Figure 7-46).

 - You can close the dialog box to review content that needs further investigation.
 - You can run the *Document Inspector* again when needed.

6. Click **Close**.

7-45 *Document Inspector* dialog box

7-46 *Document Inspector* dialog box after inspection

After you run the *Document Inspector*, a workbook property is assigned to automatically remove that metadata each time you save the file. This property can interfere with commands such as sharing a workbook. You can disable the property by clicking *Allow this information to be saved in your file* in the *Check for Issues* group in *Backstage* view.

Check Compatibility

The **Check Compatibility** command opens the *Compatibility Checker* which identifies commands, features, and objects that are not supported in earlier versions of Excel. For example, early versions of Excel did not have *SmartArt* graphics. Several Excel 2016 functions do not work in earlier versions of Excel, and select formatting features are not compatible.

The *Compatibility Checker* gives you an opportunity to edit incompatible data or objects before you save the workbook in a different file format. A few issues are significant but most are minor. When you save a workbook in Excel 97-2003 format, the *Compatibility Checker* automatically runs to alert you to potential issues. You can run the command, however, for any workbook at any time.

▶ HOW TO: Check Compatibility

1. Click the **Check for Issues** button [*File* tab].
2. Choose **Check Compatibility**.
 - The *Compatibility Checker* describes each unsupported feature (Figure 7-47).
 - Click **Select versions to show** to choose a particular Excel version.
 - The dialog box can be sized or scrolled to view all issues.
3. Click **Copy to New Sheet** to create a sheet that details the issues.
 - A new sheet named **Compatibility Report** displays and provides documentation.
 - This command is unavailable in a shared workbook.
4. If you do not copy the issues to a new sheet, click **OK**.
 - The features are unchanged and you can save the workbook in the desired format.
 - Run the *Compatibility Checker* again when needed.

7-47 The *Compatibility Checker* locates unsupported features

Define a Trusted Location

Workbooks with data from a questionable source open in **Protected View** so that you can confirm that you trust the document and its source. Workbooks from the Web open in *Protected View* as do workbooks with macros and *ActiveX* controls.

A **Trusted Location** is a folder that is identified as one that stores workbooks that are safe. When you open a workbook from a trusted location, it does not open in *Protected View* and you can avoid the protected view message. Trusted locations are identified in the *Trust Center* in the Excel *Options* dialog box.

▶ HOW TO: Define a Trusted Location

1. Choose the **Options** command [*File* tab].
2. Choose **Trust Center** in the left pane.
 - The initial dialog box explains Microsoft security features.

3. Click **Trust Center Settings**.
 - The left pane lists security categories.

4. Select **Trusted Locations** in the left pane.
 - Trusted folders for your computer are listed.

5. Click **Add new location**.

6. Click **Browse** (Figure 7-48).

7. Locate the folder to be trusted, select its name, and click **OK**.
 - Type the path to the folder if you prefer.

8. Select the **Subfolders of this location are also trusted** box.

9. Click the **Description** box.
 - Type an optional description for the folder (Figure 7-49).

10. Click **OK** to add the folder to the list of trusted locations.

11. Click **OK** to close the **Trust Center**.

12. Click **OK** to close the Excel *Options* dialog box.

7-48 *Trust Center* options

7-49 Trusted folder description

PAUSE & PRACTICE: EXCEL 7-3

In this project, you inspect a workbook, check it for compatibility, and share it. You make edits as different users and insert comments. Finally, you merge the workbooks to accept or reject the changes.

File Needed: *[your initials] PP E7-2.xlsx*
Completed Project File Names: *[your initials] PP E7-3User1.xlsx*, *[your initials] PP E7-3User2.xlsx*, and *[your initials] PP E7-3Merged.xlsx*

1. Open the *[your initials] PP E7-2* workbook completed in *Pause & Practice 7-2* and save it as [your initials] PP E7-3User1.

2. Inspect the workbook and remove sheet and structure protection.
 a. Click the **Check for Issues** button [*File* tab, *Info* group] and choose **Inspect Document**. The message box notes that you cannot inspect a workbook that has protected sheets (Figure 7-50).
 b. Click **OK** in the message box.

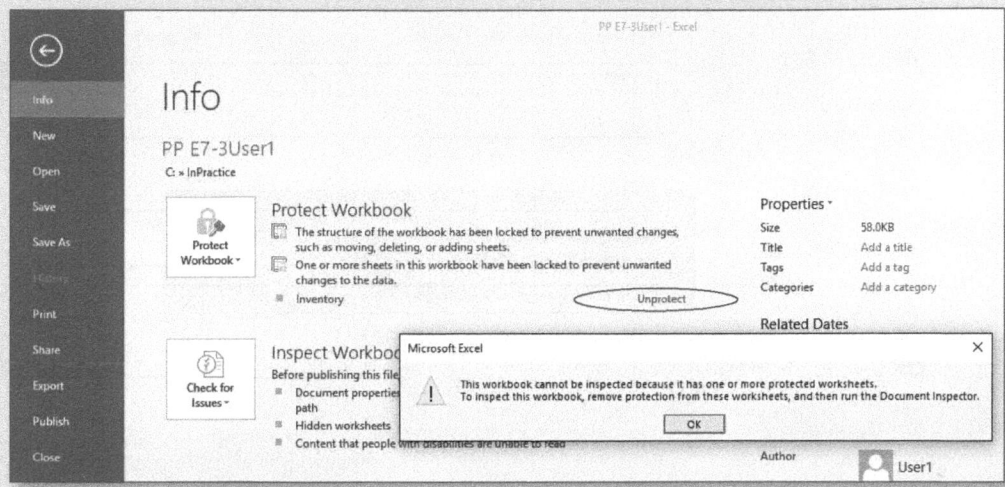

7-50 Workbook with sheet protection cannot be inspected

 c. Click **Unprotect** in the *Protect Workbook* group.
 d. Click the **Check for Issues** button and choose **Inspect Document**.
 e. Select **Yes** to save the workbook without sheet protection.
 f. Click **Inspect**. Properties and personal information that can be removed are noted.
 g. Click **Remove All** for *Document Properties and Personal Information*.
 h. Scroll the list to see the *Hidden Worksheets* tag but do not remove the sheets.
 i. Click **Close**.
 j. Click the **File** tab. Note in the *Inspect Workbook* group that personal information will be removed each time this workbook is saved (Figure 7-51).
 k. Click **Allow this information to be saved in your file**. This property must be disabled in order to share the workbook.
 l. Click the **Protect Workbook** button and select **Protect Workbook Structure**.

3. Check compatibility.
 a. Click the **Check for Issues** button [*File* tab, *Info* group] and choose **Check Compatibility**.

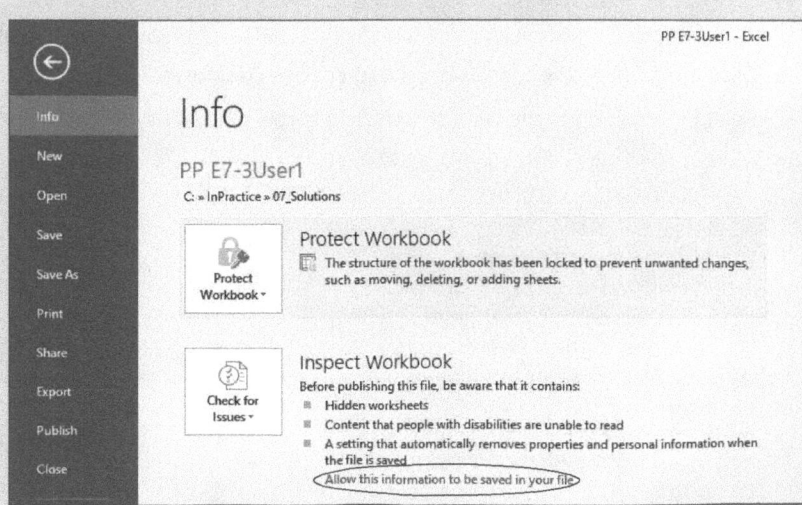

7-51 Setting changed after removing metadata

b. Review the issues in the *Compatibility Checker* dialog box.

c. Click **Copy to New Sheet**. The report displays on its own sheet (Figure 7-52).

4. Share the workbook.
a. Select the **Data Entry** sheet tab.
b. Click the **Share Workbook** button [*Review* tab, *Changes* category]. You cannot share a workbook that has an Excel table.
c. Click **OK** in the message box.
d. Click the **Guests** worksheet tab and click any cell in the table.
e. Click the **Convert to Range** button [*Table Tools Design* tab, *Tools* group].
f. Click **Yes** to convert the table to a range.
g. Select the **Data Entry** tab and click the **Share Workbook** button [*Review* tab, *Changes* category].
h. Select the **Allow changes by more than one user at the same time** box.
i. Click the **Advanced** tab.
j. Set the *Keep change history for* option to **25** days.
k. Click **OK** to close the *Share Workbook* dialog box.
l. Click **OK** to resave the shared workbook. Look for *[Shared]* at the end of the file name in the title bar.
m. Select cell **A4**.

	A	B	C	D	E	F	G
1	Compatibility Report for PP E7-3User1.xlsx						
2	Run on 3/1/2017 13:41						
3							
4	If the workbook is saved in an earlier file format or opened in an earlier version of Microsoft Excel, the listed features will not be available.						
5							
6	Significant loss of functionality				# of occurrences	Version	
7							
8	Some cells in this workbook contain data validation rules, which refer to values on other worksheets. These rules won't be saved.				1		
9					Inventory' IC5:C2	Excel 97-2003	
10							
11							
12	Minor loss of fidelity						
13							
14	Some cells or styles in this workbook contain formatting that is not supported by the selected file format. These formats will be converted to the closest format available.				33	Excel 97-2003	
15							
16	One or more cells in this workbook contain data validation rules which refer to values on other worksheets. These data validation rules will not be supported in earlier versions of Excel.				1		
17					Inventory' IC5:C2	Excel 2007	
18							
19							
20							

Inventory | Responses | Guests | Data Entry | Compatibility Report | ⊕

7-52 Documentation for unsupported commands and features

5. Make a copy of the shared workbook in the same folder.
a. Click the **File** tab and choose **Save As**.
b. Save the workbook as [your initials] PP E7-3User2 in your usual folder.

6. Click the combo box control arrow and choose **Baudette**.

7. Select cell **A4**. Enter the data shown here in row 4. Use the validation list to select the title.

Jennifer Sherman Intern 32 12

8. Insert a comment.
a. Select cell **F4**.
b. Click the **New Comment** button [*Review* tab, *Comments* group].
c. Select the default user named, type User 2:, and press **Enter**.
d. Type Jennifer spent two days in Baudette. (Figure 7-53).
e. Select cell **F3**. If the comment still displays, click the **Show All Comments** button [*Review* tab, *Comments* group] to hide it. It appears when you hover over the cell.

7-53 New comments inserted for cell F4

9. Save the workbook in your usual location and close it.

10. Open *[your initials] PP E7-3User1.xlsx*.

11. Click the combo box control arrow and choose **Walker**.

12. Click cell **A5** and type the following data:

 Alan Cronin Manager 24 10

13. Insert a comment.
 a. Select cell **F5**.
 b. Click the **New Comment** button [*Review* tab, *Comments* group].
 c. Select the default user named, type User 1:, and press **Enter**.
 d. Type Alan spent time at all locations.
 e. Select cell **F3**.

14. Save the workbook. This is the original shared workbook.

15. Add the *Compare and Merge Workbooks* command to the *Quick Access* toolbar.
 a. Select cell **A1**.
 b. Select the **Options** command [*File* tab].
 c. Click **Quick Access Toolbar** in the left pane.
 d. Choose **All Commands** from the *Choose commands from* list.
 e. Select **Compare and Merge Workbooks** and click **Add**.
 f. Click **OK**.

16. Merge copies of the shared workbook.
 a. Click the **Compare and Merge Workbooks** button on the *Quick Access* toolbar. If asked, click **OK** to save the workbook before merging.
 b. Navigate to the folder with *[your initials] PP E7-3User2* in the *Select Files to Merge Into Current Workbook* dialog box.
 c. Click the *[your initials] PP E7-3User2* file name and click **OK**. The copied workbook is merged into the workbook on screen. Cells with typed comments are indicated by a red triangle in the upper-right corner of the cell.
 d. Point to cell **F4** and then to cell **F5** to see the comments.

17. Highlight changes.
 a. Click the **Track Changes** button [*Review* tab, *Changes* group].
 b. Choose **Highlight Changes**.
 c. Choose **Not yet reviewed** for the *When* command.
 d. Click **OK**. Cells with changes display a triangle in the upper-left corner.
 e. Point to cell **D5** to see the generated comment (Figure 7-54).

7-54 All cells with changes include a triangle

18. Accept or reject changes.
 a. Click the **Track Changes** button [*Review* tab, *Changes* group].
 b. Choose **Accept/Reject Changes**.
 c. Choose **Not yet reviewed** for the *When* box.
 d. Click **OK**. The first change was the combo box selection; the linked cell for this control is cell **I2** (Figure 7-55).

7-55 First edit is identified

e. Click **3 (Original Value)** and click **Accept**. The value in cell **A2** is reset to Cass Lake, but the control is not reset until you complete the current task. The next change is the addition of a person's name in cell **A5**.

f. Click **Accept All** to accept all edits. The dialog box closes, and the combo box control is updated.

19. Save the merged workbook as *[your initials] PP E7-3Merged* and close it (Figure 7-56).

20. Remove the *Compare and Merge Workbooks* button from the *Quick Access* toolbar.
 a. Click the **Options** command [*File* tab].
 b. Click **Quick Access Toolbar** in the left pane.
 c. Click **Compare and Merge Workbooks** in the list on the right.
 d. Click **Remove** and click **OK**.

Paradise Lakes Resort Web and Phone Responses				Choose City Here First
Cass Lake				Cass Lake ▼
Name	**Title**	**Web**	**Phone**	
Jennifer Sherman	Intern	32	12	
Alan Cronin	Manager	24	10	

7-56 Completed worksheet for PP E7-3Merged

Chapter Summary

7.1 Use a template to create a workbook and save a workbook as a template (p. E7-435).

- A *template* is a model workbook that can include data, formulas, formatting, controls, and more.
- Templates are available from the *New* pane in *Backstage* view.
- Excel templates are saved in a default folder which can be changed in the *Save* pane, Excel *Options*.
- Templates saved in the default folder are listed in the *Personal* category in the *Backstage* view.
- Template workbooks have an .xltx file name extension.
- Templates are often saved with a thumbnail image, set in the *Save As* dialog box.
- When you create a workbook from a template, a new workbook opens as a copy of the template.

7.2 Set data validation, input messages, and error alerts (p. E7-437).

- *Data validation* is the process of matching data with specifications as the data is entered.
- *Validation settings* are rules applied to data as it is entered.
- Data validation settings can be statements with relational operators, choices made from lists, limits set on dates or times, or a formula.
- An *input message* is a comment box that appears as soon as a cell is selected, informing the user about the validation rule.
- An *error alert* is a comment box that appears when invalid data is entered in a cell, and the type of alert determines whether the entry is allowed.
- If data validation is set after data has been entered, you can use the *Circle Invalid Data* command to identify those cells.

7.3 Use the *Form* button and *Form Controls* (p. E7-443).

- The *Form* button creates a data entry form in a vertical arrangement for data.
- You can enter, delete, and filter data in a data form.
- The *Form* button must be added to the *Quick Access* toolbar or to a custom group on the *Ribbon*.

- A *form control* is an object or shape used to make a selection or to run a command in a worksheet.
- Form controls include option buttons, combo boxes, check boxes, and list boxes.
- The *Developer* tab on the *Ribbon* includes the *Controls* group.
- The *Developer* tab can be shown or hidden by opening the Excel *Options* dialog box and selecting the *Customize Ribbon* pane.

7.4 Set worksheet and workbook protection to manage editing (p. E7-448).

- The *Protect Sheet* command prohibits changes to cells unless they have been unlocked.
- The *Locked* property is enabled for all cells but has no effect unless the *Protect Sheet* command is applied.
- Cells that are editable must be unlocked before the worksheet is protected.
- *Worksheet protection* can be set with or without a password.
- The *Protect Workbook Structure* command allows a user to edit data but not move, copy, delete, insert, hide, or unhide sheets.

7.5 Share a workbook, track changes, and compare and merge workbooks (p. E7-455).

- A *shared workbook* is a workbook that is edited by multiple users, either at the same time on a network, or separately using individual copies of the workbook.
- Each copy must have been made from the original shared workbook and have a unique file name.
- When you share a workbook, you can set how long changes are tracked, when changes are saved, and how conflicts are resolved.
- The *Share Workbook* command maintains a *change history* for each user.
- When users have individual copies of the shared workbook, the copies are merged into a final workbook.
- The *Compare and Merge Workbooks* button must be displayed on the *Quick Access* toolbar or in a custom group in the *Ribbon*.
- In a shared or merged workbook, you can highlight, accept, or reject changes as you are working or after copies are combined.

- Changes can be highlighted in the worksheet or printed on a separate sheet.
- Each cell in a shared workbook that was edited has a **comment**, a pop-up text box that describes the change.
- You can insert a comment with a descriptive or explanatory message in any cell.

7.6 Inspect a workbook for metadata, check compatibility, and define a trusted location (p. E7-460).

- The **Inspect Document** command locates metadata and personal information that can be removed from the file.
- The **Check Compatibility** command identifies features, commands, and objects that might not work properly in an earlier version of Excel.
- The *Inspect Document* and *Check Compatibility* commands can be run as many times as necessary for a workbook.

- A **trusted location** is a folder that contains secure, safe workbooks that do not open in *Protected View*.
- You can define a folder as a trusted location in the *Trust Center* from the Excel *Options* dialog box.

Check for Understanding

The SIMbook for this text (within your SIMnet account) provides the following resources for concept review:

- Multiple choice questions
- Matching exercises
- Short answer questions

USING MICROSOFT EXCEL 2016

Guided Project 7-1

In this project, you develop a template for group instructors at Sierra Pacific Community College District (SPCCD). You create data validation with input and error messages and insert a form control. After inspecting the workbook and checking compatibility, you share the workbook.
[Student Learning Outcomes 7.1, 7.2, 7.3, 7.4, 7.5, 7.6]

File Needed: ***SierraPacific-07.xlsx*** *(Student data files are available in the* Library *of your SIMnet account)*
Completed Project File Names: *[your initials]* ***Excel 7-1Template.xltx,*** *[your initials]* ***Excel 7-1User1.xlsx,***
[your initials] ***Excel 7-1User2.xlsx,*** and *[your initials]* ***Excel 7-1Merged.xlsx***

Skills Covered in this Project

- Set data validation with an error alert.
- Set data validation with an input message.
- Insert an option button control.
- Inspect a workbook.
- Check compatibility.
- Add worksheet and workbook protection.
- Save a workbook as a template.
- Create a workbook from a template.
- Share a workbook and track changes.

1. Open the ***SierraPacific-07*** workbook from your student data files.

2. Save the workbook as a template.
 a. Click the **File** tab and select **Save As**.
 b. Choose **This PC** and click the **More options** link.
 c. Type the file name [your initials] Excel 7-1Template in the *File name* box.
 d. Verify that the **Save Thumbnail** box is selected or select it.
 e. Choose **Excel Template** from the *Save as type* drop-down box. The default templates folder opens.
 f. Click **Save**.

3. Set data validation for a range.
 a. Select cells **C5:C29**.
 b. Click the **Data Validation** button [*Data* tab, *Data Tools* group] and verify that the **Settings** tab is selected.
 c. Click the **Allow** arrow and choose **Decimal**.
 d. Verify that the *Data* option displays **between**.
 e. Type .1 for the *Minimum* and 20 for the *Maximum*.
 f. Do not click **OK**.

4. Create an error message for data validation settings.
 a. Click the **Error Alert** tab.
 b. Verify that the **Show error alert after invalid data is entered** box is selected.
 c. Click the **Style** arrow and choose **Warning** to allow an invalid entry.
 d. Click the **Title** box and type Class Points.
 e. Click the **Error message** box and type Enter a value between 0.1 and 20.
 f. Click **OK**.
 g. Select cell **C5**, type 21 and press **Enter** to display the error alert (Figure 7-57).
 h. Click **Cancel** to keep the current value.

5. Set data validation with an input message.
 a. Select cells **D5:D29** and click the **Data Validation** button [*Data* tab, *Data Tools* group].
 b. Click the **Allow** arrow and choose **Decimal** on the *Settings* tab.
 c. Verify that **between** is the *Data* option.
 d. Click the **Minimum** box and type 50.
 e. Enter 100 for the *Maximum*.
 f. Click the **Input Message** tab.
 g. Verify that the **Show input message when cell is selected** box is selected.
 h. Click the **Title** box and type Project Points.
 i. Click the **Input message** box and type Enter a value between 50 and 100.
 j. Click **OK**.

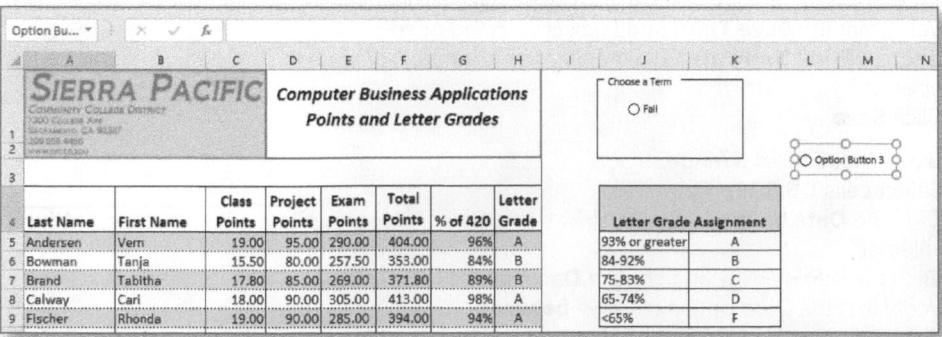

7-57 Error alert for invalid data

6. Select cells **E5:E29** and set data validation to limit the entry to any decimal number between 150 and 300. Do not use an input or error alert message.

7. Display the *Developer* tab on the *Ribbon* if it is not shown.
 a. Click the **Options** button [*File* tab] and click **Customize Ribbon** in the left pane.
 b. Select the **Developer** box in the *Main Tabs* group on the right and click **OK**.

8. Insert an option button form control.
 a. Click the **Insert Controls** button [*Developer* tab, *Controls* group] and select the **Option Button (Form Control)** button.
 b. Draw a control that covers cells **L3:M3** (Figure 7-58).

7-58 New option button form control

 c. Right-click any border of the control and choose **Edit Text**.
 d. Delete the default label and type Spring.
 e. Click cell **M1** to deselect the control.
 f. Right-click the control with the link select pointer.
 g. Point to a border of the control and click to hide the context menu.
 h. Point again to the border to display the move pointer.
 i. Drag the control to position it below the *Fall* control in the group box.
 j. Press **Ctrl** and click the *Fall* control so that both controls are selected (Figure 7-59).
 k. Click the **Align** button on the *Drawing Tools Format* tab and choose **Align Left**.

9. Insert a comment.
 a. Select cell **A4**.
 b. Click the **New Comment** button [*Review* tab, *Comments* group].
 c. Type Select and delete cells A5:E29 to begin a new grade sheet. (Figure 7-60).
 d. Select cell **F4** to hide the comment.

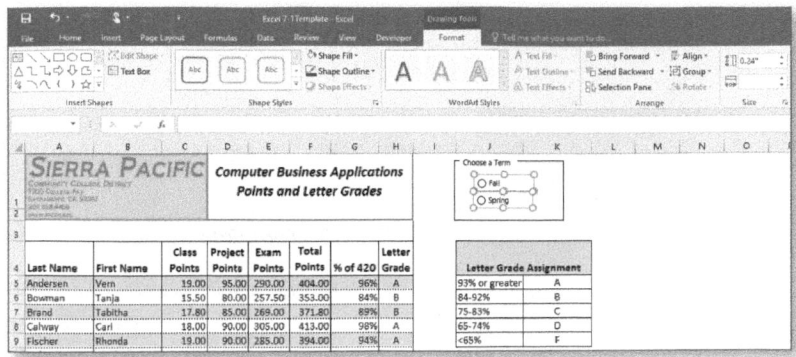

7-59 Both controls selected

10. Inspect the workbook and check compatibility.
 a. Click the **Check for Issues** button [*File* tab, *Info* group] and choose **Inspect Document**.
 b. Choose **Yes** to save the document.
 c. Click **Inspect**. Scroll the *Document Inspector* dialog box to confirm what has been found.
 d. Click **Remove All** for *Document Properties and Personal Information*. Do not remove the comment.
 e. Click **Close**.
 f. Click the **File** tab.
 g. Click **Allow this information to be saved in your file** in the *Inspect Workbook* group. This property must be disabled in order to share the workbook.
 h. Click the **Check for Issues** button [*File* tab, *Info* group] and choose **Check Compatibility**.
 i. Click **Copy to New Sheet**.

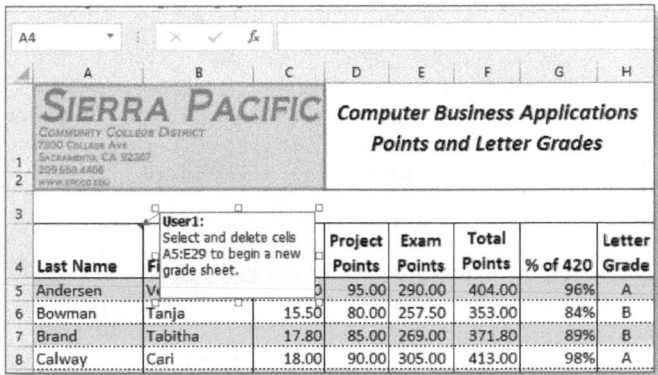

7-60 New comment in cell A4

11. Unlock cells and controls, protect the worksheet, and protect the structure.
 a. Click the **Grade Sheet** worksheet tab and select cells **A5:E29**. These are cells in which instructors enter student names and points.
 b. Right-click cell **A5** and choose **Format Cells**.
 c. Click the **Protection** tab and deselect the **Locked** box.
 d. Click **OK**.
 e. Point to the *Fall* option button control and right-click.
 f. Press **Ctrl** and right-click the *Spring* control so that both controls are selected.
 g. Right-click the *Fall* control and choose **Format Object** (Figure 7-61).
 h. Click the **Protection** tab, deselect the **Locked** box, and click **OK**.
 i. Select cell **A4**.
 j. Click the **Protect Sheet** button [*Review* tab, *Changes* group].

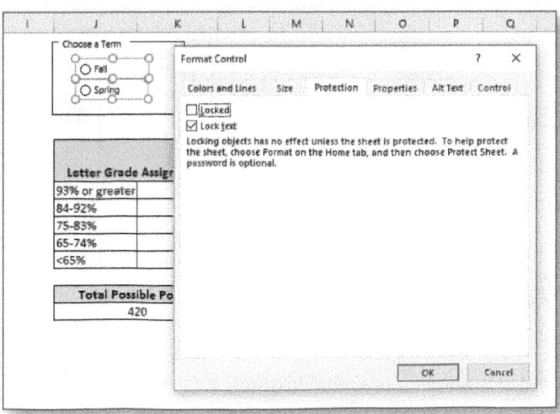

7-61 Format two controls at once

k. Allow options to select locked and unlocked cells, do not use a password, and click **OK**.
l. Click the **Protect Workbook** button [*Review* tab, *Changes* group].
m. Do not assign a password and click **OK**.

12. Save and close template.

13. Create a workbook from a template.
 a. Click the **File** tab and select **New**.
 b. Click **PERSONAL** near the top of the gallery.
 c. Click the icon for *[your initials] Excel 7-1Template* to create a new workbook.
 d. Point to cell **A4** to read the comment.
 e. Select and delete the contents of cells **A5:E29** and select cell **A5**.
 f. Save the workbook as [your initials] Excel 7-1User1 in your usual location for saving workbooks. The *Save As* dialog box displays the most recently used folder which may be your *Custom Office Templates* folder.

14. Share the workbook.
 a. Click the **Share Workbook** button [*Review* tab, *Changes* category]. (If a message box says that privacy measures are in place, click the **File** tab, and click **Allow this information to be saved in your file** in the *Inspect Workbook* group.)
 b. Verify that the **Allow changes by more than one user at the same time** box is selected.
 c. Click the **Advanced** tab and set the *Keep change history for* option to **25** days.
 d. Click **OK** to close the *Share Workbook* dialog box.
 e. Click **OK** to resave the shared workbook.

15. Make a copy of the shared workbook in the same folder.
 a. Click the **File** tab and choose **Save As**.
 b. Save the workbook as [your initials] Excel 7-1User2 in the same folder as the original shared workbook.
 c. Type the following data in cells **A5:E5**. When the error alert message displays, click **Yes** to complete the entry.

 Goldstone Violet 29 75 295

 d. Select the **Spring** radio button (Figure 7-62).

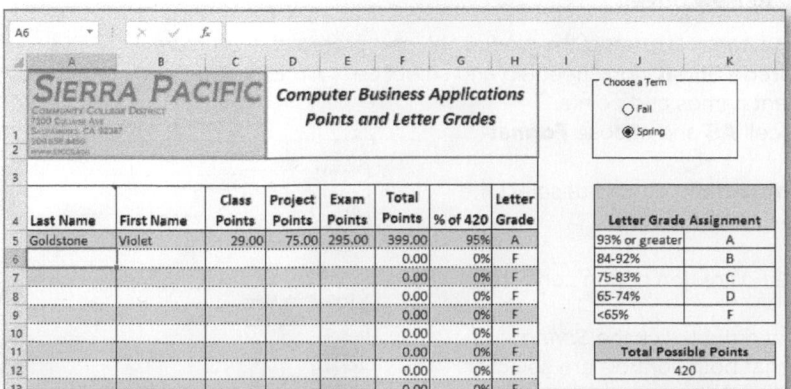

7-62 Data entry for User 2

 e. Save and close the workbook.
 f. Open the *[your initials] Excel 7-1User1* workbook.
 g. Select the **Spring** radio button.

h. Type the following data in cells **A6:E6**:

Gomez Andre 12 95 250

i. Save the workbook and leave it open.

16. Add the **Compare and Merge Workbooks** button to the *Quick Access* toolbar.
 a. Select the **Options** command [*File* tab] and select **Quick Access Toolbar** in the left pane.
 b. Choose **All Commands** from the *Choose commands from* list.
 c. Select **Compare and Merge Workbooks** in the commands list.
 d. Click **Add** and click **OK**.

17. Merge copies of the shared workbook.
 a. Click the **Compare and Merge Workbooks** button on the *Quick Access* toolbar. (Save the workbook if prompted.)
 b. Navigate to the folder with the *[your initials] Excel 7-1User2* workbook in the *Select Files to Merge Into Current Workbook* dialog box.
 c. Click the *[your initials] Excel 7-1User2* file name and click **OK**.

18. Accept or reject changes.
 a. Click the **Track Changes** button [*Review* tab, *Changes* group] and choose **Accept/Reject Changes**.
 b. Verify that **Not yet reviewed** displays for the *When* setting.
 c. Click **OK**. The first change is identified as cell **A6**.
 d. Click **Accept**. The next change is in cell **B6**.
 e. Click **Accept All**.

19. Save the merged workbook as [your initials] Excel 7-1Merged and close it (Figure 7-63).

20. Move the template from the default folder.
 a. Click the **File** tab, select **Open**, and click **Browse**.
 b. Expand the *Quick access* list in the left pane and select **Documents**.
 c. Double-click **Custom Office Templates**.
 d. Right-click *[your initials] Excel 7-1Template* and choose **Cut**.
 e. In the left pane, navigate to and select your folder for saving files.
 f. Right-click an unused area of the dialog box and choose **Paste**.
 g. Click **Cancel** to close the dialog box.

7-63 Merged workbook for Excel 7-1

21. Remove the **Compare and Merge Workbooks** button and the *Developer* tab.
 a. Select the **Options** command [*File* tab] and click **Quick Access Toolbar**.
 b. Click **Compare and Merge Workbooks** in the list on the right.
 c. Click **Remove**.
 d. Click **Customize Ribbon** in the left pane.
 e. Deselect the **Developer** box in the *Main Tabs* group and click **OK**.

Guided Project 7-2

In this project, you complete the purchase order for Blue Lake Sports by adding a data validation list and check box form controls. You protect the sheet and the workbook, save it as a template, and share it for testing.
[**Student Learning Outcomes 7.1, 7.2, 7.3, 7.4, 7.5, 7.6**]

File Needed: ***BlueLakeSports-07.xlsx*** *(Student data files are available in the* Library *of your SIMnet account)*
Completed Project File Names: ***[your initials] Excel 7-2Template.xltx, [your initials] Excel 7-2User1.xlsx,***
[your initials] Excel 7-2User2.xlsx, and ***[your initials] Excel 7-2Merged.xlsx***

Skills Covered in this Project

- Set data validation to use a list.
- Use an error alert for data validation.
- Insert a check box form control.

- Unlock worksheet cells and protect a worksheet.
- Save a workbook as a template.
- Create a new workbook from a template.
- Share a workbook and track changes.
- Accept or reject changes.

1. Open the ***BlueLakeSports-07*** workbook from your student data files.

2. Save the workbook as a template.
 a. Click the **Save As** button [*File* tab] and choose **This PC**.
 b. Click the **More Options** link.
 c. Type the file name [your initials] Excel 7-2Template in the *File name* box.
 d. Verify that the **Save Thumbnail** box is selected or select it.
 e. Choose **Excel Template** from the *Save as type* drop-down box.
 f. Click **Save**.

3. Set data validation with an error alert to use a list.
 a. Click the **Purchase Order** sheet tab, select **B17**, and click the **Data Validation** button [*Data* tab, *Data Tools* group].
 b. Click the **Allow** arrow and choose **List** on the *Settings* tab.
 c. Click the **Source** entry box.
 d. Click the **Departments** worksheet tab and select cells **A2:A14**.
 e. Click the **Error Alert** tab.
 f. Verify that the **Show error alert after invalid data is entered** box is selected.
 g. Use **Stop** for the *Style* to prohibit an invalid entry.
 h. Click the **Title** box and type Wait!.
 i. Click the **Error message** box and type Please choose from the list.
 j. Click **OK**.

4. Display the *Developer* tab and the *Compare and Merge Workbooks* button.
 a. Select the **Options** command [*File* tab] and click **Customize Ribbon** in the left pane.
 b. Select the **Developer** box in the *Main Tabs* group.
 c. Click **Quick Access Toolbar** in the left pane.
 d. Choose **All Commands** from the *Choose commands from* list.
 e. Click **Compare and Merge Workbooks** in the commands list.
 f. Click **Add** and click **OK**.

5. Insert a check box form control.
 a. Click the **View** tab and check the **Gridlines** box in the *Show* group to draw and position controls with gridlines visible.
 b. Click the **Insert Controls** button [*Developer* tab, *Controls* group] and click the **Check Box (Form Control)** button.
 c. Draw a control directly over cell **B15**.

d. Click the **Properties** button [*Developer* tab, *Controls* group].
e. Verify that the **Unchecked** radio button is selected on the *Control* tab.
f. Select the **3-D shading** box.
g. Click the **Protection** tab and deselect the **Locked** box.
h. Click **OK**.
i. Click two times near the word "Check" with the control to place an insertion point.
j. Delete **Check Box 1**, press **Spacebar**, and type Yes (Figure 7-64).
k. Click cell **E15** to deselect the control. If you accidentally placed a check mark within the control, point and click to remove it.

7-64 Edited label for check box control

6. Copy a check box form control.
 a. Point to the check box control label **Yes** and right-click.
 b. Choose **Copy** from the menu and then press **Ctrl+V** to paste the control.
 c. Point to any border of the copied control to display a move pointer.
 d. Drag the copy to cell **C15**.
 e. Press **Ctrl** and right-click while pointing to the first check box control to select both controls (Figure 7-65).
 f. Click the **Align** button [*Drawing Tools Format* tab, *Arrange* group] and choose **Align Middle**.
 g. Select cell **E15** to deselect both controls.
 h. Right-click the copied control and choose **Edit Text** to place an insertion point.
 i. Delete **Yes** and type No (Figure 7-66).
 j. Select cell **E15**. Remove check marks that were accidentally entered.

7-65 Two controls selected

7-66 Controls are aligned

7. Protect the worksheet and the workbook structure.
 a. Select **D7**.
 b. Press **Ctrl** and select cell **D9**, cells **B11:D13**, cell **B17**, and cells **A20:D28**.
 c. Click the **Format** button [*Home* tab, *Cells* group].
 d. Select **Lock Cell** to remove the *Locked* property.
 e. Click cell **D7**.
 f. Click the **Protect Sheet** button [*Review* tab, *Changes* group].
 g. Allow the options to select locked and unlocked cells. Do not use a password.
 h. Click **OK**.
 i. Click the **Protect Workbook** button [*Review* tab, *Changes* group].
 j. Do not use a password and click **OK**.

8. Save and close the template.

9. Create a workbook from a template.
 a. Click the **New** button [*File* tab] and click **PERSONAL** near the top of the gallery.
 b. Click **[your initials] Excel 7-2Template** to create a workbook.
 c. Type BLS00120 in cell **D7** and press **Tab**.

d. Type =to in cell **D9**, press **Tab** to select **TODAY**, and press **Enter**.
e. Type the following in cells **B11:B13**:

Outdoor Apparel, Inc
4232 South Water Street
Omaha, NE 68107

f. Select the check box control for **Yes**.
g. Select cell **B17**, click the data validation arrow, and choose **Apparel**.
h. Save the workbook as an Excel workbook named [your initials] Excel 7-2User1 in your usual location for saving files.

10. Inspect the workbook.
 a. Click the **File** tab. You cannot inspect a worksheet that is protected.
 b. Click **Unprotect** in the *Protect Workbook* area (Figure 7-67).
 c. Click the **Check for Issues** button and choose **Inspect Document**.

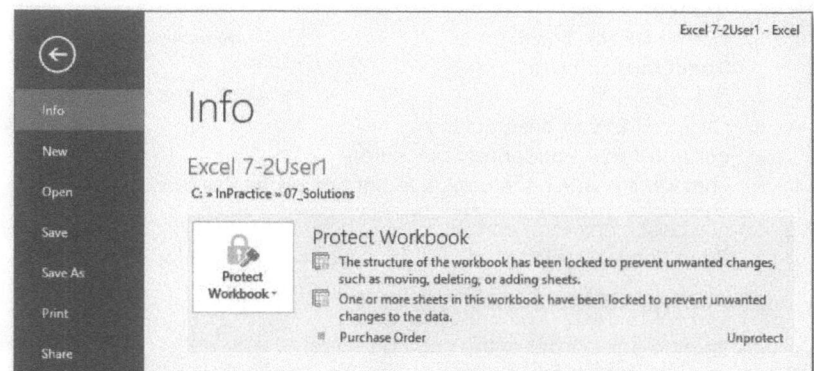

7-67 Remove protection from the *Backstage* view

 d. Choose **Yes** to save the document before inspection.
 e. Click **Inspect** in the *Document Inspector* dialog box.
 f. Click **Remove All** to remove all personal information and document properties.
 g. Click **Close**.

11. Check compatibility.
 a. Click the **Protect Workbook** button [*Review* group, *Changes* group]. In order to generate a compatibility report, the *Protect Workbook* property must be disabled.
 b. Click the **Check for Issues** button [*File* tab, *Info* group] and choose **Check Compatibility**.
 c. Click **Copy to New Sheet**.
 d. Click the **Purchase Order** sheet tab.

12. Share the workbook.
 a. Click the **File** tab.
 b. Click **Allow this information to be saved in your file** in the *Inspect Workbook* group. This property was activated when you removed metadata; it prohibits sharing the workbook.
 c. Return to the **Purchase Order** sheet and click the **Share Workbook** button [*Review* tab, *Changes* category].
 d. Select the **Allow changes by more than one user at the same time** box.
 e. Click the **Advanced** tab and set the *Keep change history for* option to **15** days.
 f. Click **OK** to close the *Share Workbook* dialog box.
 g. Click **OK** to resave the shared workbook.

13. Make a copy of the shared workbook in the same folder.
 a. Click the **File** tab and choose **Save As**.
 b. Select **This PC** and click the **More Options** link.
 c. Navigate to and choose your folder and save the workbook as [your initials] Excel 7-2User2.

 d. Type the following in cells **A20:D20**:

 Ladies Parka LP10Blue 4 87

 e. Save and close the workbook.

14. Open *[your initials] Excel 7-2User1* and select cell **A21**.
 a. In cells **A21:D21**, type the following:

 Men's Parka MP16Black 4 98

 b. Save the workbook and leave it open.

15. Merge copies of the shared workbook.
 a. Click the **Compare and Merge Workbooks** button. (Save the file if prompted.)
 b. Navigate to the folder with *[your initials] Excel 7-2User2* in the *Select Files to Merge Into Current Workbook* dialog box.
 c. Select *[your initials] Excel 7-2User2* and click **OK**.

16. Accept or reject changes.
 a. Click the **Track Changes** button [*Review* tab, *Changes* group] and choose **Accept/Reject Changes**.
 b. Verify that **Not yet reviewed** displays as the *When* option.
 c. Click **OK**. The first edit is cell **A21**.
 d. Click **Accept** to locate the next edit.
 e. Click **Accept All** and then press **Ctrl+Home**.

17. Save the workbook as [your initials] Excel 7-2Merged in your folder and close it (Figure 7-68).

18. Move the template from the default folder.
 a. Click the **File** tab, select **Open**, and click **Browse**.
 b. Expand the *Quick access* list in the left pane and select **Documents**.
 c. Double-click **Custom Office Templates**.
 d. Right-click *[your initials] Excel 7-2Template* and choose **Cut**.
 e. In the left pane, navigate to and select the folder for saving files.
 f. Right-click an unused area of the dialog box and choose **Paste**.
 g. Click **Cancel** to close the dialog box.

19. Remove the **Compare and Merge Workbooks** button and the *Developer* tab.
 a. Select the **Options** command [*File* tab] and click **Quick Access Toolbar** in the left pane.
 b. Click **Compare and Merge Workbooks** in the list on the right.
 c. Click **Remove**.
 d. Click **Customize Ribbon** in the left pane.
 e. Deselect the **Developer** box in the *Main Tabs* group and click **OK**.

7-68 Merged workbook for Excel 7-2

Guided Project 7-3

Agents for Placer Hills Real Estate (PHRE) have built a worksheet to help clients compare monthly payments. You clear and reset data validation and insert a spin box form control for the agent's ID. The workbook is saved as a template.
[Student Learning Outcomes 7.1, 7.2, 7.3, 7.4, 7.6]

File Needed: **PlacerHills-07.xlsx** (Student data files are available in the Library of your SIMnet account)
Completed Project File Names: **[your initials] Excel 7-3.xlsx** and **[your initials] Excel 7-3Template.xltx**

Skills Covered in this Project

- Save a workbook as a template.
- Find and clear data validation settings.
- Set data validation with an error alert.
- Insert a spin box form control.
- Protect a worksheet.
- Create a workbook from a template.

1. Open the **PlacerHills-07** workbook from your student data files. The #NUM error appears in three cells because data for the *PMT* formula in cell H15 is missing.

2. Save the workbook as a template.
 a. Select **Save As** [*File* tab] and choose **This PC**.
 b. Click the **More options** link to open the *Save As* dialog box.
 c. Type the file name [your initials] Excel 7-3Template in the *File name* box.
 d. Verify that the **Save Thumbnail** box is selected or select it.
 e. Choose **Excel Template** from the *Save as type* drop-down box.
 f. Click **Save**.

3. Find and clear data validation settings.
 a. Click the **Find & Select** button [*Home* tab, *Editing* group] and choose **Go To Special**.
 b. Select the option button for **Data validation** (Figure 7-69).
 c. Click **OK**. Cells with data validation settings are highlighted.
 d. Click the **Data Validation** button [*Data* tab, *Data Tools* group].
 e. Click **Clear All** on the *Settings* tab and leave the dialog box open.

4. Set data validation with an error alert.
 a. Verify that the following cells in the worksheet are selected: **C9:C12, H9, H11, H13:H14,** and **H16**. (If they are not, close the *Data Validation* dialog box, select the cells, and click the **Data Validation** button [*Data* tab, *Data Tools* group].)
 b. Click the **Allow** arrow and choose **Decimal** on the *Settings* tab.
 c. Click the **Data** arrow and choose **greater than or equal to**.
 d. Click the **Minimum** box and type 0.
 e. Click the **Error Alert** tab and verify that the **Show error alert after invalid data is entered** box is selected.
 f. Verify that **Stop** displays as the **Style**.
 g. Click the **Title** box and type Required.
 h. Click the **Error message** box and type Please enter a positive value. (Figure 7-70).
 i. Click **OK**.

7-69 Locate cells with data validation using *Go To Special*

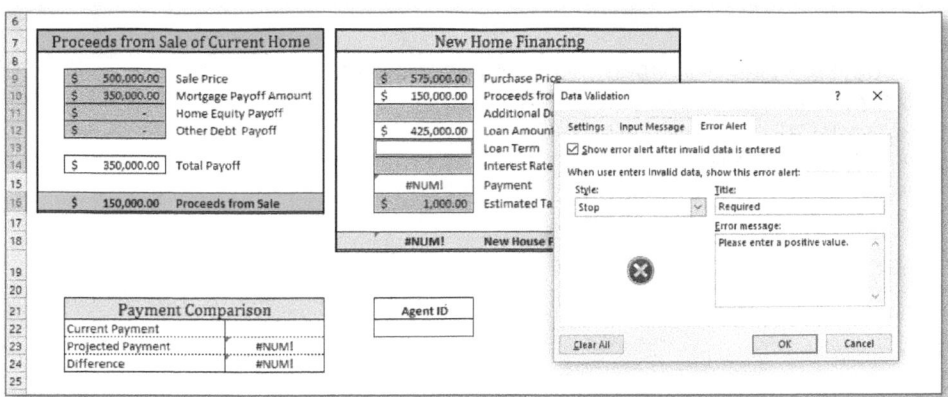

7-70 Data validation error alert

5. Display the *Developer* tab on the *Ribbon* if it is not shown.
 a. Select the **Options** command [*File* tab] and click **Customize Ribbon** in the left pane.
 b. Select the **Developer** box in the *Main Tabs* group and click **OK**.

6. Insert a spin button form control.
 a. Show the gridlines on the worksheet [*View* tab].
 b. Click the **Insert Controls** button [*Developer* tab, *Controls* group].
 c. Click the **Spin Button (Form Control)** button.
 d. Draw a control directly over cells **I21:I22** (Figure 7-71).

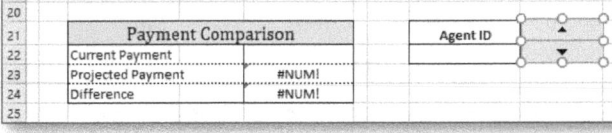

7-71 Spin button form control

 e. Right-click the control and choose **Format Control**.
 f. Click the **Minimum value** box on the *Control* tab and type 1.
 g. Set a maximum value of **8**. These are agent identification numbers (1 through 8).
 h. Click the **Cell link** box and select cell **H22**. The choice made by the spin button will be placed in this cell (Figure 7-72).

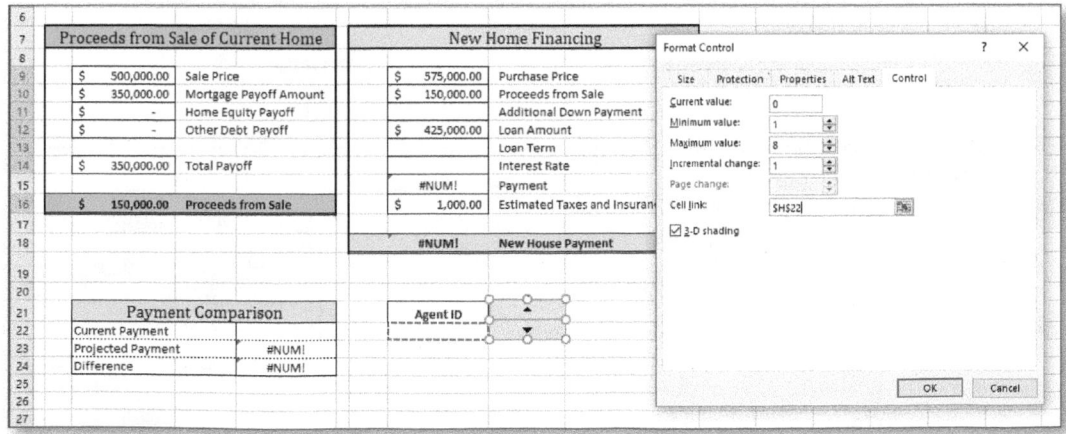

7-72 Options set for spin button control

 i. Verify that the **3D shading** box is selected and click **OK**.
 j. Click cell **D4** to deselect the control.

Independent Project 7-4

Classic Gardens and Landscapes (CGL) monitors employee hours by task and by day. The task hour worksheet has a data entry form, and the employee hours worksheet has formulas and data validation. The workbook is saved as a template for sharing.
[Student Learning Outcomes 7.1, 7.2, 7.3, 7.4, 7.5, 7.6]

File Needed: ***ClassicGardens-07.xlsx*** *(Student data files are available in the* Library *of your SIMnet account)*
Completed Project File Names: *[your initials]* ***Excel 7-4Template.xltx**, [your initials]* ***Excel 7-4User1.xlsx**,* *[your initials]* ***Excel 7-4User2.xlsx**,* and *[your initials]* ***Excel 7-4Merged.xlsx***

Skills Covered in this Project

- Create a data entry form.
- Insert a comment.
- Set data validation with an error alert.
- Save a workbook as a template.
- Create a workbook from a template.
- Share a workbook.
- Compare and merge workbooks.
- Highlight, accept, and reject changes.

1. Open the ***ClassicGardens-07*** workbook from your student data files.

2. Save the workbook as a template with a thumbnail named [your initials] Excel 7-4Template in the default *Custom Office Templates* folder.

3. Display the **Compare and Merge Workbooks** and **Form** buttons on the *Quick Access* toolbar.

4. Create and use a data input form.
 a. Select cells **A9:E17** on the **Task Hours** worksheet and click the **Form** button.
 b. Press **Tab** and type 22 for Week 1 brick and stone paving. If you accidentally press **Enter** and move to the next record, click **Find Prev** in the data form to return to the unfinished form.
 c. Press **Tab** and type 18 for Week 2.
 d. Press **Tab** and type 30 for Week 3.
 e. Press **Tab**, type 8 for Week 4, and press **Enter**. The next data form opens, and the data displays in the worksheet (Figure 7-74).

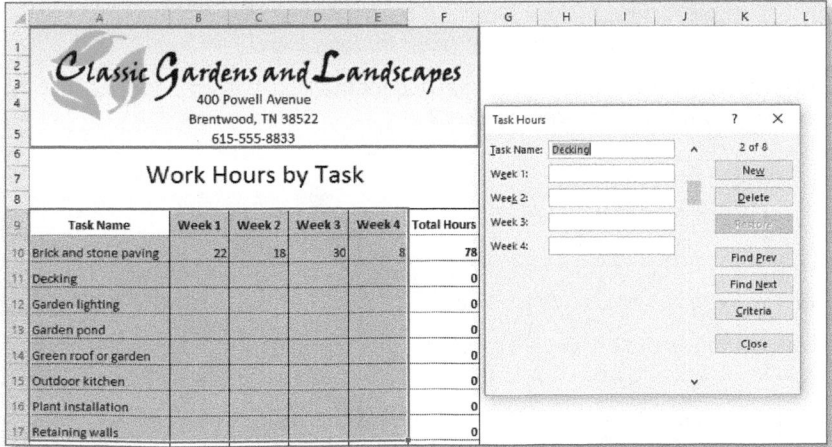

7-74 Data form to enter new records

 f. Enter data for the second task, decking:

 Week 1 15
 Week 2 28
 Week 3 0
 Week 4 12

 g. Close the data form and select cell **G1**.

5. Insert a comment in cell **G1**.
 a. Type Delete the sample data in cells B10:E11. in the comment box.
 b. Select cell **G3**.
 c. If the comment is not visible, click the **Show All Comments** button in the *Comments* group [*Review* tab] to display it.

6. Set data validation with an error alert.
 a. Click the **Employee Hours** worksheet tab.
 b. Select cells **B8:G13** and set data validation to use a decimal value less than **8.1**.
 c. Use an **Information** type error alert with the title Overtime.
 d. Type the error message Overtime pay starts at greater than 8 hours.

7. Enter *SUM* formulas for the totals in column **H** and row **14**.

8. Select cells **B8:G13** and remove the **Locked** property. Select cell **B8** to cancel the selection.

9. Protect the sheet without a password.

10. Save and close the template.

11. Create a new workbook based on the template and save it as [your initials] Excel 7-4User1 in your usual folder for saving files.

12. Share the workbook with default settings.

13. Make a copy of the shared workbook in the same folder and name it [your initials] Excel 7-4User2.

14. In ***[your initials] Excel 7-4User2***, enter the following hours for Alvarez and accept the invalid entry.

 Mon 9
 Tue 8
 Wed 7

15. Save and close *User2*'s workbook and open ***[your initials] Excel 7-4User1***.

16. As *User1*, enter the following hours for Alvarez. Accept the invalid entry and note that the days of the week are different from those entered by *User2*.

 Wed 9
 Thu 8
 Fri 7

17. Save *User1*'s workbook and leave it open.

18. Merge *User2*'s workbook into *User1*'s workbook.

19. Click the **Track Changes** button [*Review* tab, *Changes* group] to accept or reject changes. For the conflict in cell D8, select and accept **9** as the value. Accept all other changes.

20. Save the merged workbook as [your initials] Excel 7-4Merged and leave it open.

21. Click the **Share Workbook** button [*Review* tab, *Changes* group] and deselect the **Allow changes by more than one user at the same time** box. Click **OK** and then click **Yes** to unshare the workbook.

E7-483

22. Remove sheet protection.

23. Inspect the workbook and remove all comments and personal information.

24. Open the *Properties* dialog box [*File* tab], and deselect the **Show Thumbnails for All Excel Documents** box on the *Summary* tab, and click **OK**.

25. Save and close the merged workbook (Figure 7-75).

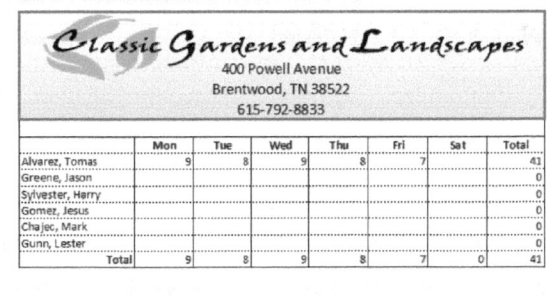

7-75 Completed worksheets for Excel 7-4

26. Remove the **Form** and **Compare and Merge Workbooks** buttons from the *Quick Access* toolbar.

27. Move the template from the *Custom Office Templates* folder to your folder.

Independent Project 7-5

In the Courtyard Medical Plaza workbook, you add items to the pharmacy inventory using a data entry form. On the Optometry worksheet, you find and correct invalid data. Finally, you inspect the workbook and check its compatibility with earlier versions of Excel.
[Student Learning Outcomes 7.2, 7.3, 7.6]

File Needed: **CourtyardMedical-07.xlsx** *(Student data files are available in the* Library *of your SIMnet account)*
Completed Project File Name: *[your initials] Excel 7-5.xlsx*

Skills Covered in this Project

- Create and use a data entry form.
- Circle invalid data.
- Inspect a workbook.
- Check workbook compatibility.

1. Open the **CourtyardMedical-07** workbook from your student data files. It is marked as final.

2. Click **Edit Anyway** in the message bar, and save the workbook as [your initials] Excel 7-5.

3. Display the **Form** button on the *Quick Access* toolbar.

4. Create and use a data input form.
 a. Select cells **A9:D24** on the **Pharmacy** sheet.
 b. Create the data entry form.
 c. Enter data for two items shown here. The currency symbol is included in format settings so you need not type it.

Product ID	Description	Cost	Retail
CMP-016	Swim ear drops	4.59	6.89
CMP-017	Peptic relief tablets (25)	2.50	3.99

 d. Close the data form.

5. Click the **Optometry** worksheet tab and circle invalid data.

6. Review the data validation settings for any cell in column A. Correct the invalid entries based on the settings.

7. Inspect the workbook. Remove personal data and document properties and hidden worksheets.

8. Check compatibility and copy the results to a new sheet.

9. Mark the workbook as final and close it (Figure 7-76).

10. Remove the **Form** button from the *Quick Access* toolbar.

7-76 Completed worksheets for Excel 7-5

Independent Project 7-6

The Hamilton Civic Center is developing a template with a calorie-tracking sheet for member exercise and a report about off-site seminars. You create the template, set data validation, complete formulas, and insert a combo box control. You create a new workbook from the template and share it with co-workers.
[Student Learning Outcomes 7.1, 7.2, 7.3, 7.4, 7.5, 7.6]

File Needed: **HamiltonCC-07.xlsx** (Student data files are available in the Library of your SIMnet account)
Completed Project File Names: **[your initials] Excel 7-6Template.xltx, [your initials] Excel 7-6User1.xlsx,**
[your initials] Excel 7-6User2.xlsx, and **[your initials] Excel 7-6Merged.xlsx**

Skills Covered in this Project

- Set data validation to use a list.
- Set data validation to use a date restriction.
- Create an error alert message.
- Insert a combo box control.

- Protect a worksheet and workbook structure.
- Check compatibility.
- Save a workbook as a template.
- Share a workbook.
- Track, accept, and reject changes.

1. Open the **HamiltonCC-07** workbook from your student data files and save it with a thumbnail image as [your initials] Excel 7-6Template in the default templates folder.

2. Select cell **D2** on the **Data** sheet and review the formula. The formula divides calories by time and rounds the results to three decimal places.

3. Select cells **D2:D10** and open the *Format Cells* dialog box.

4. Select the **Custom** category on the *Number* tab. Choose **0.00** in the sample list and edit the *Type* box to show 0.000. The number of zeros indicates how many positions display after the decimal point (Figure 7-77).

5. Select cell **D2** and click the **Format Painter** button [*Home* tab, *Clipboard* group]. Click the **Calorie Tracking** tab and paint the format to cells **E3:E33**.

6. Select cell **E3** on the **Calorie Tracking** sheet. Start a *VLOOKUP* function to lookup the label in cell **C3**. For the array, use an absolute reference to cells **A2:D10** on the **Data** sheet. The *Col_index_num* is **4** for the calories per minute column. The result of the *VLOOKUP* formula is the calories per minute for the exercise (Figure 7-78).

7-77 Custom format for values

7. Edit the formula in cell **E3** to multiply the results by the number of minutes in cell **D3**.

8. Copy the formula in cell **E3** to cells **E4:E33**. The #N/A error message displays in rows where there is no data.

9. Select cells **C3:C33** and set data validation to use the list of activity names on the **Data** sheet. Do not use an input message or an error alert.

7-78 VLOOKUP formula

10. On the **Calorie Tracking** sheet, delete the data in cells **A3:D23**.

11. Select cells **B3:B33** and set data validation to use a **Date** that is less than or equal to *TODAY* (Figure 7-79). Include a *Stop* error alert with a title of Check Date and a message of Date must be today or in the past.

12. Select cells **A3:D33** and remove the **Locked** cell property. Select cell **A3** to position the insertion point.

13. Display the **Developer** tab on the *Ribbon* and click the **Data** worksheet tab.

14. Draw a combo box control to cover cell **F8** and open its *Format Control* dialog box. Select cells **G8:G11** for the *Input range* and cell **F8** for the *Cell link* (Figure 7-80).

15. Deselect the control and then select **Second** from it. The linked cell is under the control and hidden from view.

16. Click the **Hospital Seminars** tab and select cell **D4**. This cell has *Center Across Selection* alignment applied.

7-79 Data validation for dates

7-80 Combo box settings

17. In cell **D4**, use *CONCAT* and *INDEX* to display the result from the combo box, concatenating the *Index* results to the word "Quarter."
 a. Start a *CONCAT* function [*Text* group].
 b. Use the *INDEX* function with the first arguments list as the *Text1* argument.
 c. The *Array* argument is cells **G8:G11** on the *Data* sheet, and the *Row_num* argument is cell **F8** on the *Data* sheet. The combo box control covers cell F8, so type f8 after the sheet name (Figure 7-81).

7-81 *INDEX* is nested within *CONCAT*

d. Click between the two ending parentheses in the *Formula* bar to return to the *CONCAT* arguments and type a comma , to move to the *Text2* argument. (If you accidentally clicked *OK*, click the **Insert Function** button to re-open the *Function Arguments* dialog box.)

e. Click the **Text2** box, press **Spacebar**, and type Quarter, and click **OK**. (Figure 7-82).

f. Format cell **D4** as **bold italic 16 pt**.

7-82 Space character is included with *Text2* argument

18. On the *Data* sheet, select **Third** from the combo box control, and return to the *Hospital Seminars* sheet to see the results.

19. Select cell **D4** and cells **D6:G10** on the *Hospital Seminars* sheet and remove the **Locked** property.

20. Delete the contents of cells **D6:G10** and select cell **D6**.

21. Protect the **Hospital Seminars** sheet and the **Calorie Tracking** sheet, both without passwords.

22. Save and close the template.

23. Create a workbook from the template. Save the new workbook as [your initials] Excel 7-6User1 in your usual folder for saving files.

24. Share the *[your initials] Excel 7-6User 1* workbook with the default settings.

25. Make a copy of the shared workbook named [your initials] Excel 7-6User2.

26. In *[your initials] Excel 7-6User2*, enter the data shown here on the *Calorie Tracking* sheet. Do not type the word "Yesterday" or "Two days ago," but enter date values using *mm/dd/yy* format.

Member ID	Date	Activity	Minutes
10001	Yesterday	Elliptical	45
10003	Two days ago	Water aerobics	40

27. Enter the data shown here on the *Hospital Seminars* sheet for *User2*.

	Henderson	Advocate	Mercy	Gallatin
Cardio vs. Strength	14	22	31	15
Know Your Numbers	32	21	18	21

28. Save and close the *[your initials] Excel 7-6User2* workbook.

29. Open *[your initials] Excel 7-6User1*. Starting in cell **A5** on the *Calorie Tracking* sheet, enter the following data. Enter date values and use *mm/dd/yy* format.

Member ID	Date	Activity	Minutes
10007	Today	Running	30
10003	Two days ago	High-intensity interval training	40

E7-489

30. Starting in cell **D9** on the *Hospital Seminars* sheet, enter the data shown here.

	Henderson	Advocate	Mercy	Gallatin
Pamper Your Joints	10	20	15	18
Vitamins are Best	14	31	27	15

31. Save the *[your initials] Excel 7-6User1* workbook. Then merge the *[your initials] Excel 7-6User2* workbook into it.

32. Highlight the changes and accept all of them.

33. Save the merged workbook as [your initials] Excel 7-6Merged and close it (Figure 7-83).

7-83 Completed worksheets for Excel 7-6

34. Hide the **Developer** tab and remove the **Compare and Merge Workbooks** button from the *Quick Access* toolbar.

35. Move the template from the *Custom Office Templates* folder to your usual work folder.

Improve It Project 7-7

Staff at Life's Animal Shelter (LAS) use an Excel template to maintain lists of animal adoptions. You open and edit the template to add data validation and a check box form control. In addition, you inspect the workbook, check its compatibility with earlier versions, and test it.
[Student Learning Outcomes 7.1, 7.2, 7.3, 7.4, 7.6]

File Needed: ***LASTemplate-07.xltx*** *(Student data files are available in the* Library *of your SIMnet account)*
Completed Project File Names: *[your initials] Excel 7-7.xlsx* and *[your initials] Excel 7-7Template.xltx*

Skills Covered in this Project

- Set data validation to use lists.
- Insert and format a check box control.
- Inspect a workbook and remove metadata.
- Check workbook compatibility.
- Protect a worksheet and workbook structure.
- Save a template as a different template.
- Create a workbook from a template.

1. Open the **LASTemplate-07** template from your student data files. The template has one row of sample data.

2. Press **F12** (**FN+F12**) to open the *Save As* dialog box. The *Save as type* shows *Excel Template*, but the current folder is your usual storage location.

3. Click the **Save as type** arrow and choose **Excel Workbook**.

4. Click the **Save as type** arrow again and choose **Excel Template** to reset the folder to the *Custom Office Templates* folder.

5. Type [your initials] Excel 7-7Template in the *File name* box and click **Save**.

6. Set data validation for the *Species* column to use the animal types on the **Lists** worksheet. Do not use an input or an error message.

7. Set data validation for the *City* column to use data on the **Lists** worksheet without input or error messages.

8. Build a *VLOOKUP* formula in cell **G5** to lookup the city name in cell **F5** in the array on the **Lists** worksheet and display the ZIP code. Use the sample data to verify that your formula is correct and then copy the formula (Figure 7-84).

7-84 *VLOOKUP to display ZIP code*

9. Format the cells in the *Donation* column to display **Currency** with no decimal places.

10. Format the cells in column **A** to show the **Short Date** format.

11. Determine the custom format used for *Pet IDs* on the *Animals* worksheet and then apply the same format to the *Animal ID* data on the *Adoptions* worksheet.

12. Draw a check box form control to cover cells **G2:H2**. Format the control to be unchecked with 3-D shading. On the *Colors and Lines* tab in the *Format Control* dialog box, set a **1 pt. solid black** line for the control. On the *Protection* tab, remove the **Locked** property. Edit the text in the control to display All donations cleared. (Figure 7-85).

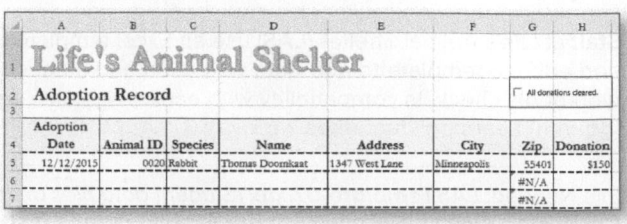

7-85 **Check box control completed**

13. Delete the test data in cells **A5:F5** and cell **H5**. Data validation is not deleted when you delete cell contents.

14. Inspect the workbook and remove all personal information.

15. Check compatibility and copy the results to a new sheet.

16. Remove the **Locked** property from cells **A5:H29** on the **Adoptions** sheet.

17. Select cell **A5** and protect the **Adoptions** sheet without a password.

18. Delete the **Animals** worksheet and hide the **Lists** and **Compatibility Report** worksheets.

19. Protect the workbook structure without a password.

20. Resave the template and close it.

21. Create a new workbook from the template and enter the following data:

Adoption Date	Animal ID	Species	Name	Address	City	Zip	Donation
2/5/17	10	Dog	John Doe	4567 Western Trail	Cass Lake		125

22. Save your workbook in your usual folder as [your initials] Excel 7-7 (Figure 7-86).

23. Close the workbook and hide the *Developer* tab.

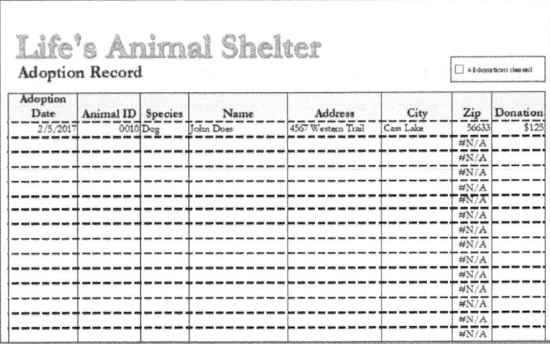

7-86 Completed worksheet for Excel 7-7

Challenge Project 7-8

In this project, you build a list of television or streaming shows and series that you regularly watch or would like to watch. You add data validation for the genre of show, inspect the workbook, and check it for compatibility. [Student Learning Outcomes 7.1, 7.2, 7.6]

File Needed: None
Completed Project File Name: *[your initials] Excel 7-8.xlsx*

Create and save a workbook as [your initials] Excel 7-8. Modify your workbook according to the following guidelines:

- In cells **A3:A12**, type the names of ten network, cable, or Internet shows, series, or specials.
- Type Title in cell **A2**. Type Network/Site in cell **B2**, Day in cell **C2**, and Time in cell **D2**. Name this sheet Watch List.

- Type a main title for the data. Apply formats based on the type of data. Add borders, shading, or other attributes to enhance the look of the worksheet.
- On another worksheet in the same workbook, create a list of network call letters, web URLs, or other identifiers for providers of your shows. Sort the data in a logical order. Then use this list to set data validation for the appropriate column on the *Watch List* sheet.
- Complete your worksheet using real or fictitious data.
- Inspect the workbook and remove personal information.
- Check the workbook's compatibility and show the results on a new sheet.

Challenge Project 7-9

In this project, you select an Excel template from the *Featured* group and create a workbook. You explore features used in the template and edit the workbook to customize it.
[Student Learning Outcomes 7.1, 7.2, 7.3, 7.5, 7.6]

File Needed: None
Completed Project File Name: *[your initials] Excel 7-9.xlsx*

Explore available templates in the *Backstage* view and choose one. Create a new workbook and save it as [your initials] Excel 7-9. Modify your workbook according to the following guidelines:

- Review sample data and formulas in the workbook.
- Unhide worksheets, columns, and rows, if they exist.
- Enter data for your own work or personal circumstances.
- Use *Find & Select* and *Go To Special* to locate existing data validation, if any. If the workbook includes data validation, edit the settings to make a change that fits the worksheet. If the template has no data validation, identify a cell range and build and apply data validation.
- Insert a form control to further personalize your workbook.
- Insert a comment to explain the purpose of the workbook.
- Inspect the workbook and remove metadata that you think can be safely removed.
- Check the workbook's compatibility and copy the results to a new sheet.

Challenge Project 7-10

In this project, you create a template to keep track of your course grades. You will include a combo box control to select the semester as well as data validation to select course codes and grades.
[Student Learning Outcomes 7.1, 7.2, 7.3]

File Needed: None
Completed Project File Names: *[your initials] Excel 7-10Template.xltx* and *[your initials] Excel 7-10.xlsx*

E7-493

Create and save a workbook as [your initials] Excel 7-10Template in the *Custom Office Templates* folder. Modify your workbook according to the following guidelines:

- In cells **A3:D3**, type the labels Code, Number, Name, and Grade.
- Format cells **A4:D9** with borders or shading to accommodate six courses per semester.
- Create and use list data validation in the *Code* and *Grade* columns. "Code" is the department or discipline indicator such as BUS, MIS, or COM; "Name" is the course title. You can type lists on another sheet or enter the list information in the *Source* entry box on the *Settings* tab for data validation.
- Type a main label in cell **A1** to indicate the purpose of the worksheet. Type a second label in cell **A2** to mark where a student enters his or her name on the sheet.
- To the right of the *Grade* column, insert a combo box control to choose the semester.
- Complete formatting for the sheet. Then copy cells **A1:D9** and the control to create a second grouping starting in cell **A12** for another semester.
- Save and close the template.
- Create a workbook from the template, complete data for two semesters, and save the workbook as [your initials] Excel 7-10.
- Remove the *Developer* tab and move the template from the *Custom Office Templates* folder to your work folder.

Exploring Data Analysis and Business Intelligence

CHAPTER OVERVIEW

Excel provides self-service business intelligence (BI) with its data analysis tools so that you can use Excel to accomplish what previously required the help of an information technology department. In this chapter, you explore scenarios, *Goal Seek*, *Solver*, data tables, and more.

STUDENT LEARNING OUTCOMES (SLOs)

After completing this chapter, you will be able to:

SLO 8.1 Create and manage scenarios for worksheet data (p. E8-496).

SLO 8.2 Use *Goal Seek* to backsolve a cell value for a formula (p. E8-498).

SLO 8.3 Use *Solver* to find a solution for a formula (p. E8-500).

SLO 8.4 Build data tables with one and two variables (p. E8-508).

SLO 8.5 Create a forecast sheet for time-based data (p. E8-511).

SLO 8.6 Get and transform data in a query (p. E8-515).

SLO 8.7 Explore *PivotTable* tools (p. E8-522).

SLO 8.8 Use the *Analysis ToolPak* to calculate statistical measures (p. E8-529).

CASE STUDY

In the Pause & Practice projects in this chapter, you create scenarios for Paradise Lakes Resort (PLR) and build a Solver problem. You build data tables to assess revenue and expense levels, create a query, and work with PivotTables.

Pause & Practice 8-1: Create scenarios and use *Goal Seek* and *Solver* to find solutions.

Pause & Practice 8-2: Build one- and two-variable data tables and create a forecast sheet.

Pause & Practice 8-3: Build a query from multiple sources, insert a timeline in a *PivotTable*, and use GETPIVOTDATA.

SLO 8.1

Creating and Managing Scenarios

A *scenario* is a saved set of values in a worksheet allowing you to vary numbers and see potential results. Scenarios are simple what-if analysis tools, often used to review best and worst possibilities.

A worksheet can have up to 32 scenarios, each one named and saved. Paradise Lakes Resort, for example, can change the value for one revenue category to calculate the effect on total revenue. Each test value is an input, is saved in the scenario, and can be shown in the worksheet.

> ▶ **MORE INFO**
>
> Because each scenario input value must be typed in the *Scenario Values* dialog box, use scenarios for data with only a few sets of values.

Create a Scenario

The first scenario that you should create is a scenario for current data so that you can always return to those values. After that, you create additional scenarios using the same cells with different values. You can display any scenario when needed, but only one scenario can be displayed at a time. Although it is optional, it is helpful to name input and result cells so that summary reports are easily understood.

You create a scenario by choosing **Scenario Manager** from the *What-if Analysis* button in the *Forecast* group on the *Data* tab.

▶ **HOW TO: Create and Show a Scenario**

1. Click the **What-if Analysis** button [*Data* tab, *Forecast* group].
2. Select **Scenario Manager**.
 - The *Scenario Manager* dialog box opens.
 - Existing scenarios, if any, are listed in the dialog box.
3. Click **Add**.
 - The *Add Scenario* dialog box opens.
4. Type a name for the saved set of values in the *Scenario name* box.
 - Name the original set of values Original or a similar name.
 - Use a short, descriptive name.
 - Use capitalization and spaces as desired.
5. Click the **Changing cells** box and select the cells whose values will be changed.
 - You can select the cell range before starting the *Scenario Manager* command.
6. Click the **Comment** box to type an optional description or explanation (Figure 8-1).
 - A default comment that includes the user name and date displays for each scenario.

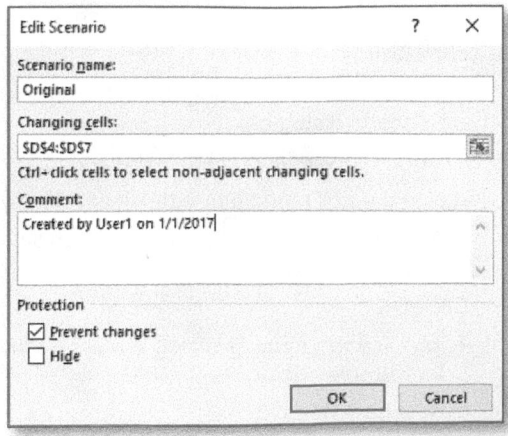

8-1 Scenario setup for original values

7. Click **OK**.

- The *Scenario Values* dialog box opens.
- The values currently displayed in the worksheet are shown for each cell address or name.
- Leave the values unchanged when creating a scenario for the original set of values.

8. Type a new value for each cell name or address (Figure 8-2).

9. Click **OK** in the *Scenario Values* dialog box.

- The *Scenario Manager* dialog box shows the scenario name.

10. Click **Show**.

- The values from the selected scenario replace the values in the worksheet.
- Select another scenario name and click **Show**.

11. Click **Close** in the *Scenario Manager* dialog box.

- The values currently displayed remain visible.

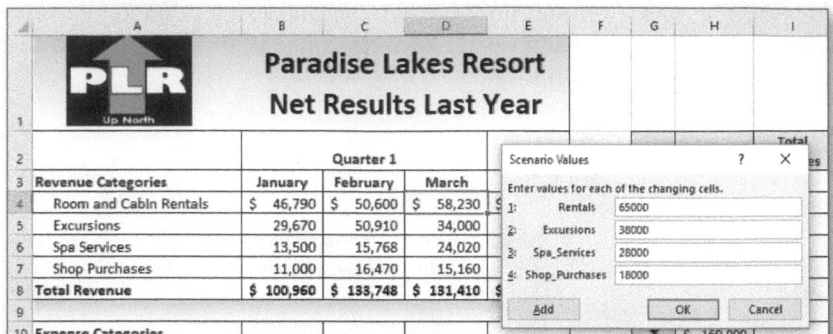

8-2 New values entered in the *Scenarios Values* dialog box

Edit a Scenario

When a scenario displays, you can change the values in the affected cells as a regular edit. The scenario itself is unchanged. To change the values saved in a scenario, open the *Scenario Manager*, select the scenario name, and click *Edit*. From the *Edit Scenario* dialog box, you can change a scenario name, redefine which cells are changed, and open the *Scenario Values* dialog box.

▶ HOW TO: Edit a Scenario

1. Click the **What-if Analysis** button [*Data* tab, *Forecast* group].

2. Select **Scenario Manager**.

3. Select the scenario name in the *Scenarios* list.

4. Click **Edit**.

- The *Edit Scenario* dialog box is the same as the *Add Scenario* dialog box.

5. Change the scenario name in the *Scenario name* box.

6. Adjust the cell range if needed in the *Changing cells* box.

- A default comment is generated each time the scenario is edited (Figure 8-3).

7. Click **OK**.

- The *Scenario Values* dialog box shows the current values for the scenario.

8. Type a new value for each cell address or range name as needed.

- You can leave some cell values as is.

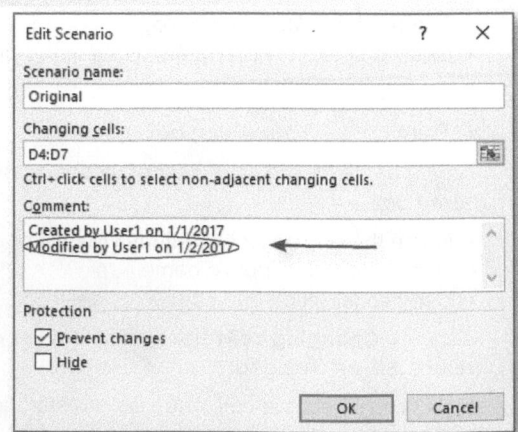

8-3 Comments are inserted each time a scenario is edited

9. Click **OK**.

10. Click **Show** to view the edited scenario in the worksheet.

11. Click **Close**.

Scenario Summary Reports

A **scenario summary report** is a generated worksheet that describes each scenario in a work-book. It is formatted as an Excel outline with two row outline levels and two column outline levels. In the report, you can hide or display details about the changing cells and the result cells. For a large worksheet with many scenarios, you can generate a scenario summary report as a *PivotTable*.

If you edit a scenario after creating a summary report, the report is not updated. You can, however, quickly generate another scenario summary report.

▶ HOW TO: Create a Scenario Summary Report

1. Click the **What-if Analysis** button [*Data* tab, *Forecast* group].

2. Select **Scenario Manager**.

3. Click **Summary**.

 - The *Scenario Summary* dialog box appears.

4. Choose **Scenario summary** as the *Report type*.

5. Click the **Result cells** box and select the cell or range (Figure 8-4).

 - These can be changing cells or cells that are affected by chang-ing cells.
 - Press **Ctrl** to select nonadjacent cells or type a comma (,) to sepa-rate cell addresses.

6. Click **OK** (Figure 8-5).

 - The report is generated on a sheet named **Scenario Summary**.
 - It is formatted as an outline in a default style.
 - You can hide or display details, delete blank columns and rows, and format the sheet as desired.

8-4 *Scenario Summary* dialog box

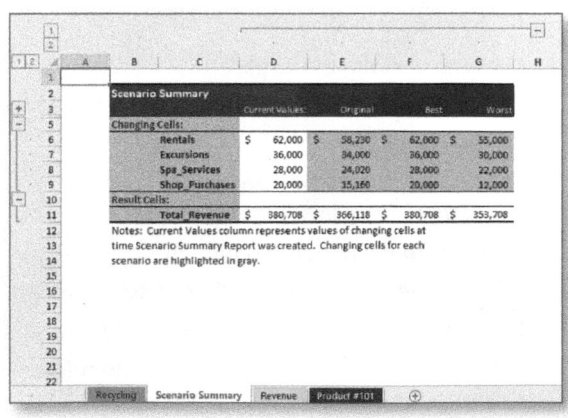

8-5 *Scenario Summary* report

SLO 8.2

Using Goal Seek

Goal Seek is a what-if analysis command that tests values in a cell to *backsolve* a formula. **Backsolving** means knowing the results and determining the value needed to reach those results. When buying a car, use *Goal Seek* to determine how much money to borrow if you can afford a $500 per month payment.

Use Goal Seek

Goal Seek solves a formula for one cell (one argument) in the formula. In the *Goal Seek* dialog box, you enter the cell reference for the formula in the *Set cell* box. You type a target or goal number in the *To value* box. In Figure 8-6, the formula in cell D4 is backsolved by adjusting the value in cell B4 so that the formula result is $50. The solution appears in the *Goal Seek Status* dialog box shown in Figure 8-7 and in the worksheet. You can accept it or keep the original value.

The *Goal Seek* command is an option for the *What-if Analysis* button [*Data* tab, *Forecast* group].

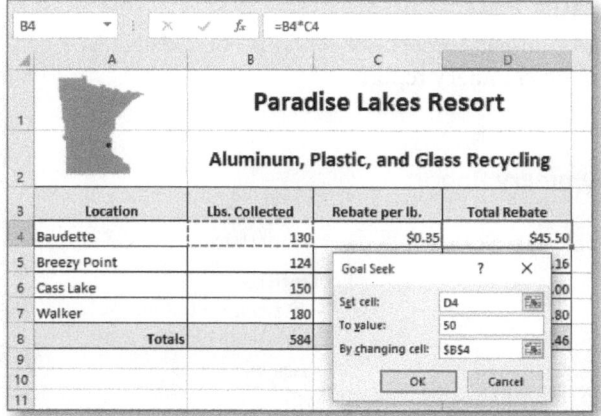

8-6 *Goal Seek* problem and dialog box

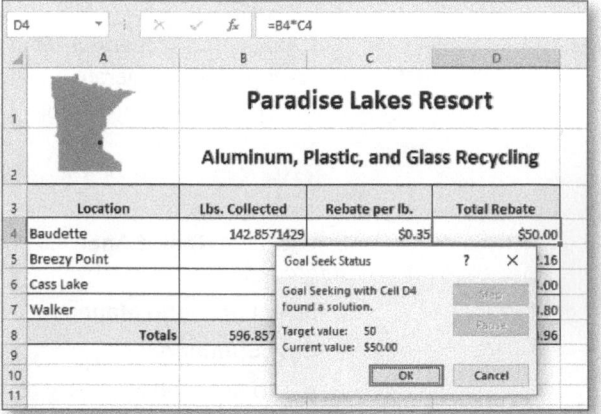

8-7 *Goal Seek Status* shows a solution

▶ **HOW TO: Use Goal Seek**

1. Click the cell with the formula.
2. Click the **What-if Analysis** button [*Data* tab, *Forecast* group].
3. Choose **Goal Seek**.
 - The *Goal Seek* dialog box opens.
 - Verify the formula address in the *Set cell* box.
4. Click the **To value** box and type the target value.
 - This is the result you want the formula to return.
5. Click the **By changing cell** box and click the cell to be adjusted (see Figure 8-6).
 - The address is entered as an absolute reference.
 - *Goal Seek* can change only one cell.
 - You can key the address instead of selecting the cell.
6. Click **OK**.
 - The *Goal Seek Status* dialog box indicates that a solution was calculated (Figure 8-7).
 - The solution displays in the cell.
7. Click **OK** to accept the solution.
 - You can also press **Enter** to accept the solution.
 - Choose **Cancel** to ignore the solution and keep the original data.

SLO 8.3

Using Solver

Solver is an analysis tool that finds the lowest, the highest, or a specific result for a formula by changing values in other cells within limitations that you set. Using *Solver* can be described as solving a problem in reverse, because you start with the desired answer and *Solver* calculates how to reach that answer. Paradise Lakes Resort, for example, might set a goal for quarterly revenue and use *Solver* to determine the best way to reach that goal by calculating a target for each revenue category.

Solver is a sophisticated analysis tool, but it may not be able to find a solution to every problem. When it cannot do so, the *Solver Results* dialog box informs you that it could not find a solution.

Install and Run Solver

Solver is an Excel **add-in**. An add-in is an enhanced command or feature that is not installed with the initial Excel setup. You can install add-ins from the *Add-Ins* dialog box in Excel *Options*.

> **HOW TO: Install Solver**

1. Select **Options** [*File* tab].
2. Click **Add-Ins** in the left pane.
 - The *View and manage Microsoft Office Add-ins* dialog box opens.
 - Applications that are currently active are listed near the top of the window.
3. Click **Solver Add-in** in the list of *Inactive Application Add-Ins* (Figure 8-8).
4. Click **Go** near the bottom of the dialog box to open the *Add-ins* dialog box.
5. Select the **Solver Add-in** box (Figure 8-9).
 - You can remove *Solver* by deselecting the box.

8-8 *Add-ins* dialog box in Excel *Options*

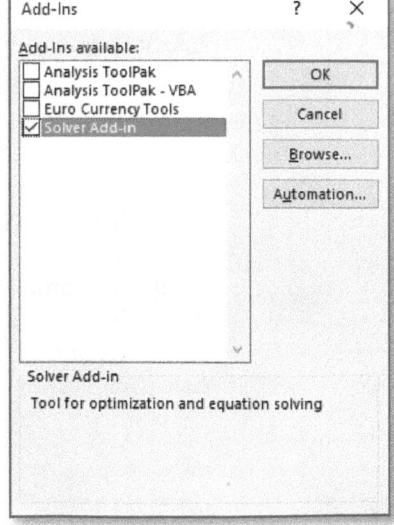

8-9 *Add-ins* dialog box

6. Click **OK**.
 - The **Solver** button is located in the *Analyze* group on the *Data* tab.

A *Solver* problem has three components, known as ***parameters***. A parameter is information used by *Solver* to find a solution. The parameters are the objective cell, variable cells, and constraints.

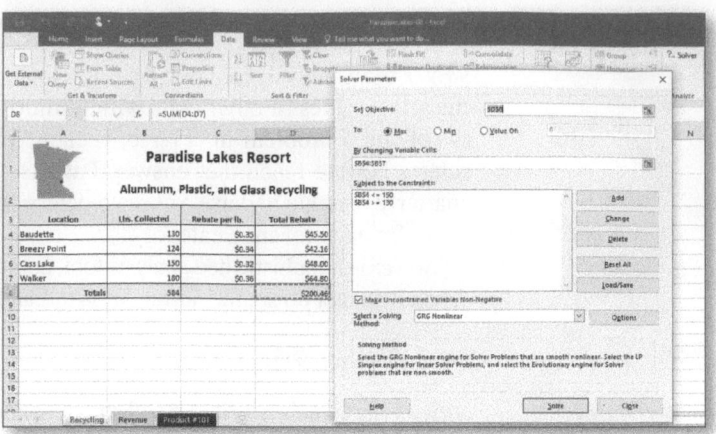

8-10 *Solver* problem for Paradise Lakes

The Objective Cell

The ***objective cell*** is a cell with a formula to be calculated to reach a desired result. It is sometimes referred to as the ***target cell***. You can set the objective cell to the maximum or minimum or to a value. In Figure 8-10, Paradise Lakes wants to determine a maximum total rebate. The formula in cell D8 is the objective cell.

Variable Cells

In order to reach the desired result in the objective cell, *Solver* changes the cells identified as ***variable cells***. These cells may also be called ***decision cells*** or ***changing cells***. In Figure 8-10, the variable cells are cells B4:B7.

Constraints

A ***constraint*** is a restriction or limitation. It could be a limitation on the formula, on one or more of the variable cells, or a limitation on other cells that are directly related to the objective cell. In Figure 8-10, a constraint for cell B4, the Baudette value, is that pounds collected cannot be fewer than 130 or greater than 150. When *Solver* cannot find a solution, it is often due to how constraints are defined.

Solving Method

Solver uses an ***algorithm***, a step-by-step procedure, to find a solution. Three solving methods are available: GRG Nonlinear, LP Simplex, and Evolutionary. For most problems, start with GRG Nonlinear. If *Solver* cannot find a solution, try either of the other methods. For sophisticated *Solver* problems with complicated constraints, identify the type of problem and explore the solving methods in detail.

To run *Solver*, click the **Solver** button on the *Data* tab in the *Analyze* group and define each parameter in the *Solver Parameters* dialog box.

▶**HOW TO:** Run Solver

1. Click the **Solver** button [*Data* tab, *Analyze* group].
 - The *Solver Parameters* dialog box opens.
2. Click the **Set Objective** box and click the cell with the formula to be solved.
 - The objective cell must include a formula.

3. Make a selection for the **To** parameter.
 - You can solve the formula for the minimum or maximum value.
 - You can choose *Value Of* and type a specific value in the entry box.
4. Click the **By Changing Variable Cells** box.
5. Select the cells that can be changed.
 - You can paste or type a range name instead of selecting cells.
 - Press **Ctrl** to select nonadjacent cells.
6. Click **Add** to the right of the *Subject to the Constraints* box.
 - The *Add Constraint* dialog box opens.
 - You can set multiple constraints for a cell.
7. Click the **Cell Reference** box and select the first cell or range that has a limitation.
8. Click the middle drop-down arrow and choose an operator.
 - The *int* operator limits the value to a whole number.
 - The *bin* operator requires a binary value, either 0 or 1.
 - The *dif* operator is used to specify that all values in a range must be different.
9. Click the **Constraint** box and enter a value (Figure 8-11).
 - You can click a cell with a value for the constraint.
10. Click **Add** in the *Add Constraint* dialog box to add another constraint.
 - If you click **OK** but want to add another constraint, click **Add** to the right of the *Subject to the Constraints* box.
11. Click **OK** in the *Add Constraint* dialog box when all constraints are identified.
 - The constraints are listed in the *Solver Parameters* dialog box.
12. Select the **Make Unconstrained Variables Non-Negative** box.
 - If you leave this box unchecked, a variable cell without a constraint can be solved to a negative number.
13. Click the **Select a Solving Method** arrow and choose a method (Figure 8-12).
 - If *Solver* cannot find a solution, try a different method.
14. Click **Solve**.
 - The *Solver Results* dialog box includes an option to keep the solution or to return to the original values.
 - You can generate *Solver* reports.
 - You can save the results as a scenario.
15. Click **OK** to keep the solution.

8-11 *Add Constraint* dialog box

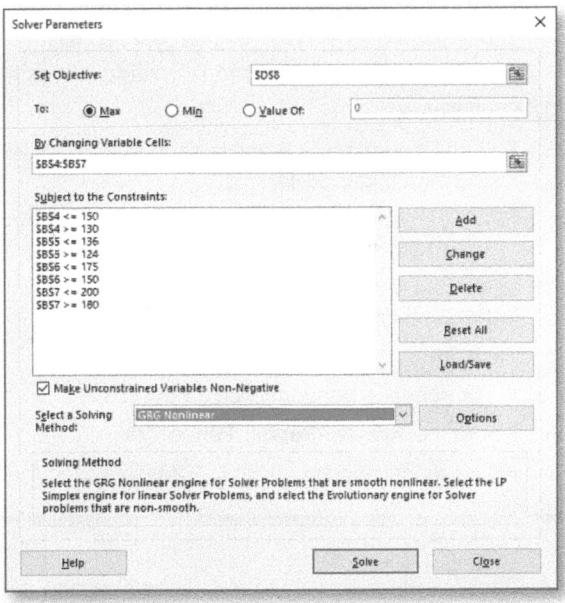

8-12 Completed *Solver* parameters with constraints

Solver Reports

Select an option in the *Solver Results* dialog box to generate statistical analysis reports about the problem and the solution. Three reports for a solved problem are listed: *Answer*, *Sensitivity*, and *Limits*. These reports are straightforward to generate, but you should have an understanding of statistical concepts and terms to understand and interpret the reports.

▶ MORE INFO

When *Solver* cannot find a solution, print the *Feasibility* and *Feasibility-Bounds* reports to help identify constraint issues.

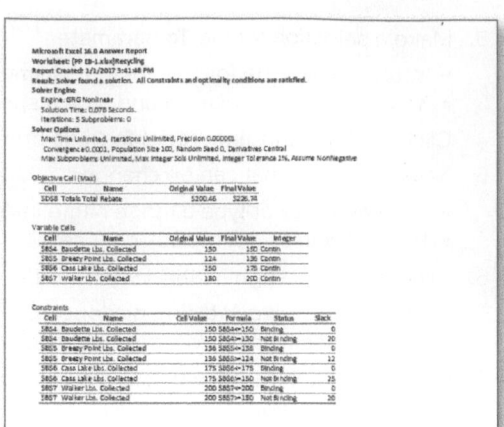

8-13 A *Solver Answer* report

Answer Report

The ***Answer report*** identifies and lists each parameter and serves as documentation of your work. The report includes original values and values suggested by *Solver* as shown in Figure 8-13.

The first *Answer* report is inserted in the workbook in a sheet named *Answer Report 1*. If you run *Solver* multiple times, you can generate an answer report each time, and the sheets are named *Answer Report 2*, and so on.

▶HOW TO: Create an Answer Report

1. Complete the *Solver Parameters* dialog box as needed.
2. Click **Solve**.
3. Select **Answer** in the *Reports* section in the *Solver Results* dialog box. (Figure 8-14).
 - You can also select *Sensitivity* and *Limits* to generate all three reports.
4. Select the **Outline Reports** box if the report should be formatted as an Excel outline.
5. Click **OK**.
 - The report is generated on a new sheet.
6. Select the **Answer Report 1** sheet tab.
 - The report documents how *Solver* reached the solution.

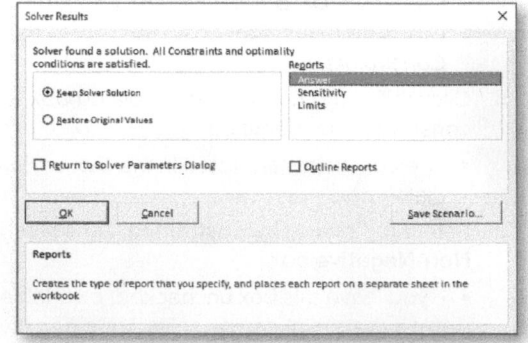

8-14 *Solver Results* window

If *Solver* returns a runtime error in a message box, uninstall the command from the *Add-Ins* dialog box in Excel *Options*, and exit Excel. Then restart Excel and install *Solver* again.

▶HOW TO: Uninstall Solver

1. Select **Options** [*File* tab] and click **Add-Ins** in the left pane.
 - The *View and manage Microsoft Office Add-ins* dialog box opens.
 - Active applications are listed near the top of the window.
2. Select **Solver Add-in** in the list of *Active Application Add-Ins*.
3. Click **Go** near the bottom of the dialog box.
4. Deselect the **Solver Add-in** box and click **OK**.

In this project, you create three scenarios for March revenue at Paradise Lakes Resort. You also use *Goal Seek* and *Solver* to analyze rebate amounts for recyclables at the current rates.

File Needed: *ParadiseLakes-08.xlsx (Student data files are available in the Library of your SIMnet account)*
Completed Project File Name: *[your initials] PP E8-1.xlsx*

1. Open the **ParadiseLakes-08** workbook from your student data files and save it as [your initials] PP E8-1.

2. Click the **Revenue** worksheet tab.

3. Create a scenario for the original data.
 a. Select cells **D4:D7**.
 b. Click the **What-if Analysis** button [*Data* tab, *Forecast* group].
 c. Select **Scenario Manager**. No scenarios exist in the workbook.
 d. Click **Add**.
 e. Type Original as the name in the *Add Scenario* dialog box. The *Changing cells* box displays the selected cells **D4:D7** and a default comment (Figure 8-15).

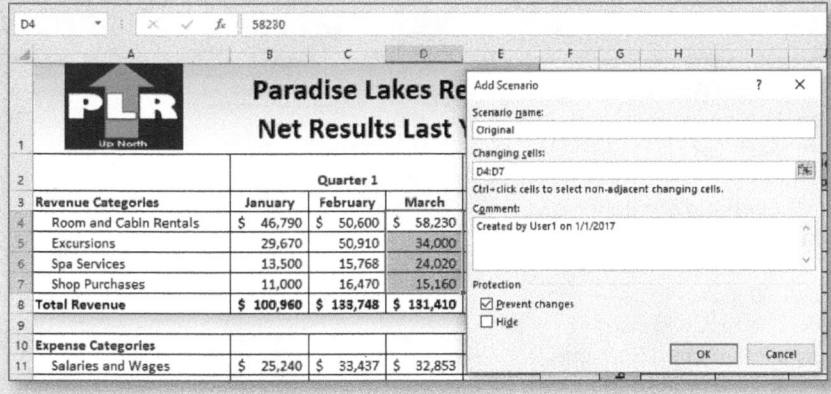

8-15 *Scenario Manager* dialog box

 f. Click **OK**. Note that the changing cells were named.
 g. Do not change any values in the *Scenario Values* dialog box and click **OK**.
 h. Click **Close**.

4. Create scenarios with new data.
 a. Click the **What-if Analysis** button [*Data* tab, *Forecast* group] and select **Scenario Manager**. The *Original* scenario name is listed.
 b. Click **Add** to add a second scenario to the workbook.
 c. Type Best as the name in the *Add Scenario* dialog box.
 d. Verify that the *Changing cells* are cells **D4:D7**.
 e. Click **OK**.
 f. Type 62000 for **Rentals** in the *Scenario Values* dialog box and press **Tab**. If you accidentally press **Enter** and return to the *Scenario Manager* dialog box, click **Edit** and **OK** to return to the *Scenario Values* dialog box.

g. Edit the values as shown here:

Excursions 36000
Spa_Services 28000
Shop_Purchases 20000

h. Click **OK** and then click **Add** to add a third scenario.
i. Type Worst as the name and click **OK**.
j. Edit the values as shown here:

Rentals 55000
Excursions 30000
Spa_Services 22000
Shop_Purchases 12000

k. Click **OK** and click **Close**. The original values are still displayed in the workbook.

5. Show a scenario.
 a. Click the **What-if Analysis** button [*Data* tab, *Forecast* group] and select **Scenario Manager**. The three scenario names are listed (Figure 8-16).
 b. Click **Best** to highlight the name.
 c. Click **Show**. The values for the *Best* scenario display in the worksheet.
 d. Click **Close**.
 e. Select cell **A2**.

6. Create a scenario summary report.
 a. Click the **What-if Analysis** button [*Data* tab, *Forecast* group] and select **Scenario Manager**.
 b. Click **Summary**.
 c. Verify that **Scenario summary** is selected as the *Report type* in the *Scenario Summary* dialog box.
 d. Select cell **E8** in the *Result cells* box.
 e. Click **OK**. The report is inserted on a new sheet named *Scenario Summary* (Figure 8-17).

7. Use *Goal Seek* to determine number of pounds of recycling.
 a. Click the **Recycling** sheet tab and select cell **D4**.
 b. Click the **What-if Analysis** button [*Data* tab, *Forecast* group] and choose **Goal Seek**.
 c. Click the **To value** box and type 50.
 d. Click the **By changing cell** box and select cell **B4** (Figure 8-18).
 e. Click **OK** to run *Goal Seek*. Recycling must increase to more than 142 pounds to reach the target.
 f. Click **OK** to accept the solution.
 g. Select cell **D5** and run *Goal Seek* to determine how many pounds are required to reach $50 for Breezy Point.
 h. Select cells **B4:B8** and click the **Decrease Decimal** button [*Home* tab, *Number* group] to display all values with two decimal places.

8-16 Scenario names in the dialog box

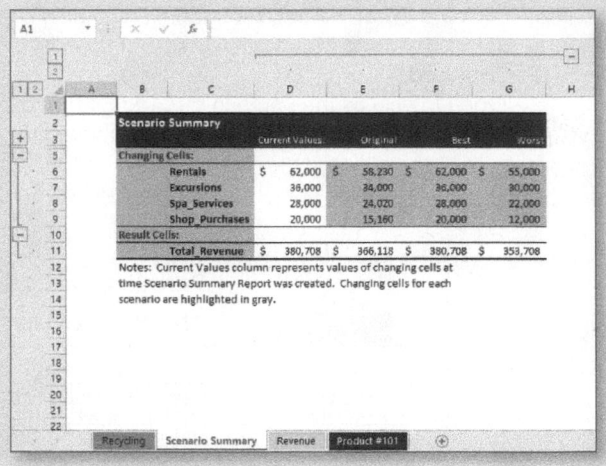

8-17 *Scenario Summary* report sheet

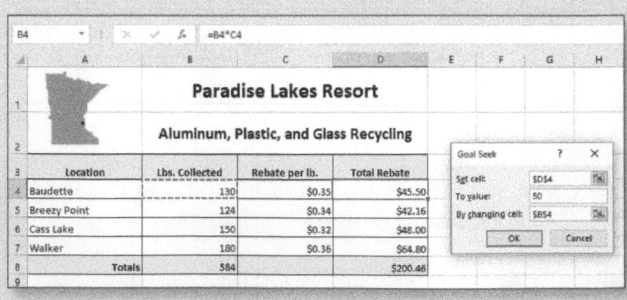

8-18 *Goal Seek* dialog box

8. Create a scenario for current data.
 a. Select cells **B4:B7** and click the **What-if Analysis** button [*Data* tab, *Forecast* group].
 b. Select **Scenario Manager** and click **Add**. Scenarios are associated with a worksheet, and this sheet currently has no scenarios.
 c. Type Current as the name in the *Add Scenario* dialog box.
 d. Click **OK**.
 e. Do not change any values and click **OK** and then click **Close**.

9. Install *Solver*. (Skip this step if *Solver* is already installed.)
 a. Select the **Options** command [*File* tab].
 b. Click **Add-Ins** in the left pane.
 c. Click **Solver Add-in** in the *Inactive Application Add-ins* list.
 d. Click **Go** near the bottom of the window.
 e. Select the **Solver Add-in** box and click **OK**.

10. Set *Solver* parameters.
 a. Select cell **D8**. This cell has a *SUM* formula.
 b. Click the **Solver** button [*Data* tab, *Analyze* group] to open the *Solver Parameters* dialog box.
 c. Verify that cell **D8** is selected in the *Set Objective* box; it is an absolute reference.
 d. Verify that the **Max** radio button is selected for the *To* parameter.
 e. Click the **By Changing Variable Cells** box and select cells **B4:B7**.

11. Add constraints to a *Solver* problem.
 a. Click **Add** to the right of the *Subject to the Constraints* box.
 b. Select cell **B4** for the *Cell Reference* box.
 c. Verify that **<=** is the operator.
 d. Click the **Constraint** box and type 150 (Figure 8-19).
 e. Click **Add** to add another constraint. If you accidentally closed the *Add Constraint* dialog box, click **Add** in the *Solver Parameters* dialog box.

 f. Select cell **B4** again for the *Cell Reference* box.
 g. Choose **>=** as the operator and type 130 as the constraint. The value in cell B4 must be equal to or less than 150 and equal to or greater than 130 (between 130 and 150).

8-19 *Add Constraint* dialog box

 h. Add the following constraints:

B5	<=	160
B5	>=	150
B6	<=	175
B6	>=	150
B7	<=	200
B7	>=	180

 i. Click **OK** in the *Add Constraint* dialog box when all constraints are identified (Figure 8-20).
 j. Select the **Make Unconstrained Variables Non-Negative** box if needed.
 k. Choose **GRG Nonlinear** for the *Select a Solving Method*.
 l. Click **Solve**. A possible solution to the problem is shown in the worksheet.

12. Manage *Solver* results.
 a. Click **Save Scenario** in the *Solver Results* dialog box.
 b. Type Max as the scenario name.
 c. Click **OK** to return to the *Solver Results* dialog box.

8-20 All constraints are listed

d. Select **Answer** in the *Reports* list.

e. Click **OK**. The generated report is inserted.

13. Create a scenario summary report.

a. Click the **What-if Analysis** button [*Data* tab, *Forecast* group] and select **Scenario Manager**.

b. Click **Summary**.

c. Verify that **Scenario summary** is selected as the *Report type*.

d. Click the **Result cells** box and verify or select cell **D8**.

e. Click **OK**. The report displays on a sheet named *Scenario Summary 2*.

14. Save and close the workbook (Figure 8-21).

15. Uninstall *Solver*.

a. Select **Options** [*File* tab] and click **Add-Ins** in the left pane.

b. Select **Solver Add-in** in the list of *Active Application Add-Ins*.

c. Click **Go** near the bottom of the dialog box.

d. Uncheck the **Solver Add-in** box and click **OK**.

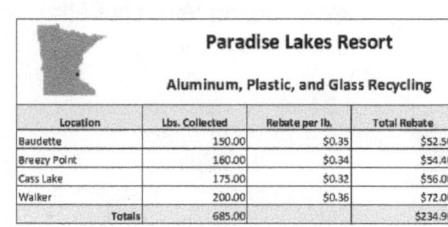

Paradise Lakes Resort
Net Results Last Year

Revenue Categories	January	February	March	Total
		Quarter 1		
Room and Cabin Rentals	$ 46,790	$ 50,600	$ 62,000	$ 159,390
Excursions	29,670	50,910	36,000	116,580
Spa Services	13,500	15,768	28,000	57,268
Shop Purchases	11,000	16,470	20,000	47,470
Total Revenue	$ 100,960	$ 133,748	$ 146,000	$ 380,708
Expense Categories				
Salaries and Wages	$ 25,240	$ 33,437	$ 86,500	$ 95,177
Administrative	15,144	20,062	21,900	57,106
Marketing	10,096	18,375	14,600	38,071
Operations and Maintenance	28,269	37,449	40,880	106,598
Total Expenses	$ 78,749	$ 104,323	$ 113,880	$ 296,952
Net Income	$ 22,211	$ 29,425	$ 32,120	$ 83,756

Paradise Lakes Resort
Aluminum, Plastic, and Glass Recycling

Location	Lbs. Collected	Rebate per lb.	Total Rebate
Baudette	150.00	$0.35	$52.50
Breezy Point	160.00	$0.34	$54.40
Cass Lake	175.00	$0.32	$56.00
Walker	200.00	$0.36	$72.00
Totals	685.00		$234.90

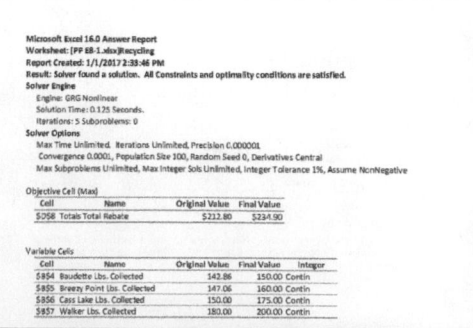

Constraints

Cell	Name	Cell Value	Formula	Status	Slack
B4	Baudette Lbs. Collected	150.00	B4<=150	Binding	0
B4	Baudette Lbs. Collected	150.00	B4>=130	Not Binding	20.00
B5	Breezy Point Lbs. Collected	160.00	B5<=160	Binding	0
B5	Breezy Point Lbs. Collected	160.00	B5>=150	Not Binding	10.00
B6	Cass Lake Lbs. Collected	175.00	B6<=175	Binding	0
B6	Cass Lake Lbs. Collected	175.00	B6>=150	Not Binding	25.00
B7	Walker Lbs. Collected	200.00	B7<=200	Binding	0
B7	Walker Lbs. Collected	200.00	B7>=180	Not Binding	20.00

Scenario Summary

	Current Values:	Current	Max
Changing Cells:			
B4	150.00	142.86	150.00
B5	160.00	147.06	160.00
B6	175.00	150.00	175.00
B7	200.00	180.00	200.00
Result Cells:			
D8	$234.90	$212.80	$234.90

Notes: Current Values column represents values of changing cells at time Scenario Summary Report was created. Changing cells for each scenario are highlighted in gray.

Microsoft Excel 16.0 Answer Report
Worksheet: [PP E8-1.xlsx]Recycling
Report Created: 1/1/2017 2:33:46 PM
Result: Solver found a solution. All Constraints and optimality conditions are satisfied.

Solver Engine
Engine: GRG Nonlinear
Solution Time: 0.125 Seconds.
Iterations: 5 Subproblems: 0

Solver Options
Max Time Unlimited, Iterations Unlimited, Precision 0.000001
Convergence 0.0001, Population Size 100, Random Seed 0, Derivatives Central
Max Subproblems Unlimited, Max Integer Sols Unlimited, Integer Tolerance 1%, Assume NonNegative

Objective Cell (Max)

Cell	Name	Original Value	Final Value
D8	Totals Total Rebate	$212.80	$234.90

Variable Cells

Cell	Name	Original Value	Final Value	Integer
B4	Baudette Lbs. Collected	142.86	150.00	Contin
B5	Breezy Point Lbs. Collected	147.06	160.00	Contin
B6	Cass Lake Lbs. Collected	150.00	175.00	Contin
B7	Walker Lbs. Collected	180.00	200.00	Contin

8-21 Completed worksheets for PP E8-1

SLO 8.4

Building One- and Two-Variable Data Tables

A ***data table*** is a range of cells that shows calculated results for one or more formulas. The *Data Table* command is an option on the *What-If Analysis* button on the *Data* tab [*Forecast* group]. It inserts the function {=TABLE(row_input, column_input)} as an array formula, because the same formula is executed in each cell in the selected range. In *SLO 6.3: Exploring Lookup & Reference Functions*, you learned about array formulas when you used *TRANSPOSE*.

Build a One-Variable Data Table

A ***one-variable data table*** substitutes values for one argument in a formula and displays results for each substituted value. Figure 8-22 shows a data table in columns H:J; column G is a descriptive label. The data table has two formulas, one for January expenses (cell I3) and one for January income (cell J3). The *Data Table* command calculates results in cells I4:J14.

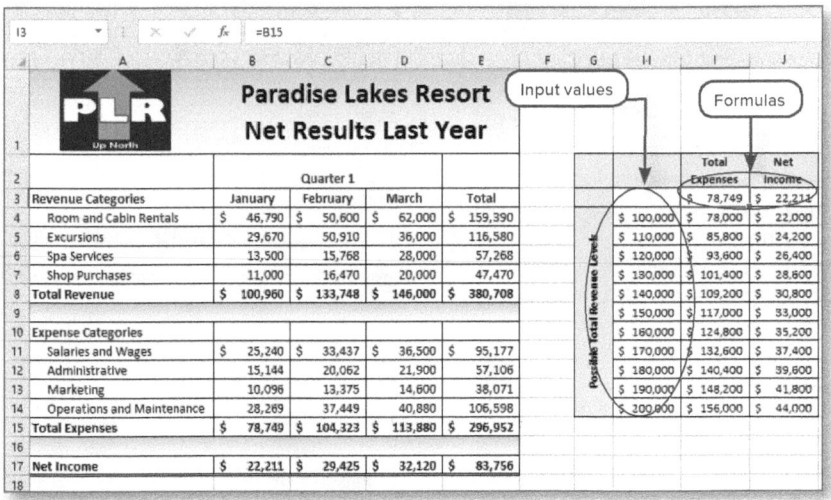

8-22 Data table shows expense and income numbers when total revenue amounts are varied

The *Data Table* command uses an ***input value***. The input values in Figure 8-22 are the revenue numbers in column H. These values are substitute values for the formula result in cell B8. In this example, each value in column H is substituted for cell B8 in the net income formula. A one-variable data table uses one input value in the command, and the substitute numbers are either in a column or a row.

When substitute input values are in a column, the data table formulas must start in the column to the right and one row above where the values start. When the data table has multiple formulas, the formulas must be in the same row. In Figure 8-22, the first formula is in cell I3. In the example, cell I3 is a reference to cell B15 so that you need not retype the formula. The second formula is in cell J3, a reference to the net income formula in cell B17. Both of these formulas have a relationship to cell B8.

> ## MORE INFO
>
> When input values are in a row, the first formula must be one column to the left of the first value and one row below.

For the *Data Table* command, select the entire data table range including the formulas, the input values, and the result cells. In Figure 8-22, the data table range is cells H3:J14.

You can edit an input value after the data table is calculated, and the results are updated. You cannot delete the contents of an individual cell in a data table, because that would "shrink" the array. You can, however, select all result cells and delete them.

▶ HOW TO: Create a One-Variable Data Table

1. Enter input values in a single column or row.
 - You can fill a series of values or key specific numbers.
2. Enter the first formula.
 - If input values are in a column, enter the formula one row above and one column to the right of the first input value.
 - If input values are in a row, enter the formula one column to the left and one row below the first input value.
 - You can type a reference to an existing formula.
 - You can type or build the formula with sample data and sample cell references.
3. Enter additional formulas in the same row (Figure 8-23).
4. Select the data table range.
 - Select all input values, all formulas, and the cells for results.
 - The top-left cell in the range is empty.
5. Click the **What-If Analysis** button [*Data* tab, *Forecast* group].
6. Choose **Data Table**.
 - The *Data Table* dialog box opens.
7. Enter a column or a row input cell reference (Figure 8-24).
 - In a one-variable data table, enter either a row input or a column input reference.
 - You can select the cell for which the input values will be substituted.
 - You can type the cell address.
8. Click **OK**.
 - The data table cells display results for each input value.
 - You can format a data table to add number styles, fill, borders, or explanatory labels.
 - The *TABLE* function is used in an array formula and is entered in each result cell.

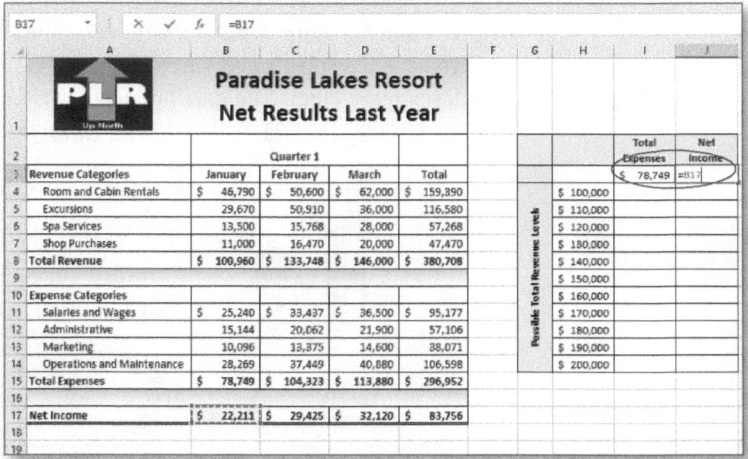

8-23 Input values are in a column; formulas are in the row above, one column to the right

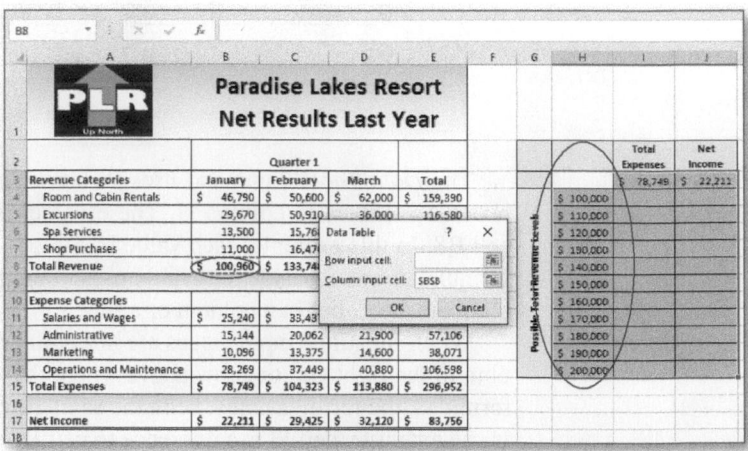

8-24 Values in column H will replace the value in cell B8 in the data table to calculate expense and income amounts

Build a Two-Variable Data Table

A *two-variable data table* uses two sets of input values, one in a column, the other in a row, and the table has only one formula. Figure 8-25 shows a two-variable data table in which January revenue *and* expenses are varied to calculate net income. The net income formula is in cell B17 and is referenced in cell H4. Substituted revenue amounts are column input values (cells H5:H17), and substituted expense amounts are row input values (cells I4:P4).

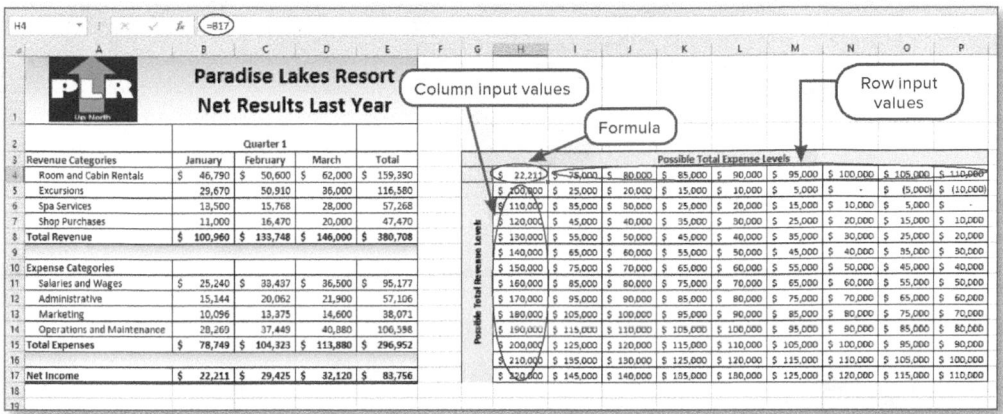

8-25 Two-variable data table

In a two-variable data table, row input values start one column to the right of the column values and one row above the first column value, cell I4 in the figure. Place the formula above the column values and to the left of the row values (cell H4 in the example).

The data table range includes the formula, the input column, the input row, and the result cells, cells H4:P17. In Figure 8-25, the column input cell for the *Data Table* command is cell B8 because revenue values are in *column* H. The row input cell is cell B15, because expense values are in *row* 4. The input values are substituted for both the revenue and expense amounts to complete the data table.

> **MORE INFO**
>
> A data table must be on the same worksheet as its formulas.

▶ HOW TO: Create a Two-Variable Data Table

1. Enter column input values in a single column.
 - Type values or fill a series.
 - You can prepare either the row or column input values first.
2. Enter row input values in a single row.
 - Start the first row value one row above and one column to the right of the first column value.
3. Enter the formula or a reference to the formula.
 - It is easier to refer to an existing formula than to re-enter the formula.
 - Place the formula reference in the cell above the column input values and to the left of the row input values.
4. Select the data table range.
 - Include the formula, column input values, row input values, and result cells.

5. Click the **What-If Analysis** button [*Data* tab, *Forecast* group].

6. Choose **Data Table**.

7. Select the row input cell.

 • You can type the cell address.

8. Select the column input cell or type the cell address (Figure 8-26).

9. Click **OK**.

 • The result cells calculate the formula results in each cell.
 • Each result cell substitutes a column and a row input value in the formula.
 • Change any column or row input value to recalculate the data table.

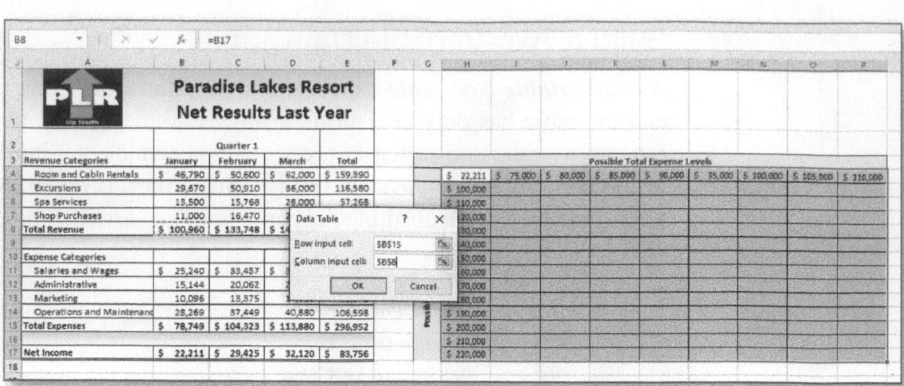

8-26 Two-variable data table setup

SLO 8.5

Creating a Forecast Sheet

A *forecast sheet* is a worksheet with an Excel table and a chart that illustrates past data and predicts future values, generated from data in the workbook. A forecast sheet can be created quickly to estimate future values for product sales, work hour requirements, or expense levels.

Create a Forecast Sheet

A forecast sheet uses two data series to build either a line or a column chart. One data series must be a date or time field, and the other series is the values used for forecasting. The date or time series must follow an interval, such as every hour, every other day, every month, and so on. The generated sheet is formatted as an Excel table and displays existing dates/times and values in adjacent columns. At the end of the table, forecast dates display with estimated values in a third column.

>
> MORE INFO
>
> A forecast sheet inserts *FORECAST* functions [*Statistical* category] in its tables. Explore these functions to learn more about them.

The *Create Forecast Sheet* dialog box has options for calculating statistics such as alpha, beta, and gamma values, and more. You can also redefine the time and value ranges if needed.

After the forecast sheet is created, format the table from the *Table Tools Design* tab. The *Chart Tools Design* and *Format* tabs are also available for limited formatting of the chart.

▶ HOW TO: Create a Forecast Sheet

1. Select the two data series.

 • One column must be a time or date field.
 • The columns need not be adjacent.

2. Click the **Forecast Sheet** button [*Data* tab, *Forecast* group].

 • The *Create Forecast Worksheet* window opens (Figure 8-27).

3. Select the line or column chart type.

 • The chart preview displays.

4. Click the calendar icon for **Forecast End** and set the ending date or time for estimated values.

5. Select the **Options** arrow to expand the window.

 • You can change the ranges used for the data series.

 • The default confidence interval is 95% which measures how likely a value is to occur within the range of forecasted values.

6. Select the **Include forecast statistics** box.

 • This option generates alpha, beta, gamma, and additional statistical measures.

7. Click **Create** (Figure 8-28).

8-27 *Create Forecast Worksheet* window

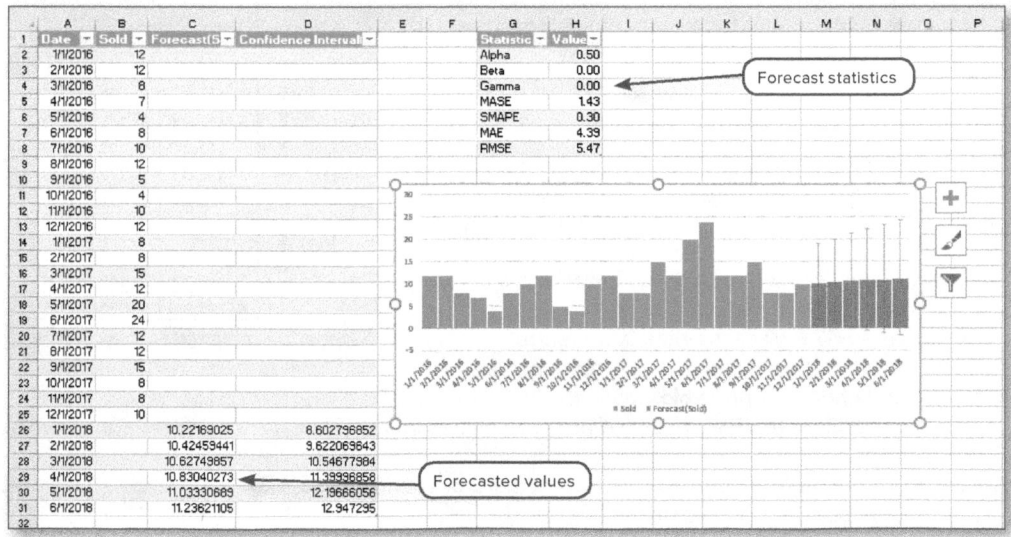

8-28 Forecast table and chart

• The forecast sheet includes the table, forecast statistics, and the chart.
• Forecasted values are at the bottom of the table.
• Forecast statistics are displayed in a separate table.

PAUSE & PRACTICE: EXCEL 8-2

In this project, you build a one- and a two-variable data table to determine revenue, expense, and income levels for Paradise Lakes Resort. You also create a forecast sheet for a product sold at PLR spas.

File Needed: **PP E8-1.xlsx**
Completed Project File Name: **[your initials] PP E8-2.xlsx**

1. Open the **[your initials] PP E8-1** workbook completed in *Pause & Practice 8-1* and save it as [your initials] PP E8-2.

2. Select the **Revenue** worksheet tab.

3. Create a one-variable data table.
 a. Select cell **I3**. This cell is one column to the right of and one row above the first input value.
 b. Type =, select cell **B15**, and press **Enter** to create a reference to the total expenses formula for January.
 c. Select cell **J3** and create a reference to cell **B17** for the net income formula (Figure 8-29).
 d. Select cells **H3:J14** as the data table range.
 e. Click the **What-If Analysis** button [*Data* tab, *Forecast* group] and choose **Data Table**.
 f. Click the **Column input cell** entry box and select cell **B8**. The total revenue amount will be replaced by the input values in column H in both formulas.
 g. Click **OK** to create the data table.
 h. Select cells **I4:J14** and format them as **Accounting Number** format with **0** decimal places.
 i. *AutoFit* columns that do not display all the data (Figure 8-30).

4. Create a two-variable data table.
 a. Select cell **H17** to place the formula one row above the column input values and one column to the left of the row values.
 b. Type =, select cell **B17**, and press **Enter** to create a reference to the net income formula.
 c. Select cells **H17:P30** as the data table range.
 d. Click the **What-If Analysis** button [*Data* tab, *Forecast* group] and choose **Data Table**.
 e. Select cell **B15** for the *Row input cell* box. The values in row 17 will be substituted for the value in cell B15.
 f. Click the **Column input cell** box and select cell **B8**. The values in column H will be substituted for the value in cell B8 (Figure 8-31).
 g. Click **OK** to build the data table. Some results are negative, meaning a net loss.
 h. Format all cells in the data table as **Accounting Number** format with **0** decimal places.
 i. **AutoFit** columns that do not display all the data.

5. Edit input values for a table.
 a. Select cell **I17** and type 75000 as a new value.
 b. Select cell **J17** and type 80000 to start a new series.

		Total Expenses	Net Income
		$ 78,749	=B17
	$ 100,000		
	$ 110,000		
	$ 120,000		
	$ 130,000		
	$ 140,000		
	$ 150,000		
	$ 160,000		
	$ 170,000		
	$ 180,000		
	$ 190,000		
	$ 200,000		

8-29 Formula reference in the data table

		Total Expenses	Net Income
		$ 78,749	$ 22,211
	$ 100,000	$ 78,000	$ 22,000
	$ 110,000	$ 85,800	$ 24,200
	$ 120,000	$ 93,600	$ 26,400
	$ 130,000	$ 101,400	$ 28,600
	$ 140,000	$ 109,200	$ 30,800
	$ 150,000	$ 117,000	$ 33,000
	$ 160,000	$ 124,800	$ 35,200
	$ 170,000	$ 132,600	$ 37,400
	$ 180,000	$ 140,400	$ 39,600
	$ 190,000	$ 148,200	$ 41,800
	$ 200,000	$ 156,000	$ 44,000

8-30 One-variable data table results

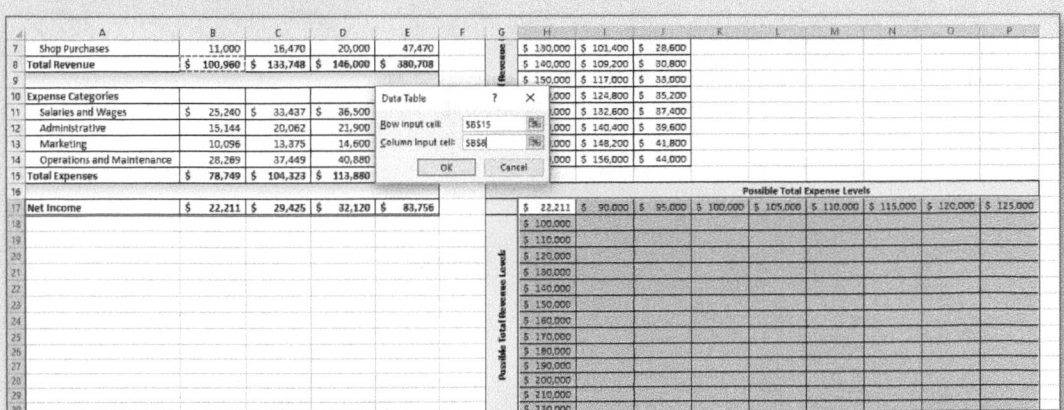

8-31 *Data Table* dialog box for a two-variable table

c. Select cells **I17:J17** and use the *Fill* handle to fill values to reach cell **P17**. The data table updates and there are fewer negative results (Figure 8-32). When revenue and expenses are equal, there is no profit, shown as a hyphen (-) in the *Accounting Number* format.

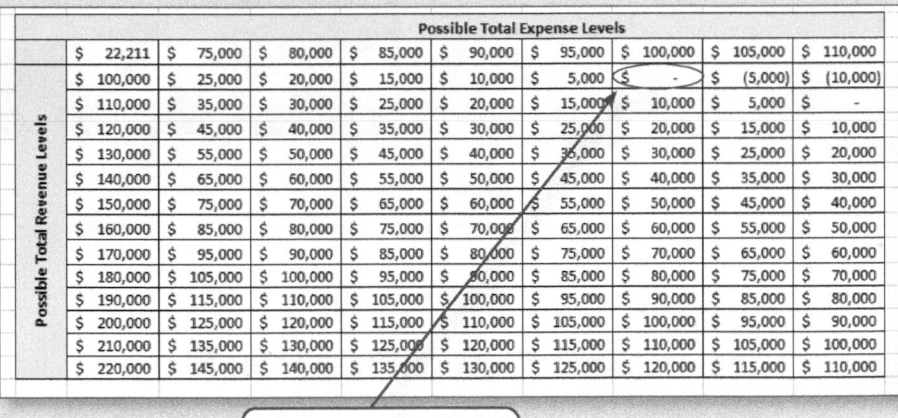

Revenue and expense are equal

8-32 Completed two-variable table

6. Create a forecast worksheet.
 a. Select the **Product #101** worksheet tab.
 b. Select cells **A4: B28** and click the **Forecast Sheet** button [*Data* tab, *Forecast* group].
 c. Click the **Create a line chart** button.
 d. Click **Create** to generate the forecast worksheet.
 e. Name the new sheet tab Forecast Sheet.

7. Format a forecast chart sheet.
 a. Move the chart to its own sheet named Forecast Chart.
 b. Format the chart with **Style 9**.
 c. Click the **Chart Elements** drop-down list [*Chart Tools Format* tab, *Current Selection* group] and select **Horizontal (Category) Axis** to select the dates along the bottom axis.
 d. Click the **Format Selection** button [*Chart Tools Format* tab, *Current Selection* group].
 e. Select the **Axis Options** button in the *Format Axis* pane.
 f. Expand the **Labels** group in the task pane and set the **Specify interval unit** at **2** to show every other month.

g. Click the **Chart Elements** button at the top right corner of the chart and insert a **Centered Overlay** chart title.

h. Edit the placeholder text to Forecasted Sales for Product #101.

i. Click the chart background to deselect the title object.

j. Point at the chart title object to display a move pointer and drag the title as shown in Figure 8-33.

8. Save and close the workbook.

8-33 Completed forecast worksheet and chart for PP E8-2

Getting and Transforming Data in a Query

You can import data from various sources in queries and transform the data to fit your Excel needs. A *query* is a combination of instructions, filters, and formats that establishes a connection to and displays data. You define and save a query once and refresh it when necessary to extract current data. You can combine queries to build an Excel table or *PivotTable* that would otherwise be impossible or difficult to create. Queries can use corporate data, online public data, or data on your computer. As for tables and *PivotTables*, data for queries is always in list-type format.

The *Query Editor* is a window that floats on top of the worksheet as shown in Figure 8-34. It opens with its own *Ribbon* and displays the *Query Settings* pane on the right. You define and organize the data for loading into Excel in the *Query Editor*. The *New Query* button is located on the *Data* tab in the *Get & Transform Data* group.

Get and Transform an XML File

XML represents *Extensible Markup Language*, a file format for exchanging data on the Web. An XML file is a text file that can be imported into many applications; it has an .xml file name extension. To create a query, you can use an XML file on your computer, on a corporate network, or in a *OneDrive* folder.

8-34 *Query Editor* window

> **MORE INFO**
>
> An XML file has a related .xsd file that provides data scheme information.

> **ANOTHER WAY**
>
> You can open an XML file in Excel and save it as a regular workbook.

▶ HOW TO: Get an XML File for a Query

1. Click the **New Query** button [*Data* tab, *Get & Transform* group] and choose **From File**.
2. Choose **From XML**.
 - The *Import Data* dialog box opens.
3. Navigate to the folder with the XML file.
4. Select the file name, click **Import**, and then click **Edit**.
 - The *Query Editor* window opens with the *Query Settings* pane at the right.
5. Click the **Expand** button next to the file name at the top of the first column (Figure 8-35).
 - All of the fields are selected.
 - You can deselect fields as desired.

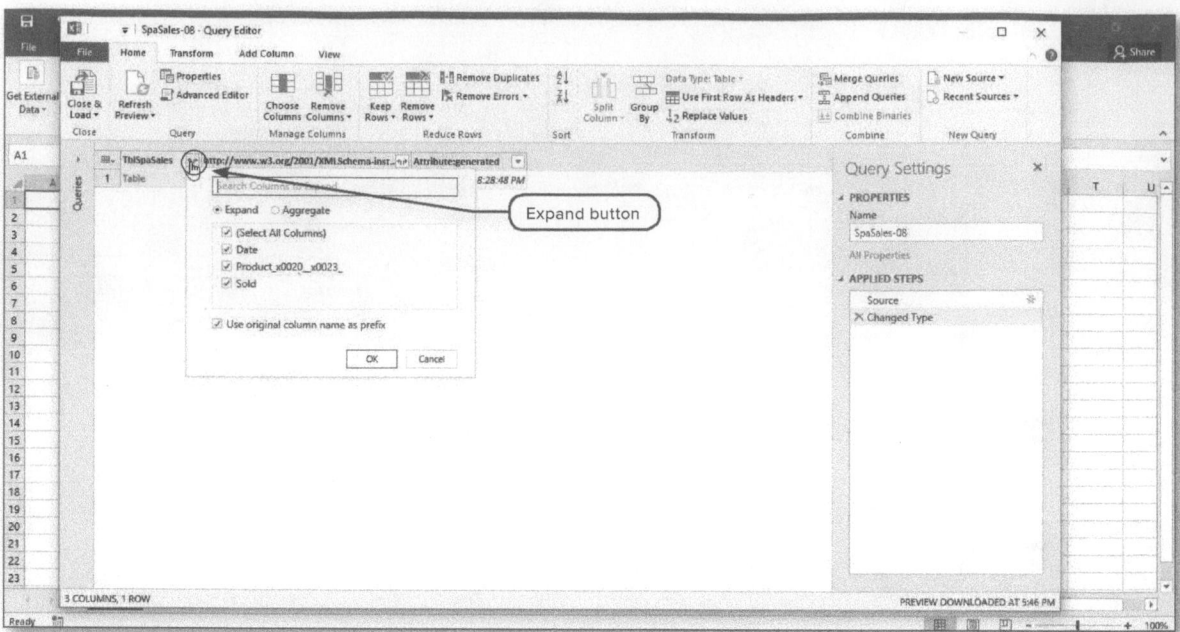

8-35 XML data is ready to be expanded

6. Click **OK**.

- Each field is expanded so that data is visible in the query sheet.
- The *Applied Steps* in the *Query Settings* pane lists each action you perform (Figure 8-36).
- You can delete steps to undo actions.

Data in a query can be "cleaned" or prepared for use in Excel. The labels, for example, can be edited to use simple, descriptive terms. You can also choose the data type for each column to match your plans for use in Excel.

Queries are named with the same name as the source file, but you can change the name in the *Query Settings* pane. Each field has a *Filter* arrow for displaying only the rows that you need for your Excel worksheet.

After you have prepared the data in the *Query Editor*, you load the results to Excel. The data is formatted as an Excel table on a new worksheet with a default name which you can edit as desired.

▶ **HOW TO: Edit and Load a Query**

1. Double-click a column name, type a new name, and press **Enter**.
 - You can also edit labels later in the Excel table or *PivotTable*.
2. Click a column name and click the **Data Type** button [*Home* tab, *Transform* group].
3. Choose the data type (see Figure 8-36).
 - If you plan to use a field in calculations, it must be a number-type field.
4. Right-click the column name for a field to be removed.
5. Select **Remove**.
 - You can also click the column name and press **Delete** on the keyboard.

8-36 Select the appropriate data type for each field

6. Click a *Filter* arrow and build a filter for a column as desired.

 • Only filtered rows are loaded to the worksheet.

7. Click the **Close & Load** button [*Home* tab, *Close* group].

 • Query results display in an Excel table on a new sheet.
 • You can rename the sheet tab as desired.
 • The *Workbook Queries* pane is open and lists existing queries (Figure 8-37).

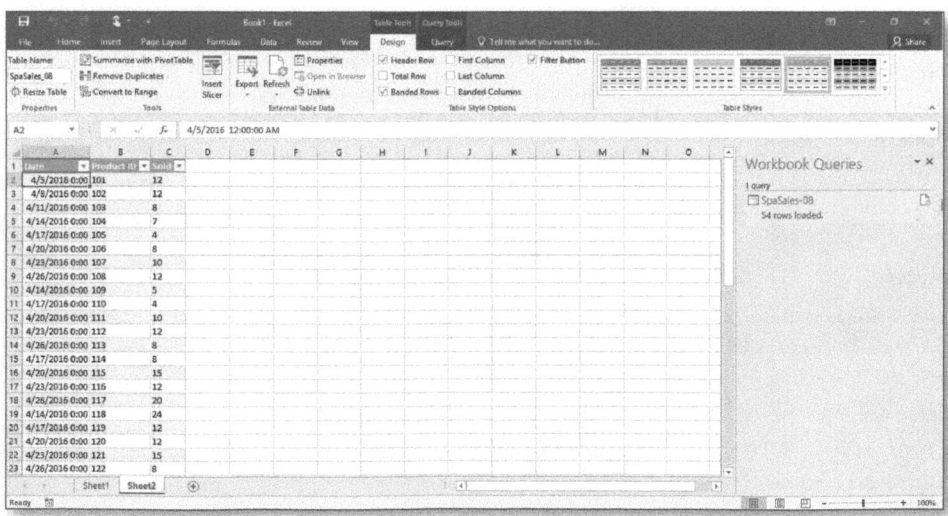

8-37 Query results and the *Workbook Queries* pane

8. Save the workbook.

Get and Transform a Database Table

Queries can be built from tables in Access or SQL databases to which you have permission. The fields are placed in the *Query Editor* with the field names used in the database, and you have the same query editing features as you have for an XML file.

▶ **HOW TO:** Build a Query for a Database Table

1. Click the **New Query** button [*Data* tab, *Get & Transform* group] and choose **From Database**.

2. Choose **From Microsoft Access Database**.
 - The *Import Data* dialog box opens.

3. Navigate to the folder with the database file.

4. Select the database name and click **Import**.
 - The *Navigator* window opens and lists the names of tables and queries in the Access database.

5. Select the name of the table or query.
 - The *Navigator* shows a preview of the data that will be imported (Figure 8-38).

6. Click **Edit** at the bottom of the window.
 - The *Query Editor* opens and displays all the fields from the selected table or query.
 - Database field names are used in the header row.

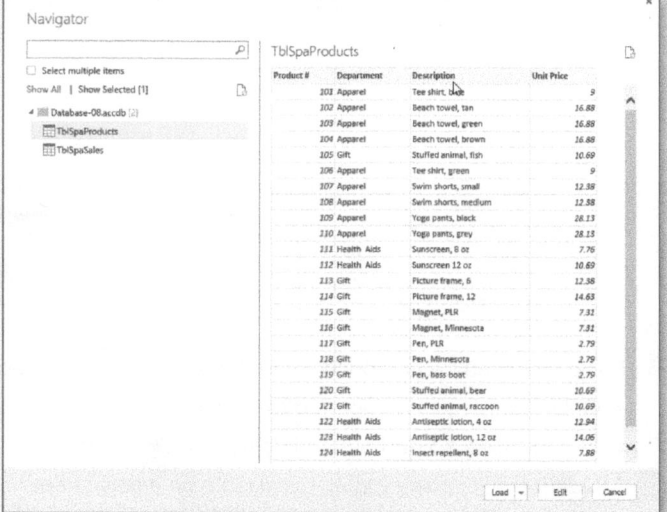

8-38 *Navigator* window for getting files from a database

7. Click a column name to select the field and click the **Data Type** button [*Home* tab, *Transform* group].

8. Choose the data type.
 - If you plan to use a field in calculations, it must be a number-type field.

9. Right-click a column name to open its menu (Figure 8-39).

10. Select **Remove**.
 - The *Applied Steps* in the *Query Settings* pane lists each action you perform.

11. Double-click a column name, type a new name, and press **Enter**.

12. Click the **Close & Load** button [*Home* tab, *Close* group].
 - Query results display in an Excel table on a new sheet.
 - You can rename the sheet tab as desired.
 - The *Workbook Queries* pane lists queries in the workbook.

13. Save the workbook.

8-39 Remove unnecessary data from the query

Create a PivotTable from Multiple Queries

Queries are part of the workbook and are listed in the *Workbook Queries* pane. The pane opens immediately after you load a query, and it can be toggled off and on from the *Data* tab. When you select a cell in a query table, the *Query Tools* tab displays as well as the *Table Tools Design* tab. From the *Query Tools* tab, you can edit the query, refresh the data, delete the query, and combine queries. From the *Table Tools Design* tab, you can create a new *PivotTable*.

You can use multiple queries to create a *PivotTable* when a common field exists in each of the queries. A ***common field*** is data that is the same in each of the queries, allowing for a relationship between the queries. Many relationships are one-to-many in which there is a key field in one of the queries. The ***key field*** is a column in which each data piece appears only once. The related query uses the same field, but it can appear many times. In a product list query, each product number appears only once with the description of the item. In a product sales query, however, the product number appears each time a sale is recorded.

> **MORE INFO**
> Relationships in Excel queries follow the same logic as database rules for relating tables.

As you create queries, Excel automatically and invisibly builds a data model. A ***data model*** is a collection of tables in the workbook available for use in creating a *PivotTable*.

▶ HOW TO: Create a PivotTable from a Data Model

1. Select a cell in one of the query tables.
 - The *Query Tools* and *Table Tools Design* tabs open.
2. Click the **Summarize with PivotTable** button [*Table Tools Design* tab, *Tools* group].
 - The *Create PivotTable* dialog box displays the name of the query and highlights the range in the sheet.
3. Select the **New Worksheet** radio button.
4. Select the **Add this data to the Data Model** box.
5. Click **OK**.
 - A blank *PivotTable* layout displays on a new sheet.
 - The *Workbook Queries* and the *PivotTable Fields* panes are open.
6. Select the fields from the active query to be shown in the *PivotTable*.
 - Fields are placed in areas in the *PivotTable* layout.
 - You can move fields as needed by dragging a field name from one area to another.
7. Click **All** at the top of the *PivotTable Fields* pane to see the related query name.
8. Select the name of the related query and expand it to see the fields.
 - The fields are available for placement in the *PivotTable*.
9. Select the fields to be shown in the *PivotTable*.
 - Fields display in the *PivotTable* layout but may not show accurate data (Figure 8-40).
 - A warning box in the *PivotTable Fields* pane states that *Relationships between tables may be needed*.
10. Click **AutoDetect**.
 - A message box notes that a relationship has been created.
 - If a relationship cannot be found, edit the queries to verify data types for related fields.

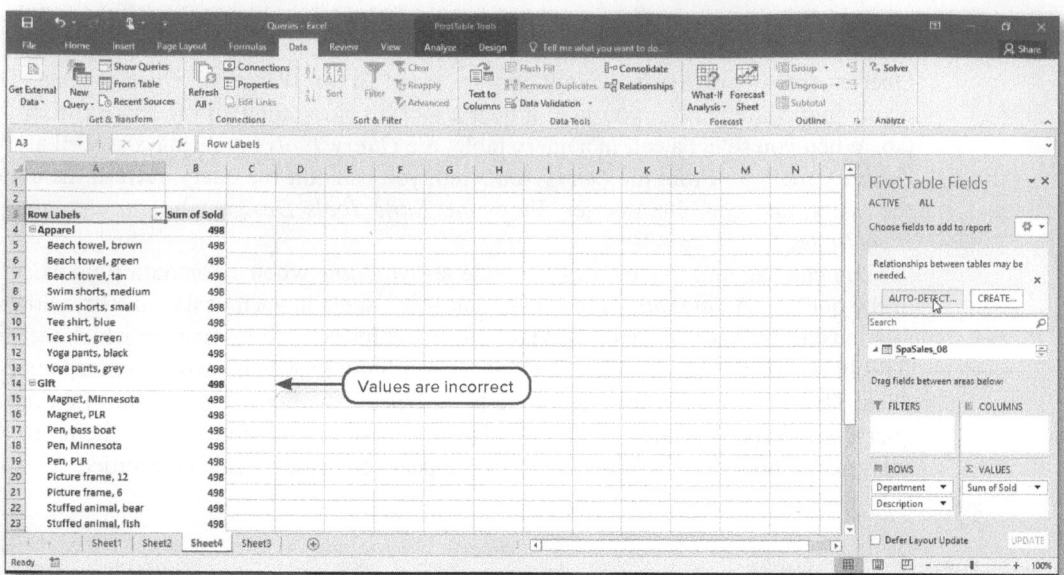

8-40 Fields in *PivotTable* are not yet matched by relationship

11. Click **Close** in the message box.
 - Data in the *PivotTable* is accurate when the relationship is valid.

12. Click the **Relationships** button [*PivotTable Tools Analyze* tab, *Calculations* group].
 - The *Manage Relationships* dialog box identifies how the queries are related (Figure 8-41).

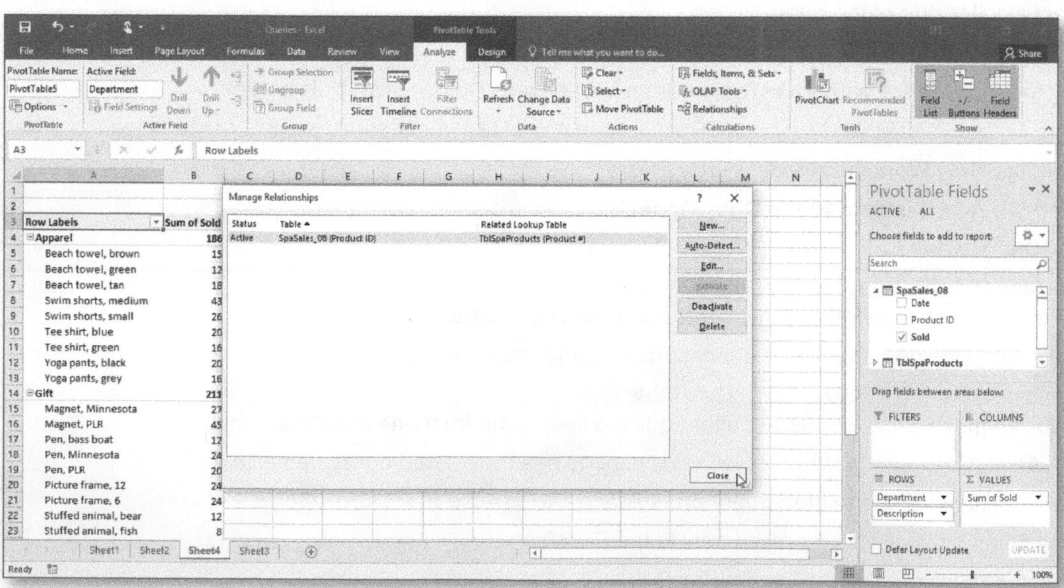

8-41 *Manage Relationships* dialog box

13. Close the dialog box.

> **ANOTHER WAY**
>
> In the *Query Editor*, you can merge queries to create another query, load that merged query to its own sheet, and build a *PivotTable* from the merged query.

SLO 8.7

Exploring PivotTable Tools

You learned in *SLO 4.8: Building and Formatting PivotTables*, how to create, format, and rearrange a *PivotTable*. *PivotTables* and *PivotCharts* have many features that allow you to manage and adjust the data. You can display a timeline for date fields, show values as ratios or percentages, or create a calculated field. A *PivotTable* and its *PivotChart* are linked, so changes you make in either are immediately reflected in the other.

PivotTable Slicers

The *Slicer* tool creates a visual filter for a field in a *PivotTable*, like a slicer for an Excel table. For a large *PivotTable*, a slicer allows you to display only the data you need at the moment. In the Paradise Lakes worksheet, for example, you can create a slicer that displays items sold by department as shown in Figure 8-42.

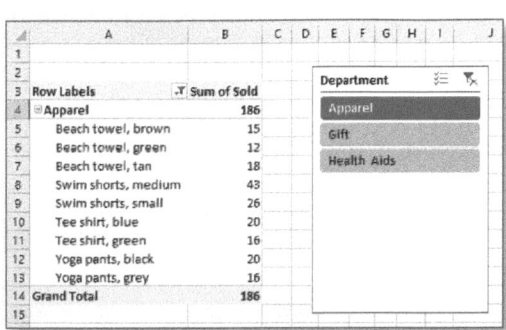

8-42 Department slicer filters data to show only apparel sales

You create a slicer by clicking the **Insert Slicer** button in the *Filter* group on the *PivotTable Tools Analyze* tab. From the *Insert Slicers* dialog box, you select fields to be displayed in slicers, each field in its own slicer window. The dialog box includes all fields used as the data range for the *PivotTable* so that you can use fields in a slicer that are not displayed in the *PivotTable*.

▶ **HOW TO:** Insert a Slicer in a PivotTable

1. Click a cell in the *PivotTable*.
2. Click the **Insert Slicer** button [*PivotTable Tools Analyze* tab, *Filter* group].
 - The *Insert Slicers* window lists each field in the data source for the *PivotTable*.
3. Select the box for each field to be used for filtering data (Figure 8-43).
4. Click **OK**.
 - A *Slicer* window opens for each field.
 - No filter applied.
 - When a slicer button is grayed out, there are no matching items in the *PivotTable*.
5. Click the item name to be used as criteria in the *Slicer* window (Figure 8-44).
 - The *PivotTable* is filtered to display data that matches your selection.

8-43 Choose one or more fields to be used in slicers

- Click the **Multi-Select** button to select more than one field, or press **Ctrl** and click each field.
- Remove a filter by clicking the **Clear Filter** button in the top-right corner of the slicer.

Slicer Tools Options

A slicer is an object that can be sized and moved. When a slicer window is selected, the *Slicer Tools Options* tab is available. It includes commands to format the slicer, change its caption, and to size and position the object.

Row Labels	Sum of Sold
⊟Gift	211
Magnet, Minnesota	27
Magnet, PLR	45
Pen, bass boat	12
Pen, Minnesota	24
Pen, PLR	20
Picture frame, 12	24
Picture frame, 6	24
Stuffed animal, bear	12
Stuffed animal, fish	8
Stuffed animal, raccoon	15
Grand Total	211

Department
Apparel
Gift
Health Aids

8-44 Slicer with filter

▶ HOW TO: Format a PivotTable Slicer

1. Select the slicer.
2. Click the **More** button [*Slicer Tools Options* tab, *Slicer Styles* group].
3. Select a style.
4. Click the **Columns** box [*Slicer Tools Options* tab, *Buttons* group].
5. Type the number of columns to be displayed in the slicer.
 - You can set a width and height for each button in the slicer.
6. Size the slicer to display the buttons in a row (Figure 8-45).
 - You can also set a width and height for the slicer window.

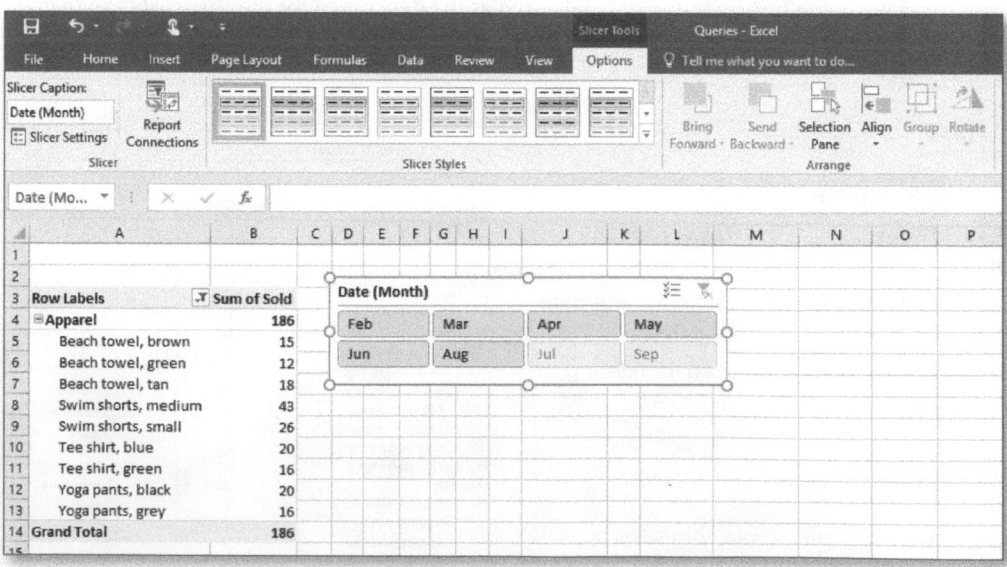

8-45 Slicer with four columns

7. Click the **Slicer Settings** button [*Slicer Tools Options* tab, *Slicer* group].
 - The *Slicer Settings* dialog box opens.

8. Click the **Caption** box and type a label for the slicer (Figure 8-46).

 - You can change the default sort order in the slicer.

9. Click **OK**.

A slicer is saved with the *PivotTable*. If you no longer need the slicer, select it and press **Delete** to remove it.

Insert Timeline

A *timeline* is a visual filter for a date field in a *PivotTable*. In a timeline, you select days, months, quarters, or years for filtering. A timeline is a selectable object that can be sized, positioned, and formatted.

The *Insert Timeline* button is on the *PivotTable Tools Analyze* tab in the *Filter* group. When a timeline object is selected, it displays selection handles, and the *Timeline Tools Options* tab appears. Timeline options include light and dark styles and height and width settings.

8-46 *Slicer Settings* dialog box

> **MORE INFO**
>
> You can insert a timeline for dates in an Excel table.

▶ **HOW TO:** Insert and Format a Timeline in a PivotTable

1. Click a cell in the *PivotTable*.

 - The *PivotTable Tools Analyze* and *Design* tabs open.

2. Click the **Insert Timeline** button [*PivotTable Tools Analyze* tab, *Filter* group].

 - The *Insert Timelines* dialog box lists date fields in the *PivotTable*.

3. Select the box for the date field to be shown in the timeline.

 - The date field for the timeline need not be shown in the *PivotTable*.

4. Click **OK**.

 - The *Timeline* object displays.
 - The *Timeline* displays months as the time level.

5. Click the **Months** arrow and choose the time level as desired.

6. Click the time group to use for filtering in the timeline.

 - The *PivotTable* is filtered to show rows based on the item selected in the timeline (Figure 8-47).

7. Click the **More** button [*Timeline Tools Options* tab, *Timeline Styles* group] and choose a style.

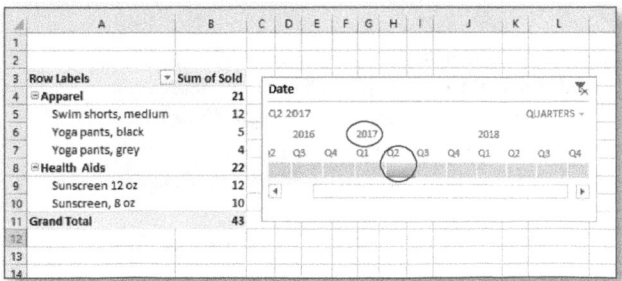

8-47 *Timeline* filter for Q2 in 2017

8. Point to a border to display a move pointer and drag the timeline object to a new location.

9. Point to a corner handle to display a size arrow and resize the timeline object.

Custom Calculations

A *custom calculation* is a built-in percentage, ranking, or ratio in a *PivotTable*. Custom calculations are listed in the *Value Field Settings* dialog box on the *Show Values As* tab. In Figure 8-48, the *Sold* field is shown twice in the *PivotTable*, once as a value (column B) and once as a percentage of the total (column C). You can see the field listed twice in the *Values* area in the *PivotTable Fields* pane.

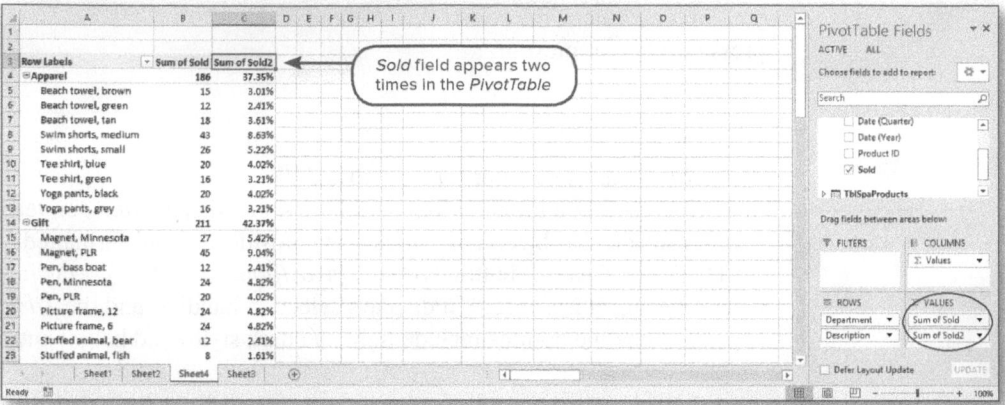

8-48 Value field displayed twice with different calculations

▶ **HOW TO:** Use a Custom Calculation in a PivotTable

1. Right-click a value in the *PivotTable* column.
2. Select **Show Values As**.
 - Custom calculations are listed.
 - *No Calculation* is the first option.
3. Choose a calculation (Figure 8-49).
 - The column in the *PivotTable* displays the custom calculation results.

8-49 Value field set to show a custom calculation

> ▶ **ANOTHER WAY**
>
> Click a cell in the *PivotTable* column, click the **Field Settings** button [*PivotTable Tools Analyze* tab, *Active Field* group] and click the *Show Value As* tab to use a custom calculation.

Calculated Fields

A *calculated field* is a field in the *PivotTable* that is not in the source data. A calculated field uses a value field from the *PivotTable's* underlying data in a formula. When you insert a calculated field, it displays as the rightmost field in the *PivotTable*, but you can move it and edit its *Value Field Settings*, too.

A calculated field can be created in a *PivotTable* based on workbook data but not in a *PivotTable* that uses data from multiple queries or online sources.

▶ HOW TO: Insert a Calculated Field

1. Click a cell in the *PivotTable*.
2. Click the **Fields, Items, and Sets** button [*PivotTable Tools Analyze* tab, *Calculations* group].
3. Select **Calculated Field**.
4. Click the **Name** box in the *Insert Calculated Field* dialog box.
5. Type a name for the calculated field.
 - The name must be unique.
6. Click the **Formula** box and delete the zero and the space after the equals sign.
7. Enter the formula (Figure 8-50).
 - Double-click a field name in the *Fields* list to insert it in the formula.
 - Fields names display within single quotation marks.
 - You can select a field name and click **Insert Field**.
 - Type an operator or a constant value to build the formula.
8. Click **OK**.
 - The calculated field is added at the right in the *PivotTable* (Figure 8-51).

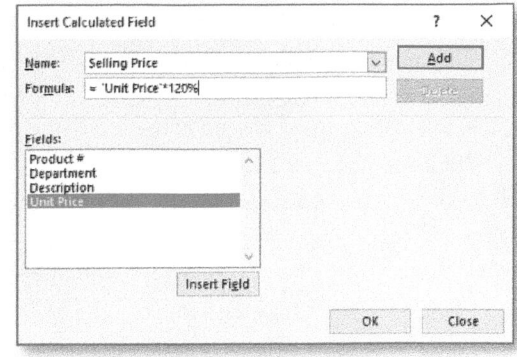

8-50 A calculated field uses a *PivotTable* field in a formula

8-51 Calculated field inserted in *PivotTable*

- The field name is included in the *PivotTable Fields* pane.
- An associated *PivotChart* is updated to include the new field.

> ### MORE INFO
>
> Delete a calculated field by right-clicking a cell in the column and choosing *Remove "Field Name."*

PivotTable Layout

The *Layout* group on the *PivotTable Tools Design* tab allows you to alter the appearance of a *PivotTable*. You can hide or display subtotals and grand totals, insert a blank row after items, or repeat row labels. The *Options* command on the *PivotTable Tools Analyze* tab opens the *PivotTable Options* dialog box which includes settings to customize display, print, and data features.

▶**HOW TO:** Adjust Layout and PivotTable Options

1. Click a cell in the *PivotTable*.
2. Click the **Subtotals** button [*PivotTable Tools Design* tab, *Layout* group].
 - Subtotals can be hidden or shown.
 - Subtotals can be placed at the top or the bottom of each item.
3. Select an option for subtotals.
4. Click the **Grand Totals** button in the *Layout* group [*PivotTable Tools Design* tab].
 - You can show grand totals for both columns and rows.
 - You can turn off the display of grand totals.
5. Select an option for grand totals.
6. Click the **Report Layout** button [*PivotTable Tools Design* tab, *Layout* group].
 - A *Compact* format places row data in one column and occupies the least amount of horizontal space.
 - An *Outline* form places row data in separate columns (Figure 8-52).
 - *Tabular* form starts row data in the same row but in separate columns.
 - *Repeat Item Labels* displays the row data in each row like an Excel table.
7. Click the **Blank Rows** button [*PivotTable Tools Design* tab, *Layout* group].
 - You can display a blank row before or after each item.
8. Click the **Options** button [*PivotTable Tools Analyze* tab, *PivotTable* group] (Figure 8-53).

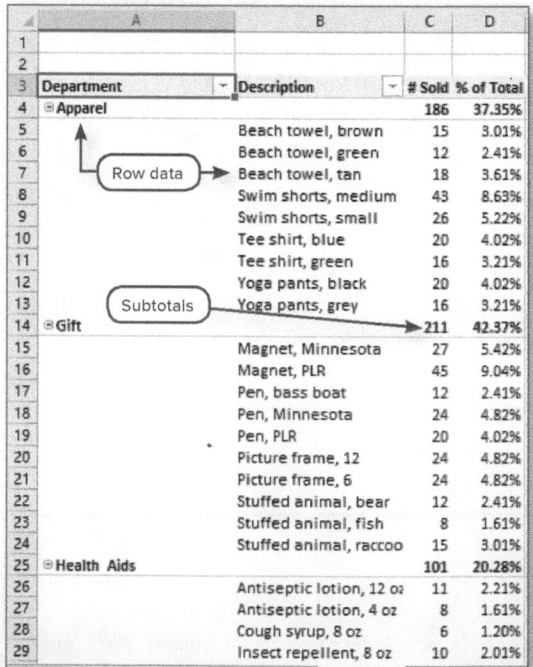

8-52 Subtotals at the top with data in outline layout

8-53 *PivotTable Options* dialog box

 - The *PivotTable Options* dialog box has six tabs.
 - Some options are also available in the *Layout* group on the *PivotTable Tools Design* tab.
9. Click **OK**.

Use GETPIVOTDATA

When you refer to a value in a *PivotTable* in another worksheet, you cannot simply click the cell because the cell content at that address may change if the *PivotTable* is rearranged. To refer to specific *PivotTable* results in another sheet, use the *GETPIVOTDATA* function from the *Lookup & Reference* category. If the *PivotTable* is pivoted to another view, your formula displays the results from the original *PivotTable* layout as long as that result is still somewhere in the *PivotTable*. GETPIVOTDATA works in *PivotTables* that are based on a range of data in the workbook, not *PivotTables* built from queries or multiple online sources.

>
> **MORE INFO**
>
> When the original data referenced in *GETPIVOTDATA* is no longer displayed in the *PivotTable*, the function returns the error message #REF!

Although you can insert the *GETPIVOTDATA* function from the *Formulas* tab, it is easier to enter a 3D reference to the cell in the *PivotTable*. The function is entered automatically with required arguments. The syntax for *GETPIVOTDATA* is:

=GETPIVOTDATA(Data_field,Pivot_table,Field,Item)

▶ HOW TO: Use GETPIVOTDATA

1. Select the cell where the *PivotTable* result should be displayed.
 - This cell is in a worksheet other than the sheet with the *PivotTable*.
2. Type = to start a formula.
3. Click the sheet tab that includes the *PivotTable*.
4. Select the cell with the desired result in the *PivotTable*.
5. Press **Enter** (Figure 8-54).
 - The focus returns to the worksheet.
 - The *GETPIVOTDATA* formula is inserted in the cell with a 3D reference to the *PivotTable* sheet name.
 - The result from the *PivotTable* appears in the cell.
6. Click the *PivotTable* sheet tab name.
7. Pivot the table to a different arrangement as desired.
 - The original result used in the *GETPIVOTDATA* formula must be shown somewhere in the *PivotTable*.
8. Return to the sheet with the *GETPIVOTDATA* formula.
 - *GETPIVOTDATA* returns the same result.

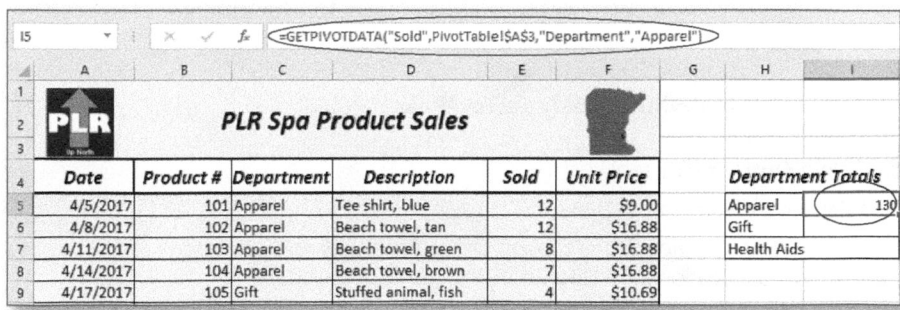

8-54 *GETPIVOTDATA* inserted in the cell

PowerPivot

When you build a *PivotTable* from multiple-source queries, not all *PivotTable* tools are available due to data storage and refresh procedures in queries. Calculated fields, for example, are not possible.

PowerPivot is a COM add-in, a compiled add-in designed to work with Excel. *PowerPivot* stores data from multiple sources for use in its own *PowerPivot* tables. It operates in a separate window and can analyze millions of records. In a *PowerPivot* worksheet, you can access and extract data from online public databases as well as company databases. *PowerPivot* is available for many, but not all, versions of Excel. It must be installed from the *Add-Ins* dialog box [Excel *Options*].

PowerPivot displays data in a *PowerPivot* table that resembles an Excel worksheet without row or column headings. You cannot edit data in a *PowerPivot* sheet, because the data is maintained at its source. You can build calculations and formulas, sort and filter data, and link tables for use in a *PowerPivot* report.

> ### MORE INFO
>
> *PowerPivot* ribbons, windows, dialog boxes, and commands are similar to the Excel *Query Editor* and *PivotTables*.

SLO 8.8

Using the Analysis ToolPak

The *Analysis ToolPak* is an Excel add-in with statistical and engineering functions. Each analysis tool performs its task when you provide the data and define the required components. For concepts such as covariance and regression, the *Analysis ToolPak* helps you analyze data with a minimum of steps and time.

Install the Analysis ToolPak

The *Analysis ToolPak* is installed from the *Add-Ins* dialog box in Excel *Options*. Its button appears on the *Data* tab in the *Analyze* group.

▶ HOW TO: Install the Analysis ToolPak

1. Select **Options** [*File* tab].
2. Click **Add-Ins** in the left pane.
 - The *View and manage Microsoft Office Add-ins* dialog box opens.
 - Active applications are listed near the top of the window.
3. Select **Analysis ToolPak** in the *Inactive Application Add-Ins* list.
4. Click **Go** near the bottom of the dialog box to open the *Add-ins* dialog box.
5. Select the **Analysis ToolPak** box.
 - You can remove the *ToolPak* by deselecting the box.
6. Click **OK**.
 - The *Data Analysis* button appears in the *Analyze* group on the *Data* tab.

Generate Descriptive Statistics

Descriptive statistics are summary measures for a data range such as the mean or average, the maximum, the minimum, and a count. Additional statistics that are generated automatically include the mode, the standard deviation, and the range. You already know how to calculate several of these measures using functions from the *Statistical* and *Math & Trig* categories.

The *Descriptive Statistics* command is a quick and easy way to prepare a summary report about a set of values. You simply select the range and indicate where results should display. The resulting report is a two-column layout of labels and values.

▶ **HOW TO: Generate Descriptive Statistics**

1. Click the **Data Analysis** button [*Data* tab, *Analyze* group].
 - The *Data Analysis* dialog box lists calculations available in the *ToolPak* (Figure 8-55).
2. Choose **Descriptive Statistics** and click **OK**.
 - The *Descriptive Statistics* dialog box opens.
3. Click the **Input Range** box and select the cell range on the sheet.
 - These are the cells with data points to be analyzed.
 - Include a column label if there is one and select the **Labels in first row** box.
4. Select the **Columns** radio button if the data is in a column.
 - Select the **Rows** button when the data is in a row.
5. Select the **Output Range** radio button.
6. Click the **Output Range** box and select an empty cell on the sheet.
 - Select a cell where there is room for a two-column report.
 - A worksheet *ply* is a new sheet tab that you can name.
7. Select the **Summary statistics** box (Figure 8-56).
 - You can include a confidence interval and *Kth* values in the report.
 - *Kth* numbers are used to order values. If you set a *Kth* Largest at 2, the result is the second largest value in the range.
8. Click **OK**.
 - The two-column report is generated (Figure 8-57).
 - The column label is the report title.
 - Format the report as desired.

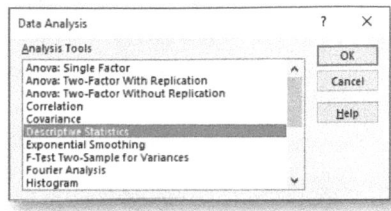

8-55 *Data Analysis* dialog box

8-56 *Descriptive Statistics* dialog box

Prepare a Moving Average

A moving average calculates a series of averages for a set of values. It is sometimes called a rolling or running average. A moving average is often used to smooth out unequal measurement periods or values in the data. Paradise Lakes Resort, for example, can determine average

	A	B	C	D	E
1					
2	**PLR Product #101**				
3					
4	**Date**	**Sold**		*Sold*	
5	1/1/2016	12			
6	2/1/2016	12		Mean	10.66667
7	3/1/2016	8		Standard Error	0.945368
8	4/1/2016	7		Median	10
9	5/1/2016	4		Mode	12
10	6/1/2016	8		Standard Deviation	4.631336
11	7/1/2016	10		Sample Variance	21.44928
12	8/1/2016	12		Kurtosis	2.135365
13	9/1/2016	5		Skewness	1.157482
14	10/1/2016	4		Range	20
15	11/1/2016	10		Minimum	4
16	12/1/2016	12		Maximum	24
17	1/1/2017	8		Sum	256
18	2/1/2017	8		Count	24
19	3/1/2017	15			

8-57 **Generated summary statistics report**

E8-530

three-month rental revenue on April 1 from January–March values. Then, on May 1, they average February–April, and so on throughout the year. At the end of a year, they can average all the averages.

The *Moving Average* command analyzes past results and predicts future values. It generates a column of averages and can also create a chart and a list of forecast errors.

▶ **HOW TO:** Calculate a Moving Average

1. Click the **Data Analysis** button [*Data* tab, *Analyze* group].
 - The *Data Analysis* dialog box lists available calculations.
2. Choose **Moving Average** and click **OK**.
 - The *Moving Average* dialog box opens.
3. Click the **Input Range** box and select the cell range on the sheet.
 - These are the values to be averaged.
 - If the values are in a row with labels directly above, select the **Labels in First Row** box.
4. Click the **Interval** box and type the number of cells to be averaged in each set.
 - An interval of 3 means that an average is calculated for every 3 values in the list.
 - An interval of 3 also means that there are no results for the first two values in the input range.

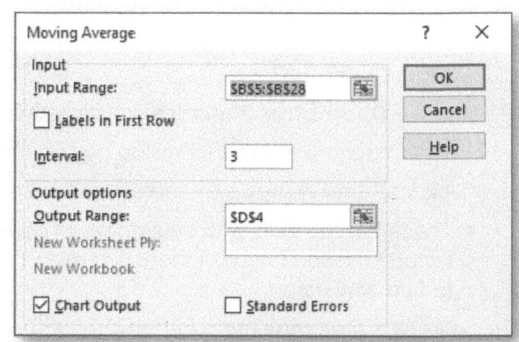

8-58 *Moving Average* dialog box

5. Click the **Output Range** box and select an empty cell on the sheet.
 - The resulting list will be at least as many rows as the input range.
6. Select the **Chart Output** box to generate a moving average chart (Figure 8-58).
7. Select the **Standard Errors** box to generate a list of deviation errors.
8. Click **OK**.
 - The list is generated (Figure 8-59).
 - You can position, size, and format the chart as desired.

8-59 Generated moving average list and chart

The **Data Analysis** button remains in the *Data* tab until you remove the *Analysis ToolPak*. You remove the *ToolPak* from the *Add-Ins* dialog box in Excel *Options*.

▶ **HOW TO: Uninstall the Analysis ToolPak**

1. Select **Options** [*File* tab].
2. Click **Add-Ins** in the left pane.
 - The *View and manage Microsoft Office Add-ins* dialog box opens.
 - Active applications are listed near the top of the window.
3. Select **Analysis ToolPak** in the list of *Active Application Add-Ins*.
4. Click **Go** near the bottom of the dialog box to open the *Add-ins* dialog box.
5. Deselect the **Analysis ToolPak** box and click **OK**.

PAUSE & PRACTICE: EXCEL 8-3

In this project, you use *GETPIVOTDATA* in a *PivotTable* and work with the *Analysis ToolPak*. So that your queries use a clean data model, you build two queries as sources for a *PivotTable* with a timeline in another workbook.

Files Needed: **PP E8-2.xlsx, Database-08.accdb, SpaSales-08.xml,** and **SpaSales-08.xsd** (*Student data files are available in the* Library *of your SIMnet account*)
Completed Project File Names: **[your initials] PP E8-3.xlsx** and **[your initials] PP E8-3a.xlsx**

1. Open the **[your initials] PP E8-2** workbook completed in *Pause & Practice 8-2* and save it as [your initials] PP E8-3.

2. Right-click the leftmost tab scrolling button to open the *Activate* dialog box (Figure 8-60).

3. Select **Combined Sales** and click **OK**.

4. Use *GETPIVOTDATA* to display results from a *PivotTable*.
 a. Select cell **I5**.
 b. Type = to start the formula.
 c. Click the **PivotTable** sheet tab, select cell **B4**, and press **Enter**.
 d. Select cell **I6** and use *GETPIVOTDATA* to display the total for the Gift department.
 e. Select cell **I7** and use *GETPIVOTDATA* (Figure 8-61).
 f. Click the **PivotTable** sheet tab and click a cell in the *PivotTable*.
 g. With the four-pointed arrow, drag the *Department* field name in the *Rows* area of the *PivotTable Fields* pane into the *Columns* area. The *PivotTable* is pivoted (Figure 8-62).
 h. Click the **Combined Sales** sheet tab. *GETPIVOTDATA* shows the same results even though the content at the original cell locations has changed.

8-60 *Activate* dialog box with sheet names

5. Format a *PivotTable*.
 a. Click the **PivotTable** sheet tab and click a cell in the *PivotTable*.
 b. Click the **More** button [*PivotTable Tools Design* tab, *PivotTable Styles* group].

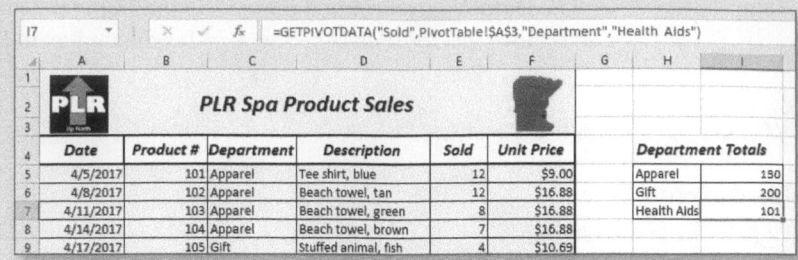

8-61 *GETPIVOTDATA* displays results from the *PivotTable*

8-62 Data in *PivotTable* is rearranged

 c. Select **Pivot Style Medium 8** in the gallery.
 d. Click the **Grand Totals** button [*PivotTable Tools Design* tab, *Layout* group].
 e. Select **On for Columns Only** to remove Column E, the grand totals column.

6. Install the *Analysis ToolPak*.
 a. Select **Options** [*File* tab] and click **Add-Ins** in the left pane.
 b. Select **Analysis ToolPak** in the *Inactive Application Add-Ins* list.
 c. Click **Go** near the bottom of the dialog box.
 d. Select the **Analysis ToolPak** box and click **OK**.

7. Calculate descriptive statistics for a data range.
 a. Select the **Product #101** worksheet tab.
 b. Click the **Data Analysis** button [*Data* tab, *Analyze* group].
 c. Choose **Descriptive Statistics** and click **OK**.
 d. Select cells **B4:B28** for the **Input Range** box.
 e. Verify that the **Columns** radio button is selected.
 f. Select the **Labels in First Row** box.
 g. Select the **Output Range** radio button.
 h. Click the **Output Range** box and select cell **E4**.
 i. Select the **Summary statistics** box.
 j. Select the **Kth Largest** box and type 3 in the entry box to calculate the third largest value in the range (Figure 8-63).

8-63 *Descriptive Statistics* dialog box

k. Click **OK**.

l. **AutoFit** column **E** (Figure 8-64).

8. Calculate a moving average for a data range.

a. Click the **Data Analysis** button [*Data* tab, *Analyze* group].

b. Choose **Moving Average** and click **OK**.

c. Select cells **B5:B28** for the **Input Range** box.

d. Click the **Interval** box and type 3 to average groups of three cells in the range.

e. Click the **Output Range** box and select cell **E21**.

f. Select the **Chart Output** box.

g. Click **OK**.

h. Select the chart object and move it so that its top-left corner is at cell **G21**.

i. Size the chart object to reach cell **P42** (Figure 8-65).

	A	B	C	D	E	F
1						
2	*PLR Product #101*					
3						
4	**Date**	**Sold**			*Sold*	
5	1/1/2016	12				
6	2/1/2016	12			Mean	10.6667
7	3/1/2016	8			Standard Error	0.94537
8	4/1/2016	7			Median	10
9	5/1/2016	4			Mode	12
10	6/1/2016	8			Standard Deviation	4.63134
11	7/1/2016	10			Sample Variance	21.4493
12	8/1/2016	12			Kurtosis	2.13537
13	9/1/2016	5			Skewness	1.15748
14	10/1/2016	4			Range	20
15	11/1/2016	10			Minimum	4
16	12/1/2016	12			Maximum	24
17	1/1/2017	8			Sum	256
18	2/1/2017	8			Count	24
19	3/1/2017	15			Largest(3)	15
20	4/1/2017	12				
21	5/1/2017	20				
22	6/1/2017	24				
23	7/1/2017	12				

◄ ... Forecast Chart | Forecast Sheet | Product #101 | Combined Sales

8-64 Generated statistics report

8-65 *Moving Average* results and chart

9. Uninstall the *Analysis ToolPak*.

a. Select **Options** [*File* tab] and click **Add-Ins** in the left pane.

b. Select **Analysis ToolPak** in the list of *Active Application Add-Ins*.

c. Click **Go** near the bottom of the dialog box.

d. Deselect the **Analysis ToolPak** box and click **OK**.

10. Save and close the workbook.

11. Open a new workbook.

12. Get and transform data from an XML file.

a. Click the **New Query** button [*Data* tab, *Get & Transform* group], choose **From File**, and **From XML**.

b. Navigate to the folder with the **SpaSales-08** XML file from your student data files.

c. Select the file name **SpaSales-08**, click **Import**, and then click **Edit**.
d. Click the **Expand** button next to the **TblSpaSales** label at the top of the first column in the *Query Editor*.
e. Select all field boxes and click **OK**.
f. Click the **TblSpaSales.Date** column label, click the **Data Type** button [*Home* tab, *Transform* group], and choose **Date/Time**.
g. Click the **TblSpaSales.ProductID** label, click the **Data Type** button [*Home* tab, *Transform* group], and choose **Whole Number**.
h. Select the **Whole Number** data type for the *Sold* column.
i. Click the **http://. . .Schema. . .** label.
j. Click the **Remove Columns** button [*Home* tab, *Manage Columns* group].
k. Remove the **Attribute:generated** column (Figure 8-66).

8-66 XML data in the *Query Editor*

l. Click the **Close & Load** button [*Home* tab, *Close* group].
m. Rename the query results sheet as XML Query.

13. Get and transform data from an Access database file.
 a. Click the **New Query** button [*Data* tab, *Get & Transform* group] and choose **From Database**.
 b. Choose **From Microsoft Access Database**.
 c. Navigate to the folder with the *Database-08* database file from your student data files.
 d. Select the **Database-08** name and click **Import**.
 e. Select **TblSpaProducts** in the *Navigator* window.
 f. Click **Edit** at the bottom of the window.
 g. Click the **Product #** column name and click the **Data Type** button [*Home* tab, *Transform* group] in the *Query Editor*.
 h. Choose **Whole Number**. This is the field that will establish a relationship between the query tables (Figure 8-67).
 i. Click the **Close & Load** button [*Home* tab, *Close* group].
 j. Rename the query results sheet as Database Query.

14. Create a *PivotTable* from two queries.
 a. Select cell **A2** in the table on the *Database Query* sheet.

8-67 Access table in *Query Editor*

b. Click the **Summarize with PivotTable** button [*Table Tools Design* tab, *Tools* group].
c. Select the **Existing Worksheet** radio button.
d. Click the **Location** box and click cell **A3** on **Sheet1**.
e. Select the **Add this data to the Data Model** box and click **OK**.
f. Select the boxes for the **Department** and **Description** fields In the *PivotTable Fields* pane.
g. Click **All** at the top of the *PivotTable Fields* pane.
h. Select **SpaSales-08** to expand the field list from the XML query.
i. Select the **TblSpaSales.Sold** box.
j. Click **AutoDetect** in the warning box to create a relationship between the tables.
k. Click **Close** in the message box (Figure 8-68).
l. Rename the sheet as Timeline.

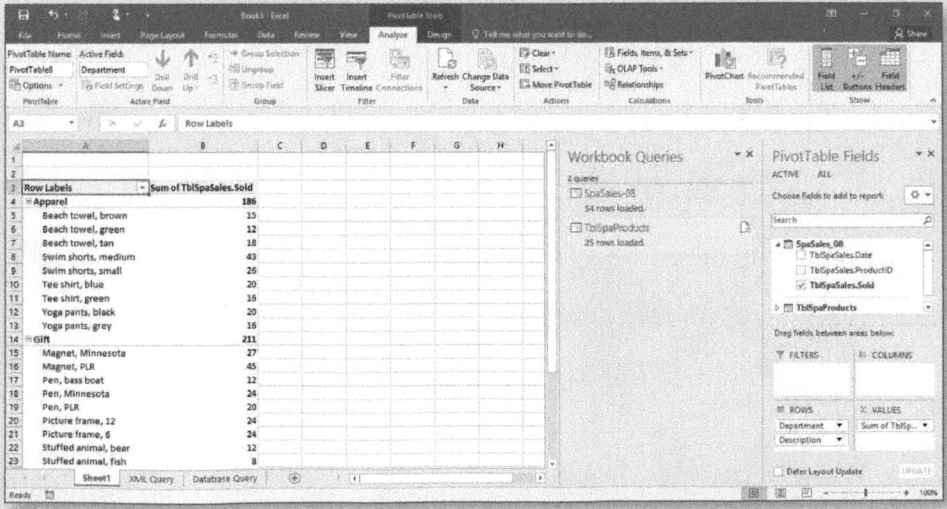

8-68 *PivotTable* created from two queries

15. Insert a timeline for a *PivotTable*.
 a. Click any cell in the *PivotTable* on the **Timeline** sheet.
 b. Click the **Insert Timeline** button [*PivotTable Tools Analyze* tab, *Filter* group].
 c. Select the **TblSpaSales.Date** box and click **OK**.
 d. Click the **Months** button in the timeline and select **Quarters**.
 e. Click **Q3** in the timeline for 2017.
 f. Click the **More** button [*Timeline Tools Options* tab, *Timeline Styles* group].
 g. Find and select **Timeline Style Dark 5** in the gallery.
 h. Position the timeline with its top-left corner in cell **C3** (Figure 8-69).

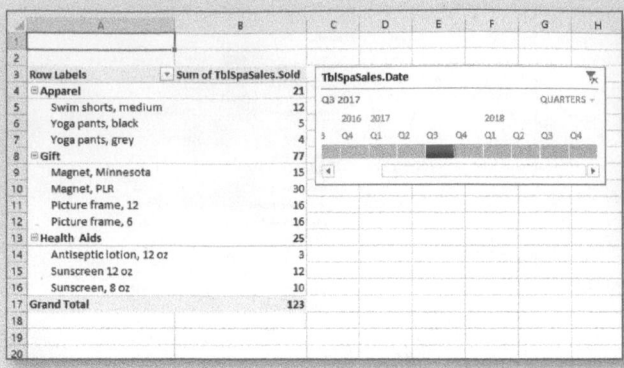

8-69 Timeline filters the data by quarter

16. Click a worksheet cell.

17. Save the workbook as [your initials] PP E8-3a and close it.

Chapter Summary

8.1 Create and manage scenarios for worksheet data (p. E8-496).

- A *scenario* is a saved set of values in a workbook.
- A *scenario* is a what-if analysis tool because it allows you to display and compare multiple data possibilities in a worksheet.
- The **Scenario Manager** command is available from the *What-if Analysis* button in the *Forecast* group in the *Data* tab.
- In the *Add Scenario* dialog box, you name each scenario and select cells to be changed.
- In the *Scenario Values* dialog box, you accept or type new values for each scenario.
- Only one scenario can be displayed in the worksheet at a time.
- From the *Scenario Manager* dialog box, you can create a **scenario summary report** that lists details about changing cells and result cells for all scenarios in a workbook.

8.2 Use *Goal Seek* to backsolve a cell value for a formula (p. E8-498).

- **Backsolving** is a problem-solving method that starts with the result and calculates the value to reach that result.
- The **Goal Seek** command tests values for one cell in a formula.
- *Goal Seek* determines what value should be in the cell so that the formula results in a specified value.
- The *Goal Seek* command is an option on the *What-if Analysis* button in the *Forecast* group in the *Data* tab.

8.3 Use *Solver* to find a solution for a formula (p. E8-500).

- The *Solver* **add-in** is an analysis tool that solves a problem in reverse.
- **Solver** determines the highest, the lowest, or a specific result for a formula by adjusting values in cells used in the formula.
- A *Solver* problem has three components known as **parameters**, identified in the *Solver Parameters* dialog box.
- The **objective cell** is a cell with a formula that will be solved for specific results. It is also called the **target cell**.

- **Variable cells**, also known as **decision** or **changing cells**, are cells that *Solver* can adjust to reach the objective.
- **Constraints** are restrictions or limitations on variable cells, the formula, or other worksheet cells that are related to the objective cell.
- The *Solver Results* dialog box includes options to keep the solution, to return to the original values, and to save the results as a scenario.
- The *Solver Results* dialog box has a *Reports* section with analysis reports that can be generated for each solution.
- *Solver* is activated from the *Add-Ins* dialog box in the Excel *Options* dialog box.
- The *Solver* button displays in the *Analyze* group on the *Data* tab.

8.4 Build data tables with one and two variables (p. E8-508).

- A **data table** is a range of cells in a worksheet that shows multiple results for one or more formulas.
- A data table is created from the *What-If Analysis* button in the *Forecast* group on the *Data* tab.
- A **one-variable data table** substitutes values for one argument in one or more formulas.
- A **two-variable data table** substitutes values for two arguments in a single formula.
- The values that are substituted are known as **input values**.
- Input values can be in a row or a column, and the formula must be entered in a specific location based on whether the table uses one or two variables.
- In the data table range, the formula can be typed or entered as a reference to the formula in the worksheet.
- In the *Data Table* dialog box, you specify a row or column input cell for a one-variable table and both for a two-variable table.
- The row or column input is the cell address in the formula that is replaced with input values.
- A *Data Table* command inserts the *TABLE* function in an array formula in each result cell.

8.5 Create a forecast sheet for time-based data (p. E8-511).

- A **forecast sheet** is a generated worksheet that uses existing data to analyze and predict results.

- A forecast sheet includes a table and a related chart.
- Two data series are required to build a forecast sheet; one series must be a date or time field.
- The date or time field must use a recognizable time interval.
- The forecast chart can be a line or a column chart.
- The *Forecast Sheet* button is in the *Forecast* group on the *Data* tab.

8.6 Get and transform data in a query (p. E8-515).

- A *query* stores instructions for getting data from an external source for display in a worksheet.
- A query can get data from online and in-house sources including database or text files, *XML* data, and others.
- A query establishes a data connection to the source so that the data can be refreshed.
- Data is cleaned or prepared in the *Query Editor* before it is loaded into Excel.
- Query results are displayed in an Excel table.
- Queries are named and saved with the workbook.
- When a *common field* exists in two or more queries, those queries can be used to create a *PivotTable*.
- The *New Query* button is in the *Get & Transform* group on the *Data* tab.

8.7 Explore *PivotTable* tools (p. E8-522).

- A slicer is a visual filter for a *PivotTable*, a small window that floats on the sheet.
- You can insert a slicer for any field in the data source for the *PivotTable*.
- A *timeline* is a visual filter for a date field in a *PivotTable*.
- The **Insert Slicer** and **Insert Timeline** buttons are in the *Filter* group on the *PivotTable Tools Analyze* tab.
- Slicers and timelines are objects that can be positioned, sized, and formatted.
- The *Value Field Settings* for a field in a *PivotTable* determine how values are summarized.

- You can change the calculation used for value fields, show custom calculations, or insert a calculated field.
- A *custom calculation* is a built-in percentage, ranking, or ratio.
- A *calculated field* is a field that is not in the data source for a *PivotTable* and is built from a formula with one of the fields in the source data.
- Insert a calculated field from the *Fields, Items, & Sets* button [*PivotTable Tools Analyze* tab, *Calculations* group].
- *PivotTable* fields can be formatted from the *Value Field Settings* dialog box or from the *Number* group on the *Home* tab.
- Layout options for a *PivotTable* include how and where totals display and the report format.
- The *GETPIVOTDATA* function displays results from a particular cell in a *PivotTable*.
- For expanded *PivotTable* functions and commands, the *PowerPivot* add-in can access millions of records for analysis in a report.

8.8 Use the *Analysis ToolPak* to calculate statistical measures (p. E8-529).

- The *Analysis ToolPak* is an Excel add-in with built-in statistical and engineering calculations.
- After the add-in is installed, the *Data Analysis* button appears in the *Analyze* group on the *Data* tab.
- The **Descriptive Statistics** command calculates and generates a list of popular measures for a data range.
- The **Moving Average** command calculates and generates a list of running or rolling averages for a set of values with a related chart.
- Other *Analysis ToolPak* commands include covariance, regression analysis, and random number generation.

Check for Understanding

The SIMbook for this text (within your SIMnet account) provides the following resources for concept review:

- Multiple choice questions
- Matching exercises
- Short answer questions

USING MICROSOFT EXCEL 2016

Guided Project 8-1

Wear-Ever Shoes uses *Solver* to analyze advertising for greatest exposure. You use scenarios, a data table, and *Goal Seek* in the analysis. You also build a query for an Access table to create a *PivotTable* that relates customer satisfaction and cost.
[Student Learning Outcomes 8.1, 8.2, 8.3, 8.4, 8.5, 8.6, 8.7, 8.8]

Files Needed: ***WearEverShoes-08.xlsx*** and ***Database-08.accdb*** *(Student data files are available in the Library of your SIMnet account)*
Completed Project File Name: ***[your initials] Excel 8-1.xlsx***

Skills Covered in this Project

- Create and manage scenarios.
- Use *Solver*.
- Use *Goal Seek*.
- Build a one-variable data table.
- Build a two-variable data table.

- Create and format a *PivotTable* with a *PivotChart*.
- Build a query to get data from an Access table.
- Use the data model to create a *PivotTable*.
- Generate *Descriptive Statistics* using the *Analysis ToolPak*.
- Create a forecast sheet.

1. Open the ***WearEverShoes-08*** workbook from your student data files and save it as [your initials] Excel 8-1.

2. Review marketing formulas.
 a. Select cell **E7** on the **Marketing Analysis** tab. The *SUMPRODUCT* formula multiplies the cost per ad (cells C7 and D7) by the number of ads (cells C13 and D13).
 b. Select cell **E10** and then cell **G4** to review the *SUMPRODUCT* formulas.

3. Create a scenario for original data.
 a. Select cells **C13:D13** and click the **What-if Analysis** button [*Data* tab, *Data Tools* group].
 b. Select **Scenario Manager**. No scenarios exist in the workbook.
 c. Click **Add**.
 d. Type Original in the *Add Scenario* dialog box.
 e. Verify that the *Changing cells* box shows cells **C13:D13**.
 f. Click **OK**.
 g. Do not edit the *Scenario Values* dialog box and click **OK**.
 h. Click **Close**.

4. Install *Solver* and the *Analysis ToolPak*.
 a. Select the **Options** command [*File* tab].
 b. Click **Add-Ins** in the left pane.
 c. Click **Go** near the bottom of the window.
 d. Select the **Solver Add-in** box.
 e. Select the **Analysis ToolPak** box.
 f. Click **OK**.

5. Set *Solver* parameters.
 a. Click the **Solver** button [*Data* tab, *Analyze* group].
 b. Click cell **G4** for the **Set Objective** box. This cell has a *SUMPRODUCT* formula.

 c. Verify that the **Max** radio button is selected to find the maximum value.

 d. Click the **By Changing Variable Cells** box and select cells **C13:D13**. *Solver* will test values for the number of TV and magazine ads.

6. Add constraints to a *Solver* problem.
 a. Click **Add** to the right of the *Subject to the Constraints* box.
 b. Select cell **C13** for the *Cell Reference* box.
 c. Verify that **<=** is the operator.
 d. Click the **Constraint** box and select cell **C15**. This constraint is that the number of TV ads (cell C13) be less than or equal to the value in cell C15.
 e. Click **Add**. (If you accidentally closed the dialog box, click **Add** to reopen it.)
 f. Select cell **E7** for the *Cell Reference* box and use **<=** as the operator.
 g. Click the **Constraint** box and type 3750 as the budget amount.
 h. Add another constraint that cell **E10** be greater than or equal to **12**. This means that the audience reach must be at least 12 million.
 i. When all constraints are identified, click **OK** in the *Add Constraint* dialog box.
 j. Choose **GRG Nonlinear** for the *Select a Solving Method* box.
 k. Verify that the **Make Unconstrained Variables Non-Negative** box is selected (Figure 8-70).

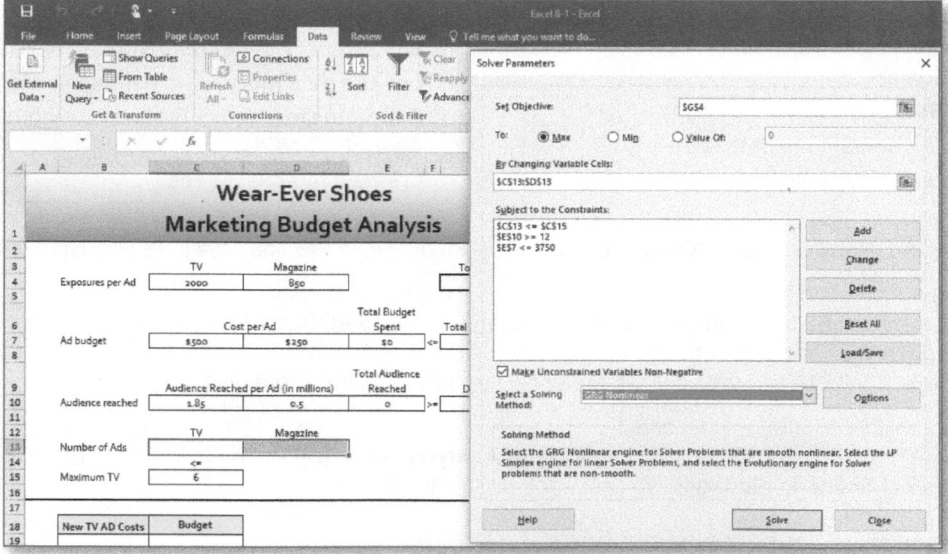

8-70 *Solver* parameters

 l. Click **Solve**. A solution displays in the worksheet, and the *Solver Results* dialog box is open. The maximum total exposure is 14,500. (If *Solver* did not return that value, uninstall *Solver*, exit Excel, restart Excel, and install *Solver* again. Then try Steps 5-6 again. If the error persists, go to Step 7f.)

7. Save *Solver* results as a scenario. (If *Solver* has not returned the indicated result, start at Step f.)
 a. Click **Save Scenario** in the *Solver Results* dialog box.
 b. Type Max Exposure as the scenario name.
 c. Click **OK** to return to the *Solver Results* dialog box.
 d. Select **Answer** in the *Reports* list.
 e. Click **OK**. The generated report is inserted, and *Solver* results are shown in the worksheet.
 f. If *Solver* has not worked as indicated, type 6 in cell **C13** and type 3 in cell **C15** and proceed to Step 7g.
 g. If *Solver* has not worked as indicated, create a scenario named Max Exposure with cells **C13:D13** as the changing cells.

8. Create a scenario summary report.
 a. Click the **What-if Analysis** button [*Data* tab, *Data Tools* group] and select **Scenario Manager**.
 b. Click the **Summary** button.
 c. Verify that the **Scenario summary** button is selected.
 d. Click the **Result cells** box, select cells **C13:D13**, type a comma , and then select cell **G4** (Figure 8-71).
 e. Click **OK** in the *Scenario Summary* dialog box. The report displays in a new worksheet.

9. Show a scenario.
 a. Click the **Marketing Analysis** worksheet tab.
 b. Click the **What-if Analysis** button [*Data* tab, *Data Tools* group] and select **Scenario Manager**.
 c. Click **Original** to highlight the name.
 d. Click **Show** and click **Close**.

10. Create a one-variable data table.
 a. Select cells **B20:B21** and fill values to reach cell **B30** as column input values.
 b. Select cell **C19**, one column to the right and one row above the first input value.
 c. Type =, click cell **E7**, and press **Enter** to reference the budget formula.
 d. Select cells **B19:C30** as the data table range.
 e. Click the **What-If Analysis** button [*Data* tab, *Data Tools* group] and choose **Data Table**.
 f. Click the **Column input cell** box and select cell **C7** to indicate that the cost per TV ad will be replaced by the input values in column B.
 g. Click **OK** to create the data table (Figure 8-72).
 h. Click the **What-if Analysis** button [*Data* tab, *Data Tools* group] and select **Scenario Manager**.
 i. Click **Max Exposure** to highlight the name and click **Show**.
 j. Click **Close**. The data table is updated.

11. Use *Goal Seek* to find the number of ads.
 a. Select cell **E10**.
 b. Click the **What-if Analysis** button [*Data* tab, *Data Tools* group] and choose **Goal Seek**.
 c. Click the **To value** box and type 15 as the target.
 d. Click the **By changing cell** box and select cell **D13** to determine how many magazine ads must be run to reach 15 million people.
 e. Click **OK**. Note the result shown in cell **D13** in the worksheet.
 f. Click **Cancel** and type the result value in cell **G23**.
 g. Select cell **E10** and use *Goal Seek* to change cell **C13** to calculate how many TV ads must be run to reach 15 million people. Do not keep the results, but type the resulting value in cell **G26** (Figure 8-73).

12. Create a two-variable data table.
 a. Click the **Inventory** worksheet tab. Current costs and increase percentages are shown at the right.
 b. Select cell **K4** to place the formula one row above column input values and one column left of the row values.
 c. Type =, click cell **J7**, type *(1+, click cell **J4**, and press **Enter**. The closing right parenthesis was necessary.
 d. Click **Yes** in the message box to accept the correction with closing right parenthesis. The formula multiplies the cost times 1 plus the percentage increase. Because cells **J4** and **J7** contain labels,

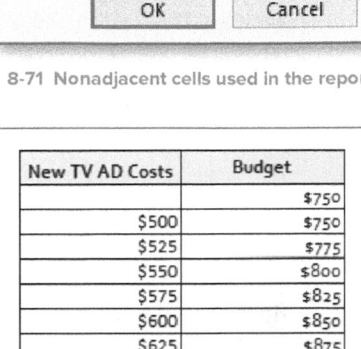

Scenario Summary	?	×

Report type
- ● Scenario summary
- ○ Scenario PivotTable report

Result cells:

=C13:D13,G4

OK	Cancel

8-71 Nonadjacent cells used in the report

New TV AD Costs	Budget
	$750
$500	$750
$525	$775
$550	$800
$575	$825
$600	$850
$625	$875
$650	$900
$675	$925
$700	$950
$725	$975
$750	$1,000

8-72 Data table results with *Original* scenario

the result is a standard error message (Figure 8-74).

e. Select cells **K4:N10** as the data table range.

f. Click the **What-If Analysis** button [*Data* tab, *Data Tools* group] and choose **Data Table**.

g. Select cell **J4** for the *Row input cell* box because the percentage values in row 4 will replace the label in cell J4.

h. Click the **Column input cell** box and select cell **J7** so that the costs in column K replace the label in cell J7.

i. Click **OK** to build the data table.

j. Format cells **L5:N10** as **Currency** with two decimal places.

k. Format cell **K4** to use a **White, Background 1** font color.

8-73 Completed Marketing Analysis sheet

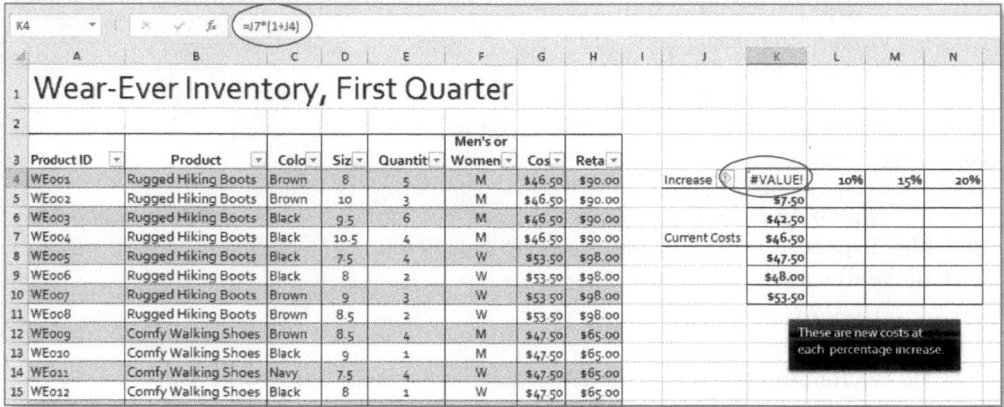

8-74 The result is an error in the placeholder formula.

13. Create a *PivotTable* for the **Inventory** data.

a. Select cell **A3** and click the **PivotTable** button [*Insert* tab, *Tables* group].

b. Verify that the **New Worksheet** button is selected.

c. Deselect the **Add this data to the Data Model** box. You cannot insert a calculated field in a *PivotTable* built from the data model.

d. Click **OK**.

e. Name the worksheet tab PivotTable 1.

f. Select the **Product ID, Product, Quantity**, and **Cost** field boxes in the *PivotTable Fields* pane. Label fields are added to the *Rows* area, and numeric fields are added in the *Values* area.

g. Right-click **Sum of Cost** in cell **C3** and select **Value Field Settings**.

h. Edit the name to display Our Cost in the *Custom Name* box.

i. Click **Number Format** in the *Value Field Settings* dialog box.

j. Choose **Currency** and click **OK**.

k. Click **OK** to close the *Value Field Settings* dialog box.

l. Edit the name in cell **B3** to show **Current Stock** (Figure 8-75).

8-75 Inventory *PivotTable*

14. Insert a calculated field.

 a. Click any cell in the *PivotTable*.

 b. Click the **Fields, Items, and Sets** button [*PivotTable Tools Analyze* tab, *Calculations* group] and select **Calculated Field**. (If *Calculated Field* is unavailable, delete the **PivotTable 1** sheet, and return to step 13. Be sure to deselect the **Add this data to the Data Model** box.)

 c. Type Total Value as the name for the calculated field in the *Name* box in the *Insert Calculated Field* dialog box.

 d. Click the **Formula** box and delete the zero and the space after the equals sign.

 e. Double-click **Cost** in the *Fields* list.

 f. Type * after =‘Cost’ in the *Formula* box to multiply.

 g. Double-click **Quantity** in the *Fields* list and click **OK**.

 h. Click **Sum of Total Value** in cell **D3** and click the **Field Settings** button [*PivotTable Tools Analyze*, *Active Field* group].

 i. Click **Number Format** in the *Value Field Settings* dialog box.

 j. Choose **Currency** and click **OK**.

 k. Change the *Custom Name* to Inventory Value.

 l. Click **OK**.

15. Insert a slicer.

 a. Verify that any cell in the *PivotTable* is active.

 b. Click the **Insert Slicer** button [*PivotTable Tools Analyze* tab, *Filter* group].

 c. Select the **Product** box and click **OK**.

 d. With the four-pointed arrow, drag the slicer so that the top-left corner is in cell **E3**.

 e. Click **Comfy Walking Shoes** in the slicer (Figure 8-76).

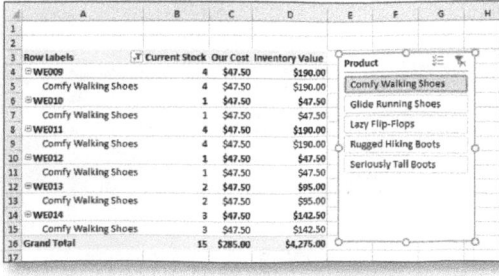

8-76 Data is filtered by the slicer

16. Create a *PivotChart*.

 a. Select a cell in the *PivotTable* and click the **PivotChart** button [*PivotTable Tools Analyze*, *Tools* group].

 b. Click **Pie** in the list, **3-D Pie** as the subtype, and click **OK**.

 c. With the four-pointed arrow, drag the *PivotChart* so that its top-left corner is in cell **I3**.

d. Point to the bottom-right sizing handle and drag it to reach cell **S24**.
e. Click **Rugged Hiking Boots** in the slicer (Figure 8-77).
f. Select cell **A1**.

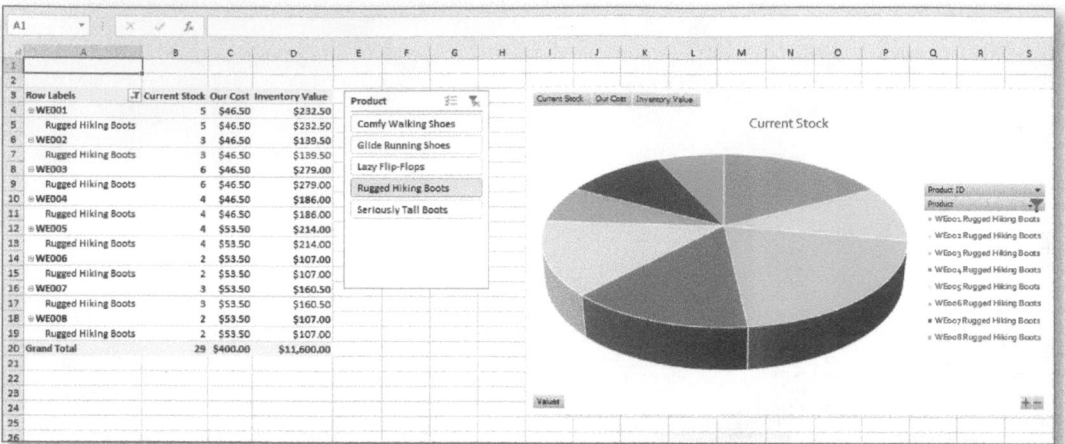

8-77 Filtered *PivotTable* and *PivotChart*

17. Get and transform data from an Access database.
 a. Click the **New Query** button [*Data* tab, *Get & Transform* group], select **From Database**, and choose **From Microsoft Access Database**.
 b. Navigate to the folder with **Database-08** from your student data files and click to select the file name.
 c. Click **Import** to open the *Navigator* window.
 d. Select **TblWearEver** in the list and click **Load**.
 e. Select the **D:H** columns headings and click the **Home** tab.
 f. Click the **Number Format** arrow in the *Number* group and select **Number** as the format.
 g. Click the **Decrease Decimal** button [*Home* tab, *Number* group] two times.
 h. Name the new sheet Ratings (Figure 8-78).

8-78 Query results are loaded without editing

18. Create a *PivotTable* from the data model.
 a. Click cell **A2** in the query results table on the **Ratings** sheet.
 b. Click the **Summarize with PivotTable** button [*Table Tools Design* tab, *Tools* group].

c. Verify that the **New Worksheet** button is selected.

d. Verify or select the **Add this data to the Data Model** box and click **OK**.

e. Expand the **TblWearEver** field list in the *PivotTable Fields* pane if the fields are not listed.

f. Select the **Product ID**, **Comfort**, **Fit**, **Style**, and **Value** boxes to place the fields in the *PivotTable* layout.

g. Click **All** at the top of the *PivotTable Fields* pane and expand the **InventoryTable** list.

h. Select the **Cost** box to add it to the *PivotTable* layout.

i. Click **Auto-Detect** to create the relationship. The *Product ID* fields from the query and the table are used to link or relate the data.

j. Click **Close** in the message box (Figure 8-79).

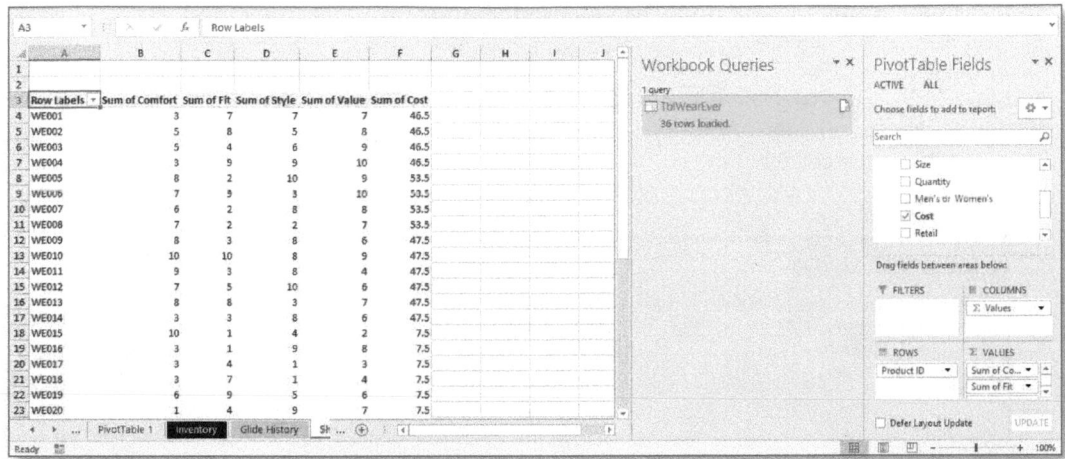

8-79 *PivotTable* from related query and table

k. Name the sheet tab PivotTable 2.

l. Close the *Workbook Queries* pane.

19. Generate *Descriptive Statistics* for a rating category.

a. Click the **Ratings** sheet tab and select cell **J1**.

b. Click the **Data Analysis** button [*Data* tab, *Analyze* group].

c. Select **Descriptive Statistics** and click **OK**.

d. Select cells **H1:H37** for the *Input Range* box.

e. Select the **Labels in First Row** box.

f. Select the **Output Range** button.

g. Click the **Output Range** box and click cell **J1**.

h. Select the **Summary statistics** box.

i. Select the **Kth Largest** box and type 3 in its entry box.

j. Select the **Kth Smallest** box and type 3 in its entry box. These settings will calculate the third largest and third smallest values in the input range (Figure 8-80).

k. Click **OK**.

l. **AutoFit** column **J**.

m. Select cell **J1** and edit the label to display Value Rating Analysis (Figure 8-81).

8-80 *Descriptive Statistics* dialog box with *Kth* values

20. Create a forecast sheet.

a. Click the **Glide History** sheet tab.

b. Select cells **A4:B16**. One data series is time-based, and the other represents values.

c. Click the **Forecast Sheet** button [*Data* tab, *Forecast* group].

d. Click the **Create a column chart** button at the top-right of the window.

e. Click the **Options** button to expand the window.

f. Set the forecast to end at 12/31/19 if it does not already show that date (Figure 8-82).

g. Click **Create** to build the new sheet and chart.

h. Select the chart object and position its top-left corner to start in cell **E2**.

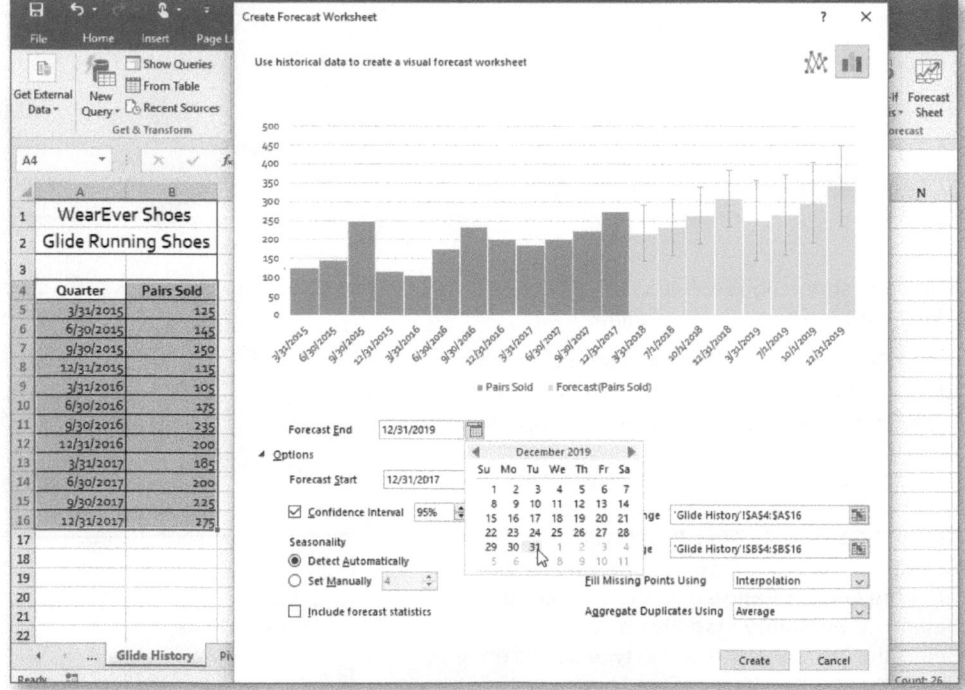

8-81 Generated statistics report

8-82 Options for a forecast sheet

i. Select a **Pairs Sold** column in the chart and change its **Shape Fill** color to **Lime, Accent 3**.

j. Select cell **A1**.

k. Name the sheet tab Glide Forecast.

21. Save and close the workbook (Figure 8-83).

22. Uninstall *Solver* and the *Analysis TookPak*.

a. Select the **Options** command [*File* tab] and click **Add-Ins** in the left pane.

b. Select **Solver Add-In** in the list of *Active Applications Add-Ins*.

c. In the *Manage* section near the bottom of the window, click **Go**.
d. Deselect the **Solver Add-in** and **Analysis ToolPak** boxes.
e. Click **OK**.

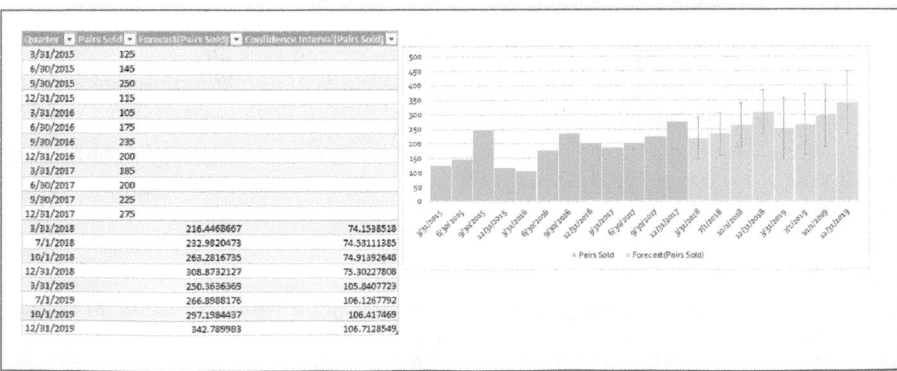

8-83 **Completed worksheets for Excel 8-1**

Guided Project 8-2

Sierra Pacific Community College (SPCC) has a worksheet for evaluating student loan offerings with data tables that you must build. You also determine how to reach a goal capacity for the freshmen orientation seminar and build a *PivotTable* to analyze departmental course fees.
[Student Learning Outcomes 8.1, 8.2, 8.3, 8.4, 8.5, 8.6, 8.7, 8.8]

Files Needed: **SPCC-08.xlsx**, **SPCC-08.xml**, and **SPCC-08.xsd** *(Student data files are available in the Library of your SIMnet account)*
Completed Project File Name: *[your initials] Excel 8-2.xlsx*

Skills Covered in this Project

- Create and manage scenarios.
- Use *Goal Seek*.
- Build data tables with one and two variables.
- Use *Solver* to determine capacity.

- Use data to create a forecast sheet.
- Calculate a moving average using the *Analysis ToolPak*.
- Get and transform XML data.
- Create a *PivotTable* from the data model.
- Use *PivotTable* tools.
- Insert and format a slicer for a *PivotTable*.

1. Open the **SPCC-08** workbook from your student data files and save it as [your initials] Excel 8-2.
2. Review the loan formulas on the **Loan Tables** worksheet.
 a. Select cell **C7**. The PMT function determines the monthly payment for a $10,000 loan at 4.5% for five years.
 b. Select cell **F4**. The total interest is the payment times the number of years times 12 minus the loan amount.
 c. Select cell **F6**. The total interest plus the loan amount are added.
3. Create scenarios in a worksheet.
 a. Select cell **C5** and click the **What-if Analysis** button [*Data* tab, *Data Tools* group].
 b. Select **Scenario Manager**. No scenarios exist in the workbook.
 c. Click **Add**.
 d. Type 5 Year as the name in the *Add Scenario* dialog box.
 e. Verify that the *Changing cells* box displays cell **C5** as the argument to be changed.
 f. Click **OK**.
 g. Do not edit the *Scenario Values* entry and click **OK**.
 h. Click **Add** to add another scenario.
 i. Type 7 Year as the name and keep the *Changing cells* as cell **C5**.
 j. Click **OK**.
 k. Change the value to 7 in the *Scenario Values* dialog box and click **OK**.
 l. Add another scenario for a nine-year loan and close the *Scenario Manager* dialog box.
4. Display a scenario in a worksheet.
 a. Click the **What-if Analysis** button [*Data* tab, *Data Tools* group] and select **Scenario Manager**.
 b. Select **7 Year** in the list and click **Show**.
 c. Click **Close**.
5. Use *Goal Seek* to find a target payment.
 a. Select cell **C7**.
 b. Click the **What-if Analysis** button [*Data* tab, *Data Tools* group] and choose **Goal Seek**.
 c. Click the **To value** box and type 125 as the target.
 d. Click the **By changing cell** box and select cell **C6** to determine the interest rate that results in this payment.
 e. Click **OK** (Figure 8-84).

6. Save *Goal Seek* results as a scenario.
 a. Select cell **C6** and click the **What-if Analysis** button [*Data* tab, *Data Tools* group].
 b. Select **Scenario Manager** and click **Add**.
 c. Type $125 Payment as the scenario name.
 d. Verify that the *Changing cells* box displays cell **C6**.
 e. Click **OK**.
 f. Do not change the *Scenario Values* entry, click **OK**, and click **Close**.

7. Create a scenario summary report.
 a. Click the **What-if Analysis** button [*Data* tab, *Data Tools* group] and select **Scenario Manger**.
 b. Click the **Summary** button.
 c. Verify that the **Scenario summary** is selected.
 d. Click the **Result cells** box and select cells **C5:C7**.
 e. Click **OK** in the *Scenario Summary* dialog box. The report is generated in a new worksheet (Figure 8-85).

8. Create a one-variable data table to calculate the payment and total interest charges based on different rates.
 a. Select the **Loan Tables** worksheet tab.
 b. Select cells **B15:B16** and fill percentages to reach cell **B23**. These are column input values.
 c. Select cell **C14**. The first formula must be one column to the right and one row above the first input value.
 d. Type =, select cell **C7**, and press **Enter** to reference the payment formula.
 e. Select cell **D14**. Additional formulas must be in the same row.
 f. Type =, select cell **F4**, and press **Enter** to reference the total interest formula.
 g. Select cells **B14:D23** as the data table range.
 h. Click the **What-If Analysis** button [*Data* tab, *Data Tools* group] and choose **Data Table**.
 i. Click the **Column input cell** entry box and click cell **C6**. The input values will be substituted for this cell in the data table formula (Figure 8-86).

8-84 *Goal Seek* results

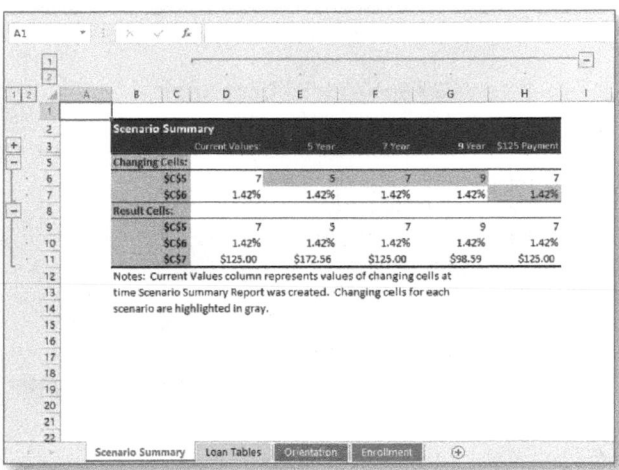

8-85 Scenario summary report results

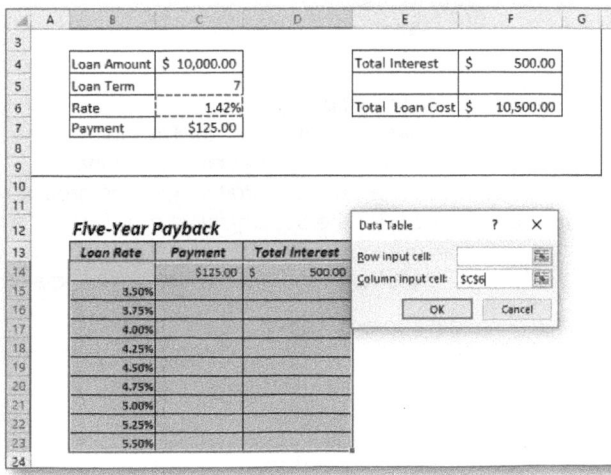

8-86 One-variable data table setup

j. Click **OK** to create the data table.

k. Format cells **C15:D23** as **Currency** with two decimal places.

9. Create a two-variable data table to calculate monthly payments at different rates and payback years.

a. Select cell **B26** to place the formula one row above column input values and one column left of row values.

b. Type **=**, click cell **C7**, and press **Enter**.

c. Select cells **B26:F35** as the data table range.

d. Click the **What-If Analysis** button [*Data* tab, *Data Tools* group] and choose **Data Table**.

e. Select cell **C5** for the *Row input cell* box. The number of years are in the row of this data table.

f. Click the **Column input cell** box and select cell **C6**. The changing interest rates are in a column.

g. Click **OK** to build the data table. The standard error message #VALUE! appears in all the cells.

h. Select **C27** and click its **Trace Error** button. An *Error in Value* results because the content in row 26 is recognized as text (Figure 8-87).

i. Click cell **C26**, type 6, and press **Tab**. The first column of the data table is refreshed.

j. Type 8 in cell **D26** and press **Tab**.

k. Correct the row input values in cells **E26:F26**.

l. Format cells **C27:F35** as **Currency** with two decimal places.

m. Format cell **B26** to use **Orange, Accent 2, Lighter 60%** as the font color.

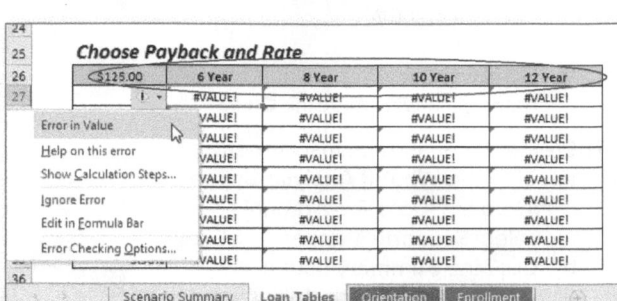

8-87 Year values were entered as text

10. Install *Solver* and the *Analysis ToolPak*.

a. Select the **Options** command [*File* tab].

b. Click **Add-Ins** in the left pane.

c. Click **Go** near the bottom of the window.

d. Select the **Solver Add-in** box.

e. Select the **Analysis ToolPak** box.

f. Click **OK**.

11. Use *Solver* to find a capacity goal.

a. Select the **Orientation** sheet tab. The college wants to maximize the number of students who can be accommodated in the orientation seminar.

b. Click the **Solver** button [*Data* tab, *Analyze* group].

c. Select cell **E9** for the *Set Objective* box. This cell has a *SUM* formula.

d. Verify that the **Max** radio button is selected for the *To* parameter.

e. Click the **By Changing Variable Cells** box and select cells **D5:D8**.

12. Add constraints to a *Solver* problem.

a. Click **Add** to the right of the *Subject to the Constraints* box.

b. Select cell **D5** for the *Cell Reference* box.

c. Use **<=** as the operator.

d. Click the **Constraint** box and type 4. The Davis campus can hold four or fewer sessions.

e. Click **Add**. (If you accidentally closed the dialog box, click **Add** to reopen it.)

f. Select cell **D5** again for the *Cell Reference* box.

g. Choose **>=** as the operator.

h. Click the **Constraint** box and type 1. The Davis campus must have at least one session.

 i. Click **Add**. Complete constraints for the problem as shown here:

 D6 <= 3
 D6 >= 1
 D7 <= 1
 D7 >= 1
 D8 <= 4
 D8 >= 1

 j. When all constraints are identified, click **OK** in the *Add Constraint* dialog box.

 k. Choose **GRG Nonlinear** for the *Select a Solving Method*.

 l. Confirm that the **Make Unconstrained Variables Non-Negative** box is selected (Figure 8-88).

 m. Click **Solve**. A solution is shown in the worksheet, and the *Solver Results* dialog box is open. The maximum number of students is 870.

 n. Select the **Keep Solver Solution** button and click **OK**. (If you see a *Solver* run-time error message, type 4, 3, 1, 4 in cells **D5:D8** so that you can continue.)

13. Create a forecast sheet.

 a. Click the **Enrollment** sheet tab.

 b. Select cells **D7:E13**. One data series is time-based, and the other is the enrollment numbers.

 c. Click the **Forecast Sheet** button [*Data* tab, *Forecast* group].

 d. Click the **Create a line chart** button at the top-right of the window.

 e. Click the **Options** button to expand the window.

 f. Set the forecast to end at **12/31/19**.

 g. Click **Create** to build the new sheet and chart. Excel supplies additional dates to smooth out the intervals.

 h. Select the chart object and position its top-left corner to start in cell **A20**.

 i. Drag the bottom right sizing handle so that the chart object reaches cell **E36**.

 j. Select the **Total** line and change its **Shape Outline** color to **Black, Text 1**.

 k. Select the **Chart Area** and set its **Shape Outline** color to **Black, Text 1** and a ½ pt **Weight** (Figure 8-89).

 l. Select cell **A1**.

 m. Name the sheet tab IMS Forecast.

8-88 *Solver* constraints for the capacity problem

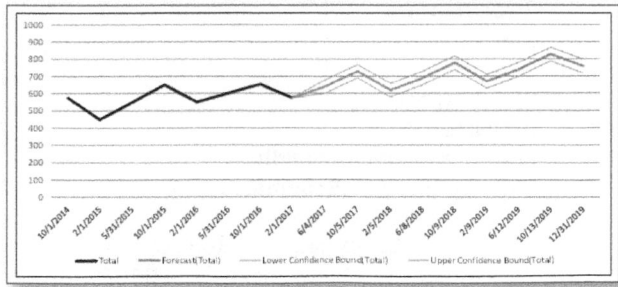

8-89 Forecast sheet and chart

14. Calculate a moving average.
 a. Click the **Enrollment** sheet tab.
 b. Click the **Data Analysis** button [*Data* tab, *Analyze* group].
 c. Choose **Moving Average** and click **OK**.
 d. Select cells **B8:B13** for the *Input Range* box.
 e. Click the **Interval** box and type 2 so that every two years are averaged.
 f. Click the **Output Range** box and select cell **B16**.
 g. Click **OK**.
 h. Click the **Data Analysis** button [*Data* tab, *Analyze* group], choose **Moving Average**, and click **OK**.
 i. Select cells **E8:E13** for the **Input Range** box.
 j. Click the **Interval** box and type 2.
 k. Click the **Output Range** box, select cell **E16**, and click **OK**.
 l. Calculate the moving average for the PHI department in column **H** (Figure 8-90).

8-90 Moving average results

15. Get and transform XML data.
 a. Click the **New Query** button [*Data* tab, *Get & Transform* group] and choose **From File**.
 b. Choose **From XML**.
 c. Navigate to the folder with the **SPCCDept-08** XML file.
 d. Select the **SPCCDept-08** file name, click **Import**, and then click **Edit**.
 e. Click the **http://...Schema...** column label in the *Query Editor*.
 f. Click the **Remove Columns** button [*Home* tab, *Manage Columns* group].
 g. Remove the **Attribute:generated** column.
 h. Click the **Expand** button next to the **SPCCDept-08** label and click **OK** to display all fields.
 i. Click the **SPCCDept-08.ID** column label, click the **Data Type** button [*Home* tab, *Transform* group], and choose **Whole Number**.
 j. Click the **SPCCDept-08.Course...** label in the third column, click the **Data Type** button [*Home* tab, *Transform* group], and choose **Whole Number**.
 k. Select the **Whole Number** data type for the **Hours** and **Sections** columns (Figure 8-91).

8-91 XML file ready to be loaded to Excel

 l. Click the **Close & Load** button [*Home* tab, *Close* group].

 m. Rename the query results sheet as XML Dept.

16. Get and transform XML data.

 a. Click the **New Query** button [*Data* tab, *Get & Transform* group] and choose **From File** and **From XML**.

 b. Navigate to the folder with the *SPCCFees-08* XML file.

 c. Select the **SPCCFees-08** file name, click **Import**, and click **Edit**.

 d. Click the **http://. . .Schema. . .** column label and click the **Remove Columns** button [*Home* tab, *Manage Columns* group].

 e. Remove the **Attribute:generated** column.

 f. Click the **Expand** button next to the **SPCCFees-08** label and click **OK**.

 g. Click the **SPCCFees-08.ID** column label, click the **Data Type** button [*Home* tab, *Transform* group], and choose **Whole Number**.

 h. Click the **SPCCFees-08.Fee** label, click the **Data Type** button [*Home* tab, *Transform* group], and choose **Currency**.

 i. Click the **Close & Load** button [*Home* tab, *Close* group].

 j. Rename the query results sheet as XML Fees.

17. Create a *PivotTable* from the data model.

 a. Click the **XML Dept** worksheet tab and select cell **A1**.

 b. Click the **Summarize with PivotTable** button [*Table Tools Design* tab, *Tools* group].

 c. Verify that the **New Worksheet** button is selected.

 d. Select the **Add this data to the Data Model** box and click **OK**.

 e. Expand the **SPCCDept-08** query list in the *PivotTable Fields* pane if it is not expanded.

 f. Select the **Dept**, **Course. . . Name**, and **Sections** boxes to place the fields in the *PivotTable* layout. Point to a long field name to see its complete name.

 g. Click **All** at the top of the *PivotTable Fields* pane and expand the **SPCCFees-08** list.

 h. Select the **Fee** box to add it to the *PivotTable* layout.

 i. Click **Auto-Detect** to create the relationship. No relationship is detected.

 j. Click **Manage Relationships** in the message box (Figure 8-92).

 k. Click **New** to open the *Create Relationship* dialog box.

 l. Click the **Table** arrow and choose **SPCCFees-08** as the table name.

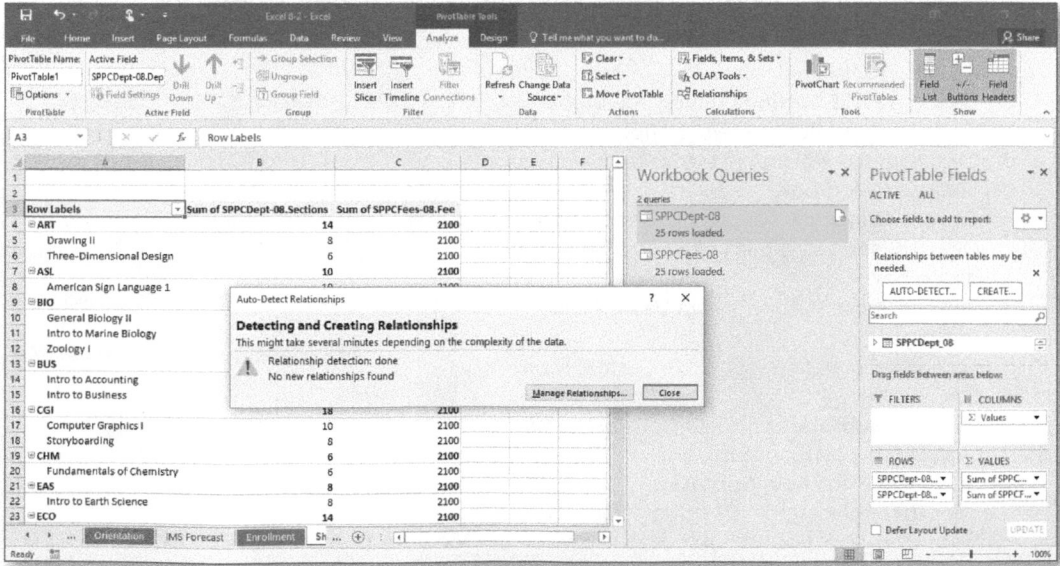

8-92 No relationship is detected

m. Click the **Column (Foreign)** arrow and choose **SPCCFees-08.ID** as the field name.
n. Click the **Related Table** arrow and choose **SPCCDept-08**.
o. Click the **Related Column (Primary)** arrow and choose **SPCCDept-08.ID** as the field name (Figure 8-93).

8-93 *Create Relationship* dialog box

p. Click **OK** and then click **Close**.
q. Name the sheet tab XML PivotTable.

18. Pivot and format a *PivotTable*.

a. Drag the **Fee** field on top of the **Section** field in the *Values* area in the *PivotTable Fields* pane to arrange the *Fee* field on the left of the *Sections* field in the *PivotTable*.
b. Select cell **B3** and type Course Fee as the *Custom Name*.
c. Click the **Field Settings** button [*PivotTable Tools Analyze*, *Active Field* group].
d. Click **Number Format** in the *Value Field Settings* dialog box.
e. Choose **Currency**, set zero (0) decimal places, click **OK**, and close the *Value Field Settings* dialog box.
f. Right-click cell **C3** and select **Value Field Settings**.
g. Type Number of Sections in the *Custom Name* box and click **OK**.
h. Click the **Subtotals** button [*PivotTable Tools Design* tab, *Layout* group].
i. Select **Do Not Show Subtotals**.
j. Click the **More** button [*PivotTable Tools Design* tab, *PivotTable Styles* group] and choose **Pivot Style Medium 1**.
k. Select the **Banded Columns** box [*PivotTable Tools Design* tab, *PivotTable Style Options* group] (Figure 8-94).

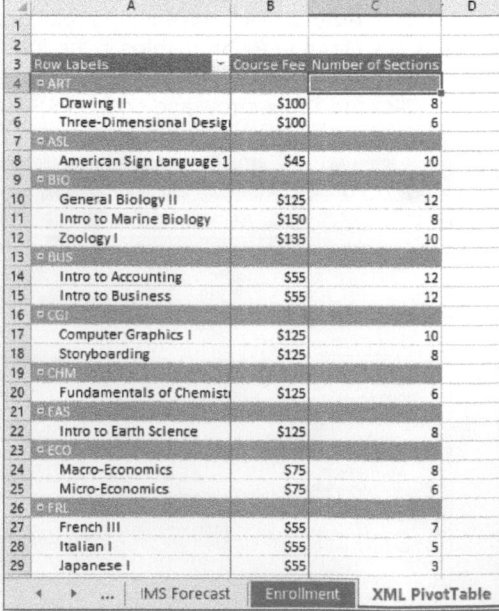

8-94 Formatted *PivotTable*

19. Insert a slicer.
 a. Click any cell in the *PivotTable*.
 b. Click the **Insert Slicer** button [*PivotTable Tools Analyze* tab, *Filter* group].
 c. Select the **SPCCDept-08.Dept** box and click **OK**.
 d. Use the four-pointed arrow to drag the slicer so that the top-left corner is in cell **E3**.

20. Format a slicer.
 a. Click the **More** button [*Slicer Tools Options* tab, *Slicer Styles* group] and choose **Slicer Style Dark 3**.
 b. Click the **Up** spin arrow for the **Columns** button [*Slicer Tools Options* tab, *Buttons* group] and to reach **4**.
 c. Size the slicer to reach column **H** and row **9**.
 d. Click **BIO** in the slicer (Figure 8-95).
 e. Click the **Multi-Select** button in the slicer.
 f. Click **CHM** and **EAS** in the slicer.

8-95 Filtered *PivotTable* and its slicer

21. Save and close the workbook.

22. Uninstall *Solver* and the *Analysis ToolPak*.
 a. Select the **Options** command [*File* tab] and click **Add-Ins** in the left pane.
 b. Select **Solver Add-In** in the list of *Active Applications Add-Ins*.
 c. Click **Go** in the *Manage* section near the bottom of the window.
 d. Deselect the **Solver Add-in** and **Analysis ToolPak** boxes and click **OK**.

Guided Project 8-3

Courtyard Medical Plaza has new worksheets for weight loss workshops. You use *Solver* with sample data and add scenarios and data tables to complete a sample set. You also create *PivotTables* to analyze dental insurance data.
[Student Learning Outcomes 8.1, 8.3, 8.4, 8.7, 8.8]

File Needed: ***CourtyardMedical-08.xlsx*** *(Student data files are available in the* Library *of your SIMnet account)*
Completed Project File Name: ***[your initials] Excel 8-3.xlsx***

Skills Covered in this Project

- Create and manage scenarios.
- Use *Solver* in a worksheet to find a solution.
- Build a one-variable data table.
- Build a two-variable data table.
- Create and customize a *PivotTable*.
- Insert a slicer in a *PivotTable*.
- Insert a *PivotChart*.
- Generate *Descriptive Statistics* for a set of data.

1. Open the **CourtyardMedical-08** workbook from your student data files and save it as [your initials] Excel 8-3.

2. Install *Solver* and the *Analysis ToolPak*.
 a. Select the **Options** command [*File* tab].

b. Click **Add-Ins** in the left pane.
c. Click **Go** near the bottom of the window.
d. Select the **Solver Add-in** box.
e. Select the **Analysis ToolPak** box.
f. Click **OK**.

3. Click the **Workout Plan** worksheet tab and select cell **E10**. Five activities are included in this plan to burn calories for weight loss. This cell includes a *SUM* formula.

4. Add scenarios in a worksheet.
 a. Click the **What-if Analysis** button [*Data* tab, *Data Tools* group] and select **Scenario Manager**.
 b. Click **Add**.
 c. Type Basic Plan as the name.
 d. Click the **Changing cells** box, select cells **D5:D9**, and click **OK**.
 e. Do not edit the *Scenario Values* and click **OK**.
 f. Click **Add** to add another scenario.
 g. Type Double as the name, keep the *Changing cells* as is, and click **OK**.
 h. Change the values to 2, 2, 4, 2, 2, doubling each current value, in the *Scenario Values* dialog box and click **OK** (Figure 8-96).
 i. Click **Close**.

5. Use *Solver* to find a target calorie burn.
 a. Click the **Solver** button [*Data* tab, *Analyze* group].
 b. Select cell **E10**, the cell with a *SUM* formula, for the **Set Objective** box.
 c. Click the **Value Of** radio button and type 3500 in the entry box.
 d. Click the **By Changing Variable Cells** box and select cells **D5:D7**. *Solver* finds how many times each activity should be performed to burn 3,500 calories subject to the constraints.

8-96 Edited scenario values

6. Add constraints to a *Solver* problem.
 a. Click **Add** to the right of the *Subject to the Constraints* box.
 b. Select cell **D5** for the *Cell Reference* box.
 c. Choose **>=** as the operator.
 d. Click the **Constraint** box and type 2. The constraint requires that the exercise be done at least twice a week.
 e. Click **Add** to add each of the five remaining constraints shown here:

 D5 <=4
 D6 <=3
 D6 >=1
 D7 <=4
 D7 >=1

 f. When all constraints are identified, click **OK** in the *Add Constraint* dialog box.
 g. Choose **GRG Nonlinear** for the *Select a Solving Method*.
 h. Confirm that the **Make Unconstrained Variables Non-Negative** box is selected (Figure 8-97).
 i. Click **Solve**. A solution displays in the worksheet, and the *Solver Results* dialog box is open.

8-97 *Solver* parameters and constraints

7. Save *Solver* results as a scenario.
 a. Click **Save Scenario** in the *Solver Results* dialog box.
 b. Type 3500 Burn as the scenario name.
 c. Click **OK** to return to the *Solver Results* dialog box.
 d. Click the **Restore Original Values** button.
 e. Select **Answer** in the *Reports* list.
 f. Click **OK**. The generated report is inserted, and the original values are restored in the worksheet.

8. Create a scenario summary report.
 a. Click the **What-if Analysis** button [*Data* tab, *Data Tools* group] and select **Scenario Manager**.
 b. Click the **Summary** button.
 c. Verify that the **Scenario summary** button is selected.
 d. Click the **Result cells** box, select cells **D5:D9**, type a comma , and then select cell **E10**.
 e. Click **OK** in the *Scenario Summary* dialog box. The report is generated in a new worksheet. Since the results cells are named, the range names appear in the report (Figure 8-98).

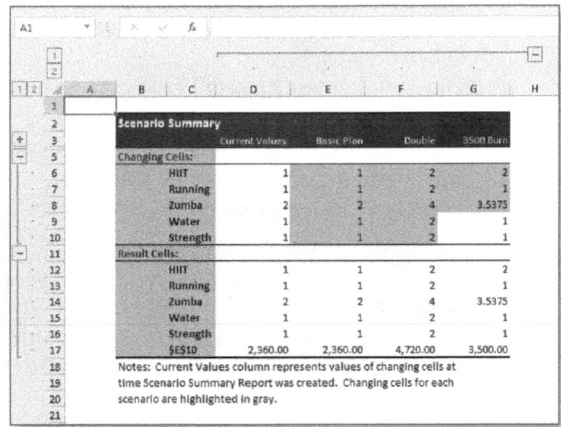

8-98 Generated scenario summary

9. Create a one-variable data table to calculate total calories if dinner calories are adjusted.
 a. Click the **Calorie Journal** worksheet tab and select cell **I5**. The *SUM* formula calculates total calories consumed per day.
 b. Select cell **E15**. The formula for the data table must be one column to the right and one row above the first input value.
 c. Type = , click cell **I5**, and press **Enter**.
 d. Select cells **D15:E23** as the data table range.
 e. Click the **What-If Analysis** button [*Data* tab, *Data Tools* group] and choose **Data Table**.
 f. Click the **Column input cell** box and select cell **G5**. The input values will be substituted for this cell in the data table formula.
 g. Click **OK** (Figure 8-99).

10. Create a two-variable data table to calculate total calories if both lunch and dinner calories are adjusted.
 a. Select cell **L15**. A two-variable table has one formula, one row above column inputs and one column left of row values.
 b. Type = , click cell **I5**, and press **Enter**.
 c. Select cells **L15:T23**.
 d. Click the **What-If Analysis** button [*Data* tab, *Data Tools* group] and choose **Data Table**.
 e. Select cell **E5** for the *Row input cell* box. Lunch calories are in the row of this data table.
 f. Click the **Column input cell** box and select cell **G5**. Dinner calories are in the column.
 g. Click **OK** to build the data table (Figure 8-100).

	Total Calories
	2,450
500	2,150
600	2,250
700	2,350
800	2,450
900	2,550
1,000	2,650
1,100	2,750
1,200	2,850

(Dinner Calories — row label)

8-99 One-variable data table with results

				Lunch Calories				
2,450	500	600	700	800	900	1000	1100	1200
500	2050	2150	2250	2350	2450	2550	2650	2750
600	2150	2250	2350	2450	2550	2650	2750	2850
700	2250	2350	2450	2550	2650	2750	2850	2950
800	2350	2450	2550	2650	2750	2850	2950	3050
900	2450	2550	2650	2750	2850	2950	3050	3150
1000	2550	2650	2750	2850	2950	3050	3150	3250
1100	2650	2750	2850	2950	3050	3150	3250	3350
1200	2750	2850	2950	3050	3150	3250	3350	3450

(Dinner Calories — column label)

8-100 Two-variable data table with results

11. Select cell **J1** and insert a page break [*Page Layout* tab, *Page Setup* group].

12. Create a *PivotTable* for dental insurance data.
 a. Click the **Dental Insurance** worksheet tab and select cells **A4:E35**.
 b. Click the **Recommended PivotTables** button [*Insert* tab, *Tables* group].
 c. Choose **Sum of Billed by Service Code** and click **OK**. Label fields are in the *Rows* area, and numeric fields are in the *Values* area.
 d. Name the worksheet tab PivotTable 1.
 e. Point to **Billed** in the *Choose fields to add to report* area and drag the field name to the **Values** area to show the field twice in the *PivotTable*.

13. Edit value field settings.
 a. Click **Sum of Billed** in cell **B3** and click the **Field Settings** button [*PivotTable Tools Analyze*, *Active Field* group].
 b. Type Total Billed as the *Custom Name*.
 c. Click **Number Format**, choose **Currency**, set **0** (zero) decimal places, and click **OK** two times to close the dialog boxes.
 d. Right-click **Sum of Billed2** in cell **C3** and select **Value Field Settings**.
 e. Type Average Billed as the *Custom Name*.
 f. On the *Summarize Values By* tab, choose **Average** as the function.
 g. Click **Number Format**, choose **Currency**, set **0** (zero) decimal places, and close the dialog boxes.

14. Use *PivotTable* tools to format the report.
 a. Click any cell in the *PivotTable* and apply **Pivot Style Medium 6**.
 b. Select the **Banded Rows** and **Banded Columns** boxes [*PivotTable Tools Design* tab, *PivotTable Style Options* group].
 c. Click the **Grand Totals** button [*PivotTable Tools Design* tab, *Layout* group] and choose **Off for Rows and Columns**.

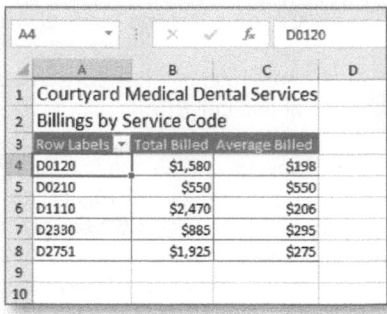

8-101 Completed *PivotTable*

15. Select cell **A1** and type Courtyard Medical Dental Services.

16. Type Billings by Service Code in cell **A2**.

17. Format both labels as **14 pt**. (Figure 8-101).

18. Create a *PivotChart*.
 a. Select a cell in the *PivotTable* and click the **PivotChart** button [*PivotTable Tools Analyze, Tools* group].
 b. Choose **Column** and **Clustered Column** as the subtype and click **OK**.
 c. Drag the chart object so that its top-left corner is in cell **E3**.
 d. Size the chart object to reach cell **M24**.
 e. Click one of the **Average Billed** columns and click the **Change Chart Type** button [*PivotChart Tools Design* tab, *Type* group].
 f. Click the **Chart Type** arrow for the *Average Billed* series and choose **Line with Markers** (Figure 8-102).
 g. Click **OK**.

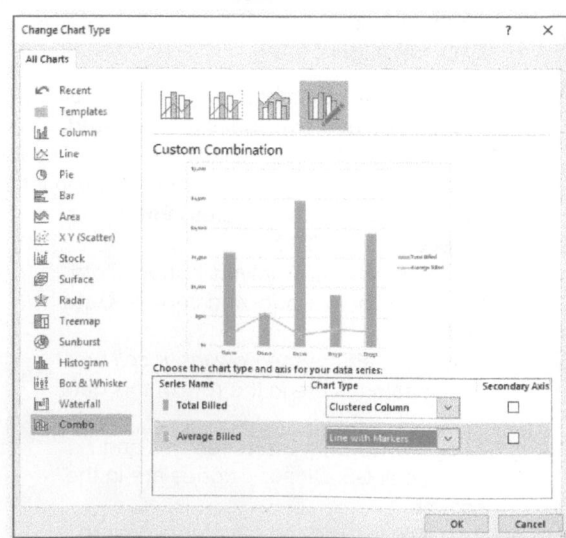

8-102 Change the chart type for one of the data series

E8-559

h. Click one of the **Total Billed** columns and change its **Shape Fill** [*PivotChart Tools Format* tab, *Shape Styles* group] to **Teal, Accent 5, Darker 25%**.

19. Insert a slicer.
 a. Click any cell in the *PivotTable* and click the **Insert Slicer** button [*PivotTable Tools Analyze* tab, *Filter* group].
 b. Select the **Insurance** box and click **OK**.
 c. Position the slicer so that the top-left corner is in cell **O3**.
 d. Format the slicer with **Slicer Style Dark 5**.
 e. Click **CompDent** in the slicer to filter the *PivotTable* and *PivotChart* (Figure 8-103).
 f. Select cell **A1**.

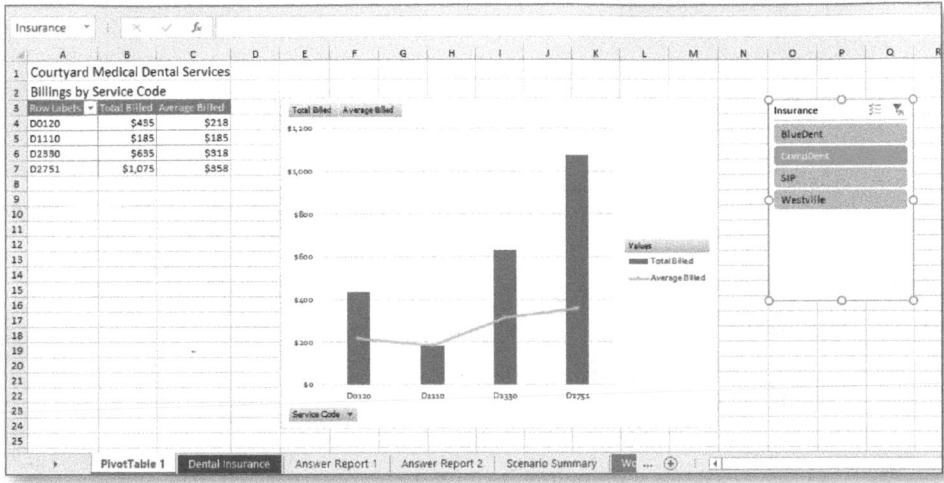

8-103 Completed *PivotTable*, *PivotChart*, and slicer

20. Generate *Descriptive Statistics* for a rating category.
 a. Click the **Dental Insurance** sheet tab.
 b. Click the **Data Analysis** button [*Data* tab, *Analyze* group].
 c. Select **Descriptive Statistics** and click **OK**.
 d. Select cells **E4:E35** for the **Input Range** box.
 e. Select the **Labels in First Row** box.
 f. Select the **Output Range** button.
 g. Click the **Output Range** box and click cell **G4**.
 h. Select the **Summary statistics** box and click **OK**.
 i. **AutoFit** column **G** (Figure 8-104).

21. Save and close the workbook.

22. Uninstall *Solver* and the *Analysis TookPak*.
 a. Select the **Options** command [*File* tab] and click **Add-Ins** in the left pane.
 b. Select **Solver Add-In** in the list of *Active Applications Add-Ins*.
 c. Click **Go** in the *Manage* section near the bottom of the window.
 d. Deselect the **Solver Add-in** and **Analysis ToolPak** boxes and click **OK**.

8-104 Summary statistics for the billed amounts

Independent Project 8-4

Central Sierra Insurance has assembled data about clients in a *PivotTable*. The data source has been updated, but the *PivotTable* has not been refreshed. You also insert a calculated field and complete formatting. You create a commission calculator with a two-variable data table and get data from an Access database file to create a second *PivotTable*.
[Student Learning Outcomes 8.4, 8.6, 8.7]

Files Needed: ***CentralSierra-08.xlsx*** and ***Database-08.accdb*** *(Student data files are available in the Library of your SIMnet account)*
Completed Project File Name: *[your initials] Excel 8-4.xlsx*

Skills Covered in this Project

- Work with *PivotTable* tools.
- Insert a calculated field in a *PivotTable*.
- Build a two-variable data table.
- Get and transform data from an Access table.
- Create a *PivotTable* from the data model.

1. Open the ***CentralSierra-08*** workbook from your student data files and save it as [your initials] Excel 8-4.

2. Click the **Client Stats** worksheet tab. Note the column labels and city and state names.

3. Click the **PivotTable1** worksheet tab. The state names on this sheet are different.

4. Click a cell in the *PivotTable*. The field name "Number of Volunteers" in the *PivotTable Field List* pane is not part of the data on the **Client Stats** sheet.

5. Click the **Refresh** button on the *PivotTable Tools Analyze* tab (Figure 8-105).

6. Edit the *PivotTable* to show # of Females and # of Males as column labels. Center align both labels.

7. Click the *Filter* arrow for cell **A5** and sort the state names in ascending order.

8. Apply **PivotStyle Light 22** and show **Banded Rows**.

9. Insert a calculated field in a *PivotTable*.
 a. Click the **Fields, Items, and Sets** button [*PivotTable Tools Analyze* tab, *Calculations* group] and choose **Calculated Field**.
 b. Type All in the *Name* box.
 c. Click the **Formula** box and delete the zero and the space after the equals sign.
 d. Double-click **Females** and type + for addition.
 e. Double-click **Males** and click **OK** (Figure 8-106).
 f. Edit the label in cell **D5** to show Total and center it.
 g. Press **Ctrl+Home**.

10. Click the **Commissions** worksheet tab and enter a formula in cell **E6** to calculate commission dollars (multiply the premium by the rate).

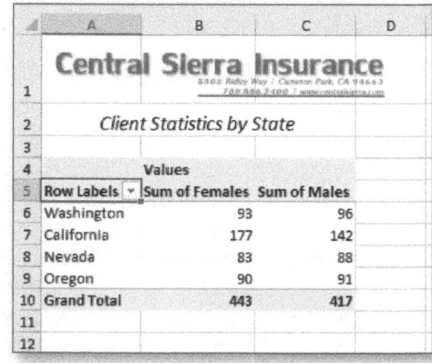

Row Labels	Sum of Females	Sum of Males
Washington	93	96
California	177	142
Nevada	83	88
Oregon	90	91
Grand Total	443	417

8-105 Refreshed *PivotTable*

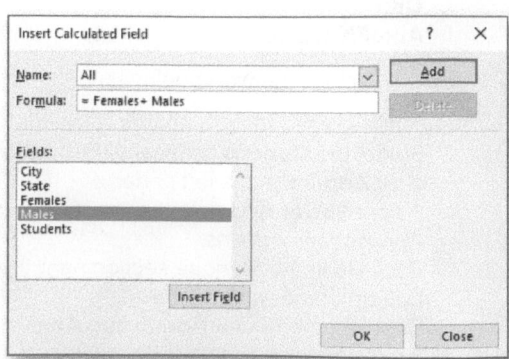

8-106 *Insert Calculated Field* dialog box

11. Build a two-variable data table to calculate commissions. Format the results as **Currency** with no decimal places (Figure 8-107).

12. Get and transform data from a Microsoft Access database.
 a. Click the **New Query** button [*Data* tab, *Get & Transform* group], choose **From Database**, and then select **From Microsoft Access Database**.
 b. Find and select **Database-08** from your student data files and click **Import**.
 c. In the *Navigator* window, select **TblCentralSierra** in the list and click **Edit**.
 d. Remove the **ID** and **State** columns in the *Query Editor*.
 e. Close the query and load it to Excel.
 f. Name the new sheet Client Stats2.

13. Create a *PivotTable* from the data model.
 a. Click cell **A2** in the table on the **Client Stats2** sheet.
 b. Click the **Summarize with PivotTable** button [*Table Tools Design* tab, *Tools* group].
 c. Add the data to the data model and place the *PivotTable* on a new worksheet.
 d. Expand the **TblCentralSierra** list in the *PivotTable Fields* pane and place all the fields in the *PivotTable* layout.
 e. Click **All** in the *PivotTable Fields* pane and expand the list for the table that includes the male, female, and student fields.
 f. Select the **Students** box to add it to the *PivotTable* layout.
 g. Click **Auto-Detect** to create the relationship. The *City* field is the common field in these two tables.
 h. Click **Close** in the message box (Figure 8-108).
 i. Name the sheet tab PivotTable2.

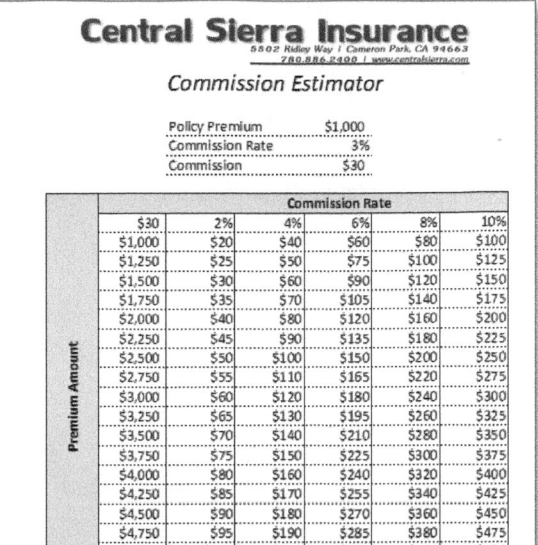

Central Sierra Insurance
5502 Ridley Way | Cameron Park, CA 94663
780.886.2400 | www.centralsierra.com

Commission Estimator

Policy Premium	$1,000
Commission Rate	3%
Commission	$30

Premium Amount	Commission Rate				
$30	**2%**	**4%**	**6%**	**8%**	**10%**
$1,000	$20	$40	$60	$80	$100
$1,250	$25	$50	$75	$100	$125
$1,500	$30	$60	$90	$120	$150
$1,750	$35	$70	$105	$140	$175
$2,000	$40	$80	$120	$160	$200
$2,250	$45	$90	$135	$180	$225
$2,500	$50	$100	$150	$200	$250
$2,750	$55	$110	$165	$220	$275
$3,000	$60	$120	$180	$240	$300
$3,250	$65	$130	$195	$260	$325
$3,500	$70	$140	$210	$280	$350
$3,750	$75	$150	$225	$300	$375
$4,000	$80	$160	$240	$320	$400
$4,250	$85	$170	$255	$340	$425
$4,500	$90	$180	$270	$360	$450
$4,750	$95	$190	$285	$380	$475
$5,000	$100	$200	$300	$400	$500

8-107 Completed data table for commissions

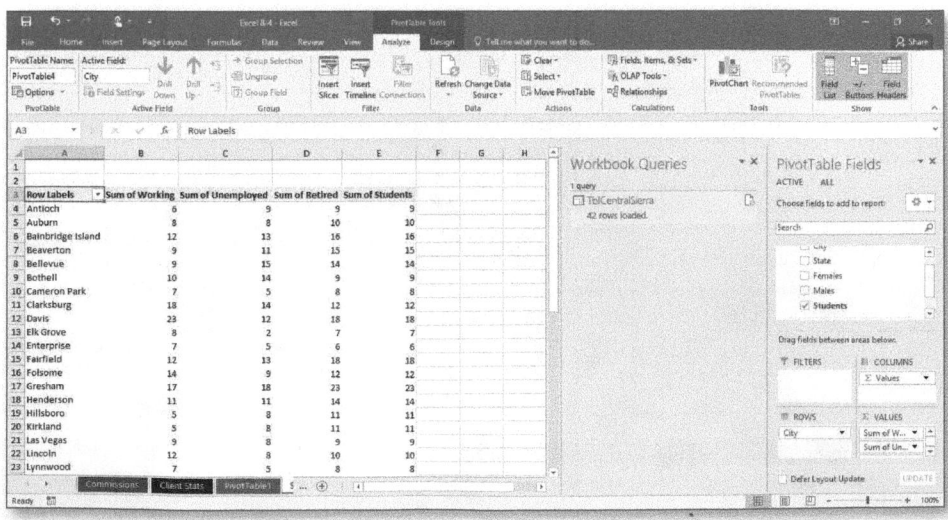

8-108 *PivotTable* from the data model

14. Edit the column labels as show here. The display label cannot be the same as the field name in the *PivotTable* list.

 B3 Employeed

 C3 Not Working

 D3 Retirees

 E3 Undergrad

15. Apply **PivotTable Style Medium 15** with **Banded Rows** and **AutoFit** each column.

16. Save and close the workbook (Figure 8-109).

Row Labels	Employeed	Not Working	Retirees	Undergrad
Antioch	6	9	9	9
Auburn	8	8	10	10
Bainbridge Island	12	13	16	16
Beaverton	9	11	15	15
Bellevue	9	15	14	14
Bothell	10	14	9	9
Cameron Park	7	5	8	8
Clarksburg	18	14	12	12
Davis	23	12	18	18
Elk Grove	8	2	7	7
Enterprise	7	5	6	6
Fairfield	12	13	18	18
Folsome	14	9	12	12
Gresham	17	18	23	23
Henderson	11	11	14	14
Hillsboro	5	8	11	11
Kirkland	5	8	11	11
Las Vegas	9	8	9	9
Lincoln	12	8	10	10
Lynnwood	7	5	8	8
Milwaukie	8	8	9	9
North Las Vegas	5	9	8	8
Oak Grove	7	5	8	8
Paradise	10	14	9	9
Parkland	8	4	2	2
Portland	10	10	14	14
Poulsbo	9	12	5	5
Redmond	8	7	5	5
Reno	9	15	14	14
Roseville	14	10	15	15
Sacramento	6	6	9	9
Spring Valley	9	5	7	7
Stockton	15	15	18	18
Tacoma	11	10	8	8
Tigard	12	13	16	16
Vancouver	10	10	15	15
Walnut Grove	12	8	13	13
Winchester	10	8	10	10
Witney	13	13	13	13
Woodland	22	20	24	24
Yakima	14	8	7	7
Yuba City	12	11	14	14
Grand Total	443	417	483	483

Central Sierra Insurance

Client Statistics by State

Row Labels	Values # of Females	# of Males	Total
California	177	142	319
Nevada	83	88	171
Oregon	90	91	181
Washington	93	96	189
Grand Total	443	417	860

8-109 Completed *PivotTables* for Excel 8-4

Independent Project 8-5

At Placer Hills Real Estate, the commission and fee split between the listing and selling agents depends on price tiers (levels). You create a one-variable data table to display commissions and net earnings for various split rates. You copy the sheet and edit it to show results for another price tier. Additionally, you create scenarios for selling price and commission, generate summary statistics, and create a forecast sheet.
[Student Learning Outcomes 8.1, 8.3, 8.4, 8.5, 8.8]

File Needed: **PlacerHills-08.xlsx** (Student data files are available in the Library of your SIMnet account)
Completed Project File Name: **[your initials] Excel 8-5.xlsx**

Skills Covered in this Project

- Build a one-variable data table.
- Use *Solver*.
- Create and manage scenarios.
- Generate descriptive statistics.
- Create a forecast sheet.

1. Open the **PlacerHills-08** workbook from your student data files and save it as [your initials] Excel 8-5.

2. Review formulas.
 a. Select cell **C14** on the **Tier 2** worksheet. The total commission is calculated by multiplying the selling price by the listing rate.
 b. Select cell **C15**. The *IFS* function checks the selling price (C12) to determine the commission split percentage (column D).
 c. Select cell **C16**. The *IFS* function checks the selling price (C12) to determine the fee percentage (column E) and multiplies the commission (C15) to calculate the fee in dollars.
 d. Select cell **C17**. The net commission is calculated by subtracting fees from the PHRE amount.

3. Build one-variable data tables.
 a. Select cell **C20** and create a reference to cell **C15**.
 b. Select cell **D20** and create a reference to cell **C17**. Both formulas in the data table refer to cell **C12**, the one variable.
 c. Use cell **D8** as the column input for the data table. (You can use any percentage from column D because its value is replaced by the possible rates in the data table.) (Figure 8-110).
 d. Decrease the decimal two times for the results in the data table.
 e. Make a copy of the **Tier 2** worksheet and name the copy Tier 1.
 f. Edit the label in cell **A23** to show **Tier 1**.
 g. Edit the selling price in cell **C12** to **$1,000,000**.
 h. Recalculate the data table with cell **D7** as the column input for *Tier 1*.

4. Name cell ranges.
 a. Click the **Price Solver** worksheet tab.
 b. Click cell **C12** and name the range **Selling_Price**. You cannot use spaces in a range name.
 c. Name cell **C14** as Total_Commission and cell **C17** as PHRE_Commission.

5. Install the *Solver Add-in* and the *Analysis ToolPak*.

6. Use *Solver* to find target PHRE net commission amounts.
 a. Build a *Solver* problem with cell **C17** as the objective cell. For the first solution, set the objective to a value of **50000** by changing cell **C12**. Save the results as a scenario named $50,000.
 b. Restore the original values and run another *Solver* problem to find a selling price for a PHRE commission of 75000. Save these results as a scenario named $75,000.

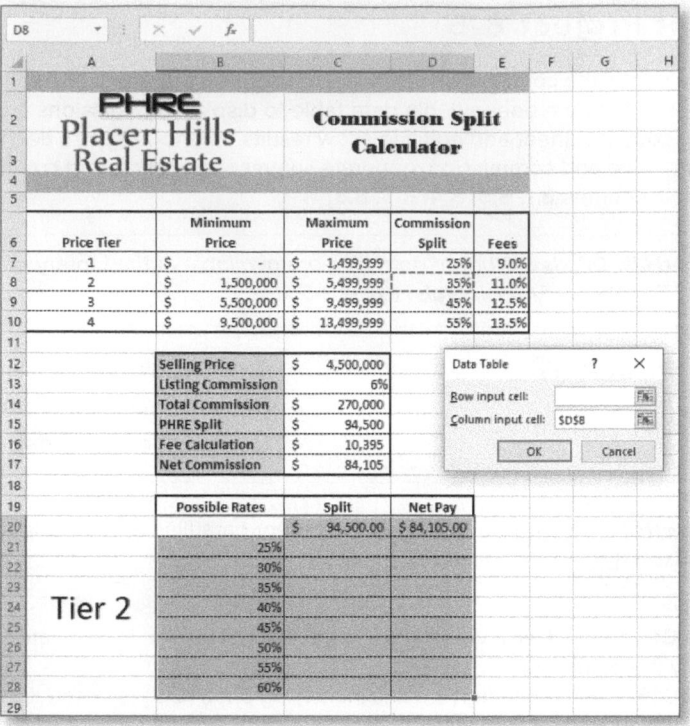

8-110 Data table setup for *Tier 2*

 c. Restore the original values and run a third *Solver* problem to find a selling price for a net commission of $100,000. Save these results as a scenario.

7. Manage scenarios.
 a. Show the **$50,000** scenario in the worksheet.
 b. Create a **Scenario summary** report for cells **C12**, **C14**, and **C17**.

8. Generate *Descriptive Statistics* for recent sales.
 a. Click the **Sales Forecast** sheet tab.
 b. Generate **Descriptive Statistics** for cells **E4:E26** and note that the label is in the first row.
 c. Select the **Output Range** button, click the entry box, and select cell **G4**.
 d. Select the **Summary statistics** box and include the largest and smallest (*Kth* values) in the report.
 e. **AutoFit** column **G** (Figure 8-111).

9. Create a forecast sheet for the date and price data on the **Sales Forecast** sheet using a column chart. End the forecast three months from the last date in the table. Position the chart object with its top-left corner in cell **E1**. Size the chart object to reach cell **P20**. Name the generated sheet as *Forecast*.

Sale Price	
Mean	370593.2
Standard Error	19986.61
Median	365000
Mode	#N/A
Standard Deviation	93745.5
Sample Variance	8.79E+09
Kurtosis	-1.23251
Skewness	0.01939
Range	294100
Minimum	228900
Maximum	523000
Sum	8153050
Count	22
Largest(1)	523000
Smallest(1)	228900

8-111 Descriptive statistics for sales

10. Save and close the workbook (Figure 8-112).

11. Uninstall the *Solver Add-in* and the *Analysis ToolPak*.

Tier 1

Tier 2

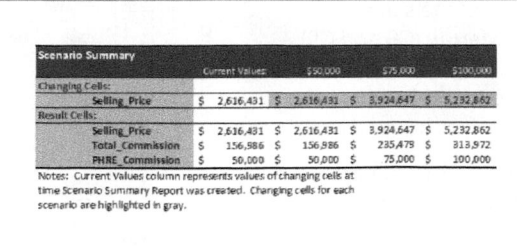

8-112 Completed worksheets for Excel 8-5

Independent Project 8-6

Wilson Home Entertainment Systems calculates selling price based on cost and profit margin. You create scenarios for the worksheet and build a two-variable data table. Other tasks include getting data from an XML file and creating a *PivotTable* and *PivotChart*.
[Student Learning Outcomes 8.1, 8.2, 8.3, 8.4, 8.5, 8.6, 8.7, 8.8]

Files Needed: ***WilsonHome-08.xlsx***, ***WilsonHome-08.xml***, and ***WilsonHome-08.xsd*** *(Student data files are available in the* Library *of your SIMnet account)*
Completed Project File Name: *[your initials] Excel 8-6.xlsx*

Skills Covered in this Project

- Create and manage scenarios.
- Create a scenario summary report.
- Build a two-variable data table.
- Create a forecast sheet.

- Use the *Analysis ToolPak* to generate a moving average.
- Use *Solver* to find a solution.
- Use *Goal Seek* to backsolve a problem.
- Get and transform XML data.
- Create and customize a *PivotTable*.

1. Open the ***WilsonHome-08*** workbook from your student data files and save it as [your initials] Excel 8-6.

2. Install *Solver* and the *Analysis ToolPak*.

3. Review pricing formulas.
 a. Select cell **F5** on the **Product Pricing** worksheet. Shipping and handling charges are calculated at 10% of the manufacturer's cost.
 b. Select cell **F6**. An insurance cost is calculated at 6% of the cost.
 c. Select cell **F7**. Total investment is the sum of the cost, shipping and handling, and insurance.
 d. Select cell **F9**. The suggested selling price is the total investment multiplied by 1 plus the margin. These results are rounded to show zero (0) decimal places.

4. Create and manage scenarios.
 a. Create a scenario named **12%** with cell **F8** as the changing cell but do not edit the value. This is the original data set.
 b. Add another scenario named **13%** and change the value.
 c. Add scenarios for **15%** and **17%** profit margins.
 d. Generate a scenario summary report for cells **F4**, **F8**, and **F9**.
 e. Edit the labels in cells **C6** and **C8:C10** in the *Results Cells* section of the summary report to display **Cost**, **Margin** (C6 and C9), and **Selling Price**. Right-align these labels.
 f. Show the **15%** scenario in the **Product Pricing** worksheet.

5. Select cell **B12** and create a reference to the selling price formula for the two-variable data table.

6. Build the data table and format results as **Currency** with zero (0) decimal places (Figure 8-113).

			Profit Margin					
		8%	10%	12%	14%	16%	18%	20%
	$133							
	$200	$251	$255	$260	$264	$269	$274	$278
	$225	$282	$287	$292	$298	$303	$308	$313
	$250	$313	$319	$325	$331	$336	$342	$348
	$275	$345	$351	$357	$364	$370	$376	$383
	$300	$376	$383	$390	$397	$404	$411	$418
	$325	$407	$415	$422	$430	$437	$445	$452
	$350	$438	$447	$455	$463	$471	$479	$487
	$375	$470	$479	$487	$496	$505	$513	$522
Manufacturer's Cost	$400	$501	$510	$520	$529	$538	$548	$557
	$425	$532	$542	$552	$562	$572	$582	$592
	$450	$564	$574	$585	$595	$606	$616	$626
	$475	$595	$606	$617	$628	$639	$650	$661
	$500	$626	$638	$650	$661	$673	$684	$696
	$525	$658	$670	$682	$694	$706	$719	$731
	$550	$689	$702	$715	$727	$740	$753	$766
	$575	$720	$734	$747	$760	$774	$787	$800
	$600	$752	$766	$780	$793	$807	$821	$835
	$625	$783	$798	$812	$827	$841	$856	$870
	$650	$814	$829	$844	$860	$875	$890	$905
	$675	$846	$861	$877	$893	$908	$924	$940
	$700	$877	$893	$909	$926	$942	$958	$974
	$725	$908	$925	$942	$959	$976	$992	$1,009
	$750	$940	$957	$974	$992	$1,009	$1,027	$1,044

8-113 Completed data table for *Product Pricing* sheet

E8-567

7. Create a forecast sheet for the data on the **Soundbar Sales** sheet with a line chart. End the forecast at the end of the third month from the last date in the data. Position the chart object with its top-left corner in cell **A20**.

8. Change the outline color for the **Values** series in the chart to **Blue-Gray, Text 2**. Change the outline color for the **Forecast** series to **Orange, Accent 4**. Select the chart area and format the outline color as **Black, Text 1**.

9. Rename the sheet tab as Forecast Sheet and select cell **A1** (Figure 8-114).

10. Create a moving average list with chart for cells **B4:B16** on the **Soundbar Sales** sheet with an interval of **2**. Output the results to cell **D4**. Position the chart object to start at cell **E4** and size it to reach cell **M18**.

11. Change the outline and shape fill color for the **Forecast** series to **Gold, Accent 3**. Select cell **A3** (Figure 8-115).

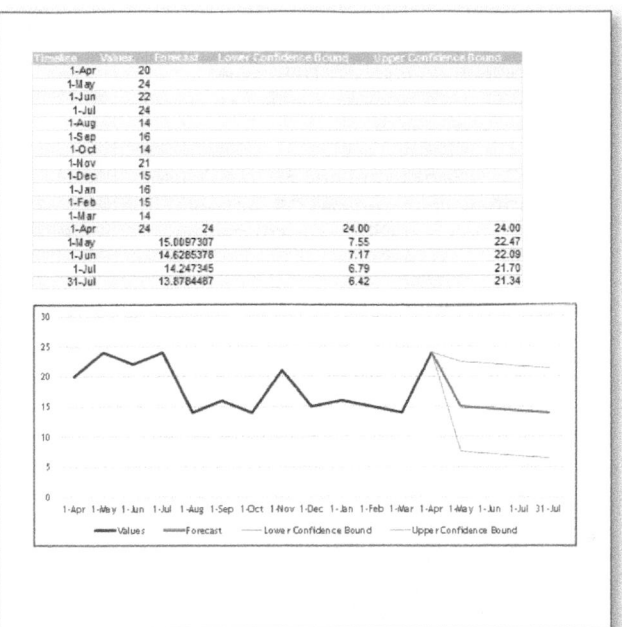

8-114 Completed forecast sheet and chart

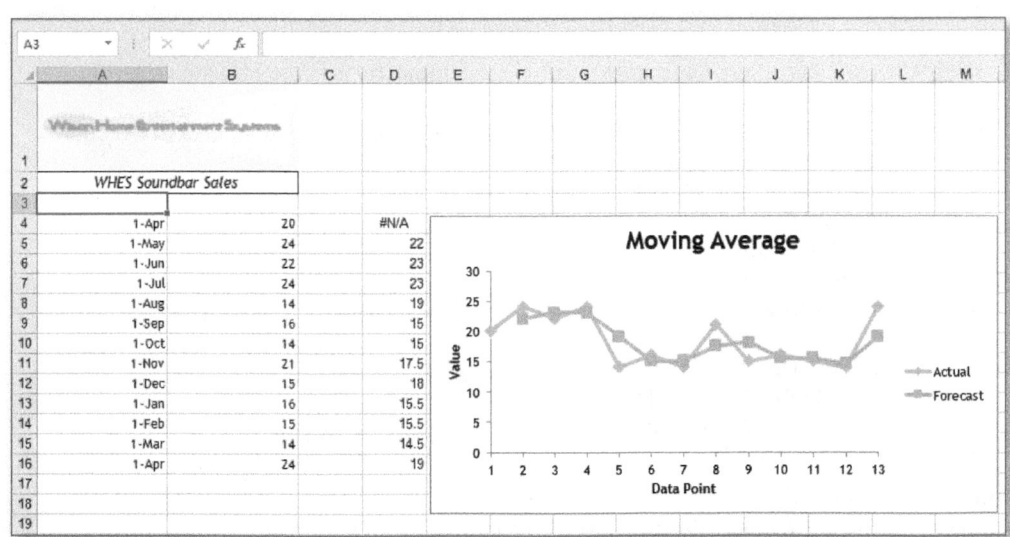

8-115 Completed moving average and related chart

12. Use *Solver* to find target total wages for one day.
 a. Click the **Man Hours** sheet tab.
 b. Select cells **C5:C8** and save the values as a scenario named **Current**.
 c. Build a *Solver* problem to find the minimum result for cell **E9** subject to the following constraints:
 C5 Between 16 and 18
 C6 Between 6 and 10

C7 Between 12 and 15
C8 Between 4 and 12
d. Save the results ($2,085) as a scenario named Minimum and show the results in the worksheet.

13. Use *Goal Seek* to set cell **E9** to a value of **1800** by changing cell **C5**. Accept the solution and save cells **C5:C8** as a scenario named $1800.

14. Create a scenario summary report for cells **C5:C8** and cell **E9** (Figure 8-116).

15. Get and transform XML data.
 a. Create a new query for the XML file **WilsonHome-08** from your student data files.
 b. Display all fields in the *Query Editor*.
 c. Remove the two generated columns at the right of the data.
 d. Set the data type to **Date/Time** for the **WilsonHome.Date** field and to **Currency** for the **WilsonHome.Price** column.
 e. Load the query and name the query results sheet as XML Sales.
 f. Select the **WilsonHome.Date** column in the worksheet and apply the **Short Date** format.

16. Create a *PivotTable* from the data model.
 a. Select cell **A2** on the **XML Sales** sheet.
 b. Create a *PivotTable* on a new worksheet and add the data to the workbook data model.
 c. Show the **ID** and **Style** fields. Drag the **Style** field to the *Columns* area in the *PivotTable Fields* pane.
 d. Click **All** in the *PivotTable Fields* pane, expand the **TableQty** list, and add the **Quantity** field to the *PivotTable* layout.
 e. Click **Create** in the *PivotTable Fields* task pane to open the *Create Relationship* dialog box.
 f. Click the **Table** arrow and choose **TableQty** as the table and **ID** as the *Column (Foreign)* field.
 g. Click the **Related Table** arrow and select **WilsonHome_08** with **WilsonHome.ID** as the *Related Column (Primary)* field (Figure 8-117).
 h. Click **OK** and then click **Close**.
 i. Name the sheet tab XML PivotTable.
 j. Close the *Workbook Queries* pane if it is open.

17. Work with *PivotTable* tools.
 a. Click any cell in the *PivotTable* and insert a timeline for the *Date* field.
 b. Format the timeline to show quarters and then display data for the second quarter 2017.
 c. Position the timeline to start in cell **F2**.
 d. Apply **PivotTable Style Medium 4** with banded columns and rows to the *PivotTable* and **Timeline Style Light 3** to the timeline.
 e. Change the label in cell **A3** to Transaction ID.
 f. Change the label in cell **B3** to Product.
 g. Select cell **A1**.

18. Use *GETPIVOTDATA* on the **Quantities** sheet to get data for column F (Figure 8-118).

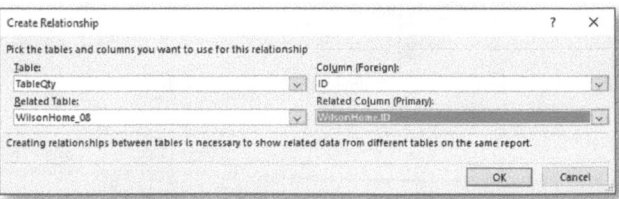

8-116 Scenario summary report after *Solver* and *Goal Seek*

8-117 *Create Relationship* dialog box

8-118 Completed worksheets for Excel 8-6

19. Save the workbook, click **Continue** in the *Compatibility Checker*, and close the workbook.

20. Uninstall *Solver* and the *Analysis ToolPak*.

Improve It Project 8-7

Pool and Spa Oasis forecasts sales for three categories of business. You create scenarios with different growth rates and build a one-variable data table. On another worksheet, you use *Solver* to find minimum total wages for a work crew.
[Student Learning Outcomes 8.1, 8.3, 8.4]

File Needed: ***Pools&Spa08.xlsx*** *(Student data files are available in the* Library *of your SIMnet account)*
Completed Project File Name: *[your initials]* ***Excel 8-7.xlsx***

Skills Covered in this Project

- Create and manage scenarios.
- Build a one-variable data table.
- Use *Solver* with constraints.

1. Open the **Pools&Spa-08** workbook from your student data files and save it as [your initials] Excel 8-7.

2. Review formulas.
 a. Select cell **D5** on the **Forecast** worksheet. The text box explains the formula which uses 3D references to the **Factors** sheet.
 b. Select cell **B12**. This is a reference to the growth factor in cell **F3** on the **Factors** sheet.
 c. Click the **Factors** worksheet tab. The company uses a general growth rate, but each category's potential is increased or reduced by an adjustment factor.

3. Create scenarios for the growth rate.
 a. Create a scenario named .15% on the **Factors** sheet for the existing data with cell **F3** as the changing cell.
 b. Add another scenario named .5% and change the value to **.005**.
 c. Add scenarios for **1.25%** and **1.75%** growth rates. In the *Scenarios Values* dialog box, you must enter the decimal equivalent of the percentage.
 d. Show the **1.25%** scenario in the worksheet.
 e. Return to the **Forecast** worksheet.

4. Complete the growth rate series for the data table in cells **D20:D27**. The formula references are already entered in row 17.

5. Build the data table with column input cell **B12**. The results are incorrect, because input values and the formula reference must be on the same worksheet.

6. Edit formulas to use a reference on the same sheet.
 a. Click cell **D5**. The data table indirectly refers to this formula which uses the growth factor in cell **F3** on the **Factors** sheet.
 b. Edit the formula to show (**1+B12**) in place of the reference to cell **F3** on the **Factors** sheet. This is the input value for the data table (Figure 8-119).
 c. Copy the formula to the cells **E5:G5** and then to cells **D6:G7**. Redefine borders as needed.

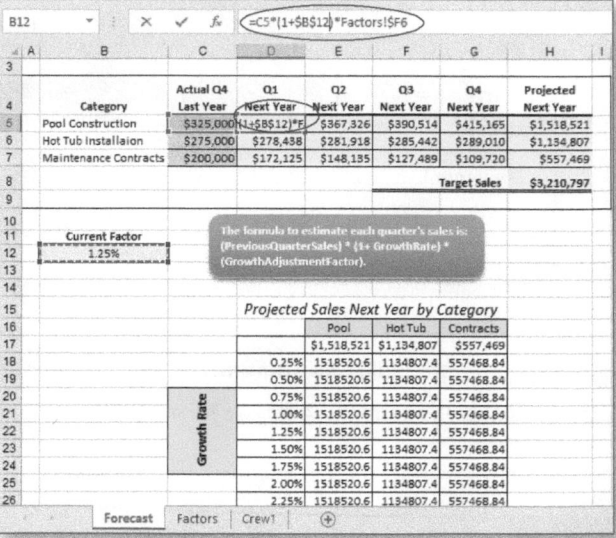

8-119 Edited formula to refer to cell on the same sheet as the data table

7. Format data table results as **Currency** with no decimal places.

8. Use *Solver* to find minimum wages.
 a. Click the **Crew1** worksheet tab.
 b. Build a *Solver* problem to find the minimum value for cell **E9** by changing cells D5:D8. Constraints for cell **D8** are already entered in the *Solver Parameters* dialog box.
 c. Add constraints for each of cells **D5:D7** that reflect the information in column C in the worksheet.
 d. Add a constraint that cell **D9** be less than or equal to 150 (Figure 8-120).
 e. Keep the *Solver* results.

8-120 *Solver* constraints for work crew problem

9. Save and close the workbook (Figure 8-121).

10. Uninstall the *Solver Add-in*.

8-121 **Completed worksheets for Excel 8-7**

Challenge Project 8-8

In this project, you create a worksheet for a carpet/flooring business. You plan to build a data table that shows cost based on total square footage and cost per square foot of the flooring product.
[Student Learning Outcome 8.4]

File Needed: None
Completed Project File Name: *[your initials] Excel 8-8.xlsx*

Create and save a workbook as [your initials] Excel 8-8. Modify your workbook according to the following guidelines:

- Enter a label in row 4 for Costs per square foot. In row 5, type the label Total square footage. In row 6, type Total cost.
- In the adjacent column enter a sample cost and square footage for carpet or wood flooring in a home. Build a formula in row 6 to calculate the cost for your sample values.
- Starting in row 9, create column input values that represent cost per square foot. Use an increment of $2. Start at an average price and fill at least 20 costs in the column.
- In row 8, type an initial row input value that reflects square footage for a single room. Use an increment of 5 and fill values so that you have 9 or 10 columns.
- Build the two-variable data table for total costs for flooring.
- Determine a name for the company and enter main and secondary titles for your worksheet. Add borders, shading, or other format attributes to enhance the interpretation of the worksheet.

Challenge Project 8-9

In this project, you use a statistical measure from in the *Analysis ToolPak* and prepare an informational worksheet to describe and demonstrate one of the calculations.
[Student Learning Outcome 8.8]

File Needed: None
Completed Project File Name: *[your initials] Excel 8-9.xlsx*

Create and save a workbook as [your initials] Excel 8-9. Modify your workbook according to the following guidelines:

- In cell A3, enter the label Statistical Measure. In cell A4, type Purpose.
- In cells B3:B4, enter the name of one of the statistical measures in the *Analysis ToolPak* that you used in this chapter. In row 4, type a brief description of its use and purpose.
- Starting in row 6, develop worksheet data that will illustrate the measure you have chosen, using work, school, or personal data. Include labels and values that clearly illustrate the goal of using your statistical measure.
- Calculate the measure.
- Format the sheet and related results in a professional manner.

Challenge Project 8-10

In this project, you create a worksheet for a trip that you are planning. Some costs are fixed, but you use *Solver* to help determine how much you can spend on lodging and meals.
[Student Learning Outcome 8.1, 8.2, 8.3]

File Needed: None
Completed Project File Name: *[your initials] Excel 8-10.xlsx*

Create and save a workbook as [your initials] Excel 8-10. Modify your workbook according to the following guidelines:

- Enter labels in column A for Airfare, Hotel, Meals, Car Rental, and two other spending categories for your trip.
- In column B, enter average values for your trip. Calculate a total and format the data in an easy-to-understand style.
- Save the original values as a scenario with the changing cells as hotel and meal costs.
- Run *Solver* with a lower total cost as your objective by adjusting the hotel and meal categories. Decide if you need to set constraints for the other categories. If *Solver* cannot find a solution, redefine constraints until it can find a solution. Save the results as a scenario.
- Run *Solver* with a higher cost as your objective. Save the results as a scenario and generate a *Solver* Answer report.
- Generate a scenario summary report for the hotel and meal categories.
- Use *Goal Seek* with the total cost cell set at an optimum cost for your trip by adjusting only the hotel cost. Show these results in the worksheet.

Microsoft Access 2016

Microsoft® Office

IN PRACTICE

access

Creating a Database and Tables

CHAPTER OVERVIEW

Microsoft Access (Access) is the leading PC-based database management system (DBMS) software in both the personal and business market. Access helps you organize and manage personal, business, and educational data in a structure known as a database. This software makes it easy for you to ensure your data are accurate, organized, and usable. This chapter covers the basics of working with a relational database and using the Access database management system.

STUDENT LEARNING OUTCOMES (SLOs)

After completing this chapter, you will be able to:

SLO 1.1 Explain data organization concepts, use the Access *Navigation Pane*, and identify objects (p. A1-3).

SLO 1.2 Create a database, set database properties, understand database object naming conventions and data types, and close a database (p. A1-11).

SLO 1.3 Create a table in *Datasheet* view, edit the default primary key, add a new field, edit field properties, save a table, and enter records into a table (p. A1-18).

SLO 1.4 Import data records from Excel (p. A1-29).

SLO 1.5 Navigate table records in *Datasheet* view and customize a datasheet by modifying field order, row height, column width, field alignment, font style and size, row colors, and gridlines (p. A1-31).

SLO 1.6 Search, sort, and filter records in a table (p. A1-41).

CASE STUDY

Throughout this book, you have the opportunity to put into practice the application features you are learning. Each chapter begins with a case study that introduces you to the Pause & Practice projects in the chapter. These Pause & Practice projects give you a chance to apply and practice key skills. Each chapter contains three to five Pause & Practice projects.

The first Pause & Practice is designed to orient you to using Access and allows you to explore the different parts of the Access interface and navigation mechanism. For this project, you

open an existing database for the College of Sciences that tracks information about classes it offers. The remaining Pause & Practice projects are designed to help you learn how to build a database for Central Sierra Insurance. Central Sierra Insurance is a multi-office insurance company that handles all lines of commercial and personal insurance policies. Central Sierra regularly hires qualified personnel, and it needs to create an effective way to organize and manage the information about its employees. Lanita McCartney has asked you to create a simple database containing information

about its employees. This database is created as a blank desktop database with one table. As you progress through the Pause & Practice projects, you incorporate many of the features you are learning in this chapter to construct and enhance this database.

Pause & Practice 1-1: Explore the tabs of the Access *Ribbon* and *Navigation Pane* in an existing database, and use *Datasheet* and *Design* views of a table.

Pause & Practice 1-2: Create a new, blank desktop database. Customize the table using *Datasheet View* to edit the primary key, add new fields, save the table, reopen the table, edit field properties, and add employee records.

Pause & Practice 1-3: Import data into the table created in Pause & Practice 1-2. Modify the table and refine the datasheet layout by modifying the field order, row height, field width and field alignment; selecting a display font and size; displaying gridlines; and alternating row colors.

Pause & Practice 1-4: Use the employee table to search for data, sort the records on a single field and on multiple fields, and filter the records using single and multiple criteria.

SLO 1.1

Understanding Database Concepts

Organizations can generate a tremendous amount of data. Think about just some of the pieces of data captured by FedEx when you send a package or envelope: the sender's first and last name, sender's street address, sender's city, sender's state, sender's ZIP code, recipient's first and last name, recipient's street address, recipient's city, recipient's state, recipient's ZIP code, date sent, package weight, and type of service (e.g., next-day air, ground service). Every day, FedEx delivers millions of packages and documents. This translates into millions of sender names, addresses, recipient names, addresses, and so forth, captured each day. To stay in business, FedEx must have an efficient and effective way to capture, process, and store these data to ensure that it delivers your package on time and to the right location.

Databases are used by many organizations to manage data. A ***database*** is an organized collection of integrated and related tables. A ***database management system (DBMS)*** is software that allows you to create a database; manage the data in the database by adding, deleting, and updating records; sort and retrieve data; and create queries and reports relating to that data. In this book, you learn about Microsoft Access, the leading PC-based DBMS software application.

Using a database management system, people can build applications to allow organizations to track orders and deliveries, manage retail sales and inventory, maintain employee payroll records, update patient data, and track student progress. Throughout this chapter, you learn more about these database concepts by using the Access DBMS to create a simple database.

Organize Data

Like the majority of the DBMSs available today, Access is a ***relational database***, which means that the data are organized into a collection of related tables. Each table stores data about one type, or grouping, of information represented in the system. For example, a database application used by a retail store contains a table with details about its customers, a table with details about the products it sells, and a table with details about the orders its customers have made for the various products. The different tables are related, or connected, to one another through common fields.

The first step in creating a database is to determine the best way to organize the required data. To do so, you need to understand the *hierarchy of data* used in relational databases. In Access, the hierarchy is organized from the smallest to the largest grouping of data. A *field* is a collection of characters that describes one aspect of a business object or activity—a single unit of data. A *record* is a collection of related data fields. A *table* is a collection of related records. Visually you see the table containing rows and columns. Each row is the equivalent of a record. A row contains many different columns or fields. A *database* is a collection of related tables. An example of how this hierarchy works for a database that a university might use is shown in the following table:

Hierarchy of Data

Unit	Description	Examples
Field	A single unit of data	Date Enrolled, Student First Name, Student Last Name, Student ID
Record	A collection of related fields	All of the fields for one student stored together
Table	A collection of related records	A record for each of the students at the university stored together
Database	A collection of integrated and related tables	The collection of the student, faculty, and course tables for the entire university

How do you know how many tables you need or which fields belong in which tables? Often the database design plan is already completed for you, and you simply need to build the design. At this point, the simplest answer to the question about how many tables you need is this: Create a separate table for each major subject or grouping of information you will store in the database. Later, in *SLO 2.6: Understanding and Designing Relational Databases*, you will learn a more formal set of steps to create a well-designed database.

The Access Interface

The interface is how you interact with Access to create, modify, delete and use different objects, or parts, of your database application. The *Ribbon* in Access contains five primary tabs: *File*, *Home*, *Create*, *External Data*, and *Database Tools*. Access also has several *contextual tabs* that become available to you when you are working on different tasks. The *Ribbon* provides the common Office functions, like copy, paste, and file management, but many of the *Ribbon* tabs are unique to Access. The *Ribbon* also contains the *Tell Me* box where you can enter text to quickly get to actions you want to perform.

> MORE INFO
>
> Depending on configuration changes made to the Access program installed on your computer, you may see a sixth tab titled *Add-Ins*.

Examine Access Objects

An Access database application typically contains many different components, such as tables and reports. In Access, these components are called *objects*. The major objects in Access are *tables*, *forms*, *reports*, and *queries*. At a minimum, your database must contain at least one table. These objects are described in the following table:

Major Access Objects

Object	Purpose	Additional Information	Navigation Pane Icon
Table	Stores data records	Once a table is created, you can begin entering data. Create a separate table for each type or grouping of information. When you view data in a table, it appears in a tabular format, very much like a spreadsheet.	
Form	Used to create an interface to view, add, update, and delete data in a table	Although you can do these tasks directly in a table, a form usually provides an easier way to interact with the data. Forms also allow you to view only one record at a time and to view fields from multiple tables at the same time.	
Query	Used to find data in your database	Queries allow you to specify criteria to locate specific records. Queries can also be used to perform actions such as updating or deleting records.	
Report	Used to view and print the data in your database	Reports allow you to create a formatted, and more professional, way to view and print the contents of your database.	

> ### MORE INFO
>
> Forms, queries, and reports provide different ways to interact with the data in your tables. As a result, they are related to the tables on which they are based.

Access contains two additional objects, **_Macros_** and **_Modules_**. These objects allow you to add functionality to the forms and reports in your database. For example, you can add a button to a form and tell Access what actions to perform when an event happens to that button. Examples of events are clicking a button or moving the pointer over a button. You can attach specific actions to each event. For example, attach an action to open a form when the button is clicked.

Use the Navigation Pane

Each object in your database application is shown in the **_Navigation Pane_**. The object is identified by its name and an icon indicating the object type.

The top bar of the _Navigation Pane_ contains the **_Shutter Bar Open/Close Button_**, which opens and closes the pane. If the pane is closed, as shown on the left side of Figure 1-1, you will only see the phrase "Navigation Pane."

- Open the _Navigation Pane_ by clicking the **Shutter Bar Open/Close Button**.
- The objects inside your database display, as shown on the right side of Figure 1-1.

> ### ANOTHER WAY
>
> **F11** opens and closes the _Navigation Pane_.

1-1 _Shutter Bar_ of the _Navigation Pane_

The *Navigation Pane* displays your objects in **groups**, which you can expand and collapse. This is useful if you have many objects in your database and wish to narrow down those that are visible. Click the **expand/collapse arrow** to the right of the group name to change the current display. When a group is collapsed, like the *Queries* group in Figure 1-1, only the name of the group displays. The objects contained within that group do not display.

You can customize what is displayed in the *Navigation Pane* and the way the objects are organized by using the **Navigation menu** (Figure 1-2). The settings shown in Figure 1-2 are the default selections.

The top half of the *Navigation* menu allows you to select a **category**, the highest organizational level in the *Navigation Pane*. The standard categories are:

- **Custom**: Groups objects based on custom categories that you create
- **Object Type**: Groups objects on the basis of their type
- **Tables and Related Views**: Groups different objects according to the tables on which they are based
- **Created Date**: Groups objects on the basis of the week associated with the date they were created
- **Modified Date**: Groups objects on the basis of the week associated with the date they were last modified

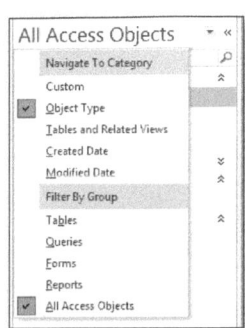

The bottom half of the *Navigation* menu allows you to filter by a specific group within that category. The choices in *Filter by Group* will change based on the selected category. The *Title* bar of the *Navigation Pane* shows the current filter selection.

1-2 *Navigation* menu

The *Navigation Pane* in Figure 1-1 reflects the settings selected in Figure 1-2; it shows all objects grouped by the category of *Object Type* and the filter of *All Access Objects*. Within a group, Access displays the objects in alphabetical order.

▶ **HOW TO: Modify the Navigation Pane Category and Group Filter**

1. Click the **Navigation Pane** arrow, shown in Figure 1-3, to open the *Navigation* menu.
2. Select the **desired category**.
 - The *Navigation* menu closes.
 - The *Navigation Pane* updates to display the objects based on your category selection.
3. Click the **Navigation Pane** arrow to open the *Navigation* menu.
4. Select the **desired filter selection**.
 - The *Navigation* menu closes.
 - The *Navigation Pane* updates to display the objects based on your filter selection.

1-3 Modify the *Navigation Pane*

Use Datasheet and Design View of a Table

Because the *Table* is the primary object of a database, it is useful to dig a little bit deeper into this object as you learn about the Access interface.

You can open tables directly from the *Navigation Pane*. Access provides two ways to open and view a table: *Datasheet* view and *Design* view.

- To open a table in *Datasheet view*, double-click the table name in the *Navigation Pane*. *Datasheet* view allows you to enter, modify, delete, or view the data records. You can also use *Datasheet* view to define or modify the structure of a table.
- To open a table in *Design view*, right-click the table name in the *Navigation Pane* and select **Design View** from the context menu. *Design* view allows you to build or modify the basic structure or functionality of an object. You see all the details, or properties, about the fields in your table in *Design* view.

To switch between views of an open table, click the **View** button [*Home* tab, *Views* group] as shown in Figure 1-4 and select the desired view.

Figure 1-5 illustrates *Datasheet* view of a table. Each row represents a record in the table and each column represents a field. The gray cell on the left of each row is the **record selector**. The *record selector* turns yellow when field(s) are selected on a particular row, indicating the active row. A rose-colored border surrounds the **active cell**. The active cell is the field where you enter or edit data. The last row in a table is the **append row**, identified with an asterisk in the *record selector* of that row. A new record is added to a table by entering the data in fields of the *append row*. The name of the table displays in the tab at the top of the datasheet.

1-4 View menu of a table

ClassID	Class Name	Dept. ID	Section	Instructor ID	Term	Units	Year	Location	Days/Time
1	General Biology	1	1	1	Spring	3	2015	NH-100	MWF 9:00 - 9
2	World of Animals	1	0	2	Spring	3	2015	LSN-122	TTH 11:00 - 1
3	General Biology	1	2	2	Spring	3	2015	AL-201	TTh 8:00 - 9:1
4	General Biology	1	3	1	Spring	3	2015	ENS-280	MWF 11:00 -
5	Introduction to General Chemistry	2	1	4	Spring	4	2015	ENS-280	MTWTH 2:00
6	Introduction to General Chemistry	2	2	4	Spring	4	2015	GMCS-333	MTWTH 4:00
* (New)		0	0			0	0	0	

Table Name tab — *Classes*

Active cell

Record selector

Append row

Record: 1 of 6 No Filter Search

1-5 Datasheet view of a table

PAUSE & PRACTICE: ACCESS 1-1

For this project, you explore a database that tracks information about classes that are offered in the College of Sciences. This database contains three tables, one query, one form, and one report. You open the database, explore the Access *Ribbon*, explore the *Navigation Pane*, and work with *Datasheet* and *Design* views of a table.

File Needed: ***CollegeOfSciencesClasses-01.accdb***
Completed Project File Name: None

1. Open the database used by the College of Sciences.
 a. Double-click the ***CollegeOfSciencesClasses-01*** file in your student data files folder. This launches Access and opens the sample database application (Figure 1-6). The *Navigation Pane* opens and the *Home* tab is selected.
 b. Click the **Enable Content** button in the *Security Warning* message bar, if prompted.

MORE INFO

Because viruses and worms may be transmitted in files, Microsoft warns you when you open a database file. If you trust the source of the file, enable the content so that you can use the database.

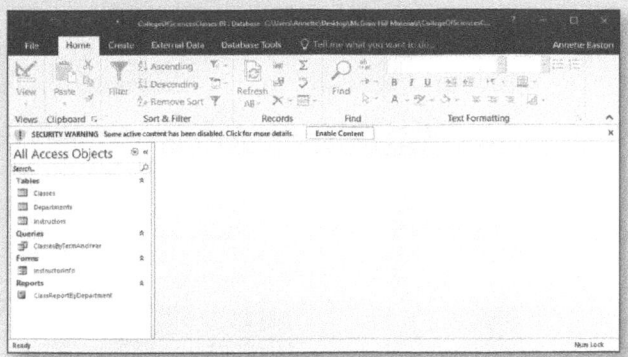

1-6 *CollegeOfSciencesClasses-01* database

2. Explore the Access *Ribbon*.
 a. Click the **File** tab to open the *Backstage* view (Figure 1-7). The *Backstage* view in Access provides file management capabilities to open, close, and save a database; create a new database; and print or publish a database.
 b. Click the arrow to return to the Access *Ribbon*.
 c. Click the **Home** tab. The *Home* tab (Figure 1-8) offers common Office functions, the ability to change the way you view an object, and searching and sorting functions.
 d. Click the **Create** tab. The *Create* tab (Figure 1-9) contains tools to create all the objects you use in your database. The icons are grouped on the basis of the type of object you need to build.

1-7 *Backstage* view

1-8 *Home* tab

1-9 *Create* tab

 e. Click the **External Data** tab. The *External Data* tab (Figure 1-10) provides functionality to link to other applications and data files. The icons are grouped on the basis of the type of connectivity arrow you need.
 f. Click the **Database Tools** tab. The *Database Tools* tab (Figure 1-11) provides information about your database and additional functions to help you manage the database.

1-10 *External Data* tab

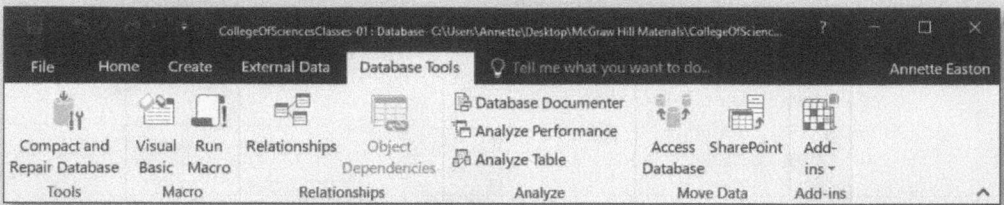

1-11 *Database Tools* tab

3. Explore the *Navigation Pane*.

 a. Click the **Navigation Pane** arrow to the right of *All Access Objects*. The *Navigation* menu should display as shown on the right side of Figure 1-12. Note that the *Navigation* menu actually displays on top of the actual *Navigation Pane* and not on the side.

 This *Navigation Pane* displays objects by the *Object Type* category, and the filter is to show *All Access Objects*.

 b. Click anywhere outside the *Navigation* menu to close the menu.

 c. In the *Navigation Pane*, click the **expand/collapse** arrow on the right edge of the *Tables* group (Figure 1-13). The *Tables* group collapses, leaving no table objects visible. The arrow has changed to an expand arrow.

 d. Click the **expand/collapse** arrow in the *Tables* group to reopen the *Tables* group and display the three tables.

 e. Click the **Navigation Pane** arrow next to *All Access Objects*.

 f. Select the **Tables and Related Views** category.

 g. Click the **Navigation Pane** arrow again.

 h. Select **All Tables** in the *Filter By Group* area. The *Navigation Pane* updates and should look similar to Figure 1-14.

 This view shows each of the tables, and all of the other objects that are associated with each table. For example, the report object named *ClassReportbyDepartment* is associated with each of the three tables. However, the form object *InstructorInfo* is only associated with the *Instructors* table.

 i. Click the **Navigation Pane** arrow.

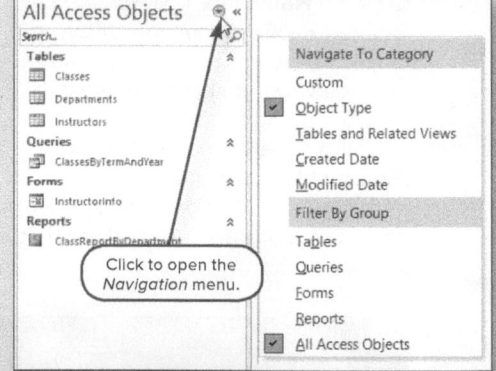

1-12 Explore the *Navigation Pane*

1-13 The *Tables* group

j. Select the **Departments** group in the *Filter by Group*. The *Navigation Pane* now shows only the *Departments* table with the query and report objects that are associated with that table.

k. Click the **Navigation Pane** arrow.

l. Click the **Object Type** category. The *Navigation Pane* should have returned to show all of your objects by the *Object Type* category.

4. Explore *Datasheet* and *Design* views of a table.

a. Double-click the **Classes** table to open the table in *Datasheet View*, as shown in Figure 1-15.

> ### MORE INFO
>
> Depending on the resolution of your monitor and the size of the Access window, you may see more or less of the table.

b. Press the **Right arrow** key nine times to navigate across the fields of the first record. You should stop at the *Days/Times* field.

1-14 *Tables and Related Views* category

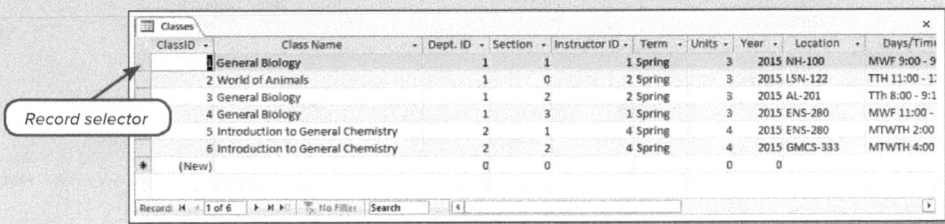

1-15 *Datasheet View of Classes* table

c. Press the **Right arrow** key once more to navigate to the *Click to Add* column. *Datasheet View* allows you to add new fields into your table at the same time that you are looking at the data values.

d. Press the **Right arrow** key once more to navigate to the *ClassID* of the second row.

e. Press the **down arrow** key four times to navigate down to *ClassID 6*, the last of the data records. If you were to navigate into the *append row*, identified by the asterisk in the *record selector*, you would be able to add a new class into the table by entering the data values.

f. Click the **record selector** of the first row. The entire row should be selected.

g. Click **View** [*Home* tab, *Views* group]. You should be able to see the two possible table views shown in Figure 1-16.

h. Click **Design View**. Your screen should look similar to Figure 1-17. *Design* view shows you the details, or properties, of the different fields in your table.

1-16 Two table views

i. Use the **scroll bar** to navigate down to the see all the fields in the *Classes* table. Look for the last field, *Days/Times*. You could add additional fields into the table by entering the *Field name* into the blank row below *Days/Times*.

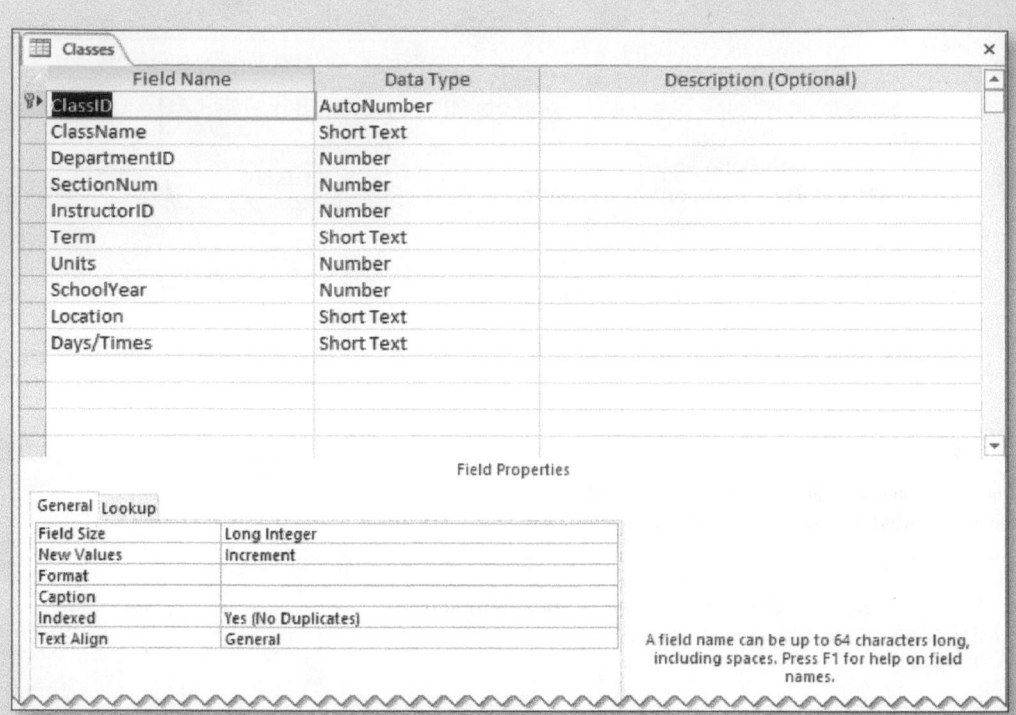

1-17 *Design* view of *Classes* table

j. Close the *Classes* table by clicking the **X** in the upper right corner of the *Classes* table window.

k. Close the *CollegeOfSciencesClasses-01* database by clicking the **Close** button [*File* tab].

SLO 1.2

Creating and Managing a Database

In Access, the database application file stores all of the separate objects that you create and use. The database file must be created before you can create and use any other objects. By default, the database file will be saved as a *.accdb* file. You can create a new database file by using a prebuilt template as a starting point, or you can create a blank desktop database if you wish to start from scratch.

Templates

A *template* is a predesigned database that contains various pre-built objects. A template provides you with a complete, ready-to-use database application. After creating a database based on a template, you can use the new database directly, or you can customize the database to better meet your needs. Templates are a great starting point if your needs are addressed in the template.

You can choose from several templates that are installed with Access. In addition, there are other templates available at Office.com.

> ▶**HOW TO:** Create a New Database Using a Template

1. With an Access database already open, if the *Backstage* view is not displayed, click the **File** tab to open the *Backstage* view.
 - If Access is closed, when you first open Access, the *Recent* page is displayed along with the list of sample templates. In this case, skip to step 3.
2. Click the **New** button. The list of sample templates displays (Figure 1-18).
3. Select the template you wish to use.
4. Type the file name in the **File Name** box.
5. Click the **Browse for a location to put your database** button (Figure 1-19) to select the location on your computer or USB drive to save the database and click **OK**.
7. Click the **Create** button.
 - The new database opens.
 - A *Welcome* form may display based on the template selected. Click the **Get Started** button on the *Welcome* form.
8. Click the **Enable Content** button in the *Security Warning* message bar if prompted.

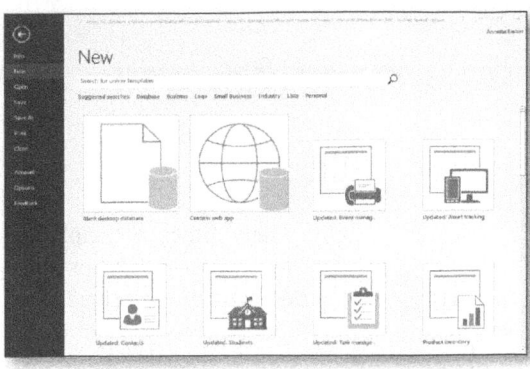

1-18 Create a new database from a template

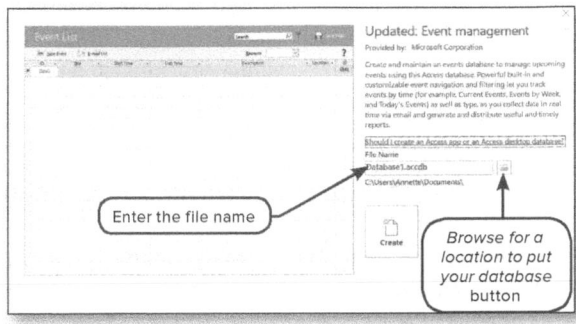

1-19 Select the file location and enter the file name

Database Properties

Every database contains details, or properties, about the database. The properties include information about the date the database was created and its author. View common file properties in the ***Database Properties*** dialog box available via the ***View and edit database properties*** link on the *Backstage* view. You can edit the properties on the *Summary* tab. However, you cannot edit properties on many of the other tabs. For example, the ***Size*** or ***Modified Properties*** on the *General* tab are automatically updated by the system.

> ▶**HOW TO:** View and Edit Database Properties

1. Click the **View and edit database properties** link [*File* tab, *Info* button] (Figure 1-20) to open the *Database Properties* dialog box (Figure 1-21).
2. Click the **Summary** tab.
3. View the properties that have been entered.

 MORE INFO

Some properties may already be completed, based on the settings selected when Office was installed on the computer.

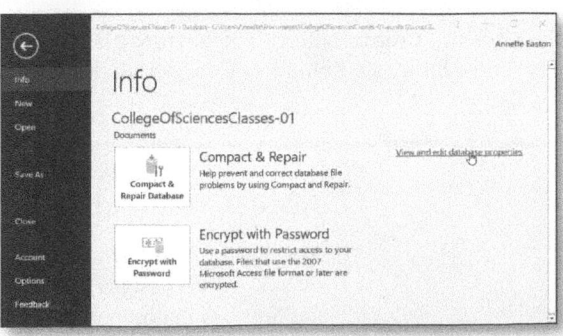

1-20 Open the database properties

A1-12

4. Edit any desired properties. Be sure to complete any properties required by your instructor.

5. Click **OK** to save and close.

1-21 *Database Properties* dialog box

Create a Blank Desktop Database

Many times a template does not exist to meet your needs, or it requires significant modifications to meet your requirements. In these cases, you can create a ***Blank desktop database***. With the *Blank desktop database* option, you create all the tables and other objects that you need. When a blank desktop database is created, Access automatically creates one new table and opens that table in *Datasheet View*.

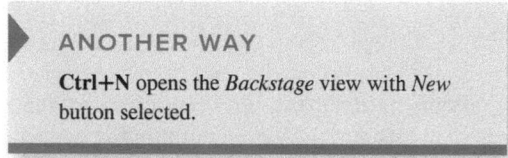

▶ HOW TO: Create a New Blank Desktop Database

1. With an Access database already open, click the **New** button [*File* tab].
 - If Access is closed, when you first open Access, the *Recent* page is displayed.

> **ANOTHER WAY**
>
> **Ctrl+N** opens the *Backstage* view with *New* button selected.

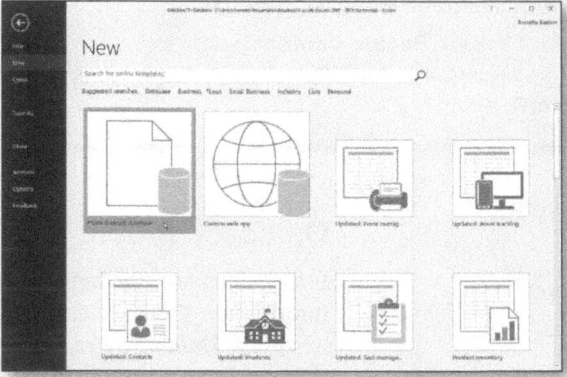

1-22 Create a new *Blank desktop database*

2. Select the **Blank desktop database** button (Figure 1-22).

3. Type the file name in the *File Name* box.

4. Click the **Browse for a location to put your database** button to select the location on your computer or USB drive to save the database and click **OK**.

5. Click the **Create** button. The database is created. A new table is automatically created and opens in *Datasheet View*.

> ▶ **MORE INFO**
>
> Access automatically suggests a generic file name for your database, such as *Database1.accdb*. Be sure to change that name to a name that is more meaningful and related to the purpose of your database.

Access Naming Rules

You need to name each of the objects you create and use in Access. When you first create an object, Access assigns a generic name, such as *Table1* or *Form1*. The first time you save an object, the *Save As* dialog box prompts you to enter a different name. Database designers strongly recommend that you use a meaningful name that describes the contents of the object. For example,

in the *CollegeOfSciencesClasses-01* database, the tables are named *Classes*, *Departments*, and *Instructors*. This makes it easy to understand the object's purpose. Each object typically contains several fields. Some objects may also have other components such as buttons or labels. These components are called controls (See *SLO 4.2: Creating and Customizing a Form in Layout View*.)

Your instructor or employer may have specific guidelines to follow when naming objects, fields and controls. In addition to those guidelines, pay attention to the following Access naming rules:

- Names can have a maximum of 64 characters.
- The characters can be letters, numbers, and spaces. You can also use special characters except a period (.), exclamation point (!), square brackets ([]), and an accent grave (´).
- The name can't begin with a space.

Although spaces are allowed within a name, most database designers avoid using them due to possible naming conflicts with other applications. Instead, when creating a compound word name, it is a good idea to start each word with a capital letter (e.g., *PhoneNumber* or *DepartmentName*). Sometimes database designers will also include a prefix in the object name (e.g., *tblAccounts* or *frmSales*). The most common prefixes are *tbl*, used for a table; *frm*, used for a form; *rpt*, used for a report; and *qry*, used for a query.

Data Types

Each field in your database must be assigned a specific **data type**. The data type determines what properties can be manipulated and how that field can be used. Before you start to create and manipulate tables, it is important to learn about the types that are explained in the following table:

Access Data Types

Data Type	Description
Short Text	Used to store alphanumeric data (text, or combinations of text and numbers). Also used to store numbers that are not used in calculations, such as phone numbers. The maximum length is 255 characters.
Long Text	Used to store text longer than 255 characters, or text containing rich-text formatting. The maximum length that displays is limited to the first 64,000 characters.
Number	Used to store numbers that are used in mathematical calculations. The number can be positive or negative. There are seven field size choices for the number data type which determine the range of possible values and amount of storage space required.
Date/Time	Used to store dates and times.
Currency	Used to store numbers representing currency values. This type does not allow rounding off during calculations.
AutoNumber	Used to instruct Access to insert a unique, sequential (e.g., increments by 1) number each time a new record is added.
Yes/No	Used to store fields with two possible values, such as Yes/No, True/False, or On/Off. Displays as a check box.
OLE Object	Used to display OLE objects (e.g., spreadsheets, documents, pictures, sounds) that were created in other programs.
Hyperlink	Used to store a hyperlink to another file or web page.
Attachment	Used to attach pictures, images, and Office files.
Calculated	Used to store the results of a calculation. Typically the equation references fields in the same table.
Lookup Wizard	Technically, this is not a data type. It is used to convert your field into a combo box that allows you to choose a value from another table or from a list of values.

Create and Save Database Objects

Databases typically contain many different objects. Each object is initially created using the *Create* tab. Once the object is created, you use one of the different views to define the object or to change the object.

▶ HOW TO: Create a New Object

1. Click the **Create** tab on the *Ribbon*.
2. Click the **object** button of the object you wish to create.
 - The button choice determines the view that displays when the object opens. For example, selecting the **Table** button opens a table in *Datasheet View*, whereas selecting the **Table Design** button opens a table in *Design View*.
 - Some buttons, such as *Query Wizard*, launch a wizard that guides you through the steps to creating that object.

To keep a permanent copy of an object, you need to save it. When an object is created, Access automatically assigns it a name. The first time you save an object, you are prompted to change the default name in the *Save As* dialog box.

▶ HOW TO: Save an Object

1. Click the **Save** button [*File* tab].
2. Type the name you wish to use in the *Save As* **Object Name** box. Instead of displaying the phrase "Object Name," Access displays the type of object you are saving. For example, Figure 1-23 is a *Save As* dialog box for a form.
3. Click **OK**.

1-23 *Save As* dialog box

Sometimes you need to make a copy of an object. This may be done to have a backup of the original object or because another object has the same initial characteristics.

▶ HOW TO: Save a Copy of an Object

1. Click the **Save As** button [*File* tab].
2. Click the **Save Object As** button in the *File Types* area and the **Save Object As** button in the *Database File Types* area (Figure 1-24).
3. Click the **Save As** button to open the *Save As* dialog box (Figure 1-25).
 - Access suggests the default object name of "Copy of" and the original object name.
 - Access selects the same object type as the original object.

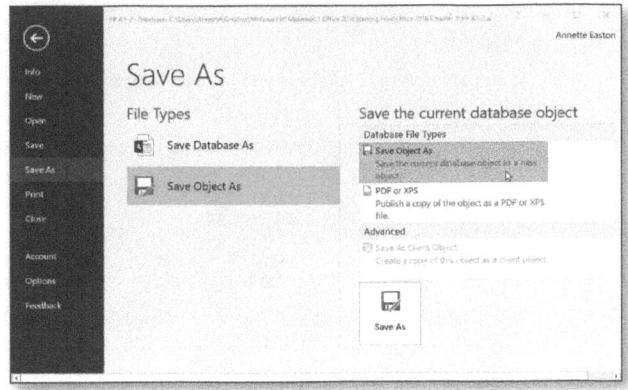

1-24 *Save Object As* button

4. Type the name you wish to use in the *Save 'Object name' to* box.

5. Select the type of object you wish to create.
 - You can make a duplicate of the object by selecting the same object type.
 - You can create a different type of object, based on the original objects settings, by selecting another object type.

6. Click **OK**.

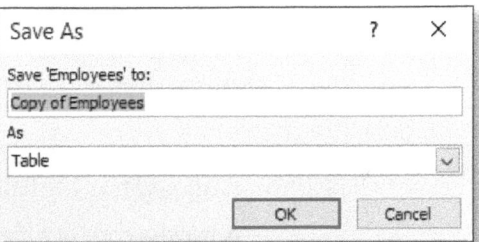

1-25 *Save As* dialog box

> **ANOTHER WAY**
>
> You can also press the **F12** function key to open the *Save As* dialog box.
>
> You can also use *Copy* and *Paste* to save a copy. Right-click the object in the *Navigation Pane* and select **Copy**. Then right-click in a blank area of the *Navigation Pane* and select *Paste* to open the *Paste 'Object name' As* dialog box.

Close and Open a Database

When you are finished working on a database, you should close the database file. You won't actually save the database file before closing it. Instead, you are prompted to save each of the separate database objects as you work on them. Access also automatically saves many changes to your database file, such as records you add into a table.

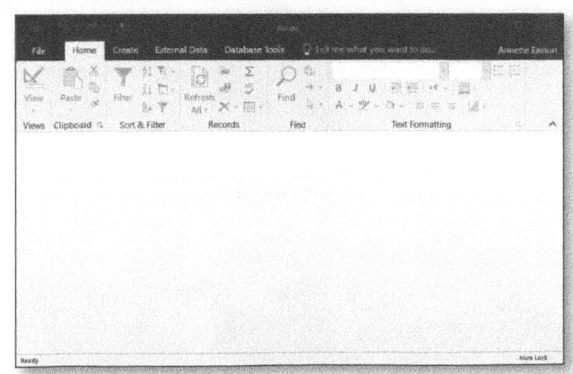

▶ HOW TO: Close a Database

1. Click the **Close** button [*File* tab] to close a database.
 - The current database closes. Access remains open, and you are positioned on the *Home* tab (Figure 1-26). Notice that the *Navigation Pane* does not display since a database is not open.

1-26 Access *Home* tab when a database is closed

> **MORE INFO**
>
> If you are closing a database and have any unsaved objects still open, Access may prompt you about saving changes to those objects.

▶ HOW TO: Open a Database

1. Click the **Open** button [*File* tab] to open an existing database.
2. Click the **Browse** button. The *Open* dialog box displays.
3. Select the database file and click the **Open** button.
 - You can also double-click the file name to open the database.

> **ANOTHER WAY**
>
> If the database name displays on the *Recent* list in the *Backstage* view, you can click the file name to open the database.

Back Up a Database

A backup copy of a database is necessary to completely restore your database. If you have several users of your database, you must be certain that all users have closed the database before you perform a backup procedure. Your organization's database administrator, in conjunction with the information systems manager, should determine a regular schedule for backups.

▶ HOW TO: Back Up a Database

1. Click the **File** tab to open the *Backstage* view.
2. Click the **Save As** button. Your screen should look similar to Figure 1-27, with *Access Database* selected in the *Save Database As* area.

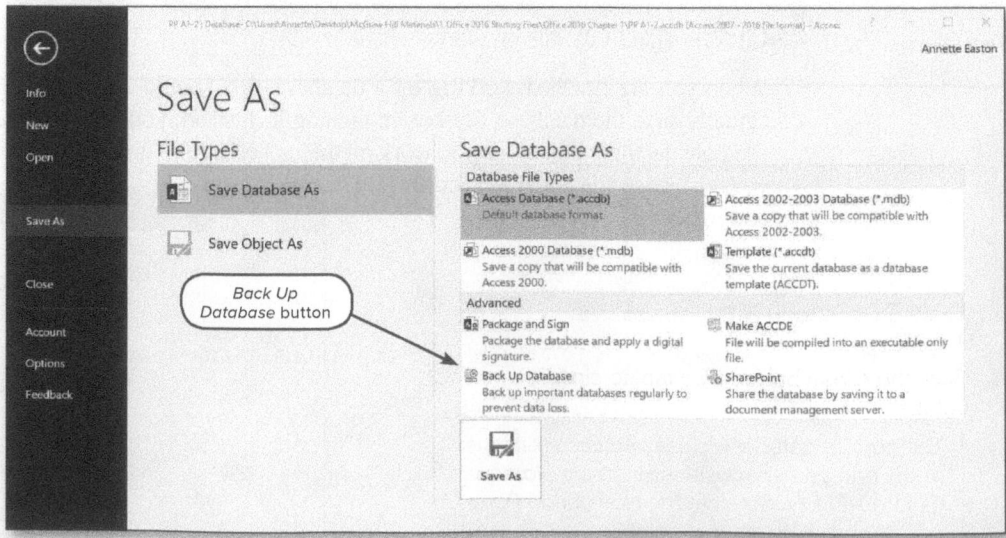

1-27 Back up a database

3. Select **Back Up Database** in the *Advanced* grouping of the *Save Database As* section.
4. Click the **Save As** button.
 - Select the desired location in which to store the backup database file.
 - Access suggests a filename, such as *PP Access 1-2_2017-09-05*, which adds today's date to the end of the file name. This is a good practice, because you can quickly determine when a backup copy was created.
 - As desired, click the **File Name** box and change the default name.
 - Click the **Save** button.

The *Back Up Database* option creates a copy of your database, but the current database file remains open and you continue to work in that file. If the original database file becomes damaged, copy the backup file to replace the original.

> **ANOTHER WAY**
>
> Use the *Access Database* file type instead of *Back Up Database* and select the **Save As** button to create a copy of the database. In this case, the open database switches to the new copy you created.

SLO 1.3 — Creating and Using a Table in Datasheet View

Recall that when you create a new, blank desktop database, Access automatically creates one table for you. You can add tables using several different methods. In this section you learn how to use *Datasheet* View to quickly create a table and enter data records. When using a database application, as you will learn later, *Datasheet* View is primarily used to enter, modify, delete, or view the data records.

No matter what method you use to create a table, you need to define the fields that are included within the table. You also need to describe the specific details, or ***field properties***, of each of the fields. The basic field properties include the field name, data type and size.

Create a New Table in Datasheet View

Databases typically contain multiple tables. You can add a new table to your database from the *Create* tab. Tables created using the *Table* button automatically open in *Datasheet* view.

▶ **HOW TO:** Create a New Table in Datasheet View

1. Click the **Create** tab on the *Ribbon*.
2. Click the **Table** button in the *Tables* group (Figure 1-28). A new table opens in *Datasheet* view.

 The *Ribbon* updates (Figure 1-29) since the *Table Tools* contextual tabs are now available, with the **Fields** tab selected.

1-28 *Table* button

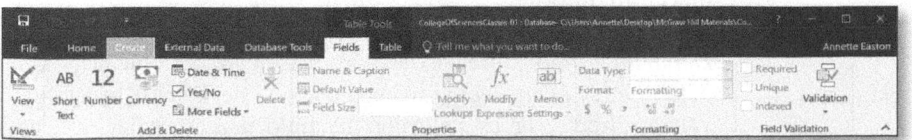

1-29 *Table Tools* contextual tabs

Edit the Default Primary Key

A **primary key** is a field that contains a unique value for each record. This is the way that one record can be distinguished from another. For example, the *InstructorID* field was designated as the primary key in the *Instructors* table in the *CollegeOfSciencesClasses-01* database, because each instructor has a unique ID number. When you enter values into a record, Access requires that you enter a value in any field designated as a primary key.

When a new table is created in *Datasheet* view, Access automatically includes one field, named *ID*, and designates it as the primary key. This field is assigned the *AutoNumber* data type to ensure that each record has a unique value.

> **MORE INFO**
>
> While not absolutely required, it is strongly recommended that each table has a field designated as the primary key.

In *Datasheet* view, you can change the following field properties of the *ID primary key* field: *Name, Caption, Description,* and *Data Type.*

▶HOW TO: Edit the Default Primary Key

1. Double-click the cell containing the **ID** *Field name* (column header) in your table (Figure 1-30).

2. Type the new name for your field and press the **down arrow** key. This action updates the change to the field name and keeps you in the same column.

3. Change the default *Data Type* of *AutoNumber* as desired.

 - Click the **Data Type** [*Table Tools Fields* tab, *Formatting* group] drop-down arrow to display the list of data types (Figure 1-31).
 - Select the desired **Data Type** property.

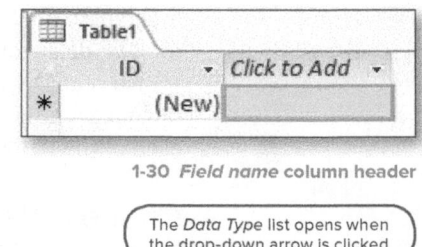

1-30 *Field name* column header

The *Data Type* list opens when the drop-down arrow is clicked

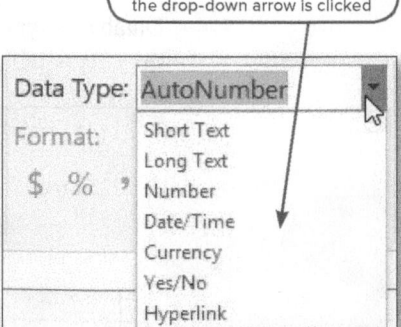

1-31 Field *Data Types*

Add New Fields

You must create a field for each of the different pieces of information you want to keep in your table. For example, *ClassID*, *ClassName*, and *DepartmentID* are three of the fields in the *Classes* table in the *CollegeOfSciencesClasses-01* database. In *Datasheet* view, you can add new fields to a table by either entering the data values directly or by entering the field names. After you have added a field, you can customize the name, caption, description, type, default value, and size properties. You can also set a few field validation properties. On numeric fields, you can set formatting properties.

Add New Fields by Entering Data

You can add new fields into a table by entering the data values. Add a new field by clicking the first cell on the *append row*. Recall that the *append row* is always the last row in the table and is identified with the asterisk icon in the *record selector* of that row.

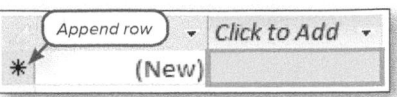

1-32 *Append row* with an *AutoNumber* field

A field on the *append row* with *(New)* displayed, as shown in Figure 1-32, indicates an *AutoNumber* data type. The data value for this field is automatically completed by Access. You can add a new field by entering data in the cell to the right of *(New)*.

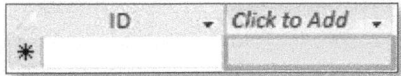

1-33 *Append row* without an *AutoNumber* field

If the *ID* field (the default, primary key) does not display *(New)* in the *append row*, the data type has been changed from an *AutoNumber* type (Figure 1-33). To add another field, first enter a value into the *ID* field and then add a new field by entering data in the *Click to Add* column.

> ▶ **HOW TO:** Add New Fields by Entering Data

1. Click the **cell** in the first *Click to Add* column.
2. Type the data value to be entered into the cell (Figure 1-34).

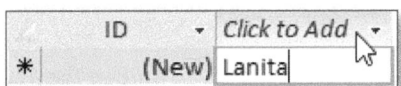

1-34 Add new field by entering data

3. Select the **Click to Add** column header to add the field.

 - The field name changes to *Field1*, as shown in Figure 1-35.
 - *Click to Add* becomes the next column.
 - Access automatically assigns a data type for the field based on the contents that you enter. As desired, you can change the data type.

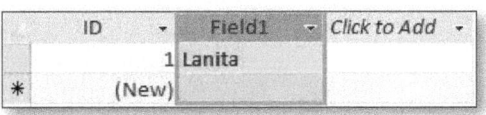

1-35 *Click to Add* becomes the next column

> ▶ **ANOTHER WAY**
>
> Press the **Tab** key to add the field and move to the next column.

4. Repeat steps 1 through 3 to add all the additional fields into your table.

Add New Fields by Entering Field Names

You can add new fields into a table by entering the field name and selecting the data type.

> ▶ **HOW TO:** Add New Fields by Entering Field Names

1. Click the **Click to Add** column header. The drop-down list of data types displays (Figure 1-36).
2. Select the appropriate **data type**.
 - The new field is added and assigned a default field name, such as *Field1*, as shown in Figure 1-37.

3. Type the desired **field name** in the column header.
 - Recall that each field name is limited to 64 characters.
 - Each field in a table must have a unique name.
4. Press the **Enter** key. You move to the next column with the list of data types displayed.
5. Repeat steps 2 through 4 to add the additional fields into your table.

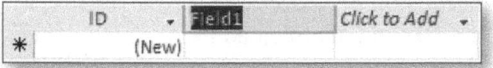

1-37 *Field name column header*

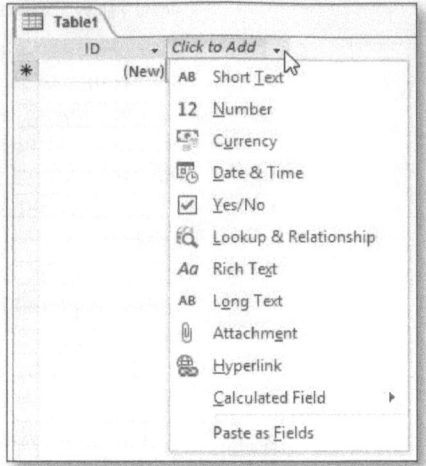

1-36 *Click to Add* data types

Use the **More Fields** [*Table Tools Fields* tab, *Add & Delete* group] drop-down list, shown in Figure 1-38, to select additional choices of the basic data type options when adding a new field.

Tehnically, these choices are not data types. Rather they assign additional formatting selections to a data type. For example, within the *Date and Time* group, there are format options for the ways to store the date or time. *Short Date* formats a date to display as 12/15/2017; *Medium Date* displays as 15-Dec-17.

The *Quick Start* group provides a set of fields that you can add by making just one choice. For example, selecting the *Phone* quick start data type adds four fields into your table: *Business Phone, Home Phone, Mobile Phone, and Fax Number.*

▶ **HOW TO: Add New Fields Using the More Fields Button**

1. Click the **Click to Add** column header.
2. Click the **More Fields** button [*Table Tools Fields* tab, *Add & Delete* group] (Figure 1-39).
3. Select the appropriate **data type**.
4. Type the **field name** in the column header.
5. Press the **Enter** key.

1-39 *More Fields* button

1-38 *More Fields* drop-down list

When using the *Click to Add* option, the new field always adds to the right of the last field in your table. Occasionally you may wish to add a field between existing fields.

▶ HOW TO: Add New Fields Between Existing Fields

1. Put your pointer on the field name of the column to the right of where you wish to insert a new field. The selection pointer appears as a black down arrow (Figure 1-40).

2. Click to select that column. The column is highlighted in blue.

3. Right-click to open the context menu.

4. Select **Insert Field** (Figure 1-41). The new field is inserted to the left of the selected field, as shown in Figure 1-42. It is assigned a default field name, such as *Field1*.

5. Double-click the **field name** to change the name.

1-40 Selection pointer

1-41 Select *Insert Field* on the context menu

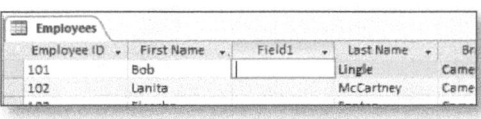

1-42 New field added with default field name

Delete Fields

You may need to delete a field from a table that was either created in error or is no longer needed in a table.

▶ HOW TO: Delete a Field

1. Place your pointer over the field name of the field you wish to delete. The selection pointer appears as a black down arrow.

2. Click to select that column.

3. Click the **Delete** button [*Table Tools Fields* tab, *Add & Delete* group] to delete the field. Access displays a message box asking you to confirm the deletion.

4. Click **Yes** to delete the field.

> ### MORE INFO
> The *Undo* button cannot be used to undo deletions of table fields.

Edit Properties in Datasheet View

In *Datasheet* view, you can change a limited number of the field properties. Recall that the properties of each field describe the field's details or characteristics. The majority of the field properties are changed in *Design* view. The properties that you can set in *Datasheet* view include:

- *Name*: Each field in a table must be given a unique name.
- *Caption*: The caption is an alternative to the field name that displays in the datasheet. Captions often include spaces and multiple words.

- *Description*: The description describes the purpose or meaning of a field if the field name by itself does not clearly convey the purpose or intended content. It displays in the lower, left corner of the datasheet.
- *Data Type*: Select a data type that matches the characteristics of the stored data.
- *Field Size*: Enter the smallest, sufficient field size to ensure best performance.

You can either edit the field properties as you add each field or after you add all the fields into the table.

▶ **HOW TO:** Edit Field Properties in Datasheet View

1. Select the cell containing the field name (column header) you wish to change.
2. Click the **Name & Caption** button [*Table Tools Fields* tab, *Properties* group].
 - The *Enter Field Properties* dialog box opens (Figure 1-43).
3. Type a new value in the *Name* property, as desired.
4. Type a value in the *Caption* property, as desired.
5. Type a value in the *Description* property, as desired.
6. Click **OK** to close the dialog box.
7. Click the **Data Type option** drop-down arrow [*Table Tools Fields* tab, *Formatting* group].
8. Select the desired **Data Type** property.
9. Type a new value in the *Field Size* property [*Table Tools Fields* tab, *Properties* group] (Figure 1-44).

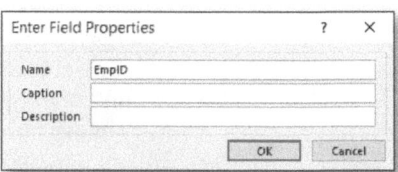

1-43 *Enter Field Properties* dialog box

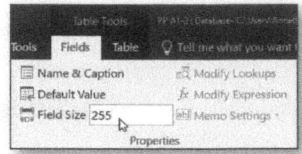

1-44 *Field Size* property

Save a Table

When a new table is created, Access automatically assigns a generic name to the table, such as *Table1*. The first time you save a table, you are prompted to change the default name in the *Save As* dialog box.

If you close *Table1* (the default table that comes with a new database) without saving it, Access deletes the table. This occurs even if you have entered data into the table.

▶ **HOW TO:** Save a Table

1. Click the **Save** button [*File* tab]. If this is the first time you are saving the table, the *Save As* dialog box displays.
2. Type the name you wish to use in the *Table Name* box.
3. Click **OK**.

▶ **ANOTHER WAY**

You can also open the *Save As* dialog box by clicking the **Save** button on the *Quick Access* toolbar or by pressing **Ctrl+S**.

If you later make changes to the table, many of those changes will automatically be saved by Access. However, it is a good idea for you to re-save the table to ensure those changes are stored. You can click the **Save** button [*File* tab], click the **Save** button on the *Quick Access* toolbar, or press **Ctrl+S** to save the changes. Since the table has been saved once, the *Save As* dialog box does not open again.

Close a Table

When you have finished using a table you should close the table. Routinely closing unneeded objects prevents you from making accidental changes to those objects.

To close a table, click the **X** (**Close** button) in the upper right corner of the datasheet. You can also press **Ctrl+W** or **Ctrl+F4** to close a table, or you can right-click the tab with the table name and select Close.

Open a Table

You can open an existing table in either *Datasheet* view or *Design* view. Once a table is open, you can easily switch views as desired.

▶ **HOW TO:** Open a Table in Datasheet View

1. Click the **Shutter Bar Open/Close Button** or press **F11** if the *Navigation Pane* is closed.
2. Double-click the table name. The table opens in *Datasheet* view.

> ▶ **ANOTHER WAY**
> Select the table in *the Navigation Pane* and press **Enter** to open a table in *Datasheet* view.

▶ **HOW TO:** Open a Table in Design View

1. If the *Navigation Pane* is closed, click the **Shutter Bar Open/Close Button** or press **F11**.
2. Select the table in the *Navigation Pane* and press **Ctrl+Enter**.

Add, Edit, and Delete Records

Datasheet view provides an easy way to add data values into your table, edit records already in the table, or delete records from a table.

Add the data by entering all the values for one record. After you finish entering the values for one record and navigate to the next record, Access automatically saves the record in the table.

> ▶ **MORE INFO**
> Your table must be saved at least once to initiate the automatic saving of data records.

If you realize you made an error in entering a value, there are several ways to make a correction:

- If you have navigated out of that field, click back into that field and change the value.
- If you are still typing in that field, click the **Undo** button to undo the typing in that field.

> **ANOTHER WAY**
>
> Press **Esc** to undo a change to the current field. If more than one field has been changed on the current record, all changes will be undone.

- If you have moved to the next field, undo a change to the previous field by clicking the **Undo** button.
- To undo all the changes to an unsaved record, click the **Undo** button twice.

Once you navigate out of the current record, the *Undo* button won't remove changes.

One benefit of a database is that it automatically verifies the contents of what you enter, based on the different properties you have assigned. For example, you are required to enter a value into the primary key field. Additionally, each primary key field must have a unique value. If you enter a primary key value that is already used, Access displays an error message. Similarly, if you enter a value that violates the data type property, Access displays an error message.

▶ HOW TO: Add Records in a Table

1. Click the first empty cell in the *append row* (Figure 1-45).

2. Type the data value.
 - The *append row* asterisk changes to a Pencil icon, indicating that you are editing a new record that has not yet been saved (Figure 1-46).

3. Press the **Tab** key to move to the next field.

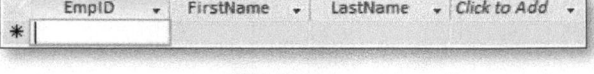

1-45 Enter new data on the *append row*

Pencil icon 1-46 Pencil icon indicates unsaved record

> **ANOTHER WAY**
>
> Press **Enter** to move to the next field.
>
> Press **Shift+Tab** to move to the preceeding field.

4. Continue entering all remaining data values for the record.

5. Press the **Tab** key to move to the first field of the next record after you enter the value in the last field
 - If you enter a duplicate value for the primary key (Figure 1-47), Access displays an error message (Figure 1-48) when you navigate out of the record.

EmpID	FirstName	LastName
101	Bob	Lingle
101	Lanita	McCartney

1-47 Duplicate primary key values

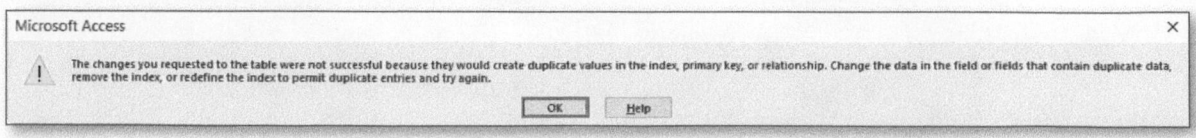

1-48 Duplicate values error message

- If you enter a value that does not match the data type, Access displays an error message when you navigate out of that field (Figure 1-49).

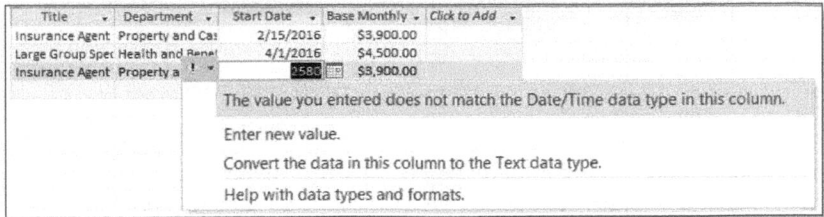

1-49 Data type error message

You can edit an existing record in a table by clicking in the cell of the field you wish to change. Make the necessary corrections in the field. When you navigate out of that field, Access automatically saves the changes.

Sometimes you need to delete a record from a table in your database.

▶ HOW TO: Delete a Record from a Table

1. Click the **record selector** cell of the record you wish to delete (Figure 1-50).

2. Click the **Delete** button in the *Records* group [*Home* tab].

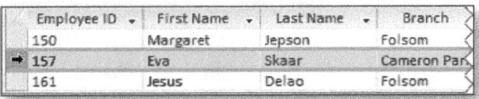

1-50 Select the record before deleting

 - Access displays a message box warning you about the record deletion and informing you that it is not possible to undo a delete operation.
 - Click the **Yes** button if you want to confirm the delete operation.

PAUSE & PRACTICE: ACCESS 1-2

Businesses regularly use databases to organize and manage data in a useful and meaningful manner. For this project, you create a database to manage data about the employees of Central Sierra Insurance.

File Needed: None
Completed Project File Name: *[your initials] PP A1-2.accdb*

1. Create a new, blank desktop database.
 a. Open Access or click the **New** button [*File* tab] if an Access database is already open.
 b. Select **Blank desktop database**.
 c. Name the database [your initials] PP A1-2 in the *File name* box.
 d. Browse to the location on your computer or storage device to save the database and click **OK**.
 e. Click **Create**. The database opens with a new table showing in *Datasheet* view (Figure 1-51).

2. Modify the default primary key.
 a. Double-click the **ID** field name (column header) in your table and type EmpID. Press the **down arrow** key to update the name and keep you in the same column.

b. Click the **Name & Caption** button [*Table Tools Fields* tab, *Properties* group]. The *Enter Field Properties* dialog box opens (Figure 1-52).

c. Type Employee ID in the *Caption* property.

d. Type Unique Employee Identification Number in the *Description* property.

e. Click **OK**.

f. Select **Short Text** in the *Data Type* option selection box [*Table Tools Fields* tab, *Formatting* group] (Figure 1-53).

g. Type 5 in the *Field Size* property [*Table Tools Fields* tab, *Properties* group].

h. Press the **Enter** key.

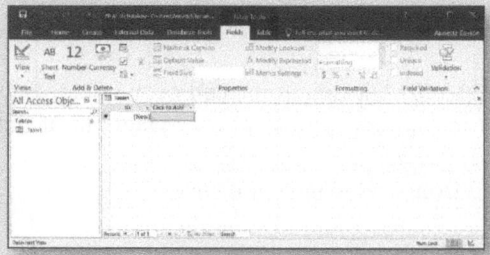

1-51 *Datasheet* view of *Table1* after a new database is created

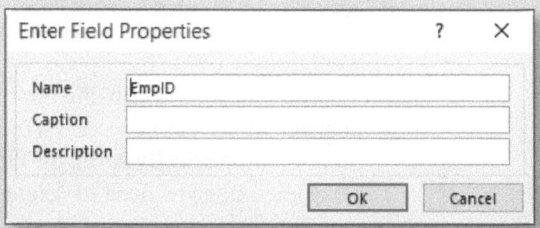

1-52 *Enter Field Properties* dialog box

1-53 *Data Type* selection box

3. Add new fields into the table.

 a. Click the **Click to Add** column header.

 b. Select the **Short Text** in the *Data Type* selection box.

 c. Type FirstName to replace *Field1*.

 d. Press the **Enter** key to move to the next column.

 e. Continue entering the additional fields in the table using the information in the nearby table.

4. Save and close the table.

 a. Click the **Save** button or press **Ctrl+S** to save all of the modifications you have made to the table.

 b. Type Employees as the new table name.

 c. Click **OK**.

 d. Close the *Employees* table by clicking the **X** in the upper right corner of the table (Figure 1-54).

Data Type	Field Name
Short Text	LastName
Short Text	Branch
Short Text	Title
Short Text	Department
Date & Time	StartDate
Currency	BaseMonthlySalary

1-54 Close the *Employees* table

5. Reopen the table in *Datasheet* view to edit the field properties.

 a. Double-click the **Employees** table to open it in *Datasheet* view.

 b. Click the **FirstName** field name.

 c. Click the **Name & Caption** button [*Table Tools Fields* tab, *Properties* group].

 d. Type First Name in the *Caption* property.

 e. Type Employee's First Name in the *Description* property.

 f. Click **OK**.

 g. Type 25 in the *Field Size* property [*Table Tools Fields* tab, *Properties* group] and press **Enter**.

 h. Continue changing the remaining field properties in the table using the following information. Repeat steps 5b through 5g for each field.

i. Click the **Save** button to save the changes to the table.

Field Name	Caption	Description	Size
LastName	Last Name	Employee's Last Name	25
Branch		Branch Assigned To	30
Title		Current Job Title	40
Department		Department Assigned To	40
StartDate	Start Date	Date Employment Started	N/A
BaseMonthlySalary	Base Monthly Salary	Current Base Monthly Salary	N/A

6. Add the employee records into the *Employees* table.

 a. Click the first empty cell in the *append row*. Recall that the *append row* is always the last row in the table. It is identified with the asterisk icon in the *record selector* of that row.

 b. Type 101 in the *EmpID* field. Remember that if you entered a caption for a field, the caption displays as the column header in *Datasheet* view. The data entry instructions reference the actual field name.

 c. Press the **Tab** key to move to the next field.

 d. Type Bob in the *FirstName* field. Press the **Tab** key to move to the next field.

 e. Type Lingle in the *LastName* field. Press the **Tab** key to move to the next field.

 f. Type Cameron Park in the *Branch* field. Press the **Tab** key to move to the next field.

> **MORE INFO**
>
> Because you have not increased the width of any fields, you may not be able to see the entire contents of some fields. Date and currency values that are too wide display with a series of pound sign symbols (######).

 g. Type Chief Executive Officer in the *Title* field. Press the **Tab** key to move to the next field.

 h. Type Administration in the *Department* field. Press the **Tab** key to move to the next field.

 i. Type 1/1/2014 in the *StartDate* field. Press the **Tab** key to move to the next field.

 j. Type 15000 in the *BaseMonthlySalary* field. Press the **Tab** key to move to the start of the next record.

 k. Continue entering the remaining records into the *Employees* table using the data values in the table below. The values that you enter are not "wrapped" in the table cells when you enter them.

Emp ID	FirstName	LastName	Branch	Title	Department	StartDate	Base Monthly Salary
102	Lanita	McCartney	Cameron Park	Chief Operating Officer	Administration	1/1/2014	12000
103	Eleesha	Santos	Cameron Park	Insurance Agent	Health and Benefits	2/10/2014	5500
104	Roy	Baxter	Granite Bay	Insurance Agent	Property and Casualty	2/11/2014	4500
115	Tami	Chan	Cameron Park	Administrative Assistant	Health and Benefits	5/7/2014	3000

7. Close the table by clicking the **X** in the upper right corner. Since the data records are automatically saved when you enter them into the table, it is not necessary to save the table before closing.

8. Double-click the **Employees** table to reopen it in *Datasheet* view. Your completed table should look similar to Figure 1-55 and display all five records.

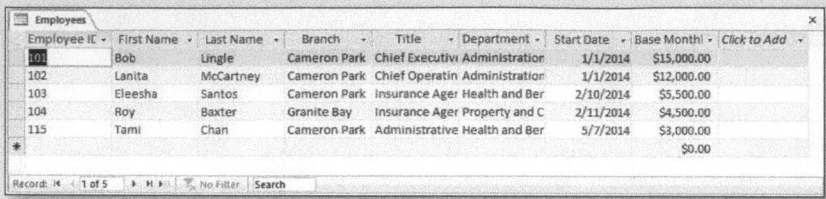

1-55 PP A1-2 completed

9. Close the table by clicking the **X** in the upper right corner of the datasheet.

10. Close the database by clicking the **Close** button [*File* tab].

SLO 1.4

Importing Data Records from Excel

You have already learned how to add data records into a table using *Datasheet* view. Sometimes companies may have their data stored in another file. In cases like this, you can import the data records into Access instead of having to enter all the data values.

In this section you learn how to import data from an Excel file into a table that you have already created. You append (add) the new data to any existing data records already in the table. Prior to importing the file you need to ensure that the Excel file is formatted correctly.

- The first row of the Excel file must contain the names of all of the fields in the Access table.
- The data fields don't need to be in the same order.
- All of the fields in the table do not need be in the Excel file as long as the *Required* property allows the field to be empty. With the exception of a primary key field, the default setting for other fields is to not require a value to be filled in. In *SLO 2.2: Setting Field Properties*, you will learn how to change the *Required* property.
- If the fields are not of the same data type (e.g., the Access field data type is *Number* but the Excel file field contains *Text*), Access still imports the file but the contents of that field is left empty. In this case, the *Required* property must allow the field to be empty.

▶**HOW TO: Import Data from Excel**

1. Click the **Excel** button [*External Data* tab, *Import & Link* group] (Figure 1-56).

 - The *Get External Data – Excel Spreadsheet* dialog box launches (Figure 1-57).

2. Click the **Browse** button to launch the *File Open* dialog box.

3. Locate and select the Excel file that contains the records you want to import.

4. Click the **Open** button. The *File Open* dialog box closes.

1-56 *Excel* button

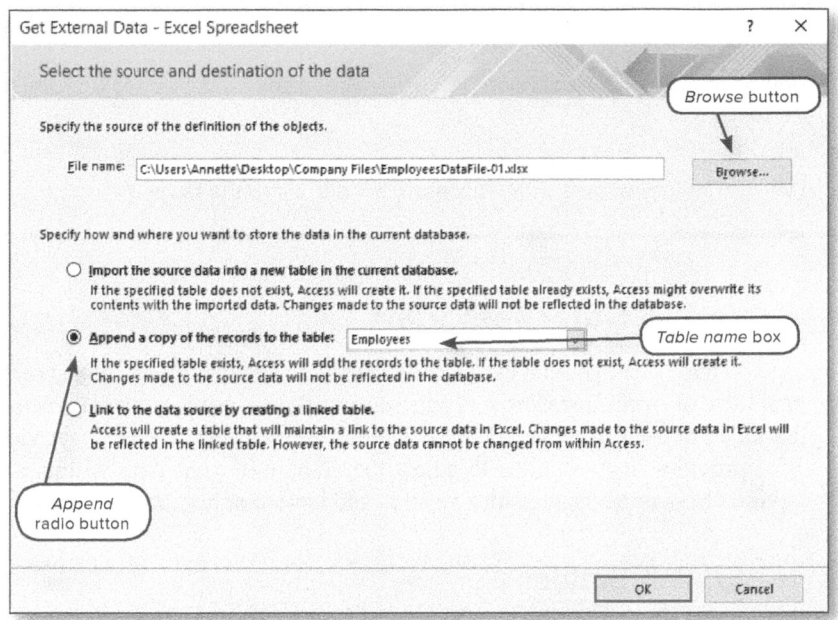

1-57 *Get External Data – Excel Spreadsheet* dialog box

5. Select the **Append a copy of the records to the table** radio button.

6. Click the **drop-down arrow** in the *table name* box and select the desired table.

7. Click **OK** to launch the *Import Spreadsheet Wizard* (Figure 1-58). The data records should display in the *Wizard* window.

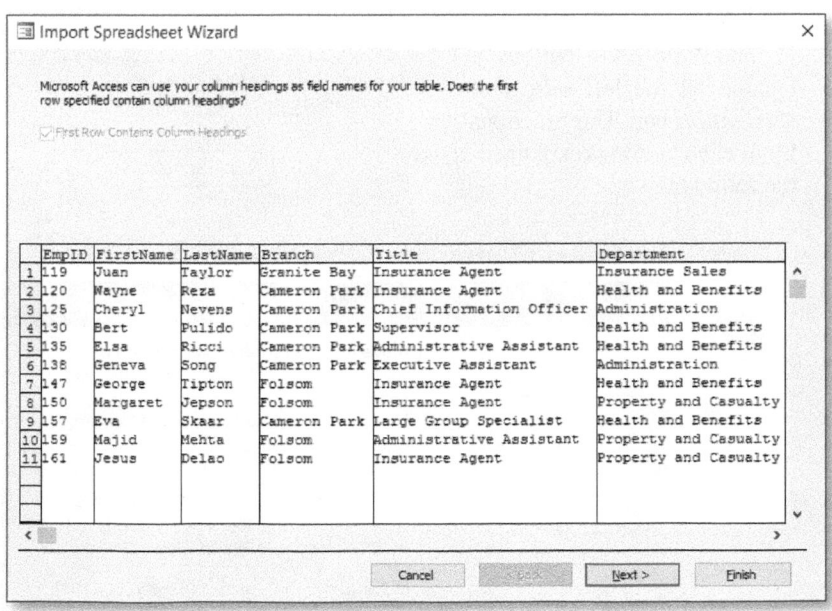

1-58 *Import Spreadsheet Wizard*

8. Click the **Next** button to advance to the next page of the *Wizard*.
 - Access confirms the name of the table to append the records.

9. Click **Finish**.

 • The *Wizard* displays the *Save Import Steps* screen.
 • If you are frequently going to repeat an import process, you can save the steps to perform the action more quickly.

10. Click the **Close** button.

11. Open the table to verify that the records were successfully added into the table.

SLO 1.5

Exploring Datasheet View

As you have seen, you can use *Datasheet* view to add new fields into a table. However, the primary use of *Datasheet* view is to add, modify, delete, or view the data records. The *Navigation* buttons are used to move among the fields and records in *Datasheet* view. *Datasheet* view also provides many options to adjust the display of your data within a table. This section reviews how to navigate among records and how to adjust *Datasheet* view display settings.

Navigation Buttons

Access provides many different ways to navigate among the data records stored in your tables. For example, you can navigate using the keyboard arrow keys and the scroll bar. This works fine on tables that do not have too many records. However, in many cases, you may want to get to a specific record more quickly.

The ***Navigation bar*** provides additional methods to move among table records. It is located in the bottom left corner of a table viewed in *Datasheet* view. The *Navigation* bar contains navigation buttons, a filter status message, and a *Search* box (Figure 1-59). Searching and filtering will be explained in *SLO 1.6: Using Search, Sort, and Filter Tools to Find Records in a Table*.

The *Navigation* buttons are located on the left side of the *Navigation* bar. The functionality of each button is explained in the following table:

1-59 *Navigation* bar

Navigation Buttons in Access

Button	Description
⏮	Move to the first record of the table.
◀	Move to the previous record of the table.
2 of 13	The number of the current record, along with the total number of records. You can type in the number of the record where you wish to move.
▶	Move to the next record in the table.
⏭	Move to the last record of the table.
▶*	Create a new record.

> **ANOTHER WAY**
>
> The *Navigation* buttons can also be found under *Go To* [*Home* tab, *Find* group].

Refine the Datasheet Layout

There are several ways to adjust the default display settings in *Datasheet* view. The settings change both the view of the table on the screen and the printed contents of a table.

Sometimes you may be given specific design guidelines based on company standards. Other times you need to use your judgment to evaluate the best way to have the data display. For example, the default column width or row height of a field may not be large enough to display the entire contents. You may wish to adjust the alignment, change the display font and size, or adjust the row colors and display gridlines.

If you make a change to the datasheet layout that you do not like, the *Undo* button cannot be used to reverse those changes. However, there are several options for making a correction:

- You can repeat the steps you made to make the changes and select the previous settings.
- You can close the table without saving your changes. Keep in mind that if you close the table without saving changes, you lose all of the changes made since the last save.

Modify the Field Order

There are times when you need to modify the order in which the fields display in a datasheet. You can move a single column or you can move a group of adjacent columns.

> **HOW TO: Modify the Field Order**

1. Place your pointer over the field name of the column you wish to move.
 - The selection pointer appears (Figure 1-60).
2. Click to select the column.
 - The cursor changes to the normal pointer (Figure 1-61).

> **MORE INFO**
>
> You can move a group of adjacent columns by selecting all of the columns at the beginning. Click to select the first column, and before you release the selected column, drag the selection pointer to the adjacent columns.

3. Click, hold, and drag the pointer to move the column to the new location.
 - A black, vertical line (Figure 1-62) moves with you to indicate the location where the column will be moved.
4. Release the pointer.
 - The column moves to the new location (Figure 1-63).

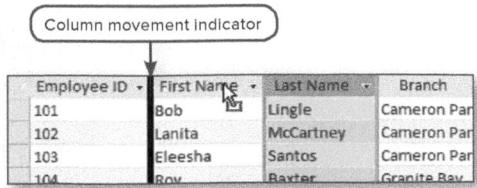

Selection pointer

Employee ID ▾	First Name ▾	Last Name ▾	Branch
101	Bob	Lingle	Cameron Par
102	Lanita	McCartney	Cameron Par
103	Eleesha	Santos	Cameron Par
104	Roy	Baxter	Granite Bay

1-60 Selection pointer

Employee ID ▾	First Name ▾	Last Name	Branch
101	Bob	Lingle	Cameron Par
102	Lanita	McCartney	Cameron Par
103	Eleesha	Santos	Cameron Par
104	Roy	Baxter	Granite Bay

Normal pointer **1-61 Pointer**

Column movement indicator

Employee ID ▾	First Name ▾	Last Name ▾	Branch
101	Bob	Lingle	Cameron Par
102	Lanita	McCartney	Cameron Par
103	Eleesha	Santos	Cameron Par
104	Roy	Baxter	Granite Bay

1-62 Column movement indicator

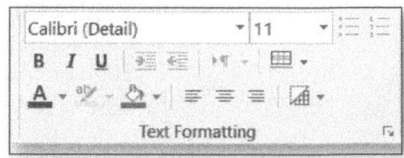

Employee ID ▾	Last Name ▾	First Name ▾	Branch
101	Lingle	Bob	Cameron Par
102	McCartney	Lanita	Cameron Par
103	Santos	Eleesha	Cameron Par
104	Baxter	Roy	Granite Bay

1-63 Moved column

Select a Display Font Face and Font Size

Access provides many of the standard text formatting options available in other Microsoft Office programs. These formatting options are found in the *Text Formatting* group on the *Home* tab as displayed in Figure 1-64.

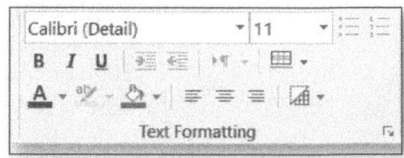

1-64 *Text Formatting* group on the *Home* tab

The *font face* specifies the shape of the text. The *font size* specifies the size of text. *Font style* options include **bolding**, *italicizing*, and underlining.

▶ **MORE INFO**

The default font face and size in Microsoft Access is Calibri and 11 pt.

Changes to a font face, size, or style are applied to the entire datasheet. If you want only specific content to have a different format, select the **Rich Text** option available on the **More Fields** button [*Table Tools Fields* tab, *Add & Delete* group] when adding the field in *Datasheet* view. Rich text is a special text format applied to a *Long Text* data type that allows you to store formatted text.

The type of change you wish to make determines the specific menu options you select.

- Change the font face by clicking the **Font** drop-down list in the *Text Formatting* group [*Home* tab] and selecting the desired font.
- Change the size of the font by clicking the **Font Size** drop-down list in the *Text Formatting* group [*Home* tab] and selecting the size.
- Change the style of the font by clicking the desired style button in the *Text Formatting* group [*Home* tab].

▶ **MORE INFO**

You can also change the default font and size in Microsoft Access.

Modify the Row Height

You can adjust the *row height* to change the amount of space that displays between rows. When you make a change to the row height in Access, all of the rows change to the new height.

▶HOW TO: Modify the Row Height

1. Place your pointer on the border of a row in your table.

 * Because your changes affect all the rows, it does not matter which row you select.
 * The resize arrow appears (Figure 1-65).

2. Click, hold, and drag the **resize arrow** to increase or decrease the height of the rows.

 * A black, horizontal line moves with you to indicate the new height (Figure 1-66).

3. Release the resize arrow.

 * The rows change to the new height.
 * The content of columns that are narrower than needed automatically wraps within the cell (Figure 1-67).

Employee ID ▾	First Name ▾	Last Name ▾	Branch ▾	Title
101	Bob	Lingle	Cameron Pa	Chief Executiv
102	Lanita	McCartney	Cameron Pa	Chief Operatin
103	Eleesha	Santos	Cameron Pa	Insurance Age

Resize arrow

1-65 Resize arrow

Employee ID ▾	First Name ▾	Last Name ▾	Branch ▾	Title
101	Bob	Lingle	Cameron Pa	Chief Executiv
102	Lanita	McCartney	Cameron Pa	Chief Operatin
103	Eleesha	Santos	Cameron Pa	Insurance Age

1-66 Row height indicator

Employee ID ▾	First Name ▾	Last Name ▾	Branch ▾	Title
101	Bob	Lingle	Cameron Park	Chief Executiv
102	Lanita	McCartney	Cameron Park	Chief Operatin
103	Eleesha	Santos	Cameron Park	Insurance Age

1-67 Changed row height

▶HOW TO: Modify the Row Height Using the Context Menu

1. Click the **record selector** of a row in your table.

 * Because your changes affect all the rows, it does not matter which row you select.

2. Place your pointer over the *record selector* and right-click to open the context menu (Figure 1-68).

3. Select **Row Height** to open the *Row Height* dialog box.

4. Type the desired height in the *Row Height* box.

5. Click **OK** to close the dialog box.

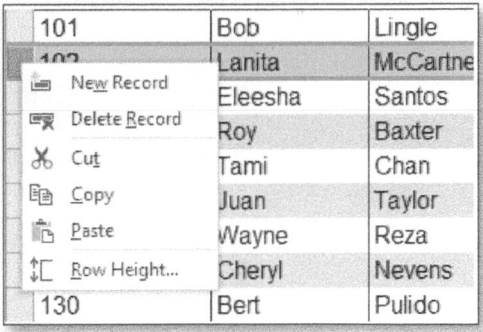

1-68 *Row* context menu

Modify the Field Width

Adjust the *field width* to change how much content displays. You can set each field to a desired width. You can also select a set of adjacent columns and set the same width to all of them in one operation.

▶HOW TO: Modify the Field Width of Selected Columns

1. Place your pointer on the right border of the field name of the column you wish to change. The resize arrow appears (Figure 1-69).

 * If you wish to change the width of adjacent columns, you must first select

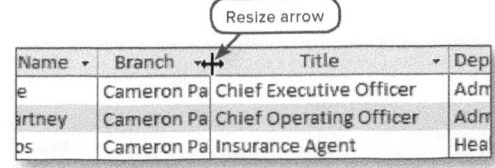

1-69 Resize arrow

all of the columns. Click and hold to select the first column, then drag the selection pointer to the adjacent columns (Figure 1-70).

- Place your pointer over the border of the right-most field.

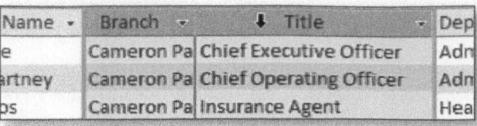

1-70 Select adjacent columns

2. Click, hold, and drag the **resize arrow** to increase or decrease the width of the field(s).

- A black, vertical line moves with you to indicate the new width (Figure 1-71).

3. Release the resize arrow.

- The field column(s) changes to the new width.

1-71 Field width indicator

> **ANOTHER WAY**
>
> To have Access *AutoFit* the column width to the widest entry, double-click instead of click and drag when the resize arrow appears.

▶ HOW TO: Modify the Field Width of All Columns Using AutoFit

1. Click the **Select All** button (Figure 1-72), in the upper left corner of the datasheet, to select the entire datasheet.

2. Place your pointer on the right border of any of the field names.

Select All button 1-72 Select All button

3. Double-click the **resize arrow** (Figure 1-73).

- All the fields automatically adjust to their widest entry or to the width of the field caption if that is larger than the contents.

1-73 Adjust field width of all columns

> **MORE INFO**
>
> If the width of the table window is not large enough to increase all the columns, some columns remain narrower.

> **ANOTHER WAY**
>
> You can also modify the column width by right-clicking the field name to open the context menu and selecting **Field Width**.

Modify the Field Alignment

The data type determines the default *field alignment*, or position relative to the edges, of each field.

1-74 *Text Formatting* group buttons

- Left-aligned data types include *Short Text, Long Text*, and *Hyperlink*.
- Right-aligned data types include *Number, Date/Time, Currency*, and *Calculated*.
- Center-aligned data types include *Yes/No* and *Attachment*. You are not able to change the alignment of fields with these Yes/No and *Attachment* data types.

Change the default alignment by selecting the field and then clicking the desired alignment button in the *Text Formatting* group [*Home* tab] (Figure 1-74). Alignment changes to a field are applied across all the database records, not just one cell. Figure 1-74 also illustrates several other buttons useful in formatting a datasheet.

Display Gridlines

Gridlines help visually frame the rows and columns in a datasheet with a border. The default settings in Access display both vertical and horizontal gridlines in a gray color.

The gridline display options include:

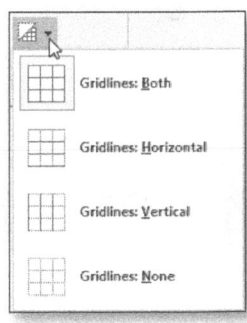

1-75 Gridlines display options

- Both vertical and horizontal gridlines
- Only horizontal gridlines
- Only vertical gridlines
- No gridlines

To change the gridline settings, click the **Gridlines** button in the *Text Formatting* group [*Home* tab] to display the gallery of gridline options (Figure 1-75), and select the desired setting.

> **MORE INFO**
>
> You can also change the default gridline settings in Microsoft Access.

Display Alternate Row Colors

Alternate row colors help you easily scan the records and fields in your datasheet. You can change the alternating colors that are displayed or remove the colors altogether.

To change the alternate row color settings, click the **Alternate Row Color** button in the *Text Formatting* group [*Home* tab] (Figure 1-74) to display the gallery of color options. Select the desired color.

Use the Datasheet Formatting Dialog Box

If you are going to make several changes to the datasheet layout, you may wish to use the *Datasheet Formatting* dialog box.

▶**HOW TO: Make Multiple Formatting Changes with the Datasheet Formatting Dialog Box**

1. Click the **launcher** [*Home* tab, *Text Formatting* group] to open the *Datasheet Formatting* dialog box (Figure 1-76).
2. Select the desired settings of the different options.
3. Click **OK** when finished.

The *Datasheet Formatting* dialog box allows you to change several other formatting options that are not available through the *Home* tab. These options include the ***Cell Effect, Background Color***, and ***Gridline Color***.

1-76 *Datasheet Formatting* dialog box

Save Changes

If you make changes to the design settings of the datasheet layout, you must save the table for those changes to be permanent. Select one of the previously discussed options for saving the design changes to your table.

PAUSE & PRACTICE: ACCESS 1-3

For this project, you import additional data into the *Employee* table. You also modify the field order, font size, row height, field width and field alignment of your *Employee* table. Finally, you enhance the *Datasheet* view by modifying the gridline settings and alternating row colors.

Files Needed: *[your initials] PP A1-2.accdb* and ***CentralSierraDataFile-01.xlsx***
Completed Project File Name: *[your initials] PP A1-3.accdb*

1. Open the *[your initials] **PP A1-2*** database file that you created in Pause & Practice 1-2.

2. Save a new copy of your database.
 a. Select the **Save As** button [*File* tab]. The *Access Database* button should be selected in the *Save Database As* area.
 b. Click the **Save As** button.
 c. Select the desired location in which to store the copy of your database.
 d. Name the database [your initials] PP A1-3 in the *File name* box.
 e. Click the **Save** button.
 f. Click the **Enable Content** button in the *Security Warning* message bar if prompted.

3. Import data into the *Employees* table.
 a. Click the **Excel** button [*External Data* tab, *Import & Link* group] to launch the *Get External Data – Excel Spreadsheet* dialog box.
 b. Click the **Browse** button to launch the *File Open* dialog box.

c. Locate and select the ***CentralSierraDataFile-01*** Excel file.
d. Click the **Open** button. The *File Open* dialog box closes.
e. Select the **Append a copy of the records to the table** radio button.
f. Click the **drop-down arrow** in the *table name* box and select the **Employees** table if needed.
g. Click **OK** to launch the *Import Spreadsheet Wizard*. The data records should display in the *Wizard* window as shown in Figure 1-77.

1-77 *Import Spreadsheet Wizard*

h. Click the **Next** button to advance to the next page of the *Import Spreadsheet Wizard*.
i. Verify that the *Import to Table* box contains the *Employees* table.
j. Click **Finish**.
k. Click the **Close** button. It is not necessary to save these import steps.

4. Open the **Employees** table in *Datasheet* view to verify that the 11 records imported correctly. The table should contain a total of 16 records and appear like that shown in Figure 1-78. Depending on the width of your Access window, you may see fewer columns.

5. Use the *Navigation* buttons to move among records.
 a. Click the **Next record** button to navigate to the second record.
 b. Click the **Next record** button three more times to navigate to the fifth record.
 c. Click the **Last record** button to navigate to the last record.
 d. Click the **Current record** box. It changes from displaying 16 of 16 to simply displaying 16.
 e. Delete the 16, type 7 and press **Enter**. The seventh record should now be selected.
 f. Click the **First record** button to navigate to the first record.

6. Change the field order.
 a. Place your pointer over the **Title** field name.
 b. Click to select that column.
 c. Click, hold, and drag the pointer to the left of the *Branch* column.
 d. Release the pointer to move the column.
 e. Move the **Start Date** column to the right of the *Base Monthly Salary* column.

1-78 *Datasheet* view of the *Employees* table

7. Change the font face and size.
 a. Click the **Font** drop-down list [*Home* tab, *Text Formatting* group] and select **Arial**.
 b. Click the **Font Size** drop-down list [*Home* tab, *Text Formatting* group] and select **12**.

8. Change the row height using the context menu.
 a. Click the **record selector** of a row in your table.
 b. Place the pointer over the *record selector* and right-click to open the context menu.
 c. Select **Row Height** to open the *Row Height* dialog box.
 d. Type 17 in the *Row Height* box.
 e. Click **OK**.

9. Change the column width of all columns using *Auto Fit*.
 a. Click the **Select All** button in the upper left corner of the datasheet.
 b. Place your pointer on the right border of any of the field names.
 c. Double-click the **resize arrow**. The column widths automatically adjust.
 d. Click any cell to release the *Select All* setting. The table should now look similar to Figure 1-79. If the width of the Access window was not large enough, some of the columns may display a series of # symbols. Most likely this will occur in the *Base Monthly Salary* or *Start Date* columns. The horizontal and vertical scroll sliders automatically display if the window is not wide enough or tall enough to display all of the rows and columns.

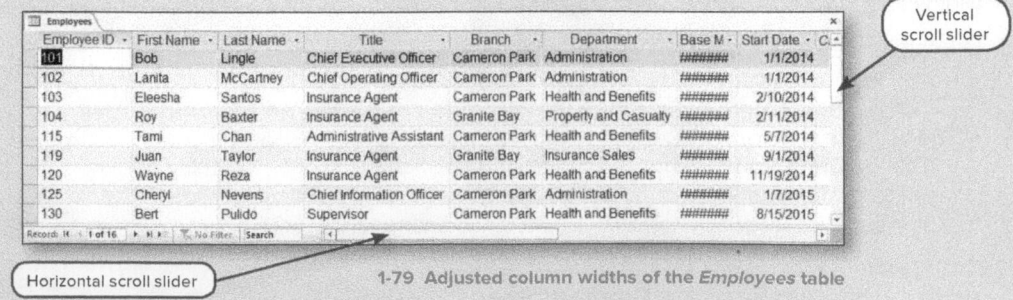

1-79 *Adjusted column widths of the* Employees *table*

10. Increase the width of any columns that display a series of # symbols.
 a. Move the **horizontal scroll slider** at the bottom of the datasheet to the right so that any column that contains # symbols moves to the middle of the window. This allows you to increase the width of this column more easily.
 b. Place your pointer on the right border of the field name.

c. Click, hold, and drag the **resize arrow** to the right to increase the column width. The column should now be wide enough to display the contents instead of the # symbols.

d. Repeat these steps for all columns that are too narrow.

11. Change the field alignment.
 a. Move the **horizontal scroll slider** all the way to the left of the datasheet window if needed.
 b. Select the **Employee ID** column.
 c. Click the **Center** button [*Home* tab, *Text Formatting* group].

12. Change the gridlines and alternate row colors using the *Datasheet Formatting* dialog box.
 a. Click the **launcher** [*Home* tab, *Text Formatting* group].
 b. Click the **Alternate Background Color** drop-down list in the *Datasheet Formatting* dialog box (Figure 1-80) and select **Blue-Gray, Text 2, Lighter 80%** (fourth column, second row in the *Theme Colors* category).
 c. Uncheck the **Horizontal** check box in the *Gridlines Shown* area.
 d. Click the **Gridline Color** drop-down list and Select **Blue-Gray, Text 2, Darker 25%** (fourth column, fifth row in the *Theme Colors* category).
 e. Click **OK** to close the dialog box.
 f. Click the *Employee ID* cell for **Employee 102** as shown in Figure 1-81. Depending on your window width, you may need to scroll to see all of the columns. The slightly darker blue color shown in the second row indicates that this is the current record.

1-80 *Datasheet Formatting* dialog box

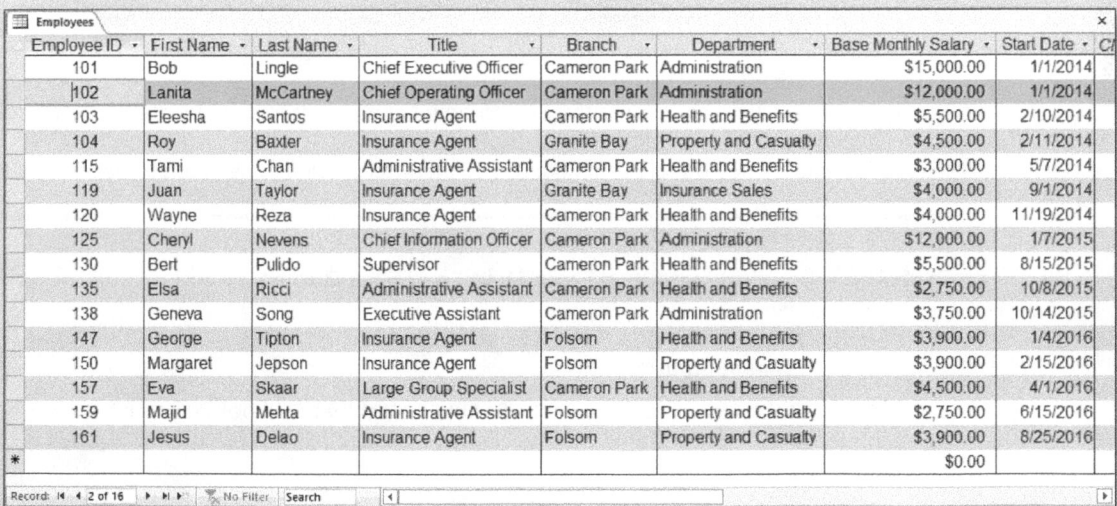

Employee ID	First Name	Last Name	Title	Branch	Department	Base Monthly Salary	Start Date	C
101	Bob	Lingle	Chief Executive Officer	Cameron Park	Administration	$15,000.00	1/1/2014	
102	Lanita	McCartney	Chief Operating Officer	Cameron Park	Administration	$12,000.00	1/1/2014	
103	Eleesha	Santos	Insurance Agent	Cameron Park	Health and Benefits	$5,500.00	2/10/2014	
104	Roy	Baxter	Insurance Agent	Granite Bay	Property and Casualty	$4,500.00	2/11/2014	
115	Tami	Chan	Administrative Assistant	Cameron Park	Health and Benefits	$3,000.00	5/7/2014	
119	Juan	Taylor	Insurance Agent	Granite Bay	Insurance Sales	$4,000.00	9/1/2014	
120	Wayne	Reza	Insurance Agent	Cameron Park	Health and Benefits	$4,000.00	11/19/2014	
125	Cheryl	Nevens	Chief Information Officer	Cameron Park	Administration	$12,000.00	1/7/2015	
130	Bert	Pulido	Supervisor	Cameron Park	Health and Benefits	$5,500.00	8/15/2015	
135	Elsa	Ricci	Administrative Assistant	Cameron Park	Health and Benefits	$2,750.00	10/8/2015	
138	Geneva	Song	Executive Assistant	Cameron Park	Administration	$3,750.00	10/14/2015	
147	George	Tipton	Insurance Agent	Folsom	Health and Benefits	$3,900.00	1/4/2016	
150	Margaret	Jepson	Insurance Agent	Folsom	Property and Casualty	$3,900.00	2/15/2016	
157	Eva	Skaar	Large Group Specialist	Cameron Park	Health and Benefits	$4,500.00	4/1/2016	
159	Majid	Mehta	Administrative Assistant	Folsom	Property and Casualty	$2,750.00	6/15/2016	
161	Jesus	Delao	Insurance Agent	Folsom	Property and Casualty	$3,900.00	8/25/2016	
*						$0.00		

Record: 2 of 16 — No Filter — Search

1-81 PP A1-3 completed

13. Press **Ctrl+S** to save the table.

14. Click the **X** in the upper right corner of the datasheet to close the table.

15. Close the database by clicking the **Close** button [*File* tab].

SLO 1.6

Using Search, Sort, and Filter Tools to Find Records in a Table

When the number of records in a database table increases, it is important to be able to quickly and easily organize and locate specific records. Access provides a number of ways to find data, change the order of how records are displayed, and limit the records that display in the datasheet.

Search Data in a Table

The search functions allow you to find data by looking for specific values. The **Search** box on the *Navigation* bar is a quick and easy way to locate the first record containing a specific value. The **Find** button in the *Find* group [*Home* tab] provides a more powerful way to search for records.

▶ HOW TO: Find Data in a Table Using the Search Box

1. Click the **Search** box in the *Navigation* bar.
2. Enter the **Search Value** you want to locate.
 - Access evaluates the criteria as you enter each character and moves to the first field that matches those criteria (Figure 1-82).

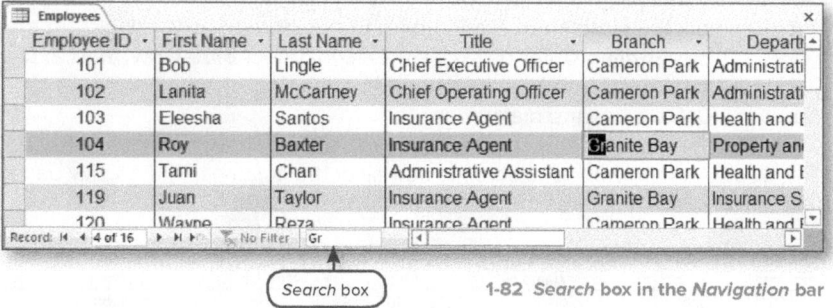

1-82 *Search* box in the *Navigation* bar

 - As you type more data into the *Search* box, Access continues to locate the first field that matches.
 - If a match is not found, the field or record that was previously selected remains highlighted.

▶ HOW TO: Find Data in a Table Using the Find Button

1. Click the **Find** button [*Home* tab, *Find* group] (Figure 1-83) to open the *Find and Replace* dialog box (Figure 1-84).
 - If you want to search only in a specific field, select that field before you click the *Find* button.

1-83 *Find* button 1-84 *Find and Replace* dialog box

ANOTHER WAY

You can also select a column and then right-click to open the context menu. Select **Find** to open the *Find and Replace* dialog box. You can also press **Ctrl+F** to open the *Find and Replace* dialog box.

> **MORE INFO**
>
> The initial settings of your dialog box may be different, depending on your previous search.

2. Enter the **Search Value** you want to search in the *Find What* box.

3. Click the **Look In** drop-down list to select either **Current field** or **Current document**. If *Current field* is selected, the search only looks for a match in the current field.

4. Click the **Match** drop-down list to select the appropriate option.

 - **Whole Field**: The *Search Value* must match the entire contents of a field. This can be used to find an exact match.
 - **Any Part of Field**: The *Search Value* must be somewhere in the field. This can be used to find a value that contains the *Search Value* anywhere in the field.
 - **Start of Field**: The *Search Value* is at the beginning of the field. This can be used to find a value that starts with a certain character or number.

5. Click the **Search** drop-down list to select **All, Up,** or **Down**. Selecting up and down searches in that direction from the current record only.

6. Check the **Match Case** check box to limit the results to the case of the search value.

7. Click the **Find Next** button to execute the search. Access searches the table to find the first record that meets the criteria.

 - If that is the desired record, click the **Cancel** button to close the *Find and Replace* dialog box or click the **Find Next** button to continue searching.
 - If the *Search Value* does not exist in the table, Access displays an information message box (Figure 1-85), indicating the record was not found.

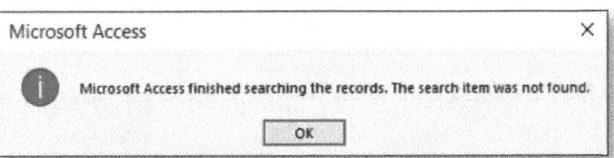

1-85 Search item not found information message

ANOTHER WAY

You can also press **Shift+F4** to find the next record that meets the criteria.

8. Click **Cancel** to close the *Find and Replace* dialog box.

As desired, you can change data using the *Replace* tab on the *Find and Replace* dialog box. Press **Ctrl+H** to open the *Replace* tab. Enter the **Search Value** in the *Find What* box. Enter the **Replacement Value** in the *Replace With* box.

Sort Data in a Table with Datasheet View

The *Sort* functions allow you to organize your data. When you open a table in *Datasheet* view, by default, Access sorts the data records in ascending order by the first field. *Datasheet* view provides you with tools to perform a simple sort. You can sort the datasheet by one field, or a set of adjacent fields, in ascending or descending order.

- *Ascending order* is *lowest to highest* for a numeric field or *A to Z* for a text field.
- *Descending order* means *highest to lowest* for a numeric field or *Z to A* for a text field.

Sort Data on a Single Field

The simplest sort is to sort the datasheet on one field. You can either use the *Ascending* or *Descending* buttons in the *Sort & Filter* group [*Home* tab], or you can open the drop-down list for the desired column.

▶ **HOW TO: Sort Data in a Table on a Single Field Using the Sort & Filter Group**

1. Click the **field name** to select the column you wish to sort.

> ▶ **ANOTHER WAY**
>
> Instead of selecting the column, you can also just click any cell in the desired column.

1-86 *Sort & Filter* group on the *Home* tab

2. Click either the **Ascending** or **Descending** button [*Home* tab, *Sort & Filter* group] (Figure 1-86).

 - The datasheet updates to show the results of the sort. Figure 1-87 shows the employee records sorted in descending order by the *Branch* field.

Employee ID ▾	First Name ▾	Last Name ▾	Title ▾	Branch ▾	Departm
104	Roy	Baxter	Insurance Agent	Granite Bay	Property and
119	Juan	Taylor	Insurance Agent	Granite Bay	Insurance S
159	Majid	Mehta	Administrative Assistant	Folsom	Property and
150	Margaret	Jepson	Insurance Agent	Folsom	Property and
147	George	Tipton	Insurance Agent	Folsom	Health and E
161	Jesus	Delac	Insurance Agent	Folsom	Property and

1-87 Employee records sorted on the *Branch* field

 - The *Field name* cell changes to display either an **Up** or **Down Sort** indicator arrow to the right of the drop-down arrow to visually indicate that the datasheet has been sorted on this field. If you want the table records to remain in this sorted order, you must save the table.

▶ **HOW TO: Sort Data in a Table on a Single Field Using the Drop-down List**

1. Click the **drop-down arrow** to the right of the field name you wish to sort.
 - The column turns blue, indicating it has been selected.
 - The drop-down list opens (Figure 1-88).

2. Select either **Sort A to Z** or **Sort Z to A** on the drop-down list.

- The datasheet updates to show the results of the sort.
- If you are sorting a numeric field, the drop-down list options are *Sort Smallest to Largest* and *Sort Largest to Smallest*.

1-88 *Sort* drop-down list

ANOTHER WAY

Press **Shift+F10** to open the drop-down list, and then type **S** for an ascending sort or type **O** for a descending sort. You can also right-click to open the context menu, then select the desired sort order.

Sort Data on Multiple Fields

Sometimes sorting your datasheet on multiple fields makes it easier to organize the data records. In *Datasheet* view, you can sort on multiple adjacent fields using the same sort order.

- The left-most selected field is sorted first.
- If there are identical items in the first field, the second field is sorted.
- This process continues for all additional selected fields.

▶ HOW TO: Sort Data in a Table on Multiple Fields

1. Click and hold the pointer over the *Field name* of the first column you want to sort. With the selection pointer still displayed, drag the pointer to the adjacent columns.
2. Release the pointer.
3. Click either the **Ascending** or **Descending** button [*Home* tab, *Sort & Filter* group].

- The datasheet updates to show the results of the sort. Figure 1-89 shows the employee records sorted in descending order by the *Branch* [Granite Bay, Folsom, and Cameron Park] and the *Department* [Property and Casualty, Insurance Sales, Health and Benefits, and Administration] fields.
- In the example shown in Figure 1-89, there is a "tie" for the *Branch*, so the *Department* field determines which record appears at the top.

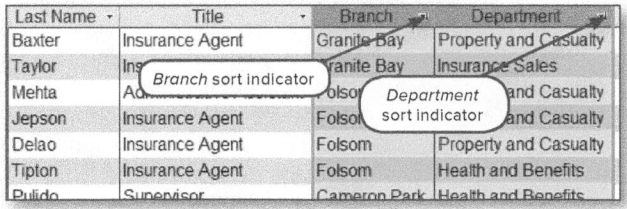

1-89 Employee records sorted on *Branch* and *Department* fields

MORE INFO

If the fields that you wish to sort together are not adjacent, you first need to move them together. Refer back to the "Modify the Field Order" section in *SLO 1.5: Exploring Datasheet View*, if necessary.

Remove Sorting Criteria

To return the records in your datasheet to their original order, remove the *Sort* criteria.

Click the **Remove Sort** button [*Home* tab, *Sort & Filter* group,] to remove all *Sort* criteria.

 MORE INFO

If you open a table with a previously saved sort, clicking **Remove Sort** removes the sort.

Filter Data in a Table with Datasheet View

The *Filter* functions are helpful in limiting the number of records that display in your datasheet. There are several different filter options available.

Create a Filter by Selection

Filter by Selection allows you to display only the records that match the value in the fields you have selected.

> **HOW TO: Filter Data Using Filter by Selection**

1. Click in the cell that contains the value you wish to filter.
 - You can select only part of the cell contents, as desired.
2. Click the **Selection** button in the *Sort & Filter* group on the *Home* tab (Figure 1-90).
 - The drop-down list shows the available filter options.
 - The available filter options depend on the data type of the field and what criterion is selected. If you only select part of a field, the beginning of the field, or the end of the field, the options differ.

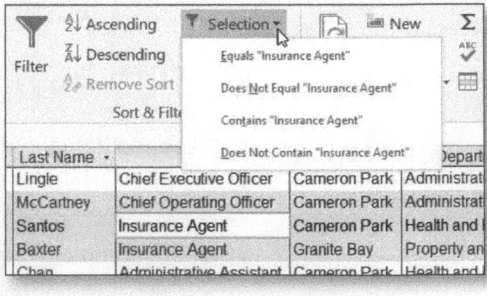

1-90 *Selection* button in the *Sort & Filter* group

3. Select the desired filter option.
 - The datasheet updates to show the results of the filter.
 - The filter status message changes, indicating the datasheet is filtered.
 - The *Field name* cell displays a *Filter* symbol to the right of the drop-down arrow, indicating this field has been filtered (Figure 1-91).
 - Once a filter has been applied, you can switch between viewing the complete dataset and the filtered results by clicking the *Toggle Filter* button [*Home* tab, *Sort & Filter* group], shown in the top image in Figure 1-92. When toggled off, the filter status message, shown at the bottom image of Figure 1-92, changes to indicate that a filter exists but is toggled off.

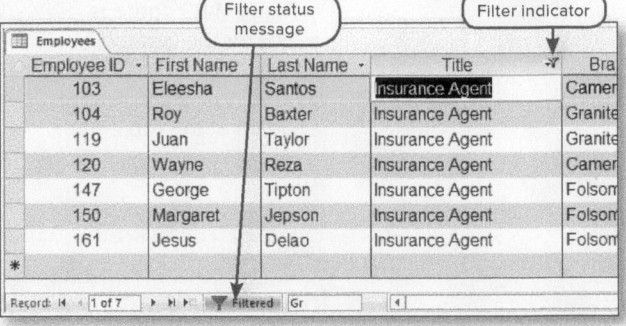

1-91 **Filtered datasheet**

> **ANOTHER WAY**
>
> After selecting the desired cell, you can also right-click to open the context menu and then select the desired filter option.

1-92 *Toggle Filter* button and updated filter status message

Create a Text Filter, Number Filter, or Date Filter

A *Text, Number*, or *Date Filter* filters the records in your database by displaying the records that match the search criteria that you enter, instead of matching criteria you have selected from a cell. Although similar to using a *Filter by Selection*, these filters provide additional options.

> ▶ **HOW TO: Filter Data Using a Text, Number, or Date Filter**
>
> 1. Click the **drop-down arrow** to the right of the field name you wish to filter.
> 2. Select **Text Filters** on the drop-down list (Figure 1-93).
> - The button name is context sensitive and determined by the type of field you are filtering.
> - The drop-down list displays the available filter options.
> - The filter options are also context sensitive and change based on the type of field.
>
>
>
> 1-93 *Filter* drop-down list
>
> 3. Select the desired filter option on the drop-down list to open the *Custom Filter* dialog box (Figure 1-94). The content of this dialog box depends on the filter option selected.
> 4. Type the word or value you wish to filter.
> 5. Click **OK**.
>
>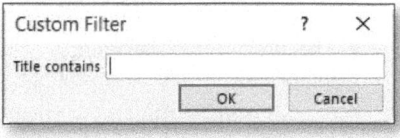
>
> 1-94 *Custom Filter* dialog box
>
> - The datasheet updates to show the results of the filter.
> - The filter status message changes, indicating the datasheet is filtered.
> - The *Field name* cell displays a *Filter* symbol to the right of the drop-down arrow that indicates this field has been filtered.

Create Compound Filter Criteria

The previous examples used filters with one search value or criterion. You can create a more complex filter using compound criteria. *Compound criteria* combine more than one search value using the *AND* and *OR* logical operators.

- *AND logical operator*: The filtered records must contain all of the criteria values.
- *OR logical operator*: The filtered records must contain at least one of the criteria values.

You can specify compound criteria on one field or you can use compound criteria across several fields in your datasheet.

▶ HOW TO: Filter Data Using "OR" Compound Criteria on One Field

1. Click the **drop-down arrow** to the right of the field name you wish to filter.
 - The drop-down list opens.
 - Initially all the check boxes are selected.
2. Click the **(Select All)** check box to clear all the check boxes.
3. Click all of the check boxes on the drop-down list that contain the desired criteria (Figure 1-95).

> **MORE INFO**
>
> Selecting multiple criteria in the same field is an *OR* condition. The returned records contain the first value or the second value or the third value, and so on.

1-95 *Filter drop-down list showing OR criteria*

4. Click **OK**.
 - The datasheet updates to show the results of the filter.

▶ HOW TO: Filter Data Using "AND" Compound Criteria on Multiple Fields

1. Click the **drop-down arrow** to the right of the first field name you wish to filter.
 - The drop-down list opens.
 - Initially all the check boxes are selected.
2. Click the **(Select All)** check box to clear all the check boxes.
3. Click all of the check boxes on the drop-down list that contain the desired criteria.
4. Click **OK**.
 - The datasheet updates to show the results of the filter.
5. Click the **drop-down arrow** to the right of the second field name you wish to filter.
6. Click the **(Select All)** check box to remove that criterion.
7. Click all of the check boxes on the drop-down list that contain the desired criteria (Figure 1-96).

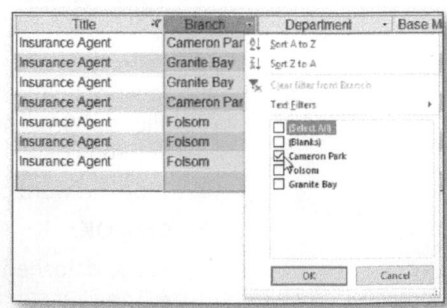

1-96 Using filters on multiple fields to create *AND* criteria

> **MORE INFO**
>
> Adding a filter to a second field is an *AND* condition. The returned records match the filter from both fields.

8. Click **OK**.
 - Only the records that meet both of the criteria display (Figure 1-97).
9. As desired, you can add a filter to additional columns by repeating the earlier steps.

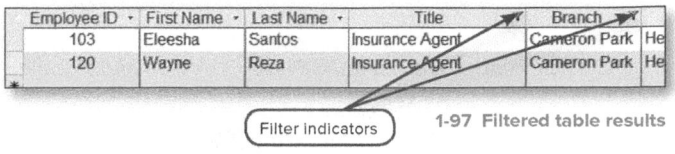

Employee ID	First Name	Last Name	Title	Branch	
103	Eleesha	Santos	Insurance Agent	Cameron Park	He
120	Wayne	Reza	Insurance Agent	Cameron Park	He

Filter indicators **1-97 Filtered table results**

Remove Filter Criteria

To return the records in your datasheet to their original unfiltered state, you must remove the *Filter* criteria. You can remove a filter from just one field or you can remove all of the filters.

▶ **HOW TO: Remove Filter Criteria from a Single Field**

1. Click the **drop-down arrow** to the right of the first field name where you wish to remove a filter.
 - The drop-down list opens.
2. Select **Clear filter from Field name** to remove the filter.
 - The phrase "Field name" will not display, but instead the actual field name that has been filtered displays.
 - The datasheet updates to show the results of this filter being removed.

▶ **ANOTHER WAY**

Click a cell of the desired field. Press **Shift+F10** to open the context menu, and then press **L** to remove the filter.

▶ **HOW TO: Remove Filter Criteria from All Fields**

1. Click the **Advanced** button [*Home* tab, *Sort & Filter* group] to open the drop-down list.
2. Select **Clear All Filters**.

PAUSE & PRACTICE: ACCESS 1-4

For this project, you search for data in the *Employees* table using the *Search* box and the *Find* button. Next, you sort the table using single and multiple fields. You also filter the records using single and multiple criteria.

File Needed: ***[your initials] PP A1-3.accdb***
Completed Project File Name: ***[your initials] PP A1-4.accdb***

1. Open the *[your initials] PP A1-3* database file you created in Pause & Practice 1-3.

2. Save a new copy of your database.
 a. Select the **Save As** button [*File tab*]. The *Access Database* button should be selected in the *Save Database As* area.
 b. Click the **Save As** button.
 c. Select the desired location in which to store the copy of your database.
 d. Name the database [your initials] PP A1-4 in the *File name* box.
 e. Click the **Save** button.
 f. Click the **Enable Content** button in the *Security Warning* message bar if prompted.

3. Open the **Employees** table in *Datasheet* view. The changes you made to the datasheet layout in Pause & Practice 1-3 should be reflected (Figure 1-98).

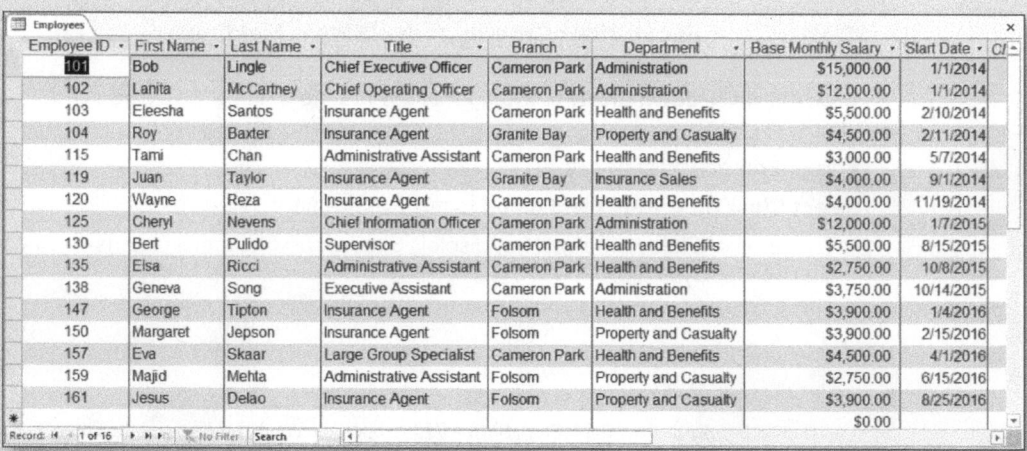

1-98 PP A1-4 Starting *Datasheet* view

4. Use the *Search* box to find records.
 a. Type Health in the *Search* box in the *Navigation* bar. The *Department* field for **Employee 103** should be selected.
 b. Type Folsom in the *Search* box. The *Branch* field for **Employee 147** should be selected.
 c. Clear the *Search* box.
 d. Click in the *Employee ID* cell for **Employee 101**.

5. Use the *Find* button to find records.
 a. Click the **Find** button [*Home* tab, *Find* group] to open the *Find and Replace* dialog box.
 b. Type Insurance in the *Find What* box.
 c. Click the **Look In** drop-down arrow and select **Current document** if it is not already displayed. Then you can look for a match in all fields in the table.
 d. Click the **Match** drop-down arrow and select **Any Part of Field** if it is not already displayed. Then you can find a match if the *Search Value* is somewhere in a field.
 e. Click the **Search** drop-down arrow and select **All** If it is not already displayed. Then you can search through all the records.
 f. Uncheck the **Match Case** check box if it is checked.
 g. Select the **Find Next** button to execute the search. The search starts from the currently selected field. Access searches the table to find the first record that meets the criteria. The *Title* field for **Employee 103** should be selected. If you had not clicked out of the *Branch* field in step 4d, the *Title* field for Employee 150 would have been selected.
 h. Click the **Find Next** button again to find the next occurrence of *Insurance*. The *Title* field for **Employee 104** should be selected.

 i. Continue clicking the **Find Next** button until the *Department* field for **Employee 119** is selected.

 j. Click the **Cancel** button to close the *Find and Replace* dialog box.

6. Sort the datasheet on a single field using the drop-down list.
 a. Click the **drop-down arrow** to the right of the *Start Date* field.
 b. Select **Sort Newest to Oldest** on the drop-down list. Employee 161, the most recently hired employee, should be in the first row of the datasheet.
 c. Click the **Remove Sort** button [*Home* tab, *Sort & Filter* group] to remove the sort criteria.
 d. Click any cell to deselect the *Start Date* column.

7. Sort the datasheet on multiple fields using the *Sort & Filter* group.
 a. Click and hold the pointer over the *Branch* field name, the first column you wish to sort. With the selection pointer still displayed, drag the pointer to the *Department* field name.
 b. Release the pointer.
 c. Click the **Descending** button [*Home* tab, *Sort & Filter* group]. Employee 104, the employee from Granite Bay in the Property and Casualty department, should be in the first row of the datasheet.
 d. Click the **Remove Sort** button [*Home* tab, *Sort & Filter* group] to remove the sort criteria.
 e. Click any cell to deselect the columns.

8. Filter the datasheet using *Filter by Selection*.
 a. Click after the "t" in the phrase "**Insurance Agent**," in the *Title* cell for **Employee 103**.
 b. Click the **Selection** button [*Home* tab, *Sort & Filter* group].
 c. Select **Equals "Insurance Agent"** from the drop-down list. The datasheet should display only the seven employees who are insurance agents.
 d. Click the **drop-down arrow** to the right of the *Title* field name.
 e. Select **Clear filter from Title** to remove the filter. The datasheet updates to show all the records.

9. Filter the datasheet using a *Text Filter*.
 a. Click the **drop-down arrow** to the right of the *Title* field name.
 b. Select **Text Filters** on the drop-down list and select **Contains** from the drop-down list.
 c. Type Assistant in the *Title contains* box.
 d. Click **OK**. The datasheet should display only the four employees who have "Assistant" as part of their title.
 e. Click the **Toggle Filter** button [*Home* tab, *Sort & Filter* group] to switch back to viewing all the records.
 f. Click the **Toggle Filter** button again to switch back to the filtered records.
 g. Click the **drop-down arrow** to the right of the *Title* field name.
 h. Select the **Clear filter from Title** button to remove the filter. The datasheet updates to show all the records.

10. Filter the datasheet using compound criteria on multiple fields.
 a. Click the **drop-down arrow** to the right of the *Title* field name.
 b. Click the **(Select All)** check box to remove that criterion.
 c. Select the **Insurance Agent** check box on the drop-down list.
 d. Click **OK**. The datasheet should display only the seven employees who are insurance agents.
 e. Click the **drop-down arrow** to the right of the *Branch* field name.
 f. Click the **(Select All)** check box to remove that criterion.
 g. Click the **Cameron Park** check box on the drop-down list.
 h. Click **OK**. The datasheet should display only the two employees who are insurance agents at the Cameron Park branch.
 i. Click the **Advanced** button [*Home* tab, *Sort & Filter* group].
 j. Select the **Clear All Filters** button. The datasheet updates to show all the records.

11. Click the **X** in the upper right corner of the datasheet to close the table.

12. Select the **No** button when asked to save changes to the design of the *Employees* table.

13. Close the database by clicking the **Close** button [*File* tab].

Chapter Summary

1.1 Explain data organization concepts, use the Access *Navigation Pane*, and identify objects (p. A1-3).

- The **hierarchy of data** helps organize the data into fields, records, tables, and a database.
- The major Access **objects** are **tables**, **forms**, **reports**, and **queries**.
- A database must contain at least one table.
- The **Navigation Pane** displays all of the objects in your database. You can open objects directly from the *Navigation Pane*.

1.2 Create a database, set database properties, understand database object naming conventions and data types, and close a database (p. A1-11).

- You can create a new database from a **template**, a ready-to-use database application that comes complete with objects already created.
- **Database properties** are details about the database including title, author, company, subject, date created, and date last modified.
- Create a **Blank desktop database** when you want to build your database application from scratch.
- Each field in your database must be assigned a specific **data type** that determines what properties can be manipulated and how that field can be used.
- In *Backstage view*, you can close and open databases.

1.3 Create a table in *Datasheet* view, edit the default primary key, add a new field, edit field properties, save a table, and enter records into a table (p. A1-18).

- Use *Datasheet* view to enter, modify, delete, or view data records.
- You can create and edit a new table using *Datasheet* view.
- Each table should have a **primary key**, a field that contains a unique value for each record.
- Add new fields in *Datasheet* view by entering data values or field names.
- The properties of each field describe the details or characteristics about the field. You can modify some of these properties in *Datasheet* view.
- Each table must be saved with a unique name.
- When entering records into a datasheet, Access verifies that the content of each field

matches the data type. After a record is entered, it is automatically saved into the table.

1.4 Import data records from Excel (p. A1-29).

- You can import data records from an Excel file into an Access table with the *Append* option.
- The first row of the Excel file must contain the field names from the Access table. The format of the fields should match or not all the data values may be imported.

1.5 Navigate table records in a datasheet and customize a datasheet by modifying field order, row height, column width, field alignment, font style and size, row colors, and gridlines (p. A1-31).

- Use the **Navigation bar** to move among records in a table.
- You can move the columns in a datasheet to change their order.
- You can change the **font face**, **size**, and **style** in your datasheet. The changes are reflected in the entire datasheet.
- You can increase or decrease the **row height** in Access, but all of the rows change to the new height.
- You can adjust each column to a unique **field width**. Numeric or date fields display a series of # symbols (#####) if the column is not wide enough to display the entire contents.
- **Field alignment** dictates how content is aligned horizontally within a cell with respect to the edges. Cells can be aligned *left, center,* or *right*.
- **Gridlines** visually frame the rows and columns in a datasheet with a border.
- **Alternate row colors** help you easily scan the records and fields in your datasheet.
- Use the *Datasheet Formatting* dialog box if you are going to make several changes to the datasheet layout.

1.6 Search, sort, and filter records in a table (p. A1-41).

- The **Search** box and the **Find** button allow you to find data with a specific value quickly.
- When you open a table in *Datasheet* view, the data records are sorted in ascending order by the first field.
- An **ascending order** sort is from lowest to highest; a **descending order** sort is from highest to lowest.

A1-51

- In *Datasheet* view, if you sort on multiple fields, they all must be sorted in the same sort order.
- The **Filter** functions display only the set of records that meet specified criteria. The available filter options vary based on the data type of the field and what criterion is selected.

Check for Understanding

The SIMbook for this text (within your SIMnet account) provides the following resources for concept review:

- Multiple Choice questions
- Matching exercises
- Short answer questions

 ## Guided Project 1-1

For this project, you create and use a new database based on the ***Event management*** template. As the vice president of events for the *Green Club* at your university, you are trying to find an efficient way to keep track of the events your club has planned this semester. After creating the database, use the *Navigation Pane* to explore the objects that exist in this database, edit field properties of the table, enter records, and modify the datasheet layout.
[Student Learning Outcomes 1.1, 1.2, 1.3, 1.5]

File Needed: None
Completed Project File Name: ***[your initials] Access 1-1.accdb***

Skills Covered in This Project

- Create a database from a template.
- Use the *Navigation Pane*.
- Edit properties in *Datasheet* view.

- Save a table.
- Enter records.
- View properties in *Design* view.
- Change the datasheet layout.
- Explore Access objects.

1. Create a new database based on a template.
 a. Open Access or click the **New** button [*File* tab] if an Access database is already open.
 b. Select the ***Event management*** template (Figure 1-99). *Note: If you experience a problem downloading the template, close the dialog box and skip to step 2.*
 c. Enter [your initials] Access 1-1 in the *File Name* box.
 d. Click the **Browse for a location to put your database** button to change the location in which to save your database and click **OK**.
 e. Click the **Create** button. The database opens.
 f. Skip to step 3.

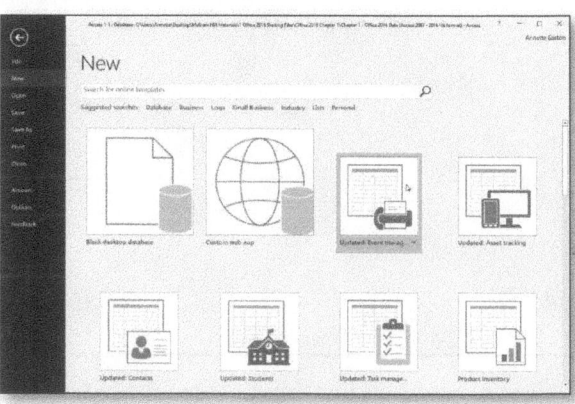

1-99 *Event management* template available online

2. Open the ***EventManagement-01*** database from your student data files.
 a. Select the **Save As** button [*File tab*]. The **Access Database** button should be selected in the *Save Database As* area.
 b. Click the **Save As** button.
 c. Select **Yes** in the message box to have Access close the open objects.
 d. Enter [your initials] Access 1-1 the *File Name* box.
 e. Select the location in which to save your database.
 f. Click the **Save** button. The database opens.

3. Depending on the selections made on your computer, the **Welcome** form may display (Figure 1-100).
 a. Click the **Play** button to view a video about using the *Events Database*.
 b. Uncheck the **Show Welcome when this database is opened** check box.
 c. Click the **Get Started** button.

4. Click the **Enable Content** button in the *Security Warning* message bar (Figure 1-101). If the *Welcome* form displays again, click **Get Started**.

1-100 *Welcome* form

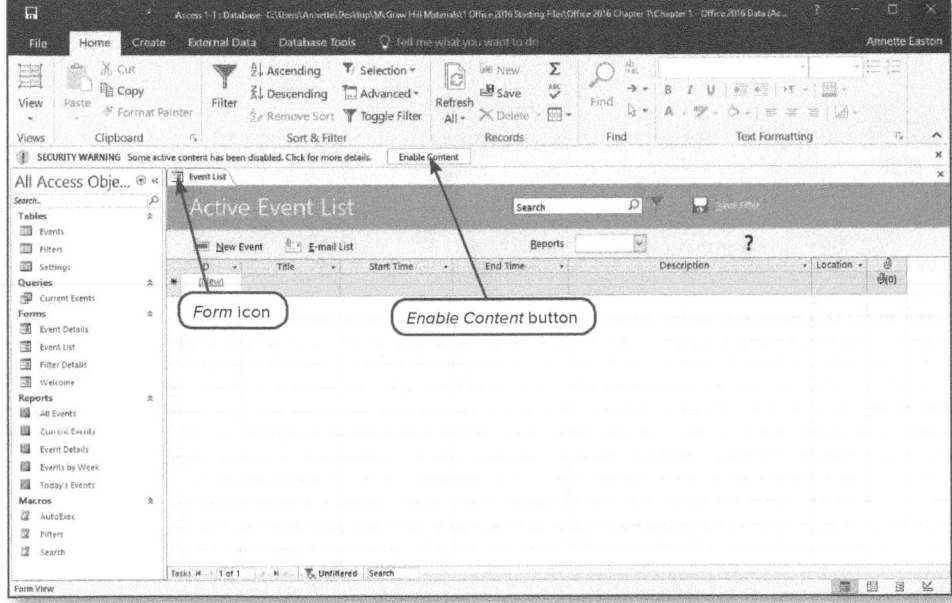

1-101 *Events Database* beginning navigation

The events database system is now ready to explore. This database contains many database objects that you have not yet used, like forms and reports. Often the objects in a template will contain more advanced database features. In the events database, when the database opens, an *Event List* form opens automatically. You know it is a form because the Form icon displays on the object tab, along with the name of the form. This form was designed to display data using a datasheet layout. You can also use this form to enter data into the database. You can now explore the database table in this template to see if it meets your needs.

5. Use the *Navigation Pane* to view the database objects.
 a. Click the **Navigation Pane** arrow next to the *All Access Objects* category to open the *Navigation* menu, shown on the right side of Figure 1-102. Note that the *Navigation Pane* is set to display all objects grouped by object type.
 b. Click the arrow to close the *Navigation* menu without making any selections.
 c. Notice that the *Events* template comes with 16 pre-built objects:
 - 3 tables
 - 1 query
 - 4 forms
 - 5 reports
 - 3 macros

The *Event List* form is linked to the *Events* table. If there are no records in the table, nothing displays in the form.

d. Close the **Event List** form by clicking the **X** in the right corner.

6. View the *Events* table in *Datasheet* view and edit field properties.

a. Double-click the **Events** table to open it in *Datasheet* view. There are no records entered into the database table (Figure 1-103).

b. Double-click the cell containing the **ID** field name (column header).

c. Type Event ID for the field name and press the **down arrow** key.

d. Click the **Table Tools Fields** tab. Remember that this contextual tab only displays when you are editing a table.

1-102 View the *Navigation Pane* display

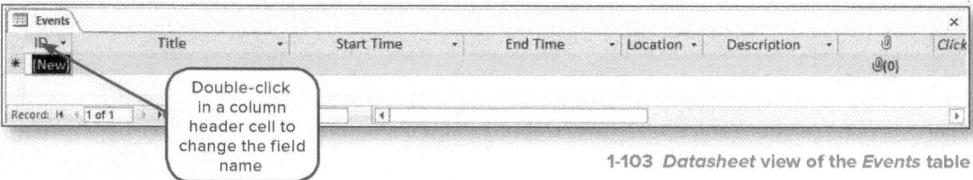

1-103 *Datasheet* view of the *Events* table

e. Click the **Title** field name.

f. Click the **Name & Caption** button [*Table Tools Fields* tab, *Properties* group].

g. Type Event Title in the *Caption* property and click **OK**.

h. Type 100 in the *Field Size* property [*Table Tools Fields* tab, *Properties* group].

i. Click the **Start Time** field name. In the *Formatting* group [*Table Tools Fields* tab], notice that the *Data Type* property is set to *Date/Time* and the *Format* property is set to *General Date*.

j. Click the **Save** button to save the changes to the table design. With the changes to the field properties saved, the table is ready for you to begin to enter data records.

7. Enter a data record into the *Events* table to test the table structure.

a. Click in the **Event Title** cell in the *append row*.

b. Type Member Welcome and Kickoff Meeting. The Pencil icon displays, indicating that this record has not yet been saved.

c. Press the **Tab** key to move to the *Start Time* field and type 7:00 PM.

d. Press the **Tab** key to move to the *End Time* field. The message box in Figure 1-104 opens. If a message box opens after leaving a field, it indicates that the data entered does not match what was expected for that field.

e. Click **OK** to return to the *Start Time* field. It appears that this template has a discrepancy in the *Start Time* field. You need to fix this discrepancy before the Green Club can use the database. Because we need to explore this field further, delete the text you entered and leave that field blank for now.

1-104 Error message box

f. Press the **Tab** key to move to the *End Time* field. Because you did not enter a value for the *Start Time*, leave the *End Time* field blank for now.

g. Press the **Tab** key to move to the *Location* field and type Recreation Center Room 202.

h. Press the **Tab** key to move to the *Description* field and type Member Meeting.

i. Press the **Tab** key to move to the *Attachment* field.

j. Press the **Tab** key because you do not have an attachment to enter. The Pencil icon no longer displays since the record has been saved.

8. Change the layout of the *Events* table.

a. Click to select the **Location** column.

b. Click, hold, and drag the pointer to move the *Location* column to the left of the *Start Time*.

c. Change the *Font Face* to **Times New Roman** [*Home* tab, *Text Formatting* group].

d. Change the *Font Size* to **12** [*Home* tab, *Text Formatting* group].

e. Click the **Select All** button in the upper left corner of the datasheet.

f. Place your pointer on the right border of any of the *Field* names (Figure 1-105).

Select All button Resize arrow

1-105 Adjust field widths in the table

g. Double-click the **resize arrow**. The width of all the fields should adjust to the needed width to display the cell contents. If the width of the Access window is not large enough, some of the fields will be smaller.

h. Click the **Save** button to save the changes to the table design.

i. Close the *Events* table by clicking the **X** in the right corner.

9. Explore the *Event List* and *Event Details* forms.

a. Double-click the **Event List** form in the *Forms* group of the *Navigation Pane*. The *Event List* form will open (Figure 1-106). The *Member Welcome* record you entered into the *Events* table displays. Recall that a form object provides a more user-friendly interface to view, add, update, and delete data in a table. It can also include additional features beyond those available in a table. For example, the *Event List* form, part of the template, has been customized to include a menu with direct links to additional forms and reports in the database.

The *Menu* bar provides links to other objects

1-106 Event List form

b. Click the **New Event** button in the *Menu* bar of the *Event List* form to open the *Event Details* form (Figure 1-107). This form provides an easy interface to enter a new record into the database. Do not enter any additional data records since the properties of the time fields are not quite right at this point.

c. Click the **Close** button to close the *Event Details* form.

10. Explore the other database objects.

a. Look at the objects displayed in the *Navigation Pane*. You should still see the same objects shown earlier in Figure 1-102.

b. Look at the *Tables* group. You see the *Events* table, the *Filters* table, and the *Settings* table. You also want your database to store information about the members of the Green Club. As a result,

you realize that this database template is not right for you yet. You recognize that you will need to learn more about how to modify existing databases to create additional tables or how to build your own database from scratch.

11. Close the *Event List* form by clicking the **X** in the right corner.

12. Close the database by clicking the **X** in the right corner of the application window.

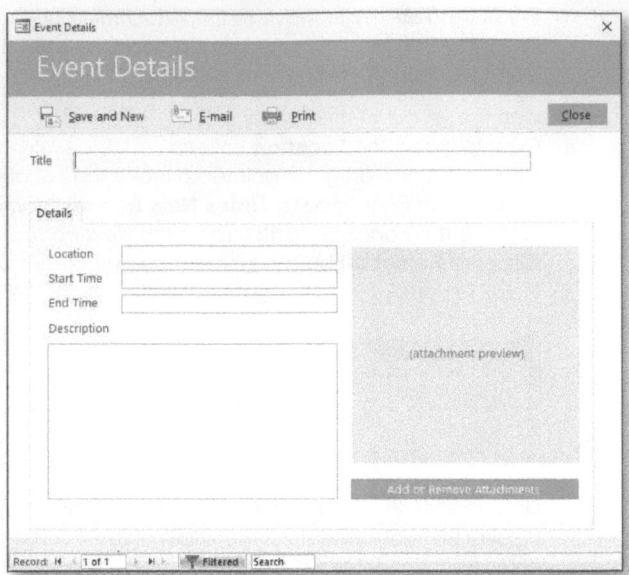

1-107 *Event Details* form

Guided Project 1-2

American River Cycling Club is a local cycling club. For this project, you create a database, containing one table, to store information about club members. After creating the database, add fields into the table, edit field properties, enter records, modify the datasheet layout, import data and sort and filter the data in the table.
[Student Learning Outcomes 1.2, 1.3, 1.4, 1.5, 1.6]

File Needed: *MembersDataFile-01.xlsx*
Completed Project File Name: *[your initials] Access 1-2.accdb*

Skills Covered in This Project

- Create a blank desktop database.
- Edit the default primary key.
- Add a new field into a table.
- Edit properties in *Datasheet* view.
- Save a table.
- Enter records.
- Change the datasheet layout.
- Import records.
- Sort data in a table.
- Filter data in a table.

1. Create a new, blank desktop database.
 a. Open Access or click the **New** button [*File* tab] if an Access database is already open.
 b. Click **Blank desktop database**.
 c. Enter [your initials] Access 1-2 in the *File Name* box.
 d. Click the **Browse** button to change the location in which to save your database and click **OK**.
 e. Click the **Create** button. The database is created. A new table is created and opens in *Datasheet* view. If a table does not display, click the **Table** button [*Create* tab, *Tables* group] to create a new table.

2. Edit the default primary key and add new fields into the table.
 a. Double-click the cell containing the **ID** field name (column header).
 b. Type MemberID in the *Field name* and press the **Enter** key. The *Click to Add* column to the right is selected so you can add the next field into the table.
 c. Select the **Short Text** data type for this new field.
 d. Type FirstName in the *Field1* column header and press the **Enter** key.
 e. Select the **Short Text** data type.
 f. Type LastName in the *Field1* column header and press the **Enter** key.
 g. Add the remaining fields into the table using the information in the nearby table. Remember that you select the data type first and then enter the field name. After you enter the last field name, *CellPhoneNumber*, press the **down arrow** key to remain in that column.

Data Type	Field Name
Short Text	Address
Short Text	City
Short Text	State
Short Text	ZIPCode
Hyperlink	EmailAddress
Short Text	CellPhoneNumber

 h. Press **Ctrl+S** to save all of the modifications you have made to the table.
 i. Type Members as the new table name.
 j. Click **OK**.
3. Edit the field properties of the *Members* table.
 a. Click the **MemberID** field name.
 b. Click the **Name & Caption** button [*Table Tools Fields* tab, *Properties* group].
 c. Type Member ID in the *Caption* property. Because the field names in this table provide a clear description of the content, it is not necessary to enter anything into the *Description* property.
 d. Click **OK**.
 e. Select the **FirstName** field name.
 f. Click the **Name & Caption** button [*Table Tools Fields* tab, *Properties* group].
 g. Type First Name in the *Caption* property.
 h. Click **OK**.
 i. Type 20 in the **Field Size** property [*Table Tools Fields* tab, *Properties* group].
 j. Change the remaining field properties in the table using the following information:

Field Name	Caption	Size
LastName	Last Name	25
Address		45
City		25
State		2
ZIPCode	ZIP	5
EmailAddress	Email	N/A
CellPhoneNumber	Cell Phone	12

k. Click the **Save** button to save the changes to the table. With the changes to the field properties saved, the table is ready for you to begin to enter data records. Remember that even though you have changed the caption that displays as the column header in *Datasheet* view, the field names have not changed.

4. Enter the member records into the *Members* table.
 a. Click the **FirstName** cell in the *append row*.
 b. Type Geneva. The Pencil icon displays, indicating that this record has not yet been saved.
 c. Press the **Tab** key to move to the next field.
 d. Type Lingle in the *LastName* field. Press the **Tab** key to move to the next field.
 e. Type 1850 Stoneridge Court in the *Address* field. Press the **Tab** key.
 f. Type Cameron Park in the *City* field. Press the **Tab** key.
 g. Type CA in the *State* field. Press the **Tab** key.
 h. Type 95682 in the *ZIPCode* field. Press the **Tab** key.
 i. Type glingle@gmail.com in the *EmailAddress* field. Press the **Tab** key.
 j. Type 780-886-6625 in the *CellPhoneNumber* field. Press the **Tab** key. The Pencil icon no longer displays. You move to the *MemberID* field in the *append row*.
 k. Tab to the next field. Enter the following information into the *Members* table. Remember that after you tab out of the *CellPhoneNumber* field you move to the *MemberID* field. Since that is an *AutoNumber* field, do not enter a value and simply tab to the next field.

FirstName	LastName	Address	City	State	ZIPCode	EmailAddress	CellPhoneNumber
Cheryl	Wilson	7105 High Street	Folsom	CA	95630	cwilson@mcc.com	916-451-8325
Ryan	Thomas	2227 Alexandra Drive	Auburn	CA	95602	rthomas@gmail.com	916-753-5586
Roy	Baxter	705 First Street	Rocklin	CA	95677	roy@centralsierra.com	780-886-2471

5. Change the layout of the *Members* table.
 a. Click to select the **ZIP** column.
 b. Right-click to open the context menu.
 c. Select **Field Width**.
 d. Type 7 in the **Column Width** cell.
 e. Click **OK** to close the dialog box.
 f. Click the **Center Alignment** button [*Home* tab, *Text Formatting* group].
 g. Click to select the **State** column.
 h. Place your pointer on the right border of the **State** field name.
 i. Double-click the **resize arrow** to adjust the *Field Width* using *AutoFit*.
 j. Click the **Center Alignment** button.
 k. Click the **Alternate Row Color** drop-down list [*Home* tab, *Text Formatting* group] and select **Blue-Gray, Text 2, Lighter 80%** (fourth column, second row in the *Theme Colors* category).
 l. Press **Ctrl+S** to save the changes to the layout.
 m. Close the *Members* table by clicking the **X** in the right corner.

6. Import data from Excel into the *Members* table.
 a. Click the **Excel** button [*External Data* tab, *Import & Link* group] to launch the *Get External Data – Excel Spreadsheet* dialog box.
 b. Click the **Browse** button to launch the *File Open* dialog box.
 c. Locate and select the ***MembersDataFile-01*** Excel file.
 d. Click the **Open** button. The *File Open* dialog box closes.

A1-59

e. Select the **Append a copy of the records to the table** radio button.
f. Click the **drop-down arrow** in the *table name* box and select the **Members** table if needed.
g. Click **OK** to launch the *Import Spreadsheet Wizard*. The data records should display in the *Import Spreadsheet Wizard* window.
h. Click the **Next** button to advance to the next page of the *Import Spreadsheet Wizard*.
i. Verify that the *Import to Table* box contains the *Members* table.
j. Click **Finish**.
k. Click the **Close** button.

7. Open the *Members* table in *Datasheet* view. Your table should contain the 14 records shown in Figure 1-108.

Member ID	First Name	Last Name	Address	City	State	ZIP	Email	Cell Phone
1	Geneva	Lingle	1850 Stonerid	Cameron Park	CA	95682	glingle@gmai	780-886-6625
2	Cheryl	Wilson	7105 High Str	Folsom	CA	95630	cwilson@mcc	916-451-8325
3	Ryan	Thomas	2227 Alexand	Auburn	CA	95602	rthomas@gm:	916-753-5586
4	Roy	Baxter	705 First Stree	Rocklin	CA	95677	roy@centralsi	780-886-2471
5	Margaret	Jepson	28861 Newca:	Fair Oaks	CA	95628	margaret@sai	780-862-9851
6	Rick	DePonte	8364 Marshall	Roseville	CA	95661	deponte@hot	916-450-3329
7	Melanie	Figueroa	4511 Johnson	Cameron Park	CA	95682	mfigueroa@p!	916-450-3336
8	Sue	Schooler	4183 Braxton	Rocklin	CA	95677	sschooler@gn	780-824-3525
9	Kelsey	Kroll	306 7th Street	Roseville	CA	95661	kkroll@hotma	780-886-2457
10	Rick	Hermenn	9035 Masi Dri	Fair Oaks	CA	95628	rickh@gmail.c	916-450-6719
11	Karen	Graves	6003 Ashland	Lincoln	CA	95648	kgraves@phre	916-450-3892
12	Robyn	Constantini	9581 Magnoli	Roseville	CA	95661	robyn@gmail.	780-886-2471
13	John	Burgess	85741 Auberr	Roseville	CA	95661	jburgess@hot	780-886-5862
14	Randy	Clemmins	7336 Lester R	Auburn	CA	95602	rclemmins@p!	916-450-3330
*	(New)							

Record: ◄ ◄ 1 of 14 ► ► ► ► No Filter Search

1-108 Members table after import

8. Sort the *Members* table.
a. Click the **drop-down arrow** to the right of the **City** field name.
b. Select **Sort A to Z** on the drop-down list. The records display in ascending order by the *City* field.
c. Click the **Remove Sort** button [*Home* tab, *Sort & Filter* group] to remove the sort criteria.
d. Click to select the **ZIP** column.
e. Click, hold, and drag the pointer to move the **ZIP** column to the left of the *Last Name* column.
f. Click anywhere to deselect the *ZIP* column.
g. Click and hold the pointer over the **ZIP** column. With the selection pointer still displayed, drag the pointer to the *Last Name* column. Release the pointer.
h. Click the **Ascending** button [*Home* tab, *Sort & Filter* group]. The records display in ascending order by the *ZIP* column. In cases of the same *ZIP* code, the records are sorted in ascending order by the last name. Your table should look similar to Figure 1-109.
i. Click the **Remove Sort** button [*Home* tab, *Sort & Filter* group] to remove the sort criteria.
j. Move the **ZIP** column to the right of the *State* column.

9. Filter the *Members* table using *Filter by Selection*.
a. Select **916** in the *Cell Phone* cell for *Member ID 2*.
b. Click the **Selection** button [*Home* tab, *Sort & Filter* group].
c. Select **Begins with "916"** from the drop-down list (Figure 1-110). The datasheet should display only the seven members who have a cell phone area code of 916.
d. Click the **drop-down arrow** to the right of the *Cell Phone* field name.
e. Select **Clear filter from Cell Phone** to remove the filter.

Sort indicator arrow

Member ID	First Name	ZIP	Last Name	Address
14	Randy	95602	Clemmins	7336 Lester R
3	Ryan	95602	Thomas	2227 Alexand
10	Rick	95628	Hermenn	9035 Masi Dri
5	Margaret	95628	Jepson	28861 Newca:
2	Cheryl	95630	Wilson	7105 High Str
11	Karen	95648	Graves	6003 Ashland

1-109 Records sorted on ZIP and Last Name

10. Filter the datasheet using a *Text Filter*.

 a. Click the **drop-down arrow** to the right of the *Email* field name.

 b. Select **Text Filters** on the drop-down list and select **Contains** from the second drop-down list (Figure 1-111). Notice in Figure 1-111 that the second drop-down list displays to the left. The exact position varies based on the width of your screen and location of the Access window.

 c. Type gmail in the *Email contains* box.

 d. Click **OK**. The datasheet should display only the five members who have *gmail* as part of their email addresses.

 e. Click the **Toggle Filter** button [*Home* tab, *Sort & Filter* group] to switch back to viewing all the records.

 f. Click the **Toggle Filter** button again to switch back to the filtered records.

 g. Click the **drop-down arrow** to the right of the *Email* field name.

 h. Select **Clear filter from Email** to remove the filter.

1-110 *Filter by Selection*

1-111 *Text Filter*

11. Close the *Members* table by clicking the **X** in the right corner. Select the **No** button in the dialog box. Do *not* save any of the changes made to the table.

12. Review the completed *Members* table.

 a. Double-click the **Members** table to view the table. The table should be similar to Figure 1-112. Note that the sorting and filtering changes were not saved.

 b. Close the table by clicking the **X** in the right corner.

Member ID ⁃	First Name ⁃	Last Name ⁃	Address ⁃	City ⁃	State ⁃	ZIP ⁃	Email ⁃	Cell Phone ⁃
1	Geneva	Lingle	1850 Stonerid;	Cameron Park	CA	95682	glingle@gmai	780-886-6625
2	Cheryl	Wilson	7105 High Stre	Folsom	CA	95630	cwilson@mcc.	916-451-8325
3	Ryan	Thomas	2227 Alexandr	Auburn	CA	95602	rthomas@gma	916-753-5586
4	Roy	Baxter	705 First Stree	Rocklin	CA	95677	roy@centralsi	780-886-2471
5	Margaret	Jepson	28861 Newcas	Fair Oaks	CA	95628	margaret@sac	780-862-9851
6	Rick	DePonte	8364 Marshall	Roseville	CA	95661	deponte@hotr	916-450-3329
7	Melanie	Figueroa	4511 Johnson	Cameron Park	CA	95682	mfigueroa@pl	916-450-3336
8	Sue	Schooler	4183 Braxton	Rocklin	CA	95677	sschooler@gn	780-824-3525
9	Kelsey	Kroll	306 7th Street	Roseville	CA	95661	kkroll@hotma	780-886-2457
10	Rick	Hermenn	9035 Masi Dri	Fair Oaks	CA	95628	rickh@gmail.c	916-450-6719
11	Karen	Graves	6003 Ashland	Lincoln	CA	95648	kgraves@phre	916-450-3892
12	Robyn	Constantini	9581 Magnoli;	Roseville	CA	95661	robyn@gmail.	780-886-2471
13	John	Burgess	85741 Auberr	Roseville	CA	95661	jburgess@hot	780-886-5862
14	Randy	Clemmins	7336 Lester Rı	Auburn	CA	95602	rclemmins@pl	916-450-3330
*	(New)							

Record: I◄ ◄ 1 of 14 ► ►I ►► No Filter Search

1-112 **Completed** *Members* table

13. Add database properties using the *Database Properties* dialog box.
 a. Click the **File** tab to open the *Backstage* view. The **Info** button should be selected.
 b. Click the **View and Edit Database Properties** link to open the *Database Properties* dialog box.
 c. Type American River Members in the *Title* area.
 d. Type Taylor Mathos in the *Author* area.
 e. Type ARCC in the *Company* area.
 f. Click **OK** to save the changes.

14. Close the database by clicking the **X** in the right corner of the application window.

Guided Project 1-3

San Diego Sailing Club is a local sailing club with a fleet of sailboats that members can rent. For this project, you create a database, containing one table, to store information about rental sailboats. After creating the database, you add fields to the table, edit field properties, enter records, import data, modify the datasheet layout, and filter the data in the table.
[Student Learning Outcomes 1.2, 1.3, 1.4, 1.5, 1.6]

File Needed: *SailboatDataFile-01.xlsx*
Completed Project File Name: *[your initials] Access 1-3.accdb*

Skills Covered in This Project

- Create a blank desktop database.
- Edit the default primary key.
- Add a new field into a table.
- Edit properties in *Datasheet* view.

- Save a table.
- Enter records.
- Change the datasheet layout.
- Import records.
- Filter data in a table.

1. Create a new, blank desktop database.
 a. Open Access or click the **New** button [*File* tab] if an Access database is already open.
 b. Click **Blank desktop database**.
 c. Enter [your initials] Access 1-3 in the *File Name* box.
 d. Click the **Browse** button to change the location in which to save your database and click **OK**.
 e. Click the **Create** button. The database is created. A new table is created and opens in *Datasheet* view.

2. Edit the default primary key and add new fields into the table.
 a. Double-click the cell containing the **ID** field name (column header).
 b. Type BoatID in the *Field name*.
 c. Press the **down arrow** key to update the field name and stay in the same column.
 d. Click the **Short Text** data type [*Table Tools Fields* tab, *Formatting* group]. Because the boats already have an ID number assigned to them, do not use the *AutoNumber* data type in Access.
 e. Click the **Click to Add** column header.
 f. Select the **Short Text** data type.
 g. Type BoatType in the *Field name* column header and press the **Enter** key.
 h. Select the **Short Text** data type.
 i. Type Length in the *Field name* column header and press the **Enter** key.

j. Enter the remaining fields into the table using the following information. Remember that you select the data type first and then enter the field name. After you enter the last field name, *ModelYear*, press the **down arrow** key to remain in that column.

Data Type	Field Name
Number	Seats
Number	Sleeps
Currency	FourHourRentalRate
Currency	FullDayRentalRate
Yes/No	GalleyWithStove
Short Text	ModelYear

k. Press **Ctrl+S** to save all of the modifications you have made to the table.
l. Type SailboatFleet as the new table name.
m. Click **OK**.

3. Edit the field properties of the *SailboatFleet* table.
 a. Click the **BoatID** field name.
 b. Select the **Name & Caption** button [*Table Tools Fields* tab, *Properties* group].
 c. Type Boat ID in the *Caption* property. Because all of the field names in this table provide a clear description of their content, it is not necessary to enter any additional information in the *Description* property.
 d. Click **OK**.
 e. Type 4 in the *Field Size* property [*Table Tools Fields* tab, *Properties* group].
 f. Select the **BoatType** field name.
 g. Click the **Name & Caption** button [*Table Tools Fields* tab, *Properties* group].
 h. Type Boat Type in the *Caption* property.
 i. Click **OK**.
 j. Type 25 in the *Field Size* property [*Table Tools Fields* tab, *Properties* group].
 k. Change the remaining field properties using the following information:

Field Name	Caption	Size
Length		8
Seats		N/A
Sleeps		N/A
FourHourRentalRate	4 Hr Rate	N/A
FullDayRentalRate	Full Day Rate	N/A
GalleyWithStove	Galley w/ Stove	N/A
ModelYear	Model Year	4

 l. Click the **Save** button to save the changes to the table. With the changes to the field properties saved, the table is ready for you to begin to enter data records.

4. Enter the data records into the *SailboatFleet* table.
 a. Click the **BoatID** field cell in the *append row*.
 b. Type 1150. The Pencil icon displays, indicating that this record has not yet been saved.

c. Press the **Tab** key to move to the next field.
d. Type Capri 22 Mk II in the *BoatType* field. Press the **Tab** key to move to the next field.
e. Type 24'8" in the *Length* field. Press the **Tab** key to move to the next field.
f. Type 6 in the *Seats* field. Press the **Tab** key to move to the next field.
g. Type 4 in the *Sleeps* field. Press the **Tab** key to move to the next field.
h. Type 65 in the *FourHourRate* field. Press the **Tab** key to move to the next field.
i. Type 89 in the *FullDayRate* field. Press the **Tab** key to move to the next field.
j. Leave the check box blank in the *GalleyWithStove* field. Press the **Tab** key to move to the next field.
k. Type 2004 in the *ModelYear* field. Press the **Tab** key to move to the next record. The Pencil icon no longer displays.
l. Continue entering the remaining records into the table using the following information. Click the **GalleyWithStove** field check box to indicate a "Y" value.

BoatID	BoatType	Length	Seats	Sleeps	4 Hr Rate	Full Day Rate	GalleyWith Stove	Model Year
1010	Catalina 270	28'4"	8	6	139	179	Y	1997
1146	Hunter 33	33'6"	10	6	299	349	Y	2003
1015	Catalina 270	28'4"	8	6	139	179	Y	1998
1185	Hunter 36	35'6"	10	6	349	389	Y	2009

m. Press **Ctrl+S** to save the table.
n. Close the *SailboatFleet* table by clicking the **X** in the right corner.

5. Import data from Excel into the *SailboatFleet* table.
 a. Click the **Excel** button [*External Data* tab, *Import & Link* group] to launch the *Get External Data – Excel Spreadsheet* dialog box.
 b. Click the **Browse** button to launch the *File Open* dialog box.
 c. Locate and select the **SailboatDataFile-01** Excel file.
 d. Click the **Open** button. The *File Open* dialog box closes.
 e. Select the **Append a copy of the records to the table** radio button.
 f. Click the **drop-down arrow** in the *Table Name* box and select the **SailboatFleet** table if needed.
 g. Click **OK** to launch the *Import Spreadsheet Wizard*. The data records should display in the *Wizard* window.
 h. Click the **Next** button to advance to the next page of the *Import Spreadsheet Wizard*.
 i. Verify that the *Import to Table* box contains the *SailboatFleet* table.
 j. Click **Finish**.
 k. Click the **Close** button.

6. Open the *SailboatFleet* table in *Datasheet* view. Your table should have the 19 records as shown in Figure 1-113.

7. Change the layout of the *Sailboat Fleet* table.
 a. Change the *Font Face* to **Times New Roman** [*Home* tab, *Text Formatting* group].
 b. Change the *Font Size* to **12** [*Home* tab, *Text Formatting* group].
 c. Click and hold to select the **Length** column.
 d. Drag the selection pointer to select the *Seats* and *Sleeps* columns.
 e. Place your pointer on the right border of the **Sleeps** field.
 f. Double-click to adjust the *Field Width* using *AutoFit*.
 g. Select the **BoatType** field.
 h. Place your pointer on the right border of the *BoatType* field. The cursor changes to the resize arrow.

1-113 *SailboatFleet* table records after import

i. Click, hold, and drag the pointer to the right to increase the width of the *BoatType* field so that you can see the entire data value in the *BoatType* column.

j. Select the **Boat ID** field.

k. Click the **Center Alignment** button [*Home* tab, *Text Formatting* group].

l. Select the **Length** field.

m. Click the **Center Alignment** button.

n. Click anywhere to deselect the column.

o. Open the *Datasheet Formatting* dialog box (Figure 1-114) by clicking the **launcher** in the bottom right corner of the *Text Formatting* group [*Home* tab].

p. Click the **Alternate Background Color** drop-down list in the *Datasheet Formatting* dialog box and select **Green, Accent 6, Lighter 80%** (tenth column, second row in the *Theme Colors* category).

q. Click the **Gridline Color** drop-down list and select **Green, Accent 6, Darker 25%** (tenth column, fifth row in the *Theme Colors* category).

r. Click **OK** to close the dialog box.

s. Press **Ctrl+S** to save the changes to the layout. The updated layout should look similar to Figure 1-115.

1-114 *Datasheet Formatting* dialog box

1-115 Formatted datasheet layout

A1-65

8. Filter the *SailboatFleet* table using compound criteria and sort the filtered results.
 a. Click the **drop-down arrow** to the right of the *Seats* field name.
 b. Select **Number Filters** on the drop-down list and select **Greater Than** from the second drop-down list (Figure 1-116).
 c. Type 8 in the *Seats is greater than or equal to* box.
 d. Click **OK**. The datasheet should display only the 15 boats that can seat at least eight people.
 e. Click the **drop-down arrow** to the right of the *4 Hr Rate* field name.
 f. Select the **Number Filters** on the drop-down list and select **Less Than** from the second drop-down list.
 g. Type 350 in the *4 Hr Rate is less than or equal to* box.
 h. Click **OK**. The datasheet should display only the 8 boats that can seat at least eight people and have a four-hour rate of less than or equal to $350.
 i. Click to select the **Length** column.
 j. Click the **Ascending** button [*Home* tab, *Sort & Filter* group] to sort the filtered results by the *Length* field. In Figure 1-117, notice the filter symbols next to the field names of the *Seats* and *4 Hr Rate* fields and the *Sort symbol* next to the *Length* field name.

1-116 *Number Filters*

1-117 *Filtered and sorted records*

 k. Click the **Toggle Filter** button [*Home* tab, *Sort & Filter* group] to switch back to the unfiltered records. Notice that the records remain sorted.
 l. Click the **Remove Sort** button [*Home* tab, *Sort & Filter* group] to remove the sort criteria.
 m. Click the **Advanced** button [*Home* tab, *Sort & Filter* group] and select the **Clear All Filters** button. The datasheet should update to show all the records.

9. Close the *SailboatFleet* table by clicking the **X** in the right corner.

10. Click the **No** button in the dialog box. You do not need to save any of the changes as a result of sorting or filtering the table.

11. Close the *San Diego Sailing* database by clicking the **X** in the right corner of the application window.

Independent Project 1-4

Courtyard Medical Plaza (CMP) is a full-service medical office complex. For this project, you create a database, containing one table, to store information about the physicians who work at CMP. After creating the database, you add fields into the table, edit field properties, enter records, import data, modify the datasheet layout, and sort and filter the data in the table.
[Student Learning Outcomes 1.2, 1.3, 1.4, 1.5, 1.6]

File Needed: *PhysiciansDataFile-01.xlsx*
Completed Project Fle Name: *[your initials] Access 1-4.accdb*

Skills Covered in This Project

- Create a blank desktop database.
- Edit the default primary key.
- Add a new field into a table.
- Edit properties in *Datasheet* view.

- Save a table.
- Enter records.
- Import records.
- Change the datasheet layout.
- Sort data in a table.
- Filter data in a table.

1. Create a new, blank desktop database.
 a. Name the database [your initials] Access 1-4.
 b. Change the location where you save the database.

2. Edit the default primary key and add new fields into the table.
 a. Change the **ID** field name to DoctorID. Keep this field as an *AutoNumber* data type.
 b. Enter the remaining fields into the table using the information in the following *Data Type* table. After you enter the last field name, *MoveInDate*, press the **down arrow** key to remain in that column.

Data Type	Field Name
Short Text	LastName
Short Text	FirstName
Short Text	OfficeNumber
Short Text	PrimarySpecialty
Date & Time	MoveInDate

 c. Save the table as Physicians.

3. Edit the field properties of the *Physicians* table using the information in the following *Field Name* table:

Field Name	Caption	Size
DoctorID	Doctor ID	N/A
LastName	Last Name	25
FirstName	First Name	20
OfficeNumber	Office	3
PrimarySpecialty	Specialty	30
MoveInDate	Tenant Since	N/A

4. Save the table after updating the properties.

5. Enter the data records shown in the following table into the *Physicians* table. Remember that the *DoctorID* field is automatically entered by Access.

Last Name	First Name	Office Number	Specialty	Move-In Date
Beyer	Robert	101	Cardiovascular Disease	2/15/2012
Scher	Elizabeth	115	Pediatrics	4/1/2014
Ostrander	Emy	101	Cardiovascular Disease	11/8/2014
Foster	Margaret	200	Pediatrics	7/1/2005

6. Save and close the *Physicians* table.

7. Import the remaining data records from Excel into the *Physicians* table.
 a. Launch the *Get External Data–Excel Spreadsheet* dialog box.
 b. Locate and select the **PhysiciansDataFile-01** Excel file.
 c. Append the records to the *Physicians* table.
 d. Launch the *Import Spreadsheet Wizard*.
 e. Finish the **Import Spreadsheet Wizard**. Close the **Wizard** after the records have imported.

8. Open the *Physicians* table in *Datasheet* view. Your table should contain 16 records.

9. Change the layout of the *Physicians* table.
 a. Change the *Font Size* to **12**.
 b. Use *AutoFit* to increase the field width of the *Specialty* field.
 c. Use *AutoFit* to increase the field width of the *Tenant Since* field.
 d. **Center-align** the *Doctor ID, Office,* and *Tenant Since* fields.
 e. Change the *Alteçrnate Row Color* to **Blue, Accent 1, Lighter 60%** (fifth column, third row in the *Theme Colors* category).
 f. Save the changes to the layout.

10. Sort the *Physicians* table in ascending order by the *Specialty* field.

11. Remove the sort criteria.

12. Filter the *Physicians* table to find the doctors who moved in on or after 1/1/2010 and who have a specialty in Pediatrics. The table should look similar to Figure 1-118.

13. Clear all the filters. The datasheet updates to show all the records.

14. Close the *Physicians* table.

15. Do not save any of the changes as a result of sorting or filtering the table.

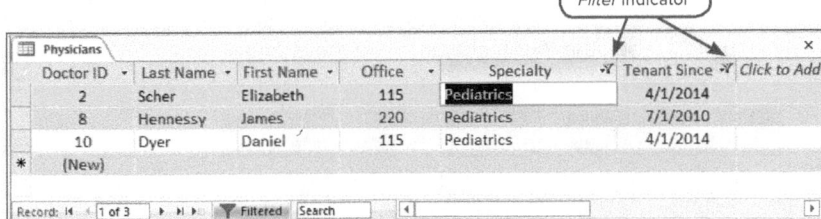

1-118 Records filtered on *Specialty* and *Tenant Since*

16. Add the following database properties.
 a. *Title*: Courtyard Medical Plaza Physicians
 b. *Author*: Caroline Rios
 c. *Company*: CMP
 d. Click **OK** to save the changes.

17. Close the database.

Independent Project 1-5

Life's Animal Shelter (LAS) is an animal adoption agency that strives to keep its expenses down and donations up and is mainly run by volunteers. LAS does not turn any animal away, and its goal is to find homes for all animals within six months of their arrival. Julie Freed, one of the volunteers, has begun building a database for LAS. For this project, you work with her database, which currently has one table that contains information about the pets currently at LAS. Add one field into the table, edit field properties, enter data into records, modify the datasheet layout, and sort and filter the data in the table.
[Student Learning Outcomes 1.1, 1.2, 1.3, 1.4, 1.5]

File Needed: *LifesAnimalShelter-01.accdb*
Completed Project File Name: *[your initials] Access 1-5.accdb*

Skills Covered in This Project

- Open an existing database.
- Use the *Navigation Pane*.
- Edit field properties in *Datasheet* view.
- Add a new field into a table.

- Save a table.
- Enter records.
- Change the datasheet layout.
- Sort data in a table.
- Filter data in a table.

1. Open the *LifesAnimalShelter-01* database from your student data files.

2. Save a new copy of your database.
 a. Select the **Save As** button [*File tab*]. The **Access Database** button should be selected in the *Save Database As* area.
 b. Click the **Save As** button.
 c. Select the desired location in which to store the copy of your database.
 d. Type [your initials] Access 1-5 in the *File name* box.
 e. Click the **Save** button.

3. Enable content in the security warning.

4. Open the *Navigation Pane*.

5. Open the *Pets* table in *Datasheet* view.

6. Edit the field properties of the *Pets* table using the information in the following table.
 For several of the fields you see a *Some data may be lost* warning message display when you change the field size. The sizes provided are large enough based on the data entered, so no data will be lost. Click the **Yes** button to make the change.

Field Name	Caption	Size
ID	Pet ID	N/A
PetName	Pet Name	15
Type		10
Breed		40
Age		8
Gender		1
Details	Why I'd make a great companion	N/A

7. Save the table after updating the properties.

8. Add a new field, to the left of the *Details* field. Remember that the field name is still *Details* even though the caption is changed to *Why I'd make a great companion*.
 a. Select the **Details** column.
 b. Right-click to open the context menu.
 c. Select **Insert Field**.

9. Edit the field properties using the following information:
 a. *Field Name*: Color
 b. *Data Type*: **Short Text**
 c. *Size*: 25

10. Save the table after updating the properties of this new field.

11. Enter the data values shown in the following table into the *Color* field.

Pet ID	Pet Name	Color
1	Abby	Black
2	Alec	Tan
3	Allie	Brown
4	Barnaby	White
5	Lilith	Black/White
6	Martin	Brown Tabby/White
7	Sasha	Tan/White
8	Tate	Black/White
9	Elsa	White/Brown
10	Hubert	White/Brown
11	Bessie	Black/White
12	Connie	Tortoise Shell
13	Topaz	Brown Tabby
14	Lady	Black Brindle/White
15	Ashley	White/Brown

12. Change the layout of the *Pets* table.
 a. Use *AutoFit* to decrease the field width of the *Pet ID, Type, Age*, and *Gender* fields.
 b. **Center-align** the *Pet ID* and *Gender* fields.
 c. Change the *Alternate Row Color* to **Gray-25%, Background 2, Darker 10%** (third column, second row in the *Theme Colors* category).
 d. Set the *Field Width* of the Details field to 60.
 e. Set the *Row Height* of the table to 110.
 f. Save the changes to the layout.

13. Filter the *Pets* table to find the **Dogs** and **Cats** with **Brown** as part of their coloring. The resulting table should look similar to Figure 1-119. Your records may display in a different order.

14. Sort the filtered results in ascending order by the *Gender* field.

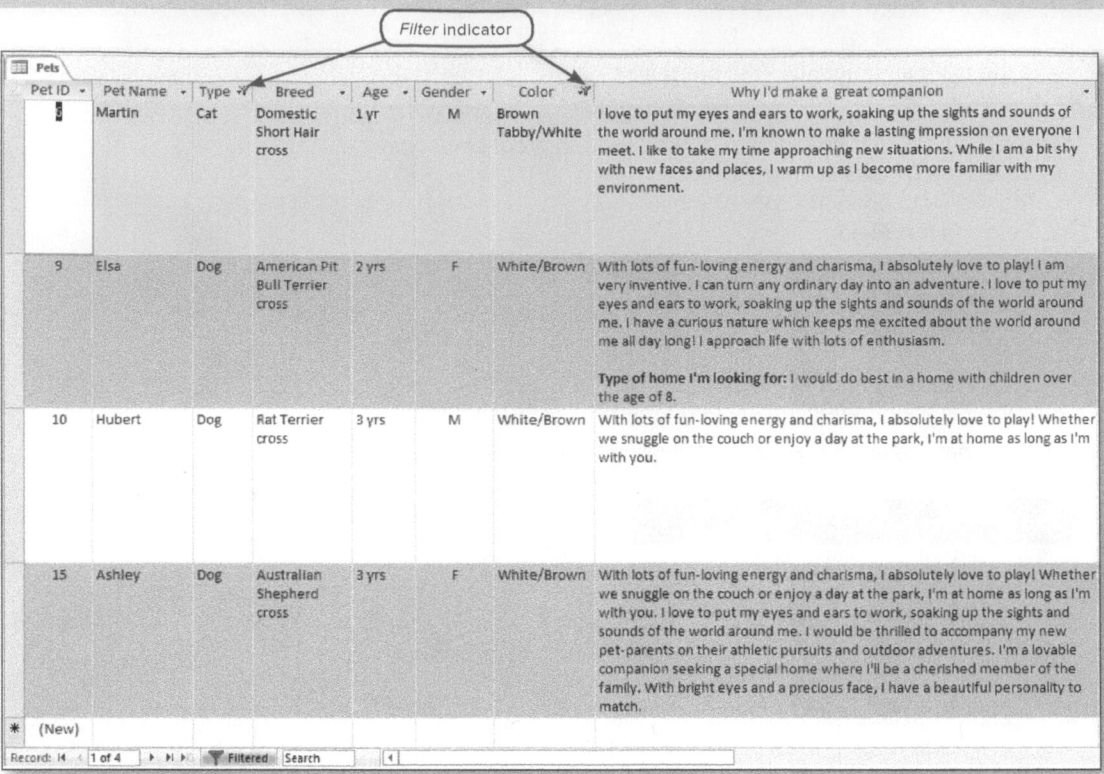

Filter indicator

Pets							
Pet ID	Pet Name	Type	Breed	Age	Gender	Color	Why I'd make a great companion
1	Martin	Cat	Domestic Short Hair cross	1 yr	M	Brown Tabby/White	I love to put my eyes and ears to work, soaking up the sights and sounds of the world around me. I'm known to make a lasting impression on everyone I meet. I like to take my time approaching new situations. While I am a bit shy with new faces and places, I warm up as I become more familiar with my environment.
9	Elsa	Dog	American Pit Bull Terrier cross	2 yrs	F	White/Brown	With lots of fun-loving energy and charisma, I absolutely love to play! I am very inventive. I can turn any ordinary day into an adventure. I love to put my eyes and ears to work, soaking up the sights and sounds of the world around me. I have a curious nature which keeps me excited about the world around me all day long! I approach life with lots of enthusiasm. **Type of home I'm looking for:** I would do best in a home with children over the age of 8.
10	Hubert	Dog	Rat Terrier cross	3 yrs	M	White/Brown	With lots of fun-loving energy and charisma, I absolutely love to play! Whether we snuggle on the couch or enjoy a day at the park, I'm at home as long as I'm with you.
15	Ashley	Dog	Australian Shepherd cross	3 yrs	F	White/Brown	With lots of fun-loving energy and charisma, I absolutely love to play! Whether we snuggle on the couch or enjoy a day at the park, I'm at home as long as I'm with you. I love to put my eyes and ears to work, soaking up the sights and sounds of the world around me. I would be thrilled to accompany my new pet-parents on their athletic pursuits and outdoor adventures. I'm a lovable companion seeking a special home where I'll be a cherished member of the family. With bright eyes and a precious face, I have a beautiful personality to match.
*	(New)						

Record: 1 of 4 ▶ ▶▶ Filtered Search

1-119 Records filtered on *Type* and *Color*

15. Remove the sort criteria. Clear all the filters. The datasheet will update to show all the records.

16. Close the *Pets* table.

17. Do not save any of the changes as a result of sorting or filtering the table.

18. Add the following database properties.
 a. *Company*: LAS
 b. *Author*: Student Name
 c. *Comments*: Pets table updated on [enter today's date]
 d. Click **OK** to save the changes.

19. Close the database.

Independent Project 1-6

Boyd Air is a national airline company. For this project, you will create a database, containing one table, to store information about the airplanes in Boyd Air's fleet. After creating the database, add fields into the table, edit field properties, import data, modify the datasheet layout, and find data using the *Search* box. [Student Learning Outcomes 1.2, 1.3, 1.4, 1.5, 1.6]

File Needed: **AirplaneDataFile-01.xlsx**
Completed Project File Name: **[your initials] Access 1-6.accdb**

Skills Covered in This Project

- Create a blank desktop database.
- Edit the default primary key.
- Add new fields into a table.
- Edit properties in *Datasheet* view.
- Save a table.
- Import records.
- Change the datasheet layout.
- Sort data in a table.
- Find data using the *Search* box.

1. Create a new, blank desktop database.
 a. Name the database [your initials] Access 1-6.
 b. Change the location to save your database.

2. Add new fields into the table.
 a. Do not make any changes to the *ID* field.
 b. Enter the remaining fields into the table using the information in the following table. After you enter the last field name, *InServiceDate*, press the **down arrow** key to remain in that column.

Data Type	Field Name
Short Text	PlaneModel
Short Text	Manufacturer
Short Text	Length
Number	FirstClassSeats
Number	CoachSeats
Date & Time	InServiceDate

 c. Save the table as Fleet.

3. Edit the field properties of the *Fleet* table using the information in the following table.

Field Name	Caption	Size
ID	Aircraft ID	N/A
PlaneModel	Model	25
Manufacturer		20
Length		7
FirstClassSeats	First Class	N/A
CoachSeats	Coach	N/A
InServiceDate	In-Service	N/A

4. Save and close the table after updating the properties.

5. Import data from Excel into the *Fleet* table.
 a. Launch the *Get External Data – Excel Spreadsheet* dialog box.
 b. Locate and select the **AirplaneDataFile-01** Excel file.
 c. Append the records to the *Fleet* table.
 d. Launch the *Import Spreadsheet Wizard*.
 e. Finish the *Import Spreadsheet Wizard*. Close the *Wizard* after the records have imported.

6. Open the *Fleet* table in *Datasheet* view. Your table should contain 17 records.

7. Change the layout of the *Fleet* table.
 a. Change the *Font Size* to **12**.
 b. Select the entire datasheet and use *AutoFit* to adjust all the fields to their correct size.
 c. **Center-align** the *Aircraft ID, First Class*, and *Coach* fields.
 d. Remove the gridlines.
 e. Save the changes to the layout.

8. Sort the *Fleet* table in descending (newest to oldest) order according to the *In-Service* field. The table should look similar to Figure 1-120.

1-120 Records sorted on *In-Service* field

9. Remove the sort criteria.

10. Use the *Search box* to find Dash8.

11. Delete the value from the *Search* box.

12. Close the *Fleet* table.

13. Do not save any of the changes as a result of sorting or filtering the table.

14. Add the following database properties.
 a. *Title*: Boyd Air Fleet Data
 b. *Author*: Marcus Sampson
 c. *Company*: Boyd Air
 d. Click **OK** to save the changes.

15. Close the database.

Improve It Project 1-7

Placer Hills Real Estate (PHRE) is a real estate company with regional offices throughout central California. Kelsey Kroll, one of the managers, began building a database. The database has one table that contains information about the real estate properties currently listed for sale. You add one field into the table, edit field properties, enter data into records, modify the datasheet layout, and sort and filter the data in the table. [Student Learning Outcomes 1.1, 1.2, 1.3, 1.4, 1.5]

File Needed: **PlacerHills-01.accdb**
Completed Project File Name: **[your initials] Access 1-7.accdb**

Skills Covered in This Project

- Open a database.
- Use the *Navigation Pane*.
- Edit the default primary key.
- Add a new field into a table.

- Edit properties in *Datasheet* view.
- Save a table.
- Enter records.
- Change the datasheet layout.
- Sort data in a table.
- Filter data in a table.

1. Open the **PlacerHills-01** database from your student data files.

2. Save a new copy of your database.
 a. Select the **Save As** button [*File tab*]. The **Access Database** button should be selected in the *Save Database As* area.
 b. Click the **Save As** button.
 c. Select the desired location in which to store the copy of your database.
 d. Type [your initials] Access 1-7 in the *File name* box.
 e. Click the **Save** button.

3. Enable content in the security warning.

4. Open the *Navigation Pane*.

5. Open the *Listings* table in *Datasheet* view.

6. Edit the field properties of the *Listings* table using the information in the following table.

For several of the fields, you see a *Some data may be lost* warning message when you change the field size. Because the new field sizes are sufficient for the existing data, click the **Yes** button to continue.

Field Name	Caption	Size
ListingID		N/A
DateListed	Date Listed	N/A
ListPrice	List Price	N/A
Address		35
City		20
SqFt		N/A
Beds		N/A
Baths		N/A
Garage		18
YearBuilt	Built	N/A
ListingAgent	Agent	25

7. Save the table after updating the properties.

8. Add a new field, to the left of the *Agent* field.

9. Edit the field properties using the following information:
 a. *Field Name*: Construction
 b. *Data Type*: Short Text
 c. *Size*: 5

10. Save the table after updating the properties.

11. Enter the data values shown in the following table into the new *Construction* field.

ListingID	Construction
10022	Frame
10023	Stone
10024	Brick
10027	Stone
10030	Stone
10031	Brick
10040	Frame
10042	Brick
10043	Stone
10044	Brick
10045	Brick
10046	Brick
10048	Frame
10052	Brick
10053	Frame
10054	Stone

12. Change the layout of the *Listings* table.
 a. Change the *Font Size* to **12**.
 b. Select the entire datasheet and use *AutoFit* to adjust all the fields to their correct size. Remember that if the width of the Access window was not wide enough, some of the columns may still be too small. You can adjust the width of those columns individually.
 c. **Center-align** the *SqFt, Beds, Baths, Built*, and *Construction* fields.
 d. Change the gridline color to **Green 5** (seventh column, sixth row in the *Standard Colors* category).
 e. Set the row height of the table to 16.
 f. Save the changes to the layout.

13. Add the following database properties and save the changes:
 a. *Company*: PHRE
 b. *Comments*: Listings table updated [enter today's date]
 c. Click **OK** to save the changes.

14. Sort the *Listings* table in descending order by the *List Price* field. *ListingID 10024* should be at the top of the datasheet and *ListingID 10053* should be at the bottom of the datasheet.

15. Remove the sort criteria.

16. Filter the *Listings* table to find the listings of homes that are at least 2000 square feet, have 3 or 4 bathrooms, and are brick construction.

17. Sort the filtered results in ascending order by the *List Price* field. Your datasheet should look similar to Figure 1-121.

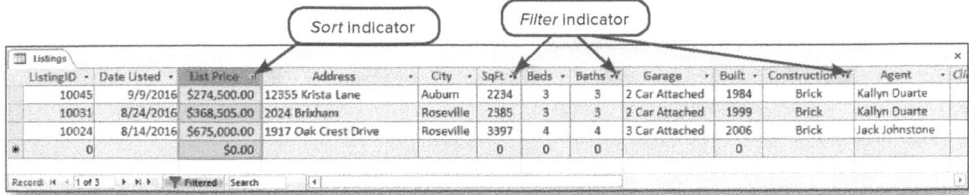

1-121 Records sorted on *List Price*

18. Remove the sort criteria.

19. Clear all the filters. The datasheet updates to show all the records.

20. Close the *Listings* table. Do not save any of the changes as a result of sorting or filtering the table.

21. Close the database.

Challenge Project 1-8

Create a database for an organization to which you belong. Add the necessary fields into the table. Be sure to edit the field properties as needed. Enter several rows of data into the table. Ensure that the datasheet layout is easy to read.
[Student Learning Outcomes 1.2, 1.3, 1.4, 1.5]

File Needed: None
Completed Project File Name: *[your initials] Access 1-8.accdb*

Create a new database and save it as [your initials] Access 1-8. Modify your database according to the following guidelines:

- Enter at least five fields into the table.
- Save the table.
- Edit the field properties to match the needs of the database.
- Enter several records into the table.
- Change the layout as desired to create a professional-looking layout.
- Sort the records by one of the fields.

Challenge Project 1-9

Create a database for a small bakery. The database should contain one table to store information about the different items sold by the bakery. Be sure to include a table field to store the item category. Examples of the content for the item categories might include cupcakes, cakes, pies, cookies, and candy. Create the table by adding fields and modifying properties. Enter data into the table. Ensure that the datasheet layout is easy to read.
[Student Learning Outcomes 1.2, 1.3, 1.4, 1.5]

File Needed: None
Completed Project File Name: *[your initials] Access 1-9.accdb*

Create a new database and save it as [your initials] Access 1-9. Modify your database according to the following guidelines:

* Add the following fields into the table: ItemID, ItemName, CostToMake, Mark-UpPercentage, and ItemCategory.
* The *ItemID* should use an *AutoNumber* data type. Select appropriate data types for the other fields.
* Save the table.
* Edit the field properties to match the needs of the database.
* Enter several records into the table.
* Change the layout as desired to create a professional-looking layout.
* Find a record where the category is *Cupcakes*, using the *Search* box.
* Use the *Filter by Selection* to find all the records for which the category is *Cupcakes*.

Challenge Project 1-10

Create a database for a travel agency. The database should contain one table to store information about upcoming cruises. Create the table by adding fields and modifying properties. Enter data into the table. Ensure that the datasheet layout is easy to read.
[Student Learning Outcomes 1.2, 1.3, 1.4, 1.5]

File Needed: None
Completed Project File Name: *[your initials] Access 1-10.accdb*

Create a new database and save it as [your initials] Access 1-10. Modify your database according to the following guidelines:

* Add the following fields to the table: TripID, TripName, NumberOfDays, DepartureCity, DestinationCity, DepartureDate, and CostPerPerson.
* The *TripID* should use an *AutoNumber* data type. Select appropriate data types for the other fields.
* Save the table as *Trips*.
* Edit the field properties, like *Field Size*, to match the needs of the database.
* Enter several records into the table for trips of various lengths. Search the web if you need help finding examples of data to enter.
* Change the layout as desired to create a professional-looking layout.
* Create a filter using compound criteria to locate all cruises that leave from a select city and have the same trip length.

Using Design View, Data Validation, and Relationships

CHAPTER OVERVIEW

In Chapter 1 you learned to use *Datasheet* view to create and view tables. Many database designers prefer to create tables in *Design* view because it is easier to change the various field and table properties. Additionally, some database properties can only be changed using *Design* view. This chapter covers the basics of creating a table in *Design* view, using data validation rules to ensure your data is valid, and creating relationships among different tables in a database.

STUDENT LEARNING OUTCOMES (SLOs)

After completing this chapter, you will be able to:

SLO 2.1 Create a table in *Design* view; add new fields; define a primary key; delete fields; save, close and open a table; and switch between *Datasheet* and *Design* views (p. A2-79).

SLO 2.2 Set field properties including *Field Size, Format, Caption, Default Value,* and *Required* (p. A2-83).

SLO 2.3 Explain data integrity and data validation concepts and options (p. A2-90).

SLO 2.4 Create field and record validation rules, test rules, create validation text, create lookup fields and define an input mask (p. A2-91).

SLO 2.5 Change field properties after records are added into a table (p. A2-104).

SLO 2.6 Explain relational database principles, understand the steps that must be taken to design a database, create relationships between tables, implement referential integrity, and delete and edit relationships (p. A2-110).

SLO 2.7 Preview and print the contents of a table (p. A2-120).

SLO 2.8 Manage a database using the *Compact & Repair Database* utility (p. A2-122).

Case Study

Mary's Rentals is a privately owned equipment rental company. For the Pause & Practice projects in this chapter, you develop a database that contains information about the company's products. As you progress through the chapter, you incorporate many of the skills you are learning to construct and enhance this database.

Pause & Practice 2-1: Create a new blank database. Customize the table using *Design*

view to store equipment information. Add new fields, define the primary key, edit field properties, and save the table.

Pause & Practice 2-2: Refine your equipment table design by adding a field validation rule and a table validation rule, adding validation text, testing the validation rules, creating a lookup field, and defining an input mask.

Pause & Practice 2-3: Add a second table to store the service history of the equipment. Define a relationship between the equipment and service history tables. Print the contents of the equipment table. Use the *Compact & Repair Database* utility to manage the database.

SLO 2.1

Creating a Table in Design View

Design view is used to create a table from scratch. When creating the table you define the fields that are included in the table and set their properties. You can also make changes to the fields in an existing table using *Design* view. This section teaches you to create a table in *Design* view, add new fields, define a primary key, delete fields, and save a table.

Create a New Table in Design View

You can add a new table into a database from the *Create* tab. Tables created using the **Table Design** button automatically open in *Design* view.

> **HOW TO: Create a New Table in Design View**

1. Click the **Create** tab on the *Ribbon*.
2. Click the **Table Design** button in the *Tables* group (Figure 2-1).

 - A new table opens in *Design* view, as shown in Figure 2-2.
 - The table is assigned a generic name, such as *Table1*.
 - The *Design* tab, a *Table Tools* contextual tab, is now available and selected.
 - The new table does not contain any fields.
 - The *Design* view window is divided into two areas. The top half displays the *Field Name, Data Type,* and *Description* for all fields in the table. The lower half displays the detailed field properties of the selected field.

2-1 *Table Design* button on the *Create* tab

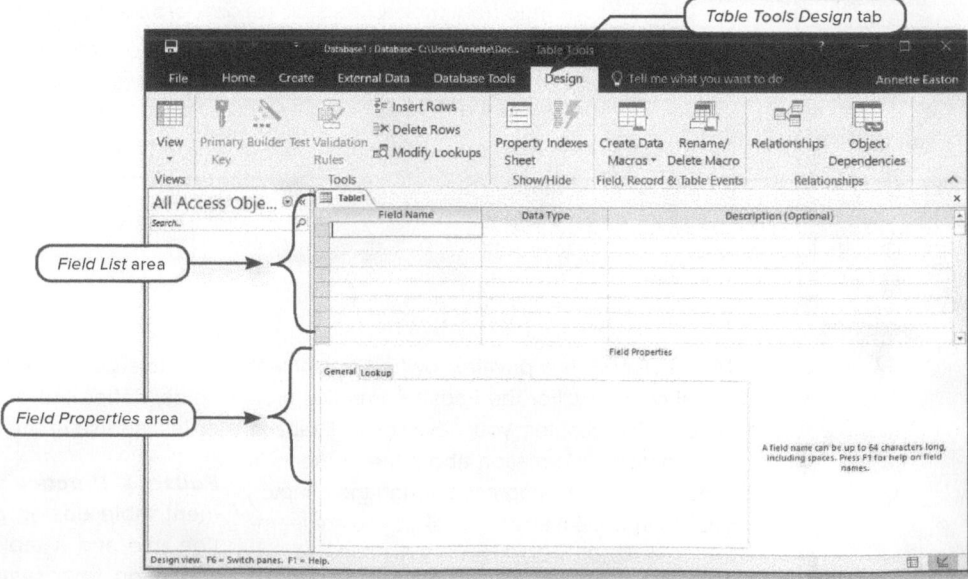

2-2 New table in *Design* view

The *Table Tools Design* tab contains buttons to perform a variety of tasks. The more commonly used buttons (*Primary Key*, *Insert Rows* and *Delete Rows*) are located in the *Tools* group (Figure 2-3) and explained in the following sections.

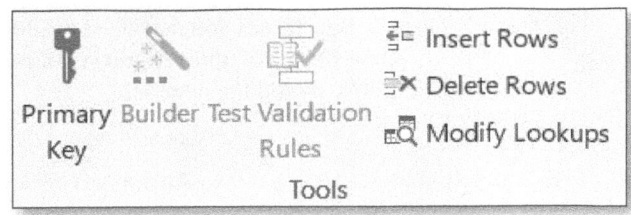

2-3 *Table Tools Design* tab, *Tools* group

Add New Fields

Add new fields into a table by entering a field name in the first empty row in the field list. When you add a new field you must enter values for the **Field Name** and **Data Type** properties. If you like, you can enter values for other available properties.

▶ **HOW TO:** Add a New Field

1. Click the **Field Name** property box in the first empty row in the field list.
2. Type the desired name in the property box (Figure 2-4).
 - Each field must have a unique name.
 - As needed, review the *Access Naming Rules* section in *SLO 1.2: Creating and Managing a Database* to ensure that you create a valid field name.
 - Use the naming conventions required by your instructor or employer.

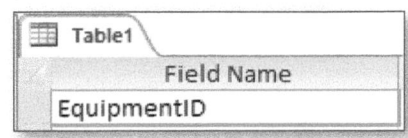

2-4 *Field Name* property box

3. Press the **Enter** key to add the field.
 - You move to the *Data Type* property with the *Short Text Data Type* selected.
 - The *Field Properties* of this field now display in the lower half of the *Design* view window.

ANOTHER WAY

Press the **Tab** key to add the field and move to the *Data Type* column.

4. Click the **drop-down arrow** in the **Data Type** property box (Figure 2-5).
 - The list of data types displays.
5. Select the appropriate **Data Type**.
6. Press the **Enter** key to move to the *Description* property box. Recall from Chapter 1 that the contents of the *Description* property displays in the lower left of the *Status* bar when the table is viewed in *Datasheet* view.

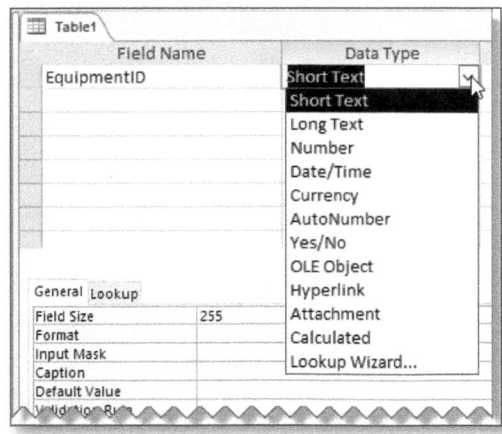

2-5 *Data Type* options in *Design* view

7. Type a value in the **Description** property box, as desired (Figure 2-6).

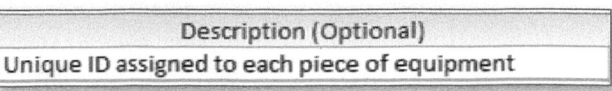

Description (Optional)
Unique ID assigned to each piece of equipment

2-6 Enter the field's description in the *Description* property

8. Press the **Enter** key to move to the *Field Name* property box of the next row.
9. Repeat steps 2–8 to add the additional fields into your table.

Sometimes you may need to add a new field between existing fields in a table. To add this new field, you must first insert a new row. After the row has been inserted, follow the steps above to add the new field.

▶ **HOW TO:** Insert a Blank Row to Add a New Field between Existing Fields

1. Click the **row selector** of the row where the new field should be added. In *Design* view, the gray box to the left of a field name is called the **row selector**.
2. Click the **Insert Rows** button [*Table Tools Design* tab, *Tools* group] as shown in Figure 2-3.
 - A new blank row is entered above the selected row (Figure 2-7).
 - Follow the steps in *How To: Add a New Field* to enter the details about the new field.

> **ANOTHER WAY**
>
> Right-click the **row selector** to open the context menu and then select **Insert Rows**.

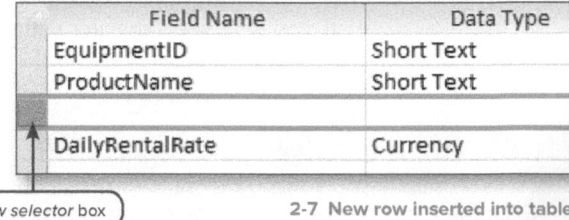

Field Name	Data Type
EquipmentID	Short Text
ProductName	Short Text
DailyRentalRate	Currency

Row selector box 2-7 New row inserted into table

Property Update Options Smart Tag

If you entered text in the *Description* property, after you tab out of that box the ***Property Update Options*** smart tag displays. Hover over the smart tag and click the arrow to display the list of options (Figure 2-8).

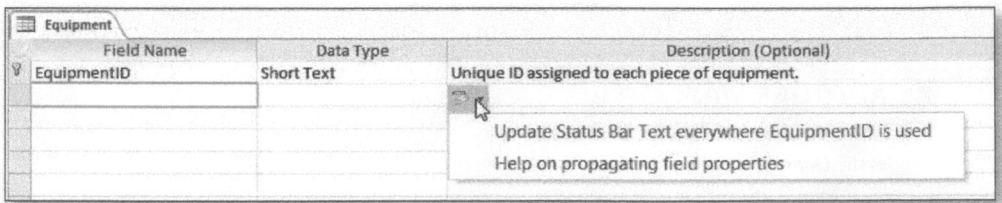

Field Name	Data Type	Description (Optional)
EquipmentID	Short Text	Unique ID assigned to each piece of equipment.

Update Status Bar Text everywhere EquipmentID is used
Help on propagating field properties

2-8 *Property Update Options* button

As desired, select the **Update Status Bar Text** option. This choice is most appropriate if you have created many different objects in your database and later make a change to the *Description* property of a field. Selecting this option updates the description in all objects containing controls linked to this field. For example, you may have a textbox control on a form object that is linked to the table field. When a field property can be passed to a control, it is called an ***inheritable property***. Not all field properties are able to be inherited. As a result, the *Property Update Options* smart tag only displays when the value of an inheritable property, such as the description, has been changed.

Define a Primary Key

Recall that a ***primary key*** is a field that contains a unique value for each record. When a table is created in *Design* view, a primary key field is not automatically assigned. You must

determine which of the fields in your table uniquely identifies each record. If needed, add an additional field with an *AutoNumber Data Type* to serve as the primary key.

▶ **HOW TO:** Define a Primary Key

1. Click the **row selector** of the desired field.
2. Click the **Primary Key** button [*Table Tools Design* tab, *Tools* group] (see Figure 2-3).
 - The *Primary Key* symbol appears in the *row selector* box (Figure 2-9).
 - The *Primary Key* button works as a toggle. Pressing it again will remove the symbol from the *row selector.*

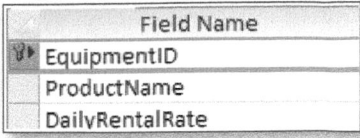

	Field Name
🔑▶	EquipmentID
	ProductName
	DailyRentalRate

2-9 *Primary Key* symbol

▶ **ANOTHER WAY**

Right-click the **row selector** of the desired field to open the context menu and then select **Primary Key.**

Delete Fields in a Table

There may be times when you need to delete a field in a table. While this is easy to accomplish, it is important to realize that this may impact other parts of your database. If you have queries, forms, and reports that contain this field, you must also modify those objects to remove this field.

▶ **HOW TO:** Delete a Field in a Table

1. Click the **row selector** of the field to delete.
2. Click the **Delete Rows** button [*Table Tools Design* tab, *Tools* group] (see Figure 2-3). If there is data in the table, Access displays an information message (Figure 2-10) asking you to confirm the deletion of the field and data in the table.

Microsoft Access	✕

⚠ **Do you want to permanently delete the selected field(s) and all the data in the field(s)?**

To permanently delete the field(s), click Yes.

[Yes] [No]

2-10 Delete field confirmation message

Save, Close, and Open a Table

The save, close, and open operations on a table work the same whether you are in *Datasheet* or *Design* view.

- Save a new table by clicking the **File** tab and then clicking the **Save** button. This opens the *Save As* dialog box. Type a new name for the table to replace the generic name assigned by Access.

> **ANOTHER WAY**
>
> Recall from Chapter 1 that you can also use **Ctrl+S**, the **Save** icon on the *Quick Access* toolbar, or the **F12** function key to open the *Save As* dialog box.

- Close a table by clicking the **X** in the upper right corner of the table. If you close a new table without saving it, Access deletes the table.
- Open a table in *Design* view by right-clicking the table name in the *Navigation Pane* and selecting **Design View** from the context menu, as shown in Figure 2-11.

2-11 Open a table from the context menu

Switch between Datasheet and Design Views

Recall that **Datasheet view** is used to enter records into a table. When creating, and later using, a table, you may find that you need to switch between looking at the data records and looking at the properties of the different fields. When a table is open, Access provides three ways to easily switch between different table views.

- Click the **View** button [*Home* tab, *Views* group] and then select the desired view option (Figure 2-12).
- Click the **Icon** on the *View* button [*Home* tab, *Views* group] to directly switch to the alternate view (Figure 2-13). The icon that displays in the *View* button is the opposite of the current view. For example, since Figure 2-13 shows the datasheet icon, this means that the current view of the table is *Design* view.
- Click the desired view icon from the right side of the *Status* bar (Figure 2-14), located at the bottom of the Access window.

2-12 *View* button

2-13 *View* button icon

2-14 Table *View* icons in the *Status* bar

SLO 2.2

Setting Field Properties

Field properties describe the specific details of each field. When you add a field into the table, you enter values for the field name, data type, and description properties. You can set many additional field properties depending on the needs of your database. The available properties vary based on the data type of the field. Field properties are grouped into *General* and *Lookup* properties, and are displayed on their respective tabs in the *Field Properties* area in the lower half of the *Design* view window. This section introduces the more common *General* tab field properties of *Field Size*, *Format*, *Caption*, *Default Value* and *Required*.

In order for the changes you make on any of the properties to be permanent, you must save the table. You can either save the table after each change or after all of your changes have been made.

Be sure to click the *row selector* of the correct field in the table before setting any of the properties discussed in this section.

Set the Field Size

The *Field Size* property determines the maximum number of characters allowed in a *Short Text* field or the range of possible values in a *Number* field.

- A *Short Text* field can have a size from 0 to 255.
- A *Number* field can have seven possible field sizes that are explained in the following table:

Number Data Type Field Sizes

Unit	Description
Byte	Stores numbers from 0 to 255. Does not use decimal places.
Integer	Stores numbers from −32,768 to 32,767. Does not use decimal places.
Long Integer	Stores numbers from −2,147,483,648 to 2,147,483,647. Does not use decimal places. This is the default field size for a number data type.
Single	Stores numbers from −3.4 × 1038 to 3.4 × 1038 with a precision of 7 significant digits.
Double	Stores numbers from −1.797 × 1038 to 1.797 × 1038 with a precision of 15 significant digits.
Replication ID	Stores a globally unique identifier (GUID) randomly generated by Access.
Decimal	Stores numbers from −1028 to 1028 with a precision of 28 significant digits.

- An *AutoNumber* field can use either the *Long Integer* or *Replication ID* field size.

The other data types do not have a *Field Size* property since their size is controlled by the database. The *Field Size* property, if available, is the first property on the *General* tab.

▶ HOW TO: Set the Field Size Property

1. For a *Short Text* field, click the **Field Size** property box and type the desired field size (Figure 2-15).

 - The default size of a *Short Text* field is 255.

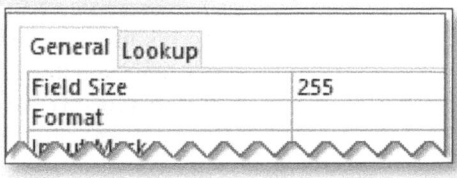

2-15 *Field Size* property

> **MORE INFO**
>
> Use the smallest field size that allows for the required processing or storage.

2. For a *Number* field, click the **drop-down arrow** in the *Field Size* property and select the desired number field size (Figure 2-16).

 - The default selection for a *Number* field is *Long Integer.*

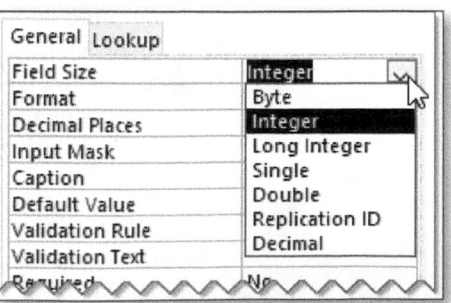

2-16 Field sizes for a *Number* data type

The Format Property

The *Format* property controls the way a field displays in a table; it doesn't change what is actually stored. The choices available vary by the data type selected. Some data types like *Number, Currency, Date/Time* and *Yes/No,* have predefined formats from which you can select. For *Short Text* and *Long Text* data types, you can create a custom format.

To enter a value in the *Format* property box, either select the predefined format or enter the desired formatting characters to create a custom format.

Number and Currency Field Formats

Click the **drop-down arrow** in the *Format* property box of a *Number* or *Currency* field to display the list of predefined formats (Figure 2-17).

If you don't select a format, Access uses the *General Number* format for a number field, although it won't display in the *Format* property box. A *Currency* field defaults to the *Currency* format.

General	Lookup	
Field Size	Long Integer	
Format		⌄
Decimal Places	General Number	3456.789
Input Mask	Currency	$3,456.79
Caption	Euro	€3,456.79
Default Value	Fixed	3456.79
Validation Rule	Standard	3,456.79
Validation Text	Percent	123.00%
Required	Scientific	3.46E+03
Indexed	No	
Text Align	General	

2-17 Predefined formats for *Number* and *Currency* data types

Date/Time Field Formats

Click the **drop-down arrow** in the *Format* property box of a *Date/Time* field to display the list of predefined formats (Figure 2-18). You can choose formats that display only the date, only the time, or both.

If you don't select a format, Access uses the *General Date* format, although it won't display in the *Format* property box.

General	Lookup	
Format		⌄
Input Mask	General Date	11/12/2015 5:34:23 PM
Caption	Long Date	Thursday, November 12, 2015
Default Value	Medium Date	12-Nov-15
Validation Rule	Short Date	11/12/2015
Validation Text	Long Time	5:34:23 PM
Required	Medium Time	5:34 PM
Indexed	Short Time	17:34
IME Mode	No Control	

2-18 Predefined field formats for the *Date/Time* data type

Yes/No Field Formats

Click the **drop-down arrow** in the *Format* property of a *Yes/No* field to display the list of predefined formats shown in Figure 2-19.

If you don't select a format, Access uses the *Yes/No* format.

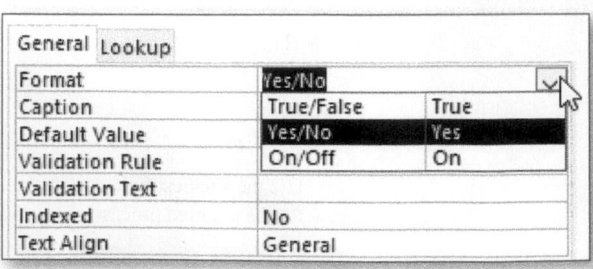

General	Lookup	
Format	Yes/No	⌄
Caption	True/False	True
Default Value	Yes/No	Yes
Validation Rule	On/Off	On
Validation Text		
Indexed	No	
Text Align	General	

2-19 Predefined field formats for the *Yes/No* data type

Short Text and Long Text Field Formats

Short Text and *Long Text* fields do not have any predefined formats. You can use formatting symbols to create a custom format and change the way the data display. More than one symbol may be used if multiple formatting effects are needed. Four common formatting symbols are described in the following table.

Short Text and Long Text Field Formatting Symbols

Character	Description
<	Characters display in lowercase. For example, if FL or Fl is entered into a field with a format of <, the entry displays as fl. This must be the first of the formatting symbols if multiple symbols are used.
>	Characters display in uppercase. For example, if fl or Fl is entered into a field with a format of >, the entry displays as FL. This must be the first of the formatting symbols if multiple symbols are used.
@	Enter one @ symbol for each character in the size of the field. If the field content contains fewer characters than the field size, the content displays with leading spaces. For example, if ABC is entered into a field of size 5 with a format of @@@@@, this entry displays as space, space, ABC.
[color]	Applies a color to this field only. The color must be enclosed in brackets. The possible colors are black, blue, cyan, green, magenta, red, yellow or white. This formatting symbol only works when applied in conjunction with one of the other formatting symbols. For example, a format of >**[blue]** displays that field's contents in upper case with a blue color.

Recall that *Short Text* and *Long Text* data types default to display left-justified. In Chapter 1 you learned to change the alignment of a field in *Datasheet* view. The @ character does not change the alignment, but when leading spaces are included for field contents that are less than the field size, the displayed contents do not appear to be left-justified.

The Caption Property

The *Caption* property contains the text that displays in the column header to identify a field in *Datasheet* views of tables, forms, queries, and reports. Captions often include spaces and multiple words as compared to the field name. Access displays the field name as the caption if you do not enter a caption value.

To enter a value for the *Caption* property, click the **Caption** property box and type the desired value.

Set the Default Value

You can use the *Default Value* property to automatically insert a specified value into a new record in a table. For example, Access can enter today's date into an *OrderDate* field. Or if most of a company's customers live in California, a default value of CA can be entered for a *State* field. Using a default value doesn't prevent the user from changing that value if needed (e.g., when a customer is from Nevada (NV) instead of California (CA)).

To enter a value in the *Default Value* property, click the **Default Value** property box and type the desired value.

 MORE INFO

The default value of *Date()* enters the current date while *Now()* enters the current date and time. The *Format* property determines how the content actually displays.

The Required Property

You can specify whether a user must enter a value into a field or whether he or she can skip the field and leave it blank. If a field must have a value, you should set the *Required* property to *Yes*. The default value for the *Required* property is *No*.

To set the *Required* property, click the **Required** property box and select **Yes**.

When building tables, you may wish to set the required property last. This allows you to more easily test different features in the table without being forced to enter a value for every field. This is especially helpful when you are adding different types of validation rules into the table. This skill is covered in the next section.

PAUSE & PRACTICE: ACCESS 2-1

For this Pause & Practice you create a new database for Ryan Thomas, operations director for Mary's Rentals. You use *Design* view to create a table to store information about the rental equipment. In addition, you modify the field properties to enhance the functionality of this table.

File Needed: ***EquipmentDataFile-02.xlsx***
Completed Project File Name: ***[your initials] PP A2-1.accdb***

1. Create a new blank database.
 a. Open Access or click the **New** button [*File* tab] if an Access database is already open.
 b. Click **Blank desktop database**.
 c. Type [your initials] PP A2-1 in the *File Name* box.
 d. Click the **Browse** button to change the location in which to save the database and click **OK**.
 e. Click the **Create** button. The database opens with a new table showing in *Datasheet* view.

2. Switch to *Design* view and save the table.
 a. Click the **View** button [*Table Tools Fields* tab, *Views* group] and select the **Design View** option. You are prompted to save the table.
 b. Type Equipment as the new table name.
 c. Click **OK**. The table displays in *Design* view with the default primary key selected.

3. Modify the default primary key.
 a. Click the **ID** *Field Name* property box in your table and type EquipmentID. Press the **Tab** key to move to the *Data Type* property.
 b. Click the **drop-down arrow** in the *Data Type* property box.
 c. Select the **Short Text** data type. Press the **Tab** key to move to the *Description* property.
 d. Type Unique ID assigned to each piece of equipment in the property box. Press the **Tab** key to move to the next row (Figure 2-20).

> ### MORE INFO
>
> The default *AutoNumber* data type was not appropriate for the *EquipmentID* field since Mary's Rentals already has assigned ID numbers to their equipment. Choose a *Short Text* data type for fields not used in arithmetic operations, even if the field contains numbers.

4. Add new fields into the table.
 a. Type ProductName in the *Field Name* property box of the second row. Press the **Tab** key to move to the *Data Type* property.

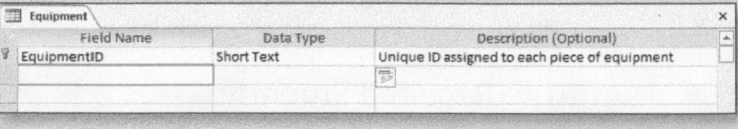

Field Name	Data Type	Description (Optional)
EquipmentID	Short Text	Unique ID assigned to each piece of equipment

2-20 Add fields into the *Equipment* table

 b. Select the **Short Text** *Data Type*. Press the **Tab** key to move to the *Description* property.

c. Do not enter a description; instead, press the **Tab** key to move to the next row.

d. Continue adding the remaining fields into the *Equipment* table using the following information.

Field Name	Data Type	Description
Category	**Short Text**	Type of equipment
DailyRentalRate	**Currency**	
WeeklyRentalRate	**Currency**	Must be greater than the DailyRentalRate
MonthlyRentalRate	**Currency**	Must be greater than the WeeklyRentalRate
DatePurchased	**Date/Time**	Date we purchased the equipment; not necessarily the date the equipment was made
Comments	**Long Text**	Additional information about the equipment

5. Save all of the modifications to the *Equipment* table.

6. Set the field properties in the *Equipment* table.

a. Click the **row selector** of the *EquipmentID* field.

b. Type 5 in the *Field Size* property box in the *Field Properties* area.

c. Click the **Required** property box and select **Yes** if necessary.

d. Click the **row selector** of the *ProductName* field.

e. Continue changing the remaining field properties in the *Equipment* table using the following information.

Field Name	Field Size	Format
ProductName	45	>[Blue]
Category	30	
DatePurchased		Medium Date

The *Required* property will be set for several of the other fields in Pause & Practice 2-2 after you have added some data validation features into the table design.

7. Save the table. Your completed table design should be similar to Figure 2-21.

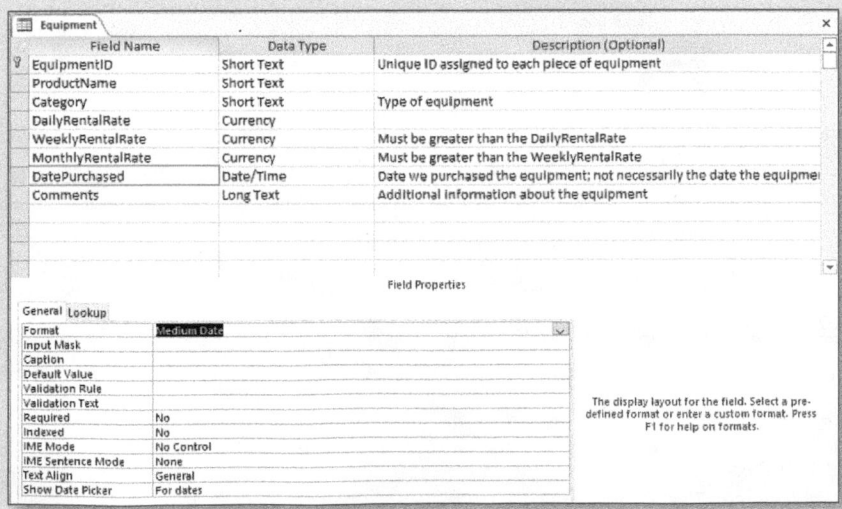

2-21 *Design view of the completed Equipment table*

8. Close the table.

9. Import the data records from Excel into the *Equipment* table.
 a. Launch the *Get External Data – Excel Spreadsheet* dialog box.
 b. Locate and select the **EquipmentDataFile-02** Excel file.
 c. Append the records to the *Equipment* table.
 d. Launch the *Import Spreadsheet Wizard*. Note that the file only contains values for the *EquipmentID, ProductName, and Comments* fields. You will adjust the properties of the other fields in Pause & Practice 2-2 before adding the additional data values.
 e. Finish the *Import Spreadsheet Wizard*. Close the *Wizard* after the records have imported.

10. Open the *Equipment* table in *Datasheet* view. The table should contain 10 records. Access automatically displays a value of $0.00 in currency data types fields that do not have any data.

11. Modify the row height of the table. Recall from Chapter 1 that you can change the row height through the context menu.
 a. Select any row in the table.
 b. Right-click to open the context menu and select **Row Height**.
 c. Enter 58 in the *Row Height* box and press **OK**.

12. Modify the field width of the *ProductName* and *Comments* columns. Recall from Chapter 1 that you can change the column width through the context menu.
 a. Select the *ProductName* column.
 b. Right-click to open the context menu and select **Field Width**.
 c. Enter 23 in the *Column Width* box and press **OK**.
 d. Repeat steps a through c to change the *Comments* field to a column width of 26.

13. Improve the formatting display of the *Comments* field. You can force a line break in a text field to have some text appear on a second line. Press the **Ctrl+Enter** keys at the point where you want the line break to occur.
 a. For EquipmentID 09863, position and click the pointer before the B in "Bucket," and then press **Ctrl+Enter**. "Bucket" now starts on a second line.
 b. For EquipmentID 10015, position and click the pointer before the W in "Weight," and then press **Ctrl+Enter**.
 c. For EquipmentID 10103, position and click the pointer before the 6 in "67"L," and then press **Ctrl+Enter**.
 d. The completed table will be similar to Figure 2-22.

EquipmentI ·	ProductName	Category ·	DailyRental ·	WeeklyRen ·	MonthlyRer ·	DatePurcha ·	Comments ·
09863	BACKHOE COMPACT ALLMAND DIESEL		$0.00	$0.00	$0.00		Lift Capacity: 2100 lbs Bucket Size: 16" only
10015	GENERATOR PORTABLE MAKITA 1000W		$0.00	$0.00	$0.00		Size: 19-1/2"L x 11-3/4"W x 17-1/2"H Weight: 55 lbs
10047	SKIP LOADER 4X4		$0.00	$0.00	$0.00		Subject to Environmental Fee
10103	GENERATOR TOWABLE POWERPRO 25KW		$0.00	$0.00	$0.00		Overall L x W x H: 67"L x 28"W x 3"H

2-22 PP A2-1 completed

14. Save and close the table.

15. Close the database.

SLO 2.3

Understanding Data Integrity and Data Validation

The usefulness of your database depends on the quality of the data being stored. It is critical that all data entered into a table is verified to make sure that it is accurate.

The process of verifying the accuracy, or integrity, of the data is known as *data validation*. Data validation uses the data integrity rules that have been defined in the field and table properties. *Data integrity rules* ensure that the data in a database is accurate and consistent. Some of the more common data integrity rules are described in the following table:

Data Integrity Rules

Rule Focus	Description
Data format	Ensures that a value entered into a field matches the data type established for that field; meets any size constraints; and meets any required formatting, such as beginning with a number or letter, or matching a month/day/year format.
Range	Ensures that a value entered into a field falls within the range of acceptable values that have been established.
Consistency	Ensures that a value entered into a field is consistent with a value in another field.
Completeness	Ensures that a field contains a value if it is required.

Data integrity rules are included as part of the *metadata*, the descriptions about what the different data fields represent and their formats. In Access, metadata is entered into the different field properties. An example of the metadata for the *Order Details* table in *Northwind Traders,* a sample database included with Access, is shown in Figure 2-23.

One of the key advantages to a database is that the DBMS automatically uses the metadata for the data integrity rules to perform data validation. Based on the metadata shown

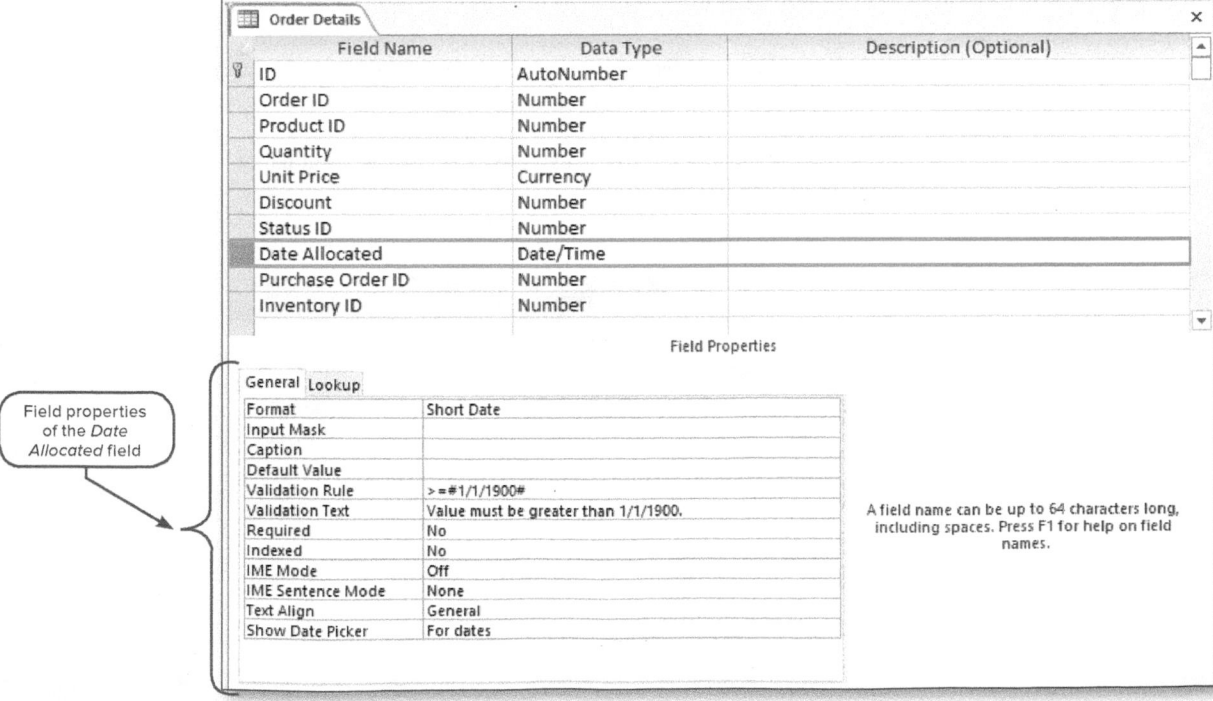

Field properties of the *Date Allocated* field

2-23 Metadata of the *Order Details* table in *Northwind Traders*

for the *Date Allocated* field, the database performs data validation using the following data integrity rules:

- The field must have *Date/Time* data and must follow the *Short Date* format (the *Data Type* and *Format* properties).
- The date must be greater than or equal to 1/1/1900 (the *Validation Rule* property).
- The user may leave this field blank (the *Required* property).

SLO 2.4 | Integrating Data Validation in Tables

You learned how to set the *Data Type* and *Required* properties in *SLO 2.2: Setting Field Properties.* Those properties are used to implement *data format* and *completeness* data integrity rules. The material that follows describes additional properties used to implement *data format, range,* and *consistency* data integrity rules. In Access, these can be created using field and record validation rules. This section explains how to create validation rules in *Design* view, although they can also be entered in *Datasheet* view. Additionally, you learn how to use lookup fields to ensure range integrity and how to use an input mask to help users enter data in the correct format. Remember to save your table after you make changes to any of these properties.

Field Validation Rules

Field validation rules are used to create *range* and *data format* integrity rules that limit entries to a certain range of values or make sure entries match a specified format. You enter the specific rule into the ***Validation Rule*** property of a field. Access checks field validation rules when a user navigates out of the field. If the data violates the rule, Access requires the user to fix the problem before he or she can leave the field.

Validation rules cannot be used on fields with data types of *Attachment, AutoNumber, OLE Object* and the *ReplicationID Field Size* choice of a *Number* field.

MORE INFO

If you want your rule to compare two or more fields, you must use a record validation rule.

In Access, the rules are called ***expressions.*** They are written using the common operators shown in the following table:

Operators Used in Access Expressions

Arithmetic	Comparison	Logical
–	<	And
+	<=	Or
*	>	Not
/	>=	Xor
^	=	
	<>	
	Between	
	In	
	Like	

The content of your expression depends on the data type of the field, along with the specific restriction you are trying to implement. Validation rules ignore the case of the text when making an evaluation. Examples of entries for validation rules, along with an explanation of their effects, are shown in the following table:

Using and Understanding Field Validation Rules

Validation Rule Example	Explanation of Effect
<5	Value entered must be less than 5.
<>0	Value entered must not equal 0.
>=#1/1/2015#	Value entered must be greater than or equal to 1/1/2015. *Tip: Dates must be surrounded by the # sign.*
"M" OR "F"	Value entered must be the letter M or the letter F. *Tip: Text values must be surrounded by double quotation marks.*
>=#1/1/2015# AND <#1/1/2016#	Value entered must be a date from 2015.
"A" OR > "M"	Value entered must be the letter A or a letter that comes after M in the alphabet.
IN ("CA", "NV", "AZ")	Value entered must be either CA, NV, or AZ
Not Null	The field must be filled in. While this can be enforced with the required property, using this validation rule allows you to include a custom validation message like "The Equipment ID field cannot be empty." *Tip: **Null** means that there is no value in the field.*

The *Yes/No* data type defaults to display data using a check box. A check indicates *Yes* while an unchecked box indicates *No*. Internally, Access stores *Yes* as a –1 and *No* as 0. Expressions written to check the contents of a *Yes/No* data type should compare the contents to either a –1 or a 0.

Use the *Like* comparison operator to find a value that is similar to (or like) another value. When using *Like,* you typically incorporate one of the *wildcard characters* available in Access. Examples of three of the wildcard characters and their effects are shown in the following table:

Using Wildcard Characters in Validation Rules

Wildcard Character	Matches	Example	Explanation of Example
?	Any single character (numbers are also considered characters)	Like "C????"	Values entered must be 5 characters long and begin with the letter C. *Tip: Even if the field size is larger than 5, this rule requires that exactly 5 characters are entered.*
*	Any number of characters	Like "MA*"	Values entered must begin with MA, but can be any length up to the maximum field size.
#	Any single numeric digit	Like "##"	Values entered must contain two numeric digits.

When using wildcards, the criteria of your expression must be enclosed in quotation marks. You can combine multiple wildcards to achieve the desired criteria.

▶ HOW TO: Create a Field Validation Rule

1. Click the **row selector** of the desired field.
2. Click the **Validation Rule** property box (Figure 2-24).
3. Type the text of the desired rule.

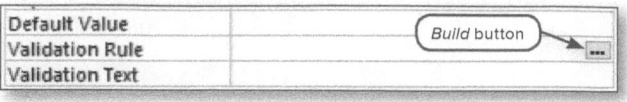

Default Value		
Validation Rule		_Build_ button
Validation Text		

2-24 *Validation Rule* property box

You can also use the *Expression Builder* to enter your validation rules. The **Expression Builder** is a dialog box that provides access to built-in functions, constants and operators. It also provides a larger window in which to type your expression. This can be useful when you have a long expression.

▶ HOW TO: Create a Field Validation Rule Using the Expression Builder

1. Click the **row selector** of the desired field.
2. Click the **Validation Rule** property box (see Figure 2-24) and click the **Build** button. The *Expression Builder* dialog box opens.

> **ANOTHER WAY**
>
> You can also open the *Expression Builder* dialog box by pressing **Ctrl+F2**, or clicking the **Builder** button [*Table Tools Design* tab, *Tools* group].

3. Type the text of the desired rule in the *Expression* box (Figure 2-25).

- You can click to expand the items in the **Expression Elements** area to display the available choices.
- Instead of typing, you can double-click choices in the **Expression Categories** and **Expression Values** areas to add them to the *Expression* box.

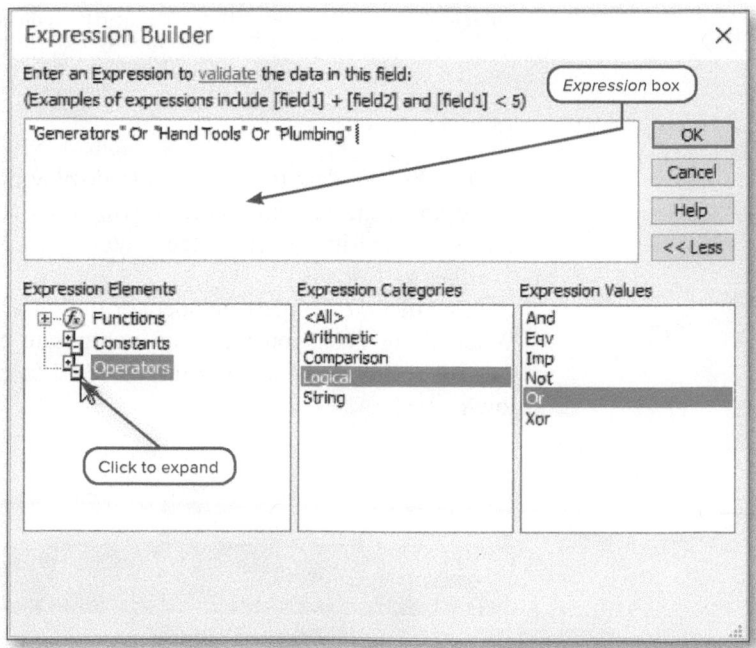

2-25 *Expression Builder* dialog box

Record Validation Rules

Record validation rules are used to create *consistency* data integrity rules that compare fields in the same table. You can also use them to create *range* and *data format* integrity rules that limit entries to a certain range of values or to a specified format. You enter the specific rule

into the *Validation Rule* property of the table. The rule is checked when a user attempts to navigate out of the record. If the data the user has entered in the record violates the rule, Access requires the user to fix the problem before he or she can leave the record.

Expressions written for a record validation rule can use the same operators and wildcard characters used in field level validation rules. However, they typically are written to compare fields. Examples of entries for record validation rules, along with an explanation of the effects, are shown in the following table:

Using and Understanding Record Validation Rules

Record Validation Rule Example	Explanation of Effect
([Field1] is Null) XOR ([Field2] is Null)	You must enter a value into either *Field1* or *Field2*, but not into both fields. *Tip: The XOR logical operator prevents both fields from having a value; both fields would be allowed to have a value if OR were used instead.*
[Field1] <> [Field2]	You may not enter the same value into both *Field1* and *Field2*.
([Field1] > [Field2]) AND ([Field2]>10)	*Field1* must be greater than *Field2* and *Field2* must have a value greater than 10. *Tip: When using the AND operator, all parts of the condition must be true.*

Substitute the actual field names in your table for the placeholders of *Field1, Field2,* etc. Be sure to include your field name inside square brackets, as shown in the examples.

▶ HOW TO: Create a Record Validation Rule

1. Click the **Property Sheet** button [*Table Tools Design* tab, *Show/Hide* group] (Figure 2-26).

 - The *Property Sheet* for the table opens (Figure 2-27).
 - This contains properties that apply to the entire table, not just a specific field.
 - The *Property Sheet* button works as a toggle. If the sheet is open and you press the button, the sheet will be closed.

2. Click the **Validation Rule** property box.

3. Type the text of the desired rule directly in the property box or click the **Build** button to open the *Expression Builder* dialog box.

 - The example validation rule shown in Figure 2-28 uses the *Date()* function, which captures the current date from the computer. This example rule requires that the value in the *DatePurchased* field is greater than or equal to the current date.

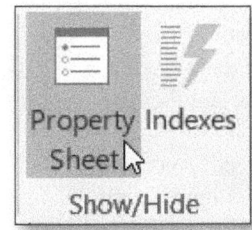

2-26 *Property Sheet* button

Property Sheet ✕

Selection type: Table Properties

General

Read Only When Disconnect	No
Subdatasheet Expanded	No
Subdatasheet Height	0"
Orientation	Left-to-Right
Description	
Default View	Datasheet
Validation Rule	
Validation Text	
Filter	
Order By	
Subdatasheet Name	[Auto]
Link Child Fields	
Link Master Fields	
Filter On Load	No
Order By On Load	Yes

2-27 *Property Sheet* of a table

Validation Rule	[DatePurchased]>=Date()

2-28 Example record validation rule

Test Validation Rules

When using validation rules it is important that you test the rules. There are two different considerations for testing.

- Test to ensure the rule is written correctly.

 These tests ensure that the logic is valid and the rule works as you intended. If several fields have validation rules, it is easiest to test each rule as you write it. This helps you focus on a specific rule instead of trying to test all of them at the same time.

 To test a validation rule you must create ***test data***, a set of data created to test an application. The test data should include a sample of every valid condition as well as samples of as many invalid conditions as possible. Several examples of creating test data are shown in the following table:

Test Data Examples for Validation Rules

Validation Rule	Examples of Test Data	Result of Test
"M" OR "F"	M	Valid (test of M condition); should be accepted.
	F	Valid (test of F condition); should be accepted.
	X	Invalid; error message should display.
>=#1/1/2016# AND <#1/1/2017#	12/15/2015	Invalid (below the range); error message should display.
	7/7/2016	Valid; should be accepted.
	2/13/2017	Invalid (above the range); error message should display.
([Field1] is Null) XOR ([Field2] is Null)	Field1 null and Field2 null	Invalid (both can't be null); error message should display.
	Field1 = 5 and Field2 = 7	Invalid (both can't have a value); error message should display.
	Field1 null and Field2 = 7	Valid (only Field 2 has a value); should be accepted.
	Field1 = 5 and Field2 null	Valid (only Field1 has a value); should be accepted.

- Test to ensure that any data already in the table is verified against the new rules.

 Test existing data by clicking the **Test Validation Rules** button [*Table Tools Design* tab, *Tools* group] (Figure 2-29).

 Access displays a message box explaining the test and alerting you to the fact that this operation could take a long time depending on the number of records of data in your table.

 If you click **Yes** to proceed, Access displays an error message (Figure 2-30) if any data is found to violate validation rules. You can select whether to continue testing other rule violations.

 If you continue testing, Access displays an error message (Figure 2-31) indicating which rule is violated.

 You must return to *Datasheet* view, locate any records that have invalid data, and then make the necessary corrections.

2-29 *Test Validation Rules* button

2-30 Validation rule violation warning message

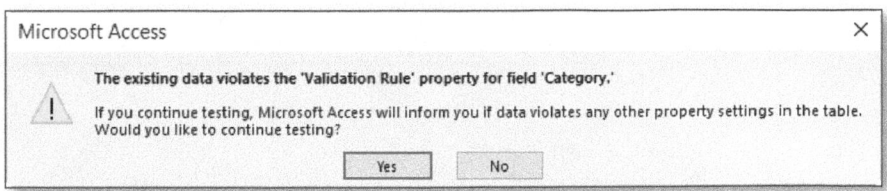

2-31 Message box for data validation errors

Create Validation Text

When data is entered that violates a validation rule, Access automatically displays a message box alerting the user to the problem. The message box text includes the condition entered into the validation rule. Unfortunately, the message, as shown in Figure 2-32, is often not very clear to a typical user of your database.

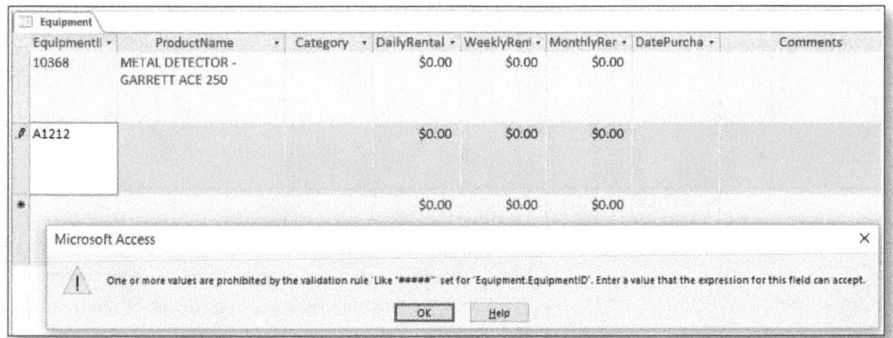

2-32 Default message when entering data that violates a validation rule

You can use the *Validation Text* property to enter a custom message that displays instead of the default message. Be clear and concise in your message. Include the reason the entry is invalid and suggest how to correct the problem. For example, "The EquipmentID must contain 5 numbers" is a better error message than "Invalid entry in EquipmentID field" or "Please enter a valid EquipmentID."

For a field validation rule, place the custom message in the *Validation Text* property of that field. For a record validation rule, place the custom message in the *Validation Text* property of the table.

▶ HOW TO: Create Validation Text

1. Click the **row selector** of the desired field or open the *Property Sheet* for the table by clicking the **Property Sheet** button [*Table Tools Design* tab, *Show/Hide* group].
2. Click the **Validation Text** property box.
3. Type the text of the desired message. An example message is shown in the *Validation Text* property box in Figure 2-33.

| Validation Rule | Like "#####" |
| Validation Text | The EquipmentID must contain 5 numbers |

2-33 Example validation text

> **ANOTHER WAY**
>
> Since the *Validation Text* property box is not very wide, you can enter the message in the *Zoom* window. The *Zoom* window (Figure 2-34) allows you to see the entire message that you are entering, which might not be visible in the smaller property box.
>
> Open the *Zoom* window by right-clicking the **Validation Text** property box and selecting the **Zoom** button or by pressing **Shift+F2**.
>
> As desired, click the **Font** button to change the default font used in the Zoom window. However, this does not affect the font that displays in the message box.

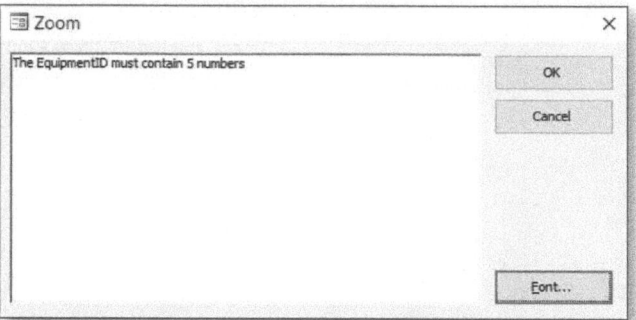

2-34 Create a custom validation text message in the *Zoom* window

Create a Lookup Field

Lookup fields display a list of data values from which the user can choose. Lookup fields are another way to implement ***range*** integrity rules and are an alternative to validation rules since they also limit what can be entered into a field. They are very helpful when the actual choices are lengthy or prone to typing mistakes. Lookup fields can be used on any field that is defined as a data type of *Number, Short Text,* or *Yes/No.* They are most commonly used on *Number* and *Short Text* fields.

The list of values in a lookup field can either be directly entered into the properties of the field or automatically filled in from values in another table or query. In this section you learn to create a lookup field by entering the list of values.

One of the choices you make when creating a lookup field is to determine the way that the list displays. This choice is made in the ***Display Control*** property on the *Lookup* tab. *Text* and *Number* fields have three options for the *Display Control* property. The appearance and behavior of the control depends on whether you are viewing the data in *Datasheet* view of a table or whether you are viewing it in a form. Since you select the type of control when creating the lookup field, it is important to understand the differences now. The three options are explained in the table below, which includes samples of how the control displays in a table or form.

Understanding Display Control Options

Display Control Choice	Explanation	Table Sample	Form Sample
Text Box	Displays the contents of a field and also allows the user to type a value into that field. This is the default choice.	Category	Category
List Box	Table view: Displays as a drop-down list. The list appears when the arrow is clicked. Form view: Displays as a box showing all possible choices.	Category Generators Hand Tools Plumbing Sawing, Cuttin Tractors	Category Generators Hand Tools Plumbing Sawing, Cutting & Grinding Tractors
Combo Box	Displays as a drop-down list in both table view and form view. The list appears when the arrow is clicked.	Category Generators Hand Tools Plumbing Sawing, Cuttin Tractors	Category

Notice that a *List Box* and *Combo Box* display the same way in *Datasheet* view of a table but are different when displayed on a form. Because the *List Box* control takes up more space on a form, and users don't always find it intuitive to understand and don't know to make a selection, you may want to opt to use the *Combo Box* display control choice.

Once the *Display Control* property is set to either *List Box* or *Combo Box,* additional properties become available on the *Lookup* tab. Several of the more commonly used properties are described in the table below.

Common Lookup Field Properties

Property	Explanation	Setting Contents
Row Source Type	Designates where the values for the different choices will come from.	Table/Query: Values will come from a table or query that you indicate. Value List: Values will come from a list of choices you enter. Field List: Values will come from a list of field names from a table.
Row Source	Contains the name of the table or query, or the actual list of values.	If the Row Source Type is **Table/Query** or **Field List**, enter the name of the table or query. If the Row Source Type is **Value List**, enter the choices.
List Rows	Contains the number of rows to display in the list. If there are more choices than rows entered, a scroll bar automatically appears. Available only if the Display Control is a Combo Box.	Enter the number of rows to display.

Continued

Property	Explanation	Setting Contents
Limit to List	Designates whether a user can enter a value into the field that is not on the list.	*Yes:* Restricts the user to picking an entry from the list.
	Available only if the *Display Control* is a *Combo Box*.	*No:* Allows users to pick from the list or enter a new value.
Allow Value List Edits	Designates whether the list of items can be edited.	*Yes:* Allows the user to change the values in the list.
		No: Restricts the user from editing the list.

If the *Allow Value List Edits* property is set to *Yes,* the **Edit List Items** button appears below the list when the user tabs into that field (see the *List Box* images in the *Understanding Display Control Options* table.) When you hover over the button, it turns gray (Figure 2-35). Click the button to open the *Edit List Items* dialog box (Figure 2-36).

> **ANOTHER WAY**
>
> Open the *Edit List Items* dialog box by right-clicking in the **lookup field** to open the context menu and then selecting the **Edit List Items** button.

2-35 *Edit List Items* button

2-36 *Edit List Items* dialog box

The *Edit List Items* dialog box allows the user to add new items onto the list, change existing items, or delete items from the list. Be cautious about giving this type of control to your users.

Since the *Combo Box* is the more common display control, we will concentrate on creating and using this type of lookup field.

▶ **HOW TO: Create a Lookup Field by Typing a List of Values**

1. Click the **row selector** of the desired field.
2. Select the **Lookup** tab in the *Field Properties* area in the lower half of the *Design view* window (Figure 2-37).

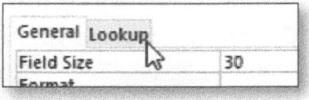

2-37 Select the *Lookup* tab

3. Click the **Display Control** property box and select **Combo Box**.
 - Based on the selection of the *Combo Box* display control, additional properties will become available on the *Lookup* tab, as shown in Figure 2-38.
4. Click the **Row Source Type** property box, click the **drop-down arrow** and select **Value List**.
 - This choice indicates that you will enter the list of possible choices.
5. Type the list of choices into the **Row Source** property box.
 - Separate each choice with a **semicolon (;)**.
 - If the choice contains a comma **(,)** as punctuation, the choice must be surrounded by quotation marks (**" "**).
6. Edit the **List Rows** property, as desired, to set the number of rows that display.

General Lookup	
Display Control	Combo Box
Row Source Type	Table/Query
Row Source	
Bound Column	1
Column Count	1
Column Heads	No
Column Widths	
List Rows	16
List Width	Auto
Limit To List	No
Allow Multiple Values	No
Allow Value List Edits	No
List Items Edit Form	
Show Only Row Source Values	No

2-38 Additional properties on the *Lookup* tab

7. Edit the **Limit To List** property, as desired.
 - Select **Yes** if you want to restrict the user to picking a choice only from the list.
8. Edit the **Allow Value List Edits** property as desired.
 - Select **Yes** if you want to allow the user to change the values in the list while entering or viewing data.

▶ HOW TO: Create a Lookup Field Using the Lookup Wizard

1. Click the **row selector** of the desired field.
2. Click the property box for the **Data Type** property and click the **drop-down arrow** to display the list of data types.
3. Select **Lookup Wizard** (Figure 2-39). The *Lookup Wizard* dialog box opens.
4. Select the radio button for **I will type in the values that I want.** (Figure 2-40).
5. Click the **Next** button.
 - The next step of the *Lookup Wizard* displays.
 - Initially there are no items in the list.
6. Click the first cell in the *Col1* column.
7. Type the first value in the list.
8. Press the **down arrow** key to move to the next row.
9. Continue typing all values in the list (Figure 2-41).
10. Click the **Next** button when done entering all items on the list.
 - The final step of the *Lookup Wizard* displays (Figure 2-42).

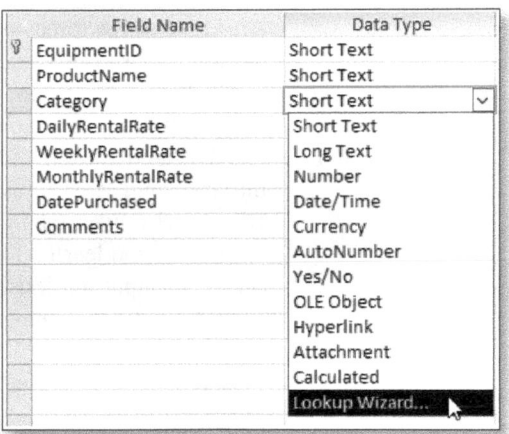

2-39 *Lookup Wizard* option in the *Data Type* property list

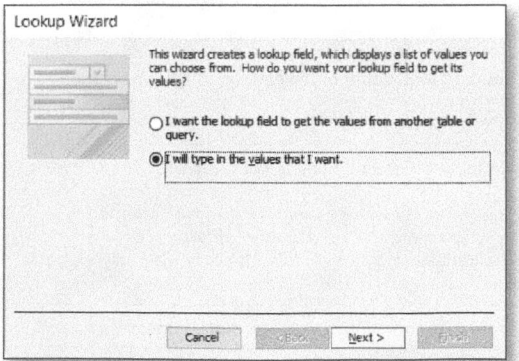

2-40 First step of the *Lookup Wizard*

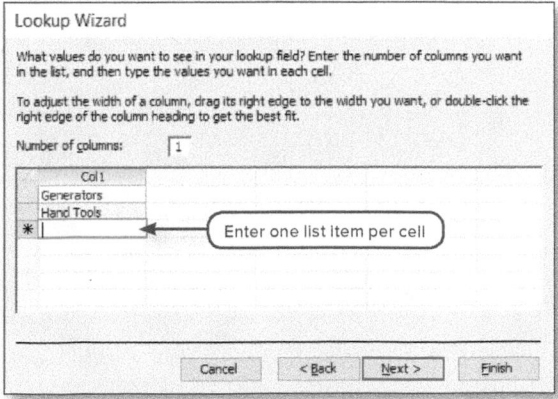

2-41 Enter choices in the second step of the *Lookup Wizard*

11. The label defaults to the original field name you entered. As desired, you can change the field name here.

12. Click the **Limit To List** check box as desired. Checking this box sets the *Limit to List* property to **Yes**.

13. Click the **Finish** button when done. As desired, you can edit the *List Rows* and *Allow Value List Edits* properties on the *Lookup* tab.

2-42 Last step of the *Lookup Wizard*

Define an Input Mask

An **input mask** forces a user to enter data using a specific format. For example, you can require a user to enter a phone number with an area code in the (123) 123-4567 format. Input masks help enforce *data format* data integrity rules.

An input mask can only be used on fields with data types of *Short Text, Number* (excluding the *ReplicationID* field size), *Currency,* or *Date/Time.* You can type the mask directly into the *Input Mask* property box or you can select the *Build* button to launch the **Input Mask Wizard**. However, the *Input Mask Wizard* only works on *Short Text* or *Date* fields.

Before you learn how to create an input mask it is important to learn some fundamental rules. An input mask uses a variety of characters that control how and what kind of data is acceptable. Some common special characters are explained in the following table:

Input Mask Special Characters

Character	Explanation of Effect
0	User must enter a number (0 to 9).
9	User can enter a number (0 to 9), but it is not required.
#	User can enter a number (0 to 9), space, or plus or minus sign, but it is not required. If not filled in, Access enters a blank space.
L	User must enter a letter (A to Z, upper or lower case).
?	User can enter a letter (A to Z, upper or lower case), but it is not required.
A	User must enter a letter or a number.
a	User can enter a letter or a number, but it is not required.
!	In a text field, when fewer characters are entered than specified in the mask, the empty spaces are placed on the left side of the field instead of the default right side of the field. This is not the same as right-justifying the field.
""	Characters entered inside the quotation marks display as written.
\	Characters following the slash are displayed as written.

An input mask contains three parts, each separated by a semicolon.

- The first part is mandatory and shows the desired formatting. Examples of the mandatory portion of an input mask are as follows.

Mask Example	Explanation of Effect
(000) 000-0000	You must enter an area code along with the phone number (0 indicates required). The phone number will be entered starting with the area code.
(999) AAA-AAAA	The phone number does not require an area code (9 indicates optional). The number portion can be numbers or digits. This mask would allow an entry of 555-STAR for the phone number.
!9999	You can enter up to four numbers (9 indicates optional). The ! symbol indicates that if fewer than four numbers are entered, the data displays right-justified with the empty spaces to the left. For example, if 12 is entered, it would display as " 12" instead of "12 ". Since 12 only contains two numbers, the two empty spaces display before the 12.
"WN "9999	The data must start with WN, a blank space, and be followed with up to 4 numbers. Since the ! symbol is not used, the numbers will be left-justified since the empty spaces will be to the right.

When you enter the mask characters, Access may add additional special characters to ensure the mask displays as desired. For example, if you enter (000) 000-0000 as the mask, Access converts it to \(000") "000\-0000. Access inserted the \ in front of the (symbol to indicate that this character displays as written. Access also inserted quotation marks around the) and space. Finally another \ was inserted in front of the — symbol to indicate that this character displays as written.

- The second part of the input mask is optional and indicates whether the mask characters, such as parenthesis, dashes, etc., are stored with the data. Not storing the characters saves space; this can be significant in large databases. If you do store the characters make sure the field size is large enough to store the data value and the characters. The two possible symbols are **0** and **1**. A **0** tells Access to store the characters; a **1** or empty tells Access not to store the characters.
- The third part of the mask is also optional and specifies what symbol displays in the mask as the user enters the data. The default symbol is the _ (underscore.) You can select a different symbol as desired. If this part of the mask is left blank, Access behaves as if the _ symbol was selected.

Based on the mask characters entered, Access may add additional special characters to ensure the mask displays as desired. Three examples of input masks follow. Recall that the semicolon symbol (**;**) separates the different parts of the mask. The parts of each mask are identified, along with displaying a sample of how the mask would appear (Figures 2-43 through 2-45).

Example 1: \(000") "000\-0000;0; Sample:

2-43 Example 1 *Input Mask* display

Part 1	Part 2	Part 3
\(000") "000\-0000	0	Empty
The \ in front of the **(** symbol, the quotation marks around the **)** and space, and the \ in front of the — symbol, indicates that these characters display as written.	The mask characters are stored along with the data. This format requires a field size of 14 to store the phone number digits and the mask characters, including the blank space between the area code and the number.	The default — symbol displays as the placeholder character.

Example 2: \(999") "AAA\-AAAA;;* Sample:

2-44 Example 2 *Input Mask* display

Part 1	Part 2	Part 3
\(999") "AAA\-AAAA	Empty	*
The \ in front of the **(** symbol, the quotation marks around the **)** and space, and the \ in front of the — symbol, indicates that these characters display as written.	The mask characters are not stored along with the data. This format requires a field size of ten to store the phone number.	The * symbol displays as the placeholder character.

Example 3: "WN "9999;1;_ Sample:

2-45 Example 3 *Input Mask* display

Part 1	Part 2	Part 3
"WN "9999	1	_
Since the database designer wanted WN and a space to appear at the beginning, she entered it inside quotation marks.	The mask characters are not stored with the data. This format requires a field size of four to store the flight number.	The _ symbol displays as the placeholder character.

▶**HOW TO: Create an Input Mask**

1. Click the **row selector** of the desired field.
2. Click the **Input Mask** property box.
3. Click the **Build** button to launch the *Input Mask Wizard* dialog box (Figure 2-46).

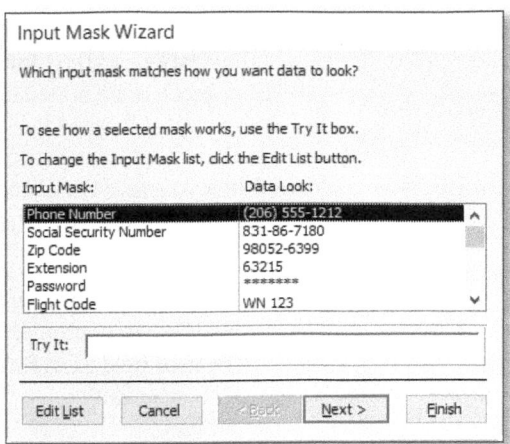

> **ANOTHER WAY**
>
> You can type the rule directly into the property box.

4. Select the pre-formatted mask you wish to use or an option that you can modify.

5. Click the **Next** button to move to the next step of the *Input Mask Wizard* (Figure 2-47).

6. Edit the **Input Mask** as desired.

7. Edit the **Placeholder character** as desired.

8. Click the **Next** button to move to the next step of the *Input Mask Wizard* (Figure 2-48).

9. Select the appropriate radio button based on whether you are storing the symbols with the data. Be sure that the field width is large enough to also store the symbol since it takes space as well.

2-46 *Input Mask Wizard, step 1*

2-47 *Input Mask Wizard, step 2*

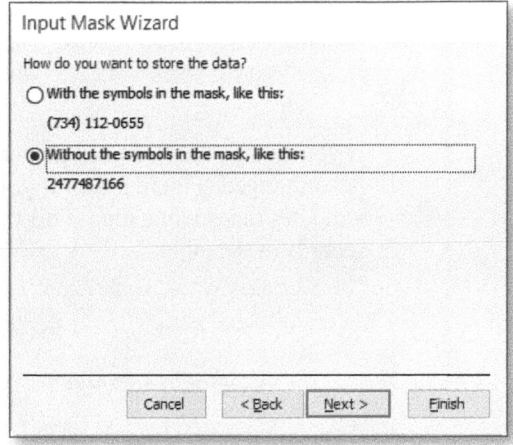

2-48 *Input Mask Wizard, step 3*

10. Click the **Finish** button.

11. Make any needed adjustments to the input mask directly in the property box.

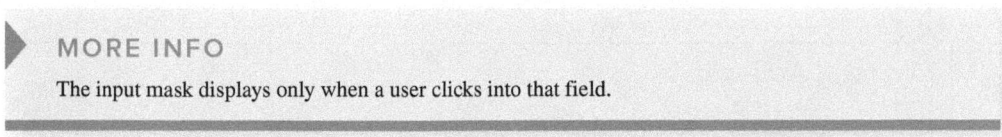

> **MORE INFO**
>
> The input mask displays only when a user clicks into that field.

SLO 2.5 Changing Field Properties after Records are Added into a Table

In Chapter 1 you learned to use *Datasheet* view to add records into a table. Ideally you will have decided on the final structure of all your tables before you begin to enter data, but there may be times you need to make a change to the field properties on a table that already contains data.

Making the change is straightforward. Open the table in *Design* view and follow the steps previously described for the specific property. However making changes to the table design after records are added must be done with caution.

You just learned that the field properties are used to specify the data integrity rules. Keep in mind that changes to several of the properties may result in unintended consequences. When you save the changes, Access displays a message box warning you about the potential problems. Examples of different problem situations and the resulting warnings include the following.

- If you reduce the *Field Size,* Access warns you that data may be lost (Figure 2-49). If you click *Yes* to continue, Access truncates the contents of any data values that are larger than the new field size. Be certain that the field is large enough that you don't lose any data since you can't undo this change.

2-49 *Field Size* change warning message

- If you change the *Required* property to *Yes,* Access warns you that data integrity rules have changed (Figure 2-50). If you click *Yes* to test the data with the new rules, Access validates the existing data. This could take a long time depending on the number of records in the table.

2-50 Data integrity rule change warning message

- If any records violate the new rule, another message box displays, similar to Figure 2-51.

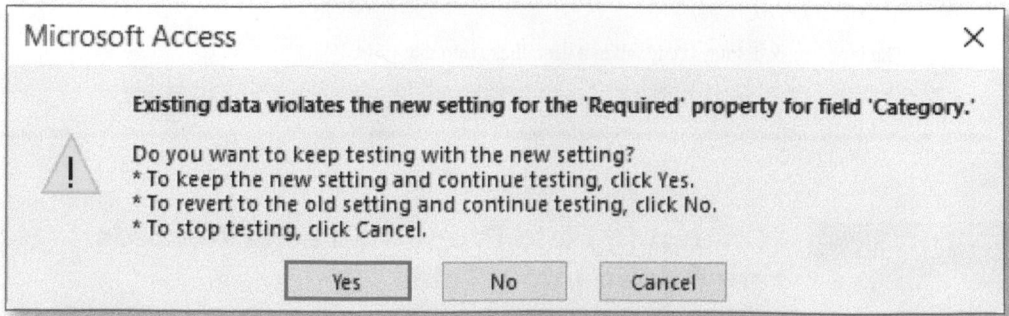

2-51 Validation error warning message

You must decide whether to keep the new rule. This message only appears once to let you know that there is data that violates the rule, not once for each record that violates

the rule. If you proceed with the change, you must open the table and individually correct each violation of this new rule.

- If you change any of the validation rules, you should test the changes as described earlier in this chapter by clicking the *Test Validation Rules* button [*Table Tools Design* tab, *Tools* group]. Again, you must individually correct each violation of a new rule.

PAUSE & PRACTICE: ACCESS 2-2

For this Pause & Practice you add features to enhance the data integrity in the *Equipment* table. You add field and record level validation rules and validation text, use the *Lookup Wizard* to create a combo box, and add an input mask. You also test the validation rules. Finally, you add data into the *Equipment* table.

File Needed: *[your initials] PP A2-1.accdb*
Completed Project File Name: *[your initials] PP A2-2.accdb*

1. Open the *[your initials] PP A2-1* database file created in Pause & Practice 2-1.

2. Save a new copy of your database as [your initials] PP A2-2.

3. Enable content in the security warning.

4. Open the *Equipment* table in *Design* view.

5. Add a field validation rule and validation text.
 a. Click the **row selector** of the *EquipmentID* field.
 b. Click the **Validation Rule** property box.
 c. Type Like "#####" in the *Validation Rule* property box.
 d. Click the **Validation Text** property box.
 e. Type The Equipment ID must contain 5 numbers in the *Validation Text* property box. The completed properties should match those shown in Figure 2-52.

6. Test the field validation rule.
 a. Switch to *Datasheet* view to test the rule. If prompted, save the changes to your table. You may also be prompted with a box that states that the data integrity rules have changed and asked whether you want to test the existing data. Click **No**.
 b. Click the **EquipmentID** cell in the *append row*.
 c. Type A1212 in the *EquipmentID* field. This value is incorrect because it contains letters. Press the **Tab** or **Enter** key to move to the next field. A message box should display the validation text message you entered in step 5 (Figure 2-53).
 d. Press **OK** to acknowledge the error.
 e. Delete the contents and type 123 in the *EquipmentID* field. Press the **Tab** key to move to the next field. This value is incorrect because it contains only three numbers. The message box should display the validation text message.

General Lookup	
Field Size	5
Format	
Input Mask	
Caption	
Default Value	
Validation Rule	Like "#####"
Validation Text	The Equipment ID must contain 5 numbers
Required	Yes
Allow Zero Length	Yes
Indexed	Yes (No Duplicates)
Unicode Compression	No
IME Mode	No Control
IME Sentence Mode	None
Text Align	General

2-52 Completed properties of the *EquipmentID* field

2-53 Error message displays validation text from a field validation rule

f. Press **OK** to acknowledge the error.
g. Type 12345 in the *EquipmentID* field. Press **Tab** to move to the next field. This value is correct and you should be moved to the *ProductName* field.
h. Click the **Record Selector** for *EquipmentID 12345.*
i. Click the **Delete** button [*Home* tab, *Records* group] to delete this test record. A message box displays. Click **Yes** to confirm the deletion.
j. Switch back to *Design* view of the table.

7. Add a record validation rule.
a. Display the *Property Sheet* for the *Equipment* table if necessary by clicking the **Property Sheet** button [*Table Tools Design* tab, *Show/Hide* group].
b. Click the **Validation Rule** property box.
c. Click the **Build** button to open the *Expression Builder* dialog box.
d. Enter [WeeklyRentalRate]>[DailyRentalRate] And [MonthlyRentalRate]>[WeeklyRentalRate] in the *Expression Builder.* Instead of typing the field names, you can double-click them in the *Expression Categories* area and add them to the *Expression* box.
e. Press **OK** to close the *Expression Builder.*
f. Right-click the **Validation Text** property box and select the **Zoom** button.
g. Type The Weekly Rate must be greater than the Daily Rate and the Monthly Rate must be greater than the Weekly Rate. in the *Zoom* window. Press **OK**.
h. Close the *Property Sheet* window.

8. Test the record validation rule.
a. Switch to *Datasheet* view to test the rule. If prompted, save the changes to your table. You may also be prompted that the data integrity rules have changed and asked whether you want to test the existing data. Click **No**.
b. For *EquipmentID 09863,* type 160 in the *DailyRentalRate* field, 160 in the *WeeklyRentalRate* field and 160 in the *MonthlyRentalRate* fields.
c. Press the **down arrow** key to leave the current record. This causes the record level rule to execute. The message box should display the validation text message (Figure 2-54) because

2-54 Error message displays validation text from a record validation rule violation

the *WeeklyRentalRate* is not greater than the *DailyRentalRate* and the *MonthlyRentalRate* is not greater than the *WeeklyRentalRate*. This test is checking if the *And Compound Condition* is working correctly.

 d. Press **OK** to acknowledge the error.

 e. Delete the contents in the *MonthlyRentalRate* field, and type 640.

 f. Press the **down arrow** key to exit the current record. The message box should display the validation text message because the *WeeklyRentalRate* is not greater than the *DailyRentalRate*, the first half of the compound condition.

 g. Press **OK** to acknowledge the error.

 h. Delete the contents in the *WeeklyRentalRate* field, and type 640.

 i. Press the **down arrow** key to exit the current record. The message box should display the validation text message because the *MonthlyRentalRate* is not greater than the *WeeklyRentalRate*, the second half of the compound condition.

 j. Press **OK** to acknowledge the error.

 k. Delete the contents in the *MonthlyRentalRate* field, and type 1920.

 l. Press the **down arrow** key to leave the current record. The record changes should be successfully saved.

 m. Switch back to *Design* view of the table.

9. Modify the *Category* field to use a *Combo Box.*
 a. Click the **row selector** of the *Category* field.
 b. Click the **Data Type** property box, click the **arrow**, and select **Lookup Wizard**. The *Lookup Wizard* dialog box opens.
 c. Select the **I will type in the values that I want** radio button.
 d. Click the **Next** button.
 e. Leave 1 in the *Number of columns* box and click the first cell in the *Col1* column.
 f. Type Generators.
 g. Press the **down arrow** key to move to the next row.
 h. Enter the values from the *Category* table.

Category
Hand Tools
Plumbing
Sawing, Cutting & Grinding
Tractors

 i. Click the **Next** button when done entering all the items.
 j. Click the **Limit To List** check box.
 k. Click the **Finish** button.
 l. Save your changes to the table.

10. Add an input mask to the *DatePurchased* field.
 a. Click the **row selector** of the *DatePurchased* field.
 b. Click the **Input Mask** property box.
 c. Click the **Build** button or press **Ctrl+F2**. The *Input Mask Wizard* dialog box opens.
 d. Select the **Medium Date** *Input Mask* (Figure 2-55).
 e. Click the **Next** button. The next screen of the *Input Mask Wizard* displays the characters used in the mask along with the *Placeholder* character (Figure 2-56).

2-55 *Medium Date Input Mask* option

2-56 *Medium Date Input Mask* characters

 f. Click the **Next** button to accept the input mask without making any changes and to accept the suggested *Placeholder character.*

 g. Click the **Finish** button.

11. Set the **Required** property to **Yes** for the following fields: *ProductName, Category, DailyRentalRate, WeeklyRentalRate, MonthlyRentalRate,* and *DatePurchased.*

12. Save the changes to the *Equipment* table. If prompted to test existing data against the new rules, click **No**.

13. Switch to *Datasheet* view and enter the following data values into the table. Remember that the *EquipmentID* value has already been entered. The values for the *ProductName* column, located between the *EquipmentID* and *Category* fields, have also been entered. Those data values are not repeated in the table below. Additionally, you already entered the rental rate values for the first record when you were testing the validation rules.

 Because you created an input mask for the *DatePurchased* field, those data values have been provided using the mask format to ease data entry.

Equipment ID	Category	Daily Rental Rate	Weekly Rental Rate	Monthly Rental Rate	Date Purchased
09863	Tractors	160	640	1920	09-Sep-14
10015	Generators	30	120	360	15-Dec-14
10047	Tractors	225	900	2700	08-Mar-15
10103	Generators	120	360	1080	20-Jul-15
10129	Hand Tools	60	240	720	02-Aug-15
10235	Hand Tools	10	30	60	01-Feb-16
10236	Plumbing	35	140	420	01-Feb-16
10237	Plumbing	200	800	2400	01-Feb-16
10283	Sawing, Cutting, & Grinding	120	480	1440	15-Mar-16
10368	Hand Tools	15	45	135	15-May-16

14. Save the table. The *Datasheet* view should look similar to Figure 2-57.

15. Close the table.

16. Close the database.

EquipmentI⏷	ProductName ⏷	Category ⏷	DailyRental ⏷	WeeklyRent ⏷	MonthlyRer ⏷	DatePurcha ⏷	Comments ⏷	Click to Add ⏷
09863	BACKHOE COMPACT ALLMAND DIESEL	Tractors	$160.00	$640.00	$1,920.00	09-Sep-14	Lift Capacity: 2100 lbs Bucket Size: 16" only	
10015	GENERATOR PORTABLE MAKITA 1000W	Generators	$30.00	$120.00	$360.00	15-Dec-14	Size: 19-1/2"L x 11-3/4"W x 17-1/2"H Weight: 55 lbs	
10047	SKIP LOADER 4X4	Tractors	$225.00	$900.00	$2,700.00	08-Mar-15	Subject to Environmental Fee	
10103	GENERATOR TOWABLE POWERPRO 25KW	Generators	$120.00	$360.00	$1,080.00	20-Jul-15	Overall L x W x H: 67"L x 28"W x 3"H	
10129	LEVEL SITE LASER	Hand Tools	$60.00	$240.00	$720.00	02-Aug-15		
10235	WHEELBARROW	Hand Tools	$10.00	$30.00	$60.00	01-Feb-16		
10236	SNAKE DRAIN 1/2" ELECTRIC	Plumbing	$35.00	$140.00	$420.00	01-Feb-16	General Brand - Easy Rooter Jr	
10237	PIPELINE INSPECTION CAMERA - 85'	Plumbing	$200.00	$800.00	$2,400.00	01-Feb-16	85' Cable	
10283	GRINDER ANGLE 7" W/VACUUM	Sawing, Cutting & Grinding	$120.00	$480.00	$1,440.00	15-Mar-16	Remove thin coatings on concrete and surface grinding of Concrete, Screed, Tile Adhesives	
10368	METAL DETECTOR - GARRETT ACE 250	Hand Tools	$15.00	$45.00	$135.00	15-May-16		
*			$0.00	$0.00	$0.00			

Record: I◀ ◀ 11 of 11 ▶ ▶I ▶✱ No Filter Search

2-57 PP A2-2 completed

SLO 2.6

Understanding and Designing Relational Databases

As you learned earlier, a database is a collection of integrated and related tables. So far we have concentrated on learning the steps to build and use a table in Access. Because most databases have more than one table, the next step is to learn how to create a collection of integrated and related tables.

Relational Principles

Recall that Access is a relational database management system. The data in a *relational database* is organized into a collection of related tables. Each table stores data about one part of the system.

Consider, for example, the Mary's Rentals database. In addition to the *Equipment* table you have been working on, Mary's Rentals needs separate tables to store details about employees, customers, customer orders, information about which equipment has been rented in each order, and the service history for the equipment.

The different tables are related, or connected, to each other through common fields. You can create these relationships and view them in the *Relationships window*. Figure 2-58 illustrates how the different tables in Mary's Rentals are connected. The lines connecting the different tables show which fields are connected to each other.

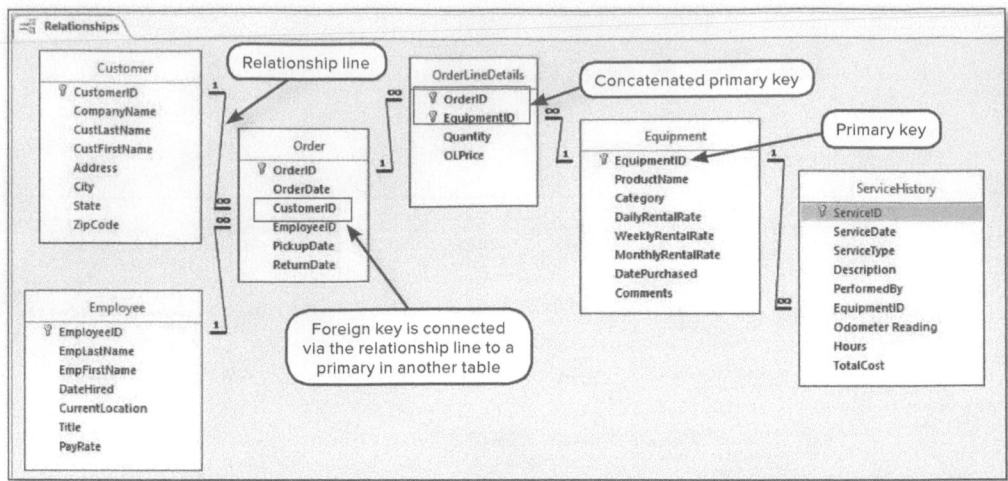

2-58 *Relationships* window for Mary's Rentals database

To be considered relational, a database must meet certain specifications. Many of the specifications are familiar to you because of the work you have already done in building tables. We use Mary's Rentals to illustrate these specifications.

- The data in the database must be stored in tables.
- The rows of the table must represent records. In the *Equipment* table, for example, each record contains the data about one particular piece of equipment.
- The columns of the table must represent fields. A field contains one specific piece of data about a record. In the *Equipment* table, *EquipmentID* and *ProductName* are the first two fields (see Figure 2-58).
- Each row must have a unique identifier or primary key. The primary key allows the DBMS to locate a specific record in the database. The primary key can either be one field in the table or a combination of several fields. If a primary key is made up of more than one field, as in the *OrderLineDetails* in Figure 2-58, it is called a **concatenated key** or **composite key**.
- Each table must have a relationship with at least one other table. In order to have a relationship, the two tables must have a field in common with each other table. This common field is created by adding the primary key field from one table into the related table. In the related table, this added field is known as a **foreign key**. After the foreign key is added into a table, you create a relationship between the two tables by linking the foreign key to the primary key. The foreign key allows you to establish the relationship with another table.

The Steps to Design a Relational Database

For a database to be of value to an organization it must be well designed. It is important to spend time early in the database development process analyzing the needs of the business so you can create a database that meets the needs of the business. The following seven steps will help you create a well-designed database:

1. **Determine the purpose of the database and the scope of the functions that will be performed**. For example, the purpose of the Mary's Rentals database is to manage inventory and customer orders. The functions that need to be performed include all tasks needed to record customers and their orders, from the initial taking of an order all the way to checking a rental return back in to the location.

While the Mary's Rentals database does contain basic information about the employees, it does not track other human resources information like sick leave or vacation time. Those functions are outside of the scope of this database.

2. **Determine the major objects that are needed in the database to support its purpose and functions**. These objects could represent people, places or things. Each object is built as a table. Having the data stored in separate tables helps to minimize the amount of duplicated or redundant data. This improves the overall data integrity in your database.

 In the Mary's Rentals database, examples of people objects are customers or employees. Thing objects are equipment and orders. While Mary's Rentals doesn't have any place objects, an example could be a warehouse or rental location should the company choose to store those in the system.

3. **Determine the specific details you need to capture about each object**. These details are the fields included in each table.

4. **Determine which field in each table is the primary key**. Remember that the primary key is a field that is unique across the different records. If none of the fields that you have identified in step 3 is unique, you may need to add an additional unique field that can serve as the primary key. Sometimes you might need to combine more than one field together to create a concatenated primary key.

5. **Determine the data type and size of each field**. Each field must be defined as containing only a specific type of data such as numbers, text, or dates. Additionally, you should decide how big each field could be.

 For example, you might allow 40 characters for a street address field while a ZIP code field should be limited to nine numbers.

6. **Determine any additional restrictions on what kinds of data can be stored in the fields**. You may wish to further limit the data that can be entered to increase data integrity.

 For example, you may determine that some fields must be filled in while others are optional, or some fields may be limited to a certain list of choices.

7. **Determine how the different tables are related to each other**. This step requires that you look at your different tables and see how they are related to each other. In this way you can create a foreign key in different tables.

 One relationship in Figure 2-58 is between the *Customer* and *Order* tables. In this case the *CustomerID* was placed into the *Order* table so that the company would know which customer was associated with a particular order. You learn how to perform this step in the next section.

Three Types of Relationships

There are three different types of relationships that may exist between tables in a database: one-to-one, one-to-many, and many-to-many. When designing your database, it is critical that you understand how your tables are related to each other and that you select the correct relationship type. One type of relationship is not better than another; a relationship is simply a reflection of the reality of how the tables are associated. The one-to-many type relationship is the most common.

> ▶ MORE INFO
>
> When describing relationships, the following shorthand notation is often used:
>
> 1:1 (one-to-one)
>
> 1:M (one-to-many)
>
> M:N (many-to-many)

Additionally, when describing table relationships, you sometimes will refer to a table based on the side of the relationship to which it belongs. For example, in a 1:M relationship, one table may be called the "1" table, while the other table may be called the "M" table. In a many-to-many relationship (M:N), the letter N is commonly used in the shorthand notation to differentiate the second side of the relationship.

One-to-One Relationship

In a ***one-to-one relationship***, one row of data in *Table A* may be associated with only one row of data in *Table B*. For example, a business may have a table containing infor-

mation about employees. Since the employees frequently travel internationally, they also have another table to store information about employee passports. Each employee has only one passport and a passport belongs to only one employee.

Figure 2-59 shows the visual representation of a one-to-one relationship in Access.

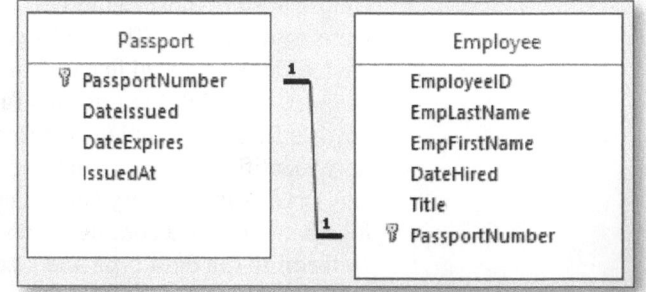

2-59 One-to-one relationship

One-to-Many Relationship

In a ***one-to-many relationship***, one row of data in *Table A* may be associated with many rows of data in *Table B*. In Mary's Rentals there is a one-to-many relationship between the *Customer* and *Order* tables. A customer can have many orders, but a particular order is associated with only one customer.

In Access, the "many" side of a relationship is indicated with the ***infinity symbol***. Figure 2-60 shows the visual representation of a 1:M relationship.

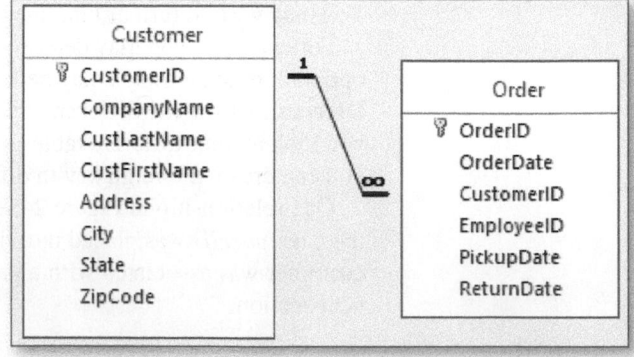

2-60 One-to-many relationship

Many-to-Many Relationship

In a ***many-to-many relationship***, many rows of data in *Table A* may be associated with many rows of data in *Table B*. In Mary's Rentals there is a many-to-many relationship between the *Order* and *Equipment* tables. An order can be for many different pieces of equipment, and a particular piece of equipment can be on many different orders (obviously not at exactly the same time).

A relational database does not directly support M:N relationships. They require the creation of a third table, *Table C*. This third table is a ***junction*** or ***intersection table*** that matches up the records across the two tables. With the creation of the junction table, the M:N relationship converts into two 1:M relationships. This results in a 1:M relationship between *Table A* and *Table C,* and another 1:M relationship between *Table B* and *Table C*.

Figure 2-61 shows the visual representation of a *M:N relationship*. The *OrderLineDetails* table is the junction table in this example. A junction table contains the *primary key* fields from each of the "1" tables. In this case, *OrderLineDetails* contains the primary key field of *OrderID* from the *Order* table and the primary key field of *EquipmentID* from the *Equipment* table. The combination of *OrderID* and *EquipmentID* creates a concatenated primary key in the junction table.

2-61 A many-to-many relationship is converted into two one-to-many relationships

Understand a Foreign Key

Recall that a foreign key is the field in common between two tables. When designing your tables it is important to know how to create a foreign key. In the seventh step of designing a database, you determine how the tables are related to each other and determine what the foreign key is. By the time you get to step 7, you already have each of the tables in your database defined.

For example, in Independent Project 1-5 in Chapter 1, you built a database containing a pet table for Life's Animal Shelter. The shelter also needs a table to store information about owners who adopt the pets. Working through step 6 of designing a database would result in the *Owners* and *Pets* tables shown in Figure 2-62. At this point there is not a field in common.

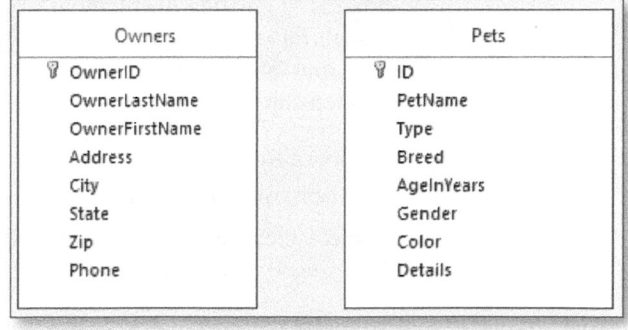

2-62 Owners and Pets tables without a field in common

Step 7 requires you to identify what type of relationship exists between the *Owners* and *Pets* tables. An owner could adopt many pets but a pet belongs to only one owner. This is a 1:M relationship.

- For a 1:M relationship, you create the foreign key by taking the primary key field from the *1* table and adding it as an extra field into the *M* table. This added field is known as the foreign key.

 In the Life's Animal Shelter example, you take the *OwnerID* from the *Owners* table and add it in as a foreign key into the *Pets* table (Figure 2-63). Although not required, many database designers prefer to start the foreign key field name with the letters *FK*.

- For a 1:1 relationship, you create the foreign key by taking the primary key from either table and adding it into the other table. You must set the **Indexed** property of the foreign key field to **Yes (No Duplicates)** for Access to recognize a 1:1 relationship.

- If you determine that you have a M:N relationship, you first need to create the junction table and convert the M:N relationship into two 1:M relationships. The junction table

contains the primary key fields from each of the *1* tables, along with any other fields that describe that junction.

Remember that the foreign key field is always the primary key of another table. Sometimes it is the primary key in both. An example of this is shown and explained later in Figure 2-67.

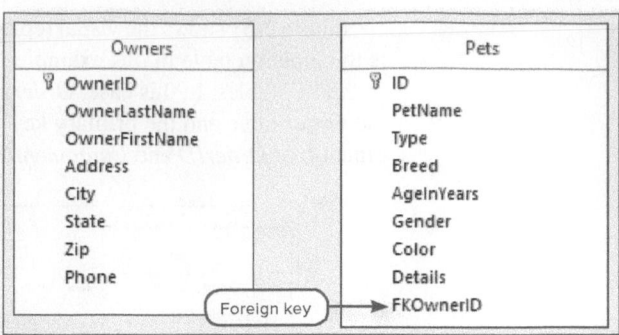

2-63 Add the foreign key into the "M" table in a relationship

The actual addition of the foreign key into the related table is done in *Design* view of the table. When adding the foreign key field, set the field properties to be the same *Data Type* and *Field Size* as the primary key in the *1* table. The foreign key field name can be anything. Often it will either be the exact same name as the primary key or the name of primary key preceded by *FK*.

Adding the foreign key into the table does not establish the relationship. This is done as a separate step, described in the next section. The addition of the foreign key just allows you to relate the tables.

Create Relationships between Tables

You can add relationships after you have added the foreign keys into the tables. Relationships should be set before any data is added into the tables that contain the foreign keys. While the process of creating the relationship is very straightforward, you need to make several decisions about how Access enforces the relationship.

Define a Relationship Using the Relationships Window

You can create a relationship directly in the *Relationships* window.

2-64 *Show Table* dialog box

> **HOW TO: Define a Relationship Using the Relationships Window**

1. Click the **Relationships** button [*Database Tools* tab, *Relationships* group].
 - If this is the first time you are establishing relationships for your database, the *Show Table* dialog box appears (Figure 2-64).
2. Select the **first table** to add.
3. Click the **Add** button.
4. Continue adding the remaining tables.
5. Click the **Close** button when all tables have been added.
 - The tables appear in the *Relationships* window.

- Sometimes the size of the table object is not large enough to display the entire field name of all of the table fields. This is the case for the *Equipment* table shown in Figure 2-65.
- If you want, you can adjust the size of the table objects to see more fields.

6. Click, hold, and drag the **primary key** field from the *1* table on top of the **foreign key** field in the related table (see Figure 2-65).

- The pointer displays a small plus sign box when it is dragged onto the related table.
- The related table is either a *1* table or a *M* table, depending on the type of relationship.

7. Release the pointer when you are positioned on top of the **foreign key** field in the related table. The *Edit Relationships* dialog box opens (Figure 2-66).

8. Verify that the field names displayed are correct. If necessary you can use the drop-down arrows to make any corrections.

9. Check the **Enforce Referential Integrity** box.

- The check boxes for *Cascade Update Related Fields* and *Cascade Delete Related Records* become available.
- As desired, check those boxes.

10. Click **Create**.

- The *Relationships* window updates with the relationship line added (Figure 2-67). The *1* and infinity symbols display indicating that referential integrity is enforced.
- As you can see in Figure 2-67, the *EquipmentID* field is the primary key of the *Equipment* table and is part of a concatenated primary key in the *OrderLineDetails* table. It also is a foreign key in the *OrderLineDetails* table since it links back to the primary key in the *Equipment* table.

11. Save the changes made to the relationships.

12. Click **Close** [*Relationship Tools Design* tab, *Relationships* group] if you are finished with all changes to the relationships.

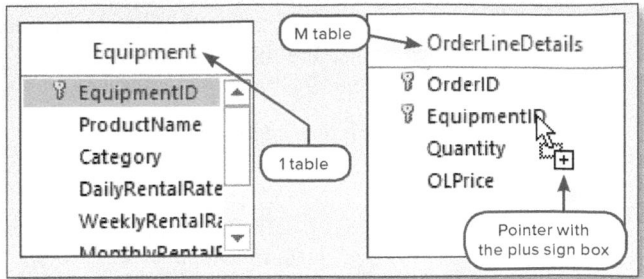

2-65 Drag the primary key to the foreign key to create a relationship

2-66 *Edit Relationships* dialog box

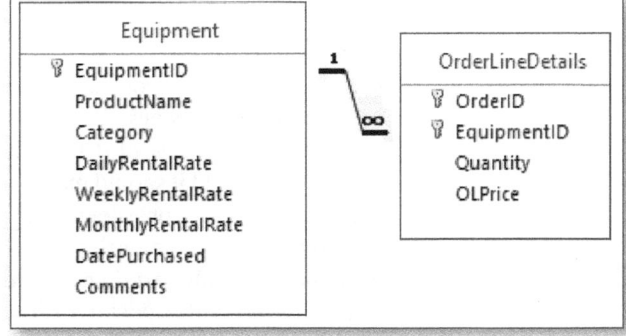

2-67 Completed relationships window

> **ANOTHER WAY**
>
> You can also create a relationship using the *Lookup Wizard*. Select the foreign key field, select the ***Lookup wizard*** data type and select the option **I want the lookup field to get the values from another table or query.**

Once a relationship has been created, when you view the *1* table in *Datasheet* view you can see the related records. A plus sign appears to the left of the first column, indicating that this table is related to another table.

- View related records by clicking the **plus sign**. The plus sign changes to a minus sign. Figure 2-68 shows the related records for *EquipmentID 10015*.

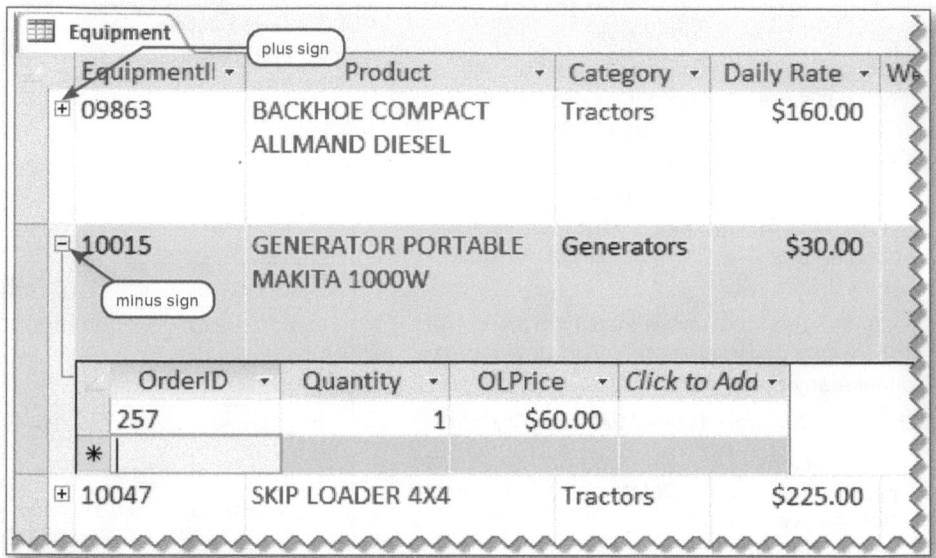

2-68 Click the plus sign to show related records in *Datasheet* view

- You can enter additional records into the related table directly from this view.
- Click the **minus sign** to hide the related records.

Enforce Referential Integrity

When creating a relationship, you must decide if you want to enforce referential integrity. *Referential integrity* ensures that records in associated tables have consistent data. For example, if you enter a row of data in the *OrderLineDetails* table, when you enter a value in the *EquipmentID* field it should match an *EquipmentID* value that already exists in the *Equipment* table. This ensures consistency and integrity of the database.

If you create a relationship and do not enforce referential integrity, you can have records in the associated table that do not match a record in the *1* table.

For example, if a doctor's office does not require a patient to declare a primary physician, the *PhysicianID* field on a *Patient* table may be left blank. While this is possible, in the majority of cases you will want to enforce referential integrity.

Enforce referential integrity by selecting the **Enforce Referential Integrity** check box in the *Edit Relationships* dialog box.

In addition to requiring that the foreign key value of a record in the associated table matches a primary key value in the *1* table, when referential integrity has been enforced Access prohibits two other actions.

- First, Access does not allow you to delete a record from the *1* table if that record has related records in an associated table. For example, at a school you may have a table with student information and another table containing information about student parking

tickets. If referential integrity is enforced, Access does not allow you to delete a student record from the *Student* table if that student has any rows of data in the *ParkingTicket* table. This ensures that all parking tickets remain linked to the student who got the ticket. This restriction means that a student can't exit the school system without first paying all their parking tickets.

- Second, Access does not allow you to change the value of the primary key field in the *1* table if that record has related records in an associated table. Assuming that *StudentID* is the primary key in the *Student* table, the student is not allowed to change the value of their *StudentID* if they have any parking ticket records in the *ParkingTicket* table.

You may determine that there are valid reasons to override these constraints. If referential integrity has been enforced, the ***Cascade Update Related Fields*** and ***Cascade Delete Related Records*** options become available.

Cascade Updates

Sometimes it is desirable to allow the primary key value of the *1* table to be changed. For example, if a *StudentID* value has been stolen, the student must be assigned a new ID. In cases like this, you want to be able to change the value of the primary key and have Access find all related records and change the value in the foreign key to match the new primary key value.

To allow the primary key value to be changed and have Access cascade updates in the related table select the **Cascade Update Related Fields** check box in the *Edit Relationships* dialog box. You can do this only if you have selected the *Enforce Referential Integrity* option in the *Edit Relationships* dialog box.

Cascade Deletes

There may be situations when you want to delete a record from the *1* table and have Access automatically delete all the related records in the associated table. For example, if a record is deleted from the *Order* table because an order is canceled, all of the records in the *OrderLineDetails* table (the specific products this customer had ordered) should be deleted as well. In cases like this, you want to be able to make this deletion and have Access delete all the related records.

To allow a record in the *1* table to be deleted and have Access delete all associated records in the related table, select the **Cascade Delete Related Records** check box in the *Edit Relationships* dialog box. You can do this only if you have selected the *Enforce Referential Integrity* option.

Save a Relationship

If you have made any changes to the relationships you need to save those changes.

Click the **Save** button on the *Quick Access* toolbar to save any changes made to the relationships.

Delete a Relationship between Tables

If a relationship has been created in error, or you need to make changes to the fields involved in the relationship, or you no longer need to have a particular relationship, you can delete it. You must close all of the tables involved in the relationship, as well as any objects that are based on those tables before you can delete a relationship.

▶ **HOW TO: Delete a Relationship between Tables**

1. Click the **Relationships** button [*Database Tools* tab, *Relationships* group].
 • The *Relationships* window appears.
2. Select the **relationship line** you wish to delete (Figure 2-69).
 • The middle part of the line thickens once it has been selected.
3. Right-click the **relationship line** to open the context menu.
4. Click **Delete** (Figure 2-70).
 • A confirmation message appears asking you to confirm the deletion. Click **Yes** to confirm the deletion.
5. Click the **Save** button to save your changes.
6. Click **Close** [*Relationship Tools Design* tab, *Relationships* group] if you are finished with all deletions to the relationships.

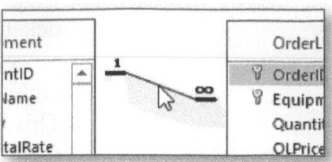

2-69 *Select the relationship line*

2-70 *Delete icon in the context menu*

Edit a Relationship between Tables

Occasionally you need to make changes to an existing relationship between tables.

▶ **HOW TO: Edit a Relationship between Tables**

1. Click the **Relationships** button [*Database Tools* tab, *Relationships* group].
 • The *Relationships* window appears.
2. Select the **relationship line** you wish to edit.
3. Click **Edit Relationships** [*Relationship Tools Design* tab, *Tools* group] (Figure 2-71). The *Edit Relationships* dialog box opens (Figure 2-72).

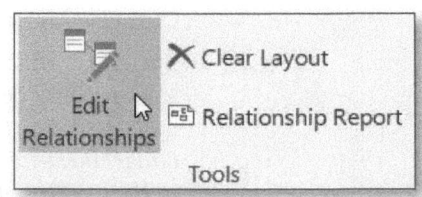

2-71 *Edit Relationships button*

> **ANOTHER WAY**
>
> Right-click the **relationship line** to open the context menu and then select **Edit Relationship.**

4. Change the referential integrity options or selected fields.
5. Click **OK**.
6. Save the changes made to the relationships.
7. Click **Close** [*Relationship Tools Design* tab, *Relationships* group] if you are finished with all changes to the relationships.

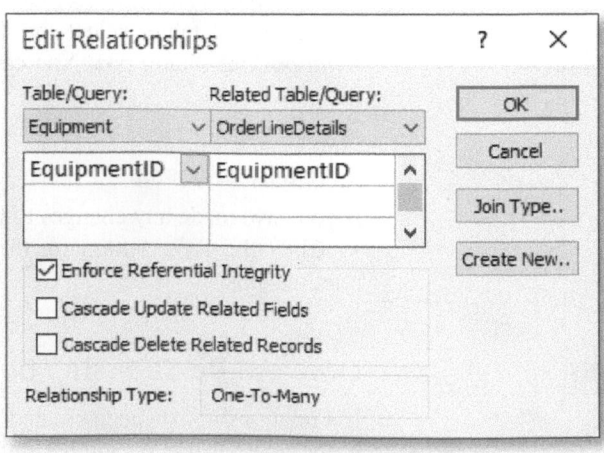

2-72 *Edit Relationships dialog box*

<table>
<tr><td>SLO 2.7</td></tr>
</table>

Printing the Contents of a Table

Occasionally you may wish to print a simple list of all records in a table. You can do this with the *Print* button on the *Backstage* view. There are three options available after selecting the *Print* button:

- ***Quick Print:*** Sends the contents of the current object immediately to the printer.
- ***Print:*** Allows you to select different print options before sending the contents to the printer.
- ***Print Preview:*** Allows you to preview the way the table records will print before actually sending them to the printer.

Preview the Data Records

Previewing the way that your table records will print is a good idea. This allows you to check that the formatting is appropriate and to make changes to any settings before printing.

▶**HOW TO: Preview the Data Records before Printing**

1. Select the **table** you want to print from the *Navigation Pane*. The table can be closed or it can be open in *Datasheet* view when you print records.
2. Click the **Print** button [*File* tab] to display the printing options.
3. Click the **Print Preview** button.
 - The *Print Preview* tab opens and shows a preview of how the table will print (Figure 2-73).
 - The default print settings include the table name and current date at the top of the report and page number at the bottom of the report. Access calls these three items *Headings*.

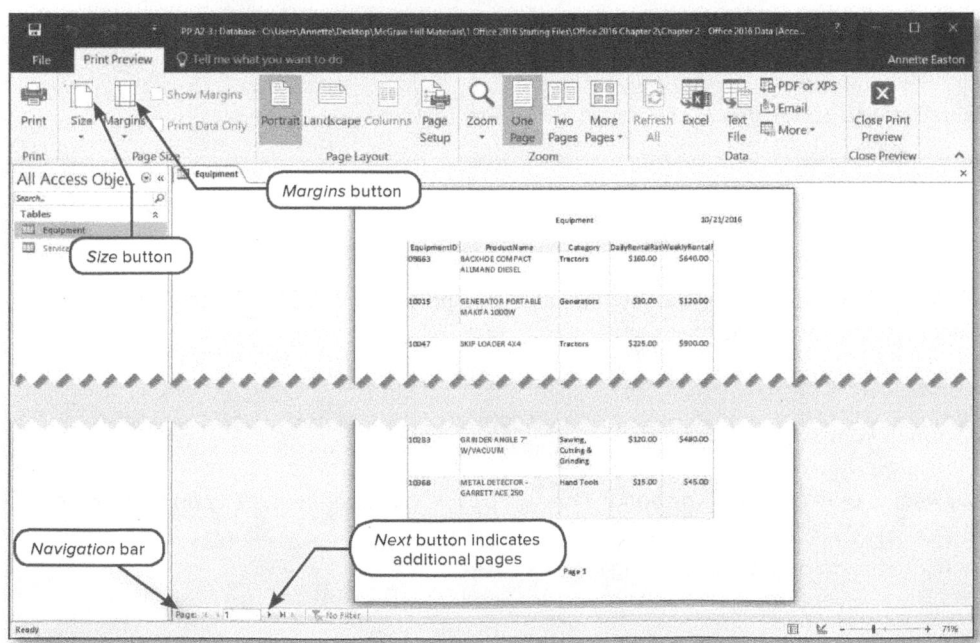

2-73 *Print Preview* of table records

4. Review the *Navigation* bar to determine if there are additional pages that will print. In Figure 2-73, the darkened *Next Page* button indicates that there are additional pages.
5. Adjust the page orientation by clicking the **Portrait** or **Landscape** buttons [*Print Preview* tab, *Page Layout* group].

6. Click the **Page Setup** button [*Print Preview* tab, *Page Layout* group] or press **S** to open the *Page Setup* dialog box (Figure 2-74).

7. Adjust the margins on the *Print Options* tab.

8. Adjust the paper size on *Page* tab. You can also adjust the page orientation on the *Page* tab.

> ▶ **ANOTHER WAY**
>
> You can set the paper size, and margins by clicking the **Size** or **Margins** buttons [*Print Preview* tab, *Page Size* group].

9. Remove the *Headings* from the printout by deselecting the **Print Headings** check box on the *Print Options* tab of the *Page Setup* dialog box.

10. Click **OK** to close the *Page Setup* dialog box.

11. Click the **Print** button [*Print Preview* tab, *Print* group] when ready to print.

 - The *Print* dialog box displays.
 - In the *Print* dialog box, you can change the number of copies, page range, and printer as desired.

2-74 *Page Setup* dialog box

> ▶ **ANOTHER WAY**
>
> Press **P** or **Ctrl+P** to open the *Print* dialog box from *Print Preview* view.

12. Click **OK** to print the table.

13. Click the **Close Print Preview** button [*Print Preview* tab, *Close Preview* group].

Print the Data Records without Previewing

If you previously previewed how the table will print you can quickly print the table records without previewing the pages.

▶ **HOW TO: Print Table Records**

1. Select the **table** you want to print from the *Navigation Pane*. The table can be closed or it can be open in *Datasheet* view when you print records.

2. Click the **Print** button [*File* tab] to display the printing options.

3. Click the **Print** button. The *Print* dialog box displays.

4. Change the number of copies, page range, and printer as desired.

5. Click **OK**.

> ▶ **ANOTHER WAY**
>
> Click the **Quick Print** button to print the table without opening the *Print* dialog box.

Queries and *Reports* provide advanced options to create more attractive and formatted printouts of table data. You can also use them to print only a subset of the table data. These objects are covered in Chapters 3 and 4.

Using the Compact & Repair Database Utility

Over time, as you use your database, the database file becomes larger. Much of this is due to additional records being added into the tables. However, some of the increased size is due to certain ways that Access operates. In order to accomplish some functions, Access creates temporary objects. These objects are not always automatically deleted when the function has been performed. Additionally, when you delete database objects, that space is not always released.

As the database file grows, it takes longer to perform tasks such as adding and deleting records, querying tables, and printing reports. With really large databases this can result in a significant decrease in processing speed.

Another concern is that a database file may become corrupted. In Access this is most likely to occur if the database is shared over a network and numerous users make frequent edits to *Long Text* fields. A corrupted database doesn't typically result in lost data; rather, some of the code or forms may be lost or become unusable.

You can use the ***Compact & Repair Database*** utility to reduce the chances of corruption and to reclaim unused space from temporary and deleted objects. Before running this process be sure to create a backup copy of your database. Additionally, if this is a multi-user database, no one can be using the database at the time the compact and repair is performed.

▶ HOW TO: Compact and Repair a Database

1. Click the **File** tab. The *Info* button should be selected.
2. Click the **Compact & Repair Database** button (Figure 2-75).

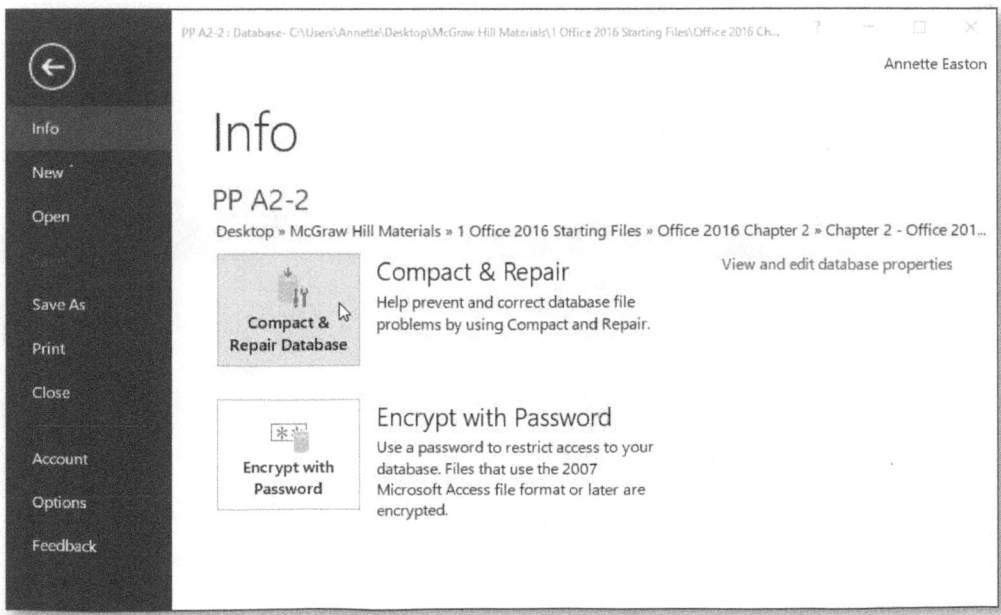

2-75 *Compact & Repair Database* button

- If Access is not able to repair everything in a corrupted database, it creates a table named *MSysCompactErrors*. This table opens automatically and contains information about the objects that could not be repaired.

 ANOTHER WAY

Click the **Compact and Repair Database** button [*Database Tools* tab, *Tools* group] to compact and repair the database.

PAUSE & PRACTICE: ACCESS 2-3

In this Pause & Practice, you add a second table to store the service history of the equipment. Next you define a relationship between the *Equipment* and *Service History* tables. You also print the contents of the *Equipment* table and manage the database using the *Compact & Repair Database* utility.

Files Needed: *[your initials] PP A2-2.accdb* and **ServiceHistoryDataFile-02.xlsx**
Completed Project File Name: *[your initials] PP A2-3.accdb* and *[your initials] PP A2-3_YYYY-MM-DD.accdb*

1. Open the *[your initials] PP A2-2* database file created in Pause & Practice 2-2.

2. Save a new copy of your database as [your initials] PP A2-3.

3. Enable content in the security warning.

4. Click the **Table Design** button [*Create* tab, *Tables* group] to open a new table in *Design* view.

5. Add new fields into the table.
 a. Type ServiceID in the *Field Name* property box of the first row. Press the **Tab** key to move to the *Data Type* property.
 b. Select the **Short Text** *Data Type*. Press the **Tab** key to move to the *Description* property.
 c. Type Unique ID number for the service request.
 d. Click the **Primary Key** button [*Table Tools Design* tab, *Tools* group].
 e. Press the **Tab** key to move to the next row.
 f. Continue adding the remaining fields into the table using the following information.

Field Name	Data Type	Description
ServiceDate	**Date/Time**	Date service was completed
ServiceType	**Short Text**	Indicates whether service was maintenance, repair, or inspection
Description	**Short Text**	General description of the nature of the service performed
PerformedBy	**Short Text**	Employee ID number of the repair person
FKEquipmentID	**Short Text**	Must match an EquipmentID value in the Equipment table – (this is the foreign key)
OdometerReading	**Number**	Odometer reading at time of repair (for vehicles only)
Hours	**Number**	Total number of hours the equipment has been in use
TotalCost	**Currency**	Cost of the service (parts and labor)

6. Click the **Save** button to save the table as ServiceHistory.

7. Set the field properties in the *ServiceHistory* table.
 a. Click the **row selector** of the *ServiceID* field.
 b. Type 6 in the *Field Size* property box in the *Field Properties* area.
 c. Set the *Required* property to **Yes** if necessary.
 d. Click the **row selector** of the *ServiceDate* field.
 e. Continue changing the remaining field properties in the *ServiceHistory* table using the following information.
 f. Save the table by clicking the **Save** button.

Field Name	Field Size	Format	Required
ServiceDate		General Date	Yes
ServiceType	15		Yes
Description	255		Yes
PerformedBy	3		Yes
FKEquipmentID	5		Yes
TotalCost		Currency	Yes

8. Modify the *ServiceType* field to use a *Combo Box*.
 a. Click to select the **ServiceType** field.
 b. Click the property box for the **Data Type** property, click the **arrow,** and select **Lookup Wizard.** The *Lookup Wizard* dialog box opens.
 c. Select the radio button for **I will type in the values that I want**.
 d. Click the **Next** button.
 e. Click the **first cell** in the *Col1* column.
 f. Type Maintenance.
 g. Press the **down arrow** key to move to the next row.
 h. Type Repair. Press the **down arrow** key to move to the next row.
 i. Type Inspection.
 j. Click the **Next** button.
 k. Click the **Limit To List** check box.
 l. Click the **Finish** button.

9. Save and close the table.

10. Create a relationship between the *Equipment* and *ServiceHistory* tables.
 a. Click the **Relationships** button [*Database Tools* tab, *Relationships* group]. If this is the first time you have established relationships for your database, the *Show Table* dialog box appears.

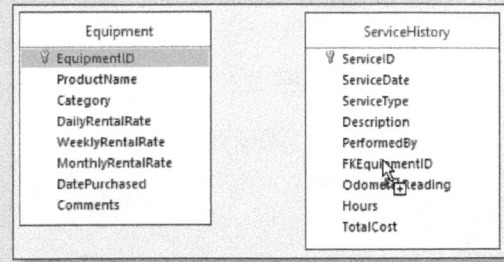

2-76 Create the relationship between the *Equipment* and *ServiceHistory* tables

 b. Click the **Show Table** button [*Relationship Tools Design* tab, *Relationships* group] if the *Show Table* dialog box does not display.
 c. Select the **Equipment** table and click the **Add** button.
 d. Select the **ServiceHistory** table and click the **Add** button.
 e. Click the **Close** button. The tables display in the *Relationships* window.
 f. Adjust the size of the table objects to see all of the fields.
 g. Drag the **EquipmentID** from the *Equipment* table on top of the **FKEquipmentID** in the *ServiceHistory* table. The pointer displays a small plus sign box when it is dragged onto the related table (Figure 2-76).

h. Release the pointer when you are positioned on top of the *FKEquipmentID* field. The *Edit Relationships* dialog box opens.

i. Verify that the field names displayed are correct. If necessary use the **drop-down arrows** to make any corrections.

j. Check the **Enforce Referential Integrity** check box.

k. Check the **Cascade Update Related Fields** check box.

l. Check the **Cascade Delete Related Records** check box. The completed *Edit Relationships* dialog box should be similar to Figure 2-77.

m. Click **Create.** The *Relationships* window updates with the relationship line added (Figure 2-78). The 1 and infinity symbols display indicating that referential integrity is enforced.

n. Save the changes made to the relationships.

o. Click **Close** [*Relationship Tools Design* tab, *Relationships* group].

11. Import data into the *ServiceHistory* table.

a. Launch the *Get External Data – Excel Spreadsheet* dialog box.

b. Locate and select the **ServiceHistoryDataFile-02** Excel file.

c. Append the records to the *ServiceHistory* table.

d. Launch the *Import Spreadsheet Wizard*.

e. Finish the *Import Spreadsheet Wizard*. Close the *Wizard* after the records have imported.

12. Open the *Equipment* table in *Datasheet* view.

a. Click the **plus sign** for *EquipmentID 09863* to display the related records. You should see the four entries in the *ServiceHistory* table for this piece of equipment (Figure 2-79).

b. Click the **minus sign** to hide the related records.

2-77 Select *Referential Integrity* options in the *Edit Relationships* dialog box

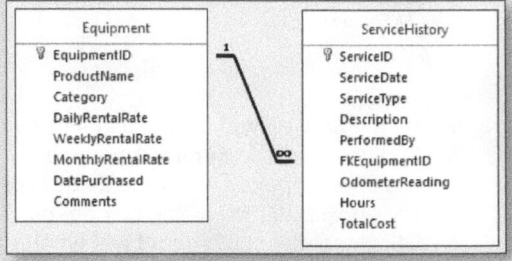

2-78 Completed relationship between the tables

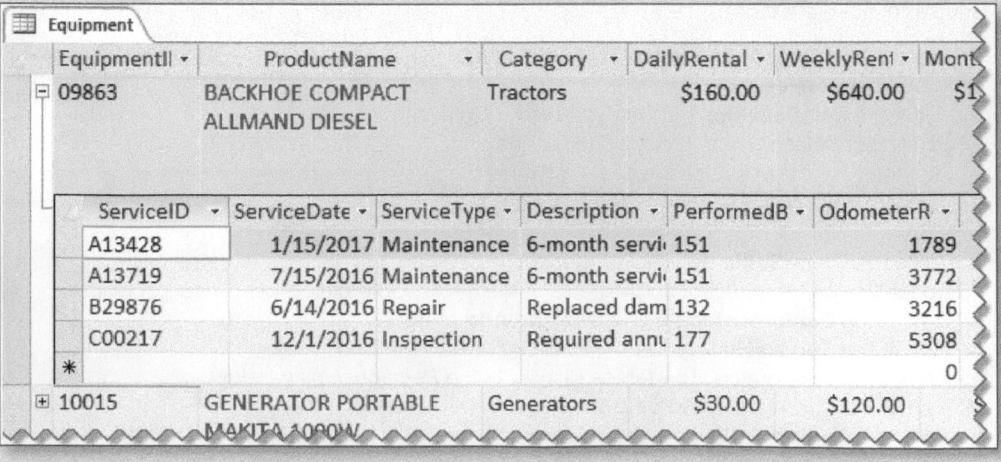

2-79 Display related records for *EquipmentID* 09863

13. Prepare to print the *Equipment* table.
 a. Click the **Print** button [*File* tab] to display the printing options.
 b. Click the **Print Preview** button to open the *Print Preview* tab and view a preview of how the table will print.
 c. Click the **Landscape** button [*Print Preview* tab, *Page Layout* group] to change the page orientation.
 d. Click the **Margins** button [*Print Preview* tab, *Page Size* group] and select the **Normal** button as shown in Figure 2-80. The report preview should appear as shown in Figure 2-81. Depending on the default font or printer settings, the *Comments* field may appear on a separate page.

2-80 *Margins* options in *Print Preview*

		Equipment					10/21/2016
EquipmentID	ProductName	Category	DailyRentalRate	WeeklyRental	MonthlyRental	DatePurchased	Comments
09863	BACKHOE COMPACT ALLMAND DIESEL	Tractors	$160.00	$640.00	$1,920.00	09-Sep-14	Lift Capacity: 2100 lbs Bucket Size: 16" only
10015	GENERATOR PORTABLE MAKITA 1000W	Generators	$30.00	$120.00	$360.00	15-Dec-14	Size: 19-1/2"L x 11-3/4"W x 17-1/2"H Weight: 55 lbs
10047	SKIP LOADER 4X4	Tractors	$225.00	$900.00	$2,700.00	08-Mar-15	Subject to Environmental Fee
10103	GENERATOR TOWABLE POWERPRO 25KW	Generators	$120.00	$360.00	$1,080.00	20-Jul-15	Overall L x W x H: 67"L x 28"W x 3"H
10129	LEVEL SITE LASER	Hand Tools	$60.00	$240.00	$720.00	02-Aug-15	
10235	WHEELBARROW	Hand Tools	$10.00	$30.00	$60.00	01-Feb-16	
10236	SNAKE DRAIN 1/2" ELECTRIC	Plumbing	$35.00	$140.00	$420.00	01-Feb-16	General Brand - Easy Rooter Jr
10237	PIPELINE INSPECTION CAMERA - 85'	Plumbing	$200.00	$800.00	$2,400.00	01-Feb-16	85' Cable

Page 1

2-81 *Print preview of Equipment table records*

14. Click the **Close Print Preview** button [*Print Preview* tab, *Close Preview* group].

15. Compact and repair the database.
 a. Click the **Save As** button [*File* tab].
 b. Ensure that *Save Database As* is selected in *File Types*.
 c. Select **Back Up Database** in the *Save Database As* area.
 d. Click the **Save As** button.
 e. Accept the default name in the *File name* box and click the **Save** button.
 f. Click the **File** tab. The *Info* button should be selected.
 g. Click the **Compact & Repair Database** button.

16. Close the database.

Chapter Summary

2.1 Create a table in *Design* view; add new fields; define a primary key; delete fields; save, close and open a table; and switch between *Datasheet* and *Design* views (p. A2-79).

- **Design view** provides the most flexibility when you are creating tables and setting field properties.
- Add new fields in *Design* view by entering the field name and selecting the data type.
- You can use the *Property Update Options* smart tag to have Access update the value of an *inheritable property* in all of the controls that are based on that field.
- Each table should have a **primary key**, a field that contains a unique value for each record.
- You can add a new field between existing fields by inserting a row, and delete a field by deleting a row.
- You must save any changes to the table design for them to be permanent.

2.2 Set field properties including *Field Size, Format, Caption, Default Value,* and *Required* (p. A2-83).

- The field properties in *Design* view are grouped into *General* and *Lookup* properties.
- The **Field Size** property sets the maximum number of characters allowed or the maximum value of a number.
- You can use the **Format** property to control the appearance of the data in a table.
- You can choose from predefined formats for *Number, Currency, Date/Time,* and *Yes/No* data types.
- You can create custom formats for *Short Text* and *Long Text* data types.
- Customize the **Caption** property to change the contents that appears as a column header.
- The contents of the **Default Value** property are automatically entered into a field when a new record is added to a table.
- Require a user to enter a value for a field by setting the **Required** property.

2.3 Explain data integrity and data validation concepts and options (p. A2-90).

- **Data validation** is the process of verifying the accuracy, or integrity, of the data.
- Create **data integrity rules** to ensure that the data is accurate and consistent.

- *Data format, range, consistency* and *completeness* are the most common types of data integrity rules.
- **Metadata** are the descriptions about what the different data fields represent and their formats.

2.4 Create field and record validation rules, test rules, create validation text, create lookup fields, and define an input mask (p. A2-91).

- **Field validation rules** create *range* and *data format* integrity rules by limiting what can be entered into a field.
- *Consistency* integrity rules compare fields in the same table. These **record validation rules** are entered into the validation rule property for the table.
- It is a good idea to create several cases of **test data** and use it to test the validation rules to ensure the rule works as desired.
- You can enter custom error messages into the **Validation Text** property. This message displays when data is entered that violates a validation rule.
- **Lookup fields** display a list of predefined choices from which the user can select.
- Apply an **input mask** to a field to require the user to enter the data in a predefined format.

2.5 Change field properties after records are added into a table (p. A2-104).

- If you change field properties after data has been added into the tables, Access warns you that the change could result in lost data or inconsistent data.
- Pay attention to the warning messages because it may be impossible to undo some of the changes and recover any lost data.

2.6 Explain relational database principles, understand the steps that must be taken to design a database, create relationships between tables, implement referential integrity, and delete and edit relationships (p. A2-110).

- A **relational database** contains data that is organized into a collection of related tables. To be considered relational, a database must meet a set of specifications.
- It is important to follow the steps to designing a relational database to ensure that your set of tables and relationships are correct.

- Relationships are the connections among different tables. They can be classified as **one-to-one, one-to-many,** and **many-to-many**.
- A **foreign key** is a field in common across tables and is the mechanism that allows tables to be related.
- Once the foreign key has been added into a table, the relationships can be established through the **Relationships window**.
- Referential integrity ensures that records in related tables are consistent.
- Depending on the needs of the business, you can decide whether to use the **Cascade Update Related Fields** and **Cascade Delete Related Records** options.

2.7 Preview and print the contents of a table (p. A2-120).

- On the *Backstage* view you can print the contents of a table.
- **Print Preview** allows you to see how the records appear before printing. In the *Print Preview* tab you can change paper size, margins, and page orientation.

2.8 Manage a database using the *Compact & Repair Database* utility (p. A2-122).

- Over time the size of your database increases due to added data as well as temporary and deleted objects.
- In larger databases, functions such as adding and deleting records, querying tables, and running reports take longer.
- The **Compact & Repair Database** utility reclaims unused space and repairs databases that have become corrupted.

Check for Understanding

The SIMbook for this text (within your SIMnet account) provides the following resources for concept review:

- Multiple Choice questions
- Matching exercises
- Short answer questions

Guided Project 2-1

Central Sierra Insurance wants to expand the database you created in the Pause & Practice 1-4 project in Chapter 1. To ensure consistency, the starting file is provided for you. For this project, you use *Design* view to create a second table, edit field properties, and integrate data integrity rules. You also create a relationship between the two tables and enforce referential integrity constraints. Finally, you view how the table records will print using *Print Preview*.
[Student Learning Outcomes 2.1, 2.2, 2.3, 2.4, 2.5, 2.6, 2.7]

File Needed: ***CentralSierra-02.accdb***
Completed Project File Name: ***[your initials] Access 2-1.accdb***

Skills Covered in This Project

- Create a table using *Design* view.
- Add fields into a table.
- Edit field properties in *Design* view.
- Define an input mask.
- Use the *Lookup Wizard* to create a drop-down list.

- Save a table.
- Enter records.
- Verify the existence of a foreign key.
- Create a 1:M relationship between tables.
- Enforce referential integrity.
- View a table in *Datasheet* view and expand related records.
- Preview table results for printing.

1. Open the ***CentralSierra-02*** database file.

2. Save a new copy of your database as [your initials] Access 2-1.

3. Enable content in the security warning.

4. Click the **Table Design** button [*Create* tab, *Tables* group] to open a new table in *Design* view.

5. Add new fields into the table and set field properties.
 a. Type Branch in the *Field Name* property box of the first row. Press the **Tab** key to move to the *Data Type* property.
 b. Select the **Short Text** *Data Type*. Press the **Tab** key to move to the *Description* property.
 c. Type Unique branch name.
 d. Click the **Primary Key** button [*Table Tools Design* tab, *Tools* group].
 e. Press the **Tab** key to move to the next row.
 f. Add the remaining fields into the table using the following information:

Field Name	Data Type	Description
Address	**Short text**	Street address of the branch
City	**Short text**	Branch city
State	**Short text**	Branch state
ZIP	**Short text**	Branch ZIP code
Phone	**Short text**	Branch main phone number
DateOpened	**Date/Time**	Date the branch first opened

g. Click the **Save** button to save the table as Branches. It is a good idea to periodically save a table when you are creating it so you don't lose your work.
h. Click the **row selector** to select the *Branch* field.
i. Type 30 in the *Field Size* property box in the *Field Properties* area.
j. Set the *Required* property to **Yes** if necessary.
k. Click the **row selector** to select the *Address* field.
l. Change the remaining field properties in the *Branches* table using the following information:

Field Name	Field Size	Format	Default Value	Required
Address	40			**Yes**
City	20			**Yes**
State	2		CA	**Yes**
ZIP	9			**Yes**
Phone	10			**Yes**
DateOpened		**Medium Date**		**Yes**

m. Save the table by clicking the **Save** button.

6. Create an input mask for the *ZIP* field.
 a. Click to select the **ZIP** field.
 b. Click the property box for the *Input Mask* property.
 c. Click the **Build** button to launch the *Input Mask Wizard*.
 d. Select the **Zip Code** *Input Mask*.
 e. Click the **Next** button.
 f. Click the **Next** button without making any changes to the *Input Mask* or *Placeholder character*.
 g. Select the **Without the symbols in the mask, like this** radio button if necessary.
 h. Click the **Finish** button.
 i. Save the table.

7. Create an input mask for the *Phone* field.
 a. Click to select the **Phone** field.
 b. Click the property box for the *Input Mask* property.
 c. Click the **Build** button to launch the *Input Mask Wizard*.
 d. Select the **Phone Number** *Input Mask*.
 e. Click the **Next** button.
 f. Click the **Next** button without making any changes to the *Input Mask* or *Placeholder character*.
 g. Select the **Without the symbols in the mask, like this** radio button if necessary.
 h. Click the **Finish** button.
 i. Save the table.

8. Enter records into the *Branches* table.
 a. Change to *Datasheet* view of the table.
 b. Enter the following records into the *Branches* table. The *DateOpened* values will display in the *Medium Date* format, DD-Mon-YY, after you enter them.

Branch	Address	City	State	ZIP	Phone	DateOpened
Cameron Park	3360 Coach Lane	Cameron Park	CA	95682-8454	530-672-3232	1/1/2014
Folsom	75 Natoma Street, #B1	Folsom	CA	95630-2640	916-458-5555	2/5/2014
Granite Bay	6132 Del Oro Road	Granite Bay	CA	95746-9007	916-791-8787	1/1/2016

c. Save and close the table.

9. Modify the *Department* field in the *Employees* table to use a *Combo Box*.
 a. Open the *Employees* table in *Design* view.
 b. Click to select the **Department** field.
 c. Click the property box for the **Data Type** property, click the **arrow,** and select **Lookup Wizard**. The *Lookup Wizard* dialog box opens.
 d. Select the **I will type in the values that I want** radio button.
 e. Click the **Next** button.
 f. Click the first cell in the *Col1* column.
 g. Type Administration.
 h. Press the **down arrow** key to move to the next row.
 i. Type Health and Benefits. Press the **down arrow** key to move to the next row.
 j. Type Insurance Sales. Press the **down arrow** key to move to the next row.
 k. Type Property and Casualty.
 l. Click the **Next** button.
 m. Click the **Limit To List** check box.
 n. Click the **Finish** button.
 o. Save the table. If prompted to test the existing data against the new rules, click **Yes**.

10. Verify the existence of a foreign key and create a one-to-many relationship between the *Branches* and *Employees* tables. The *Branch* field is the field in common across the two tables. It is the primary key in the *Branches* table.
 a. Open both tables in *Design* view and verify that the *Branch* field has the same *Data Type* and *Field Size* in both tables.
 b. Edit the *Description* property of the *Branch* field in the *Employees* table to read Branch assigned to – Must match a Branch in the Branches table.
 c. Save and close any tables that you may have opened.
 d. Click the **Relationships** button [*Database Tools* tab, *Relationships* group].
 e. Select the **Branches** table In the *Show Table* dialog box and click the **Add** button.
 f. Select the **Employees** table and click the **Add** button.
 g. Click the **Close** button.
 h. Drag the **Branch** field from the *Branches* table on top of the **Branch** field in the *Employees* table. Release the pointer. The *Edit Relationships* dialog box opens.
 i. Verify that the field names displayed are correct. If necessary, use the drop-down arrows to make any corrections.
 j. Click the **Enforce Referential Integrity** check box.
 k. Click the **Cascade Update Related Fields** check box.
 l. Leave the *Cascade Delete Related Records* check box not selected. The company does not want to delete employees just because they may close a branch. This allows them to reassign employees.
 m. Click **Create**. The *Relationships* window updates with the relationship line added. The *1* and infinity symbols display indicating that referential integrity is enforced.
 n. Save the changes made to the relationships.
 o. Click **Close** [*Relationship Tools Design* tab, *Relationships* group].

11. Enter the following record into the *Employees* table to test the new drop-down list:

Emp ID	FirstName	LastName	Branch	Title	Department	Start Date	Base Monthly Salary
200	Timothy	Hansen	Cameron Park	Insurance Agent	Health and Benefits	9/15/2016	3900

12. Save and close the table.

13. Open the *Branches* table in *Datasheet* view.
 a. Adjust the width of the fields so that the entire field contents shows for each field.
 b. Click the **plus sign** to the left of the *Branch* field for the *Cameron Park* branch. You should see the 11 employees assigned to Cameron Park.
 c. Click the **minus sign** to close the related records.

14. Preview the data records in the *Branches* table before printing.
 a. Click the **Print** button [*File* tab] to display the printing options.
 b. Click the **Print Preview** button. The *Print Preview* tab opens and shows a preview of how the table will print.
 c. Click the **Landscape** button [*Print Preview* tab, *Page Layout* group] to change the page orientation. The report preview should appear similar to that in Figure 2-82.

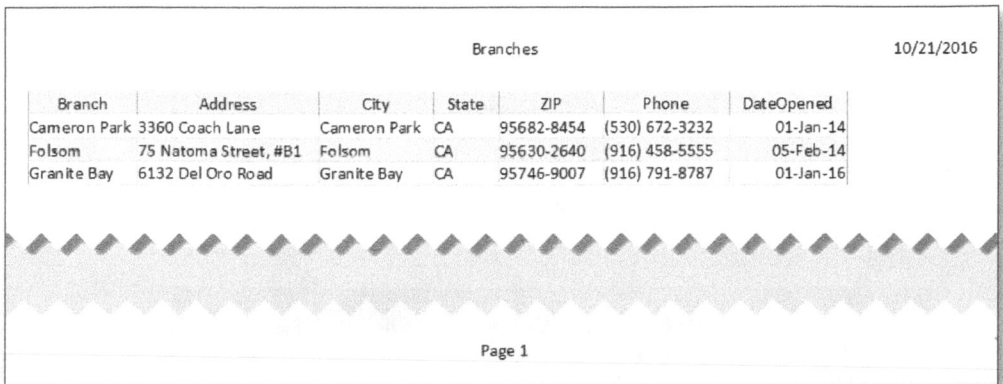

Branch	Address	City	State	ZIP	Phone	DateOpened
Cameron Park	3360 Coach Lane	Cameron Park	CA	95682-8454	(530) 672-3232	01-Jan-14
Folsom	75 Natoma Street, #B1	Folsom	CA	95630-2640	(916) 458-5555	05-Feb-14
Granite Bay	6132 Del Oro Road	Granite Bay	CA	95746-9007	(916) 791-8787	01-Jan-16

Branches 10/21/2016

Page 1

2-82 *Print Preview* of *Branches* table records

 d. Click the **Close Print Preview** button.

15. Save and close the *Branches* table.

16. Close the database.

San Diego Sailing Club wants to expand the database created in Guided Project 1-3 in Chapter 1. To ensure consistency, the starting file is provided for you. For this project, you use *Design* view to create a second table, edit field properties, and integrate data integrity rules. You also create a relationship between the two tables, enforce referential integrity constraints and preview records for printing. Finally, you create a backup, and compact and repair the database.
[Student Learning Outcomes 2.1, 2.2, 2.3, 2.4, 2.5, 2.6, 2.7, 2.8]

File Needed: *SanDiegoSailing-02.accdb*
Completed Project File Name: *[your initials] Access 2-2.accdb* and
[your initials] Access 2-2_YYYY-MM-DD.accdb

Skills Covered in This Project

- Create a table using *Design* view.
- Add fields into a table.
- Edit field properties in *Design* view.
- Create a validation rule and validation text.
- Save a table.
- Create a 1:M relationship between tables.
- Enforce referential integrity.
- Preview a table for printing.
- Compact and repair a database.

1. Open the ***SanDiegoSailing-02*** database file.

2. Save a new copy of your database as [your initials] Access 2-2.

3. Enable content in the security warning.

4. Click the **Table Design** button [*Create* tab, *Tables* group] to open a new table in *Design* view.

5. Add new fields into the table and set field properties.
 a. Type RentalID in the *Field Name* property box of the first row. Press the **Tab** key to move to the *Data Type* property.
 b. Select the **Short Text** *Data Type*. Press the **Tab** key to move to the *Description* property.
 c. Type Unique ID assigned to each rental.
 d. Click the **Primary Key** button [*Table Tools Design* tab, *Tools* group].
 e. Press the **Tab** key to move to the next row.
 f. Add the remaining fields into the table using the following information:

Field Name	Data Type	Description
FKBoatID	**Short Text**	Must match a BoatID in the SailboatFleet table
RentalDate	**Date/Time**	Date of rental
FourHourRental?	**Yes/No**	Yes is a 4-hour rental; No is a daily rental
MemberID	**Short Text**	ID number of member renting the boat

 g. Click the **Save** button to save the table as SDRentals.
 h. Click the **row selector** of the *RentalID* field.
 i. Type 5 in the *Field Size* property box in the *Field Properties* area.
 j. Type Rental ID in the *Caption* property box.
 k. Change the remaining field properties in the *SDRentals* table using the following information:

Field Name	Field Size	Format	Caption
FKBoatID	4		Boat ID
RentalDate		**Short Date**	Rental Date
FourHourRental?		**Yes/No**	Four Hour Rental?
MemberID	4		Member Number

6. Save the table by clicking the **Save** button.

7. Create a field validation rule and validation text for the *RentalDate* field.
 a. Click to select the **RentalDate** field.
 b. Click the **Validation Rule** property box.
 c. Type >=#1/1/2017#.

A2-133

d. Click the **Validation Text** property box.
e. Type The Rental Date must be greater than or equal to 1/1/2017.
f. Save the table and switch to *Datasheet* view.
g. Type 1 in the *RentalID* field. **Tab** to the *RentalDate* field and type 7/5/2015.
h. Press the **Tab** key. The message box should display the contents of your *Validation Text* property. Click **OK**. Type 7/5/2017 in the *RentalDate* field.
i. Press the **Tab** key. You should successfully move to the *FourHourRental?* field.
j. Click the **Record Selector** box to select this data record and click **Delete** [*Home* tab, *Records* group] since you no longer need this sample data.
k. Click **Yes** to confirm deletion of this record.
l. Close the *SDRentals* table.

8. Create a one-to-many relationship between the *SailboatFleet* table and the *SDRentals* table.
a. Click the **Relationships** button [*Database Tools* tab, *Relationships* group].
b. Select the **SailboatFleet** table in the *Show Table* dialog box and click the **Add** button.
c. Select the **SDRentals** table and click the **Add** button.
d. Click the **Close** button.
e. Drag the **BoatID** field from the *SailboatFleet* table on top of the **FKBoatID** field in the *SDRentals* table as shown in Figure 2-83. The *Edit Relationships* dialog box opens.
f. Verify that the field names displayed are correct. If necessary, use the **drop-down arrows** to make any corrections.
g. Click the **Enforce Referential Integrity** check box.
h. Click the **Cascade Update Related Fields** check box.

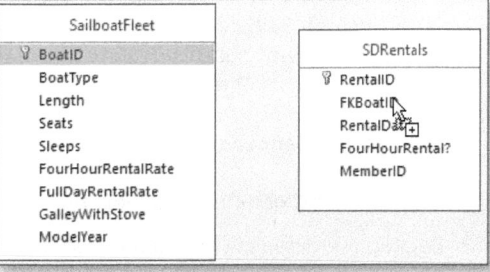

2-83 Drag the *BoatID* to the *FKBoatID* to create a relationship

i. Leave the *Cascade Delete Related Records* check box not selected. The club does not want to delete rental records just because it may take a boat out of service. This allows the club to keep a record of the rental.
j. Click **Create**. The *Relationships* window updates with the relationship line added. The *1* and infinity symbols display indicating that referential integrity is enforced.
k. Save the changes made to the relationships.
l. Click **Close** [*Relationship Tools Design* tab, *Relationships* group].

9. Enter records into the *SDRentals* table.
a. Open the *SDRentals* table in *Datasheet* view.
b. Enter the following records into the *SDRentals* table:

Rental ID	Boat ID	Rental Date	Four Hour Rental?	Member Number
08032	1152	1/15/2017	Yes	1122
08033	1146	1/15/2017		1386
08040	1010	2/2/2017	Yes	1122
08045	1010	2/9/2017		1386
08046	1152	2/9/2017	Yes	1427
08050	1152	2/15/2017	Yes	1122

c. Save the table.

10. Edit field properties in the *SDRentals* table.
 a. Click the **Design View** icon (Figure 2-84) in the *Status* bar to switch to *Design* view.
 b. Change the *Required* property for all fields except *FourHourRental?* to **Yes**.
 c. Save the changes to your table. Access displays a message box warning you that data integrity rules have changed. Click **Yes** to test your data against the new rules.
 d. Close the *SDRentals* table.

2-84 *Design View* icon in the *Status* bar

11. View the related data in the *SailboatFleet* table.
 a. Open the *SailboatFleet* table in *Datasheet* view.
 b. Click the **plus sign** to the left of the *BoatID* field *for BoatID 1010.* You should see two rentals for this boat.
 c. Close the *SailboatFleet* table.

12. Preview the data records in the *SailboatFleet* table for printing.
 a. Select the **SailboatFleet** table in the *Navigation Pane.*
 b. Click the **Print** button [*File* tab] to display the printing options.
 c. Click the **Print Preview** button. The *Print Preview* tab opens and shows a preview of how the table will print.
 d. Click the **Landscape** button [*Print Preview* tab, *Page Layout* group] to change the page orientation.
 e. Click the **Close Print Preview** button.

13. Backup the database and use *Compact & Repair Database* to reclaim unused space.
 a. Click the **Save As** button [*File* tab].
 b. Ensure that *Save Database As* is selected in the *File Types.*
 c. Select **Back Up Database** in the *Save Database As* area.
 d. Click the **Save As** button.
 e. Accept the default name in the *File name* box and click the **Save** button.
 f. Click the **File** tab. The *Info* button should be selected.
 g. Click the **Compact & Repair Database** button.

14. Close the database.

Guided Project 2-3

American River Cycling Club wants to expand the database created in Guided Project 1-2 in Chapter 1. To ensure consistency, the starting file is provided for you. For this project, you use *Design* view to create a second table, edit field properties, and integrate data integrity rules. You also create a relationship between the two tables and enforce referential integrity constraints. Finally, you import data and view the related table records.
[Student Learning Outcomes 2.1, 2.2, 2.3, 2.4, 2.5, 2.6]

Files Needed: *AmericanRiver-02.accdb* and *RaceResultsDataFile-02.xlsx*
Completed Project File Name: *[your initials] Access 2-3.accdb*

Skills Covered in This Project

- Create a table using *Design* view.
- Add fields into a table.
- Edit field properties in *Design* view.
- Use the *Lookup Wizard* to create a drop-down list.
- Save a table.
- Create a 1:M relationship between tables.
- Enforce referential integrity.
- View a table in *Datasheet* view and expand related records.

1. Open the **AmericanRiver-02** database file.

2. Save a new copy of your database as [your initials]Access 2-3.

3. Enable content in the security warning.

4. Click the **Table Design** button [*Create* tab, *Tables* group] to open a new table in *Design* view.

5. Add new fields into the table and set field properties.
 a. Type RaceID in the *Field Name* property box of the first row. Press the **Tab** key to move to the *Data Type* property.
 b. Select the **Short Text** *Data Type.* Press the **Tab** key to move to the *Description* property.
 c. Type Unique race ID number.
 d. Press the **Tab** key to move to the next row.
 e. Type FKMemberID in the *Field Name* property box. Press the **Tab** key to move to the *Data Type* property.
 f. Select the **Number** *Data Type.* Press the **Tab** key to move to the *Description* property.
 g. Type Must match a MemberID in the Members table.
 h. Click the **row selector** to select the *RaceID* field. Press and hold the **Shift** key. Click the **row selector** to select the *FKMemberID* field.
 i. Click the **Primary Key** button [*Table Tools Design* tab, *Tools* group]. The *Primary Key* symbol should appear on both the *RaceID* and *FKMemberID* fields, indicating a concatenated primary key, as shown in Figure 2-85.

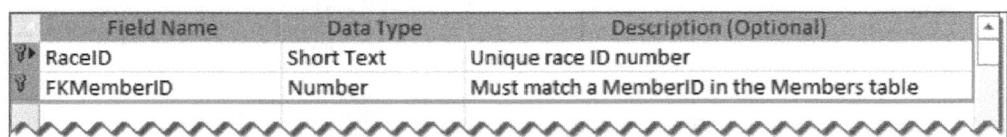

Field Name	Data Type	Description (Optional)
RaceID	Short Text	Unique race ID number
FKMemberID	Number	Must match a MemberID in the Members table

2-85 *RaceID and FKMemberID* make a concatenated primary key

 j. Click the **Field Name** property box of the cell below *FKMemberID*.
 k. Add the remaining fields into the table using the following information:

Field Name	Data Type	Description
Place	**Number**	Place finished in the race
Time	**Date/Time**	Total time
Division	**Short Text**	Division in which the member participated
AgeGroup	**Short Text**	Age group in which the member participated

 l. Click the **Save** button to save the table as RaceResults.
 m. Click the **row selector** of the *RaceID* field.
 n. Type 3 in the *Field Size* property box in the *Field Properties* area.
 o. Change the remaining field properties in the *RaceResults* table using the following information:

Field Name	Field Size	Format	Caption
FKMemberID			Member ID
Place	Integer		
Time		Short Time	
Division	1		
AgeGroup	3		

6. Save the table by clicking the **Save** button.

7. Modify the *Division* field to use a *Combo Box.*
 a. Click to select the *Division* field.
 b. Click the property box for the *Data Type* property, click the **arrow,** and select **Lookup Wizard.**
 c. Select the **I will type in the values that I want** radio button.
 d. Click the **Next** button.
 e. Click the **first cell** in the *Col1* column and type M.
 f. Press the **down arrow** key to move to the next row.
 g. Type F.
 h. Click **Next.**
 i. Click the **Limit To List** check box.
 j. Click **Finish.**
 k. Save and close the table.

8. Create a one-to-many relationship between the *Members* table and the *RaceResults* table.
 a. Click the **Relationships** button [*Database Tools* tab, *Relationships* group].
 b. Select the **Members** table in the *Show Table* dialog box and click the **Add** button.
 c. Select the **RaceResults** table and click the **Add** button.
 d. Click the **Close** button.
 e. Drag the **MemberID** field from the *Members* table on top of the **FKMemberID** field in the *RaceResults* table as shown in Figure 2-86. The *Edit Relationships* dialog box opens.
 f. Verify that the field names displayed are correct. Use the drop-down arrows to make any corrections.
 g. Click the **Enforce Referential Integrity** check box.
 h. Click the **Cascade Update Related Fields** check box.
 i. Leave the *Cascade Delete Related Records* check box not selected. The club does not want to delete race records just because a member may leave the club. This allows the club to keep a record of the race.
 j. Click **Create.** The *Relationships* window updates with the relationship line added. The *1* and infinity symbols display indicating that referential integrity is enforced.
 k. Save the changes made to the relationships.
 l. Click **Close** [*Relationship Tools Design* tab, *Relationships* group].

2-86 Drag the *MemberID* to the *FKMemberID* to create a relationship

9. Import data from Excel into the *RaceResults* table.
 a. Launch the *Get External Data – Excel Spreadsheet* dialog box.
 b. Locate and select the ***RaceResultsDataFile-02*** Excel file.
 c. Append the records to the **RaceResults** table.

d. Launch the *Import Spreadsheet Wizard*.

e. Finish the *Import Spreadsheet Wizard*. Close the *Wizard* after the records have imported.

10. Open the *RaceResults* table in *Datasheet* view. Your table should contain the 24 records shown in Figure 2-87.

RaceID	Member ID	Place	Time	Division	AgeGroup
1	1	2	2:15	F	>=20 and <30
1	2	3	2:20	F	>=30 and <40
1	4	3	2:16	M	>=30 and <40
1	5	1	2:12	M	>=30 and <40
1	8	4	2:22	F	>=30 and <40
1	11	5	2:23	F	>=30 and <40
2	1	1	0:47	F	>=20 and <30
2	8	2	0:51	F	>=30 and <40
2	11	3	0:52	F	>=30 and <40
3	1	3	1:07	F	>=20 and <30
3	2	1	1:06	F	>=30 and <40
3	5	2	1:07	M	>=30 and <40
3	6	4	1:08	M	>=30 and <40
3	7	6	1:10	F	>=20 and <30
3	8	7	1:11	F	>=30 and <40
3	10	5	1:09	M	>=20 and <30
4	1	3	0:43	F	>=20 and <30
4	7	2	0:42	F	>=20 and <30
4	10	1	0:40	M	>=20 and <30
5	1	1	2:10	F	>=20 and <30
5	3	5	2:20	M	>=30 and <40
5	8	2	2:11	F	>=30 and <40
5	9	4	2:16	F	<20
5	12	3	2:14	F	<20
*		0	0		

Record: 1 of 24 — No Filter — Search

2-87 *RaceResults* table records after import

11. Edit field properties in the *RaceResults* table.

a. Click the **Design View** icon in the *Status* bar to switch to *Design* view.

b. Change the *Required* property for all fields to **Yes**.

c. Save the changes to your table. Access displays a message box warning you that data integrity rules have changed. Click **Yes** to test your data against the new rules.

d. Close the *RaceResults* table.

12. View the related data records in the *Members* table.

a. Open the *Members* table in *Datasheet* view.

b. Click the **plus sign** to the left of the *MemberID* field for *Geneva Lingle, MemberID* 1. You should see the five races in which Geneva has participated.

c. Click the **plus sign** to the left of the *MemberID* field for the *Ryan Thomas, MemberID* 3. You should see the one race in which Ryan has participated. Your screen should look similar to Figure 2-88.

d. Close the *Members* table.

2-88 *Members* table with related *RaceResults* table records

13. Close the database.

Independent Project 2-4

Courtyard Medical Plaza wants to expand the database created in Independent Project 1-4 in Chapter 1. To ensure consistency, the starting file is provided for you. For this project, you use *Design* view to create a second table, edit field properties, integrate data integrity rules, and enter data. You also create a relationship between the two tables, enforce referential integrity constraints and import data. Finally, you preview how the records will print.

[**Student Learning Outcomes 2.1, 2.2, 2.3, 2.4, 2.5, 2.6, 2.7**]

Files Needed: ***CourtyardMedicalPlaza-02.accdb*** and ***RentInvoicesDataFile-02.xlsx***
Completed Project File Name: ***[your initials] Access 2-4.accdb***

Skills Covered in This Project

- Create a table using *Design* view.
- Add fields into a table.
- Edit field properties in *Design* view.
- Create and test a record validation rule.
- Save a table.
- Enter records.
- Create a 1:M relationship between tables.
- Enforce referential integrity.
- View a table in *Datasheet* view and expand related records.
- Preview table results for printing.

1. Open the **CourtyardMedicalPlaza-02** database file.

2. Save a new copy of your database as [your initials] Access 2-4.

3. Enable content in the security warning.

4. Create a new table using *Table Design*.
 a. Add the following fields into the table and set field properties:

Field Name	Data Type	Description
InvoiceID	**Number**	Unique invoice number
InvoiceDate	**Date/Time**	Date invoice created
DueDate	**Date/Time**	Date bill is due
AmountDue	**Currency**	Total rent amount due
FKDoctorID	**Number**	Must match a DoctorID in the Physicians table
Description	**Short Text**	Brief summary of charges

 b. Set *InvoiceID* as the primary key.
 c. Save the table as RentInvoices.
 d. Change the field properties in the *RentInvoices* table using the following information:

Field Name	Field Size	Format	Caption
InvoiceID	**Integer**		
InvoiceDate		**Medium Date**	Invoice Date
DueDate		**Medium Date**	Due Date
AmountDue			Amount Due
FKDoctorID			Doctor ID
Description	40		

5. Save the table.

6. Create and test a record validation rule in the *RentInvoices* table.
 a. Open the *Property Sheet* for the *RentInvoices* table.
 b. Type [DueDate]>=([InvoiceDate]+10) in the *Validation Rule* property for the table.
 c. Type The Due Date must be at least 10 days after the Invoice Date. as *Validation Text*.
 d. Close the *Property Sheet* window.
 e. Switch to *Datasheet* view to test the rule. If prompted, save the changes to your table.
 f. Type 1 in the *InvoiceID* field. Press the **Tab** key to move to the *InvoiceDate* field.

g. Type 1/1/2017. Press the **Tab** key to move to the *DueDate* field.

h. Type 1/5/2017.

i. Press the **down arrow** key to leave the current record. The message box should display the validation text message (Figure 2-89) since the *DueDate* is not at least 10 days after the *InvoiceDate*.

j. Delete the contents and type 1/11/2017 in the *DueDate* field.

k. Verify that the record adds successfully.

l. Delete this record since you no longer need this sample data.

m. Close the *RentInvoices* table.

2-89 Error message displays validation text from a record validation rule violation

7. Create a one-to-many relationship between the *Physicians* table and the *RentInvoices* table.

a. Open the *Relationships* window and add the two tables.

b. Drag the **DoctorID** field from the *Physicians* table on top of the **FKDoctorID** field in the *RentInvoices* table as shown in Figure 2-90.

c. Make the correct choices to *Enforce Referential Integrity* and *Cascade Update Related Fields*.

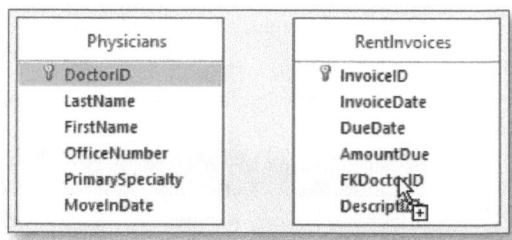

2-90 Drag the *DoctorID* to the *FKDoctorID* to create a relationship

d. Leave the *Cascade Delete Related Records* check box not selected. Courtyard Medical Plaza does not want to delete invoice records just because a doctor may move out of the office complex. This allows Courtyard Medical Plaza to keep all rental records.

e. Create the relationship.

f. Save the changes and close the *Relationships* window.

8. Import data from Excel into the *RentInvoices* table.

a. Launch the *Get External Data – Excel Spreadsheet* dialog box.

b. Locate and select the ***RentInvoicesDataFile-02.xlsx*** Excel file.

c. Append the records to the *RentInvoices* table.

d. Launch the *Import Spreadsheet Wizard*.

e. Finish the *Import Spreadsheet Wizard*. Close the *Wizard* after the records have imported.

9. Open the *RentInvoices* table in *Datasheet* view. Your table should contain 27 records.

a. Use *AutoFit* to adjust the field width of all the columns.

b. Save the changes to your table.

10. Edit field properties in the *RentInvoices* table.

a. Use *Design* view to change the *Required* property for all fields to **Yes**.

b. Save the changes to your table. Access displays a message box warning you that data integrity rules have changed. Test your data against the new rules.

c. Close the *RentInvoices* table.

11. Open the *Physicians* table in *Datasheet* view.

a. Click the **plus sign** to the left of the *DoctorID* field for *Robert Beyer, DoctorID 1*. You should see the three invoices sent to Dr. Beyer.

b. Click the **plus sign** to the left of the *DoctorID* field for the *Emy Ostrander, DoctorID 3*. Notice that Dr. Ostrander does not have any invoices. Based on the way Courtyard Medical processes billing, they only send the bill to the one doctor listed on the lease. Your screen should be similar to Figure 2-91.

c. Close the *Physicians* table.

A2-141

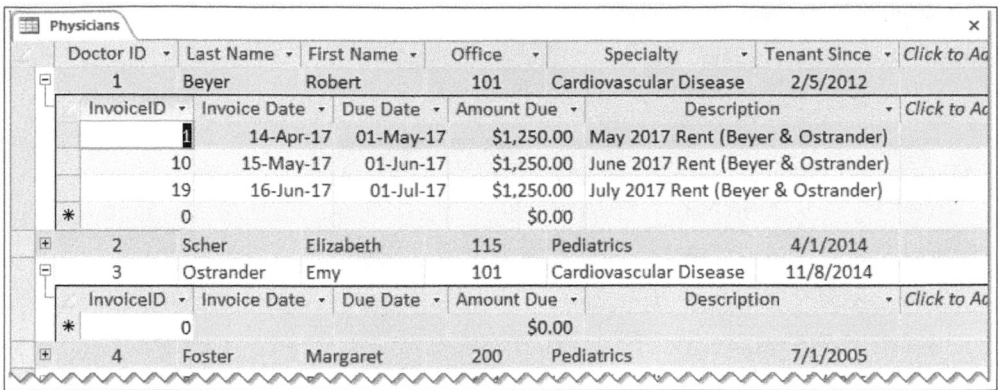

2-91 *Physicians* table with related *RentInvoices* table records

12. Preview the data records in the *RentInvoices* table for printing.
 a. Select the **RentInvoices** table in the *Navigation Pane*.
 b. Use *Print Preview* to show a preview of how the table will print.
 c. Close the *Print Preview*.

13. Close the database.

Independent Project 2-5

Life's Animal Shelter wants to expand the database created in the Independent Project 1-5 in Chapter 1. To ensure consistency, the starting file is provided for you. In this project, you use *Design* view to create a second table, edit field properties, integrate data integrity rules, and enter data. You also create a relationship between the two tables and enforce referential integrity constraints. Finally, you add data using the relationship between tables.
[Student Learning Outcomes 2.1, 2.2, 2.3, 2.4, 2.6]

File Needed: ***LifesAnimalShelter-02.accdb***
Completed Project File Name: *[your initials] **Access 2-5.accdb***

Skills Covered in This Project

- Create a table using *Design* view.
- Add fields into a table.
- Edit field properties in *Design* view.
- Create an input mask.
- Create a validation rule and validation text.

- Save a table.
- Enter records.
- Create a foreign key.
- Create a 1:M relationship between tables.
- Enforce referential integrity.
- View a table in *Datasheet* view and expand related records.

1. Open the ***LifesAnimalShelter-02*** database file.

2. Save a new copy of your database as [your initials] Access 2-5.

3. Enable content in the security warning.

4. Create a new table using *Table Design*.
 a. Add the following fields into the table and set field properties:

Field Name	Data Type	Description	Field Size
OwnerID	**Short Text**	Unique owner ID	4
OwnerLastName	**Short Text**	Last name	20
OwnerFirstName	**Short Text**	First name	20
Address	**Short Text**	Street address	40
City	**Short Text**		20
State	**Short Text**		2
ZIP	**Short Text**	ZIP Code	5
Phone	**Short Text**	Contact phone number	10

 b. Set *OwnerID* as the primary key.
 c. Save the table as Owners.

5. Create an input mask for the *Phone* field.
 a. Select the **Phone** field.
 b. Use the **Phone Number** *Input Mask*.
 c. Don't make any changes to the mask or placeholder character and select the **Without the symbols in the mask, like this** radio button.
 d. Finish the *Input Mask Wizard*.
 e. Save the table.

6. Create and test a field validation rule.
 a. Select the *OwnerID* field.
 b. Type Like "####" in the *Validation Rule*.
 c. Type You must enter a 4-digit Owner ID as *Validation Text*.
 d. Save the table and switch to *Datasheet* view.
 e. Test the rule by typing 11 in the first row of the *OwnerID* column.
 f. Move to the *OwnerLastName* field. The message box should display the validation text message (Figure 2-92) since the *OwnerID* is not four digits long.
 g. Delete the contents and type 1111 into the *OwnerID* field.
 h. Verify that you successfully move to the *OwnerLastName* field since 1111 meets the validation rule criteria.
 i. Delete this test data record.

2-92 Field validation rule error message

7. Enter the following records into the *Owners* table. Life's Animal Shelter doesn't have any data about the owners stored electronically so you are unable to import any data.

Owner ID	OwnerLast Name	OwnerFirst Name	Address	City	State	ZIP	Phone
0100	Smith	Albert	11 Lakewood Drive	Abilene	TX	79601	325-614-9333
0101	Weston	Mark	2601 Nonesuch Road	Abilene	TX	79606	325-555-1112
0102	Rivera	Angela	2548 Laney Road	Denton	TX	76208	940-321-8020
0103	Moyer	Silvia	6867 Anglebluff Circle	Dallas	TX	75248	972-380-6188
0104	Wills	Mason	2421 Klondike Drive	Dallas	TX	75228	214-224-5555

8. Save and close the table.

9. Determine the foreign key field. Currently there is not a field in common across the *Owners* and *Pets* tables. There is a one-to-many relationship between the two tables since an owner could adopt many pets, but each pet is only adopted by one owner. The foreign key comes by taking the primary key field from the *1* table and adding it in as an additional field in the *M* table.
 a. Open the *Pets* table in *Design* view.
 b. Add the foreign key field below the *Details* field using the following information:

Field Name	Data Type	Description	Field Size
FKOwnerID	**Short Text**	Must match an OwnerID in the Owners table	4

 c. Save and close the *Pets* table.

10. Create a one-to-many relationship between the *Owners* and *Pets* tables.
 a. Open the *Relationships* window and add the two tables.
 b. Enlarge the table objects, if needed, to see all of the fields.
 c. Drag the **OwnerID** field from the *Owners* table on top of the **FKOwnerID** field in the *Pets* table. Release the pointer. The *Edit Relationships* dialog box displays.
 d. Select the choices to **Enforce Referential Integrity** and **Cascade Update Related Fields**.
 e. Leave the *Cascade Delete Related Records* check box not selected. The shelter does not want to delete pet records when it deletes information about an owner.
 f. Create the relationship.
 g. Save the changes and close the *Relationships* window.

11. Enter the following data into the specified records in the *Pets* table to reflect which pets have been adopted:
 a. Open the *Pets* table in *Datasheet* view.
 b. Type *0100* in the *FKOwnerID* field for *PetID 1*.
 c. Type *0103* in the *FKOwnerID* field for *PetID 3*.
 d. Type *0100* in the *FKOwnerID* field for *PetID 12*.
 e. Type *0104* in the *FKOwnerID* field for *PetID 14*.
 f. Close the *Pets* table.

12. View the related data records in the *Owners* table.
 a. Open the *Owners* table in *Datasheet* view.
 b. Click the **plus sign** to the left of the *OwnerID* field for *Albert Smith, OwnerID 0100*. You should see the two pets adopted by Albert.
 c. Close the *Owners* table.

13. Close the database.

Independent Project 2-6

The New York Department of Motor Vehicles tracks information about drivers, including accidents in which they have been involved. The starting database file is provided for you. For this project, you use *Design* view to edit a table and integrate data integrity rules. You also create a relationship between the two tables and enforce referential integrity constraints. Finally, you view how the table records will print using *Print Preview*.
[Student Learning Outcomes 2.1, 2.2, 2.3, 2.4, 2.5 2.6, 2.7]

File Needed: ***NewYorkDMV-02.accdb***
Completed Project File Name: ***[your initials] Access 2-6.accdb***

Skills Covered in This Project

- Edit a table using *Design* view.
- Edit field properties in *Design* view.
- Create a lookup field.

- Save a table.
- Enforce referential integrity.
- View a table in *Datasheet* view and expand related records.
- Preview table results for printing.

1. Open the ***NewYorkDMV-02*** database file.

2. Save a new copy of your database as [your initials] Access 2-6.

3. Enable the contents in the security warning.

4. Edit field properties of the *Tickets* table in *Design* view.
 a. Select a **Short Date** *Format* for the *TicketDate* field.
 b. Create a *Lookup Field* for the *PrimaryFactor* field with the following choices and limit the choices to those on the list: Alcohol, Backing Unsafely, Driver Distraction, Driver Inexperience, Failure to Yield R.O.W., Passing/Lane Violations, Traffic Control Disregarded, Turning Improperly, Unsafe Speed.
 c. Change all fields to be *Required*.
 d. Save the changes to the table. If prompted to test existing data against the new rules, click **Yes**.
 e. Close the table.

5. Edit field properties of the *Drivers* table in *Design* view.
 a. Open the *Drivers* table in *Design* view.
 b. Change all fields to be *Required*.
 c. Create a lookup field on the *Gender* field with the choices of M and F. Select **Yes** in the *Limit To List* property.
 d. Assign a *Default Value* of NY to the *State* field.
 e. Save the changes to the table. If prompted to test existing data against the new rules, click **Yes**.
 f. Close the table.

6. Review table relationships.
 a. Open the *Relationships* window. Notice the *Relationship line* does not have any symbols on the end points. This indicates that *Referential Integrity* has not been enforced (Figure 2-93).
 b. Close the *Relationships* window.
 c. Open the *Tickets* table in *Datasheet* view to see the impact of not *Enforcing Referential Integrity*.

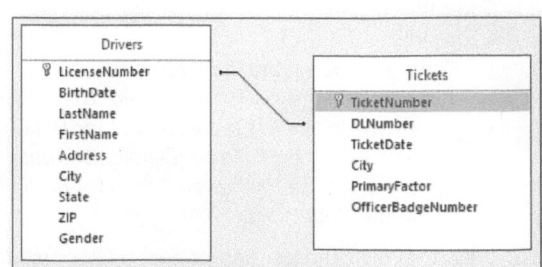

2-93 Referential Integrity is not enforced

d. Enter the following test data record into the table. Be sure to press **Enter** or **Tab** after you have entered the officer badge number so that the record is added into the table.

Ticket Number	DL Number	Ticket Date	City	Primary Factor	Officer Badge Number
12345678901	999999999	7/1/2016	New York	Unsafe Speed	123456789

e. Open up the *Drivers* table in *Datasheet* view. Keep the *Tickets* table open. Notice that there is no data record for a driver with the *LicenseNumber* of *999999999*. When *Referential Integrity* is not enforced, Access allows you to enter data records that don't need to have a corresponding record in the related table.

f. Click to expand the **plus symbol** for *LicenseNumber 10000501 (Timothy Smith)*. You should see the two tickets Timothy received. Notice that the relationship exists even if referential integrity is not enforced.

g. Close the *Drivers* table.

h. Delete the test data record from the *Tickets* table.

i. Save and close the *Tickets* table.

7. Edit referential integrity constraints.
 a. Open the *Relationships* window.
 b. Select the **Relationship line** and click **Edit Relationships**.
 c. Select the choices to **Enforce Referential Integrity** and **Cascade Update Related Fields**.
 d. Leave the *Cascade Delete Related Records* check box not selected. You do not want to delete ticket records if you delete information about a driver.
 e. Click **OK** to save the changes to the relationship.
 f. Save the changes and close the *Relationships* window.

8. Test the referential integrity constraints.
 a. Open the *Tickets* table in *Datasheet* view.
 b. Enter the following test data record into the table:

Ticket Number	DL Number	Ticket Date	City	Primary Factor	Officer Badge Number
1234567890	99999999	1/1/2015	New York	Unsafe Speed	123456789

 c. Click **OK** when Access displays a message box (Figure 2-94) indicating that you cannot add this ticket record because it requires a related record in the *Drivers* table.
 d. Press **Esc** to delete the record contents.

2-94 Error message when referential integrity is violated

9. Enter the following valid records into the *Tickets* table:

Ticket Number	DL Number	Ticket Date	City	Primary Factor	Officer Badge Number
4235895082	12394163	4/14/2016	Utica	Unsafe Speed	A00045729
4235895110	39992387	4/15/2016	Utica	Unsafe Speed	A00045729

10. Save and close the table.

11. Preview the data records in the *Drivers* table for printing.
 a. Select the **Drivers** table in the *Navigation Pane.*
 b. Use *Print Preview* to show a preview of how the table will print.
 c. Change the page to a **Landscape** orientation.
 d. Use the **Navigation** buttons to move to the second page.
 e. Close the *Print Preview.*

12. Close the database.

Improve It Project 2-7

Placer Hills Real Estate expanded the database created in the Improve It Project 1-7 in Chapter 1. To ensure consistency, the starting file is provided for you. For this project, you use *Design* view to edit properties in a table and integrate data integrity rules. You edit data records, create a relationship between the two tables, and enforce referential integrity constraints. Finally, you view how the table records will print using *Print Preview.*
[Student Learning Outcomes 2.1, 2.2, 2.3, 2.4, 2.6, 2.8]

File Needed: ***PlacerHills-02.accdb***
Completed Project File Name: *[your initials] **Access 2-7.accdb***

Skills Covered in This Project

- Edit a table using *Design* view.
- Edit field properties in *Design* view.
- Create an input mask.
- Save a table.

- Create a foreign key.
- Create a 1:M relationship between tables.
- Enforce referential integrity.
- View a table in *Datasheet* view and expand related records.
- Preview table results for printing.

1. Open the ***PlacerHills-02*** database file.

2. Save a new copy of your database as [your initials] Access 2-7.

3. Enable the contents in the security warning.

4. Open the *Agents* table in *Datasheet* view (Figure 2-95).

EmployeeN -	LastName -	FirstName -	DateHired -	Phone -
103	Bidou	Simon	Monday, May 7, 2012	5306487689
127	Weatherby	Kelly	Tuesday, November 13, 2012	9169873756
133	Burgess	John	Monday, June 23, 2014	5302784699
151	Chung	Rick	Friday, October 9, 2015	9168236940
160	Johnstone	Jack	Monday, January 18, 2016	9165551679
160	Duarte	Kallyn	Monday, February 15, 2016	9167441614
169	Montoya	Gerardo	Monday, March 21, 2016	9165345991

2-95 *Datasheet* view of the *Agents* table

A2-147

a. Look at the *DateHired* and *Phone* fields. The manager of the real estate office wants those to be formatted differently.

b. Notice that both Jack Johnstone and Kallyn Duarte have the same value in the *EmployeeNum* field. If the employee number is supposed to be unique, something must not be set correctly with the primary key in this table.

c. Change Kallyn Duarte's *EmployeeNum* to be 168, the correct value.

5. Change to *Design* view to make needed corrections to the *Agents* table.

a. Notice that the table does not have a primary key. Although Access recommends that you assign a primary key in a table, Access lets you create a table without one.

b. Set the *EmployeeNum* as the primary key.

c. Set the *Format* property of the *DateHired* field to use *Short Date*.

d. Create an input mask for the *Phone* field. Select the **Phone Number** *Input Mask*. Don't make any changes to the mask or placeholder character and select the **Without the symbols in the mask, like this** radio button. Complete the *Input Mask Wizard*.

e. Change all fields to be *Required*.

f. Save the table.

g. Switch to *Datasheet* view to ensure that the formatting shows as desired.

h. Adjust the field width of the *DateHired* field to 13. Remember that you can select the column, right-click to open the context menu and then select **Field Width** to change the width to a specific size.

i. Adjust the field width of the *Phone* field to 16.

j. Save and close the *Agents* table.

6. Open the *Listings* table in *Datasheet* view to help determine the type of relationship and the foreign key field. There is a one-to-many relationship between the *Agents* and *Listings* tables since an agent can list many different properties, but a property is listed by only one agent. The foreign key comes by taking the primary key field from the *1* table and adding it in as an additional field in the *M* table. In this case, the *EmployeeNum* should also be added into the *Listings* table. Notice that the *Listings* table has a field that stores the agent's name. However, it doesn't have the foreign key. To minimize redundant data, you will change the *Agent* field so that it will now store the agent's employee number instead of the agent's name. This requires changing the data values as well as field properties.

7. Edit the data values in the *Agent* field in the *Listings* table.

a. Click the **arrow** to the right of the *Agent Field Name* and select **Sort A to Z**. Because the employee name values begin with the first name, the sort isn't alphabetical by last name. However, the sort makes it easier to change the data values since all the property listings by the same agent are grouped together.

b. Type 169 in the *Agent* field for *Gerardo Montoya*.

c. Change each of the six records for *Jack Johnstone* to have the value of 160 for the *Agent* field. After entering the first value, you can use copy and paste to enter the remaining values.

d. Continue changing the remaining records using the information in the following table:

Number of Records	Agent Name	New Value for Agent Field
3	John Burgess	133
5	Kallyn Duarte	168
9	Kelly Weatherby	127
4	Rick Chung	151
4	Simon Bidou	103

e. Remove the sort from the *Agent* field.
f. Save the table.

8. Switch to *Design* view in the *Listings* table to edit the properties of the foreign key.
 a. Select the *ListingAgent* field.
 b. Change the field name to ListingAgentNumber. In this database, Placer Hills prefers that the foreign key have a unique name instead of choosing to use *FKEmployeeNum* as the name of the field.
 c. Change the *Description* to read Must match an EmployeeNum in the Agents table.
 d. Change the field size to 3.
 e. Save and close the table. Access warns you that the field size has been changed and that you may lose data. Your values meet this new size. Click **Yes**.

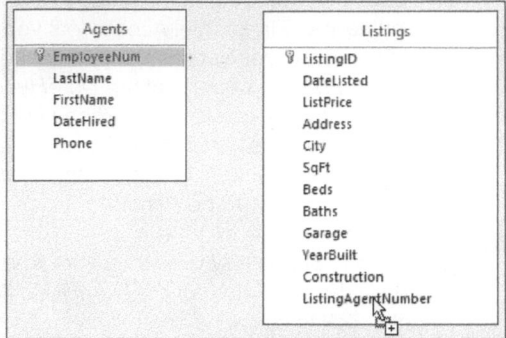

9. Create a one-to-many relationship between the *Agents* table and the *Listings* table.
 a. Open the *Relationships* window and add the two tables.
 b. Enlarge the table objects, if needed, to see all of the fields.
 c. Drag the **EmployeeNum** field from the *Agents* table on top of the **ListingAgentNumber** field in the *Listings* table as shown in Figure 2-96.

 2-96 Drag the *EmployeeNum* to the *ListingAgentNumber* to create a relationship

 d. Select the correct choices to **Enforce Referential Integrity** and **Cascade Update Related Fields**.
 e. Leave the *Cascade Delete Related Records* check box not selected. You do not want to delete property listing records just because an agent may leave the company. This allows you to keep a record of the listings.
 f. Create the relationship.
 g. Save the changes and close the *Relationships* window.

10. Open the *Agents* table in *Datasheet* view.
 a. Click to expand the records for Kelly Weatherby. There should be nine properties listed.
 b. Close the *Agents* table.

11. Preview the data records in the *Listings* table for printing.
 a. Select the **Listings** table in the *Navigation Pane*.
 b. Use *Print Preview* to show a preview of how the table will print.
 c. Change the page to **Landscape** orientation.
 d. Close the *Print Preview*.

12. Close the database.

Challenge Project 2-8

Modify the database you created in Challenge Project 1-8. Use *Design* view to edit field properties. Change any data that violates these properties, preview the table for printing, and compact and repair the database.
[Student Learning Outcomes 2.2, 2.3, 2.4, 2.5, 2.7, 2.8]

File Needed: *[your initials] Access 1-8.accdb*
Completed Project File Name: *[your initials] Access 2-8.accdb*

Open the database *[your initials] **Access 1-8*** and save a copy of it as [your initials] Access 2-8.

Modify your database according to the following instructions:

- Edit the table in *Design* view.
- Create a *Validation Rule* and *Validation Text* for at least one of the fields in your table.
- Test the validation rule.
- Add an input mask on another field.
- As appropriate, edit *Default Value* and *Required* properties for the fields.
- Test existing records against changes to the properties.
- Correct any data values that do not meet the new data integrity rules.
- Use *Print Preview* to preview the table for printing.
- Adjust the margins and orientation to create an easy to read printout. Print the table as desired.
- Use *Compact & Repair Database* to reclaim any unused space.
- Save all changes to the table.

Challenge Project 2-9

Blue Lake Sports is a nationally recognized sporting goods company. It has a growing internship program at its corporate office to offer experience to college students. You have been asked to create a database to store information about the internship program. Create two tables, create a relationship between the tables, and add data into the database.
[Student Learning Outcomes 2.1, 2.2, 2.3, 2.4, 2.6]

File Needed: None
Completed Project File Name: *[your initials] **Access 2-9.accdb***

Open a new database and save it as [your initials] Access 2-9.

Modify your database according to the following instructions:

- Create a table using *Design* view to store information about the interns.
- Add a field named InternID. Use a *Short Text* data type and designate it as the primary key.
- Add the following fields: LastName, FirstName, Phone, University, Major, and InternshipStartDate.
- Select appropriate data types and field sizes for the fields.
- Use the *Lookup Wizard* to create a drop-down list for *University* and add at least three choices to the list.
- Save the table as Intern.
- Enter several records into the table.
- Create a second table using *Design* view to store information about the different departments in which an intern can work.
- Add a field named DepartmentName. Use a *Short Text* data type and designate it as the primary key.
- Add the following fields: DeptMgrLastName, DeptMgrFirstName, OfficeNumber, and Division.
- Select appropriate data types and field sizes for the fields.
- Use the *Lookup Wizard* to create a drop-down list for *Division* and add the choices of Golf, Water Sports, and Children.
- Save the table as Department.

- Enter several rows of data. Use the following values for the *DepartmentName:* Sales-Golf, Accounting-Golf, HR-Golf, Sales-Water Sports, Accounting-Water Sports, HR-Water Sports, Sales-Children, Accounting-Children, HR-Children.
- An intern can only be assigned to one department, but a department may have several interns. Add the correct foreign key into the *Intern* table. Don't make that field required yet.
- Create the one-to-many relationship. Enforce referential integrity and cascade updates and deletes. Save the changes to the relationship.
- Edit the data records in the *Intern* table to add values into the foreign key field. Edit the *Intern* table to make the foreign key field required.
- Save all changes to the table.
- Open the *Department* table in *Datasheet* view. Expand the plus sign for several departments to see the associated interns assigned to this department.

Challenge Project 2-10

Modify the database you created in Challenge Project 1-10 for a travel agency. Your database contains a table about upcoming cruises. Use *Design* view to create a new table to store information about the different ships on which passengers can cruise. Create a relationship between the tables, and add data into the new table.
[**Student Learning Outcomes 2.1, 2.2, 2.3, 2.4, 2.6**]

File Needed: *[your initials] Access 1-10.accdb*
Completed Project File Name: *[your initials] Access 2-10.accdb*

Open the database *[your initials] Access 1-10* and save a copy of it as [your initials] Access 2-10.

Modify your database according to the following instructions:

- Create a table using *Design* view to store information about the ships.
- Add a field named ShipID. Use a *Short Text* data type and designate it as the primary key.
- Add the following fields: ShipName, CruiseLineName, DateLaunched, NumberOfPassengers, and CountryOfRegistry.
- Select appropriate data types and field sizes for the fields.
- Use the *Lookup Wizard* to create a drop-down list for *CruiseLineName* and add at least three choices to the list.
- Save the table as Ships.
- Enter several records into the table for various ships. Search the web if you need help finding examples of data to enter.
- Edit the *Trips* table you created in Challenge Project 1-10. Add the foreign key field of ShipID. It must have the same data type and field size you assigned in the *Ships* table.
- Create a one-to-many relationship between the two tables, since a ship can be used for many different cruises, but a specific cruise is only on one ship. Enforce referential integrity and cascade updates and deletes. Save the changes to the relationship.
- Edit the data records in the *Trips* table to add values into the *ShipID* field.
- Save all changes to the table.
- Open the *Ships* table in *Datasheet* view. Expand the plus sign for several ships to see the associated trips the ships are taking.

A2-151

Creating and Using Queries

CHAPTER OVERVIEW

Queries provide a powerful way to find and analyze data in databases. In Chapter 1 you learned to use the *Search, Sort* and *Filter* tools to find data. These are good tools but, over time as the number of records stored in your databases increases, those tools become less helpful. Learning to create and use queries helps you to quickly and easily access your data and manage your databases. This chapter covers the basics of creating a query, adding criteria to a query, using different query options, integrating calculated fields, and creating summary queries.

STUDENT LEARNING OUTCOMES (SLOs)

After completing this chapter, you will be able to:

SLO 3.1 Understand queries and use the *Simple Query Wizard* to create and run a query (p. A3-153).

SLO 3.2 Create a query in *Design* view, add fields, and save and run a query (p. A3-154).

SLO 3.3 Add criterion into a query, use comparison operators, and create criteria with wildcards (p. A3-159).

SLO 3.4 Integrate sorting and limiting fields and records that display (p. A3-165).

SLO 3.5 Use the *AND* and *OR* operators to include multiple criteria in a query (p. A3-168).

SLO 3.6 Create and use a parameter query (p. A3-174).

SLO 3.7 Build a query that uses a calculated field (p. A3-179).

SLO 3.8 Create and use a summary query using aggregate functions (p. A3-184).

CASE STUDY

For the Pause & Practice projects in this chapter, you develop queries for Placer Hills Real Estate. As you progress through the Pause & Practice projects, you use the features you learn in this chapter to find and analyze data in a database with queries.

Pause & Practice 3-1: Create, run, and add criterion to a query in *Design* view. Edit and save a copy of a query.

Pause & Practice 3-2: Create queries using sorting and multiple criteria.

Pause & Practice 3-3: Create queries using a parameter and calculated fields.

Pause & Practice 3-4: Create a summary query that uses aggregate functions.

SLO 3.1

Understanding Queries and Using the Simple Query Wizard

A *query* finds data in your database by allowing you to ask a question. For example, in a music database you can create a simple query that shows all the albums that you own. Some queries include a criterion to search for only specific records. For example, in a university database you can create a query to "show only the students who are taking a course in the biology department." You can also create a query that includes multiple criteria to further narrow your search. For example, a query in the Central Sierra Insurance database might use three criteria to find all of the employees who work as insurance agents in the Cameron Park branch who were hired after January 1, 2016.

You can create a query in *Design* view or with the *Query Wizard*. In this section you use the *Simple Query Wizard* option.

When you build a query you must tell Access where to find the data. The data source for a query can be a table or another query. The *Simple Query Wizard* allows you to select the specific table(s) and queries as well as the specific fields to include in the query. After you create a query, you can run it to see the results. If you need to change the query once it has been created, you can edit it using *Design* view.

▶ HOW TO: Create a Query Using the Simple Query Wizard

1. Click the **Create** tab on the *Ribbon*.
2. Click the **Query Wizard** button in the *Queries* group (Figure 3-1) to launch the *Query Wizard*.
3. Select **Simple Query Wizard** in the *New Query* dialog box (Figure 3-2).
4. Click **OK**.
 - The *Simple Query Wizard* launches (Figure 3-3).
 - The values displayed in the *Tables/Queries* box and the *Available Fields* window vary depending on the contents of your database.

3-1 *Query Wizard* button

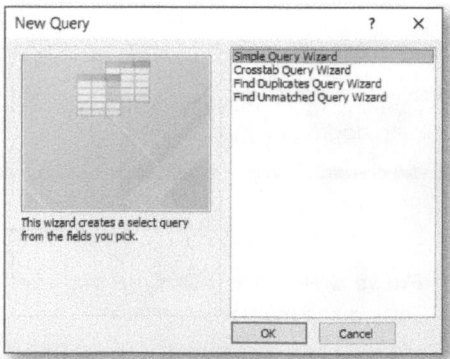

3-2 Select the query type in the *New Query* dialog box

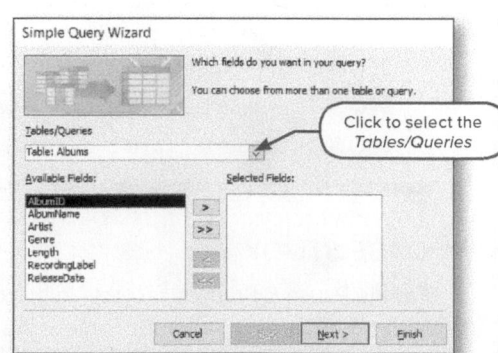

3-3 *Simple Query Wizard*

5. Click the **Tables/Queries** drop-down arrow and select the *Table* or *Query* name.
6. Select a field to include in the query from those displayed in the *Available Fields* window.
7. Click the **Move Single Field** button.
 - The field moves into the *Selected Fields* window (Figure 3-4).
 - The *Remove Single Field* and *Remove All Fields* buttons become active.

3-4 Use the *Move Fields* buttons to select the fields to display in a query

8. Continue moving all required fields, changing the selected *Table* or *Query* if needed.

>
>
> **ANOTHER WAY**
>
> Use the **Move All Fields** button (see Figure 3-4) to select all of the fields in the query.

9. Click the **Next** button when you have finished adding fields. The last page of the *Simple Query Wizard* displays.
 - The *Title* box displays a default *Query Title*. The title will also be used as the *Query Name*. The default name combines the *Table Name* with the word *Query*.
 - Since you may have several queries that use the same table as the data source, be sure to create a name that describes the function of the query.
 - If you have selected fields from related tables, the *Simple Query Wizard* may display another page to make a choice between a *Detail* or *Summary* query. Select the desired radio button and click **Next**. If shown, this page displays prior to the last page where you name the query.

10. Change the title as desired.

11. Click **Finish** to run the query. Access automatically saves and executes the query.
 - The results show in *Datasheet* view (Figure 3-5).
 - The *Query Name* displays in the *Queries* group on the *Navigation Pane*.

12. Close the query when done.

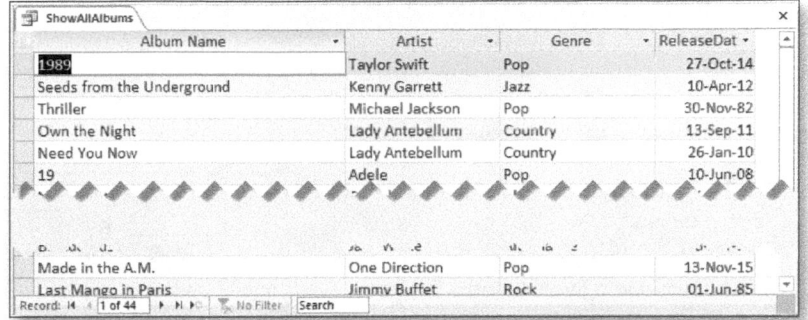

3-5 Query results display in *Datasheet* view

SLO 3.2

Creating, Running, and Editing a Query in Design View

While the *Simple Query Wizard* is useful when you want to see information quickly in your database, it doesn't allow you to take advantage of all of the options available when creating a query. As a result, the most common way to create queries is with *Query Design*. In *Query Design* you not only can specify the table(s) or queries to include, along with the fields from those objects, but you can also specify options to further restrict which records are displayed as well as how the results display. When you create and edit a query with *Query Design*, the *Design* tab, a **Query Tools contextual tab**, is available in the ribbon.

Create a Query Based on a Single Table

You can create a new query from the *Create* tab. Queries you create using the *Query Design* button automatically open in *Design* view.

▶ **HOW TO: Create a New Query in Design View Using a Single Table**

1. Click the **Create** tab on the *Ribbon*.
2. Click the **Query Design** button in the *Queries* group (Figure 3-6).
 - A new query opens in *Design* view (Figure 3-7).
 - The *Design* tab is now available and selected.

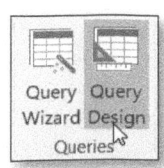

3-6 *Query Design* button

- The *Query Design* window opens.
- The *Show Table* dialog box displays with the *Tables* tab selected.

3. Select the table to use in the query.

- If your new query is based on an existing query instead of a table, first click the **Queries** tab in the *Show Table* dialog box and then select the query.
- If you accidentally close the *Show Table* dialog box and need to reopen it, click the **Show Table** button [*Query Tools Design* tab, *Query Setup* group].

4. Click **Add** to add the table into the *Query Design* window.

> **ANOTHER WAY**
>
> Double-click a table name in the *Show Table* dialog box to add it into the *Query Design* window.

5. Click the **Close** button to close the *Show Table* dialog box.

- The *Query Design* window (Figure 3-8) is divided into two sections. The top half shows the table you added into the query. The bottom half shows the *query design grid*. The **query design grid** contains the fields which have been included in the query, along with details about criteria and how the query results display. You learn to add fields in the next *How To*.
- Increase the size of the table object in the window to display all of the fields as desired.
- The **divider bar** separates the two sections. You can adjust the size of either section by moving the divider bar up or down.

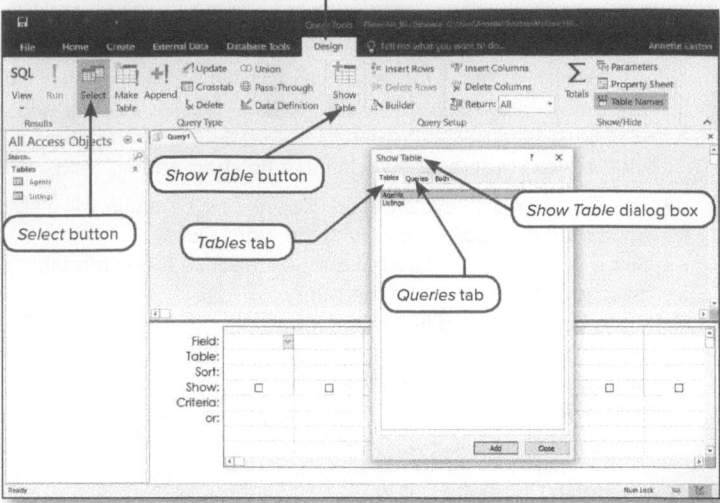

3-7 Create a new query in *Design* view

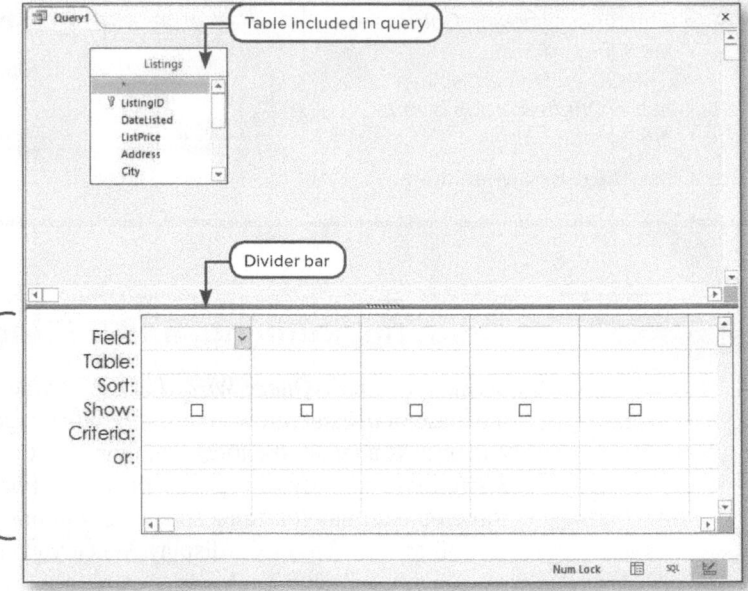

3-8 *Query Design* window

Notice that the *Select* button is highlighted in the *Query Type* group [*Query Tools Design* tab] shown in Figure 3-7. This indicates that the query is a select query. You can use **select queries** to locate, or select, data in the database. They are the most common type of query. In future chapters, you will learn about other query types that are action-based.

Add Fields into a Query

After you create a query, you need to add the fields into the query design grid. You can add as many fields as needed into the query. The query results display the fields in the order you place them into the query design grid.

There are three different ways to add fields into a query.

- Click, hold, and drag a field name from a *Table* displayed in the top part of the *Query Design* window to the first empty cell in the *Field* row of the query design grid. The *Field* and *Table* row cells in the query design grid update to display the contents (Figure 3-9).
- Double-click a field name from a *Table* in the top part of the *Query Design* window. The field is added to the first empty cell in the *Field* row of the query design grid.
- Click the **first empty cell** in the *Field* row of the query design grid. Click the **drop-down arrow** to display the list of field names. Select the desired field name (Figure 3-9).

To include all of the fields from a table in the query either select the asterisk (*) symbol from the *Table* in the top part of the *Query Design* window or select the **TableName.*** choice from the drop-down list of fields displayed in the query design grid. Remember that the text "TableName" does not actually display; instead, the name of your table displays.

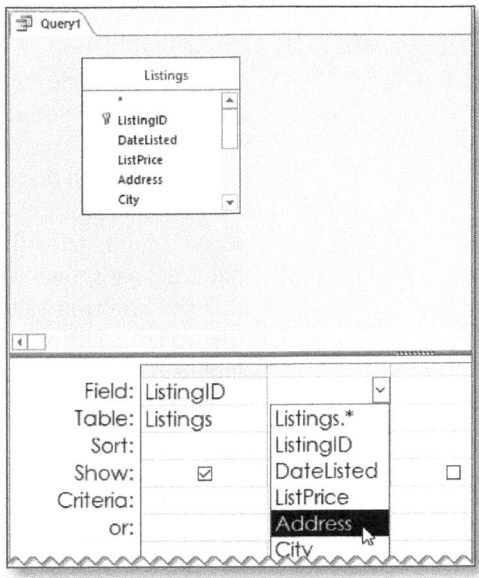

3-9 Add fields into a query

> **MORE INFO**
>
> If you want to apply criteria to individual fields, you must add each field separately instead of using the asterisk (*) symbol.

Run a Query

To see the results of a query, you need to execute, or run, the query. Running a newly written query ensures that you have created your query correctly; it is an important part of the database design and testing process.

3-10 *Run* button

- Click the **Run** button [*Query Tools Design* tab, *Results* group] to execute, or run, a query (Figure 3-10).

The results of the query display in *Datasheet* view (Figure 3-11). If the query results in more records than can display in the window, scroll bars automatically display.

Datasheet view of a query operates like *Datasheet* view of a table. This means you can change, add, and delete records in this view. Making changes to the data shown in *Datasheet* view of a query changes the actual table data.

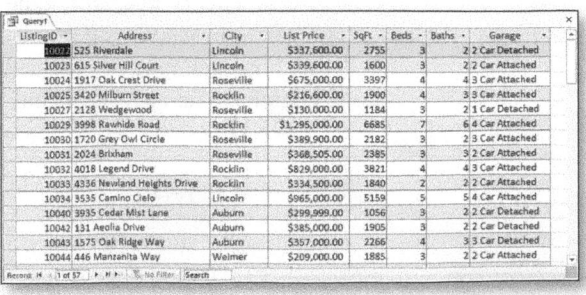

3-11 Query results display in *Datasheet* view

> **MORE INFO**
>
> Be careful about using the *Datasheet* view results of a query to add data. You will encounter error messages when you attempt to add data in *Datasheet* view if you have not included all the fields in a query but you have set data integrity properties to require all fields.

You can refine the datasheet layout using the skills you learned in Chapter 1. In *Datasheet* view of a query you can change the font type, font size, font color, column width, alternate row colors and gridlines. To further customize the appearance of the query results, you can use a form or report to display the query results. These objects are introduced in the next chapter.

Sometimes no records show when you run a query. This may be because there are no records in the table that match your query criteria. However, if you expect results to display but none are shown when you run the query, you need to explore the potential causes. Check that the criterion value entered into the query matches the way the values are entered into the table. Additionally, verify that the query design is correct. You may have accidentally included the wrong field in the query and as a result no values match the criteria entered. Finally, the data may have been entered wrong when they were added to the table.

Save and Close a Query

When you create a query, Access automatically assigns a generic name to the query, such as *Query1*. The first time you save the query, the *Save As* dialog box displays and you are prompted to change the default name.

Since you may have several queries based off the same table, change the generic name to a name that describes the function of the query.

3-12 *Save As* dialog box for a query

- Save a new query by clicking the **Save** button [*File* tab]. Type a new name for the query in the *Query Name* box (Figure 3-12) and click **OK**.

> **ANOTHER WAY**
>
> Recall that you can also use **Ctrl+S**, the *Save* button on the *Quick Access* toolbar, or the **F12** function key to open the *Save As* dialog box.

Once a query has been saved, it displays in the *Queries* group of the *Navigation Pane* (Figure 3-13).

- Close a query by clicking the **X** in the upper right corner of the query. If you close a new query without saving it, Access deletes the query. You can close the query from either *Design* view or *Datasheet* view.

Open a Saved Query

Open a saved query in *Design* view by right-clicking the query name in the *Navigation Pane* and selecting **Design View** from the context menu (Figure 3-14).

3-13 Saved queries display in the *Navigation Pane*

If you double-click a query name in the *Navigation Pane*, the query executes and the results show in *Datasheet* view.

3-14 Use the context menu to open a query in *Design View*

Create a Query Based on Multiple Tables

The vast majority of databases contain multiple, related tables. As a result, many of the questions that you want to ask about the data require that you get data from more than one table. When building a query you can add more than one table into the *Query Design* window. Be sure to include only tables that are related to each other or you may end up with more records than anticipated and records may be displayed in a way that doesn't make sense.

▶ **HOW TO:** Create a New Query in Design View Using Multiple Tables

1. Click the **Create** tab on the *Ribbon*.
2. Click the **Query Design** button in the *Queries* group to open the *Show Table* dialog box.
3. Select the first table you want to use in the query.
4. Click **Add** to add the table into the **Query Design** window.
5. Select the second table you want to use in the query.
6. Click **Add** to add the table into the **Query Design** window.
 - The *Query Design* window updates to show both tables (Figure 3-15).
 - A relationship line displays showing the relationship.
7. Continue adding all required tables.

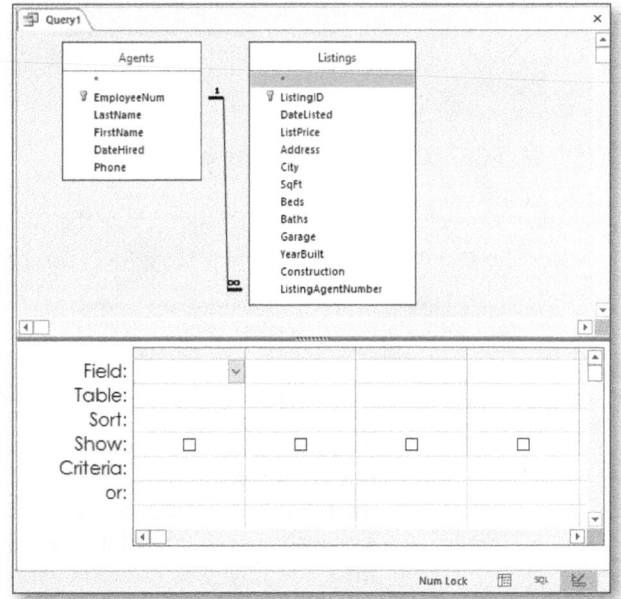

3-15 *Query Design* window displays all the tables used in a query

> ▶ **ANOTHER WAY**
>
> Select the first table name. Press and hold the **Shift** or **Ctrl** key. Select any additional table names. Click **Add** to add all the tables into the *Query Design* window.

8. Click the **Close** button to close the *Show Table* dialog box.
 - You can now add fields and run and save the query following the steps you have learned.

Edit Fields in Query Design

When building a query you may need to insert a field between two fields that already are placed in the query design grid. Alternatively, you may need to delete a field from the query

design grid if you determine it is no longer needed. The *Query Setup* group [*Query Tools Design* tab] contains the **Insert Columns** or **Delete Columns** buttons to add or delete a field (Figure 3-16).

3-16 *Insert Columns* and *Delete Columns* buttons

> ▶ **HOW TO:** Insert New Fields Between Existing Fields in a Query

1. In the query design grid, put your pointer in the small cell above the field name to the right of where you wish to insert a new field (Figure 3-17) and click the **Selection** pointer to select that column. The column is highlighted in black.

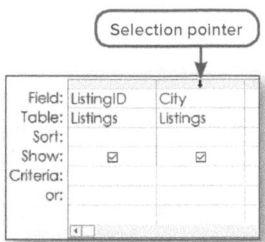

3-17 Select a column in the query design grid

2. Click the **Insert Columns** button [*Query Tools Design* tab, *Query Setup* group]. The new column displays and becomes the selected column (Figure 3-18).

3. Add a field into that column by clicking the **Field** row cell of the new column, clicking the **drop-down arrow**, and selecting the desired field name.

3-18 A new column inserted between existing fields

> ▶ **HOW TO:** Delete Fields from a Query

1. Select the column in the query design grid of the field that you wish to delete.

2. Click the **Delete Columns** button [*Query Tools Design* tab, *Query Setup* group] to delete the selected field.

SLO 3.3

Adding a Criterion to a Query

You can add a criterion into a query to search for records that meet a specific value. The type of criterion you enter, along with the way you enter the criterion, depends on the data type of the field. Use *expressions* to write the criterion. In Chapter 2 you learned to create expressions when you created a validation rule. The expressions that you write for criterion work the same way. The criterion expression can be entered directly in the criteria cell or in the *Expression Builder*.

When you enter the specific criterion value, be sure to format the value correctly based on the data type of the field.

- Criterion for *Number*, *Currency* and *AutoNumber* data types include the actual number value not surrounded by any special symbols.
- Criterion for *Short Text* and *Long Text* data types are enclosed within quotation marks. Access ignores the case of the text in the criterion when making an evaluation.
- Criterion for *Date/Time* data types are enclosed within pound (#) symbols.
- Criterion for *Yes/No* data types use either *Yes* or *No*. Use *Yes* to find records where the check box is selected and use *No* to find records where the check box is not selected.

Single Criterion

In the simplest criterion expression you only enter the criteria value. Access evaluates this criterion as an "equal to" comparison. In other words, it will find all data that is "equal to" the criterion.

▶ **HOW TO: Add a Criterion into the Query**

1. Click the **Criteria** row cell of the desired field.
2. Type the criterion expression you want to enter.

 - The criterion shown in Figure 3-19 creates a query that finds all property listings in the *City* of "Roseville".
 - As desired, you can include the equal sign in the expression. In this example, you could enter either "=Roseville" or "Roseville" since they both evaluate the same way.
 - If your criterion expression is longer than the column width, you can increase the width of the column. Position the pointer at the border of a column, in the small cell above the field name. The pointer turns into the resize arrow. Drag the resize arrow to resize the column.
 - You can also enter the criteria into the *Expression Builder*. Open the *Expression Builder* dialog box by right-clicking and selecting **Build** from the context menu (Figure 3-20) or by pressing **Ctrl+F2**.

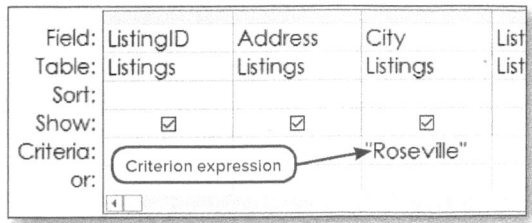

3-19 Enter a criterion into a query

3-20 Select the *Build* button to open the *Expression Builder*

When entering an expression, the ***IntelliSense*** tool may suggest a list of possible values. Figure 3-21 shows an example of an *IntelliSense* list. A description of the selected item also displays. The list automatically appears if the text you enter into an expression matches the text in a function or object name. The list updates as you keep typing additional text. You can select an item from the list, press **Esc** to hide the list, or simply continue typing your value.

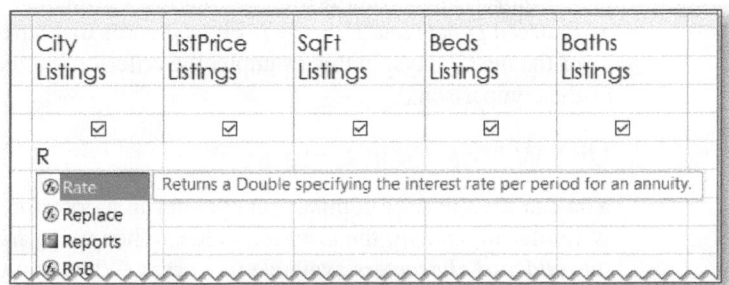

3-21 The *IntelliSense* tool suggests possible functions based on the value you have entered

After adding a criterion to a query, remember to test the query to make sure you wrote the criterion expression correctly. Test the query by running it and then comparing the results to your expected results.

If no records in the database match the query criterion, the datasheet still displays but no records appear. If this occurs and you expect that records in the table should display as a result of the query, verify that the query criterion was entered correctly or that data values were entered correctly when the record was added into the table.

Comparison Operators

When you want to search for values beyond an "equal to" comparison, you need to include a *comparison operator* in the expression. A **comparison operator** is used to compare two values in an expression. Usually the comparison operator appears at the beginning of the expression, although that depends on the exact structure of the expression.

The operators are summarized in the following table:

Comparison Operators

Operator	Explanation	Example
<	Less than	<5
<=	Less than or equal to	<=100
>	Greater than	>#1/1/2014#
>=	Greater than or equal to	>="B24"
=	Equal to	="CA"
<>	Not equal to	<>0
Between	Between these two values	Between 10 and 20
In	Contained in this list of values	In(1, 5, 10)
Like	Similar to this value	Like "C??"

A criterion can also have the value of *Is Null* or *Is Not Null*. Use *Is Null* to find records where the value is not entered for a specific field. Use *Is Not Null* to find records where the field contains a value.

Date/Time fields sometimes use a function as the criteria value. **Functions** are pre-built procedures that perform a specific task. A common function used with *Date/Time* fields is **Date()**, which returns the current date from your computer. Two criterion examples using the *Date()* function in a *ShippingDate* field are explained below.

- *<=Date()*: Finds records that have a *ShippingDate* value that is on or before today's date.
- *Between Date() and Date()+7*: Finds records that have a *ShippingDate* value that is one of the next 7 days. In this example, the criterion includes an arithmetic formula as part of the comparison.

Use Wildcards in Criteria

You can use the **Like** comparison operator in a criterion to find records containing data that is similar to, or like, the criterion value. When using *like*, you typically incorporate one of the **wildcard characters** available in Access. When you use a wildcard, the criterion of your expression must be enclosed in quotation marks, even when you use *Number*, *Currency*, and *AutoNumber* data types.

Examples of wildcard characters and their effects in a query criterion are illustrated in the following material.

The ? Wildcard Character

Use the **?** wildcard character to match any single character in a specific position. Remember that numbers are also considered characters. Review the example in the following table:

Field (Type and Size)	Example Criterion	Explanation of Example
PhoneNumber (Text, Size 10) [The input mask symbols are not stored with the data.]	Like "9?????????"	Finds records where the phone number contains 10 characters and starts with a 9.

If you use the criterion above to search the sample data shown in Figure 3-22, only the highlighted record values are returned by the query. The second record, phone number 987-3116, does start with a 9, but it is not 10 characters long.

3-22 Sample phone data

If you wrote the criterion as *Like "9???????"*, which would require a value of exactly 8 characters, no records would be returned since none of the phone numbers in Figure 3-22 contains only 8 characters.

The * Wildcard Character

Use the * wildcard character to match any number of characters, as shown in the example in the following table:

Field (Type and Size)	Example Criterion	Explanation of Example
SongTitle (Text, Size 70)	Like "love *"	Finds records where the song title starts with the word love. Note that there is a blank space after the letter "e" and before the asterisk.

Due to the blank space between the word "love" and the asterisk, this query finds only the complete word of "love" and not songs where the title contains the letters of the word "love" within a word, such as "beloved" or "lover". This criterion would find "Love for All Seasons". However, it will not find songs with the title of "Leave Love Alone" or "Make You Feel My Love" because in these titles "love" is not the first word.

If you change the criterion to *Like "* love"*, the only songs found would be those that end with the word "love". For example, it would find "Make You Feel My Love".

If you change the criterion to *Like "* love *"*, the only songs found would be those that contain the word "love" somewhere in the middle ("love" cannot be the first or last word). This query would find "Leave Love Alone".

If you are interested in finding songs that contain the letters of the word "love", you can remove the spaces. For example, the query *Like "*Love*"*, would find song titles that contain the letters of the word "love" anywhere in the title. This would find all of the songs that *Like "* Love *"* found and it would also find "She Will Be Loved" and "Lovers in a Dangerous Time".

> ▶ **MORE INFO**
>
> You must pay attention to the proper placement of the * wildcard, along with any characters and spaces, to ensure that the query returns the correct results.

Review another example in the table below used on a currency field.

Field (Type and Size)	Example Criterion	Explanation of Example
Sales Price (Currency, Size N/A)	Like "*.99"	Finds records where the sales price ends with .99.

This criterion finds records where the price is .99, 2.99, or 345.99. It will not find records where the price is 1.09 or 3.995.

You can combine multiple wildcards together. For example, using the criterion of *Like "*1?"* combines the * and *?* wildcards. Using this criterion on the *PhoneNumber* field in Figure 3-22 would return the phone numbers of () 987-3116 and (916) 744-1614. This criterion returns records with a phone number of any length, as long as a "1" is the second to the last digit.

The # Wildcard Character

Use the # wildcard character to match any single numeric digit. Review the examples shown in the following two tables:

Field (Type and Size)	Example Criterion	Explanation of Example
SqFt (Number, Size Long Integer)	Like "2###"	Finds records where the square footage starts with a 2 and contains 4 digits.

This criterion finds houses that are in the 2,000 to 2,999 square foot range. It does not find a house with 255 square feet or with 20,000 square feet since those don't meet the 4-digit specification. Remember that the comma (,) in 2,000, as an example, only displays as part of the formatting and is not stored as a character in the actual table.

Field (Type and Size)	Example Criterion	Explanation of Example
Sales Price (Currency, Size N/A)	Like "###.99"	Finds records where the sales price contains three digits to the left of the decimal point and ends with .99.

This criterion finds records where the price is 100.99 or 345.99. It will not find records where the price is .99, 2.99 or 1043.99.

PAUSE & PRACTICE: ACCESS 3-1

For this Pause & Practice, you use *Design* view to create three queries for the Placer Hills Real Estate Company.

File Needed: ***PlacerHills-03.accdb***
Completed Project File Name: ***[your initials] PP A3-1.accdb***

1. Open the ***PlacerHills-03*** database file.

2. Save a new copy of your database as [your initials] PP A3-1.

3. Enable content in the database.

4. Create a new query in *Design* view.
 a. Click the **Query Design** button [*Create* tab, *Queries* group] to open the *Show Table* dialog box.
 b. Select the **Agents** table, if needed, and click the **Add** button.
 c. Select the **Listings** table and click the **Add** button.
 d. Click the **Close** button in the *Show Table* dialog box.
 e. Increase the size of the table objects to display all of the fields.
 f. Double-click the **ListingID** field from the *Listings* table in the *Query Design* window. The field is added to the first empty column in the query design grid.
 g. Double-click the **Address** field to add it into the query design grid.
 h. Continue adding the following fields into the query design grid: **City**, **ListPrice**, **SqFt**, **Beds**, **Baths**, **Garage**, **FirstName**, **LastName** and **Phone**. Note that the last three fields come from the *Agents* table. The completed query should look similar to Figure 3-23.

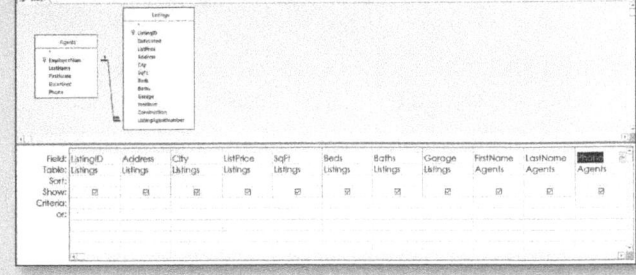

3-23 Completed query design

5. Click the **Run** button [*Query Tools Design* tab, *Results* group] to run the query. The query should open in *Datasheet* view and display 57 records.

6. Click the **View** button [*Home* tab, *Views* group] and select the **Design View** option to switch back to *Design* view.

7. Save the query.
 a. Click the **Save** button [*File* tab].
 b. Type ShowAllListings in the *Query Name* box.
 c. Click **OK**. The query name displays in the *Navigation Pane* in the *Queries* group.

8. Add a criterion to the query to find all listings in Roseville.
 a. Type Roseville in the **Criteria** row cell of the *City* field. When you enter criterion into a *Short Text* or *Long Text* field, you can either enter quotation marks around the criterion, or if you omit the quotation marks, Access automatically enters them for you.
 b. Tab out of that field. Notice that Access automatically puts quotation marks around the text criteria (Figure 3-24).

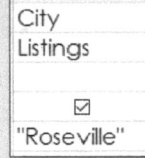

3-24 Query criterion

9. Click the **Run** button [*Query Tools Design* tab, *Results* group] to run the query. The query should open in *Datasheet* view and display the 11 listings located in Roseville (Figure 3-25).

ListingID	Address	City	List Price	SqFt	Beds	Baths	Garage	FirstName	LastName	Phone
10024	1917 Oak Crest Drive	Roseville	$675,000.00	3397	4	4	3 Car Attached	Jack	Johnstone	(916) 555-1679
10027	2128 Wedgewood	Roseville	$130,000.00	1184	3	2	1 Car Detached	Kelly	Weatherby	(916) 987-3756
10030	1720 Grey Owl Circle	Roseville	$389,900.00	2182	3	2	3 Car Attached	Simon	Bidou	(530) 648-7689
10031	2024 Brixham	Roseville	$368,505.00	2385	3	3	2 Car Attached	Kallyn	Duarte	(916) 744-1614
10049	1773 Melanzane Drive	Roseville	$599,900.00	4390	4	5	3 Car Attached	Kelly	Weatherby	(916) 987-3756
10055	954 Court Street	Roseville	$429,900.00	2580	3	3	2 Car Attached	Kelly	Weatherby	(916) 987-3756
10060	1110 Kimberly Court	Roseville	$399,900.00	3765	4	4	3 Car Detached	Kelly	Weatherby	(916) 987-3756
10080	1089 Marseille Lane	Roseville	$274,000.00	1645	2	2	2 Car Attached	Simon	Bidou	(530) 648-7689
10081	1520 Arrowwood Lane	Roseville	$340,000.00	2370	4	3	3 Car Attached	Jack	Johnstone	(916) 555-1679
10110	227 Balsam Creek	Roseville	$559,600.00	1976	4	2	1 Car Detached	John	Burgess	(530) 278-4699
10117	1924 Wildwood Way	Roseville	$279,000.00	1676	3	3	2 Car Attached	Rick	Chung	(916) 823-6940

Record: 1 of 11 No Filter Search

3-25 Query results for listings in Roseville

10. Save a copy of this query.
 a. Click the **Save As** button [*File* tab]
 b. Select the **Save Object As** button in the *File Types* area and then click the **Save As** button. Access suggests the new query name of *Copy of ShowAllListings*.
 c. Type ListingsInRoseville in the *Save 'ShowAllListings' to* box.
 d. Click **OK**. The two queries now display in the *Navigation Pane* in the *Queries* group.
 e. Close the query.

11. Right-click the **ShowAllListings** query name in the *Navigation Pane* and select **Design View** from the context menu to open the query.

12. Type Like "*Attached" in the *Criteria* row cell of the *Garage* field. This criterion will find all listings that have an attached garage, no matter how many cars.

13. Run the query. Your results should display 37 listings that have an attached garage.

14. Save a copy of the query using the name ListingsWithAttachedGarage.

15. Close the query.

16. Close the database.

SLO 3.4

Controlling the Display of Query Results

Access provides a variety of options to help control the way query results display. For example, you may wish to have the results display in a sorted order. Or you may need to include a field in a query to apply a criterion, but you don't want that field to display in the results. At other times, a query may show duplicate records and you want to show only records that contain unique values. This section describes some of the ways to control the display of query results.

Unique Values Property

A well-designed database is structured to minimize redundant data. As a result, most queries display unique records in the results. However, sometimes the structure of a particular query causes duplicated records to display.

For example, a music database may have two tables: one that stores information about each album owned and another that stores information about the songs that are on each album. The *Query* window showing those tables is displayed in Figure 3-26. As you know, it is possible for a song to appear on multiple albums. For example, "Genie in a Bottle" appears on two of Christina Aguilera's albums, *Keeps Gettin' Better: A Decade of Hits* and *Christina Aguilera*.

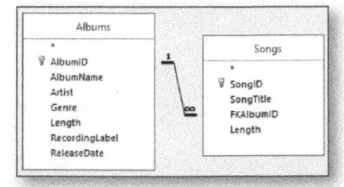

3-26 *Query* window shows the relationship between the *Albums* and *Songs* tables

If you write a query to find the names of all the songs in the database, you see that song name appear once for each album that includes this song. In the query results, this would appear as duplicated data. You can use the ***Unique Values*** property to direct Access to only display records that don't include duplicated values. Don't confuse the *Unique Values* property with the ***Unique Records*** property. *Unique Records* checks all the fields in a table (not just those included in the query).

▶ **HOW TO:** Display Unique Values in Query Results

1. Open the query in *Design* view.
2. Click anywhere in the top half of the *Query Design* window to deselect any fields that are selected.
3. Click the **Property Sheet** button [*Query Tools Design* tab, *Show/Hide* group] (Figure 3-27).

3-27 *Show/Hide* group buttons

 - The *Property Sheet* for the query opens (Figure 3-28).
 - In the *Show/Hide* group, the *Table Names* button is highlighted when the query design grid displays the *Table* row below the *Field* row. The *Table Names* button works as a toggle. Clicking it when it is highlighted removes the *Table* row from the query design grid.
 - Verify that the *Selection type* displays *Query Properties*. If the *Selection type* displays *Field Properties*, you still had a field selected before opening the *Property Sheet* and you must repeat step 2.

4. Click the **Unique Values** property box and select **Yes**.

5. Close the *Property Sheet*.

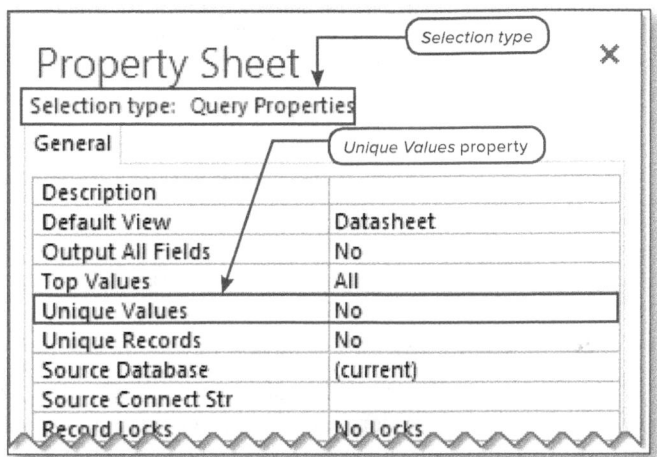

3-28 *Property Sheet* of a query

▶ **ANOTHER WAY**

Press the **F4** key to open or close the *Property Sheet*.

The usefulness of the *Unique Values* property depends on the query structure. For example, if you run the query shown in Figure 3-29 you see one record for every song in the database. Setting the *Unique Values* property to *Yes* does not reduce the number of records displayed. This is because including the field of *AlbumName* creates unique records in the results (assuming the same *SongTitle* is not included on an album twice).

The query shown in Figure 3-30 does not include the *AlbumName* field. Setting the *Unique Values* property to *Yes* on this query results in fewer records being displayed. With this query, "Genie in a Bottle" only appears one time in the query results.

Field:	AlbumName	SongTitle	Artist
Table:	Albums	Songs	Albums
Sort:			
Show:	☑	☑	☑
Criteria:			
or:			

3-29 *Unique Values* property has no impact when fields create unique records

Field:	SongTitle	Artist
Table:	Songs	Albums
Sort:		
Show:	☑	☑
Criteria:		
or:		

3-30 Not including the *AlbumName* field results in unique values

Show Option for Query Fields

Most of the time, you want all of the fields placed into the query design grid to display in the query results. Occasionally, you don't want a field to display because it would show unnecessary

or duplicated values. The query shown in Figure 3-31 displays all the songs that are on albums by "The Beatles".

This query produces a datasheet like that shown in Figure 3-32. The *Artist* field is needed in the query because you included a criterion on that field to limit the records displayed to songs by "The Beatles". But displaying the *Artist* is not really necessary here, as you know that all of these songs are by "The Beatles".

- To not show a query field in the query results, deselect the **Show** row check box in the query design grid of your query (Figure 3-33).

In order to determine if a query is working correctly, first run the query with all fields displayed so you can verify the accuracy of the query. Only after you are confident with the query design should you deselect the *Show* row check box of the appropriate fields.

Apply Sorting

Access can display the results of a query in sorted order. You can sort on one or more fields.

- To sort the results of a query, click the **Sort** row cell of the desired field.
- Click the **drop-down arrow** and select **Ascending** or **Descending** (Figure 3-34).

> **MORE INFO**
>
> To remove sorting from a field, click the **Sort** row cell, click the **drop-down arrow**, and select (**not sorted**).

Field:	SongTitle	Artist
Table:	Songs	Albums
Sort:		
Show:	☑	☑
Criteria:		"The Beatles"
or:		

3-31 *Show* row check box for fields

Song Title	Artist
All I've Got to Do	The Beatles
All My Loving	The Beatles
Bad Boy	The Beatles
Because	The Beatles
Carry That Weight	The Beatles
Come Together	The Beatles
Dizzy Miss Lizzy	The Beatles
Don't Bother Me	The Beatles
Eight Days a Week	The Beatles

3-32 Query results

Deselected *Show* check box

Field:	SongTitle	Artist
Table:	Songs	Albums
Sort:		
Show:	☑	☐
Criteria:		"The Beatles"
or:		

3-33 Deselect the *Show* row check box

Field:	ListingID	Address	City
Table:	Listings	Listings	Listings
Sort:			
Show:	☑	☑	Ascending
Criteria:			Descending
or:			(not sorted)

3-34 *Sort* option of a query

Access sorts data based on the order of the columns. If you are sorting on multiple fields, you need to decide the sorting order of the fields. For example, in a table containing a list of all properties for sale, a client may want the query results sorted by the *City*, *Construction*, and *SqFt* fields. There are many possible combinations of sorted results in this instance. Here we show two examples. The two sort examples shown here use an *Ascending* sort order on each field.

Figure 3-35 shows results sorted first by *City*, next by *Construction*, and last by *SqFt*. The highlighted cells emphasize the impact of the sorting. Because *City* is the first sort field and alphabetically Auburn is the first city in the database, this results in all properties in Auburn appearing first. Within the Auburn

ListingID	Address	City	Construction	SqFt
10042	131 Aeolia Drive	Auburn	Brick	1905
10045	12355 Krista Lane	Auburn	Brick	2234
10040	3935 Cedar Mist Lane	Auburn	Frame	1056
10069	1255 Copperdale	Auburn	Frame	1456
10177	9030 Upper Valley Road	Auburn	Frame	2635
10144	863 Holly Hill Drive	Auburn	Frame	2876
10043	1575 Oak Ridge Way	Auburn	Stone	2266
10150	423 Welterwood	Lincoln	Brick	1482
10046	1735 Andover Lane	Lincoln	Brick	1552
10052	1096 Kinnerly Lane	Lincoln	Brick	1948
10074	1827 Delouch Drive	Lincoln	Brick	2575
10072	406 E Street	Lincoln	Frame	1100
10062	2811 Cardinal Drive	Lincoln	Frame	2061
10116	611 Ledgestone Court	Lincoln	Frame	2262

3-35 Records sorted by the *City*, *Construction*, and *SqFt* fields

properties, homes made of brick appear first. Finally, within the "Auburn" and "Brick" properties, the property with the smallest square footage appears at the top of the list.

Figure 3-36 is sorted differently. In this example, the query is sorted first by *Construction*, next by *City*, and last by *SqFt*. In these results all properties with brick construction appear first. Within the "Brick" properties, those in Auburn appear first. Finally, within the "Brick" and "Auburn" properties, the smallest square footage appears at the top of the list.

ListingID	Address	Construction	City	SqFt
10042	131 Aeolia Drive	Brick	Auburn	1905
10045	12355 Krista Lane	Brick	Auburn	2234
10150	423 Welterwood	Brick	Lincoln	1482
10046	1735 Andover Lane	Brick	Lincoln	1552
10052	1096 Kinnerly Lane	Brick	Lincoln	1948
10074	1827 Delouch Drive	Brick	Lincoln	2575
10073	736 Oakdale	Brick	Newcastle	766
10166	1852 Wedgewood	Brick	Newcastle	2234
10031	2024 Brixham	Brick	Roseville	2385
10024	1917 Oak Crest Drive	Brick	Roseville	3397
10044	446 Manzanita Way	Brick	Weimer	1885
10040	3935 Cedar Mist Lane	Frame	Auburn	1056
10069	1255 Copperdale	Frame	Auburn	1456
10177	9030 Upper Valley Road	Frame	Auburn	2635
10144	863 Holly Hill Drive	Frame	Auburn	2876
10072	406 E Street	Frame	Lincoln	1100
10062	2811 Cardinal Drive	Frame	Lincoln	2061

3-36 Records sorted by the *Construction*, *City*, and *SqFt* fields

▶ HOW TO: Sort a Query Using Multiple Fields

1. Add the fields into the query design grid from left to right based on the desired sort order.
2. If the fields are already placed in the query design grid, you can rearrange the column order by moving a column.
 - Select the column to be moved. The column turns black.
 - Position the pointer in the small cell above the field name. Click and hold the pointer. A black vertical line appears to the left of the selected column (Figure 3-37).
 - Drag the pointer to the new location. The line moves with you to indicate the location where the column will be moved.
 - Release the pointer to complete the move.
3. For each of the sort fields, click the **Sort** row cell, click the **drop-down arrow**, and select **Ascending** or **Descending**.

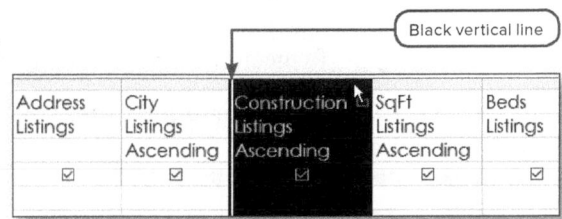

3-37 The black vertical line indicates the new location of the column

> ## MORE INFO
>
> Sometimes you may need to combine sorting and show options. For example, you may wish to have the first sort field display in a different position in the query results. In this case, you would include the field twice. The first would be included to the left of the query to designate the *Sort* selection and to deselect the *Show* box. The same field would be added a second time in the desired position to show the value.

SLO 3.5 Defining Multiple Criteria in a Query

The previous examples created queries that used at most one condition or criterion. Many times the questions that you want to ask about the data are more complex and require the use of compound criteria. **Compound criteria** combine more than one criterion using the *AND* or *OR* logical operators and allow you to ask questions using multiple conditions.

The AND Operator

The **AND** logical operator requires that a record meet all of the individual conditions specified in order to be included in the results. An *AND* condition can be used in one field or across multiple fields.

▶HOW TO: Use AND Compound Criteria in Multiple Fields

1. Click the **Criteria** row cell of the first field.
2. Type the text of the desired criterion expression.
3. Click the **Criteria** row cell of the second field.
4. Type the text of the second desired criterion expression.
5. Continue entering the criterion in the remaining fields.

 - The query shown in Figure 3-38 finds the properties in Auburn that have a list price of less than $300,000 and have more than 2,000 square feet.
 - Values entered in cells on the same *Criteria* row of the query design grid create an *AND* condition.

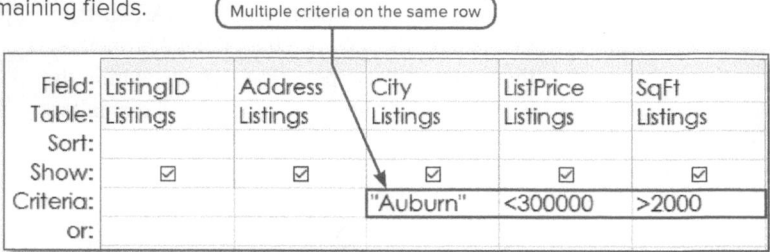

3-38 Query criteria entered on the same row creates an *AND* condition

Occasionally you need to use the *AND* operator in a single field. In these cases the *AND* operator is typically combined with another comparison operator such as *Between*, > or <. Remember that all criterion included together on a row are treated as *AND* conditions.

▶HOW TO: Use AND Compound Criteria in a Single Field

1. Click the **Criteria** row cell of the field.
2. Type the text of the desired condition, including the word "AND" between each part of the condition.

 - The query shown in Figure 3-39 finds listings with a square footage that is greater than or equal to 2,000 square feet and less than or equal to 3,000 square feet
 - This condition could also be written using the *Between* operator. The condition in Figure 3-40 uses *Between* and returns the same results as the condition shown in Figure 3-39 which uses the >= and <= operators.

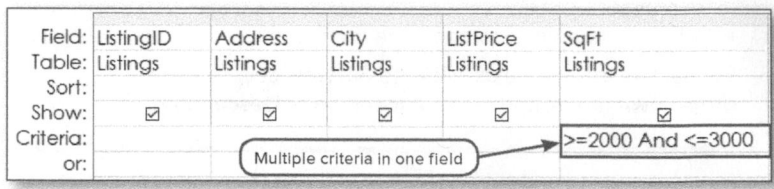

3-39 Use the word "AND" between compound critieria in the same field

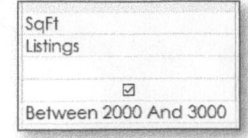

3-40 *Between* operator

> **MORE INFO**
>
> The case used to write "AND" has no impact on the query. "AND" or "And" or "and" all evaluate the same.

The OR Operator

The **OR** logical operator requires a record to meet at least one of the individual conditions specified in order to be included in the results. With the *OR* operator you can specify multiple criterion in one field or you can use compound criteria across several fields.

▶**HOW TO:** Use OR Compound Criteria in Multiple Fields

1. Click the **Criteria** row cell of the first field.
2. Type the text of the desired criterion expression.
3. Click the **or** row cell of the second field.
4. Type the text of the second desired criterion expression.
5. Continue entering criterion on the remaining fields, each time entering the value on the row below the last row you entered a value.
 - The query shown in Figure 3-41 finds the properties that are in Auburn or have a list price of less than $300,000 or have more than 2,000 square feet.

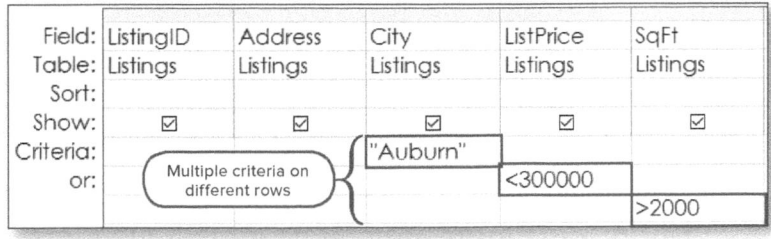

3-41 Query criteria entered on different rows creates an *OR* condition

Entering multiple criteria in the same field is an **OR** condition. The returned records match the first value *or* the second value *or* the third value, and so on.

▶**HOW TO:** Use OR Compound Criteria in a Single Field

1. Click the **Criteria** row cell of the first field.
2. Type the text of the desired criterion expression.
3. Click the **or** row cell of the same field.
4. Type the text of the second desired criterion expression.
5. Continue entering the additional criterion in the field, each time entering the value on the next row.
 - The query shown in Figure 3-42 finds the properties that are in Auburn or Roseville.
 - If you save, close, and then reopen this query, Access will have changed the criteria to read "Auburn" Or "Roseville" in the one

Field:	ListingID	Address	City	ListPrice	SqFt
Table:	Listings	Listings	Listings	Listings	Listings
Sort:					
Show:	☑	☑	☑	☑	☑
Criteria:			"Auburn"		
or:			"Roseville"		

3-42 Place compound critieria in separate rows of the same field to create an *OR* condition

cell on the *Criteria* row instead of in two cells as shown in Figure 3-42. If the query only has this type of criteria, you can type the *OR* criteria directly in one cell or on separate rows.

Combine the AND and OR Operators

You can create a query that combines both the *AND* and *OR* operators. These types of conditions can be logically complex. Keep in mind that all criterion included on a row are treated as *AND* conditions, while criterion entered on separate rows are treated as *OR* conditions.

Compare the queries in Figures 3-43 and 3-44. The query in Figure 3-43 returns all properties in Auburn that have a list price less than $300,000 and have more than 2,000 square feet or any property in Roseville, no matter the list price or square footage. The *ListPrice* and *SqFt*

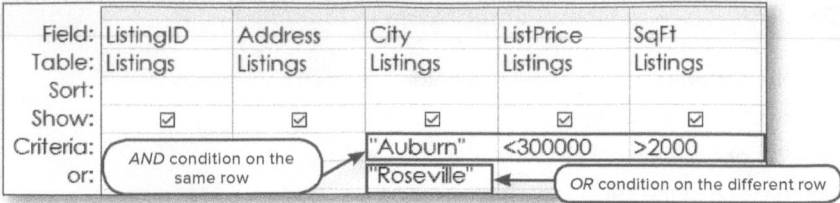

3-43 The *ListPrice* and *SqFt* criteria only apply to the city of Auburn

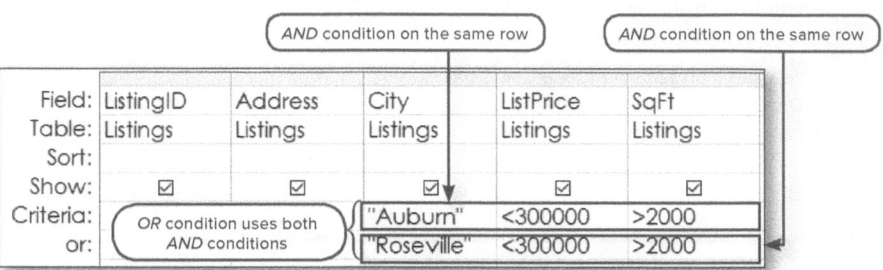

3-44 The *ListPrice* and *SqFt* criteria apply to both cities

criteria are only applied to the city of Auburn, because they are only included on the row with the *City* criterion for Auburn.

The query in Figure 3-44 returns all properties in Auburn that have a list price less than $300,000 and have more than 2,000 square feet, or all properties in Roseville, that have a list price less than $300,000 and have more than 2,000 square feet. If you want to have the *ListPrice* and *SqFt* criteria apply to both cities, you need to repeat the criteria on both rows.

Finally consider the query in Figure 3-45. This query returns all properties in Auburn that have a list price less than $300,000, or all properties in Roseville no matter their list prices or square footages, or all properties in Lincoln with square footage between 2,000 and 3,000 square feet.

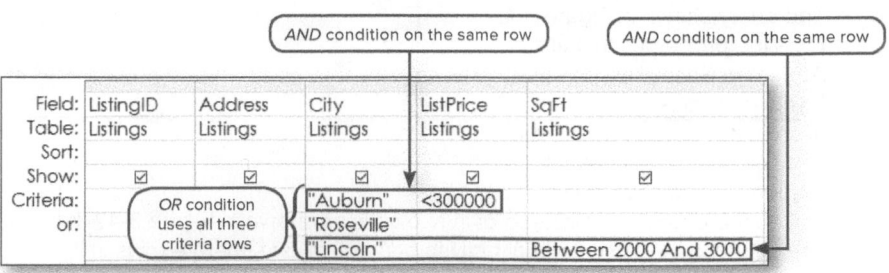

3-45 The *ListPrice* criteria apply to Auburn and the *SqFt* criteria apply to Lincoln

As these examples illustrate, compound conditions can become very complex. Spend the time to understand what you need the query to do before you attempt to build the query in Access. Now that you have learned about compound criteria, you can write more complex criteria. For example, in a music database you can now write a query to find songs where the word "I" is at the beginning, end or in the middle of the title. Using the compound criteria of *Like "I *" Or Like "* I *" Or Like "* I"* would find songs that begin, contain, or end with the word "I".

For this Pause & Practice, you use *Design* view to create two additional queries for Placer Hills Real Estate.

File Needed: ***[your initials] PP A3-1.accdb***
Completed Project File Name: ***[your initials] PP A3-2.accdb***

1. Open the ***[your initials] PP A3-1*** database completed in *Pause & Practice 3-1*.

2. Save a new copy of your database as [your initials] PP A3-2.

3. Enable content in the database.

4. Create a new query in *Design* view. The office manager wants to find all the listings by agent Rick Chung, sorted in ascending order by city and list price.
 a. Click the **Query Design** button [*Create* tab, *Queries* group] to open the *Show Table* dialog box.
 b. Select the **Agents** table. Press and hold the **Shift** key and select the **Listings** table. Click the **Add** button.
 c. Click the **Close** button in the *Show Table* dialog box.
 d. Increase the size of the table objects to display all of the fields.
 e. Double-click the **FirstName** field from the *Agents* table in the *Query Design* window. The field is added to the first empty column in the query design grid.
 f. Double-click the **LastName** field to add it into the query design grid.
 g. Continue adding the following fields into the query design grid: **ListingID, SqFt, Address, City** and **ListPrice**.

5. Click the **Save** button and save the query as ListingsByRickChung.

6. Add criteria to the query.
 a. Type Rick in the *Criteria* row cell of the *FirstName* field.
 b. Type Chung in the *Criteria* row cell of the *LastName* field.
 c. Click the **Run** button [*Query Tools Design* tab, *Results* group] to execute the query. The query should open in *Datasheet* view and display nine records.
 d. Click the **View** button [*Home* tab, *Views* group] and select the **Design View** option to switch back to *Design* view of the query.

7. Edit the query to add sorting and modify field show options.
 a. Click the **Sort** row cell for the *City* field, click the **drop-down arrow** and select **Ascending**.
 b. Click the **Sort** row cell for the *ListPrice* field, click the **drop-down arrow** and select **Ascending**.
 c. Deselect the **Show** row check box for the *FirstName* field.
 d. Deselect the **Show** row check box for the *LastName* field. Since you tested the query in step 6, you know that it only shows Rick's listings and it is not necessary to display that information.
 e. Save the changes made to the query. The query should look similar to Figure 3-46.

Field:	FirstName	LastName	ListingID	SqFt	Address	City	ListPrice
Table:	Agents	Agents	Listings	Listings	Listings	Listings	Listings
Sort:						Ascending	Ascending
Show:	☐	☐	☑	☑	☑	☑	☑
Criteria:	"Rick"	"Chung"					
or:							

3-46 *Design* view of the query criteria

f. Click the **Run** button [*Query Tools Design* tab, *Results* group] to execute the query. The query should open in *Datasheet* view and look similar to Figure 3-47.

g. Close the query.

ListingID	SqFt	Address	City	List Price
10069	1456	1255 Copperdale	Auburn	$239,600.00
10150	1482	423 Welterwood	Lincoln	$131,000.00
10180	2498	1287 Green Ravine Drive	Lincoln	$368,000.00
10078	1720	820 Hoyer Lane	Newcastle	$294,900.00
10073	766	736 Oakdale	Newcastle	$340,000.00
10075	1635	3805 Coldwater Drive	Rocklin	$299,900.00
10029	6685	3998 Rawhide Road	Rocklin	$1,295,000.00
10117	1676	1924 Wildwood Way	Roseville	$279,000.00
10099	1500	4115 Redwood	Weimar	$307,600.00

Record: 1 of 9 No Filter Search

3-47 *Datasheet* view of the *ListingsByRickChung* query results

8. Create a new query in *Design* view to help an agent locate the potential properties that meet the requirements of her client.

a. Click the **Query Design** button [*Create* tab, *Queries* group] to open the *Show Table* dialog box.

b. Select the **Listings** table and click the **Add** button.

c. Click the **Close** button in the *Show Table* dialog box.

d. Increase the size of the table object to display all of the fields.

e. Double-click the **ListingID** field to add it into the query design grid.

f. Continue adding the following fields into the query design grid: **Address**, **City**, **ListPrice**, **SqFt**, **Beds**, **Baths**, and **Garage**.

9. Save the query as ListingsForBrandonBuchanon.

10. Add criteria to the query. A client, Brandon Buchanon, is looking for homes in Rocklin or Roseville. The properties must have at least three bedrooms and at least two bathrooms and at least 1,800 square feet. Properties must have a garage, but it doesn't matter if it is attached or detached. In general, the list prices shouldn't exceed $550,000. However, if the house is in Rocklin, Brandon is willing to spend up to $600,000.

a. Type Rocklin in the *Criteria* row cell of the *City* field.

b. Type <=600000 in the *Criteria* row cell of the *ListPrice* field.

c. Continue entering the criteria displayed in Figure 3-48 into the query design grid. Note that the criterion for the *Garage* field is Like "??Car*". Because this criterion requires two characters before "Car" it will exclude Carport from the results.

Field:	ListingID	Address	City	ListPrice	SqFt	Beds	Baths	Garage
Table:	Listings	Listings	Listings	Listings	Listings	Listings	Listings	Listings
Sort:								
Show:	☑	☑	☑	☑	☑	☑	☑	☑
Criteria:			"Rocklin"	<=600000	>=1800	>=3	>=2	Like "??Car*"
or:			"Roseville"	<=550000	>=1800	>=3	>=2	Like "??Car*"

3-48 Enter the query criteria into the query design grid

11. Add sorting to the query.

a. Select **Ascending** in the **Sort** row cell for the *City* field.

b. Select **Descending** in the **Sort** row cell of the *ListPrice* field.

12. Save the changes to the query and click the **Run** button [*Query Tools Design* tab, *Results* group] to execute the query. The query should open in *Datasheet* view and display the 11 records shown in Figure 3-49.

13. Close the query.

14. Close the database.

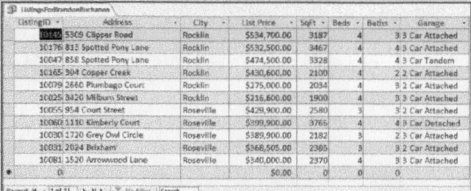

ListingID	Address	City	List Price	SqFt	Beds	Baths	Garage
10149	5309 Clipper Road	Rocklin	$534,700.00	3187	4	3	3 Car Attached
10176	812 Spotted Pony Lane	Rocklin	$532,500.00	3467	4	4	5 Car Attached
10047	858 Spotted Pony Lane	Rocklin	$424,500.00	3328	4	4	3 Car Tandem
10165	304 Copper Creek	Rocklin	$430,600.00	2100	4	2	2 Car Attached
10079	2660 Plumbago Court	Rocklin	$375,000.00	2034	4	3	3 Car Attached
10025	3420 Milburn Street	Rocklin	$216,600.00	1900	4	3	3 Car Attached
10055	954 Court Street	Roseville	$429,900.00	2580	3	3	2 Car Attached
10060	1130 Kimberly Court	Roseville	$399,900.00	3765	4	4	3 Car Detached
10090	1720 Grey Owl Circle	Roseville	$389,900.00	2182	3	3	2 Car Attached
10091	2024 Belsham	Roseville	$368,505.00	2365	3	3	2 Car Attached
10081	1520 Arrowood Lane	Roseville	$340,000.00	2370	4	3	3 Car Attached
			$0.00	0	0	0	

Record: 1 of 11 No Filter Search

3-49 *Datasheet* view of the *ListingsForBrandonBuchanon* query results

Creating and Using a Simple Parameter Query

The query examples covered so far in this chapter use criteria that has been entered into, or hardcoded into, the query. In *SLO 3.3: Adding a Criterion to a Query*, you saw a query that displayed all the property listings in Roseville—those that have a *City* listed as "Roseville". The criteria property box for that query had the value of "Roseville". What if you wanted to locate all the properties in Lincoln or all the properties in Auburn? You could create a separate query for each situation and enter in the specific criteria value into each query. But this would not be very efficient.

It is more efficient to create a parameter query. A ***parameter query*** asks you to enter the specific criteria value when you run the query. This allows you to write one query but use it for many different values of the criteria. Figure 3-50 is an example of the *Enter Parameter Value* dialog box. When you see this box, enter the specific value, such as "Roseville" or "Lincoln", click **OK**, and the desired results are shown.

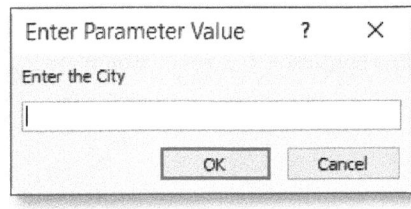

3-50 *Enter Parameter Value dialog box*

If you enter a value that is not located in the database, the query returns an empty datasheet.

To create a parameter query, you follow the same steps you learned to create a query with criteria. However, instead of entering a specific value for the criteria, you need to format the criteria expression so that Access prompts you for a ***parameter value***.

Create a Parameter

Parameters must follow a few simple rules.

- Your parameter is the specific phrase that you want to display in the dialog box, for example "Enter the City". Be sure to enter a phrase that gives clear instructions about what kind of information to enter into the dialog box, along with any formatting instructions.
- Enter your parameter into the *Criteria* row cell for the desired field.
- Enclose the parameter within square brackets.
- You can include a comparison operator, like < or >=, before the parameter.

▶ HOW TO: Create a Parameter

1. In *Design* view of the query, click the **Criteria** row cell of the desired field.

2. Type the parameter. An example parameter value is shown in Figure 3-51. You can use the *Expression Builder* to enter the parameter. This may be helpful when the parameter contains a longer phrase that is harder to enter into the *Criteria* row cell.

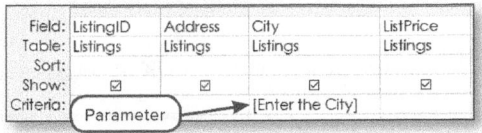

3-51 Sample parameter in the *Criteria* cell

3. Click **Run** [*Query Tools Design* tab, *Results* group] to execute the query. The *Enter Parameter Value* dialog box displays. Either press **Cancel** or enter a value and press **OK**.

> **MORE INFO**
>
> The actual phrase entered inside the square brackets has no impact on how the parameter and the query function. *[Enter the City]*, *[]* and *[City?]* all collect the same information, but the first option is more user-friendly when it appears in the dialog box.

You can include more than one parameter in the same field if you need to enter multiple values. For example, a client at the Placer Hills Real Estate Company is looking for properties between 1,800 and 2,500 square feet. You already learned how to use the *Between* operator to write a compound criteria expression. To create a more flexible query, you can incorporate multiple parameters with the *Between* operator.

▶ HOW TO: Use Multiple Parameters in a Field

1. In *Design* view of the query, click the **Criteria** row cell of the desired field.
2. Right-click and select **Zoom**, or press **Shift+F2**, to open the *Zoom* box.
3. Type the criteria expression including the parameters. An example expression using two parameters is shown in Figure 3-52.

ANOTHER WAY

The *Zoom* box is an alternative to the *Expression Builder*. It provides a larger area in which to enter an expression, but it does not show any of the *Expression Elements* displayed in the lower portion of the *Expression Builder*.

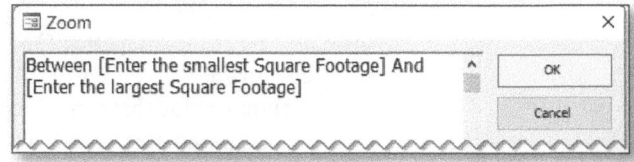

3-52 Example expression that contains two parameters in a field

4. Click **OK**.
5. Click **Run** [*Query Tools Design* tab, *Results* group] to execute the query. The first *Enter Parameter Value* dialog box displays (Figure 3-53).
6. Enter the value and click **OK**. The second *Enter Parameter Value* dialog box displays (Figure 3-54).

3-53 First Enter Parameter Value dialog box

3-54 Second Enter Parameter Value dialog box

7. Enter the value and click **OK**. After all the *Enter Parameter Value* dialog boxes have displayed, the query runs.

You can use parameters in more than one field in a query. For example, a realtor may want to locate the properties listed for sale in a specific city that have a list price less than a maximum dollar value. The realtor wants the query to prompt the user to specify the city and the maximum list price each time it runs. Figure 3-55 shows the query design grid for that query. When the query executes, the *Enter Parameter Value* dialog boxes display in the order that the fields are listed in the query. In this example, the *City* parameter displays before the *ListPrice* parameter. This example also includes the **<=** comparison operator with the *ListPrice* parameter.

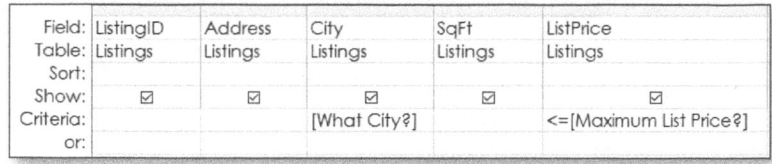

Field:	ListingID	Address	City	SqFt	ListPrice
Table:	Listings	Listings	Listings	Listings	Listings
Sort:					
Show:	☑	☑	☑	☑	☑
Criteria:			[What City?]		<=[Maximum List Price?]
or:					

3-55 Query design grid with multiple parameters

The Parameter Data Type

The *Enter Parameter Value* dialog box accepts any type of input entered by the user. However, the data type of the field determines what is valid in terms of performing the actual comparison. Consider what happens when a letter is entered into the *Enter Parameter Value* dialog box of a field with a number data type. When Access executes the query, if the value entered into the dialog box doesn't match the data type of the field, by default Access displays the following message: "*The expression is typed incorrectly, or it is too complex to be evaluated. For example, a numeric expression may contain too many complicated elements. Try simplifying the expression by assigning parts of the expression to variables.*"

The default error message, while absolutely correct in terms of content, may be confusing for a user. Also, it is problematic that even if there are multiple *Enter Parameter Value* dialog boxes, the message only shows once when the query is executed. The user doesn't know if he or she made only one mistake or several.

To make dialog boxes easier to understand, Access allows you to specify the data type that a parameter can accept. If you have specified a data type, and the user enters a value that doesn't match the data type, a more helpful error message displays (Figure 3-56).

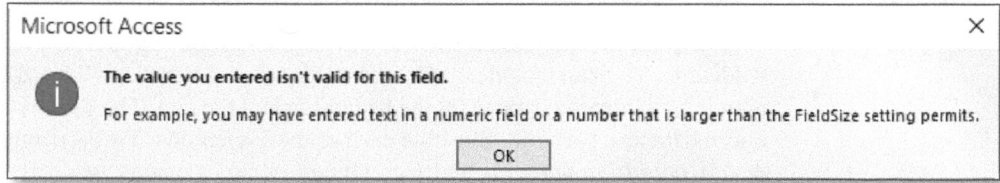

Microsoft Access ×

ⓘ **The value you entered isn't valid for this field.**

For example, you may have entered text in a numeric field or a number that is larger than the FieldSize setting permits.

OK

3-56 Error message when the data type has been specified

If you specify the data type, Access also checks the data type when you press **OK** on the *Enter Parameter Value* dialog box. If the data type is not correct, after displaying the message box, Access returns you back to the *Enter Parameter Value* dialog box to re-enter an acceptable value.

▶ **HOW TO:** Specify the Parameter Data Type

1. Click the **Parameters** button [*Query Tools Design* tab, *Show/Hide* group] (Figure 3-57).
 - The *Query Parameters* dialog box opens.
 - Recall that the *Table Names* button is highlighted when the query design grid displays the *Table* row.
2. Click the first cell in the *Parameter* column.
3. Type the name of your parameter.
 - Make sure that you enter the text as it appears in the *Criteria* property box.
 - The square brackets around the text are optional.

Σ Totals Parameters ▦ Property Sheet Table Names

Show/Hide

3-57 *Parameters* button

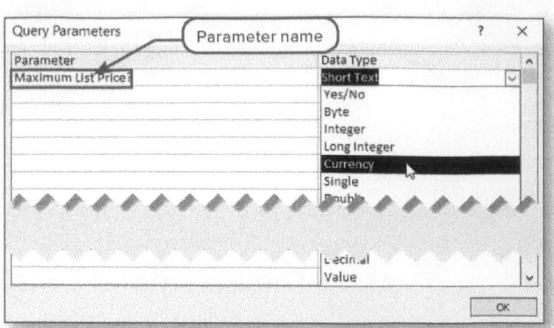

3-58 Assign a data type to a parameter

4. Click the **Data Type** cell, click the **drop-down arrow**, and select the correct data type (Figure 3-58).

5. Enter additional parameters in the dialog box, if needed.

6. Click **OK** when you are finished.

Use Wildcards in a Parameter Query

You can use the *Like* comparison operator and wildcards in a parameter when writing the query criteria. Remember the *Like* comparison operator can help you find records containing data that is similar to, or *like*, the criterion value. Recall that the * symbol represents any number of characters, the **?** represents any single character, and the **#** represents any single number.

There are three common ways to structure a criteria expression with a parameter that uses wildcards. You can include a wildcard character at the end, a wildcard character at the beginning, or a wildcard character at the beginning and the end. The following examples, using our music database scenario, illustrate each of these methods. These examples also introduce the **& *concatenation operator*** which combines, or concatenates, two text values into one.

- *Like [Enter Prompt Text Inside the Brackets] & " *"*

This parameter includes the * wildcard character at the end. It finds records where the data in the field begins with the value entered into the parameter. To limit the results to finding a complete word, the criteria includes a space before the asterisk. This treats the parameter value entered as a separate word, not just letters.

> **Example**: *Like [Enter the first word of the song] & " *"*
>
> **Explanation**: If the user enters "love" into the *Enter Parameter Value* dialog box, this query finds songs where the title starts with the word "love". For example, this query finds "Love for All Seasons" and "Love This Pain". However, it does not find the songs with the title of "Leave Love Alone", "Make You Feel My Love", or "Lovesong".

Compare the difference in the next example that removes the space before the asterisk.

> **Example**: *Like [Enter the first word of the song] & "*"*
>
> **Explanation**: If the user enters "love" into the *Enter Parameter Value* dialog box, this query finds songs where the title starts with the first four letters "love". It still finds all the songs that begin with the word "love" but will now also find "Lovesong".

- *Like "* " & [Enter Prompt Text Inside the Brackets]*

This parameter includes the * wildcard character at the beginning. It finds records where the data in the field ends with the value entered into the parameter. To limit the results to finding a complete word, the criteria includes a space after the asterisk.

Example: *Like "* " & [Enter the last word of the song]*

> **Explanation**: If the user enters "love" into the *Enter Parameter Value* dialog box, this query finds songs where the title ends in the word "love". For example, the query finds "Make You Feel My Love". It does not find "Love for All Seasons", "Leave Love Alone", or "50 Ways to Leave Your Lover".

- *Like "* " & [Enter Prompt Text Inside the Brackets] & " *"*

This parameter includes the * wildcard character at the beginning and at the end. It finds records where the data in the field contains the value entered into the parameter in the middle of the field. In this example there is a space after the first asterisk and there is a space before the second asterisk, which limits the results to finding the complete word.

Example: *Like "* " & [Enter the song word] & " *"*

> **Explanation**: If the user enters "love" into the *Enter Parameter Value* dialog box, this query finds songs with titles that contain the word "love" in the middle. For example, the query finds "Leave Love Alone". It would not find "Love for All Seasons", "Make You Feel My Love", or "50 Ways to Leave Your Lover". The phrase inside the parameter was changed just to clarify the prompt. Recall that the phrase content has no impact on the query results.

The next example removes the spaces before and after the asterisks.

Example: *Like "*" & [Enter the song word] & "*"*

> **Explanation**: If the user enters "love" into the *Enter Parameter Value* dialog box, this query finds songs with titles that contain the letters "love". This creates a very flexible query, since the user can enter only part of the parameter value. In this case, all the songs listed in the other examples would be located.

It is important to remember that the entry the user types in the *Enter Parameter Value* dialog box affects how the query functions. For example, with the criterion of *Like "*" & [Enter the song word] & "*"* , if you type "love " (with a space after the "e"), Access returns a different set of records than if the user types "love" or "love " (with two spaces).

This last example illustrates a powerful option for a database user. In addition to being able to enter all, or only part of, the parameter value to see the selected records, the user could leave the *Enter Parameter Value* dialog box blank to display all records.

For this reason, the parameter text for this option is often changed so the user knows of this flexibility. For example, in the parameter above, the parameter text could read *[Enter the song word, or Leave blank to select all songs]*.

If you don't need the complete flexibility to enter part of the parameter value or leave it blank, you could simplify the parameter by including the asterisk portion only at the beginning or at the end. Both of the following examples return all records if the *Enter Parameter Value* dialog box is left blank.

- *Like "*" & [Enter the song word, or Leave blank to select all songs]*
- *Like [Enter the song word, or Leave blank to select all songs] & "*"*

However, as you learned above, they return different records depending on the parameter value entered.

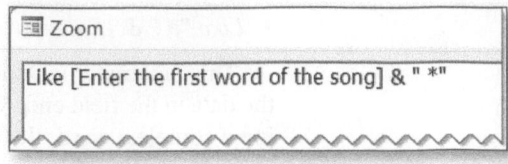

3-59 The *Zoom* box provides a large area to enter a parameter.

SLO 3.7

Adding Calculated Fields to a Query

A *calculated field* is a field that gets its value from a calculation instead of a value that is entered into the field. The calculation, or formula, can reference other fields in the database. For example, if a database that stores sales transactions contains the fields of *UnitPrice* and *Quantity*, the *Total Cost* of an item purchased is calculated by multiplying the *UnitPrice* by the *Quantity*.

Unlike a regular table field, a calculated field is not stored in the database. Why not simply store the *TotalCost* field in the database instead of having the database calculate it? To help avoid redundant data and ensure integrity in your database, most database designers recommend that you don't store fields in your database if the field can be calculated using data from other fields.

When writing a formula for a calculated field, use the traditional mathematical operators shown in the following table. Remember that Access evaluates formulas using the standard order of operations. When there is more than one operator in an equation, Access evaluates the equation from left to right, performing calculations based on their precedence level.

Order of Operations Characters and Precedence Level

Character	Operator	Order of Operation
()	Parentheses	First
^	Exponent	Second
*	Multiplication	Third
/	Division	Third
−	Subtraction	Fourth
+	Addition	Fourth

Enter a Formula in a Calculated Field

A formula for a query field has two parts that are separated by a colon (:). The first part is the name you assign to the calculated field. The second part is the formula, or what Access refers to as an expression. A generic example of a formula is written as *FieldName:Expression*. The expression can reference other fields and can include other **constants**, hardcoded values entered into a formula. The expressions must obey the following rules:

- Any fields included in the expression must be enclosed within square brackets.
- Any fields that are needed in the expression must be in tables included in the query.

For example, when you apply these rules to the *Total Cost* example described earlier, the formula for a calculated field that determines the *Total Cost* of an item is written as *TotalCost:[UnitPrice]*[Quantity]*.

> **HOW TO: Add a Calculated Field to a Query**

1. Right-click the **first empty cell** in the *Field* row of the query design grid and select either **Zoom** to open the *Zoom* box or **Build** to open the *Expression Builder*.

2. Enter the formula following the rules described above.

 - Figure 3-60 is an example of a formula that calculates the potential commission on the sale of a home.
 - Notice the formula contains the name assigned to the field, a colon, and the expression.

3. Click **OK** in the *Zoom* box or *Expression Builder* when you are finished entering the formula.

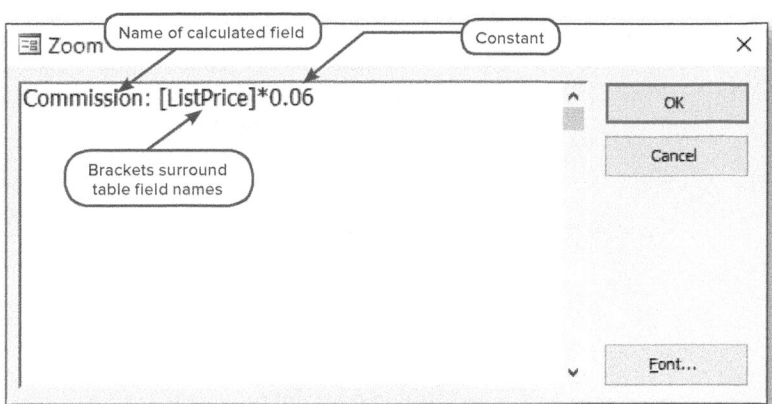

3-60 Enter the formula for a calculated field

You can adjust the *Format* properties to change how the calculated field displays.

> **HOW TO: Format a Calculated Field in a Query**

1. Click to select the **calculated field** in the query design grid.

2. Press **F4** to open the *Property Sheet* for that field.

3. Click the **Format** property box, click the **drop-down arrow** and select the desired format option (Figure 3-61).

4. Click the **Decimal Places** property box and select the desired number of decimal places.

5. Press **F4** to close the *Property Sheet*.

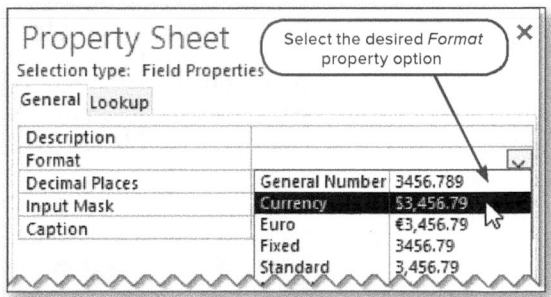

3-61 Format options

Remember to run your query to verify that your calculated field works as planned.

Troubleshoot Calculated Fields

There are three common problems you may encounter with a calculated field.

- An *Enter Parameter Value* dialog box displays when you run the query.

 If you are not expecting an *Enter Parameter Value* dialog box to display, pay attention to the contents of the parameter phrase. In Figure 3-62, the dialog box is asking the user to enter a value for "List Price".

 In *Design* view, review the formula that you have entered into the calculated field. Notice in Figure 3-63 that the field name enclosed in the square brackets is *List Price*. Recall that the field in the database was

3-62 *Enter Parameter Value* dialog box for the *List Price* field

actually named *ListPrice* (no space between *List* and *Price*).

If this occurs, edit the expression so that it includes valid field names.

- A field is missing a name.

Each field must have a name. If you forget to include a field name when you enter the formula, Access assigns the field a generic field name such as *Expr1* by default. This default field name displays in both the query design grid (Figure 3-64) and the *Datasheet* view of the results (Figure 3-65). If this happens, edit the expression and change the field to an appropriate name.

- The formula does not provide the correct answer.

In cases like this you need to review the structure of the formula. Make sure that you have used the correct fields and have written the formula correctly according to the order of operations.

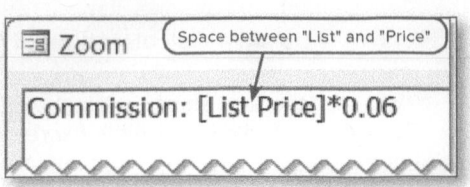

Zoom — Space between "List" and "Price"

Commission: [List Price]*0.06

3-63 Review the field name entered into the parameter

Generic field name

Field:	Expr1: [ListPrice]*0.06	ListingID	DateListed
Table:		Listings	Listings
Sort:			
Show:	☑	☑	☑
Criteria:			

3-64 A generic field name like *Expr1* is assigned by Access if you do not name the field

Expr1 ▾	ListingID ▾	Date Listed ▾
$20,256.00	10022	7/11/2016
$20,376.00	10023	8/11/2016
$40,500.00	10024	8/14/2016

3-65 The *Expr1* field name in *Datasheet* view

Functions in a Calculated Field

Access provides a variety of *functions*, predefined formulas to perform a specific task, which you can use in a formula. Access groups the functions by the type of task they perform. The following table highlights a few of the functions available in Access.

Examples of Access Functions

Function	Category	Explanation
Max	SQL Aggregate	Finds the largest value
Round	Math	Rounds the value
UCase	Text	Converts the value to upper case
Left	Text	Finds a specific number of characters from the left of the field
IIf	Program Flow	Performs a comparison and does one of two alternatives
Year	Date/Time	Returns the year portion of a date field

A function is typically included as part of a formula. This means that when you use a function, you need to follow the general rules about how to write a formula.

Some of the functions listed in this table are described in various chapters of the book but not all of the Access functions are introduced. If you are writing a complex formula, be sure to utilize the **Access Help System** to see if there is a function that might make your task easier to complete. In this section, to help you learn how to use a function in a calculated field, the *Left* function is introduced.

The **Left** function uses the format of *Left(string, length)*. Functions typically have different parameters, or arguments, that you must include with the function. The *Left* function has two parameters: **string** and **length**. The function analyzes the content of the string parameter and extracts a certain number of characters, as indicated in the length parameter, from the left of the string parameter. For example, *Left("California",2)* returns the value of "*Ca*", while *Left("California",5)* returns the value of "*Calif*".

Both the string and length parameters are required and each can be either a field or a constant. You must enclose fields in square brackets, while text constants are enclosed in quotation marks. In the example, *Left([State],2)* the *State* field is used as the string parameter.

The example in Figure 3-66 shows a formula that finds the first character of the *FirstName* field and combines it with a period, a space, and the *LastName*. This formula displays a name as "S. Bidou" or "J. Burgess".

The formula uses the *Left* function with the *&* concatenation operator. Recall that **concatentation** combines different parts of an equation together. You used the *&* operator with the *Like* special operator to combine different parts of an expression together in *SLO 3.6: Creating and Using a Simple Parameter Query*. Often concatenation is used to combine different fields together. For example, you can use it to combine a first and last name, or to combine the city, state, and ZIP code into one field.

▶ HOW TO: Use the Left Function in a Calculated Field

1. Add the fields from the database tables into the query grid.
2. Click the **first empty cell** in the *Field* row of the query design grid.
3. Right-click and select either **Zoom** to open the *Zoom* box or **Build** to open the *Expression Builder*.
4. Enter the formula, including the appropriate function.
 - The example in Figure 3-66 uses the *Left* function.
5. Click **OK** in the *Zoom* box or *Expression Builder* when finished entering the formula.

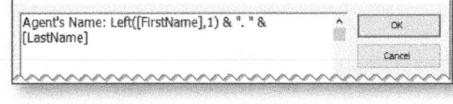

3-66 Example of a formula that uses the *Left* function

Remember to run your query to verify that your calculated field works. The most challenging part of working with a calculated field is not the actual process of entering the formula into a field. Rather it is the process of determining what the formula must do, structuring the formula correctly, verifying the results, and fine tuning the display formatting.

PAUSE & PRACTICE: ACCESS 3-3

For this Pause & Practice, you use *Design* view to create a query for Placer Hills Real Estate that uses calculated fields. Then you save a copy of that query and modify it to include a parameter.

File Needed: *[your initials] PP A3-2.accdb*
Completed Project File Name: *[your initials] PP A3-3.accdb*

1. Open the *[your initials] PP A3-2* database completed in *Pause & Practice 3-2*.
2. Save a new copy of your database as [your initials] PP A3-3.

3. Enable content in the database.

4. Create a new query in *Design* view. The office manager wants to calculate the potential commission on the listed properties. The query should display the agent's name, listing ID, and list price and potential commission for each property. The agent's name should be formatted as the first initial, a period, a space, and the last name (e.g., *J. Johnstone*). To help understand the logic behind queries, you build this query in stages.

 a. Click the **Query Design** button [*Create* tab, *Queries* group] to open the *Show Table* dialog box.

 b. Select the **Agents** table, if needed, and click the **Add** button.

 c. Select the **Listings** table and click the **Add** button.

 d. Click the **Close** button in the *Show Table* dialog box..

 e. Increase the size of the table objects to display all of the fields.

 f. Right-click the **first empty cell** in the *Field* row of the query design grid and select **Build** to open the *Expression Builder*.

 g. Type Agent's Name:Left([FirstName], 1) & ". " & [LastName] in the *Expression Builder* box.

 h. Click **OK**.

 i. Drag the **ListingID** field into the second cell in the *Field* row of the query design grid.

 j. Drag the **ListPrice** field into the third cell in the *Field* row of the query design grid. Your completed query design grid should look similar to Figure 3-67.

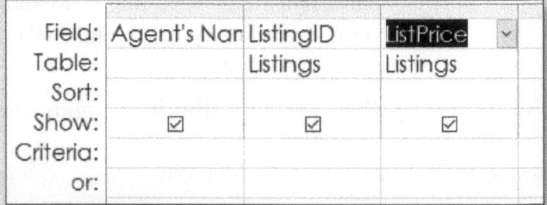

3-67 Query design grid

5. Click the **Save** button and save the query as PotentialCommissionByProperty.

6. Click the **Run** button [*Query Tools Design* tab, *Results* group] to execute the query. The query should open in *Datasheet* view and display all 57 records (Figure 3-68).

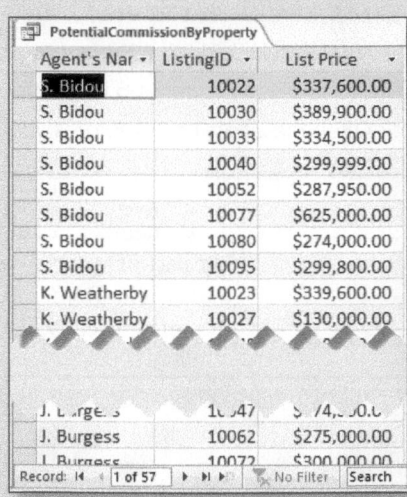

3-68 Query results

7. Adjust the width of the *Agent's Name* field.

 a. Right-click the **Agent's Name** cell to open the context menu and select **Field Width**.

 b. Click the **Best Fit** button.

8. Edit the query to add a field to calculate the potential commission and format that field.

 a. Click the **View** button [*Home* tab, *Views* group] and select the **Design View** option to switch back to *Design* view of the query.

 b. Right-click the **Field** cell of the fourth column and select **Zoom**.

 c. Type Potential Commission:[ListPrice]*.06 in the *Zoom* box.

 d. Click **OK**.

 e. Click to select the **Potential Commission** field. Verify that the **Show** check box is selected.

 f. Press **F4** to open the *Property Sheet*. If the *Show* check box was not selected, the *Property Sheet* displays the query properties instead of the field properties.

 g. Click the **Format** property box, click the **drop-down arrow**, and select **Currency**.

 h. Press **F4** to close the *Property Sheet*.

9. Save and test the query.

 a. Click the **Save** button to save the changes to the query.

 b. Click the **Run** button [*Query Tools Design* tab, *Results* group] to execute the query. The query should open in *Datasheet* view. All 57 records display, including the new *Potential Commission* field (Figure 3-69).

10. Add a parameter to find properties by agent. Because the agent's table stores the data as first and last name, you need to add those fields to the query.

Agent's Name ▾	ListingID ▾	List Price ▾	Potential Cc ▾
S. Bidou	10022	$337,600.00	$20,256.00
S. Bidou	10030	$389,900.00	$23,394.00
S. Bidou	10033	$334,500.00	$20,070.00
S. Bidou	10040	$299,999.00	$17,999.94
S. Bidou	10052	$287,950.00	$17,277.00

3-69 Updated query results

 a. Click the **View** button [*Home* tab, *Views* group] and select the **Design View** option to switch back to *Design* view.
 b. Double-click the **FirstName** field to add it into the query design grid.
 c. Double-click the **LastName** field to add it into the query design grid.
 d. Type [Enter the Agent's First Name] in the *Criteria* row cell for the *FirstName* field.
 e. Type [Enter the Agent's Last Name] in the *Criteria* row cell for the *LastName* field.
 f. Deselect the **Show** row check box for the *FirstName* field.
 g. Deselect the **Show** row check box for the *LastName* field.

11. Save a copy of the query.
 a. Click the **Save As** button [*File* tab].
 b. Select the **Save Object As** button and then click the **Save As** button.
 c. Replace the suggested name with AgentParameterPotentialCommissionByProperty and click **OK**.

12. Click the **Run** button [*Query Tools Design* tab, *Results* group].
 a. Enter Gerardo in the *Enter the Agent's First Name* box of the *Enter Parameter Value* dialog box.
 b. Click **OK**.
 c. Enter Montoya in the *Enter the Agent's Last Name* box of the *Enter Parameter Value* dialog box.
 d. Click **OK**. The query should open in *Datasheet* view and display the five records shown in Figure 3-70.

Agent's Name ▾	ListingID ▾	List Price ▾	Potential Cc ▾
G. Montoya	10144	$229,900.00	$13,794.00
G. Montoya	10145	$534,700.00	$32,082.00
G. Montoya	10176	$532,500.00	$31,950.00
G. Montoya	10191	$299,000.00	$17,940.00
G. Montoya	10192	$339,900.00	$20,394.00
*			

Record: I◄ ◄ 1 of 5 ► ►I ►□ 🔾 No Filter Search

3-70 Parameter query results

13. Close the query.

14. Close the database.

Creating and Using a Summary Query

As you now know, queries help locate data in a database by asking a question. Up to this point, the queries you have worked with have all been structured to find sets of records. But sometimes the question that you want answered involves getting summarized results. For example, you may want to know the total number of Pop/Rock albums that you own, or the average listing price of properties for sale, or the total number of dogs available for adoption. A *summary query* analyzes a set of records and displays summarized results.

Aggregate Functions

A summary query works by using an aggregate function. *Aggregate functions* perform calculations on a group of records. The most common aggregate functions are explained in the following table. When used in a summary query, the function calculates an answer based only on the records that match the query's criteria.

Common Aggregate Functions

Function	Explanation	Supported Data Types
Avg	Finds the average value of the field	AutoNumber, Currency, Date/Time, Number
Count	Counts the number of records that have a value in the field	All data types
Max	Finds the maximum value of the field	AutoNumber, Currency, Date/Time, Number, Text
Min	Finds the minimum value of the field	AutoNumber, Currency, Date/Time, Number, Text
Sum	Finds the total value of the field	AutoNumber, Currency, Date/Time, Number

> **MORE INFO**
>
> If the *Max* or *Min* function is used on a field with a ***Short Text*** data type, the smallest value is "A" and largest value is "Z."

Build a Summary Query

The basic building blocks of a summary query are the same as they are for the select queries you have already built. A summary query uses a ***Total*** row that is added into the query design grid of the query.

When you add a *Total* row, each field in the query has the value in the *Total* row initially set to *Group By* (Figure 3-71). In most cases you will change the *Group By* value to an appropriate aggregate function for at least one of the fields. If you don't change at least one of the fields, the query results show one record for each row of data. Generally, this is not your desired result in creating a summary query.

3-71 The *Total* row contains *Group By* or an aggregate function

Figure 3-72 shows the result of the query in Figure 3-71, with the *Total* row for all three fields set to *Group By*. The only difference between this query and one that doesn't include the *Total* row is that the results in this query are grouped by *City* and *Construction*.

If you change the query to use the *Avg* function in the *ListPrice* field, the query displays the results shown in Figure 3-73. Notice that the *Field Name* also changes to indicate the nature of the aggregate function. In this case, it changes to *AvgOfListPrice*.

This revised query answers the question "What is the average list price of homes, grouped by city and within each city by construction type?" Or, in other words, "By city and construction type, show the average price of the homes that are listed." Scanning through the results, you see that the highest average list price ($683,510) is for stone homes in Rocklin. The results also show that in Weimer, brick homes had the lowest average list price of $209,000.

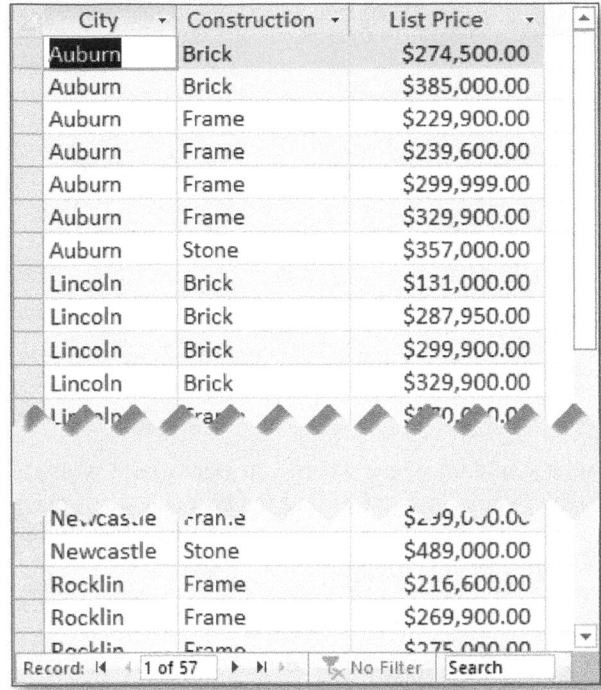

City	Construction	List Price
Auburn	Brick	$274,500.00
Auburn	Brick	$385,000.00
Auburn	Frame	$229,900.00
Auburn	Frame	$239,600.00
Auburn	Frame	$299,999.00
Auburn	Frame	$329,900.00
Auburn	Stone	$357,000.00
Lincoln	Brick	$131,000.00
Lincoln	Brick	$287,950.00
Lincoln	Brick	$299,900.00
Lincoln	Brick	$329,900.00
Lincoln	Frame	$370,000.00
Newcastle	Frame	$249,000.00
Newcastle	Stone	$489,000.00
Rocklin	Frame	$216,600.00
Rocklin	Frame	$269,900.00
Rocklin	Frame	$275,000.00

Record: ◄ ◄ 1 of 57 ► ►► ▷ 🔽 No Filter Search

3-72 Query results when all fields use *Group By* in the *Total* row

City	Construction	AvgOfListPrice
Auburn	Brick	$329,750.00
Auburn	Frame	$274,849.75
Auburn	Stone	$357,000.00
Lincoln	Brick	$262,187.50
Lincoln	Frame	$448,657.14
Lincoln	Stone	$318,300.00
Newcastle	Brick	$459,800.00
Newcastle	Frame	$264,375.00
Newcastle	Stone	$489,000.00
Rocklin	Frame	$430,446.15
Rocklin	Stone	$683,510.00
Roseville	Brick	$521,752.50
Roseville	Frame	$387,116.67
Roseville	Stone	$359,833.33
Weimar	Stone	$307,600.00
Weimer	Brick	$209,000.00
Weimer	Frame	$227,450.00

3-73 Query results with the *Avg* aggregate function

To be most effective, a summary query should include only the fields that you want to group by and the fields that you want to aggregate. For example, if you wish to find the average list price for each city, you must remove the *Construction* field from the query.

> ▶ **HOW TO: Create a Summary Query**

1. Click the **Query Design** button [*Create* tab, *Queries* group].
2. Select the first table to use in the query from the *Show Table* dialog box.
3. Click the **Add** button to add the table into the *Query Design* window.
4. Continue adding all required tables.
5. Click the **Close** button to close the *Show Table* dialog box.
6. Add the desired fields into the query design grid.
7. Click the **Totals** button [*Query Tools Design* tab, *Show/Hide* group] (Figure 3-74).
 • The *Total* row is added into the query design grid below the *Table* row.
 • The *Total* row value for each field in the query design grid is set to *Group By*.

> ▶ **MORE INFO**
>
> You cannot use the *Group By* choice in fields that have *Long Text*, *OLE Object*, and *Hyperlink* data types.

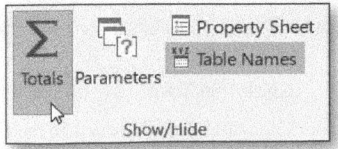

3-74 *Totals* button

Once you have created the summary query, you need to select the appropriate aggregate functions.

▶ HOW TO: Use an Aggregate Function in a Summary Query

1. Click the **Total** row cell of the desired field.
2. Click the **drop-down arrow** and select the desired aggregate function (Figure 3-75).
 - The query in Figure 3-75 answers the question "How many homes are listed for sale in each city, grouped by construction type?"
3. Repeat steps 1 and 2 for any additional fields that will be aggregated.

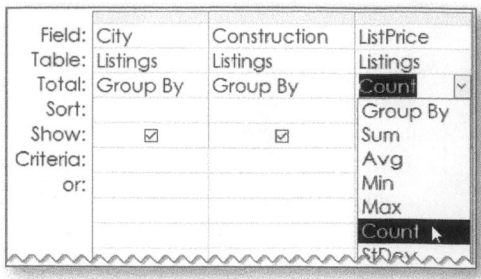

3-75 Select the aggregate function from the drop-down list

Occasionally you may want to create a summary query where you want to see multiple calculations on the same field. For example, you may want to find the best and worst place finish that each member had in a race. Or for our real estate database you might want to see the average, maximum, and minimum list price for all properties.

▶ HOW TO: Use Multiple Aggregate Functions on a Field

1. Click the **Total** row cell of the desired field.
2. Click the **drop-down arrow** and select the desired aggregate function.
3. Add the field into another column in the query design grid.
4. Click the **drop-down arrow** and select the desired aggregate function.
5. Continue adding the same field and selecting the aggregate function for as many calculations as you want to include.
 - Figure 3-76 shows an example of a query that aggregates the *Average*, *Maximum* and *Minimum* on the *ListPrice* field.
 - A sample of the query results is shown in Figure 3-77.

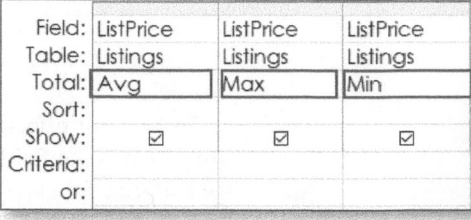

3-76 Include a field multiple times to use more than one aggregate function on the same field

3-77 Query results with multiple aggregate functions

A summary query can also include criteria to limit the results. For example, you may want to find the lowest priced three-bedroom home in a specific city, or the average price of homes listed between two dates. When you use a summary query, the way that you include criteria changes a little. You need to select the *Where* option from the drop-down list of aggregate functions, in addition to adding the specific criteria.

▶ HOW TO: Use Criteria in a Summary Query

1. Click the **Total** row cell of the field that will have the criteria.
2. Click the **drop-down arrow** and select **Where**.
 - The *Show* row check box is deselected.
 - To include the criteria field in the query results, you must add that field into another column in the query design grid, leave *Group By* as the selection in the *Total* row, and click the **Show** row check box of that field.

3. Click the **Criteria** row cell of the field and enter the criteria.

- Figure 3-78 shows an example of the query design grid that calculates and displays the *Average ListPrice* for properties listed after *1/1/2017*.
- The query results do not include the *DateListed* since the *Show* row check box is deselected and the field was not added into another column in the query design grid.

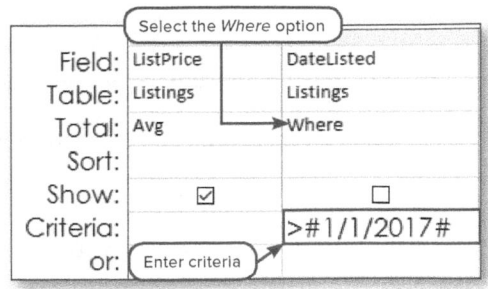

Select the *Where* option		
Field:	ListPrice	DateListed
Table:	Listings	Listings
Total:	Avg	Where
Sort:		
Show:	☑	☐
Criteria:		>#1/1/2017#
or:	Enter criteria	

3-78 Select the *Where* option in the *Total* row when using critieria in a summary query

In order to get the results you desire, you need to spend time planning the structure of a summary query before you build it. You must decide what fields to include in the query, what aggregate functions to use and any additional criteria needed to limit the results.

PAUSE & PRACTICE: ACCESS 3-4

For this Pause & Practice, you create a summary query for the Placer Hills Real Estate Company.

File Needed: *[your initials] PP A3-3.accdb*
Completed Project File Name: *[your initials] PP A3-4.accdb*

1. Open the *[your initials] PP A3-3* database file completed in *Pause & Practice 3-3*.

2. Save a new copy of your database as [your initials] PP A3-4.

3. Enable content in the database.

4. Create a new summary query in *Design* view. The Placer Hills Real Estate Company wants to know the total number of properties each agent has listed and the average list price of those properties. It wants to display the agent's first and last name, as well as the two summary fields. To help you understand the logic behind queries, you build this query in stages.
 a. Click the **Query Design** button [*Create* tab, *Queries* group] to open the *Show Table* dialog box.
 b. Select the **Agents** table, press and hold the **Shift** key, select the **Listings** table, and click the **Add** button.
 c. Click the **Close** button in the *Show Table* dialog box.
 d. Increase the size of the table objects to display all of the fields.
 e. Click the **drop-down arrow** in the first *Field* row cell of the query design grid and select **Agents.FirstName**.
 f. Click the **second cell** in the *Field* row, click the **drop-down arrow**, and select **Agents.LastName**.
 g. Click the **third cell** in the *Field* row, click the **drop-down arrow**, and select **Listings.ListPrice**.
 h. Click the **fourth cell** in the *Field* row, click the **drop-down arrow**, and select **Listings.ListPrice**. (Yes, you add this field twice!)
 i. Click the **Totals** button [*Query Tools Design* tab, *Show/Hide* group] to add the *Total* row to the query.

5. Add the aggregate functions into the query.
 a. Click the **Total** row cell of the first *ListPrice* field.

b. Click the **drop-down arrow** and select **Count**.

c. Click the **Total** row cell of the second *ListPrice* field.

d. Click the **drop-down arrow** and select **Avg**. The completed query design grid should look similar to Figure 3-79.

Field:	FirstName	LastName	ListPrice	ListPrice
Table:	Agents	Agents	Listings	Listings
Total:	Group By	Group By	Count	Avg
Sort:				
Show:	☑	☑	☑	☑
Criteria:				
or:				

3-79 Aggregate functions added to query

6. Click the **Save** button and save the query as ListingCountAndAvgListPriceByAgent.

7. Click the **Run** button [*Query Tools Design* tab, *Results* group] to execute the query. The query should open in *Datasheet* view and display 7 records.

8. Adjust the column width of the *CountOfListPrice* and *AvgOfListPrice* fields to display the entire column name.

a. Select the **CountOfListPrice** column, right-click to open the context menu, and select **Field Width**.

b. Click **Best Fit**.

c. Select the **AvgOfListPrice** column, right-click to open the context menu, and select **Field Width**.

d. Click **Best Fit**. The *Datasheet* view should be similar to Figure 3-80.

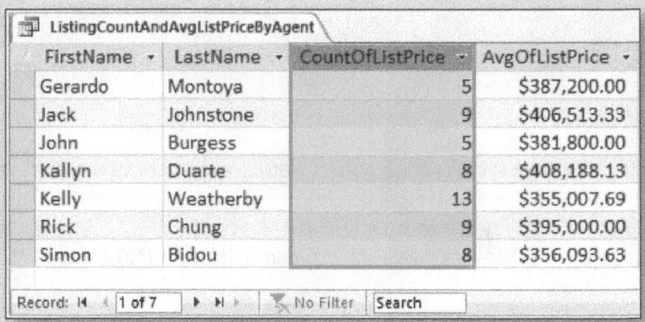

ListingCountAndAvgListPriceByAgent			
FirstName ▾	LastName ▾	CountOfListPrice ▾	AvgOfListPrice ▾
Gerardo	Montoya	5	$387,200.00
Jack	Johnstone	9	$406,513.33
John	Burgess	5	$381,800.00
Kallyn	Duarte	8	$408,188.13
Kelly	Weatherby	13	$355,007.69
Rick	Chung	9	$395,000.00
Simon	Bidou	8	$356,093.63

Record: I◄ ◄ 1 of 7 ► ►I ► No Filter Search

3-80 Query results for summary query

9. Click the **Save** button to save the changes.

10. Close the query.

11. Close the database.

Chapter Summary

3.1 Understand queries and use the *Simple Query Wizard* to create and run a query (p. A3-153).

- Use **queries** to find data in your database.
- You can build queries from tables, other queries, or both.
- Use the **Simple Query Wizard** to quickly build a query by specifying the tables or queries to use and then selecting the desired fields from those objects.
- You can edit a query created with the *Simple Query Wizard* in *Design* view.

3.2 Create a query in *Design* view, add fields, and save and run a query (p. A3-154).

- The **Query Design** button opens *Design* view to build queries.
- *Design* view provides the most flexibility when creating queries.
- Add tables or queries into the *Query Design* window by selecting them from the *Show Table* dialog box.
- You must add fields into the **query design grid** if you want them to appear in the query.
- Run a query to execute the query and have the query locate records in the database.
- Query results display in *Datasheet* view.
- Save each query with a unique name.

3.3 Add criterion into a query, use comparison operators, and create criteria with wildcards (p. A3-159).

- You can add criterion into a query to search for specific records.
- You enter a criterion **expression** into the *Criteria* row of the query design grid. You can type the expression directly into a *Criteria* row cell or enter it using the **Expression Builder**.
- Expressions can include the standard **comparison operators**.
- Combine the **Like** comparison operator with the **?, * and # wildcard characters** for greater flexibility in the criterion value.

3.4 Integrate sorting and limiting fields and records that display (p. A3-165).

- Set the **Unique Values** property to have Access evaluate the fields in the query and avoid including duplicated values.
- The **Unique Records** property checks all the fields in a table, not just those included in the query.

- Deselecting the *Show* row check box prevents a field from displaying in the query results.
- Query results can be sorted in ascending or descending order in one or more fields.
- If sorting on multiple fields, the fields must be placed into the query design grid in order of sort priority.

3.5 Use the *AND* and *OR* operators to include multiple criteria in a query (p. A3-168).

- **Compound criteria** combine more than one criterion using the **AND** and **OR** operators; this allows you to create a more complex query.
- Criteria written in different fields but on the same criteria row are evaluated as *AND* comparison.
- Criteria written on different criteria rows are evaluated as an *OR* comparison.
- You can combine *AND* and *OR* operators in one query.

3.6 Create and use a parameter query (p. A3-174).

- A **parameter query** asks the user to enter a specific criteria value at the time the query is run.
- When a parameter query is included, the *Enter Parameter Value* dialog box displays before the query executes.
- The **parameter** is the text phrase you enter into the *Criteria* row cell of the field. You must enclose the parameter in square brackets.
- A query can include multiple parameters, on one or more fields.
- If you specify the data type of the parameter, Access displays a more user-friendly message if a user makes an error when entering the parameter value.
- You can combine the *Like* comparison operator with wildcard characters for increased flexibility in a parameter.

3.7 Build a query that uses a calculated field (p. A3-179).

- **Calculated fields** get their value from a calculation instead of being stored in a table.
- Use a calculated field instead of a table field if the database can calculate the field's value using data stored in other fields.
- You can add a calculated field into the query design grid of a query.
- The formula expression for a calculated field is in the format *FieldName:Expression*.

- The formulas use the standard mathematical operators and order of operations.
- Access provides a variety of **functions**, which are predefined formulas that perform a specific task.
- You can include a function as part of an expression in a calculated field.

3.8 Create and use a summary query using aggregate functions (p. A3-184).

- A **summary query** analyzes a set of records and then displays summarized results.
- Summary queries use **aggregate functions**, functions that perform calculations on a group of records.

- Common aggregate functions include *Avg*, *Count*, *Max*, *Min*, and *Sum*.
- Summary queries can summarize several different fields or perform different calculations on the same field.

Check for Understanding

The SIMbook for this text (within your SIMnet account) provides the following resources for concept review:

- Multiple choice questions
- Matching exercises
- Short answer questions

USING MICROSOFT ACCESS 2016

Guided Project 3-1

You have built a database to store information about a friend's music collection. You want to write three queries to help answer some questions about the songs in the database. To ensure consistency, the starting file is provided for you. Use *the Simple Query Wizard* to create a query, use *Design* view to edit the query, and add criteria. After saving and testing the query, save a copy of the query to add a parameter. Finally, create a third query that includes summary query capabilities.
[Student Learning Outcomes 3.1, 3.2, 3.3, 3.4, 3.5, 3.6]

File Needed: ***MusicDatabase-03.accdb***
Completed Project File Name: ***[your initials] Access 3-1.accdb***

Skills Covered in This Project

- Create a query using the *Simple Query Wizard*.
- Edit a query in *Design* view.
- Add compound criteria to a query.
- Execute a query.
- Save a query.
- Add a parameter to a query.
- Sort query results.
- Edit a query to add an aggregate function.

1. Open the ***MusicDatabase-03.accdb*** database file.

2. Save a new copy of your database as [your initials] Access 3-1.

3. Enable content in the database.

4. Open the *Albums* table in *Datasheet* view to view the contents. You should see 44 different records.

5. Click the **plus symbol** to the left of *AlbumID 1*, to see the 13 songs that are on Taylor Swift's *1989* album.

6. Close the table.

7. Create a new query using the *Simple Query Wizard*.
 a. Click the **Query Wizard** button [*Create* tab, *Queries* group] to launch the *Query Wizard*.
 b. Select **Simple Query Wizard** in the *New Query* dialog box.
 c. Click **OK** to launch the *Simple Query Wizard* (Figure 3-81).
 d. Select **AlbumName** in the *Available Fields* window.
 e. Click the **Move Single Field** button to move the field into the *Selected Fields* window.
 f. Select **Artist** in the *Available Fields* window.
 g. Click the **Move Single Field** button.
 h. Continue moving over the **Genre** and **ReleaseDate** fields.
 i. Click the **Tables/Queries** drop-down arrow and select the **Songs** table.

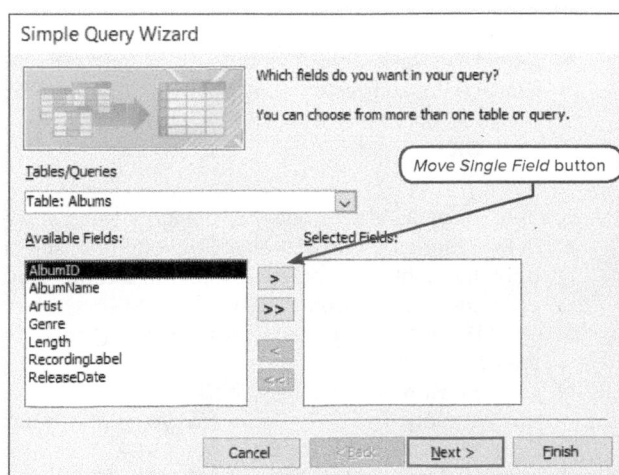

3-81 *Simple Query Wizard*

j. Select **SongTitle** in the *Available Fields* window.

k. Click the **Move Single Field** button. The completed *Selected Fields* window should match Figure 3-82.

l. Click the **Next** button. The second page of the *Simple Query Wizard* displays. Because of the relationship between the two tables, Access asks you whether you want a detail or summary query.

m. Leave the radio button selected for **Detail** and click the **Next** button.

n. Change the title in the *Title* box to SongsOnAlbums.

o. Click **Finish** to save and run the query. The query results should match those shown in Figure 3-83, displaying 561 total records.

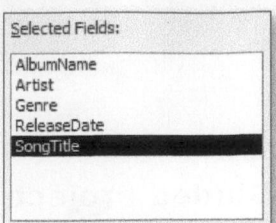

3-82 Completed *Selected Fields* window

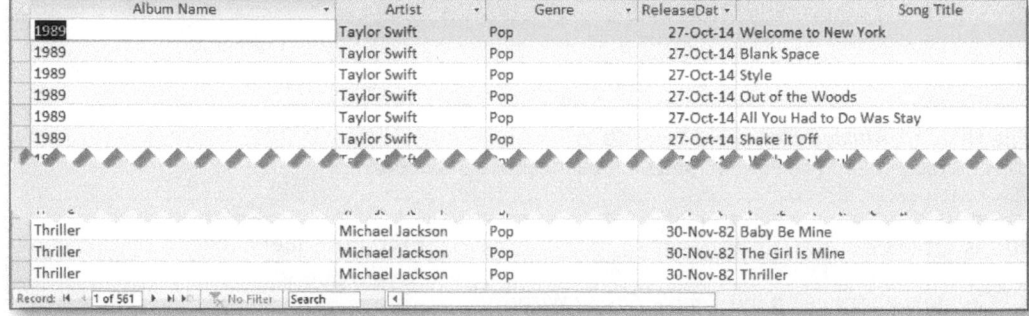

3-83 Query results of *SongsOnAlbums* query

8. Edit the query in *Design* view to add criteria to find songs on pop albums released after 1/1/2014.

a. Click the **View** button [*Home* tab, *Views* group] and select the **Design View** option to switch back to *Design* view of the query.

b. Type Pop in the *Criteria* row cell of the *Genre* field.

c. Tab out of that field. Notice that Access automatically puts quotation marks around the text criteria.

d. Click the **Run** button [*Query Tools Design* tab, *Results* group] to run the query. The query should open in *Datasheet* view and display the 155 songs that were on pop albums.

e. Switch back to *Design* view and type >=#1/1/2014# in the *Criteria* row cell of the *ReleaseDate* field.

f. Click the **Run** button [*Query Tools Design* tab, *Results* group]. The query should display 26 songs from Taylor Swift's *1989* and One Direction's *Made in the A.M.* albums.

9. Save a copy of the query.

a. Click the **Save As** button [*File* Tab].

b. Select the **Save Object As** button and then click the **Save As** button.

c. Replace the suggested object name in the *Save 'SongsOnAlbums' to* box with SongsOnPopAlbumsAfterJan2014.

d. Click **OK**.

e. Close the query.

10. Edit the *SongsOnAlbums* query in *Design* view to add a parameter for the *Artist* field.

a. In the *Queries* group of the *Navigation Pane*, select the **SongsOnAlbums** query. Right-click to open the context menu and select the **Design View** option to open the query in *Design* view.

b. Type [Show songs by which Artist?] in the *Criteria* row cell of the *Artist* field.

c. Click the **Run** button [*Query Tools Design* tab, *Results* group] to run the query. The *Enter Parameter Value* dialog box displays.

d. Type Maroon 5 and click **OK** (Figure 3-84). The query should open in *Datasheet* view and display the 57 songs on albums released by Maroon 5.

3-84 *Enter Parameter Value* dialog box

11. Edit the query to add sorting.
 a. Click the **View** button [*Home* tab, *Views* group] and select the **Design View** option to switch back to *Design* view of the query.
 b. Click the **Sort** row cell of the *ReleaseDate* field, click the **drop-down arrow** and select **Ascending**.
 c. Click the **Run** button [*Query Tools Design* tab, *Results* group] to run the query. The *Enter Parameter Value* dialog box displays.
 d. Type Maroon 5 and click **OK**.
 e. Verify that the results are displayed in ascending order on the *ReleaseDate* field.

12. Save a copy of the query.
 a. Click the **Save As** button [*File* Tab].
 b. Select the **Save Object As** button and then click the **Save As** button.
 c. Replace the suggested object name in the *Save 'SongsOnAlbums' to* box with SongCountArtistParameter.

13. Edit the query to add a *Total* row.
 a. Click the **View** button [*Home* tab, *Views* group] and select the **Design View** option to switch back to *Design* view of the query.
 b. Click the **Totals** button [*Query Tools Design* tab, *Show/Hide* group].
 c. Click the **Total** row cell for the *SongTitle* field.
 d. Click the **drop-down arrow** and select **Count**.

14. Click the **Save** button to save the query.

15. Test the query.
 a. Click the **Run** button [*Query Tools Design* tab, *Results* group] to run the query. The *Enter Parameter Value* dialog box displays.
 b. Type Maroon 5 and click **OK**. The query should open in *Datasheet* view and display the *CountOfSongTitle* on the four albums by Maroon 5.
 c. Extend the width of the *ReleaseDate* and *CountofSongTitle* columns so that your datasheet is similar to Figure 3-85.
 d. Save the changes to query.

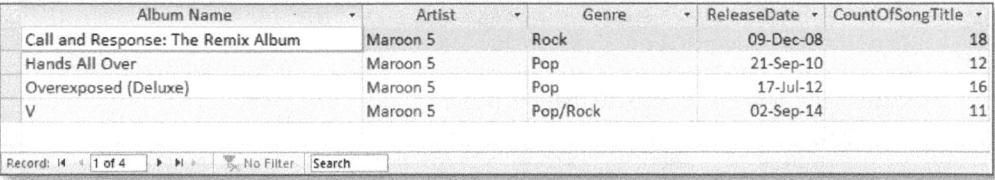

Album Name	Artist	Genre	ReleaseDate	CountOfSongTitle
Call and Response: The Remix Album	Maroon 5	Rock	09-Dec-08	18
Hands All Over	Maroon 5	Pop	21-Sep-10	12
Overexposed (Deluxe)	Maroon 5	Pop	17-Jul-12	16
V	Maroon 5	Pop/Rock	02-Sep-14	11

Record: I◄ ◄ 1 of 4 ► ►I ► 🏷No Filter Search

3-85 Query results with *Count* aggregate function

16. Close the query.

17. Close the database.

Guided Project 3-2

San Diego Sailing Club wants to create three queries. To ensure consistency, the starting file is provided for you. Use *Design* view to create, edit, add aggregate functions, and add criteria to a query to find the total dollar value of the rentals for each boat in its fleet. After saving and testing the query, create a second query that uses aggregate functions and a parameter. Finally, create a query to find which boat types have been rented.
[**Student Learning Outcomes 3.2, 3.3, 3.4, 3.5, 3.6, 3.8**]

File Needed: **SailingDatabase-03.accdb**
Completed Project File Name: **[your initials] Access 3-2.accdb**

Skills Covered in This Project

- Create a query using *Design* view.
- Add fields to a query.
- Add criteria to a query.
- Execute a query.

- Save and test a query.
- Save a copy of a query.
- Add a parameter.
- Use aggregate functions.
- Use the *Unique Values* property.

1. Open the **SailingDatabase-03.accdb** database file.

2. Save a new copy of your database as [your initials] Access 3-2.

3. Enable content in the database.

4. Create a new summary query in *Design* view. The Sailing Club wants to find out the total dollar value of the full day rentals, by boat, from the boats that have been rented. If a boat has been rented, there is a record in the *SDRentals* table.
 a. Click the **Query Design** button [*Create* tab, *Queries* group] to open the *Show Table* dialog box.
 b. Select the **SailboatFleet** table and click the **Add** button.
 c. Select the **SDRentals** table and click the **Add** button.
 d. Click the **Close** button in the *Show Table* dialog box.
 e. Increase the size of the table objects to display all of the fields.
 f. Click the **drop-down arrow** in the first *Field* row cell of the query design grid and select **SDRentals.FKBoatID**.
 g. Click the **second cell** in the *Field* row, click the **drop-down arrow**, and select **SailboatFleet.BoatType**.
 h. Click the **third cell** in the *Field* row, click the **drop-down arrow**, and select **SailboatFleet. FullDayRentalRate**.
 i. Click the **fourth cell** in the *Field* row, click the **drop-down arrow**, and select **SDRentals. FourHourRental?**.
 j. Click the **Totals** button [*Query Tools Design* tab, *Show/Hide* group].
 k. Click the **Run** button [*Query Tools Design* tab, *Results* group] to execute the query. The query should open in *Datasheet* view and display 16 records (Figure 3-86). This query only shows boats that have been rented. At most a *Boat ID* appears in two rows; one row if the *Four Hour Rental?* box is checked and another row if the *Four Hour Rental?* box is not checked.

5. Edit the query to add aggregate functions. Because you are looking only for rentals that were for a full day, use the "No" value on the *FourHourRental?* field.
 a. Click the **View** button [*Home* tab, *Views* group] and select the **Design View** option to switch back to *Design* view of the query.
 b. Click the **Total** row cell for the *FullDayRentalRate* field.
 c. Click the **drop-down arrow** and select **Sum**.
 d. Click the **Total** row cell for the *FourHourRental?* field.
 e. Click the **drop-down arrow** and select **Where**. This causes the *Show* row check box for the *FourHourRental?* field to be deselected.
 f. Click the **Criteria** row cell for the *FourHourRental?* field and enter No. The *IntelliSense* feature in Access may suggest the value of "Now" while you are typing. Press the **Esc** key to hide the list and then tab out of the field. The query window should look similar to Figure 3-87.

Boat ID	Boat Type	Full Day Rate	Four Hour R
1010	Catalina 270	$179.00	☑
1010	Catalina 270	$179.00	☐
1015	Catalina 270	$179.00	☑
1015	Catalina 270	$179.00	☐
1146	Hunter 33	$349.00	☐
1150	Capri 22 Mk II	$89.00	☑
1152	Capri 22 Mk II	$89.00	☑
1152	Capri 22 Mk II	$89.00	☐
1164	Capri 22 Mk II	$89.00	☑
1168	Hunter 33	$349.00	☐
1185	Hunter 36	$389.00	☐
1225	Hunter 36	$389.00	☑
1225	Hunter 36	$389.00	☐
1310	Beneteau 373	$409.00	☐
1401	Capri 22 Mk II	$89.00	☑
1419	Hunter 33	$349.00	☑

Record: I◄ ◄ 1 of 16 ► ►I ►► No Filter Search

3-86 Sailboat query results

Field:	FKBoatID	BoatType	FullDayRentalRate	FourHourRental?
Table:	SDRentals	SailboatFleet	SailboatFleet	SDRentals
Total:	Group By	Group By	Sum	Where
Sort:				
Show:	☑	☑	☑	☐
Criteria:				No
or:				

3-87 Query design grid for the summary query with criteria

g. Click the **Run** button. The query should open in *Datasheet* view and display eight records (Figure 3-88). The *Boat ID* now displays only once since the criteria limits the results only to the full day rentals.

Boat ID	Boat Type	SumOfFullD
1010	Catalina 270	$895.00
1015	Catalina 270	$179.00
1146	Hunter 33	$698.00
1152	Capri 22 Mk II	$178.00
1168	Hunter 33	$349.00
1185	Hunter 36	$389.00
1225	Hunter 36	$1,556.00
1310	Beneteau 373	$409.00

Record: I◄ ◄ 1 of 8 ► ►I ►* ☒ No Filter Search

3-88 Results from completed *SummaryOfFullDayRentalsByBoat* query

6. Click the **Save** button and save the query as FullDayRentalsByBoatSummary.

7. Verify that that query works correctly.
 a. Open the *SDRentals* table in *Datasheet* view.
 b. Click the **drop-down arrow** in the *Boat ID* field name cell.
 c. Select the **Sort A to Z** option.
 d. Click the **drop-down arrow** in the *Four Hour Rental?* field name cell.
 e. Select the **Sort Cleared to Selected** option. You can see that *Boat ID 1010* has five full day rentals. From Figure 3-86 you know that the full day rate for that boat is $179.00 and 5 × $179 = $895.00. This matches the results of your query.
 f. Click the **Remove Sort** button [*Home* tab, *Sort & Filter* group].
 g. Close the *SDRentals* table. If prompted, do not save the changes to the table.

8. Save a copy of the query.
 a. Click the **Save As** button [*File* Tab].
 b. Select the **Save Object As** button and then click the **Save As** button.
 c. Replace the suggested name with FullDayRentalsByBoatSummaryWithParameter. This second query will allow the Sailing Club to enter the date range for the summary query and also will count the number of rentals.

9. Edit the query to add additional fields and an aggregate function and parameters.
 a. Click the **View** button [*Home* tab, *Views* group] and select **Design View**.
 b. Drag the **FullDayRentalRate** field from the *SailboatFleet* table to the fifth column in the query design grid. (Yes, this field is in the query twice.)
 c. Click the **Total** row cell for this field, click the **drop-down arrow**, and select **Count**.
 d. Drag the **RentalDate** field from the *SDRentals* table to the sixth column in the query design grid.
 e. Click the **Total** row cell for this field, click the **drop-down arrow**, and select **Where**. This causes the *Show* row check box for the *RentalDate* field to be deselected.
 f. Click the **Criteria** row cell of the *RentalDate* field.
 g. Right-click and select **Zoom**.
 h. Type Between [Enter the Start Date] And [Enter the End Date] in the *Zoom* box to add the two parameters.
 i. Click **OK**. The query window should look similar to Figure 3-89.
 j. Click the **Save** button and save the changes to the query.

10. Test the query.
 a. Click the **Run** button.
 b. Enter 2/1/2017 in the *Enter the Start Date* box of the *Enter Parameter Value* dialog box.

Field:	FKBoatID	BoatType	FullDayRentalRate	FourHourRental?	FullDayRentalRate	RentalDate
Table:	SDRentals	SailboatFleet	SailboatFleet	SDRentals	SailboatFleet	SDRentals
Total:	Group By	Group By	Sum	Where	Count	Where
Sort:						
Show:	☑	☑	☑	☐	☑	☐
Criteria:				No		Between [Ente
or:						

3-89 Query window with aggregate functions and a parameter

c. Click **OK**.

d. Enter 2/28/2017 in the *Enter the End Date* box of the *Enter Parameter Value* dialog box.

e. Click **OK**. The query should open in *Datasheet* view and display the records shown in Figure 3-90.

Boat ID ▾	Boat Type ▾	SumOfFullD ▾	CountOfFull ▾
1010	Catalina 270	$716.00	4
1015	Catalina 270	$179.00	1
1152	Capri 22 Mk II	$89.00	1
1185	Hunter 36	$389.00	1

Record: I◄ ◄ 1 of 4 ► ►I ►☆ ⊤x No Filter Search

3-90 Query results with *Sum* and *Count* aggregate functions and parameter

f. Click the **Save** button to save the changes made to the query.

g. Close the query.

11. Review the query.

a. Reopen the query in *Design* view. Notice that Access has reordered the position of the fields. The two fields that use the *Where* option on the *Total* row have been moved to the right side of the query design grid. This does not affect the way the query runs.

b. Close the query.

12. Create a new query in *Design* view. The Sailing Club wants to find out what boat types have been rented so it can decide whether to adjust pricing or marketing on some of its boat types. If a boat has been rented, a record of that rental exists in the *SDRentals* table.

a. Click the **Query Design** button [*Create* tab, *Queries* group] to open the *Show Table* dialog box.

b. Select the **SDRentals** table, press and hold the **Shift** key, select the **SailboatFleet** table and click the **Add** button.

c. Click the **Close** button in the *Show Table* dialog box.

d. Click the **drop-down arrow** in the first *Field* row cell in the query design grid and select **SDRentals.FKBoatID**.

e. Click the **Sort** row, click the **drop-down arrow**, and select **Ascending**.

f. Click the **second cell** in the *Field* row, click the **drop-down arrow**, and select **SailboatFleet.BoatType**.

g. Click the **Run** button [*Query Tools Design* tab, *Results* group] to execute the query. The query should open in *Datasheet* view and display 28 records (Figure 3-91). Notice that in a number of instances the same *Boat ID* displays multiple times, once for each time that boat was rented.

Boat ID ▾	Boat Type ▾
1010	Catalina 270
1010	Catalina 270
1010	Catalina 270
1010	Catalina 270
1010	Catalina 270
1010	Catalina 270
1010	Catalina 270
1010	Catalina 270
1015	Catalina 270
1015	Catalina 270
1146	Hunter 33
1146	Hunter 33
1150	Capri 22 Mk II
1152	Capri 22 Mk II
1152	Capri 22 Mk II
1152	Capri 22 Mk II
1152	Capri 22 Mk II
1164	Capri 22 Mk II
1168	Hunter 33
1185	Hunter 36
1225	Hunter 36
1225	Hunter 36
1225	Hunter 36
1225 ·	Hunter 36
1225	Hunter 36
1310	Beneteau 373
1401	Capri 22 Mk II
1419	Hunter 33
*	

Record: I◄ ◄ 1 of 28 ► ►I ►☆ ⊤x No F

3-91 *BoatID* query results

13. Edit the query to display *Unique Values*.
 a. Click the **View** button [*Home* tab, *Views* group] and select the **Design View** option to switch back to *Design* view of the query.
 b. Click the **Property Sheet** button [*Query Tools Design* tab, *Show/Hide* group] to open the *Property Sheet*.
 c. Click anywhere in the *Query Window* so that the *Selection type* in the *Property Sheet* displays *Query Properties*.
 d. Click the **Unique Values** property box and select **Yes**. The query window should look similar to Figure 3-92.

3-92 Set the *Unique Values* property in the *Property Sheet* of the query

 e. Close the *Property Sheet*.
 f. Click the **Run** button. The query should open in *Datasheet* view and display 12 records (Figure 3-93). Each *Boat ID* now displays only once, but the *Boat Types* are still repeated.

14. Edit the query so the *Boat Type* displays only once. The *Boat Type* is displaying more than once because the *FKBoatID* field is different for each boat.
 a. Click the **View** button [*Home* tab, *Views* group] and select the **Design View** option to switch back to *Design* view.
 b. Click the **Sort** row of the **FKBoatID** field, click the **drop-down arrow**, and select **(not sorted)**.
 c. Deselect the **Show** row check box for the **FKBoatID** field.
 d. Click the **Run** button. The query should display the five boat types that have been rented at least once (Figure 3-94.)
 e. Click the **Save** button and save the query as BoatTypesRented.
 f. Close the query.

15. Close the database.

3-93 Query results with repeated *BoatType* values

3-94 Unique records for *BoatType*

Guided Project 3-3

The American River Cycling Club wants to run three queries on its database. The first query finds which members have participated in races and what place they got in each race. The second query is based off of the first one, which you enhance to include a parameter so the club can search only for a particular place finish. Finally, the third query displays division and age group information about the members. To ensure consistency, the starting file is provided for you. Use *Design* view and the *Simple Query Wizard* to create and edit the queries, add criteria, calculated fields, and a parameter. Save and test the queries to ensure they work correctly.

[Student Learning Outcomes 3.1, 3.2, 3.3, 3.6, 3.7, 3.8]

File Needed: ***AmericanRiver-03.accdb***
Completed Project File Name: *[your initials] Access 3-3.accdb*

Skills Covered in This Project

- Create a query using the *Simple Query Wizard*.
- Create a query using *Design* view.
- Add fields to a query.
- Add compound criteria to a query.
- Execute a query.
- Save and test a query.
- Add calculated fields to a query.
- Add a parameter to a query.
- Use *Group By* in a summary query.

1. Open the ***AmericanRiver-03.accdb*** database file.

2. Save a new copy of your database as [your initials] Access 3-3.

3. Enable content in the database.

4. Create a new query in *Design* view to find which members have participated in races and what place they got in each race.
 a. Click the **Query Design** button [*Create* tab, *Queries* group] to open the *Show Table* dialog box.
 b. Select the **Members** table and click the **Add** button.
 c. Select the **RaceResults** table and click the **Add** button.
 d. Click the **Close** button in the *Show Table* dialog box.
 e. Increase the size of the table objects to display all of the fields.
 f. Click the **first cell** in the *Field* row of the query design grid.
 g. Press **Ctrl+F2** to open the *Expression Builder*.
 h. Type MemberName:Left([First Name],1) & ". " & [LastName] into the window.
 i. Click **OK**.
 j. Double-click the **RaceID** field from the *RaceResults* table to add it into the query design grid.
 k. Double-click the **Place** field from the *RaceResults* table to add it into the query design grid. Your completed query design grid should look similar to Figure 3-95.

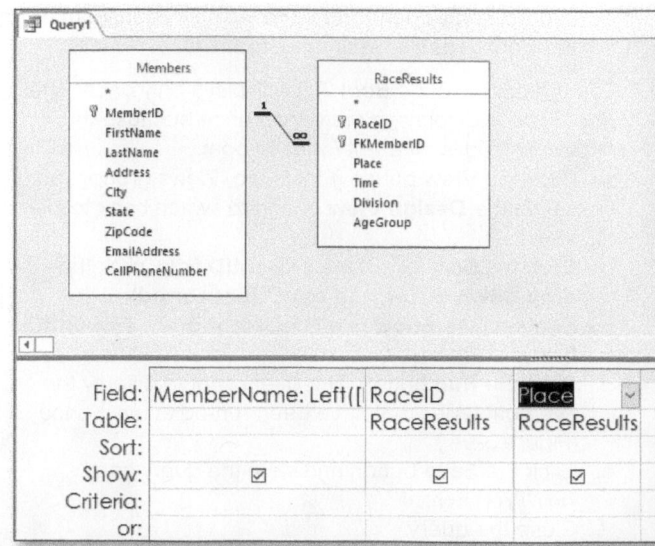

3-95 Query design grid

5. Click the **Save** button and save the query as MemberRaceResults.

6. Click the **Run** button [*Query Tools Design* tab, *Results* group]. The query should open in *Datasheet* view and display 36 records. A sample of the results is shown in Figure 3-96.

7. Save a copy of the query.
 a. Click the **Save As** button [*File* Tab].
 b. Select the **Save Object As** button and then click the **Save As** button.
 c. Replace the suggested name with MemberRaceResultsPlaceParameter.

8. Edit the *MemberRaceResultsPlaceParameter* query to add a parameter.
 a. Click the **View** button [*Home* tab, *Views* group] and select the **Design View** option to switch back to *Design* view of the query.
 b. Type [Show members who finished in what place? (Enter a number)] in the **Criteria** row of the *Place* field. You can use the *Zoom* box or *Expression Builder* to enter the parameter.
 c. Click the **Save** button to save the query.
 d. Click the **Run** button to test the query. The *Enter Parameter Value* dialog box displays.
 e. Enter 1 and click the **OK** button. The query results should display the five records shown in Figure 3-97.
 f. Switch back to *Design* view and run the query again.
 g. Click the **OK** button in the *Enter Parameter Value* dialog box without entering a value. The query results should display with no records showing since there are no records where the place value matches "null," or no value.

3-96 Query results

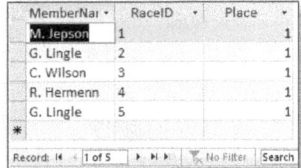

3-97 Query results

9. Close the query.

10. Create a new query using the *Simple Query Wizard*. The club wants to display division and age group information about the members, based on the races in which they competed.
 a. Click the **Query Wizard** button [*Create* tab, *Queries* group] to launch the *Query Wizard*.
 b. Select **Simple Query Wizard** in the *New Query* dialog box.
 c. Click **OK** to launch the *Simple Query Wizard*.
 d. Click the **Tables/Queries** drop-down arrow and select the **Members** table.
 e. Select **MemberID** in the *Available Fields* window.
 f. Click the **Move Single Field** button to move the field into the *Selected Fields* window.
 g. Select **FirstName** in the *Available Fields* window and click the **Move Single Field** button.
 h. Select **LastName** in the *Available Fields* window and click the **Move Single Field** button.
 i. Click the **Tables/Queries** drop-down arrow and select the **RaceResults** table.
 j. Move the **Division** and **AgeGroup** fields into the *Selected Fields* window. The completed *Query Wizard* window should match Figure 3-98.
 k. Click the **Next** button. The second page of the *Simple Query Wizard* displays. Because of the relationship between the two tables, Access asks you whether you want a detail or summary query.
 l. Leave the radio button selected for **Detail** and click the **Next** button.

m. Change the title in the *Title* box to MemberDivisionAndAgeGroup.

n. Click **Finish** to save and run the query. The query results display 36 total records, one for each of the records in the *RaceResults* table.

11. Edit the query in *Design* view to add a *Total* row. This allows you to group the records to remove the duplicate records.

a. Click the **View** button [*Home* tab, *Views* group] and select the **Design View** option to switch back to *Design* view of the query.

b. Click the **Totals** button [*Query Tools Design* tab, *Show/Hide* group]. *Group By* displays in the *Total* row for each field.

c. Click the **Save** button to save the query.

3-98 Completed *Simple Query Wizard*

12. Click the **Run** button. The query should open in *Datasheet* view and display 17 records (Figure 3-99). Notice that two records still display for Marco Guzman indicating that he has run races in two age groups. He must have had a birthday that caused him to change age groups.

13. Close the query.

14. Close the database.

3-99 Query results of *MemberDivisionAndAgeGroup* query

Independent Project 3-4

You are creating a parameter query for the music database you have worked with in previous projects. To ensure consistency, the starting file is provided for you. Use *Design* view to create the query. Edit the query to add criteria. After saving and testing the query, edit the query to add a parameter.
[**Student Learning Outcomes 3.2, 3.3, 3.4, 3.5, 3.6**]

File Needed: ***MusicDatabase-03.accdb***
Completed Project File Name: ***[your initials] Access 3-4.accdb***

Skills Covered in This Project

- Create a query in *Design* view.
- Edit a query in *Design* view.
- Add compound criteria to a query.
- Execute a query.
- Save a query.
- Sort query results.
- Add a parameter to a query.

1. Open the ***MusicDatabase-03.accdb*** database file.

2. Save a new copy of your database as [your initials] Access 3-4.

3. Enable content in the database.

4. Open the *Songs* table in *Datasheet* view to verify that the table contains 561 songs.

5. Close the table.

6. Create a new query in *Design* view. The query finds songs with lengths that are within a certain range.
 a. Add both tables into the *Query Design* window.
 b. Increase the size of the table objects to display all of the fields.
 c. Add the following fields into the query in the order listed: **AlbumName**, **Artist**, **SongTitle**, and **Length** (from the *Songs* table).

7. Save the query as 3to4MinuteSongs-ArtistORAlbumChoice.

8. Enter the following criteria in the *Length* field: Between #0:03:00# and #0:04:00#. Due to the way Access stores times, Access changes this criteria to read: *Between #12:03:00 AM# And #12:04:00 AM#*.

9. Save the changes and run the query. The datasheet should display 287 songs.

10. Change to *Design* view to edit the query and add a parameter. The parameter should allow the user to enter either the *Album Name* or the *Artist Name* to find songs.
 a. Type [Enter the Album Name] as the criteria for the *AlbumName* field.
 b. On the *Or* row, type [Enter the Artist Name] as the criteria for the *Artist* field.
 c. Copy the criteria in the *Length* field and paste it into the *Or* row cell of the *Length* field. You need the *Length* criteria to be in both the *Criteria* row and the *Or* row.

11. Sort the results to display in ascending order by song length.

12. Save the changes to the query. The completed query design grid should be similar to Figure 3-100.

Field:	AlbumName	Artist	SongTitle	Length	
Table:	Albums	Albums	Songs	Songs	
Sort:				Ascending	
Show:	☑	☑	☑	☑	
Criteria:	[Enter the Album Name]			Between #12:03:00 AM# And #12:04:00 AM#	
or:		[Enter the Artist Name]		Between #12:03:00 AM# And #12:04:00 AM#	

3-100 Query design grid of query showing multiple parameters and compound criteria

13. Run the query to verify that it works.
 a. Type Need You Now in the *Enter the Album Name Enter Parameter Value* dialog box, and click **OK**.
 b. Don't enter anything in the *Enter the Artist Name Enter Parameter Value* dialog box, and click **OK**. The datasheet should show the four (out of 11) songs from this album that meet the criteria (Figure 3-101). You can verify the song count on this album by looking in the *Songs* table for *AlbumID 5*.

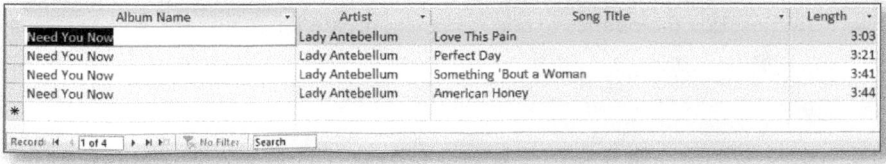

Album Name	Artist	Song Title	Length
Need You Now	Lady Antebellum	Love This Pain	3:03
Need You Now	Lady Antebellum	Perfect Day	3:21
Need You Now	Lady Antebellum	Something 'Bout a Woman	3:41
Need You Now	Lady Antebellum	American Honey	3:44

Record: ◄ ◄ 1 of 4 ► ►► ►※ ⧉ No Filter Search

3-101 Query results for *Need You Now* songs between three and four minutes long

14. Switch back to *Design* view and run the query again.
 a. Don't enter anything in the *Enter the Album Name Enter Parameter Value* dialog box, and click **OK**.
 b. Type Lady Antebellum in the *Enter the Artist Name Enter Parameter Value* dialog box, and click **OK**. The datasheet should show the 35 (out of 58) songs from this artist that meet the criteria (Figure 3-102). You can verify the song count for this artist by looking in the *Albums* table for *Lady Antebellum* and expanding the plus symbol.

Album Name	Artist	Song Title	Length
Golden	Lady Antebellum	Better Off Now (That You're Gone)	3:03
Need You Now	Lady Antebellum	Love This Pain	3:03
747	Lady Antebellum	Freestyle	3:04
747	Lady Antebellum	Sounded Good at the Time	3:06
On This Winter's Night	Lady Antebellum	Christmas (Baby Please Come Home)	3:09
Golden	Lady Antebellum	Can't Stand the Rain	3:11
On This Winter's Night	Lady Antebellum	Silent Night (Lord of My Life)	3:11
Golden	Lady Antebellum	Downtown	3:16
Golden	Lady Antebellum	All for Love	3:16
Own the Night	Lady Antebellum	We Owned the Night	3:17
747	Lady Antebellum	Bartender	3:18
On This Winter's Night	Lady Antebellum	This Christmas	3:19
On This Winter's Night	Lady Antebellum	I'll Be Home for Christmas	3:20
747	Lady Antebellum	Lie with Me	3:21
747	Lady Antebellum	She Is	3:21
Need You Now	Lady Antebellum	Perfect Day	3:21
On This Winter's Night	Lady Antebellum	The First Noel	3:23
747	Lady Antebellum	747	3:27
On This Winter's Night	Lady Antebellum	Blue Christmas	3:27
Golden	Lady Antebellum	Golden	3:27
Golden	Lady Antebellum	It Ain't Pretty	3:29
747	Lady Antebellum	One Great Mystery	3:34

Record: 1 of 35 No Filter Search

3-102 Query results for *Lady Antebellum* songs between three and four minutes long

15. Close the query.

16. Close the database.

Independent Project 3-5

The State of New York Department of Motor Vehicles wants to create three queries. The first query provides summary data on the number of tickets by city and violation. The second query summarizes the total tickets by violation. The third query provides summary data for the total fines assessed against each driver who has had a ticket. To ensure consistency, the starting file is provided for you. Use *Design* view to create the summary queries. Edit the queries to add fields, aggregate functions, and sorting. Finally, save and run the queries.
[Student Learning Outcomes 3.2, 3.4, 3.8]

File Needed: ***NewYorkDMV-03.accdb***
Completed Project File Name: *[your initials] Access 3-5.accdb*

Skills Covered in This Project

- Create a summary query in *Design* view.
- Edit a query in *Design* view.
- Add fields to a query.

- Execute a query.
- Save a query.
- Sort query results.
- Add aggregate functions.

1. Open the ***NewYorkDMV-03.accdb*** database file.

2. Save a new copy of your database as [your initials] Access 3-5.

3. Enable content in the database.

4. Create a new summary query in *Design* view. The query counts the number of tickets issued by city and violation.
 a. Add the *Tickets* table into the *Query Design* window.
 b. Increase the size of the table object to display all of the fields.
 c. Add the following fields into the query: **City**, **PrimaryFactor**, and **TicketNumber**.
 d. Add the *Total* row to the query.
 e. **Group By** the *City* and *PrimaryFactor* fields and **Count** the *TicketNumber* field.

5. Save the query as TicketCountByCityAndFactor.

6. Run the query. The datasheet should display 22 records.

7. Widen the field column widths using **AutoFit** or **Best Fit**. The datasheet should be similar to Figure 3-103.

8. Save the changes to the query.

9. Save a copy of the query as TicketCountByFactor.

10. Edit the *TicketCountByFactor* query in *Design* view. The query should show the total tickets issued for each violation factor, sorted in descending order by count.
 a. Delete the *City* field.
 b. Sort the *TicketNumber* field in descending order.

11. Save and run the query. The datasheet should match Figure 3-104.

12. Close the query.

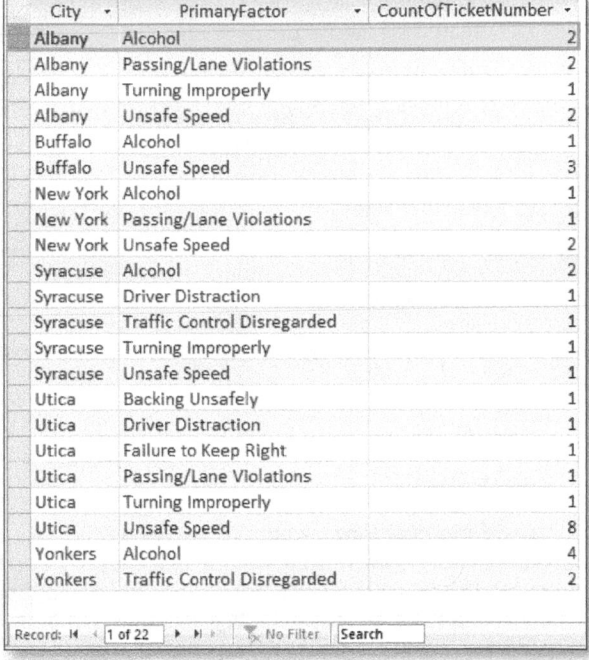

City	PrimaryFactor	CountOfTicketNumber
Albany	Alcohol	2
Albany	Passing/Lane Violations	2
Albany	Turning Improperly	1
Albany	Unsafe Speed	2
Buffalo	Alcohol	1
Buffalo	Unsafe Speed	3
New York	Alcohol	1
New York	Passing/Lane Violations	1
New York	Unsafe Speed	2
Syracuse	Alcohol	2
Syracuse	Driver Distraction	1
Syracuse	Traffic Control Disregarded	1
Syracuse	Turning Improperly	1
Syracuse	Unsafe Speed	1
Utica	Backing Unsafely	1
Utica	Driver Distraction	1
Utica	Failure to Keep Right	1
Utica	Passing/Lane Violations	1
Utica	Turning Improperly	1
Utica	Unsafe Speed	8
Yonkers	Alcohol	4
Yonkers	Traffic Control Disregarded	2

Record: 1 of 22 No Filter Search

3-103 Summary query results counting tickets by city and factor

PrimaryFactor	CountOfTicketNumber
Unsafe Speed	16
Alcohol	10
Passing/Lane Violations	4
Turning Improperly	3
Traffic Control Disregarded	3
Driver Distraction	2
Failure to Keep Right	1
Backing Unsafely	1

Record: 1 of 8 No Filter Search

3-104 Summary query results counting tickets by factor

13. Create a new summary query in *Design* view. The query provides summary data on the total fines assessed against each driver.

 a. Add both tables into the *Query Design* window.

 b. Increase the size of the table objects to display all of the fields.

 c. Add the following fields into the query: **LicenseNumber**, **FirstName**, **LastName**, **Fine**, and **TicketNumber**.

 d. Add the **Total** row to the query.

 e. **Group By** the *LicenseNumber*, *FirstName*, and *LastName* fields, **Sum** the *Fine* field and **Count** the *TicketNumber* field.

 f. Sort the *Fine* field in descending order.

14. Save the query as TicketsByDriver.

15. Run the query. The datasheet should display 24 drivers who have received tickets, sorted in descending order by the total dollar amount of their fines (Figure 3-105).

16. Close the query.

17. Close the database.

LicenseNum ▾	FirstName ▾	LastName ▾	SumOfFine ▾	CountOfTic ▾
15500786	Brian	Shin	$1,040.00	4
15503625	Corey	Norman	$800.00	2
12389049	Bonnie	Hirshman	$680.00	3
39989780	Kevin	Nguyen	$535.00	3
12344537	Austin	Davis	$520.00	2
12348692	Michael	Finch	$505.00	3
12348279	Sharon	Altier	$495.00	3
12346978	Jon	Juarez	$400.00	1
10004387	Miranda	Jones	$400.00	1
10000501	Timothy	Smith	$345.00	3
39992366	Mark	Watson	$180.00	1
12346123	Claudia	Schooler	$150.00	1
15502325	Ron	Stokes	$130.00	1
10003086	Mark	Williams	$120.00	1
12345838	Eric	Wilson	$120.00	1
18957217	Jessica	Healy	$105.00	2
15500914	Michelle	Taylor	$90.00	1
18955806	Nancy	Smith	$90.00	1
12388795	Caroline	Doiron	$90.00	1
12394163	Jake	Harvey	$90.00	1
10004372	Kathy	Brown	$90.00	1
12345678	Emily	Garcia	$60.00	1
10001786	Sanda	Johnson	$60.00	1
39992387	Kiana	Caton	$45.00	1

Record: ◄ ◄ 1 of 24 ► ►► No Filter Search

3-105 Summary query results of tickets by driver

Independent Project 3-6

Courtyard Medical Plaza wants to create a query to provide details about its tenants and their rental payment history. The starting database file is provided for you. Use *Design* view to create the query. Edit the query to add calculated fields. After saving and testing the query, edit the query to add a parameter. **[Student Learning Outcomes 3.2, 3.3, 3.4, 3.5, 3.6, 3.7]**

File Needed: ***CourtyardMedicalPlaza-03.accdb***
Completed Project File Name: *[your initials] **Access 3-6.accdb***

Skills Covered in This Project

- Create a query in *Design* view.
- Edit a query in *Design* view.
- Add compound criteria to a query.

- Execute a query.
- Save a query.
- Add calculated fields to a query.
- Sort query results.
- Add a parameter to a query.

1. Open the ***CourtyardMedicalPlaza-03.accdb*** database file.

2. Save a new copy of your database as [your initials] Access 3-6.

3. Enable content in the database.

4. Create a new query in *Design* view. The query should display the rental invoice history.
 a. Add both tables into the *Query Design* window.
 b. Increase the size of the table objects to display all of the fields.
 c. Add the following fields into the query: **LastName**, **InvoiceID**, **DueDate**, **DateReceived**, **AmountDue**, and **Discount**.
 d. Run the query to make sure it works. The datasheet should display 54 records.

5. Save the query as InvoiceHistory.

6. Edit the query to add calculated fields.
 a. Insert a column to the left of *InvoiceID*.
 b. In the inserted column, add a calculated field to concatenate the *FirstName* and *LastName* fields using the following formula: Doctor: [FirstName] & " " & [LastName].
 c. Don't show the *LastName* field. In the next step you will use that for query criteria.
 d. Insert a column to the left of *Discount*.
 e. In the inserted column, add a calculated field to determine the number of days early the rent was paid using the following formula: DaysPaidEarly: [DueDate]-[DateReceived].
 f. To the right of the *Discount* field enter a calculated field to determine the net amount of rent due with the following formula: NetRent: [AmountDue]-[Discount].

7. Save your changes and run the query. The datasheet should look similar to Figure 3-106 and display a total of 54 records.

Doctor	InvoiceID	Due Date	DateReceiv	Amount Due	> DaysPaid	Discount	NetRent
Robert Beyer	1	01-May-17	4/30/2017	$1,250.00	1		
Robert Beyer	10	01-Jun-17	5/29/2017	$1,250.00	3	$25.00	$1,225.00
Robert Beyer	19	01-Jul-17	6/30/2017	$1,250.00	1		
Robert Beyer	28	01-Aug-17	8/1/2017	$1,250.00	0		
Robert Beyer	37	01-Sep-17	9/1/2017	$1,250.00	0		
Robert Beyer	46	01-Oct-17	9/30/2017	$1,250.00	1		
Elizabeth Sche	2	01-May-17	5/1/2017	$1,100.00	0		
Elizabeth Sche	11	01-Jun-17	6/1/2017	$1,100.00			

3-106 Query results showing concatenated and calculated fields

8. Edit the query to add parameters to search either by last name or by a date range.
 a. Type [Enter the last name or leave blank to select all doctors] as the criteria for the *LastName* field.
 b. On the *Or* row, type Between [Enter the Starting Date] And [Enter the Ending Date] as the criteria for the *DueDate* field.

9. Sort the results in ascending order by *LastName* and *DueDate*.

10. Save the query.

11. Run the query.
 a. Type Flores in the *Enter the Last Name Enter Parameter Value* dialog box, and click **OK**.
 b. Don't enter anything in the *Enter the Starting Date Enter Parameter Value* dialog box, and click **OK**.
 c. Don't enter anything in the *Enter the Ending Date Enter Parameter Value* dialog box, and click **OK**. The datasheet should show the six payments received from Dr. Flores (Figure 3-107). Dr. Flores paid his rent early three months this year.

Doctor	InvoiceID	Due Date	DateReceiv	Amount Due	DaysPaidEa	Discount	NetRent
Ricardo Flores	4	01-May-17	4/29/2017	$1,350.00	2	$13.50	$1,336.50
Ricardo Flores	13	01-Jun-17	5/28/2017	$1,350.00	4	$27.00	$1,323.00
Ricardo Flores	22	01-Jul-17	6/29/2017	$1,350.00	2	$13.50	$1,336.50
Ricardo Flores	31	01-Aug-17	8/1/2017	$1,350.00	0		
Ricardo Flores	40	01-Sep-17	9/1/2017	$1,350.00	0		
Ricardo Flores	49	01-Oct-17	10/1/2017	$1,350.00	0		

Record: 1 of 6 No Filter Search

3-107 Query results when name parameter is completed

12. Switch back to *Design* view and run the query again.

 a. Don't enter anything in the *Enter the Last Name Enter Parameter Value* dialog box, and click **OK**.

 b. Type 9/1/2017 in the *Enter the Starting Date Enter Parameter Value* dialog box, and click **OK**.

 c. Type 10/1/2017 in the *Enter the Ending Date Enter Parameter Value* dialog box, and click **OK**. The datasheet should show the 18 invoices with a due date between 9/1/2017 and 10/1/2017 (Figure 3-108).

Doctor	InvoiceID	Due Date	DateReceiv	Amount Due	DaysPaidEa	Discount	NetRent
Robert Beyer	37	01-Sep-17	9/1/2017	$1,250.00	0		
Robert Beyer	46	01-Oct-17	9/30/2017	$1,250.00	1		
Juan Camacho	41	01-Sep-17	8/27/2017	$1,100.00	5	$22.00	$1,078.00
Juan Camacho	50	01-Oct-17	10/1/2017	$1,100.00	0		
Ricardo Flores	40	01-Sep-17	9/1/2017	$1,350.00	0		
Ricardo Flores	49	01-Oct-17	10/1/2017	$1,350.00	0		
Margaret Fost	39	01-Sep-17	8/29/2017	$1,350.00	3	$27.00	$1,323.00
Margaret Fost	48	01-Oct-17	9/29/2017	$1,350.00	2	$13.50	$1,336.50
James Hennes	42	01-Sep-17	9/1/2017	$1,600.00	0		
James Hennes	51	01-Oct-17	10/1/2017	$1,600.00	0		
Steven Norma	45	01-Sep-17	8/30/2017	$1,600.00	2	$16.00	$1,584.00
Steven Norma	54	01-Oct-17	10/1/2017	$1,600.00	0		
Rick Plice	43	01-Sep-17	9/1/2017	$1,400.00	0		
Rick Plice	52	01-Oct-17	10/1/2017	$1,400.00	0		
Elizabeth Sche	38	01-Sep-17	9/1/2017	$1,100.00	0		
Elizabeth Sche	47	01-Oct-17	10/1/2017	$1,100.00	0		
Robyn Singh	44	01-Sep-17	9/1/2017	$1,650.00	0		
Robyn Singh	53	01-Oct-17	9/28/2017	$1,650.00	3	$33.00	$1,617.00

Record: ◄ 1 of 18 ► ►► No Filter Search

3-108 Query results when date parameters are completed

13. Close the query.

14. Reopen the query in *Design* view. Notice that Access has moved the *LastName* field to the right side of the query design grid and also entered a copy of the *DueDate* field with the *Show* row check box deselected. This is due to the way Access processes the query (Figure 3-109).

15. Close the query.

16. Close the database.

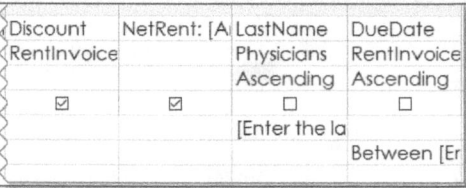

Discount	NetRent: [A	LastName	DueDate
RentInvoice		Physicians	RentInvoice
		Ascending	Ascending
☑	☑	☐	☐
		[Enter the la	
			Between [Er

3-109 Updated query design grid

Improve It Project 3-7

Central Sierra needs help with their database. One of the administrative assistants has created two queries to provide information about the employees. Unfortunately, the queries are not working correctly. For this project, determine why the queries don't work and make the necessary corrections. The starting file is provided for you. Use *Design* view to edit the queries. Use calculated fields, compound criteria, and parameters, and save the queries and test that they work correctly.
[Student Learning Outcomes 3.2, 3.3, 3.4, 3.5, 3.6, 3.7, 3.8]

File Needed: ***CentralSierra-03.accdb***
Completed Project File Name: ***[your initials] Access 3-7.accdb***

Skills Covered in This Project

- Edit a query in *Design* view.
- Add compound criteria to a query.
- Execute a query.
- Save a query.
- Add calculated fields to a query.
- Add a parameter to a query.

1. Open the ***CentralSierra-03.accdb*** database file.

2. Save a new copy of your database as [your initials] Access 3-7.

3. Enable the contents in the security warning.

4. Run the *NewSalaryCostSummary* query. The results display in *Datasheet* view (Figure 3-110). The query is supposed to summarize results by department and, within the department by title, the total salary cost and the total cost of potentially giving a 3% raise to all employees. There are several errors that need to be fixed.

First Name ▾	Last Name ▾	Title ▾	Department ▾	SumOfBas ▾	Expr1
Albert	Quiroga	Large Group Specialist	Health and Benefits	$4,500.00	4635
Bert	Pulido	Supervisor	Health and Benefits	$5,500.00	5665
Bob	Lingle	Chief Executive Officer	Administration	$15,000.00	15450
Charlene	Althouse	Large Group Specialist	Property and Casualty	$4,700.00	4841
Cheryl	Nevens	Chief Information Officer	Administration	$12,000.00	12360
Chris	Robles	Insurance Agent	Health and Benefits	$3,900.00	4017
Eleesha	Santos	Insurance Agent	Health and Benefits	$5,500.00	5665
Tami	Chan	Administrative Assistant	Health and Benefits	$3,000.00	3090
Theresa	Nguyen	Insurance Agent	Property and Casualty	$3,900.00	4017
Timothy	Hansen	Insurance Agent	Health and Benefits	$3,900.00	4017
Todd	DeRenzis	Administrative Assistant	Insurance Sales	$2,800.00	2884
Wayne	Reza	Insurance Agent	Health and Benefits	$4,000.00	4120

Record: ◄ ◄ 1 of 29 ► ► ► ▼ No Filter Search

3-110 *NewSalaryCostSummary* query results

5. Edit the query to remove the unneeded columns that cause the summary query to display too many records.
 a. Delete the *FirstName* column.
 b. Delete the *LastName* column.
 c. Save and run the query to test the results. The datasheet should now show only 14 records.

6. Edit the query to fix the calculated field name and formatting.
 a. Change the default field name of *Expr1* to SumOfPotentialNewSalary.
 b. Open the *Property Sheet* for this field and change the *Format* property to **Currency**.
 c. Close the *Property Sheet*.
 d. Save and run the query to test the results. The datasheet should show the improved calculated field (Figure 3-111).

Title ▾	Department ▾	SumOfBas ▾	SumOfPot▾
Administrative Assistant	Administration	$3,000.00	$3,090.00
Administrative Assistant	Health and Benefits	$5,750.00	$5,922.50
Administrative Assistant	Insurance Sales	$5,400.00	$5,562.00
Administrative Assistant	Property and Casualty	$2,750.00	$2,832.50
Chief Executive Officer	Administration	$15,000.00	$15,450.00
Chief Information Officer	Administration	$12,000.00	$12,360.00

3-111 Query results with improvements to calculated field and removal of name fields

7. Edit the query to fix the grouping order. The results are supposed to display the records grouped by the department, and then within each department by the job titles.
 a. Move the *Department* field to the left of the *Title* field.
 b. Save and run the query to test the results. The datasheet should show the records with the correct grouping (Figure 3-112).

Department ▾	Title ▾	SumOfBas ▾	SumOfPot▾
Administration	Administrative Assistant	$3,000.00	$3,090.00
Administration	Chief Executive Officer	$15,000.00	$15,450.00
Administration	Chief Information Officer	$12,000.00	$12,360.00
Administration	Chief Operating Officer	$12,000.00	$12,360.00
Administration	Executive Assistant	$3,750.00	$3,862.50
Health and Benefits	Administrative Assistant	$5,750.00	$5,922.50
Health and Benefits	Insurance Agent	$28,900.00	$29,767.00

3-112 Query results with improved grouping

8. Edit the query to enhance the functionality and improve the appearance. In addition to calculating the sum of both the *Base Salary* and the *Potential New Salary* fields, management would like to see the average of both of those fields, as well as the total number of employees in each area.
 a. Insert a new column to the left of the *BaseMonthlySalary* column.
 b. Click the **drop-down arrow** in the *Field* row of this new column and select **EmpID**. Set this field to use the **Count** aggregate function.
 c. Add the **BaseMonthlySalary** field into the first empty cell in the *Field* row. *BaseMonthlySalary* will be in the query design grid twice. Set this field to use the **Avg** aggregate function.
 d. Type the following formula into the first empty cell in the *Field* row: AvgOfPotentialNewSalary: Avg([BaseMonthlySalary]*1.03). Set the *Total* row cell for this field to **Expression**.
 e. Format this field to use **Currency**.
 f. Save and run the query to test the results. Adjust the column widths as necessary to improve the appearance. The datasheet should now be similar to that shown in Figure 3-113.

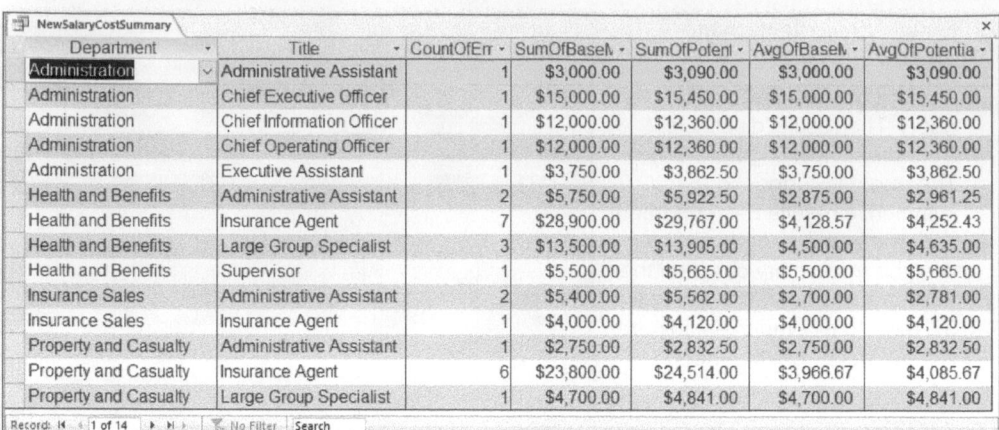

3-113 Completed *NewSalaryCostSummary* query results

9. Save any changes and close the query.

10. Run the *InsuranceAgentsBranchParameter* query. Enter Folsom in the *Enter Parameter Value* dialog box. The results display in datasheet view (Figure 3-114). The query is supposed to list the insurance agents in a particular branch or show all the insurance agents if the branch prompt is left blank. You have identified several errors that need to be fixed, including that all the insurance agents displayed even though you entered a branch.

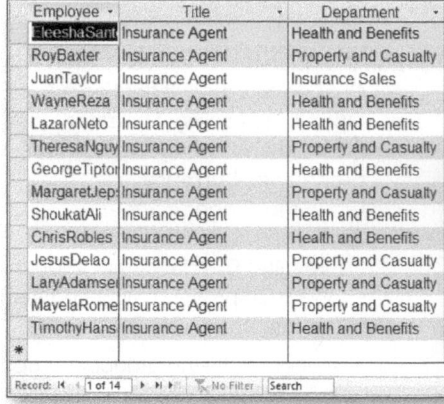

3-114 *InsuranceAgentsBranchParameter* query results are not correct

11. Edit the query to fix the parameter problem.
 a. Open the query in *Design* view. Notice that the branch parameter is actually on the *Department* field and not the *Branch* field.
 b. Change that column to contain the *Branch* field.
 c. Run the query again and enter Folsom. The results now display the branch, but you still have employees from all the branches.
 d. Switch to *Design* view to review the criteria. The *Branch* parameter is on the "or" row. It needs to be on the same row as "Insurance Agent".
 e. Move the parameter to the criteria row to fix that problem.
 f. Open the *Zoom* window to review the parameter. It isn't designed correctly, because it won't allow the field to be left blank and show all the insurance agents.
 g. Edit the parameter as follows: Like [Enter the Branch or Leave blank to select all branches] & "*".
 h. Save and run the query. Type Folsom. Only the four agents at the Folsom branch should display.
 i. Run the query again and leave the dialog box empty. All 14 agents should display.

12. Edit the query to fix the *Employee* field. Notice that there isn't a space between the names.
 a. Edit the formula in the *Employee* field as follows: Employee: [FirstName] & " " & [LastName].
 b. Run the query. Enter Granite Bay. The results should match Figure 3-115 and show only the five insurance agents at the Granite Bay branch.
 c. Use **AutoFit** to adjust the width of all the columns.

13. Save and close the query.

14. Close the database.

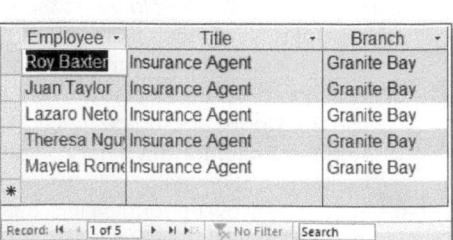

3-115 Completed *InsuranceAgentsBranchParameter* query

Challenge Project 3-8

For this project, you modify the database you built in Challenge Project 2-8. Add additional data and create two queries.
[Student Learning Outcomes 3.1, 3.2, 3.3, 3.4, 3.5]

File Needed: *[your initials] Access 2-8.accdb*
Completed Project File Name: *[your initials] Access 3-8.accdb*

Open the database *[your initials] Access 2-8* and save a copy of it as [your initials] Access 3-8. Modify your database according to the following instructions:

- Add at least 20 rows of additional data into the table.
- Create a query with the *Simple Query Wizard*.
- Add at least three of the fields into the query.
- Edit the query in *Design* view and add a criterion to one of the fields.
- Apply sorting to one of the fields.
- Save and run the query.
- Create a second query in *Design* view.
- Add all of the fields into a query.
- Add compound criteria to the query using an *OR* condition on one of the fields combined with an *AND* condition on at least one other field.
- Save and run the query.
- Adjust the width of the columns in the query so that they are sized appropriately.
- Save any changes that you made.

Challenge Project 3-9

Modify the database you created in Challenge Project 2-9 for Blue Lake Sports. Your database contains a table with information about the different departments at Blue Lake Sports and a related table with information about Interns who are working at Blue Lake. Add additional data and create one query.
[Student Learning Outcomes 3.2, 3.3, 3.4, 3.5, 3.6, 3.7]

File Needed: *[your initials] Access 2-9.accdb*
Completed Project File Name: *[your initials] Access 3-9.accdb*

Open the database *[your initials] Access 2-9* and save a copy of it as [your initials] Access 3-9. Modify your database according to the following instructions:

- If necessary, add additional data into the *Department* table so that you have at least 10 different departments.
- If necessary, add additional data into the *Intern* table so that there are at least 30 interns. When entering the value for the *DepartmentName* foreign key, don't assign all of the interns to the same department.
- Create a query with *Design* view.
- Add both tables into the query.
- Add the *DepartmentName* and *Division* fields (from the *Department* table).
- Add a calculated field to concatenate the intern's *FirstName* and *LastName* fields.

- Save and run the query.
- Edit the query to add a parameter. The parameter should allow the user to enter the division he or she wishes to query. Write this parameter using wildcards so that if the user leaves the *Enter Parameter Value* dialog box empty, the query returns all the records. You may want to review the "Use Wildcards in a Parameter Query" section in *SLO 3.6: Creating and Using a Simple Parameter Query* for help with this task.
- Save and run the query.
- Verify that the query works correctly when the user enters a specific division and that it returns all the records if the dialog box is left blank.
- Adjust the width of the columns in the query so that they are sized appropriately.
- Save any changes that you made.

Challenge Project 3-10

Modify the database you created in Challenge Project 2-10 for a travel agency. Your database contains a table with information about the different ships and a related table with information about upcoming cruises. Add additional data and create two queries.
[Student Learning Outcomes 3.2, 3.3, 3.4, 3.5, 3.6, 3.7, 3.8]

File Needed: *[your initials] Access 2-10.accdb*
Completed Project File Name: *[your initials] Access 3-10.accdb*

Open the database *[your initials] Access 2-10* and save a copy of it as [your initials] Access 3-10. Modify your database according to the following instructions:

- Add at least 10 rows of additional data into the *Trips* table. When entering the value for the *ShipID* foreign key, don't assign all of the trips to the same ship.
- Create a query with *Design* view.
- Add both tables into the query.
- Add the *ShipName*, *CruiseLineName*, and *NumberOfPassengers* fields (from the *Ships* table) and the *TripName* and *CostPerPerson* fields (from the *Trips* table).
- Add a field to calculate the potential revenue for each trip. The *Potential Revenue* is the *Cost PerPerson* times the *Number of Passengers*.
- Sort the results in ascending order by the potential revenue.
- Save and run the query.
- Adjust the width of the columns in the query so that they are sized appropriately.
- Save any changes that you made.
- Create a *Summary* query in *Design* view to count how many trips each Cruise Line has scheduled.
- Add both tables into the query.
- Add the *TripID* field and the *CruiseLineName* field into the query.
- Add the *Total* row.
- Count by the *TripID* field.
- Save and run the query.
- Adjust the width of the columns in the query so that they are sized appropriately.
- Save any changes that you made.

CHAPTER

4

Creating and Using Forms and Reports

CHAPTER OVERVIEW

Forms and reports enhance the usability of your Access database. Forms provide a user-friendly interface to view, add, update, and delete data in a database. Reports offer a professional way to view and print data, making it easier for your user to understand information in your database. This chapter introduces the Access tools that allow you to create and customize forms and reports.

STUDENT LEARNING OUTCOMES (SLOs)

After completing this chapter, you will be able to:

SLO 4.1 Create a simple form using quick create options; save, modify, and delete a form (p. A4-213).

SLO 4.2 Create a blank form, understand controls and control layouts, and customize a form in *Layout* view (p. A4-221).

SLO 4.3 Restrict a form to data entry, limit user edits and deletions on a form, add command buttons, and test a form (p. A4-227).

SLO 4.4 Create a simple report with the *Report Wizard*; save, modify, and delete a report (p. A4-234).

SLO 4.5 Create a blank report, understand controls and control layouts, customize a report in *Layout* view, and add a title, a date, and page numbers to a report (p. A4-242).

SLO 4.6 Enhance a report by adding grouping, sorting, and totals to a report in *Layout* view (p. A4-250).

SLO 4.7 Integrate conditional formatting into a report (p. A4-254).

SLO 4.8 Preview, modify print settings, and print a report (p. A4-256).

ACCESS

CASE STUDY

For the Pause & Practice projects in this chapter, you develop forms and reports for the Placer Hills Real Estate and Central Sierra Insurance databases. As you progress through the Pause & Practice projects in this chapter, you incorporate many of the features you learn in this chapter to build forms and reports used to display, add, edit, and delete data in a database.

Pause & Practice 4-1: Create and view forms using the *Form Wizard*, the *Form* button and *Split Form*.

Pause & Practice 4-2: Create a form using the *Blank Form* button. Modify the form to restrict it to data entry, add buttons, and test the form.

Pause & Practice 4-3: Create and view a report using the *Report Wizard*. Create a report using the *Blank Report* button. Modify the report to improve its layout.

Pause & Practice 4-4: Create and preview a report with grouping and conditional formatting.

Creating and Working with a Simple Form

A *form* is an object you can use to create an interface to easily view, add, update, and delete data in a database. Most forms in a database are directly connected to a table or query, the source of the data. Access calls these *bound forms* because they link to the data source. *Unbound forms*, forms that don't have a connection to a data source, can be used to help operate the database. For example, a database may have an unbound form that contains no data but has buttons that perform different actions in the database like printing reports or opening forms. In this chapter, you learn how to create forms that are bound to a table.

Forms provide flexible access to data in a database. You can create a form with fields from one or more tables or queries. The form may also contain only a subset of the fields from the table. You also can choose to display only one record at a time or multiple records. This flexibility helps you create forms that look attractive and are more user-friendly than *Datasheet* view of a table. Ideally, a well-designed form makes it easier for your user to work with the database and prevents mistakes in adding, updating, or deleting data.

Access offers three view choices for most forms. Use *Form view* to enter and view data. *Design view* allows you to change the form. *Layout view* allows you to alter the design of a form and see the effects of the changes in real time. However, not all design changes can be made in *Layout* view. Forms created with a *Datasheet* layout also have a *Datasheet view* option.

There are several different ways to create a form. These options are available in the *Forms* group [*Create* tab] (Figure 4-1). Some of the options are quick, while others take a little more effort but provide greater flexibility and allow you to create more specialized types of forms. In this section, you are introduced to three quick ways to build a form: the *Form Wizard*, the *Form* button, and the *Split Form* options.

4-1 Form creation options

The Form Wizard

The *Form Wizard* steps you through the process of quickly creating a form. When you build a bound form, you must tell Access where to find the data. Use the *Form Wizard* to select the specific table(s) and queries along with the specific fields to include in the form. You can also select the layout for the form. After you create the form, you can use the form to view data in your database. If you need to change the form once it has been created, edit it using *Layout* view or *Design* view.

When you use the *Form Wizard* to create a form based on one table, you can select from four different layout options:

- *Columnar*: The form displays the fields in one column (Figure 4-2). The field names display to the left of the field and the name of the form displays in a header section

Listings - Columnar Layout

ListingID	10022
Date Listed	7/11/2016
List Price	$337,600.00
Address	525 Riverdale
City	Lincoln
SqFt	2755
Beds	3
Baths	2
Garage	2 Car Detached
Built	2001
Construction	Frame
Agent	103

Record: I◀ ◀ 1 of 57 ▶ ▶I ▶✳ ▼ No Filter Search

4-2 Columnar form layout

at the top of the form. A columnar layout shows only one record at a time. You use the *Navigation* buttons to move from one record to another.

- **Tabular**: The form displays the fields in a table (row and column) format (Figure 4-3). The header section at the top of the form displays the name of the form and the field names as column heads.

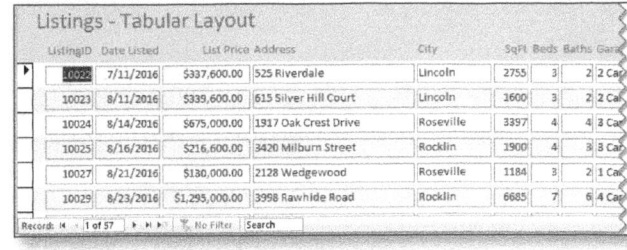

4-3 Tabular form layout

- **Datasheet**: The form displays in the Access *Datasheet* layout (Figure 4-4). The field names are the column heads.

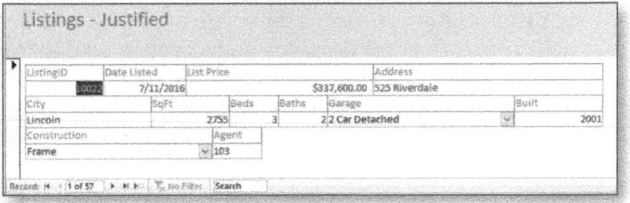

4-4 Datasheet form layout

- **Justified**: The form displays the fields in a horizontal, justified layout (Figure 4-5). The field names are above each field. The form name displays in a header section. Only one record displays at a time.

4-5 Justified form layout

▶ HOW TO: Create a Form Using the Form Wizard

1. Click the **Create** tab on the *Ribbon*.

2. Click the **Form Wizard** button [*Forms* group] to launch the *Form Wizard* (Figure 4-6).

 - The values displayed in the *Tables/Queries* box and the *Available Fields* window are based on the contents of your database.

3. Click the **Tables/Queries** drop-down arrow and select the **Table** or **Query** name.

4. Select a **Field** to include in the form from the *Available Fields* window.

 - Add fields in the order you want them to display in the form.

5. Click the **Move Single Field** button.

 - The field moves into the *Selected Fields* window (Figure 4-7).
 - The *Remove Single Field* and *Remove All Fields* buttons become active.

4-6 *Form Wizard* – step 1

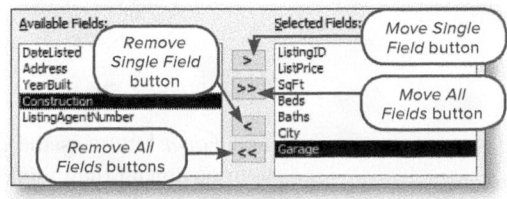

4-7 Move fields into the *Selected Fields* window

6. Continue moving all required fields, changing the selected *Table* or *Query* if needed.

> **ANOTHER WAY**
>
> Use the *Move All Fields* button (Figure 4-7) to quickly include all of the fields in the form.

7. Click the **Next** button when you are finished adding all fields. The second page of the *Form Wizard* displays (Figure 4-8).

8. Select the radio button of the form layout that you want.

9. Click the **Next** button. The last page of the *Form Wizard* displays (Figure 4-9).

10. Change the form **Title** as desired. The suggested title is the name of the table or query used to create the form. The title will also be used as the *Form Name*.

11. Click **Finish** to open the form to view the data.

- Access automatically saves the form.
- The form shows in *Form* view (Figure 4-10).
- Most of the fields appear in text boxes.
- Fields that have a lookup appear in combo boxes.
- Fields that are a *Yes/No* data type appear as check boxes.
- The size of a field depends on the data type and the field size.
- The first record in the table displays.
- The form name displays in the *Forms* group in the *Navigation Pane*.

4-8 Select the form layout

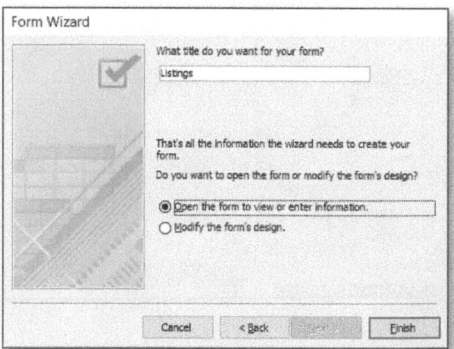

4-9 Enter the form title in the last step of the *Form Wizard*

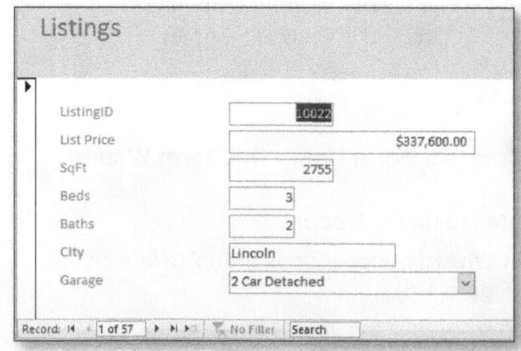

4-10 *Form* view of the completed form

12. Close the form.

The Form Button

The *Form* button is the quickest way to create a form. However, it does not give you any options during the initial creation process. After you have created the form, you can edit the form in *Layout* view or *Design* view.

▶ HOW TO: Create a New Form Using the Form Button

1. In the *Navigation Pane*, click to select the **Table** or **Query** on which to base the form.

2. Click the **Form** button [*Create* tab, *Forms* group]. Access creates the form and assigns the form object the same name as the table object. The form opens in *Layout* view (Figure 4-11).

 - *Layout* view lets you make changes to the design of the form and, at the same time, see how the form looks with data displaying.
 - The yellow selector border around a text box is an indicator that you are in *Layout* view. The *Layout View* icon is also selected in the *Status* bar.
 - The fields are placed on the form based on the order they are listed in the table.
 - Most of the fields appear in text boxes.
 - Fields that have a lookup appear in combo boxes.
 - Fields that are a *Yes/No* data type appear as check boxes.
 - All fields are assigned the same width. The height of the text boxes may be taller for fields that have a large size. The dashed border surrounding all of the fields indicates that they are grouped together to maintain uniform structure.
 - The first record in the table displays.

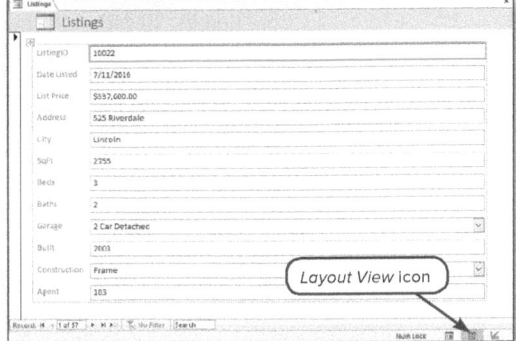

4-11 *Layout* view of a form created with the *Form* button

When a new form is created, the initial layout of the fields depends on the number of fields in the table and the size of the Access window when the form is created. A layout like the one shown in Figure 4-12 results if you have a smaller Access window before you click the *Form* button.

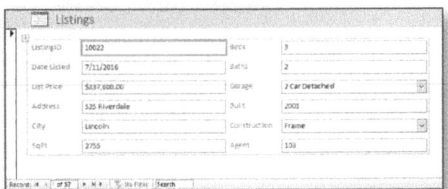

4-12 A smaller Access window results in a different field layout

The Split Form

A *split form* allows you to view data in two different ways at the same time. The top section of the form displays one record in a columnar mode while the bottom section displays a *Datasheet* view. The two sections are synchronized so when you navigate to a record, the selected record displays in the top section and is also highlighted in the lower section. This type of form allows you to see many records at once in the *Datasheet* view while giving you access to edit a single record. After you create a split form, you can use *Layout* view or *Design* view to edit it.

▶ HOW TO: Create a Split Form Using a Single Table

1. In the *Navigation Pane*, click to select the table on which to base the form.

2. Click the **More Forms** button [*Create* tab, *Forms* group] and select **Split Form** (Figure 4-13).

 - The form opens in *Layout* view (Figure 4-14).

4-13 *More Forms* button options

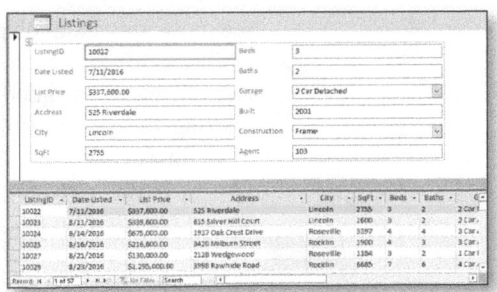

4-14 Split form in *Layout* view

Modify a Form

After you create a form using one of the three quick methods just described, you may want to make some modifications to the form. You can modify a form using either *Design* view or *Layout* view.

Design view shows you the completed structure of the form (Figure 4-15) so you can modify any aspect of a form. *Design* view has a distinctive look, but you can also tell you are in *Design* view from the *Status* bar at the bottom of the Access window. You can modify the header, detail, and footer sections of the form. *Design* view is good for adding labels and images into a form, editing text boxes, resizing the form sections, and changing some form properties. In *Design* view, the different editing choices are organized into three **Form Design Tools** contextual tabs: **Design**, **Arrange**, and **Format**.

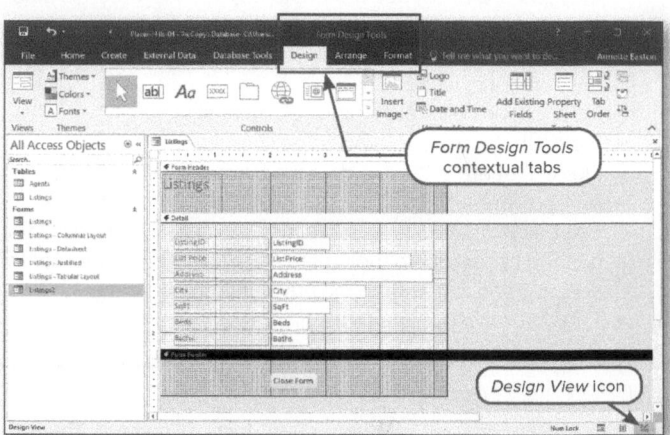

4-15 *Design* view of a form

Layout view allows you to make changes to the design of a form while seeing how the form looks with data displaying. The *Layout* view of the form in Figure 4-15 is shown in Figure 4-16. *Layout* view looks very similar to *Form* view, but you can tell what view you are in from the *Status* bar at the bottom of the Access window. While you can use the navigation buttons to move among different records, other parts of the form are not functional in *Layout* view. For example, the *Close Form* button does not work in *Layout* view.

Since you are able to see how the data displays while modifying the design, *Layout* view is good for resizing the fields or labels, changing colors or text alignment, or applying different formats. In *Layout* view, the different editing choices are organized into the same three *Form Design Tools* contextual tabs: *Design, Arrange* and *Format*. However, not all editing options are available while in *Layout* view.

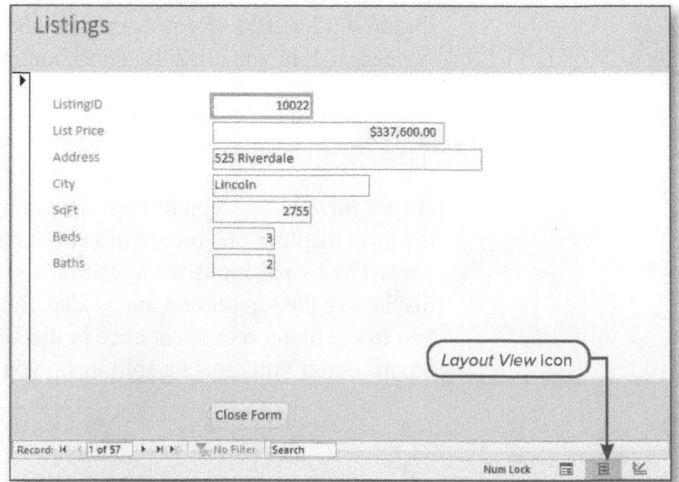

4-16 *Layout* view of a form

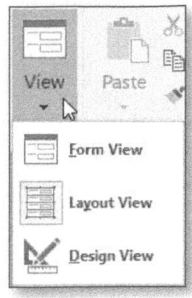

> **HOW TO: Switch Views to Modify a Form**

1. Click the **View** button [*Home* tab].
2. Select either **Layout View** or **Design View** (Figure 4-17).
3. Make any desired modifications.

> **ANOTHER WAY**
>
> Select the **Layout View** or **Design View** icons from the lower right corner of the *Status* bar.

4-17 *View* options for a form

Save a Form

When you create a form using one of the three quick methods described in this section, Access automatically saves the form during the creation process. If you have made any modifications to the design of the form you need to save those changes. Save changes to a form by pressing **Ctrl+S** or the *Save* icon on the *Quick Access* toolbar.

> **HOW TO: Save a Copy of a Form**

1. Click **Save As** [*File* tab] to display the *Save As* area.
2. Click **Save Object As** in the *File Types* options. *Save Object As* should be selected in the *Database File Types* options.
3. Click the **Save As** button to open the *Save As* dialog box (Figure 4-18).
 - The name of the current object displays in the *Save "object name" to* box.
 - In Figure 4-18, "Listings" is the name of the current object.
 - The suggested name always begins with "Copy of".
4. Type the name you wish to use in the *Save "object name" to* box.
5. Click **OK**.

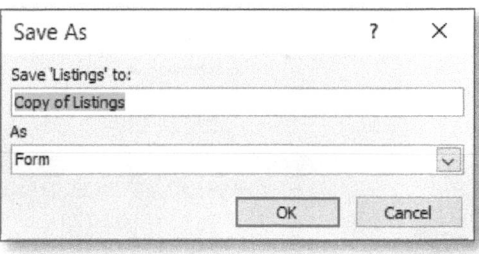

4-18 *Save As* dialog box

> **ANOTHER WAY**
>
> Press **F12** to open the *Save As* dialog box.

Once a form has been saved, it displays in the *Forms* group of the *Navigation Pane*. As you add more objects into your database, the number of objects displayed in the *Navigation Pane* increases (Figure 4-19). This is one of the reasons why it is important to use object names that effectively and immediately convey the meaning or purpose of the object. For example, in Figure 4-19 you don't know whether the *Listings* form and *Listings* report contain all the fields and information from the *Listings* table or whether there are differences, as you can see from the query names.

4-19 *Forms* group on the *Navigation Pane*

Open a Saved Form

If you double-click a form name in the *Navigation Pane*, the form opens in *Form* view. If the form was created using a *Datasheet* layout, it opens in *Datasheet* view.

Open a saved form in *Layout* view or *Design* view by right-clicking the form name in the *Navigation Pane* and selecting **Layout View** or **Design View** from the context menu (Figure 4-20).

4-20 Context menu of a form

Delete a Form

Occasionally, you have forms that you no longer need or want in the database.

Delete a form by selecting the form name in the *Navigation Pane* and clicking the **Delete** button [*Home* tab, *Records* group].

> **ANOTHER WAY**
>
> Right-click the form name in the *Navigation Pane* and select **Delete** from the context menu.

PAUSE & PRACTICE: ACCESS 4-1

For this Pause & Practice, you create three versions of a form using three quick creation methods. You create a form using the *Form Wizard*, the *Form* button, and the *Split Form* button.

File Needed: **PlacerHills-04.accdb**
Completed Project File Name: **[your initials] PP A4-1.accdb**

1. Open the **PlacerHills-04** database from your student data files.

2. Save a new copy of the database as [your initials] PP A4-1.

3. Enable content in the database.

4. Create a form using the *Form Wizard*.
 a. Click the **Create** tab on the *Ribbon*.
 b. Click the **Form Wizard** button in the *Forms* group to launch the *Form Wizard*.
 c. Click the **Tables/Queries** drop-down arrow and select the **Listings** table.
 d. Click the **Move All Fields** button to move all of the fields from the *Available Fields* window to the *Selected Fields* window (Figure 4-21).
 e. Click the **Next** button to move to the second page of the *Form Wizard*.
 f. Select the **Columnar** radio button if necessary.

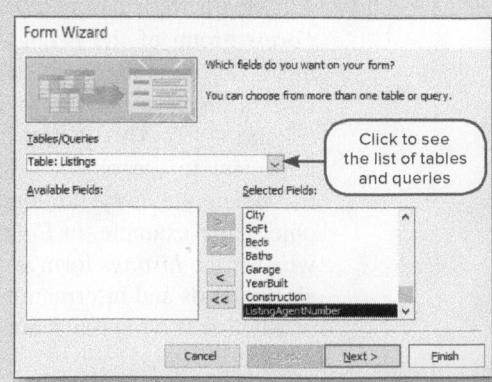

4-21 Move desired fields into the *Selected Fields* window

g. Click the **Next** button to move to the last page of the *Form Wizard*.
h. Type Listings – Form Wizard in the *Title* box.
i. Click the **Finish** button. The form opens in *Form* view (Figure 4-22).
j. Use the navigation buttons to move among records.
k. Close the form.

5. Create a form using the *Form* button.
 a. In the *Navigation Pane*, click to select the **Listings** table.
 b. Click the **Form** button [*Create* tab, *Forms* group] to create the form shown in Figure 4-23. Your layout may be different depending on the size of the Access window when you created the form.
 c. Click to select the **Listings** label in the *Header* section.
 d. Click inside the label to open the edit mode.
 e. Edit the label to read Listings – Form Button.
 f. Save the form. Enter Listings – Form Button as the *Form Name*.
 g. Switch to *Form* view by clicking the **View** button [*Form Layout Tools Design* tab, *Views* group] and selecting **Form View**.
 h. Use the navigation buttons to move among records.
 i. Close the form.

6. Create a form using the *Split Form* button.
 a. In the *Navigation Pane*, click to select the **Listings** table.
 b. Click the **More Forms** button [*Create* tab, *Forms* group] and select **Split Form** to create the form shown in Figure 4-24.
 c. Click to select the **Listings** label in the *Header* section.
 d. Click inside the label to open the edit mode.
 e. Edit the label to read Listings – Split Form.
 f. Save the form. Enter Listings – Split Form as the *Form Name*.
 g. Switch to *Form* view by clicking the **View** button [*Form Layout Tools Design* tab, *Views* group] and selecting **Form View**.
 h. Use the navigation buttons to move among records. Notice that as you change records, the selected record displays in the top section and is also highlighted in the *Datasheet* view in the lower section.
 i. Close the form.

7. Close the database.

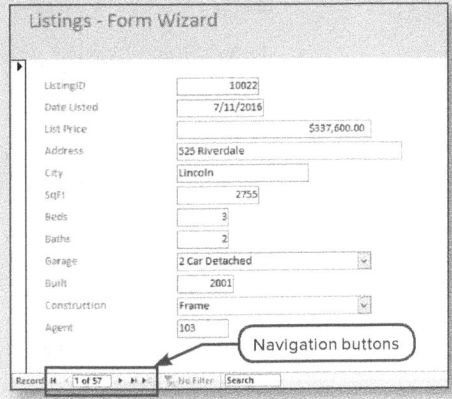

4-22 *Listings* form created using the *Form Wizard*

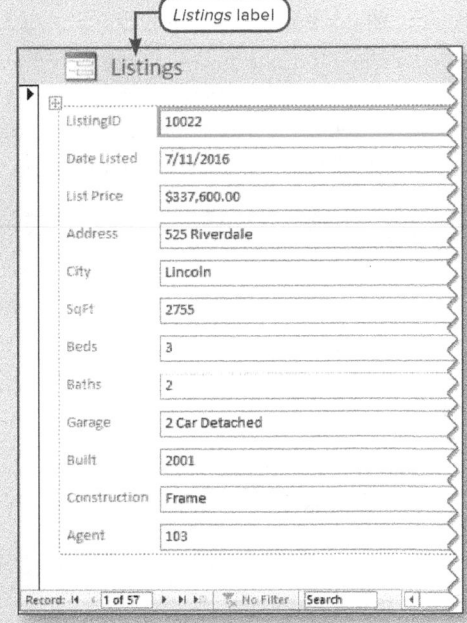

4-23 *Listings* form created using the *Form* button

4-24 *Listings* form created using *Split Form*

A4-220

| SLO 4.2 | **Creating and Customizing a Form in Layout View** |

As you have learned, *Layout* view provides an easy way to modify a form while seeing how the form looks with data displaying. The functions of the form do not work in *Layout* view. However, you can use the navigation buttons to move among different records. In this section, you first learn how to create a blank form. After that, you explore the layout of a form and learn how to make modifications using *Layout* view.

Create a Form Using the Blank Form Button

Sometimes it is easier to start with a completely blank form and add the fields, labels, or buttons that you need directly onto the form.

▶ HOW TO: Create a Blank Form

1. Click the **Blank Form** button [*Create* tab, *Forms* group].
 - A new blank form opens in *Layout* view (Figure 4-25).
 - The *Field List* pane displays. The *Field List* contains the list of the tables in your database.
2. Click the **Show all tables** link to display the database tables.
3. Click the **plus sign** to the left of a table name to see the fields in the table (Figure 4-26).

4-25 Blank form in *Layout* view 4-26 Expanded *Field List*

4. Click the **minus sign** to the left of a table name to collapse the list of fields in the table.

After you create the blank form, you are ready to start adding items onto the form. Remember to save the form and any changes you make to it.

Form Controls

In Access, the fields, labels, buttons, and so forth are all known as **controls**. You can add controls to a form in either *Layout* view or *Design* view.

The controls are located in the *Controls* group of the *Form Layout Tools Design* tab. The controls available in *Layout* view are shown in Figure 4-27.

Text box

Label Button Check box

4-27 *Controls* group for a form

Some controls are ***bound*** to a data source, like a text box that gets its value from a field in a table. Some controls are ***unbound***, which means that they are not linked to a data source. For example, a label on a form that contains a form title is an unbound control. Finally, some controls are *calculated*. For example, a text box that gets its value from an expression is a calculated control. The most common controls and their usage are described in the following table:

Common Form Controls

Control	Explanation
Text box	Used to display data on a form or to accept data from a user when entering a value.
Label	Displays the content contained in its caption property. Does not accept any input from the user. You can edit the wording in a label on the form.
Button	Used to add a command button that performs an action such as *Close Form*, *Open Form*, *Delete Record*, etc.
Check box	Used to display or accept data for a field with a *Yes/No* data type.

As you read this book you will learn more about these controls and how they are used in a database.

Form Control Layouts

Control layouts provide a structure that helps to align the different controls on your form. This gives your form a more uniform appearance. Forms are not required to include a control layout, although some of the form creation methods place all fields in a control layout by default. The two primary control layout options are tabular and stacked:

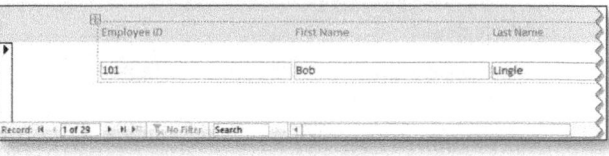

- ***Tabular***: The layout organizes data in rows and columns. Labels identifying the different fields are above the data values. Figure 4-28 shows a tabular layout in *Layout* view. The tabular layout starts with each field having a fairly large column width. This can make it difficult to see all the fields on the screen at one time.

4-28 Tabular control layout

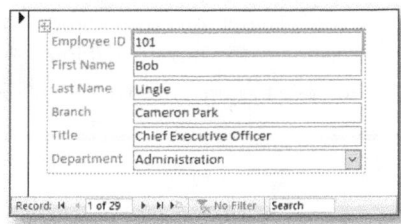

- ***Stacked***: The layout organizes data vertically. The labels are to the left of the data control. Figure 4-29 shows a stacked layout in *Layout* view.

4-29 Stacked control layout

Add Fields to a Control Layout

When a new blank form is created, no controls appear on the form. You can add any desired table fields to the form in *Layout* view.

▶ **HOW TO:** Add Fields into the Control Layout of a Blank Form

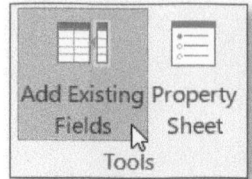

4-30 *Add Existing Fields* button

1. Open the form in *Layout* view.

2. Click the **Add Existing Fields** button [*Form Layout Tools Design* tab, *Tools* group] if the *Field List* is not open (Figure 4-30).

 ▶ **ANOTHER WAY**

 Press **Alt+F8** to show or hide the *Field List*.

3. Click the **Show all tables** link if the database tables do not show.

4. Click the **plus sign** next to the desired table name to display the fields.

5. Double-click the desired field name.

 4-31 **Add fields into a stacked layout of a blank form**

 • The field is added into a stacked layout (Figure 4-31).
 • The most recently added field is highlighted with an orange border.
 • The next field added to the form appears below the orange-bordered field.

6. Continue adding the remaining fields.

 ▶ **ANOTHER WAY**

 Click and drag a field from the *Field List* into the form window to add it into the control layout.

▶ **HOW TO:** Add Fields between Existing Fields in a Control Layout

1. Open the form in *Layout* view.

2. Click the **Add Existing Fields** button [*Form Layout Tools Design* tab, *Tools* group] or press **Alt+F8** if the *Field List* is not open.

3. Click the **plus sign** next to the desired table name to display the fields.

4. Select the desired field name to add to the form. The field is highlighted in rose.

5. Drag the field to the desired location in the control layout. A rose-colored line indicates the position of the new field (Figure 4-32).

 4-32 **Drag a field to the desired location**

6. Release the pointer to add the field.

Delete Fields from a Control Layout

As you saw in *SLO 4.1: Creating and Working with a Simple Form*, if you use the *Form* button to create a form, all table fields are automatically added to the control layout of the form. However, you may not want to keep all of the fields on the form. Although they are added together, the text box and the label are two separate controls associated with a field. If you select and delete the

text box, the label is automatically deleted. However, if you only select and delete the label, the text box control remains on the form. Additionally, deleting a label or text box control does not automatically delete the row or column that contains the control from the control layout.

▶ HOW TO: Delete a Field from a Control Layout

1. Open the form in *Layout* view.
2. Select the **text box control** of the field to delete.
3. Right-click to open the context menu.
4. Select the desired delete option (Figure 4-33). The choices work differently depending on the control layout.

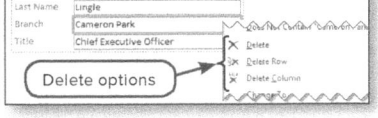

4-33 Context menu to delete a field

 - In a stacked layout, select **Delete** to delete both the text box and label, but you keep the empty row in the control layout.
 - In a stacked layout, select **Delete Row** to delete the text box, label, and row containing the controls.
 - In a tabular layout, select **Delete** to delete the text box, but the label and column are not deleted.
 - In a tabular layout, select **Delete Column** to delete the text box, label, and column containing the controls.

Customize a Form in Layout View

There are many ways to modify a form in *Layout* view. In this section, you learn how to change control layouts, adjust control widths and heights, add and delete rows and columns in a control layout, and add a title and date to a form.

These options are available through the buttons in the *Table* and *Rows & Columns* groups on the *Form Layout Tools Arrange* tab (Figure 4-34).

4-34 Customize a form layout using options in the *Table* and *Rows & Columns* groups

Change Control Layouts

When you create a form using one of the quick create options, the form starts with either a stacked or tabular layout. As you add and delete fields on the form, you may wish to change its layout.

▶ HOW TO: Change Control Layouts

1. Open the form in *Layout* view.
2. Select one of the fields in the control layout. The orange border surrounds the selected field.
3. Click the **Select Layout** button [*Form Layout Tools Arrange* tab, *Rows & Columns* group]. The orange border surrounds all of the controls in the layout.
4. Select either the **Stacked** or **Tabular** button [*Form Layout Tools Arrange* tab, *Table* group]. The form updates to show the new layout.

Adjust Control Widths and Heights

Often, the initial width of the form fields is much larger than needed. Keep in mind that in a stacked layout, all of the fields have the same width. That means that when you change the width you need to ensure that the column is wide enough to fit the largest field.

> **HOW TO: Change Field Column Widths**

1. Open the form in *Layout* view.
2. Select the **text box control** of the desired field in the control layout. The orange border surrounds the selected field.
3. Place your pointer over the right edge of the text box until it changes to the resize arrow.
4. Click, hold, and drag the **resize arrow** to increase or decrease the width of the text box.
 - The field(s) update to show the new width.
 - In a stacked layout, all fields change together to maintain the same width (Figure 4-35a).
 - In a tabular layout, you can set the width of each field individually (Figure 4-35b).

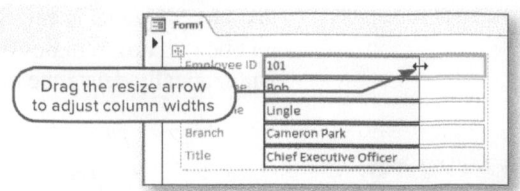

4-35a Adjust the width of all fields in a stacked layout

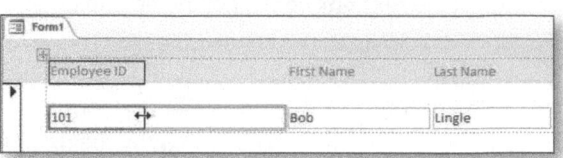

4-35b Adjust the width of a single field in a tabular layout

Change the height of a field using a very similar process. After you select the control, place your pointer over the lower edge of the control. Click, hold and drag the **resize arrow** up or down to adjust the height. If you have a stacked layout, you can set the height of each field individually. However, in a tabular layout, all fields change together to maintain the same the height.

These same instructions can be used to change the width or height of many other controls, like labels and command buttons.

You can also change the width or height of a control on the *Format* tab of the *Property Sheet*. This allows you to enter a precise value. Select the control and click the **Property Sheet** button [*Form Layout Tools Design* tab, *Tools* group]. Enter the value in the *Width* or *Height* property box on the *Format* tab (Figure 4-36). You must press **Enter** or **Tab** after entering the value so that Access recognizes a changed value.

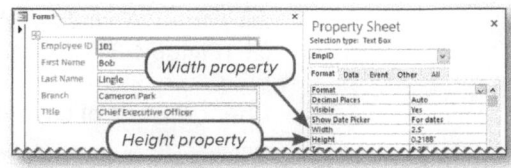

4-36 Adjust the width and height in the *Property Sheet*

Add and Delete Rows and Columns in a Control Layout

Often you want to make minor modifications to the control layout. For example, you may want to create a second column in a stacked layout, or you may want to delete a row if you removed fields from the control layout.

> **HOW TO: Add a Column to a Control Layout**

1. Open the form in *Layout* view.
2. Select a control in the column adjacent to the place where you want to add a new column.
3. Click the **Select Column** button [*Form Layout Tools Arrange* tab, *Rows & Columns* group].
4. Click the **Insert Left** or **Insert Right** button [*Form Layout Tools Arrange* tab, *Rows & Columns* group].
 - The new column is added to the control layout (Figure 4-37).
 - A light gray, dotted border surrounds each cell in the added column.

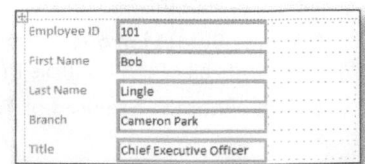

4-37 A dotted border surrounds each cell in the added column

▶ HOW TO: Add a Row to a Control Layout

1. Open the form in *Layout* view.
2. Select a control in the row adjacent to the place where you want to add a new row.
3. Click the **Select Row** button [*Form Layout Tools Arrange* tab, *Rows & Columns* group].
4. Click the **Insert Above** or **Insert Below** button [*Form Layout Tools Arrange* tab, *Rows & Columns* group].
 - The new row is added to the control layout (Figure 4-38).
 - A light gray, dotted border surrounds each cell in the added row.

4-38 A dotted border surrounds each cell in the added row

▶ HOW TO: Delete a Row or Column from a Control Layout

1. Open the form in *Layout* view.
2. Select a control in the row or column you wish to delete.
3. Click the **Select Row** or **Select Column** button [*Form Layout Tools Arrange* tab, *Rows & Columns* group].
4. Right-click to open the context menu.
5. Select **Delete Row** or **Delete Column** (Figure 4-39).

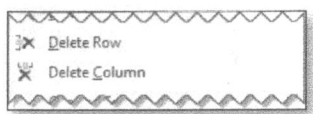

4-39 Delete options in the context menu

Move a Control within a Layout

As you make a modification to the control layout you may want to move a control from one part of the layout to another.

▶ HOW TO: Move a Control within a Layout

1. Open the form in *Layout* view.
2. Select the control that you wish to move. The orange border surrounds that control and the pointer changes to the move arrow.
3. Click the control, hold, and drag the control to the new location. A rose color highlights the destination cell (Figure 4-40).

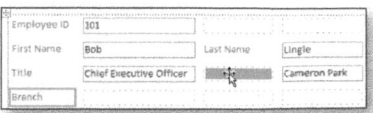

4-40 Drag a control to a new location in the form layout

> ▶ **ANOTHER WAY**
>
> Select multiple controls by pressing and holding **Shift** when you select controls.

Add a Title, Date, and Logo to a Form

It is good design practice to title each form. This helps identify the form for the user. You can also display the current date and add a logo to forms. These controls can be added to a form from the *Header/Footer* group [*Form Layout Tools Design* tab] (Figure 4-41). If the form

does not already contain a **header section**, adding any of these items automatically adds a header section to the form.

Selecting either the *Logo* or the *Title* buttons adds two controls into the header section: an **Auto_Header** control which contains the title and an **Auto_Logo** control which contains the logo.

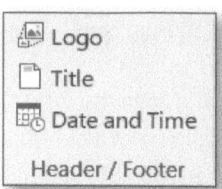

4-41 *Header/Footer* group options

> ▶ **HOW TO:** Add a Title, Date, or Logo to a Form in Layout View

1. Open the form in *Layout* view.

2. Click the **Title** button [*Form Layout Tools Design* tab, *Header/Footer* group] to add a title to the form. The title is set to the form name.

3. Click the **Date and Time** button [*Form Layout Tools Design* tab, *Header/Footer* group] to add the *Date* and/or *Time* into the header section of the form. The *Date and Time* dialog box displays (Figure 4-42).

4. Select the check boxes and radio buttons corresponding to your choices.

5. Click **OK**.

6. Click the **Logo** button [*Form Layout Tools Design* tab, *Header/Footer* group] to add a logo to the form. The *Insert Picture* dialog box displays.

7. Select the image file to use as the logo and click **OK**.

8. Click the **Auto_Header** control and edit the contents to change the title of the form (Figure 4-43).

 - In Figure 4-43, the *Date* control is selected. Notice that the width of the control overlaps onto the *Auto_Header* control.
 - If necessary, you may need to adjust the width or location of these controls.

4-42 *Date and Time* dialog box

4-43 **Controls in the header section**

> **SLO 4.3**

Facilitating Data Input with a Form

Forms allow you to view, change, or delete data already in a database or to add new data into a database. Sometimes you use a form for all these purposes, but at other times you may want to create a single purpose form. When using a form for data entry, it is important to design it to help minimize potential data entry mistakes as well as to make the data entry efficient. Use the *Property Sheet* of the form to select the desired settings to limit actions available in a form (Figure 4-44).

The following form properties control actions available in a form:

- **Data Entry**: Determines whether a form is restricted to data entry. The default setting is "No".

4-44 **Properties to limit actions available in a form**

- *Allow Additions*: Determines whether a user can use the form to add data into the database. The default setting is "Yes".
- *Allow Deletions*: Determines whether a user can use the form to delete a record from the database. The default setting is "Yes".
- *Allow Edits*: Determines whether a user can use the form to change values in a record in the database. The default setting is "Yes".

Restrict a Form to Data Entry

Restrict a form to only allow data entry when you don't want users to have access to all the data records that exist in the database. This allows you to limit some activities to authorized users. Additionally, this feature can prevent users from accidentally changing or deleting existing records in the table.

▶ **HOW TO:** Restrict a Form to Data Entry

1. Open the form in *Layout* view.
2. Click the **Property Sheet** button [*Form Layout Tools Design* tab, *Tools* group].

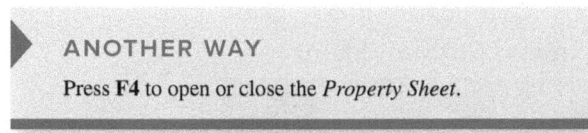

> ▶ ANOTHER WAY
> Press **F4** to open or close the *Property Sheet*.

3. Click the **drop-down arrow** in the *Selection* box of the *Property Sheet* and select **Form**.
4. Click to select the **Data** tab of the *Property Sheet* if necessary.
5. Select **Yes** in the **Data Entry** property box to restrict the form to data entry.
6. Select **Yes** in the **Allow Additions** property box.

A form that has been restricted to data entry does not show any existing records when viewed. This means that a user cannot delete or edit records. As a result, the settings in the *Allow Deletions* and *Allow Edits* property boxes don't have an impact.

Limit Edits and Deletions on a Form

Sometimes you want users to be able to view existing records in a database but not to be able to edit or delete them. You can establish these limits through the *Property Sheet*.

▶ **HOW TO:** Limit Edits and Deletions on a Form

1. Open the form in *Layout* view.
2. Click the **Property Sheet** button [*Form Layout Tools Design* tab, *Tools* group] to open the *Property Sheet*.
3. Click the **drop-down arrow** in the *Selection* box of the *Property Sheet* and select **Form**.
4. Select **No** in the *Data Entry* property box. The additional property selections you make in step 5 determine how users can access and change the data currently in the database.

5. Set the desired form properties.
 - Select **Yes** or **No** in the *Allow Additions* property box. If set to *Yes*, this will override the *Data Entry* property and allow records to be added into the database.
 - Select **Yes** or **No** in the *Allow Deletions* property box.
 - Select **Yes** or **No** in the *Allow Edits* property box.

Add a Command Button

A *command button* is a type of control that can perform a number of different actions. For example, command buttons can be set to print the current form, close the current form, navigate to the next record, or open another form. Buttons make a form more user-friendly.

The quickest way to add a command button to a form is to use the *Command Button Wizard*. The **Command Button Wizard** creates a button and attaches all of the necessary functionality to the button. The functionality is contained in a *Macro* and is attached to the **On Click** property of the button. Recall that a **Macro** is a database object that allows you to write and attach code to different objects and controls in your database.

The *Command Button Wizard* groups the available functionality into six different categories. Those categories and the available actions are shown in the following table:

Groupings of Categories and Actions in the Command Button Wizard

Category	Actions
Record Navigation	*Find Next* *Find Record* *Go To First Record* *Go To Last Record* *Go To Next Record* *Go To Previous Record*
Record Operations	*Add New Record* *Delete Record* *Duplicate Record* *Print Record* *Save Record* *Undo Record*
Form Operations	*Apply Form Filter* *Close Form* *Open Form* *Print a Form* *Print Current Form* *Refresh Form Data*
Report Operations	*Mail Report* *Open Report* *Preview Report* *Print Report* *Send Report to File*
Application	*Quit Application*
Miscellaneous	*Auto Dialer* *Print Table* *Run Macro* *Run Query*

The *Command Button Wizard* does not launch unless you first turn on the *Control Wizards* tool. The **Control Wizards** tool directs Access to launch an available wizard when adding controls to an object.

The *Control Wizards* tool uses an on-off setting. If the icon is rose-colored, the *Control Wizards* are on; if the icon is white, the *Control Wizards* are off.

> ▶ **HOW TO:** Add a Command Button Using the Command Button Wizard

1. Open the form in *Layout* view.
2. Click the **Design** tab.
3. Click the **More** arrow at the far right of the *Controls* group (Figure 4-45) to expand the *Controls* group. If the *Use Control Wizards* button does not have a rose-colored background, select the **Use Control Wizards** button to turn on the wizard (Figure 4-46).

4-45 *Controls* group

4-46 *Use Control Wizards* button

4. Click **Button** in the *Controls* group. Move the pointer to the desired location in the control layout and click the cell (Figure 4-47) to launch the *Command Button Wizard* (Figure 4-48).

 - If the *Command Button Wizard* does not launch, *Control Wizards* is not turned on.
 - Delete the button that was placed on the form.
 - Repeat step 3 to turn the *Control Wizards* on.
 - Repeat step 4 to add a button.

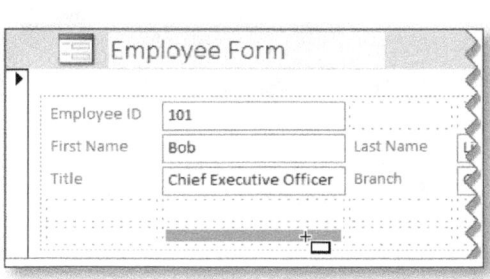

4-47 Position the button control onto the form

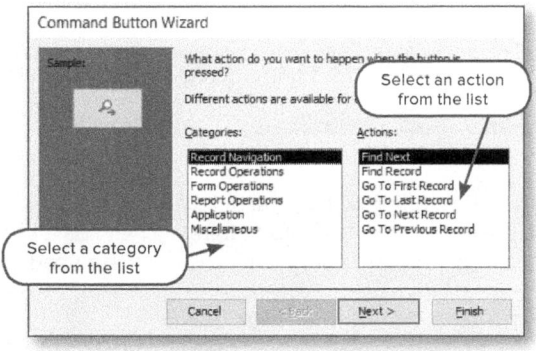

4-48 *Command Button Wizard*, page 1

5. Select a **Category** and **Action** for the button.
6. Click **Next** to move to the second page of the *Command Button Wizard*.
7. Choose whether you want the button to display words or an image (Figure 4-49).
8. Click **Next** to move to the last page of the wizard.
9. Enter a name for the button and click **Finish**.

 - The button name is important if you are going to modify the macro code attached to the button.

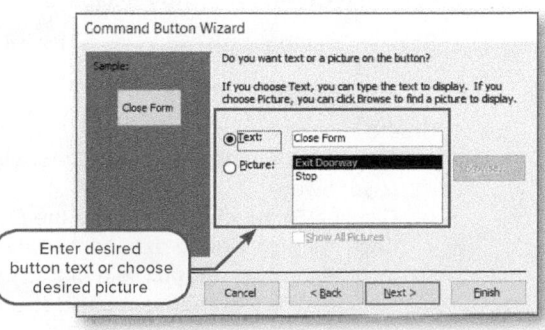

4-49 *Command Button Wizard*, page 2

- You may want the name to reference the form name and button action. For example, *EmployeeForm-CloseButton*.
- The button displays in the form (Figure 4-50).

4-50 Completed button displays on the form

Test a Form

After you have built your form, it is important to switch to *Form* view and test the functionality of the form. You may have forgotten to add or delete a field on the form or you may want to change the text in a label to make it more user-friendly. You may also realize that you selected the wrong action to assign to a button.

Switch to *Form* view by clicking the **Views** button [*Form Layout Tools Design* tab] and selecting **Form View**. If you are in *Design* view, you can also press **F5** to switch to *Form* view.
Test the functionality of the form by performing the following tasks:

- Navigate through several records ensuring that the width of the fields is appropriate.
- Review the overall layout to ensure that the structure is easy-to-use and intuitive for the user.
- Test all buttons to ensure they behave as expected.
- Make any needed corrections and re-test as appropriate.

PAUSE & PRACTICE: ACCESS 4-2

For this Pause & Practice, you build a form using the *Blank Form* button for the Central Sierra Insurance database. You modify the form to restrict it to data entry, add buttons, and test the form. This database contains an existing query and report that are used later in the chapter.

File Needed: ***CentralSierra-04.accdb***
Completed Project File Name: ***[your initials] PP A4-2.accdb***

1. Open the ***CentralSierra-04*** database from your student data files.

2. Save the database as [your initials] PP A4-2.

3. Enable content in the database.

4. Create a new form using the *Blank Form* button.
 a. Click the **Blank Form** button [*Create* tab, *Forms* group]. A new blank form opens in *Layout* view.
 b. Cick the **Show all tables** link in the *Field List* pane.
 c. Click the **plus sign** to expand the *Employees* table to see the fields in the table.
 d. Double-click the **EmpID** field to add it to the form.
 e. Double-click the **FirstName** field to add it to the form.

f. Continue adding all the fields from the *Employees* table into the form.

g. Close the *Field List*. The form should be similar to Figure 4-51.

5. Modify the control layout.
 a. Click one of the fields on the form. An orange border surrounds it.
 b. Click the **Select Layout** button [*Form Layout Tools Arrange* tab, *Rows & Columns* group]. All the cells in the layout are bordered in orange.
 c. Place your pointer over any field. Click, hold, and drag the control layout down and to the right (Figure 4-52), and then release the pointer.
 d. Select the **Base Monthly Salary** label.
 e. Place your pointer over the right edge of the label until it becomes the resize arrow.
 f. Click, hold, and drag the **resize arrow** to increase the width of the label to make the entire caption visible.
 g. Navigate to record number 10. This record contains the employee with the longest title.
 h. Click the **Title** text box. Remember that the text box control displays the actual data. In this form, the text boxes are located to the right of the label.
 i. Decrease the width of the text box to remove the excess space.

6. Add a new column and new rows to the control layout.
 a. Select the **Base Monthly Salary** text box.
 b. Click the **Select Row** button [*Form Layout Tools Arrange* tab, *Rows & Columns* group].
 c. Click the **Insert Below** button [*Form Layout Tools Arrange* tab, *Rows & Columns* group] to add a blank row.
 d. Click the **Insert Below** button again to add a second blank row.
 e. Select the **Base Monthly Salary** text box.
 f. Click the **Select Column** button [*Form Layout Tools Arrange* tab, *Rows & Columns* group].
 g. Click the **Insert Right** button [*Form Layout Tools Arrange* tab, *Rows & Columns* group] to add a blank column.

7. Adjust the height and width of the new column and rows.
 a. Select a cell in the new column.
 b. Place your pointer over the right edge of the cell until it becomes the resize arrow.
 c. Click, hold, and drag the **resize arrow** to increase the width of the cell. Make the width approximately the same as the first column.
 d. Select a cell in the bottom blank row.
 e. Place your pointer over the bottom edge of the cell until it becomes the resize arrow.
 f. Click, hold, and drag the **resize arrow** to increase the height of the cell. Make the height approximately twice as high as any other row. The completed form should look similar to Figure 4-53.

4-51 Employee form after adding all fields

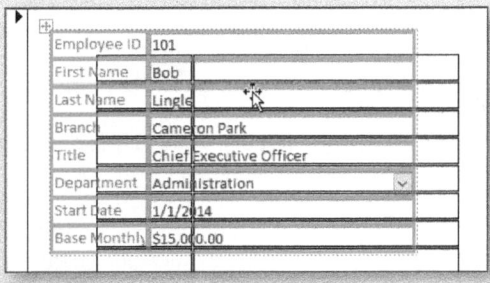

4-52 Drag the control layout to a new location

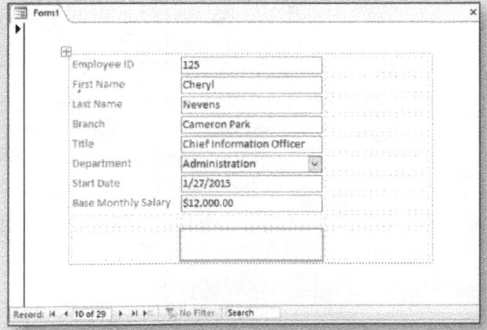

4-53 Employee form after adding and modifying rows and columns

8. Add command buttons to the form.
 a. Click the **Form Layout Tools Design** tab.
 b. Click the **More** arrow on the far right of the *Controls* group and select the **Use Control Wizards** button if it does not already have a rose-colored border indicating it is selected.
 c. Click **Button** in the *Controls* group. Click the left-most cell in the bottom row to launch the *Command Button Wizard*. If the *Command Button Wizard* does not launch, *Control Wizards* is not turned on. Delete the button that was added to the form and go back to step 8b.
 d. Select the **Record Operations** *Category* and the **Save Record** *Action* of the button.
 e. Click **Next** to move to the second page of the *Command Button Wizard*.
 f. Select the **Text** radio button and change the wording to read Save Employee Record.
 g. Click **Next** to move to the last page of the wizard.
 h. Enter AddEmpForm-SaveButton as the name for the button and click **Finish**. The button displays in the form (Figure 4-54). The text in the button wraps depending on the width of the column.

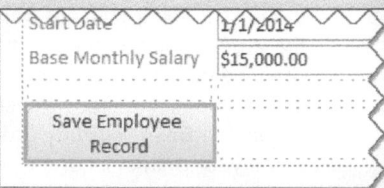

4-54 Button added to form

 i. Add a second button to the form. Place the button in the middle cell of the last row.
 j. Select the **Record Operations** *Category* and the **Add New Record** *Action* of the button.
 k. Click **Next** to move to the second page of the *Command Button Wizard*.
 l. Select the **Text** radio button and change the wording to read Add New Employee.
 m. Click **Next** to move to the last page of the wizard.
 n. Enter AddEmpForm-AddButton as the name for the button and click **Finish**.
 o. Add a third button to the form. Place the button in the right-most cell of the last row.
 p. Select the **Form Operations** *Category* and the **Close Form** *Action* of the button.
 q. Click **Next** to move to the second page of the wizard.
 r. Select the **Text** radio button and accept the existing wording of "Close Form."
 s. Click **Next** to move to the last page of the wizard.
 t. Enter AddEmpForm-CloseButton as the name for the button and click **Finish**.

9. Add a title to the form.
 a. Click the **Form Layout Tools Design** tab.
 b. Click the **Title** button [*Header/Footer* group].
 c. Change the wording to read Add New Employee. The form should look similar to Figure 4-55.

10. Restrict the form to data entry.
 a. Click the **Property Sheet** button [*Form Layout Tools Design* tab, *Tools* group] to open the *Property Sheet*.
 b. Click the **drop-down arrow** in the *Selection* box of the *Property Sheet* and select **Form**.
 c. Click to select the **Data** tab if necessary.
 d. Select **Yes** in the *Data Entry* property box.
 e. Select **Yes** in the *Allow Additions* property box if necessary.
 f. Close the *Property Sheet*.

4-55 Completed form after adding a title and three buttons

11. Save the form. Enter AddNewEmployee as the *Form Name*.

12. Switch to *Form* view by clicking the **View** button [*Form Layout Tools Design* tab, *Views* group] and selecting **Form View**. The complete form displays.

13. Test the form.
 a. Enter the data shown in Figure 4-56.
 b. Click the **Save Employee Record** button.
 c. Click the **Add New Employee** button. A blank record should display in the form. In the *Navigation* bar, you can navigate back to the record you just entered, but you cannot view any other records in the table since the form is restricted to data entry.
 d. Click the **Close Form** button.

14. Double-click the **Employees** table to open it in *Datasheet* view.

15. Scroll down to find the new record you added into the database.

16. Close the table.

17. Close the database.

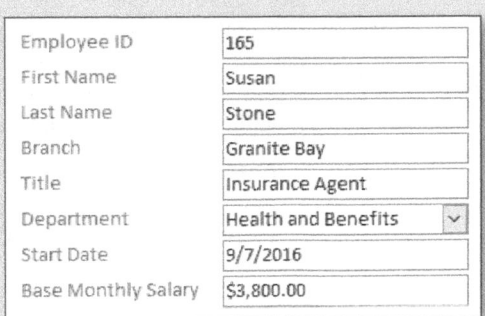

Employee ID	165
First Name	Susan
Last Name	Stone
Branch	Granite Bay
Title	Insurance Agent
Department	Health and Benefits
Start Date	9/7/2016
Base Monthly Salary	$3,800.00

4-56 Employee record values to enter in form

SLO 4.4

Creating and Working with a Simple Report

A *report* is an object you can use to create an organized and professional output of the data in a database. Unlike forms, reports do *not* allow you to modify the underlying data. The reports in your database are directly connected to a table or query, the source of the data.

In Chapter 2, you learned how to print the data records in a table. Reports provide a great deal more flexibility for viewing and printing the data in a database. A report can have fields from one or more tables or queries. Similar to a form, you select which fields from the tables or queries to include on the report. You also can select grouping and summarizing options when you are choosing how to display your records. This flexibility helps you create reports that look professional, in addition to being more user-friendly than *Datasheet* view of a table. Ideally, a well-designed report makes it easier for the user to understand the information contained in the database.

Creating reports is similar to creating forms. You can apply much of what you already learned about creating forms as you learn to create reports. Access provides several different ways to create a report. There are quick ways to create a report and some that take a little more effort but provide a great deal more flexibility when it comes to report design and specialization. In this section, you are introduced to two ways to build a report: the *Report Wizard* and the *Blank Report* options. These options are available in the *Reports* group [*Create* tab] (Figure 4-57).

4-57 Report creation options

The Report Wizard

The **Report Wizard** steps you through the process of quickly creating a report. While you will probably need to fine-tune the initial report design, it provides a good starting point. The *Report Wizard* asks you which tables and queries you want to base the report on and which specific fields you want to include in the report. Additionally, you must determine if you

want to group the data by any fields, sort on any fields, and choose the layout and orientation of the report. Your layout choices change based on whether you group the data or not.

The three layout choices for reports without grouping are columnar, tabular, and justified:

- *Columnar*: The layout displays the fields in one column (Figure 4-58). The field labels appear to the left of the data.
- *Tabular*: The layout displays the fields in a table (row and column) format. The field names display above the data (Figure 4-59).

4-58 Columnar report layout

4-59 Tabular report layout

- *Justified*: The layout displays the fields in a horizontal, justified layout (Figure 4-60). The field names display above each field.

4-60 Justified report layout

Grouping is useful when you want to organize and summarize the data in your report. For example, you could group all properties from the same city together or you could group all the songs from a particular artist together. The three layout choices for a grouped report are stepped, block, and outline:

- *Stepped*: The layout displays the fields in a table layout (Figure 4-61). The field names display in a row above the data. If the report is longer than one page, the field names appear at the top of each page. The grouped field displays in the left-most column. The data value appears in its own row at the start of each new grouping.

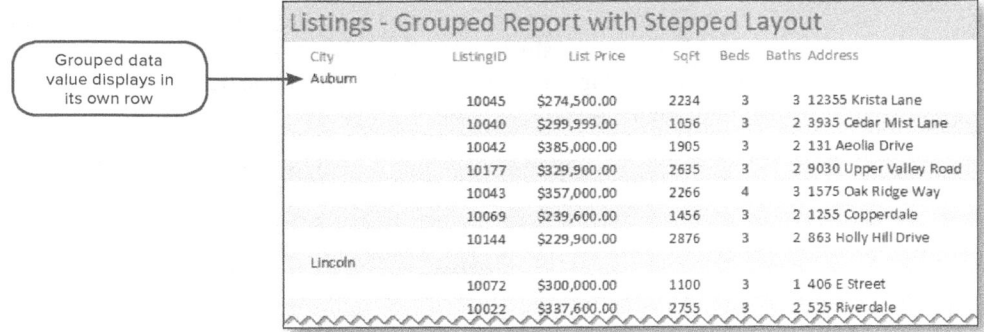

4-61 Stepped layout in a grouped report

- **Block**: The layout is very similar to a stepped layout; it has a table layout and field names at the top. The major difference is that the grouped field appears in the same row as the first record for that grouping (Figure 4-62). If the report is longer than one page, the field names appear at the top of each page. Additionally, the data rows are grouped a little more tightly together, meaning that more data can appear on each page.

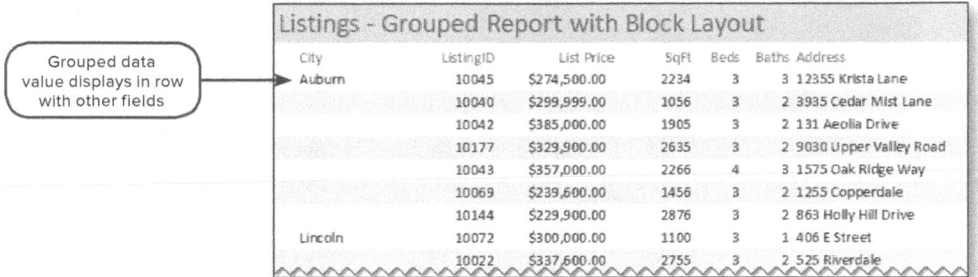

4-62 Block layout in a grouped report

- **Outline**: The layout displays the grouped field and its label on a separate row at the start of each new grouping (Figure 4-63). The field names display above the first row of data in each grouping.

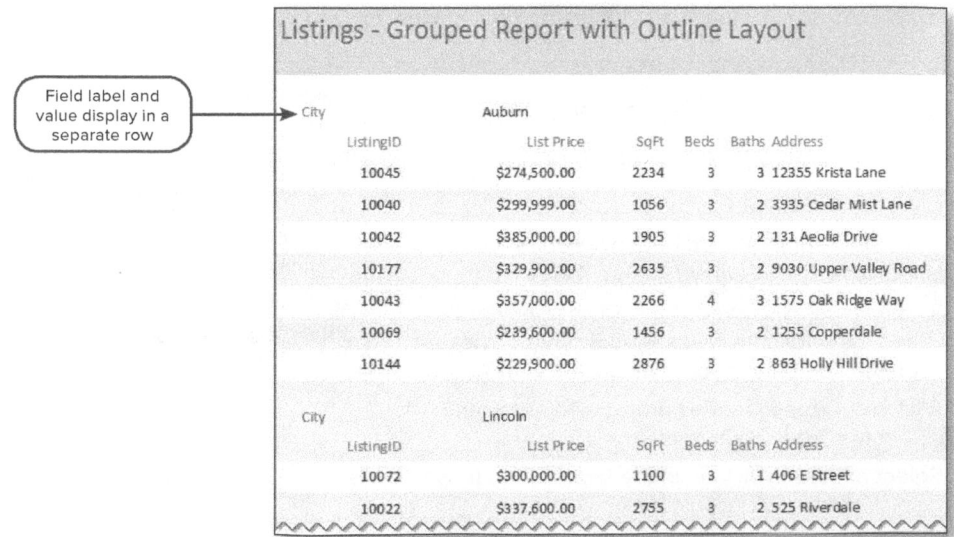

4-63 Outline layout in a grouped report

With grouped reports, you also have the option to have Access automatically calculate various summary values across the different groups. You can decide to display only the summary values (Figure 4-64) or to display both the detail records and summary values for each group (Figure 4-65).

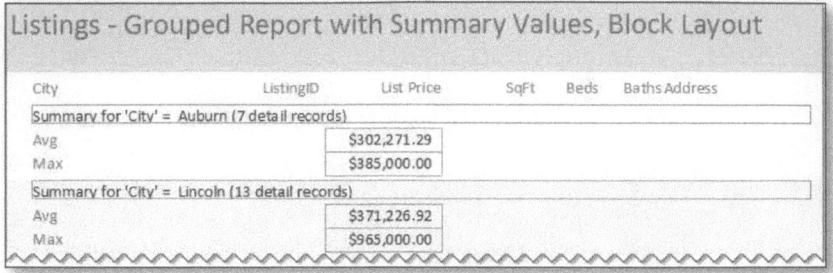

4-64 Grouped report with summary values only

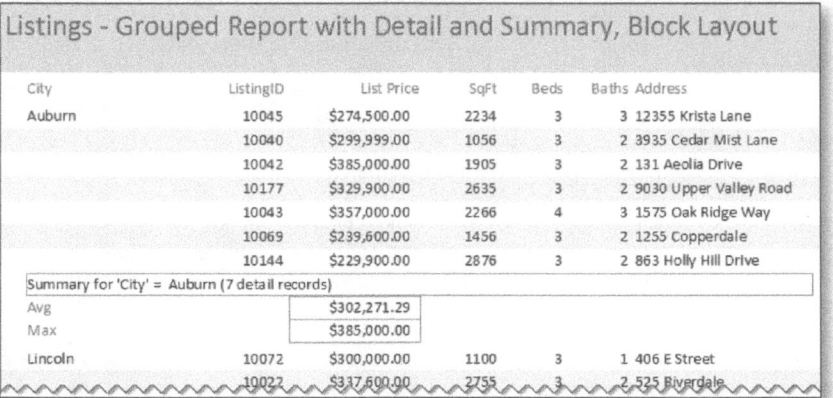

4-65 Grouped report with detail and summary values

After you have created a report using the *Report Wizard*, you can preview the report or open it in *Design* view to modify the layout. If you need to make changes to the report later, you can edit it using *Layout* view or *Design* view.

▶ **HOW TO:** Create a Report Using the Report Wizard

1. Click the **Create** tab on the *Ribbon*.
2. Click the **Report Wizard** button [*Reports* group] to launch the *Report Wizard* (Figure 4-66).
 - The values displayed in the *Tables/Queries* box and the *Available Fields* window change based on the contents of your database.
3. Click the **Tables/Queries** drop-down arrow and select the *Table* or *Query* name.
4. Select a **Field** to include in the *Report* from those displayed in the *Available Fields* window.
 - Add fields in the order you want them to display in the report.

4-66 *Report Wizard*, step 1

5. Click the **Move Single Field** button.
 - The field moves into the *Selected Fields* window.
 - The *Remove Single Field* and *Remove All Fields* buttons become active.
6. Continue moving all required fields (Figure 4-67), changing the selected *Table* or *Query* if needed.

4-67 Move fields into the *Selected Fields* window

> ▶ **ANOTHER WAY**
>
> Use the **Move All Fields** button to quickly include all of the fields in the report.

7. Click the **Next** button when you are done adding all fields. The second page of the *Report Wizard* displays (Figure 4-68).
8. Select any fields you want to use to group the data.
 - When you select fields on which to group, Access moves those fields to the left-most columns of the report.
9. Click the **Next** button. The next page of the *Report Wizard* displays (Figure 4-69).

4-68 Select grouping levels

4-69 Select sorting and summary options

10. Select any fields you want to use to sort the report and select either **Ascending** *or* **Descending** sort order.
 - The *Summary Options* button only displays if you added grouping levels in step 8.
 - Click the **Summary Options** button to open the *Summary Options* dialog box, select the fields to calculate and choose the desired functions. You can choose from the *Sum*, *Avg*, *Min*, and *Max* functions. You can also choose whether to display only summary values or both detail and summary values.
11. Click the **Next** button. The next page of the *Report Wizard* displays (Figure 4-70).
12. Select the desired layout and orientation. If you added grouping levels, the layout choices change to *Stepped*, *Block* and *Outline*.

4-70 Select layout and orientation options

13. Deselect the check box that fits all fields on one page as desired. If this box is selected, some fields may not be wide enough to display their full contents.

14. Click the **Next** button. The last page of the *Report Wizard* displays (Figure 4-71).

15. Change the title.

16. Select the radio button to either **Preview the report** or to **Modify the report's design**.

17. Click **Finish**.

- Access saves the report using the name provided in the title.
- The report shows in either *Print Preview* view or *Design* view depending on the selection made in step 16.
- Most of the fields appear in text boxes.
- Fields that have a lookup appear in a combo box.
- Fields that are a *Yes/No* data type appear as a check box.
- The size of a field depends on the data type and the field size.
- The *Report name displays* in the *Reports* group on the *Navigation Pane*.

18. Close the report.

- If the report was opened in *Print Preview* view, when you close *Print Preview* you are in *Design* view. You need to close that when you are done with the report.

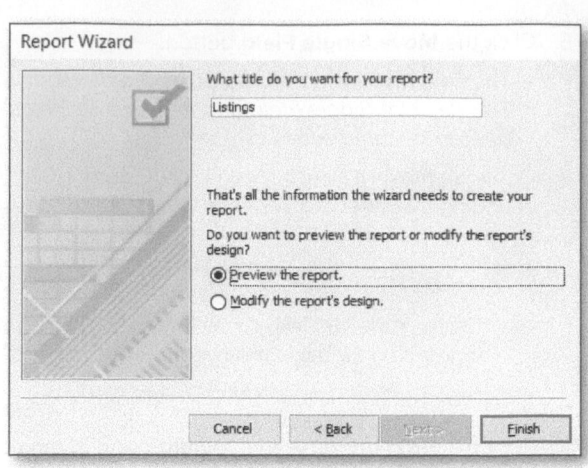

4-71 Enter the title in the last step of the *Report Wizard*

View or Modify a Report

Access provides four different view options for a report:

- **Report**: This view is used to execute the report and see the results (Figure 4-72). In *Report* view you see all the data contained in the report. However, you do not see it separated into separate pages. Use the scroll bars to see parts of the report not visible on the screen.

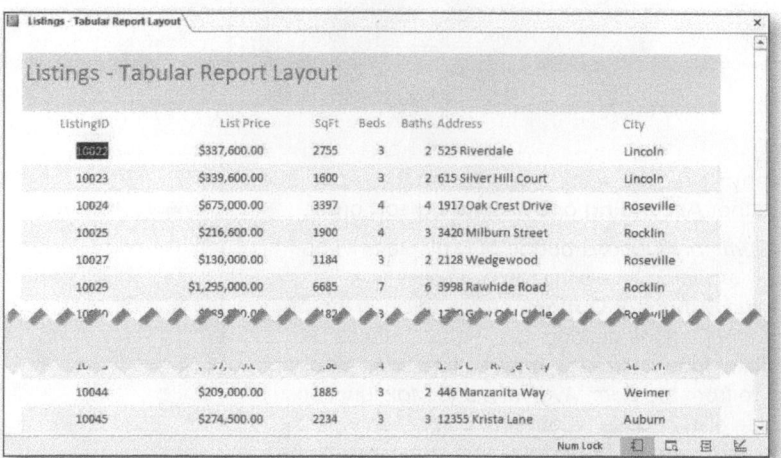

4-72 *Report* view of a report

- **Print Preview**: This view (Figure 4-73) lets you see how the report will look in print. In *SLO 4.8: Printing a Report*, you will learn to use the *Print Preview* tab to make modifications to the print settings, such as margins, page orientation, page size, and so forth.

- **Design**: This view allows you to edit the report. In *Design* view the report content is organized by the section in which it appears (Figure 4-74). The three primary sections are the **Page Header**, the **Detail**, and the **Page Footer**. Some reports have additional sections based on grouping levels that have been added.

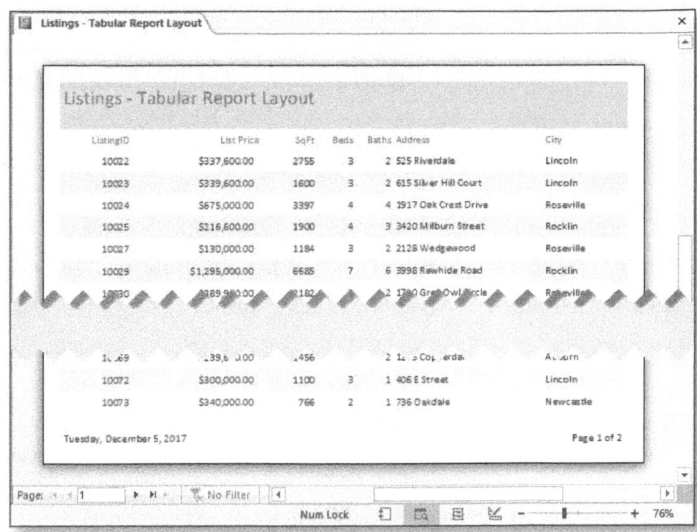

4-73 *Print Preview* view of a report

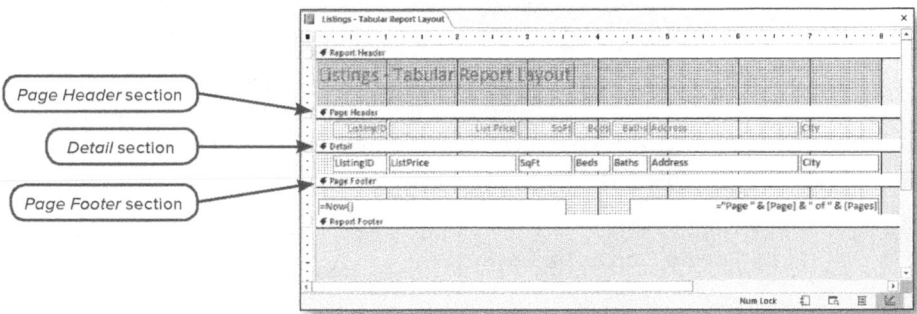

4-74 *Design* view of a report

Design view is good for adding labels and images into a report, editing text boxes, resizing the report sections, and changing some report properties. When you are working in *Design* view, Access organizes your editing choices into four **Report Design Tools** contextual tabs: **Design**, **Arrange**, **Format** and **Page Setup**.

- **Layout**: This view is a more visually-oriented mode you can use to alter the design of a report and see the effects of the changes in real time. The *Layout* view of the same report shown in Figure 4-74 is shown in Figure 4-75.

Because you can see how the data displays at the same time you are able to modify the design, *Layout* view is good for resizing fields or labels, changing colors or text alignment, or applying different formats. Like *Design* view, *Layout* view organizes your editing

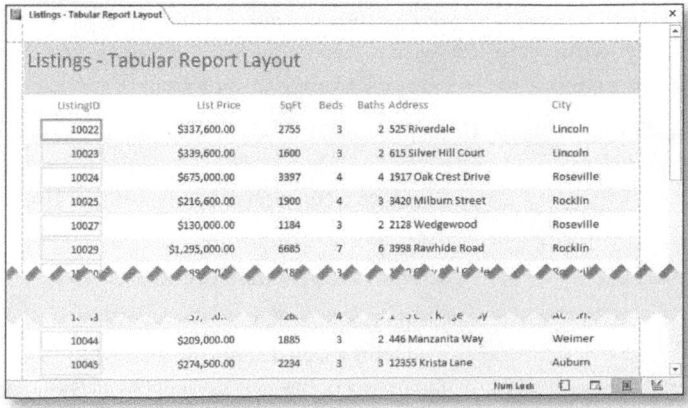

4-75 *Layout* view of a report

choices into the same four *Report Design Tools* contextual tabs: *Design*, *Arrange*, *Format*, and *Page Setup*. However, not all design options are available while in *Layout* view.

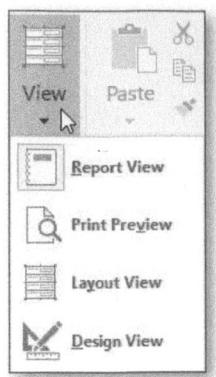

▶ HOW TO: Switch Report Views to View or Modify a Report

1. Click the **View** button [*Home* tab].
2. Select **Report View**, **Print Preview**, **Layout View**, or **Design View** (Figure 4-76).
3. View the results or make any modifications.

> ▶ **ANOTHER WAY**
>
> Select a view icon from the lower right corner of the *Status* bar.

4-76 View options for a report

Save a Report

When a report is created using the *Report* tool or *Report Wizard* options, Access automatically saves the report during the creation process. If you have made any modifications to the design of the report, or if you created the report using any of the other options, you need to save those changes. Save changes to a report by pressing **Ctrl+S** or clicking the **Save** icon on the *Quick Access* toolbar.

▶ HOW TO: Save a Copy of a Report

1. Click **Save As** [*File* tab] to display the *Save As* area.
2. Click **Save Object As** in the *File Types* options. *Save Object As* should be selected in the *Database File Types* options.
3. Click the **Save As** button to open the *Save As* dialog box (Figure 4-77).
 - The name of the current object displays in the *Save "object name" to* box.
 - In Figure 4-77, *Listings – Tabular Report Layout* is the name of the current object.
 - The suggested name always begins with "Copy of".
4. Type the name you wish to use in the *Save "object name" to* box.
5. Click **OK**.

4-77 Save As dialog box

> ▶ **ANOTHER WAY**
>
> Press **F12** to open the *Save As* dialog box.

Once a report has been saved, it displays in the *Reports* group of the *Navigation Pane*.

Open a Saved Report

If you double-click a report name in the *Navigation Pane*, the report opens in *Report* view.

Open a saved report in *Print Preview* view, *Design* view, or *Layout* view by right-clicking the report name in the *Navigation Pane* and selecting **Print Preview**, **Design View**, or **Layout View** from the context menu.

Delete a Report

Occasionally you have reports that no longer are needed in the database.

Delete a report by selecting the report name in the *Navigation Pane* and clicking the **Delete** button [*Home* tab, *Records* group].

> ▶ **ANOTHER WAY**
>
> Right-click the report name in the *Navigation Pane* and select **Delete** from the context menu.

 SLO 4.5

Creating and Customizing a Report in Layout View

In *Layout* view, you can modify a report and see how the report looks with data displaying. In this section, you first learn how to create a blank report and then you explore the layout of a report and modify the report in *Layout* view.

The Blank Report Button

Sometimes it is easier to start with a completely blank report and then add the fields, labels, or other controls.

 HOW TO: Create a Blank Report

1. Click the **Blank Report** button [*Create* tab, *Reports* group].
 - A new blank report opens in *Layout* view (Figure 4-78).
 - The *Field List* pane displays.
2. Click the **Show all tables** link to display the database tables.
3. Click the **plus sign** to the left of a table name to see the fields in the table.
4. Click the **minus sign** to the left of a table name to collapse the list of fields in the table.

4-78 Blank report in *Layout* view

After you create the blank report, you are ready to add items to the report. Save the report and any changes you make to it.

Report Controls

Recall that the fields, labels, buttons, and so forth are all known as *controls*. In a report, you can add controls in either *Layout* view or *Design* view. The controls are accessed in the *Controls* group of the *Report Layout Tools Design* tab. The report controls available in *Layout* view are shown in Figure 4-79.

4-79 *Controls* group for a report

Like controls on forms, controls on reports are either *bound* to a data value, *unbound* and are not linked to a data source, or *calculated* and their value comes from an expression. As you work through the book you are introduced to a variety of report controls.

Report Control Layouts

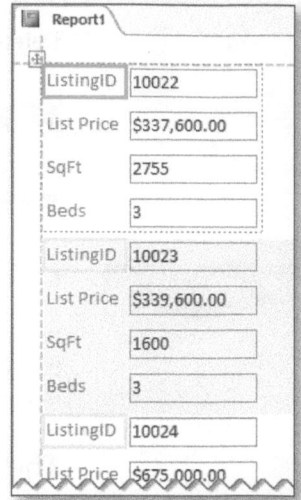

4-81 Stacked control layout in a report

Like forms, **control layouts** provide a structure to align the controls on your report. The two primary layout options are tabular and stacked:

- **Tabular**: This layout organizes data in rows and columns. Labels identifying the different fields are above the data values (Figure 4-80).
- **Stacked**: This layout organizes data vertically. The labels are to the left of the data control (Figure 4-81).

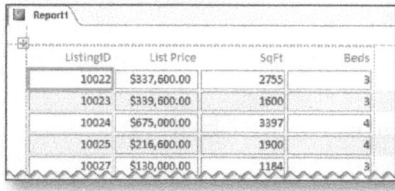

4-80 Tabular control layout in a report

Add and Delete Fields in a Control Layout

A new blank report initially has no controls. You can add table fields to the report in *Layout* view.

> **HOW TO:** Add Fields into the Control Layout of a Blank Report

1. Open the report in *Layout* view.
2. Click the **Add Existing Fields** button [*Report Layout Tools Design* tab, *Tools* group] if the *Field List* is not open.

> **ANOTHER WAY**
>
> Press **Alt+F8** to show or hide the *Field List*.

3. Click the **plus sign** next to the table name to display the fields.
4. Double-click the field name to add the field into the report.
5. Continue adding fields.

4-82 Add fields into a report

- The fields are added into a tabular layout (Figure 4-82).
- The most recently added field is highlighted with an orange border.

> **ANOTHER WAY**
>
> Click and drag a field into the report window to add it into the control layout.

▶ HOW TO: Add Fields between Existing Fields in a Control Layout

1. Open the report in *Layout* view.
2. Click the **Add Existing Fields** button [*Report Layout Tools Design* tab, *Tools* group] if the *Field List* is not open.
3. Click the **plus sign** next to the desired table name to display the fields.
4. Select the field name to add to the report. The selected field is highlighted in rose.
5. Drag the field to the desired location in the control layout. A rose-colored line indicates the position of the new field (Figure 4-83).

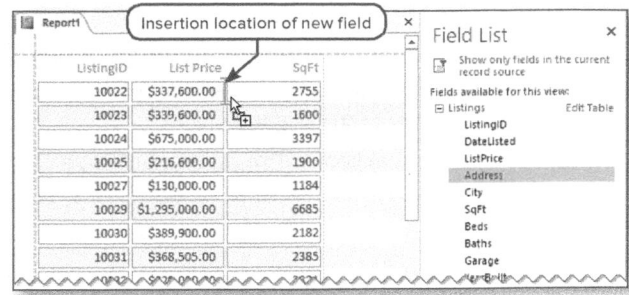

4-83 Add fields between existing fields in a control layout

 - Pay attention to the rose-colored line's placement. Reports allow rows and columns to be combined.
 - Figure 4-84 shows the new field being added into row of a tabular layout.
 - Figure 4-85 shows the resulting report. This could create a confusing report organization.

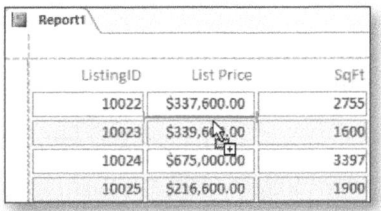

4-84 Insert a new field as a row in a tabular layout

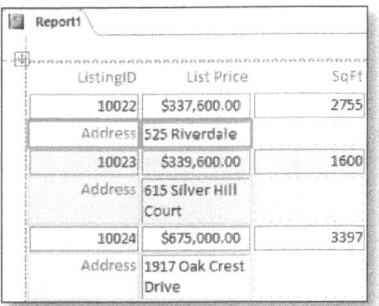

4-85 Report after new field added

▶ HOW TO: Delete a Field from a Control Layout

1. Open the report in *Layout* view.
2. Select the text box control of the field you want to delete.
3. Right-click to open the context menu.
4. Select **Delete Row** or **Delete Column**.

Customize a Report in Layout View

You can make a number of modifications to a report in *Layout* view. In this section, you explore the report controls, learn how to change control layouts, adjust column widths, add and delete rows and columns in a control layout, and add a title, date and page numbers to a report.

These options are available through the buttons in the *Table* and *Rows & Columns* groups on the *Report Layout Tools Arrange* tab (Figure 4-86).

4-86 Customize a report layout using options in the *Table* and *Rows & Columns* groups

Change Control Layouts

When you create a report, the report starts with either a stacked or tabular layout. As you add and delete fields on the report, you may wish to change its layout.

▶ HOW TO: Change Control Layouts

1. Open the report in *Layout* view.
2. Select one of the fields in the control layout. The orange border surrounds that field.
3. Click the **Select Layout** button [*Report Layout Tools Arrange* tab, *Rows & Columns* group]. The orange border surrounds all of the controls in the layout.
4. Select either the **Stacked** or **Tabular** button [*Report Layout Tools Arrange* tab, *Table* group]. The report updates with the new layout.

Adjust Column Widths

Sometimes, the initial width of the report fields needs to be adjusted. Keep in mind that in a stacked layout, all of the fields have the same width. As a result, when changing the width you need to ensure that the column is wide enough to fit the largest field. In a tabular layout, you can set the width of each field individually.

▶ HOW TO: Change Field Column Widths

1. Open the report in *Layout* view.
2. Select the text box control of the field in the control layout. The orange border surrounds that field.
3. Click the **Property Sheet** button [*Report Layout Tools Design* tab, Tools group].
4. Click the **Format** tab if necessary.
5. Type the new value in the *Width* property (Figure 4-87) and press **Enter**. Remember that a series of # symbols indicates that the column is not wide enough to display the contents.

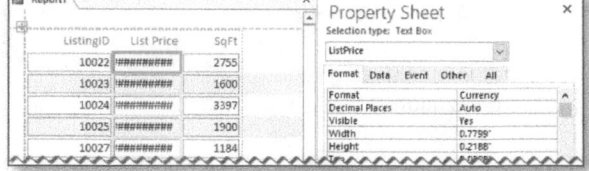

4-87 Adjust the width of a report field

Add and Delete Rows and Columns in a Control Layout

Often, you want to make minor modifications to the control layout. For example, you may want to create a second column in a stacked layout, or you may want to delete a row if you removed fields from the control layout. You can make these modifications using buttons in the *Rows & Columns* group of the *Report Layout Tools Arrange* tab.

▶ HOW TO: Add a Column to a Control Layout

1. Open the report in *Layout* view.
2. Select a control in the column adjacent to where you want to add a new column.
3. Click the **Select Column** button [*Report Layout Tools Arrange* tab, *Rows & Columns* group].

4. Click the **Insert Left** or **Insert Right** button [*Report Layout Tools Arrange* tab, *Rows & Columns* group].

 - The new column is added to the control layout (Figure 4-88).
 - A light gray, dotted border surrounds the cells in the added column.

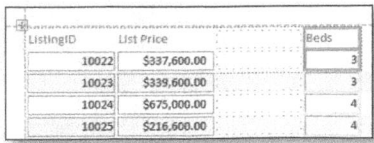

4-88 A dotted border surrounds each cell in the added column

▶ **HOW TO: Add a Row to a Control Layout**

1. Open the report in *Layout* view.
2. Select a control in the row adjacent to where you want to add a new row.
3. Click the **Select Row** button [*Report Layout Tools Arrange* tab, *Rows & Columns* group].
4. Click the **Insert Above** or **Insert Below** button [*Report Layout Tools Arrange* tab, *Rows & Columns* group].

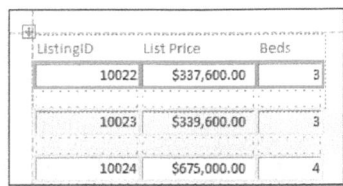

4-89 A dotted border surrounds each cell in the added row

 - The new row is added to the control layout (Figure 4-89).
 - Notice that a new row is added between each of the existing rows in the control layout.
 - A light gray, dotted border surrounds the cells in the new rows.

▶ **HOW TO: Delete a Row or Column from a Control Layout**

1. Open the report in *Layout* view.
2. Select a control in the row or column you wish to delete.
3. Click the **Select Row** or **Select Column** button [*Report Layout Tools Arrange* tab, *Rows & Columns* group].
4. Right-click to open the context menu.
5. Select **Delete Row** or **Delete Column**.

Move a Control within a Layout

As you modify the control layout, you may need to move a control from one part of the layout to another.

▶ **HOW TO: Move a Control within a Layout**

1. Open the report in *Layout* view.
2. Select the control that you wish to move.

 - The orange border surrounds that control.
 - To move the entire row or column including labels, click the **Select Row** or **Select Column** button [*Report Layout Tools Arrange* tab, *Rows & Columns* group].

3. Click the control with the move arrow, hold, and drag the control to the new location. A rose-colored line highlights the new location (Figure 4-90).

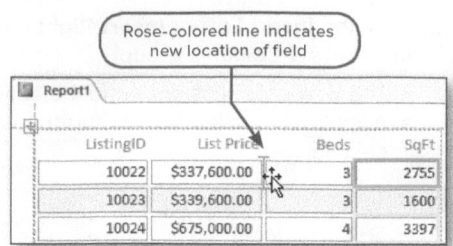
Rose-colored line indicates new location of field

> **ANOTHER WAY**
>
> Select multiple controls by pressing and holding **Shift** and selecting multiple controls. You can then move them together.

4-90 Drag a control to the new location

Add a Title, a Date, or Page Numbers to a Report

It is good database design to title each report. This allows the user to quickly understand the purpose of the report. You also may want to have the current date displayed in a report, and Access can also add page numbers to a report. These controls can be added to a report from the *Header/Footer* group [*Report Layout Tools Design* tab] (Figure 4-91). If the report does not already contain a header section, adding a title or the date and time automatically adds a header section to the report.

Selecting the **Title** button adds two controls into the header section, an *Auto_Header* control which contains the title and an *Auto_Logo* control which can contain a logo.

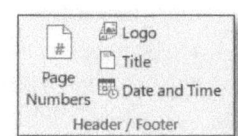
4-91 *Header/Footer* group

▶ **HOW TO:** Add a Title, a Date, or Page Numbers to a Report in Layout View

1. Open the report in *Layout* view.

2. Click the **Title** button [*Report Layout Tools Design* tab, *Header/Footer* group] to add a title into the header section of the report. The title is set to the report name.

3. Click the **Auto_Header** control to edit the report title.

4. Click the **Date and Time** button [*Report Layout Tools Design* tab, *Header/Footer* group] to add the date and/or time into the header section of the report. The *Date and Time* dialog box appears (Figure 4-92).

5. Select the appropriate check boxes and radio buttons to include the date and/or time with the desired formatting.

6. Click **OK**.

7. Click the **Page Numbers** button [*Report Layout Tools Design* tab, *Header/Footer* group] to open the *Page Numbers* dialog box (Figure 4-93).

4-92 *Date and Time* dialog box

4-93 *Page Numbers* dialog box

8. Select the radio buttons corresponding to the appropriate *Format* and *Position* of the page numbers. If the *Bottom of Page* position is selected, a footer section is added to the report as needed.

9. Select the alignment of the page numbers.

10. Deselect the check box to **Show Number on First Page** as desired.

11. Click **OK**. The title and/or date appear in the header section of the report and, based on your choice, the page numbers appear in either the header or footer section (Figure 4-94).

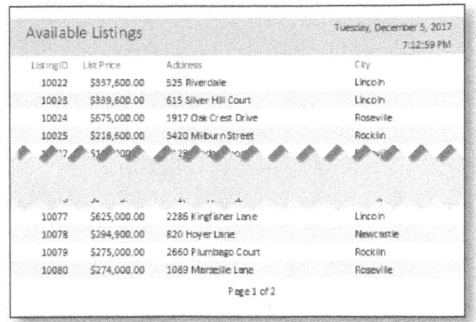

4-94 Controls in the header and footer sections

PAUSE & PRACTICE: ACCESS 4-3

For this Pause & Practice, you create two reports for the Placer Hills Real Estate database. Create one report using the *Report Wizard* and a second report using the *Blank Report* button.

File Needed: *[your initials] PP A4-1.accdb*
Completed Project File Name: ***[your initials] PP A4-3.accdb***

1. Open the ***[your initials] PP A4-1*** database file that you created in Pause & Practice 4-1.

2. Save a new copy of your database as [your initials] PP A4-3.

3. Enable content in the database.

4. Create a report using the *Report Wizard*.
 a. Click the **Report Wizard** button [*Create* tab, *Reports* group] to launch the *Report Wizard*.
 b. Click the **Tables/Queries** drop-down arrow and select the **Listings** table.
 c. Click the **Move All Fields** button.
 d. Select the **ListingAgentNumber** field in the *Selected Fields* window and click the **Remove Single Field** button.
 e. Remove the *Construction, YearBuilt, Garage* and *DateListed* fields. The *Report Wizard* should look similar to Figure 4-95.
 f. Click the **Next** button to move to the second page of the *Report Wizard*.
 g. Do not group the data. Click the **Next** button to move to the third page of the *Report Wizard*.
 h. Sort the *ListPrice* field in ascending order.
 i. Click the **Next** button to move to the fourth page of the *Report Wizard*.
 j. Select a **Tabular** layout and **Portrait** orientation.
 k. Click the **Next** button to move to the last page of the *Report Wizard*.
 l. Type Listings – Report Wizard in the *Title* box.

4-95 Select report fields

m. Click the **Finish** button. The report opens in *Print Preview* view (Figure 4-96). Notice that the *ListPrice* field moved to the left-most column because you are sorting on that field.

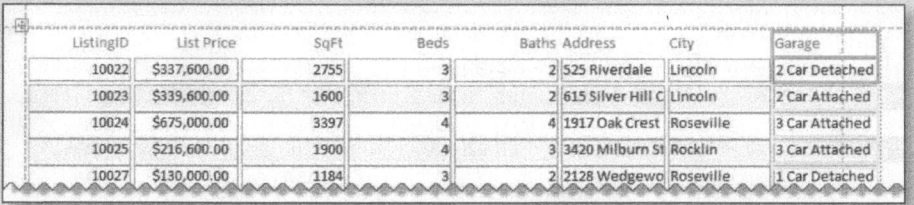

Listings - Report Wizard

List Price moved to the left-most column

List Price	ListingID	Address	City	SqFt	Beds	Baths
$104,900.00	10053	21075 Butte View Place	Weimer	914	2	1
$130,000.00	10027	2128 Wedgewood	Roseville	1184	3	2
$131,000.00	10150	423 Welterwood	Lincoln	1482	2	2
$209,000.00	10044	446 Manzanita Way	Weimer	1885	3	2
$216,600.00	10025	3420 Milburn Street	Rocklin	1900		3

4-96 Listings report created using the *Report Wizard*

n. Use the navigation buttons to move among pages.
o. Click the **Close Print Preview** button.
p. Close the report.

5. Create a report using the *Blank Report* button.
 a. Click the **Blank Report** button [*Create* tab, *Reports* group] to open a new, blank report in *Layout* view.
 b. Click the **Show all tables** link in the *Field List* pane.
 c. Click the **plus sign** to expand the *Listings* table.
 d. Double-click the **ListingID** field to add it to the report.
 e. Double-click the **ListPrice** field to add it to the report
 f. Add the **SqFt**, **Beds**, **Baths**, **Address**, **City**, and **Garage** fields to the report. The report should look similar to Figure 4-97.

ListingID	List Price	SqFt	Beds	Baths	Address	City	Garage
10022	$337,600.00	2755	3	2	525 Riverdale	Lincoln	2 Car Detached
10023	$339,600.00	1600	3	2	615 Silver Hill C	Lincoln	2 Car Attached
10024	$675,000.00	3397	4	4	1917 Oak Crest	Roseville	3 Car Attached
10025	$216,600.00	1900	4	3	3420 Milburn St	Rocklin	3 Car Attached
10027	$130,000.00	1184	3	2	2128 Wedgewo	Roseville	1 Car Detached

4-97 Add fields into a tabular layout of a blank report

 g. Close the *Field List*.

6. Save the report. Enter Listings – Blank Report Button as the *Report Name*.

7. Add a title and page numbers to the report.
 a. Click the **Report Layout Tools Design** tab if necessary.
 b. Click the **Title** button [*Header/Footer* group]. Accept the default wording of the title.
 c. Click the **Page Numbers** button [*Header/Footer* group].
 d. Select the **Page N** of **M** radio button in the *Format* group.
 e. Select the **Bottom of Page [Footer]** radio button in the *Position* group.
 f. Select **Left** in the *Alignment* drop-down list.
 g. Click **OK**.

8. Adjust the width of the report columns.
 a. Select a text box in the *ListingID* column.
 b. Click the **Property Sheet** button [*Report Layout Tools Design* tab, Tools group].
 c. Click the **Format** tab if necessary.
 d. Type .62" in the *Width* property box and press **Enter**. Don't worry if Access adjusts the actual value to a slightly different number, such as .6201".
 e. Select a text box in the *SqFt* column, type .5" in the *Width* property box and press **Enter**.
 f. Select a text box in the *Beds* column, type .5" in the *Width* property box and press **Enter**.
 g. Select a text box in the *Baths* column, type .5" in the *Width* property box and press **Enter**.
 h. Select a text box in the *Address* column, type 2" in the *Width* property box and press **Enter**.
 i. Select a text box in the *ListPrice* column, type 1.1" in the *Width* property box and press **Enter**.

9. Save the report.

10. Preview the report by selecting the **View** button [*Report Layout Tools Design* tab, *Views* group] and selecting **Print Preview**. The report should look similar to Figure 4-98.

11. Click the **Close Print Preview** button.

12. Close the report.

13. Close the database.

Listings - Blank Report Button							
Listing ID	List Price	SqFt	Beds	Baths	Address	City	Garage
10022	$337,600.00	2755	3	2	525 Riverdale	Lincoln	2 Car Detached
10023	$339,600.00	1600	3	2	615 Silver Hill Court	Lincoln	2 Car Attached
10024	$675,000.00	3397	4	4	1917 Oak Crest Drive	Roseville	3 Car Attached
10025	$521,600.00	2900		3	3490 Millburg Street	Rocklin	3 Car Attached
10077	$625,000.00	3086	3	3	2286 Kingfisher Lane	Lincoln	3 Car Attached
10078	$294,900.00	1720	3	2	820 Hoyer Lane	Newcastle	No Garage
10079	$275,000.00	2034	4	3	2660 Plumbago Court	Rocklin	2 Car Attached

Page 1 of 2

4-98 Completed listings report created using the *Blank Report* option

SLO 4.6

Adding Grouping, Sorting, and Totals

As you learned in the *Report Wizard* section, you can choose to sort records in a report on different fields, to add grouping to a report, or to add totals to a report. Add a ***group*** to a report when you want to organize and summarize your data. For example, you could group all employees from the same branch together in an insurance agency database or you could group all the songs from a particular artist together in a music database. When you create a grouping, Access can automatically calculate various summary values across the different groups. You can also combine sorting with grouping. Finally, totals can also be added to a report independent of grouping or sorting being used. The features are located on the *Report Layout Tools Design* tab.

You add grouping and sorting to a report using the *Group & Sort* button [*Report Layout Tools Design* tab, *Grouping & Totals* group] (Figure 4-99). Add totals using the *Totals* button [*Report Layout Tools Design* tab, *Grouping & Totals* group].

4-99 *Grouping & Totals group options*

Sorting

A very useful feature in Access reports is data sorting. Sorting makes it easier to read and understand reports because it places all like data together. Access allows you to sort on multiple fields, with each field having its own sort order.

▶**HOW TO: Add a Sort to a Report**

1. Open the report in *Layout* view.
2. Click the **Group & Sort** button [*Report Layout Tools Design* tab, *Grouping & Totals* group] to open the *Group, Sort, and Total* pane at the bottom of the report.
3. Click **Add a sort** in the *Group, Sort, and Total* pane.

4. Select the field you want to sort by from the field list (Figure 4-100).

- The report updates to display the data sorted in ascending order by the selected field.
- The *Group, Sort, and Total* pane updates to show how the report is being sorted (Figure 4-101).
- The default sort order is *with A on top* for text fields, *oldest to newest* for date fields, and *smallest to largest* for number fields.

5. Change the sort order by clicking the arrow to the right of the default sort order and selecting the new sort order. The default sort order in Figure 4-101 is *with A on top*.

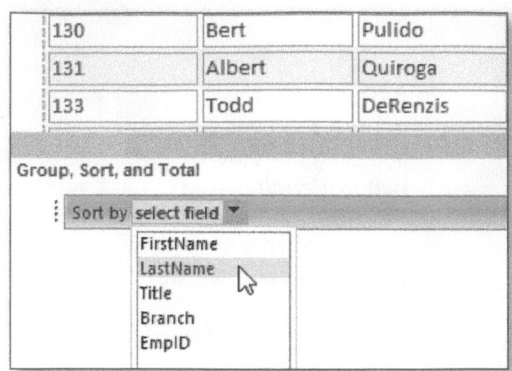

4-100 Select a sort field

> **MORE INFO**
>
> You can add additional sorting levels to a report by clicking **Add a sort** again.

6. Close the *Group, Sort, and Total* pane by clicking the **X** in the upper right corner of the *Group, Sort, and Total* pane. Be careful not to click the *Delete* symbol inside the pane or you remove the sort.

4-101 Updated *Group, Sort, and Total* pane

Add a Group to a Report

When you add a group in *Layout* view, a new section is added using a stepped layout. You can group on more than one field.

▶ **HOW TO:** Add a Group to a Report

1. Open the report in *Layout* view.
2. Click the **Group & Sort** button [*Report Layout Tools Design* tab, *Grouping & Totals* group] to open the *Group, Sort, and Total* pane at the bottom of the report.
3. Click **Add a group** in the *Group, Sort, and Total* pane.
4. Select the field you want to group on from the field list (Figure 4-102).

- The selected field moves to the left-most column (Figure 4-103).
- The report changes to a stepped layout.
- The *Group, Sort, and Total* pane updates to show how the report is being grouped (Figure 4-104).

5. Change the sort order of the grouping by clicking the arrow to the right of the default sort order and selecting the new sort order. The default sort order of the grouping in Figure 4-103 is *with A on top*.

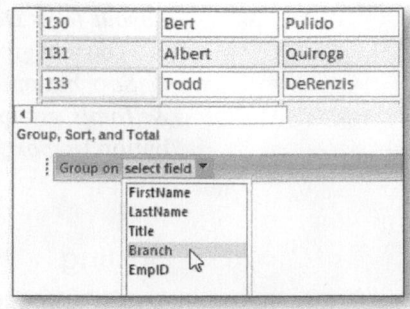

4-102 Select a group field

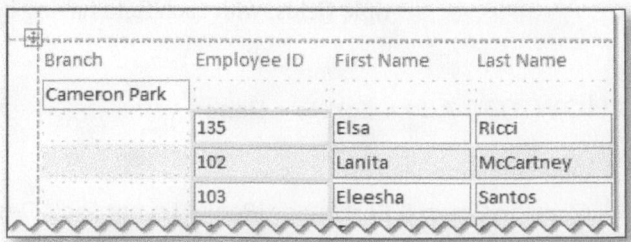

4-103 Updated report after grouping added

MORE INFO

You can add additional grouping levels to a report by clicking **Add a group** again.

6. Close the *Group, Sort, and Total* pane by clicking the **X** in the upper right corner of the *Group, Sort, and Total* pane. Be careful not to click the *Delete* symbol inside the pane or you remove the group.

4-104 Updated *Group, Sort, and Total* pane

Group and Sort Options

You can modify the report design after adding a sort or group section. You can also change the location or format of the grouping field in the control layout.

Other modifications are available. Click **More** in the *Group, Sort, and Total* pane to display the options shown in Figure 4-105 and explained in the following table. Click **Less** to close the expanded list of options.

4-105 Expanded options in *Group, Sort, and Total* pane

Options in the Group, Sort, and Total Pane

Category	Options	Explanation
Sorting	Ascending	The grouping field is sorted in ascending order.
	Descending	The grouping field is sorted in descending order.
Grouping	By entire value	The grouping is based on the entire value in the selected field.
	By partial value	The grouping is based on only part of the field. For example, in a text field, the grouping could be "by first character," which would group together all values that start with the same letter. In a date field, the grouping could be by year or month.
	Custom	The grouping is based on a specific number of characters that you provide.
Totals	Select the field and type of calculation	You choose which field in the report should be calculated, along with the calculation. Choices include *Sum*, *Average*, *Count*, *Maximum*, and *Minimum*.
	Show grand totals	Calculates overall totals for all records.
	Show group totals as percent of grand total	Displays the group totals as a percent of the grand total.
	Show in header or footer section	Determines which section displays the totals.
Title		Changes the wording in the label of the grouping field.
Header section	With a header section / without a header section	Determines whether to include a header section in the report.

Continued

Category	Options	Explanation
Footer section	*With a footer section / without a footer section*	Determines whether to include a footer section in the report.
Keep group together	*Do not keep group together on one page*	Allows a group to be split across multiple pages if it can't all fit in the space remaining on a page.
	Keep whole group together on one page	Starts a group on the following page if it can't all fit in the space remaining on a page.
	Keep header and first record together on one page	Prevents a header from printing on the bottom of a page unless at least one record of the group can also be printed with the header.

The wording for some of the options depends on the data type of the field. For example, an ascending sort for a text field is *"with A on top"* while an ascending sort for a date field is *"from oldest to newest."*

▶ HOW TO: Modify Options in a Group or Sort

1. Open the report in *Layout* view.
2. Click the **Group & Sort** button [*Report Layout Tools Design* tab, *Grouping & Totals* group] if the *Group, Sort, and Total* pane is not open.
3. Click **More** in the *Group, Sort, and Total* pane.
4. Select the **arrow** of the desired option and select the new option choice (Figure 4-106).
 - The report updates to reflect the new option.
 - The expanded list of options closes.

4-106 Expanded grouping options in *Group, Sort, and Total* pane

> **MORE INFO**
>
> You can add additional options by selecting **More** again.

5. Click **Less** to close the expanded list of options if you decide not to make any modifications.
6. Close the *Group, Sort, and Total* pane by clicking the **X** in the upper right corner of the *Group, Sort, and Total* pane.

Add Totals to a Report

You can add totals to a report to allow performance of overall calculations based on your data. Calculation options include *Sum, Average, Count Records, Count Values, Max, Min, Standard Deviation,* and *Variance.*

▶ HOW TO: Add Totals to a Report

1. Open the report in *Layout* view.
2. Select a text box in the field you want to total.

3. Click the **Totals** button [*Report Layout Tools Design* tab, *Grouping & Totals* group].
4. Select the desired calculation (Figure 4-107).
 - The report updates with the total added to the bottom of the report.
5. Repeat steps 2 through 4 to add additional total calculations to the report.

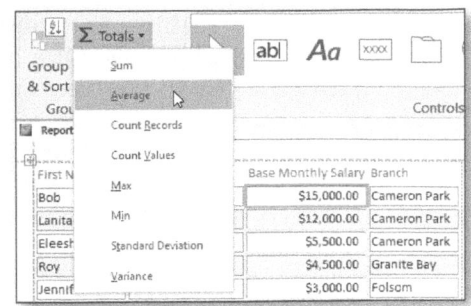

4-107 *Totals* button options

In a report with grouping or sorting, add totals by selecting the **with no totals** choice in the *Group, Sort, and Total* pane and then select the desired total options (Figure 4-108).

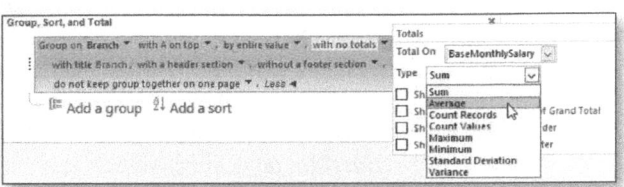

4-108 Total options in *Group, Sort, and Total* pane

SLO 4.7

Using Conditional Formatting in a Report

Conditional formatting allows you to format only values that meet a certain condition. This helps you focus the user's attention to certain records in a report.

Conditional Formatting Rules

The formatting rules are defined in the *New Formatting Rule* dialog box (Figure 4-109). When building a rule you must select the *rule type*, conditions, and the desired formatting.

The most common rule type is *Check values in the current record or use an expression*. Use the *Compare to other records* rule type to create data bars, which allow you to compare values across data records.

4-109 *New Formatting Rule* dialog box

Most formatting rules compare the value in a field. When you are building a rule, the dialog box options change based on the selection you make. For example, Figure 4-110 shows a place where you enter only one data value based on the selection of the *less than* comparison. Compare this to Figure 4-111, where you enter two data values for a *between* comparison.

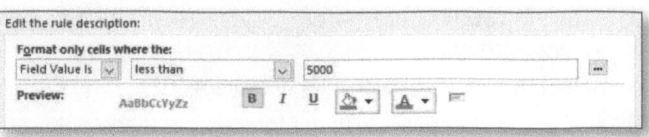

4-110 Example rule with less than comparison and one data value

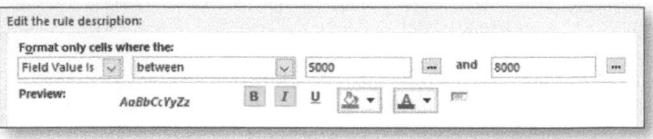

4-111 Example rule with between comparison and two data values

These figures also show examples of different formatting options.

Once you build a rule, it displays in the *Conditional Formatting Rules Manager* dialog box. You can have multiple rules in one report and even multiple rules for the same field.

When you have multiple rules, the order in which they are listed is very important, because Access stops evaluating when a match is found. For example, the rule in Figure 4-112 shows *BaseMonthlySalary* values that are less than 5,000 in blue instead of brown. That is because a value less than 5,000 is also less than 10,000. The evaluation stops after the condition in the first rule is met. To correct this situation, select the *Value <10000* rule and click the **Move Down** arrow to make it the second rule instead of the first. As appropriate, you can also click the **Move Up** arrow to change the position of a rule.

4-112 *Conditional Formatting Rules Manager* dialog box with multiple rules

Add Conditional Formatting to a Report

To add conditional formatting, you need to determine which fields will have formatting applied and the specific criteria you want to use to make the rule. Conditional formatting features are located on the *Report Layout Tools Format* tab.

> ▶ **HOW TO:** Add Conditional Formatting to a Report to Check Values in the Current Record or Use an Expression

1. Open the report in *Layout* view.
2. Select any text box in the column where you wish to apply the criteria.

> ▶ **ANOTHER WAY**
> Select multiple fields and apply the same rule to all selected fields.

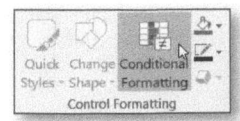

4-113 *Conditional Formatting* button

3. Click the **Conditional Formatting** button [*Report Layout Tools Format* tab, *Control Formatting* group] (Figure 4-113) to open the *Conditional Formatting Rules Manager* dialog box (Figure 4-114).

- The selected field displays in the *Show formatting rules for* box.
- If more than one field is selected, *Multiple* displays in the box.

4. Change the field to format in the *Show formatting rules for* box if necessary.

5. Click the **New Rule** button to open the *New Formatting Rule* dialog box.

6. Select **Check values in the current record or use an expression** in the *Select a rule type* box.

7. Click the appropriate **arrows** to select the desired comparison.

8. Type the comparison values into the boxes.

9. Select formatting options as desired.

10. Click **OK**. The completed rule displays in the *Conditional Formatting Rules Manager* dialog box (Figure 4-115).

11. Add another rule to either the same field or a different field as desired.

12. Click **Apply** to have Access evaluate the data in the report and apply the formatting to the values that meet the criteria.

13. Click **OK** when you are finished building all rules.

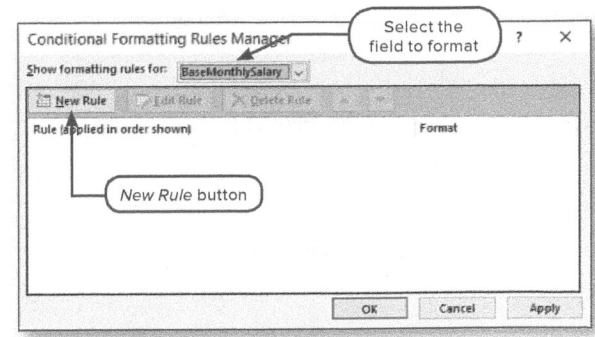

4-114 *Conditional Formatting Rules Manager* dialog box

4-115 **Completed rule**

Manage Conditional Formatting Rules

You can also edit or delete existing rules from the *Conditional Formatting Rules Manager* dialog box. The *Conditional Formatting Rules Manager* only displays rules for one field at a time. If you created rules for multiple fields, you must select the desired field first in the *Show formatting rules for* box to view the rules for that specific field.

To edit an existing rule, select the rule in the *Conditional Formatting Rules Manager* dialog box and click the **Edit Rule** button. The *Edit Formatting Rule dialog* box opens. This dialog box is similar to the *New Formatting Rule* dialog box, and you set options the same way.

To delete an existing rule, select the rule in the *Conditional Formatting Rules Manager* dialog box and click the **Delete Rule** button.

SLO 4.8

Printing a Report

Reports can be viewed on screen but most reports are designed to be printed. To ensure that your report prints as desired, take the time to review it in *Print Preview* view.

Preview a Report

Recall that *Print Preview* allows you to see how your report appears on a printed page. The options on the *Print Preview* tab let you adjust the size and margins of the page, change the orientation, and change the zoom level as needed.

▶ HOW TO: Preview a Report

1. Click to select the desired report in the *Navigation Pane*.
2. Click the **Print** button [*File* tab].
3. Click **Print Preview**.

> ▶ **ANOTHER WAY**
>
> If the report is already open, click the **View** button [*Home* tab, *Views* group] and select **Print Preview**.

4. Make any desired adjustments to the report (Figure 4-116).

4-116 Adjust printing options while viewing a report in *Print Preview*

5. If you are ready to print, click the **Print** button [*Print Preview* tab, *Print* group] to open the *Print* dialog box. Choose desired options and click **OK** to print the report.
6. Click the **Close Print Preview** button.

Print a Report without Print Preview

If you already know that your report is designed correctly, you can print the report without previewing it first.

▶HOW TO: Print a Report without Using Print Preview

1. Click to select the desired report in the *Navigation Pane*.
2. Click the **Print** button [*File* tab].
3. Choose the desired print option.
 - Click **Quick Print** to print the report on the default printer without making any changes.
 - Click **Print** to open the *Print* dialog box and customize printing options. Select a printer, desired printing options, and click **OK** to print.

PAUSE & PRACTICE: ACCESS 4-4

For this Pause & Practice, you edit a report based on a parameter query. You modify the report to add grouping and conditional formatting. Finally, you preview the report.

File Needed: *[your initials] PP A4-2.accdb*
Completed Project File Name: *[your initials] PP A4-4.accdb*

1. Open the *[your initials] PP A4-2* database file that you created in Pause & Practice 4-2.

2. Save a new copy of your database as [your initials] PP A4-4.

3. Enable content in the database.

4. Double-click the **EmployeesBranchParameter** query.

5. In the *Enter Parameter Value* dialog box, leave the value blank and click **OK**.
 a. The query executes and displays the results shown in Figure 4-117.
 b. The report you edit in this Pause & Practice was created using this query as the data source instead of a table.

Employee	Title	Branch	Base Monthly Salary
Bob Lingle	Chief Executive Officer	Cameron Park	$15,000.00
Lanita McCartney	Chief Operating Officer	Cameron Park	$12,000.00
Eleesha Santos	Insurance Agent	Cameron Park	$5,500.00
Roy Baxter	Insurance Agent	Granite Bay	$4,500.00
Jennifer Alaro	Administrative Assistant	Folsom	$3,000.00

4-117 *EmployeesBranchParameter* query results

6. Close the query.

7. Add grouping to the report.
 a. Right-click the **EmployeesBranchParameterReport** report and select **Layout View** to open the report in *Layout* view. The query executes.
 b. Click the **OK** button in the *Enter Parameter Value* dialog box without entering a value. The report opens in *Layout* view.
 c. Click the **Group & Sort** button [*Report Layout Tools Design* tab, *Grouping & Totals* group] to open the *Group, Sort, and Total* pane at the bottom of the report.
 d. Click **Add a group** in the *Group, Sort, and Total* pane.
 e. Select the **Branch** field from the *Group on select field* list (Figure 4-118).

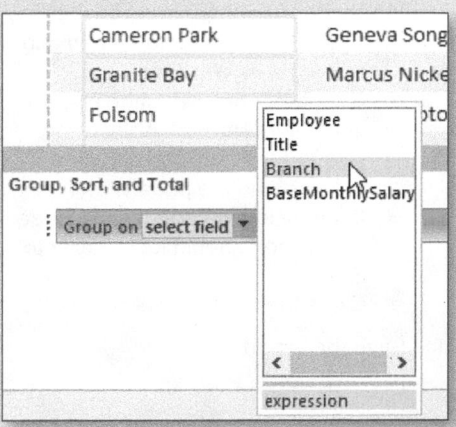

4-118 Group on the *Branch* field

f. Close the *Group, Sort, and Total* pane by clicking the **X** in the upper right corner of the *Group, Sort, and Total* pane. Be careful not to click the *Delete* symbol inside the pane or you remove the group.

8. Add conditional formatting to the report.
 a. Click any cell in the *Base Monthly Salary* column.
 b. Click the **Conditional Formatting** button [*Report Layout tools Format* tab, *Control Formatting* group] to open the *Conditional Formatting Rules Manager* dialog box. *BaseMonthlySalary* displays in the *Show formatting rules for* box.
 c. Click the **New Rule** button to open the *New Formatting Rule* dialog box.
 d. Select the **Check values in the current record or use an expression** rule type in the *Select a rule type* box if necessary.
 e. Select **greater than or equal to** as the comparison.
 f. Type 10000 into the value box.
 g. Select **Bold** and a **red** font. The *New Formatting Rule* dialog box should be similar to Figure 4-119.
 h. Click **OK**. The completed rule displays in the *Conditional Formatting Rules Manager* dialog box (Figure 4-120).
 i. Click **Apply**.
 j. Click **OK**.

9. Save the report.

10. Preview the way the report will print.
 a. Right-click in the report and select **Print Preview** from the context menu.
 b. Click **OK** in the *Enter Parameter Value* dialog box without entering a value.
 c. Click the **Zoom** button arrow and select **Fit to Window**.
 d. Click the **Margins** button arrow and select **Normal**. If a message displays that the section width is greater than the page width, click **OK** to acknowledge the message. Your report should look similar to Figure 4-121.
 e. Close the *Print Preview* of the report.

11. Save the report.

12. Close the report.

13. Close the database.

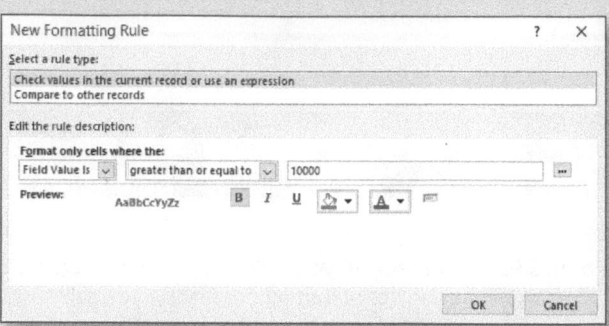

4-119 *New Formatting Rule* dialog box for *BaseMonthlySalary* field

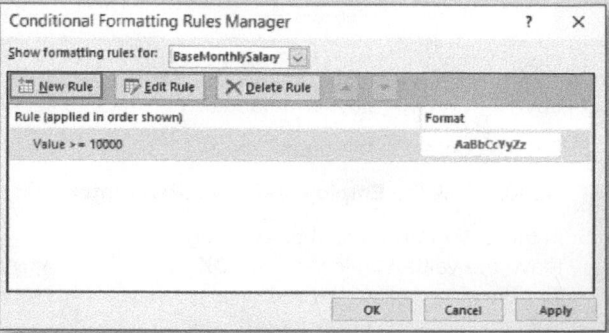

4-120 Completed rule for *BaseMonthlySalary* field

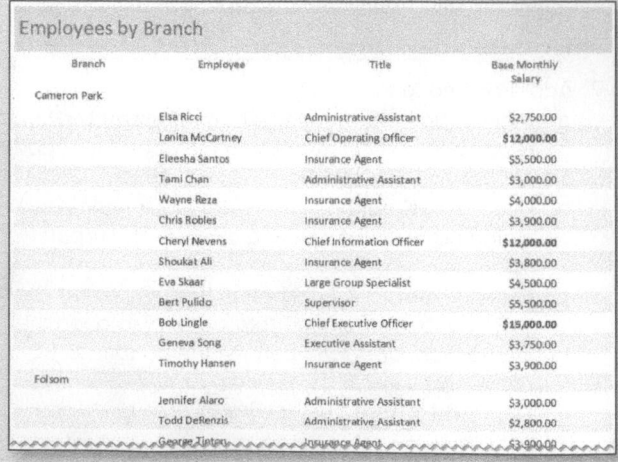

4-121 Completed report with grouping and conditional formatting

Chapter Summary

4.1 Create a simple form using quick create options; save, modify, and delete a form (p. A4-213).

- **Forms** allow you to view, add, update, and delete data in a database.
- You can build forms from tables, queries, or both.
- **Bound forms** are linked to the data source; **unbound forms** don't have a connection to a direct link to a data source.
- The **Form Wizard** lets you quickly build a form by specifying the tables or queries to use, selecting the desired fields and the desired layout of the form.
- You can use the *Form* button to create a form in one click.
- A **split form** lets you view data in two ways on the same form by combining both a columnar display and a datasheet display.
- You can edit a form in **Design view** or **Layout view** and modify any aspect of the form's design.

4.2 Create a blank form, understand controls and control layouts, and customize a form in *Layout* view (p. A4-221).

- The *Blank Form* button lets you create a new form from scratch using *Layout* view.
- The buttons, labels, fields, and so forth that you place on a form are called **controls**.
- Controls can be **bound**, **unbound** or **calculated**.
- **Control layouts** provide the structure that aligns the controls on a form.
- The two primary control layouts are **tabular** and **stacked**.
- You must save each form with a unique name.

4.3 Restrict a form to data entry, limit user edits and deletions on a form, add command buttons, and test a form (p. A4-227).

- When designing a form for data entry, choose design options that help minimize potential data entry errors and maximize efficiency for entering data.
- Use the **Data Entry** and **Allow Additions** properties of a form to restrict the form to only allow data entry when you don't want the user to be able to view data already in the database.

- Use the **Allow Edits** and **Allow Deletions** properties of a form when you want to limit the user's ability to edit or delete records in the database.
- You can add **command buttons** to a form to automate user tasks.
- Use the **Command Button Wizard** to easily add buttons to a form.
- After you build a form, test it to ensure that it functions as desired.

4.4 Create a simple report with the *Report Wizard*; save, modify, and delete a report (p. A4-234).

- Use **reports** to create an organized and professional output of the data in a database.
- You can build reports from tables, queries, or both.
- The **Report Wizard** lets you quickly build a report by specifying the tables or queries to use, selecting the desired fields, selecting any grouping or sorting options, and specifying the layout of the report.
- **Report** view executes a report and displays the results.
- **Print Preview** view shows how a report will look in print while also allowing you to make modifications to the printing settings.
- You can modify reports in *Design* view or *Layout* view.

4.5 Create a blank report, understand controls and control layouts, customize a report in *Layout* view, and add a title, a date, and page numbers to a report (p. A4-242).

- The *Blank Report* button lets you create a new report from scratch using *Layout* view.
- Control layouts provide the structure that aligns the controls on a report.
- The two primary control layouts are tabular and stacked.
- The fields, labels, and so forth that you place on a report are controls. Controls can be bound, unbound or calculated.
- It is good design practice to include titles, dates, and page numbers on a report.
- You must save each report with a unique name.

4.6 Enhance a report by adding grouping, sorting, and totals to a report in *Layout* view (p. A4-250).

- Sorting the records in a report makes it easier to read and understand the data contained in the report.
- You can sort a report in ascending or descending order on one or more fields.
- Add a **group** to a report to organize and summarize the data.
- A report can contain multiple groups.
- Within a grouping level, you can choose to include header or footer sections, integrate sorting, and include summary totals.
- Totals allow you to perform overall calculations based on the data in the report.
- Calculation options include *Sum*, *Average*, *Count Records*, *Count Values*, *Max*, *Min*, *Standard Deviation*, and *Variance*.

4.7 Integrate conditional formatting into a report (p. A4-254).

- **Conditional formatting** allows you to format only values that meet a specified condition.

- A report can contain multiple formatting rules.
- When using multiple rules, the order of specifying the rules is important because Access stops evaluating once it finds a rule that matches the data.
- You can add, modify, and delete rules from the *Conditional Formatting Rules Manager* dialog box.

4.8 Preview, modify print settings, and print a report (p. A4-256).

- To ensure that your report prints as desired, review it in *Print Preview* view.
- You can adjust the print settings related to page size, margins, and page orientation using the *Print Preview* mode.
- You can print a report directly from the *Backstage* view without using *Print Preview*.

Check for Understanding

The SIMbook for this text (within your SIMnet account) provides the following resources for concept review:

- Multiple Choice questions
- Matching exercises
- Short answer questions

USING MICROSOFT ACCESS 2016

Guided Project 4-1

In this project, you enhance the functionality of the database you built for your friend's music collection by building a form to display information about the albums and a report to show all of the songs on each album. To ensure consistency, the starting file is provided for you. Use the *Form Wizard* to create a form and *Layout* view to edit the form. Create a report using the *Report Wizard*, edit the report in *Layout* view, add totals to the report, and view the report using *Print Preview*.
[Student Learning Outcomes 4.1, 4.2, 4.4, 4.5, 4.6, 4.8]

File Needed: ***MusicDatabase-04.accdb***
Completed Project File Name: *[your initials] Access 4-1.accdb*

Skills Covered in This Project

- Create a form using the *Form Wizard*.
- Edit a form in *Layout* view.
- Add the current date to a form.

- Create a report using the *Report Wizard*.
- Edit a report in *Layout* view.
- Add totals to a report.
- View a report using *Print Preview*.

1. Open the ***MusicDatabase-04.accdb*** database file.

2. Save the database as [your initials] Access 4-1.

3. Enable content in the database.

4. Create a form using the *Form Wizard*.
 a. Click the **Form Wizard** button [*Create* tab, *Forms* group] to launch the *Form Wizard*.
 b. Click the **Tables/Queries** drop-down arrow and select the **Albums** table if necessary.
 c. Click the **Move All Fields** button to move all of the fields from the *Available Fields* window to the *Selected Fields* window.
 d. Click the **Next** button to move to the second page of the *Form Wizard*.
 e. Select the **Columnar** radio button if necessary.
 f. Click the **Next** button to move to the last page of the *Form Wizard*.
 g. Type MusicAlbums in the *Title* box.
 h. Click **Finish**. The form opens in *Form* view.
 i. Use the navigation buttons to move to record album 29. This album has the longest album name.

5. Edit the form column widths in *Layout* view.
 a. Click the **View** button [*Home* tab, *Views* group] and select **Layout View**.
 b. Close the *Field List* if it is open.
 c. Select the **AlbumName** text box.
 d. Click the **Property Sheet** button [*Form Layout Tools Design* tab, *Tools* group].
 e. Click the **Format** tab if necessary.
 f. Type 3.2" in the *Width* property box and press **Enter**.
 g. Select the **Artist** text box, type 3.2" in the *Width* property box and press **Enter**.
 h. Select the **Genre** text box, type 1.5" in the *Width* property box and press **Enter**.

i. Select the **Length** text box, type 1.5" in the *Width* property box and press **Enter**.

j. Select the **RecordingLabel** text box, type 3.2" in the *Width* property box and press **Enter**.

6. Edit the form header section.
 a. Click to select the **MusicAlbums** label in the header section.
 b. Click inside the label to open the edit mode.
 c. Insert a space between "Music" and "Albums."
 d. Click the header section outside the *Music Albums* label.
 e. Click the **Date and Time** button [*Form Layout Tools Design* Tab, *Header/Footer* group].
 f. Select the radio button to display the date using the **mm/dd/yyyy** format.
 g. Deselect the check box to **Include Time**.
 h. Click **OK**.
 i. Click the **Form View** icon in the *Status* bar. The completed form should look similar to Figure 4-122. Depending on the width of the Access window, your date field may be further to the right in your form.

4-122 Completed *MusicAlbums* form

7. Save the form.

8. Close the form.

9. Create a report using the *Report Wizard*.
 a. Click the **Report Wizard** button [*Create* tab, *Reports* group] to launch the *Report Wizard*.
 b. Click the **Tables/Queries** drop-down arrow in the box and select the **SongsOnAlbums** query. This report is based on a query instead of a table.
 c. Select the **AlbumName** field.
 d. Click the **Move Single Field** button.
 e. Continue adding the **Artist** and **SongTitle** fields. Remember that you can click the **Remove Single Field** button if you accidentally add a field that is not needed.
 f. Click the **Next** button to move to the next page of the *Report Wizard*.
 g. Choose to view the data **by Albums**. The *Report Wizard* should look similar to Figure 4-123 and click **Next**.
 h. Do not group the data. Click the **Next** button to move to the next page of the *Report Wizard*.
 i. Do not sort the data. Click the **Next** button to move to the next page of the *Report Wizard*.
 j. Select a **Stepped** layout and **Portrait** orientation if necessary.
 k. Click the **Next** button to move to the last page of the *Report Wizard*.
 l. Type SongsOnAlbums in the *Title* box.
 m. Click the **Finish** button. The report opens in *Print Preview* view (Figure 4-124).

4-123 Select to view the data *by Albums* in the *Report Wizard*

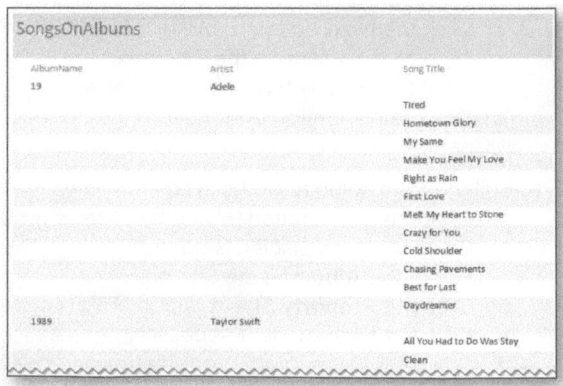

4-124 *SongsOnAlbums* report

n. Click the **Next Page** navigation button three times to move to the fourth page of the report. You should see the *Blunderbuss* album.

o. Click the **Last Page** navigation button. You should be on page 17 of the report.

p. Click the **Close Print Preview** button. The report displays in *Design* view.

10. Edit the report header section.

a. Close the *Field List* pane, if it is open.

b. Click to select the **SongsOnAlbums** label in the header section.

c. Click inside the label to open the edit mode.

d. Insert spaces between "Songs" and "On" and "Albums" so there is a space between each word.

e. Click the header section outside the *Songs On Albums* label.

11. Edit the report column widths using *Layout* view.

a. Switch the report to *Layout* view.

b. Click the **Find** button [*Home* tab, *Find* group]. The *Find* dialog box displays.

c. Type Orbit in the *Find What* box.

d. Click the **Match** drop-down arrow and select **Any Part of Field**.

e. Click **Find Next**. The "The Chieftains in Orbit (with NASA Astronaut Cady Coleman)" song from the *Voice of Ages* album by *The Chieftains* should be selected. This song has the longest song title.

f. Close the *Find* dialog box.

g. Click the **Property Sheet** button [*Report Layout Tools Design* tab, *Tools* group].

h. Click the **Format** tab if necessary.

i. Type 4.1" in the *Width* property box and press **Enter**.

j. Type 3.8" in the *Left* property box and press **Enter**. The *Left* property indicates the left position of the text box.

k. Scroll up a little so that you can see the album name, *Voice of Ages*, for this song if necessary.

l. Select the **AlbumName** text box that contains "Voice of Ages," type 1.6" in the *Width* property box and press **Enter**.

m. Type .5" in the *Height* property box and press **Enter**.

n. Select the **Artist** text box that contains "The Chieftains," type 2.5" in the *Width* property box and press **Enter**.

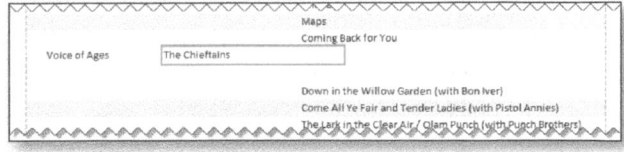

o. Type 1.9" in the *Left* property box and press **Enter**. The report should look similar to Figure 4-125.

4-125 Report fields after adjusting size and location

p. Scroll to the top of the report.

q. Select the **Artist** label, type 1.5" in the *Width* property box and press **Enter**.

r. Type 1.9" in the *Left* property box and press **Enter**.

s. Select the **Song Title** label, type 1.5" in the *Width* property box and press **Enter**.

t. Type 3.8" in the *Left* property box and press **Enter**.

12. Add totals to the report to count the number of songs on each album.

a. Click the **Report Layout Tools Design** tab.

b. Select a text box in the *SongTitle* column.

c. Click the **Totals** button in the *Grouping & Totals* group.

d. Select **Count Records**. The report updates to display the count below the last song on each album. A grand total displays at the end of the report.

13. Save the report.

14. Switch to *Print Preview* view. The complete report should look similar to Figure 4-126.

15. Close the *Print Preview* of the report.

16. Close the report.

17. Close the database.

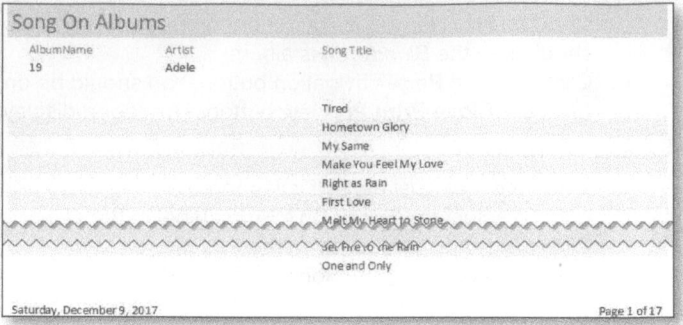

Song On Albums

AlbumName	Artist	Song Title
19	Adele	
		Tired
		Hometown Glory
		My Same
		Make You Feel My Love
		Right as Rain
		First Love
		Melt My Heart to Stone
		Set Fire to the Rain
		One and Only

Saturday, December 9, 2017 Page 1 of 17

4-126 Completed report

Guided Project 4-2

San Diego Sailing Club wants to add forms and a report to their database. To ensure consistency, the starting file is provided for you. Use the *Blank Form* button to create the form and *Layout* view to modify the form, save a copy of the form, edit form properties, and add command buttons. Create a report using the *Report Wizard* and use *Layout* view to modify the report.
[Student Learning Outcomes 4.1, 4.2, 4.3, 4.4, 4.5]

File Needed: ***SanDiegoSailing-04.accdb***
Completed Project File Name: *[your initials] Access 4-2.accdb*

Skills Covered in This Project

- **Create a form using the *Blank Form* button.**
- Edit a form in *Layout* view.
- Save a copy of the form.
- Add a title to a form.
- Add buttons to a form.
- Set form properties.
- **Create a report using the *Report Wizard*.**
- Edit a report in *Layout* view.

1. Open the ***SanDiegoSailing-04*** database from your student data files.

2. Save the database as [your initials] Access 4-2.

3. Enable content in the database.

4. Create a new form using the *Blank Form* button.
 a. Click the **Blank Form** button [*Create* tab, *Forms* group]. A new blank form opens in *Layout* view.
 b. Click the **Show all tables** link in the *Field List* pane.
 c. Click the **plus sign** to expand the *SailboatFleet* table and see the fields in the table.
 d. Double-click the **BoatID** field to add it to the form.
 e. Double-click the **BoatType** field to add it to the form.

f. Continue adding all the fields from the *SailboatFleet* table to the form. The form should look similar to Figure 4-127.

g. Close the *Field List*.

5. Modify the control layout.

a. Click one of the fields on the form. An orange border surrounds it.

b. Click the **Select Layout** button [*Form Layout Tools Arrange* tab, *Rows & Columns* group]. All the cells in the layout are bordered in orange.

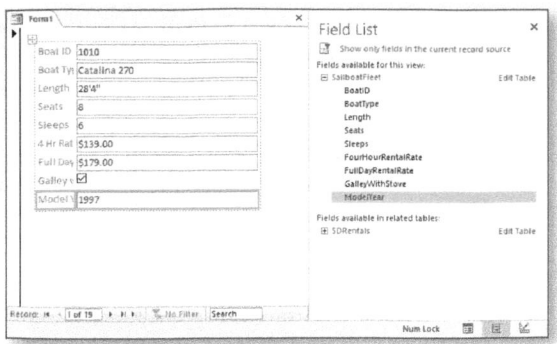

4-127 Add fields from the *SailboatFleet* table onto the form

c. Place your pointer over any field. Click, hold, and drag the control layout down and to the right, and then release the pointer (Figure 4-128).

d. Select the **Galley w/ Stove** label.

e. Click the **Property Sheet** button [*Form Layout Tools Design* tab, *Tools* group].

f. Click the **Format** tab if necessary.

g. Type 1.1" in the *Width* property box and press **Enter**.

h. Navigate to record number 4.

i. Select the **BoatType** text box, type 1.3" in the *Width* property box and press **Enter**.

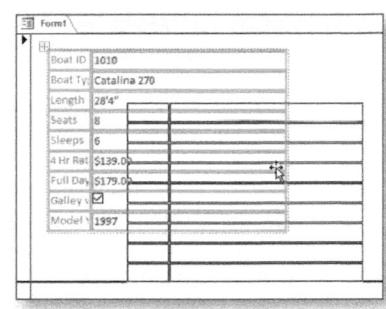

6. Add a title control to the form.

a. Click the **Title** button [*Form Layout Tools Design* tab, *Header/Footer* group].

b. Change the wording of the label in the header section to View Sailboat Fleet Data.

c. Click the form area to save the changes to the label. The form should look similar to Figure 4-129.

4-128 Move the control layout

7. Modify the form to limit user edits and deletions.

a. Click the **Property Sheet** button [*Form Layout Tools Design* tab, *Tools* group] to open the *Property Sheet*.

b. Click the **drop-down arrow** in the *Selection* box of the *Property Sheet* and select **Form**.

c. Select **No** in the *Data Entry* property box if necessary.

d. Select **No** in the *Allow Additions* property box.

e. Select **No** in the *Allow Deletions* property box.

f. Select **No** in the *Allow Edits* property box.

g. Close the *Property Sheet*.

4-129 Updated form

8. Save the form. Enter ViewSailboatFleet as the *Form Name*.

9. Test the form.

a. Switch to **Form** view.

b. Try to change the value in the *BoatID* text box. You should not be able to edit the value. Notice that the *New (blank) record* icon is not visible in the *Navigation* bar and that the *Delete Record* button is not available in the *Records* group [*Home* tab].

10. Save another copy of the form by clicking **Save As** [*File* tab] and then selecting **Save Object As** and click the **Save As** button. Enter AddNewSailboat as the *Form Name*.

11. Edit the title label of the new form.
 a. Switch to **Layout** view.
 b. Change the wording of the label in the header section to Add New Sailboat.
 c. Click the form area to save the changes to the label.

12. Add a new column and new rows to the control layout of the form.
 a. Select the **ModelYear** text box.
 b. Click the **Select Row** button [*Form Layout Tools Arrange* tab, *Rows & Columns* group].
 c. Click the **Insert Below** button [*Form Layout Tools Arrange* tab, *Rows & Columns* group] to add a blank row.
 d. Click the **Insert Below** button again to add a second blank row.
 e. Select the **ModelYear** text box.
 f. Click the **Select Column** button [*Form Layout Tools Arrange* tab, *Rows & Columns* group].
 g. Click the **Insert Right** button [*Form Layout Tools Arrange* tab, *Rows & Columns* group] to add a blank column.

13. Adjust the height and width of the new rows and column.
 a. Select a **cell** in the new column.
 b. Click the **Property Sheet** button [*Form Layout Tools Design* tab, *Tools* group].
 c. Click the **Format** tab if necessary.
 d. Type 1.1" in the *Width* property box and press **Enter**.
 e. Select a cell in the bottom blank row.
 f. Type .45" in the *Height* property box and press **Enter**. The revised control layout on the form should look like Figure 4-130.
 g. Close the *Property* Sheet.

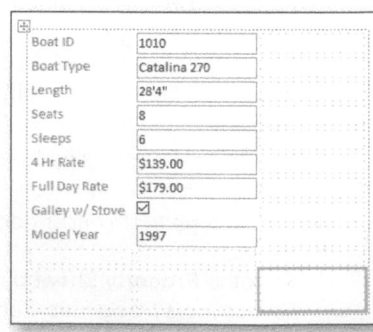

4-130 Modified control layout

14. Add command buttons to the form.
 a. Click the **Form Layout Tools Design** tab.
 b. Click the **More** arrow at the far right of the *Controls* group and select the **Use Control Wizards** button if it does not already have a rose-colored border indicating it is selected.
 c. Click **Button** in the *Controls* group. Move the pointer to the left-most cell in the bottom row of the control layout and click. The *Command Button Wizard* launches.
 d. Select the **Record Operations** *Category* and the **Save Record** *Action* of the button.
 e. Click **Next** to move to the second page of the *Command Button Wizard*.
 f. Select the **Text** radio button and change the wording to read Save Sailboat Record.
 g. Click **Next** to move to the last page of the *Wizard*.
 h. Enter AddBoatFormSaveButton as the name for the button and click **Finish**. The button displays in the form.
 i. Add a second button to the form. Place the button in the middle cell of the last row.
 j. Select the **Record Operations** *Category* and the **Add New Record** *Action* of the button. Click **Next**.
 k. Select the **Text** radio button and change the wording to read Add New Sailboat. Click **Next**.
 l. Enter AddBoatFormAddButton as the button name and click **Finish**.
 m. Add a third button onto the form. Place the button in the right-most cell of the last row.
 n. Select the **Form Operations** *Category* and the **Close Form** *Action* of the button. Click **Next**.
 o. Select the **Text** radio button and use the existing "Close Form" wording. Click **Next**.

p. Enter AddBoatFormCloseButton as the name for the button and click **Finish**. The form should look similar to Figure 4-131.

q. Save the form.

15. Restrict the form to data entry.

a. Click the **Property Sheet** button [*Form Layout Tools Design* tab, *Tools* group] to open the *Property Sheet*.

b. Click the **drop-down arrow** in the *Selection* box of the *Property Sheet* and select **Form**.

c. Click to select the **Data** tab if necessary.

d. Select **Yes** in the *Data Entry* property box.

e. Select **Yes** in the *Allow Additions* property box.

f. Close the *Property Sheet*.

g. Save the form.

4-131 Modified *AddNewSailboat* form

16. Switch to *Form* view by clicking the **View** button [*Form Layout Tools Design* tab, *Views* group] and selecting **Form View**. The complete form displays.

17. Test the form.

a. Enter the data shown in Figure 4-132.

b. Click the **Save Sailboat Record** button.

c. Click the **Add New Sailboat** button. A blank record should display in the form.

d. Click the **Close Form** button.

4-132 Sample data

18. Create a report using the *Report Wizard*.

a. Click the **Report Wizard** button [*Create* tab, *Reports* group] to launch the *Report Wizard*.

b. Click the **Tables/Queries** drop-down arrow and select the **FullDayRentalsByBoatSummary** query.

c. Click the **Move All Fields** button and click **Next**. The next page of the *Report Wizard* displays the grouping as shown in Figure 4-133.

d. Click the **Next** button to move to the next page of the *Report Wizard*.

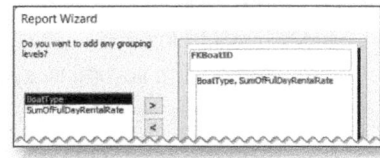

4-133 Suggested data grouping

e. Do not sort the data. Click the **Next** button to move to the next page of the *Report Wizard*.

f. Select a **Block** layout and **Portrait** orientation. Click **Next**.

g. Click the **Finish** button without making any changes to the suggested title. The report opens in *Print Preview* view (Figure 4-134).

h. Click the **Close Print Preview** button. The report displays in *Design* view.

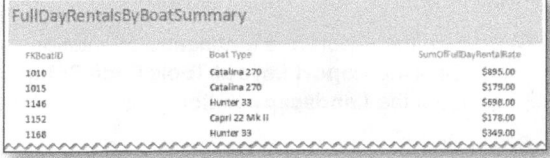

4-134 *Print Preview* view of report

19. Edit the report labels using *Layout* view.

a. Switch the report to **Layout** view.

b. Click to select the **FullDayRentalsByBoatSummary** label in the header section.

c. Click inside the label to open the edit mode.

d. Insert a space between each of the words and add Report as the last word.
e. Click the header section outside the label.
f. Edit the labels of the column headers. Change *FKBoatID* to Boat ID and *SumOfFullDayRentalRate* to Total Income from Full Day Rentals.
g. Save the report.
h. Switch to **Report** view. The report should look similar to Figure 4-135.
i. Close the report.

20. Close the database.

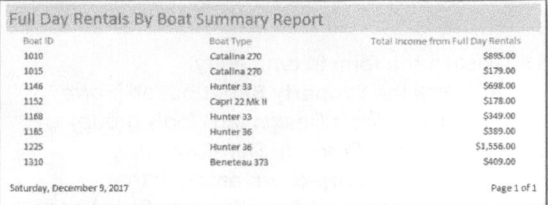

Full Day Rentals By Boat Summary Report		
Boat ID	Boat Type	Total Income from Full Day Rentals
1010	Catalina 270	$895.00
1015	Catalina 270	$179.00
1146	Hunter 33	$698.00
1152	Capri 22 Mk II	$178.00
1168	Hunter 33	$349.00
1185	Hunter 36	$389.00
1225	Hunter 36	$1,556.00
1310	Beneteau 373	$409.00
Saturday, December 9, 2017		Page 1 of 1

4-135 Completed report in *Report* view

Guided Project 4-3

Life's Animal Shelter wants to add a report and form to its database. To ensure consistency, the starting file is provided for you. You edit a report that was created based on a query. In *Layout* view, add a title, grouping, and totals. Next, add conditional formatting to the report, preview the results, and adjust print settings. Finally, you create a split form.
[Student Learning Outcomes 4.1, 4.5, 4.6, 4.7, 4.8]

File Needed: ***LifesAnimalShelter-04.accdb***
Completed Project File Name: *[your initials] **Access 4-3.accdb***

Skills Covered in This Project

- Modify a report in *Layout* view.
- Add grouping and sorting to a report.
- Add conditional formatting to a report.
- Add totals to a report.
- Preview a report.
- Create a split form.

1. Open the ***LifesAnimalShelter-04*** database from your student data files.

2. Save the database as [your initials] Access 4-3.

3. Enable content in the database.

4. Right-click the **PetsWithoutMatchingOwner** report and select **Layout View** to open the report in *Layout* view.

5. Change the report to a **landscape** orientation.
 a. Click the **Report Layout Tools Page Setup** tab.
 b. Click the **Landscape** button [*Page Layout* group].

6. Adjust the width of the report columns
 a. Select a text box in the *Why I'd make a great* companion column.
 b. Press and hold **Shift** and click to select the **Why I'd make a great companion** label.
 c. Press **F4** to open the *Property Sheet* and click the **Format** tab if necessary.
 d. Enter 3.2" in the *Width* property. You must press **Enter** or **Tab** after entering the value so that Access recognizes a changed value.

 e. Enter 7" in the *Left* property.
 f. Select a text box in the *Color* column. Press and hold **Shift** and click to select the **Color** label.
 g. Enter 1.5" in the *Width* property.
 h. Enter 5.3" in the *Left* property.
 i. Set the *Width* property of the *Gender* column and label to .6" and set the *Left* property to 4.6".
 j. Set the *Width* property of the *Age* column and label to .5" and set the *Left* property to 4".
 k. Select a text box in the *Breed* column. Press and hold **Shift** and click to select the **Breed** label.
 l. Enter 1.3" in the *Width* property.
 m. Enter 2.5" in the *Left* property.
 n. Click a text box in the *Breed* column to select only the text box and to deselect the *Breed* label.
 o. Enter .5" in the *Height* property.
 p. Set the *Width* property of the *Type*
 column and label to .7" and set the
 Left property to 1.7".
 q. Set the *Width* property of the *Pet
 Name* column and label to .8"
 and set the *Left* property to .8".
 The report should look similar to
 Figure 4-136.
 r. Save the report.

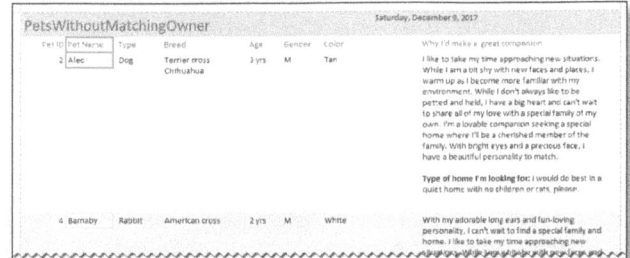

7. Edit the header and footer sections.

4-136 *PetsWithoutMatchingOwner* report

 a. Click the text box containing the *Date*.
 b. Enter 7.4" in the *Left* property.
 c. Click to select the title label and then click the label again to open the edit mode.
 d. Change the label to Pets Available for Adoption.
 e. Click outside the label to save the changes.
 f. Scroll down to the bottom of the report and select the **page number** text box.
 g. Enter 9" in the *Left* property.
 h. Press **F4** to close the *Property* Sheet.

8. Add grouping and sorting to the report.
 a. Click the **Group & Sort** button [*Report Layout Tools Design* tab, *Grouping & Totals* group] to open
 the *Group, Sort, and Total* pane at the bottom of the report.
 b. Click **Add a group** in the *Group, Sort, and Total* pane.
 c. Select the **Type** field from the *Group on select field* list.
 d. Click **Add a sort** in the *Group, Sort, and Total* pane.
 e. Select the **ID** field from the *Sort by select field* list.
 f. Click **More** in the *Group, Sort, and Total* pane.
 g. Select the **do not keep
 group together on one
 page** arrow and then select
 **keep header and first
 record together on one
 page** (Figure 4-137).
 h. Close the *Group, Sort, and
 Total* pane by clicking the **X** in
 the upper right corner of the
 Group, Sort, and Total pane.
 Be careful not to click the *Delete*
 symbol inside the pane or you remove the group.

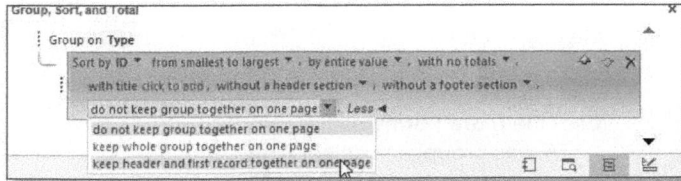

4-137 *Keep header and first record together on one page* option

 i. Scroll to the top of the report. The first record should be for "Martin", *Pet ID* number 6. Because
 the grouping uses a stepped layout, the word "Cat" appears in the *Type* column on the line
 above Martin.

9. Add conditional formatting to the report.
 a. Click any cell in the *Gender* column.
 b. Click the **Conditional Formatting** button [*Report Layout Tools Format* tab, *Control Formatting* group] to open the *Conditional Formatting Rules Manager* dialog box. *Gender* displays in the *Show formatting rules for* box.
 c. Click the **New Rule** button to open the *New Formatting Rule* dialog box.
 d. Select the **Check values in the current record or use an expression** rule type in the *Select a rule type* box if necessary.
 e. Select **equal to** as the comparison.
 f. Type M into the value box.
 g. Select **bold** and choose the **Dark Blue** font from the *Standard Colors*.
 h. Click **OK**. The completed rule displays in the *Conditional Formatting Rules Manager* dialog box (Figure 4-138).
 i. Click **Apply**.
 j. Click **OK**.
 k. Save the report.

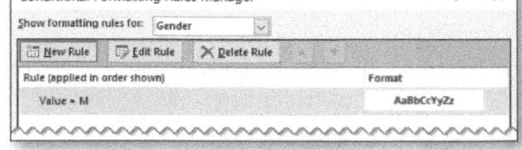

4-138 Conditional formatting rule

10. Add totals to the report to count how many of each type of pet is available.
 a. Select a text box in the **Pet ID** column.
 b. Click the **Totals** button [*Report Layout Tools Design* tab, *Grouping & Totals* group].
 c. Select **Count Records**. The report updates to show the total at the end of each group and a grand total at the end of the report.
 d. Save the report.

11. Preview the report.
 a. Select the **View** button [*Report Layout Tools Design* tab, *Views* group] and select **Print Preview**. The report should look similar to Figure 4-139.
 b. Click the **One Page** button [*Print Preview* tab, *Zoom* group] if necessary.
 c. Use the navigation arrows to move among pages.
 d. Click the **Close Print Preview** button.

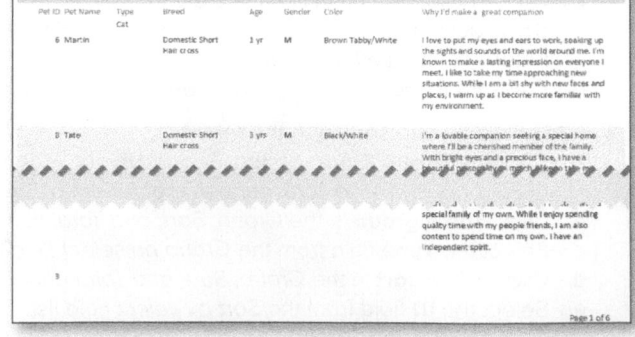

4-139 *Print Preview of completed report*

12. Close the report.

13. Create a split form.
 a. Click to select the **Owners** table in the *Navigation Pane*.
 b. Click the **More Forms** button [*Create* tab, *Forms* group] and select **Split Form** to create the form shown in Figure 4-140. Depending on the width of the Access window, your form may display the fields in one column in the top half of the form.
 c. Save the form. Accept the suggested form name by clicking **OK**.

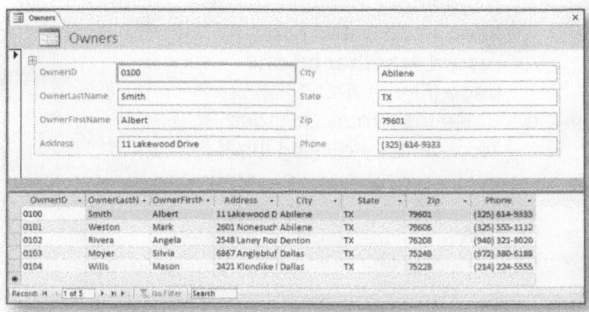

4-140 Completed split form

A4-271

 d. Switch to *Form* view by clicking the **View** button [*Form Layout Tools Design* tab, *Views* group] and selecting **Form View**.
 e. Use the navigation buttons to move among records.
 f. Close the form.

14. Close the database.

Independent Project 4-4

American River Cycling wants to add a report and form to their database. To ensure consistency, the starting file is provided for you. Create a form with the *Form* button. Edit the form in *Layout* view and add a button. Create a report using the *Blank Report* option. In *Layout* view, modify the layout and add a title and grouping. Preview the results.
[**Student Learning Outcomes 4.1, 4.2, 4.3, 4.5, 4.6, 4.8**]

File Needed: ***AmericanRiver-04.accd***
Completed Project File Name: ***[your initials] Access 4-4.accdb***

Skills Covered in This Project

- Create a form using the *Form* button.
- Edit the form in *Layout* view.
- Add the current date to a form.
- Add buttons to a form.

- Set form properties.
- Create a blank report.
- Edit the report in *Layout* view.
- Add grouping to a report.
- Preview a report.

1. Open the ***AmericanRiver-04*** database from your student data files.

2. Save the database as [your initials] Access 4-4.

3. Enable content in the database.

4. Create a form using the *Form* button.
 a. Select the **RaceResults** table and create a new form using the *Form* button. Your form should look similar to Figure 4-141, although the layout may be different depending on the size of the Access window when you created the form.
 b. Save the form as ViewRaceResults.

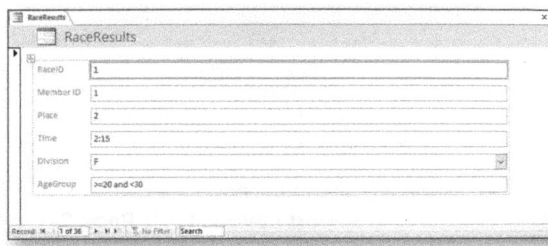

4-141 *RaceResults* form created with *Form* button

5. Edit the form in *Layout* view.
 a. Change the wording of the *RaceResults* label to read Member Race Results. Be careful to enter a space between each word.
 b. Change the *Width* of the label to 2.4".
 c. Change the *Width* of the *RaceID* text box to be 1". Remember that all the fields in this column change to the new width.
 d. Add two rows below the *AgeGroup* field.
 e. Change the *Height* of the bottom row to .4".
 f. Move the control layout down and to the right as shown in Figure 4-142.

g. Add the date to the form. Choose the *DD-Mon-YY* format. If necessary, deselect the **Include Time** check box so that only the date is added.

h. Select the **Date** control in the header and change the *Width* of the *Date* control to 1".

i. Change the *Left* property of the *Date* control to 4.75". The form should be similar to Figure 4-142.

6. Add a button to the form.
 a. Add a command button into the right-most cell in the second added row. The button should close the form [*Form Operations* category].
 b. Choose the **Text** radio button and use the suggested wording.
 c. Save the button as ViewFormCloseButton.

4-142 Completed *ViewRaceResults* form

7. Edit the form properties to limit user edits and deletions.
 a. Set the *Data Entry*, *Allow Additions*, *Allow Deletions*, and *Allow Edits* properties to **No** in the *Property Sheet* of the form.
 b. Close the *Property Sheet*.
 c. Save the form.

8. Switch to *Form* view. The complete form should look similar to Figure 4-142.
 a. Use the navigation buttons to move among records.
 b. Close the form.

9. Create a report using the *Blank Report* button.
 a. Add all the fields from the *Members* table. The report should look similar to Figure 4-143.

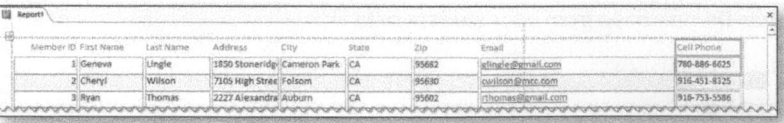

4-143 Add fields into a blank report

10. Add grouping into the report.
 a. Group the report on the *City* field.
 b. Save the report as ClubMembers.

11. Modify the layout of the report.
 a. Select the **Report Layout Tools Page Setup** tab.
 b. Click **Margins** [*Page Size* group] and select **Normal**.
 c. Change the page layout to **Landscape**. Notice the light gray, vertical dashed line to the left of the cell phone field. This indicates that the cell phone column does not fit on the same page as the other fields.
 d. Change the *Width* of the *Member ID* column to .8".
 e. Change the *Width* of the *Address* column to 1.7".
 f. Change the *Width* of the *State* and *ZIP* columns to .5".
 g. Change the *Width* of the *Email* column to 2".
 h. Add a title to the report and enter List of Club Members as the title text.
 i. Add page numbers to the bottom of the report. Use the **Page N of M** format and **Center** the alignment.

12. Save the changes made to the report.

13. View the report in *Print Preview*.
 a. Adjust the zoom to **One Page**. The report should look similar to Figure 4-144.

City	Member ID	First Name	Last Name	Address	State	ZIP	Email	Cell Phone
Auburn								
	3	Ryan	Thomas	2227 Alexandra Drive	CA	95602	rthomas@gmail.com	916-753-5586
	14	Randy	Clemmins	7336 Lester Road	CA	95602	rclemmins@phre.com	916-450-3330
	18	Dean	Teague	2112 Stonebrook Court	CA	95602	teague.dean@sac.rr.com	916-599-2222
Cameron Park								
	7	Melanie	Figueroa	4511 Johnson Court	CA	95682	mfigueroa@phre.com	916-450-3336
	1	Geneva	Lingle	1850 Stoneridge Court	CA	95682	glingle@gmail.com	780-886-6625
Fair Oaks								
	10	Rick	Hermenn	9035 Masi Drive	CA	95628	rickh@gmail.com	916-450-6719
	5	Margaret	Jepson	28861 Newcastle Road	CA	95628	margaret@sac.rr.com	780-862-9851
Folsom								
	2	Cheryl	Wilson	7105 High Street	CA	95630	cwilson@mcc.com	916-451-8325
Lincoln								
	11	Karen	Graves	6003 Ashland Road	CA	95648	kgraves@phre.com	916-450-3892
Rocklin								
	4	Roy	Baxter	705 First Street	CA	95677	roy@centralsierra.com	780-886-2471
	8	Sue	Schooler	4183 Braxton Way	CA	95677	sschooler@gmail.com	780-824-3525
Roseville								
	12	Robyn	Constantini	9581 Magnolia Way	CA	95661	robyn@gmail.com	780-886-2471
	6	Rick	DePonte	8364 Marshall Street	CA	95661	deponte@hotmail.com	916-450-3329
	13	John	Burgess	85741 Auberry Road	CA	95661	jburgess@hotmail.com	780-886-5862
	15	Amber	Harrison	488 Yale Drive	CA	95661	aharrison24@gmail.com	780-824-1111

List of Club Members

Page 1 of 2

4-144 *Print Preview* of completed report

 b. Close *Print Preview*.

14. Close the report.

15. Close the database.

Independent Project 4-5

The State of New York Department of Motor Vehicles wants to add a form and a report to its database so users can more easily view the information about drivers. To ensure consistency, the starting file is provided for you. Create a split form and edit the form in *Layout* view. Next, create a report using the *Blank Report* option. In *Layout* view, modify the layout, add a title, grouping, sorting, and totals. Preview the results.
[Student Learning Outcomes 4.1, 4.2, 4.3, 4.5, 4.6, 4.8]

File Needed: ***NewYorkDMV-04.accdb***
Completed Project File Name: ***[your initials] Access 4-5.accdb***

Skills Covered in This Project

- Create a form using the *Form* button.
- Edit a form in *Layout* view.
- Add the current date to a form.
- Move fields within the control layout.
- Test the functionality of a form.

- Create a blank report.
- Edit a report in *Layout* view.
- Add grouping and sorting to a report.
- Add totals to a report.
- Preview a report.

1. Open the **NewYorkDMV-04** database from your student data files.

2. Save the database as [your initials] Access 4-5.

3. Enable content in the database.

4. Create a split form. Recall that when creating a split form, the width of the Access window affects whether the fields are placed in one or two columns. Before creating the form, you adjust the size of the Access window to ensure that the initial layout of the form includes two columns.
 a. Click the **Restore Down** button if necessary so that the Access window is not maximized.
 b. Click the **Create** tab. If needed, reduce the width of the Access window so that there is minimal extra space to the right of the icons displayed in the ribbon.
 c. Select the **Drivers** table in the *Navigation Pane* and create a split form. Your form should look similar to Figure 4-145. If your form does not have two columns, close the form without saving. Adjust the height and width of the Access window to make it a bit smaller and then create the form again.

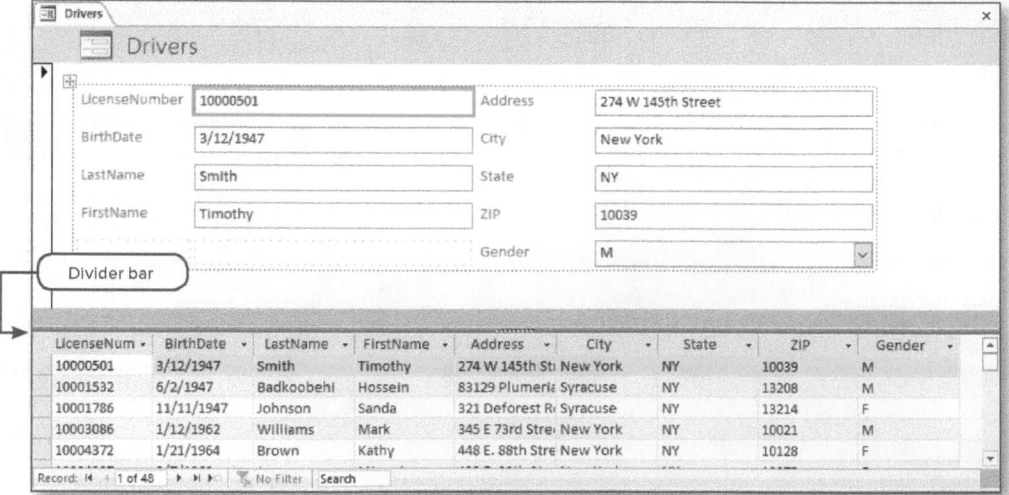

4-145 Split form based on *Drivers* table

 d. Save the form as DriverInformation.

5. Edit the form in *Layout* view.
 a. Use the resize arrow to decrease the column width of the *State*, *ZIP*, and *Gender* fields and to increase the width of the *Address* field in the *Datasheet* portion of the form. You can't use the *Property Sheet* to set the width of columns in the *Datasheet* portion of the form.
 b. Change the label for *LicenseNumber* to License# in the single record portion of the form and insert spaces between the words in the labels for *BirthDate*, *LastName* and *FirstName*.
 c. Add the date and time to the form header. Accept the suggested date and time format.
 d. Enter 6" in the *Left* property for the *Date* and the *Time* controls.

6. Move controls within the layout to customize the layout.

 a. Add two rows below the *Gender* field so you have some room to move the different fields. If necessary, you can drag the divider bar down to increase the available space in the single record portion of the form.

 b. Add one row above the *License#* field.

 c. Move the *License#* label to the cell in the top row.

 d. Move the *License#* text box to the cell below the label.

 e. Continue moving the labels and text boxes so that your fields are placed similar to those in Figure 4-146. You may need to move some labels and text boxes to a temporary location in the layout during this process.

 f. Delete any unused rows and columns in the layout.

 g. Select a cell in the left column and change the *Width* to 1.8".

 h. Change the *Width* of the middle column to 1.8".

 i. Change the *Width* of the right column to 1".

 j. Change the *Height* of the rows that contain labels to .2".

 k. Change the *Height* of the rows that contain text boxes to .25".

 l. Move the control layout from the far left so that its location is similar to the location in Figure 4-146.

 m. Save the form.

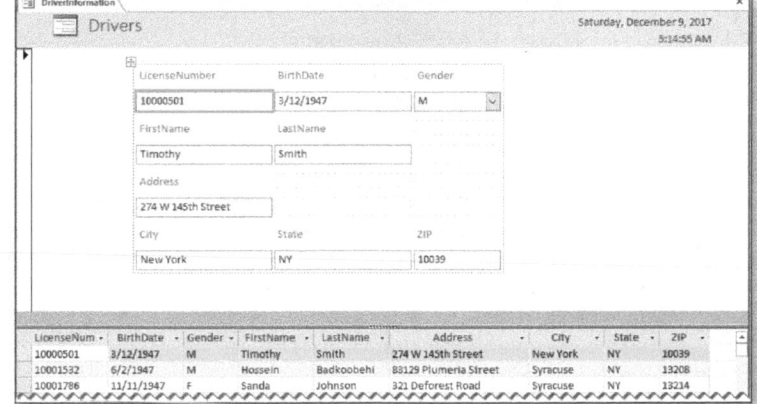

4-146 Modified *DriverInformation* form

7. Switch to *Form* view and practice using a form to add and delete records.

 a. Use the navigation buttons to move among records.

 b. Use the **New (blank) record** button in the *Navigation* bar to add a new record. Enter the following data values:
 LicenseNum#: 39992400
 BirthDate: 10/23/1997
 Gender: F
 FirstName: Patricia
 LastName: Lozada
 Address: 12846 Sandy Point Drive
 City: Utica
 State: NY
 ZIP: 13502.

 c. Navigate to the first record.

 d. Navigate back to the last record. This should be the record you added.

 e. Navigate to the seventh record. This should be Steve Miller's record.

 f. Delete the record by clicking the **Delete** button arrow [*Home* tab, *Records* group] and then selecting **Delete Record**. Click **Yes** in the dialog box to confirm the deletion.

 g. Close the form when done.

8. Create a report using the *Blank Report* button. Add all the fields from the *Tickets* table into the report.

9. Modify the layout of the report.
 a. Modify the column labels to match those shown in Figure 4-147.

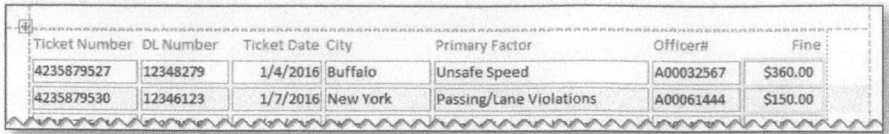

Ticket Number	DL Number	Ticket Date	City	Primary Factor	Officer#	Fine
4235879527	12348279	1/4/2016	Buffalo	Unsafe Speed	A00032567	$360.00
4235879530	12346123	1/7/2016	New York	Passing/Lane Violations	A00061444	$150.00

4-147 Adjusted column width of report fields

 b. Change the *Width* of the *DL Number*, *Ticket Date*, and *Officer#* columns to .85".
 c. Change the *Width* of the *Primary Factor* column to 2".
 d. Change the *Width* of the *Fine* column to .75".
 e. Add a title to the report header and enter Ticket Report by City as the title text.
 f. Add page numbers. Use the **Bottom of Page [Footer]** position, **Page N of M** format and **Center** the alignment.
 g. Save the report as TicketsByCity.

10. Add grouping and sorting to the report.
 a. Group the report on the *City* field.
 b. Sort the report on the *Ticket Date* field in *from oldest to newest* order.
 c. Save the report.

11. Add totals to the report.
 a. Calculate the average dollar value of the *Fine* field. The average appears at the end of each group and an overall average appears at the end of the report.
 b. Scroll to the bottom of the report. Change the *Height* of the *Fine Average* text box for both the group and the overall average to .25".
 c. Apply the **bold** format, on the *Report Layout Tools Format* tab, to the *Fine Average* text box for both the group and the overall average.
 d. Save the report.

12. View the report in *Print Preview*.
 a. Adjust the zoom to **One Page**.
 b. Navigate to the second page of the report. Notice that the Utica group of tickets is spread across two pages.
 c. Close *Print Preview*.

13. Choose **keep whole group together on one page** in the *Group, Sort, and Total* pane.

14. Save the report.

15. Preview the report again.
 a. Adjust the zoom to **One Page**. The report should look similar to Figure 4-148.
 b. Navigate to the second page. Notice that the Utica tickets are all on the second page.
 c. Close *Print Preview*.

16. Close the report.

17. Close the database.

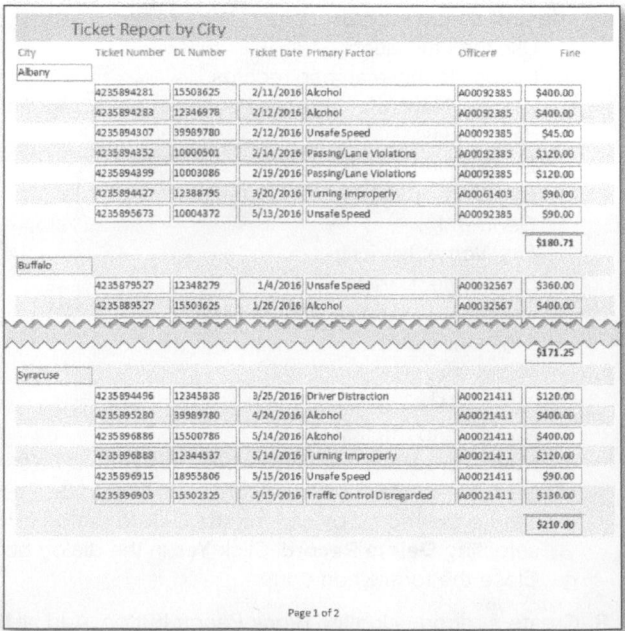

4-148 Completed *TicketsByCity* report

Independent Project 4-6

Courtyard Medical Plaza wants to add a form and a report to its database. To ensure consistency, the starting file is provided for you. Create a blank form and modify the form in *Layout* view. Edit properties to restrict the form to data entry and add buttons. Next, create a report using the *Report Wizard*. In *Layout* view, modify the layout, add sorting, and add conditional formatting. Finally, preview the results. [Student Learning Outcomes 4.2, 4.3, 4.4, 4.5, 4.6, 4.7, 4.8]

File Needed: ***CourtyardMedicalPlaza-04.accdb***
Completed Project File Name: *[your initials] **Access 4-6.accdb***

Skills Covered in This Project

- Create a form using the *Form* button.
- Edit a form in *Layout* view.
- Add the current date to a form.
- Move fields within the control layout.
- Restrict a form to data entry.
- Test the functionality of a form.
- Create a report using the *Report Wizard*.
- Edit a report in *Layout* view.
- Add grouping and sorting to a report.
- Add totals to a report.
- Add conditional formatting to a report.
- Preview a report.

1. Open the ***CourtyardMedicalPlaza-04*** database from your student data files.

2. Save the database as [your initials] Access 4-6.

3. Enable content in the database.

4. Create a form using the *Blank Form* button.
 a. Add all the fields from the *Physician* table in the following order: **DoctorID**, **FirstName**, **LastName**, **PrimarySpecialty**, **OfficeNumber**, and **MoveInDate**.
 b. Close the *Field List*.
 c. Save the form as AddNewPhysician.

5. Edit the form in *Layout* view, add a new column and new rows to the control layout, and modify their size.
 a. Add two rows below the *Tenant Since* row.
 b. Add one column to the right of the existing columns.
 c. Adjust the *Width* of each column to 1.6".
 d. Adjust the *Height* of the last row to .4".

6. Add command buttons, a title, and the date to the form.
 a. Add a button into the bottom row of the left-most column to save a record [*Record Operations Category*].
 b. Change the wording to Save Physician Record.
 c. Name the button AddPhysicianFormSaveButton.
 d. Add a second button into the bottom row of the middle column to add a new record [*Record Operations Category*].
 e. Change the wording to Add New Physician.
 f. Name the button AddPhysicianFormAddButton.
 g. Add a third button into the bottom row of the right most column to close the form [*Form Operations Category*].
 h. Use the existing wording for the button.
 i. Name the button AddPhysicianFormCloseButton.
 j. Add a title to the form header. Edit the title to include spaces between the words.
 k. Add the date to the form. Use the *DD-Mon-YY* format. If necessary, deselect the **Include Time** check box so that only the date is added.

l. Enter 1.1" in the *Width* property and 4" in the *Left* property for the *Date* control.

m. Save the changes to the form. The revised form should look similar to Figure 4-149.

7. Restrict the form to data entry.

a. Open the *Property Sheet* for the form if necessary and select the **Data** tab.

b. Click the **drop-down arrow** in the *Selection* box of the *Property Sheet* and select **Form**.

c. Select **Yes** in the *Data Entry* property box.

d. Select **Yes** in the *Allow Additions* property box. Recall that when both the *Data Entry* and *Allow Additions* properties are set to *yes*, the values in the *Allow Deletions* and *Allow Edits* properties do not have an impact

e. Save the form.

f. Close the form.

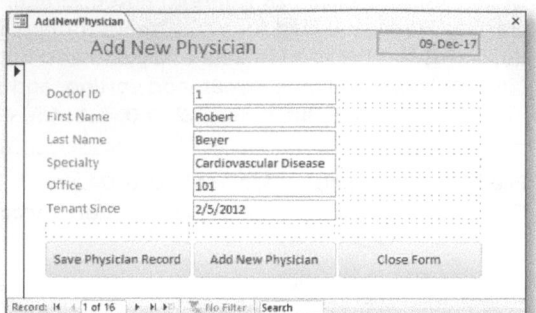

4-149 *AddNewPhysician* form

8. Create a report using the *Report Wizard*.

a. Launch the *Report Wizard*.

b. Add all the fields from the *RentInvoices* table in the following order: **InvoiceID, FKDoctorID, InvoiceDate, Description, DueDate, DateReceived, AmountDue,** and **Discount**.

c. Accept the suggested grouping by *FKDoctorID* on the second page of the *Report Wizard*.

d. Add summary options on the third page of the Report Wizard. In the *Summary Options* dialog box select the **Sum** of the *AmountDue* field and select the **Detail and Summary** radio button for the *Show* option if necessary (Figure 4-150).

e. Choose a **Stepped** layout and **Landscape** orientation.

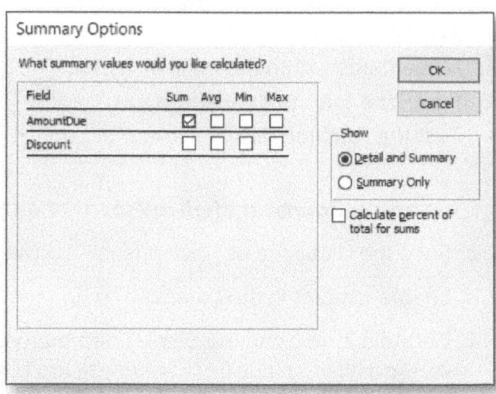

4-150 *Summary Options* dialog box

f. Click the **Finish** button without making any changes to the suggested title. The preview of the report should look similar to Figure 4-151. Don't worry if some of your fields overlap or display the **#** symbols indicating that the column width is too narrow. You resize the columns in step 9. The wording for the summary line was automatically added using the totals created by the *Report Wizard*.

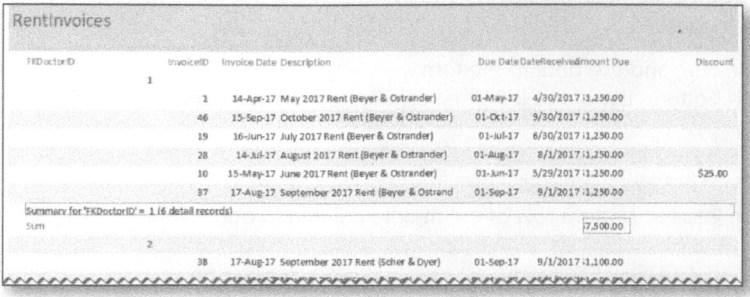

4-151 *RentInvoices* report created using the *Report Wizard*

g. Close *Print Preview*.

9. Edit the report using *Layout* view so that your report matches Figure 4-152.

a. Switch to *Layout* view and open the *Property Sheet* if necessary.

b. Select both the *FKDoctorID* text box and label and change the *Width* to .6".

c. Change the *Width* of the *InvoiceID* label and text box to .75" and change the *Left* property to 1".

d. Change the *Width* of the *Invoice Date* label and text box to 1" and change the *Left* property to 1.9".

e. Change the *Width* of the *Description* label and text box to 2.8" and change the *Left* property to 3".

f. Change the *Width* of the *Due Date* label and text box to 1" and change the *Left* property to 6".

g. Change the *Width* of the *DateReceived* label and text box to 1" and change the *Left* property to 7".

h. Change the *Width* of the *Amount Due* column to 1" and change the *Left* property to 8.3". Don't worry that you still don't see the entire value. It will be corrected when you change the next column.

i. Change the *Width* of the *Discount* column to .7" and change the *Left* property to 9.4".

j. Edit the title label and the *FKDoctorID, InvoiceID* and *DateReceived* field labels to match Figure 4-152.

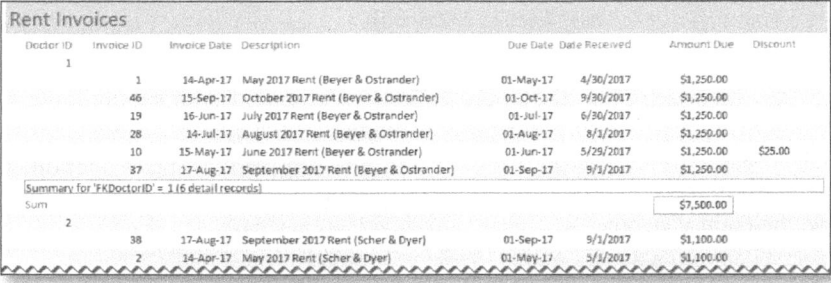

4-152 *RentInvoices* report after editing the layout

k. Change the *Width* of the text box that displays the sum of the *Amount Due* to 1".

l. Scroll to the bottom of the report. Change the *Width* of the text box that displays the grand total of the *Amount Due* to 1".

m. Save the report.

n. Switch to *Report* view. Scroll to the top of the report if necessary. The report should look similar to Figure 4-152.

o. Switch back to *Layout* view.

10. Add an *oldest to newest* sort on the *InvoiceDate* field in the *Group, Sort, and Total* pane.

11. Add conditional formatting to the report so that any *Discount* values that *are greater than or equal to $20* display in a **bold, green** font. Choose the **Green 5** font from the *Standard Colors*.

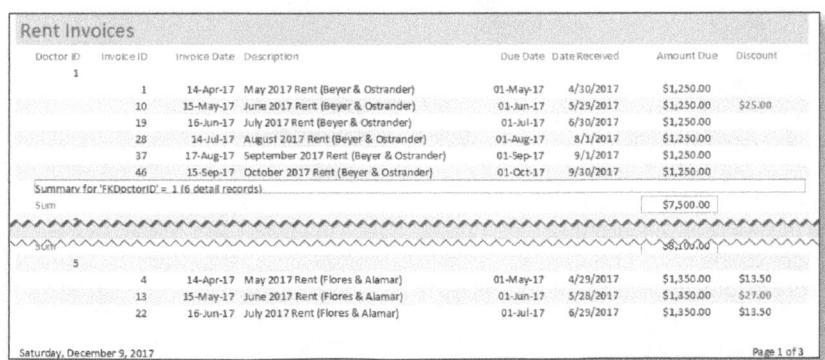

4-153 Completed *RentInvoices* report

12. Save your changes.

13. View the report in *Print Preview*.

a. Adjust the zoom to **One Page**. The report should look similar to Figure 4-153.

b. Close *Print Preview*.

14. Close the report.

15. Close the database.

Improve It Project 4-7

Mary's Rentals wants to improve its database. To ensure consistency, the starting file is provided for you. You improve the functionality of a form by editing controls on the form, modifying the layout, and limiting edits and deletions. Improve the usability of a report by modifying the layout and adding grouping and sorting. Finally, preview how the report will print.
[Student Learning Outcomes 4.2, 4.3, 4.5, 4.6, 4.8]

File Needed: ***MarysRentals-04.accdb***
Completed Project File Name: ***[your initials] Access 4-7.accdb***

Skills Covered in This Project

- Edit a form in *Layout* view.
- Add a title and date to a form.
- Move fields within the control layout.
- Set properties to limit user edits and deletions.

- Test the functionality of a form.
- Edit a report in *Layout* view.
- Add grouping and sorting to a report.
- Preview a report.

1. Open the ***MarysRentals-04*** database from your student data files.

2. Save the database as [your initials] Access 4-7.

3. Enable content in the database.

4. Edit the *ViewEquipment* form in *Layout* view so that your form matches Figure 4-154.
 a. Increase the column width of the labels to 1.5" so that the entire caption displays.
 b. Edit the label contents to insert blank spaces between the words. For example, change *EquipmentID* to *Equipment ID*.
 c. Increase the column width of the text boxes to 3" so that the entire contents displays.
 d. Add a title to the form. Enter View Equipment as the title text.
 e. Add a date to the form with the *DD-Mon-YY* format.
 f. Change the *Width* of the *Date* control to 1" and the *Left* property to 5".
 g. Move the control layout down and to the right.
 h. Increase the height of the bottom row that contains the button to .3".
 i. Fix the misspellings in the button text by changing the button to read Close Form.
 j. Select both cells in the bottom row and click the **Merge** button [*Form Layout Tools Arrange* tab, *Merge/Split* group].
 k. Save the changes to the form. The revised form should look similar to Figure 4-154.

5. Edit the form properties to restrict user additions, edits, and deletions.

6. Test the form.
 a. Save the form.
 b. Switch to *Form* view and navigate through the records.
 c. Try to change the value of one of the fields. That action should be restricted.
 d. Close the form.

4-154 Completed *ViewEquipment* form

7. Add grouping and sorting into the *ServiceHistory* report.
 a. Open the report in *Layout* view.
 b. Group the report on the *FKEquipmentID* field.
 c. Change to the option to **keep header and first record together on one page**.
 d. Sort the report on the *Service Date* field in *oldest to newest* order.

8. Edit the report in *Layout* view.
 a. Remove the *FK* from the *FKEquipmentID* label and insert a space between *Equipment* and *ID*.
 b. Edit the captions in the labels, including the title, to insert spaces between the words. Notice in Figure 4-155 that the size of the *Performed By* and *Odometer Reading* labels is wider than the corresponding text box. This was caused by inserting the space into the caption.
 c. Change the *Width* of the *Performed By* label and text box to .95".
 d. Change the *Width* of the *Hours* label and text box to .7" and change the *Left* property to 7.2".
 e. Change the *Width* of the *Odometer Reading* label and text box to 1.35".

4-155 Label sizes wider than corresponding text box

 f. Select **Center** alignment on the *Report Layout Tools Format* tab for the *Service Date* label and text box and the *Hours* label and text box.
 g. Change the *Total Cost* label to be **right aligned**.
 h. Save the report.

9. View the report in *Print Preview*.
 a. Adjust the zoom to **One Page**. The report should look similar to Figure 4-156.
 b. Close *Print Preview*.

10. Close the report.

11. Close the database.

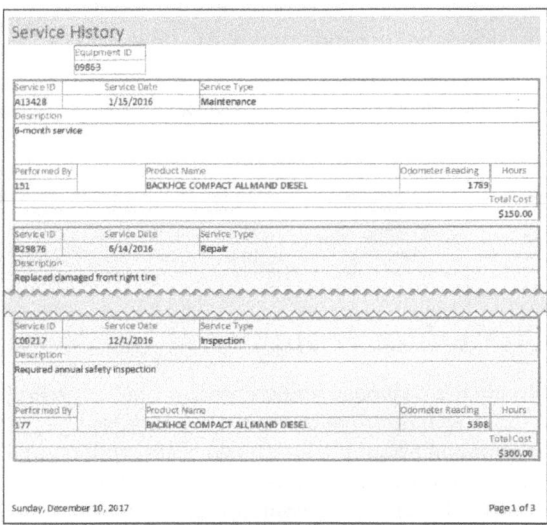

4-156 Completed *ServiceHistory* report

Challenge Project 4-8

For this project, you modify the database you built in Challenge Project 3-8, by creating one form and two reports.
[Student Learning Outcomes 4.1, 4.2, 4.3, 4.4, 4.5, 4.6, 4.8]

File Needed: *[your initials] Access 3-8.accdb*
Completed Project File Name: *[your initials] Access 4-8.accdb*

Open the database *[your initials] Access 3-8* and save a copy of it as [your initials] Access 4-8.

Modify your database according to the following instructions:

- Create a form for your table using the *Form Wizard*.
- Add all the fields to the form.
- In *Layout* view, adjust the column widths as necessary so they are sized appropriately.
- Change the form properties to restrict the form to limit user edits and deletions.
- Add one button to the form to close the form.
- Save the form and view it in *Form* view to ensure it works as desired.
- Create a report using the *Report Wizard* to show all the fields from one of your queries.
- Adjust the column widths as necessary so they are sized appropriately.
- Save the report and view it in *Print Preview* to ensure that it will print as desired.
- Create a second report using the *Blank Report* option.
- Add all the fields from the table into the report.
- Edit the layout as needed to adjust the column widths and page orientation.
- Add a title and page numbers to the report.
- Group the report on one of the fields.
- Save the report.
- View the report in *Print Preview* to ensure that it will print as desired.
- Save any changes that you made.

Challenge Project 4-9

Modify the database you created in Challenge Project 3-9 for Blue Lake Sports. Your database contains a table with information about the different departments at Blue Lake Sports and a related table with information about the interns who are working at Blue Lake, along with the query you created. Create a form for the *Department* table and a report for the *Intern* table.
[Student Learning Outcomes 4.2, 4.3, 4.5, 4.6, 4.7, 4.8]

File Needed: *[your initials] Access 3-9.accdb*
Completed Project File Name: *[your initials] Access 4-9.accdb*

Open the database *[your initials] Access 3-9* and save a copy of it as [your initials] Access 4-9.

Modify your database according to the following instructions:

- Create a form for the *Department* table using the *Blank Form* button.
- Add all the fields to the form.
- Adjust the column widths as necessary so they are sized appropriately.
- Add a title to the form.
- Add a button to the form to close the form.
- Save the form and view it in *Form* view to ensure it works as desired.
- Create a report using the *Blank Report* tool to show all the fields in the *Intern* table.

- Adjust the column widths as necessary so they are sized appropriately.
- Group the report on the *DepartmentName* field.
- Sort the records by intern *LastName*.
- Add totals to count the total number of interns in each department.
- Add conditional formatting to the *University* field. Make the font a different color for each of the university values contained in the database. You need to add several rules for the *University* field (one for each value).
- Edit the title of the report to indicate the contents.
- Save the report.
- View the report in *Print Preview* and adjust the orientation and margins as necessary.
- Save any changes that you made.

Challenge Project 4-10

Modify the database you created in Challenge Project 3-10 for a travel agency. Your database contains a table with information about the different ships and a related table with information about upcoming cruises, along with the queries you added. Add a form to allow new ships to be added into the database. Add a report to display trip information, grouped by number of days. Modify both the form and report to improve the overall functionality.
[Student Learning Outcomes 4.2, 4.3, 4.4, 4.5, 4.6, 4.8]

File Needed: *[your initials] Access 3-10.accdb*
Completed Project File Name: *[your initials] Access 4-10.accdb*

Open the database *[your initials] Access 3-10* and save a copy of it as [your initials] Access 4-10.

Modify your database according to the following instructions:

- Create a form for the *Ships* table using the *Blank Form* button.
- Add all the fields to the form.
- Adjust the column widths as necessary so they are sized appropriately.
- Add a title to the form.
- Change the form properties to restrict the form to data entry.
- Add three buttons to the form: Save a Record, Add New Record, and Close the Form.
- Save the form and view it in *Form* view to ensure it works as desired.
- Create a report using the *Report Wizard* to show all the fields in the *Trips* table.
- Group the report on the *NumberOfDays* field.
- Sort the records by cost per person.
- Add totals to calculate the average cost per person.
- Adjust the column widths as necessary so they are sized appropriately.
- Edit the title of the report to indicate the contents.
- Save the report.
- View the report in *Print Preview* and adjust the orientation and margins as necessary.
- Save any changes that you made.

CHAPTER 5

Templates, Advanced Relationships, and Macros

CHAPTER OVERVIEW

Now that you have learned the basics of Access, you are ready to learn the skills you can use to create more sophisticated databases. This chapter introduces three important skills. First, you learn more about creating and modifying databases based on Access templates. Next, you learn additional skills you can use to create table relationships, including how to create a many-to-many relationship. Finally, you learn how to create and use macros that improve the user-friendliness and functionality of your database.

STUDENT LEARNING OUTCOMES (SLOs)

After completing this chapter, you will be able to:

SLO 5.1 Analyze, create, use, and modify a database from an Access template (p. A5-286).

SLO 5.2 Create a relationship with the *Lookup Wizard*; edit a relationship; edit properties of a lookup field; delete relationships created with a lookup field; and use a lookup with multiple fields (p. A5-294).

SLO 5.3 Implement a many-to-many relationship and explore join properties between tables (p. A5-299).

SLO 5.4 Describe a macro and use the *Macro Builder* (p. A5-306).

SLO 5.5 Build a stand-alone macro, build an embedded macro, and edit and delete user interface macros (p. A5-311).

SLO 5.6 Build an event-driven data macro, build a named data macro, and edit and delete data macros (p. A5-321).

SLO 5.7 Build more advanced macros by adding conditions, build a submacro, integrate parameters, and test and debug a macro (p. A5-326).

CASE STUDY

As you progress through the Pause & Practice projects in this chapter, you will build a database from a template, implement many-to-many relationships, build user interface macros, and build data macros.

Pause & Practice 5-1: Create a database using a template, and explore and modify the database objects.

Pause & Practice 5-2: Create and edit a many-to-many relationship. Build the junction table, use the *Lookup Wizard* to create relationships, edit the relationship, and enter data into the junction table.

Pause & Practice 5-3: Build and test a stand-alone and an embedded user interface macro.

Pause & Practice 5-4: Build and test event-driven and named data macros.

A5-285

Using Access Templates

Recall from Chapter 1 that a ***template*** is a predesigned database that contains various pre-built objects. A template provides you with a complete, ready-to-use, database application. After creating a database that is based on a template, you can use the template database directly or you can customize the database to better meet your needs. If your needs are addressed in a template, it can be a great starting point.

Access Templates

You can choose from several templates that are included with Access. Additionally, other templates are available on Office.com.

Some of the Access templates are designed to work on the web. When you create a database built from one of these templates, you must link it to a ***SharePoint*** server running ***Access Services***. The web-base templates, such as Asset *tracking (SharePoint web app)*, include the phrase *(SharePoint web app)* as part of the template name. The non-web-based databases are known as desktop databases in Access, the type of database you have built in this book.

> ### MORE INFO
>
> Use the *Access Help System* to learn more about creating and using web databases.

Five of the more popular desktop database templates are described in the following table. These templates all include a ***Welcome*** form with a help video about using the database.

Access Templates

Template Name	Description	Contents
Updated: Event management	Used to track information about upcoming events.	The database contains three tables, one query, four forms, five reports, and three macros.
Updated: Asset tracking	Used to track assets within an organization, such as computers or office equipment.	The database contains four tables, three queries, seven forms, eight reports, two macros, and one module.
Updated: Contacts	Used to track information about people, such as team members, customers, vendors, etc.	The database contains two tables, one query, three forms, two reports, one macro, and one module.
Updated: Students	Used to track information about the students at a school, including details about their guardians.	The database contains six tables, five queries, eight forms, eleven reports, three macros, and one module.
Updated: Task management	Used to track information about work tasks your team needs to complete.	The database contains four tables, six queries, seven forms, nine reports, three macros, and one module.

You will find it very helpful to create sample databases based on several of these templates. This will allow you to explore the range of functionality available in Access. By doing so, you will be able to see custom menus, different form and report designs, and how all of the Access objects work together.

Create a Database from a Desktop Database Template

If you have found a template that is appropriate for your needs, you create a new database that is based on that template.

> ▶ **HOW TO:** Create a New Database Using a Template

1. Open Access to display the list of sample templates (Figure 5-1), or, if Access is already open, click the **File** tab to open the *Backstage* view and click the **New** button.

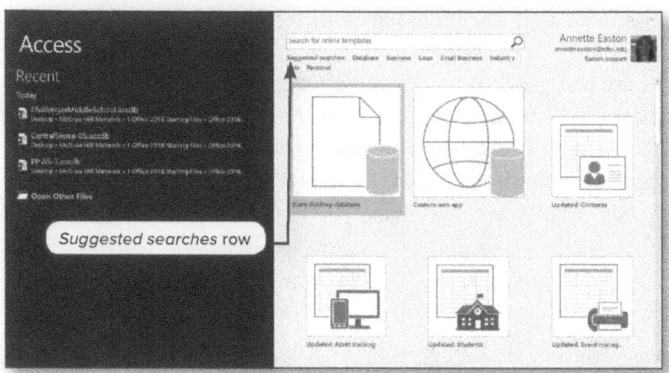

5-1 Create a new database from a template

2. Select the **template** you wish to use. A new dialog box displays where you can enter information about the data-base name and location (Figure 5-2).

5-2 Enter new database file name and location

> ▶ **ANOTHER WAY**
>
> If the desktop database templates do not display in the template listing, either click a keyword in the *Suggested searches* row or enter the key words in the *Search for online templates* box and click the **magnify** icon. Select the desired template from the available options. You can also use search to find alternate templates available on Office.com.

3. Click the **Browse** button to browse to a location on your computer or USB drive to save the database.
4. Type the file name in the *File Name* area.
5. Click the **OK** button.
6. Click the **Create** button. The new database opens.
7. Enable content in the database.

Use and Modify a Database

After creating a database based on a template, you will want to open the database to fully explore the different components and to see how it functions. Be sure to look at all of the features that have been built into the database. To help you learn what to look for within a template-based database, this section includes examples from a sample database built using the *Updated: Asset tracking* template.

Explore the Database Functionality

When a new database is created and opens, the *Asset List* form opens (Figure 5-3).

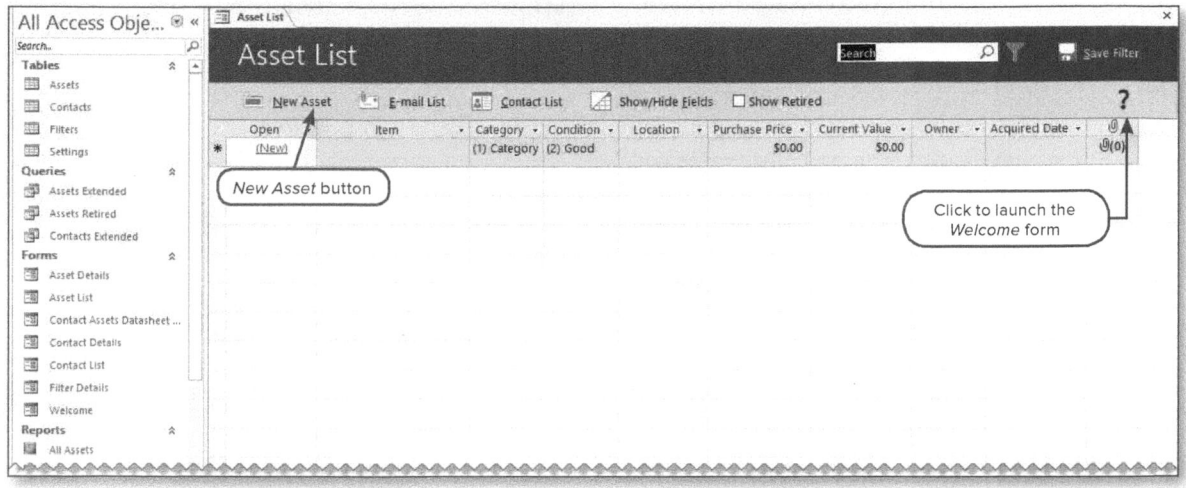

5-3 *Asset List* form in a database created from the *Asset tracking* template

This template also contains a *Welcome* form (Figure 5-4) that opens automatically when the database is opened and the content is enabled. This form contains a video on how to use the *Assets* database. When you are using templates, take advantage of any videos and other help resources. They will help you to make the best use of your database. Close the *Welcome* form when you are done. To reopen the

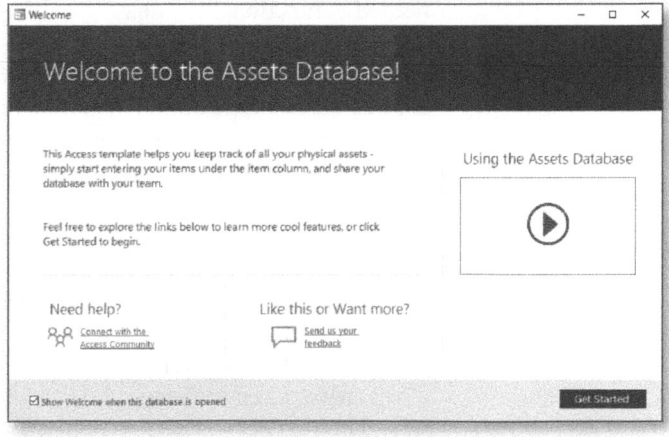

5-4 *Welcome* form

Welcome form later, either double-click the form in the *Navigation Pane* or click the **question mark** icon on the *Asset List* form.

On the *Asset List* form, note that the details of each current asset display in datasheet view. Currently no records appear since your database does not have any existing data to display. Notice the **Search** box that allows you to easily find different records.

Near the top of the *Asset List* form, a rose-colored bar contains buttons that indicate the functions available in the database. To explore the functionality of the database, click each of the buttons on the *Asset List* form.

> **MORE INFO**
>
> This template has set button properties so the buttons blend in with the form instead of having a different border color, and also so the pointer changes to a hand pointer when the user hovers over a button.

The *New Asset* button opens the *Asset Details* form shown in Figure 5-5. The *Asset Details* form is a user-friendly interface you can use to add records into the database.

Continue exploring the other forms and reports so that you are comfortable and you understand the different functions that are available in the database.

At this point you are ready to look at the objects that are used inside the database.

Explore the Navigation Pane, Objects, and Relationships

Many templates open with the *Navigation Pane* closed. Often this is because the needed functionality has been incorporated into the menu/navigation that is built into the forms. However, to analyze the database design, it may be necessary to view the contents of the *Navigation Pane*. If the *Navigation Pane* is closed, click the **Shutter Bar Open/Close Button** to view the contents.

The *Navigation Pane* should match Figure 5-6. You are already familiar with how the *Navigation Pane* groups objects (see *The Access Interface* section in *SLO 1.1: Understanding Database Concepts*).

Some of the templates have a customized *Navigation Pane* that shows the database user only certain objects in the database. This is usually so a user doesn't accidentally delete or modify objects within the database. Figure 5-7 shows the *Navigation Pane* used in the *Updated: Task management* template. It contains custom groups, such as *Tasks* and *Contacts*. In order to understand the structure of the database it helps to see all of the objects instead of the

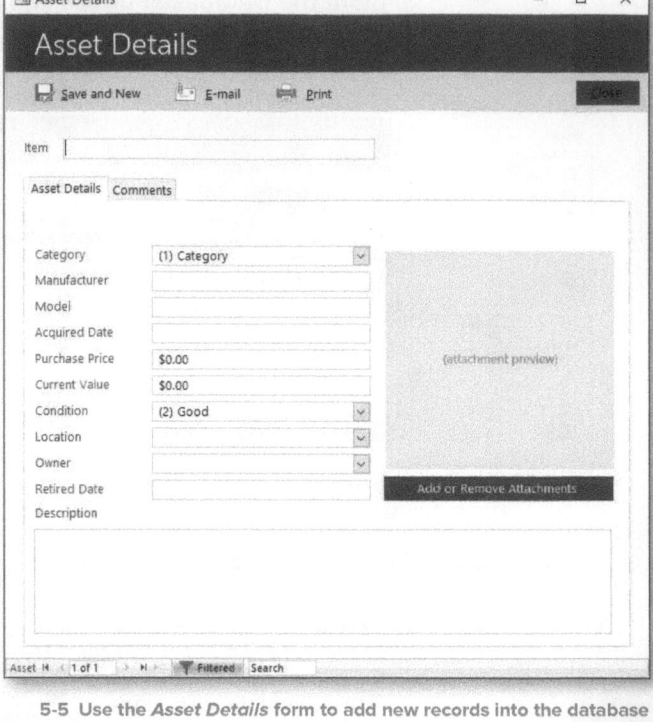

5-5 Use the *Asset Details* form to add new records into the database

5-7 Customized *Navigation Pane* in *Updated: Task management* template

5-6 *Navigation Pane*

limited set displayed in the customized pane.

To switch the *Navigation Pane* display, click the **Navigation Pane** arrow to open the *Navigation* menu (Figure 5-8). Select the **Object Type** category. The *Navigation Pane* updates to show all of the objects (Figure 5-9).

Open and view the design properties of the different tables, queries, forms and reports. You may find objects in a template database with features that are more advanced than you learned in the first four chapters of the book. When you encounter features you don't know, you can use the Access help feature to learn more about the objects.

5-8 *Navigation* menu

5-9 *Navigation Pane* showing all objects

Additionally, it is a good idea to review the relationships that exist in the template database. You can see which tables are related. You should also look at the details of each relationship to determine whether referential integrity is being enforced and whether any of the cascade options have been selected. See *SLO 2.6: Understanding and Designing Relational Databases* for a review of these skills.

It is important to note that Access databases that are built to work online are different. This includes all of the web-based templates and any databases built from these templates. For example, *Design* view is not an available option for objects in web databases. Instead, for web databases, Access provides enhanced *Datasheet* view features as well as the *Layout* view functionality. Another difference in web databases is that relationships are created and modified through a lookup field and not through the *Relationships* window, as they are in desktop databases. You will learn about lookup fields in the next section.

Modify the Database

Once you have reviewed the functionality and design properties of the database objects, you are ready to make modifications. Follow the steps you already learned in Chapters 1 through 4 about modifying the different database objects.

It is important to recognize the dependencies that different database objects have on each other, and how changes made to one object may affect another. For example, a text box on a form can be linked, or bound, to a field in a table. If you delete the field from the table, the text box remains on the form; however, the link to the table field becomes invalid. When the form displays, an error message now appears in the text box. To fix the problem you need to modify the form and remove that text box. Remember that as you make modifications to a database you must fully inspect and test all of the objects to ensure that the changes have not caused other objects or controls to no longer work correctly.

You may wish to make modifications that require skills that are covered in the remaining chapters of this book. Additionally, some of the objects in a template may even include features that are more advanced than will be covered in this book. You can use the Access help feature, or you can consult with someone who has advanced knowledge of those features.

For this Pause & Practice, you create a database using the *Desktop contacts* template. You then explore the database functionality and modify database objects.

File Needed: None
Completed Project File Name: ***[your initials] PP A5-1.accdb***

1. Create a new database based on a template.
 a. Open Access or click the **New** button [*File* tab] if an Access database is already open.
 b. Select the **Updated: Contacts** template. If the *Updated: Contacts* template is not displayed, click **Database** in the *Suggested searches* row and select the **Updated: Contacts** template. A new dialog box displays where you can enter information about the database name and location.
 c. Type [your initials] PP A5-1 in the *File Name* box.
 d. Click the **Browse for a location to put your database** button to change the location in which to save the database and click the **OK** button.
 e. Click the **Create** button. The new database opens.

2. Depending on the selections made on your computer, the *Welcome* form may display (Figure 5-10).

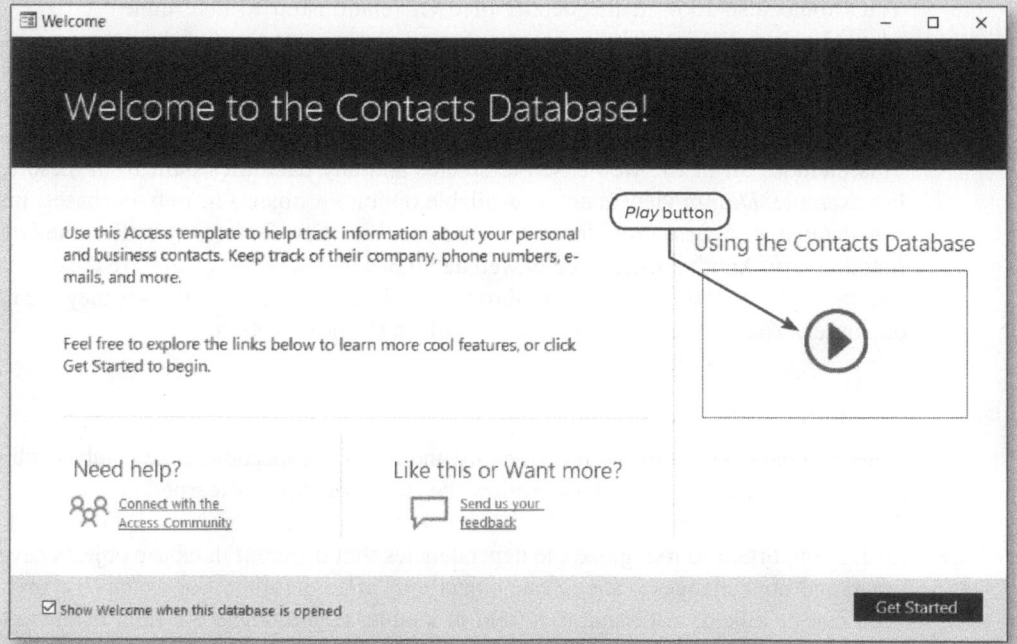

5-10 *Getting Started with Contacts* form

 a. Click the **Play** button to open the Microsoft Office web site. You need to have an Internet connection in order to open this web page.
 b. Click the **Play** button on the web page to launch the *Use the Contacts Database template* help video. Watch the video.
 c. Close the web page and close the *Welcome* form.

3. Enable content in the security warning. If the *Welcome* form displays again, click **Get Started**.

4. Add a record into the database.
 a. Click the **New Contact** button, the leftmost button in the purple menu bar, to open the *Contact Details* form.
 b. Type the information below into the form. Fields on the form that are not included below should be left blank. Add the data below into the form:
 - *First Name:* Maggie
 - *Last Name:* Nguyen
 - *Company:* Applied Materials
 - *Email:* NguyenM@AppliedMaterials.com
 - *Category:* Click the **drop-down arrow** and select **Business**
 - *Street:* 9700 Highway 290 East
 - *City:* Austin
 - *State:* Texas
 - *Zip:* 78724
 - *Business Phone:* 555-272-1234
 c. Click the **Close** button (Figure 5-11) when finished.

5. Explore the *Navigation Pane* and database objects.
 a. Double-click the **Contacts** table to open the table. The table contains Maggie's contact data you added previously.
 b. Switch to *Design* view of the table. A message box displays, informing you that another object bound to the *Contacts* table is open. Select **Yes** to open the table as read-only. Access prevents you from making changes to the design of the *Contacts* table because the *Contact List* form is open.

5-11 *Contact Details* form

> **MORE INFO**
>
> If you wanted to add additional fields to the table, or edit any of the existing fields, you would need to close both the *Contact List* form and the *Contacts* table and then re-open the *Contacts* table in *Design* view to make changes.

 c. Select the **Category** field.
 d. Click the **Lookup** tab in the *Field Properties* area in the lower half of the *Design* view window. Note the three choices in the *Row Source* property.
 e. Close the *Contacts* table.

6. Modify the *Phone Book* report.
 a. Open the *Phone Book* report.
 b. Click the **View** button arrow [*Home* tab, *Views* group] and select **Layout View**.

c. Click the **Property Sheet** button [*Report Layout Tools Design* tab, *Tools* group].
d. Click to select the **Format** tab in the *Property Sheet,* if necessary.
e. Select **Report** in the *Selection type* box. Note that the report tab displays *Phone Book by Group* (Figure 5-12). This is the contents of the *Caption* property.
f. Click the **current date** field to select the *Text Box* control shown in Figure 5-12.

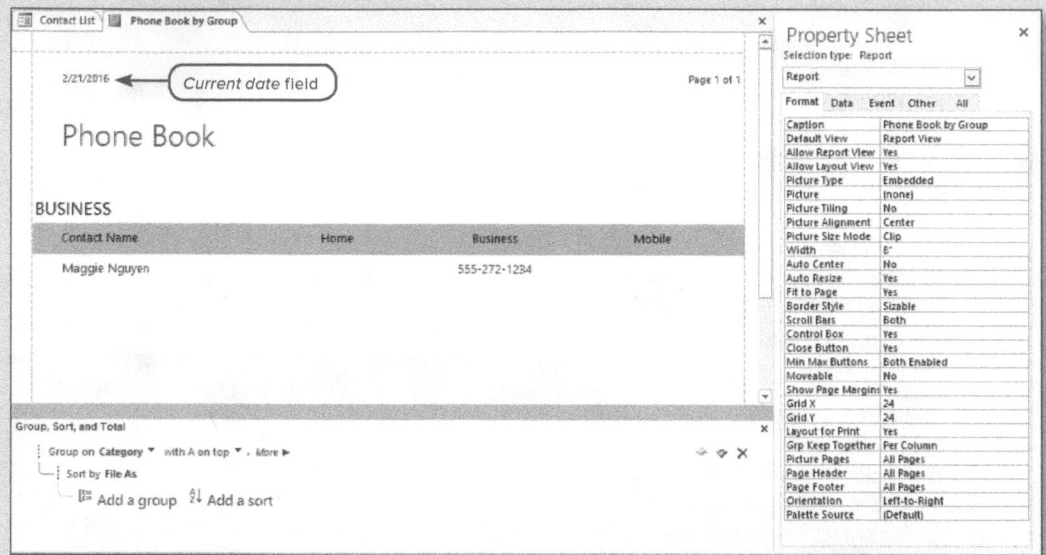

5-12 *Layout* view of the *Phone Book* report

g. Select **Medium Date** in the *Format* property box. The text box updates to display the date using this new format.

> ▶ **ANOTHER WAY**
>
> You can set the date format in the *Number* group of the *Report Layout Tools Format* tab.

h. Close the *Property Sheet.*
i. Save and close the report.

7. Explore the *Directory* report.
a. Open the *Directory* report.
b. Click the **Map** button. This button contains a macro that opens a browser and displays the contact's address in *Bing Maps*.
c. Close the web page.
d. Close the report.

8. Close the database.

SLO 5.2

Creating and Customizing a Relationship through the Lookup Wizard

In Chapter 2, you learned about relationships and how they are used to connect related tables. You also learned how to create relationships using the *Relationships* window. Recall from the *Create Relationships between Tables* section in *SLO 2.6: Understanding and Designing Relational Databases* that if you elect to enforce referential integrity when you enter data into the table, Access requires that the user enter a data value in the ***foreign key*** field that matches the value in the ***primary key*** of an existing record in the related table. This step is important to maintaining integrity of the database, but it requires that the user knows the value to enter into the foreign key field.

It may be more efficient to have your users choose the value from a drop-down list of the possible values. You can do this with a ***lookup field***. In Chapter 2, you learned how to create a lookup field in a table using the *Lookup Wizard* and entering the list of possible values. In this section, you learn to create a relationship using the *Lookup Wizard*. In addition to creating the relationship, the *Lookup Wizard* also creates a *Combo Box* for the foreign key field that displays the list of possible values from the related table.

Define a Relationship with the Lookup Wizard

You create relationships after the foreign keys have been added as fields into the related tables. While you can add data into the table on the "one" side of the relationship, you should create the relationships before any data is added into the tables that contain the foreign keys. This helps ensure that all the data in the related tables has referential integrity.

▶ **HOW TO:** Create a Relationship Using the Lookup Wizard

1. Open the table containing the foreign key in *Design* view.
2. Click to select the **foreign key** field.
3. Click the **Data Type** property box, click the **drop-down arrow** to display the list of data types, and then select **Lookup Wizard** (Figure 5-13). The *Lookup Wizard* dialog box opens (Figure 5-14).

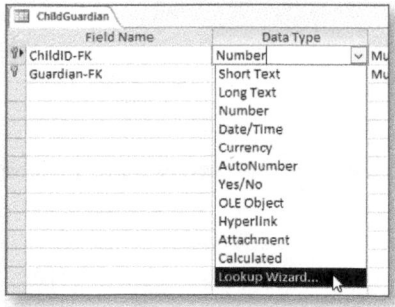

5-13 Select the *Lookup Wizard* data type

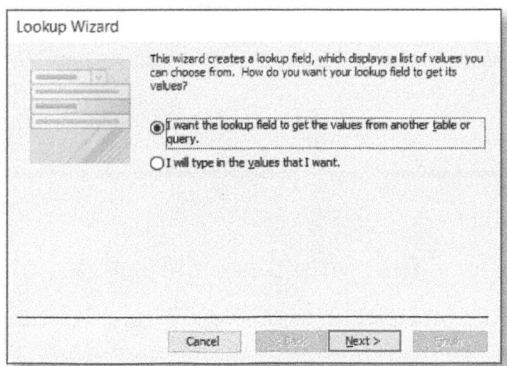

5-14 Select the related table in the *Lookup Wizard*

4. Select the **I want the lookup field to get the values from another table or query** radio button, if necessary, and click **Next** to move to the next step of the *Lookup Wizard*.
5. Select the related table from the "one" side of the relationship and click **Next** to move to the next step of the *Lookup Wizard*.

6. Select the matching field from the list of *Available Fields* and click the **Move Single Field** button to move the field into the *Selected Fields* window (Figure 5-15). Remember that the matching field is the primary key in that table.

7. Click **Next** to move to the next step of the *Lookup Wizard*.

8. Select any sort options for the lookup field.

9. Click **Next** to move to the next step of the *Lookup Wizard*. The list of current data values from the matching table displays (Figure 5-16).

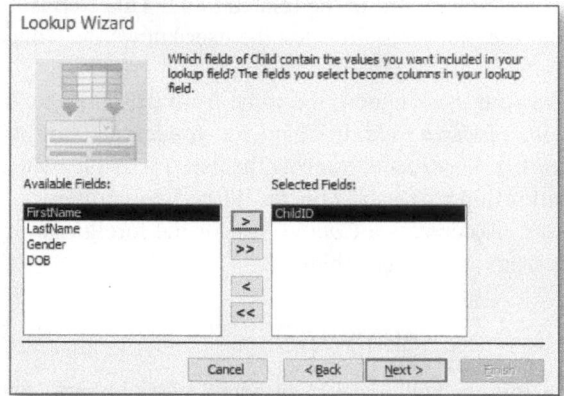

5-15 Move the matching field into the *Selected Fields* window

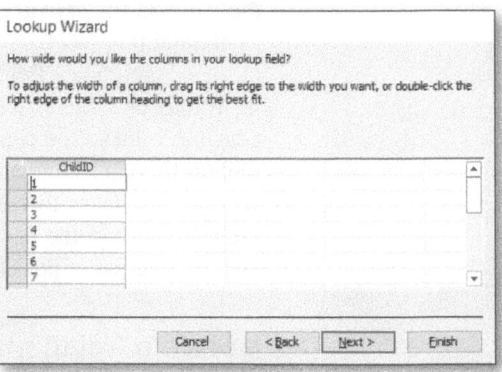

5-16 Adjust the width of the lookup field

10. Adjust the width of the column as desired and click **Next** to move to the last step of the *Lookup Wizard*.

11. Change the field label as desired. The label defaults to the original field name of the foreign key field. If you change the label contents, you also change the name of the field in the table.

12. Check the **Enable Data Integrity** check box and select either the **Cascade Delete** or the **Restrict Delete** radio buttons as desired (Figure 5-17).

13. Click **Finish** to complete the wizard. A *Lookup Wizard* dialog box displays.

14. Click **Yes** to save the changes to the table so that Access can create the relationship.

15. Close the table.

5-17 Select desired data integrity options

View, Edit, and Save a Table Relationship

After completing the *Lookup Wizard,* Access automatically creates a relationship between the two tables. However, the *Lookup Wizard* does not ask you about all the characteristics of a relationship. For example, the wizard does not ask if you want to *Cascade Updates*. As a result, you may need to view and edit the relationship. Additionally, you may want to view the relationship in the *Relationships* window to verify that you answered all the questions correctly during the *Lookup Wizard*. Finally, you may want to change the relationship if the needs of your organization change. It is important that all of the tables involved in the relationship are closed before you attempt to edit a relationship.

In Chapter 2, you learned how to edit a relationship. If necessary, review those instructions in the *Create Relationships between Tables* section in *SLO 2.6 Understanding and Designing Relational Databases* on how to view the relationship in the *Relationships* window (Figure 5-18) and how to edit the relationship in the *Edit Relationships* dialog box (Figure 5-19). Remember to save any changes you make to the relationship.

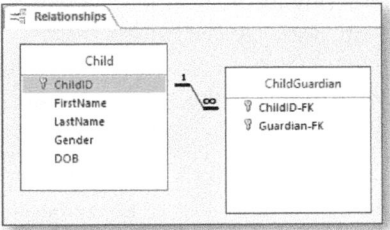

5-18 View and edit the relationship in the *Relationships* window

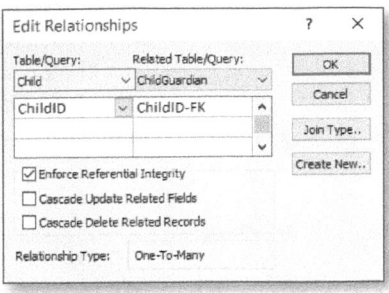

5-19 *Edit Relationships* dialog box

Edit Properties of the Lookup Field

Recall from Chapter 2 that a lookup field has many properties that you can set on the **Lookup tab**. A few of the properties are set automatically based on your answers to the *Lookup Wizard*. As desired, you may wish to modify some of those properties. If necessary, review the functions of those properties in the *Create a Lookup Field* section in *SLO 2.4 Integrating Data Validation in Tables* to determine if you need to edit any of the default settings.

Recall that the values in the *Limit to List* and *Allow Value List Edits* properties will be overridden by Access if referential integrity is enforced in the relationship. Do not change the **Row Source Type** and **Row Source** properties. These are set automatically by the *Lookup Wizard* and the set values ensure that the lookup field displays the current set of values from the related table. The entry in the *Row Source* property is written in *SQL*. *SQL* stands for **Structured Query Language**, the underlying language in a relational database system. You will learn more about *SQL* in Chapter 9.

▶ **HOW TO:** Edit Properties of a Lookup Field

1. Click to select the desired field.
2. Click the **Lookup** tab (Figure 5-20).
3. Click to select the property you wish to edit.
4. Enter the new value. Repeat steps 3 and 4 as desired.
5. Save the table when you are done editing all properties.

Field Name	Data Type	Des
ChildID-FK	Number	Must match a ChildID in t
Guardian-FK	Number	Must match a GuardianID

Field Properties

General | Lookup

Display Control	Combo Box
Row Source Type	Table/Query
Row Source	SELECT [Child].[ChildID] FROM Child;
Bound Column	1
Column Count	1
Column Heads	No
Column Widths	1"
List Rows	16
List Width	1"
Limit To List	Yes
Allow Multiple Values	No
Allow Value List Edits	No
List Items Edit Form	
Show Only Row Source Values	No

5-20 Properties of a *Combo Box* display control on the *Lookup* tab

A5-296

Delete a Relationship Created with a Lookup Field

Occasionally, you may need to remove a relationship that was not created correctly. If the relationship was the result of using the *Lookup Wizard,* you most likely will need to delete both the relationship and the lookup attached to the field.

In Chapter 2, you learned how to delete a relationship between tables (Figure 5-21). If the deleted relationship was created with the *Lookup Wizard,* you also need to change the *Display Control* property of the field so it is no longer a *Combo Box.*

5-21 Delete a relationship

▶ HOW TO: Remove a Lookup by Changing the Display Control Property

1. Open the table in *Design* view.
2. Select the field containing the *Combo Box* lookup.
3. Select the **Lookup** tab.
4. Select **Text Box** in the *Display Control* property.
5. Save your changes.

If the relationship and *Combo Box* were deleted because an error was made when creating the relationship, repeat the *Lookup Wizard* to recreate the relationship correctly.

Use a Lookup with Multiple Fields

The lookup fields you have created so far have all displayed one field in the lookup list. Access allows you to display more than one field. This is useful when the field being displayed is not very intuitive for the user. This is often the case when an ID value is used as the primary key. For example, displaying only a ChildID, as shown in Figure 5-22, may not be as helpful to the user as displaying the child's name along with the ChildID, as shown in Figure 5-23.

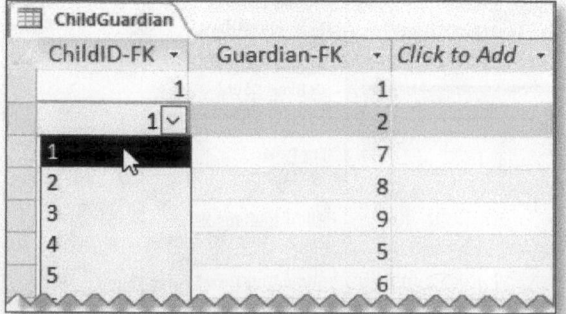

5-22 Lookup field showing one field

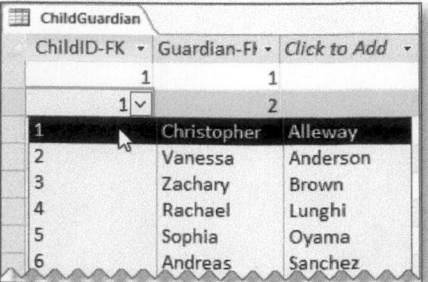

5-23 Lookup field showing multiple fields

▶ HOW TO: Use Multiple Columns in a Lookup Field

1. Open the table in *Design* view.
2. Select the desired field.
3. Select **Lookup Wizard** in the *Data Type* property box to launch the *Lookup Wizard*.
4. Select the **I want the lookup field to get the values from another table or query** radio button and click **Next**.
5. Select the related table and click **Next**.
6. Select the matching field from the list of *Available Fields* and click the **Move Single Field** button to move the field into the *Selected Fields* window. Remember that the matching field is the primary key in the table.
7. Move the additional fields into the *Selected Fields* window in the order you wish to display the fields (Figure 5-24).
8. Click **Next** to move to the next step of the *Lookup Wizard*.
9. Select any sort options for the lookup field.
10. Click **Next** to move to the next step of the *Lookup Wizard*. The list of current data values from the matching table displays.
11. Deselect the **Hide key column** check box, as shown in Figure 5-25.
12. Adjust the width of the columns as desired.
13. Click **Next** to move to the next step of the *Lookup Wizard*.
14. Select the field whose value you want to store in the table field (Figure 5-26). Most likely this should be the matching field that you selected in step 6.
15. Click **Next** to move to the last step of the *Lookup Wizard*.
 - The label defaults to the original field name you entered.
 - You can change the field name, if you like.
16. Check the **Enable Data Integrity** check box and select either the **Cascade Delete** or the **Restrict Delete** radio button, if appropriate.
17. Click **Finish** to complete the wizard. A *Lookup Wizard* dialog box displays.
18. Click **Yes** to save the changes to the table so that Access can create the relationship.

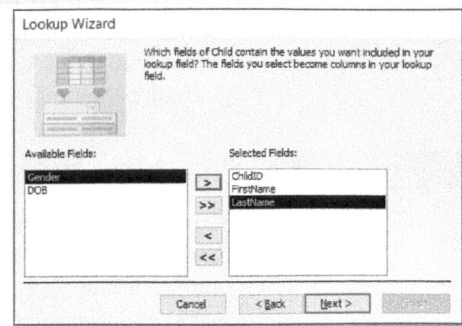

5-24 Move the matching field and any additional fields to display into the *Selected Fields* window

5-25 Deselect the *Hide key column* check box

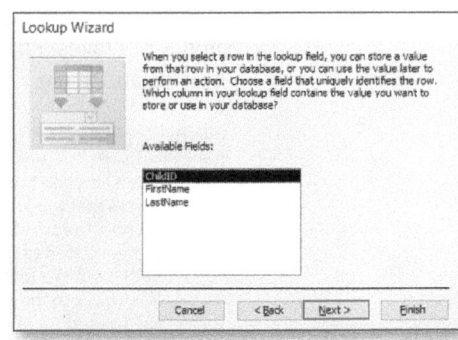

5-26 Select the field to be stored in the table field

Although Access recommends hiding the key column, it is a better design practice to actually store that key column and just display the additional fields in the list. If you do hide the key column, then that value does not display in the drop-down list or in the field column (Figure 5-27). Note that "Christopher Alleway" is the value that displays in the *ChildID-FK* field. However, the value of the key column (*ChildID* in this example) is the one that is actually stored.

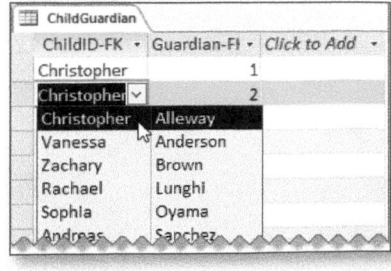

5-27 Lookup field with the key column hidden

This can be confusing, in addition to potentially creating problems. As a result, some database designers recommend against using multiple column lookup fields. Most of these recommendations are related to issues that arise when the key column is hidden. These issues include problems with queries and the sorting of records. Be sure to investigate any design guidelines that may exist at your organization prior to using lookup fields.

SLO 5.3

Working with Advanced Table Relationships

This section explores two additional concepts related to table relationships. First, you learn more about many-to-many relationships and how to implement them in a database. Second, you learn how Access actually relates, or joins, two tables together, along with the options that exist in setting the join property.

Implement a Many-to-Many Relationship

In Chapter 2, you learned that a ***many-to-many*** relationship exists when many rows of data in one table can be associated with many rows of data in a second table. Consider creating a database for a college bookstore. You need to track the books, and their authors, that will be sold by the bookstore. As you work through the database design process, you initially identify two tables, *Author* and *Book,* shown

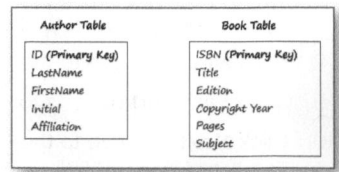

5-28 *Author* and *Book* tables

in Figure 5-28. Because a book could have many different authors and an author could have written many different books, you determine that this is a many-to-many relationship.

Relational databases, like Access, do not directly support many-to-many relationships. You must create a ***junction*** or ***intersection table*** to match up the records. A junction table changes the many-to-many relationship into two one-to-many relationships. The guidelines for creating a junction table are fairly straightforward; however, the application of these guidelines takes a little bit of practice. Follow the steps below to implement a many-to-many relationship using a junction table:

Step	Bookstore Example
1. Create a junction table. • **Recall that the junction table must contain the primary key from each of the related tables.** • **Each field is a foreign key that links back to the primary key in the related table.**	Add the *ID* field from the *Author* table and the *ISBN* field from the *Book* table into the new junction table (Figure 5-29). Each field is a foreign key. To help identify these fields, use the initials *FK* as part of the field name. For clarity of naming, the foreign key field names also include the table name. Note: *ISBN stands for International Standard Book Number. It is a unique number, and publishers use one to identify each title they publish.* 5-29 Create a junction table containing the foreign keys
2. Determine if there are any additional fields to be stored in the junction table.	If the bookstore also wants to track information about the relationship that exists between a book and the author, like the visits an author has made to promote that book, that information can be stored in this table. In the database we are describing, the junction table only provides the link, or connection, between the two tables, so no other fields are needed.

continued

Step	Bookstore Example
3. Decide on a primary key for the junction table. • If another unique field is not added into the table, the combination of the primary key fields from the tables can be used as a concatenated primary key.	Since no fields are added, the primary key is the concatenation of the *AuthorID-FK* and *BookISBN-FK*.
4. Decide on a name for the junction table. • Sometimes the new table represents a concept in the organization and the name is obvious, other times you may create a name that combines the names of the other two tables.	The new table is called *AuthorBook* because it shows which authors work on which books. The completed table is shown in Figure 5-30.

AuthorBook Table

AuthorID-FK *(Primary Key)*

BookISBN-FK *(Primary Key)*

5-30 Completed junction table

Figure 5-31 shows these three tables with sample data. For simplicity, not all of the fields in the *Author* and *Book* tables have been included. The arrows illustrate how the *AuthorBook* junction table works to provide the connection, or relationship, back to the other tables. Recall that by creating the junction table, you changed the many-to-many relationship into two one-to-many relationships. One author can have many records in the *AuthorBook* table, and one book can have many records in the *AuthorBook* table. Note that not all authors, or all books, need to have a record in the *AuthorBook* table, as indicated by the two highlighted green shaded records.

5-31 Sample data in the three tables illustrates how the junction table relates the data across the tables

After designing the tables, you still must create the tables and set the field properties in your Access database. You can do this using the skills you learned in Chapter 2. Keep in mind the following tips to ensure your database will function correctly:

- Build the tables on the "one" side of the relationship first.
- Define the primary key for each of the "one" side tables.
- Build the junction table. The foreign key fields should be the same data type and size as the matching field in the "one" side table. If the primary key in a "one" side table is an *AutoNumber* data type, then the foreign key field should use a *Number* data type. Both fields should have the same number subtype, as indicated in the *Field Size* property.
- Define the primary key for the junction table. Remember that this table represents the "many" side of each relationship.

▶ HOW TO: Define a Concatenated Primary Key

1. Click the **Row Selector** box to select the first foreign key field.
2. Press and hold the **Shift** key.
3. Click the **Row Selector** box to select the second foreign key field.
4. Click the **Row Selector** box of any additional foreign key fields that will be part of the concatenated primary key.
5. Click the **Primary Key** button [*Table Tools Design* tab, *Tools* group]. The primary key symbol appears in the *Row Selector* box of each field in the concatenated primary key (Figure 5-32).

5-32 Concatenated primary key

Recall that just building the tables, including the addition of the foreign keys into the tables, does not create the relationships. You still need to create the relationships, following the steps introduced in the *Create Relationships between Tables* section in *SLO 2.6: Understanding and Designing Relational Databases* or by using the *Lookup Wizard,* covered earlier in this chapter. If you want a lookup for each of the foreign key fields, repeat the entire *Lookup Wizard* process for each field.

Figure 5-33 shows the relationship window after the relationships are created in the bookstore database. Notice the two one-to-many relationships.

5-33 Completed relationships

Join Properties

Once a relationship is created, Access uses the properties of the relationship when a query is created. The **join type** property determines how to match the data in the two related tables. There are three different types of joins. To help understand the different joins, in the content that follows, you explore the relationship between the *Author* and the *AuthorBook* tables.

Inner Join

An **inner join** returns only records that have matching values in both tables. An inner join is the most common type of join.

In our bookstore example, an inner join would only return records for authors who have a book included in the *AuthorBook* table. Figure 5-34 shows the join line in an inner join while Figure 5-35 shows the records that the inner join would return,

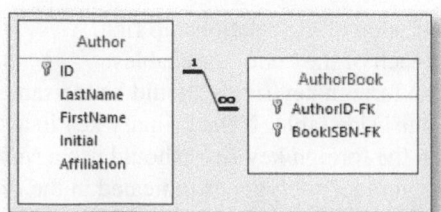

5-34 Inner join line in the *Relationships* window

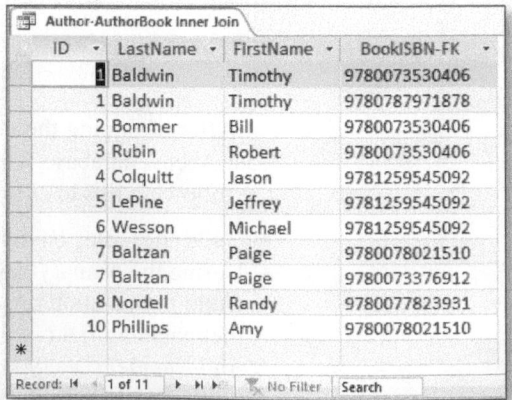

5-35 Results of an inner join show records that match in both tables

using the sample data provided earlier in the bookstore example. The record for Roger Kerin (see ID number 9 in Figure 5-31) does not display since he does not have a book included in the *AuthorBook* table.

Left Outer Join

A *left outer join* returns all the records from the table on the left side of the join and only the records that have a matching value from the table on the right side of the join. The "left" and "right" sides reference the order the tables are listed in the *Edit Relationships* dialog box, not their order in the *Relationships* window.

In our bookstore example, the left outer join would return all of the records from the *Author* table, whether or not there is a matching record in the *AuthorBook* table, but only the records in the *AuthorBook* table that match up to an author. Figure 5-36 shows the join line in a left outer join. Notice the addition of an arrow on the right side of the relationship line. The arrow points to the side of the relationship that displays only the matching rows. Figure 5-37 shows the records that a left outer join would return. The record for Roger Kerin (ID number 9) displays with an empty *BookISBN-FK* field because he doesn't have a book in the *AuthorBook* table.

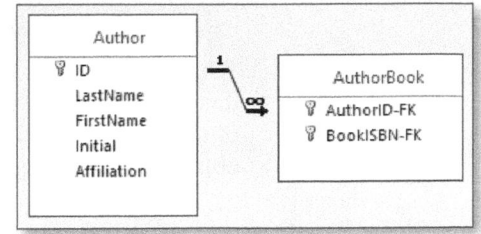

5-36 Left outer join line in the *Relationships* window

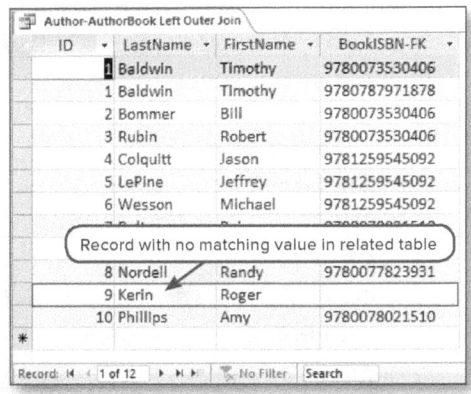

5-37 Results of a left outer join show all authors, even if they don't have a record in the *AuthorBook* table

Right Outer Join

A *right outer join* returns all the records from the table on the right side of the join and only the records that have a matching value from the table on the left side of the join.

In our bookstore example, this would return all of the records from the *AuthorBook* table, whether or not there is a matching record in the *Author* table. Figure 5-38 shows the join line in a right outer join. The arrow on the left side of the relationship line points to the side of the relationship that displays only the matching rows. Figure 5-39 shows the records that a right outer join would return, using the sample data provided earlier.

Since referential integrity is enforced in this relationship, there is no difference in the records returned from the right outer join than from the inner join. If you did not enforce referential integrity, and allowed records to be in the *AuthorBook* table without including an

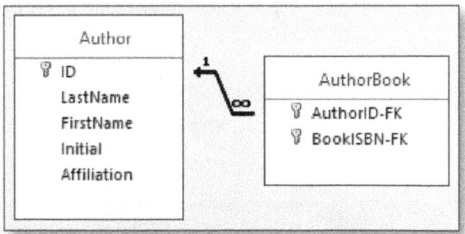

5-38 Right outer join line in the *Relationships* window

5-39 Results of a right outer join show all records from the *AuthorBook* table, even if there isn't a matching record in the *Author* table

AuthorID-FK value, the right outer join would return those records with the author information left blank.

Change the Join Type

When a relationship is created, Access assigns it an inner join type. If the queries that will use this join are more likely to need one of the other two join types, you can change the join type of the relationship. Changing a relationship's join type only affects the way queries, and any object built from a query, work.

> ▶ **HOW TO: Change the Join Type of a Relationship**

1. Click the **Relationships** button [*Database Tools* tab, *Relationships* group] to open the *Relationships* window.
2. Select the relationship line you wish to edit.
3. Click **Edit Relationships** [*Relationship Tools Design* tab, *Tools* group] to open the *Edit Relationships* dialog box.
4. Click the **Join Type** button to open the *Join Properties* dialog box (Figure 5-40).
5. Select the desired **join type** radio button.
6. Click **OK** to close the *Join Properties* dialog box.
7. Click **OK** to close the *Edit Relationships* dialog box.
8. Click **Save** to save the changes made to the relationships.
9. Click **Close** [*Relationship Tools Design* tab, *Relationships* group].

5-40 *Join Properties* dialog box

> ▶ **MORE INFO**
>
> The join type can also be set individually for a query when the query is created. The join setting in a query overrides the join setting in the table relationship.

PAUSE & PRACTICE: ACCESS 5-2

For this Pause & Practice, you create a many-to-many relationship for the River View Nursery School database. You build a junction table, use the *Lookup Wizard* to create the relationship, edit properties of the relationship, and enter data into the junction table.

File Needed: ***RiverView-05.accdb***
Completed Project File Name: ***[your initials] PP A5-2.accdb***

1. Open the ***RiverView-05*** database from your student data files.
2. Save a new copy of your database as [your initials] PP A5-2.
3. Enable content in the database.

4. Review the *Child* table.
 a. Open the *Child* table in *Datasheet* view and review the 11 data records contained in the table.
 b. Switch to *Design* view. Note that the primary key of *ChildID* is an *AutoNumber* data type with a field size of *Long Integer.*

5. Review the *Guardian* table.
 a. Open the *Guardian* table in *Datasheet* view and review the 17 data records contained in the table.
 b. Switch to *Design* view. Note that the primary key of *GuardianID* is an *AutoNumber* data type with a field size of *Long Integer.*

6. Determine the relationship type. A child can have many different guardians. For example, they may have both a mother and a father. A guardian can have many different children. The *Child* and *Guardian* tables have a many-to-many relationship.

7. Close both tables.

8. Create the junction table.
 a. Click the **Table Design** button [*Create* tab, *Tables* group] to open a new table in *Design* view.
 b. Type ChildID-FK in the *Field Name* property box of the first row.
 c. Select the **Number** data type.
 d. Type Must match a ChildID in the Child table in the *Description* property box.
 e. Type GuardianID-FK in the *Field Name* property box of the second row.
 f. Select the **Number** data type.
 g. Type Must match a GuardianID in the Guardian table in the *Description* property box.
 h. Click the **Row Selector** box to select the **ChildID-FK** field.
 i. Press and hold the **Shift** key.
 j. Click the **Row Selector** box to select the **GuardianID-FK** field.
 k. Click the **Primary Key** button [*Table Tools Design* tab, *Tools* group] to create the concatenated primary key (Figure 5-41).
 l. Click **Save** to save the table as ChildGuardian.

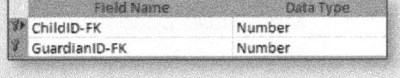

Field Name	Data Type
ChildID-FK	Number
GuardianID-FK	Number

5-41 Concatenated primary key

9. Use the *Lookup Wizard* to create a one-to-many relationship between *Child* and *ChildGuardian*. This lookup will display multiple fields.
 a. Select the **ChildID-FK** field in the *ChildGuardian* table.
 b. Select **Lookup Wizard** in the *Data Type* property box to launch the *Lookup Wizard.*
 c. Select the **I want the lookup field to get the values from another table or query** radio button and click **Next**.
 d. Select the **Child** table, if necessary, and click **Next**.
 e. Select **ChildID** from the list of *Available Fields,* if necessary, and click the **Move Single Field** button to move the field into the *Selected Fields* window.
 f. Move the **FirstName** and **LastName** fields, as shown in Figure 5-42.
 g. Click **Next**.
 h. Don't sort on any fields and click **Next**.
 i. Deselect the **Hide key column** check box and click **Next**.
 j. Select the **ChildID** field to store in the table and click **Next**.
 k. Keep the default label, check the **Enable Data Integrity** check box, and select the **Cascade Delete** radio button.
 l. Click **Finish** to complete the wizard. A *Lookup Wizard* dialog box displays.
 m. Click **Yes** to save the changes to the table so that Access can create the relationship.

5-42 Select the fields to be used in the lookup

10. Use the *Lookup Wizard* to create a one-to-many relationship between *Guardian* and *ChildGuardian*. This lookup displays only one field, to allow you to compare the two approaches.
 a. Select the **GuardianID-FK** field.
 b. Select **Lookup Wizard** in the *Data Type* property box to launch the *Lookup Wizard*.
 c. Select the **I want the lookup field to get the values from another table or query** radio button and click **Next**.
 d. Select the **Guardian** table and click **Next**.
 e. Select **GuardianID** from the list of *Available Fields* and click the **Move Single Field** button to move the field into the *Selected Fields* window.
 f. Click **Next**.
 g. Don't sort on any fields and click **Next**.
 h. Don't make any changes to the width of the column and click **Next**.
 i. Keep the default label, check the **Enable Data Integrity** check box, and select the **Cascade Delete** radio button.
 j. Click **Finish** to complete the wizard. A *Lookup Wizard* dialog box displays.
 k. Click **Yes** to save the changes to the table so that Access can create the relationship. If prompted with another dialog box informing you that changes have been made to the *ChildGuardian* table since the last time you opened it, click the **Yes** button to save your most recent changes.

11. Close the table.

12. Edit the relationship.
 a. Click the **Relationships** button [*Database Tools* tab, *Relationships* group] to open the *Relationships* window (Figure 5-43). If the tables do not display in the window, click the **Show Table** button and add the missing tables into the *Relationships* window.

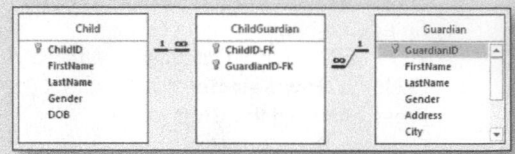

5-43 *Relationships* window

 b. Select the relationship line between *Child* and *ChildGuardian*.
 c. Click **Edit Relationships** [*Relationship Tools Design* tab, *Tools* group].
 d. Select the **Cascade Update Related Fields** check box and click **OK**.
 e. Select the relationship line between *Guardian* and *ChildGuardian*.
 f. Click **Edit Relationships** [*Relationship Tools Design* tab, *Tools* group].
 g. Select the **Cascade Update Related Fields** check box and click **OK**.
 h. Click **Save** to save the changes made to the relationships.
 i. Close the *Relationships* window.

13. Add data into the *ChildGuardian* junction table.
 a. Open the *ChildGuardian* table in *Datasheet* view.
 b. Click the **ChildID-FK** drop-down arrow in the append row, select **1 Matias DeRoche** and press **Enter**.
 c. Click the **GuardianID-FK** drop-down arrow in the append row, select **1** and press **Enter**. Note that the *GuardianID-FK* does not display any additional fields. In this case, having these extra columns in the *ChildID-FK* field makes it easier to use for data entry.
 d. Enter the remaining values from the following table. You can either type the numbers directly into the fields or you can select them from the drop-down lists.

ChildID-FK	GuardianID-FK
1	2
2	7
3	8
3	9
4	10

ChildID-FK	GuardianID-FK
4	11
5	5
5	6
6	12
6	13
7	14
7	15
8	3
8	4
9	16
9	17
10	1
10	2
11	14
11	15

14. Close the table.

15. Review the *Guardian* table.
 a. Open the *Guardian* table in *Datasheet* view.
 b. Click the **plus sign** on *Mauricio DeRoche's* record to display his matching records from the *ChildGuardian* table. Mauricio has two children in the table. If you click the **drop-down arrow** for one of the *ChildID-FK* values, the child's name will also display.
 c. Close the *Guardian* table.

16. Review the *Child* table.
 a. Open the *Child* table in *Datasheet* view.
 b. Click the **plus sign** on *Vanessa Anderson's* record to display her matching record from the *ChildGuardian* table. Vanessa has one guardian in the table. If you click the **drop-down arrow** for the *GuardianID-FK* values, no additional information displays.
 c. Close the *Child* table.

17. Close the database.

 SLO 5.4

Exploring and Building a Macro

A *macro* is a database object that allows you to write and attach code to different objects and controls in your database. Macros can perform one or more actions and can automate tasks and add functionality to your database. In this section, you learn more about the power of macros and how to build your own macros.

> **MORE INFO**
>
> Macros in Access are very different than the macros you may have created in Excel or Word. For example, Access does not have a utility that records steps to help you build a macro.

The Purpose of a Macro

In *SLO 4.3: Facilitating Data Input with a Form,* you were briefly introduced to macros when you added command buttons to your forms and attached an action to those buttons. Those actions—to open another form or add a new record—were simple macros.

Most macros execute because an event occurred in the database. An *event* is something that occurs when an action happens to an object or control. Events are occurring all of the time when you use a database. For example, when a report or form opens, the *On Open* event occurs. Likewise, when a user hovers the mouse over a button on a form, the *On Mouse Move* event occurs. Or when a user presses a button on a form, the *On Click* event occurs. Even table objects have events. For example, when a user changes a value in a field, the *Before Change* event occurs. All the events that a form or report object, or a control placed on one of those objects, can respond to are located on the *Event* tab of the *Property Sheet.* Table events are located in the *Field, Record & Table Events* groups on the *Table Tools Design* tab.

Within a typical database, most of the events that occur as a result of an action perform only the basic task of the event, like opening the form. However, with macros you can create a customized response to an event by having additional tasks occur. For example, you can choose to automatically display a message box when the form opens.

When creating a macro you need to decide on the event that will cause the macro to execute; plan out the logic behind the steps, or tasks, the macro will perform; determine the type of macro needed; and choose the best way to build the macro. It is also important to test the macro to ensure that you have developed and written the logic correctly. You will learn how to test and debug a macro in the last section of this chapter.

In Access, macros are classified by the type of object or control to which they are attached.

- *User Interface macros* are attached to objects and controls, such as forms, reports, and command buttons, that are part of the user interface. They automate actions such as opening objects, customizing form information based on a data value, and displaying message boxes.
- *Data macros* are attached to tables. These macros are used with table events such as adding, changing, or deleting data. They can help ensure the accuracy of the data in the tables by comparing values across tables or automating tasks based on a change to the data.

The Macro Builder and Macro Design

The steps to initiate a new macro vary depending on the type of macro. Those steps are covered separately in *SLO 5.5: Creating and Using User Interface Macros* and *SLO 5.6: Building and Using Data Macros.* However, independently of the way a macro is created, you write and edit the content of all macros using the *Macro Builder* (Figure 5-44).

The *Macro Builder* contains the *macro window,* the area where you enter and edit the action steps of the macro. The right side of the *Macro Builder* displays the *Action Catalog.* The *Action Catalog* contains a *Search* box, *Program Flow* folder, and *Actions* folder. Use the *Search* box to locate an action. The *Program Flow* folder contains four macro statements. A *program flow* statement provides organizational structure to the macro. The *Actions* folder contains the different actions, grouped into category folders, that are available to add into a macro. An *Action* is an individual command inside a macro. You can expand any of the category folders in the macro window to view the specific actions.

A macro contains at least one action, such as *MessageBox* to display a message box or *CancelEvent* to cancel or stop the Access event that executed the macro. The set of all the actions in a macro represents the required logic to perform a task. The macro executes the actions in the order listed, so it is important that you have planned the logic necessary for the macro to work correctly.

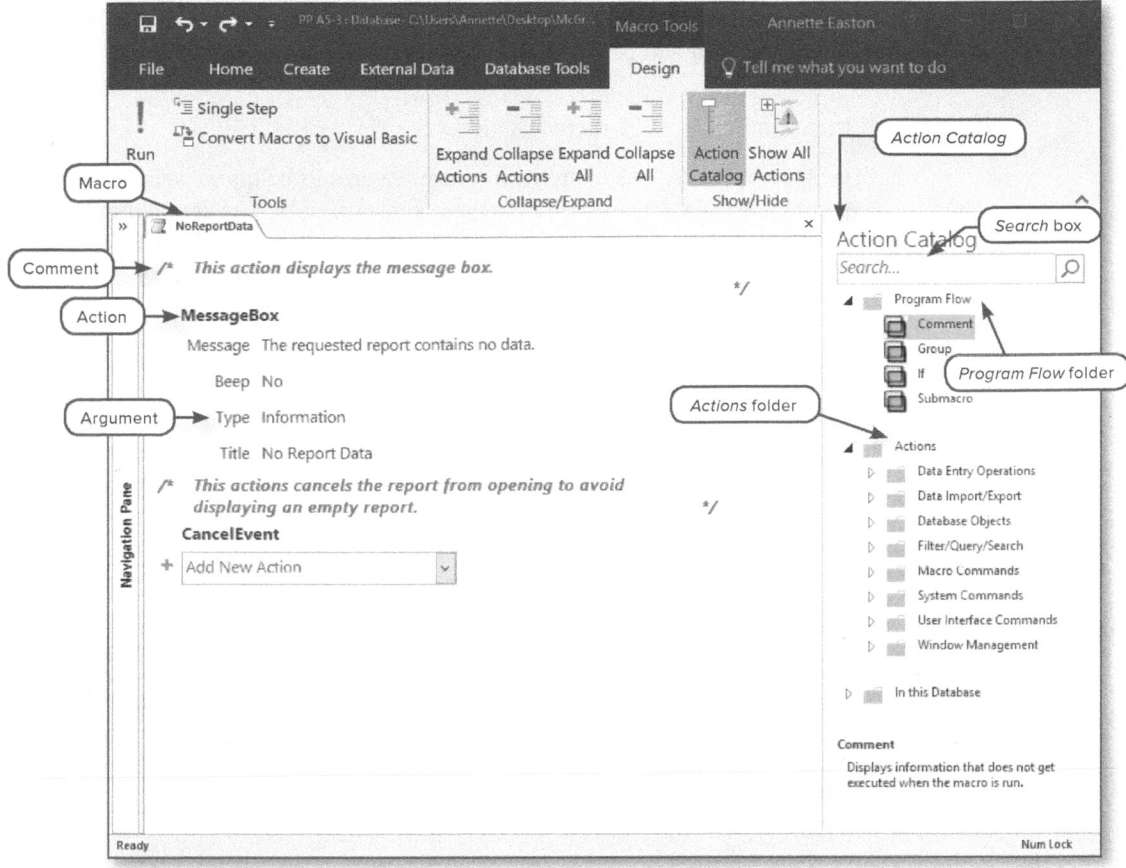

5-44 *Macro Builder*

The most common program flow statement is **Comment**. A comment is a note about the design and usage of the macro. Comments do not affect the logic or functionality of the macro and display in green text in the macro window. It is a good database design practice to include a comment above each action to briefly explain its purpose. These explanations make the macro actions more understandable, and they are useful in keeping you focused as you add many actions into a macro. Additionally, comments are very helpful when you, or another database designer, need to make changes to the database in the future.

The sample macro shown in Figure 5-44 contains two comments and two actions. Some actions contain arguments. **Arguments** are pieces of information needed to complete the action. The information entered into each argument can be a variable, a constant, or an expression. For example, the *MessageBox* action, used to display a *Message Box* in the database, contains four arguments: *Message, Beep, Type,* and *Title.* Some actions, like the *CancelEvent* action, do not have any arguments. *CancelEvent* is used to stop an event, such as opening a report, from happening.

You may consider using additional program flow statements in a macro. In a lengthy or complex macro, you can group items together. A **group** is a named block of actions. You can collapse or expand a group to make a macro more readable. You can also add an **If block** to integrate conditional logic into the execution of the macro. Finally, a user interface macro may contain submacros. A **submacro** is a named, executable set of actions that perform a specific task. Occasionally, you may have a set of actions that needs to be performed in several different macros. Instead of including the same set of actions in each macro, you can create a

submacro and call that submacro when you need to execute those steps. As you work through this chapter, you will better understand these different parts and how they are used.

Use the Macro Builder

The *Macro Builder* has many easy-to-use features to help you write a macro. The five most important tasks are adding an action into a macro, editing an action, moving an action, copying an action and deleting an action. The images shown in this section may contain some macro actions that have not yet been covered. For now, don't worry if you are not sure how the macro actions work. Instead, focus on learning how to use the *Macro Builder*.

Add a New Action

You must add all comments, program flow items, and actions into the macro window. The *Action Catalog* pane displays a list of available actions. You open and close the pane by clicking the **Action Catalog** button [*Macro Tools Design* tab, *Show/Hide* group]. Additionally, the **Add New Action** box displays a drop-down list of the available choices.

▶ HOW TO: Add a New Action to a Macro

1. Click the **Add New Action** drop-down arrow to display the list of available actions.
 - If the macro does not contain any actions, the *Add New Action* box initially displays as an empty box, as shown in Figure 5-45.
2. Select the desired action.
 - The action is added to the macro window (Figure 5-46).

5-45 *Add New Action* box

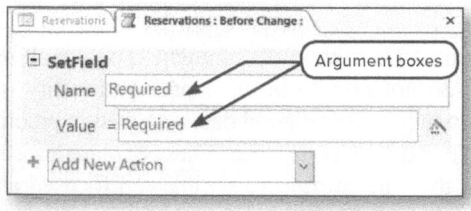

5-46 Action added to the macro window

 - Once an action has been added to a macro, another *Add New Action* box displays below the action.
3. Fill in the arguments, if necessary, by clicking the argument box and entering the appropriate value. Some of the arguments allow you to open the *Expression Builder* or have a drop-down list allowing you to select a value.

> **ANOTHER WAY**
>
> Add actions into a macro by dragging the action from the *Action Catalog* into the macro window or by double-clicking the action in the *Action Catalog*.

You can add as many actions as needed into the macro, but remember that actions are executed in the order they are listed.

When you select the *Comment* action from the drop-down list, an empty box displays in which to type comment text. Figure 5-47 shows a comment box with the text already entered. When you are done entering a comment, click outside the box. The comment then displays in green text (see Figure 5-48).

Edit an Action

You may need to change an action that you have already entered into the macro.

5-47 Example of text entered into a *Comment* action

▶**HOW TO:** Edit an Action in a Macro

1. Click to select the action. Boxes surround the arguments of the action (Figure 5-48).
2. Make any necessary changes.
3. Click outside the box to accept the edits.

5-48 Edit the selected macro action

Move an Action

In a macro containing many actions, you may need to rearrange the order of the actions.

▶**HOW TO:** Move an Action in a Macro

1. Click to select the action you want to move.
 - Green up and down arrows display in the upper right corner of the selected item (Figure 5-48).
 - If an item is at the top or bottom of the list of actions, only one arrow displays.
2. Click the **up arrow** or **down arrow** to move the item.
 - The item moves one position higher or lower.
 - Continue clicking the correct arrow until you have reached the desired location for the action.

Copy an Action

Sometimes, instead of creating a new action, it is quicker to make a copy of an existing action and edit the copied action.

▶HOW TO: Copy an Action in a Macro

1. Click to select the action.
2. Press **Ctrl+C** to copy the action.
3. Click outside the box.
4. Press **Ctrl+V** to paste the action.
5. Move the new copy of the action to the desired location.
6. Make any needed edits to the copied action and click outside the box to save the edits.

Delete an Action

If an action was entered in error or is no longer needed, you can delete it from the macro.

▶HOW TO: Delete an Action in a Macro

1. Click to select the action you want to delete.
2. Click the **Delete** icon, displayed in the upper right corner of the selected item (Figure 5-49).

Sometimes one action will actually contain several associated actions or program flow statements. In Figure 5-49, the *If* action has been selected. As you can see from the indenting of actions in the macro, this *If* action also contains one *Comment* and one *SetField* action. Deleting the *If* action also deletes the associated *Comment* and *SetField* action.

5-49 Click the *Delete* icon to delete a macro action

SLO 5.5

Creating and Using User Interface Macros

Many of the macros you build will be attached to different parts of your database's user interface. Access has two types of user interface macros: stand-alone macros and embedded macros.

- A **stand-alone macro** is a separate Access object that appears in the *Navigation Pane*. You can use a stand-alone macro independently of any other object. Additionally, you can assign it to events in many different objects, allowing you to reuse the same macro. For example, you may want to have the same message box display in many different forms or reports. Create a stand-alone macro to display the message box and then attach that macro to each form or report.
- An **embedded macro** is attached to one specific object or control on an object. Embedded macros do not display in the *Navigation Pane*. They are automatically executed by the object or control. Embedded macros are useful to automate tasks that are unique to a specific form or report in the database.

Embedded macros must be attached to an event, while stand-alone macros may be attached to an event or called independently. In Access, recall that an event is something that occurs when an action happens to an object or control. For example, events occur when you open or close a form, add a record, or click a button. Each type of object or control has a unique set of events.

In this section, you learn how to create user interface macros. In doing so, you learn about the different actions that you can include in a macro. Additionally, you explore several of the common events that can call macros.

User Interface Macros

A ***user interface macro*** can contain many different types of actions. Inside the *Macro Builder,* the available actions are grouped into eight different categories, which are explained in the *User Interface Macro Actions* table. The general purpose of each action can be inferred from the action name. For example, *DeleteRecord* deletes the current record, while *OpenReport* opens a specific report. If you click an action in the *Macro Builder,* a short description displays at the bottom of the *Action Catalo*g. In this book only a few actions are shown in the examples. Use the Access help feature to learn how to use the other actions.

User Interface Macro Actions

Actions Category Folder	Explanation	Actions
Data Entry Operations	Related to changing the data.	*DeleteRecord, EditListItems, SaveRecord*
Data Import/Export	Related to importing, exporting, sending, and collecting data.	*AddContactFromOutlook, EMailDatabaseObject, ExportWithFormatting, SaveAsOutlookContact, WordMailMerge*
Database Objects	Related to changing controls and objects in the database.	*GoToControl, GoToPage, GoToRecord, OpenForm, OpenReport, OpenTable, PrintObject, PrintPreview, RepaintObject, SelectObject, SetProperty*
Filter/Query/Search	Related to filtering, querying, and searching records.	*ApplyFilter, FindNextRecord, FindRecord, OpenQuery, Refresh, RefreshRecord, RemoveFilterSort, Requery, SearchForRecord, SetFilter, SetOrderBy, ShowAllRecords*
Macro Commands	Related to making changes to the macro.	*CancelEvent, ClearMacroError, OnError, RemoveAllTempVars, RemoveTempVar, RunCode, RunDataMacro, RunMacro, RunMenuCommand, SetLocalVar, SetTempVar, SingleStep, StopAllMacros, StopMacro*
System Commands	Related to changing the database system.	*Beep, CloseDatabase, DisplayHourglassPointer, QuitAccess*
User Interface Commands	Related to controlling what is shown on the screen.	*AddMenu, BrowseTo, LockNavigationPane, MessageBox, NavigateTo, Redo, SetDisplayedCategories, SetMenuItem, UndoRecord*
Window Management	Related to managing the database windows.	*CloseWindow, MaximizeWindow, MinimizeWindow, MoveAndSizeWindow, RestoreWindow*

Before you can write the content of a macro, you must decide how and when the macro will be used. When planning a macro, determine which object or control will use the macro and decide which specific event will execute the macro. For example, if you want a button on a form to change color when a user hovers the mouse over the button, build a macro for the *On Mouse Move* event of the button. Or if you want to have a button on a report create a PDF

of the report when the button is pressed, build a macro for the *On Click* event of the button. You can also create a stand-alone macro that executes automatically when the database is first opened.

The ***Property Sheet*** of an object or control displays all the possible events on the *Event* tab. Each type of object or control has its own set of events. Figure 5-50 shows some of the events for a command button and for a form. You will discover that several common events are shared by many objects and controls. These are explained in the table below. Some of these events have parameters that contain additional informa-

5-50 *Event* tab of the *Property Sheet* for a command button and a form

tion. For example, the *On Mouse Down* event has a parameter that indicates which mouse button was pressed. Your macro can include code to check the value of the parameter. In this case, the macro can check whether the *Left, Right,* or *Middle* mouse button was pressed.

Common Events in Access Objects and Controls

Category	Event	Explanation
Click events	On Click	Executes after the object/control is clicked.
	On Dbl Click	Executes after the object/control is double-clicked.
Focus-based events	On Got Focus	Executes when an object/control receives focus. (**Focus** refers to the status of a control or object. The active control or object is said to "have the focus." When a user tabs into, or clicks, a control, the *On Got Focus* event occurs.)
	On Lost Focus	Executes when an object/control loses focus.
	On Enter	Used only with text box controls. This event happens immediately before the text box obtains the focus. This can be used to provide instructions before that control becomes active.
	On Exit	Executes immediately before a control, on a form or report, loses the focus to another control on the same form or report. You can use the *On Exit* event to verify that an entry is correct before leaving the field. If it isn't correct, you can include an action in the macro to cancel the exit from happening.
Mouse events	On Mouse Down	Executes when the mouse is positioned over an object/control and the user presses a mouse button. The *On Mouse* Down event contains parameters to allow you to determine which mouse button was pressed, whether another key (like *Shift*) was pressed while pressing the mouse button, and the location of the mouse pointer.
	On Mouse Up	Executes when a mouse button is released after having been pressed. The *On Mouse Up* event contains parameters to allow you to determine if the user pressed another key while pressing the mouse, along with the location of the mouse pointer.
	On Mouse Move	Executes when the user moves the mouse over an object/control.
Keyboard events	On Key Up	Executes when the user releases a key that he or she was pressing. The *On Key Up* event contains parameters to determine which key was pressed and whether another key was also being pressed.
	On Key Down	Executes when a key is pressed. The *On Key Down* event contains parameters to determine which key was pressed and whether the user was also pressing another key.
	On Key Press	Executes when a key is pressed, but the *On Key Press* event only contains a parameter about which key was pressed, not whether additional keys were also pressed.

continued

Category	Event	Explanation
Form/report events	*On Open*	Executes when a form or report is opened. If an object is already open, and the user simply clicks the object to make it the active object, the *On Open* event does not occur. Use the *On Activate* event instead.
	On Activate	Executes after a form or report is already opened and the object gains the focus.
	On Deactivate	Executes when the form or report loses the focus to another object.
	On Close	Executes after a form or report is closed.

Now that you have been introduced to events and actions, you are ready to learn how to write and use a macro. To help illustrate the process, let's review a macro that solves a common dilemma. In Access, if you open a report that doesn't contain any data, the report still displays. As shown in Figure 5-51, the report shows just the header and footer, but no data. A user might think that something didn't work correctly in the database, instead of realizing that no records exist for that report.

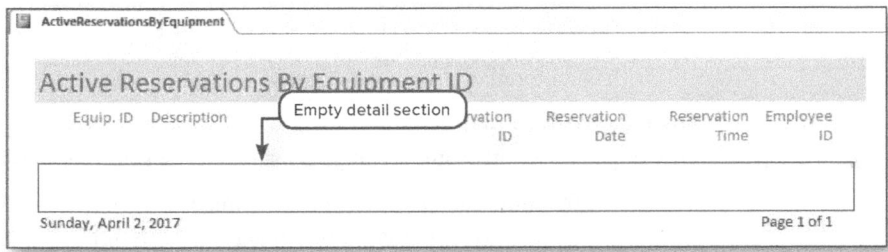

5-51 A report without data displays the header and footer

Instead of displaying an empty report, you want the database to display a message to users alerting them that the report doesn't have any data. One of the events in a report is *On No Data*. The **On No Data** event executes as part of the opening event in a report. This event occurs before a report is displayed or printed. You can use this event to display a message and then stop the report from opening.

In order to have all of your reports behave this way, you can create a stand-alone macro. This saves you the time and effort of having to create the same macro actions for each report. The ability to assign a macro to multiple objects is a key advantage of stand-alone macros.

Figure 5-52 shows the code in the sample macro. The macro contains two actions, along with comments that explain what is happening inside the macro. Let's explore the actions in this macro.

```
/*   This action displays the message box.          */
    MessageBox
      Message  The requested report contains no data.

        Beep  No

        Type  Information

       Title  No Report Data

/*  This action cancels the report from opening
      to avoid displaying an empty report.          */
    CancelEvent
```

5-52 Sample code for an *On No Data* event macro of a report

The *MessageBox* action:
As the name implies, this action causes a message box to display. The *MessageBox* action has the following arguments:

- *Message:* Enter the text that you want displayed inside the message box.
- *Beep:* Select *Yes* or *No,* depending on whether you want Access to make a sound when the message box displays.

- *Type:* Select the type of icon to display in the message box. The following table illustrates the five choices and their corresponding icon:

Message Box Types

Type	Icon
None	
Critical	
Warning?	
Warning!	
Information	

- *Title:* Enter the text that you want to display in the *Title* bar of the message box. If no title is entered, the phrase "Microsoft Access" displays in the *Title* bar.

The *CancelEvent* action:

This stops the report from opening. This action does not contain any arguments.

After you enter the macro code you must save the macro. When you save a stand-alone macro, you assign it a name. The saved macro then displays in the *Macros* group of the *Navigation Pane* (Figure 5-53).

After you create a stand-alone macro, you are able to assign it to an event of an object or control. Figure 5-54 shows the *Event* tab of the *Property Sheet* for a report. The name of the sample macro, *NoReportData,* is in the property box of the *On No Data* event. You must assign this macro to the *On No Data* event for each report in the database.

Now when the report is opened, if it doesn't contain any data, the message box shown in Figure 5-55 displays instead of the empty report. Review the message box in Figure 5-55 to see how and where the different arguments of the *MessageBox* action display.

5-53 Macro in the *Navigation Pane*

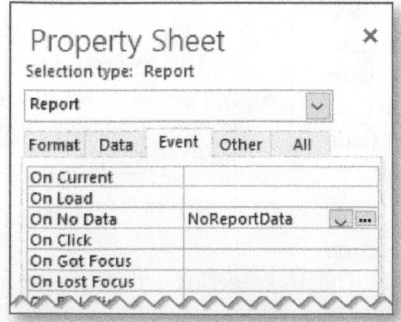

5-54 Macro called from the *On No Data* property

5-55 Message box called from the macro

Build a Stand-Alone Macro

Create a stand-alone macro when you want to call a macro from several different objects or controls or when you want to create a macro that executes automatically when the database is first opened.

Use the *Macro Builder* to create a stand-alone macro.

▶ HOW TO: Build a Stand-Alone Macro

1. Click the **Macro** button [*Create* tab, *Macros & Code* group] (Figure 5-56) to open the *Macro Builder*. The insertion point is positioned in the *Add New Action* box.
2. Click the **Add New Action** drop-down arrow and select the desired action. The action is added to the macro window.
3. Fill in arguments by clicking the argument box and entering the appropriate value.
4. Add any additional actions into the macro.
5. Add comments into the macro to explain the purpose/logic of the macro actions.
6. Save the macro.
 - The *Save As* dialog box prompts you to assign a name to the macro.
 - The completed macro appears in the *Macros* group of the *Navigation Pane*.
7. Close the macro.

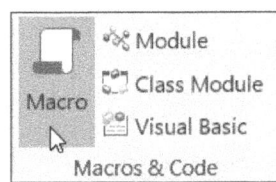

5-56 *Macro* button

▶ **MORE INFO**

Use the *Help* feature in Access to learn how each action operates and the different arguments used in a particular action.

A macro that runs when a database is first opened is an **AutoExec** macro. This kind of macro is usually set up to perform some initial actions in the database, like opening the main form in the database, modifying settings to restrict user actions, and opening a login form.

- To create a macro that executes automatically when the database is opened, save your stand-alone macro with the name *AutoExec*.
- To bypass the execution of the *AutoExec* macro, a user can press and hold the **Shift** key when opening the database.

Run a Stand-Alone Macro

There are three different ways to run a stand-alone macro:

- Double-click the macro name in the *Navigation Pane*.
- Call the macro from another macro using the *RunMacro* or *OnError* macro action. Enter the name of the macro in the *Macro Name* argument of the *RunMacro* or *OnError* action.
- Attach the macro to an event property of an object or control.

▶ HOW TO: Attach a Stand-Alone Macro to an Event Property

1. Open the object in *Design* view.
2. Select a control on the object, if you want to attach the macro to that specific control.
3. Click the **Property Sheet** button [*Design* tab, *Tools* group] to open the *Property Sheet*.

4. Click to select the **Event** tab of the *Property Sheet*.
5. Enter the macro name in the property box of the desired event.
6. Save the object.

Build an Embedded Macro

Create an embedded macro when the actions of the macro are unique to a specific object. For example, if only one report in your database might not have data to display, the macro code to display the message and stop the event could be entered into an embedded macro for the *On No Data* event for just that one report. An embedded macro is built using the actions and events previously described.

Before creating an embedded macro, you must first open the *Property Sheet* of the object or control.

▶HOW TO: Build an Embedded Macro

1. Open the object in *Design* view.
2. Select the control, if the macro will be attached to a specific control on the object.
3. Click the **Property Sheet** button [*Design* tab, *Tools* group] to open the *Property Sheet*.
4. Click to select the **Event** tab of the *Property Sheet*.
5. Click the property box of the desired event.
6. Click the **Build** button (Figure 5-57) to open the *Choose Builder* dialog box.
7. Select **Macro Builder** and click **OK**.
8. Click the **drop-down arrow** and select the desired action.
9. Fill in arguments by clicking the argument box and entering the appropriate value.
10. Add any additional actions into the macro.
11. Add comments into the macro to explain the purpose/logic of the macro actions.
12. Save and close the macro. The property box of the event property updates to display *[Embedded Macro]* (Figure 5-58).
13. Save the object.

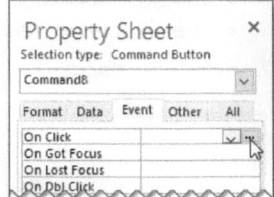

5-57 Select the *Build* button of the desired event

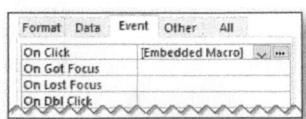

5-58 *Embedded Macro* displays in the event property

> **ANOTHER WAY**
>
> An embedded macro is automatically created when you use the *Command Button Wizard* to attach functionality to a button, as you learned in *SLO 4.3: Facilitating Data Input with a Form*.

An embedded macro automatically runs when the event to which it is attached executes.

Edit or Delete a User Interface Macro

After a macro is built, you may need to edit the macro.

▶ HOW TO: Edit a Stand-Alone Macro

1. Right-click the macro name in the *Navigation Pane* and select **Design View**. The macro opens in the *Macro Builder*.
2. Make desired edits to the macro code.
3. Save and close the macro.

▶ HOW TO: Edit an Embedded Macro

1. Open the object that contains the macro in *Design* view. If the macro is attached to a specific control on the object, select that control.
2. Click the **Property Sheet** button [*Design* tab, *Tools* group] to open the *Property Sheet* and select the **Event** tab of the *Property Sheet*.
3. Click the **Build** button in the property box of the event. The macro opens in the *Macro Builder*.
4. Make desired edits to the macro code.
5. Save and close the macro.
6. Save the object.

Delete macros from the database that have been created in error or are no longer needed. Deleting a stand-alone macro is very straightforward. Right-click the macro name in the *Navigation Pane* and select **Delete**.

▶ HOW TO: Delete an Embedded Macro

1. Open the object that contains the macro in *Design* view. If the macro is attached to a specific control on the object, select that control.
2. Click the **Property Sheet** button [*Design* tab, *Tools* group] to open the *Property Sheet* and select the **Event** tab of the *Property Sheet*.
3. Click the property box of the event and delete the phrase **[Embedded Macro]**.
4. Save the object.

PAUSE & PRACTICE: ACCESS 5-3

For this Pause & Practice, you create two user interface macros for the Challenger Middle School database. You build a stand-alone macro to display a message box instead of a blank report. You build an embedded macro to open all the reports by clicking a button on a form. You also execute each macro to ensure that it works as planned.

File Needed: **ChallengerMiddleSchool-05.accdb**
Completed Project File Name: **[your initials] PP A5-3.accdb**

1. Open the ***ChallengerMiddleSchool-05.accdb*** database from your student data files.

2. Save a new copy of your database as [your initials] PP A5-3.

3. Enable content in the database.

4. Create a stand-alone macro to display a message box instead of showing a report with no data.

 a. Click the **Macro** button [*Create* tab, *Macros & Code* group] to open the *Macro Builder*.

 b. Click the **Add New Action** drop-down arrow (Figure 5-59) and select **Comment**.

 5-59 Add a new action to the macro

 c. Type This action displays the message box.

 d. Click the **Add New Action** drop-down arrow and select **MessageBox**.

 e. Type The requested report contains no data. in the *Message* argument.

 f. Select **No** in the *Beep* argument.

 g. Select **Information** in the *Type* argument.

 h. Type No Report Data in the *Title* argument.

 i. Click the **Add New Action** drop-down arrow and select **Comment**.

 j. Type This action cancels the report from opening to avoid displaying an empty report.

 k. Click the **Add New Action** drop-down arrow and select **CancelEvent**.

 l. Click the **Save** button [*File* tab], type NoReportData in the *Macro Name* box, and click **OK** to save the macro.

 m. Close the macro.

5. Double-click the **ActiveReservationsByEquipment** report to run the report.

6. Type XXX in the *Enter Parameter Value* dialog box and click **OK**. The report should open but no records will display because no equipment has an *EquipID* of *XXX*.

7. Attach the macro to the *ActiveReservationsByEquipment* report.

 a. Click the **View** button [*Home* tab, *Views* group] and select **Design View**.

 b. Click the **Property Sheet** button [*Design* tab, *Tools* group] to open the *Property Sheet*.

 c. Click to select the **Event** tab of the *Property Sheet*.

 d. Type NoReportData in the **On No Data** property box. As you type the report name, the *IntelliSense* tool in Access recognizes the macro name and completes it for you. You can tab out of the property box to accept the value that was autocompleted.

 e. Close the *Property Sheet*.

 f. Save and close the report.

8. Test the macro.

 a. Double-click the **ActiveReservationsByEquipment** to run the report.

 b. Type XXX in the *Enter Parameter Value* dialog box and click **OK**. The message box that you created in your macro displays. Click **OK** to close the message box.

 c. Double-click the **ActiveReservationsByEquipment** to run the report again.

 d. Don't type anything into the *Enter Parameter Value* dialog box and click **OK**. The report should open and show all records.

 e. Close the report.

9. Attach the macro to the *AllReservationsByEquipment* report following the directions in step 7. Remember to open the report in *Design* view.

10. Examine the functionality of the *Execute Reports* form.

 a. Open the **ExecuteReports** form in *Form* view.

 b. Click the **Active Reservations by Equipment ID** button.

 c. Type 2 in the *Enter Parameter Value* dialog box and click **OK**. The report should open and show the eight records.

 d. Close the report.

e. Click the **All Reservations by Equipment ID** button.

f. Type XXX in the *Enter Parameter Value* dialog box and click **OK**. The message box that you created in your macro displays. Click **OK** to close the message box.

g. Click the **Preview All Reports** button. Nothing should happen.

11. Examine the macro on the *Active Reservations by Equipment ID* button.

a. Switch to *Design* view of the **ExecuteReports** form.

b. Select the **Active Reservations by Equipment ID** button.

c. Click the **Property Sheet** button [*Design* tab, *Tools* group] to open the *Property Sheet*. In the drop-down box near the top of the *Property Sheet,* notice the name of this button is *Command5.*

d. Click to select the **Event** tab of the *Property Sheet.*

e. Click the **Build** button of the *On Click* event to open the *Macro Builder* (Figure 5-60). This macro was automatically created when the button was added to the form using the *Command Wizard.*

f. Close the macro.

5-60 *On Click* event macro code of the *Active Reservations by Equipment ID* button

12. Create an embedded macro to open all four reports from a button on a form.

a. Select the **Preview All Reports** button.

b. Click to select the **Event** tab of the *Property Sheet,* if necessary.

c. Click the property box of the **On Click** event and click the **Build** button.

d. Select **Macro Builder** in the *Choose Builder* dialog box and click **OK**.

e. Click the **Add New Action** drop-down arrow and select **Comment**.

f. Type The following commands open the database reports in Print Preview mode.

g. Click the **Add New Action** drop-down arrow and select the **OpenReport** action.

h. Type ActiveEquipReservationsByMonth in the *Report Name* argument. The *Intellisense* tool should auto-complete the name as you begin to enter it.

> ▶ **ANOTHER WAY**
>
> Click the **drop-down arrow** in the *Report Name* argument and select the desired report.

i. Select **Print Preview** in the *View* argument.

j. Add three more **OpenReport** actions for the *ActiveReservationsByEquipment* and the *AllReservationsByEquipment* and *EquipmentListing* reports. Type Print Preview in the *View* argument for each report. The completed *Macro Builder* window should look like the example in Figure 5-61.

5-61 Completed macro code for the *Preview All Reports* button

k. Save and close the macro. The property box of the *On Click* event property updates to display *[Embedded Macro].*
l. Close the *Property Sheet.*
m. Save the form.

13. Test the embedded macro.
 a. Switch to *Form* view of the *ExecuteReports* form.
 b. Click the **Preview All Reports** button. The *ActiveEquipReservationsByMonth* report displays. The *Enter Parameter Value* dialog box opens for the *ActiveReservationsByEquipment* report.
 c. Do not enter a parameter value and click **OK**. The report opens in *Print Preview* mode and the *Enter Parameter Value* dialog box opens for the *AllReservationsByEquipment* report.
 d. Type XXX in the *Enter Parameter Value* dialog box and click **OK**. The *No Report Data* message box displays.
 e. Click the **OK** button. The *EquipmentListing* report opens in *Print Preview* mode. Note that you can click the tabs to switch between the different reports.
 f. Close the three reports.
 g. Close the form. Click **Yes** if prompted to save changes to the form.

14. Close the database.

SLO 5.6

Building and Using Data Macros

In contrast to user interface macros, ***data macros*** allow you to automate tasks related to the database tables. In this section, you explore different uses of data macros, create and test data macros, and understand the differences between event-driven and named data macros.

Data Macros

You can use data macros to ensure that the data in tables is accurate. Additionally, you can use them to automate tasks related to adding, deleting, or changing data. Because these macros are attached to a table, they execute any time a table's data is updated. You can create data macros to respond to any of the five events in the following table:

Data Macro Events

Event	Explanation	Additional Information
Before Change	Executes before a record is saved to validate the changes and then makes the decision to save the new values, change values, or display an error to stop the changes.	Use the *[IsInsert]* property to determine if the change is an insert or an update.
Before Delete	Executes before a record is deleted to validate the deletion, and then performs the deletion or displays an error to stop the deletion.	
After Insert	Executes after a record is added to the table.	Use the *Updated("Field Name")* function to check if a field has been changed.
After Update	Executes after an existing record is changed.	Use the *[Old].[Field Name]* to check the value of a field before the change.
After Delete	Executes after a record is deleted.	Use the *[Old].[Field Name]* to check the value of a field before the deletion.

> ### MORE INFO
>
> In addition to these five events, you can create a *Named Data Macro,* which is explained at the end of this section.

After selecting the type of event, you are ready to select the action steps that will occur inside the macro. A data macro has a more limited set of actions than a user interface macro. These actions are explained in the following *Data Macro Actions* table. An *X* in an event column indicates that you can use the action in that event.

Data Macro Actions

Action	Explanation	Before Change	Before Delete	After Insert	After Update	After Delete
CancelRecordChange	Exits an *EditRecord* or *CreateRecord* data block and does not save the current record.			X	X	X
ClearMacroError	Clears the *MacroError* object. The *MacroError* object contains information about errors that have occurred during the execution of a macro.	X	X	X	X	X
DeleteRecord	Deletes a record from an expression.			X	X	X
ExitForEachRecord	Exits the innermost *ForEachRecord.*			X	X	X
LogEvent	Adds a record into the *USysApplicationLog* table, an Access table that contains information related to data macro and application errors.			X	X	X
OnError	Contains the action to perform if an error occurs.	X	X	X	X	X
RaiseError	Notifies the application that an error has occurred.	X	X	X	X	X
RunDataMacro	Executes a *Named Data Macro.*			X	X	X
SendEmail	Sends an email using the email program installed on your computer.			X	X	X
SetField	Sets the specified field to the indicated value.	X		X	X	X
SetLocalVar	Creates or modifies a local variable used in the macro.	X	X	X	X	X
StopAllMacros	Directs Access to stop the execution of all macros currently running.			X	X	X
StopMacro	Directs Access to stop the execution of the current macro.	X	X	X	X	X

In addition to the data macro actions listed in the table, there are four additional macro actions that are classified as data blocks. A **data block** performs an action but usually requires additional actions related to the block. For example, in order to create a record, you must include actions to assign values to the different fields in the record. These four data blocks are listed in the following *Data Block Macro Actions* table. The table also indicates the event macros in which you can use these data blocks.

Data Block Macro Actions

Data Block	Explanation	Before Change	Before Delete	After Insert	After Update	After Delete
CreateRecord	Creates a new record in a table. Typically used in conjunction with the *SetField* action to assign values for the fields in the record.			X	X	X

continued

Data Block	Explanation	Before Change	Before Delete	After Insert	After Update	After Delete
EditRecord	Changes the values in the existing record. Typically will include actions to set the value of a field.			X	X	X
ForEachRecord	Repeats a set of actions for each record specified.			X	X	X
LookupRecord	Locates a specific record and performs a set of actions on that record.	X	X	X	X	X

Figure 5-62 illustrates a simple data macro. The macro is automatically named by using a combination of the table name and the event type. In Figure 5-62, the name in the tab *Members : Before Change* identifies that this is a *Before Change* event in the *Members* table. In accordance with good database design guidelines, the macro includes a comment to explain the purpose of the macro/action.

5-62 Sample code in a *Before Change Data Macro*

As you can see in the comment, this macro automatically records a date/time stamp when a record is changed. To accomplish this, the macro uses the *SetField* action. *SetField* has two arguments: the *Name* of the field in the table and the *Value* to assign to that field. The macro executes when the *Before Change* event happens in the *Members* table. The *Before Change* event automatically occurs if any of the table's fields are changed. When this happens, the actions in the macro obtain the current date and time from the computer and store them in the *LastUpdated* field. The new value in the *LastUpdated* field, along with the changed value that caused the *Before Change* event to occur, is saved into the table.

Build an Event-Driven Data Macro

Create an ***event-driven data macro*** when the actions of the macro are unique to a specific event in a table.

▶ **HOW TO: Build an Event-Driven Data Macro**

1. Open the table in *Datasheet* view.
2. Click the **Table Tools Table** tab (Figure 5-63).
3. Select the desired event button from the *Before Events* group or the *After Events* group to open the *Macro Builder*.
4. Click the **drop-down arrow** and select the desired action.

5-63 Event-driven macro buttons on the *Table Tools Table* tab

5. Fill in any of the arguments by clicking the argument box and entering the appropriate value.
6. Add any additional actions into the macro.
7. Add comments into the macro to explain the purpose/logic of the macro actions.
8. Save and close the macro.

> **ANOTHER WAY**
>
> You can build an event-driven data macro from *Design* view of a table. Click the **Create Data Macros** button [*Table Tools Design* tab, *Field, Record & Table Events* group] and select the desired event option.

After you have built the macro, the *Ribbon* of the *Table Tools Table* tab updates to highlight the event button where you attached the macro (Figure 5-64). A table can have macros attached to each of the different events.

5-64 Highlighted event button indicates that a macro exists

An event-driven data macro executes automatically whenever the specified table event occurs in the database. For example, a *Before Change* event occurs every time data is changed in the table. This could be the addition of a brand new record, or a change in the values of an existing record.

Named Data Macros

A *named data macro* is associated with a specific table, but it is not attached to any particular event. Instead, a named data macro is run by another event-driven macro or by a stand-alone macro. Named data macros have the following characteristics:

- They can use all of the data block actions and all of the event actions described in the *Data Macro Actions* and *Data Block Macro Actions* tables.
- They can use an additional action, *SetReturnVar*. *SetReturnVar* sets the value of a variable to be returned, or passed back, to the object that called the named data macro.
- They can use parameters, if needed. *Parameters* pass a value or an object reference into a macro. The name you assign to the parameter (in the *Name* box) is the name you use to refer to the parameter inside your macro.
- Named data macros are executed by using the *RunDataMacro* action to call the named data macro. Call a named data macro from an event-driven data macro or from a user interface macro.

Build a Named Data Macro

Create a named data macro when you need to have the same set of table actions executed from different objects or events, or if you want the actions to occur only from certain objects or events instead of all the time, or if you want to pass data into the macro.

Named data macros use the *Macro Builder*. However, the macro window includes an additional component, shown in Figure 5-65, which you can use to add parameters into the macro. You will learn more about parameters in the next section of the chapter.

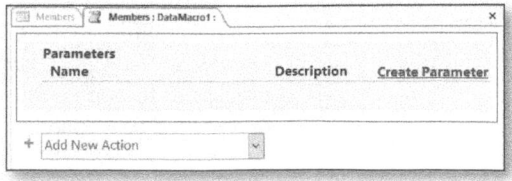

5-65 A named data macro can contain parameters

▶ **HOW TO:** Build a Named Data Macro

1. Open the table in *Datasheet* view.
2. Click the **Named Macro** button [*Table Tools Table* tab, *Named Macros* group] and select the **Create Named Macro** option (Figure 5-66). The *Macro Builder* opens.

A5-324

3. Click the **Create Parameter** link to add a parameter as desired. See *How To: Add a Parameter into a Named Data Macro* in *SLO 5.7 Building More Advanced Macros*.

4. Click the **Add New Action** drop-down arrow and select the desired action.

5. Fill in arguments by clicking the argument box and entering the appropriate value.

6. Add any additional actions into the macro.

7. Add comments into the macro to explain the purpose/logic of the macro actions.

8. Save the macro.

9. Type the desired macro name into the *Save As* dialog box and click **OK**.

10. Close the macro.

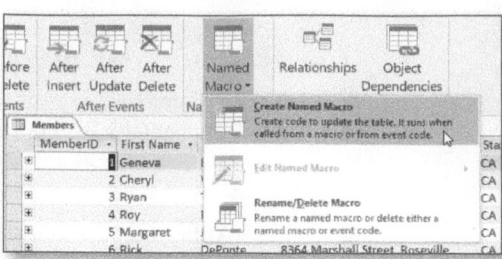

5-66 *Create Named Macro* option

> **ANOTHER WAY**
>
> You can build a named data macro from *Design* view of a table. Click the **Create Data Macros** button [*Table Tools Design* tab, *Field, Record & Table Events* group] and select **Create Named Macro**.

After you have built a named data macro, the **Edit Named Macro** option becomes active when you select the **Named Macro** button from the *Named Macros* group. A table can have many different named data macros.

▶ HOW TO: Execute a Named Data Macro

1. Add a **Run Data Macro** action to an event-driven data macro or a user interface macro.

2. Enter the data macro name in the *Macro Name* argument box.
 - You must enter the table name along with the macro name, as shown in Figure 5-67.
 - A period separates the table name from the macro name.

5-67 *RunDataMacro* action

Edit or Delete a Data Macro

After you build a data macro, there may be times when you need to edit it. Open the table in *Datasheet* view. Although the process of entering the changes into a macro doesn't vary, the process to re-open a macro does vary depending on whether it is an event-driven data macro or a named data macro.

▶ HOW TO: Edit an Event-Driven Data Macro

1. Click the event button of the macro you wish to edit from either the *Before Events* group or the *After Events* group [*Table Tools Table* tab]. The macro opens in the *Macro Builder*.

2. Make desired edits to the macro code.

3. Save and close the macro.

▶**HOW TO:** Edit a Named Data Macro

1. Click the **Named Macro** button [*Table Tools Table* tab, *Named Macros* group] and select the **Edit Named Macro** option. The names of the available macros display (Figure 5-68).

2. Select the name of the macro you wish to edit. The macro opens in the *Macro Builder*.

3. Make desired edits to the macro code.

4. Save and close the macro.

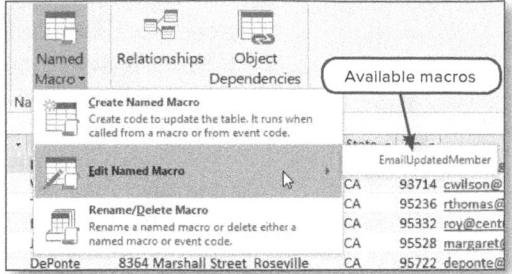

5-68 Selecting the *Edit Named Macro* option displays the list of available macros

Delete any macros from the database that you created in error or that are no longer needed.

▶**HOW TO:** Delete a Data Macro

1. Open the table in *Datasheet* view.

2. Click the **Named Macro** button [*Table Tools Table* tab, *Named Macros* group] and select the **Rename/Delete Macro** option. The *Data Macro Manager* opens (Figure 5-69).

3. Click the **Delete** option of the macro you wish to delete. A dialog box displays asking you to confirm the deletion.

4. Click the **Yes** button.

5. Close the *Data Macro Manager*.

6. Save the table.

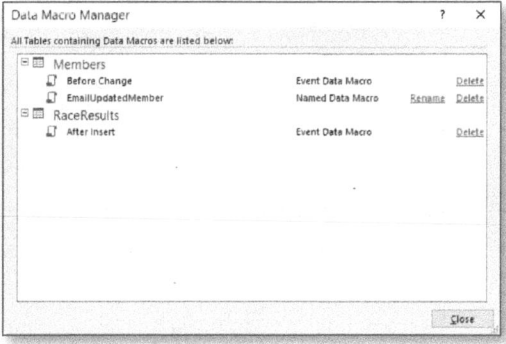

5-69 *Data Macro Manager* dialog box

> ▶ MORE INFO
>
> To change the name of a named data macro in the *Data Macro Manager* dialog box, select the **Rename** option.

SLO 5.7

Building More Advanced Macros

As you become more comfortable building and using macros, you may need to create macros that involve more advanced concepts. In this section, you learn to add conditions to a macro, create a submacro, and add parameters to a named data macro. Finally, you learn how to test and debug macros.

Add Conditions to a Macro

Many times, the task you are automating with a macro involves asking a question or making a comparison to test a condition. You can add an *If block* into a macro to allow you to test a condition and then perform different actions based on the result of the test.

Figure 5-70 shows a simple *If* statement that compares today's date, obtained with the *Date()* function, to the value in the *LastReviewDate* table field. If the difference is greater

than or equal to 20 days, then a macro action is processed. In this case, the macro action sets the value of the *EligibleForReview* field to "*Y*". If the comparison is not true (in this example, if the difference is less than 20 days), the macro exits without performing any action.

5-70 Add conditions to a macro with an *If* block

▶ HOW TO: Add an If Block into a Macro

1. Click the **Add New Action** drop-down arrow and select **If** to add an *If* block into the macro window (Figure 5-71).

2. Enter a condition into the *If* box.

3. Click the **Add New Action** drop-down arrow below the condition and select the desired action.

5-71 An *If* block contains a condition and at least one action

4. Fill in any arguments used in the action by clicking the argument box and entering the appropriate value.

5. Add additional actions into the macro as desired.

6. Select the **Add Else** or **Add Else If** links if you need to create a more complex comparison.

7. Add comments into the macro to explain the purpose/logic of the macro actions.

8. Save the macro.

9. Close the macro if you have finished adding all actions and comments.

Figure 5-72 shows an example of a ***Nested If condition,*** in which one *If* statement occurs inside another *If* statement. The actions in the green box occur only when the result of the first test is true. The first *If* tests to see whether the event that triggered the macro resulted from adding a new record into the table. The blue box contains the second (nested) *If* statement. If the result of the second test is true, the first *SetField* action is performed. If the result of the second test is false, then the *Else* part of the second *If* statement executes and the second *SetField* action is performed.

As you can imagine, the logic in

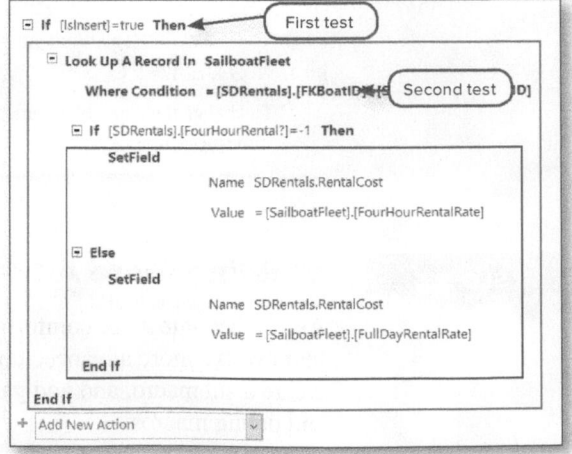

5-72 Example logic in a *Nested If* statement

some macros gets very involved. It is important to spend time in the planning and design process to ensure that you have created a macro that performs as intended. The macro in Figure 5-72 does not include any comments. Viewing a macro without comments helps illustrate the benefit of including comments. Comments not only make it easier for someone else to understand your logic, but they help you. For example, in this case comments could help you determine if you entered the correct *SetField* actions for the true versus false sides of the *If* statement.

Build a Submacro

Occasionally you may need to create a ***submacro***, which is a named, executable set of actions that perform a specific task. Once you create a submacro, you can call that submacro when you need to execute that task. Creating submacros can be a useful organizational approach; you end up with fewer separate, smaller macros when you use submacros.

You can only create a submacro in a stand-alone macro, and the submacro must appear at the end of the stand-alone macro. The only code that can follow a submacro is another submacro.

▶ HOW TO: Add a Submacro into a Macro

1. Double-click **Submacro** from the *Action Catalog Program Flow* grouping to add a *Submacro* block into the macro window (Figure 5-73).

2. Replace the default macro name by entering a unique name in the *Submacro* box.

3. Click the **Add New Action** drop-down arrow and select the desired action.

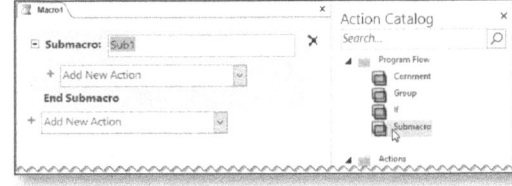

5-73 Add a *Submacro* block

4. Fill in arguments by clicking the argument box and entering the appropriate value.

5. Add additional actions into the macro as desired.

6. Add comments into the submacro to explain the purpose/logic of the macro actions.

7. Save the macro.

8. Close the macro if you have finished adding all actions and comments.

Figure 5-74 shows a macro named *WhichPetsToShow*. This macro contains two submacros that are designed to filter the records that are available to display from a table. One submacro is named *ShowAllPets* and one is named *ShowAvailable*.

The *ShowAvailable* submacro uses the *ApplyFilter* action to display only the records where the *Available* field is *Y*.

After creating a submacro you must execute it by calling the submacro. We use the *WhichPetsToShow* example to illustrate three different ways to call a submacro:

Method 1: Call a macro from within a macro using the *RunMacro* action.

- The *RunMacro* action (Figure 5-75) has three arguments.
- In the *Macro Name* box, which is a required argument, enter the name of the submacro using the following format: macroname.submacroname.
- After the submacro executes, the calling macro continues to execute.

5-74 Submacro examples in the *WhichPetToShow* macro

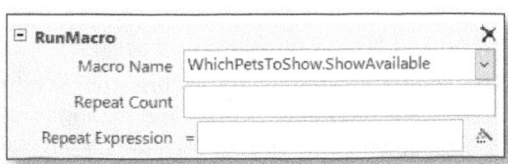

5-75 *RunMacro* action

Method 2: Call a macro from within a macro using the *OnError* action.

- The *OnError* action (Figure 5-76) tells the macro what to do if an error occurs while the macro is executing. The options for *OnError* include calling a macro, going to the next action, or stopping execution of the macro.

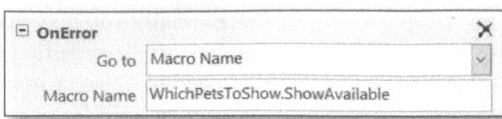

5-76 *OnError* action

- Usually the *OnError* action is the first one in the macro, although it can appear later in the macro.
- Select **Macro Name** in the *Go to* argument and enter the submacro name in the *Macro Name* argument using the following format: macroname.submacroname.

Method 3: Call a macro from an event in an object or control.

- Enter the submacro name in the property box of the desired event. In this example, the *ShowAllPets* submacro is called from the *On Click* event of a button (Figure 5-77.)

5-77 Call a submacro from an event

> **MORE INFO**
>
> In the *Go To* argument of the *OnError* action, select *Next* to advance to the next action or select *Fail* to stop the execution of the macro.

Add Parameters to a Named Data Macro

Using a parameter in a named data macro allows you to pass data into the macro. The data can come from another data macro, a form, or a user interface macro. Parameters increase the power and usability of data macros.

When you create a new named data macro, the macro window includes a ***parameter area*** at the top of the macro. You assign a name to each parameter you add. Inside the macro you refer to the data value using the parameter name.

> **HOW TO: Add a Parameter into a Named Data Macro**

1. Click the **Create Parameter** link in the parameter area. A parameter is added into the parameter area (Figure 5-78).

2. Type a name into the *Name* box.

3. Type a description into the *Description* box. This is optional but the description shows in a tool tip when the parameter is used and serves as a comment for the parameter, so it is good practice to include a description.

4. Add additional parameters as desired.

5. Click outside the parameter area, or click the **Add New Action** box when you are done adding parameters. The parameter area displays the added parameters (Figure 5-79).

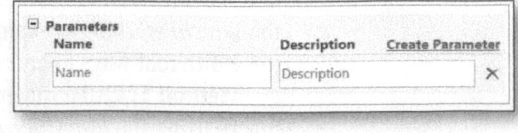

5-78 Parameter area in a named data macro

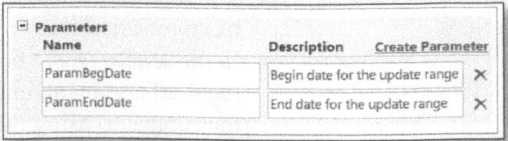

5-79 Completed parameter area

To illustrate how parameters are used, in the following material you explore a macro that changes the value of a table field if the record meets certain conditions. This macro uses two data blocks: *ForEachRecord* and *EditRecord*.

ForEachRecord Data Block

The *ForEachRecord* data block repeats the listed actions for each record. The *ForEachRecord* data block has two arguments, which we explain in the following material; only the *In* argument is required.

- The *In* argument can contain a table name, a query name, or an *SQL* statement. This argument tells Access what data to use.
- The *Where Condition* argument can contain an expression to limit the records that are affected. If this condition is omitted, all the records are processed.

As desired, an *Alias* argument can also be added. An alias provides an alternate, usually shorter name, for the table or query specified in the *In* argument.

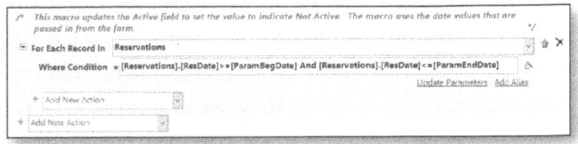

5-80 *ForEachRecord* block

In the example shown in Figure 5-80, the *ForEachRecord* block specifies that Access will use the *Reservations* table, and that only records where the *ResDate* field is between the *ParamBegDate* and the *ParamEndDate* will process. After completing the arguments, you need to add the desired actions into the *ForEachRecord* block.

Figure 5-81 shows an example of the completed macro that includes the two parameters, along with the actions that use those parameters. Notice that the *ForEachRecord* block uses an *EditRecord* data block.

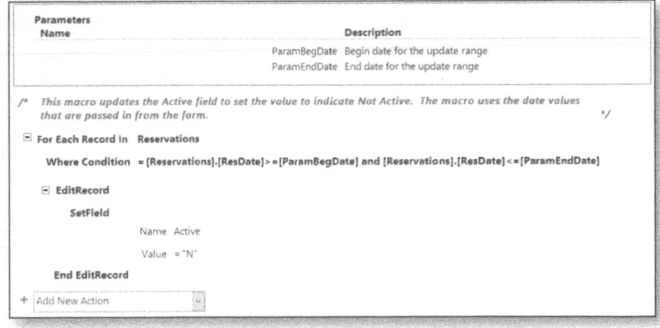

5-81 Complete macro includes a *ForEachRecord* data block and an *EditRecord* data block

EditRecord Data Block

The *EditRecord* data block edits the values of an existing record. Because this action appears within the *ForEachRecord* block, it operates on the data specified in that block. *Alias* is an optional argument that you can use to provide an alternate name to refer to the record. In the example in Figure 5-81, the *EditRecord* block uses the *SetField* action to assign a value of *N* to the *Active* field for records that meet the specified condition.

Pass Values into Parameters

Recall that named data macros are executed by using the *RunDataMacro* action inside of another macro.

In the *Macro Name* argument, if you enter a macro that contains parameters, the *RunDataMacro* action changes and requires you to fill in the values for each parameter (Figure 5-82).

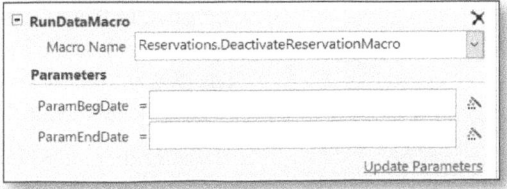

5-82 If a macro uses parameters, when you add a *RunDataMaro* command you must fill in the parameter values

As part of the macro design process, you should have already determined what fields or controls will have the parameter values. If the macro is being called from a form, it is common to have the parameter values come from text boxes on the form. If the macro is being called from a data macro of a table, then you may want the parameter values to come from the table fields.

Enter the name of the text box control or table field names into the parameter arguments (Figure 5-83). In the example shown here, the parameters come from two text boxes on a form. This macro is called from an embedded macro attached to the *OnClick* event of a button on the form.

5-83 These parameters get their values from text boxes

Test and Debug a Macro

After you create a macro, it is important to test it to ensure that it performs as planned. With some macros you may not be sure that they are performing as expected unless you develop a specific plan to test the macro. This may involve creating test data and test scenarios in your database. For example, with the *NoReportData* macro from *Pause & Practice 5-3,* we need two scenarios: Run the report once when the report would not find any data in the underlying tables and run it a second time when it would find data.

As you are developing your databases, you may need to create or modify the sample data in the table(s) in order to test all possible conditions of a macro. With some macros you may discover that a logic error results from selecting the wrong event to trigger the macro. For example, imagine that you want to create a stand-alone macro that executes whenever a form is closed. You have a *Close Form* button on every form, so it is logical to attach the macro to the *On Click* event of the button. However, you need to think of different scenarios and ways the database may be used. For example, if someone closed the form by clicking the *X* in the corner your macro would not execute. In this situation, it would be better to attach the macro to the *On Close* event for the form.

In addition to creating test data, other tools are available to help you debug macros. With user interface macros, you can debug a macro by adding error handling into a macro or by using the single step utility. With data macros, you can use error handling and the *Application Log* table.

Error Handling

Recall that one use of a submacro is to handle errors. Figure 5-84 illustrates a common design of an error-handling submacro.

- The submacro displays a message box, which will show the description of the error that occurred. In this case, the submacro also contains an action to stop the execution of the macro.
- The *OnError* action tells the macro what to do if an error occurs while the macro is executing.

Because there are hundreds of different errors, including a list of all the possible errors is not practical. They range from *"Division by zero"* to *"An expression you entered is the wrong data type*

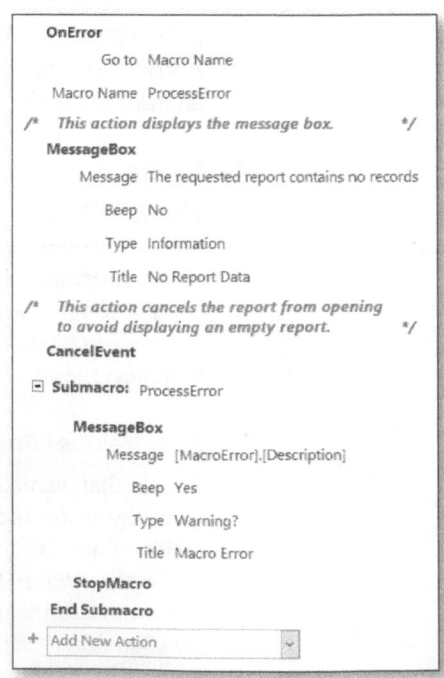

5-84 Sample error-handling macro

for one of the arguments." Use the Access help feature to research an error description. Use the help information when you review the design of the macro to fix the problem.

While submacros are not available in data macros, the *OnError* action is. A data macro can use either the *Next* or *Fail* options in the *Go To* argument (Figure 5-85).

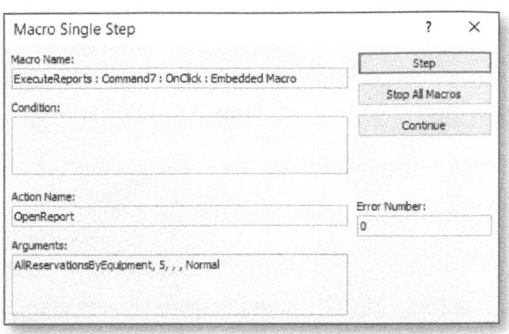

5-85 *OnError options in a data macro*

The Single Step Tool

The *Macro Builder* contains the **Single Step** tool, which can execute the macro one action, or step, at a time. When a macro executes in *Single Step* mode, the **Macro Single Step** dialog box displays (Figure 5-86). The dialog box displays the *Macro Name, Condition, Action Name, Arguments* of the action, and the *Error Number.* If no error occurred in a step, the error number is 0. The condition box contains information only when the action is part of an *If* block.

5-86 *Macro Single Step dialog box*

Depending on the information you see in the dialog box, you select one of the three buttons.

- **Step:** Advances the macro to the next step.
- **Stop All Macros:** Stops the execution of all macros that are running. This leaves the macro in *Single Step* mode the next time the macro executes.
- **Continue:** Exits *Single Step* mode and continues the execution of the macro. Since *Single Step* mode has been turned off, if you want to debug the macro in the future you need to turn it back on.

▶**HOW TO:** Use the Single Step Tool

1. Open the macro in *Design* View.
2. Turn on *Single Step* by clicking the **Single Step** button [*Macro Tools Design* tab, *Tools* group]. The *Single Step* button is highlighted in the *Ribbon*, indicating that it has been turned on (Figure 5-87).
3. Save and close the macro.
4. Run the macro. The *Macro Single Step* dialog box displays.
5. Click the *Step, Stop All Macros,* or *Continue* button.

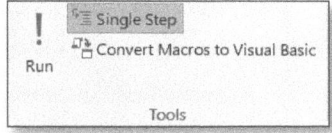

5-87 *Single Step button*

To turn off *Single Step* mode, click the **Single Step** button [*Macro Tools Design* tab, *Tools* group]. The *Single Step* button is no longer highlighted.

The *Single Step* mode is not an available option in data macros.

The Application Log table

In data macros the **Application Log** table is available to help you debug a macro. Inside a database, Access maintains a variety of tables with information about the database. These tables do not appear in the *Navigation Pane*. The *Application Log* table (Figure 5-88) contains

data related to errors encountered when executing data macros. You can refer to the information in the table to determine what happened when the macro executed.

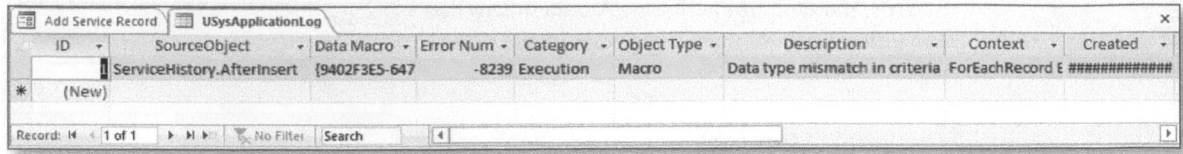

ID	SourceObject	Data Macro	Error Num	Category	Object Type	Description	Context	Created
1	ServiceHistory.AfterInsert	{9402F3E5-647	-8239	Execution	Macro	Data type mismatch in criteria	ForEachRecord E	#############
*	(New)							

5-88 *Application Log* table

To view the *Application Log* table, click the **Info** button [*File* tab] and then select the **View Application Log Table** button.

> **MORE INFO**
>
> The *View Application Log Table* button does not display on the *Info* tab until the table has been created as a result of a macro error.

PAUSE & PRACTICE: ACCESS 5-4

For this Pause & Practice you continue to work on the Challenger Middle School database. You create and test an event-driven macro to set the value of the *Active* field when a record is added. Then you create and test a named data macro that uses parameters.

File Needed: *PP A5-3.accdb*
Completed Project File Name: *[your initials] PP A5-4.accdb*

1. Open the *[your initials] PP A5-3* database file you created in *Pause & Practice 5-3*.

2. Save a new copy of your database as [your initials] PP A5-4.

3. Enable content in the database.

4. Create an event-driven data macro to set the value of the *Active* field when a user adds a record.
 a. Open the *Reservations* table in *Datasheet* view.
 b. Click the **Before Change** button from the [*Table Tools Table* tab, *Before Events* group] to open the *Macro Builder*.
 c. Click the **Add New Action** drop-down arrow and select **Comment**.
 d. Type This macro automatically sets the value of the Active field to "Y" when a new reservation record is added. The first action checks whether the BeforeChange event is the result of adding a new record (the IsInsert function would be true) versus a change to an existing record.
 e. Click the **Add New Action** drop-down arrow and select **If**.
 f. Enter [IsInsert]=True in the *If* box.
 g. Click the **Add New Action** drop-down arrow directly below the *If* action and select **Comment**.
 h. Type Use the SetField action to set the value of the Active field in the table.
 i. Click the **Add New Action** drop-down arrow directly below the *Comment* and select **SetField**.
 j. Enter Active in the *Name* argument.

k. Enter "Y" in the *Value* argument. Click outside the *Value* box. The finished macro should look similar to Figure 5-89.

l. Save and close the macro.

5. Test the event-driven macro by adding a new record using the *AddNewReservation* form. With the *Reservations* table still open in *Datasheet* view, verify that the last record is for *ResID* 25.

 a. Close the table.

 b. Open the *AddNewReservation* form. Note that the form does not have a text box to enter the value for the *Active* field.

 c. Type 2 in the *Employee Number* box.

 d. Select *Equipment ID* **1**.

 e. Type 5/25/2017 in the *Pick Up Date*.

 f. Type 9:00 in the *Pick Up Time*.

 g. Click the **Save Reservation** button (Figure 5-90).

 h. Click the **Close Form** button.

 i. Open the *Reservations* table in *Datasheet* view. Verify that the new record for *ResID* 26 has been added and that the value for the *Active* field has been set to *Y*. Also note that the reservations for November and December 2016 are still active.

5-89 Completed *Before Change* macro code

5-90 *AddNewReservation* form

6. Create a named data macro to change the value of the *Active* field to *N* for selected records.

 a. Click the **Named Macro** button [*Table Tools Table* tab, *Named Macros* group] and then select the **Create Named Macro** option to open the *Macro Builder*.

 b. Click the **Create Parameter** link to add a parameter to the macro.

 c. Type ParamBegDate into the *Name* box.

 d. Type Begin date for the update range into the *Description* box.

 e. Click the **Create Parameter** link to add a parameter to the macro.

 f. Type ParamEndDate into the *Name* box.

 g. Type End date for the update range into the *Description* box.

 h. Click the **Add New Action** drop-down arrow and select **Comment**.

 i. Type This macro updates the Active field to set the value to indicate Not Active. The macro uses the date values that are passed in from the form.

 j. Click the **Add New Action** drop-down arrow and select **ForEachRecord**.

 k. Type Reservations into the *For Each Record In* box.

 l. Type [Reservations].[ResDate]> =[ParamBegDate] and [Reservations].[ResDate]< =[ParamEndDate] into the Where Condition box.

 m. Click the **Add New Action** drop-down arrow directly below *Where Condition* and select **EditRecord**.

 n. Click the **Add New Action** drop-down arrow directly below *EditRecord* and select **SetField**.

 o. Type Active in the *Name* box.

 p. Type "N" in the *Value* box. Click outside the *Value* box. The completed macro should look similar to Figure 5-91.

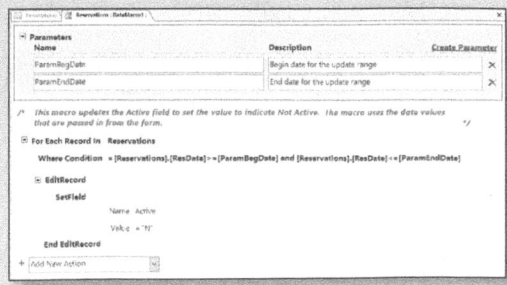

5-91 Complete named data macro code

q. Save the macro as DeactivateReservationMacro and close the macro.
r. Save and close the *Reservations* table.

7. Prepare to call the named macro.
 a. Open the **DeactivateReservation** form in *Design* view.
 b. Click to select the **unbound** text box to the right of the *Enter the Beginning Date of the range* label (Figure 5-92).
 c. Click the **Property Sheet** button [*Form Design Tools Design* tab, *Tools* group].
 d. Select the **Other** tab. In the *Name* property, note that the name of this text box is *txtBegDate*.
 e. Click to select the **unbound** text box to the right of the *Enter the Ending Date of the range* label. In the *Name* property, note that the name of this text box is *txtEndDate*.

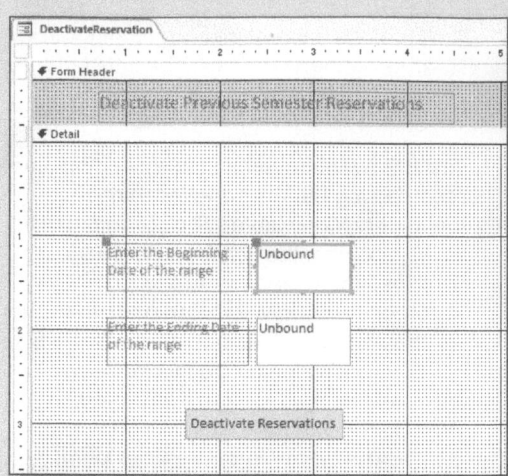

5-92 Select the text box in *Design* view of the *DeactivateReservation* form

8. Call the named macro from another macro.
 a. Click the **Deactivate Reservations** button.
 b. Select the **Event** tab.
 c. Click the property box of the **On Click** event and click the **Build** button.
 d. Select **Macro Builder** in the *Choose Builder* dialog box and click **OK**.
 e. Click the **drop-down arrow** and select **Comment**.
 f. Type This macro executes the DeactivateReservationMacro, a named data macro attached to the Reservations table. It uses two parameters that get their values from the text boxes on the form.
 g. Click the **Add New Action** drop-down arrow and select **RunDataMacro**.
 h. Click the **drop-down arrow** in the *Macro Name* argument and select **Reservations.DeactivateReservationMacro**.
 i. Enter [txtBegDate] in the *ParamBegDate* argument.
 j. Enter [txtEndDate] in the *ParamEndDate* argument.
 k. Click the **Add New Action** drop-down arrow and select **Comment**.
 l. Type The next action executes after all the updates have occurred. A message box displays.
 m. Click the **drop-down arrow** and select **MessageBox**.
 n. Type Reservations have been updated. in the *Message* argument.
 o. Select **No** in the *Beep* argument.
 p. Select **Information** in the *Type* argument.
 q. Leave the *Title* argument empty and click outside the *Type* argument. The completed macro should look similar to Figure 5-93.

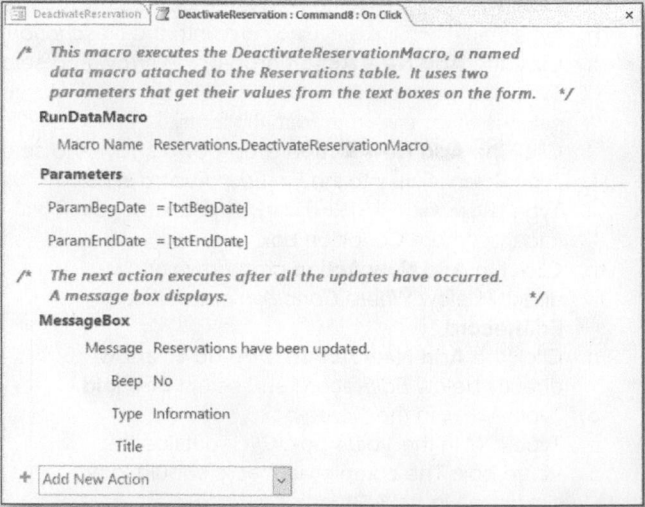

5-93 Completed *OnClick* macro code

 r. Save and close the macro.

 s. Save the form.

9. Test the macro.
 a. Switch to *Form* view of the *DeactivateReservation* form.
 b. Type 11/1/2016 in the *Enter the Beginning Date of the range* text box.
 c. Type 12/31/2016 in the *Enter the Ending Date of the range* text box.
 d. Click the **Deactivate Reservations** button. The *Message Box* displays.
 e. Click **OK** to close the *Message Box*.
 f. Open the *Reservations* table in *Datasheet* view. Verify that the *Active* field has changed to N for the records in the November and December 2016 date range.

10. Close the table.

11. Close the form.

12. Close the database.

Chapter Summary

5.1 Analyze, create, use, and modify a database from an Access template (p. A5-286).

- *Templates* are predesigned databases that provide you with a complete, ready-to-use, database application.
- There are twelve templates, covering a range of business scenarios, which install with Access.
- Some templates are designed to work on the web.
- Create a new database from a template by selecting the desired template from the *File* tab.
- After creating a database from a template, review the different objects. Make any changes needed to customize the database to fit your needs.

5.2 Create a relationship with the *Lookup Wizard;* edit a relationship; edit properties of a lookup field; delete relationships created with a lookup field; and use a lookup with multiple fields (p. A5-294).

- Use the *Lookup Wizard* to create a relationship between two tables.
- Edit the properties of a relationship in the *Relationships* window.
- After completing the *Lookup Wizard,* the foreign key field will have changed to use a *Combo Box* display control.
- Edit the *List Rows* and *List Width* properties of the lookup field to alter the way that the data displays in the combo box.
- You can set a lookup field to display multiple fields in a list.

5.3 Implement a many-to-many relationship and explore join properties between tables (p. A5-299).

- A *many-to-many* relationship exists when many rows of data in one table can be associated with many rows of data in a second table.
- To implement a many-to-many relationship, you must first create a *junction table* to match up the records in the two tables.
- A junction table has a *concatenated primary key,* which is made by creating a *primary key* that uses the primary keys from each of the two tables.

- The *Join Type* property of a relationship tells Access how to match the data in the related tables.
- Joins can be an *inner join*, a *left outer join*, or a *right outer join*.
- Change the *join type* in the *Join Properties* dialog box.

5.4 Describe a macro and use the *Macro Builder* (p. A5-306).

- *Macros* are database objects that help automate tasks and add functionality to your database.
- *User interface* macros attach to objects and controls that are part of the user interface and automate actions such as opening objects, customizing forms, and displaying message boxes.
- *Data macros* attach to tables and automate tasks that involve adding, changing, or deleting data.
- You can build macros using the *Macro Builder* utility. Macros are executed by calling them either from an event or from another macro.
- You build macros by adding various macro actions or commands.
- Some actions contain *arguments*, pieces of information needed to complete the action.
- Macros can also contain *program flow* items such as *comments*, *groups*, *If blocks*, and *submacros*.

5.5 Build a stand-alone macro, build an embedded macro, and edit and delete user interface macros (p. A5-311).

- User interface macros can perform a variety of actions related to interface objects such as importing/exporting data, searching data records, and controlling what is shown on the screen.
- User interface macros can be attached to many different types of events such as clicking a button, moving the mouse, or the opening or closing of an object.
- *Stand-alone* macros and *embedded* macros are the two types of user interface macros.
- A stand-alone macro is a separate Access object that appears in the *Navigation Pane*

and that can be assigned to events in many different objects.

- A stand-alone macro can be executed by calling it from another macro or by attaching it to an event of an object or control.
- An embedded macro is attached to an event in one specific object or control on an object.

5.6 Build an event-driven data macro, build a named data macro, and edit and delete data macros (p. A5-321).

- Data macros help ensure that the data in tables is accurate, and automate tasks related to tables.
- *Event-driven data* macros can respond to the following table events: *After Insert, After Update, After Delete, Before Delete,* and *Before Change.*
- A data macro has a more limited set of actions than a user interface macro, and the availability of those actions depends on the type of table event.
- A *named data macro* is associated with a specific table, but it is not attached to any particular event.
- A named data macro can be executed by calling it with a *RunDataMacro* action from another macro.

5.7 Build more advanced macros by adding conditions, build a submacro, integrate parameters, and test and debug a macro (p. A5-326).

- Add conditional logic into a macro using an *If* block.

- A *submacro* is a named, executable set of actions that perform a specific task.
- You can call a submacro when you need to execute a task and limit duplicated code in your database.
- Named data macros can utilize *parameters,* which allow data values to be passed into the macro.
- It is important to test the logic in your macros to ensure that they are designed and written correctly. You may need to create sample test data, as well as test scenarios, as part of the testing process.
- Add the *OnError* action into a macro to tell the macro what to do if an error occurs.
- Executing user interface macros in *Single Step* mode can help you to determine when and why an error occurs.
- Review errors that occur when a data macro executes by opening the *Application Log* table.

Check for Understanding

The SIMbook for this text (within your SIMnet account), provides the following resources for concept review:

- Multiple choice questions
- Matching exercises
- Short answer questions

Guided Project 5-1

For this project, you create a new database based on the *Faculty* template. You explore the functionality of the database, modify the table and query, and enhance the database by adding a new table and creating a relationship using the *Lookup Wizard*.
[Student Learning Outcomes 5.1, 5.2]

File Needed: None
Completed Project File Name: *[your initials] Access 5-1.accdb*

Skills Covered in This Project

- Build a database from a template.
- Review and modify template objects.
- Create a new table.

- Define a relationship with the *Lookup Wizard*.
- Use multiple columns in a lookup field.
- View and edit relationship properties.
- Edit properties of the lookup field.

1. Create a new database based on a template.
 a. Open Access or click the **New** button [*File* tab] if Access is already open.
 b. Click the **Search for online templates** box, type Faculty, and click the **magnify** icon.
 c. Select the **Faculty** template (Figure 5-94). *Note: If this template is not available in Access, skip to step 2.*
 d. Type [your initials] Access 5-1 in the *File name* box.
 e. Click the **Browse** button to change the location where you will save the database and click the **OK** button.
 f. Click the **Create** button. The database opens and displays the *Faculty List* form.
 g. Close the *Faculty List* form.
 h. Skip to step 3.

2. Open the **Faculty-05** database from your student data files.
 a. Close the *Faculty List* form.
 b. Save a new copy of the database. Type [your initials] Access 5-1 as the file name.

3. Enable content in the database.

4. Explore the *Navigation Pane,* objects, and relationships.
 a. Click the **Shutter Bar Open/Close Button** to open the *Navigation Pane.*

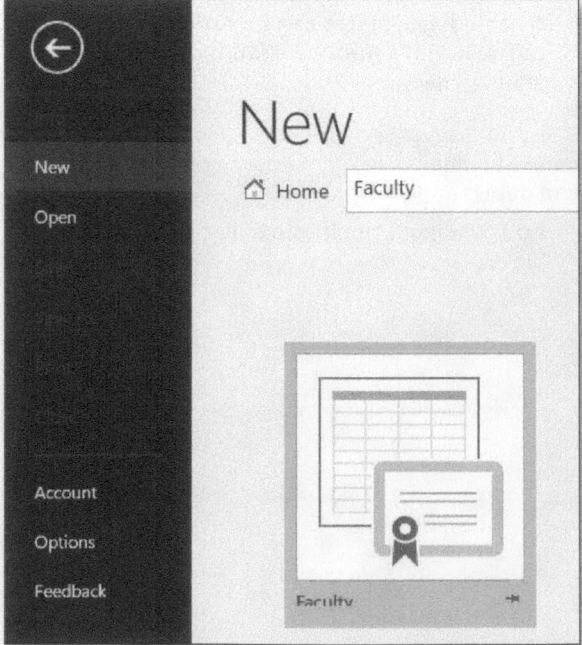

5-94 *Faculty template*

b. Click the **Navigation Pane** arrow to open the *Navigation* menu.

c. Select the **Object Type** category. The *Navigation Pane* updates to show all of the objects (Figure 5-95).

d. Open the *Faculty Details* form to get a sense of the design of this template.

e. Close the *Faculty Details* form.

f. Open the *Faculty List* form.

g. Click the **Reports** drop-down arrow on the *Faculty List* form and select the **All Faculty** report. The report displays but there are no faculty records shown.

h. Close the report.

i. Close the *Faculty List* form.

5. Modify the *Faculty* table as several fields are not needed and others require changes.

a. Open the *Faculty* table in *Design* view.

b. Select the **Company** field and click the **Delete Rows** button [*Table Tools Design* tab, *Tools* group]. Click **Yes** in the *Message Box* informing you that the index for this field will also be deleted.

c. Delete the **ID Number**, **Fax Number**, **Country/Region**, and **Web Page** fields.

d. Change the *Field Name* of the *Education Level/Degree* field to Highest Degree.

e. Select the **Department** field.

f. Click the **Lookup** tab.

g. Edit the *Row Source* property and add ;"Art"; "History"; "Music" to the list.

h. Save and close the table.

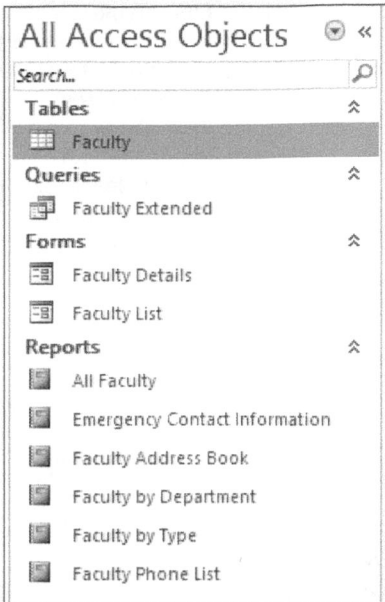

5-95 *Navigation Pane* showing all objects

6. Edit the *Faculty Extended* query.

a. Open the *Faculty Extended* query in *Design* view. This query uses the company field you deleted from the table. As a result, you need to update the query.

b. Click the **File As** cell in the *Field* row, right-click to open the context menu, and select the **Zoom** button (Figure 5-96) to open the *Zoom* window.

c. Delete **[Company],** from the expression. *Note: You must delete the comma that appears after* [Company] *for the query to work correctly.*

d. Click **OK**.

e. Click the **Contact Name** cell in the *Field* row, right-click to open the context menu, and select the **Zoom** button to open the *Zoom* window.

f. Delete **[Company]**, from the expression.

g. Click **OK**.

h. Save and run the query. The query executes but no records display.

i. Close the query.

5-96 Context menu

7. Explore the *Faculty Details* form and add records into the database.

a. Open the *Faculty Details* form. Note that the form opens in a separate window and you cannot switch to *Design* view while the form is in *Form* view. This is a result of property settings and macros attached to the form.

 b. Click the **First Name** text box and enter Bruce. Note that the *Web Page, Fax Number,* and *Country/Region* text boxes display *#Name?* because the links back to the table fields are invalid.

 c. Click the **Last Name** text box and type Elkins.

 d. Click the **Save and New** button on the form.

 e. Click the **First Name** text box and enter Charlotte. Note that the *Web Page, Fax Number,* and *Country/Region* text boxes display *#Name?* because the links back to the table fields are invalid.

 f. Click in the **Last Name** text box and type Liu.

 g. Click the **Save and New** button on the form.

 h. Close the form. Don't make any changes to remove the text boxes that are no longer valid in this exercise since you will not use this database later, although those changes must be made before putting the database into operation.

8. Add a second table into the database.

 a. Click the **Table Design** button [*Create* tab, *Tables* group].

 b. Add fields into the table using the following information:

Field Name	Data Type	Description	FieldSize
DegreeID	*AutoNumber*	Unique identifier for each degree	
ID-FK	*Number*	Must match a value in the ID field in the Faculty table	
Degree	*Short Text*	Type of degree earned	50
DegreeYear	*Number*	Year degree was awarded	.
Institution	*Short Text*	Institution granting the degree	50

 c. Designate the **DegreeID** field as the primary key.

 d. Select the **Degree** field.

 e. Click the **Lookup** tab.

 f. Select **Combo Box** in the *Display Control* property box.

 g. Select **Value List** in the *Row Source Type* property box.

 h. Type "High School Diploma"; "G.E.D."; "Bachelor's Degree"; "Master's Degree"; "Ph.D." in the *Row Source* property box.

 i. Select the **DegreeYear** field and click the **General** tab.

 j. Type #### in the *Input Mask* property box.

 k. Save the table as Degrees.

9. Create a relationship using the *Lookup Wizard.*

 a. Click the **Data Type** property box of the *ID-FK* field, click the **drop-down arrow** to display the list of data types, and then select **Lookup Wizard** to launch the wizard.

 b. Select the **I want the lookup field to get the values from another table or query** radio button and click **Next**.

 c. Select the **Faculty** table and click **Next**.

 d. Select **ID** from the list of *Available Fields* and click the **Move Single Field** button to move the field into the *Selected Fields* window.

 e. Move the **First Name** and **Last Name** fields (Figure 5-97).

5-97 Select fields in the *Lookup Wizard*

 f. Click **Next**.

 g. Don't sort on any fields and click **Next**.

 h. Deselect the **Hide key column** check box and click **Next**.

 i. Select the **ID** field to store in the table and click **Next**.

 j. Check the **Enable Data Integrity** box and the **Cascade Delete** radio button.

 k. Click **Finish** to complete the wizard. A *Lookup Wizard* dialog box displays.

 l. Click **Yes** to save the changes to the table so that Access can create the relationship.

 m. Select the **ID-FK** field and click the **Lookup** tab.

 n. Click the **Column Widths** property box.

 o. Change the entry so it reads .5"; 1"; 1". The ID column does not need to be as wide as the name columns.

 p. Save the table. If a dialog box displays informing you that the table has changed since the last time you opened it, click **Yes** to save your changes.

 q. Close the table.

10. Edit the relationship.

 a. Click the **Relationships** button [*Database Tools* tab, *Relationships* group] to open the *Relationships* window.

 b. Select the **relationship line**.

 c. Click **Edit Relationships** [*Relationship Tools Design* tab, *Tools* group].

 d. Select the **Cascade Update Related Fields** check box.

 e. Click **OK**.

 f. Click **Save** to save the changes made to the relationships.

 g. Close the *Relationships* window.

11. Add records into the *Degrees* table.

 a. Open the *Degrees* table in *Datasheet* view.

 b. Click the **ID-FK** field, click the **drop-down arrow** and select **Bruce Elkins** (Figure 5-98). The *DegreeID* column is narrower because of the property changes you made in step 9o.

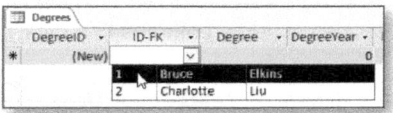

5-98 Drop-down list for the *ID-FK* field

 c. Select **Ph.D**. from the drop-down list in the *Degree* field.

 d. Type 2012 in the *DegreeYear* field.

 e. Type University of Arizona in the *Institution* field.

 f. Click the **ID-FK** field, click the **drop-down arrow,** and select **Charlotte Liu**.

 g. Select **Ph.D**. from the drop-down list in the *Degree* field.

 h. Type 2015 in the *DegreeYear* field.

 i. Type Rutgers in the *Institution* field.

 j. Save and close the table.

12. Test the cascade delete property of the relationship.

 a. Open the *Faculty* table in *Datasheet* view.

 b. Click the **plus sign** on *Bruce Elkin's* row to see his related degree records.

 c. Click the **minus sign**.

 d. Click the **row selector** box for *Bruce Elkin's* record in the table.

 e. Click the **Delete** button [*Home* tab, *Records* group]. A warning message displays alerting you that you will delete related records in another table.

 f. Click **Yes**.

 g. Close the table.

 h. Open the *Degrees* tables in *Datasheet* view to verify that the record was deleted.

 i. Close the table.

13. Close the database.

Guided Project 5-2

TextbooksRUs is building a database to store information about the books they sell. The database contains a table to store book information and another table to store author information. For this project, you extend the database functionality by modifying the database so that it can represent the many-to-many relationship between these tables. You also build and test an *AutoExec* macro to open the author and book tables when the database opens.
[Student Learning Outcomes 5.2, 5.3, 5.4, 5.5, 5.7]

File Needed: ***TextbooksRUs-05.accdb***
Completed Project File Name: ***[your initials] Access 5-2.accdb***

Skills Covered in This Project

- Determine the need for a many-to-many relationship.
- Create a junction table with a concatenated primary key.
- Define a relationship with the *Lookup Wizard*.
- Use multiple columns in a lookup field.

- Add data into a junction table.
- Use the *Macro Builder*.
- Build a stand-alone *AutoExec* macro.
- Test a macro.
- Add error handling into a macro.
- Add conditions into a macro.
- Add a submacro in a macro.

1. Open the ***TextbooksRUs-05.accdb*** database from your student data files.

2. Save a new copy of your database as [your initials] Access 5-2.

3. Enable content in the database.

4. Review the existing tables.
 a. Open the *Book* table in *Datasheet* view. View the 11 data records contained in the table.
 b. Switch to *Design* view. Note that the primary key of *ISBN* is a *Short Text* data type, with a field size of *13*.
 c. Open the *Author* table in *Datasheet* view. View the 22 data records contained in the table.
 d. Switch to *Design* view. Note that the primary key of *ID* is an *AutoNumber* data type, with a field size of *Long Integer.*

5. Determine the relationship type. A *Book* could have many different authors. An *Author* could have written many different books. There is a many-to-many relationship between the *Book* and *Author* tables.

6. Close both tables.

7. Create a junction table.
 a. Click the **Table Design** button [*Create* tab, *Tables* group] to open a new table in *Design* view.
 b. Type AuthorID-FK in the *Field Name* property box of the first row.
 c. Select the **Number** data type.
 d. Type Must match an ID in the Author table in the *Description* property box.
 e. Type ISBN-FK in the *Field Name* property box of the second row.
 f. Select the **Short Text** data type.
 g. Type Must match an ISBN in the Book table in the *Description* property box.
 h. Enter 13 in the *Field Size* property box.
 i. Click and hold in the **Row Selector** box to select the *ISBN-FK* field; drag the selection pointer to also select the *AuthorID-FK* field.

j. Click the **Primary Key** button [*Table Tools Design* tab, *Tools* group] to create the concatenated primary key (Figure 5-99).

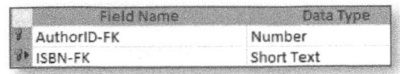

5-99 Concatenated primary key

k. Click **Save** to open the *Save As* dialog box. Enter AuthorBook as the *Table Name* and click **OK**.

8. Use the *Lookup Wizard* to create a one-to-many relationship between *Author* and *AuthorBook*. This lookup displays multiple fields.
 a. Select the **AuthorID-FK** field.
 b. Select **Lookup Wizard** in the *Data Type* property box to launch the *Lookup Wizard*.
 c. Select the **I want the lookup field to get the values from another table or query** radio button and click **Next**.
 d. Select the **Author** table, if necessary, and click **Next**.
 e. Select **ID** from the list of *Available Fields* and click the **Move Single Field** button to move the field into the *Selected Fields* window.

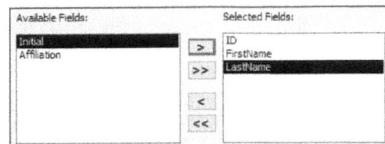

 f. Move the *FirstName* and *LastName* fields (Figure 5-100).
 g. Click **Next**.
 h. Select the **LastName** field in the first sort box and click **Next**.

5-100 Select fields in the *Lookup Wizard*

 i. Deselect the **Hide key column** check box and click **Next**.
 j. Select the **ID** field to store in the table and click **Next**.
 k. Check the **Enable Data Integrity** box and the **Cascade Delete** radio button.
 l. Click **Finish** to complete the wizard. A *Lookup Wizard* dialog box displays.
 m. Click **Yes** to save the changes to the table so that Access can create the relationship.

9. Use the *Lookup Wizard* to create a one-to-many relationship between *Book* and *AuthorBook*. This lookup displays multiple fields.
 a. Select the **ISBN-FK** field.
 b. Select **Lookup Wizard** in the *Data Type* property box to launch the *Lookup Wizard*.
 c. Select the **I want the lookup field to get the values from another table or query** radio button and click **Next**.
 d. Select the **Book** table and click **Next**.
 e. Select **ISBN** from the list of *Available Fields* and click the **Move Single Field** button to move the field into the *Selected Fields* window.
 f. Move the **Title** field.
 g. Click **Next**.
 h. Don't sort on any fields and click **Next**.
 i. Deselect the **Hide key column** check box.
 j. Double-click the right edge of the *Title* column heading to automatically adjust the field width (Figure 5-101).

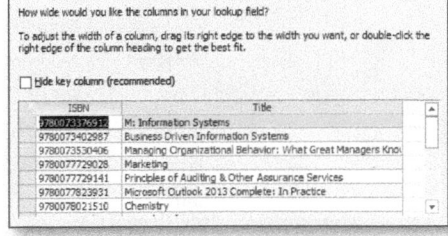

 k. Click **Next**.
 l. Select the **ISBN** field to store in the table and click **Next**.
 m. Check the **Enable Data Integrity** box and the **Cascade Delete** radio button.

5-101 Adjust the column width of the *Title* column

 n. Click **Finish** to complete the wizard. A *Lookup Wizard* dialog box displays.
 o. Click **Yes** to save the changes to the table so that Access can create the relationship. If prompted with another dialog box informing you that changes have been made to the *AuthorBook* table since the last time you opened it, click the **Yes** button to save your most recent changes.

10. Close the table.

11. Edit the relationship.
 a. Click the **Relationships** button [*Database Tools* tab, *Relationships* group] to open the *Relationships* window (Figure 5-102).
 b. Select the **relationship line** between *Author* and *AuthorBook*.
 c. Click **Edit Relationships** [*Relationship Tools Design* tab, *Tools* group].
 d. Select the **Cascade Update Related Fields** check box.
 e. Click **OK**.
 f. Select the **relationship line** between *Book* and *AuthorBook*.
 g. Click **Edit Relationships** [*Relationship Tools Design* tab, *Tools* group].
 h. Select the **Cascade Update Related Fields** check box.
 i. Click **OK**.
 j. Click **Save** to save the changes made to the relationships.
 k. Close the *Relationships* window.

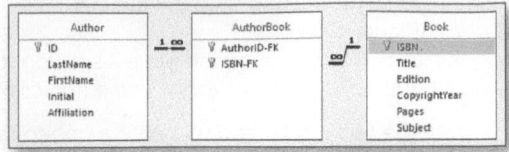

5-102 Relationships in the *TextbooksRUs* database

12. Explore three ways to add the data into the *AuthorBook* junction table.
 a. Open the *Author* table in *Datasheet* view.
 b. Click the **plus sign** on Ray Whittington's record.
 c. Click the **ISBN-FK** drop-down arrow and select **9780077729141 Principles of Auditing & Other Assurance Services**. This adds the record in the *AuthorBook* table.
 d. Close the *Author* table.
 e. Open the *Book* table in *Datasheet* view.
 f. Click the **plus sign** on 978-0-07-340298-7 Business Driven Information Systems' record.
 g. Click the **AuthorID-FK** drop-down arrow and select **10 Paige Baltzan**. This adds the record in the *AuthorBook* table.
 h. In the append row, click the **AuthorID-FK** drop-down arrow and select **21 Amy Phillips**. This adds the record in the *AuthorBook* table.
 i. Close the *Book* table.
 j. Open the *AuthorBook* table in *Datasheet* view. The three records you added display.
 k. Add the remaining nine records from the table below directly into the *AuthorBook* junction table. The table shows the values in the additional lookup fields to aid in your data entry.

AuthorID-FK	FirstName	LastName	ISBN-FK	Title
10	Paige	Baltzan	9780073376912	M: Information Systems
2	Randy	Nordell	9780077823931	Microsoft Outlook 2013 Complete: In Practice
4	Timothy	Baldwin	9780073530406	Managing Organizational Behavior: What Great . . .
6	Robert	Rubin	9780073530406	Managing Organizational Behavior: What Great . . .
7	Jason	Colquitt	9780073530406	Managing Organizational Behavior: What Great . . .
7	Jason	Colquitt	9781259545092	Organizational Behavior: Improving Performance . . .
8	Jeffrey	LePine	9781259545092	Organizational Behavior: Improving Performance . . .
9	Michael	Wesson	9781259545092	Organizational Behavior: Improving Performance . . .
18	Kurt	Pany	9780077729141	Principles of Auditing & Other Assurance Services

13. Close the table.

14. View the related records in the *Author* table.
 a. Open the *Author* table in *Datasheet* view.
 b. Click the **plus sign** on Paige Baltzan's record to view the ISBN of the two books she has in the database.

 c. Click the **plus sign** on Dhruv Grewal's record. You haven't linked him to any books in the database.

 d. Close the table.

15. Create a stand-alone macro to open the *Author* and *Book* tables when the database opens.
 a. Click the **Macro** button [*Create* tab, *Macros & Code* group] to open the *Macro Builder*.
 b. Click the **drop-down arrow** and select **Comment**.
 c. Type This action opens the Author table.
 d. Click the **Add New Action** drop-down arrow and select **OpenTable**.
 e. Click the **drop-down arrow** in the *Table Name* argument and select **Author**. Accept the default entry of *Datasheet* in the *View* argument and *Edit* in the *Data Mode* argument.
 f. Click the **Add New Action** drop-down arrow and select **Comment**.
 g. Type This action opens the Book table.
 h. Click the **Add New Action** drop-down arrow and select **OpenTable**.
 i. Click the **drop-down arrow** in the *Table Name* argument and select **Book**. Accept the default entry of *Datasheet* in the *View* argument and *Edit* in the *Data Mode* argument.
 j. Save the macro as AutoExec. The *Macros* group is added to the *Navigation Pane* and displays the *AutoExec* macro.
 k. Close the macro.

16. Test the macro.
 a. Close Access.
 b. Open the ***[your initials] Access 5-2.accdb*** database file. The database starts and opens both the *Author* and *Book* tables in *Datasheet* view.
 c. Close both tables.
 d. Select the **Book** table in the *Navigation Pane*.
 e. Right-click to open the context menu and select **Rename**.
 f. Change the name to BookTest.
 g. Close Access.
 h. Open the ***[your initials] Access 5-2.accdb*** database file. The database starts, opens the *Author* table, and displays the error message shown in Figure 5-103.
 i. Click **OK**. The *Macro Single Step* window opens.
 j. Click the **Stop All Macros** button.
 k. Close the *Author* table.

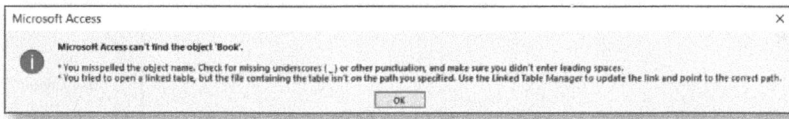

5-103 Macro error message

17. Add error handling to the macro.
 a. Right-click the **AutoExec** macro in the *Navigation Pane* and select **Design View** from the context menu to open the macro.
 b. Double-click **Submacro** in the *Program Flow* group in the *Action Catalog* to add a *Submacro* block.
 c. Enter ProcessError into the *Submacro* box.
 d. Click the **Add New Action** drop-down arrow directly below *Submacro* and select **If**.
 e. Type [MacroError].[Number]=7873 in the *If* argument.
 f. Click the **Add New Action** drop-down arrow directly below *If* and select **MessageBox**.
 g. Type Cannot find the specified table. in the *Message* argument.
 h. Select **No** in the *Beep* argument.
 i. Enter **Warning!** in the *Type* argument.
 j. Click the **Add New Action** drop-down arrow directly below the *Title* argument and select **StopMacro**.

k. Click the **Add Else** link located to the right of the *Add New Action* box below *StopMacro*.
l. Click the **drop-down arrow** and select **MessageBox**.
m. Type =[MacroError].[Description] in the *Message* argument.
n. Select **No** in the *Beep* argument.
o. Select **Warning!** in the *Type* argument.
p. Click the *Add New Action* drop-down arrow directly below *End Submacro* and select **OnError**.
q. Select **Macro Name** in the *Go to* argument.
r. Type ProcessError in the *Macro Name* argument.
s. Click the green **move up arrow** to move the *OnError* action to the top of the macro. You may need to click the move up arrow several times to move the action all the way to the top. The completed macro should look similar to Figure 5-104.
t. Save and close the macro.

18. Retest the macro.
 a. Double-click the **AutoExec** macro in the *Navigation Pane*. Because you already know that it executes when the database is opened, you can run it from within the database to see if the error handling works correctly. The message box displays.
 b. Click **OK**.
 c. Select the **BookTest** table in the *Navigation Pane*.
 d. Right-click to open the context menu and select **Rename**.
 e. Change the name back to Book.

19. Close the database.

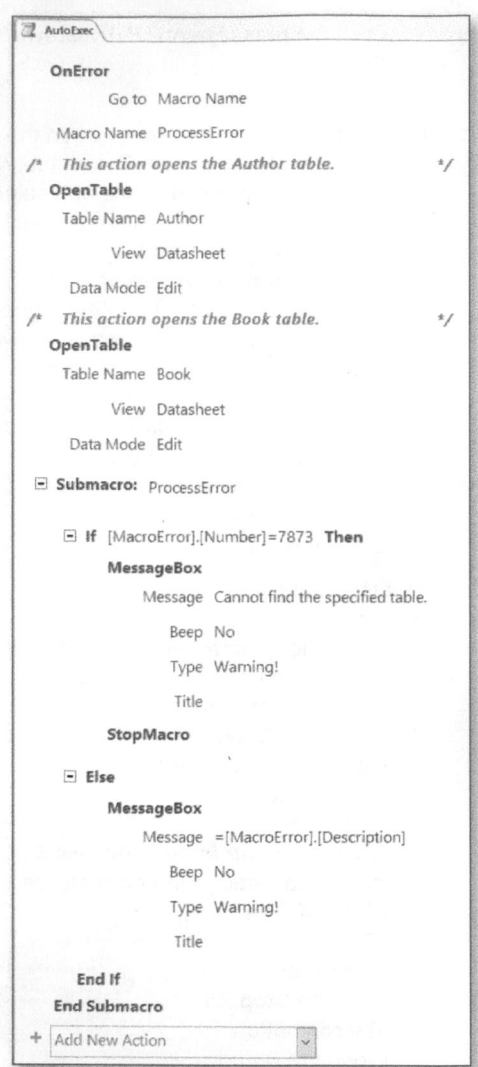

5-104 Completed *AutoExec* macro with error handling

Guided Project 5-3

San Diego Sailing wants to add a macro to its database. To ensure consistency, the starting file is provided for you. You complete an event-driven data macro to place a value in the *RentalCost* field of the *SDRentals* table. The value is based on whether the rental is a four-hour or full day rental and comes from the *SailboatFleet* table. After you test the event-driven macro, you complete a named macro to update rental rates. Finally, you complete the embedded macro that calls the named macro.
[Student Learning Outcomes 5.4, 5.5, 5.6, 5.7]

File Needed: ***SanDiegoSailing-05.accdb***
Completed Project File Name: ***[your initials] Access 5-3.accdb***

Skills Covered in This Project

- Use the *Macro Builder.*
- Edit an event-driven data macro.
- Use conditions in a macro.
- Use the *LookupRecord* action in a macro.

- Test a macro.
- Edit a named data macro.
- Use parameters in a macro.
- Use the *ForEachRecord* action in a macro.
- Edit an embedded macro to call a named data macro.

1. Open the ***SanDiegoSailing-05.accdb*** database from your student data files.

2. Save a new copy of your database as [your initials] Access 5-3.

3. Enable content in the database.

4. Edit an event-driven data macro to set the value of the *RentalCost* field when a record is added.
 a. Open the *SDRentals* table in *Datasheet* view.
 b. Click the **Table Tools Table** tab. Because the *Before Change* button is highlighted, you know that a macro already exists for this event.
 c. Click the **Before Change** button to open the macro.
 d. Click to select the **Look Up A Record In** statement. The block activates.
 e. Click the **Add New Action** drop-down arrow directly below the *Comment* in that block and select **If**.
 f. Type [SDRentals].[FourHourRental?]=−1 in the *If* box.
 g. Click the **Add New Action** drop-down arrow directly below the *If* and select **Comment**.
 h. Type Use the SetField action to set the value of the RentalCost field to the FourHourRentalRate from the SailboatFleet table.
 i. Click the **Add New Action** drop-down arrow directly below the *Comment* and select **SetField**.
 j. Type SDRentals.RentalCost in the *Name* argument.
 k. Type [SailboatFleet].[FourHourRentalRate] in the *Value* argument.
 l. Click the **Add Else** link located to the right of the *Add New Action* box.
 m. Click the **Add New Action** drop-down arrow directly below *Else* and select **Comment**.
 n. Type Use the SetField action to set the value of the RentalCost field to the FullDayRentalRate from the SailboatFleet table.
 o. Click the **Add New Action** drop-down arrow directly below the *Comment* and select **SetField**.
 p. Enter SDRentals.RentalCost in the *Name* argument.
 q. Enter [SailboatFleet].[FullDayRentalRate] in the *Value* argument. The finished macro should look similar to Figure 5-105.
 r. Save and close the macro. The *SDRentals* table should still be open in *Datasheet* view. Save the table.

5. Test the event-driven macro by adding a new record into the *SDRentals* table.

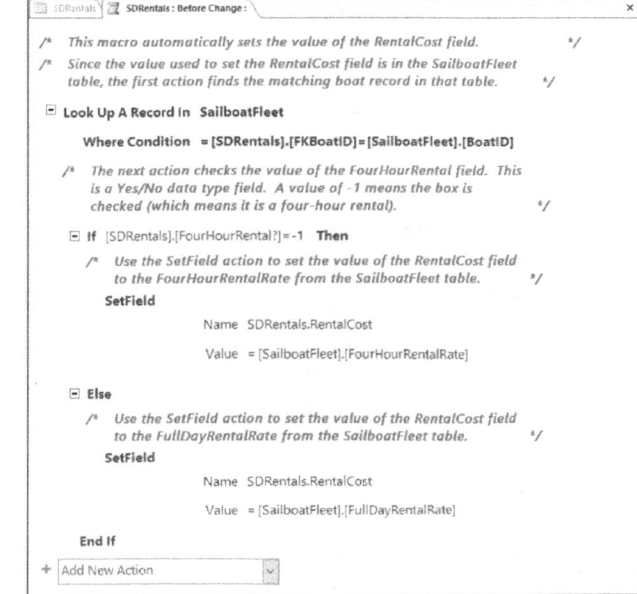

5-105 Completed *Before Change* macro code

a. Click in the **Rental ID** field of the append row of the *SDRentals* table.

b. Enter the *Rental ID, Boat ID,* and *Rental Date* data shown in Figure 5-106 into the table.

c. Don't enter anything in the *RentalCost* field. Instead, after entering the *Member Number,* press the **down arrow** key to trigger the *BeforeChange* event.

5-106 Enter the data values into the *SDRentals* table

d. Verify that the *RentalCost* was automatically updated to the value of *$179.00.*

6. Test that the macro works when a change is made to a record.

a. Click the **Four Hour Rental** field of the record that you just added to select the check box.

b. Press the **down arrow** key to leave the record and trigger the *BeforeChange* event.

c. Verify that the *RentalCost* automatically updated to *$139.00.*

d. Click the **row selector** box for rental 99999.

e. Click the **Delete** button [*Home* tab, *Records* group]. A warning message displays notifying you that you will delete a record.

f. Click **Yes**.

g. Close the *SDRentals* table.

7. Edit and finish the named data macro that updates the rental rates in the *SailboatFleet* table. This macro will be called from a button on the *UpdateRentalRates* form.

a. Open the *SailboatFleet* table in *Datasheet* view. Make a note that the *4 Hr Rate* for *Boat ID 1010* is *$139.00.* You will use that value in step 10 when you test your macro.

b. Click the **Named Macro** button [*Table Tools Table* tab, *Named Macros* group], select the **Edit Named Macro** option, and select **UpdateFleetRates** (Figure 5-107) to open the macro. The parameter section and first few lines have been entered for you. Read the comments to understand the purpose of the macro.

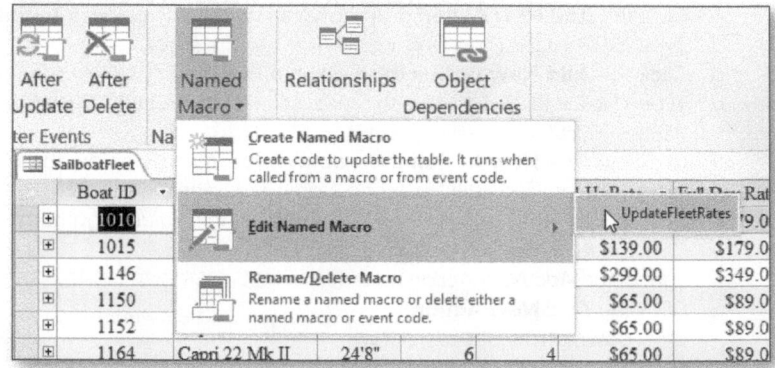

5-107 Edit the *UpdateFleetRates* named data macro

c. Click to select the **For Each Record In** statement. The block activates.

d. Click the **Add New Action** drop-down arrow directly below *Where Condition* and select **Comment**.

e. Type Perform the actions in the EditRecord block when a match has been found.

f. Click the **Add New Action** drop-down arrow below the *Comment* and select **EditRecord**.

g. Click the **Add New Action** drop-down arrow directly below *EditRecord* and select **If**.

h. Type Not IsNull([Param4HrRate]) into the *If* box.

i. Click the **Add New Action** drop-down arrow directly below *If* and select **Comment**.

j. Type Only change the field if a value was entered into the text box on the form.

k. Click the **Add New Action** drop-down arrow below the *Comment* and select **SetField**.

l. Type FourHourRentalRate in the *Name* box.

m. Type [Param4HrRate] in the *Value* box.

n. Click to select the **If** block.

o. Click the **Add New Action** drop-down arrow directly below the *End If* statement (Figure 5-108) and select **If**.
p. Enter Not IsNull([ParamDailyRate]) into the *If* box.
q. Click the **Add New Action** drop-down arrow directly below *If* and select **Comment**.
r. Type Only change the field if a value was entered into the text box on the form.
s. Click the **Add New Action** drop-down arrow below the *Comment* and select **SetField**.
t. Enter FullDayRentalRate in the *Name* box.
u. Enter [ParamDailyRate] in the *Value* box. Click outside the *Value* box. The completed macro should look similar to Figure 5-109.
v. Save and close the macro.
w. Save and close the *SailboatFleet* table.

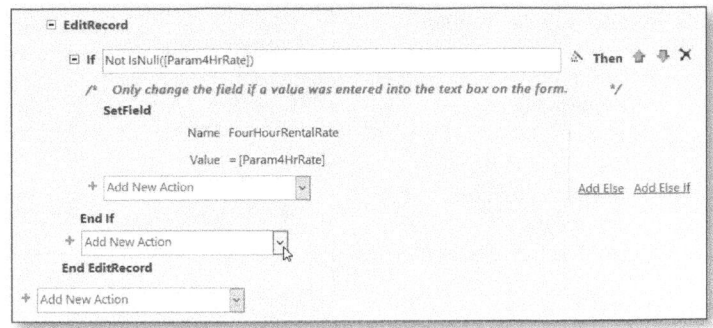

5-108 Click the *Add New Action* box below the *End If* statement

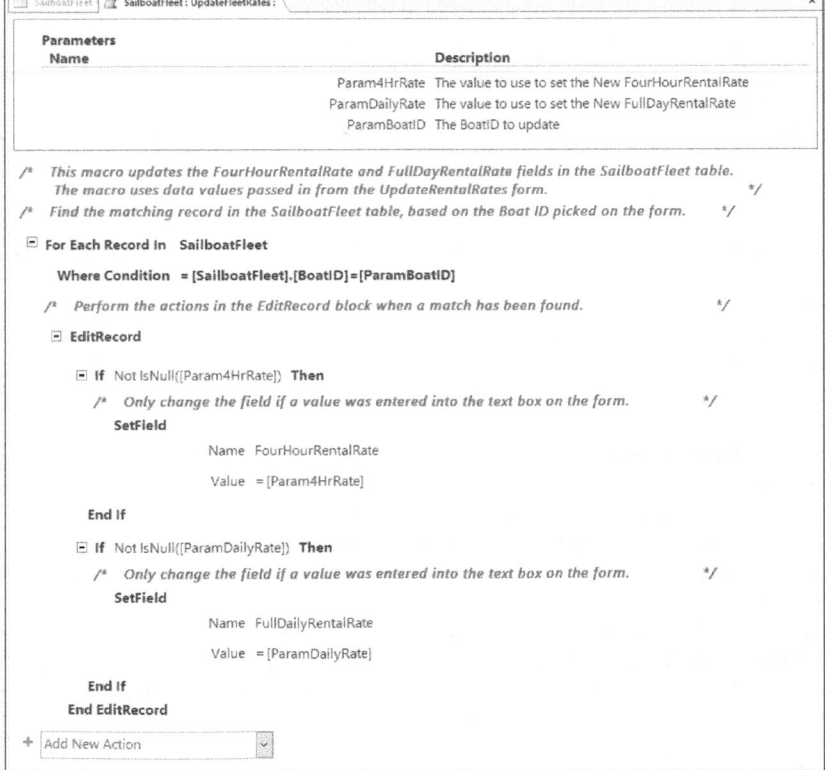

5-109 Completed *UpdateFleetRates* macro

8. Prepare to call the named macro.
 a. Open the *UpdateRentalRates* form in *Design* view.
 b. Click to select the **unbound** text box to the right of the *Select the Boat to Update* label (Figure 5-110).
 c. Click the **Property Sheet** button [*Form Design Tools Design* tab, *Tools* group] and select the **Other** tab, if needed. At the top of the *Property Sheet,*

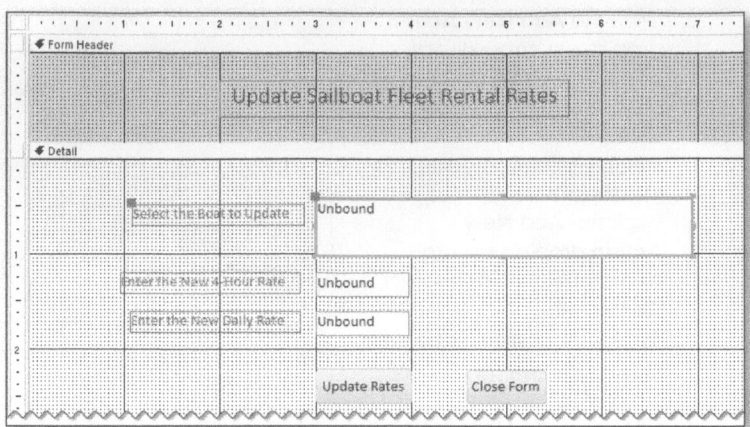

5-110 Select the top unbound text box in *Design* view of the form

 note that the *Selection type* is a *List Box.* In the *Name* property, note that the name of this list box is *LstBoatID.*
 d. Click to select the **unbound** text box to the right of the *Enter the New 4-Hour Rate* label. In the *Name* property, note that the name of this text box is *txtNew4HrRate.*
 e. Click to select the **unbound** text box to the right of the *Enter the New Daily Rate* label. In the *Name* property, note that the name of this text box is *txtNewDailyRate.*

9. Edit the embedded macro that calls the named macro.
 a. Click to select the **Update Rates** button.
 b. Select the **Event** tab.
 c. Click the **Build** button in the **On Click** event. An embedded macro opens. Some code is already entered into the macro.
 d. Click the **Add New Action** drop-down arrow and select **If**.
 e. Type IsNull([txtNew4HrRate]) And IsNull([txtNewDailyRate]) Or IsNull([LstBoatID]) into the *If* box.
 f. Click the **Add New Action** drop-down arrow directly below *If* and select **MessageBox**.
 g. Type Update not performed. Verify that rental rates have been entered and a boat selected. in the *Message* argument. Leave the other arguments as they are.
 h. Click the **Add Else** link located to the right of the *Add New Action* box.
 i. Click the **Add New Action** drop-down arrow directly below *Else* and select **MessageBox**.
 j. Enter Rental rates have been updated. in the *Message* argument. Leave the other arguments as they are.
 k. Click the **Add New Action** drop-down arrow directly below the *Title* argument and select **SetProperty**.
 l. Type txtNew4HrRate in the *Control Name* argument.
 m. Select **Value** in the *Property* argument. Leave the *Value* argument blank.
 n. Click the **Add New Action** drop-down arrow directly below the *Value* argument and select **SetProperty**.
 o. Enter txtNewDailyRate in the *Control Name* argument.
 p. Select **Value** in the *Property* argument. Leave the *Value* argument blank.
 q. Click the **Add New Action** drop-down arrow directly below the *Value* argument and select **SetProperty**.
 r. Enter LstBoatID in the *Control Name* argument.

s. Select **Value** in the *Property* argument. Leave the *Value* argument blank and click outside the *Value* box. The completed macro should look similar to Figure 5-111. Notice in this macro that there is one comment above the *If* block that explains the way the entire *If* block works. Be sure to read that comment. It will help you to understand the different macro actions you have entered.

t. Save and close the macro.

u. Close the *Property Sheet* of the form.

v. Save the form.

10. Test the embedded macro and the named data macro.

a. Switch the form to *Form* view. Note that the listing of boats displays inside the *List Box* control.

b. Click the **Update Rates** button. The message box for not performing an update displays. This is correct because no values were entered. Click **OK**.

c. Select boat **1010** in the list box.

d. Click the **Update Rates** button. The message box for not performing an update displays. This is also correct because even though a boat was selected, no rates were entered. Click **OK**.

e. Select boat **1010** in the list box.

f. Enter 129 in the text box for the *4-Hour rate*.

g. Click the **Update Rates** button. The message box indicating that the rates were updated displays. Click **OK**. The list box is deselected and the *4-Hour rate* text box is cleared.

h. Close the form. If prompted, save changes to the form.

i. Open the *SailboatFleet* table in *Datasheet* view.

j. Verify that the *4 Hr Rate* for *Boat ID 1010* has been updated to *$129.00*.

k. Close the table.

11. Close the database.

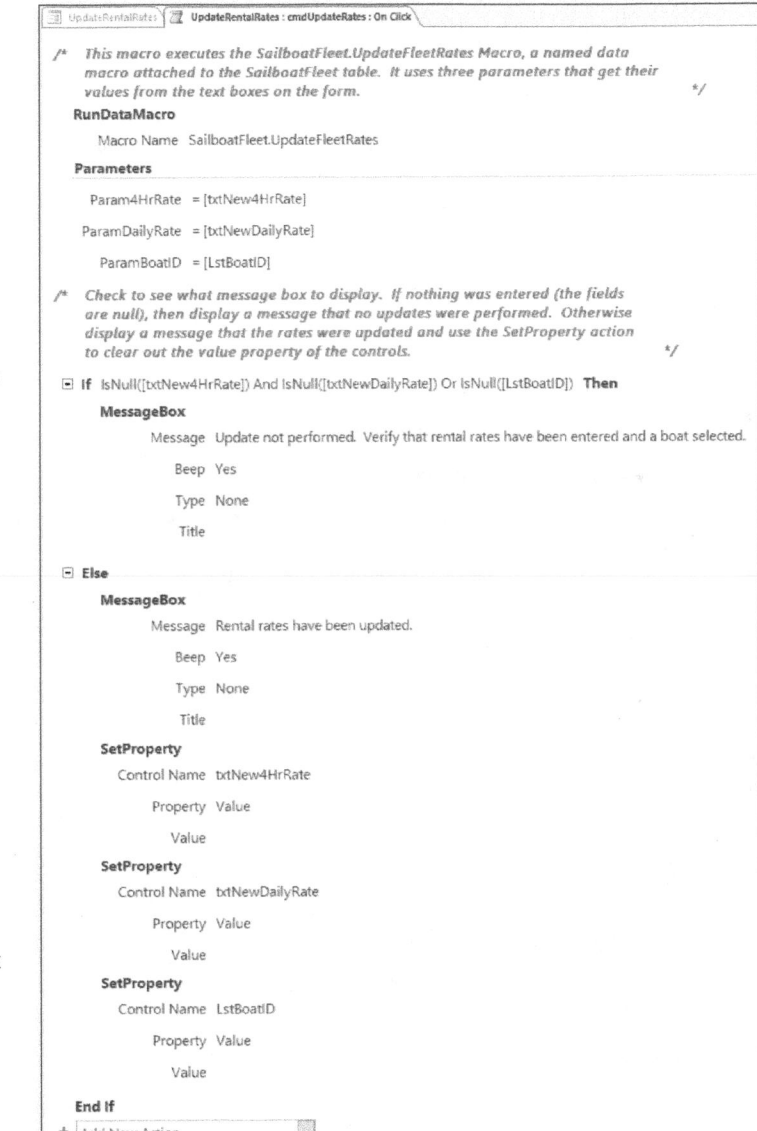

/* This macro executes the SailboatFleet.UpdateFleetRates Macro, a named data macro attached to the SailboatFleet table. It uses three parameters that get their values from the text boxes on the form. */

RunDataMacro

 Macro Name SailboatFleet.UpdateFleetRates

Parameters

 Param4HrRate = [txtNew4HrRate]

 ParamDailyRate = [txtNewDailyRate]

 ParamBoatID = [LstBoatID]

/* Check to see what message box to display. If nothing was entered (the fields are null), then display a message that no updates were performed. Otherwise display a message that the rates were updated and use the SetProperty action to clear out the value property of the controls. */

⊟ **If** IsNull([txtNew4HrRate]) And IsNull([txtNewDailyRate]) Or IsNull([LstBoatID]) **Then**

 MessageBox

 Message Update not performed. Verify that rental rates have been entered and a boat selected.

 Beep Yes

 Type None

 Title

⊟ **Else**

 MessageBox

 Message Rental rates have been updated.

 Beep Yes

 Type None

 Title

 SetProperty

 Control Name txtNew4HrRate

 Property Value

 Value

 SetProperty

 Control Name txtNewDailyRate

 Property Value

 Value

 SetProperty

 Control Name LstBoatID

 Property Value

 Value

End If

＋ Add New Action

5-111 Completed *cmdUpdateRates* embedded macro

Independent Project 5-4

Life's Animal Shelter wants you to create two macros to enhance the functionality of its database. To ensure consistency, the starting file is provided for you. You create an event-driven macro that automatically sets the value of three table fields when a new pet record is added. You then test that macro. Next, you create a stand-alone macro. This macro includes submacros that are called to determine which records display in a form. Finally, you test those submacros.
[Student Learning Outcomes 5.4, 5.5, 5.6, 5.7]

File Needed: *LifesAnimalShelter-05.accdb*
Completed Project File Name: *[your initials] Access 5-4.accdb*

Skills Covered in This Project

- Use the *Macro Builder*.
- Build an event-driven data macro.
- Use conditions in a macro.
- Create a stand-alone macro.
- Use a submacro in a macro.
- Test a macro.

1. Open the *LifesAnimal Shelter-05.accdb* database from your student data files.

2. Save a new copy of your database as [your initials] Access 5-4.

3. Enable content in the database.

4. Create an event-driven data macro to automatically set the value of three table fields when a record is added.
 a. Open the *Pets* table in *Datasheet* view.
 b. Create a *Before Change* event-driven data macro.
 c. Enter the macro code shown in Figure 5-112 into the *Macro Builder*.
 d. Save and close the macro.
 e. Save and close the *Pets* table.

5. Test the macro by adding a new record.
 a. Open the *Add New Pet* form in *Form* view. This form has been created to easily allow an employee to add the data into the table.
 b. Add the data below into the form.
 Pet Name: Scooter
 Type: Dog
 Breed: Shepherd cross
 Age: 3 yrs
 Gender: F
 Color: Tan/Black

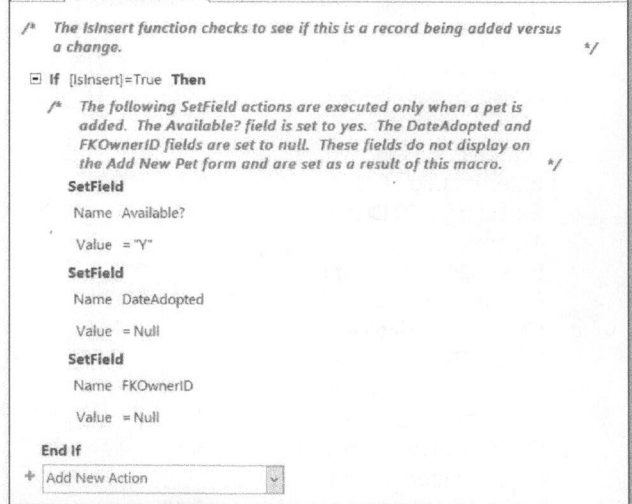

5-112 Macro code for the *Before Change* event in the *Pets* table

 Details: I am an energetic, fun loving companion. I enjoy playing with kids and adults. I love taking long walks, playing catch or running. What thrills me most is sharing my love with those around me. I can't wait to find a special family to make my own!
 c. Click the **Save Pet** button. A message box displays with the title of *Pet Successfully Added*. Do not worry about the content of the message. You will not return to the *Main Menu* since you did not start from that form. Click **OK** to acknowledge the message. The form closes.
 d. Open the *Pets* table in *Datasheet* view.

e. Scroll down to find the record for *Scooter*. The table is sorted on the *FKOwnerID* field. As a result, the pets that are not available are at the bottom of the table. The record appears right above the first pet that is unavailable (*Pet ID 1*). Verify that the *Available?* field is set to *Y* and the *DateAdopted* and *FKOwnerID* fields are *null*.

f. Close the table.

6. Create a stand-alone macro, using submacros, which will control the records that display.

 a. Click the **Macro** button [*Create* tab] to open the *Macro Builder.*

 b. Enter the macro code shown in Figure 5-113 into the *Macro Builder*

 c. Save the macro as WhichPetsToShow.

 d. Close the macro.

7. Call the submacros.

 a. Open the *ViewPets* form in *Design* view.

 b. Click to select the *ShowAllPets* button, click the *On Click* event property, and select the **WhichPetsToShow. ShowAllPets** submacro.

 c. Assign the correct submacro to the *On Click* event of the other form buttons. The *Close Form* button already has an embedded macro completed for you.

 d. Save the form.

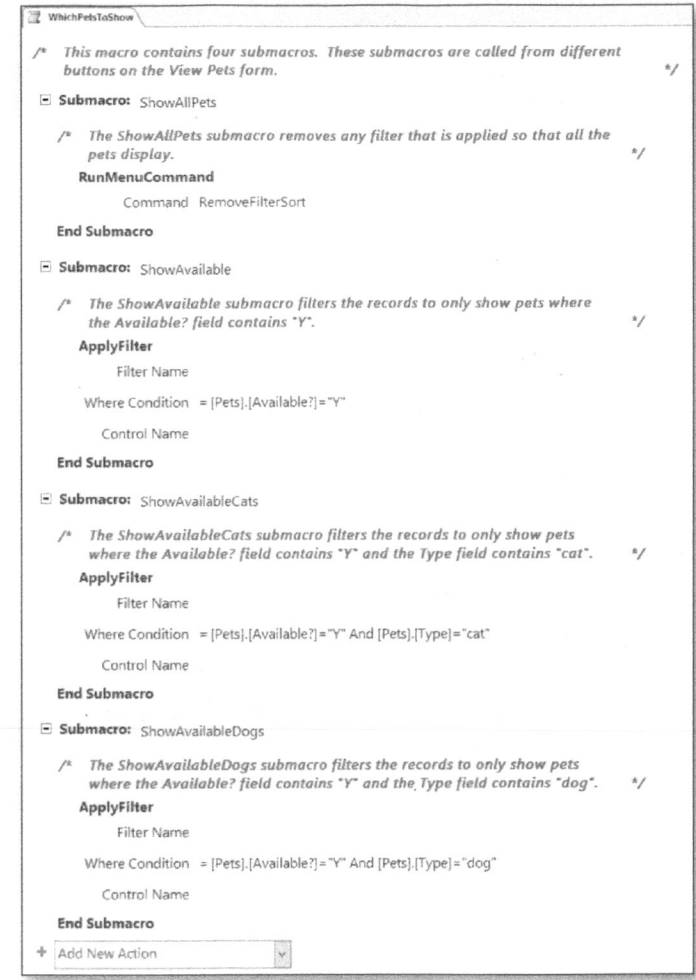

5-113 *WhichPetsToShow* stand-alone macro code

8. Test the submacros.

 a. Switch to *Form* view. The form opens displaying all of the 20 pet records.

 b. Click the **Show All Available Pets** button. The form updates to display 16 records. The *Filtered* indicator shows in the filter status message.

 c. Click the **Show Available Cats** button. The form updates to display three records. The *Filtered* indicator shows in the filter status message.

 d. Click the **Show Available Dogs** button. The form updates to display 10 records. The *Filtered* indicator shows in the filter status message.

 e. Click the **Show All Pets** button. The form updates to display all 20 records. The *Unfiltered* indicator shows in the filter status message.

 f. Close the form.

9. Close the database.

Independent Project 5-5

The New York Department of Motor Vehicles wants to extend the functionality of its database. Add a table to store information about their officers and have that table relate to the tickets table. Finally, build and test an event-driven data macro to automatically add a time-stamp when a ticket is added.
[Student Learning Outcomes 5.2, 5.3, 5.4, 5.6, 5.7]

File Needed: **NewYorkDMV-05.accdb**
Completed Project File Name: **[your initials] Access 5-5.accdb**

Skills Covered in This Project

- Edit a junction table with a unique primary key.
- Define a relationship with the *Lookup Wizard*.
- Use multiple columns in the lookup field.
- Use the *Macro Builder*.
- Build an event-driven data macro.
- Use conditions in a macro.
- Test a macro.
- Add the current date to a form.
- Preview a report.

1. Open the **NewYorkDMV-05.accdb** database from your student data files.

2. Save a new copy of your database as [your initials] Access 5-5.

3. Enable content in the database.

4. Create a new table to store officer information.
 a. Click the **Table Design** button to open a new table in *Design* view.
 b. Enter the table fields using the information in the following table:

Field Name	Data Type	Description	Field Size	Format
OfficerID	Short Text	Officer's unique ID/Badge number	9	
FirstName	Short Text	Officer's first name	20	
LastName	Short Text	Officer's last name	20	
DateHired	Date/Time	Date of employment		Short Date

 c. Designate the *OfficerID* field as the primary key.
 d. Save the table as Officers.

5. Add the data into the table.
 a. Switch to *Datasheet* view. Enter the records shown in the following table into the *Officers* table:

OfficerID	FirstName	LastName	DateHired
A00021411	Reggie	DeFrank	5/15/2015
A00032567	Alex	Rodriguez	12/20/2013
A00045729	Robert	Chung	3/17/2011
A00056591	Jackie	Markley	6/2/1997
A00057706	Rupal	Jain	2/12/2013
A00061403	Carlos	Villanueva	10/1/1995
A00061444	Amanda	Freed	9/2/2003
A00092385	Javier	Torres	5/23/2015

 b. Close the table.

6. Review the existing *Drivers* table.
 a. Open the *Drivers* table in *Datasheet* view.
 b. Click the **plus sign** to expand the first record, *LicenseNumber 10000501*, to view the related records in the *Tickets* table (Figure 5-114). Note that the *Tickets* table already has an *OfficerBadgeNumber* field.

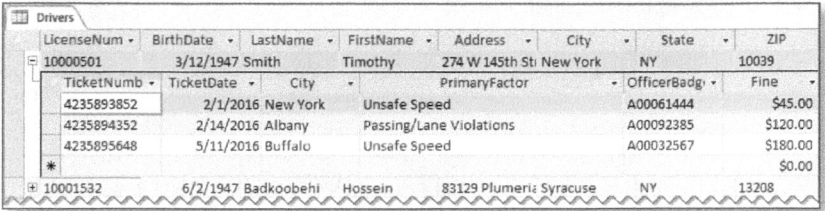

5-114 *Drivers* table and related records from the *Tickets* table

7. Determine the relationship type. A driver can have many different tickets. An officer can have written many different tickets. There is a many-to-many relationship between records in the *Drivers* and *Officers* table. This relationship is via the *Tickets* table. The *Tickets* table is the junction table.

8. Close the *Drivers* table.

9. Review the junction table.
 a. Open the *Tickets* table in *Design* view. Review that the *TicketNumber* field is the primary key. Note that this table has the two foreign keys of *DLNumber* and *OfficerBadgeNumber.* If a junction table has its own unique identifier, like *TicketNumber,* then it does not need to use a concatenated primary key. However, the foreign keys must still be in the table to provide the relationship.
 b. Select the **OfficerBadgeNumber** field.
 c. Change the description of the *OfficerBadgeNumber* field to read Must match an OfficerID in the Officers table. The description doesn't affect the database but makes the table design more understandable.

10. Use the *Lookup Wizard* to create a one-to-many relationship between *Officers* and *Tickets.* This lookup will display multiple fields.
 a. Select **Lookup Wizard** in the *Data Type* property box of the *OfficerBadgeNumber* field to create a relationship between the *Officers* and *Tickets* tables.
 b. Choose to lookup a field from the *Officers* table.
 c. Include the *OfficerID, FirstName,* and *LastName* fields in the *Selected Fields* window.
 d. Sort by the *LastName* field in ascending order.
 e. Do not hide the key column.
 f. Store the *OfficerID* field.
 g. Enable data integrity and restrict deletes.
 h. Save and close the table.

11. Edit the relationship.
 a. Click the **Relationships** button [*Database Tools* tab, *Relationships* group] to open the *Relationships* window (Figure 5-115). If all three tables do not display, click the **Show Table** button to add the missing tables into the window. Recall that you previously created the relationship between *Drivers* and *Tickets* in Chapter 2.

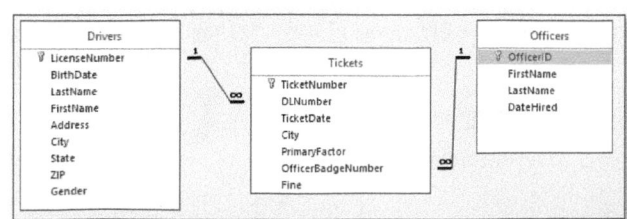

5-115 New York DMV database relationships

b. Edit the relationship between *Officers* and *Tickets* to cascade updates.
c. Save the changes.
d. Close the *Relationships* window.

12. Edit the *Tickets* table to add a date-stamp field.
 a. Open the *Tickets* table in *Design* view.
 b. Add a new field using the information in the following table:

Field Name	Data Type	Description	Format
RecordAddedTimeStamp	Date/Time	Store the date and time the record was added to the table	General Date

 c. Save the table.

13. Create an event-driven data macro to store the time stamp when a record is added to the *Tickets* table.
 a. Create a *Before Change* event-driven data macro.
 b. Enter the macro code shown in Figure 5-116 into the *Macro Builder*.
 c. Save and close the macro.
 d. Save the table.

5-116 Macro code for the *Before Change* event-driven macro

14. Test the macro.
 a. Switch to *Datasheet* view, if necessary.
 b. Add the following record into the table. When entering the *OfficerBadgeNumber,* use the drop-down list and verify that all three fields show in the list.
 TicketNumber: 4235896919
 DLNumber: 10004372
 TicketDate: 5/17/2016
 City: Syracuse
 PrimaryFactor: Unsafe Speed
 OfficerBadgeNumber: A00057706
 Fine: 90
 Press the **down arrow** key after entering the *Fine.* Upon leaving the record, the *RecordAddedTimeStamp* field updates. Most likely the field displays ####, indicating the field is not wide enough.
 c. Widen the *RecordAddedTimeStamp* field so you can see the contents. Make a note of the current value, including the time.
 d. Change the *PrimaryFactor* to Driver Distraction. Press the **down arrow** key to leave the record and have the changes saved. Verify that the contents of the *RecordAddedTimeStamp* field did not change.
 e. Save and close the table.

15. Close the database.

Independent Project 5-6

Courtyard Medical Plaza wants to expand its database. To ensure consistency, the starting file is provided for you. You create an event-driven macro to determine if a discount should be given, calculate the discount, and set the value of another table field. You then test that macro. Next, you create embedded macros to add functionality to a form and test the macros. Finally, you add error handling into a macro.
[Student Learning Outcomes 5.4, 5.5, 5.6, 5.7]

File Needed: **CourtyardMedicalPlaza-05.accdb**
Completed Project File Name: **[your initials] Access 5-6.accdb**

Skills Covered in This Project

- Use the *Macro Builder.*
- Build an event-driven data macro.

- Build an embedded macro.
- Test a macro.
- Use conditions in a macro.
- Add error handling into a macro.

1. Open the **CourtyardMedicalPlaza-05.accdb** database from your student data files..

2. Save a new copy of your database as [your initials] Access 5-6.

3. Enable content in the database.

4. Create an event-driven data macro to automatically set fields when a record is changed.
 a. Open the *RentInvoices* table in *Datasheet* view. Scroll to the far right of the table to see the *Paid* field. Scroll down through the records and note that all the records through the *Invoice Date* of 17-Aug-17 have a check mark in the *Paid* field. The October invoices for all the doctors do not have any values in the *DateReceived, Discount* and *Paid* fields.
 b. Create a *Before Change* event-driven data macro.
 c. Enter the macro code shown in Figure 5-117 into the *Macro Builder.*
 d. Save and close the macro.

5. Test the macro by adding a new invoice. Eventually all the data entry will be done through forms, but during the design process you use the table directly to test the data macro.
 a. Navigate to the append row and add the following record into the table. The macro should not activate since this is an *add* versus a *change* to the table.
 InvoiceID: 55
 Invoice Date: 10/13/2017
 Due Date: 11/1/2017
 Amount Due: 1250
 Doctor ID: 1
 Description: November 2017 Rent (Beyer & Ostrander)
 b. Tab past the *Date Received, Discount,* and *Paid* fields. Upon

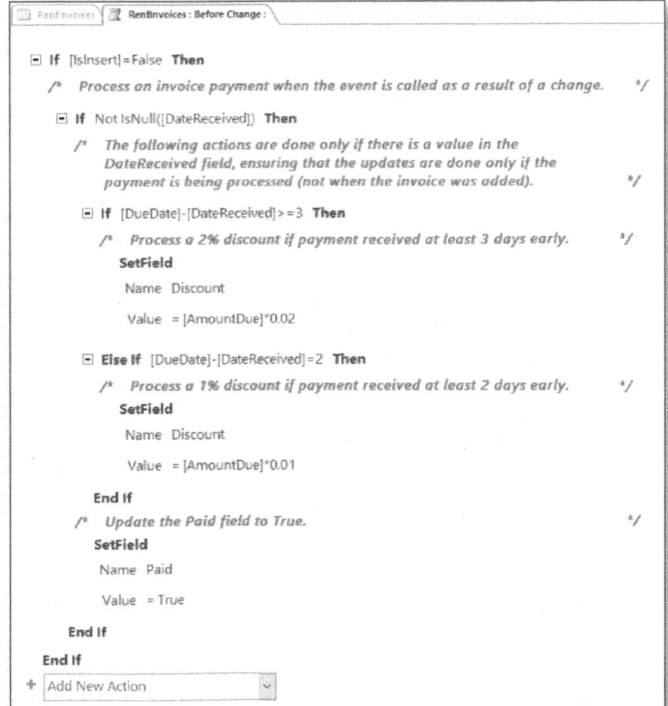

```
☐ If [IsInsert]=False Then
   /*  Process an invoice payment when the event is called as a result of a change.    */
   ☐ If Not IsNull([DateReceived]) Then
      /*  The following actions are done only if there is a value in the
          DateReceived field, ensuring that the updates are done only if the
          payment is being processed (not when the invoice was added).          */
      ☐ If [DueDate]-[DateReceived]>=3 Then
         /*  Process a 2% discount if payment received at least 3 days early.    */
         SetField
            Name  Discount
            Value  =[AmountDue]*0.02
      ☐ Else If [DueDate]-[DateReceived]=2 Then
         /*  Process a 1% discount if payment received at least 2 days early.    */
         SetField
            Name  Discount
            Value  =[AmountDue]*0.01
      End If
      /*  Update the Paid field to True.                                        */
      SetField
         Name  Paid
         Value  =True
   End If
End If
+  Add New Action                        ▼
```

5-117 Macro code for *Before Change* macro

leaving the record, verify that the *Date Received, Discount,* and *Paid* fields do not contain any values. The *Discount* field displays *$0.00* due to the currency data type.

6. Test the macro by recording a payment that should not get a discount.
 a. Select the record for *InvoiceID 55.*
 b. Enter 11/1/2017 into the *Date Received* field and navigate out of the record to save the changes. Verify that the *Paid* field is checked and the *Discount* field is empty.

7. Test the macro by recording a payment that should get a 1% discount.
 a. Select the record for *InvoiceID 55.*
 b. Change the value of the *Date Received* field to 10/30/2017 and navigate out of the record. Verify that the *Paid* field is *checked* and the *Discount* field is *$12.50.*

8. Test the macro by recording a payment that should get a 2% discount.
 a. Select the record for *InvoiceID 55.*
 b. Change the value of the *Date Received* field to 10/26/2017 and navigate out of the record. Verify that the *Paid* field is *checked* and the *Discount* field is *$25.00.*
 c. Close the *RentInvoices* table.

9. Create an embedded macro that executes when a form activates.
 a. Open the *RecordInvoicePayment* form in *Form* view. This form has been created to easily allow an employee to enter the receipt of a payment. In the *Navigation* bar at the bottom of the form, note that you can move through all 55 records of the *RentInvoices* table.
 b. Change to *Design* view.
 c. Open the *Property Sheet* and verify that the object selected is the form.
 d. Create an embedded macro for the *On Activate* Event.
 e. Enter the code shown in Figure 5-118 into the macro.
 f. Save and close the macro.

10. Test the *On Activate* macro.
 a. Change the *RecordInvoicePayment* form to *Form* view. The message box from the *On Activate* event of the form displays.
 b. Click **OK** to acknowledge the message. Note that *InvoiceID 46* is the current record and *Filtered* displays in the filter status message.
 c. Navigate through the records. The form only displays the October invoices that have not been paid.

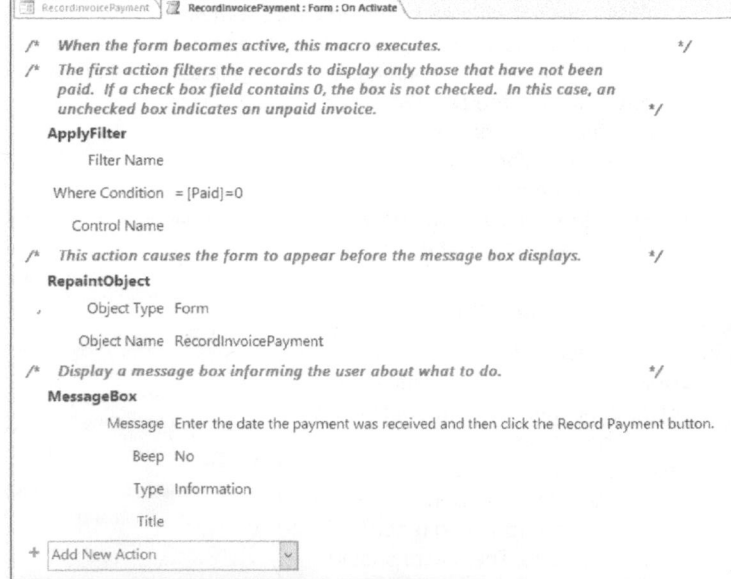

5-118 Macro code for the *On Activate* macro

11. Create an embedded macro that is used in conjunction with executing the data macro.
 a. Change back to *Design* view.
 b. Create an embedded macro for the *On Click* event of the *Record Payment* button.
 c. Enter the code shown in Figure 5-119 into the macro.

d. Save and close the macro.
e. Save the form.

12. Explore the *Go To Next Record* and *Close Form* buttons. The macros for those buttons were created with the *Command Button Wizard*.
 a. Open the embedded macro on the *On Click* event for the *Go To Next Record* button. Review the code to become familiar with the design and functionality of the button.
 b. Close the macro.
 c. Repeat these steps for the *Close Form* button.

13. Test the *Record Payment* button with the scenario that no date is entered into the text box and the *Record Payment* button is pressed.
 a. Change the *RecordInvoicePayment* form to *Form* view. The message box from the *On Activate* event displays. Click **OK** to acknowledge the message. The record for invoice 46 displays.
 b. Click the **Record Payment** button. The message box displays informing you that the invoice was processed. This should not occur since the date received was not entered. Click **OK**.
 c. Switch the form to *Design* view to fix this problem.
 d. Open the *RentInvoices* table and look at the record for *InvoiceID 46*. The *Date Received* and *Paid* fields are empty. This matches the code from the *Before Change* event-driven data macro. Recall that the changes are made only if there is a value in the *Date Received* field. However, the macro on the *Record Payment* button should not display the *Invoice Processed* message when it really was not processed.
 e. Close the *RentInvoices* table.

14. Add error handling to improve the macro.
 a. Open the embedded macro in the *On Click* event of the *Record Payment* button.
 b. Edit the macro by adding the error handling code in Figure 5-120. Because the *Add New Action* box is located at the bottom of the macro, your new code will add at the bottom of the macro. Then use the arrows to move the *Comment* and the *If* block to the top of the macro. The existing comment you have in the macro, from step 11, displays at the bottom of Figure 5-120 so you know where the new statements should be located in the macro.
 c. Save and close the macro.
 d. Save the form.

15. Retest the macro.
 a. Change the *RecordInvoicePayment* form to *Form* view. Click **OK** to acknowledge the message. The record for invoice 46 displays.

5-119 Macro code for the *On Click* event

5-120 Add error handling code into the macro

b. Click the **Record Payment** button. The message box displays informing you that you must enter the date. Click **OK**.

c. Enter 9/30/2017 into the text box to the right of the *Enter Date Received* label.

d. Click the **Record Payment** button. The *Invoice Processed* message box displays.

e. Click **OK**. The form advances to the next record.

f. Enter the data from the following table to process the following payments. You must click **OK** to acknowledge the *Invoice Processed* message box for each payment.

InvoiceID	DateReceived
47	10/1/2017
48	9/29/2017
49	10/1/2017
50	10/1/2017

g. Close the form. You do not yet have payments for the remaining October 2017 rent invoices.

16. Verify that the payments were processed correctly.

a. Open the *RentInvoices* table and verify that the *Paid* field is checked for invoices 46 through 50. *InvoiceID 48* should also have a $13.50 discount.

b. Close the table.

17. Close the database.

Improve It Project 5-7

Mary's Rentals wants to improve its database. To ensure consistency, the starting file is provided for you. You improve the functionality by debugging several macros that are not working correctly. You view and edit the *Application Log* table. After making changes, retest the macros.
[**Student Learning Outcomes 5.4, 5.5, 5.6, 5.7**]

File Needed: ***MarysRentals-05.accdb***
Completed Project File Name: *[your initials] Access 5-7.accdb*

Skills Covered in This Project

- Use the *Macro Builder*.
- Build and test an embedded macro.
- Use the single step tool to debug a macro.
- Edit an embedded macro.
- Edit an event-driven data macro.
- Use parameters in a macro.
- Use the *Application Log* table to debug a macro.
- Edit an embedded macro to call a named data macro.

1. Open the ***MarysRentals-05.accdb*** database from your student data files.

2. Save a new copy of your database as [your initials] Access 5-7.

3. Enable content in the database.

4. Review the existing tables.
 a. Open the *ServiceHistory* table in *Datasheet* view. Recall that this table contains the individual transactions related to repairs on the equipment. If you add the *TotalCost* fields of the four records for *FKEquipmentID 09863*, the total is *$982.74*.
 b. Open the *Equipment* table in *Datasheet* view. Verify that the *LifetimeMaintenanceCost* for EquipmentID *09863* is *$982.74*. Also note that there are several pieces of equipment that have *$0.00* for the *LifetimeMaintenanceCost* field.
 c. Close both tables.

5. Add an *On Activate* event to the *EquipmentListing* form.
 a. Open the *MainMenu* form in *Form* view.
 b. Click the **View Equipment List** button. The form opens. Instead, you want a message box to display before the form opens informing the user that the form is read-only.
 c. Switch to *Design* view of the *EquipmentListing* form.
 d. Open the *Property Sheet* and ensure that the selection is *Form*.
 e. Add an embedded macro on the *On Activate* event.
 f. Add code to the macro to display a message box.
 g. Type This information is read-only. Changes cannot be made on this form.
 h. Select **No** for the *Beep* and select **Information** for the *Type* arguments.
 i. Add a comment to explain what the macro action does.
 j. Save and close the macro.
 k. Save and close the *EquipmentListing* form.

6. Retest the *EquipmentListing* form.
 a. Click the **View Equipment List** button on the *MainMenu* form. The message box displays.
 b. Click **OK** to acknowledge the message. The *EquipmentListing* form opens.
 c. Close the *EquipmentListing* form.

7. Fix the *On Activate* event of the *EquipmentWithNoRepairs* form.
 a. Click the **View Equipment with No Repairs** button on the *MainMenu* form. A message box displays. Click **OK** to acknowledge the message. The form opens but no records display (Figure 5-121). You know there are equipment records that do not have any repairs.

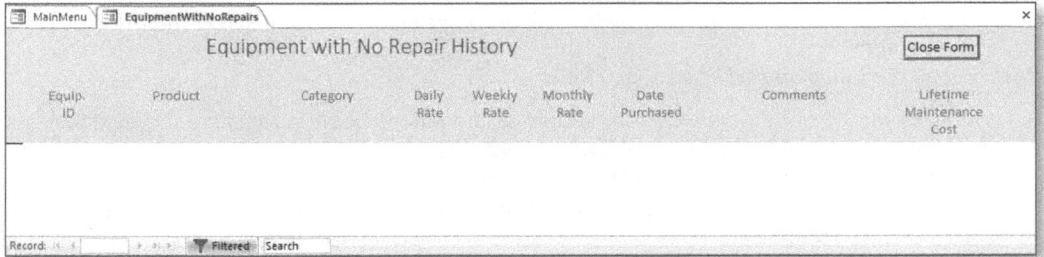

5-121 *EquipmentWthNoRepairs form*

 b. Switch to *Design* view of the *EquipmentWithNoRepairs* form.
 c. Open the *Property Sheet* if needed and ensure that the selection is the *Form*.
 d. Open the embedded macro on the *On Activate* event.
 e. Click the **Single Step** button [*Macro Tools Design* tab, *Tools* group] to turn on the *Single Step* tool to help debug a macro.
 f. Save and close the macro.
 g. Save and close the *EquipmentWithNoRepairs* form.

h. Click the **View Equipment with No Repairs** button on the *Main Menu* form. The *Macro Single Step* dialog box opens (Figure 5-122).
- In the *Macro Name* line, note that the macro being executed came from the *MainMenu,* the *cmdViewEquipNoRepairButton,* as a result of an *OnClick* event, and it is an *Embedded Macro.*
- In the *Action Name,* note that the action is *OpenForm.*

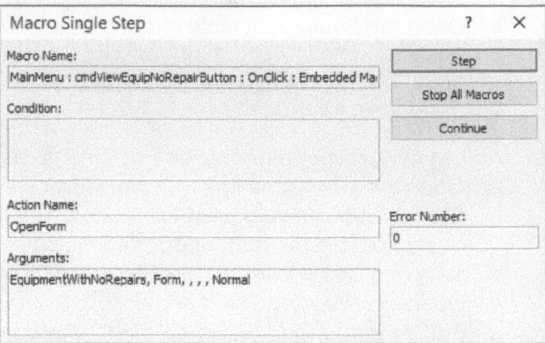

5-122 *Macro Single Step* dialog box

i. Click the **Step** button to advance. The contents of the dialog box update.
- In the *Macro Name* line, note that the *On Activate* event of the *EquipmentWithNoRepairs* form is now being executed.
- In the *Action Name* box, note that the *ApplyFilter* action is called.
- In the *Arguments* box, look at the condition. The macro is looking for a *LifetimeMaintenanceCost = Null.* That is not correct. You want to find records where the value *= 0.*

j. Click the **Stop All Macros** button. The *EquipmentWithNoRepairs* form opens in *Form* view.
k. Switch to *Design* view of the form.
l. Edit the *On Activate* event of the form.
m. Change the *Where Condition* clause of the *ApplyFilter* action to [Equipment].[LifetimeMaintenanceCost]=0.
n. Click the **Single Step** button [*Macro Tools Design* tab, *Tools* group] to turn off the *Single Step* mode since you are confident this was the problem.
o. Save and close the macro.
p. Save and close the *EquipmentWithNoRepairs* form.

8. Retest the *View Equipment with No Repairs* button.
a. Click the **View Equipment with No Repairs** button on the *MainMenu* form.
b. Click **OK** to acknowledge the message box. The six equipment records display. Note that *EquipmentID 10103* is one of the items that has no repairs. You use this *EquipmentID* later to test the database.
c. Close the *EquipmentWithNoRepairs* form.

9. Review the macros for the *ServiceHistory* table as there have been reports that the database is not working correctly when a new record is added into this table.
a. Open the *ServiceHistory* table in *Datasheet* view.
- When a record is added into the *ServiceHistory* table, the value in the *TotalCost* field should be added to the *LifetimeMaintenanceCost* in the *Equipment* table.
- When a record is changed in the *ServiceHistory* table, if the *TotalCost* of the repair was updated, that change should be reflected in the *LifetimeMaintenanceCost* in the *Equipment* table.
- When a record is deleted in the *ServiceHistory* table, the *TotalCost* of the repair should be subtracted from the *LifetimeMaintenanceCost* in the *Equipment* table.
- The change and deletions have not been a problem; however, the insertion of a new record does not work correctly.
b. Open the *After Delete* event-driven data macro in the *ServiceHistory* table. Note that this calls a data macro in the *Equipment* table named *UpdateTotalMaintenanceCost.* It passes in two parameters: one for the *ParamEID* and one for the *ParamCost.* The use of *[Old]* in conjunction with the field name allows Access to pass in the field value from the record that was just deleted.
c. Close the macro and the table.

10. Review the named data macro.
 a. Open the *Equipment* table in *Datasheet* view and open the *UpdateTotalMaintenanceCost* named macro. The code should match Figure 5-123. Note that the *LifetimeMaintenanceCost* field is updated to add to it the value of what was passed in via the *ParamCost* parameter.

5-123 Macro code in the *UpdateTotalMaintenanceCost* macro

 b. Close the macro.
 c. Close the *Equipment* table.

11. Test the *ServiceHistory* table by adding a new record.
 a. Click the **Add New Service Record** button on the *MainMenu* form.
 b. Add the following data into the form:
 Service ID: C00235
 Service Date: 12/28/2016
 Service Type: Inspection
 Description: 6-month inspection
 Performed By: 177
 Equipment ID: 10103
 Odometer Reading: Leave this field empty.
 Hours: Leave this field empty.
 Cost of Repair: 95.00
 Recall that item *10103* has no previous repairs. This will make it easy to determine if the *After Insert* macro works correctly.
 c. Click the **Save Equipment Service Record** button. A dialog box displays a *Data type mismatch in criteria expression* message, and the *Status* bar updates to reflect *New Application Errors* (Figure 5-124).

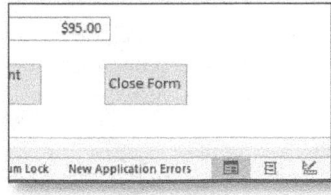

5-124 Error message in *Status bar*

 d. Click **OK** to acknowledge the message.
 e. Click the **Close Form** button.

12. Review error information in the *Application Log* table.
 a. Click the **File** tab. The *Info* button is selected.

b. Click the **View Application Log Table** button. The table opens (Figure 5-125). You may have additional records, and the value in the *ID* field may be different if you have done other activities in the database. If you have more than one record, look at the last record in the table.

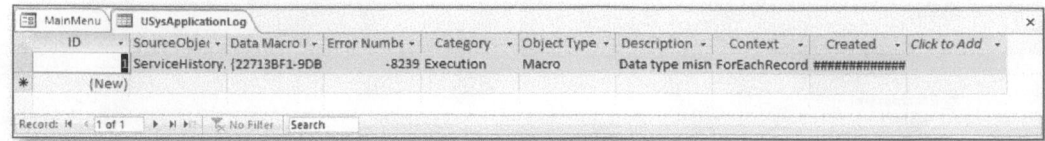

5-125 Record in *USysApplicationLog* table

- Review the contents of the following fields that give you an indication of the problem. You may need to widen some columns to read the entire contents.
 Source Object: ServiceHistory.AfterInsert
 Description: Data type mismatch in criteria expression.
 Context: ForEachRecord Equipment, [Equipment].[EquipmentID] = [ParamEID]
 Note that it appears that something is not correct with the values of the *EquipmentID* and *ParamEID* fields.

c. Close the table. You don't need to save any changes made to the table layout.

13. Review the tables.
 a. Open the *Equipment* table in *Datasheet* view. Note that the *LifetimeMaintenanceCost* for *EquipmentID 10103* is still *$0.00.* Since the *After Insert* macro had an error, the value did not update.
 b. Close the table.
 c. Open the *ServiceHistory* table in *Datasheet* view. The record was added for *ServiceID C00235,* including the *TotalCost* of *$95.* There was nothing wrong with the adding of the record, so the problem is in the *After Insert* macro.

14. Fix the *After Insert* macro.
 a. Open the *After Insert* event-driven data macro in the *ServiceHistory* table. Review the parameters. Note that both parameters are being set to the *TotalCost* value. Someone made a mistake when creating this macro and this is causing the type mismatch error.
 b. Edit the *ParamEID* parameter so that it reads =[FKEquipmentID]. The corrected *Parameters* section should be: *ParamEID = [FKEquipmentID]* and *ParamCost =[TotalCost].*
 c. Save and close the macro.
 d. Delete the record that you just added for *ServiceID C00235.*
 e. Save and close the table.

15. Correct the record for *EquipmentID 10103* in the *Equipment* table.
 a. Open the E*quipment* table in *Datasheet* view. Review the *LifetimeMaintenanceCost* for *EquipmentID 10103.* The value is *($95.00).* Obviously, that is not the correct value. This occurred because even though the *After Insert* macro didn't add the *$95.00* cost into the *LifetimeMaintenanceCost,* the *AfterDelete* macro subtracted the value.
 b. Enter 0 in the *LifetimeMaintenanceCost* field.
 c. Save and close the table.

16. Retest the macro.
 a. Click the **Add New Service Record** button on the *MainMenu* form.
 b. Add the following data into the form:
 Service ID: C00235
 Service Date: 12/28/2016
 Service Type: Inspection
 Description: 6-month inspection

> Performed By: 177
> Equipment ID: 10103
> Odometer Reading: Leave this field empty.
> Hours: Leave this field empty.
> Cost of Repair: 95.00
>
> c. Click the **Save Equipment Service Record** button.
> d. Click the **Close Form** button.

17. Verify that the record was updated.
 a. Open the *Equipment* table in *Datasheet* view. Verify that the *LifetimeMaintenanceCost* for *EquipmentID 10103* is *$95.00*.
 b. Click the **plus sign** on *EquipmentID 10103's* record to view the related service record.
 c. Close the table.

18. Close the **MainMenu** form.

19. Close the database.

Challenge Project 5-8

Modify the database you built in Challenge Project 4-8. Create a stand-alone *AutoExec* macro, add a field to a table, create an event-driven data macro to update that field, and test the macros.
[**Student Learning Outcomes 5.4, 5.5, 5.6, 5.7**]

File Needed: *[your initials] Access 4-8.accdb*
Completed Project File Name: *[your initials] Access 5-8.accdb*

Open the database *[your initials] Access 4-8* and save a copy of it as [your initials] Access 5-8.

Modify your database according to the following guidelines:

- Create a stand-alone *AutoExec* macro to automatically open the form in your database when the database is opened.
- Save and test the macro.
- Add a new *Date/Time* field into the table. The field updates with a time stamp any time the record is changed. Any of the existing records in the table do not have a value for this field since they were added prior to this new field.
- Create an event-driven data macro to store the time stamp when a record is changed in the table. Use the *Before Change* event.
- Test the macro under the conditions of adding a new record and changing an existing record.
- Make any needed corrections to the macro.
- Save any changes that you make.
- Save and close the table.

Challenge Project 5-9

For this project, you modify the database you created in Challenge Project 4-9 for Blue Lake Sports. Your database contains a *Department* table and a related *Intern* table with information about interns who are working at Blue Lake, along with the other objects created previously. Modify the *Intern* table and create an event-driven data macro for that table. The macro will set the value of a table field based on looking up related information in the *Department* table. Test the macro to ensure it works correctly. [Student Learning Outcomes 5.4, 5.6, 5.7]

File Needed: *[your initials] Access 4-9.accdb*
Completed Project File Name: *[your initials] Access 5-9.accdb*

Open the database *[your initials] Access 4-9* and save a copy of it as [your initials] Access 5-9.

Modify your database according to the following guidelines:

- Edit the *Intern* table and add a new field to store the InternshipLength.
- Save the changes to the table.
- Add a *Before Change* event-driven data macro to the *Intern* table. When creating the macro, keep the following in mind:
 - Use an *If* block using conditional logic to perform only the actions if the record is being added versus changed.
 - Use the *LookUpRecord* data block to find the matching record in the *Department* table. The *Where* condition should match the foreign key field in the *Intern* table to the primary key field in the *Department* table.
 - The logic in the macro should set the value for the *InternshipLength* field. If the *Division* is Golf or Water Sports, then the *InternshipLength* is 4 months. For all other Divisions there is a 6-month *InternshipLength*.
- Save and test the macro. You need to add several records into the database to test whether the macro works for the different sides of the condition. Also test that it doesn't make the change on an existing record.
 - Make any necessary corrections to the macro code.
 - Save any changes that you made to the database.

Challenge Project 5-10

For this project, you modify the database you created in Challenge Project 4-10 for a travel agency. Your database contains a *Ships* table with information about the different ships and a related *Trips* table with information about upcoming cruises, along with other objects created previously. Create a new *TripInformation* table that has a one-to-many relationship with the existing *Trips* table via the *TripName* field. Create the relationship using the *Lookup Wizard*. Create and test an embedded macro on the *On Activate* event of the form. [Student Learning Outcomes 5.2, 5.3, 5.4, 5.5, 5.7]

File Needed: *[your initials] Access 4-10.accdb*
Completed Project File Name: *[your initials] Access 5-10.accdb*

Open the database *[your initials] Access 4-10* and save a copy of it as [your initials] Access 5-10.

Modify your database according to the following guidelines:

- Create a new TripInformation table to store information about trips.
- Add the following fields into the table: TripName, Description, StartMonth, and EndMonth.
- *TripName* should be the primary key.
- Choose appropriate data types and field sizes.
- Save the table.
- Add data into the table.
 - Be sure to add records for the *TripName* values you already have in the *Cruise* table.
 - Search the web for samples of what to enter in the *Description* field. For example, for a *TripName* of Western Caribbean you might use a *Description* entry of "The Caribbean's warm sun, sandy beaches, and sparkling waters invite you to relax. Explore ports-of-call in the Caribbean Sea and wrap yourself in the unique culture of diverse islands."
 - Cruises typically sail in a region only during certain months of the year. In *StartMonth,* enter the month name when the season starts and in *EndMonth,* enter the month name when the season ends.
- In the *Trips* table, rename the *TripName* field TripNameFK. Use the *Lookup Wizard* to create a one-to-many relationship between the *TripNameFK* field and the *TripName* field in the *Trip* table.
- Enforce referential integrity and cascade updates and deletes.
- Save all changes to the tables and the relationships.
- Add an embedded macro to the *On Activate* event of the form. The macro should display a message box informing the user that this form can only be used to add new records into the table. Be sure that the message box displays after the form appears.
- Save and test the macro.
- Save any changes that you make.

CHAPTER

6

Creating Advanced Queries and Reports

CHAPTER OVERVIEW

As your databases continue to evolve, you will need to incorporate advanced queries and reports. This chapter addresses how to create and use action queries and how to create queries that perform more powerful tasks. In this chapter, you also learn how to use *Design* view to create and modify reports, including the use of subreports.

STUDENT LEARNING OUTCOMES (SLOs)

After completing this chapter, you will be able to:

SLO 6.1 Understand action queries; create and use *Update*, *Append*, *Delete*, and *Make Table* queries (p. A6-370).

SLO 6.2 Use the *Query Wizard* to create a crosstab query, a find duplicate records query, and a find unmatched records query (p. A6-376).

SLO 6.3 Use the top values property, explore and use date functions, and create a query with a subquery (p. A6-383).

SLO 6.4 Understand report sections, build a report and add and delete fields in *Design* view, understand the data source of a report, and create a parameter report (p. A6-390).

SLO 6.5 Use *Design* view to add a control to a report; modify the size, location, font characteristics, and formatting properties of a control; and change properties of multiple controls (p. A6-396).

SLO 6.6 Use calculations in a control on a report, create a running total in a control, and concatenate text data in a report (p. A6-402).

SLO 6.7 Understand when to use a subreport, create a main report and a subreport, add a subreport onto a main report, and customize a subreport (p. A6-409).

ACCESS

CASE STUDY

For the Pause & Practice projects in this chapter, you work on the Placer Hills Real Estate database. As you progress through the Pause & Practice projects, you incorporate skills you learn in the chapter to create action queries, implement advanced query features, create and edit reports in *Design* view and build a subreport.

Pause & Practice 6-1: Create a make table query, a delete query, and a parameter query that uses date functions.

Pause & Practice 6-2: Create and edit a report in *Design* view. Use a parameter query as the data source, and modify an existing report in *Design* view. Add calculated fields and modify several controls on the report.

Pause & Practice 6-3: Create a main report and a subreport, add a subreport onto a main report, and customize a subreport.

SLO 6.1

Creating and Using Action Queries

In Chapter 3, you learned to write a ***select query*** to locate data in a database. There is another type of query in Access, an ***action query***, which you can use to make changes to the data in a database. In this section, you learn how to create and use the four different action queries: an update query, an append query, a delete query, and a make table query.

Understand Action Queries

When creating action queries, it is important that you clearly define and understand the business task you need the query to accomplish, including knowing how frequently the task needs to be done. The following scenarios help to illustrate several different tasks, along with their frequency.

- A company closes a branch office and needs to assign employees to a different branch. This business task needs to be done only one time or very infrequently.
- A store manager needs to update the purchase cost of each item when the manufacturer who supplies goods to a store raises product prices. This business task might be part of a recurring process that happens periodically.
- At the end of every semester, a clerk in a university equipment office needs to remove the equipment reservations from the reservation table. However, the university still needs to keep the reservation records in a history table. This business task involves using several action queries together. First the clerk appends the old reservations into a history table before deleting the records from the reservation table.

You can automate each of the tasks described above using an action query. An action query makes a permanent change to the data in the database and the *Undo* button is not available to reverse the action. As a result, it is a good practice to make a backup copy of your database before you run any action query. This will allow you to restore your original data if the query does not work correctly. As additional protection, Access displays a message box (Figure 6-1) alerting you to the change before executing an action query. The exact message varies depending on the type of action query.

6-1 Action query message box

> **MORE INFO**
>
> Action queries do not display confirmation messages after the action is complete. Be careful not to execute the query a second time because that repeats the action, potentially resulting in invalid data.

It is good practice to create an action query in two steps.

1. Create and execute a regular select query to verify that you are finding the correct records.
2. Convert the select query to the desired action query, enter any required values related to the action, and execute the action query.

If you have not enabled the content in the database, you may encounter a warning message in the *Status* bar (Figure 6-2) when trying to run an action query.

6-2 Action query message in *Status* bar

If this message displays, you must enable the content from the security warning (Figure 6-3) or by opening the *Trust Center* after selecting the **Options** button from the *File* tab.

⚠ SECURITY WARNING Some active content has been disabled. Click for more details. Enable Content ✕

6-3 Security warning message

Each query type displays in the *Navigation Pane* with a unique identifying icon (Figure 6-4). For comparison purposes, Figure 6-4 also shows a sample of a select query icon.

Queries ⤒
- 📇 Append Query Sample
- 📇 Delete Query Sample
- 📇 Make Table Query Sample
- 📇 Select Query Sample
- 📇 Update Query Sample

6-4 Query icon examples

Create an Update Query

An **update query** changes data in the database. While you could open a table in *Datasheet* view and modify each record individually, an update query allows you to make the change to all records using one command.

- You can write the query to update a single field or multiple fields.
- The query can update all the records in a table or only records that meet a specific condition. For example, you can write an update query to give all employees a 3% pay raise or to give a raise only to employees in one specific department or job type.
- The query design grid includes an **Update To** row that is used to enter the new value.
- Figure 6-5 shows a query that updates the *BaseMonthlySalary* field for all the records in the *Employees* table. The formula gives everyone a 3% raise.

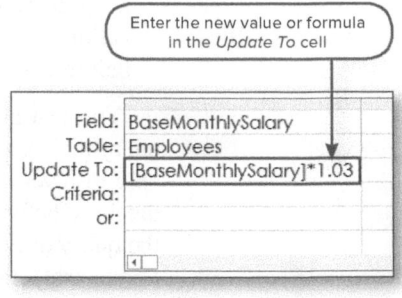

Enter the new value or formula in the *Update To* cell

Field:	BaseMonthlySalary
Table:	Employees
Update To:	[BaseMonthlySalary]*1.03
Criteria:	
or:	

6-5 Update query design grid

- Figure 6-6 shows a query that updates the *BaseMonthlySalary* field with the same 3% raise. However, in this case, the update applies only to employees whose *Title* is *Insurance Agent* and who work in the *Branch* of *Cameron Park*.

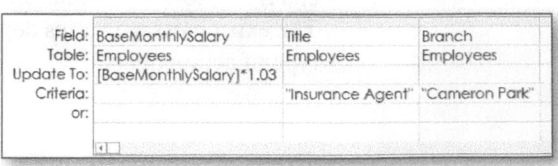

Field:	BaseMonthlySalary	Title	Branch
Table:	Employees	Employees	Employees
Update To:	[BaseMonthlySalary]*1.03		
Criteria:		"Insurance Agent"	"Cameron Park"
or:			

6-6 Update query design grid with criteria

▶ HOW TO: Create an Update Query

1. Click the **Query Design** button [*Create* tab, *Queries* group] to open the *Show Table* dialog box.
2. Double-click the first table to use in the query to add the table into the *Query Design* window.
3. Continue adding all required tables.
4. Click the **Close** button to close the *Show Table* dialog box. The *Select* button is highlighted in the *Query Type* group [*Query Tools Design* tab].
5. Add the desired fields into the query design grid. You can't use the * symbol to include all fields since each field will have a separate update value.
6. Add any criteria into the query design grid.

7. Run the query to verify that the query finds the correct records.

8. Switch back to *Design* view.

9. Click the **Update** button [*Query Tools Design* tab, *Query Type* group] (Figure 6-7) to convert the query to an update query. The *Sort* and *Show* rows of the select query are replaced with the *Update To* row of the update query.

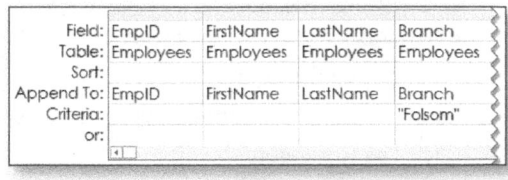

6-7 *Update* query button

10. Click the **Update To** cell of the desired field.

11. Type the new value or formula expression.

 - If necessary, you can enter the formula in the *Expression Builder* or *Zoom* dialog boxes.

12. Run the query. An Access message box displays, informing you that records are about to be changed.

13. Click **Yes** to execute the query.

14. Save the query.

> **MORE INFO**
>
> Unlike the *Criteria* row, the *Update To* row is case sensitive. Value(s) entered into the *Update To* row are added exactly as written, case included, into the records in the table.

If you execute an update query by running it directly from the *Navigation Pane*, Access displays a message box alerting you to the execution of an update query.

Create an Append Query

An ***append query*** adds records into an existing table in a database. An append query does not move the records from one table to another; rather it puts a copy of the records into the destination table.

- You can copy records from one or multiple tables into the destination table.
- You can copy all of the records from a table or only the records that meet a specific condition.
- The query design grid includes an ***Append To*** row that is used to match the fields across the tables.
- If the field names are the same in the source and destination tables, Access matches the names in the *Append To* row (Figure 6-8). You can change the name in the *Append To* row if the names do not match.
- If the field names do not match, you select the matching field names in the *Append To* row, as shown in Figure 6-9.

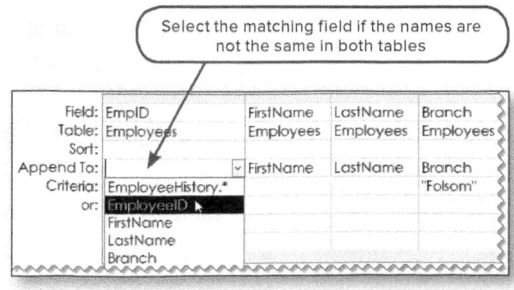

6-8 Append query design grid

6-9 Select the matching field name in the *Append To* row

▶ HOW TO: Create an Append Query

1. Click the **Query Design** button [*Create* tab, *Queries* group] to open the *Show Table* dialog box.
2. Double-click the first table that contains records that you want to copy to add the table into the *Query Design* window.
3. Continue adding all required tables.
4. Click the **Close** button to close the *Show Table* dialog box. The *Select* button is highlighted in the *Query Type* group [*Query Tools Design* tab].
5. Add the desired fields into the query design grid.
 - To include all of the fields from the table in the query, either select the * symbol from the *Table* in the *Query Design* window or select the **TableName.*** field from the drop-down list of fields displayed in the query design grid.
6. Add any criteria into the query design grid.
 - If you use criteria on a field, you must add each field individually instead of using the * symbol.
7. Run the query to verify that the query finds the correct records.
8. Switch back to *Design* view.
9. Click the **Append** button [*Query Tools Design* tab, *Query Type* group] (Figure 6-10) to convert the query to an append query. The *Append* dialog box opens (Figure 6-11).

6-10 *Append* query button

6-11 *Append* dialog box

10. Click the **Table Name** drop-down arrow and select the destination table.
11. Select either the **Current Database** or **Another Database** radio button, depending on the location of the destination table.
12. Click **OK**.
 - The *Show* row of the select query is replaced with the *Append To* row of the append query.
 - The *Append To* row contains the matching field names in the destination table.
13. Enter or edit the field names in the *Append To* row if necessary.
14. Run the query. An Access message box displays, informing you that you are about to append rows into the table.
15. Click **Yes** to execute the query.
16. Save the query.

If you execute an append query by running it directly from the *Navigation Pane*, Access displays a message box alerting you to the execution of an append query.

Create a Delete Query

A ***delete query*** deletes records from a table in a database. A delete query can save you a significant amount of time if you want to delete a number of records from a table.

- A delete query deletes the entire record. You cannot use this query to delete selected fields.
- If the table from which you are deleting participates in a relationship, be certain that you are aware of any relationship constraints that may apply, such as cascade deletes.

- The query design grid includes a *Delete* row.
- If you use the * symbol to include all fields, the *Delete* row displays *From*, as shown in Figure 6-12.
- If a field is listed individually, the *Delete* row displays *Where* so that you can enter criteria in the *Criteria* row, as shown in Figure 6-13.

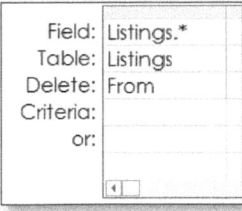

6-12 Delete query design grid

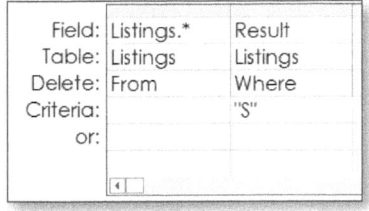

6-13 Delete query design grid with criteria

▶ HOW TO: Create a Delete Query

1. Click the **Query Design** button [*Create* tab, *Queries* group] to open the *Show Table* dialog box.

2. Double-click the first table that contains records that you want to delete to add the table into the *Query Design* window.

3. Continue adding all required tables.

4. Click the **Close** button to close the *Show Table* dialog box. The *Select* button is highlighted in the *Query Type* group [*Query Tools Design* tab].

5. Add the desired fields into the query design grid.

 - To include all of the fields from the table in the query, either select the * symbol from the *Table* in the *Query Design* window or select the **TableName.*** field from the drop-down list of fields displayed in the query design grid.
 - To include criteria in the query, add any fields that will use criteria into the query design grid.
 - When using criteria, if the table has a large number of fields, you may wish to include just a few of the fields that you can use to verify that the query criteria finds the correct records (Figure 6-14).

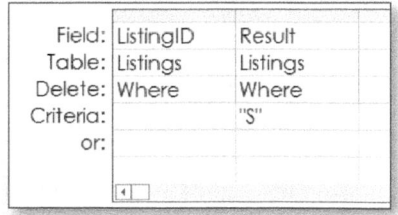

6-14 Delete query design grid with fewer fields and criteria

6. Add any criteria into the query design grid.

7. Run the query to verify that the query finds the correct records.

8. Switch back to *Design* view.

9. Click the **Delete** button [*Query Tools Design* tab, *Query Type* group] (Figure 6-15) to convert the query to a delete query.

 - The *Sort* and *Show* rows of the select query are replaced with the *Delete* row of the delete query.

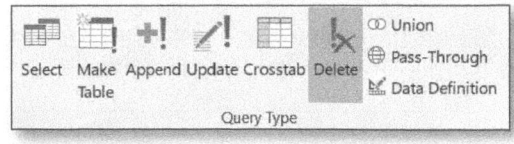

6-15 *Delete* query button

10. Run the query. An Access message box displays, informing you that you are about to delete rows from the table.

11. Click **Yes** to execute the query.

12. Save the query.

If you execute a delete query by running it directly from the *Navigation Pane*, Access displays a message box alerting you to the execution of a delete query.

Create a Make Table Query

A ***make table query*** creates a new table in a database and also copies the records into the new table. Organizations often use a make table query to create a history table, which they then use to store old records. For example, a university might store equipment reservations from previous semesters in a history table. Management could review the history table to analyze usage patterns on the equipment.

- A make table query can create the new table from fields in one or multiple tables.
- You can select which fields from a table should appear in the new table.
- You can copy all of the records or only the records that meet a specific condition.
- After the query executes, you need to designate a primary key in the new table.
- The new table you create does not have any relationships to the existing tables in the database.

▶ HOW TO: Create a Make Table Query

1. Click the **Query Design** button [*Create* tab, *Queries* group] to open the *Show Table* dialog box.
2. Double-click the first table that contains records that you want to copy to add the table into the *Query Design* window.
3. Continue adding all required tables.
4. Click the **Close** button to close the *Show Table* dialog box. The *Select* button is highlighted in the *Query Type* group [*Query Tools Design* tab].
5. Add the desired fields into the query design grid.
 - To include all of the fields from the table in the query, either select the * symbol from the *Table* in the *Query Design* window or select the **TableName.*** field from the drop-down list of fields displayed in the query design grid.
6. Add any criteria into the query design grid.
 - If you use criteria on a field, you must add all fields separately instead of using the * symbol.
7. Run the query to verify that the query finds the correct records.
8. Switch back to *Design* view.
9. Click the **Make Table** button [*Query Tools Design* tab, *Query Type* group] (Figure 6-16) to convert the query to a make table query. The *Make Table* dialog box opens (Figure 6-17).

6-16 *Make Table* query button

6-17 *Make Table* dialog box

10. Enter the name of the new table in the *Table Name* box.
11. Select either the **Current Database** or **Another Database** radio button, depending on the location of the new table.

12. Click **OK**.
13. Run the query. An Access message box displays, informing you that you are about to paste rows into a new table.
14. Click **Yes** to execute the query.
15. Save the query.

If you execute a make table query by running it directly from the *Navigation Pane*, Access displays a message box alerting you to the execution of a make table query. If the table already exists when a make table query executes, Access asks you to confirm deleting the existing table before creating a new one.

SLO 6.2

Exploring the Query Wizard

The **Query Wizard** is a tool that makes it easier to build four different types of queries. In Chapter 3, you used the *Simple Query Wizard* to create a select query. In this section, you use the three other types of query wizards—the *Crosstab Query Wizard*, the *Find Duplicates Query Wizard*, and the *Find Unmatched Query Wizard*—to create three special types of select queries. Each of these query wizard options is available in the *New Query* dialog box (Figure 6-18).

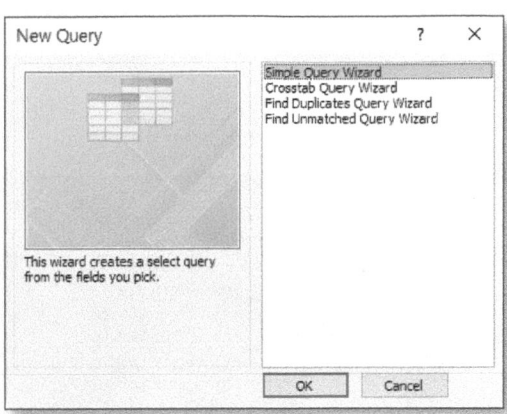

6-18 Query wizard options in the *New Query* dialog box

Understand and Build a Crosstab Query

A **crosstab query** summarizes data on two dimensions. The results of a crosstab query display in a row/column format, which makes the data easier to read and understand (compared to the results of a select query). Consider the following example. In the New York DMV database, a manager wants to find out how many tickets of each primary factor were written in each city. Figure 6-19 shows the results of a regular select query designed to show this information by sorting on primary factor and city. This query shows all 42 tickets. If you really study the results and perform some manual calculations, you can figure out how many tickets of each primary factor were written in

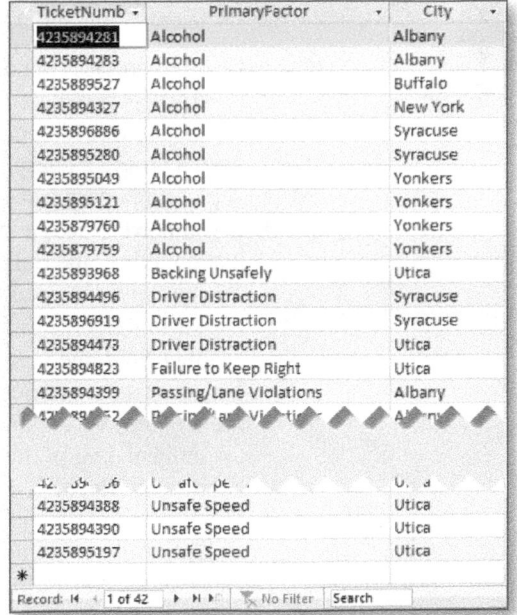

6-19 Select query showing tickets by primary factor in each city

each city. Figure 6-20 shows the results of the same query after it was converted into a summary query. Recall that a summary query includes a *Total* row used to group and aggregate the data to improve the readability. However, it still takes some effort to figure out the answer to the question.

Figure 6-21 shows the same data displayed in a crosstab query. The row/column grid makes it much easier to see how many tickets of each primary factor were written in each city.

CountOfTicketNumber	PrimaryFactor	City
2	Alcohol	Albany
1	Alcohol	Buffalo
1	Alcohol	New York
2	Alcohol	Syracuse
4	Alcohol	Yonkers
1	Backing Unsafely	Utica
2	Driver Distraction	Syracuse
1	Driver Distraction	Utica
1	Failure to Keep Right	Utica
2	Passing/Lane Violations	Albany
1	Passing/Lane Violations	New York
1	Passing/Lane Violations	Utica
1	Traffic Control Disregarded	Syracuse
2	Traffic Control Disregarded	Yonkers
1	Turning Improperly	Albany
1	Turning Improperly	Syracuse
1	Turning Improperly	Utica
2	Unsafe Speed	Albany
4	Unsafe Speed	Buffalo
2	Unsafe Speed	New York
1	Unsafe Speed	Syracuse
8	Unsafe Speed	Utica

Record: 1 of 22 No Filter Search

6-20 Select query with a total row added

Row heading in a crosstab query

Column heading displays one column for each value in the table

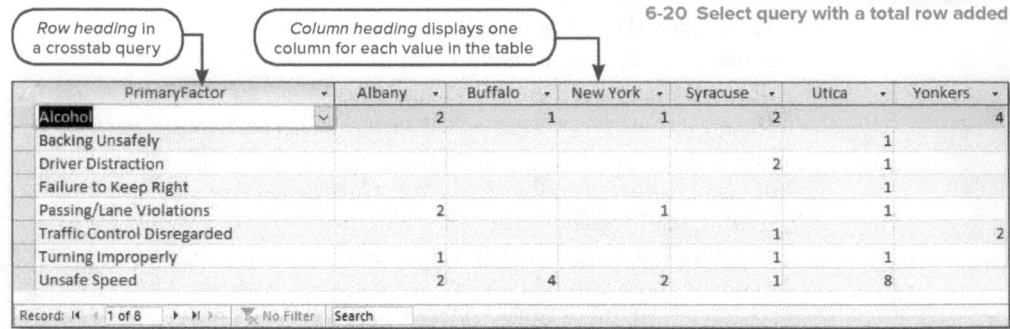

PrimaryFactor	Albany	Buffalo	New York	Syracuse	Utica	Yonkers
Alcohol	2	1	1	2		4
Backing Unsafely					1	
Driver Distraction				2	1	
Failure to Keep Right					1	
Passing/Lane Violations	2		1		1	
Traffic Control Disregarded				1		2
Turning Improperly	1			1	1	
Unsafe Speed	2	4	2	1	8	

Record: 1 of 8 No Filter Search

6-21 Crosstab query showing tickets by primary factor in each city

When creating and using crosstab queries, keep the following points in mind:

- Crosstab queries are not appropriate in all databases. You must have data that can be summarized across two dimensions.
- Unlike the resulting datasheet from a regular select query, you cannot edit the results from a crosstab query.
- A crosstab query can get its data from a table or another query.
- If you need to use fields from more than one table, you must first create a select query that combines the fields from the different tables.
- You can include up to three fields as row headings. The **row headings** are the field(s) that appear in the left-most column(s) of the grid. For example, Figure 6-21 shows one row heading field, the *PrimaryFactor*.
- You must select one column heading field. The **column heading** is the field that contains the different values that display in the heading row of the results. The *City* field is the column heading in Figure 6-21. The different values of the *City* field display as the actual column headings.
- When creating the query, you select the field to calculate and the aggregate function, such as *Sum* or *Count*, to use on that field. In Figure 6-21 the *TicketNumber* is the field to calculate and *Count* is the aggregate function.

You can create a crosstab query using *Query Design*; however, it is much easier to create the query using the **Crosstab Query Wizard**.

▶ HOW TO: Create a Query Using the Crosstab Query Wizard

1. Click the **Query Wizard** button [*Create* tab, *Queries* group] to launch the *Query Wizard*.

2. Select **Crosstab Query Wizard** in the *New Query* dialog box and click **OK**. The *Crosstab Query Wizard* launches (Figure 6-22).

3. Select the table that contains the data you want to summarize. If necessary, click the **Queries** radio button to see the list of available queries and then select the desired query.

4. Click **Next** to move to the next page of the wizard.

5. Select the field to include in the row headings from the *Available Fields* window and click the **Move Single Field** button to move the field into the *Selected Fields* window (Figure 6-23).

 - As you add fields, the sample section updates in the wizard.
 - As desired, move up to two additional fields into the row headings.

6. Click **Next** when you have finished adding fields. The next page of the wizard displays.

7. Select the field to use as the column headings. When you select the field, the sample updates (Figure 6-24). Click **Next** to move to the next page of the wizard.

8. If the field you select for the column heading is a *Date/Time* data type, the *Crosstab Query Wizard* prompts you to select an interval to use in grouping the data (Figure 6-25). Select the interval and click **Next**.

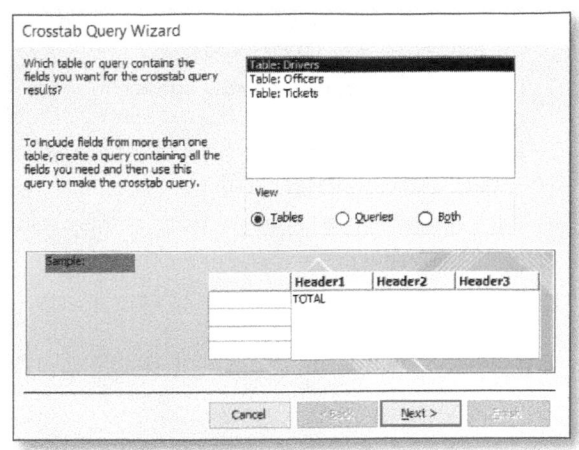

6-22 *Crosstab Query Wizard*, step one

6-23 *Crosstab Query Wizard*, step two

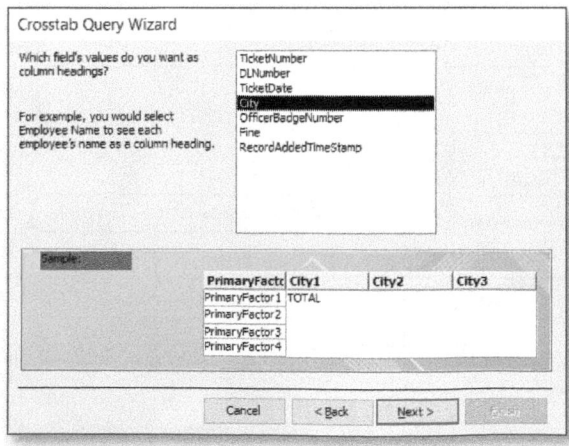

6-24 *Crosstab Query Wizard*, step three

6-25 *Crosstab Query Wizard*; select a grouping interval

9. Select the field to be used in the calculation and select the aggregate function (Figure 6-26).
10. Deselect the **Yes, include row sums** check box, as desired.
 - If row sums are included, the first column of summary data will be a total column.
11. Click **Next** to move to the last page of the wizard.
12. Enter the name of the query and click **Finish**.
 - The query executes and displays the results (Figure 6-27).
 - This example includes the total column in the results that sums each row.

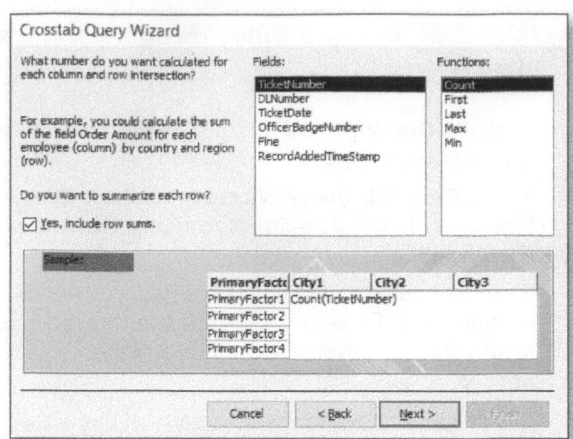

6-26 *Crosstab Query Wizard*, step four

Summary data results from including row sums

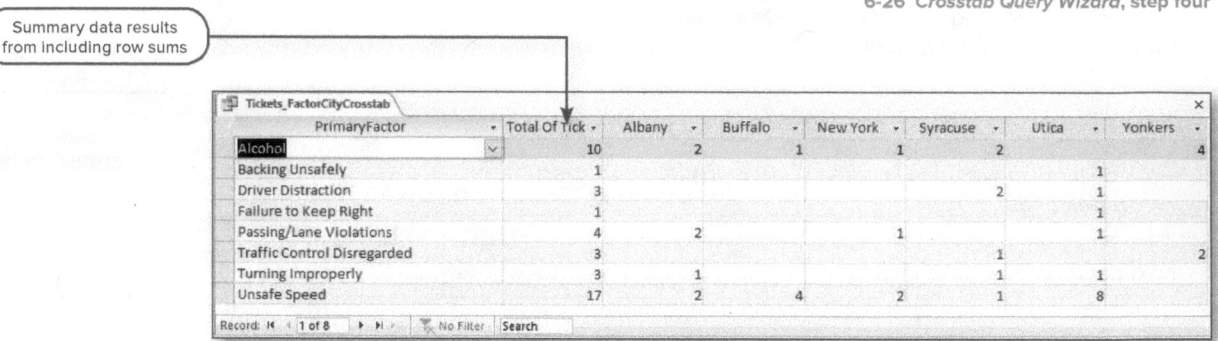

6-27 **Crosstab query results showing tickets by primary factor in each city, including row sums**

13. Close the query when done.

After you create a crosstab query with the *Crosstab Query Wizard*, you can edit it in *Design* view and make changes to any of the selections made during the wizard. You can also add criteria or sorting options to the query.

▶ **HOW TO: Edit a Crosstab Query**

1. Select the query name in the *Navigation Pane*.
2. Right-click and select **Design View** from the context menu.
 - The query opens in *Design* view (Figure 6-28).
 - Note the *Crosstab* row in the query design grid.
3. Edit the query as needed.
4. Save and close the query.

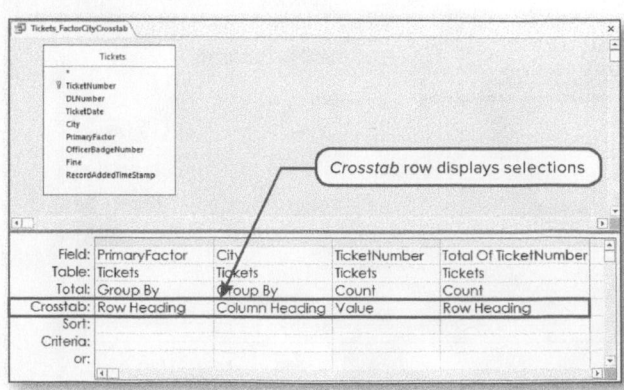

6-28 **Edit a crosstab query in *Design* view**

Find Duplicate Records

If ***duplicate records*** are present, two or more records in a table share the same values. Generally speaking, you should avoid having duplicate records in your database. When you follow good database design guidelines, you put in place features that prevent your database from allowing duplicate data. For example, when you designate a field as a primary key, Access will not allow you to have two records with the same value in the primary key field.

Unfortunately, even when you practice good database design, you still may end up with duplicated data. Consider customers who forget their login IDs and passwords and create new accounts or a salesperson who accidently enters the same order twice. Having two records for the same customer, even though the login ID is different, or two records of the same order, even though the order number is different, results in duplicate data. You need to remove duplicated records in situations like these. Additionally, sometimes you may inherit a database that was poorly designed and does not have primary keys created, or you may import data from another source that contains duplicate data. Before you can create and enforce a primary key, you need to find and remove duplicate data.

Keep in mind that all duplicated data is not bad. For example, the same product number or salesperson ID appears on multiple sales records. You want to find and correct only data that clearly is a problematic duplication of existing data. A ***find duplicates query*** locates data that is duplicated in your database. You can create a find duplicates query using *Query Design*; however, it is much easier to create the query using the ***Find Duplicates Query Wizard***.

When the query is initially created in the query wizard, Access returns only records that have a match on the entire value in a field. You can edit the query after it is created to look for partial matches by adding criteria that uses wildcards, as you learned in Chapter 3.

▶ **HOW TO:** Create a Query Using the Find Duplicates Query Wizard

1. Click the **Query Wizard** button [*Create* tab, *Queries* group] to launch the *Query Wizard*.

2. Select **Find Duplicates Query Wizard** in the *New Query* dialog box and click **OK**. The *Find Duplicates Query Wizard* launches (Figure 6-29).

3. Select the table that contains the data you want to analyze. If necessary, click the **Queries** radio button to see the list of available queries and then select the desired query instead of a table.

4. Click **Next** to move to the next page of the wizard.

5. Select the field that may contain duplicate data from the *Available Fields* window and click the **Move Single Field** button to move the field into the *Duplicate-value fields* window.

6. Move any additional fields that may have duplicated data into the window (Figure 6-30).

 • If you use multiple fields, Access checks all the fields to determine if data is duplicated. For example, two authors with the last name of "Chang" are not considered duplicates if the authors have different first names and you use both last name and first name fields.

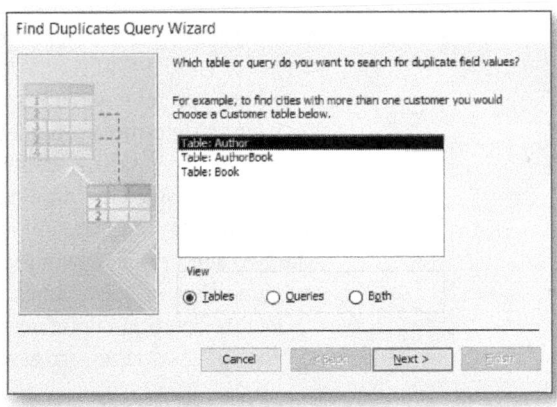

6-29 *Find Duplicates Query Wizard*, step one

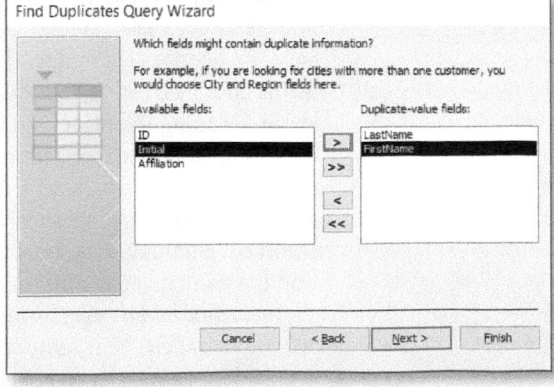

6-30 *Find Duplicates Query Wizard*, step two

7. Click **Next** when you have finished adding fields to move to the next page of the wizard.

8. Move any additional fields from the *Available Fields* window that you want to include in the results (Figure 6-31).

 - These fields may help you identify if the record really is a duplicate.

9. Click **Next** to move to the last page of the wizard.

10. Enter the name of the query and click **Finish**.

 - The query executes and displays the results of any records that contain duplicated data (Figure 6-32).

11. Review the data records to determine if any duplicates can be deleted from the database.

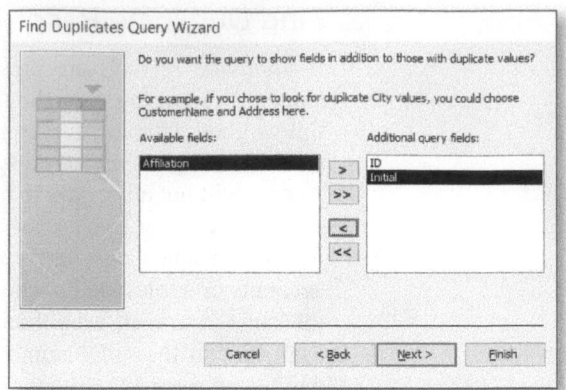

6-31 *Find Duplicates Query Wizard*, step three

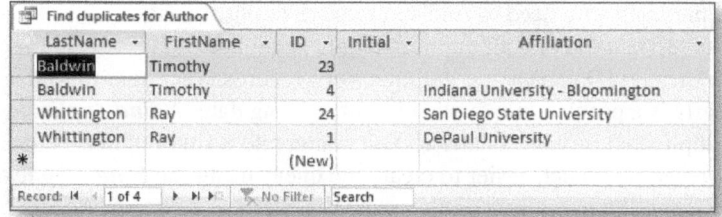

6-32 Find duplicates query results

12. Close the query.

When you review the results of a find duplicates query, you may need to conduct further analysis to determine whether the records are actually duplicates. This may involve looking at data in other tables, conducting research, or talking with employees or customers. For example, consider the duplicate records in Figure 6-32. Further research indicates that both records for Ray Whittington refer to the same person, who switched affiliations at some point. The two Timothy Baldwin records, however, refer to two different people who happen to have the same first and last names.

Before deleting duplicate records, change the foreign key connection of any related records in other tables so they are associated with the record that remains in the database.

Find Unmatched Records

Unmatched records are records in one table that do not contain any matching records in a related table. For example, imagine that San Diego Sailing wants to determine which boats have not been rented or a retail store wants to find out which products have not been purchased in the last quarter. This information can help these organizations make business decisions about reducing the price, running a promotional special, discontinuing a product, etc.

The situations described in the previous paragraph do not indicate a problem with the database design. However, as noted in the previous description of the use of the find duplicate query, sometimes you may inherit a poorly designed database. Referential integrity may not have been enforced, resulting in records that do not have valid relationships. If this happened, you need to find the unmatched records and either remove them or connect them to valid records.

An ***unmatched records query*** compares records in two tables and determines which ones are not matched. You can create a find unmatched records query using *Query Design*; however, it is much easier to create the query using the ***Find Unmatched Query Wizard***.

▶ HOW TO: Create a Query Using the Find Unmatched Query Wizard

1. Click the **Query Wizard** button [*Create* tab, *Queries* group] to launch the *Query Wizard*.

2. Select **Find Unmatched Query Wizard** in the *New Query* dialog box and click **OK**. The *Find Unmatched Query Wizard* launches (Figure 6-33).

3. Select the table that may have unmatched records. If necessary, click the **Queries** radio button to see the list of available queries and select the desired query. The data from the selected table or query displays in the query results.

4. Click **Next** to move to the next page of the wizard.

5. Select the table that contains the related records (Figure 6-34).

 - This table must have a field in common with the first table.
 - While the tables don't have to be joined with a relationship, they often are.

6. Click **Next** to move to the next page of the wizard.

7. Select the matching field in each table and click the **< = >** button (Figure 6-35). If the fields are already linked via a relationship, they may already be selected.

8. Click **Next** to move to the next page of the wizard.

9. Select any additional fields from the *Available fields* window that you want to include in the results (Figure 6-36).

 - You can only select fields from the first table selected (the one that may have unmatched data).
 - If you don't select any fields, Access displays all the fields in the query results.

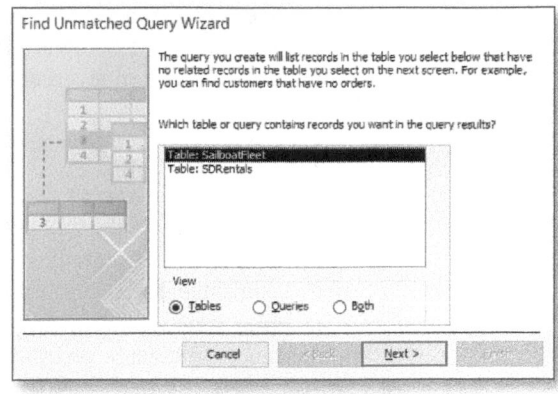

6-33 *Find Unmatched Query Wizard*, step one

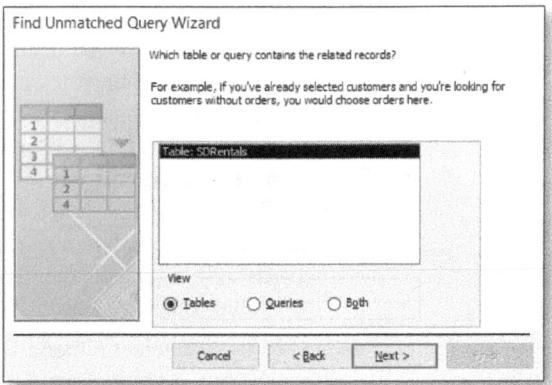

6-34 *Find Unmatched Query Wizard*, step two

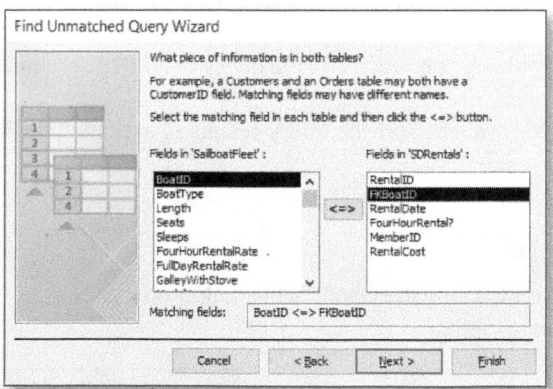

6-35 *Find Unmatched Query Wizard*, step three

6-36 *Find Unmatched Query Wizard*, step four

10. Click **Next** to move to the last page of the wizard.

11. Enter the name of the query and click **Finish**. The query executes and displays the results of any unmatched records (Figure 6-37).

12. Save and close the query.

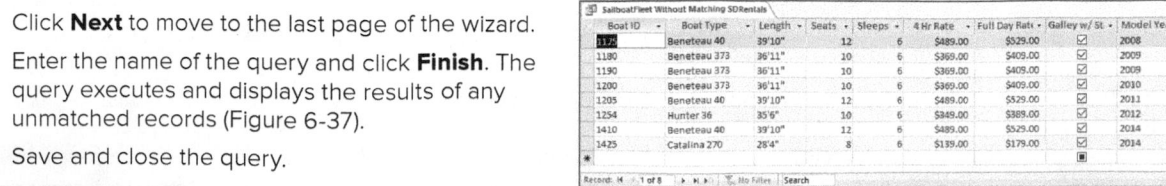

6-37 **Unmatched records query results**

If you create an unmatched records query because you are concerned about the design of your database, review the results of the query to determine appropriate action. This may involve looking at data in other tables, conducting research, or talking with employees or customers. You may determine that the unmatched records should be deleted or that they need to be matched to a record in a related table.

SLO 6.3

Creating Advanced Queries and Changing Query Properties

Queries provide a great deal of power and flexibility to help you accomplish many tasks in your database. As the number of records in your database increases, you can use query properties to limit the number of records that display in a result. Additionally, as the processing of your database becomes more sophisticated, you may need to write queries that use more complex functions or queries that use other queries as their data source. In this section, you learn how to create queries to deal with these more complex situations.

Find the Top Values in a Query

The **Top Values** query property (Figure 6-38) limits the number of records that display in a query answer. This can be helpful when you want to focus attention on certain aspects of a business. For example, an organization may want to find out who its top performing salespersons were in the past year.

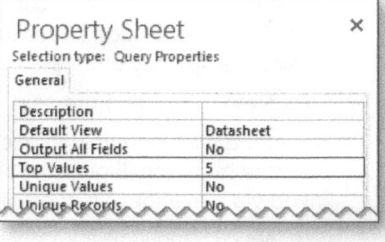

6-38 *Top Values* query property

The queries you have written so far have returned all of the records that meet the criteria. This is because the default setting of the *Top Values* property is *All*. For your top values query to function correctly, you must keep the following points in mind:

- You must select either a fixed number of records or a percentage value.
- The preset choices are *5, 25, 100, 5%, 25%,* and *All*.
- You can enter a different value if it is not one of the preset choices.
- When the query executes, the selected number or percentage of records display, starting with the first record that is in the query result.
- To have the query return the top values, you must sort the query results in descending order on the desired field.
- To have the query return the bottom values, sort the query results in ascending order.

▶ **HOW TO:** Create a Top Values Property in a Query

1. Create a new query using *Query Design*.
2. Add the tables into the query design grid and click **Close** to close the *Show Table* dialog box.
3. Add the necessary fields from the tables into the query design grid.
4. Click the **Sort** row cell of the field that determines the top values, click the **drop-down arrow** and select **Ascending** or **Descending**, depending on whether you want the top or bottom values.
5. Add criteria to the query, as desired.
6. Click the **Return** box drop-down arrow [*Query Tools Design* tab, *Query Setup* group] and select the value (Figure 6-39). Alternatively, you can enter the value directly into the *Return* box or into the *Top Values* property on the *Property Sheet* of the query.
7. Run the query.
8. Save and close the query.

6-39 Select the desired value in the *Return* box

Remember to test your query to verify that it returns the correct records. Figure 6-40 shows a sample query. The *Top Values* property, not shown in the figure, contains *5*. This query will display the agent's first and last name, along with the price, for the five most expensive properties based on the *ListPrice* field. To find the five least expensive properties, change the *Sort* to **Ascending**.

Understand and Use Date Functions in a Query

6-40 Query design grid of top values query

In Chapter 5, you were introduced to the *Date()* function, which retrieves the current date from your computer. Access has a variety of other functions that allow you to work with dates. For example, you can use date functions to write queries that find the real estate properties listed in the current month, find students who are 18 years old, or find products that are nearing their expiration dates. In this section, the date functions are explained in the context of using them with a query. However, you can also use date functions in other objects and controls that use expressions.

As you start to work more with dates, it helps to know that Access internally represents each date as a serial number. The serial number is designated by the number of days the date is from January 1, 1900. For example, the serial number for 1/1/2017 is 42736, while the number for 1/2/2017 is 42737. This format allows Access to perform date arithmetic.

Additionally, when working with many of the date functions, it is important to understand how Access represents the intervals (pieces) of a date. These are explained in the following *Access Date Intervals* table:

Access Date Intervals

Interval	Description	Value
		For 4/15/2017
yyyy	Year	2017
q	Quarter (1-4)	2
m	Month	4
y	Day of year (1-365)	105
d	Day (1-31)	15
w	Weekday (1-7)	3
ww	Week (1-52)	16

MORE INFO

Access allows you to work with time in addition to dates. The *Now()* function retrieves the current date, including the time, from your computer. Refer to the Access help system for information about using the time intervals of a *Date/Time* field.

Several of the more common date functions are described in the following *Access Date Functions* table. In this table, the *DateListed* field contains 12/17/2016 and today's date is 1/4/2017. Some of the examples use a specific date value. In those situations, the date must be surrounded by the # symbol (for example, #4/15/2017#).

Access Date Functions

Function	Description	Examples	Result
Date()	Retrieves the current system date.	Date()	1/4/2017
DatePart()	Determines a specific piece, or interval, of a date.	DatePart("q",[DateListed]) DatePart("yyyy", #4/15/2017#)	4 2017
DateSerial()	Converts values into a date value.	DateSerial(2017,2,20)	2/20/2017
DateAdd()	Adds to a date. You must specify the value along with the interval.	DateAdd("yyyy", 3, [DateListed])	12/17/2019 This example added 3 years to the *DateListed*.
DateDiff()	Determines the difference between two dates. You must specify the interval.	DateDiff("d", [DateListed], Date())	18 This example calculated how many days it has been since the property was listed.
MonthName()	Retrieves the name of the month number.	MonthName(2)	February
WeekdayName()	Retrieves the name of the weekday number.	WeekdayName(7)	Saturday

ANOTHER WAY

You can use the *Month()* and *Year()* functions to display the month and year numeric values.

Many times an expression combines several functions. For example, to display the name of today's month, you write:

MonthName(DatePart("m", Date()))

This expression uses the *MonthName* function to determine the actual name of the month. However, that function needs the month number. The month number comes from the *DatePart* function, which retrieves the month from the *Date* function. As you know, the *Date* function retrieves today's date from your computer. Don't worry; the description makes the process seem more complicated than it really is.

> **HOW TO: Use a Date Function in a Calculated Field in a Query**

1. Open a query in *Design* view.
2. Click the **Field** box of the column that will contain the calculated field.
3. Right-click and select **Zoom** to open the *Zoom* box or **Build** to open the *Expression Builder*.
4. Enter the formula, including the appropriate date function.
 - The example in Figure 6-41 uses the *DateDiff* and *Date* functions.
 - Remember to include a name for the calculated field. Enter the name first, followed by a colon (**:**).
5. Click **OK** in the *Zoom* box or *Expression Builder* when finished entering the formula.
6. Save and close the query.

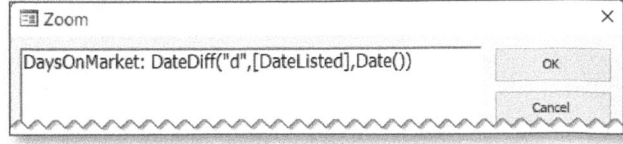

6-41 Calculated field using *DateDiff* and *Date* functions

Remember to run your query to verify that the date calculation field works correctly. Figure 6-42 shows a sample query. The query displays only properties that have active listings due to the *Is Null* criteria in the *Result* field. Recall that the *Result* field in the *Listings* table is either empty, or contains a "S" (sold), an "E" (expired), or a "C" (canceled). The *DaysOnMarket* field contains the expression shown in Figure 6-41 which calculates the number of days since the property was listed. The more you work with expressions involving date functions, the easier it becomes.

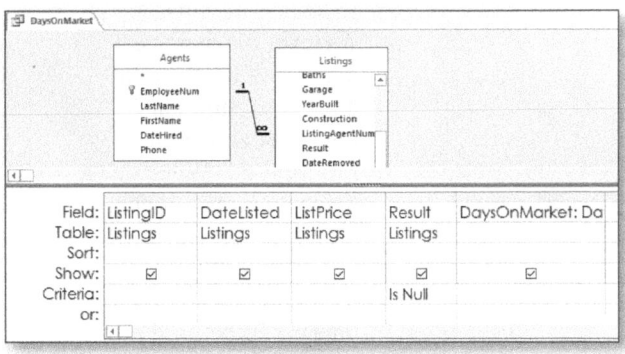

6-42 Completed query design grid

> **MORE INFO**
>
> The date functions can also be used in expressions entered into calculated controls used on forms and reports.

Create a Subquery

The query examples used so far have all used a table as the data source for a query. A query can also use another query as the data source. A **subquery** is a query that is used inside another query. Creating a query and then using it inside another query can be helpful when you have a common starting point (the original query) but want to customize it for additional purposes (the additional query). Sometimes using a subquery is a more efficient way to get the results you are seeking, but it depends on the size of the database and the design of the query.

To incorporate a subquery, you follow the general process you have learned in this book to create a query. The only thing you do differently is to select the **Query Name** from the *Queries* tab of the *Show Table* dialog box, instead of selecting the **Table Name** from the *Tables* tab.

Occasionally, you may need to use a subquery when the business question is too complex for a single query. For example, suppose Placer Hills Real Estate wants to find out which agents have listings greater than the average listing price for all properties. In the following material, you learn how to write a query to display the desired result.

- To determine the final result, first you need to have Access calculate the average listing price for all the properties. You might try to write a query structured like the one shown in Figure 6-43. However, when you try to run this query, you receive an error message because Access does not allow you to use an aggregate function in the criteria.

Field:	FirstName	LastName	ListPrice
Table:	Agents	Agents	Listings
Sort:			
Show:	☑	☑	☑
Criteria:			>Avg([ListPrice])
or:			

6-43 Incorrect query criteria using an aggregate function

- Instead, you must perform the average aggregate function in a separate summary query, as shown in Figure 6-44. When this query executes, it generates the result shown in Figure 6-45. This *AverageListingPrice* query will be used as a subquery.

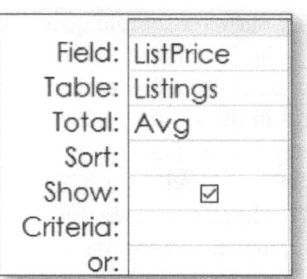

Field:	ListPrice
Table:	Listings
Total:	Avg
Sort:	
Show:	☑
Criteria:	
or:	

6-44 Query design to calculate the average list price

AverageListingPrice

AvgOfListPrice
$382,245.16

Record: ◄ ◄ 1 of 1 ► ►►

6-45 *AverageListingPrice* query results

- The last step is to create the query to display the final desired result. This query (Figure 6-46) includes the *Agents* and *Listings* tables and the *AverageListingPrice* subquery. Notice that the criteria in the *ListPrice* field has a greater than comparison to the *AvgOfListPrice* field in the subquery.

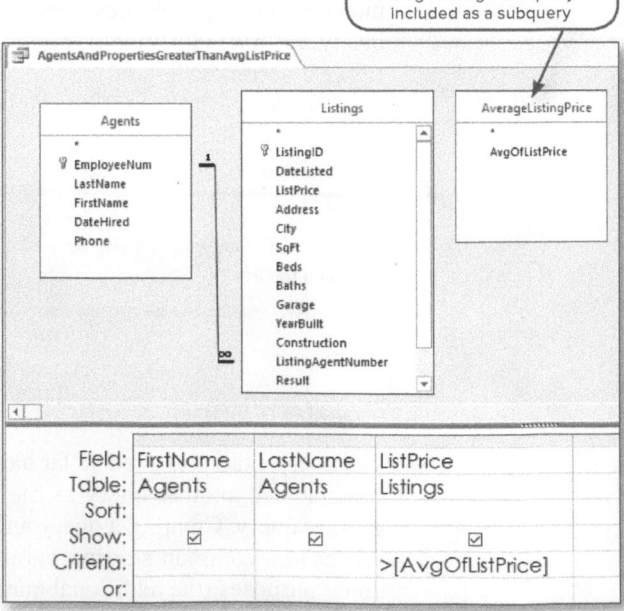

AverageListingPrice query is included as a subquery

Field:	FirstName	LastName	ListPrice	
Table:	Agents	Agents	Listings	
Sort:				
Show:	☑	☑	☑	
Criteria:			>[AvgOfListPrice]	
or:				

6-46 *Design* view of a query that uses the *AverageListingPrice* subquery

PAUSE & PRACTICE: ACCESS 6-1

For this Pause & Practice, you create three queries for the Placer Hills Real Estate database. First, you create a make table query to build a table to store the records of sold properties. Next, you create a delete query to delete the sold properties from the *Listings* table. Finally, you create a parameter query that uses date functions to display information about property listings.

File Needed: ***PlacerHills-06.accdb***
Completed Project File Names: *[your initials] PP A6-1.accdb*, *[your initials] PP A6-1_Backup.accdb*, and *[your initials] PP A6-1_Backup-2.accdb*

1. Open the ***PlacerHills-06*** database from your student data files.

2. Save a new copy of your database as [your initials] PP A6-1.

3. Enable content in the database.

4. Back up your database.
 a. Click the **File** tab to open the *Backstage* view.
 b. Click the **Save As** button.
 c. Select the **Back Up Database** button in the *Advanced* grouping of the *Save Database As* section and click the **Save As** button.
 d. Enter [your initials] PP A6-1_Backup as the file name, select the desired location, and then click the **Save** button.

5. Open the *Listings* table in *Datasheet* view to verify that the table contains 57 records. Note that three new columns have been added to the table: *Result, DateRemoved* and *SoldPrice*. As appropriate, these fields are updated when a property is sold, the listing expires, or the listing is canceled.

6. Close the table.

7. Create a make table query to create a *SoldProperties* table.
 a. Click the **Query Design** button [*Create* tab, *Queries* group] to open the *Show Table* dialog box.
 b. Double-click the **Listings** table to add the table into the *Query Design* window and click the **Close** button to close the *Show Table* dialog box.
 c. Add all of the fields into the query design grid. Do not use the * symbol since you will be adding criteria.
 d. Type "S" in the *Criteria* box of the *Result* field.
 e. Run the query. Verify that the query finds the nine records displayed in Figure 6-47.
 f. Switch back to *Design* view.

6-47 Query results showing sold properties

 g. Click the **Make Table** button [*Query Tools Design* tab, *Query Type* group] to convert the query to a make table query. The *Make Table* dialog box opens.
 h. Type SoldProperties in the *Table Name* box and click **OK**.

i. Run the query. An Access message box displays, informing you that *"You are about to paste 9 row(s) into a new table."*

j. Click **Yes** to execute the query. The new table displays in the *Tables* group of the *Navigation Pane*.

k. Save the query as MakeSoldPropertiesTable.

l. Close the query.

8. Back up your database again and enter [your initials] PP A6-1_Backup-2 as the file name. Remember, you should do this before any action that makes a permanent change to the database.

9. Create a delete query to delete the sold properties from the *Listings* table.

a. Click the **Query Design** button [*Create* tab, *Queries* group] to open the *Show Table* dialog box.

b. Double-click the **Listings** table to add the table into the *Query Design* window and click the **Close** button.

c. Add the **ListingID** and **Result** fields into the query design grid. The *ListingID* field is included to help you determine if the query works correctly.

d. Type "S" into the *Criteria* box of the *Result* field.

e. Run the query to verify that the query finds the correct records. The query should display the same nine properties that were found in the make table query.

f. Switch back to *Design* view.

g. Click the **Delete** button [*Query Tools Design* tab, *Query Type* group] to convert the query to a delete query.

h. Run the query. An Access message box displays, informing you that *"You are about to delete 9 row(s) from the specified table."*

i. Click **Yes** to execute the query.

j. Save the query as DeleteSoldProperties.

k. Close the query.

10. Open the *Listings* table to verify that the table now contains only 48 records.

11. Close the table.

12. Create a parameter query that uses date functions to display the properties listed in a specific month.

a. Click the **Query Design** button [*Create* tab, *Queries* group] to open the *Show Table* dialog box.

b. Double-click the **Listings** table to add the table into the *Query Design* window and click the **Close** button.

c. Add the **ListingID**, **DateListed**, **ListPrice**, **SqFt**, **Address**, **City**, and **ListingAgentNumber** fields into the query design grid.

d. Click the **Criteria** box of the *DateListed* field to add a parameter.

e. Right-click to open the context menu and select **Zoom**.

f. Type DatePart("m", [DateListed])=([Enter the number of the month (January = 1) to see properties listed in that month]) in the *Zoom* window and click **OK**. This criterion looks for records where the month part of the *DateListed* field is equal to the parameter value entered when the query executes.

g. Run the query to test that it works.

h. Type 9 in the *Enter Parameter Value* dialog box and click **OK**. The query should display the seven properties that were listed in September (the ninth month).

13. Edit the query to add a calculated field that uses a date function.

a. Switch back to *Design* view.

b. Click to select the empty **Field** box to the right of the *ListingAgentNumber* field.

c. Right-click to open the context menu and select **Zoom**.

d. Type DaysOnMarket: DateDiff("d", [DateListed], Date()) in the *Zoom* window and click **OK**. This calculation finds the difference between today's date and the *DateListed* field.

e. Save the query as DaysOnMarketWithMonthParameter.

f. Run the query.

g. Type 9 in the *Enter Parameter Value* dialog box and click **OK**. The query should display the records shown in Figure 6-48. The values in the *DaysOnMarket* column will vary, and may be negative, depending on the day that you run the query.

ListingID ▾	Date Listed ▾	List Price ▾	SqFt ▾	Address ▾	City ▾	Agent ▾	DaysOnMaɪ ▾
10040	9/8/2016	$299,999.00	1056	3935 Cedar Mist Lane	Auburn	103	70
10043	9/8/2016	$357,000.00	2266	1575 Oak Ridge Way	Auburn	160	70
10044	9/8/2016	$209,000.00	1885	446 Manzanita Way	Weimer	160	70
10046	9/10/2016	$299,900.00	1552	1735 Andover Lane	Lincoln	133	68
10047	9/10/2016	$474,500.00	3328	858 Spotted Pony Lane	Rocklin	133	68
10048	9/10/2016	$350,000.00	1958	900 Coyote Mountain Drive	Weimer	127	68
10049	9/16/2016	$599,900.00	4390	1773 Melanzane Drive	Roseville	127	62
* 0		$0.00	0				

Record: I◄ ◄ 1 of 7 ► ►I ►* No Filter Search

6-48 Parameter query results

h. Close the query. If you reopen the query, you will notice that Access has revised the query to put the *DateListed* criteria into a separate field. This is due to the way Access processes the query. It does not affect the way the query runs.

14. Close the database.

SLO 6.4

Building a Report in Design View

As you saw in Chapter 4, reports offer an organized and professional way to view the data in a database. While the skills you have previously learned while creating and editing reports with the *Report Wizard* and *Layout* view still apply, *Design* view provides additional flexibility and tools for creating and editing a report. In this section, you first learn about the different sections in a report and then learn how to use *Design* view to create and edit reports.

Understand Report Sections

A report can contain many different sections, explained in the *Report Sections* table. When you are viewing a report in *Layout* or *Print Preview* view, the sections are not as obvious as they are in *Design* view. You need to understand how each section works in order to build your reports correctly.

Report Sections

Section	Commonly Used To	Prints Where/When?
Report Header	Print a report title or logo.	Once, at the top of the first page.
Report Footer	Print report totals or other information at the end of the report. (In Design view, this section appears below the page footer, but in other views, and when the report is printed, this section prints above the page footer.)	Once, at the bottom of the last page above the page footer.
Page Header	Print column headings, page numbers, or dates.	At the top of every page. (Prints below the report header on page 1.)
Page Footer	Print page numbers or dates.	At the bottom of each page.
Group Header	Print the group title/value.	At the top of each group.
Group Footer	Print aggregate calculations for each group.	At the bottom of each group.
Detail	Print the fields from each record.	Once for every record.

Figure 6-49 is an example of how the report sections appear in *Design* view. This report contains two group headers and group footers: one for the *City* field and one for the *Construction* field.

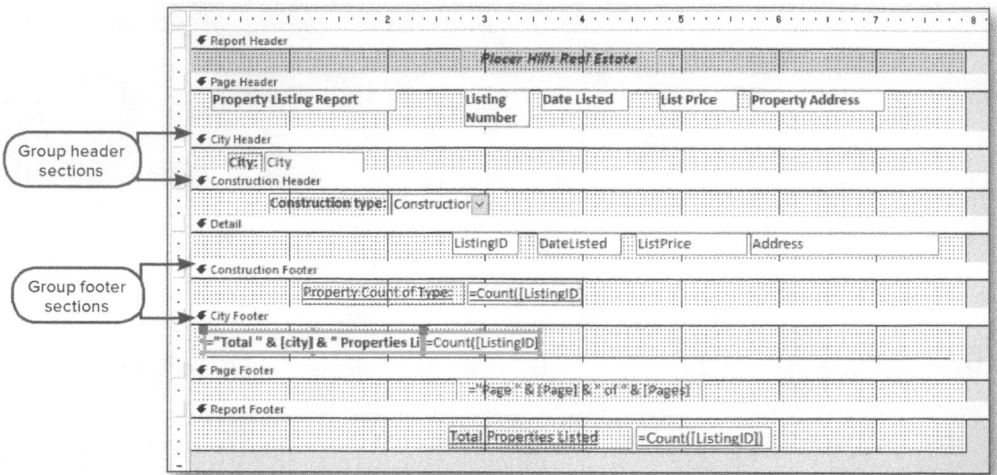

6-49 *Design* view of report with two *Group Header* and *Group Footer* sections

Figures 6-50, 6-51 and 6-52 show pages of the same report in *Print Preview* view.

Figure 6-50 shows page 1, which illustrates the *Report Header*, *Page Header*, *Group Header*, *Group Footer*, *Detail*, and *Page Footer* sections.

Figure 6-51 illustrates that only the *Page Header*, and not the *Report Header*, appears on subsequent pages.

Figure 6-52 shows the *Report Footer* displays only on the last page.

The page header and footer and the report header and footer work as matched sets. For example, when you add a page header you also add a page footer. However, if you don't need one of those sections, you can leave it empty and even reduce the space allocated to the section.

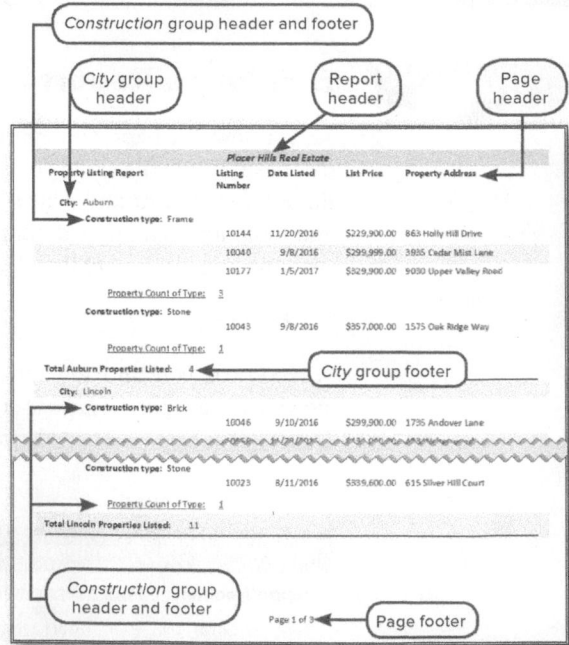

6-50 *Print Preview* view of report, page 1

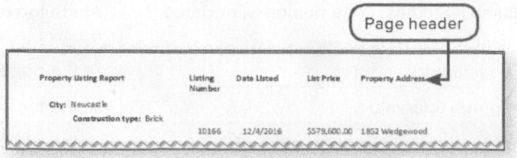

6-51 *Print Preview* view of report, page 2

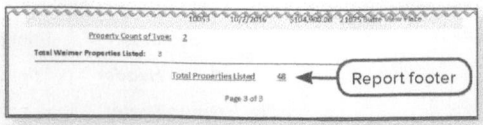

6-52 *Print Preview* view of report, page 3

Add or Delete Page and Report Sections in Design View

When you create a report in *Design* view, Access automatically includes *Page Header*, *Detail*, and *Page Footer* sections. You can add or remove sections in a report as needed.

> **HOW TO: Add or Delete Page and Report Sections**

1. Open the report in *Design* view.
2. Right-click to open the context menu.
3. Select either the **Page Header/Footer** or **Report Header/Footer** option (Figure 6-53). This selection works as a toggle.
 - If the specified header or footer is on the report and you select it, Access deletes the sections.
 - If the section is not on the report, Access adds the section.

6-53 Context menu

Add or Delete Group Sections in Design View

As you learned in Chapter 4, a report can have more than one *Group Header* and *Group Footer* section if you have multiple fields on which you want to group. Additionally, you add the *Group Header* and *Group Footer* sections independently, so you are not required to have both. Refer back to *SLO 4.6: Grouping, Sorting, and Totals* for additional information about working with group sections.

> **HOW TO: Add Group Sections**

1. Open the report in *Design* view.
2. Click the **Group & Sort** button [*Report Design Tools Design* tab, *Grouping & Totals* group] to open the *Group, Sort, and Total* pane at the bottom of the report.
3. Select the **Add a group** option in the *Group, Sort, and Total* pane.
4. Select the desired field on which to group from the field list.
 - The *Group Header* section is added to the report.
 - The *Group, Sort, and Total* pane updates to show how the report is being grouped.
5. Click the **More** button in the *Group, Sort, and Total* pane to display the available options shown in Figure 6-54.

6-54 Options in the *Group, Sort, and Total* pane

6. Click the **without a footer section** drop-down arrow and select **with a footer section** to add a *Group Footer* section.
7. Close the *Group, Sort, and Total* pane by clicking the **X** on the *Group, Sort, and Total* pane header. Be careful not to click the *Delete* button inside the pane or you will remove the group.

> **HOW TO: Delete Group Sections**

1. Open the report in *Design* view.
2. Click the **Group & Sort** button [*Report Design Tools Design* tab, *Grouping & Totals* group] to open the *Group, Sort, and Total* pane at the bottom of the report.

3. Click to select the **Group on** row of the desired field (Figure 6-55) if you have multiple grouping levels in the report.

4. Click the **More** button in the *Group, Sort, and Total* pane to display the available options.

6-55 Select the *Group on* row of the desired field

5. Choose the desired section to delete.

- To delete both the *Group Header* and *Group Footer* sections, click the **Delete** button at the far right of the *Group on* row.
- To delete only a *Group Header* section, change the *with a header section* option to **without a header section**.
- To delete only a *Group Footer* section, change the *with a footer section* option to **without a footer section**.

6. Close the *Group, Sort, and Total* pane by clicking the **X** on the *Group, Sort, and Total* pane header. Be careful not to click the *Delete* button inside the pane or you will remove the group.

Create a Report in Design View

Creating a report in *Design* view provides you with the most flexibility. After you create the report, you can edit it to add the fields, labels, or other controls that you need. You can also add or remove sections on the report, as you just learned.

- To create a report in *Design* view, click the **Report Design** button [*Create* tab, *Reports* group] (Figure 6-56). A new report opens.

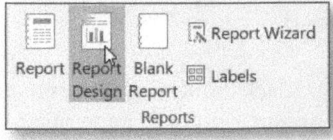

6-56 *Report Design* button

After you create the report, you are ready to start adding items to the report. It is important you save the new report and any changes made to it.

> **MORE INFO**
>
> *Design* view can be used to edit reports created in *Design* view or reports created using one of the other report tools discussed in Chapter 4.

Understand the Report Data Source

The ***Record Source*** property of a report regulates which database fields are available in the report. When a report is first created in *Design* view, the *Record Source* property is blank. When a record source is assigned, all of the fields that are included in the record source become accessible to the report. This allows you to reference the contents of a field without including it on the report. For example, consider a report in the Placer Hills database in which the *Listings* table is the record source. A text box on the report contains a formula to calculate the potential commission of a property listing. This formula uses the *ListPrice* field from the table; however, that field is not displayed in the report. Because the field is accessible through the record source, the calculation works correctly.

▶ HOW TO: Assign a Data Source to a Report

1. Open the report in *Design* view.
2. Press **F4** to open the *Property Sheet*.
3. Click the **Data** tab.
4. Click the **Record Source** property drop-down arrow and select the table or query (Figure 6-57).

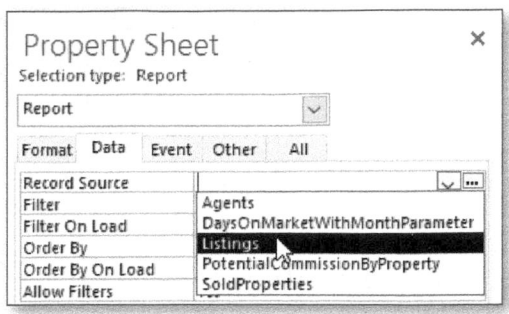

6-57 *Record Source* property can be set to a table or query

After setting the *Record Source* property, you can add fields to the report.

In *Design* view, you can also add table fields directly to the report from the **Field List** without first setting the *Record Source* property. In this case, Access automatically sets the value of the *Record Source* property to an embedded query (Figure 6-58), written in *SQL*. Recall that *SQL* stands for *Structured Query Language*, the underlying language in a relational database system. You will learn more about *SQL* in *SLO 9.6: Using SQL*.

6-58 Embedded *SQL* query is created when you add table fields directly to a report

An embedded query automatically updates as you add and remove fields from the report. Only the fields that are included in the embedded query are accessible to the report. You can also add fields to an embedded query to make them accessible without having to add them as a field on the report.

▶ HOW TO: Edit an Embedded Query in a Record Source

1. Open the report in *Design* view.
2. Press **F4** to open the *Property Sheet*.
3. Click the **Data** tab.
4. Select **Report** in the *Selection type* box.
5. Click the **Build** button in the *Record Source* property box (Figure 6-58) to open the *Query Builder* (Figure 6-59). The embedded query displays.
6. Add or remove any fields in the query. If needed, you can add or remove tables from the query design grid.
7. Save the query.
8. Click the **Close** button to close the *Query Builder*.

6-59 *Design* view of the embedded query

If a table is assigned as the *Record Source* of a report, be cautious about clicking the *Build* button. Access asks if you want to create a query based on the table. If you proceed to open the *Query Builder*, the report may become unstable unless all of the fields currently displayed in the report are added into the query source.

Add and Delete Fields in Design View

Usually, one of the first tasks in building a report is to add the data fields. The data fields can come from tables or queries.

▶ **HOW TO: Add Fields in Design View**

1. Open the report in *Design* view.
2. Click the **Add Existing Fields** button [*Report Design Tools Design* tab, *Tools* group] if the *Field List* is not open.
 - If a table or query is assigned in the *Record Source* property, the *Field List* displays the available fields.
 - If the *Record Source* property is empty, or you want to see fields in other tables, click the **Show all tables** link.
 - To add fields from an existing query, you must first enter the query name in the *Record Source* property of the report.
3. Click the **plus sign** next to the desired table name to display the fields, if necessary.
4. Double-click the desired field name to add it.
 - The field is added into the *Detail* section.
 - The most recently added field is highlighted with an orange border.
5. Add the remaining fields. You can either continue to double-click each field name or you can click and drag a field from the *Field List* into the report window (Figure 6-60).

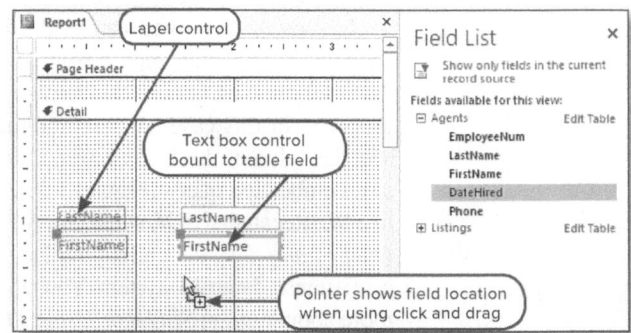

6-60 Click and drag a field from the *Field List* to the report

When you add a field into a report, both a control bound to the table field and a label are created (Figure 6-60). Visually, the label has a transparent background while the control bound to the data field has a white background. Most of the controls are text boxes, but some are combo boxes or check boxes depending on the data type of the field. Recall that a label displays the name of the field if a value has not been entered into the *Caption* property. In *Design* view, the bound control displays the field name.

▶ **HOW TO: Delete a Field in Design View**

1. Open the report in *Design* view.
2. Select the **bound control** of the field to delete.
3. Right-click to open the context menu and select the **Delete** option.

When you delete a bound control, the label associated with that control is deleted as well. You can, however, select just the label to delete only the label from the report.

Create a Parameter Report

You have learned about using parameter queries to increase the efficiency and flexibility of your database. By creating a parameter report, you can also apply those benefits to the reports in your database. A ***parameter report*** asks the user to enter the specific criteria value for a field when the report is run. This allows you to create one report but have the contents

displayed vary based on the value of the parameter that is entered. Recall that the parameter text is enclosed inside square brackets in the criteria row of the desired field. Refer back to *SLO 3.6: Creating and Using a Simple Parameter Query* if you need a review on working with parameters.

If a *parameter query* has already been created, you can assign that query to the *Record Source* property of the report. When you view the report, the *Enter Parameter Value* dialog box displays, allowing you to enter the desired value. If a parameter query does not exist, in *Design* view you can open the *Query Builder* of the *Record Source* property to add a parameter to the report.

▶ HOW TO: Add Parameters to a Report Not Based on a Parameter Query

1. Open the report in *Design* view.
2. Press **F4** to open the *Property Sheet*.
3. Choose **Report** in the *Selection type* box.
4. Click the **Record Source** property drop-down arrow on the *Data* tab and then click the **Build** button to open the *Query Builder*. If the report *Record Source* property contains a table:
 - Access displays a dialog box asking if you want to create a query based on the table
 - Click **Yes** to create a query.
 - Add all of the fields that are used in the report into the query design grid.
5. Enter the parameter into the *Criteria* box of the desired parameter field.
6. Save and close the *Query Builder*.
 - The next time the report displays, the *Enter Parameter Value* dialog box opens.

SLO 6.5

Customize a Report in Design View

After adding the required fields, you typically will want to enhance the design of the report. Common improvements include adding titles and page numbers. As appropriate, you may also want to change the size or font of fields or the size or color of sections. The information you learned in Chapter 4 about using *Layout* view to modify reports, and even forms, can be applied to making modifications in *Design* view.

Many times the modification can be made either by directly editing the control or section or by changing the corresponding property on the *Property Sheet*. The choice often depends on the precision needed, and both methods will be introduced in this section. For example, if you need a text box to be exactly 1" wide you should set the value in the *Width* property. If you just need it big enough to show the data, use the sizing handles to change the width.

Add a Control to a Report

One of the first modifications you often make is to add controls not associated with table fields. You can add *controls* such as text boxes, labels, images or lines to a report. Remember that each control you add to a report is assigned a default name that combines the type of control along with a sequential number, such as *Text3*, *Label10* or *Line8*.

> ▶ **HOW TO:** Add a Control to a Report

1. Open the report in *Design* view.
2. Click the desired control button [*Report Design Tools Design* tab, *Controls* group].
3. Move the pointer to the desired location on the report, and then click, hold, and drag to draw the control on the report.
 - For a label control, you must enter the caption into the label or Access will delete the control.
 - A text box control added from the *Controls* group is not bound to a data source.

Adjust the Size of a Control

As you continue to work with the report, you may find that you need to adjust the size of the controls. You can either use the sizing handles or set the *Height* or *Width* properties to change the size.

> ▶ **HOW TO:** Change the Size of a Control

1. Open the report in *Design* view.
2. Select the control.
3. Move your pointer to the border over a sizing handle. The pointer changes to the resize arrow.
4. Click, hold, and drag the **resize arrow** to change the size.
5. Release the pointer.

> ▶ **HOW TO:** Change the Size of a Control with the Property Sheet

1. Open the report in *Design* view.
2. Open the *Property Sheet* and click the **Format** tab.
3. Select the control.
4. Enter the new measurement in the *Width* property.
5. Enter the new measurement in the *Height* property.

Move a Control

Often you need to move a control from one location to another. You can either use the move arrow to drag the control or set the *Top* or *Left* properties to change the location. Note that the value entered into the *Top* property is relative to the particular section. For example, you can have a text box in the *Report Header* section with a .25" value in the *Top* property and a text box in the *Detail* section with a .25" value in the *Top* property. The .25" indicates the distance from the top of that section.

> ▶ **HOW TO:** Move a Control

1. Open the report in *Design* view.
2. Select the control to move.
3. Move your pointer to the border. The pointer changes to the move arrow.
4. Click, hold, and drag to move the control to the new location.
5. Release the pointer.

 MORE INFO

If you are trying to swap the exact location of two controls you will need to move the first one to a temporary location. You then move the second control to the original location of the first control, before completing the permanent move of the first control.

▶ HOW TO: Move a Control with the Property Sheet

1. Open the report in *Design* view.
2. Open the *Property Sheet* and click the **Format** tab.
3. Select the control.
4. Enter the value for distance from the top margin of the section in the *Top* property.
5. Enter the value for the distance from the left margin in the *Left* property.

 MORE INFO

Remember that the values in the *Top* or *Left* property are relative to the section where the control is located. You must consider the size of other sections in the report to know the true position on the report. Consider a report containing a *Report Header* section and a *Detail* section. The *Report Header* section has a height of .5". A control in *Detail* section with a *Top* property value of .25" will be located .75" from the top of the page.

Change the Font Characteristics of a Control

You can easily change the default font used in a label or text box using the font options in the *Report Design Tools Format* tab, *Font* group.

▶ HOW TO: Change the Font Options of a Control

1. Open the report in *Design* view.
2. Select the control.
3. Click the **Report Design Tools Format** tab.
4. Click the desired options in the *Font* group (Figure 6-61).

6-61 Font formatting options

▶ HOW TO: Change Font Options with the Property Sheet

1. Open the report in *Design* view.
2. Open the *Property Sheet* and click the **Format** tab.
3. Select the control.
4. Click the **Font Name** property drop-down arrow and select the desired font.
5. Click the **Font Size** property drop-down arrow and select the desired size.
6. Click the **Text Align** property drop-down arrow and select the desired alignment.
7. Click the **Font Weight** property drop-down arrow and select the desired weight.

8. Click the **Font Underline** property drop-down arrow and select *Yes* or *No*.
9. Click the **Font Italic** property drop-down arrow and select *Yes* or *No*.
10. Click the **Fore Color** property drop-down arrow and select the desired color.

Change the Height of a Section

Many times the initial size of a section is larger or smaller than you need it to be. Additionally, as you add controls into a section or modify the sizes of various controls, you may need to adjust the height of a section. In particular, you should pay attention to the height of the detail section since that section repeats once for each record in the report. Figure 6-62 shows the *Design* and *Print Preview* views of a report. Compare the increased height of the *Detail* section in the *Design* view in Figure 6-63 and how much additional space is required in the *Print Preview* view. If you are printing many records, this could make a significant difference in how many pages are in the report.

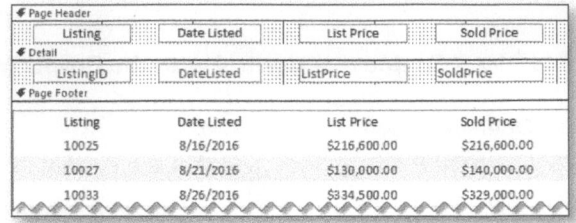

6-62 *Design* view and *Print Preview* view of a report

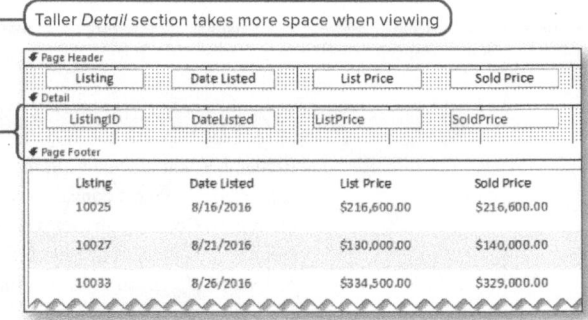

6-63 *Design* view and *Print Preview* view of a report with a larger *Detail* section

▶HOW TO: Change the Height of a Section

1. Open the report in *Design* view.
2. Move your pointer to the lower border of a section.
 - The pointer changes to the resize arrow (Figure 6-64).
 - In Figure 6-64 the size of the *Detail* section is being adjusted.
 - If a section does not have any space in it, such as the *Report Footer* section, move your pointer to the bottom of the section bar.
3. Click, hold, and drag the **resize arrow** to increase or decrease the height of the section.
 - A black horizontal line moves with your pointer to indicate the new height.
 - If a section does not contain any controls, you can adjust the height of that section not to have any space in it, as shown in Figure 6-65.

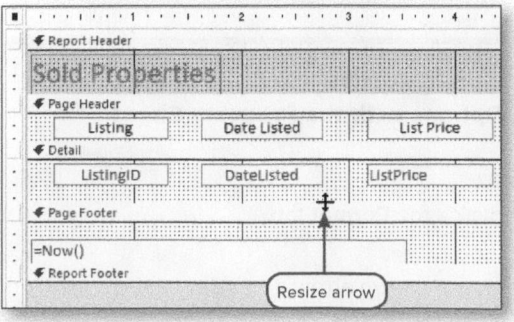

6-64 Adjust the size of report sections by dragging the resize arrow

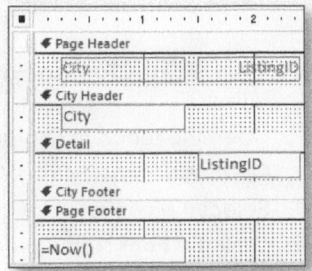

6-65 The *City Footer* section does not have any space

▶ **HOW TO: Change the Height of a Section with the Property Sheet**

1. Open the report in *Design* view.
2. Open the *Property Sheet* and click the **Format** tab.
3. Click to select the desired section header on the report. The section header updates to a black background.
4. Enter the new measurement in the *Height* property.

Change Formatting Properties of a Control

Many modifications to a control can be made directly on the control or by setting a property of the control. However, some modifications can only be made in the *Property Sheet*.

Recall that the specific properties vary by the type of control, but many controls share common formatting properties. The common properties, available on the *Format* tab of the *Property Sheet*, are described in the following table:

Formatting Properties of a Control

Property	Description
Format	Set the way the field displays in the control. Choices include *Number, Currency, Date, Time,* and *Percent*.
Decimal Places	Set a fixed number of decimal places to display.
Visible	Determines whether a control shows in *Report* view or *Print Preview* view of a report.
Back Color	Set the fill color of a control.
Border Style	Set the type of border, if any, that displays around a control.
Border Width	Set the width of the border.
Border Color	Set the color of the border.
Fore Color	Set the font color.

Change Multiple Controls Simultaneously

If you want to perform the same modification on several controls, select them all before performing the change. For example, to apply bold format to all of the text boxes, select all of the text boxes and then click **Bold** [*Report Design Tools Format* tab, *Font* group].

▶ **HOW TO: Select Multiple Controls**

1. Open the report in *Design* view.
2. Select the first control.
3. Press and hold the **Shift** key.
4. Click to select the additional controls. All of the selected controls are highlighted in orange.

You can also click the ruler to quickly select multiple horizontally or vertically aligned controls.

▶ **HOW TO:** Select Multiple Controls Using the Ruler

1. Open the report in *Design* view.
2. Move your pointer over the ruler. The selection pointer appears.
 - Use the vertical ruler to select multiple horizontally aligned controls.
 - Use the horizontal ruler to select multiple vertically aligned controls.
3. Click the selection pointer.
 - On the vertical ruler, all of the controls to the right of where you clicked are selected (Figure 6-66).
 - On the horizontal ruler, all of the controls below where you clicked are selected.

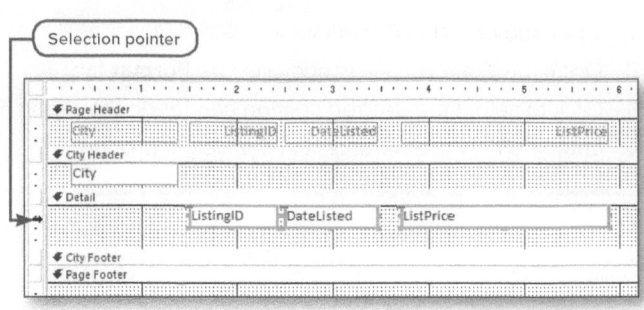

6-66 Click the selection pointer over the ruler to select multiple controls

When multiple controls are selected, the *Selection Type* in the *Property Sheet* displays *Multiple selection*. Once the controls have been selected, apply the desired changes by modifying the control or entering a new value in the desired property.

Use the Size/Space Button with Multiple Controls

The *Size/Space* button allows you to set the size or the spacing of a group of controls. For example, with the *Size* options you can change all the controls to match the tallest or widest of the group. The *Spacing* options allow you to easily adjust the horizontal or vertical spacing between the controls.

▶ **HOW TO:** Adjust the Size or Spacing of Multiple Controls with the Size/Space Button

1. Open the report in *Design* view.
2. Select all of the controls to adjust. The selected controls are highlighted in orange.
3. Click the **Size/Space** button [*Report Design Tools Arrange* tab, *Sizing & Ordering* group] (Figure 6-67) to open the *Size/Space* menu (Figure 6-68).
4. Select the desired size or spacing option.

6-67 *Size/Space* button

6-68 *Size/Space* menu

Use the Align Button with Multiple Controls

To align multiple controls to the same reference point, use the *Align* button. For example, if you want all of the text boxes to be aligned to the one furthest to the left, select them all and choose the *Left* alignment option.

> **HOW TO: Adjust the Alignment of Multiple Controls with the Align Button**

1. Open the report in *Design* view.
2. Select all of the controls to adjust. The selected controls are highlighted in orange.
3. Click the **Align** button [*Report Design Tools Arrange* tab, *Sizing & Ordering* group] (Figure 6-69) to open the *Align* menu (Figure 6-70).
4. Select the desired option.

6-69 *Align* button

6-70 *Align* menu options

SLO 6.6

Using Calculated Controls on a Report

A **calculated control** contains an expression in the *Control Source* property. You can use calculated controls to show the results of a mathematical equation, an aggregate function, or a text-based equation. You can use a calculated control in any report section. While there are several controls you can use as calculated controls, the most common choice is a text box. In *SLO 3.7: Adding Calculated Fields to a Query*, you learned how to use a calculated field in a query. The basics of what you learned will help you in this section.

Understand and Perform Calculations

Access evaluates expressions with the standard order of operations. Follow these rules when you enter an expression into a control:

- Enter the expression directly into the *Control Source* property [*Property Sheet Data* tab].
- If you need more space to enter the expression, you can open the *Expression Builder* or *Zoom* window.
- Start each expression with an equals sign.
- Assign a name to the control in the *Name* property [*Property Sheet Other* tab].
- Enclose any fields used in the expression inside square brackets [].
- If you include a function in the expression, such as *DatePart()* or *UCase()*, you must follow the usage rules for that function.

The expression is visible inside the control when the report is in *Design* view, and it also displays in the *Control Source* property if the *Property Sheet* is displayed (Figure 6-71). However, most expressions are longer than the size of the control. This means that you cannot read the entire expression in either the control or the property box. For example, in Figure 6-71 you cannot read the entire formula, which is =[SoldPrice]/[ListPrice]. To see the entire expression, use the *Expression Builder* or *Zoom* window.

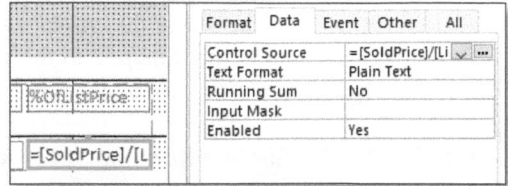

6-71 Expression displays inside the control and in the *Control Source* property box

Any fields you use in the expression must be included in the query or table used as the record source of the report. Fields that you have added onto the report are automatically included in the record source. Occasionally, you have an expression that needs to reference a field that you don't want to display on the report. In this case, you can either edit the *Record Source* property and add the field into the query or you can add the field to the report but set the *Visible* property to *No*.

You can place calculated controls in any section of a report. However, if you use an aggregate function in a control, the result of the calculation depends on where the control is placed. Recall that aggregate functions, such as *Sum* or *Count*, perform calculations over a group of records. An example of an expression using the *Count* aggregate function is =*Count*([*ListingID*]). If the control containing that formula is in a group header or group footer, the function aggregates the value of only the records that are in that group. For example, if the report is grouped by city, the *Count* function counts the total number of listings in each city. If the control is in a report header or report footer, the function aggregates the value of all the records in the report. In the previous example, the *Count* function would count the total number of listings. Do not include aggregate functions in the *Page Header* or *Page Footer* sections. If you do, an error results when you try to view the report.

Use a Running Total

A *running total* is a field that gets its value by accumulating a total over a set of records. You can use a running total field to show a running balance, cumulative total, or counting. A running total is not the same as an aggregate function. With a running total, a value shows for each record instead of just the overall total value at the end of a group.

- To create a running total, use the ***Running Sum*** property of the text box. The property has three possible values:
 - *No* is the default value in this property, indicating that the text box is not a running total.
 - *Over Group* accumulates the total within the same group level. When a new group starts, the value is reset.
 - *Over All* accumulates the total across all of the records in the report.

- Set the ***Control Source*** property of the text box to the field name you wish to accumulate. If necessary, you can also enter an expression in the *Control Source* property.

 In the sample report in Figure 6-72, the *Cumulative Repair Cost* is a running total. The *Control Source* is the *RepairCost* field. The *Running Sum* property is set to *Over Group*. Notice that when the group switches from the first *EquipID* to the second *EquipID*, the *Cumulative Repair Cost* resets.

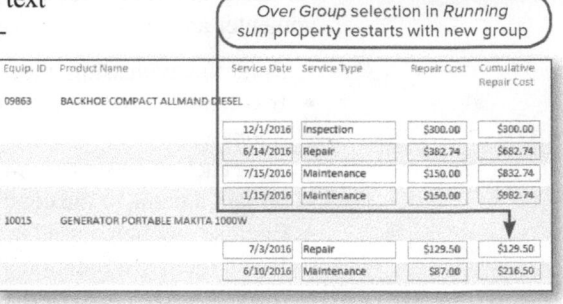

6-72 Sample report with a running total

▶ **HOW TO: Calculate a Running Total in a Text Box Control**

1. Open the report in *Design* view.
2. Add a **text box** control to the report.
3. Open the *Property Sheet* of the text box and click the **Data** tab.
4. Enter the field name to total, or an expression, in the *Control Source* property.
5. Click the **Running Sum** property box, click the **drop-down arrow** and select either **Over Group** or **Over All** (Figure 6-73).
6. Set additional properties on the *Format* tab to modify the way the control displays.
7. Enter a name for the text box in the *Name* property on the *Other* tab.

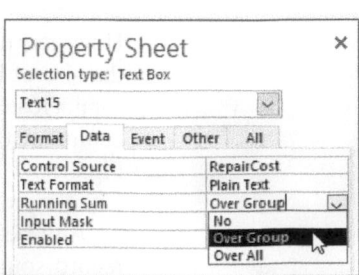

6-73 *Running Sum* property options

Number Rows in a Report

One good way to use a running total is to number the rows in a report (Figure 6-74). For the report sample shown, the text box control has the following *Property Sheet* settings:

- *Control Source* property [*Data* tab]: = *1*
- *Running Sum* property [*Data* tab]: *Over All*
- *Border Style* property [*Format* tab]: *Transparent*
- *Font Weight* property [*Format* tab]: *Bold*
- *Format* property [*Format* tab]: *. (Note that this property contains a period.)*

Listings

	ListingID	Date Listed	List Price
1.	10022	7/11/2016	$337,600.00
2.	10023	8/11/2016	$339,600.00
3.	10024	8/14/2016	$675,000.00

6-74 Running sum used to number rows

▶ **HOW TO: Use a Running Total to Number Rows in a Report**

1. Open the report in *Design* view.
2. Add a **text box** control to the report.
3. Open the *Property Sheet* of the text box and click the **Data** tab.
4. Enter =1 in the *Control Source* property.
5. Click the **Running Sum** property box, click the **drop-down arrow** and select either **Over Group** or **Over All**, depending on if you want the row numbers to restart with each group.
6. Type a period (.) in the *Format* property if you want the row numbers to be followed by periods.
7. Set additional properties on the *Format* tab to modify the way the control displays.
8. Enter a name for the text box in the *Name* property on the *Other* tab.

Concatenate Text Data

Concatenation combines different parts of an expression using the **&** operator. In a report, you may wish to concatenate different fields to improve the way the results appear. For example, combining the first and last name, or the city, state, and ZIP code together, can produce a more readable report. In Figure 6-75, the *FirstName* and *LastName* fields display as individual fields and also together because they are concatenated in the *Agent Name* text box. The text boxes use a solid border to help illustrate field sizes and how concatenation affects the resulting display.

6-75 The *FirstName* and *LastName* fields are concatenated to create the *Agent Name*

A concatenated expression can combine fields from a table or query, along with constants. Include a constant, such as a specific word or punctuation mark inside quotation marks. Recall that a constant is a hard coded value.

Examples of concatenation formulas include:

=[FirstName] & " " & [LastName]
=[City] & ", " & [State] & " " & [Zip]

Remember that you must include all required spacing and punctuation within the formula. For example, the & " " & part of the first formula example inserts a blank space between the first and last names while the & ", " & part of the second example formula inserts a comma and a blank space between the city and state.

▶ **HOW TO:** Use a Concatenation Formula in a Control

1. Open the report in *Design* view.
2. Add a **text box** control to the report.
3. Open the *Property Sheet* of the text box and click the **Data** tab.
4. Enter the concatenation expression in the *Control Source* property. As desired, click the **Build** button to open the *Expression Builder*.
5. Enter a name for the text box in the *Name* property on the *Other* tab.

Potential Problems with Concatenation Formulas

A common problem in writing concatenation formulas is misspelling the field names. If fields are misspelled, when you try to view the report in *Layout* view, *Report* view, or *Print Preview* view, an *Enter Parameter Value* dialog box displays. Remember that sometimes you have created a query where the dialog box should display when you run the query. However, if you are not expecting an *Enter Parameter Value* dialog box to display, pay attention to the name of the parameter displayed in the dialog box. In the example shown in Figure 6-76, the dialog box expects a value for *FistName*. Dialog boxes such as this one can help you determine what is wrong with the formula; in this case, the field name should have been *FirstName*.

6-76 Check the name of the parameter if you are not expecting an *Enter Parameter Value* dialog box

Hide Repeated Values

Sometimes, when you view a report, you see repeated values. Consider a report that shows property information sorted by city. Since grouping has not been done, the report in Figure 6-77 repeats the city name in each record. You can set the ***Hide Duplicates*** property so repeated values are hidden in the report, as shown in Figure 6-78.

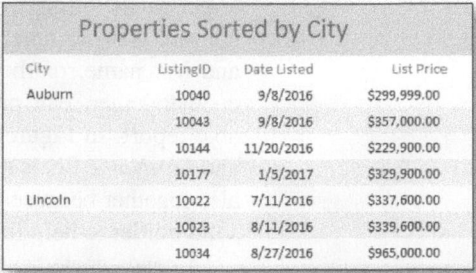

Properties Sorted by City			
City	ListingID	Date Listed	List Price
Auburn	10040	9/8/2016	$299,999.00
Auburn	10043	9/8/2016	$357,000.00
Auburn	10144	11/20/2016	$229,900.00
Auburn	10177	1/5/2017	$329,900.00
Lincoln	10022	7/11/2016	$337,600.00
Lincoln	10023	8/11/2016	$339,600.00
Lincoln	10034	8/27/2016	$965,000.00

6-77 *City* field without hiding duplicates

Properties Sorted by City			
City	ListingID	Date Listed	List Price
Auburn	10040	9/8/2016	$299,999.00
	10043	9/8/2016	$357,000.00
	10144	11/20/2016	$229,900.00
	10177	1/5/2017	$329,900.00
Lincoln	10022	7/11/2016	$337,600.00
	10023	8/11/2016	$339,600.00
	10034	8/27/2016	$965,000.00

6-78 *City* field with duplicates hidden

▶ **HOW TO:** Hide Repeated Values in a Report

1. Open the report in *Design* view.
2. Select the text box of the field that contains duplicate values.
3. Open the *Property Sheet* of the text box and click the **Format** tab.
4. Select **Yes** in the *Hide Duplicates* property.

PAUSE & PRACTICE: ACCESS 6-2

For this Pause & Practice, you create a report for the Placer Hills Real Estate database in *Design* view that uses a parameter query as the data source. You modify the design of the report to improve its appearance. Next, you modify an existing report by adding two calculated fields and modifying several controls on the report.

File Needed: *[your initials] PP A6-1.accdb*
Completed Project File Name: *[your initials] PP A6-2.accdb*

1. Open the *[your initials] PP A6-1* database file that you created in *Pause & Practice 6-1.*

2. Save a new copy of your database as [your initials] PP A6-2.

3. Enable content in the database.

4. Create a report in *Design* view, assign a data source, and add fields.
 a. Click the **Report Design** button [*Create* tab, *Reports* group] to open a new report.
 b. Click the **Property Sheet** button [*Report Design Tools Design* tab, *Tools* group] if the *Property Sheet* is not open.
 c. Click the **Data** tab if necessary.
 d. Click the **drop-down arrow** in the *Record Source* property and select **DaysOnMarketWithMonthParameter** to assign the query as the data source for the report.
 e. Click the **Add Existing Fields** button [*Report Design Tools Design* tab, *Tools* group] to open the *Field List*.
 f. Double-click the **ListingID** field to add it to the report.
 g. Add the following additional fields into the *Detail* section of the report: **DateListed, ListPrice, City** and **DaysOnMarket**. The layout should be similar to that shown in Figure 6-79.
 h. Close the *Field List* pane.
 i. Save the report as DaysOnMarketListing.

5. Modify the location of the fields and adjust the size of the *Detail* section.
 a. Click to select the **ListingID** text box.
 b. Press and hold the **Shift** key.
 c. Click to select the text boxes of the remaining fields. Each field should be surrounded by an orange border.
 d. Click the **Tabular** button [*Report Design Tools Arrange* tab, *Table* group]. The layout should change as shown in Figure 6-80.
 e. Click anywhere in the **Detail** section to deselect the controls.
 f. Click the **Property Sheet** button [*Report Design Tools Design* tab, *Tools* group] if the *Property Sheet* is not open and click the **Format** tab if necessary.
 g. Click to select the **ListingID** text box.

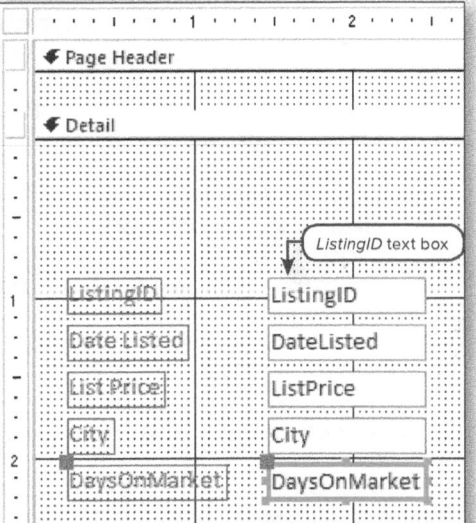

6-79 *Design* **view of report after adding fields**

6-80 **Tabular layout of fields**

h. Enter .05" in the *Top* property. All of the text boxes in the layout move to the top of the section. When entering property values, don't worry if Access slightly changes a few of the values (for example, .05" becomes .0521".)

i. Click the **Detail** section bar.

j. Enter .3" in the *Height* property.

k. Move your pointer to the right edge of the *Detail* section. The pointer changes to the resize arrow.

l. Widen the report to **8"**.

m. Click to select the **ListPrice** text box.

n. Press and hold the **Shift** key and select the **ListPrice** label.

o. Enter 1.2" in the *Width* property.

6. Add *Report Header* and *Report Footer* sections and edit those sections.

a. Right-click inside the report to open the context menu.

b. Select the **Report Header/Footer** option. The *Report Header* and *Report Footer* sections display on the report.

c. Click the **Report Header** section bar.

d. Enter .5" in the *Height*.

e. Click the **Back Color** property, click the **Build** button and select the **Orange, Accent 2, Lighter 80%** color (sixth column, second row of the *Theme* colors).

f. Close the *Property Sheet*.

7. Add a label into the *Report Header* and page numbers into the *Page Footer* sections.

a. Click the **Label** button [*Report Design Tools Design* tab, *Controls* group].

b. Move the pointer into the *Report Header* section and click to add the label.

c. Type Days on Market Report into the label. Click anywhere outside the label.

d. Click the **Page Numbers** button [*Report Design Tools Design* tab, *Header/Footer* group]. The *Page Numbers* dialog box opens.

e. Select the **Page N of M** radio button in the *Format* area and the **Bottom of Page [Footer]** radio button in the *Position* area.

f. Click **OK**. The page number is added to the report.

g. Click to select the **label** in the *Report Header* section.

h. Click to select the **Report Design Tools Format** tab.

i. Type 14 in the *Font size* [*Report Design Tools Format* tab, *Font* group], and click the buttons for **Center** alignment and **Italic** formatting.

j. Adjust the size of the label as needed so the entire label text displays.

k. Move the label so the left edge is approximately at **3"**. The *Design* view of the report should be similar to Figure 6-81.

l. Save the report.

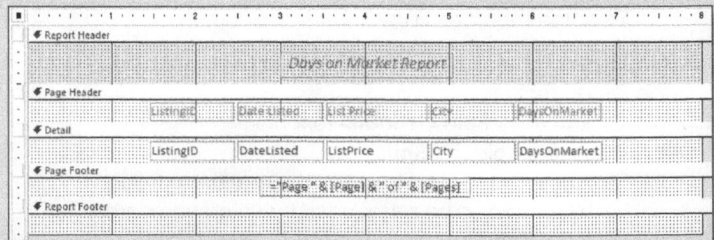

6-81 *Design* view of *DaysOnMarketListing* report

8. Test the report.

a. Switch to *Print Preview* view of the report. The *Enter Parameter Value* dialog box displays.

b. Enter 9 and click **OK**. The report should execute and look similar to the report shown in Figure 6-82. Remember that the values in the *DaysOnMarket* field differ depending on the day you run the report.

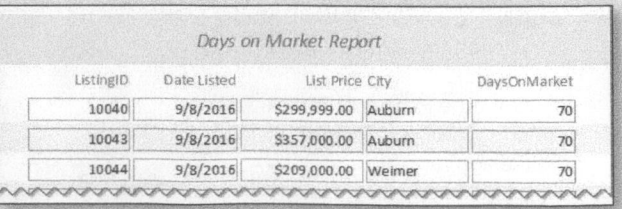

6-82 *Print Preview* view of report

 c. Close the *Print Preview*.
 d. Close the report.

9. Double-click the **SoldPropertiesListing** report to open it in *Report* view. The report should display the nine records that are in the *SoldProperties* table.

10. Change to *Design* view of the *SoldPropertiesListing* report.

11. Add calculations into two text boxes, format those text boxes, and change the captions of their labels.
 a. Click the **Property Sheet** button [*Report Design Tools Design* tab, *Tools* group].
 b. Change the *Selection type* to **Report** if necessary.
 c. Click the **Data** tab. Verify that the *Record Source* contains the table name *SoldProperties*.
 d. Select the **Unbound** text box to the right of the *SqFt* text box.
 e. Click the **Other** tab and type BedsBaths in the *Name* property.
 f. Click the **Data** tab and then click the **Build** button in the *Control Source* property.
 g. Enter =[Beds]&"/"&[Baths] in the *Expression Builder* and click **OK**. As you are typing, the *Intellisense* tool suggests the field names. Either select them from the list or continue typing them yourself.
 h. Select the **Unbound** text box to the right of the *SoldPrice* text box.
 i. Click the **Other** tab and type %OfListPrice in the *Name* property.
 j. Click the **Data** tab and then click the **Build** button in the *Control Source* property.
 k. Type =[SoldPrice]/[ListPrice] in the *Expression Builder* and click **OK**.
 l. Click the **Format** tab of the *Property Sheet*.
 m. Select **Percent** in the *Format* property.
 n. Select the **Text32** label control.
 o. Change the *Caption* property [*Format* tab] to % of List Price. Be sure to press **Enter** after typing the contents to have Access recognize the change.
 p. Enter 1" in the *Width* property.
 q. Select the **Text22** label.
 r. Change the *Caption* property [*Format* tab] to Beds/Baths.
 s. Close the *Property Sheet*.
 t. Save the report.

12. Modify the formatting of multiple controls simultaneously.
 a. Click to select the **ListingID** text box.
 b. Press and hold the **Shift** key, and then select the seven additional text boxes in the *Detail* section.
 c. Click the **Center Alignment** button [*Report Design Tools Format* tab, *Font* group]. You may need to click the button twice.
 d. Move your pointer over the vertical ruler to the left of the *Page Header* section, and then click the selection pointer to select all of the labels in the *Page Header* section.
 e. Click the **Center Alignment** button [*Report Design Tools Format* tab, *Font* group]. You may need to click the button twice.
 f. Click the **Underline** button and change the *Font Color* to **Black**.
 g. Click anywhere in the report to deselect the labels. The *Design* view of the report should look similar to Figure 6-83.
 h. Save the report.

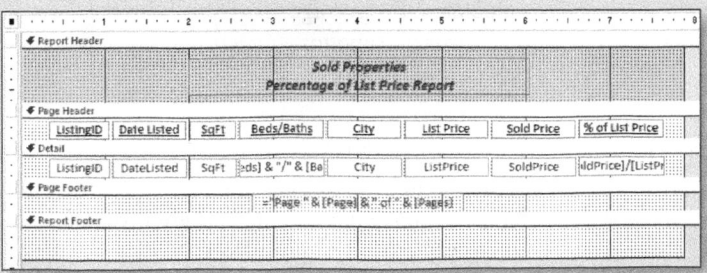

6-83 *Design* view of completed *SoldPropertiesListing* report

13. Test the report.
 a. Switch to *Print Preview* view of the report.
 b. The report should execute and look similar to Figure 6-84.
 c. Close the *Print Preview* and close the report.

14. Close the database.

	Sold Properties **Percentage of List Price Report**							
ListingID	Date Listed	SqFt	Beds/Baths	City	List Price	Sold Price	% of List Price	
10025	8/16/2016	1900	4/3	Rocklin	$216,600.00	$216,600.00	100.00%	
10027	8/21/2016	1184	3/2	Roseville	$130,000.00	$140,000.00	107.69%	
10033	8/26/2016	1840	2/2	Rocklin	$334,500.00	$329,000.00	98.36%	

6-84 *Print Preview* view of completed *SoldPropertiesListing* report

SLO 6.7

Using Subreports

Sometimes you need to create a report that shows data from tables that have a one-to-many relationship. For example, you may want to see a report of the Placer Hills Real Estate agents that also includes some data about the agents' current property listings. In this section, you learn how to use a subreport to accomplish this task.

Understand Subreports

A *subreport* is a report inserted within another report. To work correctly, there must be a relationship between the two reports. Typically, the reports represent the different sides of a one-to-many relationship. The report from the "one" side of the relationship is the *main report*, while the report from the "many" side of the relationship is the subreport.

You create the main report and subreport as two separate reports. Then you add the subreport to the main report. Once you add the subreport, it still exists as a separate object. The main report, however, contains both the original "one" side fields from the main report, plus all of the "many" side fields on the subreport.

Before you create a subreport, you need to plan the design of the finished report. Determine what tables or fields will be on the main report and what tables or fields will be on the subreport. Figure 6-85 shows an example of a finished report in which the agent information is in the main report and the property information is in the subreport. This subreport also calculates the average list price with an aggregate function.

	Placer Hills Real Estate **Agents and Current Listings**				
Employee ID 103	**Agent** Simon Bidou		**Phone** (530) 648-7689		
ListingID	Date Listed	List Price	Address	City	Built
10022	7/11/2016	$337,600.00	525 Riverdale	Lincoln	2001
10030	8/24/2016	$389,900.00	1720 Grey Owl Circle	Roseville	2002
10040	9/8/2016	$299,999.00	3935 Cedar Mist Lane	Auburn	1993
10077	10/13/2016	$625,000.00	2286 Kingfisher Lane	Lincoln	2003
10080	10/15/2016	$274,000.00	1089 Marseille Lane	Roseville	2007
10095	10/27/2016	$299,800.00	3115 Capistrano Way	Rocklin	1979
	Average List Price $371,049.83				
Employee ID 127	**Agent** Kelly Weatherby		**Phone** (916) 987-3756		
ListingID	Date Listed	List Price	Address	City	Built
10023	8/11/2016	$339,600.00	615 Silver Hill Court	Lincoln	2000
10048	9/10/2016	$350,000.00	900 Coyote Mountain Drive	Weimer	1963

6-85 Main report with a subreport

Create a Report That Includes a Subreport

You can build both the main report and the subreport using any of the report tools that you have learned. Three main tasks are involved in creating a report that includes a subreport:

1. Create the main report.
2. Create the subreport.
3. Add the subreport to the main report.

You can build the main report and the subreport in any order, but the most common approach is to build the main report first.

▶ **HOW TO:** Create a Main Report in Design View

1. Click the **Report Design** button [*Create* tab, *Reports* group] to open a new report.
2. Click the **Property Sheet** button [*Report Design Tools Design* tab, *Tools* group].
3. Click the **Data** tab.
4. Click the **drop-down arrow** in the *Record Source* property and select the table or query containing the data from the "one" side of the relationship.
5. Click the **Add Existing Fields** button [*Report Design Tools Design* tab, *Tools* group] to open the *Field List*.
6. Add the desired fields into the *Detail* section.
7. Adjust the height of the *Detail* section, but be sure to leave some space in the section for the subreport.
8. Right-click to open the context menu.
9. Select the **Report Header/Footer** option to add *Report Header* and *Report Footer* sections to the report.
10. Add a **label** into the *Report Header* section, as desired.
11. Add page numbers into the report, as desired.
12. Format any of the controls as desired to add/remove borders, adjust font characteristics, etc.
13. Save and close the report.

Figure 6-86 shows a main report in *Design* view.

6-86 *Design* view of a main report

The second task is to create the subreport. It is common to use a tabular layout for the fields. In these cases, a quick starting point is to create the initial report with the *Report* tool and then to modify it using both *Layout* view and *Design* view.

Controls in the *Page Header* or *Page Footer* sections of a subreport do not display once you add the subreport onto the main report.

▶ **HOW TO: Create a Subreport**

1. Select the table that contains the data from the "many" side of the relationship.
2. Click the **Report** button [*Create* tab, *Reports* group] to open a new report in *Layout* view.
3. Delete any fields that are not necessary by selecting the field, right-clicking to open the context menu, and selecting **Delete Column**.
4. Adjust the width of any fields by selecting the field and using the sizing handles.
5. Switch to *Design* view.
6. Select all of the controls in the *Report Header* section and delete them.
7. Select all of the label controls in the *Page Header* section.
8. Click the **Move Up** button [*Report Design Tools Arrange* tab, *Move* group].
9. Delete the page number control from the *Page Footer* section.
10. Right-click to open the context menu.
11. Select the **Page Header/Footer** option to delete the *Page Header* and *Page Footer* sections.
12. Adjust the width of the.report.
13. Format any of the controls as desired to adjust the size, add or remove borders, adjust font characteristics, etc.
14. Save the report using a combination of the table name and the word subreport. This helps you identify the report later.
15. Close the report.

A subreport in *Design* view is shown in Figure 6-87.

6-87 *Design* view of a subreport

The last task is to insert the subreport into the main report. Be sure that the *Use Control Wizards* option is selected [*Report Design Tools Design* tab, *Controls* group] before starting this activity. Use the *Subform/Subreport* button to launch the **SubReport Wizard** to add the subreport. The *SubReport Wizard* steps you through the process of adding a subreport into a main report.

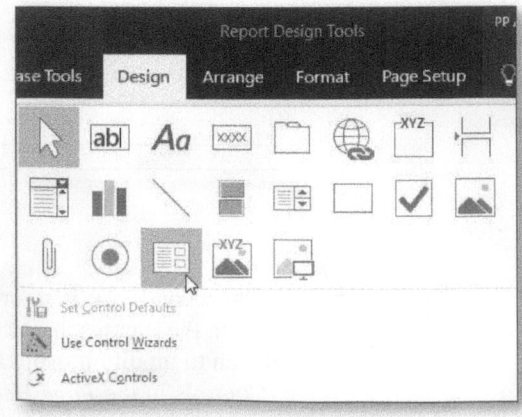

▶ **HOW TO: Add an Existing Subreport into a Main Report**

1. Open the main report in *Design* view.
2. Click the **Subform/Subreport** button [*Report Design Tools Design* tab, *Controls* group] (Figure 6-88).
3. Click inside the *Detail* section of the main report, in the upper left of where you want to position the subreport. The *SubReport Wizard* launches.

6-88 *Subform/Subreport* button

4. Select the **Use an existing report or form** radio button (Figure 6-89).
5. Select the name of the subreport from the list and click **Next**.
 - The next page of the wizard prompts you to choose how to link the subreport to the main report (Figure 6-90).
 - If there are fields in common, the wizard displays a statement that shows how the tables are related.

6-89 *SubReport Wizard*, step one

6-90 *SubReport Wizard*, step two

6. Accept the **Choose from a list** radio button and the default linking statement, and then click **Next**.
7. Accept the suggested name for the subreport and click **Finish**. The subreport is added into the main report (Figure 6-91).

6-91 Subreport added into the main report

8. Switch to *Layout* view (Figure 6-92). Verify that the subreport is correctly linked to the main report. Scroll down to verify that each grouping displays only the records that are associated with that group.

9. Save and close the report.

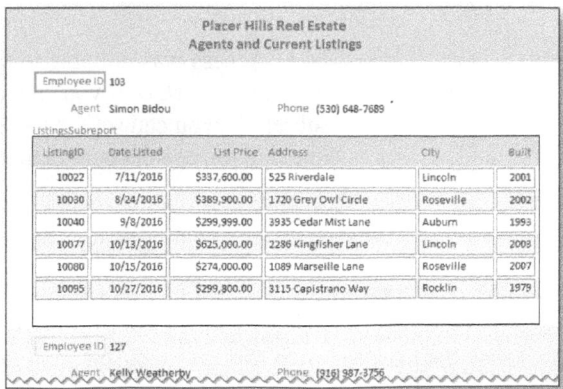

6-92 Verify that the subreport is correctly linked to the main report in *Layout* view

Instead of first creating a subreport, launch the SubReport Wizard and add a table or query into the main report. Access creates the subreport object for you and attaches it to the main report.

▶ **HOW TO:** Use a Table or Query as a Subreport in a Main Report

1. Open the main report in *Design* view.
2. Click the **Subform/Subreport** button [*Report Design Tools Design* tab, *Controls* group].
3. Click inside the *Detail* section of the main report, in the upper left of where you want to position the subreport. The *SubReport Wizard* launches.
4. Ensure that the **Use existing Tables and Queries** radio button is selected and click **Next**.
5. Select the table/query and the desired fields to use as the subreport (Figure 6-93) and click **Next**.
 - The next page of the wizard prompts you to choose how to link the subreport to the main report.
 - If there are fields in common, the wizard displays a statement that shows how the tables are related.
6. Accept the **Choose from a list** radio button and the default linking statement, and click **Next**.
7. Accept the suggested name for the subreport and click **Finish**. The subreport is added into the main report and is also created as a separate report object in the *Navigation Pane*.
8. Switch to *Layout* view. Verify that the subreport is correctly linked to the main report.
9. Save and close the report.

6-93 Select the table/query and the desired fields to use in the subreport

If Access was not able to determine the correct linking fields between the subreport and the main report, or if you created an incorrect link, you can manually establish the link. In the subreport, you can set the values of the ***Link Child Fields*** and ***Link Master Fields*** properties to make the correct connection.

▶ **HOW TO:** Set the Link Child Fields and Link Master Fields on a Subreport

1. Open the main report in *Design* view. The subreport should already have been added onto the main report.
2. Open the *Property Sheet* and click the **Data** tab, if necessary.
3. Click to select the subreport in the *Detail* section of the main report.

4. Click **Build** button in the *Link Master Fields* property box (Figure 6-94) to open the *Subreport Field Linker* dialog box (Figure 6-95).

5. Click the **Master Fields** box drop-down arrow and select the desired field, if necessary.

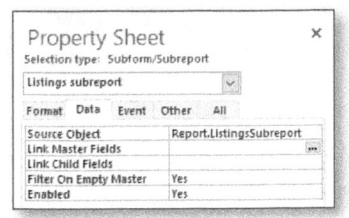

6-94 *Link Master Fields* property

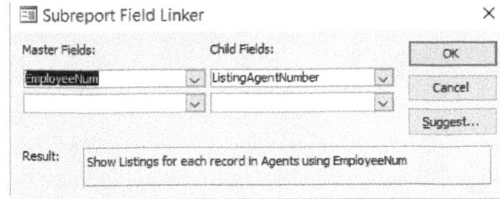

6-95 *Subreport Field Linker* dialog box

6. Click the **Child Fields** box drop-down arrow and select the desired field, if necessary.

> ### ANOTHER WAY
>
> Click the **Suggest** button to have Access attempt to determine which fields should be linked together.

7. Click **OK**.

8. Save the changes to the report.

> ### MORE INFO
>
> In some cases, you may need to edit the *Record Source* property of the subreport to include the required linking fields. Remember that the linking fields are most likely the primary key in the "one" table and the foreign key in the "many" table.

Customize the Main Report and Subreport

After you add the subreport to the main report, you should customize the overall report so that it has a professional appearance. When you open the main report, the subreport opens automatically because the objects are now attached. This allows you to edit both objects together and create a cohesive report. Alternatively, you can open the subreport separately and edit just that object.

Anticipate switching back and forth frequently between *Design* view, *Layout* view, and *Print Preview* view as you work to edit the report.

Common modifications to the report, which you already know how to do, include the following:

- Adjust the size and spacing of the text box and label controls.
- Modify font characteristics or formatting of the text boxes and label controls.
- Change the border property or back color property of the controls or sections.
- Adjust the size of the subreport or the sections on both the main report and subreport.
- Remove the label attached to the subreport.

Adding an aggregate function to a main report with a subreport involves special considerations. You can add calculated controls to a subreport using the skills you have learned. However, if you want to use an aggregate function to calculate a value over a group of records, you need to adjust the placement of that control. Your subreport most likely does not contain a *Group Header* or a *Group Footer* section. Instead, the grouping occurs as a result of the way the subreport functions when it is attached to the main report.

To use an aggregate function, place the calculation in either the *Report Header* or *Report Footer* section of the subreport. When the finished report displays, that value is calculated on each grouping in the subreport.

PAUSE & PRACTICE: ACCESS 6-3

For this Pause & Practice, you create a main report and a subreport for the Placer Hills Real Estate database. You add the subreport onto the main report and modify the design of the report to improve its appearance.

File Needed: *[your initials] PP A6-2.accdb*
Completed Project File Name: *[your initials] PP A6-3.accdb*

1. Open the *[your initials] PP A6-2* database file that you created in *Pause & Practice 6-2*.

2. Save a new copy of your database as [your initials] PP A6-3.

3. Enable content in the database.

4. Build the main report.
 a. Click the **Report Design** button [*Create* tab, *Reports* group] to open a new report.
 b. Click the **Property Sheet** button [*Report Design Tools Design* tab, *Tools* group], if necessary, to open the *Property Sheet*.
 c. Click the **Data** tab.
 d. Click the **drop-down arrow** in the *Record Source* property and select the **Agents** table.
 e. Click the **Add Existing Fields** button [*Report Design Tools Design* tab, *Tools* group] to open the *Field List*.
 f. Double-click the **EmployeeNum** and **Phone** fields to add them into the *Detail* section.
 g. Click the **Property Sheet** button [*Report Design Tools Design* tab, *Tools* group].
 h. Save the report as CurrentListingsByAgent.

5. Add a *Report Header/Footer* section and modify the report.
 a. Right-click inside the report to open the context menu.
 b. Select the **Report Header/Footer** option to add *Report Header* and *Report Footer* sections to the report.
 c. Choose **Report** in the *Selection type* box of the *Property Sheet* if necessary, and click the **Format** tab.
 d. Type 8" in the *Width* property.
 e. Click the **Report Header** section bar and enter .8" in the *Height* property.
 f. Add a **label** control into the *Report Header* section and type Placer Hills Real Estate Agents and Current Listings into the label.
 g. Select the label and enter 2.5" in the *Width* property, .5" in the *Height* property, .2" in the *Top* property, 2.75" in the *Left* property, 14 in the *Font Size* property, select **Center** in the *Text Align* property and **Bold** in the *Font Weight* property.
 h. Click the **Page Numbers** button [*Report Design Tools Design* tab, *Header/Footer* group].
 i. Select the **Page N of M** radio button, the **Bottom of Page [Footer]** radio button, and a **Center** alignment, if necessary.
 j. Click **OK**.
 k. Move your pointer to the bottom edge of the *Page Header* section, not the section bar. The pointer changes to the resize arrow. Move the **resize arrow** up to the *Page Header* section bar to remove the space in the section.
 l. Save the report.

6. Add a concatenated field and modify the *Detail* section.
 a. Add a **text box** control [*Report Design Tools Design* tab, *Controls* group] below the *Phone* field in the *Detail* section.
 b. Click the **Data** tab.
 c. Click the **Build** button in the *Control Source* property.

d. Enter =[FirstName] & " " & [LastName] in the *Expression Builder* and click **OK**.

e. Select the label that was added with the text box.

f. Click the **Format** tab of the *Property Sheet* and enter Agent in the *Caption* property, .5" in the *Width* property, 1.2" in the *Left* property, and select **Right** in the *Text Align* property. Don't worry that the label temporarily overlaps with the text box.

g. Select the **EmployeeNum** text box and enter .5" in the *Width* property, .15" in the *Top* property, and 1.8" in the *Left* property.

h. Select the *EmployeeNum* label and enter Employee ID in the *Caption* property, .9" in the *Width* property, .15" in the *Top* property, and .85" in the *Left* property, and select **Right** in the *Text Align* property.

i. Select the text box containing the concatenation formula and enter 1.5" in the *Width* property, and 1.8" in the *Left* property.

j. Press and hold the **Shift** key and select the *Agent* label. Both the concatenation formula text box and the *Agent* label are selected. Enter .5" in the *Top* property. Both controls move to the new location.

k. Select the **Phone** text box and enter 1.2" in the *Width* property, and .5" in the *Top* property, and 4.5" in the *Left* property.

l. Select the **Phone** label and enter .5" in the *Top* property, and 4" in the *Left* property.

m. Select the **Phone** text box, press and hold the **Shift** key and select the other two text boxes in the *Detail* section, and then select **Transparent** in the *Border Style* property to remove the border from these text boxes. The border displays in *Design* view but does not display when you view the report in *Report*, *Print Preview*, or *Layout* view.

n. Choose **Detail** in the *Selection type* box of the *Property Sheet* and enter 2" in the *Height* property. The report should look similar to Figure 6-96.

o. Save and close the report.

6-96 *Design view of the main report*

7. Build the subreport.

a. Select the **Listings** table.

b. Click the **Report** button [*Create* tab, *Reports* group] to open a new report in *Layout* view.

c. Select a cell in the **SqFt** column.

d. Press and hold the **Shift** key and select a cell in the **Beds**, **Baths**, and **Garage** columns, right-click inside the selected columns to open the context menu, and select **Delete Column**.

e. Select a cell in the **Construction** column.

f. Press and hold the **Shift** key and select a cell in the **Agent**, **Result**, **DateRemoved**, and **SoldPrice** columns, right-click inside the selected columns to open the context menu, and select **Delete Column**.

g. Select a cell in the **ListingID** column. Press and hold the **Shift** key and select the **ListingID** label. Enter .7" in the *Width* property.

h. Repeat this process to change the *Width* property for each of the following fields and its label: *List Price* (1.2"), *Address* (2"), *City* (1"), and *Built* (.5").

i. Switch to *Design* view.

j. Select all of the controls in the *Report Header* section and delete them.

k. Click inside the *Report Footer* section. An orange border surrounds the *EmptyCell* control that is selected. Access automatically added these controls when the report was created.

l. Right-click and select **Delete Row** from the context menu to delete these unneeded controls.

m. Select all of the label controls in the *Page Header* section.

n. Click the **Move Up** button [*Report Design Tools Arrange* tab, *Move* group].

o. Enter .25" in the *Height* property and .1" in the *Top* property.

p. Delete the **page number** control from the *Page Footer* section. You may need to scroll to the right to locate the control in the report.

q. Right-click inside the report to open the context menu.

r. Select the **Page Header/Footer** option to delete the *Page Header* and *Page Footer* sections.

s. Choose **Report Header** in the *Selection type* box of the *Property Sheet* and enter .3" in the *Height* property.

t. Choose **Report** in the *Selection type* box of the *Property Sheet* if necessary, and enter 6.7" in the *Width* property. The report should look similar to the report shown in Figure 6-97.

6-97 *Design* view of the subreport

u. Save the report as ListingsSubreport.

v. Close the report.

8. Add the subreport onto the main report.

a. Open the *CurrentListingsByAgent* report in *Design* view.

b. Click the **More** arrow at the far right of the *Controls* group [*Report Design Tools Design* tab] and verify that the *Use Control Wizards* button is selected (it will have a colored background). If it is not selected, click the **Use Control Wizards** button.

c. Click the **Subform/Subreport** button [*Report Design Tools Design* tab, *Controls* group].

d. Click inside the *Detail* section of the report, near the left border and below the fields in the *Detail* section (Figure 6-98). The *SubReport Wizard* launches.

6-98 Position the *Subform/ Subreport* icon in the report

e. Select the **Use an existing report or form** radio button.

f. Select the **ListingsSubreport** report from the list.

g. Click **Next**.

h. Accept the **Choose from a list** radio button and the highlighted **Show** statement, and then click **Next**.

i. Accept the suggested name for the subreport and click **Finish** to add the subreport to the main report.

j. Switch to *Layout* view (Figure 6-99). Verify that the subreport is correctly linked to the main report.

k. Save the report.

Placer Hills Real Estate
Agents and Current Listings

Employee ID 103

Agent Simon Bidou Phone (530) 648-7689

ListingsSubreport

ListingID	Date Listed	List Price	Address	City	Built
10022	7/11/2016	$337,600.00	525 Riverdale	Lincoln	2001
10030	8/24/2016	$389,900.00	1720 Grey Owl Circle	Roseville	2002
10040	9/8/2016	$299,999.00	3935 Cedar Mist Lane	Auburn	1993
10077	10/13/2016	$625,000.00	2286 Kingfisher Lane	Lincoln	2003
10080	10/15/2016	$274,000.00	1089 Marseille Lane	Roseville	2007
10095	10/27/2016	$299,800.00	3115 Capistrano Way	Rocklin	1979

Employee ID 127

Agent Kelly Weatherby Phone (916) 987-3756

ListingsSubreport

ListingID	Date Listed	List Price	Address	City	Built
10023	8/11/2016	$339,600.00	615 Silver Hill Court	Lincoln	2000

6-99 *Layout* view of the main report after adding the subreport

9. Customize the main report and subreport.
 a. Switch to *Design* view.
 b. Click to select the **ListingsSubreport** label.
 c. Press **Delete**.
 d. Select the subreport.
 e. Select **Transparent** in the *Border Style* property on the *Format* tab of the *Property Sheet*.
 f. Save and close the report.

10. Open the *ListingsSubreport* in *Design* view. Although you can make these changes when viewing the report through the *CurrentListingsByAgent* main report, it is easier to enter edits directly on the subreport.
 a. Add a **text box** control to the *Report Footer* section.
 b. Open the *Property Sheet* and click the **Data** tab, if necessary.
 c. Click the **Build** button on the *Control Source* property.
 d. Enter =Count([ListingID]) into the *Expression Builder* and click **OK**.
 e. Click the **Format** tab.
 f. Enter .5" in the *Width* property, .08" in the *Top* property and 6.15" in the *Left* property. When entering property values, don't worry if Access slightly changes a few of the values (for example, .08" becomes .0799".)
 g. Select the label control that was added with the text box.
 h. Click the **Format** tab of the *Property Sheet*, if necessary, and enter Total number of listings: in the *Caption* property, 1.6" in the *Width* property, .08" in the *Top* property and 4.5" in the *Left* property.

 i. Switch to *Layout* view. Because you are viewing the subreport by itself, the records are not grouped by agent. Scroll to the bottom of the report to find the text box you just added. The report should look similar to Figure 6-100.
 j. Save and close the report.

6-100 Aggregate function added to subreport

11. Open the *CurrentListingsByAgent* report in *Report* view. The completed report should look similar to the report in Figure 6-101.

12. Save and close the report.

13. Close the database.

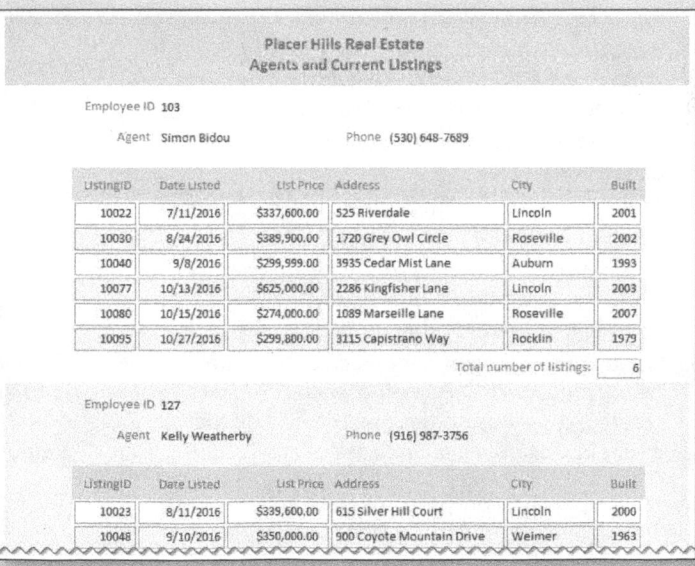

6-101 *Report* view of completed report

Chapter Summary

6.1 Understand action queries; create and use *Update*, *Append*, *Delete*, and *Make Table* queries (p. A6-370).

- You can use **action queries** to make changes to the data in a database.
- Back up your database before running an action query because action queries make permanent changes to data and cannot be undone.
- An **update query** updates data in a database.
- You can add records to an existing table with an **append query**.
- A **delete query** deletes records from a table.
- You can create a new table and copy records into that table with a **make table query**.
- To ensure your action query performs as desired, first build and test it as a normal select query, and then convert it to the desired action query.

6.2 Use the *Query Wizard* to create a crosstab query, a find duplicate records query, and a find unmatched records query (p. A6-376).

- In addition to launching the *Simple Query Wizard* to create select queries, you can use the **Query Wizard** to launch the *Crosstab Query Wizard*, the *Find Duplicates Query Wizard*, and the *Find Unmatched Query Wizard*.
- A **crosstab query** summarizes data on two dimensions.
- To locate potential duplicated data in a table, create a **find duplicates query**.
- An **unmatched records query** locates records in one table that do not have any matching records in a related table.
- While these types of queries can be created directly in *Query Design*, it is easiest to first create a query using the wizard and edit the query in *Design* view if needed.

6.3 Use the top values property, explore and use date functions, and create a query with a subquery (p. A6-383).

- Use the **Top Values** query property to limit the number of records that display in a query answer. Select from preset choices or enter your own value.
- When you use the *Top Values* property, you must sort the records in descending order on

the desired field to retrieve the top values. Use an ascending order sort to return the lowest values.

- Use the available date functions in Access to perform date arithmetic, to retrieve parts of a date, such as the year, or to retrieve the name of the month or weekday of a specific date value.
- You can use date functions in a calculated field in a query or in a text box control on a form or report.
- A **subquery** is a query that is used inside another query.

6.4 Understand report sections, build a report and add and delete fields in *Design* view, understand the data source of a report, and create a parameter report (p. A6-390).

- The sections within a report determine where and when the contents display.
- A report can contain the following sections: **Report Header**, **Report Footer**, **Page Header**, **Page Footer**, **Group Header**, **Group Footer**, and **Detail**.
- Creating a report in *Design* view allows you the most flexibility in building the report.
- The **Record Source** property specifies which database fields are available to use in a report.
- Add fields to a report by selecting them from the **Field List**.
- A **parameter report** asks a user to enter the specific criteria value each time the report is run. Add a parameter to a report by opening the *Record Source* and entering the parameter in the *Criteria* box of the desired field

6.5 Use *Design* view to add a control to a report; modify the size, location, font characteristics, and formatting properties of a control; and change properties of multiple controls (p. A6-396).

- In *Design* view, you can add **controls** to a report by selecting them from the *Controls* group on the *Report Design Tools Design* tab.
- Change the size of a control with the sizing handles or by entering a specific value in the *Height* or *Width* properties.
- Adjust the location of a control by dragging the control or by entering a specific value in the *Top* or *Left* properties.

- Modify the font characteristics of a control in the *Font* group on the *Report Design Tools Format* tab or by entering a specific value in the *Font Name*, *Font Size*, *Text Align*, *Font Weight*, *Font Underline*, *Font Italic*, or *Fore Color* properties.
- Change the height of a section with the sizing handles or by entering a specific value in the *Height* property.
- Adjust the formatting properties of a control by entering the desired value in the appropriate property located on the *Format* tab.
- Change multiple controls simultaneously by selecting all of the controls and then entering the desired value in the property.
- Use the **Align** button and the **Size/Space** button to change the size or alignment of a group of controls.

6.6 Use calculations in a control on a report, create a running total in a control, and concatenate text data in a report (p. A6-402).

- A **calculated control** contains an expression in the *Control Source* property. The most common calculation control is the text box.
- Enter the expression by typing it directly into the *Control Source* property or by opening the *Expression Builder* or *Zoom* window.
- A **running total** field accumulates a total over a set of records.

- Create a running total by setting the **Running Sum** property of the text box. Select **Over Group** to reset the total when a new group begins. Select **Over All** to accumulate a total across all the records.
- A **concatenation** formula combines the contents of fields or text boxes with constants to create a more readable value. The **&** operator combines the different pieces.
- If values in a report repeat across multiple records, you can use the **Hide Duplicates** property to hide the repeated values.

6.7 Understand when to use a subreport, create a main report and a subreport, add a subreport onto a main report, and customize a subreport (p. A6-409).

- A **subreport** is a report inserted within another report; there must be a relationship between the two reports.
- The most common situation features a **main report** that contains fields from the "one" side of a one-to-many relationship and a subreport that contains fields from the "many" side of the relationship.
- Create the main report and subreport as two separate reports. Use the **SubReport Wizard** to add a subreport onto a main report.
- To use an aggregate function in a subreport, you must place the control in either the *Report Header* or the *Report Footer* sections of the subreport.

Check for Understanding

The SIMbook for this text (within your SIMnet account), provides the following resources for concept review:

- Multiple choice questions
- Matching exercises
- Short answer questions

USING MICROSOFT ACCESS 2016

Guided Project 6-1

For this project, you enhance the functionality of the database for a friend's music collection. Recall that in Guided Project 4-1 you used the *Report Wizard* to create a report that shows all the songs on each album. For this project, you create an improved report that is grouped by artist and shows all the albums and song details. You use *Design* view to create the main report and the subreport and customize the report in *Design* view to add sections, add and edit controls, and add a running total.
[Student Learning Outcomes 6.4, 6.5, 6.6, 6.7]

File Needed: ***MusicDatabase-06.accdb***
Completed Project File Name: ***[your initials] Access 6-1.accdb***

Skills Covered in This Project

- Create a main report in *Design* view.
- Edit a report in *Design* view.
- Add a group section to a report.
- Add and edit a control in a report.

- Create a subreport using the *Report Wizard*.
- Add a subreport to a main report.
- Add totals to a subreport.
- Concatenate text data.
- Add totals to a main report

1. Open the ***MusicDatabase-06*** database from your student data files.
2. Save the database as [your initials] Access 6-1.
3. Enable content in the security warning.
4. Build the main report. To provide context for the steps in the project, view the completed report in Figure 6-106.
 a. Click the **Report Design** button [*Create* tab, *Reports* group] to open a new report.
 b. Click the **Property Sheet** button [*Report Design Tools Design* tab, *Tools* group] and the **Format** tab, if necessary.
 c. Enter 7" in the *Width* property.
 d. Click the **Data** tab.
 e. Click the **drop-down arrow** in the *Record Source* property and select the **Albums** table.
 f. Click the **Add Existing Fields** button [*Report Design Tools Design* tab, *Tools* group] to open the *Field List*.
 g. Double-click the **AlbumName** and **Artist** fields to add them into the *Detail* section.
 h. Save the report as SongListingOnAlbumsByArtist.
5. Add a group section to the report.
 a. Click the **Group & Sort** button [*Report Design Tools Design* tab, *Grouping & Totals* group] to open the *Group, Sort, and Total* pane at the bottom of the report.
 b. Select the **Add a group** option in the *Group, Sort, and Total* pane.
 c. Select the **Artist** field from the field list.
 d. Click the **More** button in the *Group, Sort, and Total* pane to display the available options (Figure 6-102).

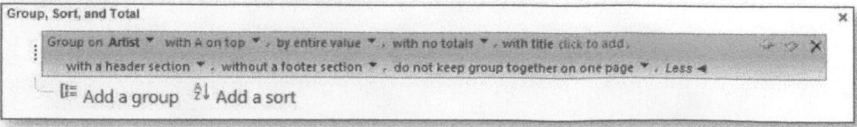

6-102 *Group, Sort, and Total* pane

 e. Change the *without a footer section* option to **with a footer section**.

 f. Change the *do not keep group together on one page* option to **keep whole group together on one page**.

 g. Close the *Group, Sort, and Total* pane by clicking the **X** on the *Group, Sort, and Total* pane header. Be careful not to click the *Delete* button inside the pane or you will remove the group.

 h. Save the changes made to the report.

6. Modify the report.

 a. Move your pointer to the bottom edge of the *Page Header* section. The pointer changes to the resize arrow. Move the **resize arrow** up to the *Page Header* bar to remove the space in the section.

 b. Right-click inside the report to open the context menu.

 c. Select the **Report Header/Footer** option to add *Report Header* and *Report Footer* sections to the report.

 d. Click inside the *Report Header* section.

 e. Press **F4** to open the *Property Sheet* and click the **Format** tab, if necessary.

 f. Enter .5" in the *Height* property.

 g. Click inside the *Artist* Header section.

 h. Enter .3" in the *Height* property.

 i. Follow the same steps to set the *Height* property of the *Artist Footer* section and *Page Footer* section to .25", and the *Detail* section to 2".

 j. Add a **label** control into the *Report Header* section and type Songs on My Albums into the label.

 k. Select the label and enter 1.8" in the *Width* property, .25" in the *Height* property, .15" in the *Top* property, 2.7" in the *Left* property, 14 in the *Font Size* property, select **Bold** in the *Font Weight* property, and **Yes** in the *Font Italic* property.

 l. Click the **Page Numbers** button [*Report Design Tools Design* tab, *Header/Footer* group].

 m. Select the **Page N of M** radio button, the **Bottom of Page [Footer]** radio button, and **Center** alignment.

 n. Click **OK**.

 o. Select the **Artist** text box. Press and hold the **Shift** key and select the **Artist** label. Both controls should be selected.

 p. Drag the **selected controls** into the *Artist Header* section. Click anywhere to deselect both controls.

 q. Select the **Artist** text box and enter 2.5" in the *Width* property, .03" in the *Top* property, and 1.5" in the *Left* property, and select **Transparent** in the *Border Style* property. When entering property values, don't worry if Access slightly changes a few of the values (for example, .03" becomes .0299".)

 r. Select the **Artist** label and enter Recording Artist in the *Caption* property, 1.1" in the *Width* property, .03" in the *Top* property, and .35" in the *Left* property.

 s. Select the **AlbumName** label and enter Album in the *Caption* property, .5" in the *Width* property, .05" in the *Top* property, and .35" in the *Left* property.

 t. Select the **AlbumName** text box and enter 3.5" in the *Width* property, .05" in the *Top* property, and 1" in the *Left* property, and select **Transparent** in the *Border Style* property. The report should look similar to Figure 6-103.

 u. Save and close the report.

6-103 *Design* view of the main report

7. Build the subreport.
 a. Click the **Report Design** button [*Create* tab, *Reports* group] to create a new report.
 b. Press **F4** to open the **Property Sheet** and click the **Format** tab, if necessary.
 c. Type 6" in the *Width* property.
 d. Click the **Data** tab.
 e. Click the **drop-down arrow** in the *Record Source* property and select the **Songs** table.
 f. Click the **Add Existing Fields** button [*Report Design Tools Design* tab, *Tools* group] to open the *Field List*.
 g. Add the **SongTitle** and **Length** fields into the *Detail* section. The *Length* text box should be selected.
 h. Press and hold the **Shift** key and select the **SongTitle** text box.
 i. Click **Tabular** [*Report Design Tools Arrange* tab, *Table* group].
 j. Press **F4** to open the *Property Sheet* and click the **Format** tab, if necessary.
 k. Enter .02" in the *Top* property.
 l. Right-click inside the report to open the context menu.
 m. Select the **Report Header/Footer** option to add *Report Header* and *Report Footer* sections to the report.
 n. Select both label controls in the *Page Header* section.
 o. Click the **Move Up** button [*Report Design Tools Arrange* tab, *Move* group].
 p. Enter .2" in the *Height* property and .02" in the *Top* property.
 q. Right-click inside the report to open the context menu.
 r. Select the **Page Header/Footer** option to delete the *Page Header* and *Footer* sections.
 s. Click the **Report Header** section bar and enter .25" in the *Height* property.
 t. Follow the same steps to set the *Height* property of the *Detail* and *Report Footer* sections to .25". The report should be similar to Figure 6-104.

6-104 *Design* view of the subreport

 u. Save the report as SongsSubreport.
 v. Close the report.

8. Add the subreport to the main report.
 a. Open the ***SongListingOnAlbumsByArtist*** report in *Design* view.
 b. Click the **Subform/Subreport** button [*Report Design Tools Design* tab, *Controls* group].
 c. Click inside the *Detail* section of the report, close to the left border, below the *Album* label. The *SubReport Wizard* launches.
 d. Select the **Use an existing report or form** radio button. The *SongsSubreport* report should be highlighted in the list.
 e. Click **Next**.
 f. Accept the **Choose from a list** radio button and the **Show Songs for each record in Album using AlbumID** statement and click **Next**.
 g. Accept the suggested name for the subreport and click **Finish**. The subreport is added into the main report.

h. Switch to *Layout* view (Figure 6-105). Verify that the subreport is correctly linked to the main report.
i. Save the report.

6-105 *Layout* view of the main report after adding the subreport

9. Customize the main report and subreport.
 a. Switch to *Design* view.
 b. Click to select the **SongsSubreport** label.
 c. Press **Delete**.
 d. Select the subreport.
 e. Enter .4" in the *Top* property, 1" in the *Left* property, and select **Transparent** in the *Border Style* property.
 f. Save and close the report.

10. Open the *SongsSubreport* in *Design* view.
 a. Open the *Property Sheet* and click the **Format** tab, if necessary.
 b. Select both the **Length** text box and label.
 c. Enter .5" in the *Width* property.
 d. Select both the **SongTitle** text box and label.
 e. Enter .2" in the *Left* property and 4.7" in the *Width* property.
 f. Select the **Report Footer** section bar and enter .3" in the *Height* property.
 g. Add a **text box** control to the *Report Footer* section.
 h. Click the **Data** tab and then click the **Build** button on the *Control Source* property.
 i. Type =Count([SongTitle]) into the *Expression Builder* and click **OK**.
 j. Click the **Format** tab, and enter .35" in the *Width* property, .02" in the *Top* property, and 4.6" in the *Left* property of the text box.
 k. Select the **label** control of that text box.
 l. Enter Total number of songs: in the *Caption* property, 1.55" in the *Width* property, .02" in the *Top* property, and 3" in the *Left* property.
 m. Save and close the report.

11. Open the *SongListingOnAlbumsByArtis*t report in *Design* view.
 a. Click the **Detail** section bar and enter 1.4" in the *Height* property.
 b. Add a **text box** control to the *Artist Footer* section.
 c. Delete the **label** control of that text box.
 d. Select the **text box**, and on the *Data* tab click the **Build** button in the *Control Source* property.
 e. Type ="Total number of albums by" & [Artist] & ":" into the *Expression Builder* and click **OK**.
 f. Click the **Format** tab, and enter 3.3" in the *Width* property, .02" in the *Top* property, .7" in the *Left* property, and select **Right** in the *Text Align* property.
 g. Add another **text box** control to the *Artist Footer* section.
 h. Delete the **label** control of that text box.
 i. Select the **text box**, and on the *Data* tab click the **Build** button in the *Control Source* property.
 j. Enter =Count([AlbumName]) into the *Expression Builder* and click **OK**.

k. Click the **Format** tab, and enter .2" in the *Width* property, .02" in the *Top* property, and 4.1" in the *Left* property, and select **Left** in the *Text Align* property.

l. Enter .25" in the *Height* property of the *Artist Footer* section.

m. Save the report.

n. Switch to *Print Preview* view. The completed report should look similar to Figure 6-106. Notice how Adele's name appears only once, at the top of both of her albums. This is because *Artist* is the grouping header.

o. Navigate to page 2 and then 3 of the report. Notice how Carly Rae Jepsen's data starts on the top of page 3 instead of at the middle of page 2. This is because *keep the whole group together on one page* is selected in the grouping options.

p. Click the **Close Print Preview** button.

q. Close the report.

12. Close the database.

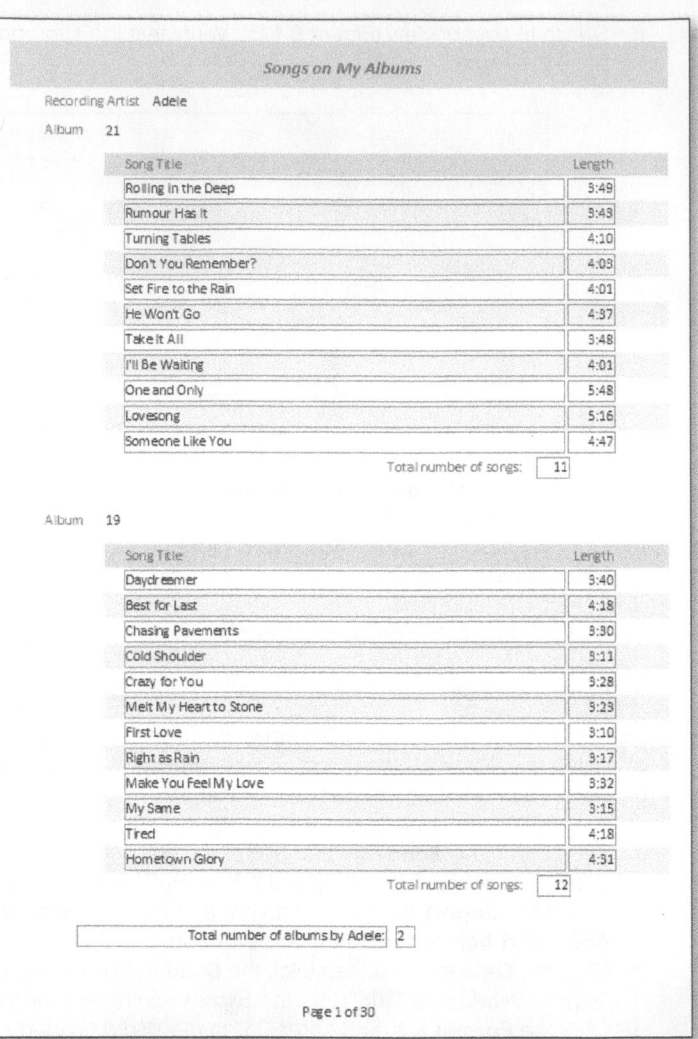

6-106 *Print Preview* view of completed report

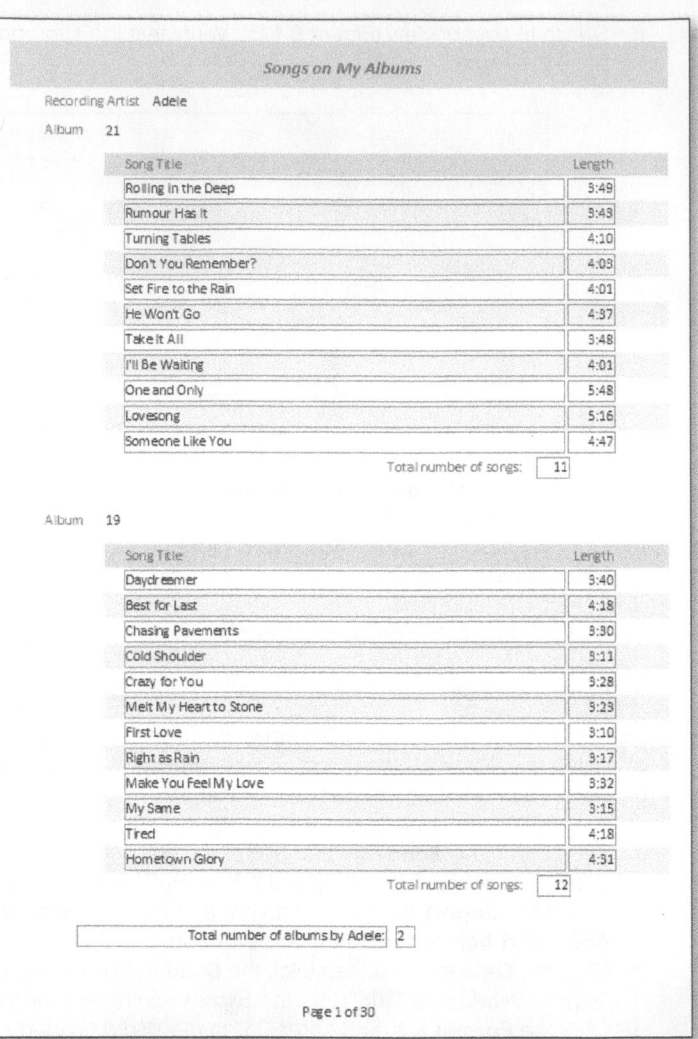

Guided Project 6-2

TextbooksRUs needs a query to find unmatched data in the database and a report to show available books in a subject area. Use the *Unmatched Query Wizard* to create a query to find which authors do not have any books included in the database. Create a query to display book information. Use *Design* view to build a report based on that query and add a parameter to the report. Finally, customize the report in *Design* view.

[Student Learning Outcomes 6.2, 6.3, 6.5]

File Needed: ***TextbooksRUs-06.accdb***
Completed Project File Name: ***[your initials] Access 6-2.accdb***

Skills Covered in This Project

- **Create a query using the** *Unmatched Query Wizard*.
- **Create a parameter report in** *Design* view.
- **Edit a report in** *Design* view.
- Hide repeated values in a report.
- Add a control to a report.
- Edit properties of a control in a report.
- Add a group section to a report.

1. Open the **TextbooksRUs-06** database from your student data files.

2. Save a new copy of your database as [your initials] Access 6-2.

3. Enable content in the security warning.

4. Build an unmatched records query to identify authors without records for books they have written.
 a. Click the **Query Wizard** button [*Create* tab, *Queries* group] to launch the *Query Wizard*.
 b. Select **Find Unmatched Query Wizard** in the *New Query* dialog box and click **OK** to launch the *Find Unmatched Query Wizard*.
 c. Select the **Author** table if necessary.
 d. Click **Next** to move to the next page of the wizard.
 e. Select the **AuthorBook** table if necessary. This table contains the related records.
 f. Click **Next** to move to the next page of the wizard. The *Matching fields* area displays *ID < = > AuthorID-FK* because these fields have already been linked via a relationship.
 g. Click **Next** to move to the next page of the wizard.
 h. Click the **Move All Fields** button to move all the fields from the *Available fields* window into the *Selected fields* window.
 i. Click **Next** to move to the last page of the wizard.
 j. Edit the suggested query name to remove spaces between the words. The query name should read AuthorWithoutMatchingAuthorBook.
 k. Click **Finish**. The query executes and displays the results of any unmatched records (Figure 6-107).

5. Edit the query.
 a. Change to *Design* view of the query. Having viewed the query results you no longer need the *Affiliation* to display.
 b. Click to select the **Affiliation** column in the design grid.
 c. Click **Delete Columns** [*Query Tools Design* tab, *Query Setup* group].
 d. Save the query.
 e. Run the query. The same records shown in Figure 6-107 display; however, the affiliation column does not show.
 f. Close the query.

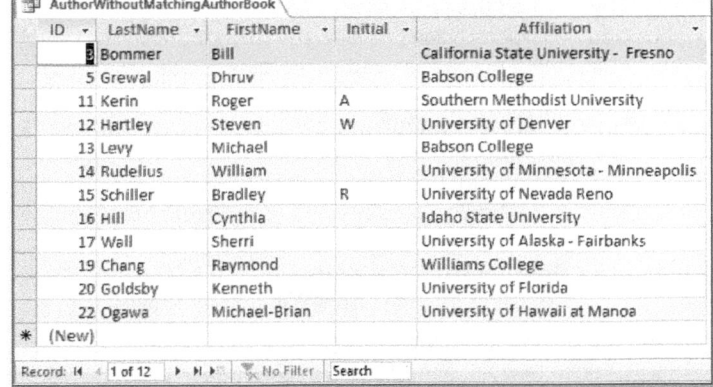

6-107 Unmatched records query results

6. Create a query to display book information.
 a. Select the **Query Design** button [*Create* tab, *Queries* group]. The *Show Table* dialog box opens with the *Author* table selected.
 b. Press and hold the **Shift** key and select the **AuthorBook** and the **Book** tables.
 c. Click **Add** to add all three tables into the query.

d. Click **Close**.

e. Add the following fields into the query design grid: **ISBN**, **Title**, **FirstName**, **LastName**, and **Subject**.

f. Click **Run** [*Query Tools Design* tab, *Results* group] to run the query. Your results should match those shown in Figure 6-108. Currently, the query results show the ISBN and title of a book each time a book has multiple authors. When you create the report you will hide the duplicated values.

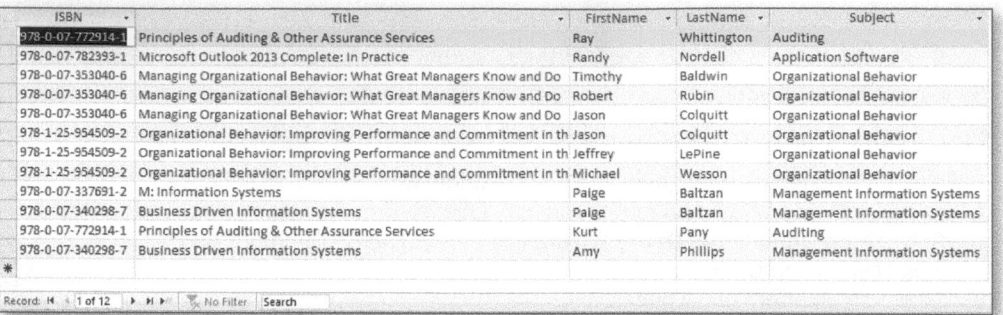

ISBN	Title	FirstName	LastName	Subject
978-0-07-772914-1	Principles of Auditing & Other Assurance Services	Ray	Whittington	Auditing
978-0-07-782393-1	Microsoft Outlook 2013 Complete: In Practice	Randy	Nordell	Application Software
978-0-07-353040-6	Managing Organizational Behavior: What Great Managers Know and Do	Timothy	Baldwin	Organizational Behavior
978-0-07-353040-6	Managing Organizational Behavior: What Great Managers Know and Do	Robert	Rubin	Organizational Behavior
978-0-07-353040-6	Managing Organizational Behavior: What Great Managers Know and Do	Jason	Colquitt	Organizational Behavior
978-1-25-954509-2	Organizational Behavior: Improving Performance and Commitment in th	Jason	Colquitt	Organizational Behavior
978-1-25-954509-2	Organizational Behavior: Improving Performance and Commitment in th	Jeffrey	LePine	Organizational Behavior
978-1-25-954509-2	Organizational Behavior: Improving Performance and Commitment in th	Michael	Wesson	Organizational Behavior
978-0-07-337691-2	M: Information Systems	Paige	Baltzan	Management Information Systems
978-0-07-340298-7	Business Driven Information Systems	Paige	Baltzan	Management Information Systems
978-0-07-772914-1	Principles of Auditing & Other Assurance Services	Kurt	Pany	Auditing
978-0-07-340298-7	Business Driven Information Systems	Amy	Phillips	Management Information Systems

Record: 1 of 12 No Filter Search

6-108 Query results

g. Save the query as BookListing.

h. Close the query.

7. Build a report using *Design* view. To provide context for the steps to build the report, view the completed report in Figure 6-112.

a. Click the **Report Design** button [*Create* tab, *Reports* group].

b. Press **F4** to open the *Property Sheet*, if necessary.

c. Click the **Data** tab.

d. Click the **drop-down arrow** in the *Record Source* property and select **BookListing** to assign the query as the data source for the report. Be sure to press **Enter** after selecting the query.

e. Click the **Add Existing Fields** button [*Report Design Tools Design* tab, *Tools* group] to open the *Field List*.

f. Double-click the **ISBN** field to add it to the report.

g. Repeat that process to add all the other fields into the *Detail* section of the report.

h. Close the **Field List** pane. The last field added into the report should be selected.

i. Press and hold the **Shift** key and select the **text boxes** of the other fields.

j. Click the **Tabular** button [*Report Design Tools Arrange* tab, *Table* group].

k. Press **F4** to open the *Property Sheet* and click to select the *Format* tab.

l. Enter .1" in the *Top* property and select **Transparent** in the *Border Style* property.

m. Click the **Detail** section.

n. Enter .8" in the *Height* property.

o. Save the report as BookListingWithSubjectParameter.

8. Add the parameter to the report.

a. Choose **Report** in the *Selection type* box of the *Property Sheet*.

b. Click the **Data** tab, click the **Record Source** property box and then click the **Build** button to open the *Query Builder*.

c. Type [Enter the desired subject area] into the *Criteria* box of the *Subject* field.

d. Save the query.

e. Close the *Query Builder*.

f. Change to *Report* view to test the report. The *Enter Parameter Value* dialog box displays.

g. Enter Management Information Systems and click **OK**. Two different books, with a total of three records, display in the results (Figure 6-109).

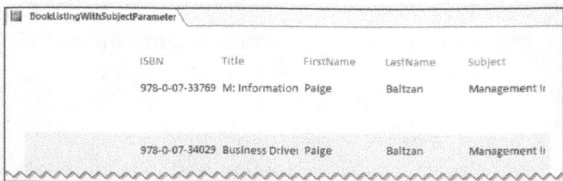

ISBN	Title	FirstName	LastName	Subject
978-0-07-33769	M: Information	Paige	Baltzan	Management I
978-0-07-34029	Business Drivei	Paige	Baltzan	Management I

6-109 Report results after adding parameter

9. Add a group section to the report.
 a. Switch back to *Design* view of the report.
 b. Click the **Group & Sort** button [*Report Design Tools Design* tab, *Grouping & Totals* group] to open the *Group, Sort, and Total* pane at the bottom of the report.
 c. Select the **Add a group** option in the *Group, Sort, and Total* pane.
 d. Select the **Subject** field from the field list.
 e. Close the *Group, Sort, and Total* pane by clicking the **X** on the *Group, Sort, and Total* pane header. Be careful not to click the *Delete* button inside the pane or you will remove the group.
 f. Save the changes made to the report.

10. Edit the *Subject Header* section.
 a. Select the **ISBN** label in the *Page Header* section.
 b. Press and hold the **Shift** key and select the remaining labels in the *Page Header* section.
 c. Click **Move Down** [*Report Design Tools Arrange* tab, *Move* group].
 d. Select the **Subject** text box in the *Detail* section.
 e. Click **Move Up** [*Report Design Tools Arrange* tab, *Move* group].
 f. Select the **Layout Indicator** to select the entire layout (Figure 6-110).
 g. Click **Remove Layout** [*Report Design Tools Arrange* tab, *Table* group].
 h. Click inside the *Subject Header* section to deselect all the items and select that section.
 i. Click the **Format** tab of the *Property Sheet* and enter .7" in the *Height* property.
 j. Select the **ISBN** label.
 k. Press and hold the **Shift** key and select the **Title**, **FirstName** and **LastName** labels.
 l. Enter .2" in the *Height* property and .4" in the *Top* property.
 m. Select the **Subject** label.
 n. Enter .6" in the *Width* property, .2" in the *Height* property, .1" in the *Top* property, and .5" in the *Left* property.
 o. Select the **Subject** text box.
 p. Enter 3" in the *Width* property, .2" in the *Height* property .1" in the *Top* property, and 1.2" in the *Left* property.
 q. Drag the **right border** of the report to **7"** wide.
 r. Save the changes made to the report. The report should look similar to Figure 6-111.

6-110 Select the *Layout Indicator*

6-111 Report after updating the *Subject Header* section

11. Improve the report design.
 a. Select the **ISBN** text box.
 b. Press and hold the **Shift** key and select the **ISBN** label.
 c. Enter 1.5" in the *Width* property, and .8" in the *Left* property.
 d. Select the **LastName** text box.
 e. Press and hold the **Shift** key and select the **LastName** label.
 f. Enter 6" in the *Left* property.
 g. Select the **FirstName** text box.
 h. Press and hold the **Shift** key and select the **FirstName** label.

i. Enter 4.9" in the *Left* property.
j. Select the **Title** text box.
k. Press and hold the **Shift** key and select the **Title** label.
l. Enter 2.3" in the *Width* property and 2.5" in the *Left* property.
m. Select the **Title** text box.
n. Enter .6" in the *Height* property.
o. Save the changes made to the report.

12. Hide the repeated values of the *ISBN* and *Title*.
 a. Select the **ISBN** text box.
 b. Press and hold the **Shift** key and select the **Title** text box.
 c. Select **Yes** in the *Hide Duplicates* property.

13. Test the report.
 a. Click the **Report View** icon on the *Status* bar. The *Enter Parameter Value* dialog box displays.
 b. Enter Management Information Systems and click **OK**. The results should match those shown in Figure 6-112.
 c. Save the report.
 d. Close the report.

14. Close the database.

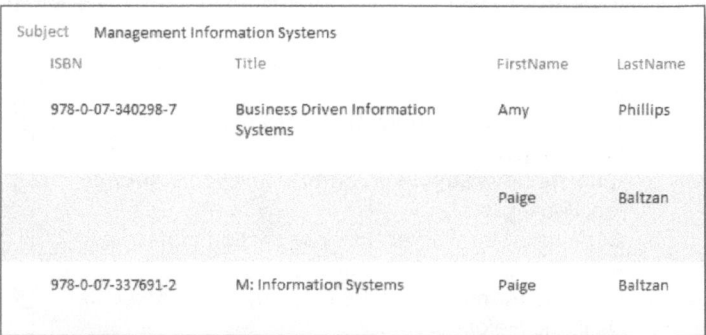

Subject	Management Information Systems			
ISBN		Title	FirstName	LastName
978-0-07-340298-7		Business Driven Information Systems	Amy	Phillips
			Paige	Baltzan
978-0-07-337691-2		M: Information Systems	Paige	Baltzan

6-112 Completed report

Guided Project 6-3

San Diego Sailing needs an update query to fix the rental dates in its database. The organization also wants a report of sailboats that have not been rented. Create an unmatched records query and then build and customize a report in *Design* view.
[Student Learning Outcomes 6.1, 6.2, 6.3, 6.4, 6.5]

File Needed: ***SanDiegoSailing-06.accdb***
Completed Project File Name: *[your initials] Access 6-3.accdb*

Skills Covered in This Project

- Create an update action query.
- Use the *DateAdd* function in a query.
- Create an unmatched records query.
- Create a report in *Design* view.

- Add *Report Header* and *Report Footer* sections.
- Add a control to a report.
- Change the font characteristics of a control.
- Adjust the size of a control.

1. Open the ***SanDiegoSailing-06*** database from your student data files.

2. Save a new copy of your database as [your initials] Access 6-3.

3. Enable content in the security warning.

4. Modify validation rule and validation text properties.
 a. Open the *SDRentals* table in *Datasheet* view. Note that all the values in the *Rental Date* column are for the year 2018. Management has realized that a data entry error was made when the records were loaded into the database and all dates entered were off by one year.
 b. Switch to *Design* view of the table.
 c. Click the **RentalDate** field. Before changing the values in this field, the *Validation Rule* must be updated.
 d. Change the *Validation Rule* property to read > =#1/1/2017#.
 e. Change the *Validation Text* property to read The Rental Date must be greater than or equal to 1/1/2017.
 f. Save the table. An Access message box displays, indicating that data integrity rules have changed. Click **Yes**.
 g. Close the table.

5. Create an update query to modify the data in the *RentalDate* field of the *SDRentals* table.
 a. Click the **Query Design** button [*Create* tab, *Queries* group] to open the *Show Table* dialog box.
 b. Double-click the **SDRentals** table to add it into the *Query Design* window.
 c. Click the **Close** button to close the *Show Table* dialog box.
 d. Double-click the **RentalDate** field to add it into the query design grid.
 e. Click the **Update** button [*Query Tools Design* tab, *Query Type* group] to convert the query to an update query. The *Sort* and *Show* rows of the select query are replaced with the *Update To* row.
 f. Enter DateAdd("m", −12, [RentalDate]) in the *Update To* box of the *RentalDate* field. The design of this *DateAdd* function will add a negative 12 months to the *RentalDate* field. The net effect is to subtract 12 months. Since the function adds to a field, the value must be written as a negative number to effectively subtract.
 g. Run the query. An Access message box displays, informing you that "*You are about to update 32 row(s)*." Click **Yes** to execute the query.
 h. Save the query as SubtractOneYearRentalDate.
 i. Close the query.

6. Open the *SDRentals* table in *Datasheet* view to verify that the dates have been changed.

7. Close the table.

8. Create a query to find the sailboats that have not been rented.
 a. Click the **Query Wizard** button [*Create* tab, *Queries* group] to launch the *Query Wizard*.
 b. Select **Find Unmatched Query Wizard** in the *New Query* dialog box and click **OK** to launch the *Find Unmatched Query Wizard*.
 c. Accept the selected **SailboatFleet** table, this is the table that may have unmatched records, and click **Next** to move to the next page of the wizard.
 d. Accept the selected **SDRentals** table, this is the table that has the related records, and click **Next** to move to the next page of the wizard. The *Matching fields* box should read *BoatID* < = > *FKBoatID* since those fields are already linked via a relationship.
 e. Click **Next** to move to the next page of the wizard.
 f. Click the **Move All Fields** button to move all the fields from the *Available fields* window to the *Selected fields* window.
 g. Click **Next** to move to the last page of the wizard.
 h. Edit the suggested query name to remove the spaces between the words. The query name should be SailboatFleetWithoutMatchingSDRentals.
 i. Click **Finish**. The query executes. Your results should match those shown in Figure 6-113.
 j. Close the query.

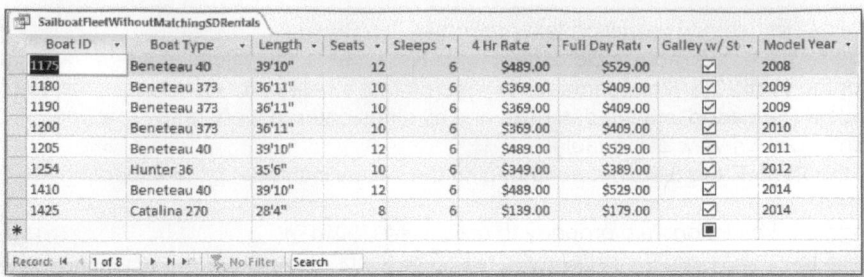

9. Create a report in *Design* view. To provide context for the steps to build the report, view the completed report in Figure 6-112.
 a. Click the **Report Design** button [*Create* tab, *Reports* group].
 b. Click the **Landscape** button [*Report Design Tools Page Setup* tab, *Page Layout* group].
 c. Press **F4** to open the *Property Sheet*, if necessary.
 d. Choose **Report** in the *Selection type*, if necessary, and click the **Data** tab.
 e. Click the **drop-down arrow** in the *Record Source* property and select **SailboatFleetWithoutMatchingSDRentals** to assign the query as the data source for the report. Be sure to press **Enter** after selecting the query.
 f. Click the **Add Existing Fields** button [*Report Design Tools Design* tab, *Tools* group] to open the *Field List*.
 g. Double-click the **BoatID** field to add it to the report.
 h. Repeat that process to add all the other fields into the *Detail* section of the report.
 i. Close the **Field List** pane. The last field added into the report should be selected.
 j. Press and hold the **Shift** key and select the **Galley w/ Stove** check box and all of the text boxes. Note that the *Galley w/ Stove* check box is to the left of its label. Be careful to select the check box and not the label.
 k. Click the **Tabular** button [*Report Design Tools Arrange* tab, *Table* group].
 l. Press **F4** to open the *Property Sheet*.
 m. Click to select the *Format* tab.
 n. Enter .15" in the *Top* property. When entering property values, don't worry if Access slightly changes a few of the values (for example, .15" becomes .1458".)
 o. Click anywhere in the report to deselect all the items.
 p. Save the report as SailboatFleetWithoutMatchingSDRentals.

10. Customize the report.
 a. Click the vertical ruler of the *Page Header* section to select all the labels.
 b. Enter .375" in the *Height* property.
 c. Select the **BoatID** text box. Press and hold the **Shift** key and select the **Boat ID** label.
 d. Enter .6" in the *Width* property and .5" in the *Left* property.
 e. Select the **BoatType** text box and label, and enter 1.3" in the *Width* property.
 f. Select the **Length**, **Seats**, **and Sleeps** text boxes and labels, and enter .5" in the *Width* property.
 g. Select the **FourHourRentalRate**, **FullDayRentalRate**, and **Galley w/ Stove** text boxes and labels, and enter .7" in the *Width* property.
 h. Select the **ModelYear** text box and label, and enter .8" in the *Width* property.
 i. Select the **Full Day Rate** and **Galley w/ Stove** labels and select **Center** in the *Text Align* property.
 j. Click the **Detail** section bar and enter .5" in the *Height* property.
 k. Choose **Report** in the *Selection type* and enter 7.5" in the *Width* property. The report should be similar to Figure 6-114.

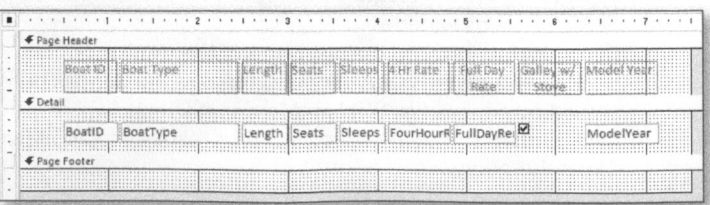

11. Add and customize *Report Header* and *Report Footer* sections.
 a. Right-click inside the report to open the context menu.
 b. Select the **Report Header/Footer** option.
 c. Click inside the *Report Header* section.
 d. Enter .5" in the *Height* property.
 e. Click inside the *Report Footer* section.
 f. Enter .5" in the *Height* property.
 g. Add a **label** control into the *Report Header* section and type Listing of Boats that have not been Rented into the label.
 h. Using the options on the *Report Design Tools Format* tab in the *Font* group, change the label font to **14 pt**. and apply **bold** and **italics**.
 i. Click the **Format** tab of the *Property Sheet*, and set the *Width* property of the label to 3.6", the *Height* property to .3", and the *Left* property to 2".
 j. Click the **Page Numbers** button [*Report Design Tools Design* tab, *Header/Footer* group].
 k. Select the **Page N of M** radio button, the **Bottom of Page [Footer]** radio button, and a **Center** alignment, if necessary.
 l. Click **OK**.
 m. Save the changes to the report.

12. Click the **Print Preview** icon on the *Status* bar to view the report. Your results should be similar to those shown in Figure 6-115.

13. Close the report.

14. Close the database.

6-115 Completed report

Independent Project 6-4

Life's Animal Shelter wants you to enhance the functionality of its database. To ensure consistency, the starting file is provided for you. First, create a make table query to build a table to store the records of adopted pets. Next, create a delete query to delete the adopted pets from the *Pets* table. Finally, add a parameter to a report, number rows in a report, and customize the report in *Design* view.
[Student Learning Outcomes 6.1, 6.4, 6.5, 6.6]

File Needed: *LifesAnimalShelter-06.accdb*
Completed Project File Names: *[your initials] Access 6-4.accdb*, *[your initials] Access 6-4-Backup. accdb*, and *[your initials] Access 6-4-Backup2.accdb*

Skills Covered in This Project

- Create a make table action query.
- Create a delete action query.
- Add a parameter to a report.
- Edit multiple controls on a report simultaneously.

- Change alignment and formatting of a control.
- Add a control to a report.
- Add a running total to number rows.
- Edit *Report Header* and *Report Footer* sections.

1. Open the **LifesAnimalShelter-06** database from your student data files.

2. Save a copy of your database as [your initials] Access 6-4.

3. Enable content in the security warning.

4. Back up your database.
 a. Open the *Backstage* view and create a backup copy of your database.
 b. Enter [your initials] Access 6-4-Backup as the file name, select the desired location, and then click the **Save** button.

5. Open the *Pets* table in *Datasheet* view to verify that the table contains 20 records. Scroll to the right and notice that some of the pets have been adopted already.

6. Close the table.

7. Create a make table query to create an *AdoptedPets* table. Refer back to *Pause & Practice 6-1* if you need additional guidance.
 a. Create a new query using the *Query Design* option.
 b. Add the **Pets** table into the *Query Design* window.
 c. Add all of the fields into the query design grid. Do not use the * symbol because you will be adding criteria.
 d. Enter "N" in the *Criteria* box of the *Available?* field.
 e. Run the query. Verify that the query finds the four pets that have been adopted (*Pet IDs 1, 3, 12*, and *14*.)
 f. Switch back to *Design* view and convert the query into a make table query.
 g. Name the table AdoptedPets.
 h. Run the query. Click **Yes** when the Access message box displays, informing you that *"You are about to paste 4 row(s) into a new table."*
 i. Save the query as MakeAdoptedPetsTable.
 j. Close the query.

8. Back up your database again. Remember, you should do this before any action that makes a permanent change to the database. Enter [your initials] Access 6-4-Backup2 as the file name.

9. Create a delete query to delete the adopted pets from the *Pets* table.
 a. Create a new query using the *Query Design* option.
 b. Add the **Pets** table into the *Query Design* window.
 c. Add the **ID**, **PetName**, and **Available?** fields into the query design grid.
 d. Enter "N" into the *Criteria* box of the *Available?* field.
 e. Run the query to verify that the query finds the same four pets that have been adopted.
 f. Switch back to *Design* view and convert the query into a delete query.
 g. Run the query. Click **Yes** when the Access message box displays, informing you that *"You are about to delete 4 row(s) from the table."*
 h. Save the query as DeleteAdoptedPets.
 i. Close the query.

10. Open the *Pets* table to verify that the table now contains only 16 records.

11. Close the table.

12. Open the *PetListingTypeParameter* report in *Report* View. The 16 pets display, grouped by the type of pet. To provide context for the steps to customize the report, view the completed report in Figure 6-116.

13. Edit the *PetListingTypeParameter* report to add a parameter.
 a. Switch to *Design* view.
 b. Open the *Property Sheet*.
 c. Change the *Selection type* to **Report**, if necessary, and open the *Query Builder* in the *Record Source* property.
 d. Click **Yes**, when prompted, to create a query based on the table.
 e. Add the **ID**, **PetName**, **Type**, **Breed**, **Age**, **Gender**, **Color**, **Details**, and **Available?** fields into the query design grid.

 f. Enter "Y" into the *Criteria* box of the *Available?* field to show only pets that are currently available. Even though all the pets in the table currently are available, those values may change in the future.

 g. Enter Like "*" & [Enter the type of pet to search for (Leave blank to search for all pet types)] & "*" into the *Criteria* box of the *Type* field. This will create a flexible parameter so users can leave the parameter blank if they wish to see all of the available pets.

 h. Save the query.

 i. Close the *Query Builder*.

 j. Save the report.

 k. Switch to *Report* view to test the changes made to the report. When prompted, enter Cat in the *Enter Parameter Value* dialog box and click **OK**. The report should show the three cats that are currently available for adoption.

14. Edit the controls in the *Type Header* section.

 a. Switch to *Design* view.

 b. Select all of the labels in the *Type Header* section. Do not select the text box that has the concatenation formula for the *Type* field.

 c. Click the **Align** button on the *Report Design Tools Arrange* tab to align all of the labels to the **Top**.

 d. Click the **Size/Space** button on the *Arrange* tab to size all of the labels using the **To Tallest** option.

 e. Change the *Fore Color* property, in the *Property Sheet*, to **Dark Blue** (the fourth column and first row of the *Standard Colors*) and the *Font Weight* property to Bold.

 f. Click anywhere in the report to deselect all of the labels.

 g. Set the *Border Style* to **Transparent** for the text box that contains the concatenation formula.

 h. Click the **Line** button [*Report Design Tools Design* tab, *Controls* group] and then click inside the *Type Header* section to the right of the text box.

 i. Select the **line control** and enter .3" in the *Left* property, 7.6" in the *Width* property, .7" in the *Top* property, and select **1 pt** in the *Border Width* property.

 j. Save the changes to the report.

15. Add a running total to number the rows.

 a. Add a **text box** control to the report below the *ID* text box in the *Detail* section.

 b. Delete the **label** that was automatically added with the text box.

 c. Select the **text box** and then click the **Data** tab.

 d. Type =1 in the *Control Source* property.

 e. Select **Over All** in the *Running Sum* property. The row numbering will not restart when a new group starts.

 f. Click to select the *Format* tab and enter a period (.) in the *Format* property, .3" in the *Width* property, .22" in the *Height* property, .05" in the *Top* property, .03" in the *Left* property, select **Transparent** in the *Border Style* property, and select **Bold** in the *Font Weight* property. When entering property values, don't worry if Access slightly changes a few of the values (for example, .22" becomes .2201".)

16. Customize the header and footer sections in the report.

 a. Click the **Report Header** section.

 b. Enter .5" in the *Height* property.

 c. Add a **label** control into the *Report Header* section and enter Listing of Available Pets by Types into the label.

 d. Select the label and enter 2.8" in the *Width* property, .3" in the *Height* property, .1" in the *Top* property, 2.5" in the *Left* property, 14 in the *Font Size* property, and select **Bold** in the *Font Weight* property.

 e. Add page numbers to the report. Select the **Page N** radio button, the **Bottom of Page [Footer]** radio button, and a **Right** alignment.

 f. Save the report.

17. Test and finalize the report.

 a. Change to *Print Preview* view to test the report. Leave the *Enter Parameter Value* dialog box empty to show all the pet types.

b. Scroll to the bottom of page 1. Notice that the header for "dogs" appears on the bottom of the page, but the records for this group start on the next page.

c. Switch back to *Design* view to adjust the grouping option.

d. Open the *Group, Sort, and Total* pane.

e. Click **More** on the *Type* group and change the *do not keep group together on one page* to **keep header and first record together on one page**. When you run the report the next time, the header for "dogs" will start on the second page along with the first dog record.

f. Close the *Group, Sort, and Total* pane.

g. Save the report.

h. Change to *Print Preview* view to test the report. Leave the *Enter Parameter Value* dialog box empty to see all the pet types. The report should resemble Figure 6-116.

i. Scroll to the bottom of page 1. Notice that the header for "dogs" no longer appears at the bottom of the page. Navigate to page 2 to see the header for "dogs" is on the second page.

j. Close the report.

18. Close the database.

Listing of Available Pets by Types

Cats Available for Adoption

	Pet Name	Pet ID	Breed	Age	Gender	Color	Why I'd make a great companion
1.	Martin	6	Domestic Short Hair cross	1 yr	M	Brown Tabby/White	I love to put my eyes and ears to work, soaking up the sights and sounds of the world around me. I'm known to make a lasting impression on everyone I meet. I like to take my time approaching new situations. While I am a bit shy with new faces and places, I warm up as I become more familiar with my environment.
2.	Bandit	16	Domestic Short Hair cross	5 yrs	M	Black/White	I'm a lovable companion seeking a special home where I'll be a cherished member of the family...
3.	Tate	8	Domestic Short Hair cross	3 yrs	M	Black/White	I'm a lovable companion seeking a special home where I'll be a cherished member of the family. With bright eyes and a precious face, I have a beautiful personality to match. I like to take my time approaching new situations. While I am a bit shy with new faces and places, I warm up as I become more familiar with my environment. **Type of home I'm looking for:** I would do best in a quiet household with older children please.

Page 1

6-116 Completed report in *Print Preview* view

Independent Project 6-5

The New York Department of Motor Vehicles wants to extend the functionality of its database. Create a crosstab query to count the number of tickets by primary factor in each city. Use the top values property in a query. Edit a main report to add a concatenation formula to a text box. Add a subreport to a main report. Customize the subreport in *Design* view and add a running total to number the rows in the report. [Student Learning Outcomes 6.2, 6.3, 6.4, 6.5, 6.6, 6.7]

File Needed: ***NewYorkDMV-06.accdb***
Completed Project File Name: ***[your initials] Access 6-5.accdb***

A6-435

Skills Covered in This Project

- Create a crosstab query.
- Find top values in a query.
- Edit multiple controls on a report simultaneously.
- Add a control to a report.

- Edit formatting properties of a control.
- Use a concatenation formula in a text box.
- Add a subreport to a main report.
- Use an aggregate function on a subreport.
- Edit *Report Header* and *Report Footer* sections.

1. Open the ***NewYorkDMV-06*** database from your student data files.

2. Save a new copy of your database as [your initials] Access 6-5.

3. Enable content in the security warning.

4. Create a crosstab query to count the number of tickets by city and primary factor.
 a. Launch the *Query Wizard* and select the *Crosstab Query Wizard*. Refer back to *SLO 6.2: Exploring the Query Wizard* if you need additional guidance.
 b. Select the **Tickets** table, on the first page of the wizard, since that contains the data you want to summarize.
 c. Move the **PrimaryFactor** field to the *Selected Fields* window, on the second page of the wizard, to use as the row headings.
 d. Select the **City** field, on the third page of the wizard, to use as the column headings.
 e. Select the **TicketNumber** field and the **Count** aggregate *function*, on the fourth page of the wizard. Leave the *Yes, include row sums* check box selected.
 f. Enter TicketsFactorCityCrosstab as the query name on the last page of the wizard. Click **Finish** to execute the query. The results should match those shown in Figure 6-117.
 g. Save and close the query.

5. Create a query to find the two most common reasons (factors) tickets are written.
 a. Open the *TicketCountByFactor* query in *Datasheet* view. The query executes and shows each of the eight primary factors along with a count of how many tickets have been written.

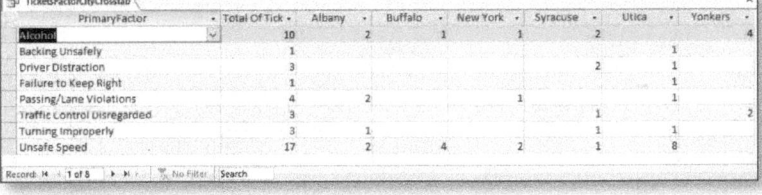

6-117 Crosstab query results showing tickets by primary factor in each city, including row sums

 b. Save a copy of that query as TopTwoTicketCountByFactor. If necessary, review the *How To: Save a Copy of an Object* in *SLO 1.2: Creating and Managing a Database*.
 c. Edit the *TopTwoTicketCountByFactor* query in *Design* view. In the *Top Values* property of the query, enter 2 to limit the query results to only the two factors that appear most frequently on all the tickets. Refer back to the *Find the Top Values in a Query* section in *SLO 6.3: Creating Advanced Queries and Changing Query Properties*, if you need additional guidance.
 d. Edit the query to not show the *TicketNumber* in the results.
 e. Save the changes to the query. Test the query. The query results should match those shown in Figure 6-118.
 f. Edit the query to change the *TicketNumber* field to an **Ascending** sort. This allows you to further explore how the sorting choice influences the query results when using the *Top Values* property.
 g. Run the query. The query now shows the two reasons that appear on the fewest number of tickets. *Failure to Keep Right* and *Backing Unsafely* should display in the results.
 h. Close the query without saving the changes since that is not what you want the query to display.

6-118 Top two ticket factors

6. Add a concatenation formula to a text box in the *OfficerTicketListing* report. To provide context for the steps to customize the report, view the completed report in Figure 6-121.
 a. Open *OfficerTicketListing* in *Design* view.
 b. Edit the unbound text box on the report. Add a concatenation formula into the *Control Source* property that will combine the *FirstName* field, a space, and the *LastName* field.
 c. Select **Transparent** in the *BorderStyle* property.
 d. Save the changes.
 e. View the report in *Report* view to ensure that the formula works correctly.

7. Add a subreport to the *OfficerTicketListing* main report. Refer back to *How To: Use a Table or Query as a Subreport in a Main Report* in *SLO 6.7: Using Subreports* if you need additional guidance.
 a. Change the *OfficerTicketListing* report to *Design* view.
 b. Use the **Subform/Subreport** button to add a subreport onto the main report. Position the subreport below the existing fields near the left side of the main report.
 c. Make sure that the **Use existing Tables and Queries** button is selected on the first page of the *SubReport Wizard*.
 d. Advance to the second page of the *SubReport Wizard* and choose the **Tickets** table and add all the fields except the *OfficerBadgeNumber* and the *RecordAddedTimeStamp* from the *Tickets* table onto the subreport.
 e. Advance to the third page of the *SubReport Wizard*, accept the **Choose from a list** radio button and the default linking statement.
 f. Advance to the last page of the wizard and edit the suggested name for the subreport so that it reads TicketsSubreport.
 g. Use *Layout* view to verify that the subreport is correctly linked to the main report. The report should look similar to Figure 6-119.
 h. Save and close the report.

6-119 *Layout* view after subreport is added to main report

8. Edit the *TicketsSubreport* in *Design* view.
 a. Open the *TicketsSubreport* in *Design* view. If needed, open the *Property Sheet*.
 b. Select the **Fine** text box and label and enter .7" in the *Width* property and 6.3" in the *Left* property.
 c. Select the **City** text box and label and enter 1.1" in the *Width* property and 3" in the *Left* property.
 d. Select the **TicketDate** text box and label and enter .8" in the *Width* property and 2.15" in the *Left* property.
 e. Select the **DLNumber** text box and label and enter .9" in the *Width* property and 1.2" in the *Left* property.
 f. Select the **TicketNumber** text box and label and enter 1" in the *Width* property and .1" in the *Left* property.
 g. Select the **PrimaryFactor** combo box and enter 2" in the *Width* property, 4.2" in the *Left* property, and select **Transparent** in the *Border Style* property.

h. Select the **PrimaryFactor** label and enter 2" in the *Width* property and 4.2" in the *Left* property.
i. In the *Caption* property of the labels, insert a space between *Ticket* and *Number*, *DL* and *Number*, *Ticket* and *Date*, and *Primary* and *Factor*.
j. Adjust all labels to be **Left** aligned.
k. Adjust the *Width* property of the report to be 7.3".
l. Adjust the *Height* property of the *Detail section* to be .3".
m. Save your changes.

9. Use an aggregate function on the subreport.
 a. Select the **Report Footer** section bar and enter .4" in the *Height* property.
 b. Add a **text box** control near the left side of the report footer of the subreport.
 c. Select the **text box** and enter =Count([TicketNumber]) in the *Control Source* property, .5" in the *Width* property, 1.35" in the *Left* property, **Transparent** in the *Border Style* property, and **Bold** in the *Font Weight* property.
 d. Select the **label** of the text box and enter Total Tickets: in the *Caption* property, .9" in the *Width* property, .4" in the *Left* property, and **Bold** in the *Font Weight* property.
 e. Save and close the subreport.

10. Edit the *OfficerTicketListing* report in *Design* view to add *Report Header* and *Report Footer* sections and ensure the report has a professional appearance.
 a. Open the *OfficerTicketListing* in *Design* view. If needed, open the *Property Sheet*.
 b. Select the **TicketsSubreport** control and change the *Width* property to 7.5", the *Left* property to .2" and the *Border Style* property to **Transparent**.
 c. Delete the *TicketsSubreport* label.
 d. Adjust the *Height* property of the *Detail section* to 1.9".
 e. Adjust the *Width* property of the report to 7.8".
 f. Add a **Report Header** and **Report Footer** section to the report.
 g. Adjust the *Height* property of the *Report Header* section to .4".
 h. Remove the *Page Header* and *Page Footer* sections from the report.
 i. Add a **label** with the *Caption* of Listing of Tickets by Officer to the *Report Header* section.
 j. Select the label and enter 2.2" in the *Width* property, .25" in the *Height* property, .08" in the *Top* property, 2.9" in the *Left* property, and 14 in the *Font Size* property. When entering property values, don't worry if Access slightly changes a few of the values (for example, .08" becomes .0799".)
 k. Adjust the *Height* property of the *Report Footer* section to .4".
 l. Add a **label** with the *Caption* of Report created by Student Name to the *Report Footer* section.
 m. Select the label and enter 2.2" in the *Width* property, .2" in the *Height* property, .08" in the *Top* property, and .15" in the *Left* property.
 n. Save the report. The completed report should look similar to Figure 6-120.

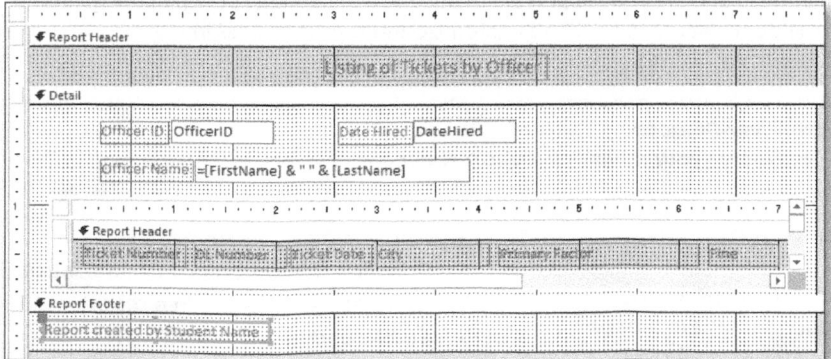

6-120 *Design* view of the completed *OfficerTicketListing* report

11. Change to *Report* view to view the completed report. Figure 6-121 shows the finished report.

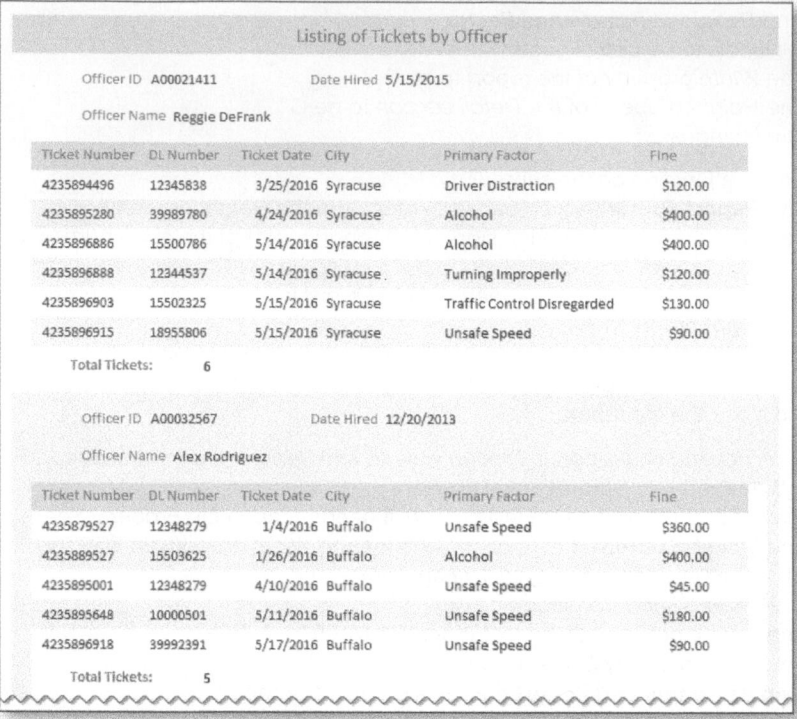

Listing of Tickets by Officer					

Officer ID A00021411 **Date Hired** 5/15/2015

Officer Name Reggie DeFrank

Ticket Number	DL Number	Ticket Date	City	Primary Factor	Fine
4235894496	12345838	3/25/2016	Syracuse	Driver Distraction	$120.00
4235895280	39989780	4/24/2016	Syracuse	Alcohol	$400.00
4235896886	15500786	5/14/2016	Syracuse	Alcohol	$400.00
4235896888	12344537	5/14/2016	Syracuse	Turning Improperly	$120.00
4235896903	15502325	5/15/2016	Syracuse	Traffic Control Disregarded	$130.00
4235896915	18955806	5/15/2016	Syracuse	Unsafe Speed	$90.00

Total Tickets: 6

Officer ID A00032567 **Date Hired** 12/20/2013

Officer Name Alex Rodriguez

Ticket Number	DL Number	Ticket Date	City	Primary Factor	Fine
4235879527	12348279	1/4/2016	Buffalo	Unsafe Speed	$360.00
4235889527	15503625	1/26/2016	Buffalo	Alcohol	$400.00
4235895001	12348279	4/10/2016	Buffalo	Unsafe Speed	$45.00
4235895648	10000501	5/11/2016	Buffalo	Unsafe Speed	$180.00
4235896918	39992391	5/17/2016	Buffalo	Unsafe Speed	$90.00

Total Tickets: 5

6-121 *Report* view of the completed report

12. Close the report.

13. Close the database.

Independent Project 6-6

American River Cycling Club wants to expand its database. To ensure consistency, the starting file is provided for you. Create a query in *Design* view to show race results for club members, and add a concatenated field to the query to combine the first and last names. Next, use *Design* view to create a report based on that query. Hide repeated values and customize the report in *Design* view.
[Student Learning Outcomes 6.4, 6.5, 6.6]

File Needed: ***AmericanRiver-06.accdb***
Completed Project File Name: *[your initials] Access 6-6.accdb*

Skills Covered in This Project

- Create a query using *Design* view.
- Use a concatenation formula in a query.
- Create a report in *Design* view.

- Add a control to a report.
- Edit formatting properties of a control.
- Hide repeated values in a report.
- Edit *Report Header* and *Report Footer* sections.

1. Open the **AmericanRiver-06** database from your student data files.

2. Save a new copy of your database as [your initials] Access 6-6.

3. Enable content in the security warning.

4. Create an *SQL* query to show race results for club members.

5. Open a new query using **Query Design**.
 a. Add both tables into the query and close the *Show Table* dialog box.
 b. Add the following fields into the query: **MemberID, City, RaceID, Place, Time, Division**, and **AgeGroup**.
 c. Save the query as MembersRaceResults.
 d. Run the query to test it. The results show 36 records.

6. Edit the query to add a concatenated field.
 a. Change back to *Design* view.
 b. Insert a column to the left of the *City* field.
 c. In the inserted column, add a calculated field to concatenate the *FirstName* and *LastName* fields using the following formula: MemberName:[FirstName] & " " & [LastName].
 d. Save the changes to the query.
 e. Run the query to test it. The results should be similar to those shown in Figure 6-122.
 f. Close the query.

7. Create a report in *Design* view. To provide context for the steps to build the report, view the completed report in Figure 6-125.
 a. Create a new report using **Report Design**.
 b. Open the *Property Sheet* and change the *Selection type* to **Report**, if necessary.
 c. Change the *Width* property to 11".
 d. Assign the **MembersRaceResults** query to the *Record Source* property.
 e. Open the *Field List*.
 f. Add all of the fields into the *Detail* section of the report.
 g. Close the *Field List* pane.
 h. Select all of the text boxes.
 i. Click the **Tabular** button on the *Arrange* tab.
 j. Click anywhere in the report to deselect all the items.
 k. Save the report as RaceResultsByMember.

6-122 *MembersRaceResults* query results

8. Customize the report.
 a. Open the *Property Sheet*, if necessary.
 b. Select the **MemberID** text box.
 c. Enter .7" in the *Width* property, .15" in the *Top* property, and .3" in the *Left* property. When entering property values, don't worry if Access slightly changes a few of the values (for example, .15" becomes .1458".)
 d. Change the **Width** of the *RaceID* text box to .4".
 e. Change the **Width** of the *Place* and *Time* text boxes to .5".
 f. Change the **Width** of the *Division* combo box to .6".
 g. Change the **Width** of the *AgeGroup* text box to 1.1".
 h. Change the **Width** of the *MemberName* text box to 1.5".

i. Change the **Width** of the *City* text box to 1.2".
j. Change the **Height** of all the labels to .4" and **Center** the alignment.
k. In the *Caption* property of the labels, insert a space between *Member* and *Name*, *Race* and *ID*, and *Age* and *Group*.
l. **Center** the alignment of the *MemberID*, *RaceID*, and *Place* text boxes and the *Division* combo box.
m. Change the **Width** of the report to 7.5".
n. Change the **Height** of the *Detail* section to .5".
o. Save the report. The design should be similar to that shown in Figure 6-123.
p. View the report in *Report* view. Notice that the records display in order of the *RaceID* field.

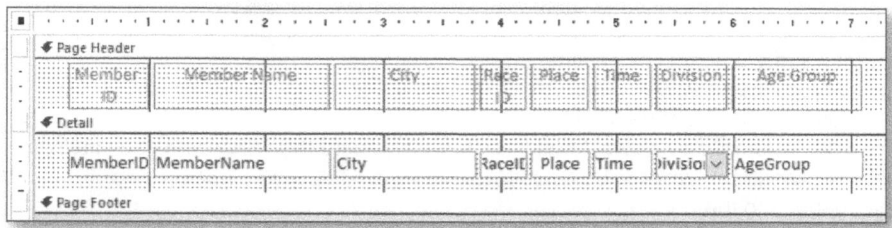

6-123 *Design* view of controls in the report

9. Change the report order and hide repeated values in the report.
 a. Change back to *Design* view.
 b. Click the **Data** tab and change the *Order By* property of the *Report* to MemberID. This causes all the records for the same member to display together.
 c. Select the **MemberID**, **MemberName** and **City** text boxes.
 d. Click the **Format** tab and change the *Hide Duplicates* property to **Yes**.

10. Add and customize *Report Header* and *Report Footer* sections.
 a. Add *Report Header* and *Report Footer* sections to the report.
 b. Change the **Height** of the *Report Header* section to .4".
 c. Add a **label** with the *Caption* of Race Results by Member to the *Report Header* section.
 d. Select the label and enter 2.2" in the *Width* property, .25" in the *Height* property, .08" in the *Top* property, 2.7" in the.*Left* property, 14 in the *Font Size* property, and **Bold** in the *Font Weight* property.
 e. Change the **Height** of the *Page Footer* section to .3".
 f. Add page numbers to the report using the **Page N of M** radio button, the **Bottom of Page [Footer]** radio button, and a **Center** alignment.
 g. Save the change to the report. *Design* view of the completed report should look similar to Figure 6-124.

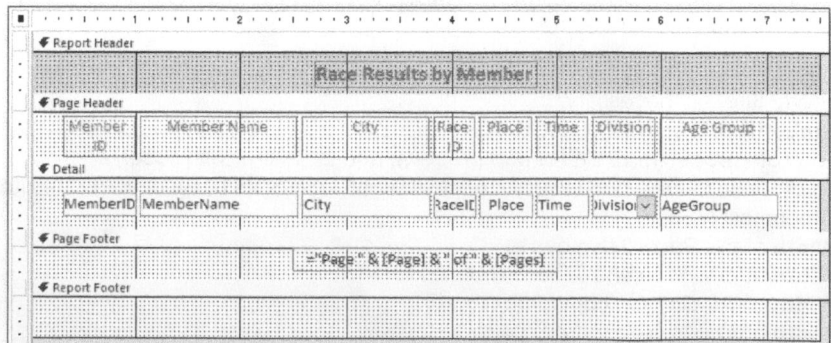

6-124 *Design* view of the completed *RaceResultsByMember* report

11. View the report in *Print Preview* view. Your results should look similar to Figure 6-125.

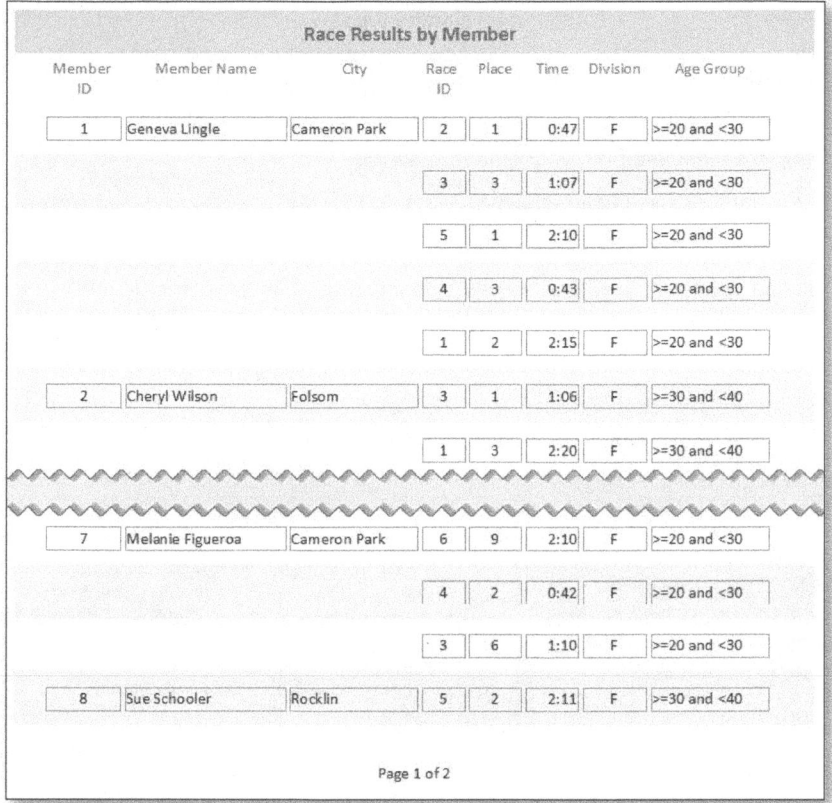

Race Results by Member							
Member ID	Member Name	City	Race ID	Place	Time	Division	Age Group
1	Geneva Lingle	Cameron Park	2	1	0:47	F	>=20 and <30
			3	3	1:07	F	>=20 and <30
			5	1	2:10	F	>=20 and <30
			4	3	0:43	F	>=20 and <30
			1	2	2:15	F	>=20 and <30
2	Cheryl Wilson	Folsom	3	1	1:06	F	>=30 and <40
			1	3	2:20	F	>=30 and <40
7	Melanie Figueroa	Cameron Park	6	9	2:10	F	>=20 and <30
			4	2	0:42	F	>=20 and <30
			3	6	1:10	F	>=20 and <30
8	Sue Schooler	Rocklin	5	2	2:11	F	>=30 and <40

Page 1 of 2

6-125 *Print Preview* view of completed report

12. Close the report.

13. Close the database.

Improve It Project 6-7

Mary's Rentals wants to improve its database. To ensure consistency, the starting file is provided for you. You improve the functionality by debugging a find unmatched query and a top values query that are not working correctly. You view and edit the *RentalsListing* report to improve the design, fix a calculated field, and add a *Group Header* section.
[Student Learning Outcomes 6.2, 6.3, 6.4, 6.5, 6.6]

File Needed: ***MarysRentals-06.accdb***
Completed Project File Name: ***[your initials] Access 6-7.accdb***

Skills Covered in This Project

- Create an unmatched query.
- Edit a top values query.
- Edit a report in *Design* view.

- Use calculated controls in a report.
- Edit properties of multiple controls simultaneously.
- Add a group section to a report.
- Add a control to a report.

1. Open the ***MarysRentals-06*** database from your student data files.

2. Save a new copy of your database as [your initials] Access 6-7.

3. Enable content in the security warning.

4. Open the *Rentals* table in *Datasheet* view. This new table contains details about the different instances that customers have rented each piece of equipment. There are 46 records in the table.

5. Close the table.

6. Click the **Relationships** button [*Database Tools* tab, *Relationships* group] to open the *Relationships* window. Notice that the *Rentals* table participates in a one-to-many relationship with the *Equipment* table.

7. Close the *Relationships* window.

8. Open the *RentalsWithoutMatchingEquipment* query. The query executes and displays no records in the results. You know there must be a problem with the query because the rental company has told you that some pieces of equipment have not been rented.

9. Review the query to identify and fix the problem.
 a. Change to *Design* view of the query. The query design is shown in Figure 6-126. The query uses a *Left Outer Join*. Recall from Chapter 5 that this join type returns all the records from the table on the left but only the records from the table on the right that match. However, the *RentalsWithoutMatchingEquipment* query also includes criteria to only find records in the *Equipment* table that have a null value in the *EquipmentID* field. Because the *EquipmentID* field is a primary key, it will never be null. This query is not designed correctly.
 b. Close the query.

6-126 *Design* view of *RentalsWithoutMatchingEquipment* query

10. Create a new unmatched records query that is designed correctly.
 a. Click the **Query Wizard** button [*Create* tab, *Queries* group] to launch the *Query Wizard*.
 b. Select **Find Unmatched Query Wizard** in the *New Query* dialog box and click **OK** to launch the *Find Unmatched Query Wizard*.
 c. Select the **Equipment** table because it is the table that may have unmatched records. Click **Next**.
 d. Select the **Rentals** table and click **Next**.
 e. Verify that the *Matching field* box displays *EquipmentID < = > EquipIDFK* and click **Next**.
 f. Move the **EquipmentID**, **ProductName**, and **Category** fields from the *Available fields* window into the *Selected fields* window and click **Next**.

g. Edit the suggested query name to read EquipmentWithoutMatchingRentals. Notice how this name reverses the order of the tables from the *RentalsWithoutMatchingEquipment* query.

h. Click **Finish**. The query executes and displays the results of any unmatched records (Figure 6-127).

i. Save and close the query when done.

6-127 Unmatched records query results

11. Open the *Top5EquipmentRentals* query. The query results display five rows containing the values for *EquipmentIDFK* of 09863 and *ProductName* of *Backhoe Compact Allmand Diesel*.

12. Edit the query to fix it so that it shows the top five products that have been rented, in order of the frequency of rentals. Note that this query does not take into account the length of time of the rentals; it only takes into account the number of times the equipment has been rented.

a. Change to *Design* view of the query.

b. Click the **EquipIDFK** column, if necessary.

c. Click the **Totals** button [*Query Tools Design* tab, *Show/Hide* group].

d. Select **Count** in the *Total* box of the *EquipIDFK* column.

e. Edit the query to change the *EquipIDFK* field to use a **Descending** sort. The completed query is shown in Figure 6-128.

f. Run the query.

g. Widen the *ProductName* field so that the entire contents are visible. The query results should match the results shown in Figure 6-129.

h. Save and close the query.

6-128 *Design* view of top values query

13. Open the *RentalsListing* report. The *Enter Parameter Value* dialog box displays asking for a value for *Rent Units*.

a. Click **OK** to leave the box empty since this should not display. The report opens and displays the data in the *Rentals* table.

b. Scroll to the bottom of the report to review the report layout. Notice that there are opportunities to improve the report by fixing the dialog box problems, adding grouping so that all rentals from the same *EquipIDFK* display together, and adjusting the controls. To provide context for the steps to customize the report, view the completed report in Figure 6-131.

6-129 Completed top values query results

14. Fix the *Enter Parameter Value* dialog box problem.

a. Switch to *Design* view. Notice that the third text box contains a field named *Rent Units*. This is the field that the dialog box referred to.

b. Select that text box and open the *Property Sheet*, if necessary.

c. Click the **Other** tab and enter RentalPeriod in the *Name* property.

d. Click the **Data** tab and open the *Expression Builder* on the *Control Source* property. Notice that the equation combines the value of *Rent Units*, a *space*, the value of *RentType*, and the word *Rental*.

e. Remove the space between *Rent* and *Units* since the field name in the *Rentals* table is *RentUnits*.

f. Click **OK** and switch to *Report* view. The *Rental Period* now displays *1 D Rental* for the first record.

g. Scroll down a little to record number *six*. The *RentalID* is *2515*. Notice that the *Rental Period* displays *1 W Rental*. Management wants the report to display the word *Day* or *Week* instead of the letter.

h. Switch to *Design* view to edit the formula.

i. Change the *[RentType]* part of the formula to read IIf([RentType]="d", "Day", IIf([RentType]="w", "Week", "Month")). This uses the Access *IIF* (Immediate If) function which is similar to the *IF* function in Excel. Based on the contents of the *RentType* field, the *IIF* function chooses the correct word to use instead.

j. Click **OK** and switch to *Report* view. The *Rental Period* now displays *1 Day Rental* for the first record.

k. Save the report.

15. Add a group section.
 a. Switch to *Design* view.
 b. Click the **Group & Sort** button [*Report Design Tools Design* tab, *Grouping & Totals* group].
 c. Select the **Add a group** option in the *Group, Sort, and Total* pane.
 d. Select the **EquipIDFK** field from the field list. The *Group Header* section is added to the report.
 e. Click the **More** button in the *Group, Sort, and Total* pane to display the available options.
 f. Change the *do not keep group together on one page* option to **keep whole group together on one page**.
 g. Change the **Height** of the *EquipIDFK Header* section to .6".
 h. Drag the **EquipIDFK** combo box and label from the *Detail* section into the *EquipIDFK Header* section.
 i. Close the *Group, Sort, and Total* pane.
 j. Switch to *Report* view. The report records now display grouped by *EquipIDFK* (Figure 6-130).
 k. Save the report.

16. Improve the layout of the controls in the report.
 a. Switch to *Design* view.
 b. Select the **EquipIDFK** label and enter Equipment ID in the *Caption* property, 1.1" in the *Width* property, .21" in the *Top* property, .125" in the *Left* property, and select **Transparent** in the *Border Style* property, and **Bold** in the *Font Weight* property. When entering property values, don't worry if Access slightly changes a few of the values (for example, .21" becomes .2097".)

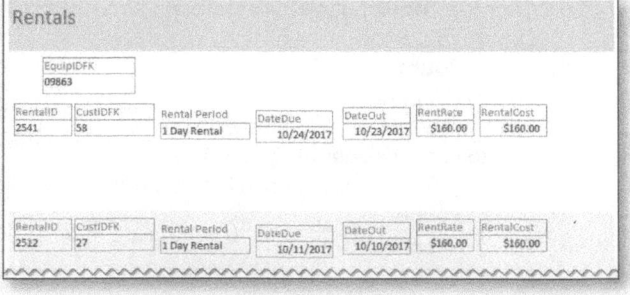

6-130 *RentalsListing* report after adding a *Group Header* section

 c. Select the **EquipIDFK** combo box and make the following changes to these properties on the *Format* tab: Enter .5" in the *Width* property, .21" in the *Top* property, 1.3" in the *Left* property, and select **Transparent** for the *Border Style* property, and **Bold** in the *Font Weight* property.
 d. Insert a **line** control in the *EquipIDFK Header* section.
 e. Make the following changes to these properties of the *line* control on the *Format* tab: Enter 7" in the *Width* property, .53" in the *Top* property, 0" in the *Height* property, .08" in the *Left* property, and 2 pt in the *Border Width* property.
 f. Select the **line** control and copy and paste the line into the *EquipIDFK Header* section. You now have two lines in the *EquipIDFK Header* section.
 g. Make the following change to the properties of this second *line* control: Enter .13" in the *Top* property and .08" in the *Left* property.
 h. Change the **Height** of the *EquipIDFK Header* section back to .6", if necessary.
 i. Select all the text boxes and labels in the *Detail* section.

j. Click the **Report Design Tools Arrange** tab, and align all of the selected text boxes and labels to the **Top** and set the spacing to **Equal Horizontal**.

k. With all the controls still selected, on the *Format* tab of the *Property Sheet*, select **Transparent** for the *Border Style* property and **Center** for the *Text Align* property.

l. Set the **Height** of the *Detail* section to .55".

m. Change the *CustIDFK label* to read Customer ID. Enter a space between the words of the other labels in the *Detail* section.

n. Change the **Width** of the report to 7.2".

o. Change the label in the *Report Header* section to read Listing of All Rentals, and change the **Left** property to 2.5".

p. Save the changes to the report.

17. Change to *Print Preview* view to show the completed report. Your report should look similar to Figure 6-131.

a. Click the **Next Page** navigation arrow to move to page 2. Notice the blank space between the last rental for equipment number 10236 and the bottom of the page. This is because the records stay together in the grouping and there isn't enough room on page 2 for all the records in the next group.

b. Continue navigating through the report pages.

c. Click the **Close Print Preview** button [*Print Preview* tab, *Close Preview* group].

d. Close the report when done.

18. Close the database.

6-131 Completed *RentalsListing* report

Challenge Project 6-8

For this project, you modify the database you built in Challenge Project 5-8. Create a regular select query to find records in your database and convert that query into a make table query. Create a delete query to remove the records from the first table that were placed in the new table. Create a report in *Design* view and modify that report to ensure it is professional in appearance.
[Student Learning Outcomes 6.1, 6.4, 6.5, 6.6]

File Needed: *[your initials] Access 5-8.accdb*
Completed Project File Name: *[your initials] Access 6-8.accdb*

Open the database *[your initials] Access 5-8* and save a copy of it as [your initials] Access 6-8.

Modify your database according to the following guidelines:

- Use *Query Design* to create a regular select query that shows all the fields from your database table. Modify the query to return a subset of the records by adding criteria to one of the fields. Test the query to ensure that it returns the correct records.
- Convert the query into a make table query to create a new table that will contain the records that meet the query criteria. Save and execute the query.
- Create, test, and execute a delete query to delete the records from the original table that were put into the new table.
- Create a regular select query to return all the fields from your new database table. Test the query to ensure that it returns the correct records.
- Create a report in *Design* view that uses the new query as the data source. Add all the fields into the report.
- Customize the report in *Design* view to adjust the formatting of the different controls, and add a report header and page numbers. Ensure the report is professional in appearance.
- Add a calculated field that counts the number of records in the report.
- Save any changes you make to the database.
- Close the database.

Challenge Project 6-9

For this project, you modify the database you created in Challenge Project 5-9 for Blue Lake Sports. Your database contains a table with information about the different departments at Blue Lake Sports and a related table with information about interns who are working at Blue Lake, along with the other objects created previously. Create a query that uses a date function to calculate the end date of the internship. Use that field to find only the intern records where the internship has ended. Convert that query into a make table query to put those records into a new table. Then, create a delete query to remove those records from the Intern table. Finally, create a report to display the records from the new table. [Student Learning Outcomes 6.1, 6.4, 6.5, 6.6]

File Needed: *[your initials] Access 5-9.accdb*
Completed Project File Name: *[your initials] Access 6-9.accdb*

Open the database *[your initials] Access 5-9* and save a copy of it as [your initials] Access 6-9.

Modify your database according to the following guidelines:

- Create a regular select query that displays all the fields from the intern table. Also add a calculated field to the query that determines the *EndDate*. To calculate the *EndDate*, use the *DateAdd* function to add the number of months from the Internship length to the *Start Date*, for example, *DateAdd("m", [InternshipLength], [StartDate])*. Test the query to ensure that it calculates correctly.
- Modify the query to return only the records of the interns who have internships that have ended. These records can be located when the *EndDate* is less than today's date. Test the query.
- Convert the query into a make table query to create an *ExpiredInternship* table. Deselect the show check box on the *EndDate* field so this field is not added into the new table. Save and execute the query.

- Create, test, and execute a delete query to delete the records from the *Intern* table for the interns whose internships have expired.
- Create a report in *Design* view that shows all the records in the *ExpiredInternship* table. Add a grouping level of the department where the students had their internships (remember that this was the foreign key field.)
- Customize the report in *Design* view to adjust the formatting of the different sections and add a report header and page numbers. Ensure the report is well designed and professional in appearance.
- Save any changes you make to the database.

Challenge Project 6-10

For this project, you modify the database you created for a travel agency in Challenge Project 5-10. Your database contains a table with information about the different ships and a related table with information about upcoming cruises, along with other objects created previously. Create a query to find the average number of passengers on all the ships. Use that query as a subquery to find all the trips on ships that have a number of passengers greater than the average. Finally, create a report based on that query. Customize the design of the report and add a calculated control to number the rows in the report. [Student Learning Outcomes 6.3, 6.4, 6.5, 6.6]

File Needed: *[your initials] Access 5-10.accdb*
Completed Project File Name: *[your initials] Access 6-10.accdb*

Open the database *[your initials] Access 5-10* and save a copy of it as [your initials] Access 6-10.

Modify your database according to the following guidelines. *(Hint: Refer to the example where you found agents with listings greater than the average listing price in the* Create a Subquery *section in* SLO 6.3: Creating Advanced Queries and Changing Query Properties).

- Create a query to find the average *NumberOfPassengers* on all the ships. Save this query.
- Create another query that includes the "average" query as a subquery. This second query should display the *TripID, TripName, DepartureCity, DepartureDate*, and *ShipName* for all trips on ships that have a *NumberofPassengers* greater than the average number of passengers. Save this query.
- Create a report in *Design* view. Use the second query as the report data source.
- Add a calculate control to the report that uses a running total to number the rows in the report.
- Customize the report in *Design* view to format the controls to ensure that the report is professional in appearance.
- Save any changes you make to the database.

Designing and Managing Databases, and Using SQL

CHAPTER OVERVIEW

Throughout the chapters in this text you have learned how to create and use tables, queries, forms, reports, and macros. Having seen how these objects work, you now understand the importance of ensuring that you start with well-designed tables—the heart of any database. In Chapter 9, you will be exposed to additional techniques you can use to ensure that your tables are well designed. Additionally, you learn how to customize the *Navigation Pane* and how to use several tools in Access to improve the performance of a database and enhance your database security. Finally, you learn more about SQL and how it defines, manipulates, and retrieves data in databases.

STUDENT LEARNING OUTCOMES (SLOs)

After completing this chapter, you will be able to:

SLO 9.1 Understand entity relationship diagrams and normalization, use the *Analyze Table* tool, and create a documentation report (p. A9-621).

SLO 9.2 Create and modify a custom *Navigation Pane* (p. A9-636).

SLO 9.3 Analyze and optimize the performance of a database (p. A9-646).

SLO 9.4 Understand front-end and back-end databases, split a database, and work with a split database (p. A9-650).

SLO 9.5 Enhance database security by encrypting and password protecting a database, packaging and signing a database, and locking a database (p. A9-653).

SLO 9.6 Understand SQL (Structured Query Language) and create and execute simple SQL statements using the *Select, From, Where,* and *Order By* clauses (p. A9-665).

CASE STUDY

For the Pause & Practice projects in this chapter, you continue to work on several different databases. As you progress through the Pause & Practice projects, you incorporate new skills to analyze and document table design, customize a *Navigation Pane*, analyze database performance, and add security to a database. You also create and execute queries in SQL.

Pause & Practice 9-1: Analyze and document table design in a database.

Pause & Practice 9-2: Create and modify a *Navigation Pane* by using custom categories and groups.

Pause & Practice 9-3: Analyze database performance, split a database, add a password to protect a database, and lock a database.

Pause & Practice 9-4: Create and test simple SQL queries.

SLO 9.1

Analyze and Document Database Design

Recall from *SLO 1.1: Understanding Database Concepts* that a relational database organizes the data into a collection of related tables. Each table is a collection of related records, and each record is a collection of related fields. As you worked on the different databases in this book, you have seen the hierarchy of data that is inherent in a relational database. In *SLO 2.6: Understanding and Designing Relational Databases*, you learned the specifications a database must meet in order to be considered relational, as well as the seven steps for creating a well-designed database.

Following those steps puts you on the right path to create a database that meets the needs of the organization. As you analyze the requirements of a business, you start to identify the various fields and the needed tables. However, as the business requirements become more complex, the number of tables and fields in a database tends to increase. This makes it harder to know exactly how many tables you need and in which table the different fields should be placed.

As the complexity of your database increases, you may find it helpful to use a formal technique to help plan the design of your database. You can also use a formal technique to evaluate an existing database to determine if improvements can be made to the design. Part of that evaluation may involve reviewing documents created by a formal technique. In this section of the chapter, we introduce entity-relationship diagrams and normalization, two of the more widely used formal techniques. In the latter part of the section, you learn how to use Access tools to analyze and document the design of your database.

Entity Relationship Diagrams

An *Entity-Relationship Diagram (ERD)* is a type of data model that graphically represents the data needs of an organization. When an ERD is created during the database design process, it can help you organize the information collected about the business needs. An ERD is a useful tool to review with database users. You can use it to verify that you have correctly identified all the data that needs to be stored in the database and that you understand how the different pieces of data are related to each other. This is a critical step to ensure that the database will meet the needs of the organization. While becoming fluent in creating ERDs is beyond the scope of this book, you most likely will encounter these diagrams in your work with Access, and it is important to know how to read and use them.

ERD Building Blocks

An ERD shows the relationships among the different entities in your database. As the name implies, an ERD contains entities and relationships.

- An *entity* is a person, place, or thing about which you want to store data. Entities are another term for the objects you identify in step 2 of the seven steps to create a well-designed database in SLO 2.6.
- *Relationships* are the associations or connections between entities. Recall from SLO 2.6 the three types of relationships: one-to-one, one-to-many, and many-to-many.

When identifying all of the entities, you also determine what details you want to know about each entity. Those details are known as *attributes*. An attribute of an entity is the same as a *field* of an object or table.

One of the attributes is used as a primary key to distinguish one instance of an entity from another. An *instance* is a single example of an entity. Consider a university database. One of the entities would be *Professor*. When you refer to Professor Gonzalez, for example,

you are referencing an instance of the *Professor* entity. Use instances when reviewing the ERD with your users. This helps them to understand the data being represented in the diagram.

Drawing an ERD

Entities are drawn as boxes on the diagram. The relationships are drawn as lines connecting the entities. Figure 9-1 shows an ERD for a small used car dealership. The symbols at the end of the relationship line show the type of relationship. A *single line* symbol indicates a one, while a *crow's foot* symbol indicates a many.

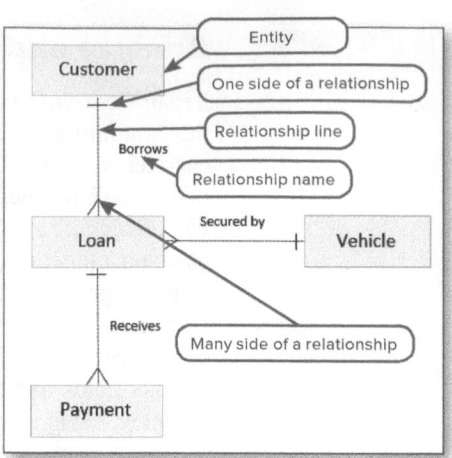

9-1 ERD for a car loan database

> **MORE INFO**
>
> The ERDs in this chapter use the *Crow's Foot* notation, one of the more common ways to represent the entities and relationships. You may encounter ERDs drawn using another notation method.

An ERD looks similar to the Access diagram used to show the relationships between the tables. One significant difference is when the diagrams are created. The ERD is created during the database design process to ensure that you have understood the business needs, while the relationships diagram is created as you implement the relationships into the database.

Sometimes ERDs also display the attributes. Figure 9-2 shows an example of the *Loan* entity with attributes included in the diagram. The entity name appears at the top and all attributes are listed below the separator line. The primary key field is underlined. If you have a significant number of attributes you may choose to include only a few

9-2 Attributes included in an entity

on the diagram. This helps your user understand what kind of data will be stored in the entity without overwhelming them by showing all of the attributes.

Reading and Using an ERD

To understand how an ERD is used, let's review the business situation of the used car dealership modeled in Figure 9-1. The dealership offers in-house financing to customers. Currently they track all of the data about the loan, customer, vehicle, and payments in an Excel worksheet. The worksheet only contains information about the car sales that involve an in-house loan. The relationships in Figure 9-1 are explained in the following *Car Loan Entity Relationship Diagram* table.

Car Loan Entity Relationship Diagram

Relationship	Type	Explanation
Borrows	One-to-many	A customer can have many different loans, but a particular loan is associated with only one customer.
Receives	One-to-many	A loan receives many different payments (typically one a month), but a payment is applied to only one loan.

continued

Relationship	Type	Explanation
Secured by	One-to-many	A loan is for only one vehicle, but a vehicle could be on many different loans. For example, this would happen if the company resold the vehicle in the future. *(Note: In most situations a vehicle will only be on one loan, but a database must be designed to allow for the "many" situation to occur, even if it doesn't happen very often.)*

> **ANOTHER WAY**
>
> As you view this example, remember that relationships reflect the way a particular business operates. Another business may have different rules and, as a result, different relationships. For example, if a company allowed co-borrowers on a loan, then the *Borrows* relationship would be many-to-many.

In ERD terminology, the type of relationship is often called the ***cardinality***. Most ERDs also include an additional set of symbols on the relationship line to show the modality. The ***modality*** specifies whether an entity must participate in the relationship. A ***single line*** symbol indicates mandatory or required participation, while a ***circle*** symbol indicates optional participation. Collectively, the cardinality and modality describe the constraints of the relationship.

Figure 9-3 shows the revised car loan database with modality added into the diagram. The cardinality symbols appear closest to each entity. The *Borrows* relationship has mandatory participation on each side. This means that each loan must be associated with a customer, and each customer must be associated with a loan.

9-3 ERD with modality symbols added

Explaining Relationship Constraints

Typically, you incorporate both the cardinality and modality when you explain the relationship. It is helpful if you think about explaining each direction of the relationship separately. Remember that one use of the ERD is to review it with your users to ensure you have correctly understood the business needs. As a result, you need to learn how to explain the relationship constraints in words that your users understand.

Figures 9-4 and 9-5 illustrate how to translate and explain the relationship constraints. You read from left to right, and always start with the assumption that you are the "one" of the entity on the left. The color-coded arrows and words help you learn where to focus as you interpret the constraints. The figures only show the symbols closest to the right-side entity, since those are the ones that are important in reading from the left to the right side.

Read the constraint statement in Figure 9-4. A mandatory restriction exists in the *Customer to Loan* constraints because the company only stores information about sales that result in a

9-4 Translating the *Customer to Loan* relationship constraints

9-5 Translating the *Loan to Customer* relationship constraints

loan. Therefore, every customer in this database must have a loan. Mandatory participation is generally read as "must."

Now you must look at the other direction of the relationship. Since we typically read from left to right, the entities have been reversed in Figure 9-5. Again, you start by being "one," or "a," loan and read in the direction of the customer. Note the "only one" explanation of the cardinality.

Figures 9-6 and 9-7 provide an example of translating and explaining a relationship with optional participation.

Optional participation exists in the *Loan to Payment* constraints (see Figure 9-6) because when a loan is first made no payments have been received yet.

9-6 Translating the *Loan to Payment* relationship constraints

Sometimes you need to modify the relationship verb to ensure that the sentences make sense to your user, as you see in Figure 9-7. In this case, when a payment is received it is applied to only one loan.

Use the relationship constraints when you actually create the relationships in Access. The constraints help you know whether to enforce referential integrity, as well as whether to cascade updates or deletes.

Once you have reviewed the ERD with your users, you are ready to start designing the database tables.

9-7 Translating the *Payment to Loan* relationship constraints

Normalization

If you followed the steps of database design in *SLO 2.6: Understanding and Designing Relational Databases*, most of your tables won't need much improvement. But you may have been unsure of whether you actually needed a separate table to store a few of the fields, or you may not have been sure where to place all the fields. Additionally, in some situations, you may inherit a poorly designed database, or you may be given a file to import that is not well structured. As a result, it is important to become familiar with **normalization**, the process of organizing attributes, or fields, into the correct tables. The goal of normalization is to create a set of tables that minimizes problems in the database.

Tables that are not well designed usually share a few common problems. These problems include having redundant data, having more than one value stored in a field, and not having the ability to store the required data. Recall from *SLO 2.6: Understanding and Designing Relational Databases* that in order to create a relational database, the tables in the database must meet a set of specifications. The specifications include:

* The data in the database must be stored in tables.
* The rows of the table must represent records.
* The columns of the table must represent fields and each field can have only one value.
* Each row must have a primary key able to uniquely identify one record from another.
* A table can have a relationship with another table by including a foreign key in its design.

Normalization involves evaluating a table against a series of rules to ensure that all of the fields describe only the entity represented in the table. The rules are known as **normal forms**. While there are higher normal forms, this section focuses on learning how to evaluate whether a table is in first, second, or third normal form. As a table achieves each subsequent level of normalization, more problems are removed from the database. Our goal is to have

each table reach third normal form. As you will see, the normal forms are often identified by initials. To learn the process of normalization, let's evaluate the data needs in the car dealership example.

First Normal Form (1NF)

To be in *first normal form*, a table must not have any repeating values. Figure 9-8 shows an example of the data from the Excel worksheet used to store the loan payment details for the car dealership. Before you can import it into Access, you need to analyze the data to see if it meets the relational specifications, identify and fix any of the common problems, and ensure it meets the normal form rules.

	A	B	C	D	E	F	G	H	I	J	K	L	M	N	O
1	Loan#	LoanDate	LoanAmt	PmtDueDate	PmtAmt	VIN	CID	LName	FName	Address	City	State	ZIP	DatePaid	AmtPaid
2	1001	1/3/2017	$ 10,800.00	2/1/2017 3/1/2017 4/1/2017 5/1/2017	$ 323.69	1HGCP25308A020571	2000	Parks	Alicia	22756 Hannah St.	Corona	CA	92883	2/1/2017 3/1/2017 3/30/2017 4/30/2017	$323.69 $323.69 $323.69 $350.00
3	1002	1/16/2017	$ 11,250.00	3/1/2017 4/1/2017 5/1/2017	$ 332.09	1HGFA15508L044187	2010	Thomas	Carl	1139 S. Baker St.	Santa Ana	CA	92707	3/1/2017 4/1/2017 5/2/2017	$332.09 $332.09 $332.09

9-8 Sample data in Excel worksheet

In reviewing the Excel worksheet, one of the first things you notice is that some of the cells (D2, D3, N2, N3, O2, and O3) contain more than one value, or repeating values. As a result, the data in this table is not in first normal form, 1NF. Notice that a table that is not in 1NF does not meet the third specification for a relational database; each field only has one value. An additional relational specification is that the table has a primary key. While not impossible to do, it sometimes is harder to identify the primary key when a table contains repeating values.

To get this table into 1NF you add in the missing information by creating a separate row for each of the individual payments. Once the table is in 1NF, you can identify the primary key. This is also a good time to assign a name to the table, so you can easily refer to it when you start building the actual database. Figure 9-9 shows the *LoanPayment* table in 1NF with the primary key underlined.

LoanPayment

Loan#	LoanDate	LoanAmt	PmtDueDate	PmtAmt	VIN	CID	LName	FName	Address	City	State	ZIP	DatePaid	AmtPaid
1001	1/3/2017	$ 10,800.00	2/1/2017	$ 323.69	1HGCP25308A020571	2000	Parks	Alicia	22756 Hannah St.	Corona	CA	92883	2/1/2017	$323.69
1001	1/3/2017	$ 10,800.00	3/1/2017	$ 323.69	1HGCP25308A020571	2000	Parks	Alicia	22756 Hannah St.	Corona	CA	92883	3/1/2017	$323.69
1001	1/3/2017	$ 10,800.00	4/1/2017	$ 323.69	1HGCP25308A020571	2000	Parks	Alicia	22756 Hannah St.	Corona	CA	92883	3/30/2017	$323.69
1001	1/3/2017	$ 10,800.00	5/1/2017	$ 323.69	1HGCP25308A020571	2000	Parks	Alicia	22756 Hannah St.	Corona	CA	92883	4/30/2017	$350.00
1002	1/16/2017	$ 11,250.00	3/1/2017	$ 332.09	1HGFA15508L044187	2010	Thomas	Carl	1139 S. Baker St.	Santa Ana	CA	92707	3/1/2017	$332.09
1002	1/16/2017	$ 11,250.00	4/1/2017	$ 332.09	1HGFA15508L044187	2010	Thomas	Carl	1139 S. Baker St.	Santa Ana	CA	92707	4/1/2017	$332.09
1002	1/16/2017	$ 11,250.00	5/1/2017	$ 332.09	1HGFA15508L044187	2010	Thomas	Carl	1139 S. Baker St.	Santa Ana	CA	92707	5/2/2017	$332.09

9-9 *LoanPayment* table in first normal form

The table uses a concatenated key that combines the *Loan#* and *PmtDueDate* because there is not one field by itself that could uniquely identify one row from another.

Unfortunately, this table now has redundant data. For example, notice how many times the *LoanDate* and *LoanAmt* repeat for each loan. If the *LoanAmt* needs to be corrected, a user might not make the change on every row. This would result in inconsistent data.

Second Normal Form (2NF)

To be in *second normal form*, a table must be in 1NF and all of the non-key fields must depend on the entire primary key. Sometimes a table may have more than one field that could be selected as the primary key. For example, if a university tracks your social security number

and also assigns you a unique student number, then two possible primary keys exist for the student table. Even though only one of them is selected as the primary key, both of them are considered key attributes. Database designers call them **candidate keys**. The definition of 2NF only applies to the non-key attributes in the table.

If a table is in 1NF and only has one field in the primary key, it automatically is in 2NF. If a table has a concatenated key, you need to look to see if some of the attributes can be identified just by knowing the value of one of the fields in the concatenated key. The arrows in Figure 9-10 help show that a *Loan#* always results in the same values in the *LoanDate, LoanAmt, PmtAmt, VIN, CID, LName, FName, Address, City, State,* and *ZIP* fields. These attributes can be determined just by knowing one part of the concatenated key. Database designers call this a **partial dependency**. In some situations, you may also have attributes that can be determined by knowing the other field in the concatenated key, but that is not true in this example. The *PmtDueDate* by itself does not give you the same value every time for any other field.

All records for *Loan# 1001* have the same values in the *LoanDate, LoanAmt, PmtAmt, VIN, CID, LName, FName, Address, City, State,* and *ZIP* fields.

9-10 Identify attributes that depend on only one part of a concatenated key

> **MORE INFO**
>
> In the limited number of records shown in Figure 9-10, it appears that the *State* field is the same for every *PmtDueDate* and even for every *Loan#*. This illustrates the need to apply common sense reasoning to your analysis. Since there could be loans with the same *PmtDueDate* made to a customer outside California, the *State* can't be identified just by the *PmtDueDate* field.

Recall that normalization helps ensure that the fields describe only the entity represented in the table. The *LoanPayment* table in Figure 9-10 contains information about the loan itself, in addition to the loan payment information. To get the *LoanPayment* table into 2NF you take the fields that depend on only one part of the key, along with the key field, and put them into a new separate table. The original *LoanPayment* table still keeps the concatenated key along with the remaining fields that depend on the concatenated key. Figure 9-11 shows the revised *LoanPayment* table and the new *Loan* table. Both tables are in 2NF.

9-11 Tables in second normal form

In the new *Loan* table, the redundancy is reduced because the loan information is stored only once. However, redundant data still exists in the first table. For example, notice how Alicia Parks' address information is repeated for each of her loans. If Alicia moves and the address needs to be changed, a user might not make the change on every row. This would result in inconsistent data.

Third Normal Form (3NF)

To be in ***third normal form***, a table must be in 2NF and all non-key fields must depend only on the primary key. If a table is in 2NF and has only one non-key field, the table is automatically in 3NF. The issue preventing 3NF has to do with a non-key field being able to identify another non-key field. Since we now have two tables, each must be evaluated for third normal form.

In the *LoanPayment* table, the *DatePaid* and *AmtPaid* fields can't determine each other. As a result, those fields depend only on the primary key and the *LoanPayment* table is in 3NF.

In the *Loan* table, *LoanDate*, *LoanAmt* and the *PmtAmt* can't determine each other. Additionally, although it seems like the Vehicle Identification Number (*VIN*) is a unique identifier, because a vehicle could be resold and appear on a different loan, it turns out this this is not a unique identifier. As a result, those fields depend only on the primary key.

However, the *Loan* table does contain redundant data, indicating we may have a problem. When a customer has more than one loan, as shown in Figure 9-11, you see that a *CID* always results in the same values in the *LName, FName, Address, City, State*, and *ZIP* fields. These attributes can be determined just by knowing the non-key field of *CID*. Database designers call this a ***transitive dependency***.

Again, remember that normalization helps ensure that the fields describe only the entity represented in the table. In Figure 9-11, the *Loan* table contains information about the customer, in addition to the loan payment information.

To get this table into 3NF you place the fields that depend on the non-key attribute into a new separate table. The original *Loan* table still remains, including the non-key attributes. Figure 9-12 shows the new *Customer* table, the revised *Loan* table and the unchanged *LoanPayment* table. All three tables are now in 3NF. In the new *Customer* table, the redundancy is reduced since the customer

9-12 Tables in third normal form

information is stored only once. The colored fields represent the foreign keys that provide the relationship to the different tables.

As you have seen in this example, normalization helps you to remove redundant data. This helps to increase the consistency and integrity of the data, which minimizes potential problems. Essentially, what normalization does is take larger tables that have problems and divide them into smaller tables that no longer have problems. As you work more with databases, you will become better at intuitively creating tables that avoid the problems. You also reduce the chances of creating an un-normalized table by following the steps to database design.

If you have inherited a poorly designed database, you may need to change the design of the tables as well as the existing table relationships. If these steps are necessary, you have learned skills to completely delete a table, delete fields within a table, and edit or delete relationships between tables.

Analyze a Table

Access includes a *Table Analyzer* tool that helps you determine if a table is well designed. The tool analyzes a table looking for duplicated data or improperly structured tables. It then makes recommendations on how to normalize the table and fix potentially inconsistent data.

You can accept the tool's suggestions, modify the suggested changes, or reject the suggestions altogether. Since the suggested changes are based on the rules of normalization, it helps to consider those rules when reviewing the analysis results.

If you allow the tool to make any changes, Access creates the new tables. The original table remains unchanged in the database. You can edit and use the new tables just as you work with tables that you created.

If you decide to keep the new tables, you should delete the original tables as you do not need them. Likewise, if you decide to keep the original tables you should delete the new tables.

It is important to keep in mind that the tool is not perfect. The quality of the recommendations depends on many factors. Relevant factors include the following:

- *The actual data in the table*: If you have very few records in a table, or if the data values don't show the duplicated fields, the tool is likely to miss some recommendations or to make incorrect recommendations.
- *Fields associated with too many different entities*: Even with sufficient data, the suggestions may not be optimal. Consider our 1NF *LoanPayment* table in Figure 9-9. That table contains fields describing three different entities. The tool is not likely to make all the needed suggestions to convert that table into the correct set of 3NF tables.
- *A concatenated key*: When a table contains a concatenated key, the tool is likely to analyze incorrectly.

▶ HOW TO: Use the Table Analyzer

1. Click the **Analyze Table** button [*Database Tools* tab, *Analyze* group] (Figure 9-13).
 - The *Table Analyzer Wizard* opens (Figure 9-14).
 - The first screen displays information about the problems that duplicated data causes. Depending on the wizard settings (see step 5), it is possible that the screens in Figures 9-14 and 9-15 will not display.

9-13 *Analyze Table* button

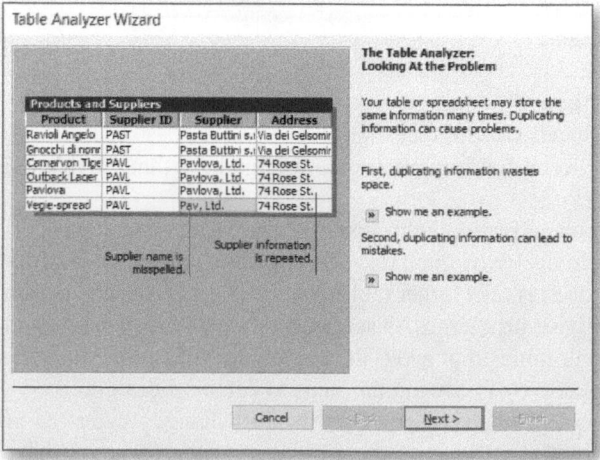

9-14 *Table Analyzer Wizard*, page 1

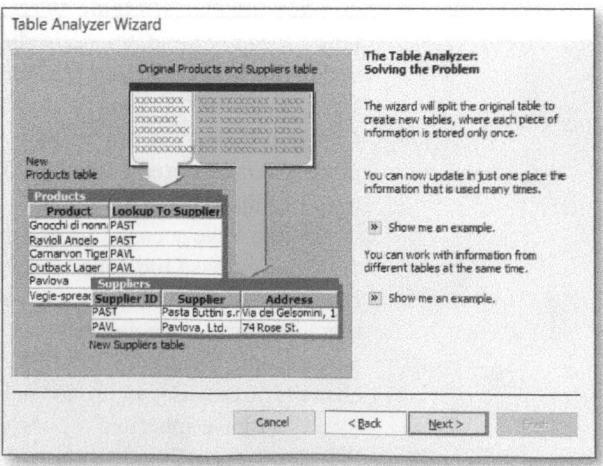

9-15 *Table Analyzer Wizard*, page 2

A9-628

2. Click the **Show me an example** button, as desired, to read more information about duplicated data.

3. Click **Next**. The second screen displays information about how the wizard splits tables to solve the problems (Figure 9-15).

4. Click the **Show me an example** button, as desired, to read more information about splitting tables.

5. Click **Next**.

 - The wizard displays the list of tables in your database (Figure 9-16).
 - This screen also has a check box which controls whether the wizard displays the introductory pages shown in Figures 9-14 and 9-15 the next time it is run.

6. Check the **Show introductory pages?** box to change the setting, as desired.

7. Select the table to analyze and click **Next**.

 - The wizard asks you to decide whether it will analyze the table or you will analyze the table (Figure 9-17).
 - If you select to have the wizard analyze for you, you are still prompted to accept or modify the recommendations.

8. Select either the **Yes, let the wizard decide** or the **No, I want to decide** radio button and then click **Next**.

 - If you selected *Yes*, the wizard displays the recommendations (Figure 9-18).
 - If you selected *No*, the wizard displays the current table.

9. Increase the size of the tables in the window to see all of the fields, if necessary.

10. Click the **Tips** button to open a dialog box containing suggested actions to take at this step of the wizard. Close the dialog box when done.

11. Select a table, click the **Rename Table** button, type the table name in the dialog box, and press **OK** to change a table name.

> MORE INFO
>
> The *Undo* button becomes available after you have performed an action on the wizard page. To undo the most recent change, click the **Undo** button.

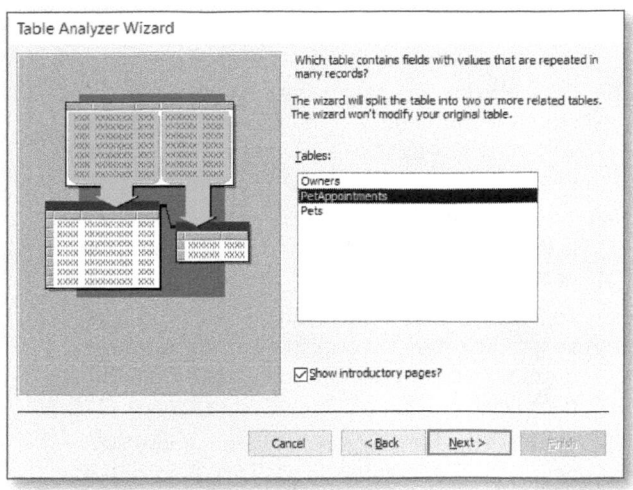

9-16 Select the table to analyze

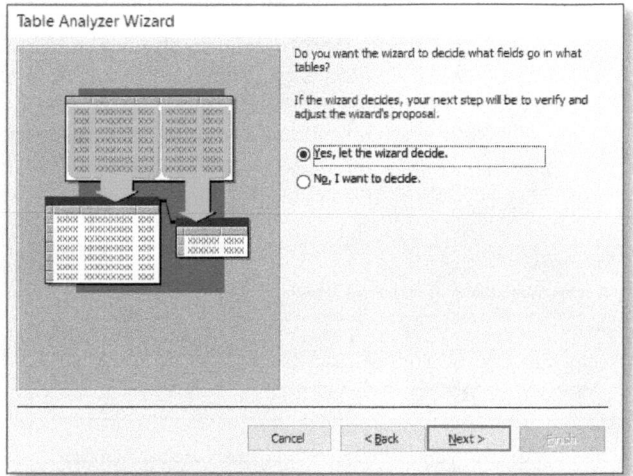

9-17 Decide if the wizard will analyze the table for you

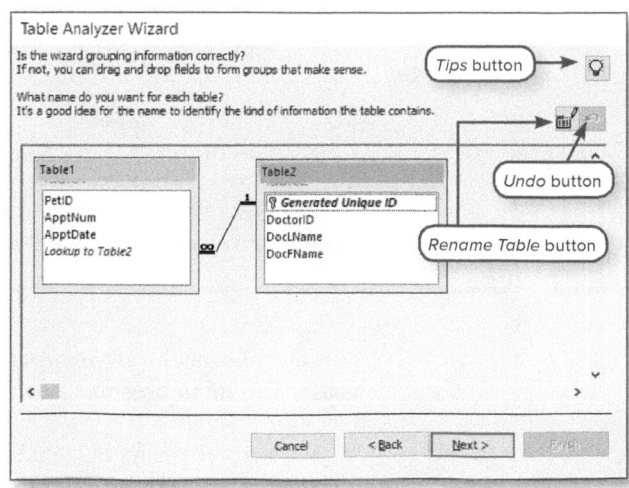

9-18 Recommended changes to the table design

12. Drag the fields to a different table or into the open window to create a new table, if necessary.

13. Click **Next** when you are satisfied with the structure of the tables. The wizard asks you to verify the selection of a primary key in each table (Figure 9-19).

14. To change the primary key in a table, select a field in the table and click the **Set Unique Identifier** button.

15. To have Access add a unique ID field into a table, select the table and click the **Add Generated Key** button. This generated key uses an *AutoNumber* data type.

16. Click **Next** when each table has a primary key selected. The information shown in Figure 9-20 displays if the wizard identified any inconsistent data. Otherwise, skip to step 18.

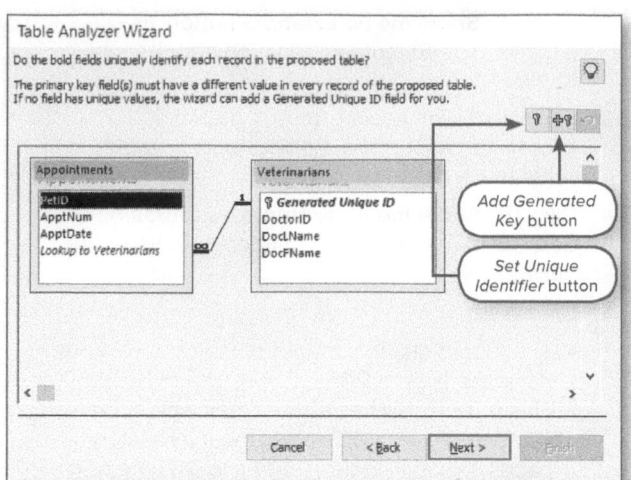

9-19 Select primary keys for each table

17. Review the data, widening any columns to see the complete contents.

 • Select the **Correct Record column** check box to indicate which data values are correct.
 • If the *Next Key* button is not dimmed, the wizard found other fields with inconsistencies. Click **Next Key** to review additional problems.
 • Click **Next** when finished reviewing all inconsistencies. The final step of the wizard (Figure 9-21) informs you that Access can create a query to join the new tables together so that you can easily see the original relationships in one datasheet.

9-20 Correct inconsistent data

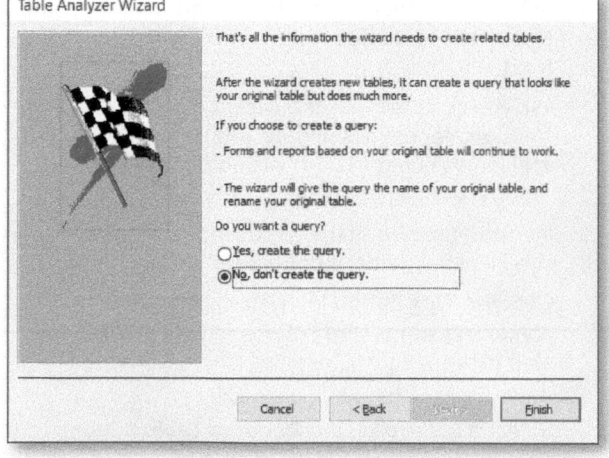

9-21 Complete the *Table Analyzer Wizard*

18. Select either the **Yes, create the query** or the **No, don't create the query** radio button and then click **Finish**.

Ideally, you should use the *Analyze Table* tool prior to creating any other objects in the database. This minimizes the changes that may need to be performed on your queries, forms, and reports.

If you accepted the recommendation of the wizard to create new tables, the *Analyze Table* tool automatically created the relationship between the new tables and enforced referential integrity. However, you should review the relationship to determine if you need to modify the

options for cascading updates or deletes. If necessary, review the *How To* topics in *SLO 2.6: Understanding and Designing Relational Databases* for help on editing, deleting, and creating relationships between tables.

Use the Database Documenter

Access contains a ***Database Documenter*** tool that allows you to view and print general information as well as detailed data about the characteristics of objects in your database. Each object in your database has its own properties. As a result, the contents of the documentation vary depending on the selected object. The *Database Documenter* tool allows you to select the level of detail displayed about the different objects in your database. You can choose to see information about the property settings of fields and relationships of tables, property settings for controls and macro code attached to a form or report, or SQL code in a query.

The *Database Documenter* creates a report containing the requested data. The report opens in *Print Preview* mode. The level of detail selected, as well as the number of fields and controls in an object, affects the number of pages in the report. Be aware that some of the reports will be quite long.

With the report open in *Print Preview* mode, you can choose to print it. As desired, you can also export the report to a PDF file or other format including Excel, Text File, Email, Word, or HTML.

▶ **HOW TO:** Use the Database Documenter

1. Click the **Database Documenter** button [*Database Tools* tab, *Analyze* group] (Figure 9-22) to open the *Documenter* dialog box (Figure 9-23).

2. Click the tab corresponding to the type of object you wish to document.

3. Select the check boxes of the objects to include in the report.

 - You can check multiple objects on a tab.
 - Click the **Select All** button to select all of the objects on a tab.

4. Click the **Options** button to modify the level of detail included in the report, The *Print [Object] Definition* dialog box displays (Figure 9-24).

 - The *[Object]* portion of the title bar changes depending on the tab selected in step 2.
 - The choices in the dialog box vary depending on what object is selected.

5. Select the check boxes and radio buttons corresponding to the level of detail you wish to view about the object properties.

6. Click the **OK** button when done. You are returned to the *Documenter* dialog box.

7. Repeat steps 2–6, as desired, to select objects from a different tab.

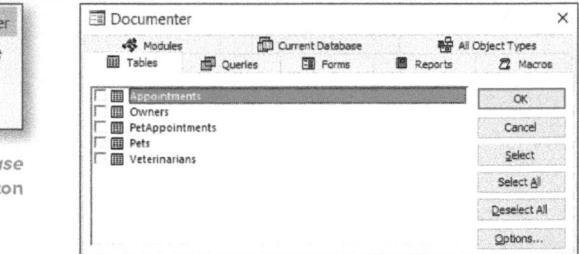

9-22 *Database Documenter* button

9-23 *Documenter* dialog box

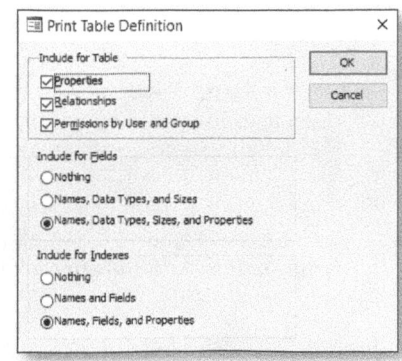

9-24 *Print [Object] Definition* dialog box

 ANOTHER WAY

To include all objects in the report, click the **All Object Types** tab and click the **Select All** button.

8. Click the **OK** button to preview the *Database Documenter* report (Figure 9-25).

- The report contents vary depending on the selections made.
- The top portion of the report includes general properties about the object.
- The remainder of the report shows specific properties about different fields or controls used in the object.
- Use the navigation buttons on the *Navigation* bar to move among the different pages of the report.

9. Export the report by clicking a button in the *Data* group corresponding to the desired format. In the dialog box that opens, browse for a location, enter the file name, and save the file.

10. Close the preview by clicking the **Close Print Preview** button [*Print Preview* tab, *Close Preview* group].

9-25 *Print Preview of Database Documenter report*

PAUSE & PRACTICE: ACCESS 9-1

For this Pause & Practice you use the *Analyze Table* tool to review a new table in the Life's Animal Shelter database. You use the rules of normalization as you review the recommendations made by the wizard. Finally, you create documentation for the *Pets* table.

File Needed: ***LifesAnimalShelter-09.accdb***
Completed Project File Names: ***[your initials] PP A9-1.accdb*** and
[your initials] LAS-PetsTableDocumentation.pdf

1. Open the ***LifesAnimalShelter-09*** database from your student data files.

2. Save a new copy of your database as [your initials] PP A9-1.

3. Enable content in the security warning.

4. Review the structure of the *PetAppointments* table.

a. Open the *PetAppointments* table in *Design* view (Figure 9-26). Note the primary key of *ApptNum*. Also note that this table contains fields about the different appointments for each pet and information about which veterinary doctor treated each pet.

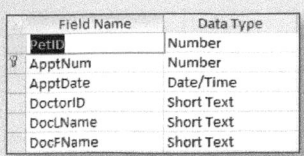

Field Name	Data Type
PetID	Number
ApptNum	Number
ApptDate	Date/Time
DoctorID	Short Text
DocLName	Short Text
DocFName	Short Text

9-26 *PetAppointments* table fields

b. Switch to *Datasheet* view.

c. Click the **arrow** to the right of the *PetID* field name and select the **Sort Smallest to Largest** button on the drop-down list. Note that several of the pets have had multiple appointments. Also note that the vet information is stored redundantly.

d. Click the **Remove Sort** button [*Home* tab, *Sort & Filter* group].

e. Close the table. Do not save changes when prompted.

5. Review existing table relationships.

a. Click the **Relationships** button [*Database Tools* tab, *Relationships* group] to open the *Relationships* window. Notice that the new *PetAppointments* table is not yet linked to the other tables.

b. Close the *Relationships* window.

6. Analyze the *PetAppointments* table.

a. Click the **Analyze Table** button [*Database Tools* tab, *Analyze* group] to open the *Table Analyzer Wizard*.

b. If the *Looking At the Problem* screen displays, click **Next** to move to the step of the wizard.

c. If the *Solving the Problem* screen displays, click **Next** to move to the next step of the wizard (Figure 9-27).

d. Select the **PetAppointments** table, if not already selected, and click **Next**.

e. Select the **Yes, let the wizard decide** radio button and click **Next**. The wizard displays the recommendations.

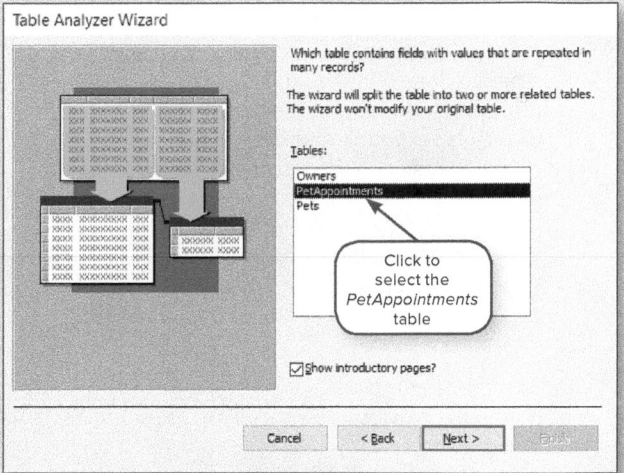

9-27 Select the desired table to analyze

f. Increase the size of the tables in the window to see all of the fields (Figure 9-28). The wizard recommends moving the fields that describe the doctor into a new table and adds a *Lookup to Table2* field to provide the relationship.

g. Select **Table1**, click the **Rename Table** button, type Appointments in the dialog box, and press **OK** to change the table name.

h. Select **Table2**, click the **Rename Table** button, type Veterinarians in the dialog box, and press **OK** to change the table name.

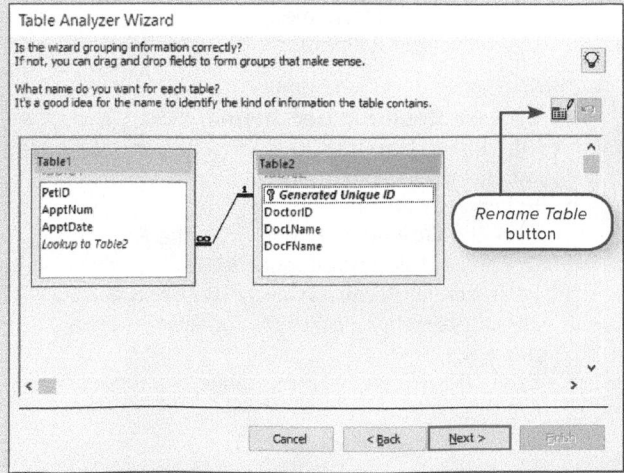

9-28 Recommended changes to the table design

i. Click **Next**. The wizard asks you to verify the selection of a primary key in each table (Figure 9-29).

j. Select the **DoctorID** field in the *Veterinarians* table and click the **Set Unique Identifier** button.

k. Select the **ApptNum** field in the *Appointments* table and click the **Set Unique Identifier** button.

l. Click **Next**. The wizard identifies inconsistent data in the spelling of Michael (Figure 9-30). Based on the number of times that it is spelled "Michael," the wizard checks the *Correct Record* box to indicate that this is the correct spelling.

m. Click **Next** to accept that correction. Access changes the incorrectly spelled data in the table.

n. Select the **No, don't create the query** radio button and click **Finish**, if needed, since you don't need to create the query. If a message box displays about the *TileHorizontally* action not available, click **OK**. Access creates and opens the new tables in *Datasheet* view and closes the *Navigation Pane*.

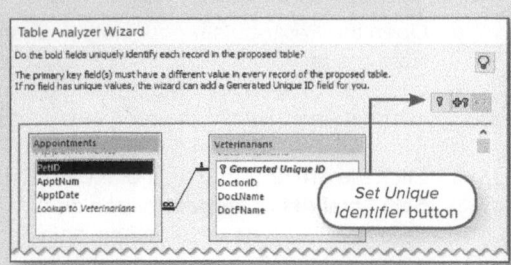

9-29 Select primary keys for each table

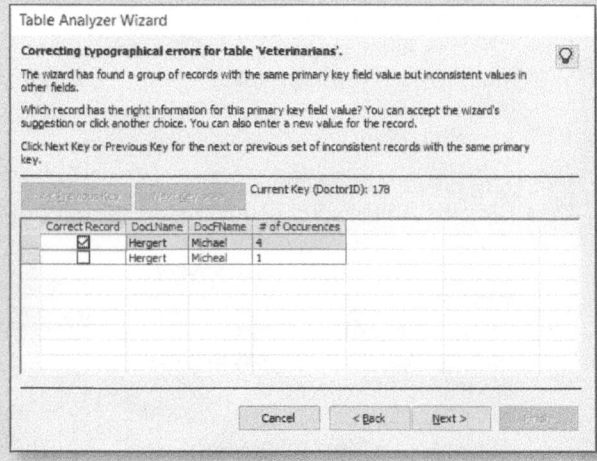

9-30 Correct inconsistent data

7. Review the new tables.

a. Open the *Navigation Pane*. The three original tables display in the *Tables* group, along with the two new tables.

b. Click the **DoctorID 160** plus sign, in the *Veterinarians* table, to display the related records.

c. Close the *Veterinarians* table.

d. Note that the *Lookup to Veterinarians* column, in the *Appointments* table, displays the doctor's ID, last name, and first name.

e. Close the *Appointments* table.

8. Create database documentation for the *Pets* table.

a. Click the **Database Documenter** button [*Database Tools* tab, *Analyze* group] to open the *Documenter* dialog box with the *Tables* tab opened.

b. Select the **Pets** check box.

c. Click the **Options** button to open the *Print Table Definition* dialog box (Figure 9-31).

d. Deselect the **Permissions by User and Group** check box in the *Include for Table* area, if necessary.

e. Click **OK**. You are returned to the *Documenter* dialog box.

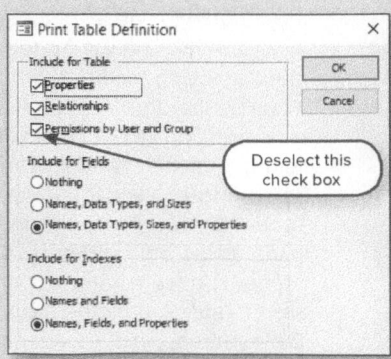

9-31 *Print Table Definition* dialog box

f. Click the **OK** button to preview the *Database Documenter* report (Figure 9-32).

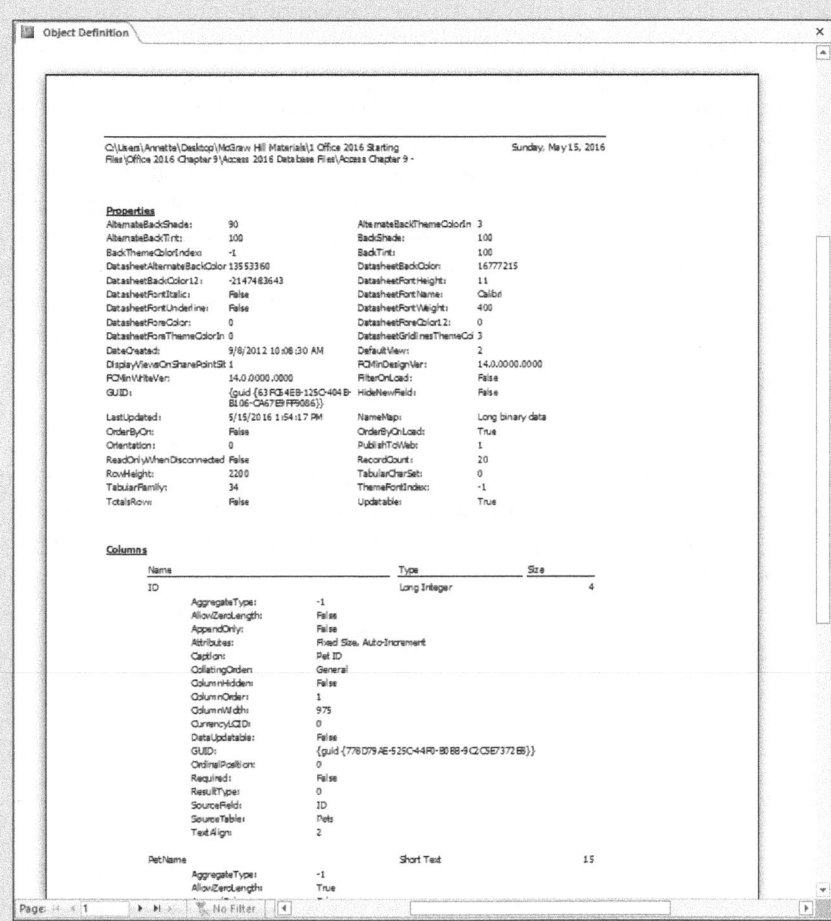

9-32 *Print Preview of Pets table documentation*

g. Use the scroll bars as needed to see the parts of the page that are not visible.
h. Click the **Next Page** navigation button five times to advance through the pages. On page 6, note the relationships section of the report.
i. Click the **PDF or XPS** button [*Print Preview* tab, *Data* group] to open the *Publish as PDF or XPS* dialog box.
j. Locate the folder where you want to save the file, enter [your initials] LAS-PetsTableDocumentation. pdf as the file name, select the **Open file after publishing** check box, if necessary, and click the **Publish** button. The PDF file opens in your PDF viewer.
k. Navigate through the pages in the PDF file to ensure it was created successfully. Close the PDF file.
l. Click **Close** in the *Export – PDF* dialog box because you don't need to save the export steps.
m. Click the **Close Print Preview** button [*Print Preview* tab, *Close Preview* group].

9. Close the database.

Customizing the Navigation Pane

The *Navigation Pane* displays the objects in your database. It is organized into categories and groups. The default settings in Access show all of the objects grouped by the type of object. You can customize the *Navigation Pane* to make a database more efficient for the users. To do this, you first create categories and groups that reflect the needs of the user. Next, you organize the database objects into the groups. You can limit the number of objects a user sees, which helps users find needed objects more quickly.

While not designed as a security mechanism, a customized *Navigation Pane* can also add a degree of security and protection to the database by hiding objects you don't want users to accidentally modify or delete. For example, a user is likely to only need to open the main form in a database that contains both a main form and a subform. In these cases, you can hide the subform object from the user. In this section, you first learn about the built-in categories and groups. Next, you learn how to create custom categories and groups and how to customize the *Navigation Pane*.

Built-in Categories and Groups

In *SLO 1.1: Understanding Database Concepts*, you learned how to change the category selection that affects the way the objects are grouped and how to change the filter selection. Figure 9-33 shows a *Navigation Pane* with the default settings. Figure 9-34 shows the new category and filter settings selected in the *Navigation* menu. Figure 9-35 shows the changes in the *Navigation Pane* after the new settings have been applied.

9-33 *Navigation Pane* with default settings

9-34 Changed settings in the *Navigation* menu

9-35 *Navigation Pane* after settings are changed

> **MORE INFO**
>
> To change the *Navigation Pane*, recall that you first open the *Navigation* menu and select a new category. The *Navigation* menu closes and the *Navigation Pane* updates. To change the filter selection, you must reopen the *Navigation* menu and select a new filter.

The name in the *Navigation Pane Title* bar reflects the filter selection made in the *Navigation* menu. For example, Figure 9-33 displays the filter selection of *All Access Objects* within the *Object Type* category. Figure 9-35 displays the filter selection of *All Tables* within the *Table and Related Views* category.

Use the *Navigation Options* dialog box (Figure 9-36) to change the options available in the *Navigation Pane*. You can modify built-in categories and groups or create new categories and groups.

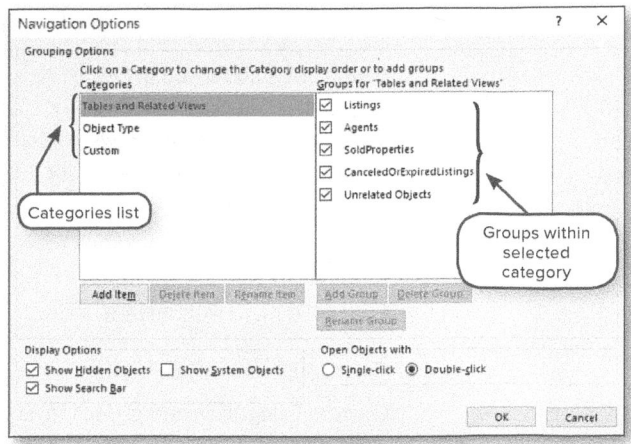

9-36 *Navigation Options* dialog box

A **category** is the highest level organizational structure of the *Navigation Pane*. A database contains five built-in categories (see Figure 9-34): *Custom, Object Type, Tables and Related Views, Created Date,* and *Modified Date*. The *Custom, Object Type,* and *Tables and Related Views* categories each contain a predefined set of groups.

A **group** is the second level organization structure of the *Navigation Pane*. The database objects display in these predefined groups.

The *Tables and Related Views* category contains a group for each table object in the database and an *Unrelated Objects* group. When the *Navigation Pane* is viewed in *Tables and Related Views* (Figure 9-35), each group displays as a heading. The table itself, and any other objects that use the table as its data source, displays within the heading. For example, within the *Agents* heading in Figure 9-35, you see the *Agents* table and the *PropertyListingsByAgent* form, because this form uses the *Agents* table as its data source. Objects that do not use a table as the data source, such as the *PlacerHillsMain* form, display in the *Unrelated Objects* group.

The *Object Type* category contains a group for each of the Access object types (Figure 9-37). When the *Navigation Pane* is viewed by *Object Type* (see Figure 9-33), each group displays as a heading. All objects of that type display within that group. If the database does not contain any objects of a certain group, that heading does not display.

You cannot rename or delete the built-in *Tables and Related Views* or the *Object Type* categories, or the groups within those categories. However, you can choose not to display a selected group (or groups) by unchecking a group's check box.

The third built-in category, *Custom*, contains two groups, *Custom Group 1* and *Unassigned Objects*. More options are available in the *Navigation Options* dialog box when this category is

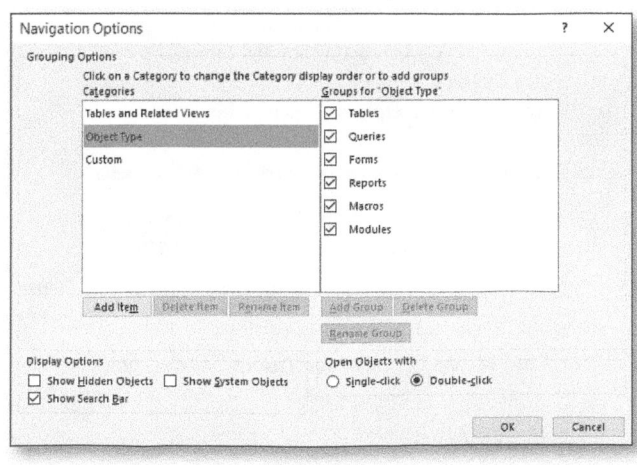

9-37 *Object Type* category and groups

selected (Figure 9-38). For example, the *Delete Item* and *Rename Item* buttons allow you to delete or modify this category. Additionally, the *Add Group* button allows you to create additional groups for this category. These options are explained in the next section.

9-38 Custom category and group

Custom Categories and Groups

Custom categories and groups in a database improve the usability of the database. A customized *Navigation Pane* can be organized to operate as a menu system for the users. Before creating the categories and groups, you will want to spend time planning the *Navigation Pane's* design, focusing on creating categories and groups that help your users perform tasks as efficiently and effectively as possible.

You can have multiple custom categories. Each custom category automatically contains an *Unassigned Objects* group. Within each category, you can create as many custom groups as you need.

To create a custom category, you can either modify the existing *Custom* category or add a new category.

▶**HOW TO:** Create a New Custom Category

1. Right-click the **Navigation Pane Title** bar to open the context menu (Figure 9-39) and select **Navigation Options**. The *Navigation Options* dialog box opens.

ANOTHER WAY

Select **Options** on the *File* tab to open the *Access Options* dialog box and select the **Current Database** button. Select the **Navigation Options** button in the *Navigation* area.

9-39 Select *Navigation Options* on the context menu

2. Click the **Add Item** button. A new custom category is added into the *Categories* list (Figure 9-40).

3. Type a new name in the category box and press **Enter**.

4. Repeat steps 2 and 3 to add additional categories.

5. Click the **Move Up** or **Move Down** arrows, as desired, to rearrange your custom categories (Figures 9-41).

 • If a category is at the top of the list, the *Move Up* arrow is dimmed. A custom category can't be moved above the *Object Type* category.

9-40 Add a new custom category

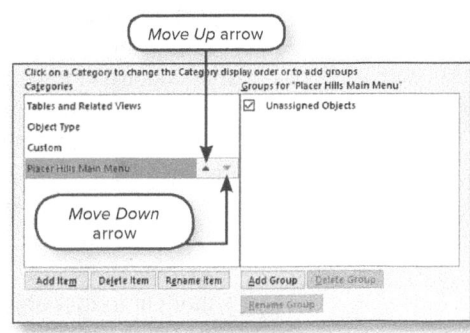

9-41 Rearrange the order of the categories

- If a category is at the bottom of the list, the *Move Down* arrow is dimmed.

6. Click **OK** when done.

After a category is created, the next step is to create custom groups within that category. Remember that your database objects will be placed into the different groups you create.

▶HOW TO: Create a Custom Group

1. If the *Navigation Options* dialog box is not open, right-click the **Navigation Pane Title** bar to open the context menu and select **Navigation Options**.

2. Select the desired category.

3. Click the **Add Group** button to add a new group in this category (Figure 9-42).

4. Type a new name in the group box and press **Enter**.

5. Repeat steps 3 and 4 to add additional groups.

6. Click the **Move Up** or **Move Down** arrows, as desired, to rearrange the groups within a category (Figure 9-43).

 - If a group is at the top of the list, the *Move Up* arrow is dimmed.
 - If a group is at the bottom of the list, the *Move Down* arrow is dimmed. A custom group can't be moved below the *Unassigned Objects* group.

7. Click **OK** when done.

9-42 Add a new group into a category

9-43 Rearrange the order of the groups

After you have created the custom categories and groups, you are ready to assign objects to the different groups.

Assign Objects to Custom Groups

You can assign the objects in your database to the custom groups. When you view a custom category for the first time, note that all objects have been moved into the *Unassigned Objects* group. You can move objects from the *Unassigned Objects* group into the desired group.

If an object does not need to be accessed by a user, don't assign it to a group. For example, some database designers believe that users should only have access to forms, reports, and queries, since these are the objects that provide an interface to the table data. These database designers do not assign tables to the custom groups. In other cases, you have objects, like macros or a query used as a report's data source, which users do not need to interact with directly. Those objects can be left in the *Unassigned Objects* group.

When an object is assigned to a custom group, Access creates a shortcut to that object. A *shortcut* is a pointer to an object in the *Navigation Pane*. A shortcut is identified by a small arrow in the lower left corner of the object (Figure 9-44).

9-44 Shortcut to an object

> **MORE INFO**
>
> The built-in categories and groups, and the *Unassigned Objects* group of a custom category, display the actual database object instead of a shortcut. If you delete an object, it is removed from the database. If you delete a shortcut, only the pointer to the object is deleted.

9-45 Custom category in the *Navigation Pane*

▶ HOW TO: Add an Object to a Group

1. Click the **Navigation Pane** arrow to open the *Navigation* menu and select the custom category.

 - The *Navigation* menu closes and the *Navigation Pane* updates to display the objects (Figure 9-45).
 - The groups in that category display.
 - Initially, all objects are located in the *Unassigned Objects* group.

2. Click, hold, and drag an object from the *Unassigned Objects* group to a different group. A shortcut to that object is created and placed in the group.

You can also right-click an object to open the context menu. Select the **Add to group** option to display the list of available groups (Figure 9-46). Select the desired group. A shortcut to that object is created and placed in that group.

As desired, a shortcut can be assigned to multiple groups. This is useful when the underlying object, like a report, has content that is relevant to more than one group.

9-46 Use the context menu to add an object to a group

▶ **HOW TO:** Add a Shortcut to Multiple Groups

1. Click the **Navigation Pane** arrow to open the *Navigation* menu and select the custom category.
2. Click, hold, and drag an object from the *Unassigned Objects* group to a different group.
3. Select the **shortcut** icon of the desired object.
4. Right-click the **shortcut**, select the **Add to group** option, and select the additional group in which to add the shortcut.
5. Repeat step 4, as desired, to add the shortcut into additional groups.

Modify Objects, Shortcuts, Custom Categories, and Groups

You can make several additional modifications to the objects or shortcuts. Additionally, you may need to rename or delete custom categories or custom groups in the *Navigation Pane*. These skills are discussed in this section.

Disable Design View

Shortcuts, in contrast to the actual database objects, have a ***Disable Design View shortcuts*** property. Use this property to prevent users from opening or switching to *Design* view for the selected object when it is opened through the shortcut. This prevents users from accidentally modifying an object.

▶ **HOW TO:** Disable Design View of an Object

1. Right-click the **shortcut** of the desired object and select the ***View Properties*** option.
 - The *[Shortcut] Properties* dialog box opens (Figure 9-47).
 - The name of the shortcut displays in the dialog box title bar along with the word *Properties*.
2. Click the **Disable Design View shortcuts** check box.
3. Click **OK**.

9-47 *[Shortcut] Properties* dialog box

▶ **MORE INFO**

Design view is only disabled when an object is opened by clicking the shortcut. If a user switches the *Navigation Pane* to display all objects, they are still able to work with the object directly in *Design* view.

Hide or Unhide Objects, Shortcuts, and Groups

You may wish to make selected objects or groups not visible to the user. For example, once you have finished assigning the objects to your custom groups, you can hide the *Unassigned Objects* group if you don't want it to display. Or you may have a few objects within a group that you don't want to display.

▶ HOW TO: Hide or Unhide an Object or Shortcut

1. Right-click the **shortcut** or **object** and select the **View Properties** option.
 - The *Properties* dialog box opens (Figure 9-48).
 - The name of the shortcut or object displays in the dialog box title bar along with the word *Properties*.
 - You can tell the object in Figure 9-48 is not a shortcut, since it does not have the *Disable Design View shortcuts* check box.
2. Select the **Hidden** check box.
 - A check in the *Hidden* check box hides the item.
 - An empty *Hidden* check box displays the item.
3. Click **Apply**.
4. Click **OK**.

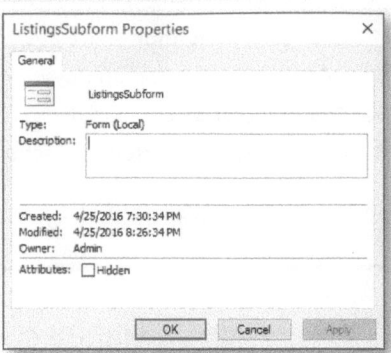

9-48 *[Object] Properties* **dialog box**

Keep in mind the following tips related to hiding or unhiding objects, shortcuts, and groups:

- To hide or unhide a shortcut or object only within a group, right-click the **shortcut** or **object** in the desired group and select the **Hide in this Group** or **Unhide in this Group** option.
- If you hide an object, all shortcuts that reference that object are automatically hidden.
- To hide or unhide a group, right-click the **group heading** and select the **Hide** or **Unhide** option.
- Groups can also be hidden or unhidden by marking the check box to the left of the group name in the *Navigation Options* dialog box.

As you would expect, objects, shortcuts and groups that are hidden do not display in the *Navigation Pane*. In some cases, you may need to unhide an item you previously hid. Before you can select the desired *Unhide* option, you must first be able to see the item.

To display a hidden object, shortcut, or group, check the **Show Hidden Objects** box in the *Navigation Options* dialog box (Figure 9-49). This displays the hidden items in the *Navigation Pane* as dimmed items (Figure 9-50). In Figure 9-50, the *Unassigned Objects* group, and any items in that group, are dimmed. When the items display in a dimmed state, you can right-click the item to choose the appropriate *Unhide* option.

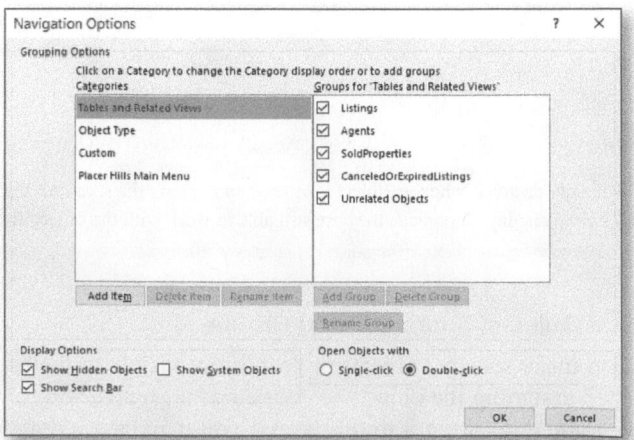

9-49 Select the *Show Hidden Objects* check box

9-50 Dimmed items in the *Navigation Pane*

Rename Objects, Shortcuts, Categories, and Groups

You may want to change the name of a custom category, group, shortcut or object.

> **HOW TO: Rename a Custom Category**

1. Right-click the **Navigation Pane Title** bar to open the context menu and select **Navigation Options**. The *Navigation Options* dialog box opens.
2. Select the desired category.
3. Click the **Rename Item** button, and enter a new name.
4. Click **OK** when done.

> **HOW TO: Rename a Custom Group**

1. Right-click the **Navigation Pane Title** bar to open the context menu and select **Navigation Options**. The *Navigation Options* dialog box opens.
2. Select the desired group.
3. Click the **Rename Group** button and enter a new name.
4. Click **OK** when done.

> **ANOTHER WAY**
>
> Right-click the group heading in the *Navigation Pane* and select the **Rename** option. Enter the new name and press **Enter**.

> **HOW TO: Rename a Shortcut or Object**

1. Right-click the **shortcut** or **object** and select either the **Rename Shortcut** or **Rename** option.
2. Enter a new name and press **Enter**.

Delete Objects, Shortcuts, Categories, and Groups

Occasionally, you may need to delete a custom category, group, shortcut or object. If you created a category in error or if you no longer need a category, you can delete it from the *Navigation* menu. Deleting a category deletes all of the groups within that category. Any shortcuts to objects contained within those groups are also deleted.

> **HOW TO: Delete a Custom Category**

1. Right-click the **Navigation Pane Title** bar to open the context menu and select **Navigation Options**. The *Navigation Options* dialog box opens.
2. Select the desired category.
3. Click the **Delete Item** button. Access displays a confirmation message box. Click **OK** to confirm the deletion.
4. Click **OK** when done.

If a group was created in error or is no longer needed, you can delete the group. Deleting a custom group removes the group from the *Navigation Pane* list. It does not delete any objects that have been assigned to that group.

> ▶ **HOW TO:** Delete a Custom Group

1. Right-click the **Navigation Pane Title** bar to open the context menu and select **Navigation Options**. The *Navigation Options* dialog box opens.
2. Select the desired group.
3. Click the **Delete Group** button. Access displays a confirmation message box. Click **OK** to confirm the deletion.
4. Click **OK** when done.

> ▶ **ANOTHER WAY**
>
> Right-click the **group heading** in the *Navigation Pane* and select the **Delete** option. Be aware that you are not prompted to confirm this deletion.

You can also delete a shortcut or an object.

- To delete a shortcut, right-click the **shortcut** and select the **Remove** option. Deleting a shortcut does not delete the actual object.
- To delete an object, right-click the **object** and select the **Delete** option. Access displays a confirmation message box. Click **OK** to confirm the deletion.

Keep in mind that, even if you have created a custom *Navigation Pane*, users can still use the *Navigation* menu to select one of the pre-built categories. To help prevent accidental changes to the database you can create a macro that locks the *Navigation Pane*. Use the Access Help system to learn how to create this macro.

PAUSE & PRACTICE: ACCESS 9-2

For this Pause & Practice you create a custom *Navigation Pane* for the Placer Hills Real Estate database. You add a custom category and groups, and assign objects to groups. You also make modifications to several of the items in the *Navigation Pane*.

File Needed: ***PlacerHills-09.accdb***
Completed Project File Name: ***[your initials] PP A9-2.accdb***

1. Open the **PlacerHills-09** database from your student data files.
2. Save a new copy of your database as [your initials] PP A9-2.
3. Enable content in the security warning.

4. Create a new custom category.
 a. Right-click the **Navigation Pane Title** bar to open the context menu and select **Navigation Options**. The *Navigation Options* dialog box opens.
 b. Click the **Add Item** button. A new custom category is added into the *Categories* list.
 c. Type Placer Hills Main Menu in the category box and press **Enter**.

5. Create custom groups.
 a. Select the **Placer Hills Main Menu** category, if not already selected.
 b. Click the **Add Group** button to add a new group in this category.
 c. Type Active Listings in the group box and press **Enter**.
 d. Click the **Add Group** button and type Sold, Canceled, or Expired Listings in the group box and press **Enter**. The *Navigation Options* dialog box should look similar to Figure 9-51.
 e. Click **OK** when done.

9-51 New category and groups in the *Navigation Options* dialog box

6. Assign objects to groups.
 a. Click the **Navigation Pane** arrow to open the *Navigation* menu and select the **Placer Hills Main Menu** category.
 b. Click, hold, and drag the **ActiveListings** form from the *Unassigned Objects* group to the *Active Listings* group.
 c. Click, hold, and drag the **PropertyListingsByAgent** form from the *Unassigned Objects* group to the *Active Listings* group. Recall that this form contains the *ListingsSubform* form, although you don't assign that form to any group.
 d. Right-click the **ListingDetails** form, select **Add to group**, and then select the **Active Listings** group.
 e. Right-click the **DaysOnMarket** report, select **Add to group**, and then select the **Active Listings** group.
 f. Right-click the **CanceledOrExpiredListings** form, select **Add to group**, and then select the **Sold, Canceled or Expired Listings** group.
 g. Right-click the **SoldProperties** report, select **Add to group**, and then select the **Sold, Canceled or Expired Listings** group.

7. Disable *Design* view of shortcuts.
 a. Right-click the **PropertyListingsByAgent** shortcut and select the **View Properties** option.
 b. Select the **Disable Design View shortcuts** check box.
 c. Click **OK**.
 d. Right-click the **CanceledOrExpiredListings** shortcut and select the **View Properties** option.
 e. Select the **Disable Design View shortcuts** check box.
 f. Click **OK**.

8. Right-click the **Unassigned Objects** heading and select the **Hide** option.

9. Drag the **divider bar** to widen the *Navigation Pane*, if necessary. The completed *Navigation Pane* should look similar to Figure 9-52.

9-52 Completed *Navigation Pane*

10. Test the custom *Navigation Pane*.
 a. Double-click the **PropertyListingsByAgent** shortcut to open the
 PropertyListingsByAgent form. In the lower right corner of the *Status* bar
 (Figure 9-53), note that the *Design* view icon is not displayed. Also note that this
 form still displays the subform, even though that object was not assigned to the
 group.
 b. Close the form.
 c. Double-click the **ListingDetails** shortcut. In the *Status* bar, note that the *ListingDetails* form allows
 the user to switch to *Design* view.
 d. Close the form.
 e. Double-click the **CanceledOrExpiredListings** shortcut. Note that the *Design* view icon is not
 displayed. Because this is a *Datasheet* form, it also does not have a *Form* view icon.
 f. Close the form.

11. Close the database.

9-53 *Status bar of form*

SLO 9.3

Using the Performance Analyzer Tool

As the number of records increases within a database, it may take longer for some tasks to be
processed. For example, it may take a while for a form or report to open and display the data,
or a query may take some time to return the desired results. The databases used in this book
have had a limited number of records and you may not have noticed any performance issues.
Keep in mind, however, that databases used by organizations may have tens of thousands of
records. The time it takes for Access to search through that many records to find the ones that
meet certain criteria can be significant.

Creating well-designed database tables is an important part of ensuring good perfor-
mance. As you learned in *SLO 9.1: Analyze and Document Database Design*, the Access
Table Analyzer tool can help determine if a table is well designed. However, other issues may
also affect the performance of a database. This section provides an overview of a few of the
more common issues and teaches you how to use an Access tool to analyze performance and
how to interpret the analysis results.

Optimize a Database

You can choose from several different ways to optimize a database. Some of them are one-
time tasks, while others need to be performed periodically. Additionally, some have tradeoffs
that limit the functionality of the database. Others may help some tasks perform more quickly
but make other tasks perform more slowly. As a result, it is important to clearly understand
the processing needs of the user in order to make the correct choices. Several of the more
common options are introduced in the following list:

- *Data Types:* While it seems obvious to say "choose the right data type for each field,"
 you should take into account many considerations when choosing data types. In general,
 keep in mind that number data types process more quickly than text data types. Within
 text data types, a *Long Text* field takes longer to search than a *Short Text* field.
 Additionally, no matter the data type, the smaller the size of a data field, the faster
 that it can be processed. For example, if you are working with *Short Text* fields, be sure
 to change the default size from 255 to a number that better matches the needs of your

data. If a field only needs to store 30 characters, don't waste space storing an additional 225 characters of blank space for every record in the table. It decreases performance and increases storage needs. Similarly, for a number field, choose the proper size, keeping in mind that the different field size options range from 1 byte of storage (for a *Byte* field size) to 16 bytes of storage (for a *Replication ID* field size).

When choosing a data type and associated field size, choose the smallest field size that can accommodate the data.

> **MORE INFO**
>
> Access recommends using a number data type for any field containing numeric data because performance is faster on number data types versus text data types. However, this contradicts the database design recommendation from *SLO 1.2: Creating and Managing a Database* to store numbers not used in calculations as a *Short Text* field. In this book, we follow the recommendations in *SLO 1.2*.

- **Relationships:** Establishing relationships between tables improves the performance of the database for any objects that use fields from both those tables.

- **Indexes:** An *index* is a list used by the database to make it easier to find data. Just like the index at the back of this book points you to a specific page to find a topic, a database index points Access to a record. To speed up performance, you can index fields that are used frequently as criteria in a query or for sorting. However, be careful not to create too many indexes or you may negatively impact performance for adding, deleting, or changing records. It is also a good idea to index the fields on both sides of a relationship join. By default, Access creates an index for a primary key field. However, you need to create the index on the foreign key.

 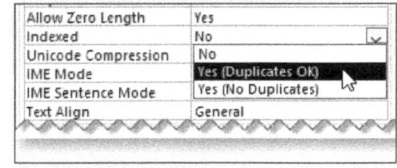

 9-54 *Indexed* property of a field

 To index a field, open the table in *Design* view, select the desired field, and select **Yes (Duplicates OK)** in the *Indexed* property (Figure 9-54).

- **Executable Files:** An *executable* file prevents users from opening forms and reports in *Design* view, prevents them from creating new forms and reports, and compiles all of the macro code. This allows the database to execute faster. In older versions of Access, an executable file was identified with the extension of *.mde*. Newer versions use the extension of *.accde*.

- **Fewer Controls:** If you include too many fields in a query, form, or report, it takes longer to return the results. Of course, if you really need to display all of the fields, you can't do much to prevent this situation.

- **Graphics:** If multiple images are included on the forms and reports in your database, performance may be impacted. Use the *Image Gallery* (see *SLO 7.5: Enhancing the Look of a Form*) to store images used on multiple forms and reports instead of storing the image separately on each form or report. Additionally, remember to save images as JPG files to save storage space.

- **Compact the database:** In *SLO 2.8: Managing a Database Using the Compact & Repair Database Utility*, you learned to use the **Compact & Repair Database** utility. Recall that this utility removes temporary objects that Access automatically creates due to the way it operates. It is important to periodically reclaim this unused space to ensure optimal performance.

Denormalize the tables: As you learned in *SLO 9.1: Analyze and Document Database Design*, normalization takes larger tables that have problems and divides them into smaller tables that no longer have problems. As a result, Access must join the tables back together when you need queries, forms, or reports to show the related data. Joining tables together takes more time than retrieving data from one table. Because of this, if a database has a significant number of tables that need to be joined, you may want to denormalize some of the tables. Denormalization is the process of intentionally returning tables to a lower normal form. This reintroduces problems you were trying to avoid with normalization, such as redundancy. You must carefully weigh the tradeoffs and make the best decision considering the needs of your users.

> ### MORE INFO
>
> Some of these modifications are quite involved and may require the assistance of someone with more experience in database systems. A ***Database Administrator*** has special training and experience in how to best optimize large databases, in addition to other skills.

The Performance Analyzer Tool

Access includes a ***Performance Analyzer*** tool that analyzes objects in the database and suggests potential solutions to improve performance.

The tool categorizes analysis results as recommendations, suggestions, and ideas, each identified with an icon (Figure 9-55).

Recommendations are solutions that can be carried out automatically by Access and do not have potential consequences on the database. Adding an index to a field is an example of a recommendation.

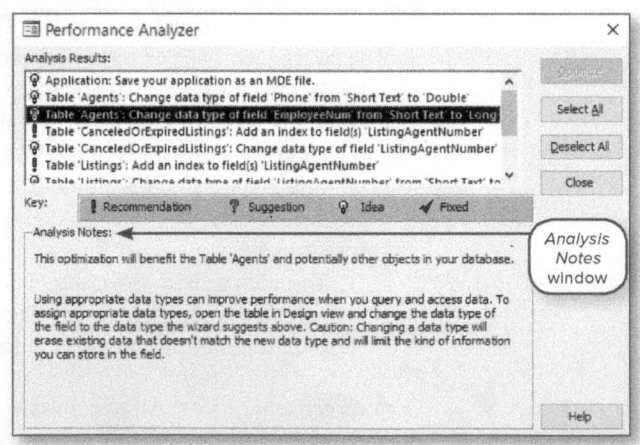

9-55 Potential solutions are suggested by the *Performance Analyzer*

Suggestions are solutions that can also be carried out automatically by Access. However, suggestions may have consequences or tradeoffs that you must consider. Creating a relationship between tables is an example of a suggestion.

Ideas are also solutions that may have consequences or tradeoffs that you must consider, but Access cannot automatically perform an idea. You must perform these changes in the database by following the necessary steps. Changing a field's data type is an example of an idea.

As you select different solutions from the list in the *Analysis Results* window, the *Analysis Notes* window updates to provide an explanation about the item.

You can have Access automatically perform recommendations and suggestions. In those cases, the icon of each item switches to ***Fixed***. To perform ideas, you must close the *Performance Analyzer* tool and complete the necessary steps to implement the idea.

It is important to keep in mind that the *Performance Analyzer* tool is not perfect, nor is it a substitute for understanding how to create a well-designed database. The tool offers limited solutions when a database contains few records. For example, it will not suggest creating an index on a field unless it determines that a sufficient number of objects use the same field

as criteria. Additionally, all potential solutions depend upon the design of existing objects in your database. A variation in how or what you have created could alter the potential solutions.

> **MORE INFO**
>
> It is a good idea to back up your database before optimizing it. This way you have the original in case the optimization causes any unanticipated problems. See *SLO 1.2: Creating and Managing a Database* to review how to make a backup copy of a database.

▶ HOW TO: Use the Performance Analyzer

1. Click the **Analyze Performance** button [*Database Tools* tab, *Analyze* group] (Figure 9-56).
 - The *Performance Analyzer dialog box* opens (Figure 9-57).
 - The dialog box shows the tab that corresponds to the selected object in the *Navigation Pane*.
2. Click the tab corresponding to the type of object you wish to analyze.
3. Select the check boxes of the objects you wish to analyze.
 - You can check multiple objects on a tab.
 - Click the **Select All** button to select all of the objects on the tab.
4. As desired, repeat steps 2 and 3 to select objects from a different tab.

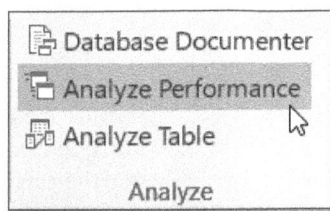

9-56 *Analyze Performance* button

> **ANOTHER WAY**
>
> To analyze all objects in the database, click the **All Object Types** tab and click the **Select All** button.

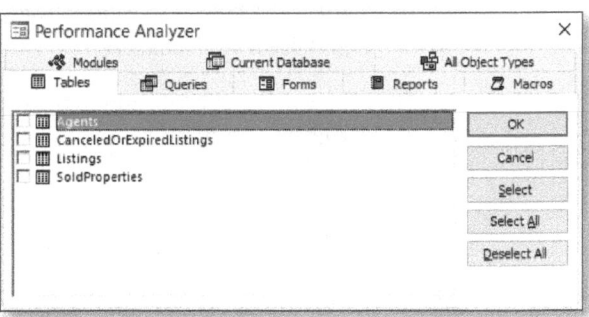

9-57 *Performance Analyzer* dialog box

5. Click **OK**. The *Performance Analyzer* dialog box updates to display the results (Figure 9-58). The results are categorized into *Recommendations*, *Suggestions*, and *Ideas*.
6. Select a potential solution from the *Analysis Results* window to review the *Analysis Notes*. If the solution is a *Recommendation* or *Suggestion*, the *Optimize* button becomes available.
7. Select a **Recommendation** or **Suggestion** and click the **Optimize** button to have Access perform the solution.

> **ANOTHER WAY**
>
> To have Access perform all *Recommendations* and *Suggestions*, click the **Select All** button and then click the **Optimize** button.

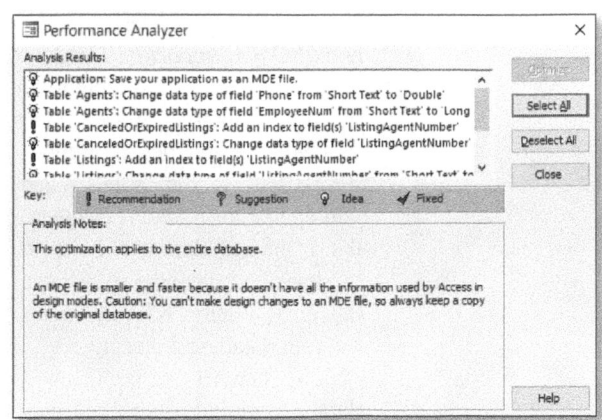

9-58 Review the *Analysis Results* and *Analysis Notes*

8. Click **Close** when you are done reviewing all of the potential solutions.

If you wish to implement any of the potential solutions classified as *Ideas*, you must perform the steps to execute the solution. If you had the tool create any relationships, referential integrity was not enforced when Access created the relationships. You should open the *Relationships* window to edit the relationship settings to meet the needs of the business.

> ### MORE INFO
>
> A common *Idea* included in the *Analysis Results* is to save the database as an MDE file. Recall that this is the older format of an executable file. You should create an ACCDE file instead.

SLO 9.4 Using the Database Splitter Tool

Some of your databases may be designed to be used by multiple users in a company. One option is to put the databases you created on a network drive. This allows multiple users to use the database at the same time. However, as the number of database users grows, this solution can result in significant performance issues and problems if different users try to update the same data at the same time. Another solution is to split the database into two database files, a front-end database and a back-end database. This technique can improve performance and security, and it allows users to create their own customized forms and reports. In this section, you learn about the front-end and back-end parts of a split database and how to create and use a split database.

Front-End and Back-End Databases

Each of the databases you have created and used in this book store all of their separate objects in one ACCDB file. When you open a database, all of the objects are available. If you split a database, you create two different parts.

The ***back-end database*** contains the database tables. The back-end database is stored on a network drive, or some other shared location, to allow multiple users to access the data.

The ***front-end database*** contains linked tables that point to the back-end database and all of the forms, reports, and queries needed to use the data. In *SLO 8.2: Importing from an Excel Worksheet* and *SLO 8.3: Importing Text Files*, you learned how to create linked tables to an Excel worksheet or a text file. A linked table to an Access database works similarly. One major difference is that when you link to an Access database you can add, delete, or modify records in the table. When you open a form, report or query, the front-end database links to the back-end database to retrieve the data. Figure 9-59 illustrates the split database concept.

The benefits of splitting a database include improved performance, customized front-ends for different users, and increased security and protection, since changes to the table structure can't be made through a front-end database.

9-59 Back-end and front-end databases

Split a Database

The Access *Database Splitter* tool creates the back-end database and moves the table objects into the back-end database. The starting database becomes the front-end database. The front-end database contains all of the original objects, except the tables, which have been replaced with linked tables.

> ### MORE INFO
>
> It is a good idea to back up your database before you split it. This way you have a copy in case you want to resume using the original database. See *SLO 1.2: Creating and Managing a Database* to review making a backup copy of a database.

▶**HOW TO:** Use the Database Splitter

1. Open the database that will be split and create a backup copy of the database, if needed.

2. Click the **Access Database** button [*Database Tools* tab, *Move Data* group] (Figure 9-60).

 9-60 Access Database button

 - The *Database Splitter* dialog box opens (Figure 9-61).
 - Review the instructions in the dialog box.

3. Click the **Split Database** button.

 - The *Create Back-end Database* dialog box opens (Figure 9-62).
 - Access suggests a default file name that combines the original database name with the ending *_be*.

 Database Splitter

 This wizard moves tables from your current database to a new back-end database. In multi-user environments, this reduces network traffic, and allows continuous front-end development without affecting data or interrupting users.

 If your database is protected with a password, the new back-end database will be created without a password and will be accessible to all users. You will need to add a password to the back-end database after it is split.

 It could be a long process. Make a backup copy of your database before splitting it.

 Would you like to split the database now?

 [Split Database] [Cancel]

 9-61 Database Splitter dialog box

4. Locate the folder where you want to save the file, modify the file name as desired, and click the **Split** button.

 - To include a path to the network location of the back-end database, enter your specific information into the *File name* box using the following format: *NetworkServerName\FolderName\Database_be.accdb*
 - If no errors occurred, Access displays a message box confirming the creation of the back-end database.

> ### MORE INFO
>
> If the location you select to save the file is not the ultimate, shared network location, you must update the table links after you move the back-end database to the shared network location.

9-62 Create Back-end Database dialog box

5. Click **OK** to acknowledge the message.
 - The front-end database remains open.
 - The *Navigation Pane* shows the linked tables (Figure 9-63). A linked Access table displays an arrow to the left of the table icon.

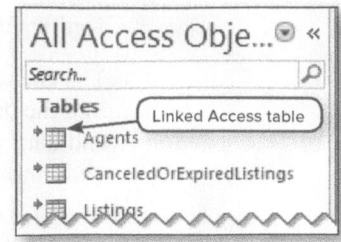

9-63 Linked Access tables in the *Navigation Pane*

Work with a Split Database

After the database has been split, you may need to perform the following tasks:

- Even if the original database was password-protected before the split, the new back-end database is not created with a password. You must open the back-end database and add a password. You learn to password protect a database in the next section of this chapter.
- Once the back-end database has been created and located in a shared network location, you must distribute the front-end database to the users. Depending on the needs of the business, the front-end for each user may look the same or they may differ. Unless you take action to prevent it, users can add new objects or modify existing objects in their front-end database. As desired, you can restrict users from being able to change any of the objects in the database by creating an executable file. You learn to create an executable database in the next section of this chapter.
- In some cases, you may create customized front-end databases for different users or groups of users. You can either save a copy of the existing front-end database and then modify it, or you can create a new blank desktop database and create the new objects.
- If you create a new database, you must create the link tables before you can add any other objects.
- When you have completed all changes in the front-end database, create copies and distribute the front-end database to each user.
- At some point during the use of the database, the back-end database may be moved to a new location, or there may be another problem that causes your users to receive an Access message indicating the back-end database file cannot be located. If this occurs, you must update the links from the front-end database to the back-end database. Use the ***Linked Table Manager*** to perform this task.

▶**HOW TO: Create a Link to a Table in Another Access Database**

1. Click the **Access** button [*External Data* tab, *Import & Link* group] (Figure 9-64). The *Get External Data – Access Database* dialog box launches (Figure 9-65).
2. Click the **Browse** button to launch the *File Open* dialog box.

9-64 *Access* button in the *Import & Link* group

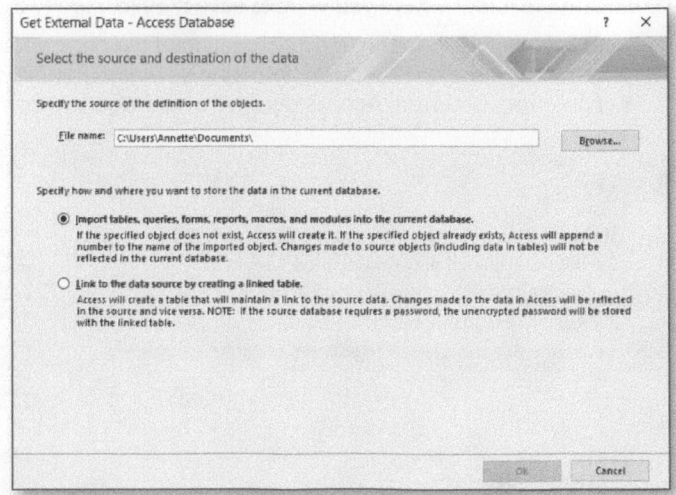

9-65 *Get External Data – Access Database* dialog box

3. Locate and select the back-end database file that contains the tables you want to link to, and then click the **Open** button. The *File Open* dialog box closes.

4. Select the **Link to the data source by creating a linked table** radio button and click **OK** to launch the *Link Tables* dialog box (Figure 9-66).

5. Select the table name. To select multiple tables, select the first table, press and hold the **Shift** key, and select the additional tables. To select all the tables, click the **Select All** button. Click **OK**.

 • If no errors occurred, Access creates the tables and adds them into the *Tables* group of the *Navigation Pane*.
 • A linked table icon includes an arrow pointing to the table icon.

9-66 *Link Tables* dialog box

▶ **HOW TO:** Update Links to a Table in Another Access Database

1. Click the **Linked Table Manager** button (Figure 9-67) [*External Data* tab, *Import & Link* group]. The *Linked Table Manager* dialog box launches (Figure 9-68).

2. Check the box corresponding to the table that needs to be relinked or, to select all the tables, click the **Select All** button.

3. Check the **Always prompt for new location** box if the tables are located in different databases.

4. Click **OK**.

 • If you checked the *Always prompt for new location* box, Access displays the *Select New Location of [table name]* dialog box. The name of your database table displays in place of *[table name.]*
 • Locate and select the back-end database file and click the **Open** button. The *File Open* dialog box closes.
 • If the tables are located in different databases, the *Select New Location of [table name]* dialog box displays again. Locate, select and open the other databases as needed.
 • If no errors occurred, Access displays a *Linked Table Manager* dialog box informing you that all linked tables were refreshed.

5. Click **OK** to acknowledge the message.

6. Click **Close**.

9-67 *Linked Table Manager* button in the *Import & Link* group

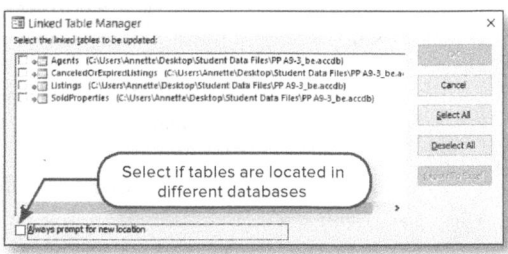

9-68 *Linked Table Manager* dialog box

SLO 9.5

Using Access Security Tools

Safeguarding your database ensures that the database continues to work and provides the needed functionality to an organization. Creating a well-designed database is an important part of this process. As you have worked on the different databases, you have created table structures that minimize redundant data. You have also integrated different features, such as data validation rules and field lookups, to enhance the integrity of the data. In *SLO 9.2:*

Customizing the Navigation Pane, you learned to customize the *Navigation Pane*, which allows you to hide objects. All of these techniques are important but even if you have used all of them, your database is still vulnerable to security breaches. In this section, you learn about several tools available in Access that can help improve the security of your database.

Encrypt and Password Protect a Database

Encryption converts data into a coded format that can't be understood unless it is decoded. If you open an encrypted file, it appears as scrambled characters and numbers. Access implements encryption through password protection. When you assign a password to a database, Access encrypts the database, saves the new file, and closes the database. When you reopen the database, you must enter the password in order to have Access decrypt and open the database.

> ### MORE INFO
>
> If you forget the password, you cannot open the database. Access does not have a mechanism to allow you to retrieve a lost password. As a result, it is a good idea to create a backup copy of the database prior to assigning a password. Be sure to store the backup copy in a secure location.

Before you can encrypt a database, it must be opened in exclusive mode. Access has four different modes in which a database can be opened:

- **Open**: Allows shared use of the database and full access to all objects. This allows you and other users to read existing data and make changes to the database. Unless settings within Access have been changed, this is the default mode.
- **Open Read-Only**: Allows shared use to see any data in the database. However, you and any other users are prevented from making any changes to the database, such as adding, changing, or deleting data. If you have opened a database as *Open Read-Only*, other users can still open the database in *Open* mode, allowing them to make changes as desired.
- **Open Exclusive**: Permits only the person opening the database to have the database open. If anyone has it opened exclusively, other users are prevented from opening the database. If anyone has the database already open, you are prevented from opening it exclusively.
- **Open Exclusive Read-Only**: Permits only the person opening the database to have the database open, but he or she is prevented from making any changes to the database.

The default *Open* mode applies when you or a user double-click an Access database file to open it from Windows or when you click the **Open** button [*File* tab] and then select a file from the *Recent* area (Figure 9-69).

In most cases, both you and any of your users, will use the default *Open* mode.

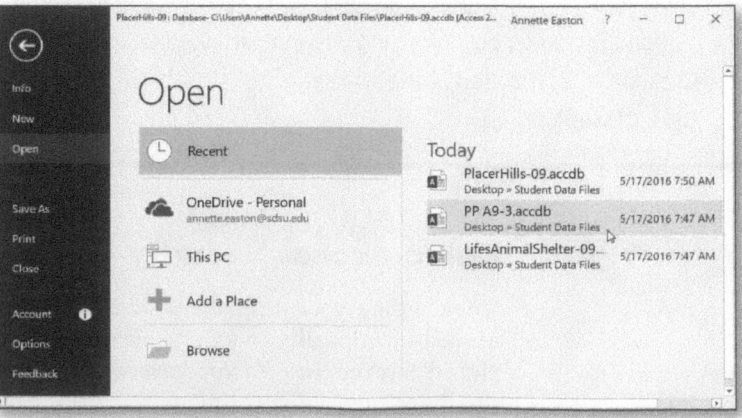

9-69 Select a file from the *Recent* area to open it in *Open* mode

▶ HOW TO: Open a Database in Exclusive Mode

1. Click the **Open** button [*File* tab] or press **Ctrl+O** to display the *Open* area in *Backstage* view.

2. Double-click **Recent**, **OneDrive**, or **This PC** to open the *Open* dialog box.

3. Browse to the location of your database and click to select the database. Do not double-click the database file name.

4. Click the **Open button** arrow and select **Open Exclusive** (Figure 9-70).

9-70 Select *Open Exclusive*

With the database opened exclusively, you can assign a password. Remember that passwords are case-sensitive. Be sure to enter a strong password, which is more difficult for someone to guess.

> **MORE INFO**
>
> To create a strong password, use at least eight characters and include at least one uppercase letter, one lowercase letter, one number, and one special character. Avoid using common words, names, or numbers that are unique to you. For example, don't use your mom's name, your street address number, or part of your social security number.

▶ HOW TO: Encrypt a Database with a Password

1. Open the database using the *Open Exclusive* option, if needed, and click the **File** tab to open the *Backstage* view.

2. Click the **Encrypt with Password** button (Figure 9-71). The *Set Database Password* dialog box displays.

3. Type a password in the *Password* box.

4. Type the same password in the *Verify* box. Note that the entries display as asterisks in both boxes (Figure 9-72).

5. Click **OK**.

 - If the passwords do not match, a message box displays. Click **OK** to acknowledge the message and then repeat steps 3 through 5.
 - If you get a message about row level locking, click **OK**.

6. Close the database.

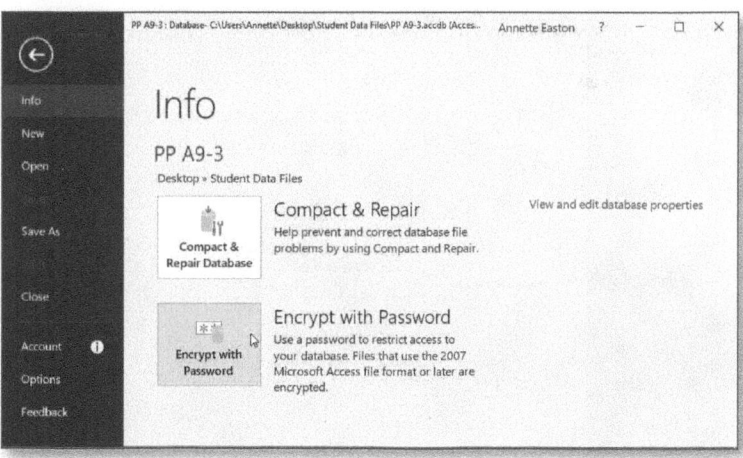

9-71 *Encrypt with Password* button

9-72 *Set Database Password* dialog box

When you open a database that has been encrypted, the *Password Required* dialog box displays (Figure 9-73). You must enter the correct password and click **OK** before the database opens completely.

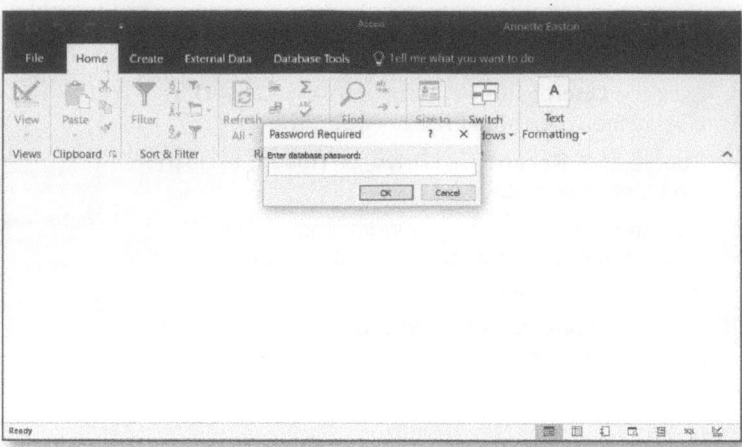

9-73 The *Password Required* dialog box displays before the database opens completely

At some point, you may need to remove the password assigned to a database, or you may need to periodically change the password as part of a good password management process. Some companies, for example, have policies that establish the frequency with which you must change a password.

To change a password, you must first decrypt the database to remove the current password and then follow the previous steps to encrypt the database to create the new password.

▶ **HOW TO:** Decrypt a Database with a Password

1. Open the database using the *Open Exclusive* option, if needed, and click the **File** tab to open the *Backstage* view.
2. Click the **Decrypt Database** button (Figure 9-74). The *Unset Database Password* dialog box displays (Figure 9-75).

9-74 *Decrypt Database* button

9-75 *Unset Database Password* dialog box

3. Type the current password in the *Password* box and click **OK**.
 - If the password is not correct, a message box displays. Click **OK** to acknowledge the message and then try again.
 - If the password is correct, Access removes the password. The database remains open in exclusive mode.
4. To apply a new password follow the steps in *How To: Encrypt a Database with a Password*. Otherwise, close the database.

Adding a password to a split database is a little more involved. While you could choose to password protect only the back-end or only the front-end, your database will be more secure if you assign a password to the back-end database and to all copies of the front-end database.

To do this, follow the steps you just learned to assign a password to a database. However, you must encrypt the back-end database first and you must recreate the linked tables in the front-end databases. The following *How To* provides a guideline for the process.

▶ HOW TO: Encrypt the Back-end and Front-end Databases in a Split Database

1. Encrypt the back-end database first by following the steps in *How To: Encrypt a Database with a Password*.
2. Encrypt the front-end database second.
 - Open the front-end database in exclusive mode.
 - Delete the linked tables. Even though the location of the tables has not changed, you cannot use them due to the new password on the back-end database.
 - Follow the steps in *How To: Create a Link to a Table in Another Access Database* in *SLO 9.4: Using the Database Splitter Tool* to recreate the linked tables. You will be prompted to enter the password of the back-end database during this process.
 - Follow the steps in *How To: Encrypt a Database with a Password* to assign a password to the front-end database.

When working with the front-end database, you must decide whether each copy of the front-end will use the same password or a different password. If they share the same password, you can assign the password before you make copies and distribute to your users. If they will have unique passwords, you need to make copies of the database first and then assign a unique password to each copy.

Package and Sign a Database

Once you have completed your database, you may wish to package and sign the database before distributing it to others. When you package and sign a database, you tell others that your database can be trusted. Recall that viruses can be transmitted inside the macro code in a database. When you first open a database, a user must decide whether he or she trusts the database. If a user does, he or she clicks the *Enable Content* button. Adding your electronic signature to the database lets others know that the database hasn't been altered.

To package and sign a database, you must have a ***digital certificate***, an authentication mechanism that contains identifying information about the creator, as well as a ***digital signature***, an electronic stamp attached to the digital certificate. You can either purchase a digital certificate from a commercial vendor or you can create a self-signed certificate. A self-signed certificate can be used on a small scale within your own organization, but if you are going to distribute the database more widely you must purchase a digital certificate from a commercial vendor. In this section, you learn how to create and use a self-signed certificate.

To create and use a self-signed certificate, you first create the certificate. This process occurs outside Access. Then you use the certificate within Access to package and sign a database.

▶**HOW TO: Create a Self-Signed Certificate**

1. Open Windows File Explorer and browse to the folder that contains your Office 2016 program files. The files should be located in the default folder, similar to *Drive:\Program Files\Microsoft Office\root\Office16*.

2. Click the **Search** box to activate the *Search Tools* tab.

3. Click **Advanced options** [*Search* tab, *Options* group] and select **System files**.

4. Type Selfcert.exe in the *Search Program Files* box. Windows Explorer locates and displays the *SELFCERT.EXE* file (Figure 9-76). It is possible that you have more than one file, depending on your installation.

9-76 Locate the *SELFCERT.EXE* file

▶ **MORE INFO**

If you have older versions of Office on your computer, the *SELFCERT. EXE* file may be located in a folder containing the earlier Office program.

9-77 *Create Digital Certificate* dialog box

5. Double-click **SELFCERT.EXE** to launch the program.

6. Type a name to assign to the certificate in the *Create Digital Certificate* dialog box (Figure 9-77) and click **OK**.

 • The *SelfCert Success* dialog box displays (Figure 9-78).
 • The message in the box displays the name of your certificate. (In the example shown here, the certificate name is "Annette Easton.")

7. Click **OK**.

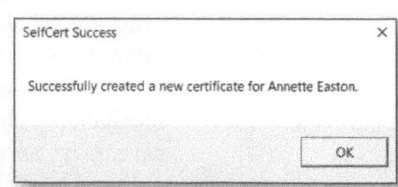

9-78 *SelfCert Success* dialog box

Once you have a digital certificate, you can use the ***Package and Sign*** tool to create a database your users know they can trust. A database that is signed and packaged has a file extension of ***.accdc***.

▶ HOW TO: Package and Sign a Database

1. Click the **File** tab to open the *Backstage* view and click the **Save As** button.

2. Click the **Package and Sign** button in the *Advanced* grouping of *the Save Database As* section and click the **Save As** button (Figure 9-79). The *Windows Security* dialog box displays listing all available certificates (Figure 9-80).

3. Select the certificate to apply to the database and click **OK**. The *Create Microsoft Access Signed Package* dialog box displays (Figure 9-81).

4. Select the location where you want to store the file. As desired, you can change the default file name but retain the extension *.accdc*. Click the **Create** button.

 - A new file is created containing the packaged database.
 - The original database remains open.

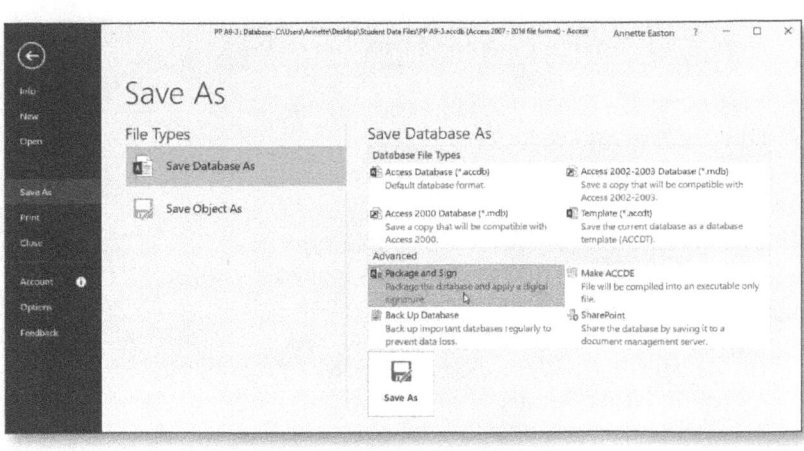

9-79 Click the *Package and Sign* button

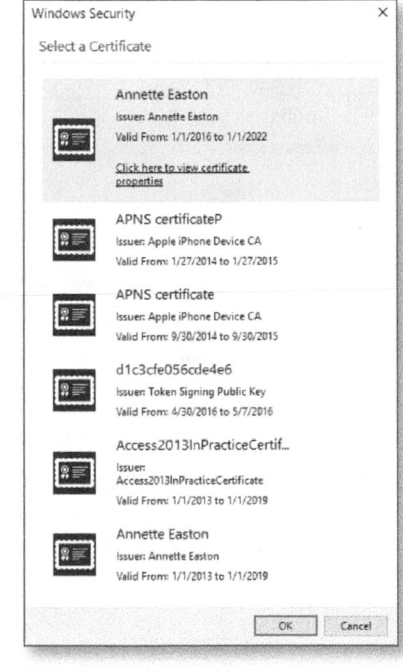

9-80 Choose the certificate to apply in the *Windows Security* dialog box

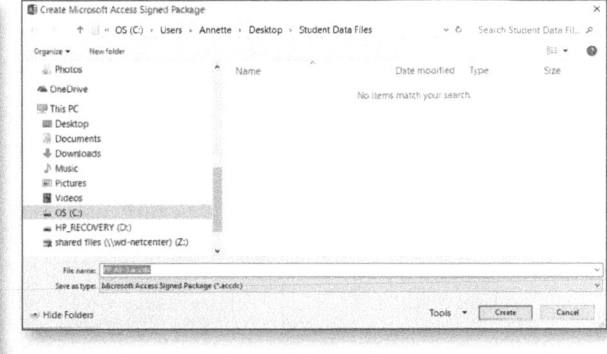

9-81 *Create Microsoft Access Signed Package* dialog box

When viewed in Windows File Explorer, the icon of a packaged database file has a small certificate added to the right-side of the normal Access database file icon. Figure 9-82 shows icons for both an *.accdb* and an *.accdc* file.

To use a packaged database, the database must be extracted from the packaged file and saved as a normal *.accdb* database. Access handles this when you open the packaged file. You are prompted to accept the digital certificate during this process.

Packaged database icon
PP A9-3.accdb
PP A9-3.accdc

9-82 Access database file icons

▶ HOW TO: Open a Packaged Database

1. Click the **Open** button [*File* tab] to display the *Open* area in *Backstage* view.

2. Double-click **This PC** to open the *Open* dialog box.

3. Change the file type by clicking the **File Type** box arrow and selecting **Microsoft Access Signed Packages (*.accdc)** (Figure 9-83).

4. Browse to the location of your database, click to select the database, and click **Open**. A *Microsoft Access Security Notice* dialog box displays information about the digital signature (Figure 9-84).

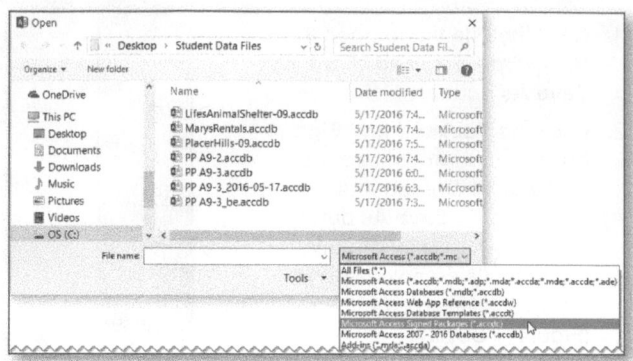

9-83 Change the file type to display signed packages

▶ **ANOTHER WAY**

Double-click the file name in Windows File Explorer instead of performing steps 1–4.

5. Click **Open** if you trust the certificate. The *Extract Database To* dialog box displays.

6. Browse to the location where you want to store the database, and then click **OK** (Figure 9-85). The database opens.

9-84 *Microsoft Access Security Notice* dialog box

9-85 Select the location to store the extracted database

Lock a Database File

Another *Save As* option in Access creates an **Access Database Executable (ACCDE)** file. An Access Database Executable file, also called a **locked** database file or an **executable** file, prevents users from making any changes to existing forms, reports, and macros or from creating any form or report objects. This additional level of security can prevent accidental mistakes. The process to create an executable file is very straightforward. Use the **Make ACCDE** tool to create an executable file.

▶ HOW TO: Create a Locked Database (ACCDE) File

1. Click the **File** tab to open the *Backstage* view and click the **Save As** button.

2. Click the **Make ACCDE** button in the *Advanced* grouping of *the Save Database As* section and click the **Save As** button (Figure 9-86). The *Save As* dialog box displays.

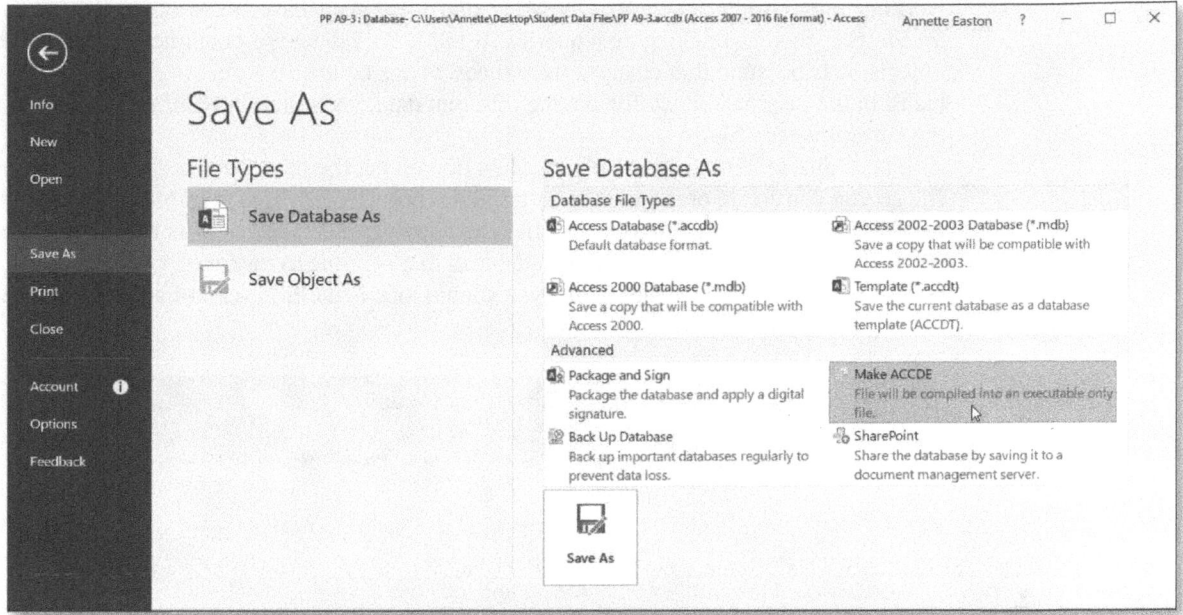

9-86 Click the *Make ACCDE* button

3. Select the location where you want to store the file. As desired, you can change the default file name but retain the.*accde* extension. Click the **Save** button.
 - A new file is created containing the locked database.
 - The original database remains open.

The icon of a locked database file includes a small lock on the right side of the normal Access database file icon. Figure 9-87 shows icons for *.accdb*, *.accdc*, and *.accde* files.

When a locked database is opened and used, all objects can be opened and used. However, *Design* view is not an available option for forms and reports. Additionally, the *Create* tab dims all of the icons in the *Forms* and *Reports* groups, as well as the *Macro* icon in the *Macros & Code* group.

9-87 Access database file icons

Be sure to keep a copy of your original *.accdb* file in a secure location. You need this file if you want to add or modify any forms, reports, or macros.

Although Access allows you to lock any database, good database design practices suggest you only lock the front-end of a split database. If you lock a non-split database containing both the tables and all database objects, or if you lock the back-end of a split database, you create a situation that is difficult to manage.

When users work in a locked database, data records are added, modified, and deleted inside of that locked database. But, Access prevents you from changing existing forms, reports, or macros or from creating any new forms or reports in the database once it has been locked. Any changes, such as creating or modifying the forms and reports, must be done in the original *.accdb* file.

However, the original *.accdb* file does not contain the most current data. Remember that all of the updates were done in the locked database (*.accde* file) that your users have been

working with. Additionally, it is possible that users may have made other changes in the *.accde* file, such as creating new queries. If the locked database contained tables as well as objects, it is possible that changes were made to the table structure. Any of these situations result in the original *.accdb* file having different data, and potentially different objects, from the current *.accde* file.

These differences create problems. How do you get the most current data into the *.accdb* file so you can create or modify the forms and reports? While it is possible to try to synchronize the data and objects across both files by copying tables and objects between the *.accdb* file and the *.accde* file, it is a complicated task that is prone to mistakes.

As a result, the only database that you should lock is the front-end of a split database.

PAUSE & PRACTICE: ACCESS 9-3

For this Pause & Practice you analyze the performance of the Placer Hills Real Estate database. To enhance performance and improve security, you split the database, add a password to the back-end database, update linked tables in the front-end database, and lock the front-end database.

File Needed: *[your initials] PP A9-2.accdb*
Completed Project File Names: *[your initials] PP A9-3.accdb, [your initials] PP A9-3_Backup.accdb, [your initials] PP A9-3_Backup_2.accdb, [your initials] PP A9-3_be.accdb*, and *[your initials] PP A9-3. accde*

1. Open the *[your initials] PP A9-2* database completed in *Pause & Practice 9-2*.

2. Save a new copy of your database as [your initials] PP A9-3.

3. Enable content in the security warning.

4. Click the **Navigation Pane** arrow to open the *Navigation* menu and select the **Object Type** category. The *Navigation Pane* updates.

5. Back up the database.
 a. Click the **File** tab to open the *Backstage* view and click the **Save As** button.
 b. Click the **Back Up Database** button in the *Advanced* grouping of *the Save Database As* section and then click the **Save As** button. The *Save As* dialog box displays.
 c. Select the location to store the file, enter [your initials] PP A9-3_Backup.accdb as the file name, and click the **Save** button.

6. Analyze the performance of the database.
 a. Click the **Analyze Performance** button [*Database Tools* tab, *Analyze* group].
 b. Click the **All Object Types** tab.
 c. Click the **Select All** button.
 d. Click **OK** to display the *Analysis Results* (Figure 9-88).
 e. Select the **Table 'CanceledOrExpiredListings': Add an index to field(s) 'ListingAgentNumber'** recommendation from the *Analysis Results* window. Read the *Analysis Notes*.

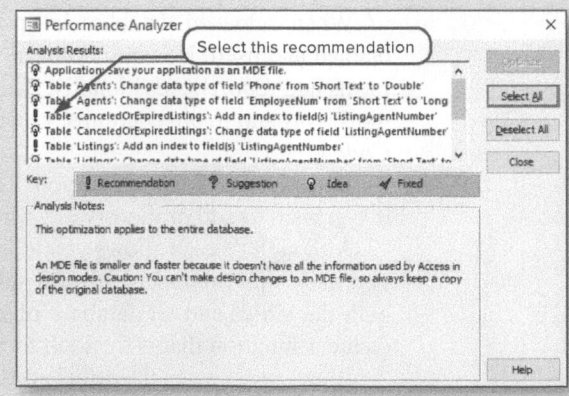

9-88 Review the *Analysis Results* and *Analysis Notes*

f. Click the **Optimize** button to have Access perform this recommendation. The icon changes to the *Fixed* check mark.

g. Scroll down to and select the **Table 'Listings': Add an index to field(s) 'ListingAgentNumber'** recommendation in the *Analysis Results* window. Read the *Analysis Notes*.

h. Click the **Optimize** button. The icon changes to the *Fixed* check mark.

i. Scroll down to and select the **Table 'SoldProperties': Add an index to field(s) 'ListingAgentNumber'** recommendation in the *Analysis Results* window. Read the *Analysis Notes*.

j. Click the **Optimize** button. The icon changes to the *Fixed* check mark.

k. Review the remaining potential solutions. You decide not to change any data types. Click **Close** when done.

7. Verify the relationship constraints.
 a. Click the **Relationships** button [*Database Tools* tab, *Relationships* group]. None of the relationships have enforced referential integrity.
 b. Select the **relationship line** between the *Agents* and *Listings* tables.
 c. Click **Edit Relationships** [*Relationship Tools Design* tab, *Tools* group].
 d. Select the **Enforce Referential Integrity** and the **Cascade Update Related Fields** check boxes and click **OK**.
 e. Select the **relationship line** between the *Agents* and *CanceledOrExpiredListings* tables.
 f. Click **Edit Relationships** [*Relationship Tools Design* tab, *Tools* group].
 g. Select the **Enforce Referential Integrity** and the **Cascade Update Related Fields** check boxes and click **OK**.
 h. Select the **relationship line** between the *Agents* and *SoldProperties* tables.
 i. Click **Edit Relationships** [*Relationship Tools Design* tab, *Tools* group].
 j. Select the **Enforce Referential Integrity** and the **Cascade Update Related Fields** check boxes and click **OK**.
 k. Save the changes to the relationships and close the *Relationships* window.

8. Back up the database (because you have made changes since the first backup).
 a. Click the **File** tab to open the *Backstage* view and click the **Save As** button.
 b. Click the **Back Up Database** button in the *Advanced* grouping of *the Save Database As* section and click the **Save As** button. The *Save As* dialog box displays.
 c. Select the location to store the file, enter [your initials] PP A9-3_Backup_2.accdb as the file name, and click the **Save** button.

9. Split the database.
 a. Click the **Access Database** button [*Database Tools* tab, *Move Data* group]. The *Database Splitter* dialog box opens.
 b. Click the **Split Database** button. The *Create Back-end Database* dialog box opens.
 c. Locate the folder where you want to save the file, accept the suggested file name, and click the **Split** button. Access displays a message box confirming the creation of the back-end database.
 d. Click **OK** to acknowledge the message. The front-end database remains open and the new linked tables display in the *Navigation Pane* (Figure 9-89).
 e. Click the **Close** button [*File* tab] to close the front-end database.

9-89 Linked Access tables in the *Navigation Pane*

10. Password protect the back-end database.
 a. Click the **Open** button [*File* tab] to display the *Open* area in the *Backstage* view.
 b. Double-click **Recent**, **OneDrive**, or **This PC** to open the *Open* dialog box.

c. Browse to the location of your back-end database and click to select *[your initials] PP A9-3_be.accdb*. Do not double-click the database file name.

d. Click the **Open** button arrow (Figure 9-90) and select **Open Exclusive**.

e. Click the **File** tab to open the *Backstage* view.

f. Click the **Encrypt with Password** button to open the *Set Database Password* dialog box.

g. Type Fufzg5o! in the *Password* box.

h. Type Fufzg5o! in the *Verify* box.

i. Click **OK**. If you receive a message about row level locking, click **OK**.

j. Close the database.

9-90 Select *Open Exclusive*

11. Update links in the front-end database.
 a. Open the *[your initials] PP A9-3.accdb* database file. Remember that this is now your front-end database.
 b. Double-click the **Agents** table. An Access message box displays informing you that you don't have a valid password. Click **OK** to acknowledge the message.
 c. Delete the **Agents**, **CanceledOrExpiredListings**, **Listings**, and **SoldProperties** tables. Click **Yes** if prompted to remove the link to the tables or asked to confirm the deletion.
 d. Click the **Access** button [*External Data* tab, *Import & Link* group]. The *Get External Data – Access Database* dialog box launches.
 e. Click the **Browse** button to launch the *File Open* dialog box.
 f. Locate and select *[your initials] PP A9-3_be.accdb* and click the **Open** button.
 g. Select the **Link to the data source by creating a linked table** radio button and click **OK**. The *Password Required* dialog box displays.
 h. Type Fufzg5o! in the *Password* box and click **OK**. The *Link Tables* dialog box displays.
 i. Click the **Select All** button and click **OK**. The tables are added into the *Tables* group of the *Navigation Pane*.

12. Lock the front-end database.
 a. Click the **File** tab to open the *Backstage* view and click the **Save As** button.
 b. Click the **Make ACCDE** button in the *Advanced* grouping of *the Save Database As* section, and then click the **Save As** button. The *Save As* dialog box displays.
 c. Select the location to store the file, accept the suggested file name, and click the **Save** button. The *.accde* file is created.
 d. Close the database.

13. Open the locked database.
 a. Open the *[your initials] PP A9-3.accde* database file. Remember that this is now your front-end database.
 b. Click **Open** if a *Microsoft Access Security Notice* displays.
 c. Open the *ListingDetails* form. Notice that you can't switch to *Design* view.
 d. Click the **Create** tab. Notice that the *Forms* and *Reports* groups are dimmed.

14. Close the database.

SLO 9.6

Using SQL

Recall from Chapter 5 that **SQL** stands for Structured Query Language. SQL is the underlying language in a relational database system such as Access. SQL defines, manipulates, and retrieves data in a database. It can be pronounced both as the initials, "S", "Q", "L", and as "sequel."

When you perform an action in your database, Access converts that action into SQL in order to execute it. Often the action in Access happens without your ability to actually see the *SQL* statement that executes. For example, when you add a new record into a table in *Datasheet* view, you are not aware of the *Insert Into* statement that actually adds the data values into the table. In another example, in *Pause & Practice 6-1* you created a *DeleteSoldProperties* query. This delete action query removed all of the records from the *Listings* table where the *Result* field value was *S*. Figure 9-91 shows the *Design* view of that query and Figure 9-92 shows the *SQL* view of that same query.

In that exercise, you initially built a select query that included both the *ListingID* and the *Result* fields so that you could test the query and ensure that it would find the correct records. Then you converted the select query into a delete query. Because a delete query deletes entire records and not just selected fields, it was not necessary to include all of the fields in the query.

9-91 *Design* view of the *DeleteSoldProperties* query

```
DELETE Listings.ListingID, Listings.Result
FROM Listings
WHERE (((Listings.Result)="S"));
```

9-92 *SQL* view of the *DeleteSoldProperties* query

When working on queries, you can switch to *SQL* view of the query by clicking the **SQL View** icon in the lower right corner of the *Status* bar.

It is not required for you to learn about all of the SQL commands. However, a basic understanding of SQL will help you work successfully with queries and the record source property in reports and forms. Additionally, queries in Access web databases are written in SQL, so understanding SQL can help you work with them.

One of the most common uses of SQL is to retrieve data from a database. The *SQL Select* statement is used in these cases. An *SQL Select* statement creates a select query, the same type of query that you have been building in many of your databases. The basic structure of an *SQL Select* statement is:

SELECT field(s)
FROM table(s)
WHERE condition(s)
ORDER BY;

This statement contains different clauses, or parts, such as the *SELECT, FROM, WHERE,* and *ORDER BY* clauses. The statement ends with a semicolon (**;**). The *SELECT* and *FROM* clauses are the only required clauses. This section provides a basic overview of these four common clauses in an *SQL Select* statement.

> **MORE INFO**
>
> To improve readability, it is a good practice to write each SQL clause on a separate line and to write the clause names in all caps. However, this does not impact how the query works and is not a requirement.

Understand the Select Clause

The *Select* clause lists the fields to display in the query result. It should contain all the fields that would appear in *Design* view of the query with a check in the *Show* box. The *Select* clause is required and it must appear as the first clause. The rules and guidelines for writing the *Select* clause include:

- You must include at least one field. If you include several fields, you need to separate them with commas.
- If you want to include all of the fields, you can use the * wildcard.
- If a field name or table name contains spaces, you must enclose the name in square brackets. For example, if the field name is *Date Hired*, you would write *[Date Hired]* in the query.
- You can use *qualified field names* as desired. A **qualified field name** includes both the table name and the field name. For example, *Agents.FirstName* specifies the *FirstName* field from the *Agents* table. You must separate the table name and the field name with a period.
- If you use the same field name in several tables, you must use a *qualified field name*.

 Review the following examples of the *Select* clause:

> **Example**: *SELECT FirstName, LastName, [Date Hired]*
>
> **Explanation:** This clause displays the *FirstName, LastName* and *Date Hired* fields. *Date Hired* is enclosed in square brackets since the field name contains a space.

> **Example:** *SELECT**
>
> **Explanation:** This clause displays all the fields.

> **Example:** *SELECT [Customer Leads].FirstName, [Customer Leads].LastName, [Customer Leads].City*
>
> **Explanation:** This clause uses qualified field names because the table name is included along with the field name. The table name, *Customer Leads,* is enclosed in square brackets since the table name contains a space.

Understand the From Clause

The *From* clause lists the tables that are needed to find the data. The *From* clause is required, and it follows the *Select* clause. The rules and guidelines for writing the *From* clause include:

- You must include at least one table. If you include multiple tables, you must separate them with commas.
- If you want to combine records from multiple tables, and you have not defined a relationship between the tables, you must specify the join type and you must also include an *ON* statement that specifies the fields used in the join. You can use either an inner join or an outer join. Recall that an inner join is the most common type of join and returns records that have matching values in both tables. Refer back to *SLO 5.3: Working with Advanced Table Relationships* to review table joins.
- If this is the last clause in the statement, end the clause with a semicolon.

Review the following examples of the *From* clause:

Example: *FROM [Customer Leads]*

> **Explanation:** This clause indicates that only one table is used in the query. The table name, *Customer Leads,* is enclosed in square brackets since the table name contains a space.

Example: *FROM Listings, SoldProperties*

> **Explanation:** This clause indicates that two tables are used. Since a join statement is not included, the tables must already have a defined relationship.

Example: *FROM Agents INNER JOIN Listings ON*
Agents.EmployeeNum = Listings.ListingAgentNumber

> **Explanation:** This clause specifies an inner join between the *Agents* and *Listings* tables. The fields that are related are identified.

Understand the Where Clause

The **Where** clause lists the expression that specifies the criteria the records must meet. It represents the constraints that would appear in the *Criteria* row in *Design* view of the query. The *Where* clause is optional. The rules and guidelines for writing the *Where* clause include:

- The expressions must follow the rules you have learned regarding how to properly write an expression.
- If necessary, you must use *qualified field names*.
- You can use the *AND* or *OR* operators to create compound conditions. If necessary, include parenthesis to ensure that the criteria are evaluated in the desired order.
- If this is the last clause in the statement, end the clause with a semicolon.

The following are examples of the *Where* clause:

Example: *WHERE Agents.[Date Hired] > "1/1/2016"*

> **Explanation:** This clause finds records where the *Date Hired* field is greater than 1/1/2016. It also uses a qualified field name and *Date Hired* is enclosed in square brackets since the field name contains a space.

Example: *WHERE LastName = "Chung" or LastName = "De La Garza"*

> **Explanation:** This clause uses the OR operator as a compound condition. Notice that a complete expression (field name, comparison operator, and value) must be written on either side of the OR. Records that meet either condition will be found.

Example: *WHERE City = "Auburn" and LengthOfResidence > 5*

> **Explanation:** This clause uses the AND operator as a compound condition. Only records that meet both expressions will be found.

Use the Order By Clause

The **Order By** clause indicates how the results are sorted. *Order By* is an optional clause. The rules and guidelines for writing the *Order By* clause include:

- The default sort order is ascending.
- Include *DESC* after the field name to sort in descending order.
- You can sort on multiple fields. If you sort on multiple fields, list the fields in the order in which you want the records sorted. Recall from Chapter 3 that additional fields affect the sort when more than one record is in the grouping.
- If this is the last clause in the statement, end the clause with a semicolon.

The following are examples of the *Order By* clause:

Example: *ORDER BY Agents.[Date Hired]*

> **Explanation:** This clause performs an ascending sort on the *Date Hired* field. It also uses a qualified field name and *Date Hired* is enclosed in square brackets since the field name contains a space.

Example: *ORDER BY Agents.[Date Hired] DESC*

> **Explanation:** This clause performs a descending sort on the *Date Hired* field. It also uses a qualified field name and *Date Hired* is enclosed in square brackets since the field name contains a space.

Example: *ORDER BY City, Construction DESC, ListPrice*

> **Explanation:** This clause performs a sort based on the combination of all three fields. The records are sorted first by *City* (in ascending order), within a city the records are sorted next by *Construction* (in descending order), and within construction by *ListPrice* (in ascending order.)

Write a Query in SQL View

In Access, you cannot create a query directly in *SQL* view. Instead you must begin by creating a query using the *Query Design* button. Once *Design* view opens, you can switch to *SQL* view to write the query. You can switch back and forth between the different query views using the icons on the *Status* bar. Remember that after you write the last clause, you must end the entire statement with a semicolon.

> **ANOTHER WAY**
>
> You can select the **View** button [*Query Tools Design* tab, *Results* group] and select either *SQL View* or *Design View* to switch views.

> **HOW TO: Write a Query in SQL View**

1. Click the **Query Design** button [*Create* tab, *Queries* group]. The *Show Table* dialog box opens.
2. Click **Close**.

3. Click the **SQL View** icon on the *Status* bar.
 - The query changes to *SQL* view (Figure 9-93).
 - The *SELECT* clause and a semicolon (**;**) are entered for you.
4. Type the desired field(s) on the *SELECT* clause and press **Enter**.
5. Type FROM and then type the desired table(s) on the *FROM* clause. If you selected table(s) before pressing *Close*, they will already be displayed on the *FROM* clause.
6. Enter a *WHERE* clause as desired.
7. Enter an *ORDER BY* clause as desired.
8. Save the query.
9. Run the query to test it.

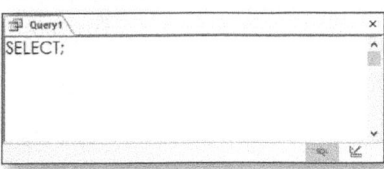

9-93 *SQL* view of a new query

Figure 9-94 shows a sample of a query written in *SQL*. Figure 9-95 is the *Design* view of the same query and Figure 9-96 shows the results of the query.

```
SELECT SoldProperties.ListingID, SoldProperties.ListPrice, SoldProperties.SoldPrice
FROM SoldProperties
WHERE (((SoldProperties.SoldPrice)>[ListPrice]));
```

9-94 *SQL* view of query

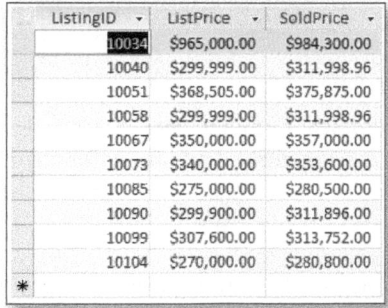

9-96 *Datasheet* view showing query results

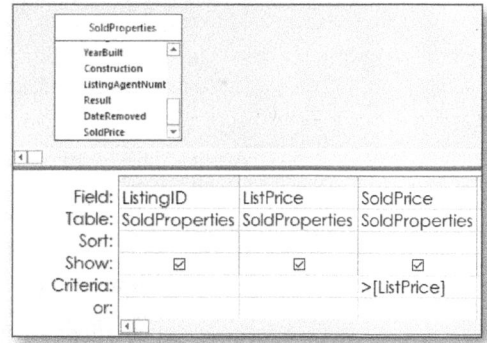

9-95 *Design* view of query

Use SQL with More Advanced Queries

You can also write SQL queries that include the more advanced query components you learned about in Chapters 3 and 6. In this section you learn to include calculated fields, parameters and functions in an SQL query.

Add a Calculated Field

You have used calculated fields in previous projects to display a value that comes from a calculation or to create criteria that limits the results returned by a query. In *Design* view, to display a calculated field in the query results, you added the calculated field into an empty column of the query design grid. The formula for the calculated field used the format of *FieldName: Expression*. An example of a formula used to calculate the potential commission an agent could earn on a property is *Commission: [ListPrice]*0.06*.

In SQL, the structure of the formula is reversed because you write the expression portion first and then define the name of the calculated field. A generic example of a formula uses the format of *Expression AS FieldName*. The potential commission formula would be written as *[ListPrice]*0.06 AS Commission*. If the *FieldName* contains spaces, it must be enclosed in square brackets. You write the formula to display a calculated field on the *Select* clause.

The following two examples illustrate using calculated fields on the *Select* clause:

Example: *SELECT FirstName, LastName, [ListPrice]*0.06 AS Commission*

> **Explanation:** The formula in this clause multiplies the *ListPrice* field by .06. The column will be named *Commission*. While not required, since *ListPrice* does not contain any spaces, it is common to include the field used in an expression inside square brackets.

Example: *SELECT FirstName, LastName, [ListPrice]*0.06 AS [Potential Commission]*

> **Explanation:** The formula in this clause performs the same calculation as above. However, the column name, *Potential Commission,* must be inside square brackets since it contains a space.

If using a calculated field as part of the criteria, the expression appears as part of the *Where* clause. You include the field name from the table, the comparison operator and the expression.

The following example uses calculated fields on the *Where* clause:

Example: *WHERE SoldPrice > [ListPrice]*1.05*

> **Explanation:** The formula in this clause finds properties where the *SoldPrice* is more than 5% higher than the *ListPrice*. The expression in the calculated field is *[ListPrice]*1.05*.

Include Functions in a Calculated Field

You can also write more complex formulas that include the & concatenation operator. Additionally, you can use Access functions, such as *Left* or any of the date functions.

The following examples illustrate several different functions that can be used in calculated fields:

Example: *SELECT [FirstName] & " " & [LastName] AS [Agent's Name]*

> **Explanation:** The formula in this clause uses concatenation to create a calculated field that combines the first and last names together, separated by a space. Because the name of the new column includes a space, it must be enclosed in square brackets.

Example: *SELECT Left([FirstName],1) & ". " & [LastName] AS [Agent's Name]*

> **Explanation:** The formula in this clause combines the *Left* function and concatenation to create a calculated field that takes the first character of the *FirstName* field and combines it with a period, a space, and the *LastName*.

Example: *SELECT DateDiff("d",[DateListed],Date()) AS DaysOnMarket*

> **Explanation:** The formula in this clause uses the *Date()* and *DateDiff()* functions to create a calculated field that displays the number of days a property has been listed. Recall that the *Date()* function gets today's date from your computer. If the value of today's date is less than the value in the *DateListed* field, the answer will be a negative number.

Example: *WHERE (DatePart("m",[DateListed]) = 8)*

> **Explanation:** The formula in this clause uses the *DatePart()* function as criteria to find records where the month of the *DateListed* field equals 8.

Include a Parameter

In *Design* view, you entered a query parameter inside square brackets in the criteria row. In SQL the parameter is written the same way. Include the parameter on the *Where* clause. When the query executes, Access displays the *Enter Parameter Value* dialog box. It is not necessary to include the field name inside parentheses, although Access defaults to write the comparison this way.

The following examples illustrate using a parameter on the *Where* clause:

Example: *WHERE (Listings.SqFt >= [Enter the minimum square footage of the property])*

> **Explanation:** This clause finds records where the *SqFt* field is greater than or equal to the value entered into the parameter dialog box. Parentheses surround the entire clause.

Example: *WHERE (((Listings.ListPrice) <= [Maximum List Price?]) AND ((Listings.City) = [What city?]))*

> **Explanation:** This clause finds records where the *ListPrice* field is less than or equal to the max price entered into the first parameter dialog box and the City field matches the city entered into the second parameter dialog box. Parentheses surround the entire clause, as well as the individual pieces and field names.

Example: *WHERE (((Listings.City) Like [Enter the City or Leave blank to select all cities] & "*"))*

> **Explanation:** This clause finds records where the *City* field matches the city entered into the parameter dialog box. Because this clause combines *Like* and the * wildcard, if the parameter dialog box is empty, all records are returned.

PAUSE & PRACTICE: ACCESS 9-4

For this Pause & Practice, you create and test four SQL queries for the Placer Hills Real Estate database.

File Needed: ***[your initials] PP A9-3_Backup_2.accdb***
Completed Project File Name: ***[your initials] PP A9-4.accdb***

1. Open the ***[your initials] PP A9-3_Backup_2.accdb*** database completed in *Pause & Practice 9-3*. You use this backup file, created prior to splitting and locking the database, since you are making changes to the database.

2. Save a new copy of your database as [your initials] PP A9-4.

3. Enable content in the security warning.

4. Build the first *SQL* query to display all the records in the *Agents* table.
 a. Click the **Query Design** button [*Create* tab, *Queries* group]. The *Show Table* dialog box opens.
 b. Click **Close**.
 c. Click the **SQL View** icon on the *Status* bar. The query changes to *SQL* view, and the *SELECT* clause and a semicolon (**;**) are entered for you.
 d. Edit the query so that the *SQL* statement reads
 SELECT *
 FROM Agents;
 Enter the text FROM Agents; on a second line to improve the readability of your query.
 e. Click the **Datasheet View** icon on the *Status* bar to run the query. Your results should include 14 records and be similar to Figure 9-97.

EmployeeN(LastName	FirstName	Multilingual	DateHired	Phone	Specialties	About
103	Bidou	Simon	Y	5/7/2012	(530) 648-7689	Luxury Properties	My Pledge – As a former teacher, I donate 10% of my net commission on all home sales originating from a school employee or a referral to your school.
109	Weintraub	Elizabeth	N	10/6/2012	(530) 633-8787	First Home Buyer Specialist	
115	Kozlowski	Carlos	N	1/19/2013	(916) 481-3840	Investment and Second Home purchases	
127	Weatherby	Kelly	Y	11/13/2012	(916) 987-3756	Land Purchases and Building Custom Homes	Kelly epitomizes integrity, energy, hard work, & creative service in every detail of your real estate transaction. She is a Sacramento native who was born and raised in a construction family. She first began her real estate career in 2005 after designing & remodeling homes. Kelly's referrals are sent to her from family, friends, and very happy clients. Let her 19 years of construction and remodeling experience assist your real estate needs.

Record: H ◄ 1 of 14 ► H ► No Filter Search

9-97 Query results to show all agents

 f. Save the query as ShowAllAgents.
 g. Close the query. Save the query, if prompted.

5. Build the second *SQL* query to display the *ListingID, DateListed, ListPrice,* and *City* for all properties over $400,000 that are located in Lincoln or Roseville.
 a. Click the **Query Design** button [*Create* tab, *Queries* group]. The *Show Table* dialog box opens.
 b. Select the **Listings** table and click **Add**.
 c. Click **Close**.
 d. Click the **SQL View** icon on the *Status* bar. The query changes to *SQL* view, and SELECT FROM Listings**;** is entered for you.
 e. Edit the query so that the *SQL* statement matches the following:

 SELECT ListingID, DateListed, ListPrice, City
 FROM Listings
 WHERE ListPrice > 400000 and
 (City = "Lincoln" or City = "Roseville");

 f. Click the *Datasheet* view icon on the *Status* bar to run the query. The query results should show 48 records and should be similar to Figure 9-98.
 g. Save the query as RosevilleLincolnProperties.

ListingID	Date Listed	List Price	City
10123	11/15/2016	$850,000.00	Roseville
10125	11/15/2016	$1,130,000.00	Roseville
10126	11/17/2016	$1,295,000.00	Roseville
10146	11/21/2016	$477,900.00	Lincoln
10156	11/25/2016	$628,000.00	Lincoln
10198	2/28/2017	$968,000.00	Lincoln
10211	3/4/2017	$477,900.00	Lincoln
10220	3/6/2017	$628,000.00	Lincoln
10253	3/16/2017	$968,000.00	Lincoln
10266	3/23/2017	$477,900.00	Lincoln
10275	3/24/2017	$628,000.00	Lincoln

Record: H ◄ 1 of 48 ► H ► No Filter Search

9-98 Query results for properties in Roseville or Lincoln

h. Switch to *Design* view to see the format of the query.
i. Close the query.

6. Build the third *SQL* query to display the *FirstName*, *LastName*, and *ListingID* for all properties listed by Boon Chatlaong.
 a. Click the **Query Design** button [*Create* tab, *Queries* group]. The *Show Table* dialog box opens.
 b. Click **Close**.
 c. Click the **SQL View** icon on the *Status* bar.
 d. Edit the query so that the *SQL* statement matches the following:

 SELECT FirstName, LastName, ListingID, ListPrice

 FROM Agents INNER JOIN Listings ON Agents.EmployeeNum = Listings.ListingAgentNumber

 WHERE FirstName = "Boon" and LastName = "Chatlaong"

 ORDER BY ListPrice;

 e. Click the *Datasheet* view icon on the *Status* bar to run the query. The query results should show 29 records and be similar Figure 9-99.
 f. Save the query as BoonChatlaongListings.
 g. Close the query.

7. Build the fourth *SQL* query to calculate the potential commission on the listed properties. The query concatenates the agents first and last name, and includes parameters to select a specific agent.
 a. Click the **Query Design** button [*Create* tab, *Queries* group]. The *Show Table* dialog box opens.
 b. Click **Close**.
 c. Click the **SQL View** icon on the *Status* bar.
 d. Edit the query so that the *SQL* statement matches the following:

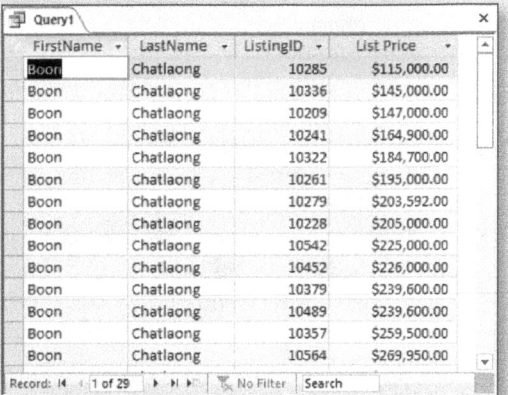

9-99 Listings by Boon Chatlaong

 SELECT [FirstName] & " " & [LastName] AS [Agent's Name], ListingID, ListPrice, [ListPrice]*0.06 AS [Potential Commission]

 FROM Agents INNER JOIN Listings ON Agents.EmployeeNum = Listings.ListingAgentNumber

 WHERE (FirstName = [Enter the Agent's First Name] and LastName = [Enter the Agent's Last Name]);

 e. Click the *Datasheet* view icon on the *Status* bar to run the query.
 f. Enter Tri in the *Enter the Agent's First Name* box of the *Enter Parameter Value* dialog box and click **OK**.
 g. Enter Ung in the *Enter the Agent's Last Name* box of the *Enter Parameter Value* dialog box and click **OK**. The query results should show 23 records and be similar to Figure 9-100.
 h. Save the query as AgentParameterPotentialCommission.
 i. Switch to *Design* view to see the format of the query.
 j. Close the query. Save the query, if prompted.

8. Close the database.

9-100 Parameter query results

Chapter Summary

9.1 Understand entity relationship diagrams and normalization, use the *Analyze Table* tool, and create a documentation report (p. A9-621).

- An *Entity-Relationship Diagram(ERD)* is a data model used to show the data needs of an organization.
- In a *relationship*, the *cardinality* indicates whether the relationship type is one-to-one, one-to-many, or many-to-many, while the *modality* specifies whether an entity must participate in the relationship.
- *Normalization* is the database design process for organizing fields into the correct table. Normalization minimizes redundant data that causes problems in a database.
- The rules of normalization are *normal forms*. Higher normal forms are better and result in fewer problems in the database.
- The *Table Analyzer* tool makes recommendations for normalizing tables.
- Create, view, export, and print documentation details about your database with the *Database Documenter* tool.

9.2 Create and modify a custom *Navigation Pane* (p. A9-636).

- You can customize the **Navigation Pane** to organize and display database objects in a way that is more efficient for the user.
- A *category* is the highest level organizational structure in the *Navigation Pane*. A *group* is the second level organization structure of the Navigation Pane. A group is used to display the different database objects.
- Access creates a *shortcut* when you assign an object to a custom group. You can disable *Design* view on a shortcut, which prevents the user from modifying the object.
- Hide objects, shortcuts, and groups as needed to minimize the number of items displayed in the *Navigation Pane* and to prevent users from using selected items.

9.3 Analyze and optimize the performance of a database (p. A9-646).

- A well-designed database ensures optimal performance.
- Choose the data type for a field that uses the smallest field size possible to accommodate

the data needs of the system. In general, number data types process more quickly than text data types and smaller field sizes process more quickly than larger field sizes.

- Objects that use fields from multiple tables process more quickly if relationships are established between tables.
- An *index* is a list used by Access to find data more quickly. To speed up performance, create an index on fields used for sorting or as query criteria.
- Limiting the number of controls used on forms and reports and storing images in the *Image Gallery* optimizes performance of these objects.
- Periodic use of the *Compact & Repair Database* utility improves performance.
- The *Performance Analyzer* tool analyzes the database objects and suggests solutions to improve performance. As desired, Access can automatically implement solutions that are classified as *recommendations* or *suggestions*.

9.4 Understand front-end and back-end databases, split a database, and work with a split database (p. A9-650).

- You can split a database into a front-end and a back-end to improve performance and security.
- The *back-end database* contains the tables and associated data.
- The *front-end database* contains linked tables that point to the back-end database as well as all of the forms, reports, and queries. You can create customized front-ends for different users.
- Use the *Database Splitter* tool to create the back-end database. The starting database becomes the front-end database.
- If you create a new front-end database, use the *Access* button to create the linked tables.
- If the back-end database is moved to a different storage location, use the *Linked Table Manager* to update the links in the front-end database.

9.5 Enhance database security by encrypting and password protecting a database, packaging and signing a database, and locking a database (p. A9-653).

- Safeguarding your database helps to ensure that the database continues to work and provides needed functionality.
- *Encryption* converts data into a coded format that can't be understood until it is decoded. You can encrypt an Access database by using the *Encrypt with Password* button to assign a password to the database. Before you can assign a password to a database, you must open it in exclusive mode. This prevents others from opening the database at the same time.
- Create a strong password that is difficult for someone to guess. Access does not have any ability to provide you with a lost password.
- Use the *Package and Sign* tool to create a database that tells others that the database can be trusted. You use a *digital certificate*, which is an authentication mechanism, to package the database. A packaged and signed database has an extension of *.accdc*.
- Create an *executable*, or *locked*, database file, to prevent users from making any changes to the forms, reports, and macros. A locked database has an extension of *.accde*.

9.6 Understand SQL (Structured Query Language) and create and execute simple *SQL* statements using the *Select*, *From*, *Where*, and *Order By* clauses (p. A9-665).

- *Structured Query Language (SQL)* is the underlying language in relational database systems. It is used to define, manipulate, and retrieve data in a database.
- A *SQL Select* statement retrieves data from a database.
- A *Select* statement contains different clauses including *Select*, *From*, *Where*, and *Order By*.
- The *Select* clause lists the fields to display in the query; it appears first in a statement and is required.
- The *From* clause lists the tables that are needed to find the data; it is required and follows the *Select* clause.
- The *Where* clause specifies the criteria that the records must meet while the *Order By* clause indicates how the results will be sorted; these clauses are optional.
- Select the *SQL View* icon to see the *SQL* view of a query.
- You can include advanced query features such as calculated fields, functions and parameters in an *SQL* query.

Check for Understanding

The SIMbook for this text (within your SIMnet account), provides the following resources for concept review:

- Multiple choice questions
- Matching exercises
- Short answer questions

Guided Project 9-1

For this project, you enhance the functionality of a database for a friend's music collection. You analyze the table structure and assess the performance of the database. Next, you create a custom *Navigation Pane* and encrypt the database with a password.
[Student Learning Outcomes 9.1, 9.2, 9.3, 9.5]

File Needed: ***MusicDatabase-09.accdb***
Completed Project File Names: *[your initials] Access 9-1.accdb* and *[your initials] Access 9-1_Backup.accdb*

Skills Covered in This Project

- Use the *Table Analyzer* tool.
- Back up a database.
- Use the *Performance Analyzer* tool.
- Create a custom *Navigation Pane*.
- Create a custom category and custom groups.
- Assign objects to groups.
- Modify shortcut properties.
- Hide objects and groups.
- Encrypt a database with a password.

1. Open the ***MusicDatabase-09*** database from your student data files.

2. Save the database as [your initials] Access 9-1.

3. Enable content in the security warning.

4. Analyze the *Albums* table.
 a. Click the **Analyze Table** button [*Database Tools* tab, *Analyze* group] to open the *Table Analyzer Wizard*.
 b. If the *Looking At the Problem* information window displays, click **Next** to move to the second information screen.
 c. If the *Solving the Problem* information window displays, click **Next** to move to the next step of the wizard.
 d. Select the **Albums** table, if not already selected, and click **Next**.
 e. Select the **Yes, let the wizard decide** radio button, if not already selected, and click **Next**. The wizard displays the recommendations.
 f. Enlarge the tables so you can read all of the content (Figure 9-101).
 g. Click the **Tips** button to open the *Table Analyzer* dialog box. Read the suggestions. In the *Table Analyzer Wizard* window, the wizard suggests moving the *RecordingLabel* and *Genre* fields into separate tables. Based on the way that you use the data, that is not a good idea because storing the lookup fields in both tables wouldn't save space and the tables would need to be joined to display the actual values.

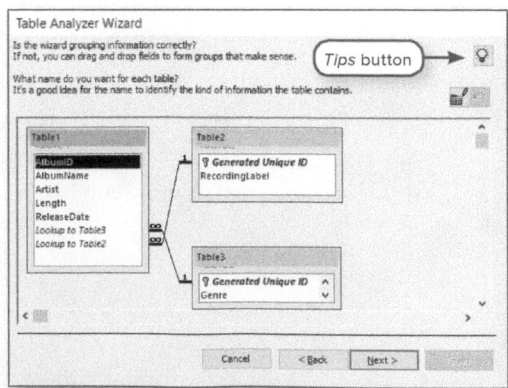

9-101 *Table Analyzer Wizard* dialog box

h. Close the *Table Analyzer* dialog box.

i. Since the wizard has no other suggestions and you determine that the *Albums* table is in 3NF, click the **Cancel** button in the *Table Analyzer Wizard* dialog box.

5. Analyze the *Songs* table.

a. Click the **Analyze Table** button [*Database Tools* tab, *Analyze* group] to open the *Table Analyzer Wizard*.

b. If the *Looking At the Problem* information window displays, click **Next** to move to the second information screen.

c. If the *Solving the Problem* information window displays, click **Next** to move to the next step of the wizard.

d. Select the **Songs** table and click **Next**.

e. Select the **Yes, let the wizard decide** radio button, if not already selected, and click **Next**. A dialog box displays informing you that the wizard doesn't recommend any splitting of the table.

f. Click the **Cancel** button to close the dialog box and exit the wizard.

6. Back up the database.

a. Click the **File** tab to open the *Backstage* view and click the **Save As** button.

b. Click the **Back Up Database** button in the *Advanced* grouping of *the Save Database As* section and then click the **Save As** button. The *Save As* dialog box displays.

c. Select the location to store the file, enter [your initials] Access 9-1_Backup.accdb as the file name, and click the **Save** button.

7. Analyze the performance of the database.

a. Click the **Analyze Performance** button [*Database Tools* tab, *Analyze* group] to open the *Performance Analyzer*.

b. Click the **All Object Types** tab and click the **Select All** button (Figure 9-102).

c. Click **OK**. The *Analysis Results* window displays one *Idea* to create an MDE executable file. Because you may add more forms and reports to the database, you will not implement this *Idea*.

d. Click **Close**.

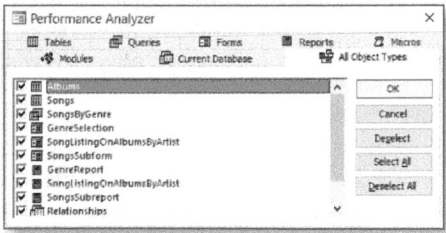

9-102 *Performance Analyzer* dialog box

 MORE INFO

The limited solutions in both the *Table Analyzer* and the *Performance Analyzer* suggest that your work on this database has followed good database design practices. However, as more data records are added, it may be a good idea to consider whether creating any indexes would improve performance.

8. Create a category and group for a custom *Navigation Pane*.

a. Right-click the **Navigation Pane Title** bar to open the context menu and select **Navigation Options**.

b. Click the **Add Item** button to add a new custom category into the *Categories* list.

c. Type My Music Main Menu in the category box and press **Enter**.

d. Click the **Add Group** button to add a new group in this category.

e. Type Music Collection in the group box and press **Enter**.

f. Select the **Show Hidden Objects** check box in the *Display Options* area, if not already selected. The *Navigation Options* dialog box should look similar to Figure 9-103.

g. Click **OK** when done.

9. Assign objects and modify the *Navigation Pane*.

a. Click the **Navigation Pane** arrow to open the *Navigation* menu and select the **My Music Main Menu** category.

b. Drag the **divider bar** to widen the *Navigation Pane*, if necessary.

c. Click, hold, and drag the **GenreSelection** form from the *Unassigned Objects* group to the *Music Collection* group.

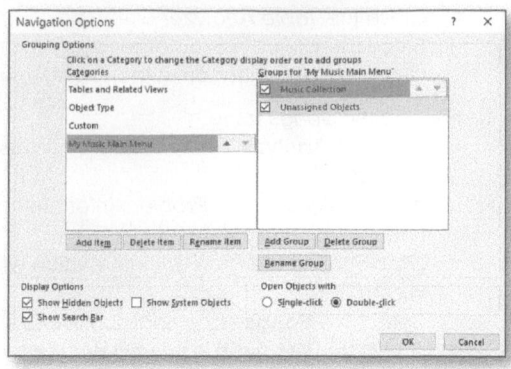

9-103 New category and group in the *Navigation Options* dialog box

d. Click, hold, and drag the **SongListingOnAlbumsByArtist** form from the *Unassigned Objects* group to the *Music Collection* group. Recall that this form contains the *SongsSubform* form, although you are not assigning that form to any group.

e. Click, hold, and drag the **SongListingOnAlbumsByArtist** report from the *Unassigned Objects* group to the *Music Collection* group. Recall that this report contains the *SongsSubreport* report, although you are not assigning that report to any group.

f. Right-click the **GenreSelection** shortcut and select the **Rename Shortcut** option. Type Open Genre Report as the shortcut name and press **Enter**.

g. Right-click the **Open Genre Report** shortcut and select the **View Properties** option.

h. Select the **Disable Design View shortcuts** check box and click **OK**.

i. Right-click the **SongListingOnAlbumsByArtist** form shortcut and select the **View Properties** option.

j. Select the **Disable Design View shortcuts** check box and click **OK**.

k. Right-click the **SongListingOnAlbumsByArtist** report shortcut and select the **View Properties** option.

l. Select the **Disable Design View shortcuts** check box and click **OK**.

m. Right-click the **Unassigned Objects** heading and select the **Hide** option. The completed *Navigation Pane* should look similar to Figure 9-104.

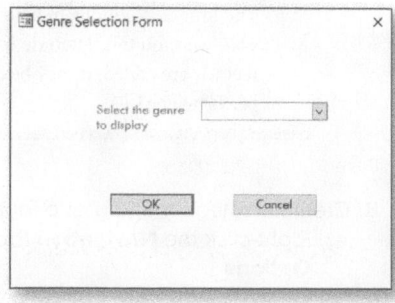

9-104 Completed *Navigation Pane*

10. Test the custom *Navigation Pane*.

a. Double-click the **Open Genre Report** shortcut. The *Genre Selection Form* opens (Figure 9-105). This form collects a parameter and opens the associated report.

b. Click the **combo box** drop-down arrow, select **Pop**, and then click **OK**. The report opens. Notice in the *Status* bar that *Design* view is still an available option. You disabled *Design* view for *Open Genre Report*, which is the shortcut to the *GenreSelection* form. This form opened the *GenreReport* object. *Design* view is still available for the report. Ultimately, you may decide to address this issue.

c. Close the report and close the database, but leave Access open.

9-105 Select a genre to display in the associated report

11. Password protect the database.
 a. Click the **Open** button [*File* tab] to display the *Open* area in the *Backstage* view.
 b. Double-click **Recent**, **OneDrive**, or **This PC** to open the *Open* dialog box.
 c. Browse to the location of your database and click to select *[your initials] Access 9-1.accdb*. Do not double-click the database file name.
 d. Click the **Open** button arrow and select **Open Exclusive**.
 e. Click the **File** tab to open the *Backstage* view.
 f. Click the **Encrypt with Password** button to open the *Set Database Password* dialog box.
 g. Type t7xL1st& in the *Password* box.
 h. Type t7xL1st& in the *Verify* box.
 i. Click **OK**. If you get a message about row level locking, click **OK**.
 j. Close the database.

12. Test the password-protected database.
 a. Open the *[your initials] Access 9-1.accdb* database file. The *Password Required* dialog box displays.
 b. Type t7xL1st& in the *Password* box and click **OK**. The database opens.

13. Close the database.

Guided Project 9-2

Courtyard Medical Plaza wants to expand its database. For this project, you use SQL to create a query to find past due invoices. Next, you back up and then split the database. You password protect the back-end database, update linked tables, and password protect and lock the front-end database. Finally, you create a PDF file of the back-end database documentation.
[Student Learning Outcomes 9.1, 9.4, 9.5, 9.6]

File Needed: ***CourtyardMedicalPlaza-09.accdb***
Completed Project File Names: *[your initials] Access 9-2.accdb, [your initials] Access 9-2_Backup.accdb, [your initials] Access 9-2_be.accdb, [your initials] Access 9-2.accde*, and *[your initials] Access 9-2_be_Documentation.pdf*

Skills Covered in This Project

- Create a query using *SQL* view.
- Edit a query using *SQL* view.
- Back up a database.
- Use the *Database Splitter* tool.
- Update linked tables in a split database.
- Encrypt a database with a password.
- Lock a database.
- Use the *Database Documenter* tool.

1. Open the ***CourtyardMedicalPlaza-09*** database from your student data files.

2. Save a new copy of your database as [your initials] Access 9-2.

3. Enable content in the security warning.

4. Create an *SQL* query to show the unpaid invoices.
 a. Open a new query using **Query Design**.
 b. Add the **RentInvoices** table into the query and close the *Show Table* dialog box.

c. Change to *SQL* view. The *SELECT* clause and the *FROM* clause are entered for you.
d. Edit the *SELECT* clause to add the following field names after the word *SELECT*: InvoiceID, InvoiceDate, DueDate, AmountDue, FKDoctorID, Description
e. Edit the *FROM* clause to remove the semicolon from the end.
f. Add the following *WHERE* clause below the *FROM* clause:

 WHERE ((Paid) = False);.

g. Save the query as PastDueInvoices.
h. Run the query to test it. The results should display 11 records.

5. Edit the query to add a calculated field to show the number of days late.
a. Change back to *SQL* view.
b. Edit the *SELECT* clause to add DateDiff("d",[DueDate],Date()) AS DaysLate, between the *DueDate* and *AmountDue* fields. Enter the contents after the comma following *DueDate* and be sure to enter the comma included after *DaysLate* in the instructions. This calculation finds the difference between today's date and the *DueDate* field.
c. Save the changes to the query.
d. Run the query to test it. The results should be similar to those shown in Figure 9-106. The value displayed in the *DaysLate* column will vary, and may be negative, depending on the day you run the query.
e. Close the query.

9-106 *PastDueInvoices* query results

6. Back up the database before analyzing the performance.
a. Click the **File** tab to open the *Backstage* view and click the **Save As** button.
b. Click the **Back Up Database** button in the *Advanced* grouping of the *Save Database As* section and then click the **Save As** button. The *Save As* dialog box displays.
c. Select the location to store the file, enter [your initials] Access 9-2_Backup.accdb as the file name, and click the **Save** button.

7. Split the database.
a. Click the **Access Database** button [*Database Tools* tab, *Move Data* group] to open the *Database Splitter* dialog box.
b. Click the **Split Database** button. The *Create Back-end Database* dialog box opens. Access suggests the default file name **[your initials] Access 9-2_be.accdb**.
c. Locate the folder where you want to save the file, accept the default file name, and click the **Split** button. A confirmation message box displays.
d. Click **OK** to acknowledge the message.
e. Close the database, but keep Access open.

8. Password protect the back-end database.
a. Click the **Open** button [*File* tab] to display the *Open* area in *Backstage* view.
b. Double-click **Recent**, **OneDrive**, or **This PC** to open the *Open* dialog box.
c. Browse to the location of your back-end database and click to select **[your initials] Access 9-2_be.accdb**. Do not double-click the database file name.
d. Click the **Open** button arrow and select **Open Exclusive**.
e. Click the **File** tab to open the *Backstage* view.
f. Click the **Encrypt with Password** button to open the *Set Database Password* dialog box.
g. Type corT!3Lekar in the *Password* box.
h. Type corT!3Lekar in the *Verify* box.
i. Click **OK**. If you get a message about row level locking, click **OK**.
j. Close the database.

9. Update links in the front-end database.
 a. Open the *[your initials] Access 9-2.accdb* database file.
 b. Delete both tables since their links are no longer valid because you added a password to the back-end database.
 c. Click the **Access** button [*External Data* tab, *Import & Link* group]. The *Get External Data – Access Database* dialog box launches.
 d. Click the **Browse** button to launch the *File Open* dialog box.
 e. Locate and select *[your initials] Access 9-2_be.accdb* and click the **Open** button.
 f. Select the **Link to the data source by creating a linked table** radio button and click **OK**. The *Password Required* dialog box displays.
 g. Type corT!3Lekar in the *Password* box and click **OK**. The *Link Tables* dialog box displays.
 h. Click the **Select All** button and click **OK**. The tables are added into the *Tables* group of the *Navigation Pane* (Figure 9-107).
 i. Close the database, but leave Access open.

9-107 Linked tables in the *Navigation Pane*

10. Password protect the front-end database.
 a. Click the **Open** button [*File* tab] to display the *Open* area in *Backstage* view.
 b. Double-click **Recent**, **OneDrive**, or **This PC** to open the *Open* dialog box.
 c. Browse to the location of your front-end database and click to select *[your initials] Access 9-2.accdb*. Do not double-click the database file name.
 d. Click the **Open** button arrow and select **Open Exclusive**.
 e. Click the **File** tab to open the *Backstage* view.
 f. Click the **Encrypt with Password** button to open the *Set Database Password* dialog box.
 g. Type #dR.Pia22a in the *Password* box.
 h. Type #dR.Pia22a in the *Verify* box.
 i. Click **OK**. If you get a message about row level locking, click **OK**.

11. Lock the front-end database.
 a. Click the **File** tab to open the *Backstage* view and click the **Save As** button.
 b. Click the **Make ACCDE** button in the *Advanced* grouping of *the Save Database As* section and click the **Save As** button. The *Save As* dialog box displays.
 c. Select the location to store the file, accept the suggested file name, and click the **Save** button. The *.accde* file is created.
 d. Close the database.

12. Open the locked database.
 a. Open the *[your initials] Access 9-2.accde* database file.
 b. Type #dR.Pia22a in the *Password* box and click **OK**. If a *Microsoft Access Security Notice* displays, click **Open**.
 c. Click the **Create** tab. Notice that the *Forms* and *Reports* groups are dimmed.
 d. Close the database.

13. Create database documentation for the back-end database.
 a. Open the *[your initials] Access 9-2_be.accdb* database file.
 b. Type corT!3Lekar in the *Password* box and click **OK**.
 c. Enable content in the security warning.
 d. Click the **Database Documenter** button [*Database Tools* tab, *Analyze* group] to open the *Documenter* dialog box.
 e. Select the **All Object Types** tab and the **Select All** button.
 f. Click the **Options** button to open the *Print Table Definition* dialog box.

A9-681

g. Mark the check boxes and radio buttons, if necessary, so they match those shown in Figure 9-108 and click **OK**. You return to the *Documenter* dialog box.

h. Click the **OK** button to preview the *Database Documenter* report (Figure 9-109).

i. Click the **One Page** button [*Print Preview* tab, *Zoom* group], if necessary, to adjust the display and use the scroll bars to see parts of the page not visible.

j. Click the **PDF or XPS** button [*Print Preview* tab, *Data* group] to open the *Publish as PDF or XPS* dialog box.

k. Locate the folder where you want to save the file, enter [your initials] Access 9-2_be_Documentation.pdf as the file name, select the **Open file after publishing** check box, and click the **Publish** button. The PDF file opens in your PDF viewer.

l. Navigate through the pages in the PDF file to ensure it was created successfully. Most likely the report contains 12 pages.

m. Close the PDF file.

n. Click **Close** in the *Export – PDF* dialog box because you don't need to save the export steps.

o. Click the **Close Print Preview** button [*Print Preview* tab, *Close Preview* group].

14. Close the database.

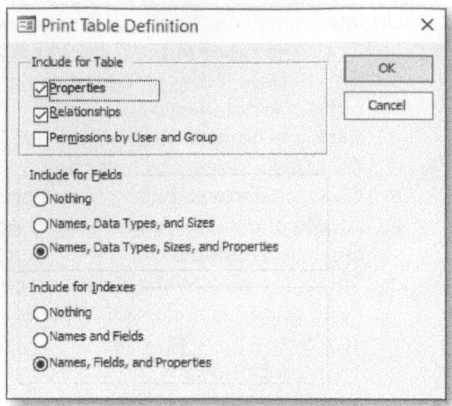

9-108 *Print Table Definition* dialog box

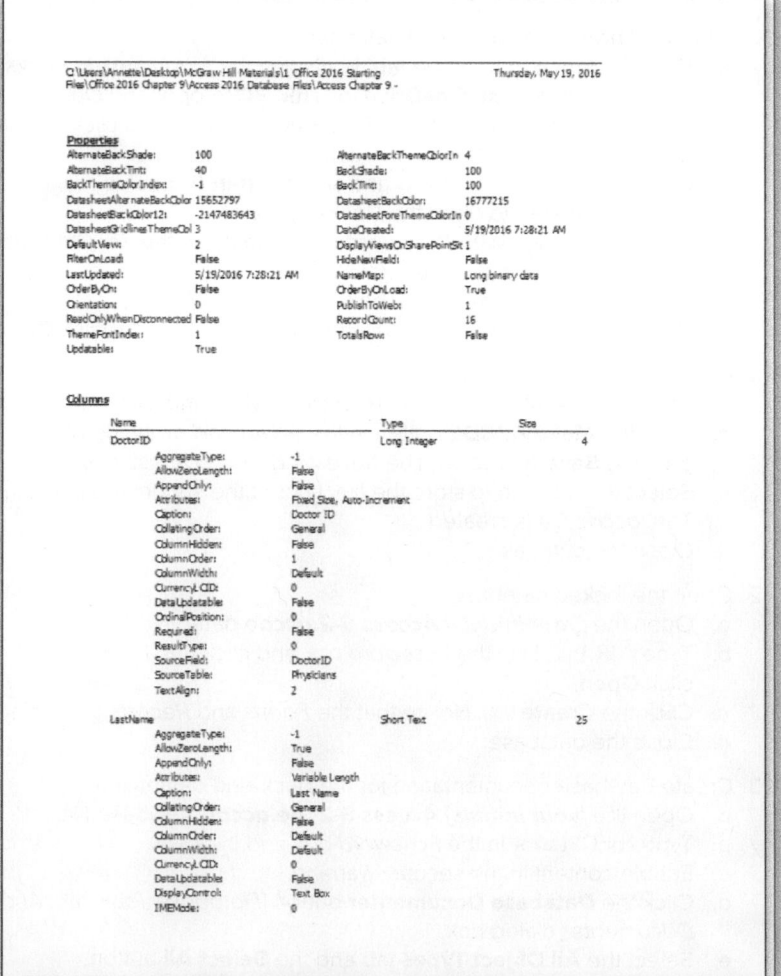

9-109 *Print Preview of the back-end* database documentation

Guided Project 9-3

San Diego Sailing wants to ensure its database is well designed. For this project, you apply the rules of normalization to the database and use the *Table Analyzer* tool. Next, you use SQL to create a parameter query to display boat details. Finally, you use the *Analyze Performance* tool and optimize the database. [Student Learning Outcomes 9.1, 9.3, 9.6]

File Needed: ***SanDiegoSailing-09.accdb***
Completed Project File Names: *[your initials]* ***Access 9-3.accdb*** and *[your initials]* ***Access 9-3_Backup. accdb***

Skills Covered in This Project

- Evaluate tables using normalization.
- Use the *Table Analyzer* tool.
- Modify a table in *Design* view.
- Use the *Lookup Wizard* to create a relationship.

- Create a query using *SQL* view.
- Add a parameter to a query using *SQL* view.
- Back up a database.
- Use the *Performance Analyzer* tool.
- Create an index to optimize a database.
- Use *Compact & Repair* to optimize a database.

1. Open the **SanDiegoSailing-09** database from your student data files.

2. Save a new copy of your database as [your initials] Access 9-3.

3. Enable content in the security warning.

4. Evaluate the *SailboatFleet* table to determine if it is in 3NF.
 a. Open the *SailboatFleet* table in *Datasheet* view (Figure 9-110). An employee added fields to track the manufacturer of each of the boats in the *SailboatFleet* table. Recall that the *Boat ID* is the primary key.

Boat ID	Boat Type	Length	Seats	Sleeps	4 Hr Rate	Full Day Rat	Galley w/ St	Model Year	MfgID	MfgName	MfgAddress	MfgCity	MfgState	MfgZIP	MfgPhone
1010	Catalina 270	28'4"	8	6	$129.00	$179.00	☑	1997	1	Catalina Yacht	21200 Victory	Woodland Hill	CA	91367	818-884-7700
1015	Catalina 270	28'4"	8	6	$139.00	$179.00	☑	1998	1	Catalina Yacht	21200 Victory	Woodland Hill	CA	91367	818-884-7700
1146	Hunter 33	33'6"	10	6	$299.00	$349.00	☑	2003	2	Marlow-Hunter	Route 441, Po	Alachua	FL	32616	386-462-3077
1150	Capri 22 Mk II	24'8"	6	4	$65.00	$89.00	☐	2004	1	Catalina Yacht	21200 Victory	Woodland Hill	CA	91367	818-884-7700
1152	Capri 22 Mk II	24'8"	6	4	$65.00	$89.00	☐	2004	1	Catalina Yacht	21200 Victory	Woodland Hill	CA	91367	818-884-7700
1164	Capri 22 Mk II	24'8"	6	4	$65.00	$89.00	☐	2006	1	Catalina Yacht	21200 Victory	Woodland Hill	CA	91367	818-884-7700
1168	Hunter 33	33'6"	10	6	$299.00	$349.00	☑	2007	2	Marlow-Hunter	Route 441, Po	Alachua	FL	32616	386-462-3077
1175	Beneteau 40	39'10"	12	6	$489.00	$529.00	☑	2008	3	Beneteau Ame	105 Eastern A	Annapolis	MD	21403	410-990-0270
1180	Beneteau 373	36'11"	10	6	$369.00	$409.00	☑	2009	3	Beneteau Ame	105 Eastern A	Annapolis	MD	21403	410-990-0270

9-110 *Datasheet* view of the *SailboatFleet* table

 b. Determine if the table is in 1NF. In any cell, do you see more than one value? The answer is no. Each cell has only one value so this table is in 1NF.
 c. Determine if the table is in 2NF. Do all the non-key fields depend on the entire primary key? Since this table only has one field in the primary key, it is automatically in 2NF.
 d. Determine if the table is in 3NF. Do all the non-key fields depend only on the primary key? Do you see redundant data? The answer is yes; you see redundant data.
 e. Analyze the redundant manufacturing data. Do you get the same set of manufacturing data values for every record by looking at the *MfgID*? The answer is yes. For example, every record that has a *MfgID* of 1 has the same value for *MfgName*, *MfgAddress*, *MfgCity*, *MfgState*, *MfgZIP* and *MfgPhone*. This is a transitive dependency; as a result, this table is not in 3NF. To fix this, you take the fields that depend on the non-key attribute and put them into a new, separate table to store the manufacturer information. You will make these changes later in the project.

f. Analyze the redundant sailboat data. Do you get the same set of sailboat values in the *Length*, *Seats*, *Sleeps*, *4 Hr Rate*, *Full Day Rate*, and *Galley w/ Stove* fields by looking at the *Boat Type*? The answer appears to be yes at first. But is this always true?

 For example, it is possible that you could get a Beneteau 373 with a different sleeping configuration? And it is possible that you could charge different rates for the Catalina 270 depending on how old it is?

 Because this variability exists, a transitive dependency doesn't exist between *Boat Type* and these other fields.

g. Close the table.

5. Evaluate the *SDRentals* table to determine if it is in 3NF.

a. Open the *SDRentals* table in *Datasheet* view (Figure 9-111). Recall that the *Rental ID* is the primary key.

b. Determine if the table is in 1NF. In any cell, do you see more than one value? The answer is no. Each cell has only one value so this table is in 1NF.

c. Determine if the table is in 2NF. Do all the non-key fields depend on the entire primary key? Since this table only has one field in the primary key, it is automatically in 2NF.

Rental ID	Boat ID	Rental Dc	Four Hour	Member t	RentalCo
08013	1146	1/5/2017	☑	1003	$299.00
08014	1419	1/5/2017	☑	1075	$299.00
08015	1146	1/7/2017	☐	1212	$349.00
08016	1419	1/7/2017	☑	1075	$299.00
08017	1168	1/7/2017	☐	1212	$349.00
08018	1146	1/8/2017	☑	1283	$299.00
08019	1015	1/8/2017	☑	1386	$139.00
08020	1419	1/8/2017	☑	1283	$299.00
08021	1168	1/10/2017	☐	1168	$349.00
08022	1185	1/10/2017	☐	1283	$389.00
08023	1015	1/10/2017	☑	1059	$139.00
08024	1200	1/10/2017	☐	1494	$409.00

9-111 Datasheet view of the SDRentals table

d. Determine if the table is in 3NF. Do all the non-key fields depend only on the primary key? Do you see redundant data? Even though the same *Rental Date* or *Boat ID* appears on multiple records, it is not redundant. None of the non-key fields can determine any of the other non-key fields. For example, when you look at *Boat ID 1146*, do you always see the same values in the *Rental Date*, *Four Hour Rental*, or *Member Number* fields? The answer is no. It appears that the combination of the *Boat ID* and *Four Hour Rental?* fields gives you the same *RentalCost*. However, the *RentalCost* is likely to change over time. Because this table doesn't have any transitive dependencies, the table is in 3NF.

e. Close the table.

6. Compare your analysis of the *SDRentals* table with the results of the *Table Analyzer* tool.

a. Click the **Analyze Table** button [*Database Tools* tab, *Analyze* group] to open the *Table Analyzer Wizard*.

b. If the *Looking At the Problem* information window displays, click **Next** to move to the second information screen.

c. If the *Solving the Problem* information window displays, click **Next** to move to the next step of the wizard.

d. Select the **SDRentals** table and click **Next**.

e. Select the **Yes, let the wizard decide** radio button and click **Next**. A dialog box displays informing you that the wizard doesn't recommend any splitting of the table.

f. Click the **Cancel** button to exit the wizard.

7. Compare your analysis of the *Sailboat Fleet* table with the results of the *Table Analyzer* tool.

a. Click the **Analyze Table** button [*Database Tools* tab, *Analyze* group] to open the *Table Analyzer Wizard*.

b. If the *Looking At the Problem* information window displays, click **Next** to move to the second information screen.

c. If the *Solving the Problem* information window displays, click **Next** to move to the next step of the wizard.

d. Select the **Sailboat Fleet** table and click **Next**.

e. Select the **Yes, let the wizard decide** radio button and click **Next**. The wizard displays the recommendations.

f. Enlarge the tables so you can read all of the content (Figure 9-112).

g. Click the **Tips** button to read about the suggestions. Close the *Table Analyzer* dialog box.

h. Note that the wizard suggests moving the manufacturing information to another table. It also suggests moving some of the fields about the boat into a separate table. Recall from step 4f that this is not a good idea.

i. Click the **Cancel** button. Although you could modify the suggested table design in the wizard, due to the differences it is easier for you to modify the table design yourself.

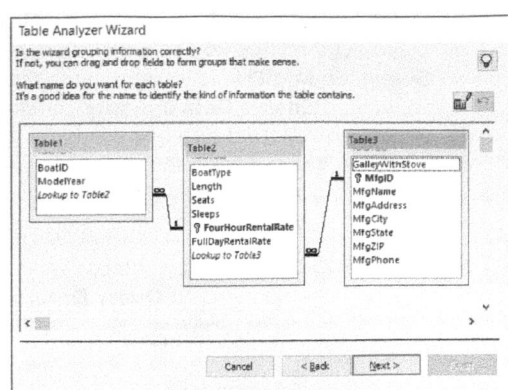

9-112 *Table Analyzer Wizard* dialog box

8. Modify the database to create the *Manufacturers* table.

a. Select the **SailboatFleet** table in the *Navigation* pane.

b. Press the **Copy** button [*Home* tab, *Clipboard* group] and the **Paste** button [*Home* tab, *Clipboard* group] to make a copy of the table. The *Paste Table As* dialog box opens.

c. Type Manufacturers in the *Table Name* box and click **OK**.

d. Open the *Manufacturers* table in *Datasheet* view.

e. Click to select the **MfgID** column and click the **Ascending** button [*Home* tab, *Sort & Filter* group].

f. Delete the records for *Boat ID* values **1015, 1150, 1152, 1164, 1230, 1240, 1401**,and **1425**. Click **Yes** in the message boxes that ask you to confirm the deletions.

g. Delete the records for *Boat ID* values **1168, 1185, 1225, 1254**, and **1419**. Click **Yes** in the message boxes that ask you to confirm the deletions.

h. Delete the records for *Boat ID* values **1180, 1190, 1200, 1205, 1310**, and **1410**. Click **Yes** in the message boxes that ask you to confirm the deletions.

i. Click the **Remove Sort** button [*Home* tab, *Sort & Filter* group].

j. Change to **Design** view.

k. Delete the **BoatID, BoatType, Length, Seats, Sleeps, FourHourRentalRate, FullDayRentalRate, GalleyWithStove**, and **ModelYear** fields. Click **Yes** in the message boxes that ask you to confirm the deletions.

l. Make the *MfgID* field the primary key of the table.

m. Save the table and switch to *Datasheet* view. The table should contain four records and be similar to Figure 9-113.

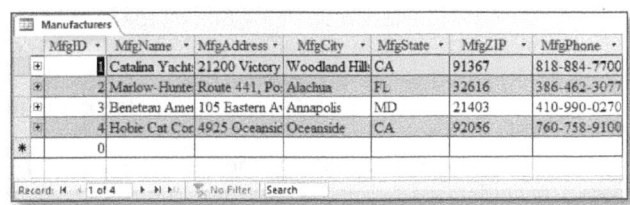

9-113 *Datasheet* view of the *Manufacturers* table

n. Close the table.

9. Modify the database so that the *SailboatFleet* table is in 3NF.

a. Open the *SailboatFleet* table in *Design* view.

b. Delete the **MfgName, MfgAddress, MfgCity, MfgState, MfgZIP**, and **MfgPhone** fields. Click **Yes** in the message boxes that ask you to confirm the deletions.

c. Change the name of the *MfgID* field to MfgID-FK.

d. Select **Lookup Wizard** in the *MfgID-FK* field *Data Type* property box to launch the *Lookup Wizard*.

e. Select the **"I want the lookup field to get the values from another table or query"** radio button, if necessary, and click the **Next** button.

f. Select the **Manufacturers** table and click the **Next** button.

g. Select **MfgID** from the list of *Available Fields* and click the **Move Single Field** button to move the field into the *Selected Fields* window.

h. Move the **MfgName** into the *Selected Fields* window and click the **Next** button.

 i. Don't sort on any fields and click the **Next** button.

 j. Deselect the **Hide key column** check box and click the **Next** button.

 k. Select the **MfgID** field to store in the table and click the **Next** button.

 l. Select the **Enable Data Integrity** check box and click the **Finish** button to complete the wizard. A *Lookup Wizard* dialog box displays.

 m. Click the **Yes** button to save the changes to the table so that Access can create the relationship.

 n. Switch to *Datasheet* view. Verify that the table is now in 3NF.

 o. Close the table.

10. Create an *SQL* query to show the boat and manufacturer information.

 a. Open a new query using **Query Design**.

 b. Add the **Manufacturers** and **SailboatFleet** tables into the query and close the *Show Table* dialog box.

 c. Change to *SQL* view. The *SELECT* clause and the *FROM* clause are entered for you. Because you added multiple tables that have an existing relationship, Access automatically specified the join type.

 d. Edit the *SELECT* clause to add the following field names after the word *SELECT*: BoatID, BoatType, Length, ModelYear, MfgName, MfgPhone

 e. Save the query as FleetDetails.

 f. Run the query to test it. The results should display 23 records.

11. Edit the query to add a parameter.

 a. Change back to *SQL* view.

 b. Edit the *FROM* clause to remove the semicolon.

 c. Enter the following *WHERE* clause below the *FROM* clause WHERE (ModelYear = [Find boats from what Model Year?]);

 d. Save the changes to the query.

 e. Run the query to test it. Enter 2014 in the *Enter Parameter Value* dialog box and click **OK**. The query results should show six records and be similar to Figure 9-114.

 f. Close the query.

12. Back up the database.

 a. Click the **File** tab to open the *Backstage* view and click the **Save As** button.

 b. Click the **Back Up Database** button in the *Advanced* grouping of *the Save Database As* section and then click the **Save As** button. The *Save As* dialog box displays.

 c. Select the location to store the file, enter [your initials] Access 9-3_Backup.accdb as the file name, and click the **Save** button.

13. Analyze the performance of the database.

 a. Click the **Analyze Performance** button [*Database Tools* tab, *Analyze* group] to open the *Performance Analyzer*.

 b. Click the **All Object Types** tab and click the **Select All** button (Figure 9-115).

 c. Click **OK**. The *Analysis Results* window displays one *Idea* to create an MDE executable file and several *Ideas* about changing the data type of different fields. Because you may add more forms and reports to the database and you want to keep the *Short Text* data type, you do not implement these *Ideas*.

 d. Click **Close**.

9-114 FleetDetails query results

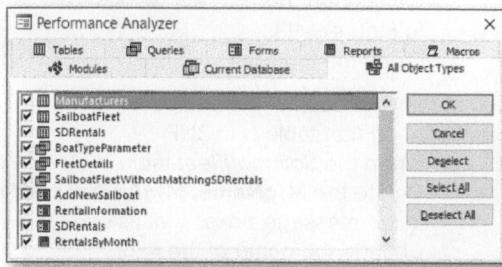

9-115 Performance Analyzer dialog box

14. Review other optimization options.
 a. Open the *RentalsByType* report. Note that the parameter uses the *BoatType* field. Click **OK** in the *Enter Parameter Value* dialog box. The report opens. Even though the *Performance Analyzer* didn't suggest it, you realize it is a good idea to create an index on the *BoatType* field.
 b. Close the report.
 c. Since you have made a number of changes to the database, you also recognize that you can optimize performance by compacting the database to reclaim unused space and remove temporary objects.

15. Create an index on the *BoatType* field.
 a. Open the *SailboatFleet* table in *Design* view.
 b. Select the **BoatType** field.
 c. Change the *Indexed* property to **Yes (Duplicates OK)**.
 d. Save and close the table.

16. Click the **Compact & Repair** button [*File* tab].

17. Close the database.

Independent Project 9-4

Central Sierra Insurance wants you to create a custom *Navigation Pane* to enhance the functionality of its database. For this project, you also encrypt the database with a password and create a PDF file of the database table documentation.
[Student Learning Outcomes 9.1, 9.2, 9.5]

File Needed: **CentralSierra-09.accdb**
Completed Project File Names: **[your initials] Access 9-4.accdb** and
[your initials] Access 9-4_Documentation.pdf

Skills Covered in This Project

- Create a custom *Navigation Pane*.
- Create a custom category and custom groups.
- Assign objects to groups.
- Modify shortcut properties.
- Hide objects and groups.
- Encrypt a database with a password.
- Use the *Database Documenter* tool.

1. Open the **CentralSierra-09** database from your student data files.

2. Save a new copy of your database as [your initials] Access 9-4.

3. Enable content in the security warning.

4. Create a category and group for a custom *Navigation Pane*.
 a. Open the *Navigation Options* dialog box.
 b. Add a new category named Human Resources Main Menu.
 c. Add a new group in this category named Employees.
 d. Add a new group in this category named Branches.
 e. Add a new category named Policies Main Menu.

f. Add a new group in this category named Policy Information.

g. Select the **Show Hidden Objects** check box, if not already selected.

h. Close the *Navigation Options* dialog box.

5. Assign objects and modify the *Navigation* pane for the *Human Resources Main Menu* category.

a. Select the **Human Resources Main Menu** category.

b. Drag the **AddNewEmployee** form, **EmployeeInformation** form, **GetBranchParameter** form, **InsuranceAgentsBranchParameter** report, and **NewSalaryCostSummary** report into the *Employees* group.

c. Drag the **Branch** form into the *Branches* group.

d. Rename the **AddNewEmployee** shortcut Add New Employee.

e. Rename the **EmployeeInformation** shortcut View and Edit Employee Information.

f. Rename the **GetBranchParameter** shortcut View Employees by Branch.

g. Rename the **InsuranceAgentsBranchParameter** shortcut to View Insurance Agents by Branch.

h. Rename the **NewSalaryCostSummary** shortcut to 3% Salary Increase Cost Summary.

i. Rename the **Branch** shortcut to View and Edit Branch Details.

j. Select the **Disable Design View shortcuts** check box for all of the shortcuts in the *Employees* and *Branches* groups.

k. Hide the **Unassigned Objects** heading.

l. Drag the **divider bar** to widen the *Navigation Pane*, if necessary. The completed *Navigation Pane* for the *Human Resource Main Menu* should look similar to Figure 9-116.

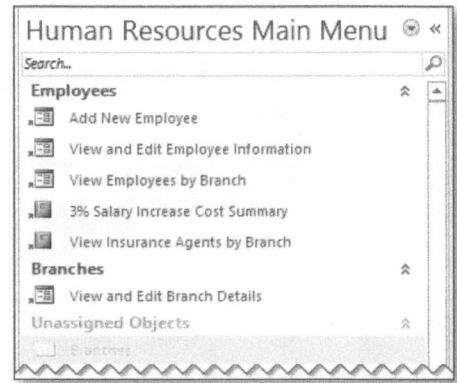

9-116 Completed *Navigation Pane*

6. Assign objects and modify the *Navigation Pane* for the *Policies Main Menu* category.

a. Select the **Policies Main Menu** category.

b. Place the **PolicyQuote** form in the *Policy Information* group.

c. Rename the **PolicyQuote** shortcut View and Edit Policy Quotes.

d. Select the **Disable Design View shortcuts** check box for the *View and Edit Policy Quotes* shortcut.

e. Hide the **Unassigned Objects** heading. The completed *Navigation Pane* for the *Policies Main Menu* should look similar to Figure 9-117.

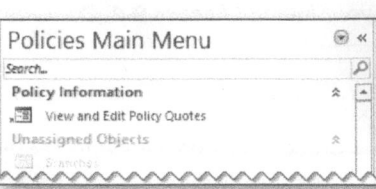

9-117 Completed *Navigation Pane*

7. Test the custom *Navigation Pane*.

a. Double-click the **View and Edit Policy Quotes** shortcut. The *PolicyQuote* form opens.

b. Close the form.

c. Select the **Human Resources Main Menu** category.

d. Double-click the **View Employees by Branch** shortcut. The *Central Sierra Employee Listing* form opens. Click **OK**. The *EmployeesBranchParameter* report opens.

e. Close the report.

f. Close the database but keep Access open.

8. Password protect the database.

a. Open the *[your initials] Access 9-4.accdb* using the *Open Exclusive* option.

b. Encrypt the database with a password. Use S8e22aRE$ as the password.

c. Click **OK**. If you get a message about row level locking, click **OK**.

d. Close the database.

9. Test the password-protected database.
 a. Open the **[your initials] Access 9-4.accdb** database file.
 b. Enter the password S8e22aRE$ when prompted.

10. Create database documentation for the database tables.
 a. Click the **Database Documenter** button to open the *Documenter* dialog box.
 b. Select all of the tables on the *Tables* tab.
 c. Verify that the options in the *Print Table Definition* dialog box match those shown in Figure 9-118.
 d. Preview the *Database Documenter* report (Figure 9-119).
 e. Export the documentation as a PDF file. Locate the folder where you want to save the file, enter [your initials] Access 9-4_Documentation.pdf as the file name, and choose to **Open file after publishing**. The PDF file opens in your PDF viewer.
 f. Navigate through the pages in the PDF file to ensure it was created successfully. The report contains approximately 23 pages.
 g. Close the PDF file.
 h. Don't save the export steps.
 i. Click **Close Print Preview**.

11. Close the database.

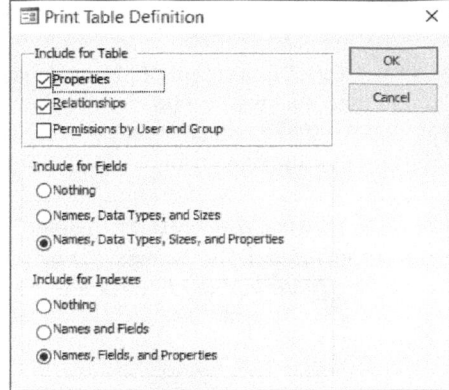

9-118 *Print Table Definition dialog box*

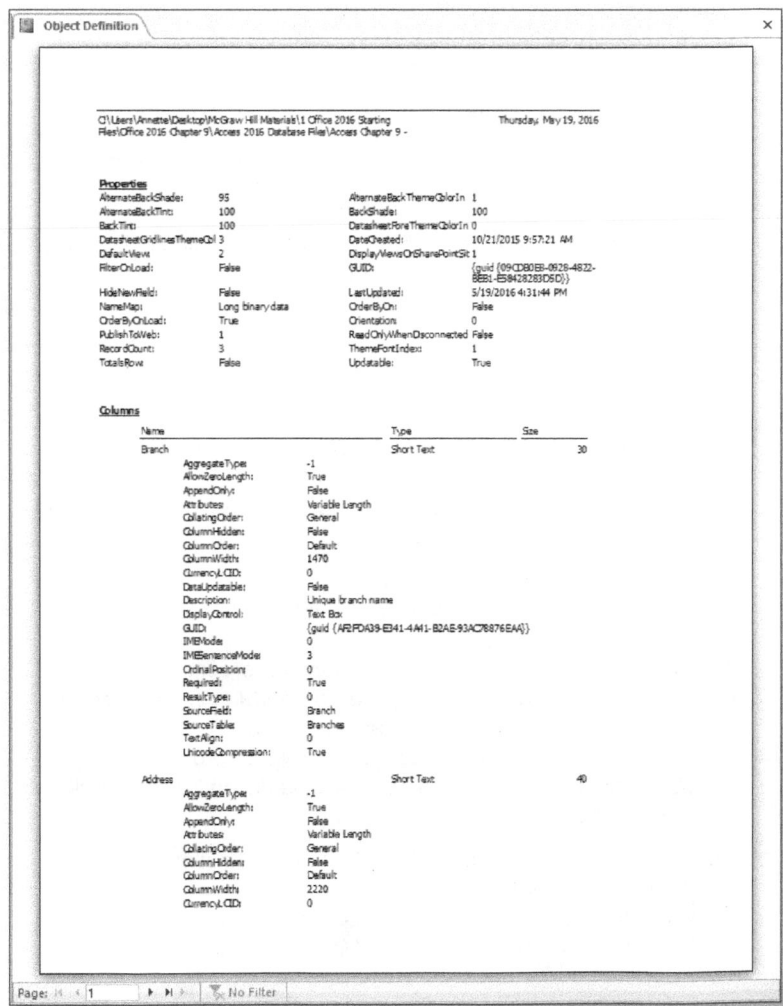

9-119 *Print Preview* of the database tables documentation

Independent Project 9-5

The New York Department of Motor Vehicles wants to improve its database. For this project, you back up and then split the database and password protect the back-end database. In the front-end database you update linked tables, create a custom *Navigation Pane*, and password protect the database. [Student Learning Outcomes 9.2, 9.4, 9.5]

File Needed: ***NewYorkDMV-09.accdb***
Completed Project File Names: *[your initials] Access 9-5.accdb*, *[your initials] Access 9-5_Backup. accdb*, and *[your initials] Access 9-5_be.accdb*

Skills Covered in This Project

- Back up a database.
- Use the *Database Splitter* tool.
- Update linked tables in a split database.
- Encrypt a database with a password.

- Create a custom *Navigation Pane*.
- Create a custom category and custom groups.
- Assign objects to groups.
- Modify shortcut properties.
- Hide objects and groups.

1. Open the ***NewYorkDMV-09*** database from your student data files.

2. Save a new copy of your database as [your initials] Access 9-5.

3. Enable content in the security warning.

4. Back up the database before analyzing the performance. Save the file as [your initials] Access 9-5_Backup.accdb.

5. Split the database.
 a. Accept the default file name of *[your initials] Access 9-5_be.accdb*.
 b. Close the database but keep Access open.

6. Password protect the back-end database.
 a. Open *[your initials] Access 9-5_be.accdb* using the *Open Exclusive* option.
 b. Encrypt the database with a password. Use 6p5Y#wrGK as the password.
 c. Click **OK**. If you get a message about row level locking, click **OK**.
 d. Close the database.

7. Update links in the front-end database.
 a. Open the *[your initials] Access 9-5.accdb* database file.
 b. Delete all three tables.
 c. Click the **Access** button to start the import process.
 d. Locate, select, and open the *[your initials] Access 9-5_be.accdb* file.
 e. Make the selection to link to the data source.
 f. Type 6p5Y#wrGK in the *Password* box when prompted.
 g. Select all of the tables in the *Link Tables* dialog box and click **OK** to add the linked tables into the *Tables* group of the *Navigation Pane*.

8. Create a category and groups for a custom *Navigation Pane*.
 a. Open the *Navigation Options* dialog box.
 b. Add a new category named NY DMV Main Menu.
 c. Add a new group in the *NY DMV Main Menu* category named Ticket Processing and another new group named License Processing.
 d. Select the **Show Hidden Objects** check box, if not already selected.
 e. Close the *Navigation Options* dialog box.

9. Assign objects and modify the *Navigation Pane*.
 a. Select the **NY DMV Main Menu** category.
 b. Put the **AddNewDriver** form and **ViewEditDriverInformation** form in the *License Processing* group.
 c. Put the **TicketCountByCityAndFactorMonthParameter** query, **DriverTicketDetails** form, and **OfficerTicketListing** report in the *Ticket Processing* group.
 d. Rename the **TicketCountByCityAndFactorMonthParameter** shortcut Ticket Summary by Month.
 e. Rename the **DriverTicketDetails** shortcut View Tickets by Driver.
 f. Rename the **OfficerTicketListing** shortcut View Tickets by Officer.
 g. Rename the **AddNewDriver** shortcut Add New Driver.
 h. Rename the **ViewEditDriverInformation** shortcut View and Edit Driver Information.
 i. Do not disable *Design* view shortcuts since you still plan to work with the users to fine-tune the objects.
 j. Hide the **Unassigned Objects** heading.
 k. Drag the **divider bar**, if necessary, to adjust the *Navigation Pane* width. The completed *Navigation Pane* for the *NY DMV Main Menu* should look similar to Figure 9-120.

9-120 Completed *Navigation Pane*

10. Test the custom *Navigation Pane*.
 a. Double-click the **View Tickets by Driver** shortcut. The *DriverTicketDetails* form opens.
 b. Close the form.
 c. Close the database.

11. Password protect the front-end database.
 a. Open the *[your initials] Access 9-5.accdb* using the *Open Exclusive* option.
 b. Encrypt the database with a password. Use 92Ae!88tE as the password.
 c. Click **OK**. If you get a message about row level locking, click **OK**.
 d. Close the database.

12. Test the database.
 a. Open the *[your initials] Access 9-5.accdb* database file.
 b. Type 92Ae!88tE in the *Password* box and click **OK**. If a *Microsoft Access Security Notice* displays, click **Open**.

13. Close the database.

Independent Project 9-6

American River Cycling wants to improve its database. For this project you analyze the table structure and the performance of the database. You create a query in SQL that uses a concatenated field. Finally, you split the database to create a back-end and front-end.
[Student Learning Outcomes 9.1, 9.3, 9.4, 9.6]

File Needed: ***AmericanRiver-09.accdb***
Completed Project File Names: *[your initials] Access 9-6.accdb*, *[your initials] Access 9-6_Backup. accdb*, *[your initials] Access 9-6_Backup2.accdb*, and *[your initials] Access 9-6_be.accdb*

A9-691

Skills Covered in This Project

- Use the *Table Analyzer* tool.
- Back up a database.

- Use the *Performance Analyzer* tool.
- Create a query using *SQL* view.
- Use a concatenated field in an *SQL* query.
- Use the *Database Splitter* tool.

1. Open the ***AmericanRiver-09.accdb*** database from your student data files.

2. Save a new copy of your database as [your initials] Access 9-6.

3. Enable content in the security warning.

4. Analyze the *Members* table.
 a. Click the **Analyze Table** button to open the *Table Analyzer Wizard*.
 b. Advance past the information windows, if necessary.
 c. Select the **Members** table and the **Yes, let the wizard decide** radio button when prompted.
 d. Enlarge the tables in the recommendation so you can read all of the content (Figure 9-121).
 e. The wizard suggests moving the *City, State* and *ZIPCode* fields into a separate table. This solution would result in less storage space. However, you do not anticipate having a significant number of member records and you are more concerned about the increased performance time it takes to join the tables back together. Do not accept this recommendation.
 f. Click the **Back** button two times to return to the wizard screen where you can select a table.

5. Analyze the *RaceInformation* table.
 a. Select the **RaceInformation** table and the **Yes, let the wizard decide** radio button when prompted. A dialog box displays informing you that the wizard doesn't recommend any splitting of the table.
 b. Click **Cancel** to choose not to split the table.

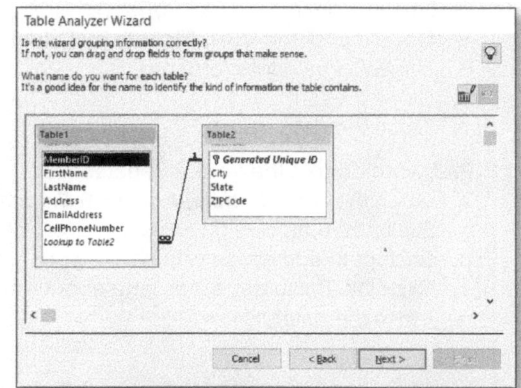

9-121 *Table Analyzer Wizard* recommendations for
Members table

6. Analyze the *RaceResults* table.
 a. Click the **Analyze Table** button to open the *Table Analyzer Wizard*.
 b. Advance past the information windows, if necessary.
 c. Select the **RaceResults** table and the **Yes, let the wizard decide** radio button when prompted.
 d. Enlarge the tables in the recommendation so you can read all of the content (Figure 9-122).
 e. The wizard suggests moving the *AgeGroup* field into a separate table. This solution could save space because the *Generated Unique ID* field would be numeric instead of text. However, you are more concerned about the increased performance time it takes to join the tables back together. Do not accept this recommendation.
 f. Cancel the wizard.

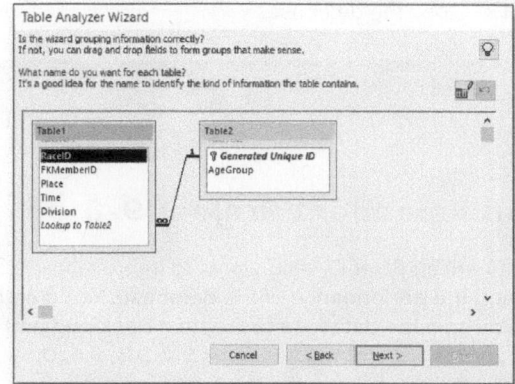

9-122 *Table Analyzer Wizard* recommendations for
RaceResults table

7. Back up the database before analyzing the performance. Save the file as [your initials] Access 9-6_Backup.accdb.

8. Analyze the performance of the database.
 a. Click the **Analyze Performance** button to open the *Performance Analyzer*.
 b. Analyze all of the objects in the database.
 c. Review the five *Ideas* and one *Suggestion* displayed in the *Analysis Results* window (Figure 9-123).
 d. Choose to have the *Performance Analyzer* optimize the *Suggestion*. Don't implement any of the other potential solutions.
 e. Close the *Analyzer*.

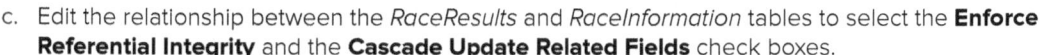

9-123 *Performance Analyzer* potential solutions

9. Edit the new relationship.
 a. Open the *Relationships* window.
 b. Open the *Show Table* dialog box and add the **RaceInformation** table into the window.
 c. Edit the relationship between the *RaceResults* and *RaceInformation* tables to select the **Enforce Referential Integrity** and the **Cascade Update Related Fields** check boxes.
 d. Save the changes to the relationships and close the *Relationships* window.

10. Create an *SQL* query to show race results for club members.
 a. Open a new query using **Query Design**.
 b. Close the *Show Table* dialog box.
 c. Change to *SQL* view.
 d. Edit the *SELECT* clause to remove the semicolon and add a concatenated field after the word *SELECT*: [FirstName] & " " & [LastName] AS [Member Name],
 e. Edit the *SELECT* clause to add the following field names after the comma following the concatenated field: MemberID, City, RaceID, Place, Time, Division, AgeGroup.
 f. Enter the following *FROM* clause below the SELECT clause FROM Members INNER JOIN RaceResults ON Members.MemberID = RaceResults.FKMemberID
 g. Enter the following WHERE clause below the *FROM* clause WHERE (Division = "F")
 h. Enter the following *ORDER BY* clause below the *WHERE* clause ORDER BY LastName;
 i. Save the query as FemaleRaceResults.
 j. Run the query to test it. The results should be similar to those shown in Figure 9-124.
 k. Close the query.

11. Back up the database, because the database has changed, before splitting the database. Save the file as [your initials] Access 9-6_Backup2. accdb.

12. Split the database. Accept the default file name of *[your initials] Access 9-6_be.accdb*.

13. Close the database.

9-124 *MemberRaceResults* query results

Improve It Project 9-7

Mary's Rentals wants to improve its database. To ensure consistency, the starting files are provided for you. The database has been split into a front-end and back-end database. You remove a weak password from the front-end database and apply a new password. You also improve the functionality by fixing a *Navigation Pane* that is not designed correctly. Finally, you update linked tables in the front-end that are not working correctly.
[Student Learning Outcomes 9.2, 9.4, 9.5]

Files Needed: ***MarysRentals-09.accdb*** and ***MarysRentals-09_be.accdb***
Completed Project File Names: ***[your initials] Access 9-7.accdb*** and ***Access 9-7_be.accdb***

Skills Covered in This Project

- Decrypt a database to remove a password.
- Encrypt a database with a password.
- Update linked tables in a split database.
- Modify a custom *Navigation Pane*.
- Assign objects to groups.
- Modify shortcut properties.
- Unhide objects and groups.
- Hide objects and groups.

1. Save a copy of the front-end database.
 a. Open the ***MarysRentals-09*** database from your student data files. Type password in the *Password* box and click **OK**.
 b. Save a new copy of your database as [your initials] Access 9-7. You are prompted to enter the current password. Type password and click **OK**.
 c. Enable content in the security warning.
 d. Close the database.

2. Save a copy of the back-end database.
 a. Open the ***MarysRentals-09_be*** database from your student data files.
 b. Save a new copy of your database as [your initials] Access 9-7_be.
 c. Enable content in the security warning.
 d. Close the database but leave Access open.

3. Remove the existing password from the front-end database.
 a. Open the ***[your initials] Access 9-7.accdb*** database file using the *Open Exclusive* option. You are prompted to enter the current password. Type password and click **OK**.
 b. Click the **Decrypt Database** button [*File* tab] to remove the current password. You are prompted to enter the current password. Type password and click **OK**.

4. Assign a new password to the front-end database.
 a. Encrypt the database with a password. Use sH@dpw#8 as the password.
 b. Click **OK**. If you get a message about row level locking, click **OK**.
 c. Close the database to release the *Open Exclusive* mode.

5. Open the ***[your initials] Access 9-7.accdb*** database file. Type sH@dpw#8 in the *Password* box and click **OK**.

6. Explore the front-end database.
 a. Select the **Mary's Rentals** category in the *Navigation Pane*.
 b. Double-click the **Employees** shortcut in the *Employees* group. An error message displays due to an invalid link to the table. Click **OK** to acknowledge the message. You fix the links to the tables in step 8.
 c. Review the *Navigation Pane*. Note that the *AddEmployees* shortcut is in the wrong group. You also have been told that not all shortcuts were created.

7. Fix the *Navigation Pane*.
 a. Open the *Navigation Options* dialog box.
 b. Select the **Show Hidden Objects** check box in the *Display Options* area, if not already selected, and click **OK**. The *Navigation Pane* updates to display the items in a dimmed state.
 c. Right-click the **Unassigned Objects** heading and select the **Unhide** option.
 d. Place the **AddEmployees** shortcut in the *Employees* group.
 e. Place the **Employees** shortcut, **Equipment** shortcut, and **RentalsSubform** shortcut in the *Unassigned Objects* group.
 f. Place the **AddCustomers** form in the *Customers* group.
 g. Move the **CustomersMain** shortcut from the *Customers* group to the *Rentals* group.
 h. Place the **Top5EquipmentRentals** report in the *Rentals* group.
 i. Place the **EquipmentDetails** form and **EquipmentServiceHistory** form in the *Equipment* group.
 j. Rename the shortcuts so they match those shown in Figure 9-125.

9-125 Completed *Navigation Pane*

8. Update links in the front-end database.
 a. Delete all five linked tables in the *Unassigned Objects* group. Confirm the deletion, if prompted.
 b. Click the **Access** button to start the import process.
 c. Locate, select, and open the *[your initials] Access 9-7_be.accdb* file.
 d. Click the **Link to the data source by creating a linked table** radio button and click **OK**.
 e. Select all of the tables in the *Link Tables* dialog box and click **OK**. The linked tables are added into the *Unassigned Objects* group of the *Navigation Pane*.

9. Verify that the database works correctly.
 a. Double-click the **Employees** linked table in the *Unassigned Objects* group. The table opens and displays the six employees. Close the table.
 b. Double-click the **View Customer Rentals** shortcut in the *Rentals* group. The form opens. Close the form.

10. Finish the *Navigation Pane* by hiding the **Unassigned Objects** heading. Do not disable design view shortcuts as you still plan to work with the users to fine-tune the different objects.

11. Close the database.

Challenge Project 9-8

For this project, you modify the database you worked on in Challenge Project 7-8. You analyze the table structure and analyze the performance of the database. You also create a custom *Navigation Pane* and document the database objects.
[**Student Learning Outcomes 9.1, 9.2, 9.3**]

File Needed: *[your initials] Access 7-8.accdb*
Completed Project File Names: *[your initials] Access 9-8.accdb, [your initials] Access 9-8_Backup.accdb*, and *[your initials] Access 9-8_Documentation.pdf*

Open the database *[your initials] Access 7-8* and save a copy of it as [your initials] Access 9-8.

Modify your database according to the following instructions:

- Use the *Table Analyzer* to analyze all the tables. Evaluate the recommendations and accept the ones that are appropriate.
- Back up the database. Save the file as [your initials] Access 9-8_Backup.accdb.
- Use the *Performance Analyzer* to analyze all objects in the database. Evaluate the potential solutions and implement the ones that are appropriate.
- Customize the *Navigation Pane*. Add at least one category and add at least one group into that category.
- Assign objects to the appropriate group.
- Modify shortcut properties to disable *Design* view.
- Rename shortcuts to make the shortcut names more helpful to the user.
- Hide the *Unassigned Objects* heading.
- Create a PDF file that contains the documentation of all objects in the database. Save the file as [your initials] Access 9-8_Documentation.pdf.
- Close the database.

Challenge Project 9-9

For this project, you modify the database you created in Challenge Project 8-9 for Blue Lake Sports. Your database contains a table with information about the different departments at Blue Lake Sports and a related table with information about interns, as well as other objects created previously. You back up and then split the database. Next, you password protect the back-end database. In the front-end database, you update linked tables, create a custom *Navigation Pane*, and password protect and lock the database. [Student Learning Outcomes 9.2, 9.4, 9.5]

File Needed: *[your initials] Access 8-9.accdb*
Completed Project File Names: *[your initials] Access 9-9.accdb, [your initials] Access 9-9_Backup.accdb, [your initials] Access 9-9_be.accdb*, and *[your initials] Access 9-9.accde*

Open the database *[your initials] Access 8-9* and save a copy of it as [your initials] Access 9-9.

Modify your database according to the following instructions:

- Back up the database. Save the file as [your initials] Access 9-9_Backup.accdb.
- Split the database. Accept the default file name of *[your initials] Access 9-9_be.accdb*. Close the database.
- Open the back-end database using the *Open Exclusive* option.
- Password protect the back-end database. Be sure to keep a record of the password you assign to the database. Close the database.
- Open the front-end database.
- Update the linked tables. You will need to enter the password you assigned to the back-end database.

- Customize the *Navigation Pane*. Add at least one category and add at least one group into that category.
- Assign objects to the appropriate group.
- Modify shortcut properties to disable *Design* view.
- Rename shortcuts to make the shortcut names more helpful to the user.
- Hide the *Unassigned Objects* heading.
- Close the database.
- Open the front-end database using the *Open Exclusive* option.
- Password protect the front-end database. Be sure to keep a record of the password you assign to the database. Close the database.
- Lock the front-end database by using the *Make ACCDE* option. Accept the default file name of *[your initials] Access 9-9.accde*. Close the database.
- Open the locked database to verify that it works correctly. You will need to enter the password you assigned to the front-end database.
- Close the database.

Challenge Project 9-10

For this project, you modify the database you created for a travel agency in Challenge Project 8-10. Your database contains a *Ships* table with information about the different ships. The *Ships* table has a one-to-many relationship with the *Trips* table, which contains specific details about upcoming cruises. The database also contains a *TripInformation* table that contains overview information about the trips. The *TripInformation* table has a one-to-many relationship with the *Trips* table. Analyze the table structure in the database. Create a custom *Navigation Pane*, password protect the database, and document the database tables.
[Student Learning Outcomes 9.1, 9.2, 9.5]

File Needed: *[your initials] Access 8-10.accdb*
Completed Project File Names: *[your initials] Access 9-10.accdb* and
[your initials] Access 9-10_Documentation.pdf

Open the database *[your initials] Access 8-10* and save a copy of it as [your initials] Access 9-10.

Modify your database according to the following instructions:

- Use the *Table Analyzer* to analyze all the tables. Evaluate the recommendations and accept the ones that are appropriate.
- Customize the *Navigation Pane*. Add at least one category and add at least one group into that category.
- Assign objects to the appropriate group.
- Modify shortcut properties to disable *Design* view.
- Rename shortcuts to make the shortcut name more helpful to the user.
- Hide the *Unassigned Objects* heading.
- Password protect the database. Be sure to keep a record of the password you assign to the database.
- Create a PDF file that contains the documentation of all tables in the database. Save the file as [your initials] Access 9-10_Documentation.pdf.
- Close the database.